W9-DFS-262

SELECTED LETTERS OF

Eugene O'Neill.

EDITED BY TRAVIS BOGARD
AND JACKSON R. BRYER

LIMELIGHT EDITIONS: NEW YORK

First Limelight Edition, October 1994.
Copyright ©1988 by Yale University.

Designed by Sally Harris
and set in Meridien type by
The Composing Room of Michigan, Inc.
Printed in the United States of America by
Vail-Ballou Press, Binghamton, New York.

Library of Congress Cataloging-in-Publication Data

O'Neill, Eugene. 1888-1953.
    (Correspondence, Selections)
Selected letters of Eugene O'Neill / edited by Travis Bogard
and Jackson R. Bryer.
    p.   cm.
Includes bibliographical references and index.
ISBN 0–87910–181–4 (alk. paper)
1. O'Neill, Eugene, 1888–1953--Correspondence.
2. Dramatists, American--20th Century-- Correspondence.
I. Bogard, Travis. II. Bryer, Jackson R. III. Title.
(PS3529.N5Z48   1994)
812'.52--dc20
(B)   94–28978
                         CIP

The paper in this book meets the guidelines for
permanence and durability of the Committee on
Production Guidelines for Book Longevity of the
Council on Library Resources.

"Choices" from *Chicago Poems* by Carl Sandburg.
copyright 1916 by Holt, Rinehart and Winston, Inc.;
renewed 1944 by Carl Sandburg, reprinted by permission of
Harcourt Brace Jovanovich, Inc.

CONTENTS

PREFACE

In preparing this edition of Eugene O'Neill's correspondence, absolute editorial and bibliographical purity has been sacrificed for readability in numerous instances. Misspellings and Briticisms, for the most part, have been silently corrected; only in the earliest letters did we leave some obvious errors in order to give the flavor of O'Neill's adolescent style. The titles of books, plays, movies, and names of ships have been italicized, although it was O'Neill's practice to place them in quotation marks; exceptions are unpublished or discarded plays, whose titles remain in quotation marks. The position of quotation marks with punctuation has been regularized to current practice. Most dashes have been standardized to one em in length, although O'Neill's custom in typing was to use a hyphen for a dash. Words that O'Neill underlined once have been transcribed as italic; if he underlined a word or phrase twice, small capital letters have been used; if three times, capitals; if four, italic capitals. The abbreviation of ordinal numbers has been regularized to *1st, 2nd, 3rd,* and so forth; O'Neill's practice in holograph was to raise and underline the letters.

The abbreviation *P.S.,* which precedes most of O'Neill's postscripts, has been regularized to appear on the same line as the beginning of the postscript; he ordinarily placed *P.S.* on a separate line. Omitted punctuation has been supplied on occasions when clarity and coherence warranted. Meaningful deletions made by O'Neill appear in the footnotes. Insignificant deletions and obliterations have not been restored, and interlineal insertions and marginal material have been transcribed as part of the letter or placed at the end of it. Conjectural readings and omitted, obliterated, or illegible words are indicated in brackets in the text.

For each item of correspondence, the return address (both printed letterhead and holograph) has been transcribed and placed within parentheses at the head of the item; where such information was not supplied in the original or was given only partially, it is given in brackets when it is known or can be determined through internal evidence. Also for each item, the spacing of salutations and closings has been compressed.

The following abbreviations describing physical form have been utilized in the headings: *ACS* (autograph postcard signed); *AL* (autograph letter unsigned); *AL (draft)* (unsigned autograph letter found only in draft form); *ALS* (autograph letter signed); *ALS(X)* (autograph letter signed found only in photocopy form); *COPY* (transcribed copy of a letter, postcard, or telegram); *TL* (typewritten letter unsigned); *TLS* (typewritten letter signed);

TLS(X) (typewritten letter signed found only in photocopy form); *WIRE* (telegram); and *WIRE (draft)* (telegram found only in draft form). The number of pages cited at the head of each item refers to the number of sides of paper on which the original letter is written, regardless of how O'Neill himself numbered the pages; occasionally he numbered only one side of a piece of stationery when both sides were used. No numbers of pages are given for some drafts because they were entered in stenographic notebooks and often O'Neill began a new draft in the middle of a page after completing another one just above it, making a page count difficult to determine.

In providing footnotes, we have attempted to steer a middle course between maximum information and sketchy identifications. Persons, places, and events have been identified only once; when they have been mentioned in the introductions, normally they are not given footnotes in the text of the correspondence. Birth and death dates are provided only for important persons. Nationalities of persons footnoted are indicated only when such persons are not American. We have not tried to anticipate the audience for this book either by footnoting all names, titles, and events or by doing so for only the most obscure of these; we hope the correspondence will interest both specialists and general readers.

The location of each item is listed in the heading in brackets; in cases where a draft, photocopy, or transcription of an item exist as well as the original, only the location of the original is indicated. For items owned by private individuals, no identification of those individuals has been provided. The following abbreviations have been used for locations:

Berg	Berg Collection, New York Public Library
Boston U.	Boston University
Bowdoin	Bowdoin College
California	University of California, Berkeley
Columbia	Columbia University
Connecticut C.	Connecticut College
Cornell	Cornell University
Dartmouth	Dartmouth College
Detroit P.L.	Detroit Public Library
Enoch Pratt	Enoch Pratt Free Library, Baltimore, Maryland
Gaylord	Gaylord Hospital, Wallingford, Connecticut
George Mason	George Mason University
Georgetown	Georgetown University
Harvard	Harvard University
Indiana	Indiana University
IISH	International Institute of Social History, Amsterdam
Library of Congress	Library of Congress
Lincoln Center	Billy Rose Theatre Collection, New York Public Library Performing Arts Research Center
Maryland	University of Maryland, College Park
Museum of City of N.Y.	Museum of the City of New York
Newberry	Newberry Library, Chicago, Illinois
NYPL	New York Public Library, Manuscript Division
NYU	New York University
Notre Dame	University of Notre Dame
O'Neill Center	Eugene O'Neill Theatre Center, Waterford and New London, Connecticut
Pennsylvania	University of Pennsylvania

Players Club	The Hampden-Booth Theatre Library, The Players, New York, New York
Princeton	Princeton University
Private	Privately owned
Stanford	Stanford University
SUNY, Stony Brook	State University of New York, Stony Brook
Tao House	The Eugene O'Neill Foundation, Tao House, Danville, California
Texas	University of Texas, Austin
UCLA	University of California, Los Angeles
Virginia	University of Virginia
Wayne State	Wayne State University
Yale	Beinecke Library, Yale University

It is possible here to acknowledge only a very few of the hundreds of persons and institutions who contributed significantly to the completion of this project. Such acknowledgments must begin at the Beinecke Library of Yale University. The majority of O'Neill's extant correspondence is there, and much of our work was conducted with the assistance of its staff, who invariably went well beyond the normal demands of assistance to a scholarly venture and did so cheerfully and expertly. Donald Gallup, the first curator of the Beinecke's extraordinary American Literature Collection and the guiding force behind its acquisition and nurturing of the O'Neill Papers, has been an inspiration and a frequent source of information and wisdom; in several instances, he even used his expert knowledge of O'Neill's shaky handwriting to help us decipher some late drafts. David Schoonover, Gallup's successor, held that position for most of the time we were working on this book and was as gracious as he was helpful during our numerous visits, phone calls, and mailed communications. Patricia C. Willis, the present curator, assumed the job just as our task was ending, only to inherit a series of last-minute questions and requests early in her tenure; she dealt with them with unfailing good humor and efficiency. Christa Sammons and Aldo R. Cupo of the Beinecke staff also extended themselves on our behalf. Traugott and Peggy Lawler provided congenial lodging during our visits to New Haven.

Many individuals helped us locate and obtain copies of O'Neill's correspondence, from which we made the selections for this edition. Arthur and Barbara Gelb, O'Neill's biographers, not only gave us their enthusiastic support but also let us see photocopies of correspondence that they had used in their research; in a number of cases these copies were of important items for which we never located the originals. Two O'Neill collectors, Bryan Sheedy and Harley J. Hammerman, were especially helpful in sharing their archives with us. Others who assisted us in tracking down frequently elusive items were: Silvio A. Bedini; Mary A. Benjamin; Jane Malmgren Bogard; Andreas Brown; Kristin Cole Brown; Frederic I. Carpenter; Ginnine Cocuzza; Joan Gruenberg Cominos; Dorothy B. Commins; Rolando Costa Picazo; Rebecca B. Desmarais; Barbara Doherty; Abdias do Nascimento; J. J. Douthit; John F. Driscoll; Richard J. Finneran; Claude Flory; Arnold F. Gates; Jere W. Hageman; Ulrich Halfmann; Adele R. Heller; Mary C. Henderson; Glenn Horowitz; Philip Horton; James M. Kee; Frederick and Joyce Kennedy; John K. King; Beatrice Laufer; Ward Lewis; Lois Erickson McDonald; Frank C. P. McGlinn; Loring Mandel; George Monteiro; Philip D. Nathanson; Maurice F. Neville; Dorothy Norman; Robert North, Jr., and the late Mrs. Robert North, Jr.; Stanley Pace; Sally Thomas Pavetti; the late John H. G. Pell; George Quimby; Kathleen C. Quinn; John Henry Raleigh; Margaret Loftus Ranald; Paul C. Richards; Paul Shyre; Ralph Sipper; Murray J. Smith; G. Thomas Tanselle; John Unterecker; Thorn T.

Welden; Robert C. Weller; Frederick C. Wilkins; Robert Wilson; George C. White; Mrs. Sophus Keith Winther; and David Wyatt.

Librarians, curators, and institutions who generously gave us access to materials and granted permission to publish them in this volume include: Lola Szladits, Curator of the Berg Collection, New York Public Library; Howard B. Gottlieb, Director, Department of Special Collections, Boston University Libraries; The Library, Bowdoin College; Bonnie Hardwick, Head, Manuscripts Division, and James D. Hart, Director, The Bancroft Library, University of California, Berkeley; Kenneth A. Lohf, Librarian for Rare Books and Manuscripts, Butler Library, Columbia University; Special Collections, Shain Library, Connecticut College; Cornell University Library; Philip N. Cronenwett, Curator of Manuscripts and Chief of Special Collections, Dartmouth College Library; Detroit Public Library Rare Book Room; Enoch Pratt Free Library; William A. Rothman, Executive Vice President, Gaylord Farm; Library of Congress Federal Theatre Project Collection at George Mason University Library, Fairfax, Virginia; George M. Barringer, Special Collections Librarian, Georgetown University Library; Rodney Dennis, The Houghton Library, Harvard University; International Institute of Social History; The Lilly Library, Indiana University; Manuscript Division, Library of Congress; Dorothy L. Swerdlove, Curator, The Billy Rose Theatre Collection, Performing Arts Research Center, New York Public Library; Donald Farren, Associate Director of Libraries for Special Collections, University of Maryland; Museum of the City of New York; The Newberry Library; Manuscript Division, New York Public Library; Frank Walker, Librarian, Fales Library, New York University; University of Notre Dame Library; Sally Thomas Pavetti, Curator, and Lois Erickson McDonald, Associate Curator, Eugene O'Neill Theatre Center Collection; Special Collections Department, Van Pelt Library, University of Pennsylvania; Louis A. Rachow, Curator, The Hampden-Booth Theatre Library at The Players; Mary Ann Jensen, Curator of the Theatre Collection, Princeton University Library; Department of Special Collections and University Archives, Stanford University Libraries; The Eugene O'Neill Foundation, Tao House; Harry Ransom Humanities Research Center, The University of Texas at Austin; Department of Special Collections, University Research Library, University of California at Los Angeles; Michael Plunkett, Curator of Manuscripts, Barrett Library, University of Virginia Library; Wayne State University Library; Patricia C. Willis, Curator of American Literature, Beinecke Rare Book and Manuscript Library, Yale University Library.

The text of O'Neill's January 20, 1935, letter to Mrs. George Pierce Baker is reprinted by permission of Dramatists Play Service, Inc., in whose *George Pierce Baker: A Memorial* it appeared. Letters to Arthur Hobson Quinn, dated April 3, 1925, and May 29, 1927, are reprinted from Arthur Hobson Quinn, *A History of the American Drama from the Civil War to the Present*, vol. 2, rev. ed. (1936; Copyright renewed 1964 by Arthur Hobson Quinn, Jr.; reprinted by Irvington Publishers, Inc., 1979); permission to reprint granted by Kathleen C. Quinn. O'Neill's December 15, 1933, letter to Sean O'Casey is reprinted by permission of Macmillan, publishers of *The Letters of Sean O'Casey: 1910–41*.

Transcribing the texts of the correspondence and readying the manuscript for the publisher could not have been done without Ruth M. Alvarez, who helped at all stages of the project; Robert Carr, Beatriz Dailey, and Terrie Hruzd, who prepared the manuscript; Brian Meyer and Juanita Rice, who provided research assistance; Mary C. Hartig, who carefully read the entire text and pointed out errors and inconsistencies before it was too late; Lawrence Dinnean, curator of pictorial collections at The Bancroft Library of the University of California, Berkeley, who helped with the photographs; and Allison Sharp, who assisted with the research and proofreading. At Yale University Press we received encouragement, support, and, above all, patience from John Ryden, the director; from Edward Tripp, our editor; and from Carl Rosen, our eagle-eyed manuscript editor.

The photographs on pages 13, 55, 237, 398, 466, 494, and 586 appear courtesy of The Beinecke Rare Book and Manuscript Library. The photographs on pages 255 and 527 appear courtesy of Culver Pictures. The photograph on page 34 appears courtesy of Mrs. Beatrice Ashe Maher. The photograph on page 136 appears courtesy of Mr. and Mrs. James Light. The photograph on page 197 appears courtesy of Joan Macgowan Faxon. The photograph on page 342 appears courtesy of The Bancroft Library, Thérèse Bonney Collection. The photograph on page 577 is by Harry Kemp.

Significant assistance for the work of the editors on this project was provided by the University of California, Berkeley; the Division of Arts and Humanities and the General Research Board of the University of Maryland, College Park; and, most generously, by a major grant from the Division of Research Programs of the National Endowment for the Humanities.

INTRODUCTION

I hate letters in a book and I think most people do.
—Eugene O'Neill to Barrett Clark, April 27, 1944

Autobiography is irresistible.
—Oscar Wilde

For a writer to whom the deepest creative privacy was as essential as water to a fish, Eugene O'Neill in his plays set his inner life at ironic odds with the personal and public contacts he made in the world around him. During his lifetime he freely dispensed romantic autobiographical glimpses of his life at sea, authenticating his Conradian-Stevensonian-Coleridgean view of a sailor's life. As a dramatist he fell into the autobiographical mode early. At the beginning of his career in the one-act play *Fog* (1914), he presented in the character of the Poet a self-portrait that was to become almost a stock figure in his plays. At the last, autobiography proved to be the manner that led him to his finest tragic statement, but it did not provide the wall of protection between writer and audience many think desirable in a created work of art. *Long Day's Journey into Night* invites close personal investigation of its author-subject: it is a wall of glass, open to the curiosity of all viewers.

Darkly through the glass there has emerged the figure of an O'Neill whose life, after an early adventurous phase, was passed in melancholy and melodrama—introspective, ghost-haunted, hag-ridden—a man who stood in relation to his children much as King Lear stood to his.

The characterization has a partial truth; O'Neill himself accepted much of it. Yet before the romantic, brooding figure be taken as the whole man, it may be well to remember that it is a construction of art and criticism, an image, not the man himself. Oscar Wilde commented on the lives of the greatest poets: "Good artists exist simply in what they make, and consequently are perfectly uninteresting in what they are. . . . A great poet, a truly great poet, is the most unpoetical of all creatures."[1] Wilde meant that in the creative center of his being where the driving force is concentrated, the artist is not possessed of "characteristics." Deep within, the artist's life and work are interlocked, personality is nearly effaced, and work becomes the totality of being.

The more than three thousand surviving letters from which the contents of this book have been chosen depict an O'Neill somewhat different from his own account or the reconstructions of his biographers. Except as he depicted himself for various journalists and critics, his correspondence contains little reminiscent romanticizing. Having been fascinated by the

---

1. Oscar Wilde, *The Picture of Dorian Gray.* In *The Complete Works of Oscar Wilde* (Twickenham, Middlesex: Hamlyn Publishing, 1986), p. 408.

melancholy figure, the reader may be surprised by O'Neill's day-to-day appearance as an ordinary man, avowing friendships, showing concern for his children, warring with the IRS, raging now with love, now hatred, swearing at Establishments, tolerating most personal contacts except from swindlers, watching over his health, going to ball games, spoiling his pets, and trying, sometimes not very successfully, to bring his diurnal existence into a reasonably coherent fiscal, personal, and spiritual order.

This rather recognizable everyman is the O'Neill in the bulk of the correspondence. Except in his most deeply felt personal letters, he was free of prosodic affectations, and even when he wrote most urgently he tended to be ironic about overwriting. Considering that his advanced education was a wasted freshman year at Princeton, he shows himself to have gained through his reading a remarkable fund of knowledge, but he displays little interest in abstract literary theory or in the intellectualized social life of the critical and literary fraternity of his time. In all his correspondence, he conveys no sense that he is writing letters of particular value to historians or to anyone other than the addressee. These are not, for the most part, studied documents. Had he possessed more tolerance for the telephone, much of their content might have been communicated orally. The great majority of the letters reflect the daily concerns of an ordinary human being talking to the inhabitants of his personal world.

Except, of course, that O'Neill was not ordinary, but the keeper of an intense flame burning out of sight of most, if not all, others. The plays were produced in silent isolation. The manuscript of the letters is open and easily read, but he wrote the plays almost as if he did not want them read, in a microscopic hand that betrays the need for the utmost privacy during their composition. His writing rooms were set high and away from the household: in a *tourelle* at the château at Le Plessis; at Casa Genotta in a room built like a ship's cabin, suggesting that he was writing far from land; and at Tao House, in a small, dark room separated from all else by three doors that silenced every sound from the outer world. In such spaces, with a concentration that was almost like self-hypnosis, writing with a finely honed, laborious muscular control, he responded to his vocation and painfully paid the debt to his genius.

In his letters—even to those closest to him—he does not speak as the keeper of a flame. No one passed the doors into the place where the plays were on brood. Once a play approached its final drafts, he was open enough about it and ready to discuss it.[2] To the act of composition, however, he never refers except indirectly and unrevealingly.[3] In his work diary he kept a matter-of-fact monthly accounting of the "W.D.'s" (Working Days) he spent at his desk, but the records carry no hint of his inner vision and excitement at what was to come.[4] Except possibly with Carlotta Monterey O'Neill, his third wife, to whom he read draft versions of works in progress, O'Neill's interior life was never shared.

Such silent dedication is the constant undersong of what the letters reflect of the surfaces of O'Neill's life. O'Neill lived as all people do, on two planes, that of the exterior man who moved in a world of time and space and pleasure and pain, and that of another, an

---

2. See for example his willingness to discuss the merits and defects of *Dynamo* before and after its production and his reiterated statement about having discussed it too much prior to its staging (letters 282, 283, 287).

3. For example: "Try a Cycle sometime. . . . A lady bearing quintuplets is having a debonair, carefree time of it by comparison" (to Lawrence Langner, letter 402).

4. See the entry announcing the onset of *The Iceman Cometh* and *Long Day's Journey into Night*: "(Read over notes on various ideas for single plays—decide do outlines of two that seem appeal most, and see—the Jimmy the P[riest].-H[ell]. H[ole].-Garden idea and the N[ew]. L[ondon]. family one.)" (Eugene O'Neill, *Work Diary*, transcribed by Donald Gallup, 2 vols. [New Haven: Yale University Library, 1981], entry for June 6, 1939, vol. 2, p. 351).

interior man, whose reality was not defined by solid objects and comprehensible obligations. For most people, the inner being is understood only in dreams and irrational longings and is either repressed and put aside or yielded to in some self-gratifying aberration. The creative artist, however, must make a tangible reality of the inner life by fashioning a work of art. To bring the work created within into the outer world is the artist's way of bringing the halves of being into harmony and wholeness, of balancing the duality of inner and outer selves, of keeping peace between the potentially warring elements that define the artist's nature.

Occasionally, as his letters reveal, the outer world intruded on O'Neill's inner life with damaging results. Impatiently waiting for Agnes, his second wife, to agree to their divorce, he fell into a frenzy of hatred for her that entirely disrupted his creative life. He wrote to remind her that the alimony settlement, scaled to his income, would be affected if he were too disturbed to write. He threatened to give up writing. To his lawyer, Harry Weinberger, he raged. And he wrote *Dynamo*, a play in which he initially had eager faith but which failed in production. He defended it in the face of its bad reviews, rewrote it for publication, and ultimately—its merits and defects being inextricably tangled with his outer life—gave it up as a job poorly done because of Agnes's delay. His fury with his daughter, Oona, when she married Charles Chaplin partly stemmed from his fear that intrusive publicity would pierce his solitude. Even his physical illnesses became enemies to his writing. At times, the inner and outer man were seemingly at irreconcilable odds, and he became a deeply divided being.

Yet even at times of greatest stress, when the surface was troubled and impassioned, what lay deep was never in doubt, and when balance was maintained, he became a whole and happy man—a justified man. To spend long, uninterrupted days of dogged writing gave O'Neill a sense of the worthiness of work, and sometimes his pride lay not only in the thing created, but in the labor required to achieve the accomplishment. In *Long Day's Journey into Night*, O'Neill portrayed his own father, the actor James O'Neill, as James Tyrone, recalling the days when he was a young, destitute Irish immigrant, struggling to survive. Then, Tyrone says in James O'Neill's words, he came to learn "the value of a dollar,"[5] and he stresses the need for his sons to follow a course in life dedicated to work. In the play, as in life, the sons find the repeated lecture tiresome and a little ridiculous, yet Eugene's later conduct reveals that he learned the lesson well. The intensity and continuity of his father's work ethic underlay many of his attitudes toward those around him. He urged Agnes to develop disciplined work habits as a writer. The letters praising and expressing love for his son Eugene, Jr., are rooted in his pride in the boy's steadily high academic accomplishment. His alienation from his second son, Shane, is directly related to his growing awareness that the boy would never value work as a means to a responsible life. In the context of World War II and Chaplin's Hollywood, Oona, whom O'Neill had scarcely known after her infancy, seemed to be living an unstable, parasitic existence, and he cast her off. Without work, life was, in his father's dying assessment, "froth."[6]

When sharp tensions between the outer and inner planes are not present, O'Neill's contacts with the outer world through the letters are open and immediate. To readers of later times the letters may often appear unsophisticated. In justice, they should be read always with an eye on the date of their composition. When, for example, O'Neill at the relatively advanced age of twenty-six writes to his beloved Beatrice Ashe, swearing to be both passionate and "pure" and sounding for all the world like Penrod in heat, the years of relative innocence prior to the sexual revolution of the 1920s must be charitably recalled. Similarly, his extraordinary hostility to Agnes as she prolonged the divorce negotiations must be

---

5. Eugene O'Neill, *Long Day's Journey into Night* (New Haven: Yale University Press, 1956), pp. 146–48.
6. See letter 107.

understood in part as stemming from period attitudes. For one thing, her delay meant that his unmarried alliance with Carlotta Monterey, a matter of little moment among the rich and famous today, could not be regularized, and they were subject to various personal embarrassments and to the inquiries of a salacious press. It was also a breach of faith. He had married Agnes with certain of the stylish ideas of the Bohemian 1920s in mind—ideas about free love and about marriage as a nonbinding agreement between free souls. If the husband or wife requested a divorce, it should be quickly and readily granted and the partnership ended. In his view Agnes failed to keep her part of the marital bargain. He had been frank, even naive, in telling her about his affair with Carlotta Monterey, showing her Carlotta's letters, encouraging the women to communicate with one another, and discussing the informal ménage à trois openly. Later, the openness turned to deception, and finally, when Agnes did not accept matters as simply as he wished, became unbounded fury at what he felt was her betrayal. The bitterness against her that endured for a lifetime and spilled over into his attitude toward Shane and Oona arose in part from the fact that a free and loving marriage had turned sour and threatened to become a society scandal.

Like his hatreds, his friendships were strong. The letters to George Jean Nathan, Kenneth Macgowan, and Saxe Commins never falter in their affection and admiration, and as the depression tightened, his concern that Commins be hired as an editor by his publisher was fine in intent and effect. To his agent, Richard Madden, and his lawyer, Harry Weinberger, he remained steadily loyal, assuming their loyalty in return and trusting them completely with the intricate details of his professional and personal life. He developed congenial, intelligent, and lasting friendships with professional associates—the critic and scholar Sophus Keith Winther, his publisher, Bennett Cerf, Lawrence and Armina Langner and Theresa Helburn of the Theatre Guild, critic Arthur Hobson Quinn, his biographer, Barrett Clark, and screenwriter Dudley Nichols. In his later years, he displayed friendly affection toward those who emerged from his past life, and he often came to their support in times of financial need. To former New London neighbors he was especially solicitous, and to strangers he was unfailingly courteous in answering requests for autographs or information.

Judging by his correspondence, his circle of friends was smaller than might be imagined for an artist of his reputation, but it was durable. Not until the end of his life were friendships shaken, ties broken. By that time, however, the core of his life was cold. When his writing was stopped by the tremor that prevented his using a pen, the force that had made his marriage to Carlotta Monterey an exceptional one diminished. Then the friends intruded and attempted to separate him from the woman who had given her life to creating and protecting the spaces of silence. They were both ill and in hospital; the break between them seemed irreconcilable. Yet his letters calling to her from his hospital bed, expressing his concern for her welfare, and begging her not to reject him attest unequivocally to his love for her. As soon as he had strength to do so, he returned to her. The friends fell by the wayside.

In his professional life in the theatre, his letters show him increasing in skill. He had a recluse's distaste for any form of public appearance—special lectures, first nights, even prefaces and puffs to the writing of his friends. Yet during the rehearsal periods of his plays,[7] even on those occasions when two of his plays were scheduled to open in the same month, he proved a knowledgeable and helpful workman. Letters from the early years—when he was

---

7. *Bound East for Cardiff*, November 3, 1916, and *Before Breakfast*, December 1, 1916; *In the Zone*, October 31, 1917 and *The Long Voyage Home*, November 2, 1917; *Where the Cross is Made*, November 22, 1918, and *The Moon of the Caribbees*, December 20, 1918; *Beyond the Horizon*, February 3, 1920, and *Chris Christophersen*, March 9, 1920; *"Anna Christie,"* November 2, 1921, and *The Straw*, November 10, 1921; *The*

coping with John D. Williams's somewhat jury-rigged production of *Beyond the Horizon*, George C. Tyler's production of *Chris Christophersen*, and the Provincetown Playhouse production of *The Emperor Jones*—show the bewilderment, querulousness, and excitement of a young playwright beginning to feel his strength. When he at last signed with Lawrence Langner and the Theatre Guild, however, he had become a fully cooperative and disciplined collaborator in the theatrical process.

These among others are the qualities of the external man shown in his correspondence. To read the letters is to gain an intimate picture of O'Neill as he moved among friends, family and acquaintances from day to day and place to place.[8] Inevitably gaps occur in the file. At times correspondence breaks off without apparent cause as with the letters to Marion Welch and to Beatrice Ashe, two early sweethearts. Some groups of letters have not been found. For example, there appears to be no surviving correspondence with John D. Williams, whose production of *Beyond the Horizon* introduced O'Neill to Broadway, very few letters to Arthur Hopkins, who produced *"Anna Christie,"* and only drafts of a handful of letters to Robert Edmond Jones. Predictably, some collectors have denied access to potentially important letters.

Nevertheless, the selection in this volume is generous and fully representative of the available whole. Only a sampling of the voluminous correspondence with Harry Weinberger and Richard Madden has been included because their concerns are largely financial—taxes, alimony, royalties, and the like. Since the complete correspondence with Kenneth Macgowan, Saxe Commins, and George Jean Nathan has been published elsewhere[9] the selection from these important letters has been cut back to permit other inclusions.

Gaps acknowledged, an amplitude remains. The very bulk of the correspondence is worth contemplation. The flow of letters was strong and continual. In his mature years he appears to have set aside time when he would draft a sizable group of letters to be typed later by Carlotta—a practice that accounts for the repetition of information in identical phrasing in some letters. The average letter is short, but some run to many pages and were written over more than one day. In 1914, for example, Beatrice Ashe, weary of receiving a daily letter, which she was always urged to answer by return mail, suggested that he write less often. He obeyed with a subterfuge, writing her daily and mailing the anthology once a week. Occasionally he wrote Agnes on the same installment plan.

What is perhaps most remarkable about the bulk of O'Neill's correspondence is that a man forced by his genius to seek undisturbed solitude should reach forth so continually to maintain contacts with the exterior world. His intimates were invited to visit; others were kept at a greater distance, yet held close in the bondage of the correspondence. By the letters, O'Neill managed to live in the outer world without entering it deeply, and by their means, he generally kept the outer and inner planes of his being in balance. The letters thus form an essential part of the complex creative process to which his life was dedicated.

First Man, March 4, 1922, and *The Hairy Ape*, March 9, 1922; *Welded*, March 17, 1924, and *The Ancient Mariner*, April 6, 1924; *Marco Millions*, January 9, 1928, and *Strange Interlude*, January 30, 1928.

8. While collecting materials for this volume, the editors have prepared a computerized index and census of all the available letters, giving full bibliographical information and an index of proper names and major topics for each letter.

9. *"The Theatre We Worked For"*: *The Letters of Eugene O'Neill to Kenneth Macgowan*, ed. Jackson R. Bryer, with introductory essays by Travis Bogard (New Haven: Yale University Press, 1982). *Love and Admiration and Respect, The O'Neill-Commins Correspondence*, ed. Dorothy Commins (Durham, N.C.: Duke University Press, 1986). *"As Ever, Gene"*: *The Letters of Eugene O'Neill to George Jean Nathan*, transcribed and edited with introductory essays by Nancy L. Roberts and Arthur W. Roberts (Rutherford, N.J.: Fairleigh Dickinson University Press, 1987).

PART ONE

BEGINNINGS

1901–1916

Perhaps you think the path ahead with me is too rough?
—*To Beatrice Ashe, March 21, 1915*

Eugene O'Neill's earliest extant letter was written in 1901 to his mother's cousin, Lillian Brennan. He was thirteen and in school in New York City. He had already experienced what a child of theatrical parents in the late nineteenth century might expect—to be transported with them as they toured the country or alternatively to be left in care of a governess or relative. Born in a New York hotel room on October 16, 1888, he was the third son of the actor James O'Neill and Mary Ellen Quinlan (Ella). His oldest brother, James, Jr., or Jamie, became a minor actor but lived the life of a Broadway sport. His second brother, Edmund, died in infancy in 1885. The difficulties of Eugene's birth caused a doctor to give his mother morphine, to which she became addicted. Her condition was a haunting, unresolved problem throughout the lives of the O'Neills, although O'Neill does not mention it in any letter.

In the early years, there was little that could be called a family life for the O'Neills. When they were not living in hotels, they resided in a small, dark house in New London, Connecticut. There, Eugene clung to the Brennans, to his neighbors, the Rippens, and to other friends about town. The letter of May 17, 1914, to Jessica Rippen is an adolescent effusion, but it also reaches out for a stable connection to a relatively uncomplicated world. He was not to find such a world in New London, but Monte Cristo Cottage—the house named after the play in which James O'Neill starred throughout most of his career—was to remain close to the center of his creative life. He returned to it obsessively in his mind if not in body. He repeatedly duplicated the arrangement of the furniture in its central room in his plays,[1] and the room itself became the scene of his nostalgic comedy, *Ah, Wilderness!* and of his greatest tragedy, *Long Day's Journey into Night*. His last home at Marblehead Neck, Massachusetts, pleased him because it reminded him of the cottage.

In 1895 O'Neill was enrolled in Saint Aloysius School at the Academy of Mount Saint Vincent in Riverdale, New York, and took his first communion in May 1900. That year, he transferred to the De La Salle Institute in New York City and thence to Betts Academy in Stamford, Connecticut. He was in attendance there until 1906, when he entered Princeton University. At the end of his first university year, his attention to his studies having been minimal, he was dismissed.

1. See Timo Tiusanen, *O'Neill's Scenic Images* (Princeton, N.J.: Princeton University Press, 1968).

At Betts Academy, the letters he wrote to Marion Welch, a Hartford girl he called Boutade ("whimsical one"), reflect a summer's flirtation, but their youthful charm masks a different education from elementary French and his other prep school subjects and activities. Now and again he tells her of trips to New York in company with Jamie and other friends of whom Boutade does not entirely approve. There, in bars and brothels, the boy's education received a sinister coloration that by 1909 had turned his course downward toward a derelict's life.

In 1909, he made pregnant a New York girl, Kathleen Jenkins. A marriage was quickly arranged, but since neither his nor Kathleen's parents approved of the match, O'Neill was hustled out of town on a gold-prospecting expedition to Honduras in the care of a friend of his father, Earl C. Stevens. The trip was short-lived. O'Neill contracted malaria and returned to the United States early in 1910.

For a short time he worked as an assistant stage manager with his father's company, touring in a sentimental romance, *The White Sister*. On May 7, 1910, his son, Eugene, Jr., was born, but O'Neill avoided seeing his wife or child and fled again, shipping out in June for Argentina on a Norwegian barque. Later, on a tramp freighter and on a transatlantic liner, he traveled to England and, he claimed, to Africa. He was made an able-bodied seaman on the American Line in 1911, but more important than this merit badge was the information about sailing vessels and steamers that proved to be of use when he had ceased running and found his vocation as a playwright.

In later years, to Carlotta Monterey, he spoke of his lifelong "seeking flight,"[2] but at this time he was only a fugitive, moving on a deliberately self-destructive course, purposeless and uncontrolled, with no destiny but death. Living on remittances from his father, he passed his days in a Raines Law hotel, Jimmy the Priest's saloon, on the New York waterfront. Some small indications of his future life were evident, such as his seeing all the plays offered by the Dublin Abbey Theatre on its first American tour in 1911; but for the most part his was a life among the down-and-outs. Early in 1912, he attempted suicide.

In July 1912 Kathleen's petition for divorce was granted. O'Neill returned to New London to work as a reporter for the *New London Telegraph*. He kept the paper supplied with verses intricate in rhyme scheme, parodying the style of well-known balladeers from Villon to Robert W. Service. The poems are exhibitionistic exercises in rhyming—diction lessons without content—but they are at least the beginnings of speech. The touch of poetry remained with him throughout his life, and although he never became a lyric singer, his way was strewn with small occasional poems, such as those he wrote lovingly to Carlotta O'Neill each year on her birthday.

He was soon to find his proper idiom. In the fall of 1912, his attention was forcibly directed to the care of his physical self. He contracted tuberculosis and in December was sent to Gaylord Farm Sanatorium in Wallingford, Connecticut. The illness made flight impossible and forced his attention to his inner being. Something of what the decay of his body meant to him can be guessed from the frequency with which characters with damaged lungs appear in his first plays. The fact of mortality and the disease's slow wasting away of his inner substance was more frightening than death had been in a romantic rebel's dream. It was time to turn in a new direction. As Stephen Murray in *The Straw* says of his self-discovery in a sanatorium, "It took T. B. to blast me loose."[3]

In the quiet of the sanatorium, under the careful guardianship of the doctor, David R.

2. Letter to Carlotta Monterey, (letter 193).
3. Eugene O'Neill, *The Plays of Eugene O'Neill* (New York: Random House, 1964), vol. 3, p. 359.

Lyman, O'Neill first came to learn the value of solitude to his creative life. In the relative isolation of the hospital, his creative energy was finally released. He began to read extensively, and then, amateurishly and tentatively, began to write. Possibly then it occurred to him that his derelict life had been little more than a series of meaningless encounters. Perhaps he also discovered that his life was divided sharply into two planes—one an existence in an outer world of things and people, the other a life of solitude where he had no choice but to dedicate himself to the dictates of his creative power—the same power that had once caused his flight but that now had defined itself and was demanding from him an irrevocable commitment.

He was discharged from Gaylord Farm on June 3, 1913, his disease arrested. He returned to New London and fell in love with a dark-haired woman named Beatrice Ashe. She was to occupy his passionate epistolary attention for the year to come. The collection of love letters to her display O'Neill at his most voluptuously romantic. At the same time they promise that he has reformed and will stay, as he put it, "pure." As the year of impassioned pleading wore on she became wary, feeling in all probability that the road with him would be "too rough." Curiously, without a signal, the correspondence broke off, as he formed a different allegiance.

More important than the romance was the beginning of his apprenticeship as a writer. Upon his discharge from the sanatorium, he wrote continually—inexpertly, melodramatically, but steadily and with a self-discipline that was obsessional. Five of his one-act plays, *Thirst, The Web, Warnings, Fog,* and *Recklessness* were published in 1914 in an edition subsidized by his father. Two full-length plays, *Bread and Butter* and *Servitude,* were added to the list, and finally there came the first play to sound the authentic notes of O'Neill's true voice, *Bound East for Cardiff.* The achievement convinced him that he had a career before him and in the fall he entered Harvard University to study with George Pierce Baker in his course English 47. "The 47 Workshop" was the first devoted to the craft of playwriting at an American university, and Baker's responsive criticism to his students' work endeared him to his graduates, many of whom would become leading figures in the American theatre.

Although he had planned to continue at Harvard for a second year, he went instead to Greenwich Village in New York, where he met intellectuals and artists elated with excitement over the new possibilities of art and politics in the United States. In the summer of 1916, he vacationed with a friend, Terry Carlin, in Provincetown, Massachusetts, where he joined with the writer George Cram Cook, nicknamed Jig; his wife, the playwright Susan Glaspell; John Reed and Louise Bryant; Wilbur Daniel Steele; Mary Heaton Vorse; Saxe Commins; Robert Edmond Jones; and others in the formation of what would become a pioneering art theatre.

A year earlier the vacationers from New York had staged four original one-act plays in one of the cottages. A second bill was performed in a shed built out over the water on a wharf. The satisfying and successful amusement encouraged the group to continue the next summer. In July 1916, their amateur production of *Bound East for Cardiff* ushered in a new era in the American theatre. The sincerity and the simple truth of the play's poetic realism was so inspirational that the group, with Cook as its leader, determined to continue producing plays in New York City that fall. At O'Neill's suggestion they called themselves "The Playwright's Theatre" and committed themselves to fostering native playwrights in order to create an American drama substantially different from what O'Neill scornfully called "the Broadway showshop." This determined, O'Neill's life became one of unremitting dedication to his writing, and the "seeking flight" came to an end.

1 • TO LILLIAN BRENNAN. ALS 4 pp. (De La Salle / 59 St. and 6th / [New York]) [Yale]

[Fall 1901]

My dear Cousin:— I was very glad to hear from you that Teddy is doing so nicely. I wish I was up there and could see him. I wonder would he remember me but I suppose he has forgotten all about me. Mama says that I may go up and spend half of the vacation we get at Christmas at Sheridans[1] and I would like to do this very much as I could see Teddy and take him out and everything. I think that if I go up there I will take Teddy back to school with me as the Director of this place says I may. He would have a nice large yard to play in and another dog for company. I would take him out in the park and let him be in the yard while the boys are in class. Jamie has made a big hit in (Albert)[2] and there are big notices about him in all the papers wherever they go. Tell Phil[3] that if I go to his house I will teach him how to play football. I wish he was boarding here as he and I would have fine fun. You want to write Agnes[4] and tell her to come and see me some afternoon. I am going to Sarah's to spend Thanksgiving and I expect to have a lot of fun. The Wilder baby has had the Chicken pox and the poor little Kid is just getting over it.

I have a bad cold and have to take bitter tasting coff medicine.

Well I must close with love to all (Teddy included).

I am Your loving cousin, Eugene O'Neill

---

2 • TO "PROFESSOR."[1] ALS 4 pp. (Stationery headed: Hotel Bellerlaire / Broadway & 77th St. / New York) [Notre Dame]

Sept. 17, 1904

Dear Professor; I hope the laxity of my letter writing will be pardoned by you for I confess to be a rather poor correspondent.

We shut up the house and came to New York about a [week?] ago Wednesday. To tell the truth I am not over joyous at leaving the dear old place especially my "Island of Monte Cristo" and the delightful moonlight rows.

Mama is here in the Hotel with me but Papa and Jamie have opened the season in Boston. Mama is very well and wishes to be remembered to all her old friends especially Sister Aloysius.

School opens on Wednesday (Alas! Woe is me! Pity t'is t'is true!) and I will have to go back to work. But "Les Affaires sont les affaires" as the French say.

I have a fine idea. If you have time write all your letters to me in French (except the address) and I will answer in it.

Hoping to hear from you soon I remain "avec beaucoup d'amour" to you and Sister Aloysius. Your true friend, Eugene O'Neill

address letter
    Betts Academy,
    Stamford,
    Conn.

1. O'Neill's second cousins, who lived in New London.
2. James O'Neill, Jr., was playing the role of Albert de Morcerf, Edmond Dantès's son, in his father's touring production of *Monte Cristo*.
3. Philip Sheridan.
4. Agnes Brennan, Lillian's sister.

1. The professor, apparently O'Neill's French teacher at De La Salle Institute, cannot be identified.

3 • TO MARION WELCH.   ALS 6 pp. (325 Pequot Ave. / New London, Conn.) [Yale]

[July 24, 1905]

Ma chère "Boutade"   You cannot imagine with what feelings of joy I received your letter this morning. All the more so, because it was unexpected, for I thought that, by this time, New London and all in it were but faint memories of the misty past to you. I am very happy to find out that I was mistaken.

I cannot say how much I missed and still miss you. New London has now relapsed into a somnambulent state which is far from pleasing and all on account of your departure. I saw Marian[1] off to that "dear old Noank" after you had left. Noank is really a fine place—to be buried in.

It must have been sacrilegious for you to sprint with that 150—Ring the bell! I miss your "windmill motion" in the row boat but, to be truthful, it was far from a windmill towards the end and more like an expert's. (Now will you be good). I have not even been up to hear the orchestra at the Pequot[2] for fear I should be overcome by pleasant memories (and the bum music).

Those pictures are exceedingly unkind to me and I hope I do not look anything like them. They are good however considering the sun was in our faces (and the subjects as you cruelly mentioned). Do not forget to send me the others and if I may ask for the millionth time for your photo "Please! Ah! Please! I think you're the meanest girl I ever knew." But all joking aside I assure you that I want it ever so much. And let us keep up this correspondence, begun with such "earnest of success." If you knew what a break it is in the dull, monotonous existence up here I feel sure you would not refuse.

I am getting to be a perfect book worm and read all morning, swim in afternoon as usual (as you said in your letter I receive no more morning baths) and read all night. Can you beat it? It has the "Cynic Tub"[3] "beaten to a pulp." Oh! Excuse me ma cherie. I forgot that was one of your sore points. However do not let it "prick your conscience." Hee! Haw!

That reminds me. I have sworn off sarcasm as a bad job as you will probably notice in this letter. It is really a very contemptible thing, don't you think so. Almost as bad as making puns.

Miss Earl tells me she expects Marian down soon. This is joyful news and I only wish you were coming too. But I may be in Hartford soon. "You never can tell." I have a mind to go to Trinity[4] just so as to be near you. Now you must acknowledge that that is a horrible sacrifice.

Miss Keeney still floats around in that hat like a nymph or a Jersey cow, I can't tell which. I guess salmon is still 25 cents a pound. Would that it would rise to 26 providing she would discard that headgear.

Well the sand in my hour glass is about run out and I must "put on brakes." Please send me your photo with the other pictures and thus make me even more than I am now. Your eternal slave   Eugene O'Neill

Given on the 24th day of July in the year of our Lord 1905.

1. Marian Flagg, a mutual friend.
2. The Pequot House, New London.
3. Reference to Greek cynic philosopher Diogenes (c. 412–323 B.C.), who advocated the simple life by discarding his possessions and living in a tub.
4. Trinity College, Hartford, Connecticut.

4 • TO MARION WELCH.   ALS 4 pp. ([325 Pequot Ave. / New London, Conn.]) [Yale]

August 5, 1905

Ma chère "Boutade":—   Received your most welcome letter with the pictures enclosed yesterday. The pictures are much better than the ones you sent before don't you think so? Thank you ever so much for your "half give-in" even though it be only a half.

Marian must have come over when I was in New York as I have not seen her. Miss Earl says she will be over soon however. Would that I might see you soon and let you complete your rowing lessons! New York was almost as slow as New London. Everyone I know was away and it was hot!! It makes me sweat to think of it.

I looked up Jean Ingelow and read "High Tide on the Coast of Lincolnshire."[1] It is fine isn't it! That parody on "Annabel Lee" is very clever. Am glad to hear you have learned the original.[2] Some of the lines express my feelings exactly especially the following:

> "And neither the angels in heaven above
> Nor the demons down under the sea
> Can ever dissever my soul from the soul
> Of the beautiful Annabel Lee"

Except her name is not Annabel Lee but M . . . W . . . . But what is it you said one time about personal remarks?

Life up here is just the same. It makes the famous "Simple Life" look like "The Pace that Kills." To say it is slow would be using language as weak as Watts Hymns for Infant Minds. But I go to Saratoga for a couple of days soon and I hope "to wake up." I was up to one of the "hops" at the Pequot last Saturday night and danced with the fair ones (not even fair). I was bored to death and said "Never again for little Eugene" and by the nine gods I never will unless you or someone else that I know are there.

I don't see how anyone can go to Darwin for enjoyment. Alex. Dumas père pour le mien. I could read every book in the world and no heroes could ever replace "D'Artagnan, Athos, Porthos and Aramis," "Monte Cristo" and "Bussy"[3] in my estimation. "Charlie Steele" however has a high place.

I am going to fix up my camera and take pictures of the New York Yacht Club when it is here. I will send you some if you would like them.

Do not let Tennis take all your thoughts because then you will forget how to row. And that would be a great misfortune in so promising a pupil. My brother and I swam the river this morning and I am some tired.

If you want to read some very pretty poems I recommend Thomas Moore to you. He has written some "peaches" and I never tire reading them and have learned a few.

You really will have to excuse this torn leaf but I found out just now that there is no more paper but this and as I am in a hurry to post it I beg of you to except my excuse.

Write soon "ma cherie" and lit up the monotonous days of   Your devoted admirer Eugene

---

1. Poem (1863) by English poet Jean Ingelow (1820–1897).
2. Poem (1849) by Edgar Allan Poe (1809–1849).
3. Characters in *The Three Musketeers* (1844), *The Count of Monte Cristo* (1845), and *The Lady of Monsoreau* (1846), respectively, by French novelist Alexandre Dumas, père (1802–1870).

Marion Welch, O'Neill's "Boutade."

5 • TO MARION WELCH.   ALS 4 pp. (325 Pequot Ave. / New London, Conn.) [Yale]

[c. August 15, 1905]

My dear Marion:—   What is the matter? I hope you have not acquired a cramp in the hand from playing tennis so that letter writing is forbidden. It is over a week since I have heard from you. You will say that is not so long. But in this modern "Sleepy Hollow" every day is composed of 24 hours, each one equivalent to ten in any other place—but why multiply details—it is centuries since I have heard from you.

The New York Yacht Club were in here over Sunday but never a bit of sun appeared so I did not take many pictures. There were some fine yachts in the harbor and I was sorry you were not here to look them over (from the seat in the stern of the boat).

L'autre Marian was over a week ago Sunday. I took her picture and she took mine. Will send you them when they are fixed. We missed you very much and especially that persuasive way of yours "Please! Ah! Pl...ease." (You see I do not forget)

The weather is so cold up here that it would cause the blush of envy and shame to mantle the cheek of an ice-berg. "And o'er the one half world Nature seems dead."

The other night it was clear and the moon was full (but I wasn't!) but the wind was blowing a gale and the sea was pretty high and "mon frère et moi" went out in the boat and rowed way out in the Sound. It was fine. The waves were so high that when we were on top of them we could see the mortgages on the houses in Shelter Island. All joking aside it was certainly rough and we enjoyed it immensely.

Do write soon and throw a little sunlight into the chasm of Despair where lies.   Your devoted slave,   Eugene

---

6 • TO MARION WELCH.   ALS 4 pp. (325 Pequot Ave. / New London, Conn.) [Yale]

[late August? 1905]

Ma chère "Boutade":—   I cannot tell you with how much pleasure I received your letter, especially after such a long wait. I find that the old maxim "Absence makes the heart grow fonder" is quite true, particularly when one is expecting a letter.

I was indeed surprised to see the postmark of your letter. It is a new one on me. I suppose you are now quite an adept at milking cows and feeding chickens.

While you were enjoying the scent of new mown hay on a farm, I was in gay Saratoga, where "the Lid" is off for good. I visited the race track and won some money on the "ponies" and then went to Canfield's Saratoga Club (a refined name for one of the most fashionable (and notorious) gambling joints in the world) and watched the rich boys throw away coin on roulette and faro. Having acquired a fever for gambling I went back to the Hotel and "rustled my pile" on the slot machines. After a while (when my cash account looked like a large minus sign) I decided that gambling was a very bad thing anyway and that hotel proprietors who keep slot machines ought to be lynched. I had a relief from the dreary solitude of New London and hated to come back. In a graveyard there is some excitement in reading the inscriptions on the tombstones but in N.L.—

Marian was over last Sunday but did not stay but a minute and I never knew she was here at all until I saw her leaving.

Your letters are the only things I look forward to now and I am sure you would write more frequently if you knew how I love to hear from you.

I am now reading *The Laughing Man* by Victor Hugo. Have you read it? I suppose you have, dear little book worm that you are. I will take your advice and read *The American*

Prisoner[1] if I can get it. I asked my brother about the other book you mentioned by Harland,[2] and he said he liked *The Cardinal's Snuff Box* better. I have not read it. *My Friend, Prospero* is another good book by the same man (and his latest).

I have met an agent for the Madison Automobile Co. and he has a 60 horse power machine worth seven thousand in which he has taken me out. We went up to Norwich and back (29 miles) in forty minutes. I have not been able to part my hair since I was so frightened.

I will send you the pictures of the N.Y.Y.C. when I get them developed and printed.

Well I guess I have "snowballed my layout" of interesting things to relate and so "Au revoir ma cherie je vous aimerai toujours et je vous baisserai en pensée."   Your devoted admirer   Eugene

---

7 • TO MARION WELCH.   ALS 4 pp. (Stationery headed: Hotel Bellerlaire / Broadway & 77th St. / New York) [Yale]

[early September 1905]

My dear Marion:—   I am very glad you took the initiative and wrote me. The reason I was so lax is because we were packing up to leave New London and I had a lot of work to do.

We arrived in New York Wednesday morning after a stormy passage on the boat, in which the fog horn kept me awake all night. I was sorry to leave New London for I was beginning to have a fine time up there.

My brother, "Con" Daly (of Yale crew fame) and myself went to see *The Prodigal Son* last night. It is a dramatization of Hall Caine's novel of that name and is very sad. In fact all the audience were crying (to get their money back). I suppose you have read the book? If not, you have a treat in store for you.

I came out to a farm in Jersey this morning and write from there. It is rented from my father by a breeder of race horses. Talk about your slow places! It has the land of the Lotus Eaters beaten to a pulp. There is nothing to do but ride horse back and dream—of you. I am going back to New York as soon as I can find a reasonable excuse to leave. That is why I write you on our hotel paper in order that you may know my New York address.

I was sorry to hear that Marian had returned to Hartford as I had hopes of seeing her before she left. If you meet her, tell her that she owes me a letter.

You say you feel funny at not going back to school. I wish I could partake of those delightful sensations.

Have just finished reading *The Man on the Box.*[1] I suppose you have read it. It is very nicely written, I thought.

Am glad you thought the pictures were good. That is more than I can say for them because so many of them had dark blotches on them. Speaking of pictures don't you think it is time to give in another half and send me your photo? "Please! Ah Please!"

I trust that you will not veto this petition if you believe in the undying affection of Your devoted admirer   Eugene

P.S. Excuse burns on paper made in drying ink.

---

1. Novel (1903) by Eden Phillpotts (1862–1960).
2. Henry Harland (1861–1905).

1. Novel (1904) by Harold McGrath (1871–1932).

8 • TO MARION WELCH.   ALS 4 pp. (Stationery headed: Betts Academy, / Stamford, Conn.) [Yale]

[c. October 10, 1905]

My dear Marion:—   I received your most welcome letter a few days ago and would have answered it sooner, but for a trip to New York over Sunday, which I made. I must again apologize for the paper on which I am writing but the Betts seal paper has not come yet and I am forced to use this.

What you said regarding my accepting Boardman's invitation would be true last year but I am glad to say he has learned a lesson and is a very good fellow. The proof of this is that he has been admitted to a very select secret society, composed wholly of what is termed, good fellows. I may mention that I also am a member and one of the framers of the constitution.

However I never had any idea of accepting his invitation (except to see you) for little old New York is good enough for me at any season. Have you any prospects of visiting there this year? If so I wish you would let me know, for I should like nothing better, than to do every thing I could to make your stay amusing and interesting.

Our football team played its first game Saturday with Stevens High School and we won 17−0. We play Yale Freshmen next Wednesday and, I beg of you, if you wish to have a good opinion of the school, do not look up the score in the paper. Richard Croker's (The Tammany chief) son is here and plays on the team. He is quite a sport. I am not playing football this year but run two or three miles every day in preparation for track.

You must have had a great time on Mt. Washington. I have never been in the White Mountains but was on top of Pike's Peak (Colorado) which is fourteen thousand feet high (if my geography has not yet gone back on me).

I stop and it is finished the bell invites me. Hear it Eugene for it is the knell that summons me to go to bed or to get—(after Shakespeare).

"Au revoir ma cherie" and write soon.   Your own,   Eugene

---

9 • TO MARION WELCH.   ALS 6 pp. (Betts Academy / [Stamford, Conn.]) [Yale]

Nov. 11, 1905

My dear Marion:—   I hope you will pardon the delay in answering your letter but I have been very busy of late and could not find time. I have started in to write to you several times but never got very far.

Boardman was laid up in football and went home so I suppose he has told you all the news of Betts by this time. Anyway he told me he would probably drop in to see you. We had a very *bum!* football team of which Boardman was a member. The season is finished for us now as we have canceled our last game.

Speaking of games I intend to join the Princeton rooters at the Yale-Princeton game a week from today. Are you going to see it? It looks as if Yale would win from form but you never can tell and I have great hopes.

I was in New York on election night and had a fine time. Broadway that night reminded me of Pequot Ave. on a rainy Sunday afternoon (Put that dog out).

We had a fine "rough house" here a few weeks ago. It was at night. All of us stuck our heads out of the windows of our rooms about one o'clock in the morning and gave four or five Betts cheers. Having awakened Mr. Betts[1] the fun began. It consisted, in the main, of wet

1. William (Billy) Betts, headmaster and son of the founder of Betts Academy.

towels and pillows and soap and pails and waste-baskets, thrown with intent to injure the visages of the Herr Professor on our floor or of any one else in the way. When Betts arrived on the scene, "mirabile dictu" all doors were shut and the snores of the sleepers would have waked the dead. When he finally did awaken us no one could give him the least information in regard to it. I am sure he would have believed himself in under the influence of an hallucination (occasioned by some of his half cooked hash) if the weapons of attack had not been laying all over the hall. But to this day he does not know who were engaged in the adventure nor is he liable to find it out. I would have liked to have gone to the fair at which you played the waitress act. But I'm afraid it would have been hard to coax me away from the restaurant and that I would have overfed myself.

Did you go to see the *Pearl and Pumpkin*?[2] If so how did you like it? I saw it in New York and did not think there was anything to it except scenery and a few songs. *Roger Bros. in Ireland*[3] is the best thing I have seen this year. If it goes to Hartford, be sure to see it. I have also seen "Houdini the Handcuff King" in vaudeville. He is fine and does a very mystifying act by unlocking seven pairs of hand cuffs, all different makes and locked upon him by detectives from the nearest station house. Anyone may bring any kind of hand cuffs and lock them on him themselves if they wish. He certainly had me guessing.

Well au revoir, write soon and in the meantime believe me to be as I have been for months and always will be, Your own   Eugene

---

10 • TO MARION WELCH.   ALS 3 pp. (Stationery headed: Betts Academy, / Stamford, Conn.) [Yale]

[c. December 12, 1905]

My dear Marion:—   It is, I suppose, useless to ask for pardon for making you wait such a long time for an answer to your letter. All I have to say is that it got here just before our Thanksgiving vacation and I forgot it in the excitement of going to New York. I just happened to find it today in my desk and determined "to do the deed before the purpose cooled" and write you immediately. I hope I am forgiven, for I cherish the remembrance of some of the happiest days of my life (passed in a rowboat in New London harbor) far too greatly to have any hitch come in our correspondence. I also have a picture of a certain girl with a dog (Teddy?) which I cherish even if it is only a half give-in.

But to throw away the pill that I was smoking and to come back to earth. Our Christmas holidays begin on the twentieth of this month and maybe I won't be glad to get to old New York again.

So you went to see old worm eaten *Monte Cristo*. It may be all right for those who have never seen it before but for me, *Back to the Bamboo*. I saw six plays during Thanksgiving vacation and we only had five days. They were all musical comedies (I always confessed to degraded tastes). Marie Cahill in *Moonshine* was about the best of all.

Have read quite a few books lately. *My Friend Prospero* by Henry Harland is fine and I like it as well as the *Cardinal's Snuff Box*. Read it by all means if you have not done so already. I have also read *The Masquerader* and *Beverly of Graustark* and *My Lady of the North*.[1] I suppose you have read all of these. I want to read *The Clansman*[2] but never can get it at the library. At

2. Musical comedy (1905) by Paul West and William W. Denslowe.
3. Musical (1905) by Max Rogers (1873–1932) and Gus Rogers (1869–1908).

1. Three novels, all published in 1904, by Katherine Cecil Thurston (1875–1911), George Barr Mc-Cutcheon (1866–1928), and Randall Parrish (1858–1923), respectively.
2. Novel (1905) by Thomas Dixon (1864–1946), on which the movie *Birth of a Nation* (1915) was based.

this time of the year when there is nothing to do in the way of sports, good books come in very handy.

Boardman said he met you at a dance during Thanksgiving and that you were as pretty as ever.

Well please do not take my delay as an example but write soon. I leave Tuesday afternoon for New York so if you don't write before then address your letter to Lexington Hotel, 47 St. between Bway and 6th.

By the way what has happened to Marian Flagg? I shall probably drop in to see Miss Earl in New York sometime during Christmas.

The "bell invites me" to go to class so "au revoir."   Your own   Eugene

---

11 • TO JAMES AND ELLA O'NEILL.   ALS 2 pp. (Tegucigalpa / [Honduras])
[Harvard]

Nov. 9, 1909

My dear Father and Mother:—   Received a letter from both of you yesterday. Also a few postal cards from Jamie from Dallas. We arrived in Amapala Tuesday and started out on mule back the next day arriving in the Capital on Saturday. This means that we travelled nearly 100 miles on mule back through the mountains in three days. I was terribly sore at first but feel all right now after two days rest. The food and accommodations along the road were better than I had imagined and everything would be O.K. if it were not for the fleas that infest the native huts and eat you alive at night. I am a mass of bites and itch all over. You can really have no conception of how damnably aggravating these pests are. The native villages are the most squalid and dirty it has ever been my misfortune to see. Pigs, buzzard, dogs, chickens and children all live in the same room and the sanitary conditions of the huts are beyond belief. However the cities—like Tegucigalpa—are fine and the climate wonderful. The temperature never hardly gets over 85° or under 70°. They have bands in all the towns— fine bands—that play on the plaza on certain nights in the week and people don't rush around like they do in N.Y. Down here they are in no hurry. If we don't do it today why we can tomorrow—that is the way they seem to feel about it. Taking it all in all I like the country and the people and think there is every chance in the world for making good. I have spells of dejection and the blues but Mr. and Mrs. Stevens[1] are very congenial and such fits do not generally last long. Mrs. Stevens is bearing up fine under all the hardships—which is more than one woman in a thousand could do.

We start out again for the property tomorrow morning at day light and expect to arrive there in the course of a week. The trails are very rough just at present and progress is slow on account of the rainy season just being over. So next week promises to be the hardest we will have to endure. You probably will not hear from me for sometime after this letter but do not worry about me for "the devil takes care of his own." We will not have any opportunity for either receiving or sending mail for at least three weeks.

Was glad to hear from Papa that he thinks *The White Sister*[2] will stay the limit. I would never have expected that it would. How is Brittain[3] making out? I suppose when I see you

1. Mining engineer Earl C. Stevens and his wife, Ann, with whom O'Neill went to Honduras on a gold-prospecting expedition.
2. Play by Francis Marion Crawford (1854–1909) in which James O'Neill, Sr., had opened on Broadway in September 1909.
3. Henry L. Brittain, for whose New York-Chicago Supply Company O'Neill had worked as a secretary in 1907–08. James O'Neill, Sr., owned stock in Brittain's company.

again that Mama will have all her money back.[4] What? Well, here's hoping that she will.

Tell Papa that there are lots of mining lands down here that can be taken up for a song and they are laying loose because no one has the capital to hold them or develop them. Holding some of them as an investment for the future would not be a bad idea. All the Americans claim that Honduras has more gold than all the States combined but on account of the difficulties of transportation etc. it has to wait until people with capital take it up.

I am as brown as a native and am growing a mustache in order to look absolutely as shiftless and dirty as the best of them. It is funny the way everyone down here struts around with a six-shooter and a belt full of cartridges on their hip—just like a 30 cent Western melodrama. So far my progress in learning Spanish has been slow as I have had no time to study it since I landed and was too lazy to do so on the boat. But out at camp I intend to take it up seriously.

Better send me down some socks—double thickness—as the kind you can buy down here are not much good and I will need them by the time they reach here.

Well good-bye. Lots of love to both of you and please write and let me know the news. Haven't seen a paper in four weeks. I must hurry to bed in order to snatch a few hours sleep before day light—if the fleas permit.   Your loving son   Eugene

P.S. Papa please tell John, the barkeep, that I received his letter and will answer it at the first opportunity I get.

---

12 • TO JAMES AND ELLA O'NEILL.   ALS 3 pp. (Guajiniquil / [Honduras])
[Harvard]

Christmas Day [1909]

My dear Father & Mother:—   Merry Christmas! For you I hope it may be merry but speaking for myself it is the most dismal and depressing day I have ever passed. I have been sick for the past week with fever and an acute bilious attack caused by the rotten food, vilely cooked, that we have to put up with. Since Nov. 11th when we left Tegucigalpa we have had absolutely no butter, bread but three or four times and milk about the same number. Nothing but beans—and lots of times we cannot even get them—*fried*, rice, *fried*, salt dried meat, *fried* (much tougher than leather) with sometimes an egg or two thrown in. But eggs are very scarce. All the natives have chickens but they are too lazy to look for the eggs. We always get "tortillas"—a heavy soggy imitation of a pancake made of corn enough to poison the stomach of an ostrich. There is the limit of your bill-of-fare—breakfast, dinner and supper—day after day—week after week. Everything they cook is steeped in grease—alike unhealthy and unsatisfying. You get terribly hungry and force down a lot of this food and the result is your stomach gets in bad condition. No fresh meat. Game is scarce and difficult to bag where we are now. The fleas are fierce and *I have never been free from bites one day since I arrived in this country*. There are also ticks that burrow in under your skin and form sores. Gnats and mosquitoes are present in abundance and do their best to make an already distressing life unbearable. From a two months experience, and after having been in all the different zones of this country, I give it as my candid opinion and fixed belief that God got his inspiration for Hell after creating Honduras. The country as far as climate and natural advantages goes is fine but the natives are the lowest, laziest, most ignorant bunch of

---

4. James O'Neill, Sr., had invested some of his wife's money in the company which was sponsoring the mining expedition.

brainless bipeds that ever polluted a land and retarded its future. Until some just Fate grows weary of watching the gropings in the dark of these human maggots and exterminates them, until the Universe shakes these human lice from its sides, Honduras has no future, no hopes of being anything but what it is at present—a Siberia of the tropics. As long as the yearly revolutions keep up foreign capital and foreigners will steer clear of the whole outfit. Even granting that the revolutions cease it will take an awful lot to get an American (who has not previously slept in a cowshed and eaten out of a trough) to live here for any amount of time. Most of those who are not crooks do not linger long. Transportation is solely by mules and it is well nigh impossible to get anything done. I will stick until the first of June when the rainy season commences and "colentura"—tropical or malignant malarial fever—is very prevalent. Nearly all the Americans return to the states at this time to escape the fever and stay until the rainy season expires and I will come home then. I don't know if I am getting any salary or not as Stevens has said nothing about it. It would sure be some shock to find out I was enduring all this for love. Better find out for me.

Since my last letter we left the camp on the upper Seale because Stevens found that the gold was finer up there than down below where he was last year—contrary to the reports of the natives—and we started to go to his old camp or below it where the gold is coarser. At this town—consisting of three houses—we met the man who had spoken last year of the "Mosquitia" unexplored country—North Coast—and he told Stevens of a river called Geneio where he said there was lots of gold. So we hired a dugout boat and Stevens, the Dago and I with two natives went four days poling down a big river called the Paducah which flows through the "Mosquitia" district until we came to the Geneio which flows into it. We went by boat five miles up the Geneio but had to land there and try to proceed on foot. This we soon found to be impossible as the tropical jungle was so dense that cutting a trail would take months. Then as we had not enough provisions to stay any longer and as the lower part of the river was too swift and would bury the gold too deep to get at so that Stevens could not tell much about it although he said the indications were that there would be lots of gold farther up the river in the mountains, we came back and arrived here last week. From here we go to the Seale where we hope to make permanent camp for the rest of the year. The delays Stevens has had to put up with from the natives would have disheartened many a man and if he is longer in getting started than he expected it is no fault of his.

You have probably read of the Revolution down here. Do not worry about it as they are of the comic opera variety and only affect Americans in that they delay the mail. *I only received your letter of Oct. 31 two days ago. Please, please* send me three pounds of Bull Durham Tobacco by mail. It is cheap and the tobacco down here is rotten except for cigars. Send this letter to Jamie when you get through with it as I do not know his route far enough ahead to write and I had lost his other one.[1] Am glad to hear you have sent some magazines. They will be more welcome than anything I know of.

Cannot tell how I miss you both. I never realized how much home and Father & Mother meant until I got so far away from them. Lots of love to you both.   Your loving son Eugene

    P.S. Menu for Christmas Dinner
        Beans
        Tortillas
        One egg
        Tea made of lemon leaves

1. James O'Neill, Jr., was touring in *The Traveling Salesman* (1908), by Canadian dramatist James Forbes (1871–1938).

13 • TO DAVID RUSSELL LYMAN.[1]   ALS 1 p. (Stationery headed: HOTEL ASCOT / 62 Madison Avenue, Cor. Twenty-Seventh Street / New York [Gaylord]

Dec. 20, 1912

Dear Sir: Have just received a letter from Dr. Miller[2] in which he states that he has written to you concerning my entrance into the sanitorium and that you have notified him of a vacancy on Dec. 24th. Therefore, I shall go to Wallingford on the afternoon of that date unless advised to the contrary by you in the meantime.

Thanking you for this early opportunity to regain my health, I remain   Sincerely yours, Eugene G. O'Neill

---

14 • TO JESSICA RIPPIN.[1]   TLS 4 pp. (325 Pequot Avenue / New London, Conn.) [Detroit P.L.]

[postmarked May 7, 1914]

Dearest Jessica:—   "Credete a me," I have meant to answer your letter long ere this but—how futile excuses sound when they are true!—I have been so beset with feverish activities such as launching boats, manicuring the front lawn of the ancestral acres, pruning the first act of my four-act drama,[2] walking to meals and back again, eating, sleeping, answering father's voluminous correspondence, (he takes a mean advantage of my knowing how to typewrite), and this and that and the other, that I have postponed answering your letter[3] day after day—and there you are. Of course it would have been possible for me to have taken my typewriter in hand and dashed off a few maunderings anent the weather and other current topics but I knew you would rather wait until I had time to stop and think. You are of a charitable turn of mind and will pardon me, will you not, for this fault and the many others, numerous as holes in the robe of Diogenes, which plague me?

As you will note by the above address I have paid my farewells to the old back porch of the Rippin chateau and am now once more ensconced in the Old Manse of the O'Neills. I find my glassed-in sun boudoir tolerably pleasant albeit Old Sol hath a vicious habit of awakening me at the unhaloed hour of six or thereabouts, for like all true believers I lie facing the east, and the sun is an early riser these days. I was possessed of a great loneliness the first few days after I left your house. I sadly missed the languid exuberance of Dolly of the Luxuriant Locks[4] as she called out a soothing good night when, bed-ward bound and bathrobe clad, I used to flit past that sanctum of charms, her room. And, is there need for me to say—(Yes, yes, go on!) what a gaping abyss was left in my life when I could no longer gather at first hand an earful of the vivacious vaporings of the loquacious Emily Belle.[5] Seriously I find my present solitude, though pleasant in the main, rather irksome at whiles, especially on days like this when the rain monotonously and fretfully patters on the roof.

1. Superintendent of Gaylord Farm Sanatorium, Wallingford, Connecticut.
2. James Alexander Miller, nationally known tuberculosis specialist to whom James O'Neill, Sr., had sent Eugene.

1. One of seven children of James and Helen Rippin. The Rippins operated a boarding house at 416 Pequot Avenue, New London, where O'Neill lived during the winter of 1913–14, while his parents were on tour.
2. *Bread and Butter*, never produced; first published in *"Children of the Sea" and Three Other Unpublished Plays by Eugene O'Neill*, ed. Jennifer McCabe Atkinson (Washington, D.C.: NCR Microcard Editions, 1972), pp. 1–84.
3. Jessica Rippin was working as a dietitian in the Philadelphia school system.
4. Grace, Jessica's sister.
5. Emily, Jessica's sister.

God weeps and men curse, and all of life becomes a tragic folly and an idiotic pose. We mouth the dregs and find their bitterness—sweet! The trees I can see from the window remind me for some ridiculous reason of homely, skinny-legged girls in drenched bathing suits which cling to their unsightly members; the river is of a doleful grayness with wind spots here and there like patches of soot on a factory window-pane; Scott's dock looks exactly like the unsightly abortion which it is, and the tug boats putter around dejectedly; my row boat is slowly filling with water which I, with many a twinge in the back, will have to bail out on the morrow, God help me, poor wretch!; Groton—oh, well, Groton looks like Groton which is anathema enough. Father is in New York and I am sitting here writing to you and freezing to death because I am too lazy and inert to light the furnace, and because— Oh, furnaces are a horrible bore anyway. Grimed with smears is he who fiddles with them. So you see my mood and the weather's mood chime perfectly. If I had not reserved the inestimable pleasure of unburdening myself to you on just such a day, life would be truly unbearable this fifth of May. I would commit suicide if I could find a tree strong enough to hang myself on without getting wet to the skin. Bloody awful, I call it, what? One can't even die decently out of doors this Spring.

I had no idea I would have to leave 416 in such haste but Father was lonely and had to solace himself with the comforting presence of his younger mistake so I collected my Lares and Penates and blew. I could hear duty calling and—Oh, damn all duty anyway, what say you? What I have been going to say all along was that there is *only one thing* to do on a day of Spring rain and that is—but why burden you with details? Suffice it to say that I cannot do it, being alone, and having no one to whom I can appeal. Nobody loves me no more since you have went. I ain't got no pashinut friends upon whose buzum I c'd lay my weary bean. I might just as well be one of those dark-complected gentry who guard the harems of Constantinople and environs. Do you wonder I am sad? I see Youth flit by while I toil not neither do I spin in the vineyard of Love. (The metaphor is a little mixed but never mind. I've never been in a vineyard so perhaps they do spin something there—lies, I know, if the wine be strong enough.) I see lovers sporting all about, I stumble over their recumbent forms as I come down through the lot o'nights, but, alas, I am as sterile as Salmacis, as barren of delights as a frog is devoid of feathers. True, my soul is ravished with a passion so etherial and spiritual that I sometimes wonder whether it really belongs to me or not. The ship of my soul has found its life harbor, in calm waters kissed by the sun of the true happiness. The love of Caesar for his wife to be is above suspicion and passeth all understanding—most of all Caesar's. Meanwhile the low-browed ape which is the flesh of me clamors for requital, as once ten thousand years ago it ran gibbering through the prehistoric gloom and sprang from tree to tree in pursuit of its female. The mud inside of me churns and bubbles. I seethe with longings; desire has me by the throat, and I—go for long rows or mow the lawn. Even Ida commences to look good. Alas it was not always thus. Rise up, ye ghosts of the past, and speak for me! O loves of old, cry aloud the tale of your delicious infamies! My soul is whitened with the scars of many old leprosies. And now—and now, forsooth, I am Sir Galahad, the Virgin Knight, sans reproach, the devil fly away with me! To refuse sin to the unrepentent sinner—that is too cruel. Lord, hear my prayer! *I would sin!* What is sin? Tell me, sweet Jessica. I think it is the bad digestion of a man of sixty, a dream of sour grapes conceived in the brain of an old maid with a hair lip. Sin and its punishment, virtue and its reward; piffle upon piffle until everything in the world is turned upside down and all that is delightful is dubbed "Bad" and all that is disagreeable and ugly "Good." The immortal Gods deliver me from Good and Evil! I tell you such values are the triumph of the commonplace, the low-browed mob at its zenith with its insolent "Thou shalt not." To be true to one-self and one's highest hope—*that is good!* To be different and hold oneself aloof from their virtue—that is

Good! To scorn them and their values; to be bad—that is Good! But to mix with them, to inhale their foul breath, their right and wrong; to bow oneself before their stupid idol; to heed their opinions, to harken to their vapid praise of all that is commonplace; to be contaminated by their approval—THAT is BAD.

And, after all, what's the difference? "We are such stuff as dreams are made on and our little life is rounded with a sleep." I and my ideal, you and your ideal, all of us poor human midges with our fretful whining cry, our feeble droning wail of impotence—dreams and thin dust of illusions which will vanish when the dreamer vanishes and be one with the same oblivion. And above and around us the ever-mocking laughter of those immortal and immoral Gods.

Volplaning down from such lofty ether of Nietzsche-Schopenhauer philosophical discussion which ends nowhere and is as aimless as life is, and returning once more to New London, the acme of all that is prosaic, I would say that I have a bone to pick with you.

As I lamp over your last epistle, as I scan the screed, as I give your script the "once-over," one thing I find in it which peeves and piques me. You say I am "very, very young." Fie! Fie! Jessica! That jibe verges perilously on the platitudinous. As if life were a question of years! Surely it is not a question of how long but of how much one has lived. If you have not learned that yet, how can you hope to teach me? Experience is the only true test of one's age. How much of life have you made a part of yourself? Have you reached out for everything, tried for everything, hesitated before no "You must not," realized *with joy* every new sensation, stripped things of their husk and picked out your own Bad and Good with a clear eye and a robust, not a sickly conscience? If you have, then you have lived much more than ninety-nine hundredths of the grey beards, whatever your age may be, and your opinion of life in general is worth infinitely more than theirs. Most people "die not, for their life was death, but cease; and round their narrow lips the mould falls close." As they grow old they sink into their pitiful rut deeper and deeper. The mob calls that wisdom. Pooh, Jessica, that remark was unworthy of you. I have lived much more than any three men in the town and you ought to know it. My ideas are hardly based on inexperience or a cloistered existence. Why link youth with fatuity?

Besides, Jessica, you're not a candidate for the Home for the aged yourself, are you? Two years—is it two?—is not such a high pinnacle from which to survey the follies of twenty-five. I hope you're not becoming sedate and settled already. That would be horrible.

As for "thinking lots of good of lots of people" as per your advice I would ask you to remember a certain remark of Horace Walpole's: "I could love my country, were it not for my fellow countrymen."

Keeping plodding? Sure I will. I don't care very much for your choice of a word to express the strivings of an impecunious young author to project the phantasmagoria of his own brain on paper, but this may be prejudice on my part. I always connect the word with Gray's "The plowman homeward plods his weary way." I'll keep on with my rainbow chasing and, who knows, I may in time find the fabled pot of gold. At any rate there is a joy in the battle itself well worth the attempt and (I will now poach on your friend Ham's[6] preserves by quoting Stevenson) "To find out where joy resides, and give it a voice far beyond singing—for to miss the joy is to miss all. In the joy of the actors lies the sense of any action."

Dolly and Emily have been to have their palms read by some Arabian seeress (probably born in South Bend, Ind.) and as she readily promised each of them a man (for fifty cents) they are jubilant to the point of hilarity. Emily's bliss is somewhat cloyed by the fact that the

6. Clayton Hamilton.

prophetess hinted strongly that the favored party was to be that worthy colleague of Potash and Perlmutter, Goodrich, the cloak-and-suiter, the boy drummer of Bolivar. Dolly's future spouse is veiled in the rosy mists of uncertainty but there is no doubt that he is to combine the pulchritude of Adonis with the magic purse of Fortunatus.

This is not a letter, it's a book, and I'm going to cut it short. There is no news, except one of our recently married neighbors has given birth to a bouncing girl six months after the official seal was put on her bed-sharing. All of which goes to show what wonderful results accrue from the salt air of the river Thames. Of course there is much evil-minded conjecture among the prying neighbors but, what would you? Such is the lot of us poor innocent mortals. Several of these cases have happened in our midst lately. The climate is really too invigorating. It's a poor child that isn't crowing and prattling lustily seven months after its parents signed the document. I am glad to know New London excels in something even if it is only the rapid pre-natal development of babies. New London's motto for the future: "Nature two months behind us."

My dear Jessica, let me wind up this shocking torrent of words with which I have deluged you by saying with all sincerity and from the bottom of my heart, that I long for July to come most ardently. Those four days you spent here a few weeks ago were merely a provocation, a hint of wonders to come, of hours which we will both be able to treasure up and ponder over when we look back in after years and wish to justify our existence to ourselves. I have told you how I long for someone in my amorous loneliness, someone who will combine in the same proportion in which I have them spirit and body; who will not be wholly of the earth earthly or of the spirit spiritually; who will have the courage of a healthy conscience; who will be a joyous animal frank in her approval of her flesh and proud, not ashamed of it, knowing that it is not in things themselves but in the eye that looks at them that guilt dwells; who will practice not deadening restraint but exultant freedom; in a word, one who will take the hour and live it fully, wholly, as if it were the last hour of her life, as if it were to be eternal. There you have it! I don't believe there is such a woman. If you want to teach me something there's an opportunity. Teach me such a woman is possible. Or don't you care to?

(Please don't be offended at the word "animal" in the above. We're all that, you know, and I don't mean it in a derogatory sense—only to distinguish that part of us which is not spiritual or mental.)

Write me soon. Tell me if you really want to be my teacher, to open up what is to me an undiscovered country, to show me a new possiblity which I have grown to lose hope in—the woman with a robust conscience, who can live without feeling guilty.

I would penetrate to the inner shrine and I hope that, as Lorenzo says in the *Merchant of Venice*: "Fair Jessica shall be my torch bearer."   Eugene

P.S. You don't object to the letter being typewritten, do you? It couldn't be squeezed into an envelope if it were in long hand. You owe me a long one in return, sabe?

---

15 • TO DAVID RUSSELL LYMAN.   TLS 2 pp. (325 Pequot Ave. / New London, Conn.) [Yale]

[Summer 1914]

Dear Dr. Lyman:—   Fearing that the answers on my question sheet may prove misleading in the case of one who is unjustly suspected of being a member of the more-or-less-Idle Poor Class, I hasten to take advantage of your charitable offer to read the egotistic spasms of former patients.

You must acknowledge that to ask a struggling young playwright with the Art of Art's sake credo how much he earns per week in terms of contaminating gold, is nothing short of brutal. It is liable to leave him in so perturbed a state of mind he will have nothing left to compute with but his imagination. Furthermore, to force him to confess that he basely befouls The Ideal by fabricating Photoplays is to put him to the blush in heartless fashion.

But such is the damning fact—to such depths of degradation have the loud and ravenous howls of the well-known wolf at times driven me. For while my adventures with High Art have been crowned with a sufficient amount of glory, I am bound to admit they have failed to be remunerative. Therefore, when I set down my earnings at thirty dollars a week, I am speaking in the main of the returns I have received from the "Movies." It is hard to form an estimate because my fortunes have been nothing if not fluctuating. One week I have been affluent to the point of purse-proud arrogance; the next week, face to face with the grisly visage of Want. So there you have it, and you must accept my figures purely as a broad estimate based on the alternate plenty and famine of the past six months.

However, let me relieve your mind of the appalling idea that you have been misled into preserving the life of a mere Motion Picture scribe—surely a thought calculated to give the most hardy conscience a jar. I can claim a little more justification for your resurrecting me than that. Five of my one-act plays are shortly to be published in book form,[1] and two of them will, I think, eventually be produced by Holbrook Blinn at the Princess Theatre, New York.[2] Also I am hard at work finishing a four-act play which, by God's grace, may see the footlights next season.[3]

But as you are naturally more interested in the state of my body than of my mind (which is robust enough, unless I am to believe those carping critics who assert that what I write proves the contrary) I will immediately come to the only reason for my pestering you with this long-winded epistle. At the risk of gaining a reputation for eccentricity before my literary fame warrants such an indulgence, I have gone in swimming in this Long Island Sound at least once a week ever since I left Gaylord last June. I haven't missed a single week. The coldest the water has ever been when I took my plunge was thirty-three degrees. I haven't had a cold (hear me rap wood) nor has the Demon Tonsilitis, formerly a familiar spirit of mine, paid me a single visit. I thought this might interest you as a "lunger's" experience. I enclose a snap-shot taken on New Year's Day.

For the rest, I can truthfully say with all the gratitude in the world to you and the Farm, that I have never felt better. My weight has varied, but never has fallen over three pounds below what I tipped the scales at when I left the San. I write steadily four or five hours a day and feel able to keep it up forever.

I am looking forward to some fine spring day when I shall be able to pay the Farm a visit. The Hart shack will have a homelike look, I know, and the verandah of the Rec. be as inviting as of yore. And although I trust all the patients I knew are now halely and heartily bucking the world, still I hope to find, among those attached to the San, some familiar face to remind me of the time I should have been cast down by my fate—and wasn't. If, as they say, it is sweet to visit the place one was born in, then it will be doubly sweet for me to visit the place I was reborn in—for my second birth was the only one which had my full approval. Sincerely your friend,   Eugene G. O'Neill

---

1. *Thirst and Other One Act Plays*, published on August 17, 1914, by the Gorham Press in Boston.
2. *The Web* and *Recklessness*, which Blinn did not produce.
3. Probably *Servitude*, which, as a three-act play, was completed in September 1914; it was first published in *Lost Plays of Eugene O'Neill* (New York: New Fathoms Press, 1950), pp. 70–144.

16 • TO GEORGE PIERCE BAKER.   TLS 2 pp. (325 Pequot Ave. / New London, Conn.) [Harvard]

July 16, 1914

Dear Sir:—   Mr. Clayton Hamilton, the dramatic critic, to whom I have frequently mentioned my ambition of becoming a playwright, has given me permission to use his name, and advised me to write to you personally regarding the possibility of my entrance, as a special student, into your several dramatic courses at Harvard University.

Let me explain my exact position. I am twenty-five years old. My university training consists of one year (Freshman) at Princeton University, Class of 1910, where I had started to take a Litt.B. course. All my life I have been closely connected with the dramatic profession. My father is James O'Neill, the actor, of whom you may perhaps have heard; so, although I have never been on the stage myself, and my direct connection with the theatre is confined to a half-season as assistant-manager with Viola Allen in *The White Sister*, nevertheless I can claim whatever knowledge there may be gained from a close association with members of the profession.

Less than a year ago I seriously determined to become a dramatist and since that time I have written one long play—four acts—and seven one-act plays. Five of the latter are shortly to be published in book form by The Gorham Press of Boston. None of my plays have as yet been submitted to any manager for production but, of course, I intend to try and obtain a hearing for them the latter part of this summer.

Although I have read all the modern plays I could lay my hands on, and many books on the subject of the Drama, I realize how inadequate such a hap-hazard, undirected mode of study must necessarily be. With my present training I might hope to become a mediocre journey-man playwright. It is just because I do not wish to be one, because I want to be an artist or nothing, that I am writing to you.

Will the Harvard regulations regarding special students permit my taking your courses—and whatever supplementary ones you would be kind enough to suggest as likely to help me? And if so, may I have your permission to enter your course?

One word more about myself: If varied experience be a help to the prospective dramatist I may justly claim that asset for I have worked my way around the world as a seaman on merchant vessels and held various positions in different foreign countries.

Hoping you may look favorably upon this very earnest desire of mine to become your student, I remain   Sincerely yours   Eugene G. O'Neill

---

17 • TO GEORGE PIERCE BAKER.   TLS 1 p. (325 Pequot Ave. / New London, Conn.) [Harvard]

July 29, 1914

Dear Sir:—   I am sending you under separate cover two one-act plays,[1] completed a short time ago, from which you will be able to form a judgment as to my suitability for taking your course.

As for my standing at Princeton, I am hardly proud of it. I went there with the idea of getting through with the smallest possible amount of work, and I succeeded in paying so little attention to the laws regarding attendance, etc. that I was "flunked out" at the end of Freshman year for over-cutting.

1. Probably *Children of The Sea* (later titled *Bound East for Cardiff*) and *Abortion*.

I do not think it would be fair to judge me by my Princeton record. I was eighteen then, but now I am fast approaching twenty-six, and the Princeton Freshman and I have very little in common.

In accordance with your suggestion, I will write to Mr. Hait as soon as I hear whether my plays fulfill your requirements or not. I don't suppose it would be any use writing to him until I could tell him that you were willing to accept me.

Thanking you for your consideration and again hoping that I may become your student, I remain   Sincerely yours   Eugene G. O'Neill

---

18 • TO BEATRICE ASHE.   ALS 3 pp. (Garden Hotel / Madison Av., & 27 Sq. / [New York]) [Berg]

[September 21, 1914]

My Own:—   If brevity be the soul of wit this epistle is going to be a screaming comedy knock-out. My room is an oven, God hasn't changed the air in it since the person last night breathed it, and I have a headache that thrusts description into the poor house. In brief Little Old Gotham, as we State St.[1] habitués speak of it, is the same sun-baked, dust-driven h--l hole as of yore.

I am dead-beat, withal. Have been on the hop—no, I don't mean that kind—since the immigrant-infested, rat-deserted fire-box dumped me on the quay this a.m. Have seen all of my people but one and reaped encouragement and deep despair in equal quantities. I'll call the day a draw.[2]

Expect to return to New London by the 8:22 tomorrow. Take a chance and meet it if you care to. I'm almost sure to connect.

My dearest dear, if you could see the obstacles in the path of the prospective playwright as I have seen them today I'm afraid you'd feel like a soldier in the forlorn hope. Many a severe jolt of discouragement awaits you down the long trail. Your love will be put to tests such as few loves are ever put to but *please, please* do stick for I have faith in the ultimate outcome, and without you—Oh, the thought is too unbearable! Your love is my whole life.

Your letter, which I read and reread on the boat last night, was the sweetest ever. I am glad you discovered my latent tenderness. How could you have doubted, that where you are concerned, I am a deep well of tenderness bubbling over.

Dear! Dear! thrice dear one! How can I whisper, my lips against your heart, the love I feel, the passion of my longing for you? Read "Upon Our Beach" and "Full Many A Cup" again.[3] They're the nearest I've ever come to it. Now I can only hold up a faded stocking and kiss it—so!—cuddle a dilapidated red bathing cap and kiss it—so!—press your three pictures to my heart and kiss them—so! so! so!

Good night, Sweet, Tender, Wonderful Little Woman! May God grant to our love a haven not too far away and as I act toward you so may he act toward me. I love you.   Gene

1. The main street of New London.
2. O'Neill was in New York trying to interest managers and agents in his plays.
3. For the texts of these two poems, see O'Neill's *Poems, 1912–1944,* ed. Donald Gallup (New Haven: Ticknor and Fields, 1980), pp. 48–54.

19 • TO BEATRICE ASHE. ALS 1 p. (1105 Massachusetts Ave., / Cambridge, Mass.) [Berg]

[September 30, 1914]

(Save your letters until I return)

My Own:— Ten million pardons for not writing to you last night but I had expected my trunk to arrive before it did and neglected to purchase writing materials until it was too late. So I had to send you a lazy man's love letter.[1]

I am settled here in a nice corner room on the ground floor with three big windows. As near as I can make out there are three other students, all Germans and graduate men, in the building. I eat with the family who all speak German and say grace before meals. S'nuff said! They also hold a little Bible reading every morning after breakfast and asked me if I cared to participate. Imagine it! I begged to be excused. However the room is good and the meals so-so—so "vive la joie!"[2]

I have just returned from my first class. Prof. Baker is a fine man with a very fascinating personality and I am sure I shall like the course very much. We are to start right away writing an adaption of some short story.

To say I am lonely would be using words as feeble as Watts Hymns for Infant Minds. I haven't a soul to say a word to, so all I do is dream of you and of those dear days of the past which memory pictures so fondly and so cruelly. The only relief I have is the certainty that I will see you again in the very near future. If it were not for this thought my agony of spirit would be truly unbearable. How I miss you! I wish I could just give you a slight inkling of the aching vacuum your absence has left in my life. The joy has gone out of everything, the sun no longer shines, all is gray and arid and sterile. Round and round my thoughts creep, lingering lovingly over all the memorable hours of "the days that are no more." I can't seem to awaken any interest in the present. Without you what is worth the tribute of a thought! The world exists only in you.

I shall probably return to you on Friday—will try to make a train around one o'clock (p.m.)—my class lets out at eleven. Will send a night letter tomorrow night and let you know definitely and you can meet me—if you care to. A long kiss, Dear! Gene

---

20 • TO BEATRICE ASHE. ALS 8 pp. (1105 Massachusetts Ave., / [Cambridge, Mass.]) [Berg]

Tuesday Night / [October 6, 1914]

My Own:— Here I am back at the old dump once more feeling more lonely and heart-sick than ever. It sure is hard to have to leave you this way, and I am fervently praying to all the Gods that the time will soon come which will bring surcease of all these soul-aches which make life so horrible and full of pain. Ah My Own, My Own, how I love you, and how the relentless hours drag their leaden feet when I am not with you!

I am thinking of last night and of all the wonder which is you, and my great desire moans from the depths of its abysmal aloneness; "Give us, ah give us but yesterday!"

Life has become for me a phantom show in which there are but two realities—you and

---

1. A telegram.
2. O'Neill shared a house with Bartley Ebel, a Mennonite from Hillsboro, Kansas, on leave from his teaching position to do graduate work at Harvard; his wife; his brother, August Ebel, who was an art student; and his brother-in-law, Daniel Hiebert, a medical student at Boston University.

my love for you. All else is misty shadow of illusion, vain fretting most valueless. I exist as I am reflected in you. I can only endure myself when I see my image in your eyes—in their gray pool does this Narcissus see himself, and admire, and feel so proud to be there.

"It's a long, long way to Tipperary" and countless aeons before my birthday when I shall again feel your soft warm lips on mine. I could shake the skies with my fruitless cries, gnash my sharp (according to you) teeth with my rage at fate—but what's the use? Time *will* pass however slowly, and again I shall hold you in my arms, O Dear One, O Most Adorable of All Women. A long kiss! Good'night.

Wednesday night / [October 7, 1914]

I went to see *Cabiria* as per schedule last night and returned with a much fairer opinion of the artistic value of the movies. The picture is simply stupendous. The acting is excellent—far above any I have ever seen done by an American company—and the scenery is wonderful. Hannibal's army crossing the Alps, the destruction of the Roman fleet at Syracuse by the reflecting mirrors of Archimedes, the temple of Moloch at Carthage, the desert expedition of the King of Cirta, the siege of Carthage by Scipio—all of these are done with the grimmest realism and are blood-stirring in their gripping action. The dame who played the naughty Princess Sophonisba—one Italia Manzini—very much resembled you and had a lot of your mannerisms. (I was enchanted.) And take it from me you needn't blush at the comparison for Italia is a bear with a capital "B." I enclose a picture of her death scene from the official score card. Her eyes are a bit too blacked up in this scene—she has just taken poison—to give you a fair idea but you can catch the resemblance—or I'm blind.

Of course it costs fifty centavos to view *Cabiria* from the ground floor and one rather expects the unusual, but I was enthusiastically surprised at that.

Our two hours session with Prof. Baker this morning was very interesting. He sure is there with the acid wit and I love to hear him discourse on the current short story and other abominations. I look forward with *horror* to the time when he trains the batteries of his biting irony on the budding efforts of his class—particularly one member I know of. The slaughter will be frightful. He hasn't picked out the stories we are to adapt yet but we are to get them Friday. Then it's ho for the real labor!

I met a very fine fellow in our class today—one Ford, a Yale grad, who had seen a review of my book in some magazine which he said was very good. He didn't remember where he had seen it, and my publisher tells me the book hasn't been generally sent out yet, so I don't know what magazine it could have been. I must have an unknown friend some place. Ford has a charmingly pretty wife whom he introduced me to and they urged me to dine with them—which I did not, being suddenly sick at heart at the sight of their happiness—and I alone and pining for a kiss from your dear lips. Down with everything! (☞ ⬅ BOMB)

Have been busy shopping all day. Ordered my suit which I hope will be a fine one, and purchased a wonderful pair of horse-hide shoes. When you next see me, I will have Solomon in all his glory looking like a tramp.

I shall now to bed after performing a short devotional exercise consisting of a long pashnut kiss implanted on your ruche. (By the way, what is a ruche and what special garment is it attached to? I am all excited!). I hope to sleep tonight—my efforts to so do last night not being crowned with any great amount of success—but OH that slumber-destroying memory of my arm about your tiny waist! It haunts me every time I pause to think for a moment.

And, oh, that time, that golden time-to-be, when dream and desire come true, when my glad mad heart shall beat against your own, when

"My lips shall sleep upon your bare soft breast
The beating of your heart their lullaby."

Good night and the long kiss!

Thursday / [October 8, 1914]

No class today, and a long and rather irksome day it has been. I wrote a poem to you this morning—a nutty sort of a lay which I hope may please my Gracious Lady. It has the merit of being peculiar, at least, and I am enclosing it to you.

Went for a swim in the tank this afternoon and feel mightily refreshed thereat. It has been close and sultry all out-of-season and the cool water was a rich relief.

I am reading *King Hunger*, a play by the Russian Andreyev which is very powerful and interesting.

Outside of these diversions I have done little but dream, pondering over the harshness of a fate which condemns us to languish apart from each other. Life, so I deem, is a bitter concoction at best but our cup seems to be unnecessarily dosed with wormwood. Things might be worse, of course,—I might lose a leg or something—but when I am not with you my optimism sort of bogs down and I see existence "as through a glass, darkly." It seems such a sorry shame that our dreams cannot be grasped and turned into realities, that we should ever be rainbow chasing after "Tomorrows" while the sun-kissed hours of Youth die swiftly one by one, never to be lived over though the heavens crack with our clamorous supplications.

I have gone over all the days of our summer together, all our wonderful hours, and I am sad this evening; sad with the knowledge that all of it is "put behind me, long ago and far away." I am sad with the oppression of fall, time of dead leaves and withered things. There is a feeling in the air of inevitable loss: of the death of warm days and caressing sunlight, of the passing of hot sand and wave-swept beaches. I want to live it all over again, every hour of it with you, and I know this is impossible. The meaninglessness of the windings of this great river of chance and change goads me into wailings of fretful impotence. I would like to "pull the pillars of my life upon me" were it not for the great certainty which rises beautiful out of the chaos and ruin—Our Love.

What a chance it offers for me to throw off my load of bitterness and take up life again as one who is reborn into a fairer greener world. To live in you, for you, by you—it is an immortality springing from the grave of my dead life. You are my happiness; I know it. I feel you calling to something in me which has never been touched before, something finer, way down in the depths of being, perhaps a soul. All of the sordid values the world has rubbed into me lose their cruel validity before your love. When I look into your eyes I feel a sense of deep shame; I want to cry out and ask your forgiveness for being what I have been, to crave your indulgence for the grimy smears on my life, to pray your pity for the tattered wings of my spirit stained with the muck of the long road. I long for some clear well of the spirit wherein I could cleanse and purify my rag of life. I would like to stand beside you with some faint hope that I was not so utterly unworthy.

Alas, I need you so much! It is you alone who can give me back the Joy of Living, who can justify my existence to myself. To make you happy, to fill your life with tender care, to call you to my aid where the ways are rough, not to shelter you—you are no Doll Girl nor shall our house be a Doll's House—but to give you a part in all my life and make my life worthy for you to take part in. All this is my ambition, my Highest Hope which must be kept holy.

And to be foiled in this great purpose by bread and butter, to be held at bay by a theory of

Economics—ah, the irony of it! Alas, I need you so much! I am weary of the hopelessness of the past and I turn to My Beatrice beseechingly for—

"There is no resting place for tired head
Like her soft breasts, there is no love like hers."

Good night. I love you!

Friday / [October 9, 1914]

Have worked pretty hard today. Baker gave us back the stories he wishes us to adapt this morning and requested us to write a scenario which we must hand in before we start on the play itself. I started right in and have written about a thousand words of mine already. Baker has injected so many "don'ts" into the work that it is fraught with difficulty to say the least. He lit into some of the stories for fair, rather unjustly, I thought, in some cases. I gave him a copy of my book and he said he would be glad to look it over. Another one of my fellow-studes asked me where he could buy a copy. I think he sort of wants to get my number as a playwright, but, wot't'ell, I should fret.

Went for a swim late this p.m. The tank at the Y.M.C.A., where I go, is better than the University Tank and not so crowded. I intend to play it strong all winter. It sure gives one the old pep.

Expect to go out to the Stadium to see deah old Harvard play Washington & Jefferson tomorrow afternoon. Should be a good game.

Have just been thinking that this time last week I was in your arms or you in mine. The world do wag on and its waggery decreases my joys instead of increasing them. Ah, that last night with my arm about your waist! You haven't forgotten it either, I know. Dear One, we have at least glorious memories of our past together which augur well for the future. It has been sweet, so sweet to me; sweet with the flavor of your adorable personality, My Own. We have a future together, I am sure, that will more than compensate for the Present's sins of omission. And yet, and yet—My God, it is so hard to wait! I try to bear it with some show of equanimity, to call a patient philosophy to my aid, but it's no use. I want you! I want you! I want you! Bee dear, my own Bee dear, I love you so, so much! Little wife, little wife,[1] I adore you!

But now, alas, when I need you so much you are worlds away from me and

"I am a prince of thwarted ecstasy
Of unassuaged desire."

But a week from tonight—Delirious thought!

Saturday / [October 10, 1914]

Have just returned from the more-or-less historic stadium where I witnessed the conflict between Washington & Jefferson and Harvard, and, having a few minutes before the welcome summons to eats, and my thought straying as per usual to your most utterly-lovable self, I resolved to take pen in hand and regale you with the quite unmomentous doings of the day.

I wrote on my scenario and the beginning of a one-act play[2] until about eleven—I rise at seven-thirty, think of it!—and then went for my daily swim. Slipped on the edge of the tank

1. O'Neill often addressed Beatrice Ashe as his wife, although they never married.
2. Possibly *The Sniper*, first published in *Lost Plays of Eugene O'Neill*, pp. 51–69.

and tried to slap all of the water out with my—er—what's the polite term—abdomen. I was quite unsuccessful and I am very sore—where I hit.

The football game this afternoon was a corker. In the first half W & J made the well known Crimson look very, very unwell. The score was 9–3 in their favor at the end of it. Harvard came back very strong in the next half and finally won 10–9, but, between you and me—I wouldn't mention it to any undergraduate—W & J had much the better team while their first string men were intact. They were beaten by lack of good substitutes. Of course Brickley and Mahan didn't play and that may account for it. W & J had the forward pass down better than I have ever seen it. They made three successful passes one after the other which netted seventy yards. In all they must have gained 150 yards on this style of play. Harvard's attempts were laughable. They won with straight football.

Tomorrow is the stupid Sabbath and I think I shall write all day to keep from remembering the fact.

I have just remembered that it was a week ago tonight you were so horribly mean to me for an hour or so. Art sorry, Sweetest Girl, now when you no longer have me to pick on? Monday also is a holiday, Columbus day or something of the sort, and I anticipate a more than usually uninteresting Cambridge for the next two days.

I had a great longing to pack my little bag and catch a rattler for New London today but I reflected that my birthday would be more appropriate and I ain't rich enough to come both times. Sure you're going to be just awful glad to see me? If you're not I'm going to come anyway and make you. I sure am looking forward to that trip and to next Friday night. Don't dare to have any subsequent dates! And remember a good, dutiful, sweet little wife should always meet the Prodigal Husband at the train.

Hope I get your letter on Monday. It will mean such a happy heart to hear from you— and your letters are much the best I ever received from anyone man or woman.

I had a wicked, wicked dream about you last night. It was very much—the afterwards. God love you as I do! A long kiss!

Sunday / [October 11, 1914]

I have just had a horrible thought and I must sit down and get it off my mind before I forget it. It came to me as I was dreaming over your picture a few minutes ago that you had threatened to take down that confidant of all our joys and sorrows, our kisses and quarrels, that most haloed of all spots—the hammock. I beg, I implore, I adjure in the name of our love, and the continued hot weather to let it remain. Spare it for the night of my birthday, at least. What if it be cold? We possess a sovereign remedy for all low temperatures—each other's arms—do we not? I promise you I will not allow you to freeze as long as your heart be warm. I really can't bear to think of sitting sedately in a room like any other fellow calling on any old girl. Besides I love every inch of that dear old floating divan. Not to find it creaking in the old place would give me a sense of personal loss. So please don't drag it in to hibernate before I see it again.

I have other reasons. Our Love is one of the open places, of the sand and sea, of moonlight and clear fresh air. We both love the open. Therefore let us stay out in it, and to the devil with the convention which decrees otherwise. Again I repeat to you, though it be ten below, be comforted, you shall not be cold!

I feel very desolate today—always do on the without youless Sabbath. My German friends are indulging in orgies of religion at some nearby sweet-smelling Baptist den. I have worked for a couple of hours but my brain seems very languid and my ideas go a-wandering you-wards. Five more days and at a little after four in the afternoon I shall dismount at the

New London station to see you waiting on the platform. Shall I? Aw, please do! It makes things seem so much like the afterwards.

Tomorrow your letter! I cannot tell you with what avidity I shall tear it from the postman's hand, with what quickened heart beats I shall open it, with what delight I shall read it nor shall I tell you where it shall rest tomorrow night. All of these things I leave to your imagination.

I suppose you are over singing in Groton this a.m., and I doubt not God looks down upon you so fondly the angels are jealous—or perhaps, in ravished wonderment, he calls the roll of the heavenly choir to find out which one is missing—for God, mid the cares of checking up the rush of German and French souls, may for a moment have forgotten that he unwillingly let you leave Paradise to become My Guardian Angel.   I kiss your dear lips, My Own!   Gene

---

21 • TO BEATRICE ASHE.   ALS 2 pp. (1105 Mass. Ave. / Cambridge, Mass.) [Berg]

[November 1, 1914]

My Own:—   Well the Sabbath is drawing to a close, thank God, for it has been long and tiresome as only the Lord's Day can be. The weather has been superfine but what's the use of fine weather when there's no place to go and no one to go with. My friends the Midinites[1] suggested that I journey to Revere Beach with them to gaze upon the sea but when I found out the children were to be taken along I backed out. A long trolley ride with a couple of playful brats is my idea of one of the tortures Dante forgot to mention in the Inferno. So I stayed at home and read in a volume of short stories by Strindberg. Worked all morning at my scrivening and attempted to continue this p.m. but my brain was peevish and soggy and I found I was using an eraser more than a pencil. So I quit.

The stories by Strindberg are in a book called *Married* and are all upon that subject. They especially harp on the fact of an insufficient income ruining so many lives by compelling them against the dictates of nature to waste their youth in waiting for each other. I think, yes I think it would make good reading for you! At any rate the stories filled me full of gloom for I could not help finding a personal application in all of them.

When it became too dark to read I went to the window and gazed out at the fragment of sunset which haloed the unspeakably dingy houses on the other side of Mass. Ave. There must have been a streak of color stolen from some old sunset of the past enjoyed with you, for I immediately fell a-dreaming of the golden days of Our Summer, and of our delightful nights together. One by one the pageant of those dear hours passed before me—Our first night, the long walk into the country Memorial Day when we picked flowers and sat on the stump together. You told me of your dream about the owl and the rabbit. I assured you I was going to do my d-est to ascend the pedestal of your Inner Shrine. Have I? I hope so, Dear One. And then the other walk we took to gather laurel. We lay in under the pine trees, do you remember? And then all the glorious days, the bathing-suit days on Our Beach!! How the few spectators used to stare when I carried you in my arms acrost the Cove! I used to put on your sneaks for you, too. I can see flashes of color in my dream: your orange stockings, your orange [illegible] around your head, your queer colored bandana handkerchief. Our Picnic Day—you haven't forgotten it I'm sure. I still have the Pall Mall box which contained your gift cigarettes. Ham ferried us back, remember? I have put that day into the casket of my soul, a jewel of a day, not to be surpassed. Have I not even written a poem about it? And

1. The Ebel-Hiebert family, who were Mennonites.

With Beatrice Ashe in New London.

about that strange quotation which kept running in my mind on Memorial Day. "In the great waste places, beyond the mountains, beyond the great Divide." Remember it? I remember all our days even unto these last sad days of Autumn.

And our nights! Why pick out one from the others when all were beautiful? Dear side porch, dear shades, dear blessed hammock! You are in my life, all of you, never to be forgotten. The night your young Lochinvar came out of Stonington and captured you and took you off in Hart's Mercer. The night you and I one-pieced[2] it together and the waves dreamed that Venus had returned to them. The first night I brought poetry to you. The night I brought my "Full many a Cup." The—

I can't continue. There are tears, real tears, rising in my eyes—from the well of my sheer loneliness, my abysmal longing for you. The Past is too sweet, the Present too bitter, the contrast too great.

Oh Bee! Bee! I love you so! I want you so! I need you so!

Our last days have been sad. The spirit of Autumn has oppressed our love with its sense of passing, of withering leaves. Our love is the spirit of Spring with a long wonderful Summer before it. The two spirits strive discordantly. We must change all that. It is all my fault. Whatever of our nights and days have been saddened or made imperfect it was always my swinishness to blame. Our next days and nights together must be perfect as the old days and nights were perfect. We must promise each other that. If not until Thanksgiving—I'll never be able to stick it as long as that—well then I shall approach you in the true spirit of the time; Thanking God for having made you; thanking Him that I love you with all my heart and soul; above all thanking Him because he has permitted you to love me. I shall love you, let the thoughts of the future go to the devil for the vacation, and be glad I am alive! It's a promise! Never again shall a day or night of ours be spoilt through me!

I love you! I adore you! Please, one kiss!   Gene

P.S. This is more of a *real* letter than I've written you in some time. It's written with my blood.

P.S. Of course shall return Tuesday if I receive ticket—which I doubt. Please, please write! Reminisce over the old days as I have done in this letter. What hours do you especially remember? What was the date of the Picnic on Our Beach? Can you figure out?

Still have my cold! Damnation!!

("God! Dear God! Please give me Bee!")

---

22 • TO BEATRICE ASHE.   ALS 1 p. (1105 Mass. Ave. / Cambridge, Mass.) [Berg]

[November 2, 1914]

My Own:—   Much tumultuous pleasure when your letter arrived this morning. It's been three whole twenty-four hours since I've heard a word from you, there being no delivery on Sunday. Evidently from your letter you hadn't yet received mine of Friday in which I waxed wicked and spoke of my return to the land of optimism. Never mind, I shall have my answer to that tomorrow, I hope.

I have been writing and reading all day. Have finished my one-act adaption and it only waits for Ken Morgan to send me a typewriter before I'll be done with the old thing—Thank God, for I took no pleasure in it at all. Stealing someone else's idea and fixing it up doesn't appeal to me when I have so many ideas of my own that I ought to be working.[1]

2. O'Neill's one-piece bathing suit, which he felt showed off his masculine physique to great advantage.

1. "Dear Doctor," O'Neill's one-act farce, later destroyed, was adapted from a magazine story; the adaptation of a short story was the first assignment in Baker's course.

Have been reading a play this afternoon which for pure unadulterated gloom just about bears off the palm. It is *The Lower Depths* by Maxim Gorki and, believe me, the depths are pretty low, to say the least.

Haven't heard a whisper from the political powers that be of New London so guess they don't care whether I vote or not. You know I can imagine nothing of less consequence to me than casting a vote, but I won't see you, that's the hell of it, unless tomorrow's mail is fruitful. If not tomorrow, then not until Thanksgiving! It's your own hard order, Little Wife! Aren't you sorry you gave it? I'll try to stick here until Thanks. at any rate. I really ought to, I suppose. But oh you are so sweet! And I need you, Bee, I need you so much!

Must rush off to a meeting of the Harvard Dramatic Club to which I have been invited. Good night and a long kiss, Onliest Girl! Will be down tomorrow if I get the wherewithal.

Kiss! here ⟶ ✗ Eugene—(12 years old)

P.S. How about the rouge print of your lips on a letter? You promised to send it to me once. Please do. I shall be able to kiss your lips good'night then.

---

23 • TO BEATRICE ASHE.   ALS 6 pp. ([1105 Massachusetts Ave. / Cambridge, Mass.]) [Berg]

Saturday / [November 7, 1914]

Have just returned from the Princeton-Harvard game and am still half frozen. Harvard, as you will know before you receive this letter, smeared up my dear almost-Alma Mater something dreadful. From my stand point the less said about the game the better. It was a sad blow to all my hopes. Princeton was outclassed from start to finish. The crowd of forty thousand was a wonderful sight. There were oodles and oodles of damsels most fair to look upon but, alas, none of them looked upon me. The cheering and singing were also something to remember.

I didn't write you a word yesterday. I received my typewriter from Ken about noon and had to pound out a whole one-act adaption which had to be handed in this morning. So you see when I plead lack of time as an excuse I am telling no more than the truth. Thank God, the adaption is now off my hands, I hope—I may have to change it if Baker so suggests—and I am free to give rein to my own creative will.

Have been a positive glutton for work these past few days. (Oh yes, I do get such industrious fits, strange as it may seem). Have written my right hand into writer's cramp several times during the past week. Have finished the original one-act play which, with an elaborate scenario, constitutes our outside work up to Christmas. So you see I am way ahead of the game and will have plenty of time to squander on the weird fancies of my brain. As a starter on the afore-mentioned fancies, I have mapped out a tentative scenario for a five act play which is nothing if not grimly realistic and to the point. If it is ever produced—and it never could be in this country—the authorities will cast me into the deepest dungeon of the jail and throw away the key.[1] But one writes what one *must*, what one *feels*. All else is piffle. I will be [an] artist or nothing.

Just think; I have been away from you now longer than any time since the memorable day in May on which you volunteered to white wash my sneaks. By the time I do see you it

---

1. Probably "The Second Engineer," later titled *The Personal Equation*. The latter is published for the first time in *The Unknown O'Neill: Unpublished or Unfamiliar Writings of Eugene O'Neill*, ed. Travis Bogard (New Haven: Yale University Press, 1988), pp. 6–75.

will have been a whole month since we were together. Oh the happiness of that time! How I hunger for it! How far away it seems!

Your last letter was very, very sweet, My Own Bee. I love it and all it means to me but I am so sorry that you should cry. As I said in my last letter I am too poor an old thing for you to waste your tears upon. But, then, there are sad tears and glad tears. I hope yours were of the latter variety.

As for loving you with a needing love you know, you must know that it is my great selfish need of you which ever stands foremost in my thoughts. I need you as my goal, my encouragement, my ambition, my end in life. I need your help to become what I want to become. Comrade and Wife, over the smooth road and the flinty trail, hand in hand, bearing one burden, sharing one happiness; under the same star, conquering or crushed by the same fate—that is it! As your song says, what matter what our destiny, "if only together." God's always in his heaven when you are with me.

Of course I *want* you, too. What a poor gray shade I would be if I didn't! The touch of your soft skin, your kisses, your hair, all your loveliness has the power to send a shivering flame through my brain. My blood seethes and fumes, and at times I have forgotten— promises and all weary things, like the rabid immoralist that I am. One cannot dam a river without letting some of it flow over. And my passion flows as fiercely toward you as any smoking rapids. I assert it! I am proud of it! Soul without body is as crippled as body without soul. Let us be proud also of our passion! Let it be frank and open, therefore innocent. Only what hides and hangs its head is guilty. Sin exists only in the consciousness of sinning. Evil is—where you see it!

Pardon this ethical philosophizing but you must understand the inherent innocence of my "I want yous." To mistake it for lust would be doing me an injustice. It is part of my love for you and is as strong and free from a sense of guilt as the love of my soul for yours.

This, I grant you, is hard to believe, especially since every one of us is taught from childhood to look with an evil eye upon the body and its functions—first fruits of that dear Christianity. But I swear to you that, above all where you are concerned, my eye is clear, can see only purity in its desire for you.

Every nerve, every atom of my body calls to yours—"I want you! Want you! Want you! And my wanting is holy!"

There you have it! And now I must say "Auf Wiedersehen" for dinner is about to enter upon the scene and I would not offend Germanic punctiliousness by being late. More tomorrow!

Good night, Dear Little Rascal. I wish to God it were three weeks from today!

My arms around you, My head on My Place—There! —Now kiss me! I am very tired of living without you.

My Declaration of Dependence—upon you—: I love you with all my heart, I want you with all my body, I need you with all my soul!

Ar't satisfied?

Sunday / [November 8, 1914]

The ever-dreary Sabbath draws to its close, praise be! A wearisome day with leaden skies, promising to rain every moment but evidently too listless to do so. One of those days when the dregs of life rise in the cup of one's soul till a longing comes to fall asleep and wake up in some fairer greener life with all prayers answered.

Not that I have idled away the hours. I have been diligent enough, all said and done. I religiously read the morning paper with its news of Princeton's defeat, religiously pounded the typewriter for a couple of hours, religiously studied one hour on the German grammar.

Oh, that reminds me; I haven't told you about the new enterprise I have engaged in, have I? I have purchased a German and a French grammar and am going to plunge in and attempt to teach myself a reading knowledge of the two. You see, so many of the best plays by writers of the two countries—and they have the best writers—are never translated; Anglo-Saxon pruddish hypocrisy being the principal reason. I will have no difficulty recovering my French. I picked up a play of Curel's[2]—*Les Fossiles*—yesterday morning and had no difficulty at all with the first act which I attempted, to find out how much I had forgotten. Of course, I missed the meaning of quite a few words but that is only natural when one considers that I haven't looked at a French word since my Princeton days. I really felt quite proud of my achievement.

With German it will be quite another matter. I doubt if I can succeed in getting away with a reading knowledge of that tongue all by myself but "daw gummit" I'm going to take a try at it anyway. You understand, I am only seeking to be able to read the books; the talking ought to be easy to pick up after that if it ever becomes necessary.

I have decided to devote one hour per day to each. Now what have you to say about the dauntless energy which has flamed up in me all at once—and, alas, if I know myself, is liable to flare out again just as suddenly! However, what a tiresome person one would become to oneself if one were the same all the time! Positively not fit to live with! I have the faculty of assuming many roles and I always feel a certain curiosity as to what I shall do under given conditions. "Know thyself!" What a mortal bore life would become if you did! It is the unexpected whims which change one's whole perspective, which make life fascinating—granting it ever could be so, what with its good'byes and separations and other abominations.

I find I am beginning to expand my letters to you into ethical essays and psychological treatises. It's just the product of my present itch for writing, for self-expression. I know these maunderings along the bypaths of my erratic fancy must bore you into a frenzy. I'll try and cure myself of such long-winded egotistical ravings and you may cease to double damn me for a garrulous nuisance who mails you pamphlets of anarchistic propaganda instead of letters. Still it's time I converted you to black radicalism, at that. "Rascals"—so called by the long-eared public—are always welcome in the ranks. Hence, q.e.d., you have all the qualifications,—barring your tendency toward green certificates which are the toys of rich, substantial, well-regulated folk and never meant for poor love-vagabonds such as us.

However since it is your will—Kismet! I bow before the dear hand which must shape my destiny. "There is no other God but Beatrice and I am her prophet!" Selah!

In my spare time today I have, as per always, been dreaming of you and Our Thanksgiving! You are, needless to relate, always in my thoughts but more so on Sunday than any other section of the week. I am going to change the name Lord's Day to Lady's Day—more appropriate in my case.

Probably all this is because on Sunday I feel my aloneness more, and my heart can only find solace for its dull pain in thoughts of Our Past, hopes for Our Future. I have taken out your blotted lips, looked and looked and looked, studied every little line of them and—kissed them! Three weeks from today I hope to improve upon this not unpleasing but rather imaginative arrangement—with my Lady's kind permission.

I've been thinking about "Your Bet" regarding a certain Night-to-be. I hate to cast a skeptical slur upon your will power but I have a sneaking suspicion that the winning of said "Bet" transcends the limits of human possibility. If you win you may have a leopard skin

2. French dramatist François de Curel (1854–1928).

coat with a spot for every orthodox sin on my soul—you look well in black. I give it out cold and clammy that it is my vain, strutting, self-hating opinion that, before the witching hour of three a.m., you and Antwerp—but why continue? I will finally defeat my own ends by plaguing you into winning that cursed bet—just for spite.

Good, night, My Own Bee, and a long kiss on your dear lips. The days pass slowly but they *do* pass somehow. Sixteen more of them and the Resurrection and the Life. I'll be back an entire week almost this next time. Think of it! Six entire days with you! No philandering with the boys, no parties, nothing but hanging around you, loving you, looking at you, until by the time the train bears me back to Boston you will be sick of the sight of me and say: "Plague take the Pest! Good riddance!"

I shall consecrate that time to loving you and being with you. Any other emotion will be greeted as an intruder.

May I? Will you give up your time to me and make no subsequent engagement? Promise!

Bye'Bye for this time! I love you! Think of me and believe in me!   Gene

P.S. Had another real wicked dream about you last night. I inform you of these physiological facts because—well, just because it's shocking and one shouldn't write such things, you know. And then I love to unburden my secrets and get you inured to your future role of keeper of my Pandora's box.

Besides the sleeping brain mirrors the day dream and—

Besides, daw gummit, an Anarchist has to feature the vulgar truth!

---

24 • TO BEATRICE ASHE.   ALS 2 pp. ([1105 Massachusetts Ave. / Cambridge, Mass.]) [Berg]

[postmarked November 12, 1914]

Dear Little Rascal Mine:—   Your letter arrived this a.m. and it sure was a welcome visitor. You are wrong to castigate me for my suggestion about the weekly letters. I mentioned it this last time because in one of your letters you hinted that the writing mood did not plague you often, and I honestly thought my proposal would make a great hit with you. I am not fond of the weekly arrangement myself. It is altogether too long a time and it was only with your comfort in mind that I proposed it. There!

Let us by all means cast this wretched plan of mine to the million devils! I will answer all your letters on the day I receive them and you can answer mine—whenever your fickle feminine fancy chooses. As always, I am your humble, much-abused slave—and glad of it! I wouldn't be anything else for anything! I kiss my fetters! I never knew true Liberty until I wore them! I love you! I love you!!

One benefit this new letter exchange will have. It will let me know whether you receive my epistles or not. I sent you a peevish special letter on Monday. Did you get it? You fail signally to mention the fact, if you did. I also sent you a long, (and I think very fair) poem a week ago. You haven't said a word about it. Either you never received it—in which case someone is snaring your letters; or the P.O. either here or in N.L. is on the bum, and I shall have to raise a yowl at the one here. Or, on the other hand, you did receive it and through pique, you have chosen to ignore it. This, you must confess, would be an unkind meanness and unworthy of you. Whether you found the poem a poor one or not makes no difference. It means something to me, I like it or I wouldn't have sent it to you, and a line to say you had received it wouldn't have hurt you much. I am serious about this. My poems mean a lot to me. I do not send the good ones to anyone but you. They are not written without mental effort. They represent, better than prose could express, the soul of a mood. You could not reveal to me in a plainer manner the fact that you do not care to have them. Very well, I shall take the hint.

Does all this sound silly? It is not so to me. I am sensitive on this one point. What I write is part of me. Praise of my work pleases me when I know it is sincere and not merely flattery; harsh criticism, when it is just, pleases me equally, for thereby I learn my mistakes and eradicate them; but indifference is unjust and an insult, for I know my work is at least worth mention.

But enough of this! If you think you are right, are punishing me for not answering a letter in which you told me not to write—"Varium et mutabile semper est femina" then go ahead. I have entered my protest and will not speak of the matter again.

Less than two weeks more! Just think of it, My Onliest Own! The return of the Prodigal Bridegroom will be an event most pleasing to the lonely heart of one EGO, whose stock of that well known virtue, Patience, is well nigh exhausted. Will he greet that Wednesday with huzzahs and other blissful acclamations? Believe me, he sure will! He has pined and ached and counted the days until all his fingers are out of joint and his soul is one great longing. He is sick with hope deferred and his mind, weary of the imaginative joy of day dreams, clamors for reality, for the wonder of the flesh and blood Bee.

Thanksgiving is the right word. Yea, he will give thanks to all the Gods when he sees his Bee again!

I am glad to hear that you and Emily[1] are becoming friendly. If Emily sings my praises, her song is reciprocated. She is a "regular" girl through and through and has always been more than kind to me—and at times when kindness meant a lot.

My work comes on apace. Although Baker suggested a few minor changes in my one-act adaption, which he read in class yesterday, his comments were very flattering. The members of the class received it enthusiastically and laughed their heads off. It really is the best, most practical, adaption turned in. Even my rivals acknowledge that. The only trouble is that the author of the short story probably stole it from a vaudeville sketch. Two of my class mates declare they have seen a play built on almost the exact subject but not treated so well. Just my accursed luck, of course! Baker said: "Well, if this has been done before it's a crime against Mr. O'Neill for I am certain this would be produced." And there you are!

I am not without honor save in my own country!

In addition to my writing I have read twenty plays in the past week or so and have spent my two hours per day on German and French. Ain't I the lazy loafer?

Good'bye for this time, Sweetest Girl. Write soon! A long kiss on your soft lips—in less than two weeks, a real one! I love you!—you know it!—I love you, Dear!   Gene

---

25 • TO GRACE RIPPIN.   TLS 1 p. (1105 Massachusetts Ave. / Cambridge, Mass.) [Boston U.]

[November 18?, 1914]

My dear Dolly:—   As the time approaches when I am to pack my little grip and fare forth for New London and the long-awaited-for Thanksgiving vacation, I am writing to request a favor of you. I will arrive in New London next Wednesday afternoon to remain until the following Tuesday afternoon—six days. Is there room for me where you are stopping? Or, more convenient still,—(Fowlers, if I remember correctly, being a long way from West Street)—will you find out from Scott whether I can stop at Forrester's?

---

1. Emily Rippin.

As my bank roll still retains its former state of perpetual leanness, the tax must not be more than ten dollars. If my bed and scoff can be arranged for less money than that, why all the better! Every dollar saved means a new book for my library, and I need the books. I rely on your gracious self to consider my poverty and make the best terms possible. Let me hear from you as soon as you have done so.

I am overpowered with all kinds of work but, false modesty aside, I am more than holding my own, and have every reason to feel satisfied with the way things are going. Am taking up French and German again to acquire a real reading knowledge of the two languages. For I am anxious to read the good foreign plays which are not translated.

Have been over to Radcliffe, the woman's college run in connection with Harvard, the past two evenings working with the dear girls at the production of a four-act play written by one of them. The fair author is also one of Professor Baker's students. The sweet young things have their own theatre, you know, which is more than the male section of Harvard can boast of. So you see life in Cambridge is not without its redeeming features, what?

My best love to that dear Emily Belle; and my best love also to your charming self. I implant the chaste kiss of brotherly passion on your most-utterly-adorable lips.

See you soon. Bye'bye. Write me all the dope as soon as you get it.   Gene

---

26 • TO GRACE RIPPIN.   ALS 1 p. (1105 Massachusetts Ave. / Cambridge, Mass.) [Boston U.]

[late November or early December 1914]

My dear Dolly:—   Another favor! Will you ask Scott to find out whether I left anything in my room at Forrester's or not? I miss from my suitcase my American Line jersey—which I would not care to lose—and two white shirts with soft collars. I must have either forgot to pack them or they were "pinched" from my suitcase when it was checked at the Crocker House. I know I haven't got them now.

Find out from Scott about the possibility of my having left them at Forrester's and I will be eternally obliged to you.

Best love to Emily and yourself. See you at Christmas.   Eugene

---

27 • TO BEATRICE ASHE.   ALS 2 pp. ([1105 Massachusetts Ave. / Cambridge, Mass.]) [Berg]

Thursday / [December 10, 1914]

Own Little Wife:—   Your "dear little tired boy" received his woodland betrothal ring this morning and has been wearing it on his engagement finger ever since. In fact he has it on his finger right now for all the world to see and wonder at. He is just crazy about it, and in his imagination he heaps kisses of thankfulness on the dear head which had such a charming thought! In fact a good bit of the peace of the woods of which his Lady spoke in her letter seemed to sink into his soul as he fondled Her gracious gift of birch-bark ring and tiny green boughs. Thanks and again thanks, O Soul of My Soul, for the sweetness of your remembrance! It brings you so strangely near me that I feel I have but to put out my arms and you will come to them. I do so. Alas, only emptiness and an ugly bare room with a stale smell of dead cigarettes. My Own, My Own, how I have missed you these past few days! How unpardonably fatuous my existence has been! I am a watch whose main-spring, a soul, has been taken out and is undergoing repairs at your dear hands, O Fair Watchmaker. Or rather you yourself are the main-spring of my life and when you are taken away—I stop!

So you rewalked our first walk together? To the place where you first knew—something? What? That I loved you? There surely could never have been a time when I didn't love you—or so it seems now. How could I have lived then! For the sin of not having loved you always I ask pardon, My Adored One. My excuse is that I didn't know you. I promise that the future will be an indication of what the past would have been—for I shall love you always.

I wish I could have sat on the old stump with you, have wished a wish for Our Future with you. Never mind, when Our Anniversary does come next Memorial Day we'll go out there and picnic and hold high carnival.

Our Future must be near? I hope so, Dear, with all my soul I hope so! Ah, it is so hard, so pitifully unjust, so damnably enraging—all this waiting!! I need you so much, Dear, I need you so much! I am so lonely! Please take me sometime soon! Please do!

Here's a quotation from a short story which is much to the point: "I sure found out that the only way in this world to play for anything you want is to be willing to go after it with all you've got—to be willing to push every last chip to the middle of the table. It don't make a bit of difference what it is. If you get a hand you want to play, play it!"

Eight days more! We'll not let our first Christmas days be anything like our first Thanksgiving ones were. We'll walk and be together all the time. For after Christmas will be a wait horrible to think of.

A week from tomorrow, remember, your husband returns! So, please, don't dance that night! And please can that Hartford thing if you possibly are able to—at least arrange to stay there as short a time as possible. I need you more than anyone else in the whole wide world!!!

Your "tired weary-hearted baby" sleeps tonight "right there"—his lips upon your breast! A Dream of Heaven-to-come!   Gene

---

28 • TO BEATRICE ASHE.   ALS 2 pp. (1105 Massachusetts Ave. / Cambridge, Mass.)
[Berg]

Saturday night / [December 12, 1914]

Own Little Wife:—   Two whole long days and not a line—nothing since Thursday morning—nothing possible, tomorrow being ye Sabbath, until Monday morning. Here am I dying of loneliness, of longing for a word even! Why hast thou forsaken me, O thou Dearest among women? I have been wishing on your bark ring all day, wishing for a letter—and now I have to wait until Monday at the earliest. Damn Sunday, say I, for the thousandth separate time. It will be a period of unutterable tedium.

Have been working like the very devil for the past week. Am typewriting the two one-act plays you know about and you shall have copies to read during our vacation hours.

Did I tell you—(Can't remember whether I did or not)—that Ford and I are going to collaborate on a long play? We have been head over ears writing out a structural synopsis of the plot, scenario of the acts, etc. and are to start on the play itself immediately after Christmas vacation. The idea is historical, founded on the fall of Babylon, and I (or we) have been reading ancient history, books on the customs, morals, etc. of ancient Babylon until I think I could find my way around if I were suddenly set down there before the temple of Bel or some other popular rendezvous in the year 650 B.C. The play will be spectacular, have a distinct Biblical atmosphere, and ought to hit the public square in the middle of their low brows.

The plot and most of its ramifications are children of my brain but Ford has all kinds of brains and is strong in spots where I am careless or frankly weak. So we ought to make a very successful combination. It sure ought to take the curse off my luck! Vive Ford & O'Neill! On to Broadway![1]

I will surely nestle in your arms with my weary bean in its own place next Friday night—provided you contract no subsequent fox-trot engagements. Also provided my stern parent ships me the wherewithal in coin of the realm.

Will'st play Little Wife in earnest this time? Will'st become my banker—for the good of my soul? Will'st let me place all my shining sequins and sesterces and rubles in your hands and then deal them out to me grudgingly, questioningly, as becometh a true wife? Honest, it sure would be a relief to me if you would. Where money is concerned I am totally irresponsible, it burns holes in my pockets, I am absolutely uneasy until it is gone. So become my banker, do! Don't shirk your just duties! Or I will be destitute before half the vacation is over—and nothing to be hoped for.

Bye'bye for this time, Sweet Little Woman. A long kiss on those soft lips which are the gates of my soul's desire—You! You! Wonderful, Adorable You! Ah, how I wish I could express what my heart and soul are crying to you—Damn the futility of words!—I can't. Just imagine your body in my arms, your arms about my neck, my lips on yours! Now, look into my eyes! There! Now, you understand—I love you!   Gene

---

29 • TO BEATRICE ASHE.   ALS 1 p. ([1105 Massachusetts Ave. / Cambridge, Mass.]) [Berg]

Wednesday night / [December 16, 1914]

Own Little Wife:—   Am so peeved this evening I would like to bite a piece out of a cement wall. Have not received a line from my dear male parent and am languishing in uncertainty as to whether I will be able to make New London on Friday or not. I might have known from previous experience that, at the crucial time, Father would dilly-dally and keep me on pins and needles. There are so many things I will have to do which cannot be done until that durned check arrives. However, I sincerely pray it may arrive some time tomorrow. If it doesn't come until Friday morning I probably won't be able to leave on that day—at least not on the four train—may be able to catch the three which arrives in New London at six. I will wire you when to expect me, at all events.

Am busy writing a brief autobiography of my life for the publishers of my book. They say they have received some inquiries about me and want to use a brief summary of my career in advertising the book. Believe me, it's a hard thing to write. If I put too much ego in it people are bound to think I am a conceited pup, and if I don't, why it won't be interesting. The Devil and the Deep Blue Sea! I hate the bloody job.

Only a few days at most and you will be in my arms again! Wonderful thought, which banishes all my irritation! Bee! Bee! I love you so!

Will save all other news to tell you when I see you. Good-night, Little Wife, and the longest of long kisses! I adore you!   Gene

---

30 • TO BEATRICE ASHE.   ALS 2 pp. ([1105 Massachusetts Ave. / Cambridge, Mass.]) [Berg]

Wednesday—noon / [January 6, 1915]

My Own Little Wife:—   Loneliness unutterable! Pain gnaws at my heart like a rat that gnaws at a beam! The memory of your face across the table last night, the look in your eyes,

---

1. O'Neill's collaboration with classmate Colin Ford was entitled "Belshazzar." The play, unproduced and unpublished, was destroyed.

haunt me—for you were very, very beautiful last night, My Own, adorable beyond all telling—And I had to leave! Damn, damn and again damn!!! The trip on the train was misery. I wanted to jump off and run back to you, to fake any kind of subterfuge just to gain a few more minutes. How hard it was to watch that old train pull in and know I had to leave on it! You will never know what a terrible pang shot through my heart when I saw it, and when I turned away from all I hold most dear in the world.

Oh My Own, my Little Wife, I love you so! And now all the gray vista of long, soggy winter weeks confronts me—and I am alone, so hopelessly alone and unhappy without you. It seems as if I never could feel the slightest interest in anything in life until I see you again. I shut my eyes and your sweet face is again across the table from me—or we are on "the rack" in your parlor and I again hold you in my arms with your heart against mine; I open my eyes and see nothing but this dreary room, and a horrible despair grips my soul.

Sweetheart, I love you so, I want you so, I need you so!!!

Beneath all this depression is a feeling of pride, pride in myself, in you, in Us, for my triumph of yesterday afternoon (or rather *your* triumph). Now indeed do you possess all my soul. You have routed the Gene O'Neill of the Past. I am born again—your very own child. Your influence in my life has ever been of the sweetest and finest. You have inspired my manhood with a great desire to be clean, and faithful to your trust in me. Your clear girlhood or womanhood has put my unwholesome cynicism to shame, has called out all the best that is in me. When I think of all the wonder which is you a sense of my own unworthiness saddens me—*but I do love you so!* At least my love is worthy. No one could love you more.

Be assured that, although you are far away, your influence is with me always. I will do nothing that I cannot look in your eyes and tell you about, without sorrow to you or shame to myself. I will make my life as you would have it—for, after all, it is *your* life.

Do you, for your part, remember my many weaknesses. I am far from strong, and if I should do this thing or that, say this thing or that which hurts you, tell me about it, and I will try to never do or say it again. Thus will my sins become fewer and fewer against you and finally, please the Gods, they will vanish completely. Whatever slips I may make, please attribute them to carelessness and not to intent, and out of the charity of your great little heart—pardon me for them. (When I say slips don't think I am referring to my promise. Nothing like that can occur. I mean minor slips in everyday matters.)

In all humbleness of spirit I lay my life at your feet—a poor gift but my best. In all gratitude of soul I thank you for your love which is making so much finer a man of me. Dear Little Wife! Sweet Little Woman of Mine! We shall, we must live out our lives in happiness— together!

Someone said: "We are as God made us, God help us!" But I say: "I am as you made me, God bless you!" A long kiss—no, a million of them!

Turn your back to me, put your feet up on the sofa, then lean back in my arms. There! I love you!

God, God, I could cry—I am so lonely!   Gene

---

31 • TO BEATRICE ASHE.   ALS 2 pp. (1105 Massachusetts Ave. / Cambridge, Mass.) [Berg]

Thursday / [January 7, 1915]

My Own Little Wife:—   The day is a beautiful one, but my spirits are out of tune with all fair weather, and I am more stuffed with gloom than yesterday. A walk with you in the open would cure me. Alas, I might just as well wish for the moon! I loathe this street with its devilish, noisy, flat-wheeled cars and I detest this wearisome suburb of a no-less uninteresting city. In fact the hours drag by slowly one by one and I sit and do nothing but brood over the interminable weeks ahead. I have tried to work but it's no use. My brain is with my heart and soul—with Beatrice.

Of course, this mood will pass by after awhile. I couldn't go on living if it didn't. Just at present I am unable to shake it off except by writing and telling you all about it—which is rather hard on you.

The day is as sunny and warm as one in Spring. My mind is as sick and dreary as a March drizzle. To quote friend Symons:

What have I lost in losing you?
Only the savour of all things.
In the same sky the same bird sings,
The same clouds darken in the blue;
Only, all's changed, in losing you![1]

How I would like to be sitting beside you on Our Beach! It was only three days ago that we were there and yet it seems like three centuries. It was only the night before last that I said good'bye, and yet I seem to have languished through years of bitterness since then. Just to see you for a minute, to kiss you again, I'd give—anything in the world! I'd like to be unmanly and weep tears which would, perhaps, wash away this melancholia but I can't even do that. I've got to sit and eat into myself.

Sweet Little Wife, I love you so, I want you so, I need you so!!!

Your letter arrived last night just as I was preparing to vault into the hay. It was just as you said it might be—like a good-night kiss. I put it in under my head and dreamed of you—before I went to sleep and afterwards, too.

It's the very fact of our last week together being so perfect which makes the present so empty by contrast. I am not intentionally gloomy. I have tried to forget the present and think only of Spring and Summer and our delightful future. But oh it's so hard, My Own, it's so hard! I long for you so intensely that I simply can't shake off this sense of aloneness which hurts me so.

All our "foolishness" comes back to me. How glorious it all was! How delightful it is to be numbered among God's fools! How happy we have been as we reveled in little things which would seem to the world to be the acme of silliness, but which were so full of meaning to us. Even unto holding hands at the Movies!

My Own, My Own, My Own, I love you so!

The one bright spot yesterday was the Baker class in the morning. He read my *The Sniper* to the class and did not hesitate to say it was "very good"—which is praise indeed from Baker.

Ford is back. He and I walked to Boston yesterday afternoon. His wife is not coming back to Cambridge—she always hated it—but is to go to Florida with Ford's mother. He is self-sacrificingly bearing up under this arrangement but I can see that he is mighty blue about it. So we walked off our devils together—or tried to. When we have both recovered our mental balance we are to start on "Belshazzar."

You won't desert me that way afterwards, will you? Even if you do like Florida?

A picture just this minute came before my mind. I could see you catching snowflakes in your mouth as on Saturday last. You utterly adorable Beatrice! How unhappy I am without you!

1. Lines taken from "Amoris Exsul—II. Loss" (1895) by English poet Arthur Symons (1865–1945).

Bye'bye for this time, Own Little Wife! Don't fail to write as often as you can! Your absence has left such a hole in my life and your letters are such a help.

Again I promise you: My life is yours and I will do my best to make it worthy of you.

Bee, Bee, Bee dear! I don't believe that anyone ever loved anyone as much as I love you! It's the very depths of my soul.

I love you, love you, love you, you wonderful, wonderful Bee!!!

Your lips, dear! There! God bless you!   Gene

---

32 • TO BEATRICE ASHE.   ALS 2 pp. (1105 Massachusetts Ave. / Cambridge, Mass.)
[Berg]

Friday / [January 8, 1915]

My Own Little Wife:—   Poor little wife! I am so sorry, so very, very sorry to hear that you are ill. I only wish that God would let me bear all the burden of illness for both of us. You really must, as you say you intend to, go to see a doctor. Things like that pain, although they may not be serious in themselves, are liable to prove serious when you take no care of them. Please be careful, for my sake, if not for your own. The thought of your suffering hurts me more than anything in the world.

If you need me, if you think having me near would help you, if you want me badly enough, let me know and I will borrow, beg, or steal the money some place and come down to you. You know there is nothing in the world I wouldn't do to save you the tiniest ache.

I am full of pity for Us—poor, lonely ones! It does seem as if God might be a little more kindly disposed, might make things a little more easy for us. Such an agony of despondency as I have been in for the past few days is horrible. Every hour I am tempted to take the first train back to you, to throw up this whole wearisome Harvard business which has separated us and made us so unhappy.

You are right. I, too, pray to God or Fate or Destiny to make the days pass quickly, to give us our Spring and Summer, to let us realize our dreams.

Sweet Little Wife, I love you so, I want you so, I need you so!!!

So my book has been admitted to our exclusive library? Well, well, that is fame indeed! Now people will be able to read it without buying it, decreasing my royalties (if there ever are any). Still every move of this kind is at least a small step in the right direction. So I am thankful; for as all roads lead to Rome, so do all my steps lead to you, My Own.

You, My Heaven, My Highest Hope, My Brightest Dream, My Reason for Being, My Soul!

I am glad the beautiful, purple-green stain remains. Every time you look at it, you will have to think of me and pity my loneliness.

The actor from *Joseph* who has joined our class tells me he received a letter from a member of the company saying they were to close at the end of this week in St. Louis.[1] If this is true it will mean my family will return to New York and maybe to New London. It will also mean that Father will be in an abominable humor and I may expect some severe judgments at his hands. Heigh-ho, t'was ever thus!

Please write to me as often as you can—until I recover my optimism, at any rate. Your letters are the only rays of sunshine in the abysmal gloom.

I shall be in the greatest anxiety until I hear that you are well and your dear self once

1. Malcolm Morley was a cast member of *Joseph and His Brethren,* a play by L. N. Parker that James O'Neill, Sr., had been performing on Broadway and on tour since the winter of 1914.

again. Please take care!!! I command it! You are mine, you know, and I simply refuse to allow you to be sick. So there!

Seriously, Sweetheart, do, do be careful! I actually believe I should go mad if you were to be seriously sick and I be forced to be away from you.

Bye'bye, Sweet Little Wife! The time will be awful long but it will pass and then—your arms once again, the sound of your dear voice once again, your kisses once again.

My Own, My Own, My Own, I love you so!

Please, Dear God, give me Bee!   Gene

---

33 • TO BEATRICE ASHE.   ALS 4 pp. ([1105 Massachusetts Ave. / Cambridge, Mass.]) [Berg]

Monday *evening* / [January 11, 1915]

My Own Little Wife:—   Have just returned from a dip at the Y.M.C.A. which I found very pleasant, although my wind is very much to the bad. The remainder of the day I have spent in writing at my play.[1] I have the first draft of the scenario for the first three acts completed but am now in a quandary as to how I shall end the daw-gun thing. I have one ending which delights my soul but—you know me, Al. I do want to strive and give it a reasonably contented ending but my perverse mind doesn't seem to want to let me.

Your letter arrived this a.m.—and it happened just as I was prying my eyes open after a very naughty, naughty dream of you. What was the use of me considering such a "promise"? If you don't "get" me while awake then your presence steals into my sleep and—the results are the same. So consider that Nature has foiled you in your effort to put restraint on the "Irish Luck Kid." It simply kinnot be did! I can't keep your picture from my brain.

I want you too much—as a part of my great love—so there! You grudging, reluctant female!

Thank you so much for your letter, dear old Sweetheart! It has filled this day with as near an approach to sunshine as is possible under the circumstances. Your recalling of the "olden time long ago" of a week past, by the keenness of the contrast, made me sad, but I was so glad to know that you had been "happy" and that you remember all of those glorious days so clearly. I was also overjoyed to hear that all your bad pains have decamped, as I have been really, earnestly praying they would. You just mustn't feel out-of-sorts for even a second. Throw your ills over to me. I am a glutton for punishment.

Do I remember your Sweetest Self a-snowflake-catching? Yes, indeedy; and I have written a booful Impressionistic poem all about it which you will receive in due time. My head is full of spritely rhythms and rhymes these days—where you are concerned—and I intend to compose some rondeau or villanelle or something on "wiping your nose." How silly this would sound to all the stiff-necked generation! But I know better. It is a beautiful, lovely, soulful, exquisite sensation to wipe *your* nose—the most adorable nose, by the way, in the whole wide world. I can think of no more deliriously happy fate than to stand by your side and wipe *your* nose for the rest of my life.

Now do you believe I love you!

Of course I remember kissing you in front of Keefe's and by Wilkinson's! Do you think for a moment a kiss of My Own's could be forgotten! I also remember the trolley, and I remember how your eyes looked. They had happiness in them and I was so proud that you were happy to be with me. I promise to ask you "Happy?" again—whenever I think you are.

1. *The Personal Equation.*

If you said "no" it would break me all up. I have Our Lucky Stone—and I have kissed it, too.

Help you to thank God for *my* wonderful love? Oh, Bee dear, you make me feel like a groveling worm when you say things like that! There is nothing wonderful about my loving you; but it would be a stupendous marvel if I didn't. You are the wonderful member of our partnership.

"My love, mine own soul's heart, more dear than mine own soul, more beautiful than God, who hath my being between the hands of her."

Consider both your hands kissed! My Own, My Own, My Own, I love you so, I want you so, I need you so!!!

If it makes you feel "heaps better" to write such delightful long letters to me, why then, Gawd blimey, I hope you take the cure as often as possible.

So you think of embracing the profession of my w. k.[2] Father? It seems to me *A Scrap of Paper*[3] is rather a difficult experiment for your Alumni. As for making you up: Who am I to dare to paint the rose? But if you'll promise to let me kiss you many, many times while so doing, I'll consent with alacrity.

Speaking of a Thespian career, I have been asked to be a "supe" with a couple of lines to say in the Jewett Players' production of *The Merry Wives of Windsor* at the Boston Opera House. There is no grand opera this year (War) and the theatre is being used by the Jewett Co. for Shakespeare productions. I would be paid a real salary for it, too. The English actor in our class[4] is to play a part and wants me to kick in also, but I don't think it is worth the time and trouble. It takes almost an hour and ten cents to get to the theatre so I fear my salary would be swallowed up in carfares and lunches. Also I care not to be an actor, and I might learn to like it. (There are many beautiful lonely dames in the Co.—so my Briton informs me.) Now ain't you worried?

Received a letter from my unworthy Father today. They closed the season in St. Louis on Saturday and should be back in New York by this time. I am satisfied not to be there to greet them. I can guess the Pater's mood and he and I would get along like a cage full of wounded wild-cats.

Also received a note from Ford—from the Waldorf—some class to friend F. He says he didn't have enough time in N.L. to phone you as the train didn't arrive until twelve and he had to hustle to snare the boat.

I am enclosing you another poem, this time a ballade, very simple but tuneful, if I may so flatter myself.[5] And—(Cries of "yes, yes, go on!") there are still more to come! Happy? Stop your kidding!

Well nighty-night, My Own Little Wife, and a million kisses! I love you, love you, love you, love you so, so————much!

Adored One! Queen of my Life! Sunshine in the Dark! Morning Light! Soul of my Soul! Thou art rightly named Beatrice, ("She who makes happy") for thou has't made me happier than any mortal upon earth! (When I am with you.)

God! Dear God who lovest love, please, please, out of the depths of Thy compassion for my loneliness, please give me Bee!

Again good-night, My World, My Happiness, My All!   Gene

---

2. Well-known.
3. Comedy (1860) by French dramatist Victorien Sardou (1831–1908).
4. Malcolm Morley.
5. "Ballade of the Two of Us," *Poems, 1912–1944*, p. 59.

34 • TO BEATRICE ASHE. ALS 2 pp. ([1105 Massachusetts Ave. / Cambridge, Mass.]) [Berg]

Wednesday night / [January 13, 1915]

My Own Little Wife:— Am so tickled to think that my poor verses pleased you so, and that they had such a curing effect on La Grippe. Am sending you another "foolish" rhyme which I hope will tickle My Lady's fancy—not her nose.[1] Am glad that "You n'Me"[2] struck your mood at just the moment it did—if you are dead sure the tears were tears of joy. I took considerable childish pleasure in composing that roundelay and it is a great satisfaction to know you loved it, too. Of course the frame of mind in which I wrote it was a tender one—I was thinking of you, Foolish! Yes, it was exactly the same feeling which prompts me to pester you with pats and pets—not to mention spankings and kisses on the nose.

I just happened to think—and chuckle to myself as I did so—of how this letter would sound to some of the straight-laced, ultra-sensible souls. "The drivelling idiot!" they would exclaim, eloquent in their staid scorn. But I snap my fingers at all such! Yea, I am a fool and Beatrice is a ninny, but what care we? Only fools see the fairies! What are words and deeds, but symbols? And the fool words and fool acts of Bee and myself are but manifestations of the great love which finds delight in foolish—to others—tenderness. Long live such folly! "Motley's the only wear!" as my lamented colleague, Shakespeare, put it.

Today has been crammed with feverish activities of one sort and another. Class in the morning. Baker telling me how he did like my Belgian play[3] and the plays in *Thirst* and saying he wished to have a private conference with me concerning them. After class, I motored to Beantown in the limousine of Elkins,[4] the millionaire kid I have told you about, and had luncheon, butler and all, at his house on Beacon St. After the feed he and his wife, his mother-in-law and I went to see the play that won the 1914 Harvard Craig prize. It is called *The Common Clay*[5] and is really very fine. After the matinee back to his house for tea, butler and all, and listen to his wife, who is very clever and charming, tell me how good she deems my plays which she has read and how my Belgian play did make her cry. (Now you know why I think she is clever.) Also his mother-in-law, all the way from Frisco, did pay me fair compliments saying she looked for great things from me in the future.

You can imagine how I returned home all puffed out like a pouter-pigeon and did strut before the glass twirling my mustache with gusto and exclaiming with admiring satisfaction: "Aha. Perhaps they were *not* kidding me. You may, with good luck, escape hanging yet."

I guarantee the enclosed rhapsody to cure you of the blues—if said monsters rule your spirit when you receive this. 'Tis a pretty thing! Tomorrow, or soon, I shall send you the last poem of the present cycle—a serious effort with more real poetry to it than any of the others except the "Impression."[6] So be on your guard!

Nighty-night, Sweetheart of Mine, and a million kisses every where—distribute them where you will and in your answer to this letter tell me how you made the distribution. Will you? Please be so foolish!

I love you, want you, need you so, My Own, Sweet, Sweet, Sweet Little Wife! Gene

P.S. This poet is the exception who proves my rule! There! Are you satisfied? Please, Dear God, give me Bee!

1. "Rondeau, To Her Nose," *Poems, 1912–1944*, p. 61.
2. "Just Me n'You," *Poems, 1912–1944*, pp. 57–58.
3. *The Sniper*.
4. English 47 classmate Felton Elkins.
5. Drama (1914) by English 47 alumnus Cleves Kinkead (1882–1955).
6. "Impression," *Poems, 1912–1944*, p. 60.

35 • TO BEATRICE ASHE.   ALS 2 pp. ([1105 Massachusetts Ave. / Cambridge, Mass.]) [Berg]

Sunday / [January 17, 1915]

My Own Little Wife:—   What a pleasant surprise your letter was this morning! I had given up all hope of hearing from you until tomorrow, and that made it all the more unexpected and sweeter.

How foolish of you to go promenading way down to the beach after such a long confinement! I can plainly see where you are greatly in need of someone—and who else could the someone be but me?—to take care of you and stifle such strenuous impulses. Poor dear little wife, what a miserable time of it you have been going through! I am so very, very sorry; so very, very mad that I cannot help you in any way.

I have officially joined you on the sick list today. Woke up this morning with a beautiful sore throat and a delightful cold in the head. Must be this infernal weather we're having. Damned old New England! Have been working on "Belshazzar" with Ford all the afternoon but didn't feel much in the mood for I have a dull headache and all the other fixings.

Loud[1] invited me to dinner with a couple of "lady friends" of his last night and I went out in all the slush, like a nut. I could feel this throat coming on at the time and I should have stayed in—but I didn't want to disappoint Loud and leave him with two fair damsels on his hands. The ladies were the "second lead" and the "ingenue" of the Craig stock company, which plays at the Castle Square theatre. We dined at the Cock Horse Tavern, a famous Cambridge feed-shop. The dames were young, clever, fair to look upon, both college grads of Smith or some place, and both were very natural and un-actressy. We escorted them to the stage door and I blew home to bed, while Loud went to rehearse in some amateur show in which he plays a part.

Quite an exciting event, n'est pas?

I worked on "Belshazzar" most of the day yesterday—all by my lonesome. I have succeeded in catching the mood in which the play should be written, very well, I flatter myself. I have also solved the difficulty of comic relief which bothered us so. I fear—and also hope—that the burden of writing most of the dialogue will fall on me. There doesn't seem to be much of the poetic fancy (creative) in Ford, and the lines in this play will have to be lifted out of every day conversation. It is only by plunging into the play myself and making Ford's conscience prick him that I have been able to arouse him from his fit of blues, and start him in working again. He sure has been wallowing in despond since his return.

And just when I am so full of energy this ghastly cold, etc. pounces on me, Gawd blast it!

Glad the "Lament"[2] pleased you. Didn't you care for my dainty rondeau anent wiping your nose?

Talk about giving your life to have me near you at the time you wrote! What would not I give to have you here now when I feel so wretched and alone! To make everything touch the summit of disagreeableness the day is Sunday and a drizzling, dirty, slushy January Sunday at that—and the town is Cambridge—and my room is what it is—In fact the whole universe is rotten!

So just try and imagine how I need you to play Mother and pet me a bit!!

Remember you have promised to be well tomorrow and you just must keep your word! One of us at a time ought to satisfy even the most revengeful God.

1. English 47 classmate Lingard Loud.
2. "Lament For Beatrice," *Poems, 1912–1944,* p. 64.

Hope you like "Love's Coming-of-Age."[3] I am sure you will.

Bye, bye for this time, Sweet Little Wife. I love you so! (Just had a cheering thought. Jan. is more than half over already.)

A million kisses on those soft, warm lips I love so well. Love me, please!   Gene

P.S. Please, Dear God, make my Bee well!

---

36 • TO BEATRICE ASHE.   ALS 2 pp. ([1105 Massachusetts Ave. / Cambridge, Mass.]) [Berg]

Sunday / [January 31, 1915]

My Own Little Wife:—   Rather was looking forward to a special from you today, since I received no letter yesterday, but so far the hope has been barren of results; but I shall not give up my pleasant expectation until I go to bed. Even then, I may be routed out.

Had a wonderful session with my dear teacher on Friday night. I went out to his house at seven-thirty and he kept me there until half past ten, talking and smoking his gold-tipped cigarettes. He has a beautiful home on Brattle St. and the finest study I was ever in. We sat in front of the enormous open fire-place where a log fire was burning, and he made me open up and tell him the story of my life and adventures along the Ragged Edge. I did so with the plainest frankness and I saw that even he was forced to acknowledge that I have knocked about a bit. I did most of the talking and I held his interest all right for it is almost unprecedented for him to give up a whole evening to one student.

Of course we discussed my plays which he has read and he told me my faults and my virtues—said that while everything he had seen of my work was eminently worth while and above the ordinary, there were certain tendencies I would have to look out for. He seemed confident that I had it the "stuff"[1] in me and that time and hard work would grind it out.

Altogether it was the most pleasant evening I have spent in a long time, and I got more value out of it than of all the classes put together.

Am busy making the changes in my Belgian play which Prof. Baker suggested, and life has again become one typewritten page after another.

Today is the last of January! One detestable month "gone glimmering through the dream of things that were." Thank God! And good riddance! The hour of our deliverance seems much nearer to me now that Jan. is out of our way. Soon, soon will come April! "April! April! Laugh thy girlish laughter, and the moment after weep thy golden tears."

Bye-bye for this time, Little Wife. I love you! I kiss your soft lips.   Gene

P.S. Please, Dear God, remind Beatrice O'Neill about my request in regard to her red flannel—(censored), or her nightie, or her pajamas, or her undershir—(cens.) or something.

---

3. Edward Carpenter's *Love's Coming of Age: A Series of Papers on the Relations of the Sexes* (Manchester, England: Labour Press, 1896), which includes chapters on, among other subjects, "The Sex—Passion," "Woman—On Freedom," and "The Intermediate Sex" (Homosexuals).

1. "The 'stuff'" is added above the line with a caret, which indicates where the phrase is to be inserted.

37 • TO BEATRICE ASHE.   ALS 3 pp. ([1105 Massachusetts Ave. / Cambridge, Mass.]) [Berg]

Tuesday / [February 9, 1915]

My Own Little Wife:—   Nary a word from you since Sunday, Oh hard-hearted person! Today I hoped and hoped from mail to mail, but the last one has came and went and my box is still empty.

Don't you know how terribly anxious I am to hear that you are again well in body, and resigned in mind to Our cruel situation? Really, don't you give me credit for enough tenderness and love for you, to be very much worried about my Beatrice O'Neill? Then I think you're a hussy not to write just a line to let me know there is nothing serious the matter with you.

I have been up to my very ears in hard work—eight hours Sunday, nine hours yesterday, and five hours so far today with the long night still before me.

Have been writing a scenario on a new idea of mine for a four-act play. I completed one but after it was all finished I decided to change the whole thing—so I had to sit down, tear ten hours work up, and start in all over again. "Fancy that, Hedda!" (Hedda is a good name for you in your present mental state.)

You know I told you a few weeks ago about my giving one scenario for a long play to Baker. It was on the subject of abortion and was written with my peculiar mental twists in plain evidence.[1] He said he thought it would make a very powerful play but advised me not to write it for this course. It would stand no chance of production in this country or England, he said—only on the Continent. But he told me to write it by all means as the idea was great, but to lay it aside for the nonce, so t.s.[2] Hence my recent feverish activity at new scenarios. He has also asked me to make changes in two of my one-act plays—two which you haven't seen. So I am a busy, busy bee these Feb. days.

I am the original impoverished author. I haven't had a sou, literally not even one penny to my name since the middle of last week, and I won't have for a week more. I even have to graft the stamps from Ford to mail your letters with. Talk about the destitution of the Belgians! You might knit a few socks for me. If I didn't have so much work to do I'd be nuts—what with longing for you, and the pangs of poverty.

Please don't be so "mortally bored" with me and yourself and everything in general, My Hedda Gabler! I love you so and I do so want you to be well and your old self again.

Again I ask it, when do I get the something which has nestled close to your warm flesh? I tell you my lips are parched with thirst for it.

Please, please bring Beatrice O'Neill back to herself, Oh Aphrodite! (I'll try a pagan deity and see if my prayer works better.)

I kiss your lips, Dear Little Wife of Mine.   Gene

---

38 • TO BEATRICE ASHE.   ALS 4 pp. ([1105 Massachusetts Ave. / Cambridge, Mass.]) [Berg]

Saturday / [February 13, 1915]

I received your valentine this morning. Awful cute! I love it! I had forgotten all about Valentine's day, or rather I never did know when it was, until yours came. Would send you

---

1. Probably an expansion of the one-act play *Abortion*, which O'Neill wrote in the spring of 1914.
2. To speak.

one but I have to even graft stamps—haven't a penny to my name and won't have till next week.

Your program of the Y.M.C.A. orgy sure is a scream. I have showed it to Ford, Loud and Elkins and we have laughed ourselves into a fit. Who in the name of all the devils wrote the poetry for the ads? Ye Immortal Gods!! I have read much bad poetry, even some advertising rhyme, but I hereby wish to doff my sombrero to the author of those scintillating gems. I crown him King of all Bad Versifiers, past, present, or future—The Rottennest Poet the world has ever known! Hail! All Hail! I also recommend—and my three classmates sanction the proposition—that he be boiled in oil, drawn and quartered, and then guillotined or hung. He is much too ethereal for this prosaic, not to say mundane, sphere. Off with his head!

Some of the poses of the characters caught by the camera surely never could have been achieved by sane human beings with brains capable of controlling the action of their bodies. I can only think of a scare-crow in the last stages of St. Vitus dance. What bloody fools most of them look! You are the only one of the whole lot whose picture reveals a sense of what the "profesh" call "stage presence"—that is, the art of being consciously unconscious of what one is doing. You really look as if the pose belonged to you, not as if you had been jammed into it by the photographer. And you have grace, My Own, as all my friends agreed without knowing anything about you, while all the others are hereby elected life-long members of the awkward squad.

Speaking of Grace, Ford remarked—(I'll blame it on him)—that from the expression on her face they had made a mistake in the way they spelled the Muse she represented. He opined they should have used an "i" and put the accent on the first two syllables! D'yuh get me? It's not a nice joke to tell a young girl like you but I think it rather states the case. She sure does look as if something were all wrong.

(By the way, when do I get my crimson scarf?)

As for the Egyptian frieze girls—well—words fail me! Only I know now why Moses led the Israelites out of the land of Egypt. He must have had rather an eye for beauty, that old guy! Oh my God! every time I look at that picture, I nearly die. Friezes, eh?

In your picture the señorita next to the end on left (as you look at it) reminds me of a very accurate cartoon of Kid Broad about to deliver his famous left to the solar plexus. She has the same wide-open guard as the famous Kid. But who is she going to hit, and why?

Seriously, Bee, why in the devil do you mingle in such monumental bunk? You're not interested in Christian young men. (I hope!). It seems to me you've been making yourself nervous and irritable for piffle, wasting your health and strength *and energy* on the most worthless variety of inanity. You don't accomplish anything worth while, it isn't a step onward in any sense of the word. (Hear the man preach!) Just think if you had devoted that time to typewriting—(Ah-ha, now we see!). Really, Bee, long walks would be much better, no?

As for *A Scrap of Paper*, take my advice—"which I know you will not" as Kip. says—and CAN it! *A Scrap of Paper* is a hard play for professionals to get over. It requires good acting, and by good I mean experienced. There *are* good amateur companies—one at Toy theatre in Boston—but they are few and far between and the members are used to the stage, to each other, and to playing all kinds of parts in all kinds of plays.

Why, in the name of God, do the leather-heads who select the plays always pick out such hard ones? Why don't they select some broad comedy or farce where the lines carry the play along in spite of anything? (I mean high-class farce—A. W. Pinero's *The Magistrate* for example.) Instead they insist on Shakespeare or Sardou—thereby making those authors thankful to be beyond such earthly vexations.

No matter how good *you* are you are going to appear bad. Not even Maude Adams could play *A Scrap of Paper* with the W.M.I.[1] and get by, for the majority make or break and the majority are bound to be rotten. People will applaud, of course—but for one of three reasons 1—relatives in cast. 2—No sense, anyway. 3—Because it is so funny, or ridiculous, I should say.

Does all this enrage you? I'm sorry, dear. I don't mean to under value *your* ability a bit. Only when you write saying you are ill, a nervous wreck, worked to death, up all night, headaches, etc. I am naturally sore at the cause thereof. Of course if you're getting fun out of it, if it amuses you, why the more the merrier. But if you're doing it from a sense of duty—as your letters would indicate—why *don't*, that's all! It isn't worth it.

It's terrible late, My Own, so nighty-night and a long kiss! I love you!

Sunday / [February 14, 1915]

Your special arrived this a.m. and I sure was surprised and delighted. To have you write to me "I love you"—well, it means encouragement, happiness, and, alas, bitter longing. I need you so much!

How did you like the letter I mailed to you Friday night and which you must have received Saturday?[2] I am very proud of it. It's one of the best I ever wrote, and one of the most satisfying to me, for it exactly expressed what I felt then, and always feel, but cannot always put into words. I like it so well that I am going to put two of the last lines into the mouth of Belshazzar as he makes love to his Princess Istara.

I didn't "compose" that letter either. It just trailed from the end of my pen, in one of those moments so satisfying to a writer when his feelings and thoughts come out of his brain all properly attired in words, not naked as is their usual wont. And what a task it is to fit words on to a naked, and beautiful, idea! There are times when one cannot find a dress of words becoming to the thought. No matter what one picks out, it looks dowdy. Those are the times when I pluck hair from my mustache in frenzy and curse till the Germans in the next room shudder at the vengeance of the Lord.

Have been working on "Belshazzar" all of past two days and have first two acts well under way. The idea of collaboration is ridiculous but I have let myself in for it and there you are. I will write the whole play and Ford will get half the credit—if there ever is any. Of course he is much too fine a fellow and too good a friend of mine for me to ever let him have an inkling of this but, really, as far as the creative work goes, it will be all mine. He hasn't anything in this romantic, semi-poetic drama line which I cannot beat him at by many miles. Of course he knows this and acknowledges it. Reminds me it isn't fair, I am doing it all, etc. All of which I deny emphatically—and then write all of [the] dialogue when I am alone.

On the other hand, I may be all wrong about this. Difficulties may arise of different nature where I will be all at sea and he will be life-saver. At any rate I am perfectly happy to continue the arrangement. Don't mistake this for a grumble! It isn't! Merely a statement of fact, that's all, to prove how I am working—for you!

The German medical student[3] has a fine Kodak and he took several pictures of me today. Two at my table writing—(soft shirt, Windsor tie, all the properties)—and two in a—well, how shall I say it?—well, in nothing but what the Indians used to wear—not feathers, silly!—around their loins. The artist[4] wanted them for help in his studies of the nude. (I am now a model, wot?)

1. Williams Memorial Institute, a high school for women in New London.
2. This letter apparently does not survive.
3. Daniel Hiebert.
4. August Ebel.

At his desk in Cambridge.

Shall I send you *all* of them if they are good? There's really nothing immodest about the nude ones you know—not nearly so much as my one-piece suit ones. I run the risk of losing your love by this offer. You may take one flash at me, unadorned—and say: "So this is what they give green certificates with! Take it away!" Promise not to or I won't send them. (They'll probably turn out bad, anyway.)

When, when, when do I get that "something" which had caressed your soft skin? Pig!

Bye'bye, Own Little Wife, I love you so! Feb. is half over, thank God! A million kisses! Please write me the "real" letter, you promised. I am so lonely!   Gene

Please, God dear, make the days hurry! I want my Beatrice, God! Thou knowest how it is for Thou dost love her too!

---

39 • TO BEATRICE ASHE.   ALS 3 pp. ([1105 Massachusetts Ave. / Cambridge, Mass.]) [Berg]

[February 17?, 1915]

Dear Actress-Wife:—   I suppose by this time the New London Day et Telegraph have heralded the brilliance of a new comic opera star in the theatrical firmament—"Beatrice O'Neill" on an electric sign for all the world to look at and admire.

Musical comedy is not in my line but if you'll stick to the legitimate I'll write plays for you and we can form a combination similar to that of Laurette Taylor and her husband[1]—I forget his name for the moment—who wrote *Peg o'my Heart.* Is it a go?

I am sure the dire forebodings in your last letter about everyone miscueing and being "rotten" were not justified. All professional companies are usually the last word in ultimate cheese at their dress rehearsal. Playing to empty benches is not inspiring but when they get before an audience they always buck up and put the stuff across. And I suppose it was much the same with you.

Please write and tell me about your triumph—for I know it was one, if the members of your audience had any taste at all—in your first spare moment. I know how little time you are having to yourself and I am resigned to a week of lonely waiting for the "real" letter you promise me. Ain't I the original gracious hubby? I give my wife to the public—not without pangs of jealousy, be it understood—for this week, but only on condition that my Beatrice O'Neill return to me promptly at the expiration of that time, with all her aforetime sweetness and love for me intact.

I too, am not having any time for much aimless drifting. I wrote one scenario for my long play, I typed it, I tore it up; I wrote another scenario, I typed it, I found flaws in it, I tore it up. I have just finished my third and this time I think I have hit upon a *real* idea for a *real* play with possibilities of production. Honest, I am tickled to death with it. It pleases me more than any idea I have ever had, I think.

Have also worked a wee bit on "Belshazzar" and rewritten two one-act plays. I have worked consistently for seven or eight hours a day for the past week and, after much disappointment, have really accomplished something which in my humble opinion, is eminently worth while.

I'm so glad to hear you are better mentally and physically. Better rest up after this strenuous week is over.

Please, please remember how a long, long time ago you promised me a "something" which had nestled near to you! In that "spare" moment, I mean.

Bye'bye, Own Little Wife, and a long kiss! Please don't forget me amidst all the adula-

1. J. Hartley Manners (1870–1928).

tion you are receiving. Remember I am the most ardent and humble of all your worshippers.

God bless you!   I love you!   Gene

---

40 • TO BEATRICE ASHE.   ALS 4 pp. ([1105 Massachusetts Ave. / Cambridge, Mass.]) [Berg]

Thursday morning / [February 18?, 1915]

My Own(?):—   Your last letter in answer to my special was a revelation, and yet not so much of a revelation, for I had guessed intuitively what was taking place in your mind. However, it is well that the matter is at last clearly stated, for the situation, as it stood, was impossible for both of us.

It is up to you to choose for once and for all time!! It is up to you to make a decision for once and for all time!! In justice to me, I ask it. If you love me, as you say, then *bury your dead!!* How often have I implored you to do that! You must! You must! I will have none of these specters of your past arising to mock my love and make me miserable!! I cannot and I will not bear it! I have work to do, work which must be done, and these phantoms come between me and my work, fill my heart with agony and my soul with misgiving, stifle inspiration and all creative joy. I will not bear it!

My past is dead. There is not a single thread that binds me to it. I stand before you, I am yours free and unfettered! There is no room for doubt. I am yours. Not a single emotion remains. I have buried my dead because I thought, I felt, it would be unworthy of you not to do so. No ghosts can arise at my feast. My cosmos contains nothing, or rather no one, but you.

I demand the same of you. I am worth, my love is worth, all of you or nothing at all! Though to the world at large my value may be small, yet to myself I am all I have. I will not give myself for a part of you! All or nothing! If I were content with less I would be unworthy of myself, and of my love for you.

I have no former loves, under the guise of friends, to steal my thoughts away from you. All my former loves are now my enemies as it is natural they should be. However I have accomplished my purpose. The slate is clean. Never again could they love me or I love them. We are dead to each other, and our lives have definitely separated.

All this trouble, all this agony in your own mind and mine, is caused by the fact that you have not thrown away the past. You have not seen the utter impossibility of transforming someone who has really loved you into a friend. The history of a thousand broken lives proves my contention: It cannot be done! Their supposed friendship is, at best, only a subterfuge behind which the old love hides and looks out with envious eyes.

I love you!! You know it!! You know I would not say it, in this letter above all, if it did not come from the depths of my soul! But again I say, I want all of you, freed from the past, or I want nothing. If you are unwilling to lay these ghosts which make me unhappy, then your love is the merest mockery. Free as I am free, hand in hand, with eyes fixed on the Future of Our Dream, ready, glad to endure and strive for each other, reborn by the force of Our Love into new lives which are divided from the past by a wall of determination which no old ghost may chink!! Either that or nothing!

You love me, you cry? Very well, then. Write to whatever-his-name-is and tell him in such a way that he cannot doubt, that he is out of your life forever. Be cruel! It will be the greatest kindness you can do him. It will be but simple justice to me who love you and am living and building for you. It will ease your own mind and free it from uncertainty. It is the one solution.

If you love him and do not love me, why marry him in May, as he suggests. And I—well, I promise you neither you nor anyone else will realize the extent of my pain, or see the wounds on my soul.

If you love me, and still are lured by the manifold attractions of Canadian lodges and ridiculous mahogany groves in Liberia—(As if mahogany grew in groves! And as if Liberia were not the jumping-off place of the world, unfitted by climate, etc. for any but niggers to live in! (See Encyclopedia Britannica.)) If you are so fascinated by these things that, in spite of your love for me, you allow him to write you letters proposing to *"forgive"* your *"affair"* with me, and urging you to forget me, and then you consider his proposition seriously, and think of selling your love for me and mine for you, for a "miserable ease," a platter of bread & butter glorified into a Canadian lodge, a house on Montauk Ave. masquerading as a castle in Liberia,—why then, I release you, I don't want you, I urge you as my greatest revenge to marry him in May! I shall take great delight in watching life punish you for being untrue to your own soul. It will fill my life with bitterness, it will convince me that my judgment of women in the past was justified, but it will not hurt me! If you, confessing that you love me, were to marry him, you would be in my eyes such a mean and pitiful caricature of my ideal of you, that only hate and disgust would remain of my love!!

I have nothing but my love for you, my need of you, my life, to offer you! Put in the balance against his Canadian lodge et al., I confess it makes a poor showing. If I add my brains, my power of creation, my dream children whose future no one knoweth, will it balance? Then choose! All or nothing for either one of us! As far as your love is concerned, one of us must die! There is not room there for him and me!

I am enclosing a picture of myself. It is a good picture. Look at it and then at his. Which of us will win the most in the end? Which of us belongs to the future? Which of us can give you a home and servants, etc.? Which of us expects you to do your share, to work and win with him, to fight and endure with him? Which of us contains the most "man?" Which of us loves you the most? Look into our eyes! Who will be your lover and who your husband down the long trail which leads from the green certificate? Who has the most poetry,—and therefore, the greatest capacity for emotion, in him? Then choose! For all time! All or nothing for either one of us!

It is up to you. Either one of us must die and die *for all time!* You must not put the choice up to me by imploring me to forget you because you are unworthy. You are not unworthy. You are the sweetest little woman in all the world. You are all I said of you in my Valentine letter and more. And I love you with all my soul! Be true to yourself, the real Bee! Don't ask me to forget you, to love someone else, unless you have ceased to love me, and that is your way of letting me down easy. The truth! I must have the truth! If you love me, bury your dead! And, hand in hand, we will start forward again, with all this tumult of soul forgotten! Our Dream depends on you! Our Future is in your hands to wreck or cherish as you see fit! You are worthy of it in every way, Foolish Little Woman, if you but love it and me, and *bury your dead!* My love for you demands a love for me which is as undivided as itself. You are too wonderful to share! All or nothing! For all time!

If you love me, promise me to put the others out of your life! Please! There will be no lasting happiness for us until you do.

I love you, Sweet Little Wife (Or must I cease calling you that?) and I need you! Before you shatter this sorry scheme of things be sure you can rebuild it nearer to your soul's desire!—with the Other One.

I love you so, Own Sweetheart! But you must choose. There is not room enough in your life for that man and me!

So he promised to "forgive" your "affair" with me! May God damn him for an imperti-nent numbskull! Ah, these Philistines!   I love you! Choose!   Gene

P.S. Please, dear God, make B. O'N. choose me! Thou knowest thou madest us each for each! Else why hast thou told me so, O God?

---

41 • TO BEATRICE ASHE.   ALS 2 pp. (([1105 Massachusetts Ave. / Cambridge, Mass.]) [Berg]

Monday night / [March 1, 1915]

My Own Little Wife:—   Have just been mooning over your picture, kissing your garter and the tangled hair from your comb,—in fact have been performing a lot of seemingly foolish stunts which are dear to my heart because they bring you so near to me. Thus do I, your forlorn lover, seek solace in my loneliness.

I hoped for one of your dear comforting letters this morning but none came and so it has been a cheerless day. But, thank God, it was not anything like yesterday, which I certainly must acknowledge was the most utterly miserable twenty-four hours I have ever put in in my whole life.

You know all about it by this time for you must have received my letter of yesterday evening, and were undoubtedly able to read my agony between the lines, if not in them. I went to bed at ten-thirty last night and sleep "which covereth all things," "the balm of hurt minds" etc. never came to me until I had heard the janitor come in and make the fires at five-thirty this morning! Think of it! I rolled and tossed, I turned from side to side, I called on your name aloud in the darkness until the Germans in the next room must have thought I was mad—and I wasn't far from it. My thoughts went eternally round in the same circle of dismal pain until I know my fettered brain plumbed the depths of every separate, lonely hell a lover's heart can hold.

Imagine, as I described in my letter of that afternoon, my abandon to that devil's mood when I could throw myself face-downward on my bed and just give sway to one paroxysm of sobs after the other for a whole half-hour. Why I haven't done a thing like that since I was a wee, small child. It isn't like me at all. I usually suffer in sullen silence. This time when I started sobbing I just couldn't stop. My self-control was a thing of some distant past.

Pardon me for dwelling on this incident so. Your tearful little boy is not trying to excite sympathy for his weakness. I merely speak of it because the whole affair is so unprecedented that it has shown me more clearly than anything else could how impossible life would be without you. (I hope you are interested to hear this proof, Dear.)

Don't worry at all about me! Don't think my health is not all it should be! It isn't that; but those lonely longings have been massing in my brain ever since I left New London and yesterday they charged and carried my defenseless emotions at the point of the bayonet, so to speak. If there had been any place I could have gone to, if Ford had been in, or even one of the Germans, I might have distracted my mind for a few minutes until the crisis was past. Everyone was out, however. I hadn't a soul to turn to. So that mood of the devil just grabbed me by the throat, and got me down, and held me there for twelve hours. And, by God, Bee, it was the most horrible, nerve-tearing torture I have ever been through!

The cause of it all is the same old cause: We love each other, want each other, need each other—yet the stone wall stands between! We are so near to each other and yet so com-pletely separated! When my mind is healthy and sane I know that this wall can be crossed, must be crossed, will be crossed! My belief in the haven of our Blessed Future is so strong usually that I accept our wait with more-or-less philosophy, knowing it to be but the price we poor, ill-starred humans must pay for ultimate happiness.

But there are moments, as you yourself know well, when that wall which separates at some time in life every man and woman from their highest hope, seems adamant; when our heads are so confused with battering at the barrier that we cry out in anguish: "How long, O Lord, how long?" That was my yesterday.

Please pardon me this dissertation which I know must bore you. But I know you are my Own Wife, Mother and Comrade in One, and that you will understand and pity me. The mood is past now. I am not happy—How could that be without you?—but I am more resigned and confident.

I have told you all this, My Own, that you may know how complete my love is. I glory in my pain, for it proclaims to all: "I love her! Love her! love her!" Who could doubt it now?

A long kiss, Wonderful, Beautiful Wife!   Gene (my "something?")

---

42 • TO BEATRICE ASHE.   ALS 3 pp. ([1105 Massachusetts Ave. / Cambridge, Mass.]) [Berg]

Tuesday / [March 2, 1915]

My Own Little Wife:—   Your two letters arrived this morning and I cannot tell you what comfort and happiness they brought to my heart. Bless you, Dear One, for writing them! You seemed to guess just what I *needed* you to say and you said it in just the dearest, sweetest way imaginable. You are a *Dear*, that's all there is to it! I feel so proud that you love me, so proud that you are My Own, My Wife, that I could shout with the jubilation of it. Most Adorable of all women, I love you so, so much! You have been the Pal in Need this time, the strong Comrade where I was so pitifully weak and had such need of you. Again bless you! Bless you! I am all unworthy of your wonderfulness but I thank God from the bottom of my heart that I have gained your love, and I promise Him I will give every moment of my life to my love for you—that it shall always be my religion, my whole existence.

Your proclamation of me as your husband-to-be will undoubtedly create quite a stir in the placid circles of Groton. Please remember to tell me all you hear about it. Let's hope all will concur in that young girl's "terribly dear" opinion—but I have my doubts.

Indeed, indeed Our Spring is at hand. Only nineteen more days before the first of Spring, and after that not such a long time before we will be in each other's arms again. And then we will be amply repaid for all this waiting and hoping. I promise you I will be the most ardent lover who ever loved, the most abject adorer who ever burnt incense of prayer before his goddess, the most humbly thankful of all whom the Gods have blessed beyond their merit. (And my "evil lips"—(that adjective is rather hard on them, isn't it?)—will kiss your eyes, your hair, your lips, your ears, your nose, your neck, your breast—and, in token of befitting humility, every small toe on your littlest feet! There!)

I enclose a clipping from the Harvard Crimson about the one-act play competition. Three girls from Prof. Baker's advanced course—what I would take if I came back next year—won the award. I, and another girl from R. got honorable mention; so I am the only male in Harvard to get among the honored few. Baker told me this a.m. that Pritchard Eaton & Goodman[1] had both favored *The Sniper* but that he has cast the dissenting vote because, although he thought it a stronger play than any of the others, he did not think it judicious for the Harvard Dramat. to put on a war play. And there you are! I always miss by inches. Still I am well content. Those amateur butchers on the Dramat. would murder *The Sniper*. And

---

1. Playwright Jules Goodman (1876–1962).

Harvard spirit and taste runs to the sort of clever plays women usually write. (Sorehead!) I'm not sore, really, for I entered *The Sniper* without a hope and am pleased rather than disappointed at its reception by Goodman (author of *Mother* and Otis Skinner's new play)[2] and Walter Pritchard Eaton, one of [the] best dramatic critics in U.S.

Phone it in to the *Evening Day* and let my knockers know how I flourish and wax illustrious. Ask for Joe Smith. I appoint you my press-agent.

Of course we shall share everything, Dear Heart, even unto the tiniest joy or sorrow. It is generous for you to propose that for you are the one who is always giving—and I have nothing to give but my love, my self.

I'm glad you cried too! For every tear you shed I promise you an hour in which you will desire to cry with the joy of living and loving. You promise, too? Ah Bee! Bee! Bee! How I love you, dear! How I wish I could show you, tell you how much! My whole being bursts with it. I am become a great desire, an enormous tenderness, a gigantic crying need, which wastes itself in futile strivings.

But I did show you a little of how much I loved you the last time I was down, did I not? Please say yes! I want so that you should nevermore doubt me—or yourself. There is such a power of wonder and happiness ahead. Yea "Beyond the Alps, lies Italy!"

For that green rosary of twelve kisses, I hereby wish on you a robe of jewels, clinging tight to every inch of your lovely body, representing the millions of kisses my longing spirit breathes to you!

I promise not to be too unhappy. Whenever that mood appears I will conjure up your dear image so strongly that all the sad weeks will disappear and you and I will again be lying in Our Hammock, in the soft summer and spring nights in the moonlight, dreaming in each other's arms.

Ah beautiful nights of old! With what sweet charm does your memory come back to me! And yet the nights to be will be twice as wonderful! Let us promise ourselves that, Bee dear. We know each other so much better now. Our love has been purified by long suffering of soul and I know it is finer and nobler for it.

I know that now there is nothing in the world I would not do for you, no sacrifice I would not make to render your happiness complete and flawless. You are beyond and above everything, a Dream of All Dreams, a Desire of All Desires. You are the craving of my soul for the joy of living, the Ideal, the uttermost star beyond which is nothing. My world looks out at me from your eyes. To be your lover and husband combined in one—why, I search my mind for its every emotion, but I find all combined and consumed in that. The Meaning of My Life—that's what you are.

The happiness that comes to me when you are in my arms! Can you guess it? No, for I can't even explain it to you. It's just a feeling of being at harmony with Life itself, of having found the Thing-In-Itself, of having reached the ultimate goal of all my striving. I become a part of God and He of me. For are you not—my God?

And also, even better, my Mother whose loving pity reaches out in her letters and draws her own tired Child back to the haven of her arms where there is ease for bruised heads and anodyne for sorrow.

I love you, yes; but you are above me, Lovely One, and so I lay at your feet, "one hand clasped round your ankle," and adore you!   Eugene

Write to me! Write to me!

Dear God, please make Bee O'Neill send me that "something" soon. I'm going to take it

2. Goodman's *The Silent Voice*, starring Otis Skinner, had opened at Broadway's Liberty Theatre on December 29, 1914.

to bed with me, God, and kiss it, and hug it close, and sleep with it in under my head, and even say my prayers to it; but You won't be jealous, will you, God?, for You know I never believed in You till I loved Bee and she loved me.

---

43 • TO BEATRICE ASHE.   ALS 2 pp. ([1105 Massachusetts Ave. / Cambridge, Mass.]) [Berg]

Friday night / [March 12, 1915]

My Own: Your letter with the returned pictures arrived this morning. It sure was good to hear from you again after such a long wait. You needn't have gone to the trouble of looking up those films for me. Spring Recess would have been time enough.

I have sent *The Sniper* to my father in New York asking him to take it around and see what he can do with it. Don't know whether he will accept the job as my agent or not but I hope he does. It's about time for something to break my way in some manner or other.

If you are busy with *The Scrap of Paper* and the trials and tribulations of dress-hunting, you have nothing on me. I have finished the first draft of "Belshazzar"—complete in all its seven act glory! Ford and I are now typewriting it. We are going to hand it to Baker and get his opinion on it. Of course there will be lots to do with it yet, but you can imagine how I have labored to get this much completed in so short a space of time. Am also in a frenzied state of mind about my "Engineer" play[1]—can't seem to fix in my mind what final form it will take. I know all the pangs of child-birth.

Also they have wished a job on me for Saturday, Monday and Tuesday nights at the Radcliffe theatre. They are giving two plays over there for what Baker calls his English 47 Workshop, trying them out to see if they have the stuff in them. Someone must have informed the management that I was once connected with the real stage for I am elected to go over and assist the actors and actorines with their make-up—put on their rouge for them, etc. Some job, what! I attended the dress rehearsal last night and met lots of the dear girls. The two plays, written by last year students (Radcliffe, of course) of Baker's course, are very good. And the novel scenic and lighting effects introduced by Baker make the evening's show a better one than could be bought for real money in Boston. The acting is also surprisingly excellent—due to Baker's coaching. Also some of the girls I met last night were surprisingly pretty—("Surprise" being the right word when a Radcliffe belle is pretty.) What ho!

Ford, wife and I took a trip to Nantasket Beach yesterday p.m. Some beach—makes New London's look like a thin strip of nothing. Beautiful surf rolling in with slumbrous roar. I just stood and drank it in. We got away out on a ledge of rocks where the breakers crashed below our feet. Took pictures. Will send you some if they are good.

Take care of yourself! Don't let the strenuous life wear you down! Don't overdue it! How about that "something?" Or are you too busy to think of me? Nighty night!   Gene

---

44 • TO BEATRICE ASHE.   ALS 2 pp. ([1105 Massachusetts Ave. / Cambridge, Mass.]) [Berg]

Tuesday p.m. / [March 16, 1915]

My Own Little [Wife]:—[1]   Yes, I'm assistant "make-up" man at the Radcliffe workshop, daw gummit, but tonight is my last night on the job, for the present spasm at any rate. The two plays they are giving are really very good, and the staging and acting are excellent. (Of

1. *The Personal Equation.*

1. Tear on original letter has necessitated conjectural readings.

course the make-ups are fine.) It's quite a pleasure to work with such an enthusiastic bunch of people.

I believe you intended sarcasm when you spoke of your "Faithful Husband." You are wrong. Never was he any more faithful, never did he long for his Beatrice any more than at the present. It is she who has been forgetful of him. She would not let him know she was sick, and allow him to claim his rightful part of her suffering as his just due as her Comrade. No, rather did she give him the impression that she was in the best of health and spirits but too taken up with a round of social duties to waste a thought upon him. Therefore must she acknowledge that she is to blame, in part at least, for his negligence in not writing when he received no letters from her.

I am awfully, awfully sorry, Bee dear! I told you how sorry I was in my letters yesterday and I repeat it again. If I had only known! Please forgive me! You know I love you so. I feel all kinds of a beast for not having written when you were ill. But you must realize by this time that the whole thing was a rank misunderstanding of the true state of affairs.

As for my Radcliffe job, it's all in the day's work. Prof. Baker asked me to lend a helping hand—and there you are. Three-fourths of the casts in both plays are males so you could hardly call it [a] precarious situation by any stretch of the imagination.

I had quite a young time last evening after the show. I met Elkins and wife between the acts and was introduced to his wife's sister, one of the most beautiful girls I have seen in a long time. She is here from San Francisco paying them a visit. They invited me to have supper with them and we all motored down to the Georgian—best restaurant in Boston— where we had some eats and sat around listening to the music and talking until after twelve. (O Wild Debauchery!) The sister, whose name is Josephine, is a very intelligent, interesting type. She had a million dollars worth of clothes and furs on, and certainly made them all sit up and take notice when we breezed into the Georgian.

Another thing: Elkins is a great friend of Marc Klaw of Klaw and Erlanger.[2] He— Elkins—is very enthusiastic about *The Sniper* and he asked me if I would care to have him send it to Klaw. Of course Klaw doesn't bother with one-act plays but it will be interesting to have the opinion of one of theatredom's grand moguls, so I jumped at the chance. Elkins was going to mail it to Klaw, but the fair sister-in-law, who is going to New York in a few days, has volunteered to see Klaw, whom she knows well, and give him my play in person. I hope her good will will take the curse off my luck.

I am going to have supper with them at Elkins' house again tonight after the show. Oh yes, life is just one revel after another! This will be the second time I have been out at night later than ten since my return from New London. I really am working hard, believe it or not!

You wanted a newsy letter. Well, this is it. Newsy letters are hard to write here in Cambridge where nothing new ever happens—to me at least. That's why I haven't written one before.

Please write and tell me you're your old dear self again. Spring is in the air! You must be well and happy and love me a little, for I love you so, so much, Own Little [Wife]![3]   Gene

---

45 • TO BEATRICE ASHE.   ALS 2 pp. ([1105 Massachusetts Ave. / Cambridge, Mass.]) [Berg]

Thursday / [March 18, 1915]

O Deirdre of the Sorrows!—   Fain were I that my Beatrice could have her lover "in all the courses of the sun and moon." Her lover can think of no bliss more ecstatic than that—for

2. Producer A. L. Erlanger (1860–1930).
3. Word supplied from context because of a tear on the page.

him. And some day so shall it be! Let but his Beatrice have faith and hope and love him a little, and the land of heart's desire will become a real land, the dream will awake in the kingdom of its longing.

Somehow I have a joyful feeling that you are much better today, that you are your old self once again—Beatrice O'Neill! I am sure this hunch of mine cannot be a mistaken one. You *are* well today, aren't you, Dear? I wish you would write a long letter and tell me all about it instead of leaving me the prey of endless misgivings.

You simply must get well and wax fat again. Three days and Spring will be here—Our Spring! Let us both greet it with hearts beating high with hope, with a love for each other confident in its ultimate destiny. Let us greet it as the end of a winter of long and bitter separation, as a beginning of new and finer things. Will you?

Four weeks from tomorrow and I shall be with you again. It will not seem long. The worst is over and done with. Let us look forward, not back. Therein lies happiness and health and all the blessings I would wish upon you.

Wish yourself well, and take care of yourself, and you will blossom forth in Spring like any other beautiful flower. It is Nature's will that you do so, and you must. Banish from your mind all that sickly morbidness which seems to have taken possession of you lately. The sun is shining! You have love and hope and Our Future, and Our Dream which depends as much on you as on me for its realization. Up! Up! We have work to do side by side, hand in hand, a kingdom to conquer!

Cure your mind of its unhealthy hypochondria and your body will soon burst through your clothes. It is enough that one periodical victim of melancholy introspection should exist in Our Family. Let me corner that market for us both.

My social whirl continues. I am getting to be the Beau of Beacon Street, what! Again tonight do I dine with the Elkins and after that we go to see Mrs. Patrick Campbell in G. Bernard Shaw's *Pygmalion—and the treat is on me!* As I have four orchestra seats which would ordinarily set me back eight dollars, this necessitates explanation, does it not? Well I met the manager of the show in Boston. He is an old friend of mine—was manager of *The White Sister* when I was assistant-manager years ago. He volunteered to give me the seats in spite of Boston's rigid theatrical law against "dead-heads." And there you are! Some luck, what? It will serve to return in part the many favors the Elkins have done me lately.

Mrs. Elkins has roped me in to assist her in some charity work she is doing. She belongs to some Christian organization which makes it a practice to visit members of the "deserving" poor, pay their doctor bills, investigate conditions, etc. And I am elected to accompany her and the beautiful Josephine on their round of visits some time next week. The fair Josephine is prolonging her visit with them and I don't know exactly when she will leave for New York. She has asked me for an autographed copy of my book which she likes very much—(so she says.)

Bye'bye for this time, Own Little Girl. Please write me a real letter soon and send me my "something" for which I have waited so long. Please do!   I love you!   Gene

---

46 • TO BEATRICE ASHE.   ALS 6 pp. ([1105 Massachusetts Ave. / Cambridge, Mass.]) [Berg]

Sunday / [March 21, 1915]

Dear Bee:—   Your special arrived a short time ago and I have just finished reading it. After careful consideration I must reiterate my statement about morbid introspection being the ailment you are suffering from. You are seeking to analyze love, and love is an emotion which will not stand analysis—except by the mere spectator. You have become so preoccupied with your own moods that you have let everything—and me, into the bargain, go to the devil.

As for not writing, and neglect, don't you know that I have written, since my return from New London, nearly twice as many letters as you have? Come, do me justice, at least!

I don't understand why you should not send my "something"—when you know I want it so; I don't understand why you should say you do not *feel* my love—I *feel* it, my love for you, (though I have every reason to doubt yours for me after your past four or five letters). I try and write it to you every way I can, I put into my letters all of my love for you. If I didn't feel it, I wouldn't waste time writing it. Believe it, for God's sake, and put aside these everlasting doubts of yours which only tend to make us both unhappy—and which are such foolish, uncalled for doubts.

Don't take your moods and every thought you have with such tragic seriousness! That way madness lies. You seem to have completely lost your sense of humor where Bee Ashe is concerned. If I set out to take seriously and be influenced by every emotion I have in 24 hours, I would be mad in a week. One must laugh—*above all at one's self,* or there is no salvation!

As for jealousy—if I were to be jealous of every man who holds your hand so long that it has a meaning, of every man into whose eyes you smile provocatively, etc., where would I be? Yet I am never unfaithful to you in even the smallest things.

It seems to me you are again letting a mood run away with you as you did before I came down last time. You know you realized how wrong it all was—when I was there. You know you *did not, could not* doubt my love then. You swore you never would again. You swore by Our Future and your confidence in it! You *knew* Our Love was all it should be! And now— why? why? why? I don't understand! Can a few weeks of absence cause that difference? Then your love—your "mother-love" even—is not worth the name, but is more correctly "whim."

If you do not believe I love you, it is your fault absolutely; because I do! I do! I do! and, if I didn't mean that, do you think for a minute I'd say it, or write it? What for? Why should I?

And "My Dear Little Wife" makes you skeptical? By all the Popes, past, present, and future I swear I wouldn't put down a syllable of it I didn't feel. If I didn't mean all that phrase contains I wouldn't write at all. *I* don't want you for a friend. All or nothing!

I have looked forward to our Spring Recess together ever since Christmas. I have dreamed of it, longed for it, counted the days! You are doing your best to make it all meaningless! You are doing your best, it seems to me, with your silences, your doubts, your suspicions, your eternal preoccupation with the moods which you allow to rule you, to kill my love for you. Certainly I would not permit myself to love anyone who did not love me, whom absence can make forget so easily.

I say "I LOVE YOU!" Am I a liar, then? Why should you think I am? I don't understand!

I don't understand some parts of your letter—your invocation to God, par example. Your mother-love, for another thing. Of course, a great part of every woman's love for a man is mother-love. Why not? Am I not a child, in great part, and every other man also? What is strange in that?

I don't understand what you mean by "what THEY say." "If it comes to pass that no baby-child of your own shall you ever hold in your arms"—well, then, hold me! I promise to always be your child. Where you are concerned, like Peter Pan, I shall never grow up. Have I not always told you I shall be Husband, Lover, Comrade and Child in one? Why not believe something I say, *for a change,* instead of doubting everything? It might awaken a little of your old love for me if you did.

What do you mean when you say you shall not worry until you hear from me? Well, now you've heard from me, are you worrying? About what? I don't understand! Do you think your announcement could make any difference to me or my love? Do you think I would marry you for breeding purposes, or what?

I have felt you in my arms too often to believe your statement about loving only in the mother-way. I know you too well for that.

If you're changing, it's not a progressive change. You're not growing out; you're going back into your shell, eating into yourself.

Perhaps you think the path ahead with me is too rough?

Go ahead then! Pick flaws in Our Love where there are none, look at it with suspicion, have no faith in it or me, blame me for every bump in the road, pity, oh pity yourself, attribute to me every unkindness, expect me to be a hybrid of mind-reader and servant, be unjust, make promises to me and break them for a moment's whim, become obsessed with the constant thought: "What am I thinking of now, and why, and wherefore, and perhaps this, perhaps that."—do all this and you will accomplish your purpose. You will reduce our love to such a mean and shameful common, every-day emotion that neither of us will harbor it, any more. Our Love! The wonderful dream and life-purpose of mine made tawdry! Good God, Bee, think! All for groundless suspicion and self-questioning. It was all decided when I left New London. Why resurrect the issue?

If the intention of your letter was to make me miserable with your uncertainties, you have succeeded wonderfully well. Although it was hardly necessary, for I felt rotten enough without your added digs—Had just returned from a visit to the Doc's. My sore-throat developed into tonsilitis, as per usual, and the Doc has ordered me to stay in my room for a couple of days. All of which I shall certainly not do, the damned old fool. My room is impossible enough when I'm well but when I feel rotten it's unendurable. Besides, I have an engagement with Elkins to-night to drive down to the Seamen's Institute and get some dope for my play.

However if some parts of this letter sound peevish you can blame fever and headache and general grouchiness. Do you know what I'd love to do now? I'd love to give you a good spanking, my mother-child! Honestly I can imagine nothing in the world which would give me more satisfaction—except to kiss you. I'd show you then whether to doubt my love for you or not! I'd make you *feel* it then, you silly little girl, you!

I am trembling with rage at the idea—or is it rage?   Consider yourself spanked, Mother! Gene

P.S. I love you! God d—n it, if you don't believe that, it's only your obstinacy! Please make a Spring resolution to trust me and my love for you.

Afternoon

Am going out now and will mail this letter. Feel very, very p-u-n-k!

Please stop dissecting your love for me—trying to dope out how much is mother-love, how much [illegible] love, etc. I am satisfied if you *do love* me!

Or else save all those arguments to tell me when you see me and I can answer back and fight for My Own.

This is the first day of Spring, Our Spring! For God's sake, try and trust me a little more! If you do not trust or believe in me, then you do not love me, and—Finis! I want to be certain you do love me, or—well, things and conditions of life would change a lot.

Do you ever stop to think of all I am refusing because I love you? No, you don't; you couldn't understand. Still I am giving up everything which, in my past, has made life bearable to me and given me pleasure. And I am proud to do so because I love you, and a sin now would be a sin against our love—and so, unpardonable!

Am I selfish? Ah no, you know I am not. I have made over my life that it might be worthy of you, and in return you give me—moods and uncertainties! It is never so when I am with you. You know you are happy then. Why now?

Enough! Either you love me or you don't. There are no mediums which are not unhappy—mother-loves and brother-loves, etc. ad n.[1] If you love me you will be generous, and brave, and have faith—and you will not nag at me in your letters, or pick old arguments out of the dust-bin of the past.

When I left New London the last time I felt sure in my soul that *you were sure,* and that in your love for me I had a firm foundation on which to build my happiness. And behold, the foundations already begin to crumble into mother-loves and other neutral material, on which nothing can be reared with certainty.

I don't want mother-loves or brother-loves or anything of the sort. I want love, real love, or nothing! There can be no question in your mind of my meaning. You are twenty and I am twenty-six. There is only one love possible between us—all else is piffle and you know it. I don't want to be your father or uncle or brother. I want to be lover and husband—or nothing.

I am giving up a lot—though you seem to give me no credit for it. I demand a red-blooded love in return, not a milk-and-water family-relation affection. I will not be played with or be mocked at by half-tones. I love you! And I am too proud of that love to exchange it for a futility.

Decide in your mind, or rather in your heart, what you want me to do—whether you love me now as you did in my arms only four weeks ago today. If I am to build my dreams, my hopes, my future on your love I must be sure of it. Do not answer this letter until you have arrived at certainty. I have misery enough without any more of your torturing letters. If you, my ideal, are but illusion, then—I shall return to the beast hunt of old times, which, at least, is not illusion.   Remember! I love you!   Gene

---

47 • TO BEATRICE ASHE.   ALS 2 pp. ([1105 Massachusetts Ave. / Cambridge, Mass.]) [Berg]

Sunday / [March 28, 1915]

My Own Little Wife:—   My spell of tonsilitis is almost completely gone, thank God!, and I feel more in tune with the joy of Spring than I have at any time since that festive season commenced. Not that there has been much to jubilate about as far as weather is concerned here in Boston and environs—a cold wind that would blow one's head off, etc., but still it *is* Spring. Our Spring, and I feel it in my blood.

Have been working on my "Engineer" play, the first scenario of which you read, but the main theme has undergone such changes in my mind and wandered into such unforseen ramifications and complications, that it has me bewildered and a bit peeved. However I hope it will all iron out in the writing.

The fair Josephine has gone to New York—left a couple of days ago—we all were down to see her off. She took my play of *The Sniper* and I had a letter from her yesterday saying she had seen him and given it to him—(Klaw being the him)—and that she would write and let me know his verdict in the near future. She is to return to Boston for a further visit later on in the Spring.

1. Ad nauseum.

Had a letter from my father recently. *The Sniper* has made a big hit with all the people he has had read it but they all say the vaudeville censors would not allow it unless I omitted all reference to Prussians, French, Belgians, etc. I also had a personal letter from Holbrook Blinn in which he speaks very highly of the play and assures me he will seriously consider its production if I send it to him after the war.

I have also had some very flattering comments written to me from several others in New York—Cowles, the writer,[1] Wm H. Thompson,[2] and others. So you see I do progress even if it be only at a disheartening snail's pace.

Your "undervestie" has been the source of infinite "wanting," and longing for you, and provocation! I always lie in bed at night with it on the pillow beside me, and dream the old wonderful dreams over and over again. Ah, My Own! My Own! I need you so! I *do love you so much,* (even if you do cast slurs at the truth of that statement, Old Miss Skepticism!)

Ah well, it's less than three weeks now—think of it! Only nineteen more days! How I do hope the weather will be fine and warm.

Think I will go to the Rippin's if their house is open by that time. It would be rather an imposition to stay at my cousins for so long a period. Besides the Rippin's is beside the sea I love so well and I intend to start in bathing if the water is not too horribly frigid.

Bye'bye for this time, Old Sweetheart, and a long kiss! I love you! Please write! Gene

P.S. I am wearing your wedding ring. It just squeezes on my left little finger.
Did you receive letter with pictures I sent you Thursday?

---

48 • TO BEATRICE ASHE.   ALS 2 pp. ([1105 Massachusetts Ave. / Cambridge, Mass.]) [Berg]

Wednesday night / [May 12, 1915]

Own Little Wife:—   Your letter was quite the delightful surprise, Old Sweetheart! I never expected to hear from you so soon and it was more than dear of you to be so thoughtful. It—the letter—came just in time to ward off one of my moods of deep despondency.

Ah the great longing and the great loneliness! How can I tell you of them? I can't; they are deep in the soul where words may not intrude. You know! You know! You must feel them crying for you out of the depths of their desolation. I can feel your spirit near me now as I write. I can feel you bending over my shoulders and reading. You understand what is in my heart. You read what is written in letters of flame over my page of life:—"I love you!" Therefore I will be chary of words which are so impotent when one would express a yearning of the innermost being. My old prayer comes nearest: "My Own, I want you so! I need you so! I love you so!"

I hope that tormenting fear of yours has disappeared—even when in the dark. Feel me near you! Call to me! Stretch out your arms and I will answer the cry of your spirit and come to you out of the darkness, into your room. I will hold you close to me, gently, tenderly, more of the husband than the lover this time, more of the comrade in need. I will kiss your eyes softly, and you will sigh and fall asleep, and the silly old fear will slink from your room and haunt you no more.

It seemed good to be having a meal in my own home once more. It is only when one has been deprived of such a privilege for a long time that one gets the true valuation.

1. Probably the poet Albert Abernethy Cowles (1845–1916).
2. Actor William H. Thompson (1852–1923).

But I have a better thought than that. A toast, O Beatrice O'Neill! To the first meal when we face each other across the table in Our Home, be it even a mud hut!

This summer of Ours—it is to be Our Summer—will be wonderful; must be! We are going to be very happy, You and I. We are going to be content with what the Gods have given us, and do our best to wait philosophically for what they still withhold. There are golden days and nights of stars, and nights of silver which await us. We are going to bind them to us with memories of delight, make them ours. They will be milestones along the road of Life. We have Youth and Love and the hush of moonlight, sun and wind and the kiss of the sea. All Nature will bless us and be kind to our great longing. How can we help being happy— even if we dare not the consumation? Our love is greater than mere desire, will prove itself so. You love and trust me? Content you! I will be worthy.

"Yea, I will kiss the dust beneath thy feet,
Nor ask to share the wine-cup in thy hand;
I am a slave, who waits on thy command,
And lo, a slave who finds his bondage sweet!"
My heart rebels, and cries, "A beggar be.
And haunt her door with supplicating cry.
Perchance she may give ear, and, drawing nigh,
Give thee sweet alms out of her charity."

Ah Sunday night! Monday night! Nights most glorious! I revel in thee, I bring back every moment of delight! Hail! All hail! And I kiss—*yes, I kiss!*—my fine tresses of memory! Ar't blushing? Do not; for I am, the spirit of Love, triumphant, daring, unafraid, exulting in its foolishness, proud of its abandon! It is proud humility which prompts my kiss. Do you understand? Please, when you write again, answer this letter.

Own Little Wife who art my God—Good night. A kiss!   Gene

---

49 • TO FELTON ELKINS.   TLS 2 pp. (325 Pequot Avenue / New London, Conn.)
[Stanford]

[June? 1915]

Dear Felton:—   I read your scenario soon after I received it, but I knew you were in no hurry to get it back, and I haven't really had time to write what with the boat race[1] and similar festivities disturbing the even tenor of New London existence. However, now that the last college cheer is silenced, and the last stewed student has hied hence with his hangover, I take my pen in hand, etc.

I wish to discount my criticism before I begin. It's damned hard to criticize scenarios justly, as you know. They never express exactly what is in the author's mind.

If your play is meant for melodrama, it's there. If you mean it for tragedy, it's not. From the scenario I don't "get" any of the characters as characters. They're simply types—types I have met before in the theatre. Then it seems to me your whole theme and the method of developing it are somewhat sentimental and trite. Perhaps this is because there has been so much in the newspapers lately about prison reform, inequality of sentence, and the rest of the subject matter of your play.

The scenario proves in every way how much you gained from [English] 47 in the past

---

1. The annual Harvard-Yale crew races, held on the Thames River in New London.

year. The play doesn't compare with any of your other stuff I have seen or heard, in idea or in technique.

My advice is: Keep the main idea—the injustice of Justice. It's big. It's fundamental. Too much can't be said about the farcicality of man-made laws. Can the sentiment. Write impartially and make your facts, your characters, drive home the point. Galsworthy's *Justice* is a model of what I mean.

Of course I'm criticizing it all from the stand point of tragedy. As melodrama I don't see why you shouldn't stick to the plot you have now. You have material and strong situations enough but too many scenes. It seems to me you could make four straight acts of it with your present fourth act as tableau-epilogue.

Accept this attempt at criticism for what it is worth—which probably isn't much. I may have missed your point entirely. As I said before, scenarios are no true indications.

Thank you for giving me the opportunity of meeting Miss Jones.[2] I like her very much. On short acquaintance she seems to be all kinds of a regular person. It's a delightful treat to meet a girl whose bean is not simply a rendezvous for hair, and who is trying to do something worth while. Most of the God-bless-'ems in this locality have a large To Let sign painted on their more-or-less lofty brows. The only thing that ever enters their heads is food—not for thought.

I was lucky enough to have two Yale friends of mine as my guests over boat race. One of them possesses a large car and we motored to the Griswold on race day and ran into Clayton Hamilton and wife. I asked Ham for Miss Jones and, lo and behold, she and her mother were right there with them. Introductions followed all around and the result was that we all went in the car to see the finish. Unless a lot of polite lying was indulged in everyone had a fine time, as such times go. I know I did.

Clayton Ham reviewed my book in *The Bookman* for April[3] and *The Nation*—a weekly— of date unknown. I enclose the review—extremely flattering coming from him. He's hardly the kind to say anything he doesn't think. Please send the clipping back to me for it's the only one I've got.

I also received a good review from the Baltimore *Sun*.

No other news worth mentioning. Have loafed so far but intend to dig in from now on. Wrote you a long, almost-a-book letter which must have crossed your last to me. Did you receive it? If so, put that old right hand to work. No welching on the letter stuff! Profit by my good example. "You know me, Al." Adios,   Gene O'Neill

---

50 • TO DANIEL HIEBERT.   ALS(X) 2 pp. (325 Pequot Ave. / New London, Conn.)
[Private]

[postmarked September 22, 1915]

Dear Dan:—   It sure was good to hear from you, and I would have answered your letter sooner if I had not been so busy helping to close our house for the summer.

I am coming back to Harvard to enter Professor Baker's second year course. Will arrive Monday about 2:15 p.m.[1]

I have a favor to ask of you. I wish to get a room and board some place for about two weeks until I can look around Boston and find a place to settle in for the winter. I want to

---

2. Nina Jones, a young woman from California who was studying playwriting with Clayton Hamilton and summering in the New London area.

3. "A Shelf of Printed Plays," *The Bookman* 41 (April 1915): 182. No other reviews of *Thirst* have been located.

1. O'Neill did not return to Harvard, later attributing his inability to do so to a lack of financial resources.

locate in Boston this year. Cambridge is too darn dead. Do you know of any place I can go for the two weeks? Are the Professor and August still at 1105, and, if so, do you think they could put me up for that time—or, at least, board me? Is there any place near you at Wellesley you could recommend?

If you will find out about this for me I will be everlastingly obliged to you. I know you're busy and I hate to bother you, and you mustn't inconvenience yourself to do this for me.

All I want is some definite place to head for when I leave the South Station.

Thanking you for this kindness in advance and hoping to hear from you in regard to it as soon as possible, I remain   Sincerely your friend   Eugene O'Neill

P.S. All the news when I see you!

---

51 • TO BEATRICE ASHE.   ALS 4 pp. (Provincetown, Mass.) [Berg]

[postmarked July 25, 1916]

My Own—   No one realizes better than I do the difficulty of the position you are in. I can sympathize with all my heart with your indecision. It is hard to go and just as hard to stay. The time has come, the inevitable moment which confronts everyone of us at some period in our lives, when you stand at the crossroads. One way or the other, choose you must. You may mark time undecidedly for a space while Youth dances past and beckons you un-heeded, but postponement is of no avail. The choice is finally thrust upon you.

I think the time has arrived when you are compelled, in justice to yourself and to all those who love you, to make your decision—and irrevocably. The blind selfishness of parents is appalling, the more appalling because it is prompted by love and excites our sympathy for that reason—thus weaving another of the ties that bind. Who can blame them? We are all creatures of selfish emotions and in their place we would doubtless feel and think likewise. We are forced to love their love for us even though that love stands between us and freedom.

My advice is always the same. I can remember talking myself hoarse on this same subject on more than one occasion. To my idea, happiness is the one aim we all seek to achieve and there is no happiness outside of self-development. One's duty to one's self must forever stand first of all duties.

You are far too splendid a creature, you have too much of the Joy-of-Living spirit in you to permit your vibrant youth to wither and grow stale in the vapid atmosphere of a New England small town. Why are you loitering, Glorious One, among those dull lives, those small hopes, those mean ambitions? You have eyes to see great distances. What use will you put them to—on State Street! You have a soul and a voice that sings. What are you doing among those deaf ones whose cheap familiarity is a species of contempt? You have a fine spiritual beauty and a keen brain. But those grey moles will always speak only of your body.

To be misunderstood by them, to be stung by their poisonous bites, that is a distinction, a proof of worth. To continue to live among them, that is criminal folly.

Beware! There is a time when the constant, deadening pressure of environment breaks the will of the strongest one. In hopeless apathy one ceases to resist and sinks back, one of the herd.

Bee! Bee! If you want to become an artist you must come out of your shell. There is so much to see, so much to experience which will all be new to you. There is so much moral excess baggage you will have to throw overboard before you can gain the comprehension which is indispensable to true art. How can comprehension be born without a multitudinous experience? You must come out and scratch and bite, and love and hate, and play and sing and fly, and earn your place in the sun. You will have to starve and weep and know great sorrows and great joys and great sacrifices. You will have to thrill with the eternal ecstasy of a self-surrender which scorns compromises and counts no cost. Only by throwing yourself away will you realize your own worth and find your soul. Only by standing on the grave-mound of the Past will you see the vision of the future clear before you, alluring in its possibilities.

Does this all sound as if I were making a plea for myself? Do not misunderstand me. I am trying to forget for the moment how much I love, want, need you! I am writing to you as I would write to any girl in your cruel predicament whose soul is crying to be free. If I did not know you at all and was only familiar with the details of your case, I would write you the same words, and love you in a general, human way—for I love all those rare ones who love the things I love, and who struggle for self-expression through the medium of art.

I think you are prone to exaggerate your parents' concern over your departure. They are afraid of the vague possibility. It is a horrible phantom which haunts them. Make it real, concrete fact! *Make them feel it is inevitable!* (My old song!) Explain to them it does not mean eternal separation or anything of the sort. Show them your happiness, your future depends on it. Talk about it constantly. Make them familiar with the idea. They will protest, of course. There will be arguments, and sentimental scenes, and tears at parting, etc. But one month after you are gone (—I predict from my knowledge of human nature—and it doesn't mean they will love you any the less)—they will be getting used to the situation, and six months after it will be a part of their lives. Three hours distance by train is not a thing even a parent continues to despair over.

Bee! Bee! You mustn't stay! Think what it means! Can you see yourself, wild, wayward bird-soul that you are, caged in a home, propagating with a husband-man? Or clutching your virginity to the miserable, stagnant end? Or after years, in a moment of bitter despera-tion wasting your wonderful self on some lover of the moment who would be too conven-tionally small-minded and moral to value the depth of your sacrifice? These seem to me the three alternatives New London holds out.

No! No! No, Bee! God damn me (and the oath reveals how intensely I feel about it) you must save yourself; and I pledge you in advance the sympathetic aid of all us others who work and struggle and starve and are happy in the fight for greater freedom in life, in Art, in everything.

What work to do? How about singing? Can't Weld help you to get church work in N.Y. or something in that line? Then there's posing; but that's hard. I should think Weld could fix you up all right. If you make six a week it will be enough. Among my people there is no dress or show and that eliminates a lot of expense. I can help you all in the world down there but can't do anything from up here.

Promise to try it, at all events, in the fall. I know you will make good. It will be strange at first but you will love it after a time. Try it! You must! You can always go back—but *you* never would.

Now I have finished talking like an interested adviser and I beg leave to return to my own self—your lover who is willing to put his life in your dear hands and live and love it out with His Lady in such manner and under any conditions which are pleasing to her.

There, you sweet, foolish old fish! Tristan could not have said more to his Iseult, or Paolo to his Francesca.

News of myself? I am half through the first act of a three-act comedy[1] which I have

1. *Now I Ask You*, first published in *"Children of the Sea" and Three Other Unpublished Plays by Eugene O'Neill*, pp. 107–87.

hopes for in the producing line when completed. Have been busy directing rehearsals of my play *Bound East for Cardiff* which the Provincetown Players are to produce next Friday and Saturday nights. The cast is good—several professionals are summering here and many of the Washington Square Players. The theatre is a delightfully quaint place—an old store-house on the end of a long dock owned by Mary Heaton Vorse, the writer. Of course we make all our own scenery, music, costumes, etc. Have people in the Players who are up on all those things. It's very interesting.

Also have written much poetry—free verse—in past months and think a lot of it will eventually land in *Poetry, The Little Review, The Masses, Blast, The Flame* or some of the other radical publications. Used to write for *Revolt,* the Anarchist Weekly which was suppressed by the Federal police after running three months. That was last winter. I was one of the group who helped get the paper out every week. We all narrowly escaped getting a bit to do in the Federal pen.

I will sometime write you or tell you—for your ears alone!—a story entitled—"The Passing of Hutch Collins."[2] His debut and finish in G. Village life were lamentable. He had every chance to make good, too. I was a fixture there when he arrived and knew everyone and was popular, if I do bouquet myself. I introduced him and took him everywhere. At the end of a few months one after another of my best friends came to me and protested about him: "Is *he* a friend of yours?" They condemned him as stupid, "nothing to him," etc. and they were disgusted with his grafting. Hutch went at Bohemia as if he thought it was a place where you sponged without gratitude and made no pretense of return. Honestly, Bee, it was a shame! No one would have minded if he had ever shown he appreciated their kindness but he only acted like a surly, silent bore, and so anathema is his name.

When you were in New York I asked him to bring you down to Christine's restaurant[3] for dinner—I had the money then and I wanted oh, so much to see you! I didn't dare go to you myself for I thought you must hate me. He promised to do so but I forget what the excuse was. If you had come down it would have saved me many nights and days of hell when I longed for you so hopelessly. I would have cried in your arms and you would have forgiven me, Dear Old Big Heart, as you have now.

Did he ever speak to you about it? I suppose not. I trust his friendship as far as I can throw this house, exactly.

Do you think you could make a trip up here this summer? Know anyone in Boston? How are the finances? I would go to New London for a day or so to see you—God! To see you again!—but—the usual Tale—Broke! If you came up here you could stay at the house of Jack Reed, the author & war correspondent, and his wife[4] would act as chaperon as far as outsiders would know. They live right across from us. Or you could stay with Mary Heaton Vorse,[5] or a dozen other households with females presiding.

Try! Lie a little to be happy much! You'd love it here.

Will tell you all about the place and the celebrities and their scandalous lives when I write next. This letter is already a four-decker novel and I know the most boo'ful eyes in the world are already tired peering at my dwarfed handwriting.

---

2. Actor Charles Hutchinson Collins (d. 1919), who appeared in the Provincetown Players's premieres of O'Neill's *Fog* (1917), *The Long Voyage Home* (1917), and *Ile* (1917).
3. The Sixty at 60 Washington Square South, run by Louis Holladay, whom O'Neill met at Princeton; Christine Ell was the cook there.
4. Louise Bryant (1890–1936), then living with John Reed (1887–1920), did not become his wife until several months later.
5. Vorse (1881–1966), novelist, memoirist, journalist, and champion of labor, had resided in Provincetown since 1907; it was on her wharf that the Provincetown Players first held public performances in 1916.

The long kiss, Own Sweetheart, and the old cry of my whole being, but ten times more poignant and lonely than of old— I love you, I want you, I need you so!   Gene

P.S. This poem of Carl Sandburg's from *The Little Review* expresses something of the spirit I have tried to put into this letter.

> *Choices*
> They offer you many things,
>   I a few.
> Moonlight on the play of fountains at night
> With water sparkling a drowsy monotone,
> Bare-shouldered, smiling women and talk
> And a cross-play of loves and adulteries
> And a fear of death
>   and a remembering of regrets:
> All this they offer you.
> I come with:
>   salt and bread
>   a terrible job of work
>   and tireless war;
> Come and have now:
>   hunger
>   danger
>   and hate.

P.S.(2) A million congratulations about your song. Did not see that page of your letter till just now.

PART TWO

APPRENTICESHIP

1917–1920

God stiffen it, I am young yet and I mean to grow!
—*To George Jean Nathan, June 20, 1920*

By 1917, O'Neill's days of wandering were nearly over. He still drank heavily, and his associates were not always entirely respectable, but his life centered on the Playwrights' Theatre, where, in a converted brownstone house on Macdougal Street in Greenwich Village, George Cram Cook led the Provincetown Players toward idealistic theatrical goals. The work was serious, the aims clear, the means simple, and the Players provided O'Neill with an atelier while he learned his craft and defined his individual voice. They staged *Before Breakfast, The Moon of the Caribbees, The Long Voyage Home, Fog, The Sniper,* and *Ile.* Branching out in an untried direction O'Neill began a series of short stories based on his life at Jimmy the Priest's. Only "Tomorrow" was completed, but its publication by Waldo Frank in *The Seven Arts* was a beginning. Shortly thereafter, H. L. Mencken and George Jean Nathan accepted *The Long Voyage Home, Ile,* and *The Moon of the Caribbees* for publication in *The Smart Set,* evidence enough that his voice was being heard. In Nathan, O'Neill made a lifelong friend.

In these years, the free, easy, exciting world of the Greenwich Village bohemians provided heady company. Maxwell Bodenheim, Theodore Dreiser, Charles Demuth, George Bellows, Emma Goldman, and John Reed, together with an array of friends of less substantial accomplishment but equal in joviality and creative energy, were his companions. He had an affair with Louise Bryant, John Reed's wife, but she broke it off to follow Reed to Russia, where Reed's experiences would lead to his writing *Ten Days that Shook the World.* Somewhat on the rebound, O'Neill began an affair with a young writer, Agnes Boulton, who resembled Louise. Their affair was conventionally unconventional—two individuals living together, committed to one another but without irrevocably binding ties to hamper their individual freedom. In April 1918, however, the two were married in Provincetown. There, the following year, their son, Shane Rudraighe O'Neill, was born.

The period in Provincetown was one of astonishing creativity for O'Neill. Plays poured copiously from his imagination, and the stockpile of unpublished and unproduced works grew bulky. Increasingly essential to his intensive labors was solitude. To find it, he moved from Provincetown to a former Coast Guard station on the edge of the sea at Peaked Hill Bar. Solitude here was guaranteed. The station was several miles south and west of Provincetown and could be reached only by a long walk over sand dunes. Mail was delivered by the Coast Guard passing from town to their new station. Unless they so desired it, the young family, augmented by Shane's nurse, Fifine Clark, were required to see no one. The exterior life was simple—swimming far out in the Atlantic or paddling in a treasured kayak. For the first time, there was nothing to interfere with his writing. O'Neill's career as a dramatist began in earnest.

As his skills improved, O'Neill began to seek a scope greater than that permitted by the one-act play. In 1918 and 1919 he completed three full-length plays: *Beyond the Horizon*, *Chris Christophersen*, and *The Straw*. The first two were optioned by important Broadway producers, John D. Williams and George C. Tyler respectively. O'Neill found that his affairs were growing sufficiently complicated for him to engage a lawyer, Harry Weinberger, and to sign with the American Play Company, where Richard Madden became his agent. The two men remained his lifelong friends.

The productions of the Provincetown Players were amateur endeavors. In their early years, the author, an actor, or whoever was around and willing would direct the play and often design it and act in it as well. The Players were notably insouciant about critical reception of their offerings. They tended to sneer at the "commercialism" of a rival Village organization, the Washington Square Players, headed by a patent attorney named Lawrence Langner, because they hired directors and courted reviewers. Before long, however, the anarchy of amateurism was forced to give way to the demands of the group's increasingly skilled writers and actors. Then the professional appeared among them. Nina Moise, for example, was one on whom O'Neill relied for knowledgeable control of his productions, and through a lifetime's friendship, he wrote her revealingly about his theatrical concerns. He relied equally on "Fitzie," M. Eleanor Fitzgerald, the business manager of the Players.

O'Neill quickly moved beyond the amateur level. With two of his long plays under professional management, his demands for the highest standards of production understandably increased. John D. Williams staged *Beyond the Horizon* to critical and popular success in 1920. Hard on its heels, *Chris Christophersen* failed out of town. There were no producers for *The Straw*, the play based on O'Neill's experiences at Gaylord Farm. *Beyond the Horizon*, however, was proof enough that a powerful dramatist had arrived, and many critics felt the play to be a harbinger of a new life in the twentieth-century American theatre. It won the first of O'Neill's four Pulitzer Prizes, and its production, as the correspondence concerning a possible London staging suggests, was the beginning of O'Neill's European reputation.

O'Neill's personal life was satisfactory. The letters written to Agnes from New York while he was attending to production matters echoed the passionate correspondence with Beatrice Ashe, displaying many of the same attitudes, even speaking in the same phrases. The echoes, however, were paler than their source in the Ashe letters, and before long the amorous tone became domesticated and a little matter-of-fact. As O'Neill attended rehearsals and conferences on his plays, the gypsy began to die. A tweed suit and overcoat were purchased at Lord and Taylor, and the few ventures into the saloons of yesteryear were not convivial successes. Far more interesting were the evenings drinking absinthe with expensive people.

As his life curved toward an outer respectability, his relationship with his parents, especially his father, changed. The two grew closer and found values in one another neither had suspected. In August 1920, James died in agonizing pain from intestinal cancer with Eugene at his bedside. He had lived long enough to see his renegade son's success with *Beyond the Horizon* and to rejoice in the knowledge that earlier antagonisms had died away.

By November 1920, when the Provincetown Players's production of *The Emperor Jones* became the season's sensation, O'Neill was acknowledged as a dramatist of the first rank in the United States. He responded to the interest the newspapers showed in him with a certain protective irony but also with a shrewd recognition of the valuable copy that his picaresque background provided. He was excited by his new work in the theatre, and as his letter to Agnes written on January 28, 1920, during rehearsals of *Beyond the Horizon*, makes evident, he was thrilled when for a short time he occupied the command post of the director: "For two days now I have occupied that position so unattainable to most playwrights—the only man in the auditorium, director of my own play. . . . At the end of each scene . . . every member of the cast who has been in that scene lines up at the footlights while I—a lone figure in a vast auditorium—go from one to one, praising or panning. . . . Can you imagine!" His was still the joyful voice of the amateur, but the excitement quickly abated. When *Chris Christophersen* began rehearsals, he made excuses to absent himself. Agnes was ill, he said, and he could not leave her alone in the wilds of Peaked Hill Bar to attend out-of-town tryouts in New Jersey. He returned to Cape Cod and let the play sink without his help.

Agnes's illness may have been a reality, but the pressure of his imagination was a more urgent reason for leaving the theatrical turbulence of New York to return to the isolation of the sea and sand dunes. The practical Broadway theatre was all very well. He would ultimately understand it thoroughly, but he instinctively knew that only in solitude could the growth in his work that he urgently sought take place. His profession was not to be that of a "lone figure in a vast auditorium."

52 • TO WALDO FRANK.[1]   TLS 1 p. (Provincetown, Mass.) [Pennsylvania]

March 26th, 1917

My dear Mr. Frank,   I am enclosing the only other copy of my story, "To-Morrow," about which Louise Bryant spoke to you. It is a bit battered, due to its being a working copy, but I hope still presentable.

I am not able to send you any of the plays Louise mentioned, because at present they have not been translated from my longhand, but I can and do threaten you with a deluge of two or three as soon as I have them typed.

Hoping "To-Morrow" may prove to be something in the line of what you are looking for,   I remain,   Sincerely yours,   Eugene G. O'Neill

---

53 • TO WALDO FRANK.   ALS 1 p. (Provincetown, Mass.) [Pennsylvania]

March 31, 1917

My dear Mr. Frank: I spent all this afternoon and evening going over "Tomorrow" with a view to eliminating the imperfections you mentioned in your letter, and I think I have done so in a great many cases at any rate.

The postscript goes overboard. You are quite right about it. When I first wrote the story I planned it as the first of a series of Tommy the Priest's[1] yarns in which the story-teller was to hog most of the limelight—a sort of Conrad's Marlow—and once I had that idea I couldn't let go, and it rode me into the anti-climax. I see all this now but didn't when, under the influence of said obsession, I jammed in that postscript.

I hope I have sharpened the story. At least I have shortened it about a thousand words.

I must ask your pardon again for sending back the old faithful M.S.S. to you. The cuts have been made in pencil so you can see exactly what has been pruned and whether the changes accord with your ideas or not.

Also my typewriter has not come yet; also there is no typist in this hamlet; also, if there were, I could not pay her!

The last reason having it, I remain   Apologetically yours   Eugene G. O'Neill

---

54 • TO WALDO FRANK.   TLS 1 p. (care of John Francis[1] / Provincetown, Mass.) [Pennsylvania]

[April 1917]

My dear Mr. Frank: As I don't know exactly what you want for your "Notes on Names," and as there is no copy of *The Seven Arts* to be had in this hamlet to give me any information on the subject, I am simply sending you a list of different things I have done in their chronological order, leaving it to you to pick out whatever you think suitable.

Born, New York City—28 years old—One year—freshman—at Princeton Univer-

---

1. Frank (1889–1967) edited, with James Oppenheim, Louis Untermeyer, and Van Wyck Brooks, *The Seven Arts* magazine (1916–17).

1. Barroom locale of the story, which was modeled on Jimmy the Priest's, a New York saloon and flophouse where O'Neill lived between sea voyages in 1911–12.

1. O'Neill was living in a rented room above John Francis's grocery store on Commercial Street in Provincetown.

sity—Secretary, mail-order firm in N.Y.—Gold prospecting expedition in Spanish Honduras (six months)—Assistant-manager of theatrical company on road tour in U.S.—Ordinary seaman, Norwegian barque, Boston to Buenos Aires, (65 days)—Draughtsman for Westinghouse Electrical Co., Buenos Aires—Job in wool house, Swift Packing Co. in La Plata, Argentine—then with Singer Sewing Machine Co. in Buenos Aires—worked on cattle ship, Buenos Aires to Durban, South Africa, and return—Back to New York from B.A. as ordinary seaman on British tramp steamer—To England as able seaman on American Line—Actor in *Monte Cristo* sketch on Orpheum circuit in U.S.—Reporter on morning paper in New London, Conn.—Book of my one-act plays published under the title of *Thirst*—One year in Harvard University, Professor Baker's course in the drama—since then, writing, plays, mostly.

Four of my plays were produced by the Provincetown Players in New York last season—*Bound East for Cardiff, Before Breakfast, Fog,* and *The Sniper.* The Cardiff play is to be put on by the Greenwich Village Players at their new theatre next winter.

That's about all. Excuse my thrusting a young autobiography on you but it's the only way I can figure out to give you something of what you may want. Hoping I have done so, I remain   Sincerely yours   Eugene G. O'Neill

P.S. Am going to send you some one-act plays this week.[2]

---

55 • TO H. L. MENCKEN.[1]   TLS 1 p. (Provincetown, Mass.) [Enoch Pratt]

May 26, 1917

Dear Mr. Mencken: I am taking advantage of your kind letter asking to see more of my stuff to enclose two one-act plays.[2] They are units in a series the first of which was *Bound East For Cardiff,* produced in New York last season by The Provincetown Players. They deal with merchant-sailor life on a tramp steamer as it really is—its sordidness inexplicably touched with romance by the glamor of far horizons.

Each play is complete in itself and does not depend in any way upon the others. I merely use some of the same characters in each because, from my own experience as a sailor, I thought I had, in the majority of cases, picked out the typical mixed crew of the average British tramp.

I have never seen anything of this kind in *The Smart Set* and I have small hope of it being the type of material you desire. But I do hope, and hope it strongly, that you will read them. I want these plays, which to me are *real,* to pass through your acid test because I know your acid is "good medicine."   Sincerely yours,   Eugene G. O'Neill

---

56 • TO DAVID RUSSELL LYMAN.   ALS 1 p. (325 Pequot Ave. / New London, Conn.) [Yale]

[Summer? 1917]

Dear Doctor Lyman:—   My father received your letter yesterday inquiring as to my whereabouts. Any communication to the above address will reach me. Someone must have

---

2. "Tomorrow" was published in the June 1917 issue of *The Seven Arts;* the magazine later accepted O'Neill's one-act play *In The Zone* but ceased publication before it could appear. "Tomorrow" is reprinted in *The Unknown O'Neill: Unpublished or Unfamiliar Writings of Eugene O'Neill,* pp. 311–31.

1. The critic H. L. Mencken (1880–1956) coedited *The Smart Set* magazine with George Jean Nathan.
2. *The Long Voyage Home,* published in the October 1917 *Smart Set,* and *The Moon of the Caribbees,* published in the August 1918 issue.

blundered somewhere, as I left orders at the post office here where my mail should be forwarded.

I have been intending to write you personally about a matter upon which I am very uncertain. I claimed exemption in the draft on the grounds that I was an arrested tubercular case. Will I have to have a certificate from you to prove this?

I am not trying to dodge service but, from what I hear, conditions in the camps and at the front are the very worst possible for one susceptible to T.B. Is this so? I would be very grateful for your advice. I want to serve my country but it seems silly to commit suicide for it.

Also I distrust an army surgeon's knowledge of T.B. I had my experience with the ordinary doctor before I was sent to Gaylord. It was not one calculated to inspire respect for their insight into the G.W.P.[1]

I tried to enlist in the Navy but was refused for minor defects which will not count in the draft, I understand.

Would you mind telling me your opinion about all this?   Sincerely, and always gratefully, yours   Eugene G. O'Neill

---

57 • TO NINA MOISE.[1]   TLS 2 pp. (Provincetown, Mass.) [Yale]

April 9, 1918

Dear Nina: I am very glad to hear from Susan[2] that you are to direct *The Rope*. That is exactly as I would have it. I had hoped you would be able to. You know my work and understand the spirit underlying it as few people do. Therefore I have complete confidence in your direction. I know you will let me know of any cuts which may appear advisable. You know I'm no stickler when it comes to cuts when I can *see* them.

I can't get down myself until probably the preliminary dress rehearsal. When will that be? I've forgotten. I have many other things to do which make the trip imperative—see *Ile*— see Nathan—present my long play to J. D. Williams,[3] etc. At present I'm slaving on the latter part of the last act of the long play. I've been working like the devil on it—six and seven hours a day. If I can make it what I dream, and cram it down the managerial throat—well— wait and see!

Speaking of *Ile* I have a favor to ask of you. Probably your time is so taken up you won't be able to grant it but here goes: I have written Conroy[4] I couldn't get down before opening but told him I would try and get someone familiar with *Ile* to look over one or more of his rehearsals. This for my own interest so that I can learn from a neutral source how the atrocity is being perpetrated. Do you think you could get over? Would it interest you to do so? You know *Ile* so thoroughly. If you can't manage it, who of the bunch could, do you think?

This shows I've my nerve with me, but what can a poor absentee do? I really must get my long play in to Williams—I've promised him—and, to do so, I've got to remain here and slave instead of hastening in quest of first-night clamors for Author—if *Ile* doesn't get the

---

1. The Great White Plague, i.e., tuberculosis.

1. Director of the Provincetown Players's premieres of O'Neill's *The Sniper* (February 16, 1917) and *Ile* (November 30, 1917), Moise was scheduled to direct the Players's premiere of *The Rope* on April 26, 1918.
2. Playwright and novelist Susan Glaspell (1882–1948). She and her husband, George Cram (Jig) Cook (1873–1924), were instrumental in founding the Provincetown Players.
3. Broadway producer John D. Williams (1886?–1941), to whom O'Neill wanted to submit *Beyond The Horizon*.
4. Frank Conroy, actor and a founder of the Greenwich Village Players, who revived *Ile* on April 18, 1918.

well known raspberry instead! Anyway, if you can't make it, suggest something! I'm that practical(?), as you know, but I'm not beyond advice.

Susan writes you are having difficulties casting *The Rope*. It's too bad about Hutch. He would make a fine Luke. Can't he be beguiled in some way? The parts have to be well acted or *The Rope* is likely to hang itself. Do let me know what the prospective cast is when you get a moment's writing spell.

By the way, how do *you* like *The Rope*?

Ssshh! Secrets between us! Don't let Ida[5] play the child!

I'm sorry I didn't get a chance to have that long talk with you before I left—or, rather, I'm not sorry. What use for Mr. Hyde to discuss Dr. Jekyll (if that's the way you spell him) or vice-versa? I might as well try to account for the leopard's spots as for my own. The more-or-less good God put them there—probably, as in the leopard's case, for camouflage so that I may dream on my branch—unhunted!

One part of me fiddles betimes while Rome burneth and while the other part perishes in the flames—a martyr giving birth to the soul of an idea. One part of me is the author of my life-play tearing his hair in a piteous frenzy as he watches his "worser" half playing the lead and distorting the theme by many strange grimaces. Believe me, from line to line, the poor wretch can never tell whether the play is farce or tragedy—so perverse a spirit is his star.

Enough! This all reads like Jabberwocky but it's the best I can do with "Little I Myself." There's the germ of the truth in it somewhere, I feel.   My very best, Nina!   Gene

P.S. Pardon the machine but our one pen is scarcely capable of signatures.

---

58 • TO NINA MOISE.   TLS 2 pp. (Provincetown, Mass.) [Yale]

Sunday / [April 14, 1918]

Dear Nina: Have just finished looking over the script with the cuts marked on it. Some of them, as you will see, I have reinstated. It isn't in character for old Bentley to cut the sequence of phrases of his biblical quotations. He learned and repeats them by heart. Also it spoils the rhythm. I don't agree with you about the exposition. It's dramatic exposition if I ever wrote any, and characterized, I flatter myself. It's up to the actors. If they are bad—I refer especially to the woman—then the extensive cuts are justified under the circumstances. Make the woman talk as fast as she can in a flurry of petty, nagging rage. It's part of her to keep always nagging at the old man on account of the hated step-mother she has never forgotten. Sweeney is half-drunk and in a garrulous mood when he tells her about his trip to town. Also he loves the sound of his own voice. Make him that sort of person. If the thing is acted naturally all that exposition will come right out of the characters themselves. *Make them act!* Don't let them recite the lines. Of course it will drag if they do that.

I've made quite a few cuts myself, as you will see. Tried to quicken the scene at the end and think I've succeeded. Let me know how it works out. I've also shortened the scene between Sweeney and wife. I really—(between us)—don't think such cutting would be necessary in an A 1 acting production where the actors could hold the attention by the vividness of their characterization—but—oh, well—you know.

Your personal objection to the prospective branding of father does credit to your gentle soul, Nina; but isn't it exactly what a drunken Luke would immediately think of, feeling the grudge he does—and with his sweet mother's influence squirming in his heredity?

5. Ida Rauh (1877–1970), who had appeared in the Provincetown Players's premieres of O'Neill's *The Sniper* and *The Long Voyage Home*.

On the level, Nina, I haven't time to rewrite even if I thought it required it. I am up to the ears in work getting the long play in shape for Williams. Besides, I don't exactly see what you mean. On reading it over I think I have done what I wanted to do. Of course, I might use a lot of cleverness to make the exposition smoother but I really want just raw character in this play. You see, I see the exposition as a perfectly logical outcropping of the mood the different characters are in. Every word, I think, is just what they would say. If the actors make definite speeches of exposition which don't come out of the way they're supposed to feel—then, adios! But I insist the play isn't written that way. I think you've misunderstood what I was driving at.

Many thanks for your kindness in regard to *Ile*. It takes a load off my mind. I trust not producers—oh—ah—but of course—you know—save one.

Agnes[1] and I are deeply grateful to you for your wishes of happiness to us. May your wish prove father to the fact itself! Yes, past tense is correct. We were married two evenings ago—in the best parlor of a parsonage by the most delightful, feeble-minded, Godhelpus, mincing Methodist minister that ever prayed through his nose. I don't mean to sneer, really. The worthy divine is an utterly lovable old idiot, and the ceremony gained a strange, unique simplicity from his sweet, childlike sincerity. I caught myself wishing I could believe in the same gentle God he seemed so sure of. This sounds like sentimentality but it isn't. It's hard to describe—the wedding of two serious children he made out of it; but it was startlingly impressive. The meaning behind the lines "got across with the punch" to both of us. (And just think we were intending to have a Justice perform but, luckily, there isn't one in town with the requisite authority.)

Agnes sends her best love. Give our joint finest to all the bunch we know and like. Bye'bye for this time.   Gene

P.S. Go easy on the script, for Gawd's sake! I haven't had time to browbeat my wife into doing my typing yet. Try and get the P.P. to have a copy made—if possible. The authors should get that.

---

59 • TO EDWARD GOODMAN.[1]   TLS 2 pp. (Provincetown, Mass.) [Virginia]

June 28, 1918

My dear Eddy: I had heard through Susan of Lucy and you playing leads in that fatal "I do" dialogue but waited to hear from you before bursting into congratulations. However, my tumultuous applause, though belated, is none the less there with the punch. All the luck, health, success—and consequently, happiness—in the world be yours! The bleedin' best is none too good, is wot I says!

Or, to put it in fewer words, may you be as happy as Agnes and I have been and feel assured of being to our ultimate gasp! Which is the thanwhichest of wishes!

As for another *In The Zone*, I have it not nor do I expect to write one this summer. To be candid, I am rather fed up with the one-act play at present and am starting a new long one. The news that three of my best, after bringing me in the magnificent sum of thirty seeds apiece, had fallen into the hands of a garden-worm vaudeville producer who would take up

1. Agnes Boulton.

1. Goodman (1888–1962), schoolteacher and free-lance journalist, and his wife, Lucy Huffaker, were among the founders of The Washington Square Players. Goodman also directed the Players, who presented a production of *The Rope* on May 13, 1918. The Players had produced the premiere of O'Neill's *In the Zone* on October 31, 1917.

the W.S.P.[2] contracts and so only be compelled to pay me 15 per on a five year tie-up—and even if God is good and they aren't put on anywhere at all, they will still be locked in for a year more—hardly inspired me with any desire to plunge into new short plays, at least not during the vicissitudes of war time.

Furthermore, next season I anticipate having to make appeals to the Authors League every week or so to protect me from the brigandage of Lewis & Gordon[3]—my opinion, based on what correspondence we have had to date, being that, like all the rest of their kind, they are crooks from the word go. Also I will have to subscribe to *The Dramatic Mirror*, the *Clipper*, *Variety*, etc. and read them from cover to cover to find out where my plays are playing regardless of their author.

No, my next one-act play is going to be started the day peace is signed—when you're back on the job again.[4]

Am damn glad to hear things are not as bad as you expected up there; and good luck attend the Ontario Players. If I had a play along the line of what you want I would send it to you, but I haven't the heart to start one now when I'm just getting interested in my new long one. You can readily understand that.

Again my best to Lucy and to you!   Pip-pip!   Eugene G. O'Neill

---

60 • TO NINA MOISE.   ALS 2 pp. (West Point Pleasant, / New Jersey) [Yale]

January 17, 1919

Dear Nina: What ho! It was some surprise when I discovered who the Frisco letter with the forbidding—(to those "broke")—Red Cross insignia attached came from. I had forgotten your daughtership to the Great Mother. But much welcome to your letter, whatever the stationery!

First to answer your question regarding plays: You can have any you want of the ones which *are* mine. *Cardiff* comes under this head, so go to it. *Before Breakfast* is another. *The Long Voyage Home* and *The Moon Of The Caribbees* will return to me after April first as there is small chance of Lewis and Gordon, to whom the W.S.P. kindly(?) handed over my contracts, producing them before that time. *The Rope* is nailed to them for five years—and of course they will never use it! Some business! *Ile* you will have to seek via Barney Gallant of the G.V.T.[1]

I have several new plays, notably *Where The Cross Is Made* which appeared on the opening P.P. bill this year with great success. It's one of my best. I have no copy of it, however, at present. The P.P. maimed or lost two scripts and the one remaining is out on duty just now. Will send it to you later.

My other new short plays are untyped so far. There's small encouragement to go to that trouble these days. The one-act play is dead in N.Y. this season, but for the P.P.

We—meaning the P.P.—and I especially have missed your "pep" very much this year. The direction of both my plays on the first and second bill was "punk." Ida did the first[2] and also played a part in it—very bad handicap to try two things at once. They put on *The Moon* on their second bill, and what with the small stage, the large cast—(which was never large at

2. Washington Square Players.
3. Albert Lewis and Max Gordon (1892–1978), O'Neill's agents, who had sold *In the Zone* to the Orpheum vaudeville circuit.
4. Goodman had recently joined the armed forces.

1. Greenwich Village Theatre.
2. *Where the Cross Is Made*, which opened on November 22, 1918.

rehearsals, as you can guess), and the difficult set, well—just use your imagination! The director[3]—I forget his name—couldn't do anything under such conditions, and didn't have personality enough to overcome them.

So hasten East! I'll keep the two newest plays untyped till you come. There's a threat for you!

My luck, after touching only the high spots last Spring, has become a mole. *In The Zone* staggered through the influenza, with a six weeks lay-off, only to fall a victim to the premature hand of Peace-on-Earth-good-night-to-war-plays. At present it is billed only In The Zones of the Spirit from which no royalty accrues. And it *was* booked for forty weeks!! Sherman got the wrong pig by the ear. *Peace* is Hell!

The date of production for my long play *Beyond The Horizon* is still indefinite. Williams has had his bumps this season and he can't seem to get the cast he planned to get. *In confidence* I may mention that he hoped to have the two Barrymores play the two brothers. A grand notion, surely! But John has made such a hit in *Redemption* under Hopkins[4] that it's extremely unlikely that he'll be available for many moons, if ever by Williams. In the meantime, things drift and nothing is done. So there you are! It's especially hard from a practical standpoint when the New York season is booming along at a record attendance. Ah well! I'm not the first author to buck that game of watchful waiting.

Would be glad to send you a copy of the play but only have one and simply must keep that right by me to have in case of a sudden emergency. You're so far away. Wait till you come East and you shall have it immediately.

Agnes and I are living in the house she owns out here—a fine quiet place for work, in the midst of pine trees, and only a half-mile from the ocean. We are going to Provincetown next summer, I guess, if our present plans go through.

Worked hard this summer and fall in P'town. Have another long play all finished to my credit but untyped yet.[5] Am working on the outline of another now which I hope to complete this winter.[6] You can't keep a squirrel on the ground.

Agnes is well, and sends her love to you. We both hope you'll soon hit the rails this ward. When you do be sure and come down here. It's only two hours from N.Y.

Write again and let me know all your R.C.[7] trials and tribs.

Success to the new theatre!   Sincerely your friend,   Gene

---

61 • TO JESSICA RIPPIN.   ALS 2 pp. (West Point Pleasant, N.J.) [Private]

Feb. 4th 1919

Dear Jessica: What ho! Greetings and salutations! Your letter came as unexpected as a bolt from the well known blue, but it was thrice welcome in that it brought back to me a thousand memories of the good old times at the Villa Rippin. Those days hadn't been forgotten. Indeed not! They were merely enjoying the hearty sleep which is the record of days well spent; and it needed the jolt of your letter to wake them to conscious life again.

Well, how are you and how are all the clan of Rippin? Reveling in the best there is, I hope, and giving Time the battle of his life. How is your Mother? And Father? And where is Dolly now and what doing? And Emily—has she added to her heirs in the year and more I've missed? And Nelly? And Percy? And your other two brothers? And yourself? You see

3. Thomas Mitchell (1895–1962), later a famous movie actor.
4. Producer Arthur Hopkins (1878–1950).
5. *The Straw.*
6. *Chris Christophersen,* an early version of *"Anna Christie."*
7. The American Red Cross.

you let yourself in for it, and now you will have to write me an honest-to-Gawd long letter giving me all the dope on the above questions. I asked my mother about all of you when I saw her this fall but what she knew was fragmentary and not very satisfying. So it's now up to you. Go to it! And remember also that I haven't had a bit of current New London gossip in ages. Of course, I know all of my old loves are safely married into the hero class—(U.S.N.—U.S.A.)—but that was to be predicted, and I failed to be astonished by the news.[1] Neither—ain't we men fickle?—was I driven into any heart-broken, sleepless nights thereat. You see, I had beaten at least one of them to the deadly deed myself. But let me hear all the "dirt" as I haven't talked with anyone from New London in a century, it seems.

As for myself—well—it's a long story. I look about the same, act about the same, and am hardly at all as "famous" as you are flattering enough to make out. All I can hand myself is that I have worked like the devil for the past three years with but few let-ups for celebration, and I am glad to be able to say that this hard labor is at least showing some results and winning for me a bit of recognition. Most of my time, until this winter down here in a place of my wife's, has been spent in Provincetown—a fishing village at the end of Cape Cod, hard to get to and get out of, but a grand place to be alone and undisturbed when you want to work. There's an art colony up there and I rented a small studio on the beach. Hearing the waves all the time, I was often reminded of the winter at your mother's when I first started my pen-pushing in earnest. At any rate, I've never worked harder or with pleasanter surroundings than I did those *cold* months in the Packard. Your family gave me the most real touch of a home life I had had up to then—quite a happy, new experience for an actor's son! I've never forgotten to be grateful to all of you for it—above all, to your mother.

As for my work, I continue hard at it. A new book of my latest short plays is to be published in spring—this time by a *regular* publisher.[2] Most of the plays have been produced in New York on the stages of the so-called Little Theatre groups. A long play is under contract to John D. Williams. I hope it will be put on this season but, owing to the difficulty of casting it as he has planned to do, it might have to wait until next fall. I trust not, however. I have another new long play under optional contract to Williams which will probably be produced next winter.[3] So you see the future will tell, and the present is nothing. And that's enough drool about my work for this time!

Mother probably broke the news to you of my marriage last April. After nearly a year's experience with double harness I can state in all honest sincerity that my former existence by my lonesome was not living at all. In short, I am very happy and as much in love as on the first day. One couldn't ask more, what? My wife, your mother will be tickled to hear, was born in London of English-American parents. (Damn those English! They always have taken possession of Ireland!) She is a writer like myself, only her specialty is short stories. So we're interested in exactly the same things and have small excuse for flinging the plates about. We have a beautiful place down here—hers—quite a distance removed from the town, off by itself in a fringe of pine woods about a quarter of a mile distant from the ocean. Our summers we will continue to spend in Provincetown.

Oh—I was forgetting—yes, Agnes is very pretty. As I have other opinions less prejudiced than my own might be to back me up in the matter, I give you the above statement as a fact. You'll all see her sometime—and agree with me.

And now you've got all the statistics of the changes I have undergone in the interval

1. Two of O'Neill's former girl-friends, Maibelle Scott and Beatrice Ashe, married members of the armed forces.
2. *The Moon of the Caribbees and Six Other Plays of the Sea,* published by Boni and Liveright on April 23, 1919.
3. *The Straw.*

since I last saw you. They look dry and uninteresting enough when written down in green and white but living them has been a lot of fun. I'll wind up the autobiography by adding that, though toned down, I'm still unreformed and will strive to continue so.

In response to your request for an autograph I can only say that why anyone should want mine, except as an example of what not to do in penmanship, is beyond me. As for the "sentiment" you mention—the devil mend you! The only one I can think of is that if my handwriting was as beautifully clear as yours I'd write letters to myself requesting an autograph. However, if your friend really wants it, I'll be glad to do the signature end of the trick. Signing checks has hardly become so usual with me that I'm becoming affected with writer's cramp from it. So send me a blank card, or whatever he wants it written on, in your reply to this, and I'll do my John Hancock with glee! I haven't anything here but typewriting paper.

Be sure to give my best love to your mother when you see her next. Also, my best to all the Rippins when you see or write to them. Tell the ones I knew best I'd be more than glad to get a line from them if the time and the inclination to write ever hits them together.

And now I'll sit back and wait for your *long* reply. Give me all the news of you and yours—and all the N.L. "dirt," remember! Pip-pip!   Eugene

P.S. Perhaps this will do for your friend if snipped off   Eugene G. O'Neill

---

62 • TO BARRETT H. CLARK.[1]   ALS 1 p. (West Point Pleasant, N.J.) [Yale]

April 30, 1919

Dear Mr. Clark: I really can't vouch for the Mencken story although it may very well have happened as he relates. I remember I sent a script of the play to Williams and Nathan at the same time. It is quite probable that Nathan saw him before he had looked at his. However that may be, I can say that my debt of gratitude to both Nathan and Mencken is great. From the first time they read two of my sea plays they have given me many a boost in spirit by their fair criticism and words of encouragement. It was Nathan who directed Williams' attention to my work. And to this day I have not met either of them personally—Nathan or Mencken, I mean.

My book should be out any day now, the publisher tells me. Some trouble with printers has caused the delay, I believe. I wrote Boni and Liveright to send you a copy as soon as the volume appeared and they have said they would do so.

It is certainly kind of you to have your *European Theories*[2] sent to me. I am very grateful and look forward to reading it with the greatest interest.

I'm glad the stuff I sent you will fill the bill. I was rather afraid it looked as if I were making a Jack London hero out of myself—whereas, strive as I may, I cannot recollect one heroic passage in those experiences.

I expect to be in New York for a few days about the middle of May—a stop-over on my way to Provincetown—and shall be only too pleased to call you up on my arrival, or drop you a line beforehand, and take advantage of your luncheon invitation.

1. Clark (1890–1953), critic and author, was gathering background information for a review of the *Moon of the Caribbees* collection that he published in the *New York Sun* on May 18, 1919.
2. *European Theories of the Drama—An Anthology of Dramatic Theory and Criticism from Aristotle to the Present Day* (Cincinnati: Stewart and Kidd, 1918).

Am mailing a letter today to the American Play Company asking them to send you the script they have of *Beyond The Horizon*. They are my agents—(managerial delays and subterfuges drove me to them)—and possess my only presentable copy. I sure hope you will like the play. At least, I feel confident it will interest you.

Looking forward to the pleasure of meeting you in the near future, I remain, with very best regards   Very sincerely yours,   Eugene G. O'Neill

---

63 • TO BARRETT H. CLARK.   TLS 2 pp. (West Point Pleasant, N.J.) [Yale]

May 8, 1919

My dear Mr. Clark: It was welcome news to hear that you gained such a favorable impression from *Beyond The Horizon*. But I by no means agree with you in your high estimate of *In The Zone*. To me it seems the least significant of all the plays. It is too facile in its conventional technique, too full of clever theatrical tricks, and its long run as a successful headliner in vaudeville, terminated only by the Flu and the armistice, proves conclusively to my mind that there must be "something rotten in Denmark." At any rate, this play in no way represents the true me or what I desire to express. It is a situation drama, lacking in all spiritual import—there is no big feeling for life inspiring it. Given the plot and a moderate ability to characterize, any industrious playwright could have reeled it off. Whereas, *The Moon Of The Caribbees,* for example—(my favorite)—is distinctively my own. The spirit of the sea—a big thing—is in this latter play, is the hero. While *In The Zone* might have happened just as well, if less picturesquely, in a boarding house of munition workers. Let me illustrate by a concrete example what I am trying to get at: Smitty in the stuffy, grease-paint atmosphere of *In The Zone* is magnified into a hero who attracts our sentimental sympathy. In *The Moon,* posed against a background of that beauty, sad because it is eternal, which is one of the revealing moods of the sea's truth, his silhouetted gestures of self-pity are reduced to their proper insignificance, his thin whine of weakness is lost in the silence which it was mean enough to disturb; we get the perspective to judge him—and the others—and we find his sentimental posing much more out of harmony with truth, much less in tune with beauty, than the honest vulgarity of his mates. To me *The Moon* works with truth, and *Beyond The Horizon* also, while *In The Zone* substitutes theatrical sentimentalism. I will say nothing of the worth of the method used in the two short plays save that I consider *In The Zone* a conventional construction of the theatre as it is, and *The Moon* an attempt to achieve a higher plane of bigger, finer values.

But I hope to have this all out with you when we meet. Perhaps I can explain the nature of my feeling for the impelling, inscrutable forces behind life which it is my ambition to at least faintly shadow at their work in my plays.

Will arrive in New York next Wednesday afternoon. Thursday I have a lot of details to attend to which must be cleared away before I can have a free hand. Will you write me where and when on Friday, if that day proves suitable to you, I can meet you? Or on Saturday?

Again let me thank you for your book which reached me a few days ago. I won't attempt to do it the injustice of a reading at present. Spring cleaning, preparations for moving, etc. have me in a state of mind where my mental range bogs down before anything more weighty than Watts Hymns for Infant Minds.

With very best regards,   Very sincerely yours,   Eugene G. O'Neill

May 9, 1919

My dear Professor Baker: Not once but a dozen times since our chance meeting in Provincetown two years ago have I determined to write you, but each time I hesitated, reflecting: Better wait until you have something real to relate. Not that the possession of any grand achievement emboldens me at present writing; but at least the burden of a yowl at Fate gives me ballast.

I have been hoping all during the past theatrical season to be able to give you the date and all other data of a forthcoming production of my long play, *Beyond The Horizon,* which has been under contract to John D. Williams since last spring. It is a play of two brothers, and Williams was sure he would produce it with the two Barrymores in the cast—a fair hope, that!—as soon as *Redemption*[1] petered out, as the consensus of wise opinion decreed it must. *Redemption,* however, refused to peter. And now comes *The Jest*[2]—a very mocking irony of a title, it seems to me—which promises to beat all records for endurance.

That, in brief, is my plaint; and who can gainsay its justice when he sees this native-son steam-rollered by that foreign invasion? True, Williams has renewed the contract and promises a production before next December, and is still full of hope that in the end his devout wish will be consummated. Ah yes—in the end! But my system has absorbed so much hope in the past six months that I am now immune. I turn a callous, cauliflower ear to all managerial fair promises. I have ceded my winter home in Spain for a permanent residence in Missouri.

Since you last saw me I have completed three long plays. The first, finished a year ago, was immediately taken by Williams—with the resultant blighted dreams recorded above. The second, *Chris. Christophersen,* is now awaiting the verdicts of both Hopkins and Belasco.[3] I really have every confidence that, in spite of the fact that it is far removed in nature and treatment from the usual run of acceptable plays, it will eventually find a producer. The third play, the last act of which I have just finished rewriting, is still untyped.[4] It is the best of them in my opinion but, on account of its subject matter, I anticipate a long period of waiting— unless the Theatre Guild crowd like it enough to face the music.

I wish you could read these three plays. They would interest you, I feel sure, because they are sincere and because they demand a freshness of treatment and a widened scope for the playwright's subject material. Will you let me send one or more of them to you sometime this summer? I know you are at your busiest just now. In truth, it has been the conviction that you have no season that isn't busy that has prevented my sending them to you as they were finished.

I hope you escaped seeing the production of my one-act plays by the Washington Square Players and Greenwich Village Theatre a year ago this season. You would have acquired a false opinion from these productions of the worth of the plays as written, I am sure. And as for *In The Zone* as mutilated by the vaudeville folk—it ran for over thirty weeks

1. Play by Russian novelist and dramatist Leo Tolstoy (1828–1910), produced by Arthur Hopkins and starring John Barrymore (1882–1942).
2. Play by Italian dramatist Sem Benelli (1877–1949), produced by Arthur Hopkins and starring John and Lionel Barrymore (1878–1954).
3. Producer, actor, and playwright David Belasco (1859–1931), known primarily for his dedication to realism in the theatre.
4. *The Straw.*

until peace and the Flu intervened—I had better turn the page. Well, a vaudeville audience never reads an author's name, anyway.

Under separate cover I am sending you a copy of the book of my one-act plays just published. All of the seven have been produced in New York, most of them originally by the Provincetown Players. I wish very much for you to have this book as a small token of my remembrance of all I owe to my year under your guidance. Let me only hope that these plays will justify that year in your eyes. I realize I must have seemed woefully lacking in gratitude because, seemingly, I have never had the decency to write—and I know the interest you take in the work of your former students. But I'm really not as bad as that. In all honesty, I have waited more out of a small boy ambition than anything else. I was confident that the night would come when I could approach you with that digesting-canary grin, and, pointing to the fiery writing on the wall of some New York theatre, chortle triumphantly: "Look, Teacher! See what I done!"   Very sincerely yours,   Eugene G. O'Neill

P.S. I hope you will pardon the typewriting; but I realized that this letter is long, and my handwriting is small, and your time is short.

---

65 • TO GEORGE PIERCE BAKER.   TLS 1 p. (Provincetown, Mass.) [Harvard]

June 8, 1919

My dear Professor Baker: Please pardon my delay in acknowledging your kind letter, but I have been busy moving from New Jersey to New York to my new place in Province-town, and you can imagine what a continual upset that has meant.

I tried hard to get a script of *Beyond The Horizon*—the play Williams promises to produce in the fall—to you by May 31st; but retrieving a borrowed script seems to be more difficult than selling the play. As it is, I have written a very unfriendly letter to a friend who "was so anxious to read the play" and I'm sure one copy will get back to me shortly. Will you have time to read it now and, if so, to what address shall I send it?

My agent has sold my latest long play—*Chris. Christophersen*—which was completed this spring, to George Tyler for production this fall. As Tyler has known me since I was a kid, is a fine all round man, and has given me a contract which leaves nothing to be desired, I anticipate a square deal in every way—which is luck!

Of course, I very much want to have you read *Chris*, too; but, as *Beyond The Horizon* is the first real long play I have written since leaving your class, I would rather you saw it first. *Chris*, I hope, will receive your verdict in its due order.

A word of explanation as to why I failed to come back for your second year. I wanted to. It was none of my choice. I just didn't have the money, couldn't get it, and had to take a job as New York dramatic critic on a new theatrical magazine which never got beyond the promotion stage, although I was religiously paid a small salary for doing nothing for three months or so. But please do not believe for an instant that my failure to report was caused by any doubt as to your helping me further. I was too well aware of the faults in my work to harbor any such erroneous idea of my own self-sufficiency. My one year helped me tremendously—in more ways, perhaps, than you can imagine—and I was not blind to the fact that without the short-cut of your advice I would have to learn (if I have learned!) by a laborious process of elimination. Oh, indeed, I wanted to come back! I'm a lazy guy.

Have you had time to look over the book of one-act plays yet?   With very best regards,   Very sincerely yours,   Eugene G. O'Neill

June 8, 1919

My dear Mr. Tyler: Have been busy getting settled in my new place up here and haven't had time to breath so far; but now I'm all fixed to "stay put" and expect to start work on the change in *Chris* at once. I've got it all mapped out in my head and it shouldn't take long. Will send it on to you as soon as it's completed and typed.

The telegram from Farnum[2] sounds encouraging. Did you send him the script? I'm anxious to hear what he'll have to say when he has read it. Somehow, I have doubts as to his willingness to accept such an unheroic, character part.

My place up here is some unique and I wish you could see it—an old U.S. life saving station fixed up wonderfully inside by Sam Lewisohn, the millionaire, as a sort of strange toy of which he soon grew tired—hence my present ownership. The Atlantic for a front lawn, miles of sand dunes for a back yard, with not a house within miles except the new U.S. station down the beach about half a mile away. No need to wear clothes—no vestige of the unrefined refinements of civilization—much manual labor and consequent health—great stuff! If you tour up Cape-ward this summer, be sure and pay us a visit. The place is worth the three mile walk up and down sand dunes which is one of the penalties for communication with the world of people.

With very best regards,   Very sincerely yours,   Eugene G. O'Neill

---

67 • TO GEORGE C. TYLER.   TLS 2 pp. (Provincetown, Mass.) [Princeton]

July 20, 1919

Dear Mr. Tyler: It was a keen disappointment to learn that you think the revised last scene of *Chris* still weak, as I had hoped the change had lifted the end to its due proportion with the rest of the play. To be out and out candid, so that you will clearly understand how I feel about it, I don't believe I agree with you. It seems to me that the only logical culmination is worked out in the only possible way. It is a darned hard scene to write, that last one— darned hard to carry on what has gone before to *the* one inevitable conclusion without becoming artificially theatrical and falsifying characters that have been built up with so much care in the scenes preceding. Then again, the possibilities for the meeting of the three people, their probable courses of action, leave but little choice to the writer since the circum- scribed life aboard ship necessarily prohibits much variation if one would stick to truth. The way I feel about it is that Chris and the two lovers could not come together in any other place or way, and that, having come together, they would have reacted to the situation in just the way I have made them.

Do not take the above to mean that I am "up stage" about my last scene or cocksure of my own infallibility. I just wanted you to know exactly what my reaction is at present writing. I'll promise to think hard and keep thinking hard and preserve an open mind to any hint for improvement which the God of playwrights may deign to whisper. But for me to

---

1. Tyler (1867–1946), producer.
2. Actor William Farnum (1876–1953), whom Tyler hoped to interest in the title role of *Chris Christopherson*.

deliberately rack my inventive powers to strengthen the scene would be a false move. I know this from experience, and I also know you will understand the why of it. Whenever I haven't seen my way and yet have forced myself to invent—even when I've felt myself there was something radically wrong to be remedied—the result has been false and futile, and in the end always had to be discarded for the original. In this case any such tinkering would waste your time and mine to no purpose. But I'll try hard to *feel* what you do—and pray for light.

In the meantime, it would help a lot if you could write me at more length as to just where and why the scene sags in your estimation. Doesn't the change do away with your former objection to Chris' too lengthy inactivity? Don't you think that, acted, perhaps the struggle of Chris to keep his daughter, his increasing anguish as he sees her turn from him and realizes that even his own arguments merely make matters worse—don't you think if you *saw* this happening instead of reading it it would acquire the necessary tragic poignancy to make the scene "big?" And his attempt at suicide is, I believe, exactly what the Scandinavian Chris would do.

I feel it would be very difficult to follow your suggestion of discovering a completely new idea which would allow the retention of the brief finale. The whole play was constructed and written with the plan of this last scene in view and I'm afraid any complete change in it would involve a rewriting of previous scenes which might destroy the unity of the play.

It's too bad Farnum is so dilatory. It probably means he can't see himself in the part—or else he hasn't even read the play yet!

Rely on me to do my damndest to see this thing your way and if I do find a weakness to correct it. At present I feel confidence in the scene as it is. This is a delightful sensation for an author—to be cherished with care for it seldom lives long.

With my very best regards,   Very sincerely yours,   Eugene

---

68 • TO GEORGE C. TYLER.   ALS 1 p. (Stationery headed: Peaked Hill Bar Provincetown Massachusetts) [Princeton]

July 29, 1919

Dear Mr. Tyler: After careful consideration and rereading I have come to the conclusion that you are right and that the last scene can be much improved by an extensive revision. I am not changing the main place of the scene, however—which I still think to be the only possible one—but simply introducing at the very beginning a scene between Chris and his daughter, very dramatic in its scope, that cannot fail to intensify the significance of what follows. This addition will also give me a chance to do some much needed condensing further on without appreciably shortening the length of the whole.

I expect to have all this finished and typed by the end of the week and I will send it down for your consideration immediately. This new construction seems to me a hundred percent improvement and I feel confident you will find it so, too.

Farnum's wire doesn't strike me as bubbling over with enthusiasm. Perhaps the letter he speaks of will reveal his attitude more satisfactorily.

With very best regards,   Very sincerely yours,   Eugene

69 • TO JOHN PETER TOOHEY.[1]   TLS 1 p. (Provincetown, Mass.) [Connecticut C.]

August 4, 1919

My dear Mr. Toohey: To have pictures taken of the house and self by a regular camera man is beyond my scope at present writing—for reasons, not too subtle, connected with the minimum luxury law which applies to playwrights still awaiting production. But a friend of mine recently devoted several rolls of film in his very excellent Kodak to snapshotting this man's manse and its inhabitants. The results are not in yet. Would you care to have a look at the good ones—if there are any? If so, let me know.

My "temperamental diffidence"—you've said it!—must remain deaf to all persuasion when it comes to posing pen-in-hand with the sea as a background. Come now, Mr. Toohey, that's a bit thick, isn't it? Put yourself in my shoes. Have a heart and allow me to remain natural. My self-preservation as an honest-to-God human being is "vital" to me above all things. There are so many others just watering at the mouth for that weapon-in-mit close-up that I won't be missed. In fact, in my opinion, to "shoot" an author in one of those moments of profound absent-mindedness when he lapses into a he-man, to catch him penless, desk-less, his chin unaccountably kept in place without the prop of a sensitive hand, his hair looking like hair and not like a back drop to accentuate his troubled-by-my-last-act brow, his eyes temporarily soulless but betraying a keen interest in dinner—such a photo ought to establish forever his rep. as a "sad bad glad mad," eccentric Nut, a defier of all our cherished traditions—and make him A One copy!

In New York I'm a religious *Post* fan but up here it's next to impossible to get it. The few copies received in the hamlet are usually gobbled up before my weekly visit; but I'll leave an order and catch some of your stories, at any rate. I certainly look forward to reading them with the greatest interest. I can congratulate you all the more sincerely for placing a whole series with that weekly because I know by experience how difficult it is to break in with a single story.[2] I've tried them twice without success—the veto being "too gloomy"—one which you, knowing my work, can well imagine I receive with some frequency.

I hope you won't think my "beef" about the picture the result of up-staginess or any similar conceit. I honestly feel very strongly on the subject. An author whose work is sincere and honest should see to it that he remains likewise. In order to do this his best place is—out of sight in the wings.

With very best regards,   Very sincerely yours,   Eugene O'Neill

---

70 • TO GEORGE C. TYLER.   TLS 1 p. (Provincetown, Mass.) [Princeton]

August 6, 1919

Dear Mr. Tyler: It was gratifying to learn from Farnum's letter that he liked the play so well. Whether it would be worth while holding up the production for him all depends, I should think, on what he will have to say when you see him. If he is sincerely interested enough, he ought to be willing to give some iron-bound guarantee that he will appear in the

---

1. Tyler's press agent and a writer who contributed short stories to the *Saturday Evening Post* and other magazines.
2. Four of Toohey's stories, "Pie for the Press Agent," "Her Son," "Jimmy Aids the Uplift," and "The Water's Fine," appeared in the *Saturday Evening Post* between June 21 and November 8, 1919.

play in early winter. I think it would be a mistake to keep the piece idle for any length of time in what promises to be a boom year unless he can bind himself absolutely to a concrete proposition. I suppose all this "dope" sounds unnecessary and self-evident to you, and I merely give it to show what my opinion is.

In casting the small parts of *Chris*, I have someone to recommend for your serious consideration. His name is William Stuart, and he has played the lead in several of my one-act sea plays down at the Provincetown Players with real merit and a genuine distinction. He is distinctly a type apart from the usual run of amateur—one I persuaded to act in my plays myself—a Scotchman, a wood-carver by trade, a bit of a rough-neck naturally. He has seen the "hard" side of the world, knows ships and the men on them by heart, and is the only actor of my sea plays—I include professionals in this statement—who ever really looked and acted like a "salt" instead of an actor in war paint. He is anxious to act and displays that genuine feeling for the stage which is so hard to find in amateurs.

This is high praise, you will say; but I think it is deserved in Stuart's case. As for looks, he is an ideal type—a tall, brawny, big-featured, sandy-haired Celt who could slip into dungarees and step on in a ship scene without make-up. He speaks with a Scotch accent naturally but has spent a long time in Ireland and knows the real brogue. At present he is a teacher of wood-carving in Mrs. H. P. Whitney's school in Greenwich Village, but he has written me asking if there is any chance for him in *Chris*. I have told him to drop you a line and you would let him know.

I assure you no mere friendship consideration would influence me to recommend anyone. I care for my play too much for that. But Stuart can carry the atmosphere of the forecastle, of the waterfront, with him on the stage and I believe—if he can run true to past form, of course,—that as one of the sailors in either the first or fifth scenes he might prove a valuable asset. Actors usually make such "stagey" seamen that it would be worth while having someone who knew to pitch the right key for them. Will you give Stuart a chance? At any rate, have a look at him and see what you think.

With very kindest regards,   Very sincerely yours,   Eugene

---

71 • TO GEORGE C. TYLER.   ALS 1 p. (Provincetown, Mass.) [Princeton]

Sept. 25, 1919

Dear Mr. Tyler: I am tickled to death to hear Emmett Corrigan is to play "Chris." He is a corking actor and should do it splendidly. To be quite candid, I think he is a much better choice from an artistic standpoint than Farnum. I very much doubt if the latter would have played up to his old form. Years of the crass characterization of movie work must have left their mark.

As to when I expect to be in New York—did the Governor tell you he was expecting a grandchild? Well, he is—we are—any day now. So you can well imagine that under the circumstances I desire more than anything else in the world to stay up here with my wife as long as I possibly can. I will rely on you to let me know fairly well before the time just when my presence will be an imperative necessity.

My expectations were that I would be called to the city long before this for the *Beyond The Horizon* rehearsals—but—the same old story—the announcement stage is as far as that play has reached up to date. I am so hardened to disappointments in that direction I no longer expect anything.

With very kindest regards,   Very sincerely yours,   Eugene

72 • TO GEORGE C. TYLER.   TLS 1 p. (Provincetown, Mass.) [Princeton]

Oct. 27, 1919

My dear Mr. Tyler: Many thanks for your long letter. I judge from what you say that there is little chance of *Chris* seeing the footlights before the holidays. This, at least, is definite even if it doesn't add much to the alleged joy of living. I won't pretend that the news isn't disappointing; for I had counted on *Chris* for an early home-coming with the glory bacon—not to mention the fat ham of royalty which hangs in the box office and sustains authors on tours to Bermuda during a winter of coal shortage. "Ah, dream too bright to last, etc." But the facts in the case seem closed to argument and I accept them in a spirit which, if it rises not to Job, at least sinks not to Jeremiah. Even though you are the manager, I can't see my way clear to reviling you with the customary curses. I'll admit I'd like to. When the first blizzard finds me in flannel underwear panning out the corners of an empty coal bin and dreaming of sun-drenched coral islands, I probably will anyway, regardless of reason. Nevertheless, even then, I'll continue at bottom to have implicit faith in your good judgment, knowing that you have the success of the play as sincerely at heart as I have, and confident that the final results will rebuke my present impatience.

It's a shame about Corrigan. Let's hope he will still be available. I don't know anything about Gaul.[1] The part demands a *real* he-actor with at least a near-star name, I should think. My not knowing Gaul's work proves nothing. I've been out of touch with actors for years and it would be unjust for me to judge.

I'm grateful for the information you give because it sets me free to go on with my work. I've been holding back, afraid to make definite plans, expecting to be called away. One can't work in that frame of mind. Now, unless Williams' plans for *Beyond The Horizon* come to life, I can see clear water ahead. I've several plays mapped out. The first—*Gold*—will prove a perfectly corking play for Farnum unless I'm much mistaken—if he decides to go in for the legit next season.

I'll rely on you for as early a reading of *The Straw* as you possibly can give. It will impress you, I'm confident of that. Has Mr. Toohey read it? If so, I'd be very grateful for his candid, honest-to-God opinion if he cares to confide it to me.

My sincere thanks for your good prayers for the Heir. When he—or she—arrives I'll give them to—It.   With all best wishes,   Eugene

---

73 • TO GEORGE JEAN NATHAN.[1]   TLS 1 p. (Provincetown, Mass.) [Cornell]

Nov. 4, 1919

My dear Mr. Nathan: Your letter and the script arrived by the same mail. That you found genuine merit in *The Straw* is the most encouraging boost to my spirits I have received since the play was written. Your stamp of approval gives me renewed confidence in my own valuation.

The Theatre Guild[2] have seen the play and rejected it. They said it was most excellent

---

1. George Gaul.

1. The critic Nathan (1882–1958) coedited with Mencken *The Smart Set* and, after December 1923, the *American Mercury*.

2. New producing organization, established in early 1919 by playwright Lawrence Langner (1890–1962), director Philip Moeller (1880–1958), actress Helen Westley (1879–1942), and others from the disbanded Washington Square Players.

but not the kind of play for their public. Since *John Ferguson*[3] inoculated them with the virus of popular success—quite contrary to their expectations—I'm afraid they've become woefully worried about the supposed tastes of "their public." I speak not only from my own experience. Before *Ferguson* set them on horseback they had decided to do Susan Glaspell's *Bernice* this season. But now they have discovered "their public" would never—And the latest I hear is that James K. Hackett is to star for them in *Silas Lapham.* My God! The trouble seems to be that you can't eliminate the weakness of the old Washington Square Players by merely changing the name.

No, even Al Woods[4] is preferable to a success-ridden Guild. He, at least, has few inhibitions. And, although I know *The Straw* stands but small chance with them, I'll have to put my trust in Tyler, Hopkins and Williams. Williams has stated that he is willing to reopen negotiations for the play in case I should not sell it elsewhere. As I told you, he was much taken by it, wanted it, but was very vague as to when he could produce.

In the light of the Guild's rejection for popular reasons, I'm sure you'll be interested to know that the Selwyns[5] almost took the play. In a moment of aberation the agent submitted a script to them and they actually hovered on the brink of acceptance for days. They were quite impressed by its possibilities, it seems. They and Williams are the only commercial managers to pass on it so far.

I'm in daily expectation of a Tyler decision. I wish Hopkins would give it a hearing but my experience with *Chris* makes me think it's next to impossible to get him to read a play. However, I'm going to have a try at him.

Boni and Liveright are to publish both *Chris* and *Beyond The Horizon* this winter. Perhaps they might do *The Straw* later.[6]

I don't expect to be in New York before the middle of next month but will surely drop in when I do come.

My sincerest gratitude for your words of encouragement. They certainly mean a lot to me!   Cordially,   Eugene O'Neill

---

74 • TO JOHN PETER TOOHEY.   TLS 2 pp. (Provincetown, Mass.) [Connecticut C.]

Nov. 5, 1919

My dear Mr. Toohey: Many thanks for your kind letter. I'm glad you liked *The Dreamy Kid* and that it was done so well.[1] Of course, I by no means rate it among my best one-act plays for genuine merit, but I did think that it would prove theatrically effective and go over with a bang to an audience—thanks partly to the trick, which I acknowledge.

I'm particularly glad to hear how well you liked *The Straw.* I put a lot into that play and am willing to stand or fall by it. I only hope George C. is sufficiently impressed to—take the chance. I honestly believe that the American managers are lagging behind their public in regard to the worth of their plays. I think that there is now a numerous and growing

3. Play by Irish dramatist and critic St. John Ervine (1883–1971) that opened on May 13, 1919, with a nonunion cast during an Actor's Equity strike and became an unexpected success.

4. Producer Albert H. Woods (1870–1951).

5. Producers Archibald (Arch) Selwyn (1877?–1959) and Edgar Selwyn (1875–1944), who in 1924 would coproduce O'Neill's *Welded.*

6. *Beyond the Horizon* was published by Boni and Liveright on March 10, 1920. *The Straw* appeared, with *The Emperor Jones* and *Diff'rent*, in a volume published by Boni and Liveright on April 7, 1921. *Chris Christophersen* was not published until 1982 by Random House.

1. O'Neill's one-act play, directed by Ida Rauh, premiered in a Provincetown Players production on October 31, 1919.

audience, in the big cities anyway, who really demand something more than just a couple of hours amusement, and that, on the strength of this audience, any manager can afford [to] produce plays that would have been impossible before we got into the war. How about *The Jest, Redemption,* and *John Ferguson?* I don't believe that, even with the Barrymore increment in the case of the first two, any of these three would have stood a burglar's chance three years ago. The psychology of the average audience member has changed a lot in two years—and is changing.

I take it that the principal objection to *The Straw* on popular grounds would be the T.B. element;[2] but I believe that the idea of tuberculosis is now too familiar to the people at large to be fraught with the old ignorant horror. The Great White Plague is more of a household companion than most people realize. There are few families that haven't come in touch with it either through themselves or their friends. You meet people every day who have had it, have caught it in time, and are now going around as good as new. I refer you to statistics to prove all this must be so.

I honestly believe my play would have a good fighting chance because it is at bottom a message of the significance of human hope—even the most hopeless hope—and that is something we all want to believe in. For we know deep down in our souls that, logically, each one of our lives is a hopeless hope—that failure to realize our dreams is the inexorable fate allotted to us. Yet we know that without hope there is no life, and so we go on pursuing our dream to the last gasp, convinced in spite of our reason that there must be some spiritual meaning behind our hope which in some "greener land" will prove it was all justified.

All of which sounds scrambled, and forgive me for the wordy dissertation. The nurse in the end of the play puts what I mean more lucidly.

I'd love to have Mr. Bissing take charge of the play for the Continent, especially as he thinks so well of it, but I'm afraid The American Play Co. have it for all countries. I don't know exactly. I'm writing Madden[3] about it. Will see if he has any intention of doing anything with it over there and if he hasn't I don't doubt that I'll be free to place it under Mr. Bissing's wing. I'd certainly like to, after reading what you wrote of him.

I'll be sure and catch the *Post* this week. You've sure chosen a subject that you must know from the inside out.[4] They must have been great sport for you to write.

Yes, it's a boy.[5] If you've got a mob scene rehearsing, I'd like to place him. His Grandpa's voice! Sincerely, Eugene O'Neill

---

75 • TO GEORGE C. TYLER.   TLS 1 p. (Provincetown, Mass.) [Princeton]

Nov. 9, 1919

My dear Mr. Tyler: Your note has put me into that torturing state popularly known as "up in the air." I sure am glad to hear that *The Straw* made such a favorable impression on you. I have always felt confident that it would. But in your letter you seem to have made no definite decision as to whether you would produce it or not. Naturally, I am frenziedly hoping that the Ayes will have it. I am drawing hope from the fact that you don't say you

2. The play was based on O'Neill's stay at Gaylord Farm Sanatorium.
3. Richard Madden (1880–1951), O'Neill's agent, who was one of the partners in the American Play Company. Aside from O'Neill, Madden also represented W. Somerset Maugham, Sean O'Casey, T. S. Eliot, and Cole Porter, among others.
4. "The Water's Fine," *Saturday Evening Post* 192 (November 8, 1919): 16–17, 186, 189–90, 193–94.
5. Shane O'Neill had been born on October 30, 1919.

won't; for I feel sure you would not mince matters if you felt that way about it but would come out with a plain negative.

I am heartily in accord with what you have to say about the play's chances of success being enhanced by holding it back until after *Chris* has paved the way. That has always been my own idea. Under no circumstance would I want it to go on before *Chris* had come into its own. I think also that the Williams production of my *Beyond The Horizon* in Chicago with Bennett[1] in the lead, which now seems a practical certainty for around the first of the year, will give my work the authority which will be so great an asset as a background for a *Straw* production.

I am in the devil of a hurry to place *The Straw*, it is true, because it is my pet play and I am anxious to hug to my heart the certainty that it *is* going to be done. However, I am in no such flurry of haste when it comes to production and am quite prepared to wait any length of time that the best interests of the play would seem to me to demand. For instance, I realize that it would require time and the most careful selection to secure a woman who would be fit to play Eileen.

Whether what I have written above will influence your final decision or not, I don't know; but your letter sort of suggests that you think I am after an immediate production for the play and I want you to know that is not the case. I am too keenly aware myself that *The Straw* needs all the authority behind it it can get to insure it a favorable hearing.

You will let me know definitely the next time you write, won't you?

With very kindest regards,   Sincerely,   Eugene

---

76 • TO AGNES BOULTON O'NEILL.   ALS 1 p. (*On the train*) [Harvard]

[November 30?, 1919]

Own Dearest: What ho! This is the time I fool you. You won't expect this one, will you, after what I said—with malice aforethought. I'm hoping it will make you happy and also lonely.

It's writing under difficulties, though. The train seems to give an extra jerk at every word.

We're only just past Truro[1] but I already feel that pang of a great emptiness which always gnaws way down at the roots of my soul as soon as I become sickeningly aware of the vacant spot by my side where you should be. I love you so, My Own! You must believe that and also that I need you, your help and sympathy and love, as I have never before needed you. You said you thought my need had grown less, but that is mistaken nonsense. (Nonsense!) It has grown day by day, hour by hour, as you crept into my inner life, my finer self, until now that part of me is your creation, the soul of me which is all you and yours. You are wife of all of me but mother of the best of me. So ignore my bad moods and my irresponsible tongue. They are the leopard's spots; and, after all, a leopard isn't such a bum creation, taking bum all in all, and he wouldn't be a leopard if he were spotless.

The above is incoherent but you'll get me, I know. Kiss Shane for me. I *do* love him—"in my fashion." My best to Mrs. Clark[2] and tell her I rely on her to fatten you up with early hours—and much "eats."   A long kiss, Own Sweetheart!   Gene

1. Richard Bennett (1873–1944), prominent actor whose interest in *Beyond the Horizon* was instrumental in causing Tyler to produce it.

1. Town adjacent to Provincetown; O'Neill was on his way to New York by train and boat (from Fall River, Massachusetts) to visit his parents and to try to hasten the productions of his plays.
2. Fifine Clark, nicknamed Gaga, who had recently been hired by the O'Neills as a nurse-housekeeper.

77 • TO AGNES BOULTON O'NEILL.   ALS 4 pp. (Stationery headed: Prince
George Hotel / Fifth Avenue & 28th Street / [New York]) [Harvard]

Monday—6 p.m. / [December 1?, 1919]

My Own: Well, we arrived! Yes, finally, we got here! It was some long night! About twelve the purser passed out bunk numbers to us and we went below to have a look. Jig quit at the end of the look, but I resolved to have a try at it. I crawled into the bunk and tried to go to sleep; but too many people had taken off their shoes in the compartment. I and those nude feet simply couldn't live in the same world. So finally, in spite of my foc's'tle training, I had to throw up the sponge and join Jig on an uncomfortable chair in the salon. Jig was already uneasily asleep but I didn't get to that point until three a.m. In the meantime the night watchman took a fancy to me, sat beside me, and unfolded his family troubles—just why his wife and his sister couldn't live in the same house in Fall River. After I had condoled with him, a Jewish gentleman, who also had missed a stateroom, woke up long enough to feel of his feet and confess to me how he suffered from corns and, in detail, the different cures he had tried ineffectually.

Be the trip what it might, I got one long kiss of "the bleeding lips of suffering humanity." On the outside I must certainly look to be a sympathetic soul—(and perhaps they're right (?)).

Jig and I had breakfast on the good ship at six a.m. and I've been home ever since we landed. Mama and I have been shopping all afternoon. I got a tweed suit—65.00—and an overcoat—85.00—shirts—collars—all at Lord and Taylors. Hope you will like me when you see me again. I thought I might as well stick to L. & T. as Mama knows everyone there and there would be no chance of the double-cross. Also, on second thought, I decided that pure sport clothes were a luxury one couldn't afford before laying the foundation of a regular, bread-and-butter costume. After *Chris* brings home the bacon will be time enough for me to exhibit my strange fancies. Not that the present clothes are the absolute usual. They have too much class for that.

Most of the p.m. has been spent in the P.G.[1] chatting with the Old Governor & Mama who both appear extremely glad to see me—especially after the detective work at the greeting failed to find my breath guilty. They are full of thous. questions concerning the baby and crazy to see him.

The hope of unlimited booze at the Old Homestead is another yen hok[2] gesture. Papa had only *one-quarter of one bottle* left of the treasure when I arrived—and that is now gone, need I add? *And he is at a loss where to get more!* Honestly! He still loves Wilson[3] but hates his native land—U.S.—and swears to beat it home with all his gold to some country where gentlemen may still be ungentlemanly. I've talked Bermuda to him and he says he is willing to buy a place and settle down there. Perhaps the fact that I told him good Scotch sold in the British dominions for 10 shillings may have something to do with his eagerness. At any rate I have him interested—and Bermuda would be a good old winter home to go to. I speak interestedly.

Have had three drinks and that is all I'm liable to get during my stay. The Garden[4] is dry as dry.

1. The Prince George Hotel.
2. Underworld slang for the needle used to cook opium. Here probably suggests the idea of a pipe dream.
3. President Woodrow Wilson.
4. The Garden Hotel, located in the vicinity of the Prince George.

My clothes won't arrive until tomorrow p.m. so can't start on my round of calls till Thursday morning.

Feel terrifically done up by the awful night on the boat. I honestly needed the drink Papa was thoughtful enough to proffer when I arrived. I was all in.

There's lots more in the way of home gossip to relate but it's unimportant and will wait for my next.

I've been wishing so much today that you were here! I've felt so punk generally—although the jesting tone of this letter might lead you to believe differently. New York looks rotten to me, and I'll be giving a loud cheer when the train pulls in to P'town again. I'm not joking. There's nothing for me here now that Prohib. is in force. Of course, it did make me happy to see Paw 'n' Maw again, and I suspect I'll spend most of my time right under their wing. So don't worry about me! I'm a good, good boy!

A long kiss, Own Sweetheart of Mine! And one for Shane! It won't be long now till—our honeymoon!   Bye'bye for this time.   Gene

Write!

---

78 • TO AGNES BOULTON O'NEILL.   ALS 3 pp. (Stationery headed: Prince George Hotel / Fifth Avenue & 28th Street / [New York]) [Harvard]

Tuesday a.m. / [December 2?, 1919]

Own Wife: Last night about ten I made a voyage to the Hell Hole[1] to see how it had survived the dry spell. Lefty, Jim Martin, Joe Smith and quite a populous mob of the old bunch were there along with a lot of new "guerrillas" to whom I was presented as "our old pal, Gene." There was no whiskey in the house and Joe Smith told me they couldn't get it more than two days a week now—and then it had to be stolen by some of the gang out of a storehouse, and sold to Tom Wallace[2] afterward. All hands were drinking sherry and I joined this comparatively harmless and cheap—20¢ per drink—debauch right willingly. There was just enough kick in the wine to make everyone feel jovial and that's all. Some "hard" ladies of the oldest profession, who seemed to know me, were in the back room along with a drunk. Where this latter got his jug, I don't know. He had a huge roll of money and was blowing the house. I suspected he was being "framed" for a "frisk" and kept my eyes to myself. To support this theory of mine, I noticed that several parties after visits to the rear, came back with money to purchase further drinks.

There was much talk of the bike race[3] and finally a party of about 20, in which I am included, arranged to go up and see it tomorrow night. This ought to prove real fun for me. They're going to have several quarts of sherry to pack on the hip and even that "ladies" booze is not to be sneezed at in the New York of today. Believe me, Prohibition is very much of a *fact*.

Scotty[4] had told Lefty[5] of the Josephine song[6] being in *Chris* and the latter is tremen-

---

1. The Golden Swan saloon, which O'Neill frequented regularly in 1915–16 and which later became one of the models for Harry Hope's bar in *The Iceman Cometh*.
2. Owner of the Golden Swan.
3. The six-day bike races held at Madison Square Garden.
4. William Stuart, woodcarver and Hell Hole regular who also acted in Provincetown Players productions.
5. Lefty Louie, Hell Hole bartender.
6. "My Yosephine [Josephine]," sung by Chris in the original version of the play and in *"Anna Christie."* See Travis Bogard, "'My Yosephine': The Music for *Anna Christie*," *Eugene O'Neill Newsletter* 8 (Winter 1984): 12–13.

dously elated. Also, to my astonishment, he swears—(and I believe him)—that Josephine is his own stuff, a song he made up when he was singing in a tough Wop cabaret—"my own bull s--t," he explains proudly. That it is to be heard on Broadway is a great event in his life. He offers, as soon as rehearsals start, to go up for a couple of hours every morning to instruct Corrigan how to sing it—without desiring pay for his services! All he wants is two seats to take his girl to surprise her with his song—on Broadway!

This little incident of the song seems to me quite touching in a way. Don't you think so? And quite characteristic. It sounds rock-bottom and I think all the hours seemingly wasted in the H.H. would be justified if they had resulted in only this.

Lefty and Joe Smith seem as delighted with Shane's arrival as if they were godparents. They urged me to send all their blessings to you on "the little girl."

It was quite an "old time" night down there—minus drunkenness—and I thoroughly enjoyed it. No Villager came to spoil the atmosphere, thanks be!, and the Hell Hole was itself again.

I'm wondering what you're doing today and all the time since I left. Expected a letter this morning but was disappointed. What about your promise to write? Oh Sweetheart, how I wish you were here with me! I sort of feel empty and hollow—a body without a soul—and, except for a few moments here and there, I've been fairly aching with loneliness. But in a few days I'll be back in your arms, My Own, and be your other—and firstborn!—baby again!

This afternoon, I'm slated to continue the shopping ordeal under Mama's guidance. Still need a hat, shoes before I start my business calls tomorrow.

Send me or Mama the size of your bean so she can get that hat.

Haven't been near the P.P. yet but expect to go down tonight long enough to submit my play, at any rate. And all dolled up in new store clothes—if they come in time.

A million kisses, Beautiful! And a gentle one for my son—so it won't wake him up.

More later!   Your   Gene

---

79 • TO AGNES BOULTON O'NEILL.   ALS 4 pp. (Stationery headed: Prince George Hotel / Fifth Ave. & 28th Street New York) [Harvard]

Monday evening / [January 5?, 1920]

Heart's Desire: A busy day after a night of comparative comfort—(compared to my last cruise with Jig)—in which Hutch and I sat up in a deck stateroom[1] and theorized the universe to sleep until about midnight. I have grown to love Hutch. He's a peach!

My firebrand letter to John D. produced immediate results—a messenger boy to the P.G. this morning with a reply. He is stirred to the heart, it seems, and rather sore, I judge. I enclose his note to save quoting. He also phoned Madden saying "O'Neill didn't know how much he (W) had done for the play." He's a great joker, surely, is Mr. Williams. Madden and I are to see him tomorrow and get down to brass tacks. We have agreed that he must "show us" or give up the play.

Went up to Tyler's at two. He is extremely anxious to get Tearle[2] for the part of "Chris." It seems from what I have heard on all sides that Tearle, even in a play that was a flat failure, has scored the knockout hit of the season as far as acting is concerned. All the managers are after him. Tearle told me he had read at least fifty American plays sent to him by Belasco, etc.

1. After returning to Provincetown for Christmas and the New Year, O'Neill went back to New York to resume efforts to get *Beyond the Horizon* and *Chris* into rehearsal. He was apparently accompanied on his trip by the writer Hutchins Hapgood (1869–1944).
2. Godfrey Tearle (1884–1953), who was starring in *Carnival* at the Forty-fourth Street Theatre.

but none was artistic enough to make it worth his while staying in this country. He had his passage booked back to England—then read *Chris* and decided to stick around a while.

He seems a corking chap—not a bit actory—about 35—tall and good looking. He claims it has always been his ambition to play a character part. The only reason he hesitates on the *Chris* matter is because he is afraid he may not realize my conception of the part. We had a long talk together. I convinced him it made no essential difference whether Chris was tall or short as long as he was Chris in spirit. He is taking the play to go over it again tonight and give a final decision to Tyler tomorrow. I hope he decides to do it, not only because I liked him personally but also because, on account of his great popularity in London, he would make an English production a certainty.

Tyler has a new scheme. His Helen Hayes, now in *Clarence*,[3] is soon to be starred in a new play which is to go for a run in Boston in the spring. Tyler wants her to put on one special matinee of *The Straw* in that city. The idea is to try her out and see if she can play the part. Tyler claims she is going to prove *the* great emotional actress of the future—(she is only 19 now)—and wants to see if she's up to doing *The Straw* this early. If she is, he argues, it will be a great asset, as he thinks the part requires *real* youth and not some old actress pretending to be young, to be effective. I agree with him in this, and think the whole scheme for a Boston matinee is a fine one. If she fails, one matinee in Boston will not hurt the value of the play, and if she succeeds it will mean that the play, with her, will come right to New York next year.

Had an hour's chat with Madden. He is strong for Tearle as Chris and also approves of my stand with Williams.

Here's a bit of news: Lord Dunsany[4] had read my book of plays and asked Hopkins where he could read my long stuff. Hopkins phoned Tyler who in turn phoned Madden and Madden sent a script of *Chris* to H. to give to Lord Dunsany to read on his return voyage. His Lordship has promised to return same from England as soon as he has perused it. The Lord evidently has a better idea of me than I have of him. Folks tell me, however, that he's a charming person to meet.

Father has been pretty sick and looks bad but is getting better. Mama is O.K. I'm having dinner with the two of them up in the room shortly.

That's enough news for one day. Bye'bye for this time, Own Sweetheart, and a long kiss! I love you, love you, love you!!! I'll be back to you the first second I can skip away! A kiss for our Shane from me, and all the love of his grandparents who are crazy to see him.

More tomorrow, s'help me!   Another Kiss!   Gene

P.S. (To Mrs. Clark) Has Agnes gained a pound yet?

---

80 • TO AGNES BOULTON O'NEILL.   ALS 3 pp. (Stationery headed: Prince George Hotel / Fifth Avenue & 28th Street / [New York]) [Harvard]

Tuesday night / [January 13?, 1920]

Own Dearest: Just a few lines tonight and this is why: Have been up at Williams' office with Madden all afternoon. Had a terrific battle with him over *Beyond* but finally came to a compromise. The old contract is to be torn up and a new one more fair to me made. *Beyond* is due to go on at the Morosco three weeks from yesterday—one performance first at Stam-

3. Play (1919) by Booth Tarkington (1869–1946).
4. Dunsany (1878–1957), English playwright, poet, and short-story writer, was greeted as an international celebrity on his first American lecture tour in 1919–20.

ford, I guess. The first week it is to go on at special matinees—four of them. Then it is to play regularly the latter half of each week on night performances. The idea of a preliminary week of special matinees is to get the finest cast possible by taking people out of different N.Y. shows. This way they can play in *Beyond* without conflicting with their regular engagements. Helen McKellar[1] and Strong[2] of *The Storm* are to play Ruth & Andrew in this first week. Afterwards, the regular Williams cast will go on for the split-week night run.

It's a long story and I'm not going to try to tell it here. Tonight I've got to go over all the W. cuts and have the script back by noon tomorrow. Some work!

So you'll forgive me for not writing more, won't you? As soon as I get time I'll write you fully about all this. I've a million things to tell you but simply have to get to work on the *Beyond* script if I don't want to stay up all night.

Old Sweetheart, forgive me!—but you'll understand, won't you?

Your letter reached me when I got back from W. It was a Godsend of peace and security after my hectic experience this afternoon. I love you, My Own Own!

A million kisses for you to divide with Shane!   I love you!   Gene

---

81 • TO AGNES BOULTON O'NEILL.   COPY 5 pp. (Prince George [Hotel] / [New York]) [Harvard]

Jan. 14, 1920

Own Sweetheart: Have just returned from a second interview with Williams. Saw the models for *Beyond* sets by Hewlett.[1] They are very fine and quite in the right spirit. Madden and I handed him the bad news—for him—the new contract which is exactly the same as my Tyler ones. It further has clauses which limit his option on my plays to two years, requires a decision within 30 days, and generally do away with all the faults of the old agreement— my royalty to be 5, $7\frac{1}{2}$, and 10 instead of the former 3, 5, and 6—a big difference! Also he is not to deduct any of the thousand advance until *Beyond* is running by itself in consecutive performances at night. This means I will get paid my part of the matinees, etc., at once.

Things in the *Beyond* matter are not so bad, taking it all in all. I was not strong for the matinee idea and am not; but good actors are scarcer and hard to get these days and the matinees will at least enable W. to cast the play for its opening in a way he could not do by any other scheme. Also he has already laid out a lot of money in the production and it would be a dirty trick to make him lose all of it by taking away the play, even if I had another buyer for it. And I don't want to wait longer for a hearing. As things now stand it's a compromise with both of us giving in a lot. Let's hope it will turn out right. The split-week idea can't be helped. We can't get another theatre. *For the Defense*[2] is making money and without it W. would have no theatre at all.

I labored until 2 A.M. on the cuts. Finished up the first two acts. A great many made by W. are all right but some are very silly and I will not stand for them. He leaves that up to me,

1. Helen MacKellar played the role of Ruth Atkins when *Beyond the Horizon* opened on February 20, 1920.
2. No actor named Strong is listed in the credits of Langdon McCormick's *The Storm* or *Beyond the Horizon*. Actor Edward Arnold acted in *The Storm* and portrayed Andrew Mayo in the matinee performances of *Beyond the Horizon*.

1. Possibly J. Monroe Hewlett (1868–1941), architect, mural painter, and scene designer.
2. Melodrama by Elmer Rice (1892–1967); Williams proposed that *Beyond the Horizon* play with the cast of *For the Defense* at special matinee performances.

however. In spite of my grudge against him I can't help liking him personally and we shall probably end up as good friends.

The play has already been rehearsing a week. I'm to attend regularly as soon as my revisions of the cuts goes into effect—day after tomorrow, I guess. Tomorrow, I have a session with Williams to go over the entire script with him. *Beyond* will go on Monday P.M., Feb. 2nd.

Tyler has not yet heard finally from Tearle who is evidently giving himself a private try-out in the part before deciding. If he turns it down, Corrigan will be called in. I've been busy on that too, making plans for the scenes for the artist to go by. I'm also due to have a confab soon with Stanhope,[3] the director, to go over the play.

So you see I'm a busy little bee these days.

Dr. Aspell, the "high up" specialist who operated on Mama so successfully and who has been attending Papa (the old man has been very sick, so serious that Mama was going to summon the priest and wire for Jim and me at one time. Aspell pulled him through, and he's now much better and on his feet again)—came in and gave me a quick once-over. I told him of my nerves. He said "Keyed up tight as a string. You'll snap it if you don't take care. Let down! Don't worry! Forget your work and rest!" Good advice, maybe, but how the hell can I keep it at this stage of the game? I'm to go to him on Saturday for a complete physical examination. Perhaps, after that's over, he'll know if there's really any physical cause back of it all or whether it's all just mental. I've confidence in Aspell. He has a personality full of strength.

The night before last was a scream. Tyler and Will Connor[4] called on the old man. They were both well "boiled" when they arrived. The old man brought forth a jug from hiding— the first I knew about it—and they had more and I had four which made me quite "squiffy." Tyler and Connor had a brawl over whether *Ile* or *The Rope* was the best one-act play ever written, Tyler cheering for *The Rope* and Tyler and I "went to the mat" on what was or was not the matter with the American theatre. They never left till one A.M. It was quite fun. The old man didn't drink but the excitement cheered him up just the same. Tyler, in spite of his "bun," was astonished to find I could be talkative.

Tell Susan I spoke to Tyler about her play[5] and that he is genuinely eager to have a look at it. He said he had seen three of her plays at different times at the P.P.—*Bernice, Woman's Honor* and one other. He said "that *girl* has a real touch of genius"—(he evidently thinks Susan is about as old as Helen Hayes), and he added with a questioning misgiving: "If the damned Greenwich Village faddists didn't get her into the radical magazine publications class." I didn't disillusion him about Susan being 19 and at the mercy of the faddist world—it was too funny—but I did say she was married to a very sensible man. Upon which Tyler heaved a sigh of relief and ceased to "view with alarm."

The funny end of it aside, her play will be received with gratitude at the Tyler office and given a quick reading, I'm sure of that. She of course knows that she can submit a copy to every manager at the same time if she wants to. The magazine ethics in this regard don't apply here in the theatrical game. So she can try Hopkins, Tyler, etc., simultaneously and let the best man win. If she judges it would be any use, if she will send me the play (I'd like very much to read it myself, of course) I will put it in Tyler's hand myself and keep asking him if he's read it, to get action. I'll be seeing him every day pretty soon. You can at least assure her for me that Tyler, personally, is a fine straight guy—and that's a lot in this man's business!

3. Frederick Stanhope.
4. William F. Connor, longtime business manager and friend of James O'Neill, Sr.
5. Possibly *Inheritors* or *The Verge*, written in Provincetown in 1919–20.

And he sincerely wants—on the strength of her work he has seen and liked immensely—to get a chance to read her play. The outcome is in the lap of the gods of course.

Finish that comedy![6] I'll get it read immediately and I really believe it has a grand chance. Get busy, now!

We'll all have to go down to Boston and see that matinee of *The Straw* even if Mrs. Clark has to come along to take care of the baby. It'll happen in spring sometime.

Both *Clarence* companies are turning them away in N.Y. and Chicago and Tyler is clearing about two thousand a week profit on them.

Met Bill Farnum on Broadway for a few minutes this morning as I was heading for the W. office. He inquired about *Gold,* is anxious to read it. He said: "I've more money than I'll ever know what to do with and I want to get out of the movies and *act.* That's all life means to me now." He's now getting 8,000 a week from the movies, Tyler told me—52 weeks in the year! He's a damn nice quiet chap, as I've always told you.

This is a very newsy letter and sounds cheerful. However, I feel punk physically, as if a mine were about to go off inside me, but Aspell, I know, will see the way out of that. So don't worry. The disease that'll kill me hasn't been discovered yet.

I'm sorry poor old Timmy[7] misses me. Ask him "Where's Gene?" and see what he does.

Mama is all in a sweat to see Shane's pictures. Hurry them up.

The old man was a headliner in the papers this A.M. I enclose the *Telegraph* clipping, quite a tribute from Reinold Wolf, showing that stage folk aren't all wrong.[8]

I'd like to lay my tired buzzing old head on its own old place, own little wife! When I'm lonely I close my eyes and feel your arms about me, and I *know* you're here!

A kiss on Shane's adorable grin, and a kiss for you!   Gene

P.S. My best to Mrs. Clark.

---

82 • TO AGNES BOULTON O'NEILL.   ALS 4 pp. (Stationery headed: Prince George Hotel / Fifth Ave. & 28th Street New York) [Harvard]

Jan. 17, 1919 [1920]

Dearest Own Wife: A million pardons for my not writing yesterday, but when you know the circumstances, I'm sure you'll forgive me. Thursday night I went to Williams' office at 11:30 to meet Bennett. He called in a taxi with his wife—Adrienne Morrison—and we went down to his house on Eighth St. between 5th and Macdougal. He's got a perfectly corking place, wonderfully and artistically fitted up. The servants being a-bed, Adrienne—(a quite charming woman, by the way, but an actress from toe to scalp) made scrambled eggs for us. They both know Felton Elkins very well. He has praised me to the skies to them—also Nina Jones—and so I was treated as one of the 400. When his wife left us to our labors in Bennett's study, he turned to me and said impressively: "Do you like absinthe?" I said yes but what good does a liking do me. There isn't any real Pernod in this country. Yes, there is, quoth Bennett; I have fifty cases. Jack Barrymore and I are the only people in the country who have any. Produce, I returned avidly, I knew I was going to like you from the first moment we met.

---

6. O'Neill continually urged Agnes, who before their marriage had published short stories, to continue writing. None of her plays were produced.

7. O'Neill's dog.

8. The *New York Telegraph* correspondent called James O'Neill, Sr., "one of the American stage's most brilliant actors" and reported that he was seriously ill.

He dug down in the old oak chest and a quart of *real Pernod* was the result. He mixed frappie in large, tall glasses and we sipped them as we worked on the play line by line with Richard reading aloud. Don't think I'm going to describe an absinthe orgy. We had one frappies to an act. If we hadn't had it we couldn't have kept awake. Do you know what time the work was finished? 7:30 a.m.! We were both dead, and I came home and slept all day and felt so rotten when I woke up that I didn't feel up to writing you.

So you will forgive me, won't you, Old Dear?

When I came home I was too tired to get to sleep—you know that feeling—and in addition my brain was full of subtle fireworks from the queer poison of absinthe. I sat down and wrote a prose poem.[1] I'll send it to you. Want to get it typed. When I wrote it the whole world was shot through with White Logic and I seemed to see through the whole game. Looking over it now, I think it's fine and nutty. Be sure and show it to Terry[2] when you get it. He'll be interested in it as an absinthe product.

Am glad the *Beyond* script is now straightened out. Will start in attending rehearsals on Monday at the Playhouse.

Today I spent the p.m. with Stanhope. Like him immensely. He dragged me to the Standard theatre to see *The Whirlwind*[3] because they were considering the star of that play—Laura Walker—for Chris' daughter.

Oh, boy! Of all the rotten plays! As I said to Stanhope when we left the theatre at the end of the second act, everything in the play is so rotten—acting, sets, directing, dialogue, plot—that it's really a perfect thing without a false moment in it. (This remark is due to travel all over Broadway as Stanhope nearly died laughing at it.)

Toohey has blood in his eyes these days and prowls around me with his press-agent nose sniffing the wind. Pretty soon he'll begin to bay—and then watch the papers for news of your dear husband. You'll probably read some startling lies.

I seem to have lost a lot of my self-consciousness. Wander about New York regardless, walking everywhere I have to go.

Mama is "nuts" about the pictures of Shane but wants one "with his eyes open." Of course, she thinks he looks like me.

Christine[4] phoned me and asked me to come down to a farewell John Barleycorn party at the P.P. after the show tonight. I'm going—couldn't very well get out of it, she was so nice—but I'm not going in for any orgy. I've been drinking almost every day but, outside of the 4 absinthes with Bennett, have done it all up in the room with Papa—four drinks or so a day. So don't worry about my making a fool of myself. I'm a wise guy—when I know it's necessary. But it would be silly for me not to drink. Everyone I'm associated with does—Tyler, Williams, Bennett, Stanhope, Toohey and they'd simply think me a prig if I didn't.

Bye'bye for this time—and all my love! I wish you were here, My Own—but you will be later on. I'm fixing that now.

XX for Shane—and all of me to you!   Gene

---

1. See "62.," *Poems, 1912–1944*, pp. 92–94; the date of composition is there incorrectly given as September 1919.

2. Terry Carlin, incurable alcoholic whom O'Neill had met in Greenwich Village in 1915–16 and who first introduced O'Neill to the Provincetown Players group in the summer of 1916. Carlin occupied a shack in the dunes near Peaked Hill Bar and was eventually immortalized by O'Neill in the character of Larry Slade in *The Iceman Cometh*.

3. Play by George C. Hazleton (1868?–1921) and Ritter Brown.

4. Christine Ell.

83 • TO AGNES BOULTON O'NEILL. ALS 3 pp. (Stationery headed: Prince George Hotel / Fifth Avenue & 28th Street / [New York]) [Harvard]

Jan. 22, 1920

My Own: Your "lecture" letter seems to me unkind and unreasonable. Those sort of letters are not the kind that do any good and in this case I see no justification whatever for it—especially as I have been home here without leaving the P.G. ever since Monday doing a severe penance for my crimson-ink sins of Sat. night and Sunday. I assure you my sojourn in the Village—with the exception of about 2 hours at the P.P., was entirely spent at the Hell Hole where no one is trying to "drag me down." The night I slept there Lefty, Leo, Chuck and I camped in one bed! Imagine! That was the only way we could keep warm in Tom's zero flat. Now what in hell is effete Village stuff—or "party"—in that? Rather it was good old healthy H.H. days back again and I had a good time—of that kind. The red ink, though, is poison. I cashed a check for twenty dollars—the only money I have drawn since my arrival—and sent out for a quart of real whiskey at twelve dollars per. As there were about ten of us present in the back room that meant 2 small drinks apiece for each of us; but it *was real* bonded Bourbon. As I had been drinking their wine up without any money for twelve hours it seemed to me the least I could do.

No more lecture letters, please! You never used to be a moralist, and I've never in my life stood for that stuff, even from my Mother. My ethics of life forbid that in any conduct based upon emotional reaction, even Christ or Buddha should tell the lowest slave what he should do. That slave has something actuating him that they can never understand.

As for letters, you should have received one Monday a.m. and another Wednesday p.m. Is that so bad? Have a heart, won't you, and don't expect too much, especially when I'm feeling punk.

There is no news, as I told you in my last. And be assured that what you evidently think is my feeble mind is not losing any golden opportunities. Business is slack and I'm waiting.
Gene

---

84 • TO AGNES BOULTON O'NEILL. ALS 6 pp. (Stationery headed: Prince George Hotel / Fifth Avenue & 28th Street / [New York]) [Harvard]

Jan. 23, 1920

Own Sweetheart: Your letter of Thursday arrived this a.m. Thanks for it! It gladdened my heart wonderfully. Own Little Wife of Mine, I miss you so!

No more of the lecture letters! And forgive my own of yesterday in answer to it. I didn't mean to be so harsh—but I wrote mine on the spur of the moment. I felt so sick when your letter arrived—and so it seemed more inconsiderate than it really was.

No more of that stuff—between you and me. Remember we're "pals"—first of all!

To tell you the truth I've been sick from more than the after-throes of "red-ink." I've had a bad cold. They thought for a time it was the "Flu." I must have caught it that night at Tom Wallace's—sleeping with overcoats over us and no bed clothes on the bed. I didn't want to write you about it with the return of the "Flu" headlined in the newspapers. Now you needn't worry. I'm much better.

I had a letter from Adele Holladay[1]—special—yesterday. She wanted to borrow $25

1. Mother of Louis and Paula (Polly) Holladay, O'Neill's friends from Greenwich Village days of 1915–16.

immediately. "Fancy that, Hedda!" Such is fame! If I really believed she needed it I'd give it to her in spite of her poisonous tongue which has had no good word for you or me or Jim[2] since her last Provincetown stay. But I think she and her coterie of "fairies" are on a spree, and I'm not supplying them with booze in these dry days. Outside of her being Louis' mother, she has no claim on me. So I've decided to pay no attention to her letter.

Madden is out of town until Monday. So is Tyler. Tried to get either Williams or Bennett on the phone today—no use. The Doc. says I can't go out of the P.G. until Monday, with the danger of "Flu" in the air. I still feel pretty bum and I'm not sorry to lay off although I'd like to get a slant at the *Beyond* stuff. Still I'll have a week of it—and that's about all an author ought to have to stand of rehearsals. After all, once the script is in shape, he's a mere figurehead— and God knows Bennett and I worked hard enough on that.

I'm sick of *Beyond* and convinced that I must forget it. In my judgment there won't be an ounce of Fame or a cent of money in it for us. All I want to do is get done with it and throw the script into "the deep blue sea." I'd never go near a rehearsal if I didn't have to—and I'll certainly never see a performance. Those people will never—can never—be my Robert, Ruth, and Andy—and what would be the use of my watching another lot of actors per- form—after all these years of watching them?

Perhaps this is the pessimism of sickness—"Quién sabe?"

Tearle decided not to do *Chris.* Held the script for four days and then brought it to me, not to Tyler. Said: "I've gone over the part ten times—gone down to the waterfront to try and get the lingo. I'd be a failure, Mr. O'Neill—and I don't want to spoil the only real artistic play I've ever read or seen by an American, in his own country, at that." He's a fine chap— and sincere—is Tearle. He's sailing for England in a week—asked me very cordially to be sure and look him up when I came to London.

I thought I'd written you all this before. I have a distinct recollection of writing a letter just about Tearle's refusal. Either I or the U.S. Mail has missed a step.

Corrigan is to play *Chris.* Perhaps it's better. Tearle would have been a gamble (in this part, I mean) while C. is sure fire.

I enclose Nina's[3] letter. Read it and you will like her for what she is—a naive, childish- simple soul and a lady of real breeding combined. I think it would be more perfect courtesy—and please her more—if you wrote a few lines first. Do it, won't you? If we ever decide to go to So. California, she would be a willing slave at looking up a place, making all arrangements, etc. The place they live—Montecito—is the most beautiful town in all California, Mother says—and that's saying something! But these practical considerations are nothing! She's one of the few genuine ones—(it's so easy to make fun of them)—and I think you'd find you'd like her, and that she'd prove one of the best friends you ever had.

Bye'bye, Sweetheart! This is a long letter for an "unwell" gentleman. A long kiss for you and Shane!   Gene

P.S. About your coming down—all depends on *Beyond*—What can I talk with now?

---

85 • TO AGNES BOULTON O'NEILL.   ALS 3 pp. (Stationery headed: Prince George Hotel / Fifth Avenue & 28th Street / [New York]) [Harvard]

Sunday / [January 25?, 1920]

My Own: Your letter of Friday received when I got up this morning. Perhaps a lot of the points you make in it are true enough—from your standpoint—But, Oh God!, My Own, the

2. James O'Neill, Jr.
3. Nina Moise.

tragedy which overwhelms me in all our bickering is this: If you and I, who love each other so much, who have been through so many fundamental life-experiences successfully together; if, at this so crucial moment of our union, we cannot keep petty hate from creeping into our souls like the condemned couples in a Strindberg play; if our letters are to become an added torture to our hearts already tortured by separation and by the mishaps of outside shame; if we cannot stand back to back to face failure or the equally fatal possibilities contained in success; if the morale at home cannot reinforce the morale at the front when that falters, and vice-versa—then we are lost; and my only remaining hope is that the "Flu," or some other material cause, will speedily save me the decision which would inevitably have to come at my own instance. If you and I are but another dream that passes, then I desire nothing further from the Great Sickness but release.

I am supposed to make some little cuts on the first scene of *Chris* today. Your letter has put over the K.O. I'm "out" temporarily—until I get another letter from you and, let me hope, a kinder one. You don't have to be hypocritical to be kind, do you? Your letter may have been true; but, where love is concerned, isn't kindness greater than truth? And do you think that greater kindness is a product of—a "flat surface wife?" There may be depths—of love—in that——

As for my letter to you which drove you to the response you made, if you had written your good advice first and the way you felt last, I would have remembered only the last. As it was—vice-versa—I wrote on the spur of the moment remembering only the good advice—(which we all hate!). You might have known all this—if you knew me.

The "Flu" has already caused an official regulation of theatre opening hours. You can imagine what it is doing to the attendance. Ah well, there has been all through history a curse which, after minor victories, through no fault of their own, always smites the O'Neills at the wrong moment. The Curse of the Red Hand of Ulster!

But all this is puerile—and aside. Your letter was gall when I prayed for wine. You always have kicked me when I was down,—do you realize that!—you did not mean to, of course, but you always have.   Gene

---

86 • TO AGNES BOULTON O'NEILL.   ALS 6 pp. (Stationery headed: Prince George Hotel / Fifth Avenue & 28th Street / [New York]) [Harvard]

Jan. 28, 1920

Dearest Sweetheart: Have just returned from my second *Beyond* rehearsal. It was a stormy session. Bennett and I "went to the mat" with a loud bang at the close of Act II Scene I. He had his own idea of what he should do—(Williams, the damn idiot, had inspired it)— but I rebelled and insisted on the directions for reading the lines as per the text. He tried to get away with some learned remarks as to the true nature of the hero in tragedy. This was a bad mistake for him because I know more about that than he ever dreamed of and I showed him up before the whole company, who were now assembled at the ringside to see the scrap. He was stung, and resorted to sarcasm anent my inexperience in Broadway productions. But no one can beat me at that game and I came back with a remark about his inexperience in playwriting. Finally, furious, he yelled: "Will you be responsible for the failure of this scene if we play it your way?" And I said yes, I'd be responsible for its artistic success and that was all I cared about. Then they went over it and he played Robert faithfully—(I'll hand him that)— as I wanted. After it was done he turned to me enthusiastically and said "By God, you're right! Let's have a few more fights and this play'll pick up 100%." So it all ended in the most friendly manner. He's sincerely fighting for the play as much as I am and so, no matter what tiffs we have, we'll remain friends; and he's as frank to acknowledge when he's wrong as I am.

For two days now I have occupied that position so unattainable to most playwrights—the only man in the auditorium, director of my own play! And I don't think I've made such a fizzle of it either! They all showed a noticeable improvement today, and also a marked improvement in their respect for me. At the end of each scene Bennett calls "Suggestions!" and every member of the cast who has been in that scene lines up at the foot lights while I—a lone figure in a vast auditorium—go from one to one, praising or panning, and not excepting Bennett himself.

Can you imagine! No, you can't—or any one of the P.P. either. For at every one of their rehearsals I was "pickled" and not myself. You can bet that doesn't happen nowadays.

Tomorrow Williams is due to be present and there may be fireworks between him and me. But he, too, sincerely loves the play and any brawls will be forgotten if *Beyond* profits thereby. He has been down at Atlantic City putting on the Brieux-Lionel Barrymore play—*The Letter of the Law*.[1]

I am getting to be great friends—now don't be jealous!—with Helen MacKellar. She read *The Straw* when the script was in Williams' office and liked it immensely—(so she says!). She is the best person in the play—excluding Bennett—and I think will do Ruth quite well. She sure is one ambitious hustler, playing in one play and rehearsing in another at the same time—which means 11 in the a.m. to 11 p.m., and after, with few intermissions. She isn't more than 25, I should judge.

Altogether *Beyond* is not so very bad off. Things might be worse. It has a splendid cast—from a Broadway standpoint, at any rate—and I have no cause for complaint on that score. They are not my ideals but they are good.

You would miss a lot of the text in the play. Nothing has been written in or substituted but it sure has been cut. That had to be. It was over half an hour—30 theatrical pages—too long. That was my fault. However I'm sure that by my supervision of the cutting, the meaning of the play has not suffered by consequence. It seems to me to benefit by it, rather. You know I always knew *Beyond* was too long. At least the cutting makes it much more thrilling.

All this about *Beyond!* Well, *Beyond* takes up all my time these days—and will. Tomorrow rehearsal with sets for the first time—all day—next day, ditto—Saturday—half-day with the rest devoted to going over *Chris* with Stanhope. Sunday, dress rehearsal of *Beyond* from 3 p.m. until 3 a.m. (I guess, knowing dress rehearsals) and Monday, first performance in Yonkers—Tuesday, first N.Y. showing at the Morosco.

There you have it! I'm a busy bee. Just as soon as *Beyond* gets on I'm going to Tyler and arrange to get away for a time—back to you! God, how I need you and want you! The whole thing is without meaning without you! Talk about missing my arms at nights—God, if I haven't wanted yours in my dingy cell on the Prince George court where eternal twilight is a fact! And my bad, bad dreams—but they were all of you, My Own, showing that the Nightingale[2] has not forgotten. He sends his love to Her and asks Her not to forget him but to just wait and He will soon—Ah, My Own, how much I want you!

Kiss our Shane for me. And to you—All of me!   Gene

1. Play by French dramatist Eugène Brieux (1858–1932).
2. The Nightingale (Eugene) and Miss Pussy (Agnes) were the sexual pet names the O'Neills used with one another.

87 • TO AGNES BOULTON O'NEILL.   ALS 6 pp. (Stationery headed: Prince George Hotel / Fifth Avenue & 28th Street / [New York]) [Harvard]

Jan. 29, 1920

My Dearest: This is just a few lines. I've this minute finished dinner here in the room with Papa after putting in from 11 a.m. to 5:30 p.m. at the Morosco Theatre with *Beyond*—not an interval for lunch, even, for me who had to be there every moment of the time. Today we rehearsed in the gents smoking room downstairs while they were rehearsing the sets on the stage above. I had to be on one floor one minute, and on another the next, to give my opinion. After it was all over—(I thought)—about 4:30, Bennett takes it into his head to take me into his dressing room and go over the whole part of Robert speech by speech. I arrived home in a taxi at 6 p.m.—*Dead Tired!*

To make matters at this epoch still worse, as an after effect of the grippe—or, I guess, of my being in the house so long—I have the most terrible insomnia. I simply can't sleep any more. Every night I stay religiously with the family—have only been away from home one night since I got down here—play "rummy" with the "old man," have two or three drinks of rum, and go to bed about 11:30. I try to sleep, pitch and toss, and finally do sleep about 5 or 6 a.m. It's frightful! I've never had it before. And I have to be up, bright and smiling, at 8:30! For the past week I've averaged about 4 hours per night. Last night I took veronal—with the only result that I didn't get to sleep til 6:30 this a.m.! Got up at 8:30—at theatre at 10:45—and then an all day grind. The funniest thing about it is that I don't feel bad, only a bit woozy.

Listen now! The following is important, VERY, and I rely on you to get action and let me know at the very earliest moment. Williams asked me today if I could suggest any names to him of people to whom *Beyond* might appeal, to use in advertising—that is, to send personal announcements of the special matinees to. I didn't think of any at the time but since then it has occurred to me that if I could get a list of P.P. subscribers, it might help a lot. He wants a selected audience for the matinees and for the first performances generally—people who can appreciate the play. He thinks they will speak about it to their friends and thus be the best ad. in the world. Now I'm not especially friendly with the queer gang—except Jimmy[1]—who are at present pervading the P.P. I want to go down for that list with authority at my back. So tell this to Jig and Susan. I want their consent to it. Futhermore, they have read the play and know they are not backing any unknown quantity. It seems to me only fair that I should have the benefit of the list which my plays, on 14 out of 28 bills, have done their part to build up. Ask Jig, as President, to write a letter to the Secretary to that effect—and *immediately!* And you let me know what Jig and Susan say—also *immediately!*

After all, it is only a question of getting the address of people to send a card of announcement to.

Ads. for *Beyond* will begin in all N.Y. papers Saturday.

Rehearsals look better. I think the play has a good chance for artistic success—beyond that, hope nothing!

All my love, Own Sweetheart! The N. sends his last gasp to Miss P.[2]

Only a little while now, Own Little Wife!   Gene

P.S. (later) Just opened the box. A ton of hungry gratitude from all the family! Mother loves the jelly and cakes, Father craves the cold bird, and I—all! And we're all so grateful for

---

1. James Light (1894–1964), leading member of the Provincetown Players since late 1917, who acted in or directed many of their productions.
2. The N. (Nightingale) and Miss P. (Pussy).

and proud of the pictures of Shane! The Old Man bubbles over! And I—you both look so beautiful, My Own, that I'm afraid you can't be mine, I feel so unworthy. I want to get back to you and see—and prove my claim. Tell Shane his poor Daddy is as busy these days as a centipede with St. Vitus dance but as soon as he gets one hook free for a reflective hour, he'll certainly answer that letter. In the meantime tell him my advice as one Sein Fein to another: Never trust a woman, or depend on her, especially—as Shane the Proud will be sure to whisper out of the subconscious—a woman born in London, surely!

---

88 • TO AGNES BOULTON O'NEILL.   ALS 4 pp. (Stationery headed: Prince George Hotel / Fifth Ave. & 28th Street New York) [Harvard]

Jan. 31, 1920

My Own: Never got home this p.m. until seven. Rehearsal at the Morosco, 11 to 1:30, 2 to 6:30 at the Lambs' Club going over the script of *Chris* with Stanhope. At that we only got through the first two acts—one still to do, the third. Stanhope left it absolutely up to me and I found many cuts to make. I'm a lot wiser now than when I first went to *Beyond* rehearsals. Honestly, I've learned a tremendous lot that I wouldn't miss for worlds—knowledge that will be of *real* worth to me hereafter. I don't mean knowledge of the technique à la Broadway—*Beyond* isn't being put on like that—but *real* stuff as to the theatrical medium. Bennett is really a liberal education all in himself. He has brains and he uses them every second and, outside of some misconceptions, he has really been a great help to the play. And even from his mistakes, I have learned a hell of a lot. I'm a better playwright already; I feel it. This whole experience has been invaluable to me as an artist who ought to know his medium from top to bottom. And Bennett represents the best there is in this country. He, at least, knows all the plays of all countries and is far from the type of usual ignorant, egotistical star.

I got your wire about the list of P.P. subscribers on my return. When I see Williams tomorrow I'll tell him Susan's suggestion about sending down an addresser. John, with all his faults, is a gentleman and I know he would take no unfair advantage of any favor granted him.

Thank you for being so prompt in attending to my request. You're a peach, Little Sweetheart!

You won't mind if I don't write tomorrow, will you? I don't see how I'll ever get the time. The dress rehearsal starts at one and it is their intention to run that through and then start another trial performance at 8 p.m. Now I know something of dress rehearsals, and if I get out of that theatre before 3 a.m. Monday, I'll be a surprised prophet. But I will write at length after I get back from Yonkers Monday.

It doesn't look as if I'd be able to get back to you as soon as I expected. I thought I'd be able to get out of the *Chris* preliminaries and first rehearsals, but Stanhope says he'd much rather have me at first and let me off for the middle week or ten days.

The N. droops and languishes at this news. He has been pestering me to death at every thought of you. He's a very vexatious fellow when he has his mind set on something. But he sends word to Her that he's damn well going to make up for all this lost time when he finally does see her—and you can tell her that's a promise!

My dearest love to our Shane. I'm so glad to know he's flourishing and full of smiles. Kiss him for me.

Dear Wife of Mine, how I wish you were here! I'll be back the first second I possibly can, My Own, I swear to you; but I don't want to go and then get a wire to come back at the end of 24 hours. I want to be sure of ample time for a real, wee honeymoon with you. You understand, don't you, Dear?   Your   Gene

89 • TO AGNES BOULTON O'NEILL.   WIRE 1 p. ([Prince George Hotel / New York]) [Yale]

4 FEB 1920

HAVE WRITTEN BUT THIS IS JUST A LINE SO YOU WILL NOT WORRY *BEYOND* IS A TRIUMPH ALL I EXPECTED WILL BE HOME TO YOU FIRST SECOND I CAN VERY SOON NOW ALL MY LONELY LOVE TO YOU AND SHANE   EUGENE

---

90 • TO AGNES BOULTON O'NEILL.   ALS 3 pp. (Stationery headed: Prince George Hotel / Fifth Avenue & 28th Street / [New York]) [Harvard]

Feb. 4, 1920 / 11:30 p.m.

My Own: This is the very first second I've had in which to draw a free breath—and not so damn free either because I *have* to go to see *Clarence* tonight. It's the last night Helen Hayes is to be in the cast and Tyler insists on my giving her the once over.

Have been up at the *Beyond* matinee all the p.m. We made some further cuts and rehearsed them this a.m.—meaning that I have been at the Morosco since 10:30 this a.m. until my arrival home a few minutes ago.

I explain all this to show you that my negligence in writing is not my fault. I think of you—oh, I swear to you, all the time!—but I hate to sit down unless I have time to write you at least a pretense of a real letter.

The first performance was hell! I sat through it as I couldn't shake Williams and he planted me beside him. I suffered tortures. The waits were terrible and the show never ended until ten of six. I went out convinced that *Beyond* was a flivver artistically and every other way. That's why I didn't write you last night—I was too depressed. I dreaded to see this day's papers. When I did—lo and behold, in spite of all the handicaps of a rotten first performance, *Beyond* had won. You never saw such notices! There was not a single dissenting voice—so far, at any rate. Even old Towse, who has always panned my plays to a frazzle, came to life in the *Evening Post* with a big boost.[1] Woollcott is to run a special on Sunday with quotes from the script in the *Times* and photos of the play.[2]

Today the play went great—not a whisper in the house from start to finish, but many in tears. Ida was there, and Jimmy Light, and Grace Potter[3] and Rob Parker.[4] They all liked it. Ida even kissed me in the lobby in her enthusiasm. Lewisohn of the *Nation* was there. He liked it immensely, Jimmy told me.[5]

I'd send you notices but you'll get them all from Romecke[6] before you get this, I suppose.

They're are a million other things to tell you. Will try to do it all in a long letter tomorrow.

I got yours from Miss P. this a.m. Oh, Sweetheart Wife, I want you so! It's a torture of longing at night when I'm in bed alone—result, insomnia. I'll be home to you, and the N. to Her, very, very soon now—the very first second I can. Believe that, won't you? A kiss to Shane, and you—and Her!   Gene

1. J. Ranken Towse, "'Beyond the Horizon,'" *New York Post*, February 4, 1920, p. 11.
2. Alexander Woollcott, "The Coming of Eugene O'Neill," *New York Times*, February 8, 1920, sec. 8, p. 2.
3. Member of the original Provincetown Players group.
4. Robert Allerton Parker (1889–1970), writer and Greenwich Village friend of O'Neill.
5. Ludwig Lewisohn's very positive review, "An American Tragedy," appeared in *The Nation* on February 21, 1920.
6. The clipping service that sent O'Neill copies of reviews.

ALS 6 pp. (Stationery headed: Prince
George Hotel / Fifth Avenue & 28th Street / [New York]) [Harvard]

Feb. 4, 1920 / 11:30 p.m.

My Ownest Own: Have just returned from *Clarence* with Mother and now that I am in
my dark hole-on-the-court room, the voice of Mr. N. becomes insistent and he demands that
he be put into instant communication with Miss P., or at least, poor lonely bird that he is!,
that he send a message by me to her which you are to tell her in the still hour before you fall
asleep. So here goes—my own Fuzzy-Wuzzy, he says, if you find it HELL to be away from me
then I find it triple-plated HELL not to have you beside me in the long, lonely nights! But
wait, only WAIT, my little Sweetheart, and in a few days now I will be back to you. For my
master is going to tell Mr. Tyler that he simply must get away as near immediately as he can
be dispensed with. And then your mistress and he, and you and I, what a sweet honeymoon
we'll all have! Be patient, Own P., for just a wee while longer. The reunion will be all the
more intense for the enforced wait.

That's what he says, the poor forlorn Nightingale!

Oh My Own, My Darling Agnes, My Own Little Wife, I want you, and need you, and
love you so! It's been HELL, I've been so lonely. My family are all right, and as kind as kind
can be, but they are not You—beautiful, adorable, lovely wife of mine! I've been tempted to
send for you, to wire, a thousand times I've never mentioned to you. It was only the thought
of the Flu danger to you and Shane which kept me level-headed. And, after all, it's better for
us to reunite in our own home, with our own dear child, where we can be alone—and not in
a rotten hotel room.

I swear to you I'll be back to you the first moment I can! I know you wouldn't want me
to play coward—(it takes courage to stay!)—to Us, Our future, *Chris,* and Tyler; and my
experience with *Beyond* has convinced me that there are certain things an author must see to
right at the start or they'll never be done right—notably the sets. Stanhope wants me to go
with him and the artist to visit tramp steamers at the Bush docks in Brooklyn and barges in
Erie Basin. Also we have the last act of the script still to go over. Also Corrigan has to be
taught the Yosephine song. These three things I simply *have* to attend to personally before I
leave. I want to go back to you with a mind free from the worry that things such as cropped
up in the *Beyond* production are not going on behind my back. I want to have You—and my
happiness which is You!—without a disturbing thought.

Believe me, Own Sweetheart, it is from a standpoint of our happiness—Us Three!—
that I make all decisions. God, it has been hell not to have you with me in this hour of
consummation. You remember what I used to tell you in the old days when realization of
each other was first peeping through our love—that paraphrase of a line of Louis XV in
DuBarry[1]—"The stars are only stars, Sweetheart, when I can hang them in your hair!" Well,
I still feel the same—only more so!

You'll see what a knockout *Beyond* was when you get the Romecke clippings. It's
positively stunning! Whatever it may or may not do in a financial way, it has done all I ever
expected of it already—and more. It's useless to prophesy the money end. It'll take a week
yet to get any dope on that.

And it's a tremendous ad for *Chris.*

I'll not tell you any more news in *this* letter, My Own. It isn't meant to be newsy. It's a
letter from the soul of me—the soul and heart of a lover—which will always be the first of

1. Play (1901) by David Belasco.

me to spring to your love, even should we both be in our nineties. Your lover, always to the end of time—that's me!

A long kiss, My Darling, and be patient—(and Miss. P. too!)—I'll be back soon. You know what Robert says in *Beyond*—"It's hard to stay—and harder to go, sometimes." You are my life!   Gene

---

92 • TO AGNES BOULTON O'NEILL.   ALS 3 pp. (Stationery headed: Prince George Hotel / Fifth Ave. & 28th Street New York) [Harvard]

Monday / [February 16?, 1920]

Sweetheart: I have nothing to report except more physical trouble so this shall be brief. Expected to go to *Chris* rehearsal today. Woke up at 4 a.m. with the most terrible pain in my side, just over my heart. I thought first: "this is cases," and afterwards "it's pleurisy." The pain was so fierce whenever I moved that I couldn't get out of bed to the phone to call up Mama. I had to lie there until 11 a.m. when the chamber maid opened the door and I got her to go to Mama's room—about fifty feet away—and sound the S.O.S.

Well, it was a case of Doctor again, and he found that I didn't have pleurisy—only neuralgia of some nerve connected with the heart. This was cheering, but doesn't alter the fact that the pain was among the worst I've ever bumped into. It will return off and on for some time, he blandly confesses, unless I take an electric massage treatment.

I seem to be reaping the whirlwind of I know not what wind—unless it be the long nervous tension of this fall and early winter. At any rate both King and Aspell[1] unite in declaring that I am worn down to the last notch, without resisting power, open hospitably to all ills. Stripped, I look like a medical student's chart, every muscle outlined and every bone and bit of sinew. I weigh about 125, I estimate.

And I feel—well, only a drink makes me feel alive at all and drinks come about one every other day. Even the Old Man is "dry" as a bone these days—not even port wine any more.

I hate to write you these pathological letters, but what can I do? Life with me now consists in wondering: "What new ill is going to hit me tomorrow?"

Just think! I haven't been out of this hotel since the Friday after *Beyond* opened! And all "the honor and glory" passes by in the street below. And I haven't even the comfort of your presence! Life is a sweet thing, is it not?

But I've gotten to that stage now where nothing can hurt or anger me. Like the Old Woman in *Riders to the Sea*[2] I feel I've won to that spent calm where neither joy nor sorrow over anything exist.

Don't mind the above, Agnes. I'm sick, that's all. I want you—need you—and yet, with Shane, what is the use of my heart crying. It's all so impossible. I love you!   Gene

---

93 • TO AGNES BOULTON O'NEILL.   ALS 6 pp. (Stationery headed: Prince George Hotel / Fifth Ave. & 28th Street New York) [Harvard]

Wednesday / [February 18?, 1920]

Own Sweetheart: Forgive me for not writing yesterday. One reason for my not doing so was the neuralgia in my chest would start in raising hell every so often and, besides,

1. The doctors who had examined O'Neill.
2. Play (1904) by Irish dramatist John Millington Synge (1871–1909).

although I'm still tied down to the room there's always something over the phone to keep me on the hop.

Stanhope had me on the wire for a long talk, principally about Scotty.[1] To come down to cases, Scotty is to be fired! No, not for drinking or any sort of misbehavior but just because he hasn't made good. He hasn't the instinct for the stage, so Stanhope says. They've given him every chance to pick up but he just simply can't make it. In his scene with Corrigan at the end of Scene One—very important, if you'll remember—Scotty has failed absolutely to "hold up." Corrigan, of course, is wild as he can't carry the whole burden of the two parts himself.

The damnable part of the whole business is that they've been afraid to fire Scotty on account of his being my choice, as they thought. On the other hand, Scotty has lost his old job and is very much up against it and was relying on this to save his life. But there is more than that to it. He's been so proud of playing the part, he's had such a genuine enthusiasm and confidence in himself, that this throw down is due to break him all up. There isn't even a smaller part for him as all the cast is engaged and each one has made good.

But you see what I mean by its getting me in wrong, can't you? The management cursing me for foisting a bum actor on them, Scotty probably thinking by now that I could save his skin if I wanted to—Well, never again! No more of that friendship game in business!

Williams has picked Helen Freeman to play Ruth when *Beyond* goes on at nights.[2] As I've never seen her work, I pass judgment until I do. It's very hard to get any one at this stage of the season. The receipts for three matinees week before last were $2,600. As the capacity of the Morosco is $1,700 for one performance at 3.50 prices and as *Beyond* is playing 2.75 you'll see that's pretty fine. Friday matinees for the past two weeks have been well over $1,000—which means practically capacity. What it will do when it goes on regularly, the devil alone knows.

Worry not and gnash not your teeth over the "blond beauties." They come not, no, not one, to sit beside my couch. Helen MacK. has written me several letters of commiseration over my illness, but that is all. As, in private life she is Mrs. McQuarrie, and I know her husband—a corking big fine chap that I don't blame her for being so much in love with, I hardly think her kind letters can be regarded jealously—even by one as green-eyed as Agnes O'Neill. (You will remember I spoke of meeting McQuarrie at rehearsals and of how much I liked him. At that time I suspicioned that he was Helen's lover, or, more conventionally, her intended; but it turned out that the two Canadian Scots were quite prosaically married, even as you and I.)

If you saw me now you'd believe the interviewer's "sad-eyed & delicate." I look like a ghost who is all eyes. The Flu simply knocked hell out of me.

I wouldn't worry about their believing I'm sad because of an unhappy home life. They're much more liable to guess the truth—that it's being away from my home that makes me sad.

Tell Susan her script is now at Tyler's office awaiting his first breathing spell. It's a bad time for quick action from him. He's made three new productions in the last ten days—Phil Moeller's play[3] among them—and is busy as a bird dog with fleas. If she had sent it to me two weeks before she did——

---

1. William (Scotty) Stuart.
2. Evening performances of *Beyond the Horizon* began on February 23, 1920, when the play moved to the Criterion Theatre.
3. *Sophie*, which opened on March 2, 1920.

Helen Hayes in *Bab*[4] in Boston seems to have made a big hit. Rehearsals for *The Straw* are to start up there very shortly.

Did you see Lewisohn's criticism in *The Nation?* A corker, the best I have received.

The book of *Beyond* is held up by trouble with the printers. Liveright is tearing his hair but hopes to have it out within a week.

Am reading *Jurgen*[5]—a wonderful, beautiful book! The boneheads who suppressed it ought to be hung! The Lady Interviewer of the *Theatre Magazine*[6] loaned it to me—said that Cabell and I had the same feeling behind our writing. At any rate, I'm "nuts" about *Jurgen*. It doesn't sound American a bit—reads more like Anatole France than any one. I wish you could read it but it can't be got anymore except at $25.00 a copy when you buy it on the sly, like booze.

The L.I. also loaned me another book—short stories of the Malays—by some Englishman who died unsung,[7] the book being now out of print. It is called *The Farther Side of Silence*. Some title, eh? I haven't read them yet.

Well, this is some letter for you! Bye'bye, My Own, and a long kiss! The date of my return now depends first on the old Doc. The neuralgia still gives me hell at night when I lie down but my cough seems much better. Well, cheer up, pretty soon I'll have had every thing and then I'll have to get well.

All my love to you & Shane! Be patient with me! I'm doing my best to get well and back to you. I'm so lonely and unhappy here!   Gene

---

94 • TO ST. JOHN ERVINE.   ALS 3 pp. (Stationery headed: Prince George Hotel / Fifth Avenue & 28th Street / [New York]) [Private]

Feb. 22, 1920

Dear Mr. Ervine: I will not attempt to tell you how very much your note of appreciation meant to me. Praise from a man whose work I admire as sincerely as I do yours is praise indeed! Your letter was the most gratifying and happy event that the production of *Beyond The Horizon* has brought to me.

We owe you a tremendous lot—the few of us in this country who are trying to write *honestly* for the theatre. I don't believe you can realize just how very significant *John Ferguson* was to us here. The general appreciation of it as a work of art, the fact that the public *kept on* going to see it—a really fine play!—why, it was an impossible dream come true, a grand big omen that put new heart in us and made us believe that the despaired-of dawn of finer possibilities had actually broken at last.

And I am certainly proud that it took an Irishman to wake up our public and give us writers new hope! (Yes, I'm of undiluted Irish blood on both sides of my family.)

I am just tottering through the last stages of influenza, but as soon as I cease to be a coughing nuisance to myself and every one else I hope to see *Jane Clegg*. In the meantime all my cheers are with it.

Again let me thank you for the kindness of your note. Such an act of genuine consideration I can never forget. Sincerely,   Eugene O'Neill

4. Play by Edward Childs Carpenter (1872–1950).
5. Controversial novel (1919) by James Branch Cabell (1879–1958).
6. Alta M. Coleman, whose essay-interview, "Personality Portraits: No. 3, Eugene O'Neill," appeared in the April 1920 issue of *Theatre Magazine*.
7. By Sir Hugh Charles Clifford (1866–1941).

Feb. 27, 1920

My Own: Failed to write you yesterday because, to tell the truth, I was too "pickled" to write anyone. Whereon hangs a tale, and this is it. Wednesday night I was frightfully nervous. Life cooped up in these hotel rooms, feeling rotten anyway, has been steadily getting my goat and I was due to crack. Well, Wednesday night the two female pests of the Western World, my cousins,[1] called. I had no chance to get out of the way. Well, after an hour of them I felt that I must shriek, go mad, jump out of the window—or get out of the hotel. I grabbed my hat and coat and set out for the Hell Hole where I found a big "bust" of the "rough-necks" just starting. I was welcomed as a brother. They had whiskey—of a kind!—and I was soon as full as a tick. I spent the night as a bed-mate of the First Division doughboy, Chuck, and returned home last night.

The funniest part of all this is that on this jamboree I lost my neuralgia and also my cough. I feel 100% better—except for my nerves which are somewhat tattered as an after effect. But what would any doctor say was the cause of my being cured of my cough and the pain in my chest, I wonder, after all medicines had failed. Alcoholic Christian Science is my only dope!

Am going to *Chris* rehearsal tomorrow. The Flu and I are now quits and I can get back on the job again.

Yes, I'll have to go to Atlantic City. The dress rehearsal is to be there. Also three performances. I've asked Tyler and he says it's imperative for me to be there. Why do you ask about this so particularly? Is there any chance of your coming down to Point Pleasant and being able to make the show at A.C. from there? It's a great scheme if it can be worked.

Honestly, Agnes, there's no chance I can make out of getting any place here. We have had Mrs. Phillips,[2] the Connors, all our friends on the trail. Mama has also followed up all the newspaper ads. that sounded good. There seems to be nothing under 200 a month—and all, without exception, won't rent unless you lease until Oct. 1st. New York is jammed with people, an unprecedented situation, and every hotel is booking their rooms 3 weeks in advance.

I enclose the check for 450.00. It was delayed in transit by Madden. Shove it in and send me a few blank checks, will you? The ones I had I cashed for a total of sixty-four dollars—not so bad for seven weeks.

I'm unhappy as hell and my whole being is one big ache of loneliness for you. Never again! No more separations, My Own! I've learned my lesson. Life without you is—impossible! Well, one way or another, the trial will soon be over. All my love to you and Shane. Eugene

---

Monday / [March 1?, 1920]

Own Dearest: Well, we've been having one hell of an awful time at home here for the past forty-eight hours! Not one wink of sleep in all that time for yours truly. Papa's condition,

---

1. Agnes and Lillian Brennan.
2. Identified as "an old friend of the family" by Louis Sheaffer, *O'Neill: Son and Artist* (Boston: Little, Brown, 1973), p. 83.

which had seemed to be improving, suddenly took a bad turn for the worse. The night before last he was on the very fringe of death, following another slight stroke. We had Doctor Aspell in at once and he just managed to keep life in Papa. Then he told Mama and me the truth. Papa, it seems, is doomed. He has a growth in the intestines which is bound sooner or later to prove fatal. It ought to be operated on at once but this is impossible in his case as his heart is so bad he would die at the first sniff of ether.

And Mama and I have to go around nursing him, watching his every movement, and pretending to kid him and cheer him up! Can you imagine it? And I've also had to hold sessions with Stanhope on *Chris* every morning, ten to 11:30, as I can't leave the hotel to go to rehearsals. As if I gave a damn about *Chris* or any other play now!

To have this happen just at the time when the Old Man and I were getting to be such good pals!

I'm not going to write any more. I'm all broken up and begin to cry every time the meaning of it all dawns on me.

It can't be more than a little over a week now before I'll see you. I'll send detailed dope on *Chris* as soon as I see Tyler.

Be brave, My Own! This is a bad bit of road for us both but we have our love and we'll soon be together to fight back to back again.   All my love!   Gene

P.S. Sent you wire this noon.
P.S. Did you receive special with check?[1]

---

97 • TO GEORGE C. TYLER.   TLS 1 p. (Provincetown, Mass.)[1] [Princeton]

March 10, 1920

My dear Mr. Tyler: Have gone over the third scene carefully since your telegram arrived and have just wired you at length what my suggestion is regarding it. This suggestion that the scene end with Chris' defiant challenge "Dat ole davil, sea, she ain't God" and then out of the distance the sea's answer, the whistle of the steamer that is to run them down, seems to me to be very much in keeping with the whole meaning of the play. Also I think that if it is done with that impressive pause at the end it will carry all kinds of suspense at the fall of the curtain. At any rate, I think this scheme ought to be given a fair try-out.

As I read the scene over, it struck me forcibly that the trouble with the very end is that it is all out of key. The scene is one of awe, of mystery, of something of a doom impending in the silence and its effect on the minds of the two people. All that scrambling about, that physical action at the end destroys this, in my opinion, and distracts the audience's mind from the main theme of the play to a mere side issue—the details of how they are to be saved, etc.—things that the audience will take for granted as having happened when the next scene opens—or when they look at their programs, for that matter. I believe the scene should be done with all the suggestion of mystery and awe that can be crammed into it, and with the matter-of-fact stuff serving only as a momentary discordant break to emphasize the other. I mean that there ought to be some of the spirit of Maeterlinck's[2] earlier plays about it—the idea of these two little human beings lost in the fog, awaiting the fate which is about to seize them, with Chris' futile gesture of defiance at the end followed by the definite reply from fate,

1. This postscript appears at the top of the first page of this letter.

1. After his father's condition improved slightly and he got word that Agnes was not well, O'Neill told Tyler that she was seriously ill and, avoiding the out-of-town previews of *Chris*, returned to Provincetown.
2. Belgian playwright, poet, and short-story writer Maurice Maeterlinck (1862–1949).

leaving him crushed by the coincidence and his daughter, youth, excited, elated, expectant, eager for the new life whatever it may bring.

I do not think anything needs to be written in at the end. Let the whistle close the scene. Surely Corrigan and Fontanne[3] are artists enough to convey the effect the whistle has on them without words, and enough has been said by Chris in the first part to let the audience know of the danger they are in from steamers.

My wife is still very ill and she is all alone up here. I cannot leave her and the baby to the mercies of a Portuguese servant when there are a million things that have to be done; and a trained nurse is a luxury unknown in these localities. Otherwise I should now be on my way to New York. I hope you will understand this and the damnable position I am in—not to speak of my own mental condition with the worries of the past few weeks all coming at once and at a time when I am far from well myself.   Eugene

---

98 • TO BARRETT H. CLARK.   ALS 2 pp. (Provincetown, Mass.) [Connecticut C.]

March 13, 1920

My dear Mr. Clark: Your note, forwarded from the Prince George, reached me here this afternoon. I had mailed a letter to you this morning which crossed yours.

I will write John D. Williams at once about the seats for Thursday, March 18th. Will tell him either to send them to you or, if my letter reaches him too late for that—(you can't count on the mail either leaving or arriving up here in this weather with the prevailing floods, wash-outs, etc.) I'll tell him to have the seats left in the box office in your name. As Williams is a great little absent-minded forgetter, I think it would be a good idea if you gave him a ring Thursday to make sure. I'm damn sorry I'm not in town to see to this myself.

I'm very glad you find *Beyond* worthy of an article. It is one of my high hopes that *Beyond* may be done in London and I know your article will be of tremendous help in calling their attention to it over there.

You remember when you read *Beyond* you remarked about its being "an interesting technical experiment."[1] Why is it, I wonder, that not one other critic has given me credit for a deliberate departure in form in search of a greater flexibility? They have all accused me of bungling through ignorance—whereas, if I had wanted to, I could have laid the whole play in the farm interior and made it tight as a drum à la Pinero. Then, too, I should imagine the symbolism I intended to convey by the alternating scenes would be apparent even from a glance at the program.

It rather irks my professional pride, you see, to be accused of ignorance of conventional every day technique—I, a Baker 47 alumnus! Professor Baker himself, whose opinion I value as much as any man's in the world, has both read and seen *Beyond* and is delighted with and proud of it. He never mentioned my "clumsiness." Perhaps he saw it but appreciated the fact that it was intentional.

Well, well, how I do go on! But I've been longing to protest about this to someone ever since I read the criticisms by really good critics which blamed my youthful inexperience— even for the poor scenery and the interminable waits between scenes! I'll have a lot more to tell you about this, and what my good intentions were, when we finally do meet. Cordially,   Eugene O'Neill

---

3. Lynn Fontanne (1887–1983), who played Anna.

1. The alternation of exterior and interior scenes in the play.

March 17, 1920

My dear Mr. Tyler: The press notices of *Chris* opening in Philly[1] reached me today. I had been led to expect by your last letter that the play would come in for an unmerciful panning, neck and crop, from all the critics; so the notices, though they were hardly what you would call hysterically enthusiastic, were nevertheless favorable enough to furnish me with a pleasant surprise. At least all of them got the idea that I was trying to do something new and outside of the carpentered flip-flap that constitutes the usual American play. To me this is the highest tribute and flattery that I desire. And if the Philadelphia public refuse to be interested in any unconventional form of drama—well, after all, who could expect them to, and in the middle of Lent at that.

Everyone who has read *Chris* has unreservedly declared it to be a fine play. You bought it because that was your opinion, and because you thought it was different from the ordinary run of plays. Now that very reason seems to be just the fault found with it—that it isn't a play in the accepted Broadway sense. As for the "glass of water" criticism[2] I think the water in question must have been on the critic's brain. Anyone who so characterizes the psychological struggle that goes on in a man's mind against his own fate is merely a booby too empty-headed himself to recognize any form of drama more subtle than *East Is West*.[3] All of which leads up to the debated question which has no answer: When is a play not a play? If you answer, when the American public doesn't like it, then you bar out nearly every really fine play that has ever been written.

But I don't want to appear peevish and sore-headed when I am honestly not that way at all. I've had a hunch ever since I have reread the script up here that *Chris* could not bring home the bacon in its present form, and your letter did not come as an unexpected blow. I am glad you were so frank about it. I realize as well as anyone that the fault is primarily mine in making the stupid mistake of misjudging the length of the play so completely. The intensive cutting that this rendered necessary has taken all the quality and a lot of the guts out of the play. You can't cut a play in which the whole plot is a study in character built up bit by bit down to bare essentials of story without losing your play in the process. As I say, I know the blame for this cutting is mine, due to my own silly mistake in thinking my typed pages were one-minute instead of one and a half. I realize too that the last scene is weak and that the love affair in the play is piffling and undramatic. But, outside of the changes in the last scene which I suggested in my last letter, I can think of no way of improving the play at present writing. Perhaps the method of doing this will come to me in time; but I have a keen suspicion that dickering too much with the present script would only make a bad matter worse. After all, all the scenes in which the love affair does not enter are good and necessary to the general scheme. To attempt to limit the play to three sets, as you suggest, is in my opinion an impossibility unless we completely change the story, keeping only the big, main idea of Chris, his daughter, her lover, with the sea as the fate in the background which molds their lives.

---

1. After several performances in Atlantic City, where it opened on March 9, 1920, *Chris* toured to Philadelphia on March 15, where it closed after a brief run.
2. Reference to *A Glass of Water*, by French playwright Eugène Scribe (1791–1861), whose work is synonymous with the "well-made" play, in which action is mechanically plotted but little attempt is made at psychological insight.
3. Comedy (1918) by Samuel Shipman and John B. Hymer, critically dismissed as absurd hokum but a great hit.

Which means, to write a completely new play and throw the present play in the ashbarrel. Candidly, that is the idea which strikes me as promising the most chances of future success, both artistic and financial. In the back of my mind there are already inklings as to how this could be done but they have not yet formed themselves into any definite plan that I could tell you. Suffice it to say that of the present play I would keep without change only the character of Chris—I'd give you a real daughter and lover, flesh-and-blood people—and the big underlying idea of the sea.

When I could do this, I don't know, as it would all depend on the back of my head which works independently of urgings and won't be forced to turn out ideas. So you see this scheme would require a great deal of faith on your part. However I feel enough confidence in my nut when it once gets started on a thing to say that I think I should be able to work out the new play and have the final script for you by next fall.

Let me know what you think about this scheme. It is the very best I have to offer.

The possibility of my getting away to Philadelphia is very slim. My wife is still bed-ridden, very weak, and she will not be fit to take up the burden of this man's establishment on her shoulders for some time to come. And even if I could go, what would be the use? Up here I see the real faults inherent in the play itself—my faults. But the only thing I ever get out of seeing a presentation is the actors' faults which never fail to set me in a rage. I'd rather keep a pleasant memory of the *Chris* cast than to have to hate at least fifty percent of them for the rest of my life. I am perfectly open to any suggestion anyone has to make which meets your approval and I can act on any such suggestion a hundred times quicker and keener-minded up here than if I were in some city, for up here I live in the work atmosphere.

Chris cost me five months hard labor from first to last, and I suppose it has cost you a devil of a lot of money. I'm sorry for both of us for we both of us thought it was a good play. I still think, with the last scene changed, that it's a good play as originally written. If only an American audience would sit a bit longer in the theatre for something besides Jack Barrymore, I think *Chris* would pick up the trail of *Beyond The Horizon* in New York with a very fair chance of success.

But no more post-mortems!   Sincerely,   Eugene

P.S. Madden is going to Philly as my proxy.

---

100 • TO GEORGE C. TYLER.   TLS 2 pp. (Provincetown, Mass.) [Princeton]

March 26, 1920

My dear Mr. Tyler: The enclosed clipping from the *Transcript* of March 15th leads me to hope that you have given up the idea of a special matinee of *The Straw* in Boston. I am very glad for I have been dead set against that plan ever since you first mentioned it to me. My reasons for this opposition are many. In the first place I am firmly convinced that Helen Hayes is not old enough either in stage or life experience for the part. The role of "Eileen" is so tremendous in its requirements that only one of our very best and proved dramatic actresses should be allowed to attempt it, in my opinion. You must confess that the choice of Hayes is in the nature of a hunch bet, a radical experiment, a gambling on the unknown. Even more radical was your idea of trying out a farce actor in the role of "Murray," and letting him also direct the play although you acknowledged that he had had no previous experience in that line. Now all of this was fine for Hayes and the actor. They had everything to gain. But I think it's unjust to what I consider the best play I have written—better even than *Beyond The Horizon*. The subject of the play is experiment enough. Everything else about it, especially the casting, should be rock-bound certainty. I know you said the matinee would not be regarded as a test of the play—but it would just the same. You couldn't help so regarding it.

So I'm glad *The Straw* is not to undergo what its author deems a very unfair test. I know that you want to give it the best chance possible—if you produce it at all—just as much as I do; for unless produced with the very finest cast obtainable—and it would be worth waiting long for that!—a play of its character will be made hopeless at the start.

I'm also glad there will be no matinee because I would have to be at all rehearsals. *The Straw* can't go on without me—if I have to be taken there on a stretcher. I'm the only one who can tell the cast of that play what, how, and why they ought to behave. And there's another thing: Wouldn't it be unfair to have to give up a month's hard work at creative writing for one experimental-acting matinee?

I'm trying to be absolutely frank with you in this letter and I hope you won't be offended by it. It's only right you should know how I feel about this play. I'm certainly not fussy about most productions—after years with the Provincetown Players—but I sure must be about *The Straw*.

As for *Chris*, I think a mistake was made in believing that it could be treated and launched forth as a general popular success possibility. *Chris* was a special play, a technical experiment by which I tried to compress the theme for a novel into play form without losing the flavor of the novel. The attempt failed. Perhaps such a bastard form deserved to fail. Perhaps I was attempting the impossible. Certainly *Chris*, play or novel, was badly written toward the end, and the author can blame no one for that but himself.

I've received over half a dozen letters from people in Philly who have seen *Chris*, several of whom have read the original script. Also, I may mention that they are all from people of intelligence who have a wide knowledge of the written drama. They liked the play when they read it—you did, too—we all did—but they said the performance indicated that my experiment wouldn't hold the interest except of some special audience who knew what I was driving at. Without exception they panned the acting of Fontanne, Ashley, Hampden and the Captain.[1] This did not surprise me. I know it is the truth from what I saw at rehearsals. I protested against three of these people being in the cast the last time I saw you. The letters stated that the best acted scenes were the first and fifth. Three of the letter writers are artists. These condemned the unreal realism of the sets. The letters spoke of the play having been cut injudiciously—they could not follow the sense of the scenes at times. One of them said that the curtain rang down before 10:30. Madden also wrote me that so it must be fact. Phew! No wonder the curtain rose and fell rapidly. That must allow about 15 minutes per scene. Of course such cutting might have been justified but my character sketch must have gone to hell in the shuffle.

So I don't think all the blame for the fiasco of *Chris* can be laid at my door, although I think I've shown that I'm only too aware of the faults in the play itself which are my fault.

I'd go to see *Chris* this week if I could—not because I think it would accomplish anything or because I have the slightest desire to see the play, but because you seem to demand that I go. I'd willingly oblige you if I could but it's impossible. If it lasted another week I might make it, but I can't leave here yet under any circumstances.

I've carefully timed *The Straw*, reading aloud, and I've gone over the script speech by speech and done all the cutting that will ever need to be done, I feel sure. Next week I'm going to start in on *Gold*—not for Williams or anyone else but because it's a play that has

1. Arthur Ashley, who played Paul Andersen; Mary Hampton, who played Marthy; and Roy Cochrane, who played Captain Jessop.

been in my mind ever since last fall demanding to be written and I want to write it. I ought to finish it in two months. Then I'll start the new *Chris*. By that time I'll have the whole play worked out in my mind. I couldn't write it just now even if I had nothing else to do first. The catastrophe is too recent.   Sincerely,   Eugene

---

101 • TO GEORGE C. TYLER.   TLS 2 pp. (Provincetown, Mass.) [Princeton]

March 30, 1920

My dear Mr. Tyler: I remember quite well when Westley[1] played in the *Three Of Us*[2] with Carlotta Neilson. I saw the play. But it must have been some ten years ago and his success was that of a boy actor. However, my objection was principally to his not having had experience in directing. I think anyone, no matter who, who tries to play Murray and direct the play at the same time is certainly cutting out work for himself. But if you are convinced he can do it and that Miss Hayes can do it, then my objections cease. I think it ought to be understood, however, that the special matinee should be a test of them and not of the play. That is, if we don't think they fill the bill, then the play must be recast before it sees New York next season. I refuse to consider Boston's verdict on the play itself to be worth a damn as far as its New York chances are concerned—anymore than I believe that the judgment on *Chris* in A.C. and Philly gave any indication of what its fate would have been in New York. I think *Beyond The Horizon* proves to any unprejudiced mind that New York is interested in my plays as my plays. It is the town where I am known. My name is worth something to my manager there. There, and there alone, will be found the special audience which can be relied on as a sure basis on which to build up a general appeal. *Beyond The Horizon* has proved this. It would not have played to one thousand dollars a week in Atlantic City nor would it have done any better in Philly. I think to produce a play so drastic in its subject matter as *The Straw* in a town as conventional and hide-bound as Boston is to reduce the play's chances to a minimum. Without the sanction of New York first applied, they will never stand for it. This is my sincere conviction. And the report coming down from Boston that the play is a frost will do much to kill it in advance in New York—with the critics, at least.

What I honestly can't get through my skull is: What is this one special matinee in Boston for, and what is it going to prove? It's so late in the year, too. What does it lead up to? My main objection is not to the casting—I'd cheer with all my might for Miss Hayes and Westley for their own sakes, and they may be all you claim for them for all I can prove to the contrary—it's simply that I cannot "get" the reason for Boston. I don't see why you don't wait and do what you are planning for this late spring in New York next fall. Surely Miss Hayes is liable to play *Bab* in New York for a long time—which, by the way, would limit *The Straw* to special matinees as long as she was cast in it, especially if she made a hit. What answer is there to this? If she makes a hit in *The Straw* and in *Bab* in New York—then what?

Perhaps I am asking a lot of questions I have no right to ask, but you have never told me what future plans you have in mind for *The Straw* after that Boston matinee. If I could get the connection, things would be much clearer to me. As it is, I don't see where I stand. The fear in my mind is that you will accept the Boston verdict, which I know will be adverse, and that you will expect me to make changes in the play on the basis of how it goes in Boston. This, I warn you in advance, I will absolutely refuse to do, for I am convinced that as it is now

1. John Westley (1878–1948).
2. Play (1906) by dramatist Rachel Crothers (1878–1958).

written it should stand or fall. With *Chris* it is a different matter. I can plainly see the faults in my script and that is why I am willing and eager to rewrite.

I hope all of this doesn't sound unreasonable and temperamental to you. I don't want to kick, I don't want to quarrel with any man's judgment, especially do I want to avoid all friction with your ideas, since I recognize how friendly an interest you have shown in my work—*but*—I do want to be sure that my play is being given for my play's sake and with its best interests placed above all other considerations. This is no more than fair. My plays demand this treatment if they are to have a chance of success. *Beyond The Horizon* received it—and justified it! Richard Bennett even sunk his stardom to make that play a success—and gained new laurels thereby. I don't think I am asking too much when I demand for all my plays the same standard of excellence in acting and directing.

Will you tell me, to satisfy my doubts in the matter, just what will happen next fall if Miss Hayes makes a big hit in *Bab* in New York and then at special matinees *The Straw* and she both score? Will you be willing to throw *Bab* aside as Williams and Bennett threw *For The Defense?* If not, then you are not giving me as fair a show as the author of *Bab* receives. Through the medium of special matinees I have proved my right is as good as any author's in America to ask for my own regular production—and I don't want to be condemned to special matinees forever when there is no reason for it.

And tell me what this Boston matinee is for. When is it to be given, by the way?

I withdraw all objections to Miss Hayes and Westley. Let them go to it with all my blessings, provided they show in rehearsals they can make good. Only I do think you ought (and I hope you will see the value of the arguments therefor in this letter) to postpone this production until next fall in New York—with trial performances in the p.m. in Yonkers and Stamford, say, just before the N.Y. opening.

I must deny saying in my last letter that you were "in the main responsible for the failure of *Chris.*" I never thought that or wrote it. It failed because Atlantic City is Atlantic City, because Philadelphia is Philadelphia, and because *Chris,* as written, has many faults. It failed because it is an experiment and New York and Chicago are the only cities that will endure experiments. Finally, I don't believe it failed and I won't until, rewritten and strengthened, it has had its New York chance.

Westley has written me. He thinks he and I should get together as soon as possible if he is to direct the play. I'm up to my ears in work just now and I don't see how or where it would be possible.

With all best wishes,   Sincerely,   Eugene

---

102 • TO CLAYTON HAMILTON.   ALS 3 pp. (Provincetown, Mass.) [Berg]

April 6, 1920

My dear Clayton Hamilton: Ever since I read your fine tribute to *Beyond The Horizon* in *Vogue*[1]—forwarded to me by the family—I have wanted to try and express my deep gratitude to you; but now that I'm "all set," pen in hand, I find I can't—without slopping over. I would like to tell the truth and say that what you have written makes me feel very humble, very much "non sum digno"; but these statements are so connected in one's mind with the usual blather of unblushing insincerity that I despair of making them sound to you like truth.

Well, darn it, they *are* true in this case; for although, respecting your critical judgment as I do and always have done, your high verdict on my work might be humanly calculated to

1. "Seen on The Stage," *Vogue* 55 (April 1, 1920):89, 156, 158.

change the size of my hat—well, it hasn't so far. Rather it makes me say to myself: "Now, by God, you've got to work! You don't deserve this but you've got to do work which shall deserve it!" So the nearest I can come to defining the reaction your article produced in me is to say that I feel you have given me a star to shoot at—and I'll promise to keep on shooting!

I want to tell you of two things you did in those first days of my self-finding which, as I look back, had an extraordinarily far-reaching effect in keeping me going. Probably you have forgotten them. The first was when you reviewed my *Thirst* book of one-act plays—for *The Bookman*, I think. Do you know that your review was the only one that poor volume ever received? And, if brief, it was favorable! You can't imagine what it meant, coming from you. It held out a hope at a very hopeless time. It *did* send me to the hatters. It made me believe I was arriving with a bang; and at that period I very much needed someone whose authority I respected to admit I was getting somewhere.

The second boon you would never guess in a million years. It was one day I met you down at the R.R. station in New London. I had just sent off the script of what was really my first long play[2] to some manager or other. I innocently expected an immediate personal reading and a reply within a week—possibly an acceptance. I asked you for information regarding the reading habits of managers, the chances of scripts from unknowns, etc. You handed me the desired data—with both feet! You slipped me the unvarnished truth and then sand papered it! You wound up in words to this general effect: "When you send off a play remember there is not one chance in a thousand it will ever be read; not one chance in a million of its ever being accepted—(and if accepted it will probably never be produced); but if it is accepted and produced, say to yourself it's a miracle which can never happen again." I wandered off feeling a bit sick and thinking that you were hardly a fit associate for budding aspirations. But finally I reflected that you knew whereof you spoke, that I was up against a hard game and might as well realize it and hew to the line without thought of commercial stage production. Your advice gradually bred in me a gloomy and soothing fatalism which kismeted many a rebuff and helped me to take my disappointments as all an inevitable part of the game.

So all my gratitude for your invaluable help, past and present. Your tribute to *Beyond The Horizon* is the most intensely gratifying thing the production of that play has brought to me. If I can't say more, it's because the right words fail me.

I am sending you a copy of the book of the play which I hope you will accept as a token of my sincere appreciation of your interest in my work.

May I look you up when next I come to New York? I meant to last time but there was such an orgy of sickness in the O'Neill clan—I was laid up with flu for four weeks—that I hardly escaped from the hotel except for rehearsals.

My very kindest regards to Mrs. Hamilton.   Sincerely,   Eugene O'Neill

P.S. I've been married since I last saw you, did you know? Have a son, Shane, six months old.

---

103 • TO GEORGE C. TYLER.   TLS 1 p. (Provincetown, Mass.) [Princeton]

April 7, 1920

My dear Mr. Tyler: After having met and talked with Mr. Westley and gone over the whole script of the play with him I think you have made a very good choice. I believe he will

---

2. *Bread and Butter*, which O'Neill had submitted to George C. Tyler in the spring or summer of 1914.

make a very good "Murray"; and, from the sympathetic insight he seems to possess into the whole spirit in which the play is written, I also believe his direction will be an asset to the piece.

There seem to be several drawbacks to this Boston production, however. In the first place, the play cannot be played without real children. To use midgets would simply turn the whole thing into farce of the most absurd description. Mr. Westley agrees with me that it would be much better not to do the play at all if the child labor people cannot be persuaded to relent in this respect.

Neither do I think that makeshift scenery, drawn from the storehouse, is liable to do anything but injury. It is hardly likely that sanitorium sets will be found in the boneyard and, as the interior of a san. is very distinctively itself and not like anything else, I don't see how the effect can be accomplished with repainted, old material. However, Mr. Westley seems to believe this can be done, and I am perfectly willing to be shown.

To use members of the *Bab* cast who are absolutely suited to play parts in *The Straw* is one thing; but to engage people for my play simply because they are in *Bab* is another. Westley tells me two of the *Bab* cast are absolutely impossible for the parts you thought they might do, and by the time you receive this I suppose he will have informed you to the same effect. To me it is equally important that even the smallest part in *The Straw* should be cast with as great care as "Eileen" and "Murray." It is a play that will prove no stronger than its weakest link. The part of the old man, "Carmody," demands the finest kind of an actor and I understand this role is uncast as yet. So does the part of the nurse demand a first-rate actress.

The obstacles in the way of a telling performance in Boston seem to me to be very difficult ones. Perhaps they may be overcome—and they *must* be overcome! The play is not just the two principal characters. It is every smallest detail of it. I am just as determined that the patients shall be patients as I am that Miss Hayes shall be Eileen. I sweat too much blood in the writing of the play and I love it too much to permit it to run the slightest avoidable risk, even in a special matinee performance. Either it should be done *right*, down to its smallest detail, or it should not be attempted at all. I have set my heart on this play and I must be convinced that it is receiving the best there is, and is being played as it was written. This was done in the case of my *Beyond The Horizon* (the poor outdoor sets being the one exception to my statement) and the results are plain for anyone to read.

With very kindest regards,   Sincerely,   Eugene

---

104 • TO GEORGE C. TYLER.   TLS 2 pp. (Provincetown, Mass.) [Princeton]

June 3, 1920

My dear Mr. Tyler: I was sorry to have missed seeing you on my last trip to New York. Will Connor was at the hotel the first night I was down and told me you were in Chicago. I only remained in the city a few days and devoted most of that time to sticking around the apartment with the Governor and my Mother. Mr. Westley called or called up, Jamie told me, but at that time I was in New Jersey with my wife visiting her people there.

Madden writes me that you have a plan for "trying out" *The Straw* for a week in Atlantic City in July. I can hardly credit this—after the *Chris* experience. How is it humanly possible for an audience of A.C. summer mob to appreciate a play such as *The Straw?* I cannot see how this kind of try-out week will afford anyone concerned with any line at all on the play's New York qualifications. I know that I will never consent to change or cut one word of the play on the verdict of Atlantic City, which I regard as worse than worthless. I only wish my judgment counted for something with you in this matter of my play—in which case I would suggest that you start the piece in the only place in the country where it will be sure of a fair hearing and a discriminating audience for its first performances. I mean New York. Even if it had to start there with special matinees, as *Beyond* did, I would still be strong for this idea. In my humble opinion, a week in A.C. is bound to be a failure, this failure bound to have a bad effect on the cast, and bound to make you ask for changes, rewriting, etc., which I will not consent to. In short, I think it will mean a bad break at the very start for everyone connected with the production.

Another thing: Jamie told me that when you were down at the hotel to see Father you spoke of *The Straw*—said it was a "Romeo and Juliet" play, and that all the "coughing and spitting," and the weighing business in the first scene of Act Two would have to be cut out. Now let us understand each other on this important matter now and thus avoid any misunderstandings later. *The Straw is not* a Romeo and Juliet play, and was never so intended by me, and cannot be produced as such. It is a play of the significance of human hope and the T.B. background of the action is as important as the action itself in bringing out my meaning. Secondly: There are only about three coughs in the whole play and not one spit. A careful reading of the script will show you this statement is true. Thirdly: As I took great care to impress upon Mr. Westley, I regard the weighing scene as one of the very best, technically and artistically, that I have ever written and, outside of a few cuts in the dialogue which may prove necessary, I will not consent to any change in it.

The trouble seems to be that you are not thinking of producing *my* play, the play you bought, but some other play that you have in mind that my play ought to be made into. This is all very well for you but you can hardly expect me to consent to it—especially as I regard *The Straw* as the best thing I have done and have the opinion of some of the foremost critics in the country, who have read the script, to back me up in my estimate. A Romeo and Juliet version would doubtless be very much easier for Miss Hayes to approach than the real Eileen of the real play; but I cannot consider Miss Hayes or anyone else in this affair except myself and my play. I cannot, and square with my own conscience.

Finally, if you now consider that the play as written has no chance of popular approval, and are unwilling to produce it according to the script which I cut myself and went over with Mr. Westley, then I can only suggest that, to avoid the inevitable clash which is bound to come if you want to remake my play into something foreign to its intention, that you allow me to pay you back the advance you paid on it and regain my sole right to the script. I have no hope that it would be produced elsewhere in any immediate future; but I do know that I can get it published in book form, and I would rather have it judged that way than have my whole meaning misrepresented.

This letter is written with no feeling of bitterness or any animus whatever. I write it because I think it is better to be frank from the start. You sincerely think one thing about this play. I just as sincerely believe another, and that you are absolutely wrong, root and branch. After all, I wrote it and I intend to fight for my play, line for line as written, no matter with whom.   Sincerely,   Eugene

---

105 • TO GEORGE C. TYLER.   TLS 2 pp. (Provincetown, Mass.) [Princeton]

June 6, 1920

Dear Mr. Tyler: My letter was *not* based on any "imaginings" but on the statements of people whom I thought I had every reason to believe.

No, I have never considered that Miss Hayes was ideal for Eileen, and I have never pretended that I did. As for knowing very little about her, I saw her in *Clarence* and I know what her past performances have been. I am very well acquainted with Barrie's *Dear Brutus*[1] and with the part she played in it—the exact antithesis of all Eileen should be. I have discussed her with several people who know her work and have also read *The Straw*—but all this is immaterial. Where Miss Hayes was concerned I have always been of an open mind and quite willing to be shown that my doubts, based on her youth and comparative inexperience, were groundless. The one thing I have keenly felt in this connection from the very first is that ever since you got the idea of casting her in the role you have been primarily interested in *The Straw* as a starring vehicle for Miss Hayes, and not in a rounded production of the play as a whole.

My contempt for Atlantic City may be traced in part to a remark in one of your letters that *Chris* could not be fairly judged by the reactions of an audience "principally composed of tango lovers and chewing gum sweethearts"—(I quote verbatim). If not *Chris*, then how *The Straw*, a much more serious play? You call *The Straw* a "splendid serious drama," but you had much the same idea of *Chris* before a week in Atlantic City completely reversed your opinion and convinced you that it wasn't a play at all! Have I not just reason to fear, therefore, that another week in that same frothy cesspool, where I deem it inevitable that *The Straw* must absolutely fail, would cause you again to blame the play and demand a revision which I could not, in all conscience, consent to?

No, I have no impression of your being an "idiot manager," blind to the artistic side of the theatre and caring only for financial success. I know too much of what you have done in the past—Irish Players, Shaw-Daly, Loti-Gautier,[2] etc., etc., etc.—to harbor any such fool notion. And I realize quite well that you care nothing about money-grubbing. *You* read this implication into the sentence you quote from my letter. It is not there. The real implication is plain as day. If, as I had heard, and as I had grown to suspect ever since my interview with Mr. Westley,—(and I hereby apologize, as I properly ought, if my suspicions were too hastily conceived on unsound evidence)—you wanted the weighing cut out, the T.B. element weakened to nothing, the emphasis put on the love interest as a thing in itself and not as a poignant revelation of a deep spiritual meaning in human hope, then I think the quoted sentence is easy to understand: "The trouble seems to be that you are not thinking of producing my play, the play you bought, but some other play that you have in mind that my play ought to be made into." I did not think for a moment that you were judging the play only from a money-popularity standpoint. I gave you credit for sincerely believing that it would be a better play your way. I objected because I know the play as written is *the truth*, and that any change in emphasis would falsify it and distort its significance. As for rehearsals in Boston, I never knew there were any. I was never notified in any way, shape or form. I saw a notice in the *Boston Post* saying they had started and I wrote to Mr. Westley, care of the *Bab* manager, asking him if it were true. I never received a reply. When I saw Westley up here he did not know for certain when rehearsals would start—if they started at all—on account of the child labor law obstacle, the difficulty in picking a cast from Boston productions, etc. That was the last I heard either from you or him about rehearsals. I had told Westley to send for me as soon as he felt I could be of use.

You have no reason whatsoever from any act or statement of mine to suspect that I would accuse you of returning *The Straw* to me because you didn't think it would make any

---

1. Play (1917) by Scottish dramatist James M. Barrie (1860–1937).

2. In 1911, Tyler had brought Dublin's Irish Players to New York, and O'Neill later claimed to have seen "everything they did" (Arthur and Barbara Gelb, *O'Neill* [New York: Harper, 1962], p. 172). In 1904, Tyler had produced several plays by Irish dramatist George Bernard Shaw (1856–1950), directed by and starring Arnold Daly (1875–1927); and in 1912, he presented *The Daughter of Heaven,* adapted by George Egerton from *La Fille du ciel* (1911), by French novelists Pierre Loti (1850–1923) and Judith Gautier (1850–1918).

money; nor have you any reason to say I inferred you were an idiot. What I do infer from this last letter is that you are a manager who, when a playwright rises up in protest against what he believes is to be an injustice to his work, loses his temper and resorts to abuse. Such remarks as "idiotic things—in your mind," "perfectly stupid conclusion," your sneer at *Chris,* a play about which you once had an all-so-high opinion—these things are personal affronts but they are not arguments.

Even if I were in a position where I could afford to do so, I would certainly refuse to refund one cent on the Boston affair. I was always opposed to it and, after my interview with Westley in which I raised many objections to the whole scheme as planned—as he must have told you—I never was kept in touch with it. Any rehearsals that took place in Boston did so without my knowledge. (It is true, however, that I told Westley that I was very busy and did not want to come down until he really needed me, but would gladly come as soon as he did. Perhaps this may account for the fact that he never notified me. I do not wish to seem to be blaming him in any way for anything, especially as ever since his trip here I have had a high opinion of his ability to direct the play and to portray Murray.)

In view of the above, you will have to keep the play the allotted time, produce it or not just as you see fit. Besides, on second thought, if it is not worth a thousand dollars to me, it is not worth five hundred—or five cents. For me it is now deader than John Brown's body, and all that I ask is that I never hear of it again for years, except as a book. No play is worth all this unpleasantness, and *The Straw* is no such great matter that I shall allow my summer isolation to be poisoned by any further thought about its production, or give an actor's damn whether it is produced at all or not. All that is written and will be as it must. For me to fret and fume and quarrel and argue is silly and untrue to my real nature which is that of an interested but distant spectator.   Sincerely,   Eugene

---

106 • TO GEORGE JEAN NATHAN.   TLS 2 pp. (Provincetown, Mass.) [Cornell]

June 20, 1920

Dear Mr. Nathan: I mailed a letter to you on a trip to the village yesterday—after which I bought the July *Smart Set* and read your article on American playwrights.[1] *After,* s'help me! I underline that word because my letter of yesterday might well appear to you in its too-aptness to have been inspired by what you wrote; and I do not want you to suspect, even for a second, that I would mask my rebuttal that cunningly.

Your criticism of me and mine in the magazine is sure *invigorating*—grateful as keen salt breeze after much hot air puffing from all sides. If my sublime head were bumping the stars askew, your acid test would sure put a blister of truth on my heinie that would disturb any squatting at ease even on the softest complacency. However, I honestly don't need blister-ing—on that account. My head retains its proper proximity to sea level, I think. But your weighing in the balance is a tremendous lift to me in other ways. For one thing, it gives me the added urge of attempting to make you out a false prophet—in ten years or so. For I refuse to accept your serious doubt, but rather snatch at your "But it may be—that I am wrong" and will try to prove it to you, given the time.

In this connection, I would like to make you my confession of faith where my work is

---

1. "The American Playwright," *Smart Set* 62 (July 1920): 132–33, which called O'Neill "the one writer for the native stage who gives promise of achieving a sound position for himself."

concerned. Honest confession. I am familiar enough with the best modern drama of all countries to realize that, viewed from a true standard, my work is as yet a mere groping. I rate myself as a beginner—with prospects. I acknowledge that when you write "He sees life too often as drama. The great dramatist is the dramatist who sees drama as life" you are smiting the nail on the head. But I venture to promise that this will be less true with each succeeding play—that I will not "stay put" in any comfortable niche and play the leave-well-enough-alone game. God stiffen it, I *am* young yet and I mean to grow! And in this faith I live: That if I have the "guts" to ignore the megaphone men and what goes with them, to follow the dream and live for that alone, then my real significant bit of truth and the ability to express it, will be conquered in time—not tomorrow nor the next day nor any near, easily-attained period but after the struggle has been long enough and hard enough to merit victory.

In The Zone—your "vaudeville grand guignolism"[2] is my own verdict—but I am out of that zone now, never to return. As for *The Rope*, I do believe that is sound enough, although it's a year or more since I looked at it and perhaps I'd agree with you now. But where did you get the idea that I really valued *Where The Cross Is Made?* It was great fun to write, theatrically very thrilling, an amusing experiment in treating the audience as insane—that is all it means or ever meant to me. You will see by my last letter how I came to write it, that it was a distorted version of a long play idea and never intended for a one-act play in my mind. And, by the way, it was not *Where The Cross Is Made* that you advised me to tear up for reputation's sake. You must have confused it with another I submitted to you—"Honor Among The Bradleys"[3]—a very false and feeble piece of work which you "bawled me out" for writing—now in limbo.

To make sure of my accuracy in this matter of *Where The Cross Is Made* I have been looking up your old letters and I find this in one written in October 1918: "I have read *Where The Cross Is Made* and like it very much indeed. It would please me to print it in *The Smart Set*. But I fear that the performance of the play by the Provincetown Players around the first of December would interfere with such a publication. It would be impossible for us to use the play before our January issue"—etc. So you see you have confused *The Cross* with that other play. I am at pains to state all this merely to show you that it was not *The Cross* you advised me to destroy.

Your scheme of measurement to the contrary, I would like to stand or fall by *Bound East For Cardiff*—(with due consideration that it was written in 1914)—*The Long Voyage Home*, *The Moon Of The Caribbees, Beyond The Horizon, The Straw, Gold*—because these plays are my *sincerest* at different stages. They were written purely for their own sakes. The others had their contributing causes. There are so many intermediate reasons that enter into the writing of a play between the two serious extremes of art and money. Such intermediate dramas are but an instructive form of recreation when one cannot remain inactive—and it takes time to get over the itch to put everything on paper, regardless.

In the light of what you say in your article that you hope I may top my writings from year to year, your later opinion that *Gold* is a better piece of work than *Beyond The Horizon* is more than ever welcome to me.

Let me again urge you to try and make the trip up here with John Williams. I'd sure love to have you.

---

2. The phrase, which Nathan used in his July 1920 article, refers to the type of sensational short plays with surprise endings and scenes of violence and horror that were popular in Paris at the end of the nineteenth century.
    3. A one-act play that O'Neill wrote in the fall of 1918 but later destroyed. See *Eugene O'Neill at Work: Newly Released Ideas for Plays*, ed. Virginia Floyd (New York: Frederick Ungar, 1981), pp. 2–3.

And again let me thank you for your estimate in *The Smart Set*. Those are the things that count. A prod in the rear and a pointing to a distant goal, not without hope—that is what it means to me.   Sincerely,   Eugene O'Neill

---

107 • TO AGNES BOULTON O'NEILL.   ALS 4 pp. (Stationery headed: Lawrence and Memorial / Associated Hospitals / New London, Connecticut) [Harvard]

Thursday, p.m. / [July 29?, 1920]

Own Sweetheart: Am writing this at the hospital.[1] Papa is lying in bed watching me, his strange eyes staring at me with a queer, uncanny wonder as if, in that veiled borderland between Life and Death in which his soul drifts suspended, a real living being of his own flesh and blood were an incongruous and puzzling spectacle. I feel as if my health, the sun tan on my face contrasted with the unearthly pallor of his, were a spiritual intrusion, an impudence. And yet how his eyes lighted up with grateful affection when he first saw me! It made me feel so glad, so happy I had come!

The situation is frightful! Papa is alive when he ought to be dead. The disease has eaten through his bowels. Internal decomposition has set in—while he is still living! There is a horrible, nauseating smell in the room, the sickening, overpowering odor of a dead thing. His face, his whole body is that of a corpse. He is unspeakably thin and wasted. Only his eyes are alive—and the light that glimmers through their glaze is remote and alien. He suffers incredible tortures—in spite of all their dope. Just a few moments ago he groaned in anguish and cried pitifully: "Oh God, why don't You take me! Why don't You take me!" And Mama and I silently echoed his prayer. But God seems to be in His Omnipotent mood just now and not in His All Merciful.

One very pitiful, cruelly ironic thing: He cannot talk plainly any more. Except when he cries out in pain it is impossible to understand him. And all through life his greatest pride has been in his splendid voice and clear articulation! His lips flutter, he tries so hard to say something, only a mumble comes forth—and then he looks at you so helplessly, so like a dog that has been punished it knows not why.

Death seems to be rubbing it in—to demand that he drink the chalice of gall and vinegar to the last bitter drop before peace is finally his. And, dear God, why? Surely he is a fine man as men go, and can look back to a long life in which he has kept an honorable faith and labored hard to get from nothing to the best attainment he knew. Surely the finest test of that attainment is the great affection and respect that all bear him who knew him. I don't believe he ever hurt a living thing intentionally. And he has certainly been a husband to marvel at, and a good father, according to his lights. I know those are the conventional virtues that are inscribed on tombstones—but he is the one person in a million who deserves them. Perhaps these virtues are so common in cemeteries because they are so rare in life. At any rate, looking at it dispassionately, he seems to me a *good* man—in the best sense of the word—and about the only one I have ever known.

Then why should he suffer so—when murderers are granted the blessing of electric chairs? Mankind—and myself—seem to me meaningless gestures, to be mocked at with gales of dreary laughter. The last illusion—the soft beauty of Death—"gone glimmering through the dream of things that were"—one result of this present visit.

1. James O'Neill, Sr., had suffered a relapse on May 14, 1920, which necessitated his admission to St. Vincent's Hospital in New York. He was transferred to a New London hospital on June 10, and Eugene was summoned as the end neared.

There is a man on the floor above—an automobile accident case—who is howling monstrously & with every expulsion of breath—ticking of the clock of agony. He is dying, too, it seems. Like a wounded jackal he bays uncomprehendingly at the setting moon of Life. These hollow cries reverberate echoingly through the wide, cool halls where the nurses march from room to room—fat, buxom, red-armed wenches, mostly. They walk quietly on their rubber soles—insistently efficient with a too-fleshy indifference.

I'm afraid you'll find this letter a false note of drama. It isn't. It's sincere as hell! Perhaps I'm too keyed up to write convincingly. When the Ultimate plucks you by the sleeve and you stand confronted by a vast enigma—brought home—what more can you do than—stutter! But I hope I've conveyed something.

Later—He was asleep when I was writing the above. Then he woke up and called me over. He made a dreadful effort to speak clearly and I understood a part of what he said, "Glad to go, boy—a better sort of life—another sort—somewhere"—and then he mumbled. He appeared to be trying to tell me what sort—and although I tried my damndest I couldn't understand! (How appropriate! Life is at least consistent!) Then he became clear again: "This sort of life—froth!—rotten!—all of it—no good!" There was a bitter expression on his poor, sunken face. And there you have it—the verdict of a *good* man looking back over seventy-six years: "Froth! Rotten!"

But it's finely consoling to know he believes in a "better sort—somewhere." I could see he did—implicitly! He will die with a sigh of relief. What queer things for him to say, eh? They sound like a dying dialogue in a play I might have written. Yet I swear to you I am quoting verbatim! He didn't mention God, I am sure. His "somewhere" didn't appear to be a Catholic Heaven. He tried to tell me and I couldn't understand! Isn't it ghastly?

Oh My Own, we just mustn't fight and hurt each any more! *We mustn't!* It's the unforgivable sin—a crime against the spirit of our love! I can see that the great thing my father hugs to his heart as a something vital, not froth or rotten, is my mother's love and his for her. He has thrown everything else overboard but that remains—the real thing of the seventy-six years—the only meaning of them—the justification of his life because he knows that, at least, is fine and that it will go with him wherever he is going—the principal reason he is not afraid to go, I believe!

So let us protect our love against ourselves—that we may always have the inner courage, the faith to go on—with it to fall back on. All my love.   Gene

P.S. Am keeping my promise. So don't worry—and *rest!*

P.S. again. They expect Father to go any moment now. It can't be long postponed—and they can't be any more definite. His pulse is almost out. I'll write all developments.

Am staying at my cousin's with my Mother.

---

108 • TO AGNES BOULTON O'NEILL.   ALS 3 pp. (Stationery headed: Lawrence and Memorial / Associated Hospitals / New London, Connecticut) [Harvard]

c/o Mrs. Mary Sheridan, / 55 Channing St.[1]
Friday p.m. / [July 30?, 1920]

Own Sweetheart: Again at the hospital. Father is just the same—hanging on by the merest thread. The doctors expect it to happen any moment—but it doesn't. The head one

1. O'Neill added by hand this return address, that of his cousins the Sheridans, where he was staying while in New London.

says it is only Papa's *marvelously strong heart* that is keeping him alive! And that fool in New York was afraid to operate on him months ago because he claimed his heart was *weak!* Isn't it all a ghastly joke? Who could ever trust a doctor's word after this revelation of their criminal ignorance.

How long it will keep me here, I can't tell; but now that I am here I'll have to "stay put" until the finish. There's no help for it when they tell me it's liable to happen at any hour. I believe myself it is only a question of hours. If you could know how horribly he has failed since my last trip, you'd realize why I'm so sure of this. There is Death written on his face.

When I'm not enduring the ordeal of the hospital, I'm stupidly watching the hours drag. There's nothing to do but hang about and wait. The town and the people are dead. I despise both. Tried to work on the *Gold* script last night but didn't get much done. Can't concentrate, naturally. Feel better physically, though. My hives seem to have gone, thank God—and Hiebert's[2] medicine which I have been religiously taking.

The Old Man's business affairs are in a hellish tangle and my Mother is worried sick. I'm afraid when the end comes and the tension she is under relaxes, she'll collapse.

Oh, My Own, I miss you so in the long, long hours! I hope you're resting and keeping your promise to me as I'm keeping mine. I love you so, and want so much for you to feel fine and your old self again. And I'm praying that the other thing has come around all right or will very soon.

We've taken a solemn oath in the name of our love that we won't fight any more, haven't we? Remember! It's so silly—and criminal—for us to wound each other in that vicious fashion.

Got my suit—60.00—and low black shoes—Hanan's—14. Still have hat and socks to get.

All my love to you and Shane, Dear Little Wife of Mine! Remember me to Cecil & Mrs. C.   Gene

P.S. I'll be back the first second I can. Burial will be soon after death on account of his condition.

Oh, by the way, if you have to get Cooky to start engine, tell him not to monkey with anything. She works fine as she is. Show him how to hold finger over hole to start her.

I discover I have checkbook. Put it in pocket that day you & I started—so keep track of any checks you write. Again adios—and a long kiss, Sweetheart!

---

109 • TO AGNES BOULTON O'NEILL.   ALS 2 pp. (c/o Mrs. Mary Sheridan / 55 Channing St. N.L. Conn.) [Harvard]

Sunday eve. [August 1?, 1920]

Own Little Wife: Have just finished the "once-over" revision of the *Gold* script on which I have been laboring all afternoon. And now I don't know whether to be glad or sorry it's done—because what in hell am I to have now to take up my time and make me forget for a moment or so the intense loneliness which gnaws me. I tried to make today shorter by staying in bed late, but some atrocity-monger has presented the Congregational Church nearby with a new set of chimes—so I had to get up to escape their damn racket. They play five different hymns, the tunes of which I now know by heart—and loathe most mightily.

Father's condition remains exactly the same. He scarcely notices any of us any more—

2. Daniel Hiebert, O'Neill's friend and housemate from Harvard days, who was now a physician in Provincetown.

seems sunk in a coma, and tries to speak only at rare intervals. All of those "in the know" at the hospital expect him to depart every night—morning, rather—between two and five, the hours of least resistance. Every morning they seem astonished to find him still alive. His case appears to be unprecedented in their experience, and they have given up any attempt at further prophecy except to remark vaguely that "it may happen any moment, that human flesh and blood cannot hold up much longer,"—which they have been saying for a month!

All of which puts me in a hellish quandary. Shall I continue to stay on, or shall I go back to you as my heart longs to every waking minute? It would be some reconciling satisfaction if I could know that my presence here *means* something to Father. I am sure hoping it does; but judging from his actions—or rather, lack of action—I should say he was too far removed from life to value with its values.

On the other hand, what a futile thing for me to return to Peaked Hill Bar if I am liable to be called again immediately! I haven't spoken of the trip before but it is sure a long, tedious ordeal and one I would like to avoid a repetition of. I so much want to be sure that when I get back to you and my work again, I'll be able to devote all my time unreservedly to both of you.

So you see in what a perplexing mess I'm in! Try and feel sorry for me a bit. The life, the people I meet, everything in New London—my cousins excepted—bores me to a nervous sweat with the incredible inanity which makes up so large a part of a town of this size. Talk about intellectual stagnation! Oh boy!

I sure hope there'll be a letter tomorrow morning! If there isn't I don't know what I'll do! I'm so lonely, Own Little Girl! I want you so, love you so, *need* you so!!! Life is just simply meaningless without you!

A million kisses, Sweetheart! All my love to you and Shane.   Your lonely   Gene

---

110 • TO MARY SHERIDAN.   ALS 3 pp. (Old Peaked Hill Bar, / Provincetown, Mass.) [Private]

August 20, 1920

My dear Mrs. Sheridan: Now that this section of the O'Neill clan has taken up its ocean-bound life where it left off and everything is running smoothly again, I can do what I have wished ever since Agnes and I said goodbye—write and try to tell you how very much we appreciated your kindness to us and how exceedingly grateful we are to all the Sheridans, root and branch.[1]

To me, who have never known a home in the true sense in which yours is one, it was much more than a mere pleasure to be in such close contact with you and yours at so poignant a crisis—it was an eye-opening privilege; for your family by their genuine kindness to all of us restored in me a faith in human beings that was on the wane. You taught me what a real home was like, what I would wish my own, now in the building, to become in the future. You and Agnes and Bessie and Irene, Phil, Mat and Dan gave Agnes and I a domestic star to shoot at. To put it more concisely, we'd like to be like you; for we think that, by and large, you're the finest, biggest-hearted, kindest family ever grouped together under one roof—and we back that bet against the world!

The above is only a small part, poorly expressed, of the large amount I would like to say well. Where feeling is strongest, words come like pulling teeth. But I hope you'll read between the lines what I'm trying to "get off my chest" and judge accordingly.

1. James O'Neill, Sr., died on August 10, 1920, and Agnes came to New London for the funeral, staying at the Sheridans' with her husband.

We don't want to lose you now that we've found you, no matter how many miles may ever separate us. We want to be adopted too, as you have adopted Mama. We want, whenever we get within hailing distance of New London, to send you a wire: "Bed down some straw in the attic. Put two portions of water in the soup. We cousins are coming!" And we want any or all of you to regard our home as yours at any and all times—whenever you need or want a change or a rest.

I'm sending you my *Beyond The Horizon*; and when I get a copy of the book of short plays I'll send that also. No house is quite furnished without my complete works. And Phil need have no fear that I'll ever "back up the wagon."

Agnes sends all of you her best love; and I, mine. God bless you all!   Eugene

P.S. If I have not mentioned Lou's kindness it's only because I suppose she will have left for Cinci before you receive this.

Oh, and if you want to see several bum photos and read many large lies about Ag, the baby, our home and me, get the Sunday *Boston Post*—(if this reaches you in time). They sent down two men day before yesterday and I was interviewed and snapped for a Sunday special article until I was dizzy. I am sure it will hand you all a laugh. If it shouldn't happen to be in this week, it will next.

---

111 • TO NINA MOISE.   ALS 3 pp. (Provincetown, Mass.) [Yale]

August 29, 1920

Dear Nina: I won't amuse you with any elaborate excuses as to why I haven't answered your previous letters—not that I haven't really legitimate ones, however, as such things go. This winter was an orgy of ills for the O'Neills. First my mother had the flu, then just after *Beyond The Horizon* opened I got it and was laid up in the hotel for a month, then my father was taken down with what proved to be his fatal illness—and there you are.

I sure am grateful to you for your kind note of condolence. My father's death leaves a big hole in my life. He and I had become great pals in the last two years. My one reconciling thought is that he suffered such incredible tortures the last three months of his life that death was for him a true release—and peace. His disease was cancer of the intestines—so you can imagine what he went through. It was terrible for my mother, brother, and me to have to stand by and watch him suffer and not be able to help in any way. For two months the doctors expected him to die every day but his grand old constitution kept him going and forced him to drain the cup of agony to the last bitter drop.

Yes, it was the greatest satisfaction he knew that I had made good in a way dear to his own heart. And I thank "whatever gods may be" that *Beyond* came into its own just when it did and not too late for him. He was in a box at the opening matinee and wept his eyes out.

My winning the Pulitzer Prize of one thousand dollars for the best American play also pleased him immensely. (Can you imagine me at the point where Columbia University actually confers one of its biggest blue ribbons on me? And the funniest part of it is that I never knew such a prize existed until I received a wire this June saying I had won it!)

I'm darn glad you like *Beyond* so well, and I'm sorry you could not have been in New York to see the original matinee cast. Helen MacKellar as "Ruth" was the best thing in it—a perfect portrayal if there ever was one. Of course, when the play boomed and received a theatre of its own for a regular run, she had to quit as she was playing in *The Storm* and under contract with Broadhurst.[1] Perhaps you will get a chance to see it yet. It may reach the Coast

1. Producer George Broadhurst (1866–1952).

The Coast Guard Station at Peaked Hill Bar.

this year on its tour. The present cast is good enough. Richard Bennett is really very fine as "Robert."

I have two new ones going on this year—*Gold* and *The Straw*—both of which I consider better plays than *Beyond*. *Gold* is to be put on by Williams, and Lionel Barrymore is talked of for the lead, but I don't know whether that will go through or not. *The Straw* will be a Tyler production with Helen Hayes as the particular light. I consider this play the very best thing I have done so far. The whole action takes place in a T.B. sanatorium. Imagine my selling it to a Broadway manager! It will be hard to put across, but, goll durn it, I made 'em like it once and perhaps I can do it again.

At any rate, I'm sure you'll be pleased to know that I am not compromising but "hewing to the line," and not trying to get too wealthy although, as you can imagine, the opportunities to sell myself have not been lacking of late.

Enough of the w.k. Profesh! Did you know that Agnes and I have a son—Shane Rudraighe O'Neill—now almost ten months old? Well, we have, and he's a perfectly good healthy person who howls with his deceased grandfather's far-famed voice. We also have acquired a place of our own on the Atlantic Ocean with two miles of sand dunes separating us from inquisitive neighbors. The house was formerly a U.S. Life Saving Station. Sam Lewisohn bought it, Mabel Dodge[2] and Robert E. Jones—(no less!)—fitted it up inside. Lewisohn got bored with his toy and sold it to me for a song. It's really a bear of a place— different from any other in the world, I'll bet. I wish you could see it. Why don't you come East next summer—or this fall, for that matter? Haven't you had enough Coast for a while?

This letter sounds horribly egotistical—all my doings, etc. You must pay me back with a letter telling me all your trials and tribs. What are you doing these days. The last time I heard of you was some rumor to the effect that you were bound for Australia as directress of some touring Little Theatre idea. Any truth in it? Probably not, as it came from a Village source, if I remember rightly.

Agnes joins with me in wishing you all the best there is! Write to us!   Sincerely your friend,   Eugene O'Neill

---

112 • TO GEORGE C. TYLER.   TLS 1 p. (Old Peaked Hill Bar, / Provincetown, Mass.)
[Princeton]

Oct. 24, 1920

My dear Mr. Tyler: For some devilish reason your note of Oct. 16th got mislaid by the Coast Guards who usually bring out our mail and I never received it until yesterday morning. Since you wrote it *Bab* has opened up and, if I may judge by the only review of the play I have seen—*The Times*—it must now be a rousing success and Miss Hayes has scored a great personal triumph. I am very glad if this is indeed so—glad in the sense that it will mean a fine break in the bad luck you had been complaining of. However, I am not glad to lose Miss Hayes for *The Straw*, and I judge from your letter that that is what a big hit for *Bab* means.

What other woman are you thinking of for *The Straw*? My only suggestions are Helen MacKellar and Laurette Taylor. MacKellar's performance as Ruth in *Beyond The Horizon* was one of the best I have ever seen, and I think she is one of the future greats. But I suppose she is

---

2. Dodge (1879–1962), patron of the arts, was hostess of a famous New York artists' salon and summer resident of Provincetown. Her stormy love affair with John Reed was the subject of one of the first plays performed by the Provincetown Players, *Constancy* by Neith Boyce (1915).

tied up to *The Storm*[1] and Broadhurst, and that Taylor is sentenced for life to her hubby's dramas. By the way, didn't you tell me once that Miss Taylor had read *The Straw?*

I hardly think I shall be in New York for some time to come unless the unexpected calls me down. I am working like the devil on some new things for the Provincetown Players who are promising to bloom forth with a renewal of their old spirit of adventure into new fields this year. I have what I consider a very unique piece of drama going on their opening bill— *The Emperor Jones.*[2] I wish you could find time to drop down and see it. I think you will find it interesting enough to be worth an evening downtown.

You spoke in your first letter of an important idea that you wished to see me about. Can't you tell me what it is by letter, or shall I wait until I do see you?

With all kindest regards,   Sincerely,   Eugene

---

113 • TO GEORGE C. TYLER.   TLS 1 p. (Provincetown, Mass.) [Princeton]

Nov. 28, 1920

My dear Mr. Tyler: I was in New York for a few days a couple of weeks ago and meant to get in and see you, but I was so tied up with *The Emperor Jones* and other affairs downtown that I missed it. Also I knew that you were "up to your ears" in the revival of *Erminie*[1] and probably would not want to be bothered.

In your last letter, which I received just before going to the city, you said there would be nothing definite to say about Miss Hayes and *The Straw* until *Bab* had been given another three or four weeks to show just how it stood up. It is about that now. Is there anything new to tell of plans for my play?

I promised you last spring that I would have a brand new play around the old theme of *Chris* ready to submit to you this fall. I haven't mentioned it since because I wanted to wait until the play was an accomplished fact. I finished it just before I left for New York. Madden has been having copies made of my script which, I believe, are ready now. So you may expect to receive one any day now—if he hasn't already sent you one by the time you get this letter. The new play is much stronger than the old—in four acts, no scenes—and Chris is now the third part with the daughter as the principal character.[2]

As for your idea about a new version of *Monte Cristo,*[3] I'm frankly not very enthusiastic about it. I have a sort of grudge against that play—perhaps because I once had to act in the tabloid vaudeville version. But I should like very much to talk it over with you and learn just what your idea is.

My Mother, who is up here with Jim taking a Thanksgiving rest with us, tells me that she heard through Will Connor that you were still under the weather. I am very sorry to hear this and hope it's just one of those false reports.

We all send our very best to you.   Sincerely,   Eugene

1. Melodrama by Langdon McCormick (1873–1954).
2. The Provincetown Players production of *The Emperor Jones* opened at the Playwrights' Theatre in Greenwich Village on November 1, 1920.

1. Musical (1886) by Englishmen Harry Paulton and Edward Jacobowski, which was revived on Broadway in January 1921.
2. This new version, initially called "The Ole Davil," was eventually produced by Arthur Hopkins as "*Anna Christie*" in November 1921.
3. Play by English actor Charles Fechter (1824–1879) and Arthur LeClercq in which James O'Neill, Sr., starred for twenty-nine years.

PART THREE

CERTAINTIES

1920–1926

All I ask . . . is new actors, new directors and a new
theatre for my new plays to be worked by and with!
—*To Kenneth Macgowan, August 23, 1926*

By 1920 O'Neill's reputation was firm, and he wrote with assurance in ways that would change the traditional patterns of the American theatre. He worked with speed, energy, and unflagging creativity. The joy and excitement of writing called forth a kind of ecstacy. "I have recovered my creative élan," he told Oliver Sayler, Arthur Hopkins's press agent, "and have started *The Hairy Ape* with a mad rush."[1] He became as well known for his experiments in stagecraft, ranging through a variety of theatrical styles from the realism of a Galsworthy to the far reaches of Expressionism, as he was for his dramatic statement, but the experiments were more than novelties. Each experiment was justified by its use in the development of the play and for the most part succeeded. He had a remarkable series of successes. Between 1921 and 1925, *Gold, The First Man, The Fountain,* and *Welded* failed, but in roughly the same period, the successes—"*Anna Christie,*" *The Hairy Ape, All God's Chillun Got Wings, Desire Under the Elms,* and *The Great God Brown*— became landmarks in the history of the drama in this country and abroad. Rapidly, as O'Neill mastered his craft, he found a public awed by his theatrical devices and responsive to his themes.

The copious flow of "creative élan" brought responsibilities and problems. His letters often reflect the need for greater income to support his family. Camping out at Peaked Hill Bar was pleasant for a young Bohemian couple, but less so for a writer who was beginning to have complex professional commitments. Furthermore, the old Coast Guard station was tenable only in summer, and wintering at the house of Agnes's parents in New Jersey was wholly unsatisfactory. He felt a need to buy more stately mansions: in 1922 a large house, Brook Farm in Connecticut, and in 1926 Spithead, a home in Bermuda that required expensive remodeling.

To support the new establishments the plays had to be produced, but often production was hard to achieve. Neither Williams nor Tyler, after unsuccessful productions of *Gold* and *The Straw,* staged another of his plays. The Theatre Guild, which had evolved from the old Washington Square Players, continually turned down his scripts, although Lawrence Langner, one of the Guild's directors, offered O'Neill a subsidy so that he could be entirely free to write. O'Neill responded coldly that the only "subsidy" he wanted was for the Guild to

---

1. Letter to Oliver Sayler, (letter 136).

produce his plays, and for a time communication between the playwright and the producer broke off. Arthur Hopkins, one of the period's most creative directors, as his staging of Shakespeare with the Barrymore brothers proved, was to accept nothing of O'Neill's after "*Anna Christie*" and *The Hairy Ape*. Other commercial managers were intrigued but wary of plays that were so out of the line of surefire commercial fare. Then too, with the exception of Hopkins and Williams, commercial managers brave enough to undertake an O'Neill play bungled the staging. Thus whatever merits the plays might have had were obscured by indifferent casting and run-of-the-mill direction. At the Provincetown Playhouse he was safe, but as his plays grew larger, the limited facilities of the Macdougal Street Theatre could not accommodate them.

With the difficulty both of finding a creative outlet and of keeping a reasonably steady income, O'Neill, not surprisingly, tried to develop his own theatre. By 1920, the Provincetown Players had become the victim of their idealism. The astonishing success of *The Emperor Jones* washed away the charmingly earnest theatre of amateur players. Thereafter, their challenge was to develop fully professional controls of production. Their leader, George Cram Cook, refused the challenge, saying that the Players should either hold to their creative first principles, unfettered by commercial considerations, or they should disband. As the members of the group fell out among themselves, Cook turned his back on his theatre and went to Greece with his wife, the playwright Susan Glaspell, to live among the shepherds on the slopes of Mount Parnassus in Delphi. There, in 1924, with some bitterness of heart at the course the Players were taking, he died.

His death served to divide the Players into sharply opposed factions. One headed by Edna Kenton, a devoted worker under Cook's direction, attempted to keep alive Cook's ideals for the Players as a spiritual commune. The other, which included O'Neill, advocated a more sophisticated modern theatre, dedicated to experiment and to innovative stage production. O'Neill was supported by the critic Kenneth Macgowan and the designer Robert Edmond Jones. Together, as a triumvirate, they formed "The Experimental Theatre" at the Provincetown Playhouse. The new regime opened in 1923 with a production of Strindberg's *The Spook Sonata*, directed and designed by Jones. The following season, they produced at both the Playhouse and the Greenwich Village Theatre. Their work aroused critical interest and a considerable public following, but it lasted only three seasons. O'Neill's foray into theatrical management ended with the production of *The Great God Brown* in January 1926, and matters were left much as they had been before.

Part of the problem was the nature of the plays O'Neill had in hand. Nothing like the new turn his theatre was taking had happened before, except possibly in the productions of Max Reinhardt in Germany. Only a manager of unusual courage would consider a satire in eight acts, *Marco's Millions*,[2] which demanded a large and elegantly costumed cast and settings of extraordinary Oriental opulence. Nor could producers eagerly see their way to risking a fortune on a massive pageant-style play on biblical themes, *Lazarus Laughed*, which would require about 165 actors in a variety of masks. O'Neill had yet to face the problem of finding a producer for his work-in-progress, *Strange Interlude*, written in an unprecedented nine-act length.

In the early 1920s O'Neill's exterior life became more orderly. His mother had broken free of her morphine addiction, and after the death of her husband, "in fine health," as O'Neill wrote to George Tyler on December 9, 1920, she took charge of the problems of James O'Neill's estate. Jamie, who had been in danger of drinking himself to death, gave up

---

2. The text of the eight-act version of *Marco Millions*, entitled *Marco's Millions*, is published in *The Unknown O'Neill: Unpublished or Unfamiliar Writings of Eugene O'Neill*, ed. Travis Bogard (New Haven: Yale University Press, 1988), pp. 195–307.

alcohol and stayed by her side. O'Neill also cut back on drinking, seeing clearly that it was a case of drink or write. He spent some time in Rochester, New York, having his teeth repaired by a friendly dentist whom he had previously met in the Village and on Cape Cod. The sessions brought about a close friendship with the dentist, Saxe Commins, who was to become his amanuensis and ultimately his editor, first at Horace Liveright, later at Random House.

Relief from the burden of the problems of his mother and brother was only temporary. On a trip to settle some property matters in Los Angeles, Ella died. Jamie, who would himself die in a sanatorium for alcoholics the following year, immediately began to drink again. O'Neill rejected the responsibilities forced on him. With Jamie in a drunken stupor, the train bearing Ella's body arrived in New York City on the night *The Hairy Ape* opened. O'Neill refused to meet it and fled from his obligation both to his family and his play. He would not fully face the situation until at the end of his life he wrote of Jamie and his mother in the central confessional scene in *A Moon for the Misbegotten.*

O'Neill's reputation was developing rapidly in several countries. He became the subject of a full-length critical study by Barrett H. Clark. Serious critics, principally Nathan and Joseph Wood Krutch, were listening to him with interest. Briefly he came to know Hart Crane and tried but failed to write a preface to Crane's *White Buildings.* Most of his friendships, however, were not with the literary establishment but with his working associates in the theatre and at his publisher, Horace Liveright.

His marriage to Agnes lessened in ardor, but he seemed contented with their life together. His affection for young Shane was warm. In 1925, in Bermuda, his daughter Oona was born, but perhaps the most important familial development in these years was his meeting with his elder son, Eugene, Jr. An affection grew between them, and his letters to the boy, dutifully signed "Father," indicate an assumption of responsibility for the boy's welfare.

Although the deaths of his mother and brother weighed the scale toward shadows, the balance was up, toward success and contentment. A tension remained between his inner and outer lives, but the plays were compelling and the arduous work seemed to be worth doing. Conditions, however, were to change rapidly over the next three years. In Maine in 1926, vacationing at Belgrade Lakes, he met again the actress who had played Mildred in *The Hairy Ape* when it moved from the Village to a Broadway theatre. He was attracted to her, an affair began, and when he returned to Bermuda in the fall, it was with a sense of loyalty sharply divided between Agnes and his children and Carlotta Monterey.

Dec. 6, 1920

My dear Mr. Toohey: I am darn glad to have your opinion on the new play around the old *Chris* theme, and darnder glad that it is such a favorable one. Having finished it so recently, I'm much too close to it myself to be able to see and judge the play as a whole, and I'm very grateful for any criticism on it. It's particularly welcome to me to hear you like the character of Burke so well—because I'm quite stuck on him myself. Yes, it sure is a play that will require acting of the most intelligent sort to get at the quality of the three principals, and so overcome the surface sordidness of their lives. But the acting profesh ought to greet a play of this kind with loud cheers, I should think. They're always complaining that they never get a chance to show how good they can be.

The *Emperor Jones* promises to get its chance uptown in the near future, via special matinees, at least, if the present dickerings of the Players don't fall through. Didn't you think that Gilpin was fine?[1]

I'm glad to know you intend to see *Diff'rent*.[2] It is one of the best things I have ever done, I believe. Margaret Wycherly is directing it, and if the acting material she has to work with is anything at all, she ought to turn out a good performance. But I'm afraid any of our home talent will look mighty sick with the memory of Gilpin's work so fresh in everybody's mind. And *Diff'rent* is a play that will have to be well and subtly done—or blooey!

I am sure glad to hear of your play—and you have all my sincerest best wishes for its success in every way. Is it the one you were thinking of writing, founded on the idea in your story of the actress and her son? I hope so. I always thought that would make a corking play.

Again thank you for your letter.   Sincerely,   Eugene O'Neill

---

Dec. 9, 1920

Dear Mr. Tyler: I am anxiously awaiting your verdict on the new Chris play, curious to know what you will think of it. Mr. Toohey seems to agree with my opinion that it is an infinitely better play than the old one.

In thinking over your *Monte Cristo* idea, I can only imagine one way in which the project could call forth any genuine creative interest on my part. If I could say to myself: Throw everything overboard—all precedent, all existing dogmas of what is practicable and what is not in the theatre of today, all well-regulated ideas of what a play is or isn't, etc. Create your own form just as you did in *The Emperor Jones*. Rely on and *demand,* as you did in that play, a new ingenuity and creative collaboration on the part of the producer—a new system of staging of extreme simplicity and flexibility which, combined with art in the lighting, will permit of many scenes and instantaneous changes, a combination of the scope of the movies with all that is best of the spoken drama. But keep all this strictly within the realms of theatrical possibility as you understand it. Don't write a closet drama. And, above all, make the Count and the others *human beings* which they never are in either book or old play—that is, don't touch the thing at all unless you can write something better than the novel, (which,

---

1. With black actor Charles S. Gilpin (1872–1930) as Brutus Jones, *The Emperor Jones* was so successful that it was transferred from Greenwich Village to Broadway, opening at the Selwyn Theatre on December 27, 1920.

2. The Provincetown Players production of *Diff'rent* opened at the Playwrights' Theatre on December 27, 1920, directed by Charles O'Brien Kennedy (1879–1958).

as romantic melodrama, is fine; but romantic melo. is not art), and a play far surpassing any of the old pure melodrama versions.

Not that I've figured any of this out. The above is merely a preliminary filing off of shackles. I feel I could never be interested, were all the gold in the world forthcoming, unless I could make an original thing of the *Monte Cristo* plot, make it mine and tell Dumas, Fechter, and Co. to go to the devil. Of course, the revenge motif of the theme would remain the same. It is only the treatment I refer to.

My direst grudge against *Monte Cristo* is that, in my opinion, it wrecked my father's chance to become one of our greatest actors. Since he did not mince this matter himself but confessed it to me during our very close "palship" last winter, I feel free to state it. *Monte Cristo*, he often said with great bitterness as he lived over his past out loud to me, had been his curse. He had fallen for the lure of easy popularity and easy money—and he suffered as a retribution in his old age the humiliation of supporting such actor-yokels (by comparison) as Tynan, Allen, Fredericks, Elliott,[1] etc. How keenly he felt this in the last years, I think I am the only one who knows, the only one he confided in. He felt also that he had made a bad bargain. The money was thrown away, squandered in wild speculations, lost. He was leaving my Mother with the barest sufficiency. Even now, she is having difficulty in getting his messed-up estate into a sane condition where it can maintain her with a fair degree of comfort. The treasures of *Monte Cristo* are buried deep again—in prairie dog gold mines, in unlubricated oil wells, in fuelless coal lands—the modern Castles in Spain of pure romance.

My father died broken, unhappy, intensely bitter, feeling that life was "a damned hard billet to chew." His last words to me—when speech had almost failed him—were: "Eugene—I'm going to a better sort of life. This sort of life—here—all froth—no good—rottenness!" This after seventy-six years of what the mob undoubtedly regard as a highly successful career! It furnishes food for thought, what? I have quoted his words verbatim. They are written indelibly—seared on my brain—a warning from the Beyond to remain true to the best that is in me though the heavens fall.

All the above is, of course, confidential. As so old and close a friend of his and ours I thought the facts would interest you.

My Mother is in fine health. His leaving her to untangle his chaotic affairs has proved to be the most merciful thing in the world. She has had no time to think or brood. And, although this may sound strange to you, she is developing into a keenly interested business woman who seems to accept this unfamiliar responsibility with a great sense of relief. Under her hand, I honestly have a hunch that some dividends may finally accrue from the junk buried on the island of M.C.

I will hope that some unforseen stroke of fortune will provide a theatre for *The Straw* in the near future. It would be fine if it could come in on the tail end of all this publicity that *The Emperor* has received—before it dies out. It would help *The Straw* immensely, don't you think?

Gold also is held up for diverse reasons. I begin to think that where the "a curse it is upon me" stuff is concerned, I provide a fit running mate for The Lady Of Shalott.   All my best to you.   Eugene

P.S. I'm glad to hear you don't book in Shubert houses. They closed up *Beyond The Horizon* in Chicago just when it had commenced to pick up.[2] It played to over seven

1. Brandon Tynan and Pauline Frederick, with whom James O'Neill, Sr., played in *Joseph and His Brethren* in 1913–14; Viola Allen (1867–1948), with whom he played in *The White Sister* in 1910; and William Elliott, with whom he played in *The Wanderer* in 1917.
2. Lee Shubert (1873?–1953) and J. J. Shubert (1878?–1963), the powerful theatre owners and

thousand the second week at the Princess and promised to enjoy a profitable run—(this was just two weeks before election, too). That sudden closing was a fine financial jolt to yours truly who had been fatuously counting on it taking hold out there.

---

116 • TO JOHN V. A. WEAVER.   ALS 3 pp. (Provincetown, Mass.) [Boston U.]

Jan. 13, 1921

Dear John Weaver: I've been meaning to write to you ever since my return from New York—but always saying "tomorrow," as I suppose most of us do where our good intentions are concerned. The arrival of your book[1] on the p.m. mail just now threw the proper bomb into my "tomorrows"; so with a million curses at my damnable laziness, here I am pen in hand.

To begin with, thank you for your book. It was very kind of you to think of me and I am darned glad to have it. I haven't given myself a chance to look into it yet—it arrived about ten minutes ago—but I'm anticipating a real pleasure when I do get to it.

And now for the thing I've been going to write you about for the past month or so: Mrs. O'Neill tells me that your brother—the last time we were down—seemed to think when he talked with her that, because I had not called up, I did not want to see you. And I wouldn't have you believe that for anything in the world *because it is not so!* I can say in all sincerity that there is no one I would rather renew friendship with than you, that my memory of our 47 colleagueship is a very green one, and that I did mean to get in touch with you on each of my visits to town—but—

The explanation of how I missed out is complexly simple. On each occasion, after the ordeals of dress rehearsals were over, I have hilariously hurled my sombrero in the cuspidor and gone romancing forth upon an anti-Volstead orgy during which I exuberantly forgot every single thing I was supposed to do. It usually took about two days of the poison masquerading as whiskey to get in its good work. Upon which I was sick in bed for two days. After which I hated New York and all in it and beat it back here with the "Brooklyn Boys" sounding the full brass band of Remorse after me.

The trouble with me seems to be that I can't get over the old sailor feeling that I am "making port" when, after several months of sober and industrious labor up here, I land ashore from the old Fall River Line. At any rate, the results of my last two relaxings have been so venomous that I have taken the holy New Year oath to remain henceforth on the wagon, N.Y. or no N.Y., as long as I'm in the U.S., so help me Wheeler!

But now I hope you understand, and will pardon, my failure to get in touch with you. When one forgets everything, how can one remember anything? I might easily have run into you, I suppose, at Christine's or someplace; but, after some years in the past of the G. Village artistic life from soup to nuts, I have conceived a great loathing for same and flee from it as from a plague—(which it is!). I know that you are not identified with it in any way; and that, take it from me, is a damn good thing, not on moral grounds but on artistic ones. However, enough of that talk! It sounds like good advice, God pity me!

I do want to see you the next time—which, let me pray, will be soon for it will mean that rehearsals of one of my long plays—(scheduled for production last fall!)—have called me

---

prominent producers, had forced the closing of the road tour of *Beyond the Horizon* in Chicago because they wanted the theater for one of their own productions.

1. O'Neill's classmate in English 47, Weaver (1893–1938) had recently published *In American—Poems* (New York: Alfred A. Knopf, 1921).

down. Write to me here, will you, and let me know just how, when, and where to reach you? There are a million things I want to talk to you about. In the meantime, if you ever get a chance to spend a few days with us up here, grab your little bag, wire or write us to expect you, and come a-running. Take this seriously for I mean it! Until then   Sincerely your friend,   Eugene O'Neill

---

117 • TO ST. JOHN ERVINE.   ALS 2 pp. (Provincetown, Mass.) [Private]

Jan. 23, 1921

My dear St. John Ervine: I am greatly disappointed to learn of Sidgwick & Jackson's adverse decision. I was hoping they would do it. Thank you for your suggestion about the Talbot Press. I'm writing my publisher over here to get in touch with them. As for the preface—if the book ever does get published!—I sure want you and no one else but you to write it, and I am very grateful to you for wanting to do so.[1]

I read, in the *N.Y. Times*, I believe, about your dramatizing the Wells' story. I've never read it and so I can look forward to a brand new experience when I see the play. I hope it will be done in New York in the near future.

You ought to see Margaret Wycherly in *Mixed Marriage*.[2] She is corking. As for the rest, I still retained a vivid memory of the play as done by the Irish Players the first year they were over here and hardly found this production as good. But the play certainly shines through and holds one! It is fine and encouraging to know that New York likes it so well. We are fellow special mat. playwrights these days for my *The Emperor Jones* is at the Selwyn.

Just how is the Everyman Theatre in London making out? I have given permission—as far as it in me lies—for them to produce *Beyond The Horizon*. It is now only a question of terms, in which they will find my people reasonable enough, I think, because there seems no chance of a strictly commercial production.

There also seems to be a good chance that *The Emperor Jones* may be done in London. There are numerous inquiries, at any rate. I'm mailing you under separate cover a copy of the January *Theatre Arts* in which the play was published. I'll wait anxiously to learn what you think of it—also of the short plays in the book you got.

Three of my long plays are under contract but held up on different excuses. I'm praying for a production before the season is too far gone.

Lawrence Langner[3] and I had several sessions together just before he sailed. There was some prospect of the Guild doing one of my plays by arrangement with the present contract holder but the plan seems to have fallen through.

However, enough of my woes! Would that I could get over to meet you and see your new play in London, but there seems no possibility of it. The waiting-for-something-to-start game has me lashed down here indefinitely. All success to the play!   Sincerely, Eugene O'Neill

---

1. O'Neill was apparently trying to find an English publisher for *The Moon of the Caribbees and Six Other Plays of the Sea*. It was published in England in April 1923 by Jonathan Cape with an introduction by Ervine.
2. Play by Ervine that opened on December 14, 1920, at the Bramhall Playhouse.
3. Langner, a founding member of the Theatre Guild, later would become one of O'Neill's closest personal and professional friends.

Jan. 28, 1921

Dear Kantor: Oh well, *Diff'rent* seems to have aroused the ire of all the feminists against me. Susan Glaspell told me that Ruth Hale objected strongly to the play on those grounds—as if the same theme could not have been woven with equal truth about a man, with a different reaction, of course. As for the main criticism, it was bound to come from someone. The accusation of always seeing things black has been hurled against the best of them in all countries—Ibsen, Strindberg, Hauptmann, Andreyev, who not—so I am in good company. It is a very obvious criticism to make, especially in this 100% optimistic country, and it is only good old human nature, after all, that it should be made.

However, I think it damned unfair that Broun should allow the thing[2] to appear under his name unless he entirely agrees with it—and before he has seen *Diff'rent*. The article is due to prejudice people against that play just before it opens uptown. This is the sort of thing that makes dramatic criticism contemptible in this country. Broun, I had always thought, was one of the best and above such evasive tricks. The only way I can account for it is to think that he holds the late Nathan controversy[3] against me. Certainly, all there is left for him to do now is to permit his wife to write up *Diff'rent* for him. He is sure to go to the play with a definite prejudice against it.

And why does Broun always date me from Harvard? I had written many plays—notably *Bound East For Cardiff*—and had a book of them published before I ever went there. Also I had lived more before I saw Cambridge than most Harvard men ever do in all their lives.

However, all this sounds as if I were very peeved and I really am not. The circumstances are a bit phony in this case, that is all, and I do object to that.

The above is, of course, confidential. The whole affair is no great matter one way or t'other. I merely confess to you how I feel about it.

I haven't *The World's Illusion*.[4] It was loaned to me. It's in two volumes, published by Harcourt, etc., I think. Why don't you grab it for review in the *Trib.?* I'm sorry I haven't it. If I had, you'd get it at once—but I am going to get it. It's one of those worth owning.

By the way, someone wrote that there was an article about my stuff in the *Trib.* last Sunday. Is it true? No one has sent me it, if there was.

I hear that *Gold* is honestly to start rehearsing soon—this from my agent. In which good luck, I will be in N.Y. in the near future and shall hope to see you. In the meantime, do write again whenever you get the chance.   All my best. Mrs. O'Neill sends hers also.
Eugene O'Neill

1. Kantor (1900–1961), free-lance newspaperman, whom O'Neill met and befriended in Provincetown. Kalonyme was his pen name.

2. Journalist Heywood Broun's negative review of *Diff'rent* appeared in the *New York World*, February 1, 1921. O'Neill, having apparently heard of its view ahead of publication, inferred that it was to be written by Ruth Hale, Broun's wife. *Diff'rent* began to play matinees at Broadway's Selwyn Theatre on January 21 and was due to begin regular performances at the Times Square Theatre on February 4.

3. Perhaps Nathan's criticism and praise of O'Neill expressed in "The American Playwright," *Smart Set* 62 (July 1920).

4. Novel (1919) by German Jakob Wassermann (1873–1934), published in English by Harcourt, Brace and Howe in 1920.

Jan. 31, 1921

My dear Miss Helburn: You have doubtless heard by this through Mr. Madden that Williams has no intention of letting *Gold* go but is to produce it himself in the near future. Even if he had been willing to forego his rights, you would not have had the next chance at it for I had unofficially committed myself to submitting it to Hopkins in that eventuality. I did not even know that you were considering *Gold*—and this is an instance of what Mr. Madden characterized as your hydra-headedness. Mr. Langner mentioned *Gold* the first time I saw him. The next day he said you had definitely decided against it and that the *Ole Davil* was what you were interested in. Mr. Moeller and Mr. Simonson[2] also gave me to understand that *Gold* was no longer in question. Shortly afterward Mr. Hopkins showed his interest in it and I made up my mind to give the play to him in case Williams lost it. Until Madden's letter of a few days back I had no idea you were considering *Gold*.

I cannot help but doubt the predisposition in favor of my work among you that Mr. Wertheim[3] alludes to in his letter. The facts are rather against it. You could have had *The Straw*, you could have had *The Emperor Jones*, you can have *The Ole Davil*—but something always goes wrong, certainly not through my fault. I have had no such experience with any other management—quite the contrary—and yet, from the character of my plays, one would think it would be the other way around.

I say you can have *The Ole Davil* with justice. Mr. Tyler's proposition to you, via Madden, was merely a tentative one on which to begin negotiations. He has written assuring me that he is open to any fair arrangement. He is doing this not because he wishes to get rid of the play which he likes extremely, but because, as a very old friend of mine, he sees the unfairness to me in holding the piece until next winter when he already has *The Straw* to put on in the meantime.

My future plays are already tied up for the next year by one reading option, as you know. I would not care to add another to that, except in recognition for a present production. Of course, I realize that such options can be easily gotten around by the author when terms for production must be mutually agreed on, but all that takes a lot of time. In short, I want my plays to be free in future until such time when the experience of an actual production has been of such a nature that I am convinced that that producer and I can continue indefinitely to work together without friction.

This is meant for no "kick" against the Guild. That would be too silly. It is merely a feeling on my part that perhaps your Committee and I are inevitably bound to disagree. My plays, as written, have not satisfied you in the past and I am doubtful if they would in the future.

With all best wishes,   Sincerely,   Eugene O'Neill

---

1. Helburn (1867–1959), producer, cofounder, and executive director of the Theatre Guild.
2. Lee Simonson (1888–1967), set designer and member of the governing committee of the Theatre Guild.
3. Maurice Wertheim (1886–1950), stockbroker and member of the governing committee of the Theatre Guild.

Feb. 1, 1921

My dear Mr. Nathan: Your criticism certainly probes the vital spot.[1] The devil of it is, I don't see my way out. From the middle of that third act I feel the play ought to be dominated by the woman's psychology. And I have a conviction that with dumb people of her sort, unable to voice strong, strange feelings, the emotions can find outlet only through the language and gestures of the heroics in the novels and movies they are familiar with—that is, that in moments of great stress life copies melodrama. Anna forced herself on me, middle of third act, at her most theatric. In real life I felt she would unconsciously be compelled, through sheer inarticulateness, to the usual "big scene," and wait hopefully for her happy ending. And as she is the only one of the three who knows exactly what she wants, she would get it.

And the sea outside—life—waits. The happy ending is merely the comma at the end of a gaudy introductory clause, with the body of the sentence still unwritten. (In fact, I once thought of calling the play "Comma.")

Of course, this sincerity of life pent up in the trappings of theatre, is impossible to project clearly, I guess. The two things cancel and negate each other, resulting, as you have said, in a seeming H. A. Jones[2] compromise. Yet it is queerly fascinating to me because I believe it's a new, true angle.

One thing that I realize, on a rereading of the last act, is that I haven't done enough to make my "comma" clear. My ending seems to have a false definiteness about it that is misleading—a happy-ever-after which I did not intend. I relied on the father's last speech of superstitious uncertainty to let my theme flow through—and on. It does not do this rightly. I now have it in my mind to have the stoker not entirely convinced by the oath of a non-Catholic although he is forced by his great want to accept her in spite of this. In short, that all of them at the end have a vague foreboding that although they have had their moment, the decision still rests with the sea which has achieved the conquest of Anna.

Do you think this would help—in the way of holding up the theme at the end? I sure pine to talk over this play with you, but just how soon I will be able to get to town again is uncertain.   My sincerest thanks for your letter!   Eugene O'Neill

---

Feb. 5, 1921

My dear Jig: We've just read your note and the clippings, and another one that someone else sent us, and we're both as tickled to death by the glad tidings as if Shane were the author of *The Spring*—than which no two fond parents can say mucher![1] I rejoice mightily at this success, not only as an old friend and fellow member of the P.P., but because there has been nothing I have hoped for more, as an observer sticking out for the eternal fitness of things, than that you, who have labored so long and unselfishly for the work of others, should enter

1. Nathan, having read the script of *"Anna Christie,"* judged the ending to be a conventional happy ending—a sellout to the audience.
2. British playwright Henry Arthur Jones (1851–1929).

1. The Provincetown Players opened Cook's play *The Spring* at the Playwrights' Theatre on January 31, 1921. Despite good reviews, it was not a great success, but it was moved uptown to the Princess Theatre for a series of special matinees.

into your own kingdom. In fact, this is quite perfect from all angles and I hope you are as satisfied by it as I am.

My only fear has been that the critics of the newspaper genus would, as is their usual custom, find something irresistibly comic in the mere mention of the psychic and give vent to the loud hoots of the empty-minded. But they seem to have risen nobly to the occasion—which is certainly not the least tribute to the intrinsic dramatic power of the play.

Well, the P.P. are sure coming into their own this season, what? We had a hunch they could and would last summer, remember? Now it only remains for Susan's play[2] to finish us up in a blaze of glory. Which it will, depend upon my newly-proved gift of prophecy. After which I shall be inclined to pat Destiny on the rump approvingly with the remark "well done, thou good and faithful tyrant."

Agnes and I sure hope to get down in the near future and see the play. I have been expecting a call for *Gold, The Straw*—but that is an old and meaningless story. The P.P. are the only reliable management, say I.

The uptown scribes seem to have been piqued at *Diff'rent* for not being different, thereby proving that Emma is fundamentally human. They all seem to have Freud on the brain—and not in it.

Again, all felicitations! I am glad as hell! Come up and have a needed rest with us, Susan and you, alone or together, as soon as you can sneak away.   Gene

---

122 • TO LAWRENCE LANGNER.   TLS 1 p. (Provincetown, Mass.) [Yale]

Feb. 9, 1921

My dear Lawrence Langner: Your letter reached me here today. I am sure grateful for what you are doing to bring *The Emperor Jones* and *Beyond The Horizon* into notice over there,[1] and I am hoping mightily that something will come of it.

I am sorry to tell you that the negotiations between the Guild and this author have come to an end with no advantage on either side. To be frank, I do not think they have treated me in a fair, above-board manner. When you left, for example, it was understood that *Gold* was no longer in consideration. My session with Moeller and Simonson confirmed me in this idea. It was *The Ole Davil* that was henceforth to be argued about. Now when I came back up here I wrote Miss Helburn just what changes I was willing to make in that play to overcome your committee's happy ending objection. For three weeks no answer came to this. Then I receive a letter saying that the committee had decided to take *Gold* if they could get it! Now fancy! There I had been waiting for three weeks thinking about changes in a play they were not even considering while they were voting on a play I could have told them they could not get—for Williams had assured me he was going to hang on to it.

I cannot see the use of giving your committee a reading option on future plays when they treat my present ones with such indifference. My plays are already tied up until 1922 on one reading option, and I would have to be well assured of a frictionless combination before I could tie another anchor to my work. Your committee has said they cannot get *The Ole Davil*—that Tyler's terms are prohibitive. But Tyler writes me he is willing for any half way fair arrangement. The truth is that whoever the boob was who introduced the old *Chris* to the Guild set them all to rewriting both plays—with the result that they don't want my play.

2. *The Inheritors,* which opened at the Playwrights' Theatre on March 21, 1921.

1. Langner was in London trying to interest British producers in O'Neill's work.

I am sorry things have turned out so. If you had been here, I know nothing of the sort would have happened.

All best wishes, and all thanks for what you have done over there in my behalf.[2]   Sincerely,   Eugene O'Neill

---

123 • TO KENNETH MACGOWAN.[1]   TLS 2 pp. (Provincetown, Mass.) [Yale]

March 18, 1921

Dear Kenneth MacGowan: I have finished the first draft of my new long play, *The First Man*, and am now going to set it aside to smoulder for a while in the subconscious and perhaps gather to itself a little more flame therefrom. It looks so good now, I'm afraid of it. At this stage of the development, they all look fine, I've found.

But to my muttons. I want to ask a favor of you. I intend to start right in now with the preliminary work for the Fountain of Youth play[2] and stick right to it until I get at least a tentative first draft of it done. Could you suggest any books to read that might be of help in the way of atmosphere, mood, method or myth? If you can, it will be a great favor. I am thinking a reading of Frazer's *Golden Bough*[3] might be the best background spiritually that I could get. I have always wanted to read it anyway.

I have asked Bobby Jones[4] also to suggest reading for me. I am hoping that he will be able to come up here either before or after his trip abroad. By that time my idea of the whole play ought to have more form and substance—and he could tell me just how the thing appeared to him from his angle—and we might combine. It would be an intensely interesting experiment, I believe, to work this thing out in harmony from our respective lines in the theatre—one not done before, as far as I know. For my part, a clearer understanding of what he is striving for would be of inestimable value.

You are not to forget that you have promised to visit us this spring, summer, or fall—and to bring Mrs. Macgowan and your heirs with you. We will have plenty of room, once we have migrated to our ocean shore home, which will be about May 1st. Perhaps you could fix it so that you folks and Bobby could make it at the same time. That would be fine if you could. I want all your suggestions on this *The Fountain* opus that you can give, you know.

I never got to writing the letter on *Macbeth* you spoke about.[5] Just after our return here, our heir, Shane Rudraighe, accomplished an attack of the measles with resulting upset to the household. Then whenever I thought of the letter, I discovered that someone else had already spoke my piece for me. Then again, my principal reaction to the production was a rage at Barrymore that wasn't fit to print. He got between the production and me, darn him. It was only when he was off the stage that I could become aware of anything else. That is my

2. Writing in the margin of this letter, Langner instructed Theresa Helburn, his fellow Theatre Guild director, to "Please read this [O'Neill's letter] to the Committee. The trouble with you people is that you don't understand O'Neill's temperament. O'Neill is perfectly easy to get along with if you treat him as a friend. If your relations are *impersonal*, you'll get nowhere. (Why doesn't Maurice [Wertheim] get up a booze party for him?)"

1. Macgowan (1888–1963), critic and theatrical and film producer, became one of O'Neill's closest professional and personal friends.

2. *The Fountain.*

3. *The Golden Bough* (1890) by Scottish classicist and anthropologist James George Frazer (1854–1941).

4. Robert Edmond Jones (1887–1954), set designer who worked with the Provincetown Players and Washington Square Players and, for nineteen years beginning in 1915, with producer Arthur Hopkins.

5. Macgowan apparently asked O'Neill to write a public letter in defense of the controversial production of *Macbeth*, starring Lionel Barrymore, for which Jones designed sets. It opened on February 17, 1921, and ran for only twenty-eight performances.

main trouble in theatre-going, by the way, and the real reason why I avoid the show-shops. I can't help seeing with the relentless eyes of heredity, upbringing, and personal experience every little trick they pull as actors. Thus the actor is ever present to me and the character is lost. Thus in the most tense moment of a play I am struck—with amusement or disgust as the case may be—by the sly, insidious intent—plain to me—of a gesture, a fillip, a change in tempo, a body wriggle. The actor stands revealed, triumphant in his egotistic childishness, his brazen—to me—disharmony,—and the drama goes skidding down the Golden Mountain. "The dead cling to Rosmersholm"—that's my tragedy as an audience member.

Well, all the above is beside the mark enough, Gawd knows, and I wonder that I bore you with it. Where is Dave Carb[6] these days? I wrote to him at the Harvard Club over a week ago but have received no reply. I know he was planning to go away somewhere and surmise that my letter hasn't been forwarded.

I want you to read *Diff'rent* when it comes out in the book.[7] I honestly believe you'll find something in it you haven't before when you do. To me its dialogue from curtain to curtain is the very completest I have achieved—and has its rounded rhythm.

Well, adios. All my best to you. It is a great pleasure to have finally gotten to know you. I feel, somehow, as if I'd known you for a long time and that we were fated for a real friendship.   Sincerely,   Eugene O'Neill

---

124 • TO MRS. EDMOND T. QUINN.[1]   ALS 2 pp. (Provincetown, Mass.) [Yale]

April 1, 1921

Dear Mrs. Quinn: I crave a favor of you. April 12th will mark the third anniversary of Agnes' and my matrimony, and I want to make her a present upon said date. A kimono seems to be what she most desires. Now I know naught of kimonos and can gain no experience of them in the P'town shops, to which they are equally foreign. So will you pick out one for her in New York? I hate to trouble you thus but you are the only one I can appeal to with any confidence in the result. You know her tastes, size, what would be becoming to her, etc.

Of course, all this is to be a dead secret, a stunning surprise. When you write me about it, address the letter not to me but to Mrs. Fifine Clark, 199 Bradford St., Provincetown, and have the kimono also sent to her. This lady, our dame of all work, I have taken into my confidence and she will see that the matter is kept hidden from Agnes.

I am enclosing a check with the amount blank for you to fill in. In the depths of my ignorance I haven't the least idea whether good kimonos cost ten, twenty, thirty, forty or fifty dollars. My only idea is to get her a fine one with which she will be tickled to death.

Agnes, I know, has written you expressing our great gratitude for your hospitality on our last trip to town. Let me take this opportunity of telling you of my deep individual appreciation of it. I shall never forget your kindness. You and Mr. Quinn made your house seem like a home to me where I felt perfectly at ease, where I knew I "belonged"—and the quality of kind and sincere friendliness which such hospitality implies is a rare and infinitely grateful boon to me. If I were sure of the quotation, I'd venture "I was a stranger and ye took me in." At any rate, you'll know what I mean.

6. Carb, a member of the original Provincetown Players, played the Captain in the premiere production of O'Neill's *Bound East for Cardiff* in July 1916.

7. *Diff'rent* was published in a volume with *The Straw* and *The Emperor Jones*, by Boni and Liveright on April 7, 1921.

1. Wife of sculptor Edmond T. Quinn; the Quinns were friends of Edward Boulton, Agnes's father.

All my best to you and Mr. Quinn. And thank you in advance for your aid in this, my kimono quandary.   Eugene O'Neill

---

125 • TO AGNES BOULTON O'NEILL.   ALS 1 p. (Stationery headed: Five Twenty Nine Mercantile Bldg. / Rochester, N.Y.) [Harvard]

(Send letters—and forwarded mail—here. Saxe says it's quicker delivery)
Thursday—noon / [April 21?, 1921]

Own Little Wife: Arrived O.K. after a sneezy night on the "rattler" during which I thought I was acquiring a bad cold—but guess I didn't as no real symptoms have appeared as yet.

Have been out to Saxe's house and met his mother and father—fine, lovable old people. Then down to his office where I am now after having a bum wisdom tooth pulled.[1] It was some difficult job, Saxe declares, although I felt little pain but do feel a bit "woozy" now that the ordeal is half an hour over. He says he can bridge work me all the rest—no need of plates—which will please you, I know—and me, too! No need for further extractions, he says.

This is just a line, Dear One. I do feel a bit "off my oats," as you can imagine, but want to get this off to you. I miss you horribly. I want to lay my head on your breast for comfort, as always when in trouble or pain—but I'm glad for your sake you're away. I wouldn't be a very pleasant companion—(worse than my usual breakfast grouch!)

A kiss to Shane! My life to you! I'll write in full when I'm normal. Sweetheart, I love you so!   Gene

---

126 • TO AGNES BOULTON O'NEILL.   ALS 2 pp. (c/o Doctor S. Commins, / 529 Mercantile Building, / Rochester, N.Y.) [Harvard]

Saturday, p.m. / [April 23?, 1921]

My Own: It has been a long, hard morning with Saxe drilling away at my teeth preparing for the bridge he is to put in on the right side. To add to the general discomfort, I had a note from Stella[1] with a clipping from the *Tribune* stating that Williams is to open up *Gold* at the Frazee theatre on May 23rd with the famous Willard Mack, erstwhile playwright of melodramas and hubby of Pauline Frederick, as the lead. I cannot believe this, it is so outrageously inept—and yet, damn it, I have a sneaking suspicion that it's a fact. It's just the sort of thing that Williams would play as a desperate last card. And if he does, he will pretty well have my hands tied as far as objections that would hold good in the eyes of the law are concerned. The clause in the contract which refers to the quality of production states: "To produce and represent in first-class theatres and in a first class manner, with a competent cast to be approved by the author, *as all these terms are generally understood in the theatrical profession*"—etc. Now the Frazee is undeniably a new, first-class theatre, and Mack a well known and excellent actor according to current standards. However, you can rest assured I will fight this production tooth and nail—if the story turns out to be true. I have wired

---

1. O'Neill was in Rochester to have his teeth fixed by dentist Saxe Commins (1892–1958), whom he met in 1915 in Greenwich Village and who became his close friend and, after 1931, his editor.

1. Stella Commins Ballantine, Saxe's sister, who was married to Edward J. (Teddy) Ballantine (1888–1968), a New York actor who had been cast in *Gold*.

Madden to let me know at once if there's anything in it. It'll sure be a hell of a mess if it's true, what? God damn Williams, anyway!

Received a letter from Warren[2] that Mrs. Clark had sent on—but none from you so far. I guess it takes quite a while longer to reach P'town from this burg—and vice-versa—than we usually count on with N.Y. letters. Please send me Warren's address when you write next. His former letters are in my letter case. He does not give it in this last letter and I ought to write him.

With but little intermission, it has been raining ever since I arrived here. Today is especially wet and I am twiddling my thumbs out at the Commins' home without ambition to work or read or do anything but lie on the bed and dream of you and count the days until I can feel your sleep-walking feet reach out and scratch at mine again. (Yes, they do too!). I feel quite intolerably lonely and I miss you in every atom of me. It is only my iron resolve to get this teeth business done thoroughly for once in a way that keeps me from buying a ticket and grabbing the first train back to you. I simply can't live—really live—without you any more. I'm lost. And yet you say at times that you feel as if I no longer needed you! Dear Foolish One, if you only realized how much I do—more every minute I breathe!

I hope you're not having the weather we are. It's hardly the right variety for moving day. We're practically house-bound. Saxe and I have had a couple of walks but that's all. We read. He took me to the Athletic Club but I don't dare risk swimming when I'd have to come out into the wet afterwards. So you see life is hardly exciting. How I long for this to be over and be back at Peaked Hill with you once more!

Answer all the letters for me you can, will you? It would be a great help to me. That one you got for an interview from the *Musical Review,* for example. Tell them I can't. There's a true and valid excuse this time. Saxe's machine is a Remington and I can't manage it. Also my face is still swollen and pains and I'm in no mood to write letters except to you. If you'll help me this way, I'll be ever so grateful, Dear One.

All my love to you, Own Little Wife! I love you more than man ever loved a woman, I know I do! You are everything! Think of me once in a while, kiss Shane for me, *and do write.* I'm so utterly lonely!   Gene

---

127 • TO AGNES BOULTON O'NEILL.   ALS 1 p. (Stationery headed: Five Twenty Nine Mercantile Bldg. / Rochester, N.Y.) [Harvard]

Wednesday / [April 27?, 1921]

My Own: A million thanks for your long letter received yesterday. I was feeling completely all in—much pain—and it cheered me up a lot. Saxe extracted some old abscessed roots on Monday and we both had a frightful ordeal of it. They had grown in under the next tooth and simply refused to be yanked out—had to be cut out bit by bit—and the anesthetic didn't work right and—well, it was hell on wheels, believe me. Poor Saxe! He honestly suffered more than I did about it. I'm a fine sight—jaw all swollen—and glad you can't see me. No woman could love this face.

That was the principal reason I only wired yesterday and didn't write. I was done up and my nerves all gone. Also things in the Commins family have been rather hectic. Saxe's brother & wife arrived from Los Angeles. I wrote you about their child dying a week ago. It is terribly tragic. Saxe and I have moved out to his sister Miriam's place in the country on the outskirts of town. Very nice out there. I like it better than the town place.

2. Probably James C. Warren, a lawyer who had represented Kathleen Jenkins in her divorce action against O'Neill in 1912.

Williams has written me two long letters. His dope doesn't sound so bad. At any rate, there's nothing to be done but let him go ahead and gamble with him. His cast sounds very good—especially Teddy who will be able to keep me posted from the inside.

Saxe expects to be finished with me in about a week—with good luck. My idea is then to set forth for N.Y.—and for you to meet me there, Sweetest One—or as near that time as you can make it. Let me know what you think of this as a general plan and any suggestion you have to make.

This is a short letter but I'm feeling "mighty low." So forgive me this time, Own Little Wife. All love to Shane & you.   Gene

---

128 • TO AGNES BOULTON O'NEILL.   ALS 2 pp. (Stationery headed: Saxe Commins, D.D.S. / Five Twenty Nine Mercantile Bldg. / Rochester, N.Y.) [Harvard]

Thursday (late p.m.) / [April 28?, 1921]

Own Sweetheart: I wrote you rather a hurt little note this morning because no letter had come from you. Later—about 2 p.m. it arrived—must have been delayed. I'm awfully sorry for being so hasty. Your letters mean so much when I'm down in the mouth—("In the mouth" is right!)—and I was so disappointed at not hearing. Your letter was lovely. Poor little girl, to have so much damn moving work thrust on you. Wish I were there.

Just had another extraction. Didn't hurt as bad as others—but bad enough. Feel a bit groggy. I'll let you know by wire or letter the exact date and hour of my departure hence just as soon as Saxe can tell me.

For Christ sake, don't think of the movie writing.[1] My God, you have a soul to express which will create beauty in your novel, etc. if you will only work hard and give it a chance. The films would ruin all that chance—and what for? A mess of garbage! For God's sake, be your beautiful self and live out your life in the light. You may think you can trifle with the film and still do your real work but you can't. The experience of everyone else is against it. Let the Clara Bs of the world do their contemptible scribbling. They can't do any better and they'd like everyone else to "get that way."

Be yourself! God stiffen it, you're not a movie writer! I'll hate you if you go in for it, honestly!

If the above sounds rather excited, pardon me! I just have a tooth pulled and then your letter comes hinting you'd like to become a movie writer! These are grey days. Where is your novel?   All my love, Sweetheart   Gene

---

129 • TO AGNES BOULTON O'NEILL.   ALS 1 p. (Stationery headed: Five Twenty Nine Mercantile Bldg. / Rochester, N.Y.) [Harvard]

Monday, p.m. / [May 2?, 1921]

Own Sweetheart: Two letters from you this forenoon. I am just as happy as can be! But I feel guilty because I failed to get one off to you yesterday. It was a case of too much Jewish family—crowds and crowds of them, seven or eight children running and shouting about—Talk, Talk, Talk!—a general pandemonium at the Commins home all yesterday afternoon and evening. Twelve or more sitting at dinner! I nearly went "nuts," and writing was out of the question. But I was sort of guest of honor and had to stick it out.

1. Agnes had been encouraged by a visitor, screenwriter Clara Baranger, to consider writing for the movies.

I am wiring you to expect a letter with definite dope. I can't give it in this but will write later on—this eve—when I have had a chance to look up train connections. I think, unless a hurry call comes from N.Y. in the meantime, that I will come to Provincetown—if any sort of connections can be made—leaving here either Wednesday or Thursday night, this depending on Saxe. Then I will stay there—with YOU!!—until Monday or Tuesday when we can go down together to N.Y.

Damn your suggestion of Harvard Club! Is there a wife Agnes there? What I need is a few days rest and quiet in the open air—and you, you, YOU!!! My Own Love, My Little Sweetheart Wife, the thought of seeing you so soon again just drives me foolish with joy! I've missed you so horribly all these long, painful, rainy days.

I'll wire or write exact data later!   A million kisses!   Gene

---

130 • TO SAXE COMMINS.   ALS 1 p. (Provincetown, Mass.) [Private]

Saturday, / [May 6, 1921]

Dear Saxe: Well, I did miss that damned connection in Boston. On account of daylight saving they had switched the train to 6:30 instead of 7:30 and our train was half an hour late. 'Nuff said. I had to bum around a hotel until 3:30 in the p.m.

Your wish for fine weather for me is losing by a mile. It rained Thursday, yesterday, and is pouring today. Wind right in from old mother Ocean, surf roaring in our front yard all wild and woolly. But it's great to lie back and rest, safe in the knowledge that I have no appointment to have my teeth beaten up today. They feel fine, by the way, and eating is again becoming the popular indoor sport it used to be of yore.

I am enclosing notes for you to give to your Mother and Miriam. I feel enormously grateful to all of you for your corking, "homey" spirit of hospitality to a guest who bounced in at such an unfortunate time. You can bet your house and your folks in general will be among my dearest memories of fine human beings as long as I live.

And as for you Saxe, I can't say all I feel for you of friendship and gratitude for fear it would sound "sloppy." It's simply that you are my friend, in the finest sense of the word, and that it means a hell of a lot to me that you are.

Be sure to try and make the opening of *Gold!!!*[1] Write via Stella and let me know. Agnes and I are going down on Tuesday, I guess.

This letter probably won't be mailed until Monday. I am going to stick out here until then and there isn't any chance of the Coast Guards going in in this weather to act as postmen for us.

Agnes sends her kindest—and I all my best to all of you.   Gene

---

131 • TO RALPH BLOCK.[1]   ALS 1 p. (Stationery headed: Eugene O'Neill / Provincetown, Mass.) [Player's Club]

June 10, 1921

Dear Ralph Block: This is an unpardonably late date for me to be answering your letter, but if you have seen the atrocity now being perpetrated on my *Gold*, I know you will imagine

---

1. *Gold* opened on June 1, 1921, produced by John D. Williams at Broadway's Frazee Theatre, and it closed in ten days after thirteen performances.

1. Ralph Block (1889?–1974), movie producer, writer, and critic.

my state of mind for the past month and a half and make due allowance for a mental stupor incapable of writing a line. I gladly remember that you have read that play and are not liable to judge it by Mack's mightly extemporized version.

Indeed I am interested in what you say of planning for a new latitude in screen expression. I saw *Caligari*[2] and it sure opened my eyes to wonderful possibilities I had never dreamed of before. So count me in, by all means. Why not a picture Little Theatre movement—at least for one theatre in New York? Of course, I realize the production costs would be tremendous compared to anything the speaking Little movement had to buck—but still, darn it, it *ought* to be done somehow.

I meant to drop in on you when I was in N.Y. but I felt so damned depressed all the time I didn't care to inflict my presence on anyone. I foresaw from my first rehearsal what was to happen to *Gold*. I fled after a week of it, got good and "pickled" to chase the memory of it away, and beat it back up here to regain sanity and await the crash. It isn't that I object to *Gold* failing. It probably would have anyway, financially. But one does like one's own play to fail with integrity. I feel like paraphrasing Rolla's line into: "Don't cry, my child, and I will take you to see an actor boiled in oil."

All best to you. Remember I'm greatly interested in what you are trying to do—and cheering my loudest. I'll look forward to the *Century* article.[3] Drop me a line when you know what number it is to be in, will you?   Eugene O'Neill

---

132 • TO EDWARD KEEFE.[1]   ALS 2 pp. (Stationery headed: Eugene O'Neill / Provincetown, Mass.) [O'Neill Center]

Monday / [November? 1921]

Dear Ed: I've meant to answer your letter a dozen different times—but, you know, good intentions. I sure was darn tickled to hear from you—that you liked *The Straw* so well. I meant to get up to N.L. for the opening but some work on the other play had me tied up in New York. It was rather a hectic, nerve-wracking time for me—what with the two of them going on within a week of each other.[2]

The Straw received quite a surprisingly fair reception in N.Y., taking it all around. I thought on account of the subject matter that they would rip my hide right off. But it had improved immensely since you saw it. Kruger[3] instead of Westley made an enormous difference. I don't think it will go financially—but I never nourished that foolish hope anyway. *"Anna Christie,"* on the other hand, seems to have a very good chance. But you never can tell in this generally disastrous season. *"Anna"* deserves to go; for, leaving the play itself out of the question, it's one of the best acted I have ever seen, and the best set.

It was funny, *The Straw* opening in N.L. when there is so much autobiographical stuff in it connected with that town. When I wrote it three years ago of course I never dreamed of that coincidence—or I would never have lazily picked up actual names which, even if the

2. *The Cabinet of Dr. Caligari* (1919), German expressionist film.
3. "Movies versus Motion Pictures," *Century* 102 (October 1921): 889–92.

1. New London friend of O'Neill with whom he spent time in New York in 1907–08, when Keefe was an art student; Keefe was an architect in New London.
2. While O'Neill was in New York attending rehearsals of *"Anna Christie,"* which opened at Broadway's Vanderbilt Theatre on November 2, 1921, and ran for 177 performances, Tyler presented *The Straw* for one pre-Broadway performance in New London on November 4. *The Straw* opened in New York on November 10 and ran for twenty performances.
3. Otto Kruger (1885–1974), who replaced John Westley as Stephen Murray shortly before *The Straw* opened.

stage folk were altogether different from the living, must have sounded rather mirthful. "Doctor Gaynor" for Doc. Gayney, for example—and "Doctor Stanton."

À propos of this, let me tell you something that I know will tickle you: My cousins, the Brennans, are infuriated at me. They take the old harridan step-mother as an insult direct aimed at their mother whom they insist is a lady and not the creature of the play at all—all because of the name, "Brennan!" Can you beat it! I've tried to explain that every city directory is pretty full of Brennans but it's no use.

Well, bye-bye for this time, Ed. Remember whenever I've seen you in N.L. you've always promised a visit up here with us sometime. Anytime you can get away is fine for us. And now that you've started writing, make it a habit. I'll promise to reciprocate.

All luck and success to you—and my best to everyone I know.   Gene

---

133 • TO GEORGE C. TYLER.   ALS 1 p. (Stationery headed: Eugene O'Neill / Provincetown, Mass.) [Princeton]

Dec. 2, 1921

Dear Mr. Tyler: Better luck next time! I'm sorry *The Straw* did not last longer. I honestly wanted very much to see it and was coming down this week for that very purpose. Honestly! Everyone whose opinion I value had nothing but the most glowing praise for the production, acting, etc. As you say, the fault must lie in the subject matter. Having been so close to its background once, I was never able to feel any shudder about it, but I guess most people did. So the fault for the failure, if there is fault in it, is all mine. The play, I feel, had every chance that any producer could possibly give it. And I want to express my gratitude to you for staking everything on a play that any other manager would have turned down as a "hopeless hope." I know you must have always appreciated how little chance for financial success the play had; and yet you went ahead because you believed it a good play that deserved a hearing. Not many men would have done that. It was fine of you and I shall never forget it. Perhaps I'll be able to bring you a success sometime that will make up for *Chris* and *The Straw*. I sure hope to!

Give all my best to Mr. Ford[1] when you see him. He did wonders in the time I was there and I feel a tremendous respect and admiration for him as a director. I also liked him immensely personally and hope we are friends.   Again, all my gratitude to you!   Eugene

---

134 • TO MALCOLM MOLLAN.[1]   ALS 2 pp. (Provincetown, Mass.) [Connecticut C.]

Dec. 3, 1921

Dear Moll: The stuff you sent is corking—far and away the best thing of its kind that has ever been done about me. This is fact, not flattery. I'm immensely pleased with it and think you've snared a new fresh slant that ought to make it interesting copy anywhere. The only criticism I have to make is that you perhaps lay too much stress on the sociological bias in back of my work. I'm not a propagandist—not consciously, at any rate—in any sense of the word. I'm a dramatist through and through, that's the answer. What I see everywhere in life

1. Hugh Ford (1868–1952), who, although not listed in reviews, apparently directed *The Straw*.

1. City editor of *New London Telegraph* when O'Neill worked there as a cub reporter in the summer of 1912. Now a free-lance journalist, he had sent O'Neill his draft of an article on O'Neill for which he asked the playwright to interview himself.

is drama. It's what I instinctively seek—human beings in conflict with other human beings, with themselves, with fate. All else is a side issue. Of course, an author is a bad judge usually of what his things reveal as their motive to others. I just set down what I feel in terms of life and let the facts speak whatever language they may to my audience. To get to the point of this involved statement, it is just life that interests me as a thing in itself. The why and the wherefore I haven't attempted to touch on yet.

So what I suggest is that you make it plainer that the sociological significance you attach to the plays is your own interpretation, knowing me so well, etc., and not any conscious intent of mine. This will be the truth. Perhaps there is that in them, perhaps not. An author, if he is frank, will acknowledge he doesn't know. For him, if he is an artist, there is no conscious aim in the work except the perfection of the work itself. I don't know whether I make my meaning clear or not. I hope so.

But this is merely a matter of personal attitude and, on just rereading your latter part, it seems to me as if my objection had no point, that you had already done what I've been talking about. It is your own interpretation. So let it pass. At any rate, don't change any of it. It's corking stuff. Reread it and see if you think my point needs any added emphasis. If you think so, do so. If not, don't. I'll leave it up to you.

I'm filling out the rest as best I may but it would help me if you'd send on some questions. I don't know what to ask myself, honestly. Send on some that you'd ask if you were talking to me. It will make it a lot easier for me to come out of my shell. I'm not one of these fluent guys when it comes to being interviewed—even when I'm the whole dialogue myself.

I'm darn sorry to hear that things have been breaking badly for you, Moll. If there is any other way whatsoever that I can be of service, don't fail to speak up. I assure you I would consider it a privilege.

Yes, I know that I have, and always have had, your loudest cheers. And believe me they mean a lot.

All best. Send on your questions. I'm returning all except your lead-up page herewith.   Gene

P.S. If you want any human interest dope, let me know. My wife is writer also—short stories—in O'Brien's book best American s.s. last year[2]—my son, Shane etc.—that kind of thing.

---

135 • TO MALCOLM MOLLAN.   TLS 5 pp. (Provincetown, Mass.) [Connecticut C.]

Friday, / [December? 1921]

Dear Moll: Well, here is all the dope I can muster up. You will note I have only answered the last three questions because I thought that the replies to the first two would be contained in the other three. Of course, the stuff will have to be joined together to keep the semblance of a spoken interview. And if you find it needs any editing—it probably does—why use your old blue pencil.

I think I know why the *Times* and *World* said no. It's because they can get lots of stuff about me free of charge from the press dept. of the Hopkins office. For instance I recently, at

---

2. No story by Agnes Boulton was reprinted in *The Best Short Stories of 1920,* ed. Edward J. O'Brien (Boston: Small, Maynard, 1921), but her "Hater of Mediocrity" (*Smart Set,* July 1920) was listed in the book's "Roll of Honor For 1919 and 1920" (p. 380).

Hopkins' request, had to do a short article on the ending of *"Anna Christie"* for the *Times*.[1] It will probably be in next Sunday. That is the reason I don't enter much into that discussion in your interview. It will be stale.

Wouldn't one of the big news syndicates be a possibility for you?

But the Sat. edition of the *Post* is second to none in real worth. I don't know about the money end.

This is in much haste to catch the noon collection—the only collection, I might add. Let me know what you think of enclosed. You may find it possible to do a lot of cutting in the repetitions of what I say and what you say about me. Never mind sending it back when you've joined it together. I know it's good—your part of it—and I know you're in a hurry. I hope it will sell for you. It sure ought to. Your own angle is fresh and interesting, and what I have to say I haven't ever said before—in public.[2]

All best. Be sure and write me that "cabbages and kings" letter.   Gene

Answer to question three:

Nearly all the critics accused me of dragging in a happy ending to *"Anna Christie."* Where they got the idea that the ending is happy I don't know, unless it be that there is a kiss and a mention of marriage in the last act. As a matter of fact there is no ending to *"Anna Christie"* at all, either happy or unhappy. The final curtain falls just as a new play is beginning. At least, that is what I meant by it. A naturalistic play is life. Life doesn't end. One experience is but the birth of another. And even death—

But far be it from me to carp at the critics. Ingratitude is a base sin, and taking them by and large they have been more than fair to me.

But to return to the last section of your question: Sure, I'll write about happiness if I ever happen to meet up with that luxury and find it sufficiently dramatic and in harmony with any deep rhythm of life. But happiness is a word. What does it mean? Exaltation, an intensified feeling of the significant worth of man's being and becoming? Well, if it means that—and not a mere smirking contentment with one's lot—I know that there is more of it in one real tragedy than in all the happy ending plays ever written. It is a present-day judgment to think of tragedy as unhappy. The Greeks and the Elizabethans knew better. They felt the tremendous lift to it. It roused them spiritually to a deeper understanding of life. Through it they found release from the petty considerations of every day existence. They saw their lives ennobled by it.

But it might be easier to sum the whole matter up in a few words and say: A work of art is always happy; all else is unhappy.

One critic—and an eminent one, and justly so—has said tragedy is not native to our soil, has no reason for being as *American* drama. I take most strenuous exception to this statement. If it were true, it would be the most damning commentary on our spiritual barrenness. Perhaps it was true a decade ago but America is now in the throes of a spiritual awakening. The signs of it are on all sides for even the maddest joy-rider to read. A soul is being born, and where a soul enters, tragedy enters with it. Supposing someday we should suddenly see with the clear eyes of a soul the true valuation of all our triumphant, brass band materialism, see the cost—and the result in terms of eternal verities? What a colossal, ironic, 100 percent American tragedy that would be, what? Tragedy not native to our soil? Why, we *are* tragedy the most appalling yet written or unwritten!

1. "The Mail Bag," *New York Times*, December 18, 1921, sec. 6, p. 1.
2. Mollan's interview-article appeared as "Making Plays with a Tragic End: An Intimate Interview with Eugene O'Neill, Who Tells Why He Does It," *Philadelphia Public Ledger*, January 22, 1922, magazine sec., p. 3.

Answer to Question Four

If there are any people who picture me thusly—and I hate to believe it—then you can tell them I've guessed their secret. They are romanticists and all is romance to their eyes, especially queer people like authors. I'll expect to hear next that I'm an inveterate homebrew hound, an opium smoker, or a hasheesh eater. Authors, particularly the "gloomy" ones, ought to go in for that sort of thing, you know. However I'll succumb to all the vices in their fairy tales if they'll go to see my plays.

As for the dive in the Atlantic, say I do it often. I find it some times bitter cold but never to a suicidal degree—quite the contrary, most invigorating.

Answer to question Five

I love life. I always have. If, for the superficial, I have appeared not to, it is only because they cannot understand diffident folk who don't wear their hearts on their sleeves. But I don't love life because it's pretty. Prettiness is clothes-deep. I am a truer lover than that. I love it naked. There is beauty for me even in its ugliness. In fact, I deny the ugliness entirely, for its vices are often nobler than its virtues, and nearly always closer to a revelation.

I like human beings as individuals—(as any kind of crowd from a Rotary Club to a nation they are detestable)—but whether I like them or not, I can always understand and not judge them. I have tried to keep my work free from all moral attitudinizing. To me there are no good people or bad people but just people. The same with deeds. Good and Evil are stupidities, as misleading and outworn fetishes as Brutus Jones' silver bullet.

But what ho! How I do go on! Let's call it a day and tea up a bit. No? What else? Oh yes. Is the nature of my work likely to change? you asked. In form, yes—and in content, again yes. Wait until you see *The Fountain*, a play quite unlike any I have written before. I intend to use whatever I can make my own, to write about anything under the sun in any manner that fits, or can be invented to fit, the subject. And I shall never be influenced but by one consideration: Is it the truth as I know it—or better still *feel* it—or isn't it? If so, shoot and let the chips fall where they may; if not, not. All of which sound bold and brave but isn't. It simply means I want to do what gives me pleasure and worth in my own eyes, and don't care to do what doesn't. I don't deserve any credit for this noble stand because there is no temptation for me to compromise. My "unhappy" plays have done very well, considering— quite well enough for a person to whom Rolls-Royces and similar tittibations mean less than nothing and who desires no greater extravagance than food and lots of it——

Which reminds me: Let's go see when do we eat.

---

136 • TO OLIVER SAYLER¹ TLS(X) 1 p. (Provincetown, Mass.) [Private]

Dec. 10, 1921

My dear Oliver: I am not leaving for sunnier parts yet awhile. In fact, don't know exactly when will go—not until after the holidays at the earliest. I insinuated to Hopkins that I wished to leave at once because I thought thereby I might jimmy some definite info. out of him in regard to *The Fountain*. It was fruitless. His reply was nothing if not enigmatic. But Madden writes he has it on good authority that Jack B.² has read the play. What I was after was to find out what B's opinion was. Have you heard anything of this? If so, a word, even a rumor, would be appreciated for I am all in the dark.

1. Press agent for Arthur Hopkins.
2. John Barrymore, whom O'Neill was trying to interest in playing the lead role of Ponce de Leon in *The Fountain*.

As to Aley's[3] publishing the play, that would draw a loud howl from Horace Liveright. He has no right to howl, however. And I suspect I would get more for it from the *Century* than the royalties of a book would bring in. Liveright would include the play in his next book of mine, whatever happened. But he labors under illusions that he ought to be the sole, possessive hog at publishing my stuff.

But does Aley know how long it is? It would eat up most of his magazine. I will probably be in town the latter part of next week and we can talk it over then.

I have recovered my creative élan and started *The Hairy Ape* with a mad rush. Think I have got the swing of what I want to catch and, if I have, I ought to tear through it like a dose of salts. It is one of those plays where the word "inspiration" has some point—that is, you either have the rhythm or you haven't and if you have you can ride it, and if not, you're dead. I'm not keen for running the risk of breaking this mood up by a trip to N.Y. but my mother and brother are leaving for California to be gone six months and I have to see them before they leave.

The news about *"Anna"* is indeed gorgeous. I am prepared for the regular before-Christmas slump. As long as it rebounds with a virile leap, all is well.

But what puzzled Woollcott[4] about my article? I can't figure out.   All best to you-all from us-all.   Gene

---

137 • TO GEORGE JEAN NATHAN.   TLS 2 pp. (Stationery headed: Eugene O'Neill / Provincetown, Mass.) [Cornell]

Jan. 2, 1922

Dear Mr. Nathan: I have been up here for the past six weeks or so working on my latest, *The Hairy Ape*. The first draft is now completed, with typing and revising still to be done. It is one of those themes where, if the right rhythm is in your system, the whole play just spills forth without interruption save for writer's cramp.

I believe you are going to be very much interested in this play whatever your verdict may be on the complete result. It is a large experimental departure from the form of all my previous work. Perhaps it follows the method of *Jones* closer than any other. But it does not fit into any of the "isms" although there is a bit of all of them in it. I feel confident I have succeeded in what I set out to do but in doing so I have not hesitated to use everything I could find in the theatre or life which could heighten and drive home the underlying idea.

This play is promised to the Provincetown Players but I hope that Hopkins, after he has seen it, will take it uptown after three weeks down there. The production, however, will be pretty well out of the hands of the P.P. Kennedy,[1] a Hopkins man, will direct; Wolheim,[2] a Hopkins actor, will play the lead, I hope. He is the only actor I know who can look it, who has by nature the right manner. Whether he can act it or not, I doubt; but I also doubt if any actor can act it. It is a tremendous part. Finally, Bobby Jones will do the eight sets which must be in the Expressionistic method. So you see it will not be an amateur affair but can be relied on to achieve results. I doubt if any commercial manager, especially this bad year, and including even Hopkins, would be daring enough to give it a thought.

3. Maxwell Aley (1890?–1953), managing editor of *Century*.
4. Alexander Woollcott (1887–1943), drama editor of the *New York Times* to whom O'Neill addressed his letter about *"Anna Christie."*

1. Charles O'Brien Kennedy, who had directed *Diff'rent*.
2. Louis Wolheim (1881–1931), who played Yank in the Provincetown Players production of *The Hairy Ape*, which opened at the Playwrights' Theatre on March 9, 1922.

No, I haven't had any word of *The Fountain* being done in the near future. There is no one to play it. Ben-Ami[3] is scratched for the present on account of his Yiddish accent but he is furiously going after English and voice culture and wants to play the part. Jack Barrymore is supposed to have read it but Hopkins is vague on that outcome. J.B.'s frau, I understand, is dead against his acting again—except in the films! It is too bad. He is the real man for it, of course. Well, he isn't definitely out of the running yet, so I will nourish hopes.

Genuine Pilsner! Business of a playwright smacking his lips. It makes me want to grab the first train—but duty demands that I stick here until my *Ape* is typed and revised, a matter of three weeks or so. Will be sure to see you then. In the meantime, if you ever feel so inclined, drop me a line on your opinion of the two plays. I would like to hear what you felt was wrong with the mistitled *Oldest Man*[4] and if you detected many false spots in *The Fountain*. So many folk have objected to the blank verse rhythm in this latter, on the grounds, seemingly, that it is not beautiful verse. Whereas, of course, I used it to gain a naturalistic effect of the quality of the people and speech of those times, to place them, with little care for original poetic beauty save in the few instances where that is called for. I wanted to make ordinary speech of ordinary thoughts stilted, bigoted, narrow, sentimental and romantic, pretentiously ornate.   All best to you.   Eugene O'Neill

---

138 • TO HAROLD DEPOLO.[1]   TLS 2 pp. (Provincetown, Mass.) [Virginia]

Jan. 10, 1922

Dear Harold: What ho and again what ho![2] I was sure damn glad to get your letter. Frankly, I had thought that the reason I never heard from you was because you might be sore at my lack of response when Helen wired me last winter—but honestly, Harold, when I wrote Helen how impossible it was I was telling the Gawd's-honest truth. That was a slack time for me with nothing on hand but debts and nothing in the way of asset but the hope that *The Emperor Jones* would make good on its regular night run. The bets were all against this as it had not done so at special matinees. So you see. But let's forget it.

I can't understand your dope about Jim. I was with him in New York a lot while my plays were rehearsing in Oct. and Nov. but, as I remember, he said he hadn't heard a word from you in a long time. Perhaps you tried New London when he was in N.Y.—but even then the word ought to have been forwarded. There's some mistake about it somewhere, you can bet. No, of course Jim isn't sore about anything. You know him better than that. One bit of news about him will surprise you. He hasn't had a drink in almost a year and a half now! Fact, I swear to you! My mother got him to go on the wagon and stick—and he *has* stuck. Another bit of info. will more than surprise you. His sobriety has had a wonderful effect on his judgment of the ponies. He follows a system of his own with religious rigidity, has accumulated quite a small bankroll in reserve, and spends hours a day in intensive doping. He has been beating them for the past year almost. Well, is your credulity overtaxed?

---

3. Jacob Ben-Ami (1890–1977), who later played Michael Cape in the 1924 premiere production of O'Neill's *Welded*.
    4. *The Oldest Man*, copyrighted on October 13, 1921, was first presented on March 4, 1922, as *The First Man* at New York's Neighborhood Playhouse.

    1. Pulp magazine writer whom O'Neill had met and befriended in New York in 1915–16.
    2. The habitual salutation of James O'Neill, Jr.

But I swear by my grandmother's beard I am telling you naught but exact, however amazing, fact!

You won't be able to get in touch with him for some time to come. He left with my mother for Los Angeles only a week ago. They are stopping over at New Orleans for a week. Fine for Jim with the track running! It's some business of the Old Man's that is taking them to Cal. He had some property near Los A. which we deemed worthless but it seems the city has boomed that way and there's something doing. My mother is going out to investigate. They won't be back until spring, I think, as she has decided to dodge the cold as long as the trip is necessary anyway.

I don't remember missing any dates with you but there is probably an alcoholic reason for this. If you tried to locate me this fall via the P.P., there is a good answer why you failed. I was keeping my whereabouts a dead secret from the Villagers. I had to. With two plays rehearsing at the same time I was busy as hell all day and too worn out at night to be good company for anyone. Also I was strictly dry. But if you had written me here, the letter would have been forwarded and I sure would have been glad to see you. I don't mean that I was in complete seclusion, but I did try to arrange it so the bores would be barred. I know you can imagine how I am pestered by this brand, now that I have become notorious. If I had been drinking I would have told them all to go to hell—but being sober, I hid.

After the plays were once on—in fact before *The Straw* with which I was thoroughly disgusted was on—I emerged on a brief debauch and romanced around for a couple of days. But I'm a rube in N.Y. now, I don't know one place where they sell *real* booze so I have to fall for the synthetic poison and that makes me so damn sick that I quit in disgust after a short battle. Honestly, I'm so fed up with the rotten deal you get drinking now in this U.S. that my sentiments waver between all dry and foreign residence.

But—hold!—I take back all prohibition leanings if your tale of Johnson and the Bourbon be true. I'll confess I can't help but doubt it. It listens too damn good. Are you in Arcady or where? But I'm sure going to give you a chance to prove it. I expect to get to New York in about a month and will be only too tickled to take advantage of your invite and come out. Where is Harmon[3] and how does one get there?

The above is joking, of course. Bourbon or vinegar highballs, I want to see you. I feel that there has been some sort of misunderstanding between us, caused probably just by the fact that we haven't been able to get together in so long for one of the old talks. You and I have been too good pals ever to let either devil or deep blue sea touch us. Circumstances have changed, the damn country and city have changed, we are both older—in short, the old days can't be recovered. But friendship is one thing that time ought not to be able to change or weaken. And when you have that the past is never quite past but can be called back in a moment.

All of which sounds rather involved—but I know that you will "get" me. What I mean, after all, is just that I damn well want to see you again!

Bye'bye for this time. Agnes joins in all best to Helen, the heirs, and yourself. We don't know yet whether she will be down with me in Feb. or not—all depends on situation up here, whether she can get away. We are all in the pink. Shane is hale and husky and talking a lot with a small vocabulary. I am working like the devil on another. P'town looks the same. That's about all the news.   Again all best!   Gene

---

3. Harmon, New York, north of New York City, where DePolo lived.

139 • TO LAWRENCE LANGNER. ALS 2 pp. (Stationery headed: Eugene O'Neill / Provincetown, Mass.) [Yale]

Jan. 10, 1922

Dear Lawrence: Indeed I'll be glad enough to talk it all over with you when I get to Town again—the first part of February probably. I'll confess your proposition has me puzzled.[1] Granted its generous intent, it yet seems to me inconsistent. I am in no dire straits for money, as you must know. Even if I were, my poverty-stricken years of past are proof enough that there is no danger of my street-walking along Broadway. I simply ain't that kind of a girl.

But, after all, all that part of it is immaterial. I know what you were driving at and, as I have said, I appreciate the intent. However, the whole thing, to my mind boils down to this: Either you have faith in my plays, or you haven't. If you have, you produce them. If not, not. And you have turned down three of mine already—(I am not counting in *The Emperor Jones* mix-up of a year ago). In rejections of my work you have a clear lead over any other management. These facts, you must acknowledge, are a bit inexorable.

Your Committee's judgment is not in question here. Perhaps they were right, perhaps wrong. A jury of our peers might well disagree forever on that point. And certainly they— the Com.—were entitled to their verdict made in good faith. The thing is, how do you expect me to reconcile your adverse judgments with your alleged appreciation? It is all very well to talk of my future work, but if everyone had done that I would have no past nor present to build a future upon. The only help I need or would accept from anyone is a hearing—a fair hearing as in *Jones* or *"Anna Christie."* And my obligation, both as a man and as a playwright, lies toward those who have helped me to that hearing and thereby proved their faith in me in the one way it can be proved.

So there you have my side of it; and it seems to me there is little else that can be said.

All this without any trace of hard feeling on my part, I know I don't have to tell you that. It is merely a question of unprejudiced disagreement, but I am afraid the evidence indicates that your Com. & I are doomed forever to disagree. *The Oldest Man* matter only counts as an added indication, not as anything important in itself. The play will be done sometime by somebody and, if it is well done, I feel confident it will justify its producer both artistically and financially.

All best to you. I'll hope to see you and hear your end of the tale when I get down. Sincerely,   Eugene O'Neill

---

140 • TO HARRY WEINBERGER.[1] TLS 1 p. (Provincetown, Mass.) [Yale]

Jan. 26, 1922

Dear Harry: The proposition of the movie rights to *Jones* is not open at present. I am working out a scheme for its filming along Expressionistic lines with the husband of my aunt-in-law—an Italian who worked for years as director of one of their biggest film companies over there. He has done some remarkable work in Italy along the line that I would like to have *Jones* developed for the screen, and I think this play may give him an opportunity to

---

1. Langner had proposed that Maurice Wertheim finance O'Neill for two years so he would be free of financial worries and could concentrate on his writing.

1. Weinberger (1888–1938) was O'Neill's lawyer. He had also represented radicals Emma Goldman and Alexander Berkman in their fight against deportation and acted as attorney for the Provincetown Players.

gain a foothold as a director over here. Of course, he could easily get a job with one of our companies if he were willing to submit to their dictation as to what's what but he does not want this. His idea is to make a startlingly new film in a startlingly new way—and that's my idea, too. I would not be interested—outside of the money—in having *Jones* spoiled as they ordinarily ruin everything they touch.

Of course, this thing may fall through. Bianco may not be able to raise the backing for his undertaking, or there may be some other slip. In which case, I will be open to all your plans.

I'll be in town within a week and we can have a talk then.   All best.   Gene

---

141 • TO JAMES O'NEILL, JR.   WIRE (draft) 1 p. ([36 West 35th St., New York]) [Berg]

[c. February 20, 1922]

No question of temperament. Be fair. Specialist says means complete nervous collapse if undertake trip present condition. Would not help Mother or you?[1] Also you wire she is unconscious, will not know me. Want to help any possible way. Everything I have at your command. Wire me what and how. Just consulted Jelliffe[2] famous specialist here on Mama's case. He says hopeless but last resort call consultation best man on Coast, Samuel D. Ingham, Los Angeles. Mention Jelliffe. My plans depend on health. Would leave immediately if able. You must accept truth. I am in terrible shape.   Eugene

---

142 • TO GEORGE PIERCE BAKER.   TLS 1 p. (Stationery headed: Eugene O'Neill / Provincetown, Mass.) [Harvard]

April 3, 1922

Dear Professor Baker: This may well seem to you an unpardonably late date to be answering your note, but fate has been giving me a hard time of it during the past month and I have been in a state of mind where it was difficult for me to attend to anything. On top of the strain of two productions which opened within a week of each other in New York came the news of my Mother's sudden death out in Los Angeles.[1] Well, I have been pretty well broken up ever since.

I am going to try and stop over in Boston on my next trip to New York about a week from now. Not that I have any desire to see *The Emperor Jones* which, they tell me, shows very sadly the effect of the road on cast, scenery, and lighting and the effect of too much alcohol and actor's swell head in its leading character; but I do want very much to see you and have a talk. The only thing that may prevent me is that I am liable to be called to New London any minute, or even out to Los Angeles. There is no end of a legal mix-up over my Mother's will and the states of Cal. and Conn. are calling each other names. It promises to be a field day for the lawyers, damn 'em. But I suppose, like all bad dreams, it will come to an end someday. In the meantime, however, I am at their beck and call and cannot count a day ahead as my own.

England, I think, will soon give me a real chance. The first volume of plays is [to] come

---

1. Ella O'Neill had suffered a stroke early in February.
2. Smith Ely Jelliffe, New York psychoanalyst.

1. Ella O'Neill had died on February 28, 1922.

out over there in a month and that will help.[2] The productions of *In The Zone* and *Diff'rent* at the Everyman were very much artistic successes in their way. And a year from now both *Jones* and *"Anna Christie"* are scheduled for production in London.

As for the Continent, Copeau[3] says he will do *Beyond The Horizon* next season, and Yessner[4] (if that's his name) is contemplating putting on *Jones* in Berlin in the same period. But more of all this when I see you.

Be sure and take in *The Hairy Ape* on your next visit to New York. Hopkins will bring it uptown to the Plymouth theatre on April 17th. It is, with the possible exception of *The Fountain* to be done by Hopkins next season, my best play, I think—and a stab in a new direction.[5]

---

143 • TO MARJORIE GRIESSER.   ALS 2 pp. (Stationery headed: Eugene O'Neill / Provincetown, Mass.) [Yale]

May 5, 1922

My dear Mrs. Griesser: I was very glad indeed to receive your letter. Sincere intelligent criticism such as you were kind enough to offer is always grateful—and always a help, too, whether I agree with it or not.

Certainly, I meant the "Ape" to have universal significance—that is, that he should reach back step by step as the play goes on until in the last scene he attains it. But the play is also very much a protest against the present. I meant many things in the play and am satisfied if an audience "gets" even one of the many. One cannot expect too much. The big, universal meaning in back of the whole thing is sensed, emotionally felt, by a great many people, I believe, even if their intelligences fail to grasp it. And that is what I had hoped for. So I have felt no "sense of profound failure"—quite the contrary, I have been agreeably surprised. You see I have had quite a large experience now with critics and audiences and I know their limitations by heart. *The Hairy Ape* is a startling dose for them to swallow. Considering the demands it makes, I think the reaction from critics & public has been more intelligent and hopeful than that given to any play of mine so far. Most of them are *trying* in this case. Usually they don't take that much trouble.

Again, thanks for your letter.   Sincerely,   Eugene O'Neill

---

144 • TO MILTON SALSBURY.[1]   TLS 2 pp. (Stationery headed: Eugene O'Neill / Provincetown, Mass.) [Private]

May 17, 1922

Dear Milton: It was good to hear from you. I have received no letter from your Mother up to date. Did she send it to the Plymouth? Then possibly it has been mislaid and will be forwarded later. This has happened before.

At the time of my Mother's death, Will Connor and I tried to locate your family via the phone book but with no success. I wished very much to have your Mother—all of you—

---

2. *Plays: First Series, The Straw, The Emperor Jones, and Diff'rent,* published by Jonathan Cape in May 1922.

3. French director Jacques Copeau.

4. German director Leopold Jessner.

5. The rest of this letter is missing.

1. O'Neill's cousin.

present at the services which were held in New York. My brother, after his terrible trip across the country alone with her, was completely prostrated. Also, to make matters worse, everything seemed to go wrong on that trip, connections, etc. Will Connor and I did not know until the very last moment just when they would arrive—or anything about it—with the result that everything had to be arranged on the spur of the moment. But I do wish your Mother to know that I thought of her, that I knew it would be my Mother's wish that she should be present, and that I did try to get in touch with her but had no means of finding out her whereabouts. And then you can imagine that I was pretty well broken up myself and hardly knew what I was doing. The news of her death came right on top of the strain of rehearsing two plays at once, just as they were about to open, and I was on the verge of a nervous breakdown, anyway. Her body arrived the day *The Hairy Ape* opened.

But I must seem a bit morbid to you to be going into all these details.

No, my Mother's estate has not been settled yet and I doubt if it will be for some months to come. Those affairs have a way of hanging fire. But, as Jim and I are the only heirs and the will specifies an equal division, the shares will eventually be evenly divided. However, I suppose for the present there is no use signing the proxies.

I will have to appeal to you for some information about the Milner Cattle Co., for I must confess I know absolutely nothing about it. So I'll take the liberty of asking a few questions: Did the attempt to strike oil ever result in anything? What is the present state of their cattle business? What would be the value of the shares now, do you think? Doesn't the Company issue a yearly statement to stockholders? Will there be any dividend declared this year? If the answers to these last two questions are affirmative, then the Company should send same to Frank W. Dart, 138 Vauxhall Street, New London, Conn. who is the administrator of the estate.

I hope you will pardon my wishing this large amount of inquisitiveness on you but you are the only one to whom I can appeal, and as in the near future I will be a stockholder it rather behooves me to find out what the pieces of paper I will be given stand for.

I am tickled to death to learn that your Mother and you liked the play so well. It is a frank experiment along new lines—for this country, at least—and is so radical a departure in many ways that no one has been more surprised than I that it ever was taken uptown. My astonishment has been doubled by the fact that it is doing extremely well there, the lateness of the season, etc. considered.

I am worried about your Mother's letter. When did she write? You see, up to a couple of weeks ago we were jumping here and there every week or so—to New York, to New London, to Boston, back here, etc.—and we seem to have missed quite a few letters that were forwarded at that period. I hope hers was not one of them.

All sincere regards to you and yours. If any of you ever get down Cape Cod, be sure and look us up. It would sure be a pleasure to meet you again.   Sincerely,   Eugene O'Neill

---

145 • TO OLIVER SAYLER.   TLS(X) 1 p. (Provincetown, Mass.) [Private]

May 25, 1922

Dear Oliver: Yes, I seem to be becoming the Prize Pup of Playwriting, the Hot Dog of the Drama. When the Police Dept. isn't pinning the Obscenity Medal on my Hairy Ape chest, why then it's Columbia adorning the brazen bosom of Anna with the Cross of Purity.[1] I

---

1. *"Anna Christie"* won the Pulitzer Prize, O'Neill's second, at just about the same time that the New York Police Department, in an attempt to close *The Hairy Ape* after it moved uptown, filed a complaint with the

begin to feel that there is either something all wrong with me or something all right. Both the *Tribune* and *Solidarity*—the I.W.W. organ—praise me editorially—both for something I didn't mean.[2] "It's a mad world, my masters!" Lincoln, evidently, made a too hasty assumption. It is possible to fool them all all the time—at least as long as the "meanings" hold out. In fact, you don't have to fool them. They will most hilariously do that for themselves. This seems to be a sound psychological tip for all ambitious politicians. There is nothing which *has to be* so fascinatingly open to a personal interpretation as the obvious truth your subconscious can't allow you to see. Which sounds rather opaque, but I think I know what I mean.

I hope all this outcry has boosted business—and hurt the censor hounds. It ought to, I should think.

Are the circulars of the *Ape* out yet? If so, would like to have a copy or two.

I am about to hike the dunes for a visit to the dentist—and I feel just as one does under those circumstances—not entirely nonchalant. So adios.   Gene

P.S. Oliver, as a friend I love you as a brother; but as a publicity man, a certain uneasy suspicion forces me to hand you the following insult: The above is not for the public prints. As you must know what an utterly depraved, conscienceless character you are in that role, I know you will not take this in bad part.

---

146 • TO M. ELEANOR FITZGERALD.[1]   TLS 2 pp. (Peaked Hill Bar, / [Provincetown, Mass.] [Texas]

Saturday, / [May 27?, 1922]

Dear Fitzie: Many thanks for your kind letter. Yes, we are all "in the pink"—Terry, Shane, Agnes, dog, cats, and self—and having a wonderful time. It is great out here now— no flies, mosquitos—the best time of the year. Why don't you come and pay us a visit this coming month? Try and make it. A real rest will be fine for you and we'd love to have you.

This Provincetown P. situation sort of gives me a pain. I have a long letter from Jimmy Light relative to next year and the future in general and asking my cooperation. (Keep this under your hat.) I have replied sort of hinting that his plan is impossible—legally. The whole situation puts me in a hell of a position where no matter which way I jump or don't jump I tread upon a friend's corns. It makes me sick—this mess. Primarily, as you undoubtedly will agree, it is all Jig's fault. As I look back on it now, I can see where he drove all our best talent, that we had developed, away from the theatre for daring to disagree with him—this in a supposed group democracy! Then beat it to Greece leaving a hollow shell as a monument to his egotism. Just consider the *Ape*. What would that production have been except for the outside talent called in—I include in this category the old P.Ps like Jimmy who are on the outs with the present organization. Why the play couldn't have been done at all! It is really only about a one-fifth P.P. production.

But what's the use? I think the only thing to do is absolutely to reorganize from top to bottom as soon as Jig and Susan return. Otherwise, ignoble death by slow—or sudden—

---

magistrate's court charging that the play was "indecent, obscene and impure." The chief magistrate read the script and dismissed the complaint.

2. "The Hairy Ape," *New York Tribune*, April 20, 1922, p. 10; and R. Robbins, "The I.W.W. on the Stage," *Industrial Solidarity*, April 8, 1922, p. 2.

1. Long-time employee of the Provincetown Players, who first joined them on a part-time basis in 1918 to do bookkeeping and handle the box office and eventually became the company's business manager.

starvation. A meeting should be held in which all those who had ever been important P.Ps since the founding should be present. Everything in the past and everything for the future should be threshed out openly, let the chips and insults fall where they may. And then a secondary meeting where everyone should be invited who is interested in our future—everyone with talents, ambitions, ideas, like Bobby Jones, Kenneth Mac., Bel-Geddes[2] etc., for a fine experimental theatre and who are eager for opportunities to express themselves. These people ought to be allowed—urged—to come in with us on an even basis, to become part of us. New blood—lots of it—or death. That's the alternative as I see it.

Jig will probably oppose this. He will see it as a deliberate attempt to further ruin him by taking *his* theatre out of *his* hands. But unless something of this kind is done a year from now, I am going to resign instanter. There is no good sitting up with the corpse. And I will be making the plea not on my own behalf—for through Hopkins I now have an outlet where he has assured me I can shoot at the moon, demand changes in the theatre, etc.—but because I think it for the best of all concerned. Well—we shall see. But Greek wine cables are not encouraging symptoms of recovery. We have not heard from either of them since Gibraltar. Where does one address them, by the way? I'd like to write Susan.

Let anyone rent the theatre who can pay the rent. That's the way I feel about it. I don't want to hear about it again for a year.

But if Jimmy should be able to organize a group to take it over I think—in spite of Jig's probable objections—that he should be encouraged to do so. After all he has worked hard with and for us and in all justice should be given the preference over Goodman or anyone else, and if we have any principle left in this tangle we ought to do our best to support him with everything but the taking over of the P.P. name.   All best to you! Try and come up.   Gene

P.S. How about *Jones* road tour next year from P.P. angle? Is it worth while their hanging on to that half share—or would it be more profitable to sell out to Klauber[3]—I mean, withdraw the P.P. fund, etc.? Better have Madden or someone who knows look over the booking carefully and decide accordingly.

No one has written about *Chains Of Dew.*[4] Whatever happened to it anyway? I am interested to know. Remember to tell me when you write next.

---

147 • TO ARTHUR HOBSON QUINN.[1]   TLS 2 pp. (Stationery headed: Peaked Hill Bar / Provincetown, Mass.) [Pennsylvania]

June 13, 1922

My dear Dean Quinn: I wish to apologize for this late reply to your letter but I have been on a tramping tour up the Cape where mail could not reach me and did not receive your letter until my return yesterday.

As for the autobiography, I'll give it to you in brief herewith: Born Oct. 16, 1888. Spent my first seven years mainly in the larger towns all over the U.S.—my Mother accompanying my Father on his road tours in *Monte Cristo* and repertoire, although she was never an actress

2. Set designer Norman Bel Geddes (1893–1958).
3. Adolph Klauber (1879–1933), coproducer of *The Emperor Jones*.
4. Play by Susan Glaspell, which opened on April 28, 1922, at the Provincetown Playhouse.

1. Quinn (1875–1960), theatre historian and dean of the college at the University of Pennsylvania, was preparing an article on O'Neill, which appeared as "The Significance of Recent American Drama" in the July 1922 issue of *Scribner's*.

and had rather an aversion for the atmosphere and people of the stage in general. After that, boarding school for six years in Catholic schools—then four years of prep. at Betts Academy, Stamford, Conn.—then Princeton University for one year (Class of 1910)—was an attempt at a "sport" there with resulting dismissal. Then worked for over a year as secretary of mail order house, a small affair, in New York City. The firm went into bankruptcy. I never took it seriously. Then discovered a chance to work off some of my latent romanticism—went to Spanish Honduras with mining engineer on prospecting expedition—at the end of eight months or so got the fever, malarial, so bad had to be sent home. Much hardship, little romance, no gold. Arrived back in States, got position as assistant manager *The White Sister*— toured from St. Louis back through Middle West to Boston with them. Had read Conrad's *Nigger of the Narcissus* some time before—also Jack London—got the urge for the sea, sailing ships. Sailed from Boston for Buenos Aires on Norwegian Barque—65 days out of sight land. Then remained in Buenos Aires for year or so—worked with Westinghouse Electric Co., Swift Packing Co., Singer Sewing Machine Co., at different times (This was in years 1910–1911). Worked on cattle boat voyage from Buenos Aires to Durban, South Africa and return. Then was "on the beach" for considerable period in Buenos Aires, no job, eating and place to sleep intermittent. Finally returned home, ordinary seaman on British tramp steamer to New York. After period in New York loafing became able seaman on American Line, steamers New York and Philadelphia. This was my last experience as sailor. Became actor in my father's company, *Monte Cristo* sketch touring Orpheum circuit, Far West. Then worked as reporter on morning paper New London, Conn. for six months or so. Then health broke down with a slight touch of pulmonary T.B. resulting. Spent six months in sanitarium. After I was released, started to write for first time—this was in 1913, latter part I think. In that winter, 1913–14, wrote eight one-act plays, two long plays. Of these *Bound East For Cardiff* only one worth remembering. In 1914–15 went to Baker's 47, Harvard. Winter 1915–16 in Greenwich Village. Summer 1916 came to Provincetown, joined Provincetown Players, acted in own plays, *Bound East For Cardiff* and *Thirst* at theatre shed on wharf here. When they opened first season in New York *Cardiff* was on opening bill.

So much for the autobiography. I'll try now to answer your other points although in all cases I cannot give exact data. *The Emperor Jones* after its season in New York, last season played thirty-five weeks on the road, touching at about every decent sized city from St. Louis east. It made two ventures into the South proper—Richmond and Norfolk and was well received there, but I believe the management and Gilpin were warned by the Ku Klux jackasses not to venture further—and they haven't so far. Next season I believe they go to the Far West—and a year from now I hope London will see the play along with *"Anna Christie"* and *The Hairy Ape.*

Yes, another negro played the part for one performance at the Little Theatre in Indianapolis. Permission for this was given when the play was still downtown with no thought of its moving further in N.Y. or elsewhere. Long, I think the man's name was. At any rate, he made a big hit in it although only an amateur. So also did the negro who played it for Howard University in Washington a year ago this early spring. Which goes to prove my conviction, founded upon a large experience with plays, actors, and theatre, that "Brutus Jones" is what is called "actor-proof" and that any negro with ordinary acting sense can do it as well, or almost as well, as Gilpin. What they would lose on the beneficial end of experience they would gain by their freedom from Gilpin's cheap theatrical tricks.

In The Zone was produced in London at the Everyman June 15, 1921. *Diff'rent*—Oct. 4, 1921. Both ran the regular repertoire four weeks. Since then *Ile* has been produced there at same theatre, April 17, '22. Also my first book came out there last month—*Jones, Diff'rent, Straw*—published by Jonathan Cape.

In The Zone was first play to receive what might be called professional production by Washington Square Players at Comedy theatre, Nov. 1, 1918—but *Beyond The Horizon* was first simon-pure professional. *Beyond* saw Chicago for two poor weeks in late October, 1920—never went to Boston—closed after Chicago.

Diff'rent was produced by P.P. Dec. 27, 1920 (I think).

"*Anna Christie*"—Vanderbilt, Nov. 2.—Chicago, Cort Theatre, April 9.

The Hairy Ape—Plymouth theatre—April 17.

And that, I think, covers all your points. I hope it will be satisfactory to you.

I was very grateful for your letter to Mr. Hopkins, and I will surely look forward to reading your article in *Scribner's* next month.

With all best wishes to you, Sincerely, Eugene O'Neill

---

148 • TO MAURICE SPEISER.[1]   ALS 1 p. (Stationery headed: Peaked Hill Bar / Provincetown, Mass.) [Pennsylvania]

June 15, 1922

My dear Mr. Speiser: I appreciate deeply your offer to bring my *Hairy Ape* to the attention of Dr. Blei in Munich, and I would like nothing better. However, the situation in regard to this play and the other two you mention is somewhat involved just at present where Germany is concerned. Robert E. Jones & Kenneth Macgowan, who are now making a tour of the theatres in that country, took my plays with them when they left to try and interest the German and other Continental producers in them. Whether they have done anything definite or not up to date in Munich or elsewhere I haven't heard. They will be back here in three weeks or so—but in the meantime I don't feel that I can do anything about it which might in any way conflict with any arrangements they might have made—I don't mean "conflict" in any financial sense, of course. It is no more a question of that with them than with you.

I will write you again as soon as I have talked with them.

Again, all my gratitude for your interest in helping my work to a German hearing. That is one of my big ambitions now—to get a real production of a real translation there. Sincerely,   Eugene O'Neill

---

149 • TO KATHLEEN JENKINS PITT-SMITH.[1]   ALS 2 pp. (Stationery headed: Peaked Hill Bar / Provincetown, Mass.) [Yale]

June 26, 1922

Dear Kathleen: I have been in Cambridge for the past week nearly and did not get your letter until my return here Saturday.

As it turns out, the time you suggest for Eugene's visit is hardly the best at this end. Up to ten days ago I would have said fine—then came a letter from Hopkins saying *The Fountain* would open up in September, that he, R. E. Jones, the scenic designer, and Lionel Barrymore, who is to star in the play, would all be up here to get busy on the preliminary work on the play during, or soon after, the first week in July. This will mean that our none-too-big

---

1. New York theatrical attorney who had contacts with overseas producers.

1. Kathleen Jenkins (1889–1982) was O'Neill's first wife. He married her on October 2, 1909, and they were separated shortly thereafter. Seven months later she gave birth to Eugene O'Neill, Jr. O'Neill and Kathleen were divorced in 1912 and their son met his father for the first time in May 1922. In 1915 Kathleen married George Pitt-Smith.

establishment will be packed to the roof. But that in itself isn't the most important thing. We could find room for Eugene even if I had to sleep in an outhouse. The main difficulty is that I will be busy all day, every day, will have to be under the circumstances, and would have no time to be much with Eugene if he were here. This is hardly what I would want. I want to have an opportunity to get to know him, to convince him I am his friend as well as his father. Neither would it be safe for him if, as you say, he wanders about alone and cannot swim well. The ocean here is not especially dangerous but it *is* the ocean and not the Sound and one not used to it has to learn the ropes, particularly where canoes are concerned.

How would any time from the last week in July on suit you for his visit? Then I could promise him my undivided attention as I will be free to vacation a bit myself then.

You need not worry about any danger to him. I will not allow him to go out in a canoe alone, or swim alone. On some days, however, the ocean is so mild that even Shane, who isn't three yet, wades in up to his waist or sits down in the wash when there is someone on the beach to watch him. I can't say more for our Atlantic's good behavior—and I think this ought to reassure you.

Another objection to the visit on July 7th—from Eugene's standpoint. I doubt it he likes a lot of strange people all talking the strange lingo of the theatre. I think he would be bored— and I don't want that at all.

The best way for him to come when he does would be Fall River boat, I guess—but will look all ways up and let you know later. I don't believe I've ever made the trip either to or from N.Y. in summer and, as the whole schedule is changed, I'm rather hazy.

All kindest regards and my love to Eugene. I hope this different plan will be as satisfactory to you as the one you proposed. And, believe me, if I could arrange things your way, I sure would. But a playwright's life is never his own as long as a play is under contract for production "sometime before a certain date."   Sincerely,   Eugene O'Neill

---

150 • TO ARNOLD DALY.[1]   TLS 1 p. (Stationery headed: Peaked Hill Bar / Provincetown, Mass.) [Virginia]

August 13, 1922

Dear Mr. Daly: I hope you will pardon this tardy reply to your very kind letter, but I have been away on a tramping tour where no mail was forwarded to me and I did not receive your note until my return yesterday.

It will give me the greatest pleasure to inscribe the copy of *Beyond The Horizon* to M. Rostand.[2] I am doing this now and mailing the volume to you under separate cover.

May I take this opportunity of expressing to you my deep appreciation of many years standing for all you have done in, and for, the theatre? And much gratitude to you for bringing my work to the attention of M. Rostand. It is naturally one of my big ambitions to have a play produced in France. There has been some talk of it—by Copeau—but nothing definite ever seems to happen.

With all best wishes,   Sincerely,   Eugene O'Neill

1. Daly (1875–1927) was a prominent actor, director, and producer of the day.
2. French playwright Edmond Rostand (1868–1918), author of *Cyrano de Bergerac* (1897).

151 • TO MAURICE SPEISER. TLS 1 p. (Stationery headed: Peaked Hill Bar / Provincetown, Mass.) [Pennsylvania]

Sept. 3, 1922

Dear Mr. Speiser: Copeau has been considering a production of *Beyond The Horizon* for some time—in fact, he now has an option on that play, I hear from my agents. And Maurice Bourgeois, the French author, is translating four of the other plays. In addition to this, as a result of the Drama League vote, both *"Anna Christie"* and *The Hairy Ape* have been sent to M. Gemier at the Odeon. So I think the French end is pretty well taken care of. All of this has transpired since your departure.

As for Germany, Bobby Jones and Kenneth Macgowan saw many people over there and discussed the plays. I am to meet Reinhardt[1] when he comes over here in November and think it's advisable for me to do nothing in any German direction until I have the benefit of his advice. What he suggested to Jones when over there was that Bobby and I could make some arrangement whereby we could go over and do our own productions there of the plays we wanted under the auspices of different German theatres in different cities. What may come out of that, I don't know.

Let me assure you again of my gratitude for your interest in wishing to help my work to a hearing over there. I surely appreciate it.

With all best wishes, Sincerely, Eugene O'Neill

---

152 • TO EARL STEVENS. ALS 2 pp. ([Peaked Hill Bar / Provincetown, Mass.]) [Private]

Oct. 22, 1922

Dear Earl Stevens: It was a pleasure indeed to hear from you! And please pardon the delay in this reply which is due to your letter being mislaid by the Coast Guards who form our only connecting link with civilization.

Yes, I often hark back in memory to the Rio Siale days. It's hard now to imagine them really happening and they hand me a thrill—of hunger for real food, principally—each time I recall them. No, I've never used anything from them in my plays yet—but probably I shall sometime. Myself, for example, loaded down like an arsenal with ammunition, knives, and firearms would make a first rate comedy hero of romance, especially if my faithful (?) mule could also play a part.

By the way, don't believe any lurid tales of my Honduras experience you may happen to read are the product of my imagination. I have simply stated the autobiographical fact of my having been there. The dear interviewers do the rest. They have to make a "story" of everything and the facts don't bother them a bit.

As for your proposition in regard to the mine, it sure listens good but unfortunately I am absolutely unable to do anything about it at present—or for some time to come. My Mother's estate is not settled yet and will not be for six months or so, it seems; and all of the available money from my plays has gone—and is going—into payment for a home I have recently bought near New York.[1] Then too, even in the ordinary course of things, this is

---

1. Austrian producer and director Max Reinhardt (1873–1943), director of Berlin's Deutsches Theatre.

1. O'Neill had bought Brook Farm, a thirty-acre estate in Ridgefield, Connecticut.

nearly the leanest time of the year for me. The non-productive summer is only just over and returns from the new season are just starting to come in. So you see, I simply couldn't afford it now. Later, I might—although you can't prophesy in the theatrical business. But if this thing continues open, you might write again about mid-Winter. It sure sounds good.

All my very kindest to Mrs. Stevens and you! I shall never forget how very good you both were to me—and at a time when I must have been a pretty trying-on-the-nerves specimen! I hope all luck and success are, and will be, yours.   Sincerely your friend,   Eugene O'Neill

P.S. Have just remembered something—

My Father lost those photos of Honduras you gave him to give me. Have you any copies? I'd sure like to have them.

---

153 • TO WILLIAM LYON PHELPS.[1]   ALS 1 p. (Stationery headed: Peaked Hill Bar / Provincetown, Mass.) [Yale]

Oct. 27, 1922

My dear Professor Phelps: I am very grateful to you for the honor of your invitation but I have never lectured and don't believe I ever will. Frankly, there is a certain prejudice in my mind against it. It seems to me that authors should neither be seen nor heard outside of their work—(not this one, at any rate, for I'm quite certain my plays act better than I ever could—which is faint praise for them indeed!). So, both from the standpoint of personal discretion and of Christian charity toward the audience, I feel bound to decline.

But again, all gratitude to you for the honor of selecting me. I appreciate that immensely and regret that I cannot accept.   Faithfully yours,   Eugene O'Neill

---

154 • TO MARY HEATON VORSE.   TLS 2 pp. ([Brook Farm / Ridgefield, Conn.]) [Wayne State]

[November? 1922]

Dear Mary: I know your letter should have been answered sooner, but I have been sick, so forgive me. As a matter of fact I am going in to New York today to see a specialist, and try and find out just what is the matter.

In regard to the fifteen hundred, matters are so terribly complicated with me just now, that I am going to ask you to let me have two or three weeks to let you know in. First, as you know, if I possibly can manage it, I want to. I guess that is understood. But this is how things are: we have just bought this rather expensive place here, as Harry may have told you, and I have just made one big payment, and will have to pay $2500 on Jan. 25th, and another large payment before the year is up. Then, there is not a stick of furniture in the place, and Agnes and I find that to furnish it is going to cost a lot more than we expected: you see we got this place as an investment, not only as a winter home: we will have to rent it every summer, and so it will have to have the right sort of furniture, otherwise I dare say we could manage with very little for a while, but as it is it means an immediate outlay of cash: just how much we are

1. English professor at Yale University.

trying to figure out now. That much for that! Then there is also the State and Federal income tax which I will have to pay, coming right now; and I haven't any idea how much they will come to, until I figure it out, which I expect to do within the next week or so.

I expected to be able to get through the above without having to worry—this at the beginning of the winter when I bought the place. However, things have not gone as we expected—*The Fountain* has not gone on, *The Hairy Ape* closed in Chicago—although playing to $9000 the closing week!—and an offer from the movies, that looked as though it might materialize, is still in the very distant air. Also, which is even more important, my mother's estate, from which I absolutely counted on getting some cash, has not been closed yet, and matters there are so complicated, owing to the sudden death of the executor, that it may be a year or more before I get a cent from it.

So there you see how matters are—and why I want you to let me have a couple of weeks to see how much cash I will have on hand. In the meantime, if you can manage it elsewhere, so much the better, as you can see. But if you can't, you can rely on me to do my darndest!

(Of course I realize that it would be a good investment; the question is, as you can see from the above, that I don't know if or not I can afford an investment just at this moment.)

And forgive this letter if it seems a little jumbled—I'm really not even feeling up to writing a letter these days. In the meantime, come up and see us as soon as we get a little furniture, which I hope to God will be sometime next week.

Very best wishes from us both,   As ever,   Gene

---

155 • TO GEORGE JEAN NATHAN.   ALS 2 pp. (Stationery headed: Brook Farm / Ridgefield, Connecticut) [Cornell]

May 7, 1923

Dear Nathan: Nevertheless, I am convinced *Welded* is the best yet. I'm glad to get Mencken's letter but I must confess the greater part of his comment seems irrelevant as criticism of my play. To point out its weakness as realism (in the usual sense of that word) is to confuse what is obviously part of my deliberate intention.

Damn that word, "realism!" When I first spoke to you of the play as a "last word in realism," I meant something "really real," in the sense of being spiritually true, not meticulously life-like—an interpretation of actuality by a distillation, an elimination of most realistic trappings, an intensification of human lives into clear symbols of truth.

Here's an example: Mencken says: "The man haranguing the street-walker is surely not a man who ever actually lived." Well, he surely is to me and, what is more to my point, he is also much more than that. He is Man dimly aware of recurring experience, groping for the truth behind the realistic appearances of himself, and of love and life. For the moment his agony gives him vision of the true behind the real.

I can't agree that the speeches in this scene are "banal" or the ideas "rubber stamp." In fact, I'm positive it's the deepest and truest, as well as the best written scene I've ever done. Perhaps it isn't "plausible"—but the play is about love as a life-force, not as an intellectual conception, and the plausibilities of reason don't apply. Reason has no business in the theatre anyway, any more than it has in a church. They are both either below—or above it.

But I won't rave on. I'll grant this much for your criticisms—that parts of the dialogue are still, I find, "speechy" and artificial but that will all be gone over and fixed. It's the slopping-over of too much eagerness to say it all.

Thank Mencken for me for reading it. I'm sorry it didn't "knock him dead" to repay him for his trouble.

Well, just wait until you see it played![1] (if it's done right) I'm hoping that may make you recant.

My best to you both.   Sincerely,   Eugene O'Neill

---

156 • TO JONATHAN CAPE.   ALS 2 pp. (Stationery headed: Brook Farm / Ridgefield, Connecticut) [Detroit P.L.]

May 15th, 1923

Dear Mr. Cape: Thanks very much for your letter about the *"Anna Christie"* opening. I should have replied long before this, I know, but I've been on the go so constantly during the past weeks I've let everything slip.

The success of *"Anna"* in London came as rather a surprise. I had thought it might do well enough to last a while but not that it would prove any sensation at all. I hope there will be some interest left over for my plays that I consider a good deal more important than *"Anna Christie"*—*The Hairy Ape* and *The Emperor Jones,* etc.

I trust this doesn't sound like treachery to *"Anna."* It only means I do not regard that play as highly as some others of mine. I wouldn't want to be judged by it alone.

But I do resent those of your critics who think the end a compromise with integrity. Of course, it *is* a compromise, I mean it to be, just the sort of compromise those characters would have arranged for themselves in real life. It would have been so easy to have killed them off—one, two, or all three—so tragically easy! But realistically false—theatrical! They wouldn't have suicided, or murdered, or done anything at all but make exactly the pitifully humorous gesture in the direction of happiness I have allowed them to make. For that last act is their doing, not mine. I have no patience with such quibbling as theirs. I told them they ought to die rather than give in to such weakness. But they were stubbornly resolved. They even insisted their last pitiful groping has a deep significance as being a symbol of what most of us have to do—at any rate, *do* do—every now and then, in this decision or that, in order to keep on living. Which makes life even more a tragedy, when you come to think of it.

But enough of that. There was the same argument over the ending when the play was in New York. I suppose it's inevitable. Perhaps it's the fault of the play and what I mean fails to convince because I've not done it right. I don't know. When I read the play it seems clear enough.

Thank you for sending me the proof of the advertisement. I hope the books of the plays will justify your faith in them.

I think I shall surely come to London next fall sometime. It will be a pleasure to talk with you again then.

With all best wishes,   Sincerely,   Eugene O'Neill

P.S. I wired the photographer to send you photos for advertising. You should have received them by the time you get this letter.

---

1. *Welded* was produced by O'Neill, Macgowan, and Jones in association with producer and playwright Edgar Selwyn (1875–1944) at Broadway's Thirty-ninth Street Theatre on March 17, 1924.

[May? 1923]

Dear Mike Gold: Sure, I'll be only too tickled to read the play[2]—with the more interest since I've always argued that John Brown was one of the few historical Americans who demanded a real play to be done of him. So ship it on pronto and I'll read it at once and give you all the dope as it hits me whenever I think of anything that might be valuable. I know the feeling well of being so close to a play you hardly can tell what it's about, and I know from frequent experience that it's just at that time when a word from a neutral sometimes is worth the asking.

It's damn good news that you are writing again and I'm glad the leisure came your way. (Not that I mean you haven't been writing but I allude, with a true dramatist's prejudice, to *plays*.)

Yes, Gilpin is all "ham" and a yard wide! Honestly, I've stood for more from him than from all the white actors I've ever known—simply because he was colored! He played Emperor with author, play & everyone concerned. There is humor in the situation but I confess mine has worn out. I'm "off" him and the result is he will get no chance to do it in London. He was drunk all of last season and, outside of the multitude of other reasons, I'd be afraid to risk him in London. So I've corralled another Negro to do it over there (when it's done)—a young fellow with considerable experience, wonderful presence & voice, full of ambition and a damn fine man personally with real brains—not a "ham."[3] This guy deserves his chance and I don't believe he'll lose his head if he makes a hit—as he surely will for he's read the play for me and I'm sure he'll be bigger than Gilpin was even at the start.

No, I don't think Gilpin's color had much—or anything—to do with the "warping" you speak of. He's just a regular actor-brain, that's all. Most white actors, under the same circumstances, would have gone the same route. The point is, none of them would have *dared* go so far. Gilpin lived under the assumption that no one could be got to play his part and took advantage accordingly.

Yes, *The Fountain* is due to go on in October with Fritz Lieber in the lead. It is a play totally different from any of my others but the same Hairy-Ape, human quest of "belonging" is the real subject of it—although on the surface it's a far cry from "Yank" to Ponce de Leon, Grandee of Spain.

And I've finished another, *Welded*—an attempt at the last word in intensity in the truth about love and marriage. Quite an undertaking, eh? Not that I pretend to have succeeded but I think the result is interesting.

We're attempting to get a new live group started using the Provincetown Player name again. Kenneth Macgowan & Irving Pichel[4] (from the Coast) would be active heads, Pichel directing. Fitzie retained in office. I would be one of a few directing policy of theatre which would be, when lack of interesting new plays, to give radical productions of old, revolutionary adaptions of classics, new forms of all kinds—in brief, to give the emphasis to the actor &

1. Gold (1894–1967), novelist, radical journalist, and playwright, had been a friend of O'Neill since their days together in Greenwich Village in 1917–18.
2. Gold's *Life of John Brown* was published in 1924; written with Michael Blankfort, his play *Battle Hymn* (with John Brown as its subject) was first produced in 1936.
3. Paul Robeson (1898–1976), who first played Jones in a May 1924 Provincetown Players revival, later went on to play the role in London and in the 1933 film version.
4. Irving Pichel (1891–1954), stage and screen actor, created the role of O'Neill's Lazarus.

director for a time and to quicken some of the fine old stuff into modern life. A theatre of this kind is an immediate need. I'm sure its experiments, if successful, would result in a widening of possible scope of expression for everyone connected with the American theatre. Indirectly it should be a tremendous incentive to playwrights, I believe.

But enough. Send on the play. Later on when you're satisfied with it and say "go!" I'll be glad to do what I can to hasten a hearing. My influence consists only in an ability to get Hopkins to read anything I suggest—but, as he's the best, that counts something. He'll dare anything for anything he likes, I'm sure.

Agnes joins in all best. Luck to you!   Gene O'Neill

---

158 • TO KENNETH MACGOWAN.   ALS 4 pp. (Peaked Hill Bar / [Provincetown, Mass.]) [Yale]

Friday / [June? 1923]

Dear Kenneth: Many thanks. Only too tickled to have been in a position where I could. But what is the extra ten about? Do you really owe me that for something or other I've forgotten—or is it simply a grand gesture to prove to an author that *that's* the kind of manager *you're* going to be? Well, in either case, I am impressed and grateful.

Your ideas of how I can help on the P.P. sound reasonable.[1] As I wrote before, I'd like to take as active an interest as my work—(meaning actual writing time)—permits. This would mean a good deal more active interest than I ever showed in the old P.P. except during their first year—and even then my participation was alcoholically erratic. Physically and every other way, I feel up to more in a cooperative sense than I believe I ever have before—constructively speaking. Also, barring the chance of a trip to Europe, I'll be in Ridgefield where I can come in any time—or anyone come out.

As for actual writing, there is the "Homo Sapiens" Express. effort[2] which I have felt at times very much like doing and which I may do if I ever feel that way again. Not very definite, that, but with a mind full of *Polo* I'm sort of "off" everything else original at the moment.

There's "The Ancient Mariner"[3] adaption might be worked out as a novel form of recitative, pantomime, Express. set drama—and one of the Norse sagas (of Eric the Red, for example), if I remember their quality aright. These in addition to what you mention as possibilities for experiments in new treatment.

I'd be very much interested, I feel sure, in *The Gilded Age* thing.[4] Dig up the play along with the book and bring them when you come. We could go over them together.

The other (Sologub)[5] doesn't hit me from the bare idea as you've told it to me.

My greatest interest in this venture, as I guess you know from what I've said, would be as a person with ideas about the how & what of production rather than original writing—I mean there are so many things outside of my own stuff that I have a creative theatre hunch

1. Macgowan had proposed that the Provincetown Players—in the absence of Cook, who went to Greece after having declared the original Players group disbanded in 1922—be run by a triumvirate of O'Neill, Jones, and himself, with disputes to be settled by Macgowan as manager.

2. A discarded idea for a play called "The Homo Sapiens," which was to be done in the Expressionistic style. See *Eugene O'Neill at Work: Newly Released Ideas for Plays*, pp. 38–40.

3. O'Neill's dramatization of Coleridge's poem, produced by the triumvirate, opened at the Provincetown Playhouse on April 16, 1924. It was first published in the *Yale University Library Gazette* 35 (October 1960): 61–86 and is reprinted in *The Unknown O'Neill: Unpublished or Unfamiliar Writings of Eugene O'Neill*, pp. 169–90.

4. Possibly the dramatic adaptation by Mark Twain, based on an outline by Gilbert S. Densmore, of the Twain novel written in collaboration with Charles Dudley Warner in 1873.

5. Penname of Russian poet, novelist, and playwright Fyodor Kuzmich Teternikov (1863–1927).

about as being possibilities for experiment, development, growth for all concerned in work-ing them out. Perhaps I'm mistaken about myself in this capacity. At any rate, I'm willing to work these out with whoever is interested & pass them on to whoever is interested—to work as one part of an imaginative producing scheme, if you "get" me from this jumble. You see, all these ideas of mine are being incorporated into my own plays bit by bit as they fit in but I can't write plays fast enough to keep up with the production-imagination section of my "bean." It would be suicidal to attempt it particularly at this time when I am reaching toward the artistic wisdom that in order to keep moving I've got to treat each play with more & more concentration of mind & effort over a longer period of time. In other words, if I wish my work to grow steadily more comprehensive & deeper in quality, I've got to give it more & more of my possible sum-total.

"M. Polo" is proving grand pleasure. I have tentative plans drawn—floor plans—for all of it about. Am reading & taking millions of notes, etc. A lot of what the actual writing must be is now clear—and a lot isn't but will, God willing! I'll soon start a lengthy scenario of the whole to find out just how & where I stand—then get right after the writing, I hope. There's a lot of reading still to be done. I feel satisfied with the development—elated, even! The child will be either a surpassing satiric Beauty—or a most Gawdawful monster. Beauty, I fondly opine. Satiric or not remains to be seen—but Beauty must be the word!

You speak of "directors" for your theatre. I don't just "get" you. "Director" in what sense—theatre or organization? Here's a hunch for your Senate of this theatre—(you to be permanent First Consul,—Pichel other—not bad idea Roman Republicanism, for theatre perhaps)—Two actors, Roland Young (comedian) and Ben-Ami (tragedian) (if he has learned to think in American (best sense) yet)—one actress, Clare Eames[6] (?) (Don't know her or work. Take her on what I've heard—woman with brains & imagination)—Two playwrights, your humble & (?) devil take me if I know! You want a playwright who loves the theatre outside of his own plays, who is interested in the theatre as theatre—a writer of comedies & lover of them preferably. Who is? You will know, if anyone. I think it is harder to find an intelligent selfishness here, imaginative enough to realize how unselfish love loves itself, than in any other of the capacities named. With the others it's simpler and more direct returns. But to continue, last but not least Bobby & Norman who stand for such equally fine but totally distinct aspiration plus accomplishment. You to preside over this august body—eight in all—plus Pichel, of course, nine—function of this body being to discuss what to do, how & who to do it along general plan for each production as whole—powers limited to this government of general scheme embodying ideal of this theatre.

But enough. This is merely a suggestion which may prove nonsense. At any rate, what I think you need is an imaginative body back of you & Pichel who will cooperate where they can and be out of the way when they can't. But you ought to be absolute head with an absolute veto. To hell with democracy! As Director—with a cap. D!—you'll need to use all you can extract of theatre blood from our eager frames but never let anyone think his blood is what keeps the theatre going. Each one of the old P.P. got to think that. When each became sure of it the theatre up and died of anemia—which insulted each so each blamed everyone else!

Tuesday

The above has lingered on my desk since Friday. I'll wind it up right here & now and save the airing of any further of my views until I see you—otherwise the letter'll never get off!

6. Jacob Ben-Ami, Roland Young (1887–1953), and Clare Eames (1896–1930), stars of the Broadway stage who later agreed to be guest-players at the Provincetown Playhouse.

This about Djuna B's play.[7] Read it by all means! I think it's one of the finest pieces of work by an American in any line of writing. A real deep original play! It's too wordy maybe and marred by her old fault of the consciously bizarre & ultra-sophisticated in a few spots but as a whole it's corking stuff—and it's practically certain it will probably never get a chance except through a theatre such as you plan. (The Guild wanted to rewrite it for her!)

Late August will be fine—or any time a'most you-alls can arrange it. Only give us warning.

All best to *Masks & Demons!*[8] I'm looking forward to reading it.   Love to Eddy & you from us.   Gene

---

159. TO MARY A. CLARK.[1]   ALS 2 pp. (Stationery headed: Peaked Hill Bar / Provincetown, Mass.) [Yale]

August 5, 1923

My dear Miss Clark: Your letter was certainly a welcome surprise! (I didn't get it until yesterday as I've been off motoring and the mail wasn't forwarded.) Though I've thought of you many, many times I had no idea of your whereabouts. I'm glad to know. But you must write again and give me all the "dope" on just where Eagleville is, for if I can ever get anywhere near it I want to pay you a visit. (I'm taking your invitation for granted, you see— my blackmail on you for publishing my poem!)

Seeing the poem[2] again gave me great pleasure—the pleasure of bringing back to mind your kindness to me at Gaylord—a very grateful memory, I assure you. As for the opus itself, well, I can admire its intent and spirit even though I have no illusions about my ability as a poet. And if you like it as *your* poem, then I certainly like it too. But—whisper!—I think as a poet I'm a very good playwright.

It would be a wonderful treat for me to have a long talk with you—or a letter from you if you ever have time—about all the folks we used to know at the Farm and particularly about yourself and what has happened to you in the years between. You mention Miss Murray.[3] How and where is she now, do you know? I remember her interest in my writing, her genuine friendship for me. I also remember her sending me "The Hound of Heaven"[4] which I had never read before—surely just cause for my gratitude!

I've never been back to Gaylord though I've thought of going lots of times. Something always prevents—fate or laziness or something. Indirectly I heard from Dr. Lyman & Mrs. B.[5] at the time of *The Straw* production. I sent the director up to them to be shown that a San. wasn't necessarily a gloomy place. He returned quite cheered up about the play. Sometime I'll write—or tell—you all about *The Straw*—its intent, its writing, its production, its fate. You will be amused, I know, at parts of the tale—disgusted (as I was) at other—the latter— parts.

Sometime—when I have them around—I'd like to send you copies of my various

---

7. Possibly *The Dove*, by American novelist and playwright Djuna Barnes (1892–1982), published in *A Book* (New York: Boni and Liveright, 1923). The Provincetown Players had produced three of Barnes's one-act plays during the 1919–20 season.

8. *Masks and Demons* by Macgowan and Herman Rosse (New York: Harcourt, Brace, 1923).

1. A nurse at Gaylord Farm Sanatorium upon whom O'Neill based the character of Miss Gilpin in *The Straw*.

2. Probably "Ballade of the Birthday of the Most Gracious of Ladyes," *Poems, 1912–1944*, p. 41.

3. Katherine Murray, a nurse at Gaylord Farm Sanatorium.

4. Poem (1893) by English poet Francis Thompson (1851–1907), which O'Neill often recited aloud in the back room of the Hell Hole in 1915–16.

5. Florence R. Burgess, head of nursing at Gaylord Farm Sanatorium.

"works" duly signed & sealed by the author—if you'd care to have them. I know you're impervious to what they are pleased to call my "pessimism"—I mean, that you can see behind that superficial aspect of my work to the truth. I'm far from being a pessimist. I see life as a gorgeously-ironical, beautifully-indifferent, splendidly-suffering bit of chaos the tragedy of which gives Man a tremendous significance, while without his losing fight with fate he would be a tepid, silly animal. I say "losing fight" only symbolically for the brave individual always wins. Fate can never conquer his—or her—spirit. So you see I'm no pessimist. On the contrary, in spite of my scars, I'm tickled to death with life! I wouldn't "go out" and miss the rest of the play for anything!

But how I do go on! I didn't intend to let you in for a dose of "words."

All kindest regards to your sister & you. Do write when you get the time.
Eugene O'Neill

---

160 • TO SAXE COMMINS.   ALS 2 pp. (Stationery headed: Peaked Hill Bar / Provincetown, Mass.) [Private]

August 7, 1923

Dear Saxe   It was sure good to hear from you. I'm damn sorry you won't get up this summer but perhaps it's just as well. Things up here promise to be uncertain from now on—I mean I'm liable to be called away for this or that. For one thing my brother Jim is now in his second sanitarium of the year. He was "nuts complete" when taken there but is sane again now but very sick with alcoholic neuritis. Also *he is almost blind* from bad booze and the *best* they hope for is to get his sight back to *50 percent normal only*. What the hell can be done about him is more than I can figure. He'll only get drunk again, I guess, after he gets out and then he'll be all blind.[1] In the meantime his antics have tied the estate up more than ever and I begin to doubt if we'll ever get a cent out of it.

I believe I remember the Calhern you speak of. Didn't he play in *Roger Bloomer?*[2] If so, I thought he was damn fine, although the play itself carried its study of adolescence to the extent of being adolescently badly written and thereby bored me, for I came expecting to see something. However, the evening was made well worth while for me by the performance of the actor who played the Yale man. As I remember his name was Calhern or Calhoun or something similar. If that's your friend, I'm all for him.

It's great news about Stella![3] Teddy wrote me about it. Your mother must certainly be pleased. How is she now? Fine, I hope. Give her all my most affectionate best—but also to your father, your sister & her husband—to all your family who were so kind to me when I was there.

When I wrote above "just as well" you can't get here, I meant you can come to Ridgefield instead. You can surely arrange to manage that for a week-end, if for no longer. We'll be settled there by *Fountain* time.

I've a favor to ask. Our playful heir has lost the bulb to our Kodak—unscrewed it on the beach and it's in the sand somewhere. Now it's impossible to replace here and I don't know where to write exactly. Could you ask them to send one C.O.D.—also a portrait attachment for that sort of camera & a tripod. I wouldn't trouble you but I've lost their booklet which

---

1. James O'Neill, Jr., died at the age of forty-five on November 8, 1923, of arteriosclerosis and cerebral apoplexy induced by chronic alcoholism.
2. Play by John Howard Lawson (1894–1977) that opened on Broadway in March 1923 with Louis Calhern in the cast.
3. Stella Ballantine was pregnant with her first child.

came with the Kodak and am all at sea. Now I don't want you to go to any extra trouble about this—just wait till you happen to be around an Eastman supply place and tell them to send collect.

All best to Charlie Kennedy. Has he found any place in Rochester as good as Gilhooleys?

I'll promise to send you some snapshots when we get some good ones—if you'd like them.

Agnes joins in all best to you!   Gene

---

161 • TO UPTON SINCLAIR.[1]   ALS 1 p. (Peaked Hill Bar, / Provincetown, Mass.) [Indiana]

August 12 '23

My dear Upton Sinclair: Thank you for sending me *Hell*. I'll look forward to it—but just now I'm "off" reading as all my time is mortgaged to a new play I'm in the midst of which I want to finish before leaving here.

I'm sure glad to know you're a "fan." It's reciprocated, believe me! I've been one of yours ever since way back in *Jungle* days, and I think I've read everything of yours—except *The Goose-Step*—since then.   All sincere appreciation and respect to you!   Eugene O'Neill

---

162 • TO KENNETH MACGOWAN.   ALS 4 pp. (Peaked Hill [Bar / Provincetown, Mass.]) [Yale]

Sunday / [late September? 1923]

Dear Kenneth: Frankly, things are happening a bit as I had dreaded, and I already see a wild-eyed Jig Cook returning hot-foot from Greece to denounce the kidnapping of his child. But if you insist upon having the name, you'll have to accept a bit of the old game—no help for it.

This is my very emphatic advice, Kenneth! I've never really favored continuing the P.P., even though in name only. I by no means share in the belief about the commercial value of "P.P." They were absolutely dead financially when the *Ape* came—and no one knew that better than the subscribers. I believe the name will be a hindrance rather than an asset. Personally, the mere idea of being *actively* associated where any of the old bickering has a legal right to operate kills all my interest instanter. I won't be mixed up in any organization which has to straddle the old and new.

Make it entirely a fresh effort! To hell with the old name! Any name will do if you've got the stuff. For example, did *Sun-Up*[1] need P.P. affixed to it? Or *God of Vengeance?*[2] There's really no reason, except a doubtful financial one, for wanting the name—yet the name will share in all credit for your success and be absolved of all blame for a failure! (de mortuis nihil nisi bonum!). I think you ought simply to lease the Provincetown theatre and then take into

---

1. Upton Sinclair (1878–1968), most famous for his social protest novels: *The Jungle* (1906); *The Money Changers* (1908); *King Coal* (1917); *Boston* (1928); and the eleven-volume Lanny Budd series. *The Goose-step* (1923) is a social and political study; *Hell* (1923) is a verse drama and photoplay.

1. Play by Lula Vollmer (1895–1955) that opened as an outside production at the Provincetown Playhouse on May 24, 1923.
2. Play by Polish-born Yiddish novelist and dramatist Sholem Asch (1880–1957) that opened as an outside production at the Provincetown Playhouse on December 20, 1922.

your new group what little of value there was left in old P.P. but under an entirely new understanding.

In short: Either start off entirely and absolutely on your own feet—or postpone the opening of the new organization until you can. After all, when it comes down to it, I feel this new thing has no right to the P.P. name. It's a false pretense. The new group stands for an entirely opposed policy to the old—or so I have understood it—and the freer it is from all the old connotations which will inevitably arise in people's minds at the mere sight of the name, the greater your opportunity for achievement.

I hope this doesn't sound like a belated howl for I argued—with Fitzie and, I think, also with you—along these same lines last spring. What persuaded me otherwise was the idiotic notion that the financial help of the name could be inherited as a free gift—a blessing upon your undertaking—from the dying P.P. But there's nothing so unreliable as a corpse that doesn't believe in death—or so unbenevolent!

As for your manifesto, I don't like some of it, to be frank. First, I agree with Edna[3] that if you're to be the P.P., then your cover is presumptuous for the accent ought always to be on the organization when it is an established thing. I think people would be quick to criticize this cover—and justly so. If you decide on "canning" P.P., I still think the names ought to come at the end. I may be wrong but the publicity of this front page is won at the expense of dignity, in my opinion. Everyone in the B'way theatre is following Hopkins and getting out personal "announcements"—Gest,[4] etc. Then I think another name ought to be added—that of an actress, preferably, to represent what is intended to be an actor's theatre also. Then again it is *your* announcement, Kenneth—not Bobby's and mine. We are to figure, as I understand it, as active aids in consultation with you as are Bel-Geddes, etc. but this is to be *your* theatre where your final word is to govern absolutely. I want to help, to contribute all I can of the best I can, but I don't want the responsibility of an authority implied by that first page. It would weigh down and obstruct the work I can do. I haven't the ability of that sort or the time. I think I outlined all I felt I could do in my long letter of early summer. I'm looking for a director of new—or old-new—things in the theatre but I only wish to be a worker therein myself, a consulting engineer, as it were.

All this above deals only with your first page—the thing implied by it as I see it. The rest of your announcement is O.K. except "American play" by me. Cut out the "American." What that signifies is an original "all-my-own" play and, as you know, that isn't my idea—at least, I mean, I can't promise it. Again, I don't think it is good policy—or publicity—to announce any definite plays as "3 Amer. plays," *Karamazoff*,[5] etc. Just give them a promise that something mysterious, new, daring, beautiful and amusing is going to be done by actors, authors, designers—that the purpose of this theatre is to give imagination and talent a new chance for such development—ask them to subscribe because you promise them things which they *can't* see anywhere else—and then keep your promise to them! It seems to me this is the one and only reason for this theatre, Kenneth—and unless they can be promised that, it has no excuse much. I think this kind of announcement, backed up by all the names you can really depend on to contribute, is a sure way to arouse genuine interest, publicity, and subscriptions. Your manifesto is too meekly explicit, the plays you list too much what might be found on the repertoire of a dramatic club. I think you ought to inject a

---

3. Edna Kenton (1876–1954), one of the original Provincetown Players who was hostile to the new project.

4. Russian-born producer Morris Gest (1881–1942).

5. Macgowan had suggested producing an adaptation of *The Brothers Karamazov* for the 1923–24 Provincetown season.

lot of the Kamerny[6] spirit into your statement with the emphasis on imaginative new interpretations, experimentation in production. That's what that theatre ought to mean in New York today, Kenneth! That's what N.Y. lacks right now! That's the gap we ought to fill. And that idea is the idea we've been interested in, it seems to me. But where is it in your manifesto? Nowhere! And do you know why? Because that old man of the sea, P.P. is on your neck. You're trying to collect subscriptions in the name of a dead issue, in the spirit of a straddling compromise.

Don't get sore at the above. I'm raving because this isn't developing as you, Bobby & I dream—as Bel-Geddes & others dream—and unless it's going to be that dream, or at least, approximate it in spirit, then what's the use? If this is going to be just another repertory Guild on a smaller scale, what's the use? If it's going to be anything of anything that is or has been in N.Y., again what's the use? The opportunity is for the unique or nothing.

This is the way I feel—that your plea for subscriptions ought to rest on a pledge of originality, of daring experimentation, of imaginative reconception, of a unique theatre—as unique as the P.P. group was at its inception. And I'm also absolutely convinced that such an idea can succeed down there again—as it did then—both financially & artistically, but I doubt if any other idea can—or ought to.

Here's some ideas for plays: *Menschen* or *Jenzeits* of Hasenclever[7] as example of essence of Expressionism in acting, scenic, everything. I think Philip Goodman[8] would give us rights to these easily. *The Black Maskers* by Andreyev for wonderful use masks, etc. also very fine play—or *King Hunger* by the same author.[9] *Erdgeist* by Wedekind[10] done entirely with masks as by a lot of mannequins! Strindberg's *Spook Sonata* with masks—or his *Dance of Death*,[11] the two plays joined together with each act cut and intensified into a scene—one play of eight scenes (there are four acts in each play of 2 parts as I remember) etc., etc.—there are lots and lots of plays that would lend themselves to imaginative new treatment besides what we've already talked about together.

I'll write Harry[12] at once to tell him to see Edna. I'll tell him just what I've told you in regard to the P.P. name—that my dope is for you to go ahead without it. Otherwise, my honest opinion is that, especially with Fitzie away, you'll be in for a lot of interference, well-meaning but hard to take. But if you insist on P.P. I'll tell him my vote is that if the committee—or whatever the hell it is—approves of your program then there must be no strings attached to the presentation of the custody of the name.

I thought last spring there were only the five on the old Executive Committee to be considered—of which Edna, Fitzie & I were three—but it seems that's "out" and there's now seven on some other board or other of incorporation, three of whom are in Europe. Well, it's great stuff but I must confess I don't quite "get" it. I've a letter from Harry today, too, but it only suggests waiting for a meeting when I get down in a week or ten days. Well, I'm agreeable. Then we can thrash it all out. As I see it, no one seems to understand just exactly what the other is getting at.

---

6. The Kamerny Theatre in Moscow, founded by Alexander Tairov in revolt against the naturalism of Stanislavski's Moscow Art Theatre.

7. *Die Menschen* [1920; Humanity] and *Jenseits* [1920; Beyond] by German expressionist poet and playwright Walter Hasenclever (1890–1940). *Beyond* was presented at the Provincetown in January 1925.

8. Goodman (1885–1940), New York producer, held the American rights to Hasenclever's plays.

9. *Chyornye maski* [1908; Black masks] and *Tsar golod* [1906; Tsar hunger] by Russian short-story writer, novelist, and playwright Leonid Nikolayevich Andreyev (1871–1919).

10. *Der Erdgeist* [1893; Earth Spirit] by German playwright Frank Wedekind (1864–1918).

11. *Dodsdansen* [1900; The Dance of Death] and *Spoksonaten* [1908; The Spook Sonata] by Swedish novelist, poet, short-story writer, and playwright August Strindberg (1849–1912).

12. Harry Weinberger.

All best to Eddy & the heirs from all of us! Don't mind if this letter is a bit carping in spots. I'd like to see this a real Big Thing, Kenneth, for you as much as for myself, for the Theatre more than for either of us, and I hate to think that any mistake now might ruin the Main Chance—for which we can afford to wait, if necessary.

All best! Yours with writer's cramp.   Gene

---

163 • TO EUGENE O'NEILL, JR.   COPY 1 p. (Stationery headed: Brook Farm / Ridgefield, Connecticut) [Yale]

Monday / [January 21, 1924]

Dear Eugene: I am enclosing a note for you to present at box office at the Playhouse at 133 Macdougal St. Friday night. It's just south of the southwest corner of Washington Square—very easy to locate. Be sure and go. I've written them to expect you. You'll see an unusual play unusually produced in an unusual theatre by my friends and associates.[1] The experience will be of use to you in your writing. Strindberg is one of the greatest of moderns.

I think you and I will be great pals—that, in fact, we almost are now, considering how little we've seen of each other. If you feel this way too, you must come out as often as you can manage.

All of us join in all best! Remember me to Mr. Furness[2] and thank him for his letter to me which I should have answered so long ago.

It was fine having you with us!   Your   Father

---

164 • TO EDNA KENTON.   TLS(X) 1 p. (Stationary headed: Brook Farm / Ridgefield, Connecticut) [Private]

May 26, 1924

Dear Edna: If you had been willing last fall to be generous and turn over the theatre without any strings to it to the new organization, if you hadn't held out so obstinately for retaining everything possible of the old Provincetown Players so that the old corporation might still have some show of power over the new scheme, there would be no need for Susan's letter,[1] no need for your note to me, no need for this to you. I always wanted, as everyone knows and as my letters of that time show, a complete cleavage between the old idea and the new—name, game, and everything. I held out for it and was overruled. Parts of Susan's letter might be quotes from my letters of that time.

What Susan does not take into consideration is that for a year we have operated under "Provincetown Playhouse." Our idea is no longer confused with the old P.P. anymore than the Kausers[2] was who made full use of Provincetown as indicating the theatre itself. It is easy to rechristen a group. A theatre is an entirely different matter. We should have to put

---

1. *The Spook Sonata*, which opened at the Provincetown Playhouse on January 5, 1924.
2. According to the holograph notes of Eugene O'Neill, Jr., written in 1949 on this copy of his father's letter, Clifton Joseph Furness was his English teacher at the Horace Mann School in New York who had "encouraged me to write."

1. Influenced by Edna Kenton, Glaspell, when she returned from Greece after Cook's death on January 14, 1924, wrote O'Neill asking that the name of the theatre be changed because it no longer held to the aims of the original Provincetown.
2. Play broker and agent Alice Kauser (1872–1945), who leased the Provincetown Playhouse in 1922–23 with her brother Benjamin.

elaborate directions how to get there—to the new named theatre—for years to come and even then all the regulars would still refer to it as Provincetown Playhouse. I simply don't see where sentiment can enter where the name of a building is concerned. It seems to me the theatre under that name is rather a monument to Jig and I feel sure there is no experiment we have made this season in which he would not have felt our sincerity and artistic intention and, granting the old P.P. dead, been glad to have had presented in a theatre originated principally by his untiring effort. If there has been any insult done to Jig, it was in renting the theatre to the Kausers the season before and permitting them to drag "Provincetown" into the commercial gutter.

Susan seems to have heard a lot from people who are "agin us." When she gets at the real facts I am confident she will feel differently. The whole trouble and confusion lies in the fact that we were forced to operate under the old corporation and old name while in spirit and intention we had nothing in common with either. Susan does not understand this and I'll admit it has always been equally bewildering to me.   As ever,   Gene

---

165 • TO SUSAN GLASPELL.   ALS 2 pp. (Stationery headed: Brook Farm /
Ridgefield, Connecticut) [Virginia]

May 26, '24

Dear Susan: I am enclosing a letter I wrote to Edna in answer to a note from her enclosing your letter to the P.P. members. It will serve as a brief, incomplete explanation of my attitude. Frankly, I blame her actions of last fall—and Harry's—for the whole confused situation. And I hope to explain everything to you in full when I see you so that you will realize that I tried my damndest to have everything worked out as I knew you and Jig would have wished it.

But I feel at the same time that it is a damn shame that you should be pestered with our bickering. And I'm not going to write another word about it.

As for Jig—when I heard of his death, Susan, I felt suddenly that I had lost one of the best friends I had ever had or ever would have—unselfish, rare, and truly noble! And then when I thought of all the things I hadn't done, the letters I hadn't written, the things I hadn't said, the others I had said and wished unsaid, I felt like a swine, Susan. Whenever I think of him it is with the most self-condemning remorse. It made me afraid to face you in New York.

The above is futile. I haven't said it at all. But I hope you'll understand. This is a late day to be writing you but I couldn't before.

You mustn't believe we forgot him so completely. We were planning even then a memorial tablet to be set up in his theatre. After all, he wouldn't want to "fill in" a program—which is about all the other stuff amounts to.

I'm sure if Jig can look into the hearts and minds of Bobby, Kenneth, and me he sees an integrity toward the creation of beauty in this theatre with which he can be content.

As for patrons, bonds, etc. I'll admit it sounds cumbersome and silly. But that's only necessary outside nonsense. The inside is absurdly simple and smooth. Bobby, Kenneth and I fit into each other and run the whole works from within.

This is a frightfully poor attempt at writing what I want to say to you. Forgive it. I wish you could have come out to see us here. Why didn't you? It made us feel you didn't want to see us. You would have loved it here, I know. There is wonderful peace in these woods and hills.   All our love.   Gene

166 • TO DAVID BELASCO.   ALS 1 p. (Stationery headed: Brook Farm / Ridgefield, Connecticut) [Private]

June 3, 1924

My dear Mr. Belasco: This is an unpardonably late date for me to be thanking you for sending me the books[1] but I hope you'll pardon my remissness on the grounds of the spring cold I have been enjoying, plus all the worry and fret of the production of *All God's Chillun* (with His Honor the Mayor officiating as chief botherer).[2]

I've read the two volumes with the greatest interest—all the more because I found my father so often mentioned, and also such an illuminating account of the production of *The Passion Play.*[3] And, needless to remark, I was more than a little intrigued by Winter's account of your early struggles and successes about which, up to this time, I knew only what I remembered of what my father had told me. The story of your life is the best history of the American theatre that has been written.

It was a pleasure indeed to meet you. I hope I may have that pleasure again when I get back to town.

Again, my deep gratitude for your gift.   Sincerely,   Eugene O'Neill

---

167 • TO OLIVER SAYLER.   ALS(X) 2 pp. (Peaked Hill Bar, / Provincetown, Mass.) [Private]

July 2, 1924

Dear Oliver: *Welded* was produced by Macgowan, Jones & O'Neill in association with the Selwyns. If we could do it over, without the Selwyns & without the cast, in the light of what we learned, perhaps the play might shine through. Which it didn't last winter![1]

I finished a new one, *Desire Under The Elms* in June. It will open our season at the Greenwich Village Theatre. My adaption of "The Ancient Mariner" followed *All God's Chillun*[2] with this *Desire* play next. The Marco Polo opus I worked on all last summer, am working on now and think will be finished by fall. It required a lot of work in preliminary reading, blocking out, etc. and that took a lot of time. But it's coming fine now and seems up to all my expectations.

In connection with this play, would there be any chance, do you think, of interesting the Gest-Reinhardt combine in it when the latter comes over again?[3] As a production it might be right "up his alley" and he would probably welcome all the collaboration our principals downtown like Bobby, Kenneth and self could give on some cooperative basis. It's

1. William Winter's two-volume *The Life of David Belasco* (New York: Moffat, Yard, 1918).
2. *All God's Chillun* opened at the Provincetown Playhouse on May 15, 1924, amid considerable controversy regarding its depiction of an interracial marriage. At the opening performance, director James Light was forced to read the first scene to the audience, because the Mayor's office refused to grant the customarily routine permit required to employ child actors.
3. Play by Salmi Morse (d. 1884) first produced in San Francisco in 1879, directed by Belasco and starring James O'Neill, Sr., as Christ.

1. The production had closed after twenty-four performances.
2. *The Ancient Mariner*, in actuality, had opened on April 6, 1924, at the Provincetown Playhouse, before *All God's Chillun.*
3. Sayler edited *Max Reinhardt and His Theatre* (1924), a collection of materials by and about Reinhardt, and was in touch with the director and with producer Morris Gest, who in January 1924 had presented the first American production of Reinhardt's *The Miracle.*

a tremendous big thing to stage with lots of crowds, silent and otherwise, to be trained perfectly—or they'll fall flat. In fact, it involves everything a theatre can be made (let us hope) to give, and it will take *some* directing!

I put this pertinent question to you because, as you probably know, I'm rather "off of" Hopkins. His dilatory course with *The Fountain*, his failure to follow up the big chance he had in London with Lord[4] and my plays, his missing out on everything generally, have convinced me that he's not the right sort of Santa Claus for me to believe in. And this is too big for us to attempt to handle downtown. So let me know what you think.

I've also got all prepared for the dialogue stage a very experimental new one, *The Great God Brown* which I'll do in the fall and early winter. *Desire Under The Elms* is experimental—it follows my line of development through *Jones—Ape—Chillun*—but not to the extremes of *Brown*. I wish I had a script of *Desire* to send you. It's my very completest best so far, I'm sure.

We've been up here for the past three weeks. Yes, I know it "shouldn't be." I want to see you, too. I'll call you up as soon as I get back—Sept. In the meantime, write when you get a chance.   All our best to all of you!   Gene O'Neill

---

168 • TO OLIVER SAYLER.   ALS(X) 2 pp. (Stationery headed: Peaked Hill Bar / Provincetown, Massachusetts) [Private]

August 8, '24

Dear Oliver: Frankly, next week isn't so good. We're due for a lot of visitors, and also Kenneth expects to bring up Mary Morris then to read for *Desire* and go over lots of our downtown affairs. So you see it'll be rather a jam. Couldn't you make it later after *The Miracle* is started on its way? It would be fine to have you here.

I didn't mean to sic you on to Gest in behalf of *Marco Millions*—(this is one of several possible titles)—but merely to ask what you thought might be Gest's reaction. Reinhardt, I feel sure, will be much interested by both theme and production possibilities. I ought—with good luck—to get a first draft of the thing done by Sept. 1st. The reason I suspect Gest might see it is because it turns out in the writing—the Polo family's end of it—to be a great deal funnier than I had imagined. True, it is dire satire but at the same time it isn't bitter. I find myself quite affectionately fascinated by my Homo Boobus and they are spanked with a somewhat "for your own good, my boy" paternalism. Also, the poetic beauty of the Kublai Kaan-China part is holding up well. So you see.

By all means, bring it to Gest's attention if you care to go to that much trouble—and much gratitude from me for your intercession! But maybe you better wait until we've had a long talk over it and I've showed you all the scheme for staging it I've evolved and read—or let you read—what I've done on it so far. If you can pay us a visit here later on, that will be just "the cheese." Is *The Miracle* going to Boston soon—I mean, will your business take you up there at all in the near future? It's easy to make it from there here as you know.

Agnes joins in all best to Lucie, her mother & yourself.   Gene

P.S. Don't think the Glencairn cycle will be much.[1] It's been very hard for Shay to get big cast of men to stick. He's only giving 3 of the plays—with *In The Zone* out.

---

4. Pauline Lord (1890–1950), who played the title role in *"Anna Christie"* for both its New York and London premiere productions.

1. Writer and bookstore owner Frank Shay (1888–1954) opened the Barnstormer's Barn Theatre in Provincetown and presented *Bound East for Cardiff, Moon of the Caribbees,* and *Long Voyage Home* as *S. S. Glencairn.* The cycle premiered on August 14, 1924.

169 • TO KENNETH MACGOWAN.   ALS 4 pp. (Stationery headed: Peaked Hill
Bar / Provincetown, Massachusetts) [Yale]

Aug. 19, '24

Dear Kenneth: I'm sorry you didn't get up here. There is a lot I wanted to talk over—principally financial. Are you sure the Straight Secy. dame[1] understood about the other thousand? I had a note from her the other day in which she signally failed to mention it. I don't want to bother you again about this—or her—but I need to know where I stand—and prepare. Next month is a bad one—with the income tax installment, my son, Eugene's, quota for schooling as per contract with my former frau, and the summer's bills, and—but why go on? Her thou. would just about cover the first two items. Meanwhile, this firm is rapidly drifting toward insolvency. There has been nothing coming in of any account now in over a year and my back is beginning to creak under the strain. *Welded* the biggest asset, didn't bring enough to pay the income tax on the last year's prosperity. Fact! I know of nothing more irritating—and astonishing!—than an income tax which is way beyond one's incoming means. The O'Neill estate continues quiescently in probate. An endeavor to auction off a choice bit of New London real estate to pay off the lawyers & administrators failed lamentably. A large crowd gathered, they say, but they evidently thought it was a philanthropical outing for the highest bid was thousands below real value and the estate bid it in. No one profited but the auctioneer, and the estate is more balled up as to any definite end of its present uselessness than ever.

All of which moves me to the heartless inquiry as to a possible advance on *Desire,* provided your backing for the G.V. enterprise[2] is now available. Needs must when the devil drives! And that theatre really ought to advance to its playwrights anyway.

I must overcome my reluctance, I guess, and pay a visit to Otto the Magnificent, the Great Kahn,[3] when I get to town and see if he won't help me in this estate matter—on good security—or at least advise me what to do. There must be a way out, if one had the tired B.M.'s[4]—and not the weary author's—instinct to see it.

Seeing the *Glencairn* cycle of one-act plays—(which, by the way, were well done (considering) and which proved very popular. They go together in great shape and would make a good paying bet for the G.V. sometime, I'm convinced!)—makes me homesick for homelessness and irresponsibility and I believe—philosophically, at any rate—that I was a sucker ever to go in for playwriting, mating and begetting sons, houses and lots, and all similar snares of the "property game" for securing spots in the sun which become spots on the sun. Property, to improve upon Proudhon,[5] is theft of the moon from oneself.

However, I'm not so "glumy" as this sounds. Though landsick, we do work, swim, eat, and other perquisites, with hearty appetite for more. "Mister Mark Millions" moves apace and I hope to have a first draft around Sept. 1st. Also I have new ideas—one for a play to be called *Dynamo,*[6] queer and intriguing. So all is well enough.

I've been going over, with the English translations of the separate plays as a trot, the combination made by Wedekind himself of *Erdgeist & Pandora's Box* which he called *Lulu.*

---

1. Secretary to Mrs. Willard Straight, one of the Provincetown's leading financial backers.
2. The triumvirate was planning to present some of their productions at a second theater, the Greenwich Village, where *Desire Under the Elms* opened on November 11, 1924.
3. Otto Kahn (1867–1934), New York financier and philanthropist and one of the earliest supporters of the Provincetown Players.
4. Business Man's.
5. Pierre Proudhon (1809–1865), a French anarchist.
6. O'Neill did not actually begin writing *Dynamo* until 1928.

Margot Kelly[7] dug a copy of it up in Library of Congress. It looks good. I'm strong for it, provided we can get a good translator. I'll even promise to help on the dialogue. This *Erd-Pandora* work of Wedekind's ought to be done somehow. It's the best thing of its kind ever written and we ought to do it at the P.P. My sole objection to our program for this year is that it ought to be much more adventurous. Some of our choices don't seem to me very imaginative or original—as *our* selection, mind!—or to offer very imaginative opportunities for Bobby—etc.—but perhaps here I am wrong. But the shameless fact remains that there isn't a play on either of our lists to represent any of the "Big Men" we recognize as the Masters of Modern Drama, whatever the reason may be. And whatever the reason is, bum translation or whatever, we ought to find some method of dealing with it. Two plays by Stark[8] and two by Wilson[9] and two by me and none by Strindberg, none by Wedekind, none by Hauptmann,[10] none by Ibsen, none by Andreyev, etc. doesn't seem right to me. However, I don't mean to kick. This is mostly self-reproach.

A wire from Jimmy says *God's Chillun* opened to a full house & much enthusiasm.[11] Good enough! But it wants more than anything a lot of shrewd press-agenting to let people know about it. Why not bring that suit against the Mayor and the Gerry Society,[12] what?— on the grounds that now it's in a public house, their refusal constitutes a direct injury to receipts. After all, it is true. Who is doing the press work now? Louis Kantor might be a good bet here. A reopening simply must have a foxy press-agent to get it any attention, as you know.

Arthur wired me some time ago asking if I would revise my father's *Monte Cristo* for Bill Farnum. As I need the jack, I wired back for details which haven't come. The idea of it rather tickled my sense of irony. It might be amusing to play with. It was a grand old romantic melodrammer, and might make a pile with Farnum, I think, as it would hit his Movie public just right. But alas, poor Arthur! But it's a million times more interesting (as it is even) than *Virginius*[13] ever was—so Arthur's taste is showing slight improvement.

You should have come here for the *Glencairn* cycle. You'd have been surprised, as I was, how the plays were held together and given a continuity by the characters persisting from one to another. Also the whole effect was of a single-complete play about sailors. It really gave a feeling of a new sort of thing. An artist in town did exceptionally well with the sets considering the frightful handicaps he worked under. In fact, the whole affair pleased me very much, although I went under protest expecting to be bored stiff.

The water's fine. So are we. Try & come up.   Our love to all of you.   Gene

P.S. I'm glad to hear about Mary Morris being so good. Tell Jimmy L. & Bobby I'll write soon—and thank Bobby for sending drawing.

If you see Lee, or any Guild folk, from now on ask about *Fountain*, will you? Is Theresa Helburn back yet?

7. Actress who later starred in the title role of *Lulu* when it opened at New York's Forty-ninth Street Theatre in May 1925.

8. Stark Young (1881–1963), critic and playwright, whose *The Saint* opened at the Greenwich Village Theatre on October 11, 1924.

9. Edmund Wilson (1895–1972), critic and playwright, whose *The Crime in the Whistler Room* opened at the Provincetown Playhouse on October 9, 1924.

10. Gerhart Hauptmann (1862–1946), German novelist, poet, and playwright.

11. After a successful run at the Provincetown Playhouse, *All God's Chillun Got Wings* reopened at the Greenwich Village Theatre on August 8, 1924.

12. The New York Society for the Prevention of Cruelty to Children and its president, Elbridge Gerry, assisted the mayor's office in refusing to permit the first scene of the play to be presented as written—with child actors.

13. Play (1820) by Irish dramatist Sheridan Knowles (1784–1862), once a star vehicle for James O'Neill, Sr.

170 • TO DJUNA BARNES. ALS 2 pp. (Stationery headed: Peaked Hill Bar / Provincetown, Massachusetts) [Maryland]

August 25, '24

Dear Djuna: Crazy yourself! Charlie[1] must have gotten Kenneth's and Bobby's opinions mixed up with mine for I never made no such criticism of *Ann.*[2] In fact, I don't believe I've ever cast any critical aspersions on it at all. I like it too darn well, and have cheered right along for us to do it, as Fitzie can testify.

No, Fitzie hadn't told me—or written me—about your letter so I had to send your note on to her to "get" your meaning about Charlie's remarks. She writes she has written you a long letter a few days ago so you'll have all the news before you receive this.

I'll look forward to reading the new play.[3] When are you coming back to us? Never, I suspect you hope. But aw, come on over!

Agnes joins in all best to you. She & the child and I are all "in the pink." We swim miles, bake in the sun, walk, eat & sleep. I am become so eccentrically normal I haven't even smoked for two months. It is also very draughty in these parts—fine for the play crop. Fraternally, Gene

P.S. I treasure your book.[4] It is great stuff. I read all I'd read before over again. Someday I'll get revenge on the pests who pester me by asking you to autograph it. I know how the author's emotion feels but I'd like to see how it looks when complying with such a request.

---

171 • TO DAVID BELASCO. ALS 2 pp. (Stationery headed: Brook Farm / Ridgefield, Connecticut) [Dartmouth]

Nov. 22, 1924

Dear Mr. Belasco: This is rather a late day to be thanking you for your wire on the opening of *Glencairn,*[1] but my gratitude is none the less sincere for being delayed. It was certainly kind of you and I appreciate it deeply.

But to thank you is not the sole purpose of this note. As per my promise to you last spring, I now have a play to submit to you—my latest, which I had thought in final shape until I reread it a week ago. Since reading it over, I seem to find it needs some readjustment— still, I would regard it as a great favor if you would give it a reading now and write me what you think.

It has these defects from a production stand-point: It is costly to put on, involving a forestage, music, many scenes, large crowds, etc.—and also *it seems to last two nights*—to be *two* plays, in fact!

Now for its merits: I believe it is *comedy satire by an American* of our life & ideals—(although ostensibly written about Marco Polo and the late 13th century)—and I am confident it possesses in its background of the East and its love story, *real* poetic beauty and philosophy.

I'm sailing on Saturday for Bermuda but I'm asking Madden to get the script to you. At least, I'm confident you'll find it not uninteresting reading. With all sincere respects, Eugene O'Neill

1. Possibly Charles O'Brien Kennedy.
2. Probably *Anna of the Portuguese.*
3. *The Biography of Julie von Bartmann.*
4. *A Book.*

1. *S. S. Glencairn* opened at the Provincetown Playhouse on November 3, 1924.

172 • TO MR. PERLMAN. COPY 1 p. (Campsea / South Shore, Paget W., / Bermuda) [Yale]

Feb. 5, '25

My dear Mr. Perlman: Playwrights are either intuitively keen analytical psychologists— or they aren't good playwrights. I'm trying to be one. To me, Freud only means uncertain conjectures and explanations about truths of the emotional past of mankind that every dramatist has clearly sensed since real drama began. Which, I think, answers your question. I respect Freud's work tremendously—but I'm not an addict! Whatever of Freudianism is in *Desire*[1] must have walked right in "through my unconscious."

Your other questions can't very well be answered without writing a regular article. To be brief, I have begun plays with an idea or a character or a story—never with a situation, I don't think. And sometimes I write a scenario, sometimes I don't—(my work stands about fifty-fifty in this respect)—which means that some ideas develop fully and clearly before a word is written, others won't. But, here's the queer part, having written a detailed scenario, I rarely ever look at it when writing the play or follow it at all except in the bare framework— and rarely in that! Which proves something, I suppose, but what, I don't know—unless it be that for me scenarios are written to get rid of all the mistakes before starting by putting them in writing. Sincerely, Eugene O'Neill

---

173 • TO SISTER MARY LEO.[1] ALS 3 pp. ("Campsea" / South Shore, Paget W., / Bermuda) [Yale]

Feb. 6, '25

Dear Sister Mary Leo: Your very kind and welcome letter finally reached me here some days ago after being forwarded and reforwarded—so I shall not apologize for the delay in this reply, for there, at least, I have a good conscience.

Your letter interests me extremely. I remember that one of my father's leading ladies in *Monte Cristo*—Grace Raven—left the stage to enter a convent of the Good Shepherd (I think) and later became the Mother Superior there. But I have not heard of her in years and perhaps she may be dead by this. She could hardly be the pupil to whom you refer, I judge.

The stage, I believe, is not so unlike other market places as you appear to think. In any market the best is merely incidental. Few buy it because few can appreciate it. What is on display is the most salable ware, be it good or bad. If the public had a taste for "rotten lillies" every flower market would contain little else. And so it is with the stage—the commercial stage, I mean. The producers and managers, to use their own Broadway lingo, "give 'em what they cry for." And one cannot blame them. That is their business.

My writing is not of the commercial theatre. When plays of mine succeed in it, it is in spite of all the commercial dogmas which never consider the theatre as a medium for Art. So I cannot believe any of your strictures were intended for me, although because I write of the spiritually & physically disinherited whom Jesus loved better "than those that are fair and comely" (as your letter describes them), silly and shallow critics have accused me of "look-

---

1. *Desire Under the Elms* had opened at the Greenwich Village Theatre on November 11, 1924, where it ran for 208 performances.

1. Sister Mary Leo Tierney, O. P., who was teaching at Rosary College, River Forest, Illinois.

ing only on the dark side," and similar banalities. I write tragedy. Tragedy is what it is. It is only those who are ignoble in themselves who cannot appreciate the nobility of tragedy. It is only by suffering in the suffering of others that we can save ourselves, is it not so?

I must reread the *Lives of the Saints*, following your valuable suggestion. Certainly I know from memory that there are wonderful plays in them. Whether I could be the one to write them, however, seems doubtful to me. For this reason, because I must confess to you that for the past twenty years almost, (although I was brought up a Catholic, naturally, and educated until thirteen in Catholic schools), I have had no Faith. Therefore, my interpretation of the lives of the Saints would be purely of their nobility as men and women, their essential characters as human beings, without bias either one way or another as to the truth of their doctrine. I'm afraid such a neutral attitude would be liable to be misinterpreted by Catholics in general, especially if they were aware that the author had once professed the same Faith as theirs. Such resentment would be only human on their part.

In conclusion, let me again express my gratitude for your letter. It gave me a great deal of pleasure. And I would dearly like to have you for a friend, and to be remembered in your prayers—that is, if one who has confessed himself such a shameless heathen and sinner has any title to such a request.

With all grateful best wishes,   Your friend,   Eugene O'Neill

---

174 • TO MICHAEL GOLD.   ALS 2 pp. ("Campsea" / South Shore, Paget W. / Bermuda) [Dartmouth]

Feb. 12, '25

Dear Mike Gold: Your letter was a long time being forwarded—never reached me until last Monday. I'm glad to know you're back and hope we can get together for a real session when I hit New York again in June.

Yes, I got your letter from Moscow—and took the liberty of letting them quote your description of "*A.C.*" in Moscow in the *Evening Sun*. Then when *Desire Under The Elms* opened and I had some time to myself I found your letter had been lost somewhere and I had no address. By the way, have you seen *Desire* yet? I rank it as one of my very best.

I'm glad Moscow is a revelation in stage-craft for Germany certainly isn't—judging from photos and the reports of eyewitnesses, the German producers—and I've had some of their alleged best—ought to come over to Broadway in a body and go to school. They have certainly made a shoddy, unimaginative stock-company hash of the six or more productions of my stuff. The sets, etc. were dull beyond words! If I didn't have the photos, I couldn't believe it! We did better at the P.P. in the old first days and our productions of *Emperor Jones* and *The Hairy Ape* were worlds beyond theirs. I would think it just bad luck if the same thing hadn't happened with different plays and at different cities.

By the way, is there any way my agents, the American Play Co., could get after the Russian producers of "*Anna Christie*"? As I remember you said they could well afford to pay.

And did you see *The Hairy Ape* at the Kamerny? I had a letter saying they were to do it soon after Shaw's *St. Joan*. I'm very interested to find out some details of it somehow.

I'm glad you're going to settle down to writing plays and I hope you'll give us first shot at them. By all means let me see them as soon as you've finished them. And don't drop *John Brown* for good! There's a wonderful play there and some fool will run across the idea and ruin it for everyone else—temporarily, I mean—if you don't get busy! I don't mean you ought to shoot until you're ready—but give your unconscious the hint to get ready!

I don't know anything about the *Processional*[1] production—or about the play. Several of our organization read it, I remember, but thought it too much German patent American goods. I saw his *Roger Bloomer*. It had fine spots but was mostly an adolescent's idea of adolescence—which isn't very deep or stimulating.

I'm sorry but I don't know anyone on *Vanity Fair*.[2] But go and see Kenneth Macgowan. Say I sent you. Or Fitzie could have you meet. He'll be able to help you in this matter more than anyone. He's a fine fellow and a real lover of the theatre—also one of the editors of *Theatre Arts*—and knows everyone of importance on the others.

All luck to you! I'm darn glad you're back. Write again when the spirit moves. Agnes joins in best to you.   Gene O'Neill

---

175 • TO GRACE DUPRE HILLS.   ALS 1 p. ("Campsea" / South Shore, Paget W. / Bermuda) [Berg]

March 21, '25

My dear Mrs. Hills: Your very interesting letter deserved an answer long before this, and would have had one if I hadn't lost yours. It got mislaid among my papers and never turned up until a few days ago. I am very sorry.

No indeed, no ceremony surrounds me and I'm not half as secluded as any ordinary business man in his office. It costs much too much in the way of wages to secretaries, etc. to build an impenetrable wall about oneself. It isn't for a writer of tragedies to aspire to such grandeur! The best I can do is to live in a home which is a long walk from any place and where there isn't even an R.F.D.! Such are the trials of true art, oh woe!

Yes, my Collected Plays are honestly limited to 1200 copies[1] and as there was a much greater demand than that, you will find that already you could sell yours at quite a premium. They are publishing *Desire Under The Elms* in a separate volume, I believe, soon—thanks to the stupid censorship uproar in New York.[2]

Desire, briefly, is a tragedy of the possessive—the pitiful longing of man to build his own heaven here on earth by glutting his sense of power with ownership of land, people, money—but principally the land and other people's lives. It is the creative yearning of the uncreative spirit which never achieves anything but a momentary clutch of failing fingers on the equally temporal tangible. This, in brief, is the background of the drama in *Desire*. Of course, there's more to it than that, and the above is so crude as to misrepresent, but it's the best I can do. I love to write plays but I hate to write about them.

As for my philosophy, that's a hard one. I have so many brands depending so much on the weather and the state of my digestion. Call me a tragic optimist. I believe everything I

1. Expressionistic play by John Howard Lawson that opened at the Garrick Theatre on January 12, 1925.

2. Sophisticated magazine devoted to literature and the fine arts, edited by Frank Crowninshield.

1. *The Complete Works of Eugene O'Neill*, 2 vols. (New York: Boni and Liveright, 1924).

2. After a successful run at the Greenwich Village Theatre, *Desire Under the Elms* moved uptown to Broadway's Earl Carroll Theatre on January 12, 1925. District Attorney Joab H. Banton, having been frustrated in his attempt to close *All God's Chillun Got Wings* the previous year, threatened to seek an indictment from the grand jury unless *Desire Under the Elms*, which he called "too thoroughly bad to be purified by a blue pencil," was closed. Kenneth Macgowan proposed inviting a "citizens' play-jury" to a performance and agreed to abide by their decision, at which point Banton dropped his case. On March 13, 1925, the "Jury" attended the play and acquitted it of all charges; the resultant publicity considerably increased the production's box-office receipts (Sheaffer, *O'Neill: Son and Artist*, pp. 165–66). Capitalizing on this publicity, O'Neill's publisher, Boni and Liveright, which had included the play in volume 2 of his *Complete Plays*, issued it in a separate volume on April 11, 1925.

doubt and I doubt everything I believe. And no motto at this moment strikes me as a better one than the ancient "Hew to the line and let the chips fall where they may!"   Sincerely,   Eugene O'Neill

---

176 • TO ARTHUR HOBSON QUINN.   ALS 2 pp. ("Campsea" / South Shore, Paget W., / Bermuda) [Pennsylvania]

April 3, '25

Dear Dean Quinn: Your letter didn't reach me here until two days ago. I don't expect to return to New York until the middle of July. An heir is expected—(rather, another heir)—to this branch of the Red-Handed O'Neills sometime this spring, and Mrs. O'Neill and I have decided that in order to mitigate the chances of he, or she, devoting "its" entire life to serious drinking, "it" had better be born outside the U.S.[1] It's a case of the Family taking precedence over the State!

I should like nothing better than to have a talk with you before you do your article.[2] It's not in me to pose much as a "misunderstood" one, but it does seem discouragingly (that is, if one lacked a sense of ironic humor!) evident to me that most of my critics don't want to see what I'm trying to do or how I'm trying to do it, although I flatter myself that end and means are characteristic, individual, and positive enough not to be mistaken for anyone's else or for those of any "modern" or "pre-modern" school. To be called a "sordid Realist" one day, a "grim, pessimistic Naturalist" the next, a "lying Moral Romanticist" the next, an "immoral, violent Expressionist" the next, etc., etc., is quite perplexing—not to add the *Times* editorial that settled *Desire* once and for all by calling it a "Neo-Primitive," a Matisse of the drama, as it were! So I'm really longing to explain and try and convince some sympathetic ear that I've tried to make myself a melting pot for all these methods, seeing some virtues for my ends in each of them, and thereby, if there is enough real fire in me, boil down to *my own* technique.

But where I feel myself most neglected is where I set most store by myself—as a bit of a poet who has labored with the spoken word to evolve original rhythms of beauty where beauty apparently isn't—*Jones, Ape, God's Chillun, Desire* etc.—and to see the transfiguring nobility of tragedy, in as near the Greek sense as one can grasp it, in seemingly the most ignoble, debased lives. And just here is where I am a most confirmed mystic, too, for I'm always, always trying to interpret Life in terms of lives, never just lives in terms of character. I'm always acutely conscious of the Force behind—(Fate, God, our biological past creating our present, whatever one calls it—Mystery, certainly)—and of the one eternal tragedy of Man in his glorious, self-destructive struggle to make the Force express him instead of being, as an animal is, an infinitesimal incident in its expression. And my profound conviction is that this is the only subject worth writing about and that it is possible—or can be!—to develop a tragic expression in terms of transfigured modern values and symbols in the theatre which may to some degree bring home to members of a modern audience their ennobling identity with the tragic figures on the stage. Of course, this is very much of a dream, but where the theatre is concerned, one must have a dream, and the Greek dream in tragedy is the noblest ever!

All the above sounds a bit confused—it's just scribbled off—but I know it will accom-

---

1. Oona O'Neill was born in Bermuda on May 14, 1925.
2. "Eugene O'Neill: Poet and Mystic," *Scribner's* 80 (October 1926): 368–72, which was later incorporated into Quinn's two-volume *A History of the American Drama from the Civil War to the Present Day* (New York: Crofts, 1936).

plish its purpose of giving you some inkling of a lot I'd say if we could talk—as we surely must sometime.

In the meantime, if your article can't wait, you might send me some questions to be answered.

With all best wishes,   Sincerely,   Eugene O'Neill

---

177 • TO AGNES BOULTON O'NEILL.   ALS 2 pp. (Stationery headed: Hotel Lafayette / University Place / New York)[1] [Harvard]

Wednesday night / [July 22, 1925]

My Own Aggie: Just got your wire on my return with Bobby from a long session with Belasco. The Old Master is very long-winded when he starts reminiscing over his past but sharp and direct enough when it comes to practical present details. He certainly admires *Marco*, God bless him! He showed us over his place—a truly amazing museum and packed with wonderful stuff he collected.

I tried to write you last night but the flesh was weak. It was the hottest ever! My hand stuck to the paper and I gave it up.

I got a nice wire from John Barrymore today saying he'd look forward to reading the play.

Had lunch with Walter Huston. I like him better every time I see him. Bobby and I now agree we ought to try him on the part in *Fountain*. Atwill[2] has been acting like a true "ham"—demanding all sorts of impossible money, comparing himself to Irving & Mansfield[3] & Barrymore—in short, playing the jackass—and we all feel "off him." He just doesn't belong with us and Huston does. But whether Jones & Green[4] can be made to see this is another matter. I hope so.

So much for news.

I'm damn lonely! Every second I spend alone in the room I miss you like the devil—and I miss Oona over on the couch. I really love her! Never thought I could a baby! And I love you, my dear wife and pal, more than I have power to say! When you leave me I really feel a sensation of having had some vital part of me removed—my heart, probably—it's with you in Nantucket!

Good night, Darling! My love to Shane & Oona and kisses for all of you!   Gene

---

178 • TO KENNETH MACGOWAN.   ALS 2 pp. (Nantucket, Mass.) [Yale]

Sept. 28, '25

Dear Kenneth: You needn't thank me for my wire. I meant it plumb sarcastic! In fact, frankly, I'm feeling as disgruntled about our G.V. theatre venture as Bobby was when he hit Bermuda.—and this in spite of fine, sober, smokeless health and ideas bubbling over!

---

1. After returning to the United States for the summer, O'Neill remained briefly in New York to be treated for a nervous condition and to oversee theatrical ventures while Agnes, Shane, and Oona (born May 14, 1925) went to Nantucket, where the family was to spend the next few months.

2. English actor Lionel Atwill (1885–1946).

3. English actor Henry Irving (1838–1905) and German-born actor Richard Mansfield (1854–1907).

4. Producers A. L. Jones and Morris Green, who had underwritten the costs of moving *Desire Under the Elms* from Greenwich Village to Broadway and with whom O'Neill and Macgowan apparently were involved in coproducing *The Fountain*.

O'Neill, Robert Edmond Jones, and Kenneth Macgowan in Bermuda.

(*Lazarus*[1] is elaborately scenarioed—wonderfully, I believe—also ditto my woman play[2] and I'm enormously excited over both—will be able to start right in on either or both as soon as I've unpacked in Ridgefield. Also *Fountain* work is all done and well done, I think.) So I ought to be happy or contented or resigned about things theatrical but——

Am not! First, the Anderson opus at present succeeding in our theatre.[3] I've read it. It's all right—good enough stuff, turned out well enough, meriting success—but, so it seems to me, with no depth, not half as possible as Gold's play which has real atmosphere and truth, and totally without significance as far as what Bobby or you or I imagined we wanted in the theatre. Then why? Nothing better we had the capacity or ability to produce? Then let's be honest and either give up the ghost or give up pretending to mean anything new or deep or significant. This start is to me worse than *The Saint*. *The Saint* had a real idea. Late for me to be talking like this? Maybe—but what difference would it have made when I have no actual authority in the organization except as a negotiable asset whether I had read it before and said no or not? Bobby, according to what he told me, never liked the play or thought we should do it.

And now a Galsworthy second-rater![4] What the hell are we, anyway? Why, compared to this, our first season at the P.P. was ten years in advance of what we are now! It seems to me we're nothing but another New York theatre. Candidly, Kenneth, I'm not interested in such an idea. I certainly wouldn't be interested in continuing with it next year. I'd rather go back to the P.P. The acting there might be more amateur—but so would the spirit be. We've become too professional. I think McKaig must have infected the G.V. with some of the grave mold from the Frohman office.[5]

The thing that galls me most is this—We've had *Brown* since June. *Brown* is important, we believe. Nevertheless *Brown* isn't cast yet and we don't know when it will be. Now no one can tell me that if we'd been paying half the attention to *Brown* we've been giving to all this other crap—I include in this road companies of *Desire* and recasting bickerings—we'd have had a cast for *Brown* long ago. At any rate, we *ought* to be able to do our stuff that way. If we can't it simply means we're no better than the others, and less powerful. I again say the old Provincetown idea is better. There a cast for *Brown* from the old group could be fixed right now and preliminary work started on masks of the cast. Perhaps the cast might not be as technically right as we'll get at the G.V. but I'm sure we'd collect more brains than Eldridge, Harrigan,[6] etc. are liable to have. Why so much fuss about Harrigan, by the way? He may be good but the fact remains that he's been on the stage for quite a while and is still nothing much.

But no more of this beef. I'll be down and talk the rest of it in a week—leave here next Sunday—have to stop off in New London—will be in N.Y. about Wednesday.

1. *Lazarus Laughed*, which O'Neill finished in 1926, was not produced until April 9, 1928, at the Pasadena (California) Community Playhouse. It was first published in book form by Boni and Liveright in 1927.
2. *Strange Interlude*.
3. *Outside Looking In* by Maxwell Anderson (1888–1959), which had opened at the Greenwich Village Theatre on September 7, 1925.
4. Macgowan was apparently considering a Galsworthy play for the next bill, but no Galsworthy play was subsequently produced.
5. Alexander McKaig, the business manager of the Greenwich Village Theatre, had once worked for Daniel Frohman (1851–1940) and Charles Frohman (1860–1915), commercial Broadway producers.
6. William Harrigan, who was in the cast of *Desire Under the Elms* when it opened, and Florence Eldridge (1901–), who was not.

The selections for *Don Juan*, except Dale,[7] I've never heard of. It requires a fine actor—two fine actors—or I feel very sorry for Rostand's ghost—and even sorrier for the G.V. for we'll get unmercifully panned.

Naturally I wouldn't permit *Brown* to go on in March or April. I believe it has a real fair success in it if done right and, if I belong in this theatre, it owes it to me to give my plays the preference in position, other things being equal. If there doesn't seem any probability of casting it adequately so it can be done by the first of the year, I'd much prefer to do it with Jimmy at the P.P. before then. If we must have poor acting let's have it there where the audience is somewhat willing to make allowances in that respect.

Eldridge's point about the mask change is no point at all it's so obvious.[8] Naturally anything so arbitrary may confuse an audience for a second but by the end of the scene they will have accepted it. It has never so far bothered anyone who read it—and lots of all kinds have up here this summer.

Well, day-day! See you soon. The crew of the good ship G.V.T. ought to have a drastic meeting then. I fear that just as the fair wind starts to blow we're liable to sink. At any rate, give an ear to my above yawp of indignant distress. I somehow feel we're going bad and have become a young organization with a brillant past.   Gene

---

179 • TO EDWARD SHELDON.[1]   ALS 1 p. (Stationery headed: Brook Farm / Ridgefield, Connecticut) [Harvard]

Feb. 21, 1925 [1926]

Dear Edward Sheldon: I was immensely grateful for your wire about *Brown*.[2] Your continued generous appreciation of my work during the past years has meant a great lot to me, has been one of the very few things that have gratified me and satisfied me deep down inside. I say this—and I want you to *know* I say it!—with the deepest sincerity. Your *Salvation Nell*, along with the work of the Irish Players on their first trip over here, was what first opened my eyes to the existence of a real theatre as opposed to the usual—and to me then, hateful—theatre of my father, in whose atmosphere I had been brought up. So, you see, I owe you this additional debt of long standing.

My inner conviction has always been that you are one of the rare ones who really understand and have a spiritual right to speak, and be listened to, whether of praise or blame. And I have always felt that we should be, and would be, friends—(not that you haven't proved very much of a friend already as far as my work is concerned!)—if my good fortune should ever be to meet you. And I shall look forward to that good fortune, if I may, on my return from Bermuda in spring.

With your "every good wish" right back at you a thousand fold!   Eugene O'Neill

---

7. Possibly James Dale, but no one named Dale was in the opening night cast when *The Last Night of Don Juan*, by Edmond Rostand (translated by Sidney Howard), opened at the Greenwich Village Theatre on November 9, 1925.

8. Macgowan sent Eldridge a copy of *The Great God Brown* in an effort to interest her in playing the role of Margaret Anthony. After reading the script, Eldridge wrote Macgowan that the play "seems to me almost perfect until the third act—third scene—when reality and symbolism merge to a point of (to me) confusion. . . . From the time that Brown assumes Dion's mask I become slightly bewildered."

1. Sheldon (1886–1946), a playwright, was an early successful pupil of Baker's in English 47 and was a role model for O'Neill and others who later took the course.

2. *The Great God Brown* had opened on January 23, 1926, at the Greenwich Village Theatre and, after a successful five-week run, moved uptown to the Garrick Theatre on March 1 and then to the Klaw Theatre on May 10.

March 22, '26

Dear Manuel: Much, much gratitude for your long letter! I really wouldn't have dared make those many requests to you if I thought you would go to so much trouble about them. I'll reply herewith in brief:

G. G. Brown and *Brook Kerith*[2] arrived by the same mail as your letter. I'm damn glad to have the latter, especially in that fine edition. By next mail came *Chips*[3] of Mueller and *Legacy & Pageant of Greece.*[4] These latter look very much like what I want. I would like also to get the short history of *Greek Literature* by Murray and *The Greek Commonwealth* by Zimmern and *Critical Study of Greek Philosophy* by Stace.[5]

I'll make due allowance for Mueller's prudery. I only want him for his religious historical stuff. I have several of his other books (on the East).

If you haven't already got *The Alchemist,*[6] never mind it. Someone sent it to me in the Mermaid series.

Frazer's *Golden Bough* in one volume will be welcome. I'll hope to hear more on watership through other channels—if there are any!—however.

I'll trust to Nietzsche for an interpretation as to what the Greeks thought of laughter. I agree with him even if he is wrong! I'd like Freud's book.

As for Rome, *The Legacy of Rome*[7] sounds good. I'd like to have that. The others sound beside the mark I'm after except *The Conflict of Religion in the Roman Empire* by Glover[8] which I would also like to get. I would also like to get a good translation each of the Talmud and the Koran.

I'm going in very heavily these days for the study of religion along certain definite lines I have mapped out as a sort of large background for certain work in the future I have in mind. Am also starting to study Ancient Greek which I never "took" at college or prep. If in three or four years I'm able to read Greek Tragedy in the original and enjoy it—the sound as well as the meaning—I'll have made a grand refuge for my soul to dive deeply and coolly into at moments when modern life—and drama—become too damn humid and shallow to be borne.

I wish you & Mrs. Komroff could only visit us here. We have a peach of a place—a real bargain, too! But may you have a wonderful time—and rest—in Europe. By "rest," I mean rest in doing your own work, of course. Write when you're in the mood and let me know how everything is with you!

Well, "bon voyage" and all that stuff, if you don't hear from me again before you sail. When do you sail—oh yes, I see you've told me—I got you mixed with Bobby Jones who hasn't told me but who I know sails in early April.

Again, all best to you! In which Mrs. O'N. joins. It has been a privilege to have gotten to know you both. We are your real friends, we hope!   In all friendship,   Eugene O'Neill

1. An editor at Boni and Liveright.
2. Novel (1916) by the Irish writer George Moore (1852–1933).
3. *Chips from a German Workshop* (1867–75) by British Orientalist F. Max Mueller.
4. *The Legacy of Greece* (1921) and *The Pageant of Greece* (1923) by R. W. Livingstone.
5. *A History of Ancient Greek Literature* (1897) by Gilbert Murray, *The Greek Commonwealth* (1911) by A. E. Zimmern, and *Critical History of Greek Philosophy* (1920) by W. Stace.
6. Play (1610) by English dramatist Ben Jonson (1572–1637).
7. *The Legacy of Rome* (1923), edited by Cyril Bailey.
8. *The Conflict of Religions in the Early Roman Empire* (1909) by T. R. Glover.

181 • TO GEORGE JEAN NATHAN.   ALS 2 pp. (Stationery headed: "Bellevue" /
Paget East, Bermuda) [Cornell]

April 17, '26

Dear Nathan: I anticipated the Miller verdict—but not the rejection of Hopkins, the
news of which reached me in a note from Madden by the same mail as your last. My hope
was that Arthur might take it on, especially as Bobby Jones is so keen to do the sets. His
reasons for a negative I haven't heard yet—he is extra uncommunicative with agents!—but
Madden says he is writing me, and that he admitted *Marco* was fine writing. At all events,
that is that. Harris, I believe, was impressed but unwilling to tackle such a new proposition
on his own.[1]

As for Selwyn, I really know so little about what he does and how he does it that my
opinion is worthless. An interview he gave out in London in which he condescendingly
pooh-poohed my plays and said not one of them had ever made any money—a rather
startling statement in view of the fact that no less than six (*Brown* will be the seventh) have
had runs in New York of over one hundred performances within six seasons. (and comparatively few of these performances were given in the P.P., too!)—rather prejudiced me
against him. Besides being what he must have known was a lie, such spoofing in a foreign
land by a brother playwright is not cricket. Perhaps I am unduly irritable about the "regular"
theatre cant on how nothing that pretends to art can make a dollar. There is too much
inferiority and envy peering through the busted seams of that old dogma of Managers and
Lambs. One reason for my disgust is that I honestly believe the propagation of that theory has
done a lot to discourage writers of real sensibility—but who must live—from ever tackling
the theatre. And in my case, the notion is completely refuted. I must confess to having made
a darn good thing out of my plays financially—a much better thing for the six years I am
confident, than nine out of ten of the professional crafty playwrights of gamblers' guesses at
trade goods! Why even one of my sailor one-acts (*In The Zone*) with a large cast, all men, no
love interest, no star, ran successfully as a headliner for from 30 to 40 weeks on the Keith &
Orpheum line and paid me good royalties—on which I got married!—way back in 1918!
Knowing vaudeville, what greater triumph for the serious playwright can the ages offer? It is
true rumors occasionally reached me at the time that the direction had my Cockney stop the
show at a crucial point and do a specialty hornpipe and sing "The Old Kent Road," that my
Irishman had a few of Jimmy Thornton's[2] stories arranged in his past, etc. but—well, you
cannot prove it by me for I never saw it.

I seem to have gone off on a tangent. Aside from the above, Selwyn is O.K. to me but my
inner hunch is he wouldn't look at it with any considering eye. How about Dillingham? Or
Ames?[3] They have the money, I know, but have they anything else? Do you know of their
possibilities? I might try Gest. Or perhaps Walter Hampden—although I have him in mind to
submit my Lazarus play to when completed.

We are sorry about your not coming to Bermuda this year. Still, if your London plans
are still unfixed, we'll keep on hoping.

Much gratitude for your efforts on behalf of *Marco!*   Eugene O'Neill

P.S. My felicitations to Comrade Mencken! It's a case of hands across the continent—

1. Producers Gilbert Miller (1884–1969), Sam H. Harris (1872–1941), and Arthur Hopkins had all
turned down *Marco Millions*.
2. James Thornton (1861–1938), songwriter and actor famous for humorous monologues.
3. Charles Dillingham (1868–1934) and Winthrop Ames (1870–1937), New York producers.

while they are at him in Boston[4] (where they have refused to allow *Desire* to play, by the way) they are climbing my frame in great shape out in Los Angeles—for having my Abbie appear in a flannel nightgown, no less! There ought to be a grand quote for Americana[5] in that trial out there as reported in the L.A. papers.

---

182 • TO DAVID BELASCO.   TLS(X) 1 p. (Stationery headed: "Bellevue" / Paget East, Bermuda) [Private]

April 28th, 1926

My dear Mr. Belasco: I was very glad to receive your letter. There is no question of any controversy. However, there seems to be a misunderstanding. I have never heard of your wanting any more time on the play[1] except that once last fall. I replied then through Mr. Madden that you could have all the time you wanted on a new contract with exactly the same royalty terms, but I thought it was only fair that whatever had been advanced should be forfeited. A manager has no right to hold up scripts for a year or more without paying some rental. As it usually works out, more money is given to the author as a further advance and ultimately it all comes out of his royalties. I have never believed that this was fair. If you will pardon my saying so, you have the reputation of holding plays for a long, long time. My only endeavor was to try and persuade you to get to work on it at once.

Mr. Roeder[2] certainly gave Mr. Madden to understand that the reason for your unwillingness to produce the play was due solely to the cost involved which you did not think you could afford on top of the losses of a season, which up to the production of *Lulu Belle*,[3] had been unfortunate for you. This I accepted as a very natural explanation. Certainly if you wanted more time, something more should have been said about it during the past four or five months and some compromise agreement could have probably been reached between us, (or could still be reached, for that matter!). I certainly never meant to take the play away from you, but I thought it was up to you to show some definite signs of going ahead with it.

I, too, am sorry that you decided not to do my play. All this with the most cordial best wishes to you, and my deep regrets that our association should have been terminated so abruptly.   Cordially,   Eugene O'Neill

---

183 • TO BARRETT H. CLARK.   ALS 2 pp. (Stationery headed: "Bellevue" / Paget East, Bermuda) [Yale]

April 28. [1926]

Dear Barrett Clark: Herewith are the proofs which I have carefully gone over. Before I go into anything else, let me sincerely compliment you on your critical estimate of the plays.

---

4. *The American Mercury*, coedited by Nathan and H. L. Mencken, was having trouble with censors in Boston (see *The Editor, The Bluenose and The Prostitute: H. L. Mencken's History of the "Hatrack" Censorship Case*, ed. Carl Bode (Boulder, Col.: Roberts Rinehart, 1988).

5. Mencken's regular column in the *American Mercury*, in which he ridiculed American words and events.

1. *Marco Millions*.

2. Ralph Roeder, an actor and writer who was an associate of Belasco.

3. Play by Charles McArthur (1895–1956) and Edward Sheldon, which, produced by Belasco, opened in February 1926.

1. Clark's *Eugene O'Neill* (New York: Robert M. McBride, 1926) was the first on its subject and presented a brief biography followed by analyses of each play. Updated editions entitled *Eugene O'Neill: The Man and His Plays* appeared in 1929, 1933, 1936, and 1947.

That main part of the book[1] is excellent in every way—a damn good piece of work—real criticism! Not that I agree with you at all points where you take exception—or where you praise. There is plenty I would like to argue with you about. But even where I disagree most I admire the fine intelligent quality of both thought and writing.

The first part of the book—the personal side—seems to me to sort of fall between two stools. It's too long and intimate for a sketch, and too sketchy for a real picture. My advice would be to make it more of a synopsis. It seems to repeat somehow, to need cutting—this in addition to the marks I have taken the liberty to make on it by way of suggestion and criticism. You will find a lot of these. You see when you speak in the script of my having helped on the details of it, you make me a bit responsible, so I've waded right in, even to the extent of suggesting word changes which I thought better expressed the truth.

And when all is said and done—and this is, naturally, no conceivable fault of yours—the result of this first part is legend. It isn't really true. It isn't I. And the truth would make such a much more interesting—and incredible!—legend. That is what makes me melancholy. But I see no hope for this except someday to shame the devil myself, if I ever can muster the requisite interest—and nerve—simultaneously! The trouble with anyone else writing even a sketch is that I don't believe there is anyone alive today who knew me as intimately in more than one phase of a life that has passed through many entirely distinct periods, with complete changes of environment, associates, etc. And I myself might not be so good at writing it; for when my memory brings back this picture or episode or that one, I simply cannot recognize that person in myself nor understand him nor his acts as mine (although objectively I can) although my reason tells me he was undeniably I.

Well, enough of that. But I think my suggestion of still further pruning—in the interest of a more concise and interest-catching piece of writing—will stand your consideration. I don't claim to be absolutely right here but it was a feeling I got.   All best to you!
Eugene O'Neill

P.S. How about a photo for the book? I would like an O.K. on that as some of the photos used of me are very poor. Steichen[2] took some fine ones this winter. Perhaps you could get *Vanity Fair*'s permission (he takes exclusively for them) to use one of these. If not, I strongly suggest you use Muray's[3] enlargement of his photo taken on the "lookout" of our house at Peaked Hill, Provincetown. This is by far best of all old ones and really represents me.

---

184 • TO KENNETH MACGOWAN.   ALS 2 pp. (Stationery headed: "Bellevue" / Paget East, Bermuda) [Yale]

May 14th [1926]

Dear Kenneth   A cable from McKaig arrived via phone some time since, our Semgambian[1] tells me, saying something about royalty being paid—which is cheerful news—but I assure you even before that I had decided to forgive. Pardon my impatience in return. Not getting paid any royalty *by anyone* had gotten me as crochety as any other philanthropist.

The Actors' Theater combine[2] looks fine from what you tell me. The point I felt doubtful on was whether they would put you in the saddle without loading you down with dead

2. Photographer Edward Steichen (1879–1973).
3. Photographer Nickolas Muray (1892?–1965).

1. A reference to one of the native servants the O'Neills employed in Bermuda.
2. Macgowan had proposed a merger of the Greenwich Village Theatre with the Actors' Theater, a group unofficially sponsored by Actors' Equity, which had presented plays by Ibsen, Wilde, and Shaw on Broadway, with Macgowan to head the combined groups.

weight from their old organization. The idea of getting the new Channing theatre[3] sounds especially good to me. As you know, I have never been over fond of the G.V. as a theatre. One of the most important things about the new Channing, if you have anything to say about it, should be to insist on perfect acoustics. Those deaf spots are always bad work.

Why don't you amble down here on a ten day vacation once matters are set, if you're all worn out? Try to. It would be grand to see you.

Lazarus Laughed was finished—first draft—the 11th, but there will be lots to do on it once Budgie[4] gets it all typed. In the meantime, I am going to get started on the lady play *Strange Interlude*, if I can—and my creative urge is all for going on.

As for *Lazarus*, what shall I say? It is so near to me yet that I feel as if it were pressed against my eyes and I couldn't see it. I wish you were around to "take a look" before I go over it. Certainly it contains the highest writing I have done. Certainly it *composes* in the theatre more than anything else I have done, even *Marco* (to the poetical parts of which it is akin although entirely different). Certainly it is more Elizabethan than anything before & yet entirely non-E. Certainly it uses masks as they have never been used before and with an intensely dramatic meaning that really should establish them as a sound and true medium in the modern theatre. Certainly, I know of no play like *Lazarus* at all, and I know of no one who can play "Lazarus" at all—the lead, I mean. Who can we get to laugh as one would laugh who had completely lost, even from the depths of the unconscious, all traces of the Fear of Death? But never mind—I felt that about *Brown*. In short, *Lazarus* is damned far from any category. It has no plot of any sort as one knows plot. And you had better read it and I had better stop getting more involved in explaining what I can't, for the present, explain to myself.

I have many new ideas—for a play similar in technique & length to *Emperor Jones* with Mob as the hero—or villain rather!—done with masks entirely—showing the formation of a lynching mob from more or less harmless, human units—(a white man is victim of this lynching)—its gradual development as Mob & disintegration as Man until the end is a crowd of men with the masks of brutes dancing about the captive they are hanging who has reverted (a Jones but *white*) to a gibbering beast through fear. That is, it is the same lust and fear that made him commit his crime that takes possession of them and makes them kill him in the same spirit—of enjoyment, of gratified desire. (This is a botched explanation—but you get me. Not a pretty theme—but very true! I have a fine ironic title for it "The Guilty Are Guilty.")[5] The masks could be equally well used in a vice-versa scheme to this.

And many more new ideas. They will wait.

Your letter sounds wilted. Come down and get budding again—you & Eddy—lots of room. If it's money holds you back can keep the passage dough back out of my royalty indefinitely and I will howl not at all!

Agnes joins in all love to all of you!   Gene

P.S. I meant to cable Clara[6] to wait for the photos Kundren, (the steward on boat she knows about) took. They were much better than ones I sent. Too bad.

---

3. No theatre with this name existed at this time in New York; O'Neill was probably referring to Chanin's Forty-sixth Street Theatre, which had opened in 1925.
4. Probably Agnes's sister Margery.
5. See *Eugene O'Neill at Work: Newly Released Ideas for Plays*, pp. 174–75.
6. Clara A. Weiss, who worked in press relations for the Greenwich Village Theatre.

185 • TO EDWARD W. BOULTON.[1]   ALS 1 p. (Hamilton, Bermuda) [Berg]

June 3rd. [1926]

Dear Teddy: I've been meaning to drop you a line for a long time but I'm such a damned lazy correspondent I haven't been able to bring myself to a boil on it.

Agnes tells me when she went to see you that you felt pretty comfortable at Shelton. I am awfully glad. I would certainly like to see it again and look over all the improvements that have been made since I was there. When we come back to the States in late summer one of the first things we will do will be to drive out and see you.

It's getting pretty hot down here now but the bathing is the most wonderful you can imagine. The water is so warm and the air so soft that you can sport around in the water and on the beach in the moonlight as pleasurably as in sunlight. Shane is in the water all the time and Oona wades about in it.

This is just a note as Agnes says you don't feel up to reading much. I surely send you all my heartiest cheers along the long road to ultimate recovery. It is a rotten hard battle but with your courage and spirit you must win out in the end.   All love to you,   Gene

---

186 • TO ISAAC GOLDBERG.[1]   ALS 2 pp. (Bellevue / Paget E., Bermuda) [Harvard]

June 14th. [1926]

Dear Goldberg: I've just been going over the final script of *Lazarus Laughed* in order to get it off my hands before leaving here—(we sail tomorrow)—and I've let all correspondence go to, in the meanwhile.

I can't for the life of me recall much about my first meeting with Nathan. It was with John D. Williams at some restaurant, I believe, and I was three-fourths "blotto." I remember thinking how much he looked like an old friend[2] of mine who wrote animal stories at that era for Street & Smith. The second meeting was, if memory serves—mine is damn bad on such matters, let me add!—at the Royalton in his apartment, and I still have a letter somewhere written by Nathan a few days later in which he speaks of being gratified at discovering that I was as proficient at drinking cocktails as at concocting dramas. So you see. Suffice it that I found him warm and friendly and human where I half-expected an aloof and caustic intelligence completely enveloping and hiding the living being. *Half*-expected—for his letters to me had given me an inkling. And a point to make is that we had corresponded—at rare intervals, it is true—for some years before we met, and I had sent him all my scripts for criticism as soon as the plays were written.

We will be at Belgrade Lakes in Maine this summer (near Augusta somewhere) and if you can get up that way, be sure to visit us and we'll have a talk.   All best wishes—in haste.   Eugene O'Neill

---

1. Agnes's father, who had contracted tuberculosis and was at the same state sanitorium in Shelton, Connecticut, to which O'Neill had been sent in December 1912.

1. Critic and editor who was doing research for his biography, *The Theatre of George Jean Nathan* (New York: Simon and Schuster, 1926).

2. Possibly Harold DePolo.

187 • TO MICHAEL GOLD.   ALS 2 pp. (Stationery headed: Loon Lake[1] / Belgrade
Lakes, Maine) [Dartmouth]

July 2nd—[1926]

Dear Mike Gold: I wanted to get to talk to you in N.Y. but was only there three days
altogether and had a million things to do—including many hours at the dentist! But we must
get together when I come down again.

I saved the play[2] until the trip up from Bermuda when I could give it my undivided
attention. The first act I liked immensely—corking, amusing new stuff! After that, frankly,
my interest grew less and less. The last two acts seemed somehow terribly scrambled in
form—but most important to me your theme lost its novelty, your chief character his unique
lovableness—(characters, I might say, the others too)—and what followed seemed both in
its technique and content to be so much like so many other things I've read at one time or
another. My real grievance was that you'd hit me so hard with the freshness and charm and
humor of the first that the last part seemed doubly out of the picture with its familiar
propaganda set in the familiar Xpressionistic (I use the term because it's [the] only one)
model.

Don't get me wrong. My quarrel with propaganda in the theatre is that it's such damned
unconvincing propaganda—whereas, if you will restrain the propaganda purpose to the
selection of the life to be portrayed and then let that life live itself without comment, it does
your trick. But this is platitude. Gorky's *Lower Depths* is a good example of what I mean. And
your Mexican play[3] is much better propaganda than the last two acts of this one.

Another thing, if you want Constructivist sets, I think you ought to write more Con-
structivistically—that is, in constant theatrical terms of your characters' actions in relation to
the set. It really needs dialogue & pantomime written exactly in keeping.

I wish I could talk to you and discuss all this. You've got the making of a darned fine new
amusing play. For Pete's sake, don't let it slide. If you want my most candid dope, I think you
ought to keep the artist, Mike Gold, and the equally O.K. human being, the Radical editor,
rigidly segregated during their respective working hours. I advise this in the name of flesh &
blood propaganda!

See you before long & let's talk. You could have a grand second act with Sam's experiences with the circus—a grand 3rd act when Sam, the circus man, comes home in his
glory—all this in the tempo & medium of your first. This struck me when reading. I give it for
what it may be worth.   All best!   Gene

P.S. Am sending back script to Kauser.

---

188 • TO KENNETH MACGOWAN.   ALS 2 pp. (Loon Lodge, / Belgrade Lakes,
Maine) [Yale]

This, after living in "Bellevue" all winter, makes me suspect that God is becoming a symbol-
ist or something![1]

---

1. O'Neill inserted this above the printed stationery heading.
2. *Hoboken Blues*, which opened at the New Playwrights' Theatre on February 17, 1928.
3. *Fiesta*, which opened at the Garrick Theatre on September 17, 1929.

1. O'Neill drew an arrow from this sentence to the return address at the head of the letter.

Dear Kenneth: I've been laid up with a rotten bad combination of cold in the head and sore throat for the past week—still have it—and have been feeling peevish enough to bite nails. Had just gotten started again on *Interlude,* too, when it came on. Tough luck, for the damn thing seems hard to shake and keeps me from bathing and everything else. Still, it's the first bad cold I've had since around the opening of *Desire* so I suppose I shouldn't beef too much.

Your idea about Reinhardt sounds grand.[2] But will he be tempted? I doubt it. I imagine America means enormous money to him or he won't play. At any rate, try it out.

Don't waste a script in Barrymore's[3] direction unless you find out absolutely that he's definitely looking for a return from the films. Why not see if you couldn't make some team-up arrangement with Hampden?[4] Madden says he—H—is very sore I didn't send him a script.

I don't know enough about the work of most of the men you cite to have an opinion. George Gaul sounds good as an "L" possibility—Tyrone Power,[5] Conroy,[6] Hohl[7] for Tiberius—Keith, Morgan, Hull[8] for Caligula. Don't know Ames'[9] work—or that of any of the others except I know that if MacQuarrie[10] can play Tiberius, I can play the Virgin Mary.

What I really need to be sure of as soon as possible is, are we going to have the backing to do *L*? It simply can't be done "economically," you know that. McKaig is quite right, I think, in his estimation of its chances as written. If it were a question of sets, but it isn't. Crowds, especially when they are such an integral part of the play-scheme as my crowds, have got to have size and volume or be absurd. Remember how vocal they are.

"Speaking of Bobby," I think it would be the wrong dope for us to urge him further. I wrote him at length from Bermuda saying how I wanted—needed is better—him for *L* etc. and I've just had a note similar to yours saying he couldn't get back before first of year and almost certainly not until long after that. Also that he feels his career is "shot," etc., and really feels his resignation is imperative for his peace of mind—not in those words but he puts it strongly. So I see nothing to do but accept what he is very evidently determined on and simply explain it on the grounds that he has to remain in Europe and isn't willing to "belong" until he can actively participate. I think to urge him further—by letters—would only make him the more obstinate. At all events, my last letter to him, referred to above, did my best. Let's wait till he "comes out of it."

The Lakes are fine and we have a good camp, good rowboat & canoe and fish abound. I had just settled down to enjoying it when this damn cold threw me out. Eugene is here & Barbara[11] so we're a fat family.

Do keep me up on the financing of *L*. It's important because the Guild & Hampden both want to see it—now—and if we can't swing it, I want to get in hooked up elsewhere

2. Macgowan was trying to interest Max Reinhardt in staging *Lazarus Laughed.*
3. John Barrymore.
4. Walter Hampden (1879–1955), who served for many years as president of the Players, the most important American theatrical club.
5. Power (1879–1931) was a Shakespearean actor and father of the movie star.
6. Probably Frank Conroy.
7. Arthur Hohl.
8. Robert Keith (1898–1966), Ralph Morgan (1883–1956), and Henry Hull (1890–1977).
9. Possibly Robert Ames (1889–1937).
10. Benedict or George MacQuarrie.
11. Barbara Burton, Agnes's daughter by her first marriage.

immediately for, if I wait too long, I'll get no production next year at all—*Marco* looking very dubious in spite of all the wonderful encomiums from Ames and others who shudder at the cost. Has Skinner[12] read *L*? Is there any latest about *Brown* on road?   All best!   Gene

P.S. Don't give too many scripts of *L* out. We want to keep "inside" talk on that down to a minimum.

---

189 • TO KENNETH MACGOWAN.   ALS 9 pp. (Belgrade Lakes, / Maine) [Yale]

August 7. [1926]

Dear Kenneth: My wire crossed your letter. Your wire arrived this a.m. It's hellish that everything remains so indefinite about *Lazarus*. It ought to be cast and the work on the masks for the crowds (so that they could be used in rehearsals of the crowds right from the start) well under way by the first of September. Otherwise, the whole thing will only be hurried and bungled as everything usually is—for you can't produce *Lazarus* later than the first of the year, hardly, with any fair chance of return. I feel very much as Bobby does that it's pretty hopeless to attempt to accomplish anything fine under these conditions in a theatre. I feel very discouraged about this Actors combine. Combine? As far as I can see the G.V. has been simply swallowed up by a vastly inferior, quite brainless organization! You made one grand mistake when you let them keep the name of Actors' Theater and all the paraphernalia of their ridiculous letter-head staff![1] What have we gained, for Christ's sake? We have no money to do any real work with, we haven't even got a theatre to plan ahead with, and we've lost our absolute control! Who has gained by this? Certainly not Bobby—if he had elected to stay in, for he would be more cramped than before. Certainly not I! On the contrary, I feel deeply humiliated by being swallowed by an organization for which I have no respect and which gives me nothing in return in the way of advantages for production of my plays! What authority have I in this "combine" of a theatre—the G.V.—which sprung from the P.P. and which my plays certainly did a big part in creating? I tell you candidly, Kenneth, if it weren't for our friendship I'd be out of this Combine—script of *L* and all—as fast as I could get to the telegraph office! And what have you gained? More money, perhaps, which undoubtedly you ought to have, but no added prestige. Director of the G.V. was more than this is. And you have to beg for coin as insistently as before. So what the hell? I'm not denying the G.V. was finished financially and that something had to be done but I think we have been cheated into giving our good names for nothing, and that the wherewithal to achieve new things has not been placed at our disposal, and therefore we are doomed to artistic failure before we start—just another of those theatres a good deal inferior in possible scope to the Guild and many others.

What can be done? Well, I think if you start to raise a howl—in my name, which will let you out of the responsibility—it may have some salutary effect. Tell whoever should be told that my decision, as laid down in this letter to you, is that if the Actors' Theater, with which I am supposed to be combined for mutual benefit, cannot raise the money to insure time and material for a proper production of either *Marco* or *Lazarus* (Simonson claims *M* can be done beautifully at not-too-great cost), then I feel cheated and I wish to be publicly announced as out of it, just as Bobby is.

12. Catholic critic Richard Dana Skinner (1893–1941). O'Neill and Macgowan were trying to interest religious organizations in financing *Lazarus Laughed*.

1. The Board of Directors of the Actors' Theater, which was listed on the letterhead of the new combine, included Ethel Barrymore, John Barrymore, Laurette Taylor, John Drew, and Jane Cowl, among others.

As the Director of this new theatre, I can't see why it is up to you to shoulder the responsibility of raising the money. A Director isn't that, certainly.

And I might go on and on indefinitely, for a deep sense of "insult and injury" has been growing & brewing in my mind ever since I've realized how little we've got in exchange for the G.V. labors. I'm sick of your having to beg money from these tin-horn bastards, Catholic or Jew, for my plays. I'm sick of your submitting them to them, whose opinion is worthless. It's humiliating for you and for me. It cheapens us both and it cheapens the plays in the minds of cheap people—and the less they respect us the less money you'll ever get from them, you can bank on that, human nature being what it is. This putting my stuff up for auction in the slave-market spoils the game for me. The regular commercial managers have their lousy disadvantages but I'm not sure if they're not less insulting to one's self-respect. Certainly our dealings in a money way with the Selwyns (*Welded*) and with Jones & Green (*Fountain*) proved that, compared to Kahn, say, they were generous gentlemen, good losers, and much more sincere patrons of the "best in the theatre," whatever that is. I am sure, if we were what we were, or independent, we could get backing from the commercial theatre itself for *Marco* or *L*—somewhere—perhaps not—at any rate, it would be a clean-cut business, with no favors asked.

But enough. Only it occurs to me that our progression from the P.P. to the G.V. to the Actors' to—what? is not any progress toward the sort of theatre we want and should stand for but rather a reversion to show-shop type. And like Yank in the *H.A.*, I question the moon above Broadway dolefully "Where do I get off at? Where do I fit in?"

And in fairness to a friend, I think you should set me free to submit *L* to the Guild now so that I may get quick action there in case, as seems to me quite possible, you can't raise the coin at the Actors' to do it. For, unless the improbable happens, *Marco* is out of it for next season and, even if you get the backing and a possible route booked for *Brown & Beyond*,[2] the road is too uncertain to count on for anything—in which case, with *L* tied up by contract or held up until too late for production elsewhere, I would be "in the soup." This would not be nice. Of course, it will probably not be greeted with howls of acceptance elsewhere. But there is a chance with the Guild and Hopkins and a few others.

The decision of the Catholics, I knew all along, having once been one myself. Skinner must be a dull boy—or a bad Catholic—to imagine, after he'd read it, that they'd fall. If they are not stupid, it should hit them as a flat denial of all their fundamental dogmas. So after all——! As for the Christian S.[3] I fear they will feel the same, old top, although I'm not familiar with their particular brand of salvation-hootch. The point is that if *L* is anything, it's absolutely non-sectarian. And to the members of a sect that's more anathema than even the doctrine of a rival creed. As for Wall street, I imagine they're not good enough judges of plays or religions or what have you down there, to see it as a profitable stock gamble.

What would set me more "in the soup," in case of the failure of a *L* production, is that there is no chance of *Strange Interlude* being ready for next season. My experience with it so far—I did most of a second scene two separate times and tore them up before I got started on the really *right* one!—is that there's going to be more work on it than on any previous one— much more—with no end to the going over & over it, before I'll be willing to call it done. If I get it—and the 1st draft of some new one—done by next June I'll think it a good year. The point is my stuff is much deeper and more complicated now and I'm also not so easily satisfied with what I've dashed off as I used to be.

2. The Actors' Theater was planning to revive *Beyond the Horizon*; it opened on November 30, 1926, at the Mansfield Theatre.
3. Christian Scientists.

Naturally, until I hit my stride—or rather found *the one* action & place for the 2nd scene—I felt rather sour (one reason why I haven't written before, but don't blame this letter on that for I'm "all set" now.) on life generally. But the swimming & boating, etc. are grand and we all love the lake. Also motoring about this interesting Maine country is pleasant. Perhaps I could do with less progeny about for I was never cut out, seemingly, for a pater familias and children in squads, even when indubitably my own, tend to "get my goat." However, they have their recompensing sides too. But I do feel that A. & I could do with more real friends to talk with—especially I feel that I could for, my days of rum being, I am quite confident, over forever in this world, I rather feel the void left by those companionable or (even when most horrible) intensely dramatic phantoms and obsessions, which, with caressing claws in my heart and brain, used to lead me for weeks at a time, otherwise lonely, down the ever-changing vistas of that No-Mans-Land lying between the D.T.s and Reality as we suppose it. But I reckon that, having now been "on the wagon" for a longer time—a good deal—than ever before since I started drinking at 15, I have a vague feeling of maladjustment to this "cleaner, greener land" somewhere inside me. It is not that I feel any desire to drink whatever. Quite the contrary. I rather wonder that I ever had sought such a high-priced release, and the idea of it is (what must be fatal to any temptation!), dull and stupid to my mind now. But it is just like getting over leprosy, I opine. One feels so normal with so little to be normal about. One misses playing solitaire with one's scales.

I have been pondering over the theatre and I have tentatively worked out a scheme that I want to put up to someone—Jimmy L. or someone who is foot-loose. This would solve for me the problem of my permanent relationship to the theatre both as writer & worker-in, and I believe might be profitable, if given a decent stake to start with. It's an idea founded upon an O'Neill repertoire and a permanent co. for chief roles as follows: Start Oct. 1st with a revival of *"Anna Christie"* (with Lord, if possible—perhaps with last act revised, or playing alternate last acts for novelty) for three to four weeks—then *The Straw* for 2 weeks—then *Emperor Jones* 3 weeks until last week in Nov.—then opening of my new play each year whatever it was, this to run 4 wks or less if only half-liked and, if a big success, not more than 8 wks (1st of Feb.) at our theatre before being moved—then an experimental new production of a classic with the emphasis on the acting, for four weeks—then four weeks of either an original modern play or a revival of a modern play with the emphasis on originality of production. (This would take the season to either Mar. 1st or April 1st, depending on how long my new play had run.) Then two to 3 weeks of *All God's Chillun*, (with it being played on alternate nights by an all-white and an all-colored casts, or some novel touch like that), followed by 4 to 5 weeks of *Hairy Ape*, with a chance of getting Wolly[4] that late in season. The next season would be

Beyond the Horizon	—3 to 4
Gold	—2 to 3
Great God Brown	—3 to 4
New Play	—4
Classic Revival	—4
Welded	—1
Glencairn cycle	—2
Desire Under The Elms	—4 to 5

4. Louis Wolheim, who had had great success in creating the role of Yank in the original 1922 production of *The Hairy Ape*.

I would work for this theatre all during summer with whoever was Director for certain hours outside my writing daily and would be at all rehearsals practically from start of season till 1st of year, by which time everything would be planned to last detail for remainder of season. New and original productions of all these old plays, in the light of past errors, would be in order and this, together with the entirely new productions, would give the Director his chance. And the actors would certainly have theirs.

Now I may be dumb but it seems to me such a theatre would pay for itself, once given a fair start, and it is an even business proposition. Also I can see how, from it, by gradually including more of other people's plays in future years, while sticking to my proven standbys, by gradually sticking in split weeks, then a week with a different play each night, a repertory theatre might finally grow from it. And also, I feel this is absolutely—as things appear now— the only possible chance for one growing up as a self-supporting unit. And Jimmy L. I feel, is certainly the best available man for a Director (not connected with raising the money).

What do you think of this? You see, I've got to have a chance to grow in the theatre and make it grow. I've got something I ought to contribute beyond plays. This Actors' Theater promises no such opportunity—much less than I have enjoyed hitherto—and I can't help being convinced that, for me, it is a backward step. I also feel you are going to find that your absolute dictatorship will be double-crossed the moment you step on their prejudices. Honestly now, you simply *can't* believe that anything can evolve out of a theatre where the Director has to give consideration to what Francis Wilson[5] and similar people have to vouchsafe? And if you think you *don't* have to give consideration to such birds if you don't want to, then just try it a few decisive times!

But that's your affair, of course, and none of my business. I merely state it as a prophecy.

No more of that stuff. I sure hope the *Brown-Beyond* Tour will go through somehow— that *Brown* will at least get a Chicago chance. Aren't Jones & Green interested at all? Eldridge or Mary Ellis would be fine. Who is Clifford Sellers?[6] Helen Freeman wouldn't do. I saw her toward the end in *B.T.H.* She was bad. Also, she always felt miscast and I doubt if she'd want to do it. You want the same woman for Marguerite & Ruth,[7] don't you? Hogarth[8] would be ideal.

Sorry but I think your swell idea of a prize play is a bad hunch. Prizes are another way of becoming banal and, besides, I doubt if you'd get anything worth 2500 out of it. And it's bad advertising, this offering prizes. It "places" you.

Here's something important. Of that 1500 borrowed from Mrs. S. 1000 remains to be paid. It must be due now and I think Bogue[9] will soon be on my tail about it. Now the organization still owes me 500 advance of Gold's play and 500 of the 1000 I gave at the *Brown* opening. So will you take up this note for me with her? Undoubtedly, you can exchange a note of the New Co. for it and thus avoid paying me the 1000, which I should presently be clamoring for, and at the same time get me out of her debt. How about it? It looks to me a good solution for all of us.

The Prague-*Desire* pictures were amusing. Did the *Hairy Ape* ones ever come out in *World*, as you said they would?

---

5. Wilson (1854–1935), author, actor, and manager, was the first president of Actors' Equity and also served as president of the Actors' Theater.

6. Actress who appeared as William A. Brown's mother in the Greenwich Village Theatre production of *The Great God Brown* (1926) and also in a 1925 revival of *Diff'rent*.

7. O'Neill means Margaret (Anthony), the leading female character of *The Great God Brown*, who was intended to resemble Marguerite in *Faust*; Ruth Atkins is the leading female character in *Beyond the Horizon*.

8. Leona Hogarth, who played Margaret in the premiere production of *The Great God Brown*.

9. Mrs. Willard Straight's secretary.

This seems rather a tough letter to be imposing on you—but, as a friend, I know you want to know just how I feel about things.

Agnes sends her love to Eddy and the kids—and mine also—why don't one or all of you come up in the Ford for a visit? Eugene Jr. & Barbara are leaving on Wednesday next.   All best!   Gene

P.S. Will you give enclosed to Clara and ask her to have B & L send the lady the book she asks for and Clara send her the mimeoed data (which I haven't) she asks for?

P.S. I don't think there's a chance with Reinhardt really. If he could read English, yes—but not after it's been transposed through Kommer's[10] cropped bean, whether his report be good or ill.

---

190 • TO HART CRANE.[1]   ALS 3 pp. (Belgrade Lakes, / Maine) [Columbia]

August 21st [1926]

Dear Hart: I was certainly damn glad to get your letter! I've been going to write you a lot of times about that introduction business—have been really afraid you might get the wrong angle on the position I took and that it might in some way put a spike in our friendship, or at least introduce a feeling of resentment.

So let me explain once and for all: I've never felt that I was the right one to do that introduction. It has been my opinion right along that I wasn't qualified for it—that, considering the difficult nature of the poems for the layman-reader, you needed a poet or a critic of poetry who could not only understand your purpose sympathetically (I could do that) but also make a clear, well-devised statement of your use of means to your end. This I felt, no matter how good my intentions, I might bungle because, after all, the writing of good articles or introductions requires practice and I have never done any and lack confidence in myself. And my conviction was that a poor introduction would hurt you, hurt me and, in the long run, not even help the sales of the book a damn bit. If your poems had been of a kind where I could have written a very personal introduction, talking about you, etc. and giving my enthusiastic opinion that the poems were damn fine and beautiful stuff, etc., I would have done it in a minute but a reading of them over again convinced me that this would only sound like ballyhoo and, as introduction, be worthless. But for the jacket of your book, where an arresting opinion can do some good in attracting attention and selling—(I don't believe anyone ever reads an introduction before buying a book)—why I'll still be there "with bells on."

And another angle of the affair made me increasingly sore! It is an angle that concerns the publishing game in our U.S. and many of the writers thereof. I felt that it was a humiliating injustice to you as the author of such poems for the proposition to be put up to you that the publisher would only publish if I wrote an intro.—the publisher not giving a damn if my opinion of your poetry is worth a valid damn or not but thinking only of the business end of the notoriety-publicity value of my name. And I felt that it was an injustice to me that the publisher should say, in effect, either you write this intro. for your friend or his book won't

---

10. Rudolf K. Kommer, Austrian journalist and translator, who was Reinhardt's representative in the United States.

1. Poet Crane (1899–1932), whom O'Neill met in 1923 and whose first collection of poems, *White Buildings*, for which O'Neill originally offered to write a foreword. The volume, published by Liveright, appeared late in 1926 with a preface by Allen Tate and a dust jacket blurb by O'Neill.

get published by me. This position faced both you & me from the start and it made it exceedingly difficult for both of us, if you ask me, to go over the situation frankly together. Now I don't mean to blame Liveright. He is really, in all my many dealings with him, a good, white guy and I've felt all along that, if given time enough, he'd finally publish the book on its own with the right intro. from Tate and with me doing my bit where I know it would be of most use. The fault was his who first put it into Liveright's mind that I would write the intro. And I don't doubt that was done in all good faith. So it was nobody's fault!

To state finally in brief my principal feeling. I felt my introduction might prove a damn poor piece of work and a poor piece of writing, no matter how glowing its praise, is never justifiable on any occasion because it always defeats its purpose.

Enough! I'll love to have the inscribed copy! You know that. And I'm damn glad *The Bridge* is coming along so well. When you talked of the Isle of Pines it always sounded like the right place for work to me. I've found Bermuda hits me better than any spot heretofore. I can relax there, get rid of nerves, be more free to free myself—and still keep from losing the needful pep. I imagine that's what you're finding, isn't it?

Agnes joins in all the best. Write again when you have nothing better to do. We'll be up here—these Maine lakes aren't bad, either—until Oct. 15th—then New York.   Gene

---

191 • TO KENNETH MACGOWAN.   ALS 4 pp. (Belgrade Lakes, / [Maine]) [Yale]

Monday / [August 23?, 1926]

Dear Kenneth: All right, old top! The Ayes have it! Still and all, my principal grudge remains—against this or any other old theatre—this particularly because I belong to it which I assure you I wouldn't to any other—that we ought to be able to start work on *Lazarus Laughed* far enough ahead, with the full certainty of where, how, when & with whom. Such a play demands that from any producer. (Belasco was going to give it to *Marco*, no? I mean, when he meant business.) If we'd been able to start as soon as I got back we'd have had six months (or five) to work on masks, etc. *knowing L* would be the second bill or third bill. I'm not claiming under the circumstances it *was* possible. But it ought to be where such a play is concerned. And you know as well as I that no theatre in America will be worth bothering one's bean about until such a step in advance can be made for it is obvious that without that step nothing new or old can be done except in the established hit-or-miss way. I give you two examples from our past. Do the masks in *Brown* do what the script requires of them? They do not. They only get across personal resemblance of a blurry meaninglessness. Whose fault? No one's! Not enough time to see them. Perhaps the result the script calls for is impossible to attain by the method by combination masks the script describes. I think I see this now. With more time on masks in their proper lighting, I—we—would have seen it then. Then again, *Desire*. Has it ever been produced as I wrote it? Never! (I'm leaving acting out of this dope, as a necessary uncertainty.) There have never been the elm trees of my play, characters almost, and my acts were chopped up into four distinct scenes through lack of time to get the changes perfected in black-outs, the flow of life from room to room of the house, the house as character, the acts as smooth developing wholes have never existed. You know this.

Now these two plays were well done, as things go. But if you are "getting tired" of conditions in the show-shop from your end as a director, I am certainly getting God damn tired of them—of eternally putting up with inexcusable—in the sense of avoidable in a true theatre with more time and preparation—*approximations* to what I've written. Put yourself in this playwright's position. I stand for the playwright's side of it in this theatre. What's the use of my trying to get ahead with new stuff until some theatre can give that stuff the care and opportunity it must have in order to register its new significance outside of the written page in a theatre? It makes me feel hopeless about writing except for my own satisfaction in a book (and, as in the old past, never going near rehearsals or taking any interest—except financial—in the production). What I want now—when I am able and eager for it—is a theatre I can give my best to in every way. I'm sick and tired of old theatres under old conditions, of new theatres handcuffed by old conditions, of "art" theatres with fuzzy ideals and no money or efficiency—in fact, of *the* American theatre as it exists. I've had exactly ten years of it as a playwright—considerably more than your three as director—and my ambition to see my stuff performed on any stage I know (never very avid!) is beginning almost to cease, and this at a time when I *know* I have most to give to a theatre.

I write the above principally to a friend, a good deal to a co-idealist and fellow-worker, hardly at all to the director of a certain old (G.V., P.P., A.T. what matter?) theatre. So don't get your managerial back up! From your angle, you might kick in almost the same words. We are both tired. And no wonder. But where I claim the right to be especially concerned is that *Marco* has already passed by the few who might do it even adequately, that the theatre I'm in can't do it at all, that *Laz* is uncertain, that I'm deep in a new one even more difficult, if not so costly, that still more difficult ones—except for a *new* theatre—are in my brain, and that, looking this over, it seems I as an artist have a lot to "view with alarm."

My objection to *your* position is most certainly *your own.* You are—and have been, except a little that 1st P.P. year—not getting any chance to give what you have to give toward a new theatre, you are not getting any chance to work creatively with me in the art of the theatre, to dream and plan the executing of dreams, you are not becoming what I urged you—(how you must bless my interference there, at times!) to take over the P.P. & dictatorship for, you are being forced into the job of a manager instead of a European director, it seems to me, and I hope you can give me credit for being unselfishly resentful against conditions because of this in addition to my resentment against them on my own account.

And therefore your postscript is unjust, I think. "Time & troubles" have not affected my courage as a playwright and are hardly liable to, and although my patience frequently bogs down it has an elastic quality yet. And my feeling for you and confidence in you as a co-worker for and in a new theatre remains as unsinkable as of yore, and then some! So what have you? All I ask is that we be able to work together and let someone else do the roll top desk stuff. And *all* I ask in addition is new actors, new directors and a new theatre for my new plays to be worked by and with!!! Surely a simple matter! There must be a Maecenas somewhere in the U.S. if we could but find him who would have the faith and generosity to gamble artistically for a few years on my new plays & revivals of old ones as a basis and give us the chance to start clean, clear of old people & old conditions, and "do our stuff." I may be a fool but I believe in this. I believe if we knew how to go after this opportunity, we'd find it. (Baker found Harkness.)[1] In fact, I don't believe much in anything in the theatre but this dream. It is this theatre I'm writing for.

Consider "the thunderstorm" over. If it has brought back a little ozone of our old idealism, it was a good one. It has to me.

Why don't you try and get up over a week-end? Bar Harbor X'press—sleep & you're here at 8 a.m. Great fishing, swimming, canoeing, rowing—golf course ¼ mile off only. Plenty of room now. Eugene & Barbara gone.   Luck!   Gene

---

1. George Pierce Baker had gone to Yale University in 1925 to head a newly formed drama department and to preside over a new theatre center, which had been established with a one million dollar gift from Standard Oil heir Edward S. Harkness.

P.S. Who do you think of for directing *Lazarus* if Reinhardt not?

P.S. I think your idea of 50000 or over for *Lazarus* is not necessary. Seems to me it should not cost more than 25000 to get on—set severely simple, costumes are inexpensive, depend a great deal on arbitrary lights. The running expenses of crowds will be high, of course, but the play will be on a week before this starts. Will masks be very expensive?

We don't want any "spectacular," as such is usually termed, quality to this. A severe simplicity of outline, a formalized grouping—no hint of excess—if you get me, it's hard to explain.

If *Fountain* only cost 18000 to get on——

PART FOUR

CARLOTTA

1926–1928

It was as if your presence became suddenly apparent
in my cabin and I could hear your voice saying
that "everything will come out as we wish it."
And now I am full of faith again.
—To Carlotta Monterey, November 27, 1926

Between October 1926 and April 1928, O'Neill's inner
and outer lives reached major turning points. In his writing he was striving after greater
wisdom and depth than he had shown before, and in his personal life he was called upon to
display the same qualities of mature judgment and control. He was not at first successful.

Following their vacation in Maine, and after a brief "second honeymoon" in New York,
Agnes returned to Bermuda, leaving O'Neill to seek backers for *Marco Millions* and *Lazarus
Laughed*. That fall, the attraction he felt for Carlotta Monterey deepened beyond a summer's
flirtation. She was beautiful, sophisticated, and emotionally responsive to his evident interest in her. She was also protective and unexpectedly capable of taking charge of practical
matters—coping with New York department stores, for example—that he usually avoided.
Shortly he began to feel that he needed her in a way he did not need Agnes, and their affair
evolved quickly and passionately. While his love letters to Agnes often seem to lack genuine
feeling and sometimes read like watered-down versions of the letters to Beatrice Ashe, his
letters to Carlotta, written after he returned to Bermuda in late November, are of an introspective and confessional nature, love letters that are also self-exploratory.

The quality of O'Neill's letters to Carlotta may have been caused in part by the introspection resulting from a short-term psychoanalytic counseling O'Neill received from Gilbert V.
Hamilton. O'Neill and several of his friends had responded to questions concerning their
personal marital relationships for Hamilton's study *A Research in Marriage*. Hamilton had
repaid each of the participants with a short counseling session. The results were beneficial for
O'Neill. Thereafter, he all but gave up drinking and seemed better able to come to grips with
the effect of his early family background on his present life.

The affair with Carlotta, however euphoric, forced O'Neill to confront distressful domestic problems. Aglow with naive honesty he told Agnes all about Carlotta. Carlotta wrote
to Agnes, whose response is not recorded. O'Neill could not easily choose between the two
women, the one exciting, loving, and new and the other companionable, occasionally
shrewish, but in place as the mother of his children and as part of his domestic world. With
the duality of the protagonists of *The Great God Brown* in mind, he cried out to Carlotta: "If I
could only live at the same time in two worlds! But what a shamefully inadequate gift of half

to offer you—or Agnes. And yet each of those halves is really a whole me! See *Brown*. I *am* two—absolutely!"[1]

Carlotta removed herself for the waters at Baden Baden, thinking perhaps that absence might help in its usual way to resolve dilemmas of the heart. Agnes left Bermuda briefly to tend to her sick father, and the letter written to her on April 16, 1927, is one of his most impassioned protestations of love. Spithead, he said, will be their "old English family estate." It must be entailed as a "background" for their children, a haven to which they have won after much "struggle," an "ultimate island where we may rest and live toward our dreams with a sense of permanence and security that here we do belong." The letter, protesting too much, is undercut by the irony of Carlotta's silent presence, out of sight, but not out of heart.

In the fall of 1927, there arose what O'Neill called "nervous bickerings and misunderstandings" with Agnes, and the dramatist inevitably responded badly to the turmoil of their relationship. The situation was not helped by the continuing financial problem brought on by his failure to find producers for *Lazarus Laughed* and *Marco Millions*, now cut down to a compassable four acts. Moreover, in the writing was a play that would surpass even these spectacles in length, complexity, and technical originality. He worked on *Strange Interlude* sometimes as long as eleven hours a day, shutting away the world and putting out of his thoughts the possibility that like the others, it would not find a stage. Only the success of *The Great God Brown* enabled them to continue with the restoration of Spithead. The home in Connecticut, for which they could find no buyers, became a burden, and O'Neill, uncertain of his income, refused to support members of Agnes's family beyond what he had already given for her daughter by her previous marriage.

Domestic difficulties aside, his reputation continued to grow. *Desire Under the Elms* was produced in Moscow; Reinhardt showed interest in *Lazarus Laughed;* the American producers with whom he discussed productions were among the most respected in New York, far removed from those who dominated the run-of-the-mill Broadway offering or the amateurs on whom he once relied. Among his new acquaintances were a number of wealthier New Yorkers, Otto Kahn, Norman Winston, Maurice Wertheim and Robert Rockmore. Through Nathan, he became friendly with Lillian Gish, who expressed interest in playing the Princess Kukachin in *Marco Millions*. Benjamin and Bio De Casseres, two avant-garde writers, became his friends. Arthur Hobson Quinn and Joseph Wood Krutch listened to him with respect.

In March 1927, his artistic and financial problems were resolved when Lawrence Langner, managing director of the Theatre Guild, arrived in Bermuda. By the mid-1920s the Guild had become one of the most respected producers in New York, the one most firmly committed to the best in play selection and production. Ruled by a formidable board of directors—the actress Helen Westley, the financier Maurice Wertheim, the designer Lee Simonson, the stage director Philip Moeller, and as executive director, Theresa Helburn—the Guild was the answer to O'Neill's production problems. Langner had arranged that the Guild would become Bernard Shaw's American producers, and major American playwrights, among them Robert Sherwood and S. N. Behrman, were regularly represented on the Guild's stage. Langner, certain that O'Neill belonged in the Guild's stable, came courting, determined to resolve earlier differences. He read *Marco Millions* with interest; the unfinished *Strange Interlude* set him on fire. In relatively short order, the Guild directors accepted both plays for production in early 1928. The success of *Marco Millions* was as anticipated—a respectable late season run. The success of *Strange Interlude*, in nine acts with "thought-

1. Letter to Carlotta Monterey, (letter 201).

asides" whereby the characters revealed the substance of their inner lives, was not so predictable. With its unusual running time—a 5:15 curtain and a ninety-minute dinner break at 7:30 after act 5—the play became a sensation. Like *The Emperor Jones* at the Provincetown Playhouse, it became almost more than the Guild could cope with. Published, it became the first drama to achieve best-seller status, and it won O'Neill his third Pulitzer Prize. It was the climax of O'Neill's early career, and the income quickly resolved his financial difficulties.

Strange Interlude also served indirectly to resolve O'Neill's emotional problems. In New York, awaiting the final decision about casting and scheduling the two plays, O'Neill again saw Carlotta. The relationship that had faded a little in the previous months revived. In late 1927, the letters to Agnes in Bermuda become angry and accusatory as if O'Neill were looking for a reason to break with her. In November, he wrote that he felt that there was no longer any love between them. In December, he began to try to get his scripts and other literary valuables out of Bermuda, and on the day after Christmas, he told her that he loved "someone else."

Agnes came to New York. There was a moment's flare-up of former passion, but it was not enough. The day belonged to Carlotta, and she and O'Neill sailed for London, leaving Harry Weinberger to work out the details of the divorce. It was to prove an embittering experience. Agnes, he came to feel, had betrayed the code of their marriage, which honored the freedom of each individual within the matrimonial circle. Should either ask release from the marriage, the liberty should be freely granted with no claim of ownership. Agnes, with two children and an uncertain financial future, was less than enthusiastic about the Bohemian idealism she once had championed. Furthermore, she claimed she was pregnant. O'Neill denied he had fathered the child.

192 • TO CARLOTTA MONTEREY.   ALS 2 pp. (Stationery headed: Harvard Club /
27 West 44th Street / [New York]) [Yale]

Saturday night / [October 23, 1926]

Dear Carlotta:

And your fine note did me more good than you can imagine! To know that our luncheon meant something to you means a lot to me. The shoe is on my foot. I am the one to be grateful!

Don't *you* talk about "extra veronal!" You *are*! You don't—or at any rate, you shouldn't! —need those futile embellishments we others have to adorn our egos with in order to strut successfully before our mirrors. *You're* splendid!

I'm sorry I can't make the luncheon. I will miss not seeing you. But let's get together again soon. I'll call you up tomorrow—I mean Monday—morning and try to catch you. I tried it this a.m. and yesterday. What do you do going out so early? I suspect you must be in love with a milkman! Or am I a late-riser?

You shall have a script of the play[1] as soon as I can lay hands on one. Just gave my one out to have copies made.

We might do something together—unusual, bizarre and revolutionary—like taking a walk over on the Drive and breathing healthy, carbon-monoxideless air, if any, some fine morning. I used to be young up around the Drive many years ago and have never been there since. I suppose the air isn't as fresh as it used to be—(it never is!)—but, if you crave healthy exercise, we might try it.   Yours,   Gene

---

193 • TO CARLOTTA MONTEREY.   ALS 3 pp. ([Aboard the *Fort St. George* en route
to Bermuda]) [Yale]

Saturday / [November 27, 1926]

Dearest: She's starting to roll now, off the Hook.[1] I remember in my sailor days what a thrill of living it gave me, that first feel of the great ground swell of ocean heaving under me. It meant a release then, an end of an old episode and the birth of a new. Life then was simply a series of episodes flickering across my soul like the animated drawings one sees in the movies, and I could not then see how the continuity of my own seeking flight ran through them as a sustained pattern. Now that old thrill is gone. The ground swell is just a swell. The rhythm is lost. The self that it excited to dreams was long since buried at sea. But there are times when, lolling on deck as a passenger I can feel it swimming under the keel of the ship, the haunting soul of a drowned one, wailing lamentable sagas of the past and mocking me in the blasphemous irony of the forecastle: "What did they give yer, Gene the Yank, in place of the sea?" "Oh," I answer with forced airiness, "There's a little fame, you know; and I once heard that someone once told someone that fame is sweet to taste." "It don't go down with me, that tale," he retorts, "and it don't go down with the sea neither, 'ceptin' down in it to drown and dissolve." "Well," I say defensively, "I've got a little money and a little house and a little security and ease." "And cauliflowers in the front yard? But there's roses deep in the sea," he answers. "Aw hell, what has it got yuh? This thing's still in your inside but it ain't your belly. It's way down—" etc. And so on. Quite like the Hairy Ape, that long-drowned

1. Probably *Lazarus Laughed*.

1. O'Neill sailed from New York to rejoin his family in Bermuda; Sandy Hook is barely out of New York Harbor.

self of mine, who comes back to haunt my loneliest bitterest hours. Today I said to him: "There's Carlotta." And I hear him give what sounded like a grunt of approval and say something like "Even a god-damned fool sometimes finds his rightful harbor at last." And he went away.

But, unhumorously speaking, I feel pretty much in hell right now, dear—a hell of lonely longing for you. And a desperation too blindly suffering for the saving vision of any hope. God has turned his back and slammed the door and all the prison is in darkness.

Tomorrow I trust my courage will again lift its flattened ears and wag the tail from between its legs and bark with hope at the ghosts that now inspire it with such cringing dismay.

But what a sad letter to be writing to you, Dear One, when of all things I don't want to bring you sorrow of which you've already had your dose, God knows. Forgive me. It's rank ingratitude for the great rare joy your love has given me—and I don't mean it—only just now you seem so far away, so lost to me. If I could only kiss you again, Carlotta———

Sunday eve / [November 28, 1926]

Your Marconigram came at just the right moment this morning. It was darling of you to send it. It was as if your presence became suddenly apparent in my cabin and I could hear your voice saying that "everything will come out as we wish it." And now I am full of faith again. To quote from the *G. G. Brown* I feel "You will never die till my heart dies. I will feel you stirring in your sleep forever under my heart."

I hope the roses pleased you. I wanted each one to be a prophecy to you of an hour to come to us.

You must write me what you really feel. I can't bear the thought of your writing letters—guarded letters—that you know someone else may see. It is too horribly cruel. I simply will not allow anyone else to see them.

I think I shall have to tell the truth right from the start down here. It will be kinder to all in the end. I am a bad liar, even by omission and I can't live a lie. My silences have a way of being more damning than words. And there is no such thing as the saving lie. Only the truth can save. But the horrible facts here are that some people won't believe truth. Oh, I don't know what I'll do. I'm so tortured now I can't trust my own judgment. I'll have to try and wait until I can push things a little away from myself so I can see them. What did—or do— you think I ought to do? Please tell me! You have a much better head for this than I. You are strong and cool when you want to be. I should have asked you. It seems now I was so unpardonably vague. It was all so beautifully cataclysmic for me. Everything in the world but you seemed as remote as if it were in another life, a past life. But now mile by mile it grows exigently into a present that I must live and grin and work in—attempt to, at least— for what?—we will all be dead so soon and good deeds and bad will become but a faint echo of one same deed, heard for a moment or two. Oh hell, Carlotta, "it's all wrong, get me." "I can't t'ink." "I don't belong!"[2] Yet I do believe "everything will come out as we wish it"— but how to get it started so it will come soon? Try and tell me, Beloved One, whose heart is now my heart, whose wish is my wish, whose will and way are my will and way!   My love, I adore you! Do not forget me!   Gene

P.S. Forgive the pencil. My fountain pens are always dry. My possessing them is a mere literary affectation, I guess. And I haven't been out of my cabin yet—and won't till we dock. The fellow countrymen one sees on these boats make one aghast at all the breeding that is

---

2. These are phrases used several times by Yank in *The Hairy Ape.*

being done among the natives of Brooklyn and Newark. It will soon become a race question, I'm sure.

---

194 • TO CARLOTTA MONTEREY.   WIRE 1 p. (At head of wire: SS FT ST
GEORGE EASTHAMPTON NY) [Yale]

NOV 28 [1926]

IT IS LONELY MY LOVE   GENE

---

195 • TO KENNETH MACGOWAN.   ALS 2 pp. (Spithead, / Warwick, Bermuda)
[Yale]

Thursday / [December 1926]

Dear Kenneth: Well, here we are—stopping temporarily at a cottage near our place, the smaller house of which is not quite ready for occupancy yet nor the furniture for it yet arrived. Our Spithead will be a wonder of a spot once it's done. It's ideal for me. I've been in swimming every day and the sea is the same old sea.

Yet I'm not what you would call perfectly at peace with God. The two days' voyage was a beautiful little inner hell. The high cost of living seemed horribly exorbitant. One was tempted to refuse to pay the bill. I envy those simple souls to whom life is always either this *or* that. It's this *and* that, the this-that desire,—more than desire, need!—that slow-poisons the soul with complicated contradictions. Vague? Well, you get me, I hope. But be silent about what you get, I need not warn you. And do not mistake my nebulous cries for whinings. Beauty, either here or there, is worth whatever price one has to pay for it, here or there. Yes!, as friend Lazarus says. Oh very much so!

Your wire about *Beyond* was encouraging. Let's hope the business will keep step.

Be sure and have Clara have Muray send me those photos of me as soon as possible. I liked them so much and I'm anxious to have Agnes see them. She is fine. So are the heirs. And it is good to be home again. And lucky I left when I did—for I love her and them and my home and nothing could ever take their place—but oh Christ, there are also other things— "on the other side of the hills"—the curse of being an extremist is that every ideal remains single and alone, demanding all-or-nothing or destruction.

Oh balls! "What hunted, haunting ghosts we are." Pardon my getting maudlin. But it relieves me to tell someone—I mean not someone but that rare privilege, a friend.

Let me know about Chicago—and anything you may hear. Are the gossips on my trail? I am a poor intriguer. Everything I do always seems—for the moment—so proudly right I never dream of concealments.

Try to get me a letter as soon as you've leisure. One ship is laid up now and for the next 2 weeks there's only one mail per.

And try and get down!   All best!   Gene

---

196 • TO HARRY WEINBERGER.   ALS 3 pp. (Hamilton, Bermuda) [Yale]

Dec. 7th [1926]

Dear Harry: The enclosed bunch of trouble explains itself. You will note that the two Massachusetts notices threaten to "collect same according to law" within fourteen days, so something ought to be done about them at once. They seem to ignore the application I made through you to have my alleged, wholly fictitious residence in that State for the years mentioned wiped off their books. But, as I told you the last time I saw you—, two weeks before I had had a notice from them that that application was filed for consideration. What is one to do about such people? Their right hand doesn't seem to know what their left hand does. What can they do about collecting? Can they attach any money or property of mine outside of Mass.? If so, I ought to remove all my little available dough down here at once. All I own in Mass. are the Peaked Hill buildings—the title to the property is doubtful and there is still (technically) a chattel mortgage on the furniture (which I paid off long ago but never had stricken from the town records). There are also a bunch of my original longhand scripts in a safe deposit box in the bank at P'town. Do what you think best about this, will you?

And now for the Federal branch. As I feared this happens just after my departure. The summons is for Dec. 3rd, as you will note, so this also ought to be taken care of right away. You had better explain to them that I am down here under doctor's orders to rest & stay put, suffering from a complication of nervous disorders that have resulted in an almost complete loss of memory as far as my income tax returns are concerned. Lay it on thick that I am, like all artists, half-crazy, impractical, with no sense of money, that I have kept no books, no receipted bills, that I can't locate any canceled checks on account of having moved so many times (all this is true enough)—that I never dreamed anybody but business men had to keep books, that the only records I—or my different secretaries—have ever kept have had to do only with theatrical royalties. If they ask anything about the sale of property from the estate, explain that that was all handled by the administrator and I know nothing about it except that the Hulls wrote me there was nothing for me to file in my return.

I'm enclosing the copy of my return for 1924—the year they are after—and my explanation of the expenses, etc. claimed on it, as I wrote when calculating them. This is about all in the way of explanation I can give. 1924 is a long way off and I simply couldn't remember details about it for God or the State or anyone. And they'll have to act accordingly. They've picked out the one year I had only a small tax to pay. The year before I paid them a couple of thousand and 1925 another couple. It isn't square of them. My income for 1924 was small but my expenses kept up. In fact, I had to borrow money to get through that summer on.

Well, see what you can do. I'm just starting to get to work and these damn fools pester me to death. Probably if they look into the records closely they'll find they owe me more money for mistakes than I do them. This past year they've already sent me back 180.00 I didn't have to pay.

All best from all of us! Let me hear from you!   Gene

(P.S.) If you want some corroboration for my nervous state I can refer them to Doctor G. V. Hamilton of the Rockefeller Foundation who has been treating me for two years. He is at 47 E. 61st St.

I simply can't come up to appear in person, make them get that.

It seems to me they ought to have a pretty good general notion of what the expenses of a man in my position, etc., legitimately should amount to, and ought to judge by this.

Dec. 8th [1926]

Dear Mr. Gorelik: I'm glad you were excited by *L.L.* And I entirely agree with you about the danger of a non-robust production—also about the rotten position a scenic designer is in in doing sketches on spec. But I don't know what you mean about Hopkins. I suppose you must mean Arthur H—but he has not got the play—no one has—no definite production is in sight except a possible one in Chicago at the Goodman next spring (or late winter), and a production by Danchenko[2] in Moscow on his return, and one by Reinhardt in Berlin. There is also a possibility that R. might do it in N.Y. a year from now but it's a very mere possibility. So you see I can hardly be very definite to you about it. My big worry is first, who the hell can play the lead even if anyone does it?

But about Chicago? Do you know Gering, the Russian who worked with Meyerhold[3]— directed Kaiser's *Gas*[4] in Chicago last spring? He will direct *L* if done out there. Why not see him? If you don't know him, get in touch with Kenneth and he'll arrange to have you meet. They have money out there and I don't believe he has any prejudices about "better known designers." Tell him it's my idea your getting in touch with him. Perhaps something you'd want might come of it—but it seems to be a lousy bad year in the theatre for all concerned—including, thank God, the commercial wise-pickers!   All best to you and Good luck!   Eugene O'Neill

---

Dec. 10th. [1926]

Dear Carlotta: It was grand to get your two letters by the last boat. The steamer service to this isle is for some reason temporarily disrupted and there is only one mail a week—so one looks forward to it with double expectation.

I have read your letters many times. Evidently they were written before you had received either of mine. They were very good medicine for me. They brought me back to earth. They imparted to me some of your own calm—which I badly needed to get back to "living as usual" and setting to work again. You see I had a training the exact opposite to yours. It was extremely undisciplined. I was allowed—or allowed to allow myself!—to become what you might call an excessivist, battered about from emotion to emotion, always demanding the extreme reward or the extreme penalty—or nothing. This makes for an exciting life, as my past will bear lamentable witness, but it is hard on sound sleep, sane judgment and the other requisites for peace of mind. I have always been either hilariously shooting in on the crest of a wave or else bogged down up to my neck in a swamp. The dry, warm, sure-footed middle ground was the one place where I never was taught to walk. So I finally escaped on to the plane of my work where I can always dance and drown and be reborn to dance and drown again. When work wouldn't come I had to escape via masks of solitude, alcoholic and otherwise, provided only they were excessive.

So calm comes hard. However, I'll try it—indeed, *must* try it, things being as are. And I'll begin by trying to write to you calmly.

1. Set designer and author of *New Theatres for Old* (1940).
2. Vladimir Nemirovich-Danchenko, Russian director who split off from the Moscow Art Theatre.
3. Marion Gering and Russian director and producer Vsevolod E. Meyerhold (1874–1940), who led the revolt against naturalism in the Russian theatre.
4. *Gas I* (1918) and *Gas II* (1920) by German dramatist Georg Kaiser (1878–1945).

We are still all living in a rented place, our furniture not having put in an appearance yet. It is not too uncomfortable but there is no right place for me to work—but one room or another has never bothered me much and I've been laboring all week at going over the script of *Marco Millions* to send to Liveright. Production or not, I'm going to let him publish it in the spring.[1] I've got to get some sort of hearing for that play.

By the way, speaking of scripts, will you send me the *Lazarus* one when you get it back from the man you loaned it to? I'm trying to get back all the scripts I can because I want to go over *Laz* in the near future and trim it up a bit.

I'm feeling wonderfully again—physically speaking. The swimming and the lying in the sun can do wonders to me in even a few days. New York always shoots me full of holes in a few days. I'm afraid that cities are not for me to live in. I've just had an awful thought—does your present bad come-back from too much sun mean that you will never be able to enjoy the beach in a bathing suit again. I hope not! I have dreamed of you beside me on beaches like these down here. But perhaps we could compromise on moonlight and moonlight bathing.

It is wonderful to know you have again "faith in your heart and dreams in your head"— but what is that faith and what are those dreams? I would so love to know. You must write me about them sometime when, if ever, you feel the need to. You say that so often the most beautiful things are spoiled by people trying painfully to explain what they mean and feel. But I don't think I agree with you there. Rather I should hold to the opposite notion, being an inveterate author eternally on the itch to say just that last thing that can never be said.

I long to be put in that chair and hear you "go on and on" about what you are to do in your strange life. Has it been so strange? From the expression I've seen sometimes in your eyes I should imagine so—but I really know so precious little—but that little *is* precious— about you, do you know it? While I must be to you an open book—or rather five open books! Have you read *The Great God Brown* yet? I'm anxious to have you like that. As I've told you, it is my pet of all the published plays. There is so much of the secret me in it.

Help you to be sensible and womanly and real? But you are womanly—and you are real, aren't you? And as for sensible, I should be the pupil there and not the teacher. I should say no one could be more real than you, when you want to be.

The photographs got held up in the mail down here and we only got them yesterday. It is good to see us together although I shouldn't say either picture flattered either of us, what?

This letter sounds stilted and self-conscious. I was never meant to be "wise and adult," I guess. I'd rather, if I could, be very young and unwise—or very dead. None of these choices are easy, however.

Good night, Carlotta—and my love.   Gene

P.S. Hamilton, Bermuda is the best address. We have a box there and get our mail quicker that way.

---

199 • TO CARLOTTA MONTEREY.   ALS 3 pp. (Hamilton, Bermuda) [Yale]

Dec. 15, 1926

Dearest Carlotta: Well, these one-a-week mails lead to a crossing of our letters that certainly mixes things up! On the last one, inspired by your letter of the previous week, I had

1. It was published by Boni and Liveright on April 23, 1927.

written praising your calm and striving to imitate it myself, and now by the same mail I receive one revealing that you have been suffering too. I am afraid that if you are in the same mood when my last letter arrives you will find it sounds a bit callous and flat. If so, forgive me. I was trying to do as I thought you wished.

I can't bear to think of you so full of despair. What is it that happened during the week between your letters that made your world suddenly grow so black? Before, you were so confident, you felt so sure of yourself. Not make any effort to go on? No talent, no inspiration to give the world? Your life as a woman grey and vapid! Carlotta! You are a nut! There is no other word for it! You ought to be spanked! You who are so beautiful inside and out to go on denouncing yourself in that way! I will not have it! I will not listen to you! You who have so much that is rare and precious to give, weeping that you have nothing: It's incredible! And why should you believe you have made such a mess of life? And why is the future outlook so terrible? And how do you know you will be lonely? You accuse me of being vague—but your letters really give me no clue to what, definitely, is behind them. I have to guess—and hope my personal hopes, realizing at the same time that all you are thinking and feeling may by now have little to do with me. Almost three weeks is a long time—and people forget so easily even the things they desire to remember the most.

What did I mean when I wrote I had been perfectly frank? Just that! As soon as I reached here I told Agnes exactly how I had felt about leaving you. I said I loved you. I also said, and with equal truth, that I loved her. Does this sound idiotic to you? I hope not! I hope you will understand. If you should not, it means we had better—stop, while forgetting is not so horribly impossible as it might be, (for me) later. It is possible to love like that. Perhaps you know this as well as I. You are not one of the simple, one-track ones who are so lucky as always to be able to know but one thing at a time. And there are people and things one cannot tear out of one's life without leaving a wound behind that sickens not only one's own future but the future of everyone whose life is close to one afterward.

But surely you realized all this two weeks ago Friday night—why I could not stay in N.Y. although going made me suffer so terribly too. It was not a sense of duty or anything of that persuasion. It went much deeper—or else that night—but you know—and I would still be in New York—and you might already be frightfully weary of me!

But I suppose you are curious about Agnes. She has been very fine about it. She has offered to do anything about it I want—to set me free, etc., etc. However, it is ridiculous to imagine one can ever set another person free—and it is equally as asinine to imagine one can set oneself free by one's own efforts. Either the thing resolves inside one in silence, and the freeing moment comes—or it doesn't. And who can foretell?

And what would I do with freedom? And what would you do with my freedom, Strange Carlotta—granting, which I have no particular reason to expect, that you would want to be bothered with it at all? It is true I love you but I do not know you. You are so strange and beautiful to me. And I am horribly confused about all this. If I am vague it is only because I cannot be clear—yet. It takes time—time—time—to remember—or to forget—to take this road—or that.

Besides, I find it terribly hard, Carlotta, to believe you love me. I do, honestly! And I do not want to be hurt for the fun of it.

So now, you in your turn be frank when next you write. There is no reason you shouldn't be.

I wish I could see you—and talk—but perhaps that would only make things harder. On the other hand—who knows?

Good night, Dear! Sometimes I seem to smell your hair again, to feel your lips—. Those are wonderful times—but torturing.

I hope you get my flowers on Christmas. They are a symbol of what might have been—or may be. Roses are as wonderful—or as banal—as love. It all depends what we make of them.   Gene

---

200 • TO EDWARD W. BOULTON.   ALS 2 pp. (Hamilton, Bermuda) [Berg]

Dec. 20th [1926]

Dear Teddy: I have been meaning to drop you a letter for the past week or so but have been so busy trying to get moved into our new place and to get at work again, that my good intentions have gone the way they usually do.

And this isn't the letter. This is just a note to get to you in time for Christmas and to wish you the Merriest you can have under the circumstances.

It was with deep sorrow I heard the news that you have been so sick. I have always, as I hope you know, had a very soft spot for you in my heart and a deep affection. I have always felt we were genuine friends and, without the necessity of saying much about it, understood each other. And it pained me like hell to realize that T.B., my old enemy, had taken a fall out of you. Also I know, from my own experience, what you must be going through now. The first weeks at a San. or a hospital are the devil's own for getting one at the bottom of depression. But never mind! After that it gets better and better until you begin to find a new and interesting life going on around you. And Doctor Lyman's reports to me have been most encouraging. It is a matter of time—a longer time than one likes to give, perhaps—but all's well that ends well. So keep up your courage and the old "pep" will be back before you know it. I honestly didn't mind my six months in a San—after the first one was over—and I think you will find your experience will be similar.

Again, all my love and cheers to you! And anything that I can do in any possible way to help make the path easier, let me know! It will be a privilege for me!   Your friend,   Gene

---

201 • TO CARLOTTA MONTEREY.   ALS 3 pp. (Hamilton, Bermuda) [Yale]

Dec. 29th [1926]

Dearest Carlotta: I feel like a dog for not having gotten off a letter to you sooner but it was honestly not entirely my fault. I had intended to write you last Friday—then suddenly found out the boat sailed that morning instead of, as usual, on Saturday—and it was too late. A lazy man's excuse! I should not have waited until the last moment. I know—but please forgive me!

Three of your letters have arrived since my last to you. I have read and reread them—and gotten myself into a terrible state of guilty conscience and self-loathing. It seems at times as if all the suffering I find in your letters were my fault—that I ought to tell you to forget about me, to go on with your life as if I had never come into it. And yet I can't do that! Can't! The thought of losing your love is unbearable! But equally unbearable is the thought that that love is making you suffer, that, even innocently, I have brought more pain into a life already so full of pain and which, if there were any justice, or if I could have my deepest desire for it, would be only full of beauty and peace and tenderness. So I keep asking myself the same unanswerable questions over and over: What can I do? What must I do? Haven't you any answer, Dear One? I know it is difficult to ask you this but you must have thought about it and if there is any solution clear to you, for God's sake write it to me! I don't want you to suffer any more on my account—for one reason, (not the only one!) because your suffering makes me suffer.

Parts of your letters I do not quite understand. In your long one (the earliest of the three) you speak about fighting alone against all the things that you want to do, chances for happiness, joys of being yourself and indulging in self-expression, etc. My answer to that is, do not fight them—at least, not for my sake. I am not able to hold out to you any certainty of happiness for which I could with any justice ask that you give up the slightest possibility of joy elsewhere. I wish to God I were in a position to do so! Then I would demand sacrifices—for I could promise you a little joy, I think.

Yes, I know you have been much—"what men call loved." And I am jealous of those "strange hours and months." It is a pity every love cannot be that first love which is alone without regret. Afterwards, there is always the past—the past of each which lives a sinister new life in the other's mind! Even when you know that there was never a love of "gentleness & sweetness & exultation and spiritual fire" in that past. But one must be critical of one's remembrance here. In retrospect, perhaps no love ever seems to have possessed those qualities—except when death interrupted it at its height. "For a moment" you felt it? When was that moment? Tell me the exact second, won't you? That might explain much that is troubling to me, and why you wonder, "was it real."

I still dream of beaches and rest—and everything—with you. Will they never be more than dreams? Quien sabe? Woman disposes! Are you not a woman?

Yes, one might very well sum up the meaning of *Brown* as my search for God in this life. But I don't quite get you when you speak about the "physical man" of me not being in it. Or rather I agree with you that perhaps it isn't. But *Brown* isn't autobiography. There is simply a lot of my past and my consequent "insides" in it, but none of the actual relationships of the people in the play have any direct connection with any of my past ones. Dion goes down because he is the creative spirit balked of expression, turned self-destructive. That is not my case. Physically, you might say (using your wider meaning), he is weak and frustrated and derisive—Christian virtues. But I feel a large part of me—the sea part—the love of the sea—and the sea is a woman to me—is pagan and physically exultant in itself. What made you doubt—that? Would you have ever loved me if you had not intuitively known that about me? I think not. But to give one's paganism, one must be free inside—unless one is all animal and without a sternly-judging imagination.

Oh, it is hell to try and write those things. They escape or words distort them into self-mocking caricatures. But you know, Sweetheart!

I hope there was no slip-up and that you got my roses on Christmas—the symbols of my prayers for may-be! Oh Carlotta, Beautiful Dear One, how I long to see you! Sometimes that longing is like your fingers on my throat, choking me into another consciousness, another world where you are! If I could only live at the same time in two worlds! But what a shamefully inadequate gift of half to offer you—or Agnes. And yet each of those halves is really a whole me! See *Brown*. I *am* two—absolutely.

Agnes thought your note to her fine. And I—I can't tell you how fine I think your attitude is about all this. You make me feel like some particularly helpless species of worm!

You say "I wonder" about my love for you! Don't, Carlotta! That hurts me. You must believe that!

Pinchot[1] is here. He will tell you I swim, row, etc. and feel fine—also that our house will be a peach when finished off—(if the money lasts that long!). Shane is eagerly awaiting your

---

1. Ben Pinchot, a portrait photographer for whom Carlotta often posed.

gift. The books haven't arrived yet—nor the candy—it seems everything was sent by mistake to some parish sub-post office. Christmas demoralizes the service down here.

I am working hard—just finished going over *Lazarus* cutting loose ends, concentrating, clarifying. It is now a much better play. I start ahead on the new one[2] tomorrow.

If you want to do me a favor will you get me some gents writing paper—single sheet—to write you on? Impossible to buy down here.

Good'bye, Dear! Forgive me for loving you, for your love for me. It seems to have brought you nothing but pain. But I couldn't help it! You shouldn't be—so you!

(Write!)   Gene

---

202 • TO KENNETH MACGOWAN.   TLS 2 pp. (Hamilton, Bermuda) [Yale]

Dec. 30. [1926]

Dear Kenneth: Your letter with the news about the new Gering arrangement I had proposed, going through all right was welcome. I had begun to think from Madden's silence that the deal was all off—and I sure hated to see that five thou. get away from me, what with the high cost of renovating houses in Bermuda. I hope there will be no further hitch.

Now here is something that is damned important—*damned* important! I have been laboring for the past two weeks like hell on *Lazarus* and I have made what are very grave alterations and cuts—especially in the first scene which I have taken out of the Bible—all the Saint John Gospel stuff out, etc.—and most of Lazarus talk, relying on a few sentences of his and his laughter. The scene has now, I think, real mystery and power—is much shorter, of course. It was always, to my mind, the weakest in the play. There was too much in it that reminded one of a regular Biblical play—a bad start for *Laz*. I have also paid particular attention throughout to getting the chants of the Chorus and Crowd into a more definite sound pattern. And I have cleared up Caligula at the end and trimmed all the loose ends throughout. It is now, I think, a much better play. But you know me when I get after my own stuff—after I've had time for perspective and you will know what to expect. Now this new script *must* be used for the Chicago production. So will you have Madden cable me the moment they sign the contract and I will get this script off to you by the first boat thereafter. I don't want to send it until I am sure they are on. I have only the one. When you get the script will you have copies made at once? They will have to be done by a damn good careful stenographer, and the copies gone over afterwards for errors. How about that girl who used to be at the Actors' office? At any rate, put someone you can trust on it, who will take an interest and be absolutely accurate. I am so tired of getting scripts through Madden that are full of the most absurd errors afterwards. I have to go over them line for line—it's as much of a job as typing them myself. And hang on to the script when you get it as you would your life. I would go entirely nuts if anything happened to it after the hard work I have put in on it. Send two scripts to me. Let the Chicago crowd get their own made. Send one at once to Kommer to show Reinhardt, and give one to Fitzie to send Berkman[1] for his Russian translation.

---

2. *Strange Interlude.*

1. Alexander Berkman (1870?–1936), Russian expatriate intellectual and anarchist. He was also a translator and friend of M. Eleanor Fitzgerald (Fitzie), the triumvirate's business manager, with whom he had worked on the anarchist publication *Blast*. O'Neill was interested in having Berkman translate *Lazarus Laughed* into Russian for the planned Danchenko production.

I am intending to start work on *Strange Interlude* tomorrow—the 31—hunch—one year on the wagon, my boy! I am going to drink fifty lime squashes watching the new year in and, at least, put my lunch in memory of the good old days.

It is good news about *Beyond*. I sure hope it holds up and runs along. As for *The Straw* and Pauline Lord, that sounds like a damn good idea, if you can get her. But if *Beyond* holds its own why not do the Lord thing separately—not close *Beyond* to do it? I am sure *Straw* with Polly in it would make money. And I could go over it again, if the proposition goes through.

Did you get my check for twenty-five I sent you some weeks ago?

I have sent *Marco* to Liveright after throughly going over it and cutting. The next to the last scene I cut out entirely and I switched the whole scheme of acts, scenes into a much better plan. The play is now much shorter and more wieldy.

I do not know just what to make of the Reinhardt situation. It seemed from both your letter and Madden's to be fairly uncertain as far as New York is concerned. Perhaps when he gets the play in detail things will be different. For I think this new version is some play! I have a real swelled head about it.

Well, I guess that's about all—except to say that we are having a hell of an overcrowded time of it in the little house, that I am working in a bedroom with children, carpenters, plumbers, masons and whatever else you have doing all sorts of telling chorus work in the near vicinity, and it doesn't bother me much which proves that I can't really be as artistic as the prints would have it. Also we are discovering that the average Bermuda artisan more than makes up for his lower wages by the longer time he takes. It is a scream to watch them doing "stills" of men at labor—but the scream is of laughter only when they are working on the place next door. But the place will be a wonder when it is finally fixed up—absolutely ideal for me and will surely pay me big dividends in the work I shall do here. I love it. Shane and Oona and Agnes are all fine. You and Eddy *must* come down and see us once we get settled and have a house—or at least half a one to place at your disposal.

All our best to all of you! Happy New Year!   Gene

P.S. I'm worried about something. I sent you a check for 25 to get roses for Carlotta for X'mas. Did you ever get it? The letter was addressed care of Mansfield Theatre or to Charlton St.—was mailed two weeks or more ago. Hope it's O.K.

There is lots I don't write. Emotionally I'm still up in the air. Perhaps this will be good for *Interlude* (author's thought!) but otherwise it hain't purty.

---

203 · TO MRS. WILLIAM BUTLER YEATS.[1]   TLS(X) 1 p. (Hamilton, Bermuda)
[SUNY, Stony Brook]

January 6, 1926 [1927]

My Dear Mrs. Yeats: I have been intending to write to you for the past fortnight since your letter arrived. I hope my cable reached you safely.

I am only too pleased that the Dublin Drama League wants to do *The Emperor Jones*. I wish I could get to Dublin to see your production. Perhaps I can. I will certainly try to. It is about time, I think, for although I am all Irish on both sides of my family, I have never been nearer to Ireland than the harbor of Queenstown—when I used to be a sailor on transatlantic liners.

1. Wife of the Irish poet and playwright, who was apparently assisting him with the Dublin Drama League. Yeats had cofounded the League in 1919 to broaden the scope of the Abbey Theatre by presenting plays by non-Irish writers.

I am very glad you finally got in touch with me through Mr. Colum.[2] I cannot understand the agent, Campbell's, replies to your inquiries during the past three years. He had absolutely no authority to tell you the rights were not obtainable—in fact he had every reason to know that this was not the case. But Mr. Campbell seems to have handled my stuff very stupidly all around, until I finally had to tell my American agents that they must pick another London agent for my plays. At present Mr. Golding Bright is acting in that capacity.

The last time I heard from Dr. MacCartan[3] must have been about eighteen months ago in a letter forwarded to me by Dr. Maloney.[4]

I sincerely hope you will do more of my things now that you know that any one of them you care to try is available.   Yours truly,   Eugene O'Neill

---

204 • TO MRS. WILLIAM BUTLER YEATS.   TLS(X) 1 p. (Hamilton, Bermuda)
[SUNY, Stony Brook]

January 16, 1927

My dear Mrs. Yeats: Your last letter must have crossed one of mine to you. I am very much pleased to hear that Mr. Robinson[1] is to direct *Jones*. I have always had a very great admiration for his work as a playwright.

May I make one suggestion? The title is *The Emperor Jones* and not just simply *Emperor Jones*. This difference seems to me to have something quite vital to do with the innate love of grand titles of the negro of Jones' type.

As for your being grateful for the permission, I feel that that is all on my side. I am immensely pleased that you are going to do it. It will be a favor if you can find time to let me know how the production goes.   Yours faithfully,   Eugene O'Neill

---

205 • TO CARLOTTA MONTEREY.   ALS 3 pp. (Hamilton, Bermuda) [Yale]

Jan. 23rd [1927]

Dear Carlotta: As you will note, the paper has arrived and it is fitting a letter to you should be the first to be written on it. It pleases me immensely. I love the texture of good paper either in books or stationery. Will you let me know in your next how much it cost so I can send you a check? They had a value of fifteen dollars on it but I don't know whether this is right or not, as they put false values on things sent here frequently to get by the duty.

What do you mean, anyone who keeps letters should be shot? I have kept yours. Must I turn the old Colt automatic loose on myself for wanting that consolation in my loneliness? Seriously, if you really feel that way about it, I will destroy them—but it would cause me a most awful heartache, and I can hardly believe you want to be so stern.

What you say about the Venetian portrait painter and the German etcher sounds interesting. I sure hope one or the other—or both—get something worth while of you. It seems to me I've never seen anything that did you any sort of justice. Don't you feel yourself this is true?

2. Padraic Colum (1881–1972), Irish critic, poet, and playwright, whom O'Neill met through sculptor Edmond T. Quinn and his wife.

3. Patrick McCartan (1878–1966), Irish physician, who fought for Irish causes in America.

4. O'Neill's New York physician.

1. Lennox Robinson (1886–1958), Irish playwright, director, and critic, who became a producer at Dublin's Abbey Theatre in 1910 and remained associated with it until his death.

All your talk about growing old leaves me skeptical. It isn't flattery, it's only a fact to remark that, until you told me, I didn't think you were thirty yet. You may feel terribly old inside at times but your face will certainly never confess it. And you say about yourself "*has been* desirable." Has been! May the devil confound you for such a libel on yourself as that past tense!

What you say about sophistication is perfectly true—but like all other words it has two meanings. You're thinking of it in its best sense and I was of its worst. I've known many sophisticated people and undoubtedly they were bad specimens of the type for when their layer of sophistication was peeled off or run out—there was nothing left but an appalling boredom with sophistication. As for the primitive, honest soul when dealing with it at least we know that if it causes us suffering it can be made to suffer in return. And that is something by way of consolation. However, I hold no brief for the primitive honest body. He is a dull lot, too—and he is usually too self-conscious of his simplicity to be primitive, and doesn't know enough about life to be honest about it. In brief, another fake. But surely there is a happy medium—who is always unhappy because life is not so simple to him as to the other two. You belong to it, don't you? And don't I? Or are we fakes too?

Yes, to know life one must live with people—but not too long, one must know when to quit—it is like a training in stock for an actor—or else they get as blurred and unfamiliar and too close to one as those perfect strangers who are one's father and mother and wife and children. The trouble with people is that if you live too long with them you get to look and act and think like them and you forget Infinity and the sea and earth and moon and stars and begin to believe that life is people—which is too egotistically idiotic. No, I am not sure that God is life but I'm perfectly certain men aren't life!

But that's about enough of that! It sounds as if I were giving a Daddy's Philosophical Bedtime Secret for Today!

I am keeping my days full of work and sun and sea. As for thinking, it always came hard to me so I don't have to worry much about that. I can remember when I was a boy, my Mother, whenever she would see me thoughtful, would ask suspiciously "What are you doing, Eugene?" "Thinking," I would say portentiously. "What is the matter with you—do you feel sick?" she would ask with a naive maternal solicitude that used to exasperate me. But now I know she was deeply right about it. She guessed the truth. Only sick people think. Well people live. Thinking is a quack medicine invented by the first ape who felt too sick to climb trees. He thought of a reason why all apes should give up climbing to the heights.

But I drivel, I drool on. Good night, Carlotta. My love always. When shall we be able to talk? Never, if we stop to think about it, maybe. Well, Life knows when. But we *will* talk, won't we? There's a million things—in one thing—to say. I speak for myself. You've forgotten.   Gene

---

206 • TO ALEXANDER BERKMAN.   TLS 1 p. (Hamilton, Bermuda) [IISH]

January 29, 1927

My dear Berkman,   I was very glad indeed to get your letter—and very glad to have your good opinion on *Lazarus Laughed*. I have been immensely pleased ever since I talked with Fitzie about your doing the translation. Most of my stuff, I believe, has not been very well done into foreign languages, and as I have a very meager knowledge of them myself, I have been in no position to check up. It has been all a gamble. But with you I feel secure, naturally.

As regards royalties, the agreement Mr. Madden is proposing is only for your protection in case we do manage to get some out of Russia. I am writing directly to Lunarcharsky,[1] as author to author, in the hope that he will do something about it. I have no great hopes of this, but since the production of my *Hairy Ape* in Moscow they seem to regard me as a pure proletarian writer. There may be some chance for us. And I have let them steal three of my plays already, without making any protest.

Yes, it is a long time since that night at Romany Marie's![2] But I am quite sure that you do not remember me better than I do you. I have a very clear picture of you in my mind to this day. I had had a very deep admiration for you for years, and that meeting was sort of an unexpected wish fulfillment. As for my fame, (God help us!) and your infame, I would be willing to exchange a good deal of mine for a bit of yours. It is not so hard to write what one feels as truth. It is damned hard to live it!

I asked Kenneth Macgowan to give Fitzie a revised script to send to you as soon as he had some made, and I will check up on this and find if one has been sent. If not, I will get one mailed to you in the near future.

All kindest regards to you. Write to me again sometime if you feel in the mood.   Yours, Eugene O'Neill

---

207 • TO CARLOTTA MONTEREY.   ALS 3 pp. (Hamilton, Bermuda) [Yale]

Feb. 10th [1927]

Dear Carlotta: I've been meaning to write to you for the past week but I've honestly been slaving so hard on *Strange Interlude*—working from eight-thirty in the morning until three or four in the afternoon, staying in bed and having my breakfast and lunch sent up to me to insure against disturbing interruptions—that for the remainder of the day, after my daily swim to keep fit, I've felt too done up and dull-witted to attempt anything beyond browsing around in books. This play, *Strange Interlude*,—and it is really two plays, being nine acts in all, and will have to be done—if ever!—on two consecutive nights—justifies the "strange" part of its title. It is so strange to me at times that I feel as if something inside of me were writing about something inside the lives of people that gets beyond any of the usual psychological evaluations. I seem to hit on things that, dramatically at least, have never been touched before. This is my proud feeling in my good moments. In the black slack-water periods—and they are black indeed!—I see myself falling so short of my mark, involved in such insoluble and inexpressible complications of the soul, that I groan with despair and curse the day I ever attempted such a grinding impossibility. But it does go on and I go on with it, sometimes pushing and sometimes being pulled! When it is done—and by this I mean even the first draft of it—I shall emit a frantic shriek of joy and deliverance that, if you be but cocking a responsive ear at the time, will be heard above the rattle of brains and taxicabs in N.Y.

A question before I forget it. When did you send Shane his boat-builder present? I ask because it did not arrive here until last Monday's boat. He is having all kinds of fun with it and asks me to state that he will be writing to you soon, via Gaga who takes his dictation for him, and thank you in his own words.

As for your letters, all right, since you appear to be so set on it. I will destroy them as you do mine. All the same I think you are unduly sensitive and apprehensive about them—and

1. Anatoly Lunacharsky (1875–1933), Russian playwright.
2. Greenwich Village restaurant that O'Neill frequented in 1916–17.

rather hard on me. But if you will send me a photo of the portrait I'll forgive you. I'll certainly love to have that, Carlotta; and much gratitude to you!

A news photographer down here, a friend of mine, formerly a ship's steward, has been taking snaps of me in my Kayak (Eskimo canoe model), rowboat and swimming. Some of them I am tickled to death with. They look and "feel" like me. I'm going to send you some prints soon. The ones Muray took of me that day in his studio have rather provoked me. He couldn't leave them alone and the retouching is badly done and can be plainly seen. And you heard me make him promise he'd leave them alone, didn't you? It's too bad. They would have been good pictures, if given a chance. Why will he do this?

I wrote to Kenneth and mentioned you for "Pompeia" in *Lazarus Laughed* at Chicago but said I thought you were disgusted with the stage. Even if you weren't, Carlotta, much as I would love to have you in it, I don't know enough and haven't faith enough in this Chicago group to advise you to be interested. They offered me a five thousand dollar bonus to permit the play to be done in Chicago first—and I had to have the money and that's the answer. I figured that Chicago means nothing in my life and if the production is a fiasco it can't hurt the play much or for long as far as New York is concerned. It's humiliating to have to do such things but our place in Ridgefield didn't sell—and hasn't—and we had counted on that money to pay for fixing up Spithead—and, briefly, I was in a hole and still am. No one at the American Play has been able to pry the film magnates loose from any gold for my stuff—and *Beyond The Horizon,* due to the stupid juggling of the man who took it over from the Actors' Theater, has gone "blooey." So you see. The smell of all money, as Vespasian said, is sweet— at times—even Chicago money. However, the situation isn't dire at all. I'm not bewailing— only explaining Chicago to you. It also explains why I'm not likely to come to New York in the near future or go out to Chicago for any rehearsals or performance—that and the fact that I *must* finish *Strange Interlude* before going any place. But I'm never very keen on seeing any of my plays anyway. By the time I'm through all my writing of them they've been produced—under ideal conditions, of course!—in the theatre of my mind, and all that comes after is a more-or-less commercial necessity and a disillusioning anti-climax.

So, if you're sailing for Europe on June 15th, God knows when we will see each other again! Probably not until you return in the fall. It is quite possible, for the financial reasons stated above, that it will be incumbent on us to spend the summer here at Spithead where there is no rent to pay. Moving a family from place to place comes high.

And yet I want so much to see you again! Your last letter—but one—sounded so unhappy and lonely. I wish we could talk together. There is something rotten and wrong about all this. I feel as if you were going out of my life forever and that there was nothing I could do, in fairness, to hold you. We write and write and we never mention love except as a conventional tail to letters, and act like two shy defensive people who are in deadly fear of being wounded. Do I dare believe you still love me—that you ever did love me? I look at your letters and wonder and doubt and am afraid and slink back into myself. Do I dare ask you if you do? But your answer, I am afraid, would be evasive and by its evasion, wound. You are afraid your letters would be seen. They aren't—but what difference if they were? Of what have you or I to be ashamed? Why should we be so damned cautious? We have no common ground of meeting where absolute frankness could console us. Yet I want you in my life but I know I am losing you. If I do, well at least remember me without bitterness. Perhaps the only happiness we ever really possess wholly is the dream that was too rare to be owned. I speak for myself. You are rare. And I have loved you deeply as Carlotta—but now Carlotta leaves me and becomes a dream whose letters I interpret for signs of my Carlotta— not without unhappiness.

God give you what you want—and need!   Gene

March 4th [1927]

Dear Carlotta: Well, at last I've finished it. *Strange Interlude* is now an accomplished fact—at least, the first draft of it is—for better or worse. I'm still much too near to it to be able to view it with any dispassionate judgment and tell how successfully I've accomplished what I set out to do. Now it will be typed—then put away to rest until sometime in late spring when I've recovered perspective and am capable of going over it critically. All my feeling about it now is confined to a deep joy that such a "work" is out of my system. I'm exhausted and pining to rest. I've been driving myself—or more correctly being driven by it—to the limit during the time since my last letter, working as much as eleven hours on some days, from eight-thirty in the a.m. until 5 in the p.m. and afterwards in the evening. My face—my eyes especially—is all caved in as if some vampire had been "scoffing" my life up! Well, not to be too melodramatic about it, I'm damned tired and determined to take a lengthy vacation with much sun bathing and loafing in the sea and tennis.

Yes, I'll admit nine acts and two evenings do sound a bit impractical but I don't think they will be. I need a producer with courage, not necessarily one with much money. It isn't an expensive production. Honestly, I sincerely believe this play can be a financial as well as an artistic success. A two-play play has never been so before because no playwright has ever really written in that form. They have always either written two distinct plays with no real connection except that they are about the same characters; or else they have written one play that is simply two plays in length. But mine is really two plays in one play. I know that anyone who sees the first will want to see the second—*won't be able to help* seeing the second, I think! Of course, the Broadway dogmatists of what's done in the theatre will shudder and cry impossible, but they've been doing just that, on one ground or another, ever since I wrote *The Emperor Jones.* The real truth is I was practically born in the theatre and I couldn't do anything that wasn't practical in a theatre if I tried. I'm too wrapped up in the theatre as a medium. I've simply made it a bit broader, higher and deeper than the usual show-shop but what I write always *can* be done. I've never yet written a closet drama. My only mistake is in always assuming that there are actors who can play roles, like "Lazarus," for example, when of course there are not.

The photo of the painting hasn't arrived yet. I hope it will soon. By separate cover I'm sending you some of the outdoor ones of me taken about a month ago.

What does *Strange Interlude* make you think of? No, there is nothing of us in it—at least, it was all planned out even before we met at Belgrade. Of course, there's almost everything in it that makes people mad with rapture or tortured beyond belief—emotions out of my own experience but principally, in this play, out of my experience with others' experiences as I have known them and suffered or been happy in or with them. There is no one character in it who, as "Dion" in *Brown,* or a number of my characters, partly reproduces phases of my character or experience. This whole play is I, my experience, you might say, but the characters in it individually more closely resemble many, many men I have known. There is a lot of you in the woman, I think (come to think of it) and yet she is wholly unlike you. And there you are!

And I am hungry to talk to you, Carlotta! Yes!, as Lazarus says.

I am awfully sorry you have to go to Europe alone. I wish I had an aura or a ghost or my soul or something—but that wouldn't be very satisfying, would it?   Always   Gene

P.S. Sure I'll give you a script of *Lazarus*—when I get one! Haven't a one here now.

March 27, 1927

Dear Carlotta: The photograph of your portrait is grand! I am immensely pleased to own it and am going to have it framed for my study. The painting itself must be beautiful. I look forward to seeing it. I can imagine how the colors you have described give it life and intensity. My only criticism is that as a likeness it makes the lower part of your face appear too heavy. Don't you think so? But the artist has captured your general quality faithfully.

Speaking of likeness, the little passport one you enclosed strikes me as being a lot better than most of the Muray ones.

Yes, I do look pretty ghastly in those Bermuda Trade Development Board pictures that appeared in the *Times,* etc. Not to add glum! They were taken more or less under duress. Such is the fate of one so notorious as to become an advertising medium! But it has its compensations. The steamship people are extra obliging and reasonable in their rates to us— and so on and so forth. All of which helps in bad years when my plays are noticeably unproduced. I'm glad you liked the Greyflex ones I sent. In my opinion they are damned good—more like the real me than all the studio-posed stuff.

After finishing *Strange Interlude,* I turned right around and went all over it. This turned out to be a tough job and took me much longer than I thought. Since then—with intervals of much moving from one house to another and trying to get many years of accumulated papers sorted and filed in my study—I've been taking a vacation and doing a great deal of all-day boating and tennis and swimming. And it has developed into quite a social time too—that is, for me. A number of people we know, or who know people we know, have been down on trips. The last to appear was Lawrence Langner of the Guild whom I have known slightly for a number of years. The Guild are again considering doing *Marco Millions* next season. I hope something will come of it. With their company and theatre they could probably do better with that play than anyone else. But I have my doubts about the deal going through. There seems to be always some hitch between the Guild and my stuff.

There has been an interesting gal visiting our next door neighbors (the Hubers, a young couple from Philadelphia, extremely social but likable in spite of it). The gal is Delphine Dodge, the sole female driver of high speed motor boats who drove in last year's Gold Cup race. She is a daughter of Horace Dodge, one of the two brothers who owned and invented the Dodge motor car. She is far from fair to look at but is a good sport and full of a queer driven intensity, like one of her racing boats. You would be interested in her, I think.

Your diet doesn't sound very appetizing. I can't, for the life of me, imagine you as sick even in the most minor degree. You have always seemed to me so strong and full of vitality and health that I'd as soon believe a steam engine could be sick! This is a rather dastardly failure to sympathize, what? Well then, you'll have to grow thin and wan and give up your Viking's-daughter body! Just what is the cure at Marienbad—taking waters or what? I've heard about it and read about it so many times but haven't the ghost of an idea.

Eugene is down here now on his spring vacation. He has grown enormously since last summer and must be six feet now. I find him a son I can well take a paternal pride in. He is my sort.

Write when you feel in the mood. I wish to God we could have a long talk together, Carlotta.   Ever,   Gene

A portrait of Carlotta.

210 • TO ALEXANDER BERKMAN.   TLS 2 pp. (Hamilton, Bermuda) [IISH]

April 14, 1927

Dear Berkman: I received your letter a few days ago with your letter to Mr. Madden enclosed. Do not mind his not having sent you the agreement before this. Agents are a slow lot, especially where something connected with Russia is concerned and they see no money in it. You can consider the agreement as already made and binding with me, and I really do most of my own arranging myself. Madden simply acts more or less as a collector—a very necessary thing where American managers are concerned.

I have no definite idea myself how things stand with Danchenko and *Lazarus*. All I know is what I heard through Fitzie, Kenneth Macgowan and Bulgakov,[1] the Moscow Art Theatre actor who is now associated with the Provincetown group, and who is a friend of Danchenko's. As I understand it, he told them all he wanted to do *Lazarus Laughed* as soon as he got through with his year's contract with the movies, which ought to expire next fall, I believe.

I will send your translation to Bulgakov when you send a copy to me. He is a great admirer of the play, and he also knows English fairly well. As for me, I feel absolutely confident that you will do a grand job with it. This is a satisfying feeling, believe me, after my hit-or-miss experience with German translations.

Did you ever hear anything of the stir raised in Moscow when they did *Desire Under the Elms* at the Kamerny? It seems they held a public trial of the character "Abby" in the play, on the charge of having murdered a child. An audience of the intelligentsia were the jury. I believe Korolenko[2] presided and Lunacharsky had something to do with it. All the prominent critics testified for or against, and she was finally found entirely innocent by unanimous vote because, it was argued, under the curse of private property and inhibited by New England morals she was forced into it. I got all this information from quotations from the *Izvestia* and other papers which have been quoted in the American press. It evidently must have created a bit of a stir in Moscow or they would never have given it this exceptional public notice, would they? I would be glad to hear of any details you may have heard of it.

I have just finished a new play, and am now taking a bit of a vacation. This new play is a two-nights-long piece, *Strange Interlude,* in which I attempt to do in a play all that can be done in a novel. I will send you a copy sometime when I get some extra ones made, if you would care to read it. I think it would interest you.

Mrs. O'Neill and I are both "in the pink." She joins me in all best wishes to you. Sincerely yours,   Eugene O'Neill

---

211 • TO AGNES BOULTON O'NEILL.   ALS 1 p. ([Hamilton, Bermuda]) [Yale]

Friday evening / [April 15?, 1927]

Own, Own Wife: God, how I miss you![1] And how horribly alone I have felt ever since returning here! I actually broke down on the bed in our room in a fit of hysterical crying when I first went up there. I know this is unreasonable, a bit absurd when you are only going to be gone a week, but my whole control seems gone and my inner being is in pretty

---

1. Michael Bulgakov.
2. Vladimir G. Korolenko (1853–1921), Russian short-story writer and journalist.

1. Agnes went to Connecticut to visit her father, who was dying of tuberculosis.

shattered shape. *I need you, need you, need you!*—intensely more now than ever before in our married life. I feel—it's so hard to attempt to explain—as if this were a crucial period in my life, an ordeal, a test on which everything I have built depended—God knows what!—and our lives were in the balance. And it's so bitterly hard to be alone—although I know your love is here with me and in that faith I can come through.

This sounds incoherent. Well, I feel that way. But don't be frightened. There's no danger of anything you might fear. I'm just alone and miserable, and will be until your return.

Because I love you! Remember and think over our talk last night.

I kiss your dear lips and body. Your Lover always   Gene

---

212 • TO AGNES BOULTON O'NEILL.   ALS 6 pp. (Spithead / [Bermuda])
[Harvard]

Saturday night / 4/16/27

My Own Aggie: Well, I've certainly been feeling lost since that moment when your dear familiar beautiful face blurred out into the background of the receding *Fort Victoria* and I about faced and took up my burden of a wifeless life for a spell. There was nothing of the slightest interest in the remaining mail at the post office—and it wouldn't have interested me any if there had been. So, after finding the Grays office closed, I drove right back to Our Home. *Our Home!* I feel that very much about Spithead, don't you? That this place is in some strange symbolical fashion our reward, that it is the permanent seat of our family—like some old English family estate. I already feel like entailing it in my will so that it must always be background for our children! I love Spithead—and not with my old jealous, bitter possessiveness—my old man Cabotism!—but as ours, not mine except as mine is included in ours. The thought of the place is indissolubly intermingled with my love for you, with our nine years of marriage that, after much struggle, have finally won to this haven, this ultimate island where we may rest and live toward our dreams with a sense of permanence and security that here we do belong. "And, perhaps, the Hairy Ape at last belongs." I have, as you know, never felt this deep peace of permanence about any place where we have lived before. Perhaps, a lot of this feeling is due to the change in me. In the old—and how really far distant and improbable those days seem to me now!—alcoholic times there could be no confidence in the security of anything. Perhaps we should rechristen Spithead Water Wagon Manor! It is certainly connected in my mind with sobriety and sane living.

But what I started out to say was that it is a very lonely home right now. I miss you so much, Dearest! It isn't a keen stabbing pain, because I can keep telling myself that, after all, ten days are not so horribly long, but a dull aching longing as if the Familiar Spirit of our home whose presence alone gives it meaning and makes it *my* home, were gone from it. It is now just a large empty house in which I sit alone at my desk and am desolately conscious that I am alone, that no matter how late I stay up there will be no sound of your coming along the empty rooms to my room, that when I go to bed there will be no other half of me lying beside me and spiritually completing me—without the necessity of saying a word or making a movement, the sound of your breath, sleeping, is enough, it is my breath too, without it my heart stifles and beats laboriously as if it were only hitting on one lung! And it is! We are the two lungs that give one life its life—our life which we have slowly created out of our separate lives.

You seem to think I never have such thoughts any more. But I do! Many, many times. Perhaps I should tell you of them more than I do, as I used to do in more hectic shifting days, but the reason I don't is that I have come to accept them as a recognized part of my being, that

I seem to feel them in you too and that I expect you to feel them in me, that they are of the soul and sound bald and shallow when forced into words, that here silence, the silence of a love that knows itself loved in return, is the only eloquent speech.

I love you! For over nine years I have loved you and you alone, loved you with my whole being, without reservation given you my life, with joy in that giving even at times when everything else in the world was joyless. That is all I can say to you, now or ever, in that utterance all is uttered, it is the deep whole from which all my emotions flow, from you out to the world and back to you at last.

I seem to hear a single doubt, an exception, a sorrowful suspicion creeping into your mind to destroy its peace. You will think of Carlotta. Don't. Dear One! Please! If you could only look into my heart and mind and see how little trace is left there of that incident, you would never give it a thought, much less an apprehensive thought, again! You would find in me only an amused—yes, ironically amused!—memory of an outcrop of childish vanity by that Playboy part of me. Also, an astonishment—an amazement at myself for my utter lack of a sense of humor at that time! You would be amused too! Honestly you would! For I was never in love with her. That was nonsense. I was simply dramatizing a gratifying shot in the arm of my vanity! As for your fear that there could ever, under any circumstances, be a recurrence of the symptoms, I swear to you that's ridiculous. When you begin to smile at the ghosts in yourself they never materialize again. Mine don't, I know. You give the lady credit for too much intriguiness—and ability at it. After all, am I an ass? Or an innocent, with my life behind me? One hair of your head is more to me than the whole body and soul, liver and lights, of any other woman! If I lost your love, I'd go mad with grief! Am I liable to long for any such exchanges of peace and fulfillment with you for torture and frustration? No, thanks! I love you and only you, now and always. You should forgive my one amusing (yes, it is!) gesture of a virginal Casanova—as you would forgive Shane kissing Peggy Ann to show what a little man he was!—and then banish it from your mind, except when you want a laugh!

I let you into my deepest inner secrets! This is bad policy even with a wife one loves! One should keep one's posing before the mirror of oneself in decent obscurity. It is an awfully adolescent, undeveloped nakedness I am revealing to you! But I do want you to laugh at that incident, to see it clearly for what it was. *Was!* "Dead for a ducat, dead!" as Hamlet says.

All this about C.—which I write because I so earnestly and with justice want to relieve your mind of the slightest consideration about it—again makes me think to warn you that if, as is most improbable, any malicious person, alleged friend or otherwise, should bring to your ears any tattle about it, that you shut them up at the first word. For I told you the whole inside truth of it, all there is to be told, when I came down. And I know there are so many people, mostly "friends," who would get a mean satisfaction out of "getting your goat" by some innuendo or other, that it's just as well to be ready for them. After all, we've got to remember I'm in the "show business" and a good subject to hang any rag of scandal upon for the multitude of the failures and the envious ones. And she did come to rehearsals twice!

When I write the above, I feel bitterly ashamed of myself, ashamed of having been such an ass as, even innocently, to have ever allowed myself to do anything that could lay you open to being wounded. It was rotten of me! It was stupid and meaningless! Forgive me again! It will never happen again, I assure you!

But enough of that! I certainly never intended to speak of it when I sat down to write you. All I want to do is get it out of your mind when it is so entirely forgotten and out of mine! The fact that you recur to it so often has made me feel guilty toward you even yet.

Well, the bold Dan hasn't showed on the lot yet. I had a solitary day—swam, took a nap, practiced tennis strokes, played with Oona for a while and gave her your present. She went to sleep tonight without protest except to call for you wonderingly and beseechingly a few times. She was tired out—but healthily tired, she is in fine shape, don't worry about her. Shane I allowed to go to the matinee of *Rin Tin Tin* with Peggy Ann and their nurse who invited him in Mrs. Huber's name. He returned all steamed up about it. He evidently got a great thrill out of it.

Well, it's bedtime. Good-night, Sweetheart! I love you so damned much! We must get away alone to beaches and places when you return. We don't do enough of that. We ought to have our private life together as well as our life in our family. Kisses & kisses, Dear!

(I'll add some to this tomorrow and let you know anything new.)

Sunday / [April 17, 1927]

Awoke this morning feeling pretty poorly. My detestable hives seem to have come back on me with a bang overnight—in spite of diet and everything. It is ridiculous that this petty ailment should keep on making so many fine days miserable for me. There must surely be something that can be done to stop them altogether, once and for all, if one only knew what that something is. You might speak to Hamilton about it—or call up Doctor Eugene Du Bois whose address was 1215 Park Ave.

I have been thinking of Teddy. I feel guilty because I haven't written him—but you know how one keeps postponing from week to week the important things one ought to do. I hope you will tell him, if he is strong enough to care about listening, that my intentions at least have been good—and of how sincerely sorry I am. You know that I have always felt a real affection and respect for Teddy. If there is anything more that can be done to make his lot easier where I can be of help, by all means do it.

Oona & Shane have been looking for Easter eggs that Gaga had hidden about the grounds—and getting a lot of fun out of it. They are both fine.

A depressing bit of news is that our water in the barrels is now all gone. This morning Simons and Johnston began getting some from the tank in buckets but there's very little there and it's hard to get at, so I suppose we had better see about ordering some from Wathington's. There's no sign of rain.

It has seemed horribly lonely here today and I miss you damnably. The fact that I feel so rotten makes it less bearable, of course, but that's only a tiny part of it. Dearest One, I love you so! Maybe it is tonic to have you go away every once in a long time. It makes me realize how much I do love you, how tremendous and deep a part you have in my life, and how beautiful and sweet you are! But one day of that loneliness would be enough! Ten is too much! I'm already counting the days before you get back. What joy your return will mean to me! Please don't let anything keep you one hour more than you planned, if you love me! I should be too horribly disappointed!

Your prognostications about Harold[1] have been wrong so far. He hasn't showed up at all. Hurn was here for a short time this afternoon. This morning I worked at reading the Sagas but didn't find much that works in with my scheme.

I can't understand not having heard from Harry on the Ridgefield mortgage transfer. I hope when you get in touch with all those people in New York it will result in your getting some good news to bring back to me. God knows we need it!

Don't forget Evangeline![2]

Again all my love, Own Sweetheart! I can't tell you how much I long for you to be here again! Kisses!   Your   Gene

---

1. Harold DePolo.
2. Evangeline Adams, a New York astrologist whom Agnes visited at her husband's behest.

P.S. Don't forget to mail those four letters I gave you, if you have not already done so.

Monday noon / [April 18, 1927]

Can't resist the temptation of dropping you a word more. It's stormy and blowing a gale today, but no rain, worse luck! A new crop of hives sprung out on me during the night in spite of my taking soda and the diet and all. Can't understand it. It's laughable in a way but I can't quite appreciate the joke, so if you get a chance to consult anyone who savvys the secret why and wherefore of this affliction be sure and get all the dope you can. I know this is an imposition when you have so much to do and worry about so if it's too much bother, don't worry about it.

Oona and Shane are fine so there's nothing for you to be anxious about there. I hope you got my Marconigram to the *Victoria* in answer to yours.

If there is any very important mail today I'll get another letter off to you by the supplementary. I'm sending this in this afternoon.

I'm so lonely, Dearest! It's hard to think there's a full week more to wait before you'll be back again! I certainly hope I won't have to go up and leave you for a long, long time. You can explain to Langner how unwilling I am to go unless it's a case of absolute necessity— unless I have absolute guarantees that they're going to do something of mine, not just argue about it.

I hope you had a good passage and were not sick. Good'bye for this time, My Own Sweetheart! I love you! Come back to me soon! I'll cable if I don't get any cables about anything.   I kiss your dear lips!   Gene

---

213 • TO AGNES BOULTON O'NEILL.   ALS 3 pp. ([Hamilton, Bermuda])
[Harvard]

Friday / [April 22?, 1927]

Dearest Aggie: I'm writing this in pencil because I'm laid up in bed with a rotten sore throat—quit smoking abruptly for two days and this is result—or perhaps just a coincidence. I've just answered your second cable in answer to mine of yesterday. I know mine was harsh and unreasonable but I had been counting the days and was frightfully disappointed—and was sick in the bargain and dejected about Ridgefield and financial worry in general—and because I'd heard from Arthur[1] turning down *Lazarus* and it seemed as if our tough luck would never break and, looking ahead, that we're heading for a most frightful cropper unless something turns up soon. So forgive my cable. I need you, that's all.

Your cable of today sounds hectic. I cannot imagine what new trouble your folks can have gotten into. But I feel compelled to say something—and if I'm talking about things that never entered your head, I hope you'll forgive me because I absolutely feel it's necessary to guard against these possibilities right now for the sake of your happiness and peace of mind and my own and my power to work. Firstly, don't bring Budgie or anyone of them back with you. It would be fatal to all concerned. Speaking for myself, I simply couldn't be fair about it. I feel too strong a resentment in the matter. Nothing could be solved by it. It would only be an added complication. And just now I owe it to myself—and you owe it to me—to have comparative peace of mind or I shall go bugs entirely and there will be no work done. Even your going away has thrown me completely out. I haven't written a line on anything, and I see no hope of doing so until you get back and life gets regular again.

1. Producer Arthur Hopkins.

Secondly, look out how you involve me financially. You know what our situation is. We simply cannot do it. People have got to help themselves or get help elsewhere. It is morally unfair for anyone to look to us at this juncture beyond what we are doing for your father. And as long as your people own property like Point Pleasant which is salable I cannot help but look upon their holding on to it while they accept gifts from others who are themselves in difficulties as not honorable and an imposition. Even in the case of helping your father, I'll admit I have felt this. It goes against my grain somehow. And you know I am no niggard. But just now my foot is down. It has to be in self-preservation. I'm doing all I can or will do.

Now don't get sore at the above. I think I am speaking within my rights as your husband and for the peace of our relationship. If none of my suppositions have any basis, then all the better, I apologize. They are only inspired in me by your cable. I feel damn resentful and disgusted that in addition to your worry about your father, they should bother you with other matters. It is weak. I think if they did not have a lazy feeling that if the worst comes to the worst they have always you to fall back on, it would be a damn sight better for them and for you. And as far as I am concerned—and in the end it always comes down to me through you—you can be absolutely frank with them about the way I feel—*am compelled to feel.* If I was flush and flourishing it wouldn't matter, any more than it ever has mattered.

Another week to wait! It will be a long one, Dear. I was all pointed to meet you Monday a.m. I miss you terribly.

Oona & Shane are both grand. The shutters are being fitted and painted (first filler coat). You want same final color as shutters to your balcony and the window trim throughout, don't you? You'd better cable Yes to this. I'm afraid to let them go ahead on it without your O.K. although that color has proved good and I think the shutters should be same logically. No more news from Smith—no estimate yet—am going to call up.

Don't fail Wednesday or I shall never have faith in anything you ever say again! You will have been gone 2 weeks.   All best love!   Gene

Miss Sergeant[2] was going to give *Interlude* script to Bobby. That is all right. Ask Bobby [to] send it to Nathan at Royalton. Kenneth can get it from Nathan and after reading, give to Hamilton who can give it back to Miss Sergeant. I'll write her whom to send it to—Jimmy Light. He could call and get it and give back to her. That will about use up those I want to read it before it's hawked about. Get this straight!

---

214 • TO LAWRENCE LANGNER.   TLS 2 pp. (Hamilton, Bermuda) [Yale]

May 1st. [1927]

Dear Lawrence: The outline of your proposition has come from Madden and Agnes has told me all you had to say to her and it seems to me that nearly everything is satisfactory. However there are a few reservations I would like to make which I am confident the Guild will see the weight of when you come to consider it from my angle.

In the first place I think the option on the three plays should be made conditional on the actual production, and not merely the sale of *Marco Millions,* and also on your definite acceptance of *Strange Interlude.* I am perfectly willing to accept what I consider the pretty small advance on *Marco Millions* and *Strange Interlude* which you offer and also to forego

2. Elizabeth Shepley Sergeant (1881–1965), a writer who first met the O'Neills in Maine in the summer of 1926, when she interviewed the playwright, and then spent six weeks during March and April 1927 at Spithead, recuperating from an auto accident.

asking for any money for the option on the three plays. This I feel shows my eagerness to work with the Guild, particularly as it is all going out and nothing coming in with me at present and I direly need all the cash I can grab. But a similar eagerness on the Guild's part will be best shown by giving me an actual production at the earliest possible date. Therefore it is only fair the option on future work should be made conditional on production.

And on your definite acceptance of *Strange Interlude*. The way Madden outlines it your position about that play remains vague to me—a half-acceptance that must be as unsatisfactory to you as to me. Surely now that you have all read it and know the dramatic guts of it and its new method you ought to be able to make a definite decision. All it needs is an intensive cutting of words, phrases, sentences, speeches, from first act to last, such as I always do on all my plays—but certainly no drastic reconstruction is called for. And I don't feel that I should be called on, as Madden says you suggest, to submit this cut script to you in order to get a decision. I have offered you the essential play and I don't want to do more work on it until I have the incentive of knowing it's going to be produced. What I mean is that you should have enough confidence in my ability to trim this play down to be able to predict for yourselves what the final product will be. After all, you are not dealing with any novice in the theatre, and anyone who has ever worked with me—Bobby, Kenneth, Arthur, etc.— will testify that I don't have to be urged but am always on the lookout for helpful cuts right up to the last week of rehearsals. And the legend that I don't attend rehearsals is all rot. I didn't in the old P.P. days because I was never in New York and when I was I was never "on the wagon." But of late years it has been different. Except in cases where I saw that my play was being given no chance and it didn't matter whether I was there or not, I have been very much on the job. *Beyond The Horizon, "Anna Christie," Hairy Ape, All God's Chillun, Glencairn* cycle, *Desire Under The Elms* and *G. G. Brown* are examples of when I was. And I should most decidedly be there from first day to last if I were doing stuff with you people because I would be genuinely interested.

To get back to *Strange Interlude*, here is another thing. You will agree that it is important to do it as soon as possible. Though I have sworn everyone who has read it to secrecy about the method still it is bound to leak out and if it waits too long there is always a chance that some half-and-half attempt at the same form will be suggested to another playwright and produced before mine, thereby taking off a lot of its edge. Don't you think so? So you see I need a prompt decision so that I can try for quick action elsewhere if you should not see your way to it. Even a production at the P.P. might be preferable, under the circumstances, to having the play in the air too dangerously long. I have no idea what tentative plans you may have made, in case you accept the play. Will you let me know this—cable me or have Madden do so. (Now that they have taken off one-half the boats it may take ages for you to get a letter to me.) So much depends on this.

I don't want you to get the idea that this is an attempt on my part to force your hand. Rather my own hand is being forced by imperative financial circumstances. In case *Marco* fails I must have another production to fall back on. The *Lazarus*-Reinhardt deal, as far as the U.S. is concerned, is off apparently and its Chicago production is extremely problematical and, even if done, will probably be a blundering wash-out for all concerned. And there is hardly a producer left—you and Arthur having passed it—to whom I care to submit *Lazarus*. So you will realize, to speak plainly, that the advances you offer me under this contract are not liable to keep me eating very long and that my present position, after an empty season, is such that I have to do some tall pondering on my future financial security.

Of course, all of this needs a lot of talking over but I want to make my position clear to you so that you will be able to decide whether, under these circumstances, you still think there is a basis on which we can talk. If so, I will come to New York as soon as I possibly can. I have tried to arrange it for the 7th (sailing from here) but things have come up that make that impossible. The next steamer leaves on the 14th. I can make it then. How is that with you?

Agnes joins me in all best to you.　　Eugene O'Neill

---

215 • TO ARTHUR HOBSON QUINN.　　ALS 1 p. (Hamilton, Bermuda)
[Pennsylvania]

May 29 '27

My dear Dear Quinn:　　Your letter arrived here when I was up in New York[1] and I did not get it until my return. And as there is only one mail a week from this remoteness now this reply will be late in reaching you.

Your appreciation of the two plays[2] is deeply gratifying and I share in your estimate of the place of *Lazarus Laughed* in my work—that is, leaving my latest, *Strange Interlude*, out of the consideration, for I set great store by that, too. As to whether you have understood my meaning in *L.L.* I can only reply by giving you my idea of the deep underlying idea of the play:

The fear of death is the root of all evil, the cause of all man's blundering unhappiness. Lazarus knows there is no death, there is only change. He is reborn without that fear. Therefore he is the first and only man who is able to laugh affirmatively. His laughter is a triumphant Yes to life in its entirety and its eternity. His laughter affirms God, it is too noble to desire personal immortality, it wills its own extinction, it gives its life for the sake of Eternal Life (patriotism carried to its logical ultimate). His laughter is the direct expression of joy in the Dionysian sense, the joy of a celebrant who is at the same time a sacrifice in the eternal process of change and growth and transmutation which is life of which his life is an insignificant manifestation, soon to be reabsorbed. And life itself is the Self-affirmative joyous laughter of God.

So much for it in a few clumsy words. I could carry this explanation on endlessly without making clear all I mean in *L.L.*, but you have the gist of it above.

All kindest regards to you.　　Eugene O'Neill

---

216 • TO BENJAMIN DE CASSERES.[1]　　ALS(X) 3 pp. (Spithead, [Bermuda])
[Virginia]

June 22 '27

Dear De Casseres:　　Your long letter was a treat. Here in Bermuda one rarely gets the chance, especially now in the slack season, to say a word to a human being above the intellectual and spiritual level of a land crab and this solitude gets damned oppressive at times. But it's a fine place to get work done, I've found, and that's why I'm here. Also the climate suits me for I'm able to live at all times the amphibious sort of life I love.

What you say of *Lazarus Laughed* deeply pleases me—particularly that you found something of *Zarathustra*[2] in it. *Zarathustra*, although my work may appear like a pitiable

---

1. O'Neill went to New York for several days in mid-May to give Theatre Guild officials a revised script of *Strange Interlude;* the Guild placed that play and *Marco Millions* under option.
　2. *Marco Millions* and *Lazarus Laughed.*

1. De Casseres (1873–1945), critic, poet, and essayist with whom O'Neill became close friends when he returned to New York later in 1927.
　2. *Thus Spake Zarathustra* (1883–1892) by German philosopher Friedrich Nietzsche (1844–1900).

contradiction to this statement and my life add an exclamation point to this contradiction, has influenced me more than any book I've ever read. I ran into it, through the bookshop of Benjamin Tucker, the old philosophical anarchist, when I was eighteen and I've always possessed a copy since then and every year or so I reread it and am never disappointed, which is more than I can say of almost any other book. (That is, never disappointed in it as a work of art, aspects of its teaching I no longer concede.)

I was also very much caught by what you said of the identity of No! and Yes! and as a result I'm going to put back in the first scene some lines that I had cut out of the last version you read. It is Lazarus' first speech in answer to the Crowd's "What is beyond?" He says "I heard the heart of Jesus laughing in my heart. There is Eternal Life in No! And there is the same Eternal Life in Yes! Death is the Fear between! And my heart reborn to love of life cried Yes and I laughed the laughter of God!" These lines now appear to me indispensable, the keynote to the whole of the character of "Laz" and I feel an awful jackass for having deleted them. Maybe I would have put them back anyway in the course of an intensive going over before publication or production. And then again, I mightn't have! So much gratitude to you for the present inspiration to do so!

You are right to ask who can play "Laz." No one that I know of who has ever played in the States except Chaliapin.[3] He would be magnificent, I think, but he is quite money-mad and impossible to interest (except commercially), so they say. And he doesn't know English. But I wouldn't care about that. He could speak the lines in Russian. The average audience would probably get just as much out of them that way! All in all, I'm not expecting much from an American production of this play but I do think they will do well by it in Russia— that there are actors there who have the talent, and have had the training, to play Lazarus. All the Russians who have read it or had it read to them—Danchenko, for example—have been particularly keen about it. Their strong religious feeling about life, I suppose.

I'm glad you are going to read Brown. It is one of my own favorites. I quite understand the masks confusing you when you saw it. They were never right and we had neither the time nor the money to experiment and get them right before we opened—the old story that prevents anything really fine from ever being done in the American theatre! When you read what I wanted those masks to get across—the abstract drama of the forces behind the people—as it is suggested in the script you will remember more clearly how wrong they were. They suggested only the bromidic, hypocritical & defensive double-personality of people in their personal relationships—a thing I never would have needed masks to convey. They became an unnecessary trick. Perhaps I was demanding too much, and it can't be done—but I'm sure with the right masks my meaning would get across, that the play would be mystic instead of confusing—and I'm sure, given the money and time, the right masks could have been made.

I like tremendously the two things you enclosed. I was overcome with amazement when I read what you wrote about only five of your books out of twenty having been published. It seems too incredible! What the hell's the matter with the publishers, anyway? And I had no idea you had written so much. The only books of yours I have are The Shadow Eaters, which was what I knew you by for many years, & Chameleon.[4] I'd like very much to read the Merry Comedy of Hamlet—a grand title!—and be sure and send me your wife's The

---

3. Feodor Chaliapin (1873–1938), Russian basso who was an exceptionally fine actor.
4. The Shadow Eaters (New York: Alfred and Charles Boni, 1915), a book of poetry; and Chameleon (New York: Lieber and Lewis, 1922), a collection of essays.

Boy of Bethlehem,[5] as you kindly offer to do. And I'll hope when I get back in the fall you'll let me take some of the unpublished books. All best wishes to you! Eugene O'Neill

---

217 • TO JOSEPH WOOD KRUTCH.[1] ALS 2 pp. (Stationery headed: Spithead / Bermuda) [Yale]

July 15th '27

My dear Mr. Krutch: I would have answered your letter long before this but one of those damned summer colds has had me feeling too sour to do anything.

Your appreciative criticism of *Strange Interlude* was deeply gratifying—especially that you found that there was something of a novel's comprehensiveness in it. What you say about the slightness of even the best modern plays is exactly the way I feel. To me they are all totally lacking in all true power and imagination—and to me the reason for it is too apparent in that they make no attempt at that poetic conception and interpretation of life without which drama is not an art form at all but simply tricky journalism arranged in dialogue. But on the other hand, even the best of modern novels strike me as dire failures in another direction. They are all so wordy, so padded with the unimportant and insignificant, so obsessed with the trivial meaning of trivialities that the authors appear to me as mere timid recorders of life, dodging the responsibility of that ruthless selection and deletion and concentration on the essential which is the test of an artist—the forcing of significant form upon experience. No, I think the novelists are worse than the playwrights—they waste more of one's time!

As for the "complexes" of the characters in *Strange Interlude*, I must confess that before or in the writing I never thought of them as such in any Freudian sense and that's probably why no exposition of them obtruded. I'm no great student of psycho-analysis although, of course, I do know quite a bit about it, without ever having gone in for a complete analysis myself, and I'm enormously interested to see what will eventually emerge as science out of all these theories and the Behavioristic ones. My position is sort of half in one camp and half in the other. But to get back to *S.I.* I feel that, although it is undoubtedly full of psycho-analytic ideas, still these same ideas are age-old to the artist and that any artist who was a good psychologist and had had a varied and sensitive experience with life and all sorts of people could have written *S.I.* without ever having heard of Freud, Jung, Adler & Co. This doesn't apply in my case, of course. I'm simply making this statement because it seems to me that there is a tendency now to read psycho-analysis into an author's work where ordinary psychology offers a sufficient explanation—let alone imagination and intuition. All the author's pet thunder will be stolen soon if it keeps up!

Yes, I like "Marsden" in the play very much myself—next to "Nina." I've known many Marsdens on many different levels of life and it has always seemed to me that they've never been done in literature with any sympathy or real insight.

I'm almost finished with the cutting and minor revising of the play. Your scheme is about the one I had been following in making the cuts. My fear in writing a first draft is always of omitting something, so there are bound to be many repetitions. I usually have a

5. Bio (Terrill) De Casseres's novel about Christ (New York: Christopher Press, 1926).

1. Krutch (1893–1970), critic, whom O'Neill met through Langner in New York in May 1927 and who later wrote many articles and reviews on the playwright's work.

first draft at least one-fourth too long—almost intentionally, for I've gotten so cutting is a labor of love with me and I get a keen satisfaction out of it second only to the actual creating.

The Guild are going to do *Strange Interlude* next season, or I will have to get it done elsewhere. Their option, on my insistence, is only for a next season's production. I can't afford to wait. Waiting years for production while your mind passes on to other things is the most trying experience—financially trying too, let me add!

As for productions of my stuff in the past, I only hope the Guild will do as well by me as the P.P. & G.V. did in *The Moon of the C, Jones, Hairy Ape, Desire & Brown.* But there can be no such thing as a really good production in the American theatre and I gave up all hope of ever getting one years and years ago! I am tickled to death if a play of mine is done adequately! I expect bad productions. In a theatre run as a commercial gamble—or in enforced competition with such a business—where more than four weeks rehearsal is a dangerous financial risk, where directors, actors and actresses have no chance for any real training and no background or tradition of artistic feeling for their own calling, where—but why go on?—you know the facts as well as I do—it is simply a proof of congenital imbecility in a dramatist to expect a good production. The producer may mean as well by him as may be but you can't build temples out of rotten wood. When we can afford time in the American theatre, then and then only will things begin to pick up. Until then we'll only have well-intentioned gestures. And in order for that time to come we'll have to dig up some Lorenzos who aren't of the self-ballyhooing, jitney variety of the Great Kahn, Otto!

All best to Mrs. Krutch & you! I'll hope to see you soon. There is so much I would like to discuss with you.   Again, thanks for your letter.   Eugene O'Neill

---

218 • TO CARLOTTA MONTEREY.   ALS 3 pp. (Spithead, / Hamilton, Bermuda) [Yale]

July 15th. [1927]

Dearest Carlotta: It has been the devil of a long time since I have written you and I feel horribly ashamed of myself, particularly as it is difficult to explain why I haven't even to myself. To tell you the truth I have been in a strange disorganized state where it seemed as if it were impossible to concentrate on even the slightest thing outside of my writing, on which I have labored with a sort of feverish intensity as though that were the one anodyne for all the instability and drab insecurity of the reality of my every day existence.

For one thing I haven't been at all well for the past month. One cold followed another—or perhaps the same old one recurring—until I finally had to take to my bed for ten days with a genuine attack of Bermuda flu, high fever and all the fixings. I'm just recovering from that now but still have a rotten cough which has hung on like a plague for three weeks.

But I guess the real reason behind all this sickness is really a psychic one—and the reason for the psychic one I will leave you to guess! How I wish I could talk to you! See you! It seems so damned long ago and so far away. And I've felt a curious diffidence about writing you, a deep sense of the unfairness of asking you to remember when I have so little to give. I have tried to make myself hope that you would forget all about me, that you would fall in love with someone over there, that even though it meant pain to me you would let me pass out of your life without regret, oblivious in some new-found happiness. For I do want you to be happy, Carlotta! You know that, don't you? And how can I make you happy?

But enough of that! It is too torturing to think about. I've thought about it too much. That's what has been the matter with me. And perhaps I haven't written for the pure, selfish reason that writing would force me to be so keenly aware of my loneliness and my ineffectual dodges to escape or hide from that loneliness! It has been a trying summer. Perhaps it is my mood but the weather has seemed intolerably oppressive and I've found little zest in anything I used to take pleasure in. Even the sea has failed me. It is such a tepid, lukewarm ocean now, there is no life or sting to it, the only reaction one gets from it is a new lassitude. I would never spend another summer down here on a bet. It really is just too boring! But it had to be done this year or we would never have got the new dock built for hurricane protection. These lads of color down here don't labor much unless your eye is on them and you can't trust the contractors to get anything done right when you're absent.

Jimmy Light and his new wife have been down here since the first of the month visiting us. That has been a bit of a treat and relaxation for me, having him to talk to. Jimmy is one of my oldest friends and he has one of the few imaginative minds connected with the theatre.

But I wish I could go away on a vacation someplace—Baden-Baden by preference! I have gotten Godawful stale down here and I feel the need of a change. My visit to New York in May was far too short! I wish I could have stayed there longer.

I see you mention having talked about the American "Art" theatre in Paris. I've had a letter from that damned fool, Sturgis, telling me all about his grand chaotic plans and he mentions having talked with you. I say "damned fool." I judge him by his rather asinine letter. Perhaps he isn't as bad as all that. But I think saving the American theatre via Paris is a stupid notion no matter what genius may be back of it. It will be saved in New York or not at all. Probably not at all. But it's a cinch that the French theatre is far more limited than ours.

If you hear anything regarding me or my plays in Germany be sure and relay it on to me. I have gotten an awfully unfair deal over there in the way of translations and productions and it has given me a black eye, I think, except among those of the literati who know my stuff in English.

I hope you are having a good time and that the baths will really be beneficial. I wish I could see you. Oh, hell! Please don't forget me! Or, for your sake, please do!   Good'bye for this time, dear. All love, Carlotta.   Gene

---

219 • TO KATHARINE CORNELL.   ALS 2 pp. (Stationery headed: Spithead / Bermuda) [Lincoln Center]

July 25th [1927]

Dear Miss Cornell: Your letter reached me here a few days ago. It was particularly gratifying to hear that you and Mr. McClintic[1] thought so well of *Strange Interlude* and I am anxious to have a talk with you both about it. I have done a lot of work on the script you saw—which, as I explained, was a first draft—and have cut it down until it is now where I want it to be—and, undoubtedly, a much better play. In its present form, as near as one can figure out playing time in a piece of this kind (where figuring a page to a minute is foolish), the first play should be about two hours and a quarter, the second around an hour and three quarters.

I will go into some detail about the situation in regard to its production because I have not yet lost *all* hope that you may be able to do it. I should hate to relinquish all hope of that because to my mind there is absolutely no one else who could touch what you could do with "Nina."

The Guild have an option on it and, I think, will probably do it next season. Their

---

1. Guthrie McClintic (1893–1961), Katharine Cornell's husband, who directed many productions in which she starred.

option, at my insistence, is only for a next season's production. If they find they cannot fit it in with their plans for the coming year, then I will look for another producer—but I have every reason to believe the Guild will do it. If they do, their idea is to put it on as a special feature event quite outside of their regular repertory—(by this I don't mean "special" in the sense of matinees or anything of that sort. I would never allow that. The play is eminently practicable and can stand on its own feet as a regular theatre attraction. In fact I'm confident that, if done reasonably well, it will prove the biggest all around success of any of my plays). The Guild's scheme—and my own—would be to do it in Bayreuth fashion—start at six or six-thirty, then allow an hour or an hour and a half for dinner between the first and second plays. I feel sure this will work.

Of course I know you are going to do *The Letter*[2] and I am sure you will make a tremendous personal success of it, judging from what I know of the play and the part through English papers and periodicals. Also, because I like Maugham's work and liked him very much the one time I met him, I hope the play will score a hit—than which, under the circumstances, no gent could be more nobly unselfish! But if the Guild do *Interlude* they will not do it until mid-season or later, and by that time you might feel you needed to play a new part—and the Guild, I know, are strong for your doing *Interlude* and I am sure, if they thought there was any chance of his having that time off from the directorship of the Actors' would be equally eager to have your husband direct it.

So, as I say, I still hope and I'll hope to have a talk with you both soon as I'm coming to town in about a week.

And even if this hope comes to nothing, I'll still hope again that we'll get together on something else of mine before too long.

Mrs. O'Neill joins in all best to you both.   Cordially,   Eugene O'Neill

P.S. George Jean Nathan is writing something about *Interlude* for the August *Mercury*[3] which you might be interested to read.

---

220 • TO J. O. LIEF.[1]   ALS 3 pp. (Stationery headed: Spithead / Bermuda) [NYU]

August 7th [1927]

Dear Doctor Lief: I haven't answered your letter before because I've been expecting to go up to New York again any day and I was going to drop up and see you—but now it turns out I've got to stay here until Sept. 1st.

I meant to drop in on you on my last trip but I was the Guild's guest, living at Langner's house, and they kept me busy all the time the few days I was there.

But I'll see you soon now. We were sorry you didn't make Bermuda. Better luck next year! We hope Mrs. Lief and the children are now "in the pink."

Many thanks for the *Punch* clipping.[2] I hadn't seen it. It is surprisingly fair, considering I'm a Yank. They don't like Americans to presume to be artists over there. They regard it as rather a similar manifestation of uncivilized impertinence as a drunken Indian in a plug hat and spats.

Brown, in general, has enjoyed quite a fair—and surprising to me—amount of appre-

2. Play (1925) by English novelist and playwright W. Somerset Maugham (1874–1965), in which Katharine Cornell opened on Broadway on September 26, 1927, with McClintic directing.
3. "The Theatre: O'Neill's Finest Play," *American Mercury* 11 (August 1927): 499–506.

1. O'Neill's dentist in New York and a friend as well.
2. Joseph T[horp], "At the Play," *Punch* 172 (June 29, 1927): 717–18.

ciation among the high-brow papers and periodicals. Of course, they don't exactly think it's a play—(what it is, if not, they don't state)—and they do say it's Expressionism—(without saying what they think *that* is!)—but they do commend it as writing and they admit to being emotionally and intellectually stirred. As for the newspapers, most of their critics were frankly outraged. That a bleedin' Yank should presume to think was bad enough, but that he should have the shocking bad taste to expect an audience of English gentlemen to think with him—an act of God that hasn't happened in the English theatre since the Restoration!—was an atrocity only to be compared to the rape—or whatever it was—of Edith Cavell by the late Huns. St. John Ervine, former playwright and present critic on the *Observer*, lays all my degeneration from the time of *Beyond The Horizon*, which he liked, to my present total decay, to the influence of Stark Young and Macgowan and other rabid destructive rebels of the American scene![3] Well, well!

I go into this so lengthily because it has amused me more than a little—especially the strange forms Mr. Ervine's self-disappointment takes. I am Irish enough at heart to love to see the English make damn fools of themselves, I guess. Ervine is an Orangeman. That makes it even more toothsome!   I'm glad you liked *Marco*!   All best to Mrs. Lief and the kids and to your brothers.   Sincerely,   Eugene O'Neill

---

221 • TO AGNES BOULTON O'NEILL.   ALS 2 pp. (S.S. Fort St. George [en route to New York]) [Harvard]

Sunday a.m. / [August 28, 1927]

Dearest One: Well, the voyage so far has been an exceedingly calm one—and I've spent quite a little time out on deck.[1] Got a chair with the Whitneys and have enjoyed talking with him. He's an interesting and likable chap and it is a shame that someone with his decidedly above the average qualities and appreciations should have been trapped into the Bermuda rut (which at least he hates).

Mayor Dall's wife is also on board with a couple of children. The rest of the passengers look to be a dreary lot. They might all come from some New Jersey suburb, but as various of them shriek and applaud viciously when the orchestra plays "Dixie," I judge these are from South Brooklyn.

My report on the infection for this a.m. is that it is no worse—and no better. So I continue to be worried. It is perhaps too easy to expect final results from Orton's medicine but I had hopes—. I'll await your message on his second analysis with a good deal of anxiety. I had a grand long sleep last night and feel rested today but even the slight roll of the ship in this fair weather keeps me a bit uneasy in my innards. Truly I am not the doughty sailor man I once was!

I hope you got my Marconigram last evening and that you deciphered the message I intended. I meant "Remember our front of house steamer chair love." I wanted you to have pleasant longing thoughts of me my first night away as you remembered the night before! Did you blush when it came to you over the phone?

Dear One, I do miss you so much and wish so longingly that you were here with me! Everything seems so right in our relationship now after all the nervous bickerings and

---

3. O'Neill is probably referring to Ervine's "Mr. Eugene O'Neill," *Observer* (London), October 31, 1926, p. 15.

1. O'Neill was returning to New York to confer with the Theatre Guild about their impending productions of *Marco Millions* and *Strange Interlude*.

misunderstandings of the summer. I feel deeply at peace now about you and me, as if we had reached a new understanding of our married life together, a fresh faith to carry us on together through the rest of our lives with a love that will grow tenderer and be freed from all bitterness as the years pass. And this feeling is a great consolation in my loneliness for it keeps you near to me in spirit even though you are so far away in the flesh. Never mind, Dear One! It won't be long before I'll come down or you will come up. And I feel when we see each other again we will love as never before! Is that a promise? In the meantime, don't worry about anything—except hurricanes, and I'm hardly liable to be caught in any emotional storms again!

One request: As I'm going to see Owen Davis,[2] will you send me by return mail the scripts of my movie scenarios of *The Hairy Ape* and *Desire?* It would be a good thing to have him read them, I think, don't you? Show him I *can* write that way. You will find them somewhere in the *top drawer* nearest the door of my cabinet.

Kiss Oona & Shane for me. Don't let them forget me. Love to Gaga & my best to Lily, Johnston, Powell[3] & the rest.

And a million kisses to all of your dear self, Own Wife of Mine!   Gene

P.S. Get latest *Mercury*. Read first story "We Rob A Bank" written by a bank robber now serving a life sentence in Folsom prison, California. Read first his life history as given at the back of the magazine. Interesting stuff! True story of a bank robbery written from the bandit's point of view.

Later (Sunday eve)

I'm going to mail this now. Have been reading all day. All love to you again, Darling!

---

222 • TO AGNES BOULTON O'NEILL.   ALS 8 pp. (Stationery headed: Hotel Wentworth / 59 West 46th Street / New York) [Harvard]

Sept. [8?, 1927]

Dearest Aggie: This is to warn you to be on the lookout for a most gawgeous present for your birthday which I purchased today and which they promised would get off to you by this same boat. Perhaps this may seem a bit previous to you but I wanted to be on the safe side and get it there earlier rather than later—and to be guiltily candid I don't remember the exact date, only know it's in the 'teens. You'll have to pay duty on it, which is rather a dirty trick but I don't see how to get around it unless you charge me with it.

As for the present itself, I certainly liked it and I hope you will. Let's hope it won't be damaged in transit—but they will insure it, of course. As for its nature, please regard it as a gentle hint that I miss you and want you and need you and that I'm longing most damnably for the time when you'll be in my arms again. I do love you so much, Own Little Wife! Remember that always and don't worry about anything! Promise?

I've felt much better the past two days because some of my physical worry has been cleared from my mind. Yesterday I saw Doctor Gile, former Princeton wrestler, now a prostate specialist. He reported me O.K. in every way in that respect. Today I got most of a general exam. from a shark called Barach (better than the Loeb I wrote you about, Doctor Murray finally decided) and so far he hasn't found anything the matter although he immediately saw my nerves were all shot. It looks as if I would have to put up with them

2. Davis (1874–1956), playwright, who won the 1923 Pulitzer Prize for *Icebound* and was the author of many plays as well as movie and radio scripts during a prolific career.
3. The O'Neills's servants at Spithead.

philosophically as the inevitable paying the piper for my past, and that everything else that is wrong with me is all mental and up to Hamilton[1] & Co. However, I'm very much relieved. I also got a real kick out of meeting these three Docs—all young men, college grads, already in the top ranks of their profession. There was something so high grade and genuinely fine and big about their personalities. They're so damned healthy and strong and sane compared to most of the people I know. I wish I could get to know them better—as friends. Murray I could except that he's moving to Boston. He is a former Harvard varsity oarsman.

Yesterday I had tea with Nathan and Lillian Gish. At the Ritz, no less! And let me say right here that I fell for the Ritz (at five p.m. at least). We sat in a room with a fountain and a pool and were the only people there! I liked Lillian and can understand why people make such a fuss about her (Bobby for example). She surprises you by being the exact opposite of all you imagine when you say "movie queen." She's quiet and has real brains and is nothing startling to look at except that she has fine eyes. I talked to her about my Lucretia Borgia movie idea and she was enthusiastic, said she has always wanted to play Lucretia and has read a great deal about her—a lot more than I have! So something may come out of it. At any rate I'm to see her with Nathan again before long. Nathan suggested she play the Princess in *Marco*. She certainly could make up to look it and it seems she wants to do something on the speaking stage. But I suppose there's nothing much in the idea—just one of his notions. The Guild would probably throw a fit at the idea!

Tomorrow I'm going up to get X rayed at the Presbyterian Hospital—then to Lief's to get my teeth X rayed. Doctor Barach wants this done. I hope to God my teeth won't show anything! An extraction now would be almost more than my nerves would stand.

Knock on wood before you read the following! It looks as if I might sell Ridgefield right away—through Kelly of the Bessell drugstore who has a rich Jew in tow who seems to mean business. Kelly was in to see me twice today and it looks good. However, it's unlucky to count chickens before they're hatched! But I expect a definite decision within the next few days. Let's pray! I'm holding out for 35 and but will sell if I can get the price I paid (32,500) in cash. I've decided I ought to.

Here's a question: Supposing the luck is good and it does sell and he wants immediate possession? I couldn't afford to risk losing the sale by saying he couldn't have it for a month or more (waiting until you could come up, I mean). Do you think I could manage the superintending of the packing of furniture? Better let me have all the dope on who did the packing before, how long they took, etc., etc. That is, if you get (or have gotten by the time you receive this) a cable from me that the sale has gone through. Get this dope back to me by return mail—also any advice, instructions, etc. you have to offer. Is there any inventory around that I could show a packing co. to get an estimate? In the meantime, I'll pull whatever wires I can to find some friend of a friend of some packing place, etc.

I sound hopeful but from what Kelly told me there is reason to be. God I hope this doesn't fall through! It would solve our Spithead fixing up, wouldn't it, and we'd be settled at last!

I sure hope you're feeling "in the pink" again by this time. Please take care of yourself, Dear One! If all our troubles blow over we really must have a wonderful time together either when you come up to join me or when we come up together after I've been down to Bermuda again, however it works out (I discussed the alternatives in my last). But for God's sake let's stick together and try and make it a real honeymoon and be selfish about ourselves and not let any outside worries or family or friends intrude to keep us from being absorbed in each other. What I mean is what we had a ten days taste of last fall in New York. Those were

---

1. Psychotherapist Gilbert V. Hamilton.

wonderful days, weren't they? Then let's go after a month or more of those this time! Promise? There are so many things we can do together—(one thing above all, what!)

There's no new news on the plays. Haven't heard from the Guild since I wrote last. They're reading *Marco* but Simonson is still out of town. Helburn is strong against publishing *S.I.* before it is produced—if they do it. Some sort of compromise will have to be reached— by me!—between them and Liveright. I can't afford to lose either of the chances for getting some coin.

Friday / [September 9?, 1927]

Just a line. This is another of my bad days—feel like the wrath of God, completely done up and nervous as hell! This feeling punk four or five days per week is no fun. Of course, the answer is simple. New York never did agree with me and I ought to be out in the country, especially in this weather. I never get a bit of exercise now and there's no fresh air. When I got weighed this morning at Dr. Barach's I found I was *almost fifteen pounds underweight*—I only weighed 137 with all my clothes on! This is serious—and yet they can't find anything wrong with me so far but it may be something latent that hasn't made itself apparent as yet.

The Ridgefield deal is hanging fire. The man wants to go out with his wife and look it over again. I'm no longer optimistic about it.

The *Lazarus*-Jewish Art theatre scheme has come to nothing. They were afraid down there it would offend their Orthodox audience.

No chance of getting any definite decision from the Guild until Lawrence Langner comes back on the 26th, I'm afraid. It is a matter of their discussing whether they can cast and direct and fit it in with their other plans. He'll have to be in on this discussion. In fact, it's wise for me to wait until he is.

So there's no good news to give you—and small prospect of there being any for some time.

You evidently don't read my letters through. I'm sorry if they bore you. Of course I realize how entirely your attention is monopolized by Spithead and perhaps I should be more considerate and not bore you with any letters at all! I wrote you some time ago to send movie scripts of *Hairy Ape* and *Desire*, it was important, but haven't got them yet. They are in left top drawer near door of the cabinet in study.

Oh, hell! I feel rotten about everything! It seems as if we manage things in the exact way to make everything turn out all wrong—and this fall's mess certainly draws the prize! You must have framed it up with the idea of becoming a widow!   Gene

P.S. Forgive this! But I do feel sick and despondent.

---

223 • TO SHANE O'NEILL.   ALS 4 pp. (Stationery headed: Hotel Wentworth / 59 West 46th Street / New York) [Harvard]

[September? 1927]

Dear Shane: Your Daddy—meaning myself—was certainly tickled to death to get your nice letter! It is very lonely for me living in this hotel where I don't know anyone and I often think of you and Oona—and I miss you both like the devil! You mustn't tell Oona this, though—at least, when you tell her you must say "like the deuce" instead of "like the devil" for it isn't polite to say "devil" to ladies and Oona, let us hope, is a perfect lady!

I was glad to hear you caught eight of "them yaller grunts" the other day. You are certainly the prize fisherman of the O'Neill family. You have us all beat! And it sure is a

With Agnes, Shane, and Oona in Bermuda.

surprise to hear you've been diving off the springboard already. I thought that would be too high for you. You'll get to be such a good swimmer that one of these days I expect you'll turn into one of "them yaller grunts" yourself and swim out and leave us, and then we'll have to set the fish pot to catch you and bring you home again!

It's cheering to know Bowser came home by himself this last time. It's about time he was getting enough sense to know his way home, don't you think so, if he doesn't want to be a fool dog all his life? You tell him for me I'm sorry he's chained up but it serves him right for being such a fool dog and I hope it teaches him a lesson to be good in future.

Keep on with your lessons. What I saw in your copy books was fine. If you keep on that way it won't be long before you can learn to typewrite and be my secretary and write down all my plays and I'll pay you a big salary and you'll be able to buy a big boat of your own or anything you like.

You take good care of Mother & Oona & Gaga while I'm away. You're the only O'Neill man down there now and I'm relying on you to see that none of those fool women get into trouble! However, they can't help being that way because it isn't their fault they were born girls—so I guess you better kiss all three of them for me because they really are nice to have around, even if they are crazy, and you realize that when you're far away from them and all alone in a big city and exposed to temptation like I am now! But maybe you better not read Mother this part of my letter. She might get mad and raise hell with me when I get back. Remember us men has got to stick together!

Give Gaga my thanks for her letter. It was awful nice of her to write me and I appreciate it.

I'm terribly homesick and I hope it won't be long before I can get back to Spithead again.

Write to me again. Much love to you and Oona and Mother & Gaga from   Your Daddy

---

224 • TO AGNES BOULTON O'NEILL.   ALS 7 pp. (Stationery headed: Hotel Wentworth / 59 West 46th Street / New York) [Harvard]

Sept. 11th [1927] / *eve.*

Dearest Aggie: I have again been feeling vile, physically and mentally, ever since I wrote you Friday, and have had to drag myself around to keep my various dates. This evening I feel much better—for the good reason that I've stayed in all day, seeing no one, resting and reading. What I need is rest in the country but where or how to find that is a problem. So I'll stick on here until the end of the month or later—whenever I get a decision on *Interlude* from Guild. If they don't take it, Liveright will and will start rehearsing as soon as he can cast it. In that case I'll have to stay on. I hope not. I'm not up to it and it would make *Interlude* open just as *Marco* started rehearsing. In which case, by the time *Marco* opens I can confidently predict that I will exit from the last dress rehearsal to enter some nice quiet sanitarium in the country.

There is very little for me to do here now and time hangs heavy. For every interesting thing I do I get trapped into about five uninteresting ones. It's the same dull old game. Outside of my one meeting with Gish and meeting the doctors (who are only professional acquaintances) I haven't seen a fresh face. Kenneth is out of town writing the golf book,[1] Bobby is head over heels in a new Hopkins production, even Jimmy is all tied up with the de

---

1. Kenneth Macgowan and Charles Blair Macdonald, *Scotland's Gift—Golf* (New York: Charles Scribner's, 1928).

Acosta play.[2] The Guild bunch are swamped with getting 2 road companies out, and new productions rehearsed. I haven't seen one of them in ten days.

Carlotta is back. I saw her yesterday—had lunch with her. The cure at Baden-Baden seems to have done her a lot of good—in appearance and nerves. She remarked on how thin and badly I looked compared to when she saw me last. She's quite right. I wish Hamilton were here. These other medicos are simply going to find that all my organs are intact, and that will be that—except that I'll be just where I was!

Last night I went for dinner and the evening down to Patti's[3] sister's (the musician). About ten people were there—a dreary lot! Paul Robeson sang, but I'm about fed up with negro spirituals. I talked with him about his doing *Lazarus* when he gets back from his tour in Europe. Don't laugh. It's a good hunch. A face (white) of Lazarus could be designed for him and his face built up to fit it. White folks make up to play negroes and there's no reason why the reverse shouldn't be practiced. He's the only actor who can do the laughter, that's the important point. It would be good showmanship, too—no end to the publicity it would attract. I think it's a fine hunch, don't you? Now all we have to do is raise the money!

I *am getting* some things accomplished. Through Rockmore,[4] (Jimmy's partner) I got in touch with a real estate shark (pal of R's) and we three went to look over my mansion at 53 Columbus.[5] It is rather a sordid hole but there's a lot of building starting up around it and, as no one can build on the corner without buying my place, ought to be worth real money some day. This real estate guy handles Rockmore's property—gives individual attention to each place he takes hold of. He claims the Joseph Day people have a bad rep. for flimflamming absentee owners with high expenses, etc. I believe him! The check with their last statement was for 20 dollars! I'm going to take it out of their hands the last of this month.

Nothing more on Ridgefield. Harry W. is arguing with the guy's lawyers. Something may still come of it.

I'm having dinner here with Ben de Casseres tonight. Haven't seen him so far but am looking forward to talking with him.

It continues muggy and hot in N.Y. I'd give a lot for a swim and the sun on a beach. I'd let everything slide and hop down to Bermuda right now but the thought of the heat down there stops me. I want sea & country but not that kind. It's staying down there that is responsible for the state I'm in, I'm sure. Never again, no matter how much more it costs to come up here! It's bad dope! Perhaps this year it couldn't be helped—but it's a damned shame that I have paid and am paying and must continue to pay for it with my health! That's not economy. It would be cheaper to buy new clothes for you & the kids than to pay doctors. I suppose my bills to the docs. are already over two hundred and it's costing me at least 150 a week to live here. And supposing I get good and sick and can't work this winter? What will it profit then, this economy?

Well, I hate to go off on that tack again—but somehow it sticks in my gorge and won't down! Every time I sit alone in this stuffy room looking out over the dirty, smelly roofs and streets, feeling low and sick and depressed and lonely, I'm overcome by bitterness and a feeling that something is all wrong when you deliberately sacrifice me for your own designs and convenience. It isn't your work. You could have worked at Ridgefield. It isn't the sale of the place. Even if it were sold while we were there we could have put a limit before a purchaser could take possession. It isn't economy. Between my expenses and yours—two

2. *Jacob Slovak*, which opened October 5, 1927, at the Greenwich Village Theatre.
3. Patti Light, James Light's wife.
4. Robert Rockmore, a New York lawyer who wanted to be a theatrical producer and was collaborating with James Light in some theatrical ventures.
5. Family property O'Neill still owned in New York City.

establishments—it's costing more than R'field (or any place we could rent near N.Y.) would. (I haven't counted the extras all over the place in my weekly estimate.) It isn't healthy. You're making our children run the risk of the hurricane down there. Supposing it is a really terrible hurricane like the Florida one? Perhaps you don't worry about this but I do! It's just another worry piled on when I already have enough! I won't feel right about it until I know the hurricane is over and you're safe! Perhaps this is morbid but the point is that you know how liable I am to such fears at this period! And if anything happens to either of the children I swear I will never forgive you! Then there's my health, living in New York, wasting time, sick, doing no work, getting no vacation or enjoyment.

I sit and try to figure out why all this should be happening to me. What have I done to you that I should be treated this way? There's no reason I can figure out except that you must have a lover down there as I suspected before! If so, I wish you'd be fair enough to be honest about it and let us quit! I simply can't imagine, for example, why you should deliberately put me in this lonely and distracted situation where I long for love and care and tenderness (knowing as you did what the particular temptation as it exists now would be) unless you are in love with someone down there and don't care what I do or who I love! It's simply unbelievable that you could have done such a ridiculous thing except for some good reason of your own! You know damn well I'm not interested in little sex affairs for sex's sake alone, that it is love or nothing! Do you want me to love someone else?

Oh hell again! What sort of a game is this you're playing, Agnes? Either I'm crazy or you are! Probably I am, anyway. Or, at any rate, I wish to Christ I could escape from this obscene and snaily creeping tedium of dull days, and empty hours like nervous yawns, into some madness—of love or lust or drink or anything else! This camel's back is beginning to crack and snap under the strain!

Oh well, I suppose it isn't as desperate as it feels now. I'm simply on edge, that's all. As I said before, coming to N.Y. under these trying circumstances, all alone, was like jumping from the frying pan into the fire! What I needed was a healthy change, a fresh outlook, but this is hardly it. Still perhaps it had to be. You may be right. I can't think straight now. I feel too much like The Hairy Ape "It's all dark, get me? It's all wrong!"

I dread the thought of that hurricane! Be sure and cable me as soon as it's over. I hope the damn dock holds up!

I'll phone to Barlow soon and reserve passage for the first week of next month or thereabouts. I can always cancel it, if necessary. If Ridgefield sells when could you come up to see about furniture—in case I can hold off the taking possession until Oct 15th or Nov 1st. Or would you want me to do it?

To offer a synopsis of this long story: I'm not well. I'm lonely. I love you. That's the whole case in a nutshell.

Tomorrow will be full of doctors and a dentist.

Kiss the kids for me!   Your   Gene

---

225 • TO AGNES BOULTON O'NEILL.   ALS 7 pp. (Stationery headed Hotel Wentworth / 59 West 46th Street / New York) [Harvard]

Monday, Sept. 19th [1927]

Dearest Aggie: I went out to the races at Belmont with the Rockmores on Saturday—it was Futurity Day, the biggest day of the year at the track—and then had dinner with them & Jimmy & Patti and after that Paul Green came to their place to meet me (he is a nice guy even if he is a playwright), so I didn't get your cable until I got home about one. I sent an answer, deferred rate, yesterday morning. Hope you got it all right and that my last letter which you will get today will explain. I am in much better shape now and there is no need for you to give up all your plans to come up, especially as I'm planning to come back to Bermuda as soon as I possibly can. But I sure am grateful to you, Dearest One, for your willingness to sacrifice your own ideas—which are undoubtedly a good deal wiser than my overwrought, morbid notions of feeling abused have been!—to come to my rescue. Now that I'm healthier I can be fair and see how fair you have been.

I ought to be able to sail home the first week in October—or, at the latest, the second week. Lawrence is due back the 29th and although the Guild definitely decided to do *Strange Interlude* at a meeting they held Friday night without needing his vote—(that's one item of good news for you! It also means five hundred bucks!)—still they must wait for him for a full meeting to decide the where, when, how, the possible casting, etc. and I simply must be in on it. Naturally they won't be able to do it at once—even if they could cast it—but there is the possibility that they'll get it on before *Marco*. At any rate, I'm sure to have enough time before rehearsals start to come to Bermuda for a while, thank God!

Other reasons that would keep me here until the first of next month are that Lief is working on my teeth, Doctor Barach has to have a couple of weeks more to discover by experimenting just how much thyroid is the right dose for me to take each day, and I still have two more prostate treatments (they come a week apart) to get from Doctor Gile. I want to get this all off my slate on this trip so that when I come to Bermuda and come back for rehearsals I will be "in the pink" and have nothing like that to worry about but be free to concentrate on the job. This seems to me essential. With *Marco & Interlude* coming close together it is going to be a long hard drive.

I'm having a pleasant time now—nothing hilarious but pleasant enough. The Rock-mores have been very kind. I have enjoyed their invites to the races. You certainly must come with me to the track sometime! You'd love it! And if one restrains one's gambling instinct it isn't so expensive. I split even on my little bets (I didn't risk much, naturally!) on Saturday.

Komroff had lunch with me yesterday and spent the afternoon—a damned nice fellow! I like him very much.

I'm due to have dinner with Lillian Gish this week sometime. That will be interesting—all except the dinner part! Why do people always want to meet to eat?

I've seen Carlotta a couple of times. I won't go into that now but wait until I see you. As a matter of fact, there's nothing much to go into—so, whatever you do, don't get to worrying about that. She's been damned nice to me and I've enjoyed being with her—but that's the all of it from both sides.

Another reason I couldn't go down right away is that through Wertheim I have got in touch with the big hydro-electric people and am going to visit one of their plants soon.[1] Unfortunately there isn't one anywhere near New York! They want me to go to Niagara Falls where there is one of the finest in the world. I thought I might get Larkin (if he would do it cheap) to go with me and drive up. It would make a nice four or five day trip through beautiful country there and back. I wish you were here to do it with me! It really isn't 100% American not to do a honeymoon to Niagara Falls! I shall have to advertise for a temporary wife!

But I hope they'll dig up a plant nearer N.Y. I can't afford to be away from town five days now.

---

1. O'Neill visited this plant as background for preliminary work on *Dynamo*.

I had dinner with Helen MacKellar & George[2] & Sessue Hayakawa, the Jap actor & his wife, at her place a while ago. Perhaps I've already mentioned this. His wife was interesting but he is very much movie-actor.

The Emperor Jones road tour has gone blooey—a bad luck item. I thought something might come in from this.

There's not a peep about Ridgefield, damn the luck! Although another hundred and fifty dollars has been wasted advertising it.

Moran was down and spent evening talking over things. He expects to get the 1750 from Packer before long—there's been a delay at the bank of some sort—but the deal for the corner is off (of course!) and there's no other sale in sight. He says things are pretty bad up there. So you can count New London out! An auction wouldn't do at this time, Dillon advised. Everyone up there is hard up.

And that's about all the news. I'm sorry there isn't more cash in it!

Darling, I do wish you were here! But don't come! It would break us entirely just now with the bankroll so low, getting the kids up and rigged out and everything. *You were right!* But I'll be down just as soon as I can make it, I promise you! October is less than two weeks off, after all! And then let's really honeymoon! We're always promising ourselves to do this and we never do—except for that ten days last fall!

Kiss Oona & Shane for me. Love to Gaga. All my love to you, Darling.   Gene

P.S. Did my present ever arrive? You haven't said thank you yet. Perhaps you didn't like it?

Later (Monday eve)

Your letter arrived a while ago and it has made me terribly depressed and hopeless again. I feel it is most unkind. I acknowledge you have a right to feel peeved at that letter of mine but not to that "God damn" degree. After all, you might have taken into consideration that I have been palpably not myself mentally for the past few months and, as everyone up here noticed as soon as they saw me and as the doctors' diagnosis have proved to be so, physically sick. And why remember the bitter things I said and did? You said and did things just as wounding—more so!—to me and I assure you that I love you enough to have completely forgiven them and not to hold them against you.

My expression of gratitude for your cable in my return cable and in the first part of this letter seem to be misplaced. I thought you wanted to come up to help me but evidently you're merely doing it out of anger and, if you do come, I have only to expect a wife who will hate me! And similarly, what reception can I expect if I return to Bermuda?

It had all become so simple and I was looking forward to the *happiness* of being with you again—but now it's all so hopeless I don't know what to do. Good Christ, why can't we understand each other, why couldn't you see that it was at bottom my loneliness and love for you that made me write as foolishly as I did?

Sweetheart, what the hell is the matter with us, anyway? We act like a couple of children and we ought to be ashamed of ourselves!

Tuesday a.m. / [September 20, 1927]

I've just cabled you again to postpone your decision until you get this letter. The point is I'm planning to sail for Bermuda so soon—want to get something of *Dynamo* done down there—and this will throw all my plans out. It seems to me the logical thing now—consider-

---

2. George D. MacQuarrie, Helen MacKellar's husband.

ing finances, etc.—for you to wait and then come back up with me when I return for rehearsals. I hope you will see it that way. Otherwise we'll soon go cash broke.

All love, Sweetheart. Forgive that crazy letter and forget it, please do! Remember we both desire so much to start a new life together.   Gene

P.S. Can't understand present not having arrived!

---

226 • TO SHANE O'NEILL.   ALS 2 pp. (Stationery headed: Hotel Wentworth / 59 West 46th Street / New York) [Virginia]

Sept. 25th [1927]

Dear Shane: I was awfully glad to get your last letter and I have meant to answer it long before this but I have been so busy that there has been no chance to write except to Mother.

I was terribly sorry to hear you have been sick. You must take good care of yourself because I want you to grow up to be big and strong and to row on the crew and be on the swimming team when you go to college. And I am sure Mother does too. Are you practicing your crawl stroke? You ought to do that every day and then pretty soon you'll find you'll be able to beat me.

I wish I could have been there when you caught that big porgie and that big shark! I don't see how you ever landed them without getting pulled overboard! I'll bet they fought like the dickens and were awful hard to land! I'm very proud of you! You are the A 1 fisherman of the family, as I told you before. Did Mother take pictures of you with those fish? I hope so because I'd certainly like to see what they looked like. And I wish I could have been around to see those whip morays. I've never seen one.

It's good news that Oona's sores are all gone away. She must look very pretty now her skin's all right again. Those sores don't look very good on anyone and they completely spoil a lady's complexion.

I am glad you miss me because I miss you an awful lot, too, and I think a lot about you and Oona every day, usually when I'm lying in bed and the light is out, just before I get to sleep.

I went out in the country the other day and went in swimming in a lake like the one near our house in Ridgefield. I haven't had a swim since I left Bermuda and it felt good to get in again but it was fresh water and it seemed cold and dirty compared to the water in Bermuda.

Kiss Mother and Oona and Gaga for me. I'm coming back to all of you very soon now—two weeks at the longest—and it will certainly feel fine to be with you all again because it's awful lonely living here in a hotel when you're all so far away.   All love to you!   Daddy

---

227 • TO AGNES BOULTON O'NEILL.   ALS 6 pp. (Stationery headed: Hotel Wentworth / 59 West 46th Street / New York) [Virginia]

Thursday / [September 29?, 1927]

Dearest Wife: I've just got your letter with the enclosures and I'll send the check as you direct.

Sweetheart, I do long for you so much these days! Now that the time is growing shorter and I know I'll see you in two weeks, I'm simply eaten up by impatience and actually counting the days! How's that for a nine years husband amid the wiles and glamours of N.Y.? I think I'm pretty close to being a model! It will be so marvelous to take you in my arms and kiss you again! As I write this an image of your beautiful face comes close to mine and I seem to feel and smell your body touching mine and I get goose flesh all over—not to mention other things which I won't make you blush by mentioning! Two weeks becomes a hellish long ordeal, and all the supposedly useful activities that keep me here appear as most frightful bores. I only hope you are half as anxious to have me back as I am to get there! Please answer this, if only by one line, by supplementary mail and tell me you are! I do want you and love you so!

Tomorrow I go out by car—with Larkin—to the hydro-electric plant in Conn.—an all day affair. It will be fun to drive the car again.

Speaking of cars I had a ride yesterday in an Hispano-Suiza. Some boat! And whose do you think it was? Arthur Hopkins! He's had it three years, he says—*What Price Glory*[1] money, I suppose. I had lunch with him yesterday at the Lotus Club. He's the same old Arthur—a bit more beaming because his *Burlesque*[2] is the biggest hit in town (28000 a week!) and he also has another play that is a big out-of-town hit but hasn't come to N.Y. yet.

I'll try and see Evangeline A. next week.

The note from Jarboe was amusing. So that's how it was! Have you had any word from Burland or from Hill? I suppose not. I wonder what Hill[3] has got up his sleeve to spring on us—if anything.

This morning I went up to Barach's for one of those long before breakfast gland tests. My thyroid remains subnormal in spite of my having taken $\frac{1}{2}$ a grain daily for the past two weeks, so he started me today on a full grain. It's a tiresome business—takes so long for them to determine exact reactions—but another two weeks ought to show what my right dose is.

A word about finances. Liveright again has strong hopes of the "book-of-the-month" for December for *S.I.* He ought to know definitely before I leave. If *S.I.* gets it then that means we can count on so much money from it without fail, and then you can go ahead with your plans on the house. As it is, I think we perhaps ought to make ourselves afford the work of painting and fixing up big room, etc. At least, we could go ahead to the tune of one thousand and trust to luck. What do you think? Do you think it may be better to wait until I get down and we've talked it over? Let me know. God, I sure wish I was coming in a week but I don't see how I can possibly make it! How I wish you were here now, Dearest!

(If this letter sounds a bit fleshly desirous—well—I am!—of you! I feel like turning out the lights and taking your picture to bed! Maybe I will!)

Langner arrived this a.m. I hope to see him tonight. Now that he's back I ought to get a little more exact forecasts out of the Committee—(casting of *S.I.*, etc.). Alice Brady is reading it.

Cornell opened in *The Letter*. It didn't do her rep. so much good. No one thought anything of the play except as cheap melodrama but it will probably make money. She's a damn fool! She'll ruin herself.

Bunny[4] is to see me again. He said something about paying me when I saw him but haven't heard from him since.

Elsie Sergeant is still up at Peterboro, I believe.

I'm glad the weather down there has changed and that you're able to work again. I'm awfully keen to see what you've done with the article.

I've seen Eugene twice.

---

1. Highly successful 1924 play by Maxwell Anderson and Laurence Stallings, which Hopkins produced and directed.
2. Comedy by George Manker Watters and Arthur Hopkins.
3. Frederick P. Hill, the contractor chiefly responsible for renovating Spithead. Jarboe and Burland were possibly workmen involved in the renovation of Spithead.
4. Edmund Wilson, who apparently owed O'Neill money.

When are the Hubers coming down, do you know? I happened to think it would be fine if they were sailing the 12th—company down.

I've been going to call up Delphine D. but can't locate her in phone book. Do you know her address? I'd like to have a peek at that apartment—might need it for my work sometime.

Don't let the arrival of Harold and Helen[5] get you flustered or off work? Be firm about writing when you feel like it, and not being disturbed by anyone. It's the only way.

Not so long now, Darling—(but much too long!)—and then——! Adios for this time, Dearest. I have a date with your picture!   Your lover,   Gene.

(Later)

P.S. Just remembered this—

The Gish-*Marco* thing is developing and may happen! I'm to see her again soon. She is genuinely excited—offers to work on voice with Carrington[6] and says she will come to Bermuda get house with her mother (who is ill) and work on the part with me if I will help her before actual rehearsals start. That would be good stuff. She is a "real guy." You'd like her immensely. She & Nathan seem to be very amoured of each other, if I'm any judge, so he'd probably make a trip down too while she was there.

But this will probably all blow up. I can't believe she's serious about *M*—or brave enough to take such a chance!

---

228 • TO CARLOTTA MONTEREY.   ALS 2 pp. (Stationery headed: Spithead / Bermuda) [Yale]

Monday / [October 24, 1927]

Dearest Shadow Eyes[1] (which *cannot* go out!):   God, how I long for you! There is little else to write you, Heart's Desire! That would be the burden of all my rimes. I am horribly lonely for you. The sun and the sea are good. They bring me peace of a kind—peace in which to dream of the peace that is in your arms—and to hope and count the days before I can see you again. Not long—but so damned long!

Everything here is unchanged. I have had nothing at all to say so you need not worry about my "shooting the works." There seems a very good chance that when I come up again it will be alone—for a while, at least.

Do you remember what you told me of Mike S. having a studio. I have thought of that— such a practical lover, what?—and it sounds to me like a solution of possible future difficulties. Think it over—whether you don't think you would like one?

Dear, there is nothing to write except the same thing over and over: I love you! There is only a great empty ache for you left of me! Remember that ache! It is yours.

I am getting all brown again. I lie in the sun and dream of you in the warm air—your warmth. "Where her last kiss still warms the air"—that is true, "Lucidé"—air of my life warmed to new life by your sweetness and beauty!

Kisses, Shadow Eyes!   As always,   Gene

P.S. I hope you got a letter I sent up to be mailed in N.Y. by one of the ship's officers. You ought to get it tomorrow.

5. Harold and Helen DePolo.
6. Margaret Carrington, voice teacher who had coached her brother, actor Walter Huston, for the role of Ponce de Leon in *The Fountain* (1925).

1. O'Neill's nickname for Carlotta, which may have been derived from Arthur Symons's translation of Baudelaire's "Le Flambeau Vivant" or Symons's own "Impression" or "Disguises."

229 • TO KENNETH MACGOWAN.   ALS 2 pp. (Stationery headed: Spithead / Bermuda) [Yale]

Oct. 27, '27

Dear Kenneth: I'm taking advantage of your kind proffer of aid. Herewith is a check and a note. With the one will you purchase flowers—roses—or use your own judgment or the florist's as to what would be best—I don't know flower lingo—and send to Carlotta at 20 East 67th Street with the enclosed note attached. Many thanks!

Back around the fifteenth. I'll hope to see a lot more of you this next time than the last now that you're settled in town. In the meantime, here's wishing you "all the breaks!"[1] It seems as if that were about the best wish one friend could make another in the show-shop game. (Let us not add, in the game of life—we who are trying so hard to believe in something hidden in either flesh or spirit—oh dear me, no, let us not admit, for another twenty years at least, that life is merely—and perhaps at its highest and holiest!—a game in which the best winning of the greatest winner is in regarding with a self-contempt the pain of his inevitable loss—a game of greater and lesser losers!)

Selah! Daddy's Bedtime Secret for Today! I need a little of the glue of God, I'm afraid—a bit broken.[2] See you soon.   Gene

---

230 • TO CARLOTTA MONTEREY.   ALS 3 pp. (Stationery headed: Spithead / Bermuda) [Yale]

Oct. 27, '27

Dearest Lady: Evening of Thursday—around six—I'm thinking of you at home before your fire for a spell reading my last mail's letter which should have got to you by this. I hope some of the warm love I felt when I wrote it goes out to you and makes you say again with that adorable half-joyous, half-regretful happy groan "Oh, you've gone and done it! I love you, damn it!"

I sent you a cable two days ago—just the word "remember"—oh please do that, Carlotta!—and then we will seize happiness out of this stinking world in which all that is truly fine is so soon forgotten! No time is too long to wait—if one can remember clearly and passionately enough. Remember all I said to you on that last day!

I'll be back so soon! November is almost here and the 15th is only two weeks. I am sure I will be coming up alone.

Everything here is unchanged. I swim, row, tennis, bike, etc.—feel most husky & healthy—wonderful weather—have cut out smoking the past three days and am a bit ratty and on edge as to nerves.

God but I'm lonely! When I dream of those hours of ours—it hurts but at the same time is my only solace. And I can't even expect an open letter from you for comfort. I hope mine are a little to you! But perhaps you've decided you really ought to forget me by this time! Don't!   Your   Gene

---

1. Macgowan's first production with his new partner Sidney Ross, Noel Coward's play *The Marquise*, opened at Broadway's Biltmore Theatre on November 14, 1927.

2. References to William Brown in act 4, scene 1 of *The Great God Brown*: "This is Daddy's bedtime secret for today: Man is born broken. He lives by mending. The grace of God is glue!"

Dearest: Just got the mail with your note of last Saturday. God, if you knew what a thrill just the sight of your handwriting, touching the paper your fingers had touched, gave me! "You damned Dane,[1] you've gone and done it, damn it!"—to paraphrase your wail, Miss Monterey—except I'm so most horribly glad about it!

I've tried to read all I want to hear you say from between the lines of your note—and I hope you mean all I'm reading—a deuce of a lot!

Oh remember our hours, Carlotta—and believe! Kisses! This is just a line! Adios, Darling. Be with you soon.   Gene

---

231 • TO CARLOTTA MONTEREY.   2 pp. (Stationery headed: Spithead / Bermuda) [Yale]

Sunday Oct 30th [1927]

Dearest One: The little volumes of Keats & Verlaine came yesterday. Much gratitude! Were you thinking of us in the taxi in the rain and of my quoting—or probably misquoting!—"It weeps in my heart As it rains on the town" when you picked out the Verlaine for me? I am sure you were. Dear One, it is so sweet to remember you! Certain flashes of your beauty, of your face in this light and that, turned toward me or in profile in a taxi, walking along a street, across a table, in a theatre—or . . . —and your lips and eyes so expressive, smiling or sad, gentle, outraged when you force them to be cold and hard. All the photos of you really miss you—the beautiful real you—so damnably! It's a shame! You are so marvelous and you should be put on record, you know! You better come with me to Pinchot's and let me pose you—that is, whisper in your ear just what you are to think about and lose yourself in for a minute—so you of the Shadowy Eyes in which are love and pain and a fierce hurt bewilderment & defiance and a great tenderness, may be captured on the plate? Will you let me try this?

It still "weeps in my heart." The weather has been in tune the past few days—much downpour. Everything here is the same—most unsettled. It is lonely. I am most silent. I am planning to sail from here on the 15th—unless the Guild makes some decided change in plan. This will mean I can see you on the 17th—if I may. May I? I will probably be alone in the Great City again for the first few weeks. We must do a lot together. May we? You can't say I'm not letting you know ages in advance!

"Nor can your eyes go out!" And don't let mine—for you! Kisses to you! I love you! Remember us!

I hope you've gotten all my letters, cable, flowers, etc. I seem to be developing into the Complete Lover, what? Your beneficent influence! It must be love!

You shall have *Ulysses.*

One mail a week from now on as they're taking off one boat—you better look it up in your newspaper before you write. Do write! If it's only your handwriting it's a blessing—but anything is quite safe. Honest! Certain attitudes *have* changed that way & I am unread and will be. But you know best!   Gene

---

1. Carlotta's real name was Hazel Neilson Tharsing; her father was born in Denmark.

[November 27?, 1927]

My only social diversions have been more or less connected with my business—that is, with the exception of a philharmonic concert Carlotta took me to last Thursday, and even that was, in a sense, because I was told to hear Debussy as being the kind of note needed for the first scene (Prologue—Music of the Leaves) and they played Debussy and Stravinsky that night. I was up at the Wertheim's for dinner one night, met Stieglitz and Georgia O'Keefe there and liked them both immensely. At Langner's for dinner another night to meet Alice Brady who was then being considered for *Interlude*. She is a good scout but rather a rough neck, a real daughter of her eminent father, Bill.[2] Then I went to the opening of Shaw's *Doctor's Dilemma* at the Guild, to see the same cast in it as there will be in *Marco*, and also Lynn Fontanne. I think she will give a very adequate performance in *Interlude* but she will be far from being my "Nina." However, who would be? I've simply got to be philosophical about it and make the best of the material at hand. The men, at least—Powers, Anders and Larrimore[3]—should be splendid. And Lunt[4] should make a remarkable "Marco." He is a fine actor. So the cloud has its bits of silver lining. One can't have everything in our American theatre. The Guild is our best and they are certainly doing their best by me.

Last night I had dinner with Elizabeth Sergeant and Bobby and spent the evening. Bobby will probably do the sets for *Interlude*. It is only a question of their paying his price. Both Sergeant and Bobby again concentrated on urging me to go to Taos, that I simply *must* go. I was a great deal impressed this time. After all they told me I really feel I ought to go, as if there was something down there I needed and that would give me something. Perhaps I might be able to go down for a few weeks after the plays get on. I've been thinking of this and it seems like a good plan to me. I certainly won't feel in any mood to start writing a new one for some weeks after this ordeal is over, my nerves and vitality will undoubtably be all shot, and some weeks in the desert might prove a wonderful reviver. What do you think?

I'm sending this check to Gaga. I'm also enclosing the check for five hundred to you herewith.

A few reviews of *Lazarus Laughed*[5] have appeared, one in *Tribune* a week ago today, very fine, by Lewis Mumford—one in *Times* today, one in last evening's *Sun*—all fine.[6] So that's hopeful.

I've got to end this—date with Phil M.[7] for dinner and work with him afterward. Much love, dearest, kiss Oona and Shane for me.   Gene

P.S. Just got your cable about house a few minutes ago. I'll have Harry get in touch with Crane tomorrow.

1. The first part of this letter is missing.
2. William A. Brady (1863–1950), prominent Broadway producer.
3. Tom Powers (Charles Marsden), Glenn Anders (Edmund Darrell), and Earle Larimore (Sam Evans), who were in the cast of *Strange Interlude* when it opened on January 30, 1928, at the John Golden Theatre.
4. Alfred Lunt (1892–1980), who played Marco Polo when *Marco Millions* opened on January 9, 1928, at the Guild Theatre.
5. Published by Boni and Liveright on November 11.
6. Lewis Mumford, "Lazarus Laughs Last," *New York Herald-Tribune Books*, November 20, 1927, pp. 1, 6; Brooks Atkinson, "Man's Challenge to Death in Lazarus Laughed," *New York Times Book Review*, November 27, 1927, p. 5; Edwin Bjorkman, "A Dramatist of Moods," *New York Sun*, November 26, 1927, p. [11].
7. Philip Moeller.

Just got your two letters and am writing a line before going to the Guild. I'll send the check to Bedini.[8] I'm going to sell R'field for 30,000—get rid of the damn place even at a loss. Got your cable about Denton—had Harry phone Winstead to find out what it was about. Later I got this telegram from Winstead: "Have accepted Mrs. O'Neill's offer for two puppies." Signed "Denton." What the hell does that mean? You're not buying more dogs are you, at this time?

I'm so damn busy I'm nearly off my nut, but feeling not so bad, considering the pressure. I'm sorry about no letter on last mail. I'll try and do better after this.

Must run now. Love—   Gene

---

233 • TO AGNES BOULTON O'NEILL.   ALS 4 pp. ([Hotel Wentworth / New York]) [Harvard]

Friday evening / [December 2?, 1927]

Dearest Aggie: I've had no time to really sit down and write until now—and I guess it's too late to catch the mail if I mail it from here so I'll send it over to Gray, the purser, by messenger and have him mail it the first thing when they land.

This week has been spent mostly in hearing people read for all the innumerable small parts in *Marco.* You would think they would be easy to cast but they're not—or else the available brand of actor and actress is particularly poor. It has been a long boring business and the opening has been postponed until the 9th of Jan. instead of 6th, so that the *real* rehearsals start next Monday instead of last. But I feel as if I'd already had a full week of them! I haven't met either Lunt or Fontanne yet. From what I hear they are both pretty dull in the old bean—but that hardly astonishes me. At any rate, they both *can* act. I've also been doing a lot on *Interlude* with Phil. Bobby finally backed out of doing the sets of *Interlude*— had a fit of arty temperament and decided he couldn't work with the Guild people. I suppose he asked Arthur's advice! Well, it's his own funeral.

And now about the house in Ridgefield. I sold it, as I cabled you, for 30000 less an agent's commission of 1000 (Harry jewed Crane down to that)—which means that all I will get is 14000 out of the deal—which means, considering the money I've put in out there plus the price paid, a loss of at least ten thousand! Not a bright business deal! But I thought it best to sell and get the white elephant off my conscience. I hope you felt properly relieved when you got my cable. All of this money I'm going to put back into stocks to pay back into my capital what we've used of the cash from the sale of New London stuff in fixing up Spithead which, as you know, was to be considered as a loan until Ridgefield was sold. I'm sure you will agree that this is the sensible thing to do. Until we're sure what the fate of the plays is going to be, we really mustn't be so foolish as to put any more money into Spithead than what we've already agreed upon—the sum from the stocks I sold for that purpose. We have, counting the 10000 paid in the sale, already got 35000 sunk in Spithead and that's aplenty for an artist who is trying to stick to being an artist. So please, if you think anything of my peace of mind, don't go making plans for Spithead beyond what we've already agreed on,

---

8. Vincent Bedini, who worked for the O'Neills at Brook Farm.

just because Ridgefield is sold. Later on, it may be a lot different but for the present the only sensible thing to do is to stand pat and have a good reserve for me to work on in peace in case the plays flop.

The time limit before the buyer gets possession is until February 1st and he says we can leave the furniture there later than that if we like as he isn't going to start any work on the place (he plans a lot of renovating) until the winter is all over and the weather right. So you know where you stand on that and can plan accordingly. In this connection let me say that you mustn't think I will be horribly hurt if you can't arrange it to come up in time for the opening of the plays. I understand your feeling about first nights. They are the bunk! And at least with Guild productions you can be sure, even if the worst happens, that you'll be able to see both plays for six weeks after they open! And it's your seeing them that is the important thing and not the opening night fiesta, at which I certainly shall not be present, anyway. So do what you think best about this according to your own inclination.

What plans are you making about coming up? You don't say in your letters. Is your Mother going down?

Now here is something that is *very very important* and that I wish you would attend to *without fail* as soon as possible. Liveright has spoken to Rosenbach,[1] the big dealer, about my original scripts and Rosenbach is very much interested and wants to see what he can do about them *but* he must first see them and make sure that I really have a complete set—also their condition, etc. etc. It is no question of an immediate sale but, given the time, he thinks he can work them up to a big price. The point about your sending them immediately is that he is going away in two weeks—to Coast or Europe, I forget which—and I want him to see them before he goes. Now will you find out what is the best possible way—safest—to send them? Perhaps giving them to the purser to lock up for the voyage and for me to call for—or to insure them *very* heavily and send by mail—or maybe there will be someone coming up whom you can trust. (But it must be someone you *can absolutely trust!*) You will find them all in the second drawer from top of the cabinet nearest the door. If not in this drawer, then in one below it—at any rate, in the drawer the steel box with most of them in it is in. And please send *all the contents* of that drawer so there can be no mistake! But do please take the greatest care about all this. Remember this may be a big "ace in the hole" for us and the kids. I really ought to have them in a safe deposit box—fire-proof—up here anyway so they'd be absolutely safe.

And here's another thing I wish you would do—in connection with the R'field sale. I must get all the insurance policies to Harry at once. Will you go through my contract drawer (top drawer in the middle, I think) and get any insurance thing relating to R'field? They must be there, if I have them.

Be careful in packing those scripts! Better ask the Furness people the safest way to send them. And be sure to send everything you find. I've got to convince R. the set is complete.

I've been trying to write Shane—will find time soon—tell him to forgive a busy Daddy—and have him dictate to me. Kiss Oona for me. Bye bye for this time, Dearest, and much love! I know my letters must sound like a stock broker's to his frau but I'm really so damn up to my neck in business that that's all I've got to write about.   Kisses!   Gene

P.S. I'm sending this by boy down to General P.O.—it can be in time for mail there.

---

1. A. S. W. Rosenbach, a prominent rare books and autographs dealer and collector.

ALS 5 pp. (Stationery headed: Hotel
Wentworth / 59 West 46th Street / New York) [Harvard]

Tuesday / [December 20?, 1927]

Dearest Aggie: Some lines before going to rehearsal. I have been working like hell the
past few days trying to cut some time out of *Interlude*. It turned out to be much longer than I
thought and I've simply got to get it down. But it isn't easy. Nor grateful work. Added to
everything else, it's almost too much. I've had a hell of a cold and am worn out and
depressed. Still this cutting must be done—otherwise the play couldn't be done in an
afternoon-evening and that would be fatal. And, at that, I think the cutting will help it as a
playing play. The book is a different matter.

Rehearsals of *S.I.* are coming along fine. Real enthusiasm among the company. *Marco* is
also blooming—except for the man who is playing the Kaan.[1] So far he is pretty poor but we
hope he will finally get it. Otherwise it will be a mess.

Excuse me for speaking so much about my plays. I realize that it's tactless on my part.
It's quite evident to me that you're not interested since you never mention them.

I hope the scripts in the steel box will arrive by the next boat. I was terribly worried
when one package came and the box didn't. I thought my letter had been very explicit and
that you must have sent them and they must have gotten lost or stolen. A pretty appalling
thought for me! If they were lost, I'd go off my nut!

I'm enclosing a check for one hundred for you for Christmas. I've honestly tried damn
hard to get you a present—gone to stores when I should have been at rehearsal. But I
couldn't see or think of anything. Mrs. Winston[2] sent me down to a Chinese importing
house. I thought I'd get you a jade necklace, but the only decent ones were five hundred and
up and that's out of present reach. They had cheaper ones but I didn't like them and was
pretty sure you wouldn't. I explain all this because I don't want you to believe that the check
is only a lazy man's easy gift. But you'll probably believe that anyway.

You never say a word about your plans. Are you coming up—and, if so, when? I don't
mean for the openings—or one of them. Leave them as entirely out of your considerations
as, if you are frank, you must acknowledge they are out of your mind. Think of your own
pleasure in making this trip or not making it. If you'd rather stay where you are with the
children, if you're having a fairly amusing time down there, don't feel there's any obligation
to come. N.Y. is far from pleasant these days, I warn you. The weather has been hellish. In
short, what I mean by all this talk is, please feel free to do as you wish without any
compunction about hurting my feelings. I honestly don't care. You can't hurt me any more,
thank God! You've tortured your last torture as far as I'm concerned. Something in me is so
damn utterly dead that I don't care about anything any more—except doing my work. I am
so damn tired with the bitterness and futility of all my dead dreams that, as the Senator says
in *Laz*, "I could welcome my own death as an excuse for sleeping."

A gloomy letter for Christmas? Well, it really shouldn't be for you. You are still young
and beautiful and, with any sort of an even break from fate, you should have every chance
for a real happiness before you—a happiness that it has become indubitably evident I never
did and never can give you. And I certainly wish you to be happy, Agnes—from the bottom

1. Baliol Holloway.
2. Mrs. Norman Winston, wife of a wealthy shoe manufacturer whose husband had contributed to the
Provincetown Playhouse.

of my heart—remembering our years of struggle and the deep friendship that ought, no matter what, if we are decent human beings, to exist between us for the rest of our lives. For what has happened is neither your fault nor mine. It is simply the curse of the soul's solitude, the grinding, disintegrating pressure of time, that has destroyed Us. If we are not vicious and mean, we can only sadly pity each other. We both tried—and tried hard!

So my Christmas present to you is really to give you back your absolute liberty in any way, by any method, you may desire. I will always do anything you wish to make you happy. I will always be your friend—your very best friend, I hope! I can be that—in fact, as a friend I can be "the works" while as a husband I'm afraid I've been a miserable misfit.

Please believe that everything I have written is an explanation of something that has happened in me. No outside circumstance has anything to do with it. And no one is to blame. Any other supposition would be shallow and absurd. You know well enough that, when it comes to profound inner convictions I am not swayed by anything but my own searching of my own life. And this is a time when, in justice to us both and our children, I have searched deeply. And you are free!

Look into your own heart and face the truth! You don't love me any more. You haven't for a long time. Perhaps you feel a real affection, as I do for you, but marriage, as I wanted it and can live with it, cannot go on on that.

But there's no use going into it. It is. We don't love each other. That's evident to anyone. So, as friends who wish each other happiness, what are we going to do about it? As far as I'm concerned, anything you wish. It doesn't matter to me. Nothing matters. I'll work someplace or other—California, New Mexico, Florida, it doesn't matter a damn. I can rely on myself to do my stuff and outside of that life is meaningless to me, anyway.

Kiss the children for me. I hope they like their presents. I love them more than you give me credit for. But what do you understand of me or I of you? And for their future happiness I am sure it's better for me to be more a friend and less a father than the reverse.   God bless you and give you happiness!   Gene

---

235 • TO AGNES BOULTON O'NEILL.   ALS 6 pp. (Stationery headed: Hotel Wentworth / 59 West 46th Street / New York) [Harvard]

Monday eve. / [December 26?, 1927]

Dearest Agnes: I just got your cable a while ago, saying you understand. I wonder if you really do. Well, I will not beat about the bush but come to the point at once. I love someone else. Most deeply. There is no possible doubt of this. And the someone loves me. Of that I am as deeply certain. And under these circumstances I feel it is impossible for me to live with you, even if you were willing I should do so—which I am sure that you are not, as it would be even a greater degradation to your finer feelings than it would to mine to attempt, for whatever consideration there may be, to keep up the pretense of being husband and wife.

We have often promised each other that if one ever came to the other and said they loved someone else that we would understand, that we would know that love is something which cannot be denied or argued with, that it must be faced. And that is what I am asking you to understand and know now. I am sure that I could accept the inevitable in that spirit if our roles were reversed. And I know that you, if for nothing else than that you must remember with kindness our years of struggle together and that I have tried to make you happy and to be happy with you, will act with the same friendship toward me. After all, you know that I have always been faithful to you, that I have never gone seeking love, that if my love for you had not died no new love would have come to me. And, as I believe I said in my last letter, if you are frank and look into your own heart you will find no real love left for me in it. What has bound us together for the past few years has been deep down a fine affection and friendship, and this I shall always feel for you. There have been moments when our old love flared into life again but you must acknowledge that these have grown steadily rarer. On the other side of the ledger moments of a very horrible hate have been more and more apparent, a poisonous bitterness and resentment, a cruel desire to wound, rage and frustration and revenge. This has killed our chance for happiness together. There have been too many insults to pride and self-respect, too many torturing scenes that one may forgive but which something in one cannot forget and which no love, however strong, can continue to endure and live.

I am not blaming you. I have been as much as you, perhaps more so. Or rather, neither of us is to blame. It is life which made us what we are.

My last letter did not mention being in love because, even if I were not so deeply and entirely in love with someone else, I think we ought to end our marriage in order to give us both a chance, while we are both at an age when there still is a chance, to find happiness either alone or in another relationship. Soon it would be too late. And if in the end we have failed to give happiness to each other, then all the more reason why each of us owes the other another chance for it.

Looking at it objectively, I am sure freedom to do as you please will mean a lot to you. You can go to Europe, for instance, as you have always wished—live there or anywhere else you like. You can have the use of Spithead exclusively for the rest of your life as a permanent home. I will never go to Bermuda again. You can be reasonably sure, unless catastrophe beans me, that you will always have enough income from me to live in dignity and comfort. You know I am hardly a stingy person, that I will do anything that is fair, that I will want to do all I can for you. And, above all, you will have your chance of marrying someone else who will love you and bring you happiness. I am happy in my new love. I am certain that a similar happiness is waiting for you. It seems obvious to me that it must be.

When I say I am happy now, it is deeply true. My only unhappiness is what I expressed in my last letter—a bitter feeling of sadness when I think over all our years together and what the passage of time has done to us. At such moments I feel life-disgusted and hopeless. It gives me the intolerable feeling that it is perhaps not in the nature of living life itself that fine beautiful things may exist for any great length of time, that human beings are fated to destroy just that in each other which constitutes their mutual happiness. Fits of cosmic Irish melancholia, I guess! Otherwise I am strangely happy. Something new in me has been born. I tell you this in the trust that your friendship may understand and be glad and wish me luck—and set me free to live with that happiness.

I mean, divorce me. That is what we agreed we would do if the present situation ever occurred, isn't it? It is the only fair thing—fair to you as to me in that it gives us both freedom. A separation is only for people with religious scruples. It is a ruinous thing because it divides and keeps joined at the same time. It forces each party into all sorts of sneaking love affairs. It turns a possible friendship of people who have agreed to disagree into the hatred and revenge of bitter enemies.

But I don't want to go into what should be done in this letter—I mean, arrangements about this and that and the other. As for the children, what I said in my last letter is true and need not be repeated. When you come up all this can be talked over.

This letter is merely to say that you *must* realize this decision is final, that we can never live together again, that I am never coming to Bermuda again, that when you come up we must live separately, that we must try to meet as friends who want to help each other, that we must avoid scenes and gossip and cheap publicity, that we must keep our mouths shut and make the world mind its business and not use our unhappiness for shiny copy, that we must remember our children will forgive us parting and understand it but won't forgive or understand—and they would be right—if we let ourselves get dragged in the dirt. In short, we must act like decent human beings, realizing that we are both hot-tempered and sensitive to take offense at each other's words or looks or whatever, that we can and must, for our own and our children's sake, remain friends who wish each other happiness. I know how I would act if I were in your place—how I would force myself to act even if I loved you and your decision crushed me. I confidently expect you to do the same by me. You don't love me and it should not be hard.

If you can see your way to it, I'd be eternally grateful if you postponed coming up until after my openings. It isn't going to be easy for us, what we've got to do, and for me it would make it terrifically difficult even to think of plays just when they need my thought most. But if you feel you must come up now, why come along. I don't want to be selfish about it.

This is a long letter! It is horribly hard for me to write these things to you—it is horrible to face the end of anything one has hugged to one's heart for years—but the truth is the truth and it must be told in justice to both of us, to give us both a chance to live our lives again.

Kiss Shane and Oona for me. My deep affection to you!   Gene

---

236 • TO AGNES BOULTON O'NEILL.   ALS 4 pp. (Stationery headed: Hotel Wentworth / 59 West 46th Street / New York) [Harvard]

Thursday / [January 19?, 1928]

Dearest Agnes: As I cabled you, your cable didn't reach me until afternoon yesterday—after the boat had sailed. I went out the afternoon before with Winston and stayed overnight at the place of a friend of his near Greenwich—when I got back next morning went directly to rehearsal without coming to the hotel. I'm awfully sorry. I'm enclosing the check for five hundred plus the Christmas present herewith. Meant to give it to you before you left. Why didn't you remind me then? I'm also enclosing the trunk key.

Also enclosed—if I get it in time tomorrow—will be the draft of an agreement between us that Harry has drawn up. I think we ought to get something of the sort signed and sealed before I go away, for God knows just when I will come back, once I've started off. It is really principally for your protection that this ought to be done. Once this agreement is signed you will know that you can absolutely depend on at least five hundred a month, that it is legally your right. It goes, as per our verbal agreement, from a minimum of six thousand a year to a maximum of ten thousand, depending on what I can afford. When I leave I will give Harry my power of attorney and he will see that you get this the first of every month so there will be no need for you to worry. When you come up in April or May, Harry will have full authority from me to provide for the trip you plan.[1] So you see that I am really trying to arrange everything so you will not have to fret. But I do beg of you, in fairness to me, to arrange your life on a five hundred a month budget. Anything I can afford beyond that you will get. You know I have never been tight on money matters and that you can trust me to do my best by you and the children. But you must look the facts in the face. Six thousand a year three years ago was over one-half my income, the next year it was one-fourth (that was a good year), last income tax year (I mean 1926) it was a good deal more than one-third of my income (if you leave out the sale of property—capital asset—the money from which went into Spithead) and for 1927 (a bad year with only a few weeks of *Beyond The Horizon* from

1. Agnes had agreed to go to Reno, Nevada, to get a divorce.

production) you will find it was also a good deal over one-third. So you see. I doubt on the basis of the above facts that any court would allow you as much as five hundred a month (especially considering I have Eugene to support) if you should sue for it. So does Harry. I merely explain the above to you to point out that it is wise for you to be economical, but that I am not trying to stint you. You talked a lot about my fine position to grow rich now with the Guild but, even if *Interlude* goes well, you must remember that it's late in the season, that both plays will be off by the end of June, that *Marco* plays only two weeks out of every four (on a low royalty scale too), that probably neither play can be taken on the road, that *Interlude* will have only 6 performances a week (no matinees). You must also remember that for almost a whole year now we have been living, with the exception of what came in from books, almost entirely on my capital and my children's, from the sale of property from my estate.

I know you hate talk about money but for my sake and your own and our children's, you've got to face these facts. Remember, if I don't write a play between now and fall there won't be any money coming in next year for you or anyone else—and I've got to have peace of mind and a chance for happiness in order to do my stuff. So don't let fools advise you to be as hard on me as you can. It's to your advantage in the long run to respect my desires—provided they're not obviously unfair, which you know me well enough to know they won't be. And don't run up outside bills—or I will have to take drastic measures to protect myself! Do you know what your hotel bill was for the last *two days* you were here? 122.00!—85 of it cash! Now I ask you! If that's playing fair, then I must be all wrong!

I'm going to New Mexico and California, I guess. Thought of Europe for a few days but changed my mind. *Lazarus Laughed* is to be done for a week at Pasadena around April 1st and I'd like to be there for some rehearsals—can live near there and still be on the ocean and doing my writing.

Will you send up my father's *Monte Cristo* script for the museum[2] (middle drawer, middle row) and the scripts of the scenarios for *The Hairy Ape* and *Desire*—top drawer, nearest door—to show Reinhardt? You remember I spoke about this. Please send right away—also all the letter files in my desk—lower drawer on right—and in the filing cabinet. I'll need these to refer to in case anything turns up. I also wish you'd pack and send me the complete set of all my books ever published that is on the shelf on the beam in what was my study. Please take good care of everything in that room, will you, and don't let worms get into the books, etc. It would be the best thing, especially as you will probably want to use the room for something else, if you will pack everything in it and send it up as soon as possible—especially all the books in there—to the Manhattan Storage people to be stored there in my name. Will you do this?

Speaking of the Manhattan Storage people, I'll pay them as soon as my first *Marco* money comes in—may get the Guild to advance me some. Last week's royalty disappeared in the 1000 advance I had had. And I'm practically broke, now that I've sent this check to you, until I get money from the R'field sale. Did you sell any of the furniture?

So have a care with the bankroll, Mrs. O'Neill! There isn't much of it and you can't get blood out of a stone, by process of law or any other way.

I hope you will soon write me that you are really at work again on your real stuff. This isn't a mercenary wish—it's a wish for your happiness!

I am tired out but I have peace of mind and certainty again—and I feel confident that nothing will disturb my deep feeling of calm and security. So you can plan accordingly. I know you wish my happiness as much as I do yours. We can be friends and we will be.

2. The Museum of the City of New York to whom O'Neill gave the *Monte Cristo* script.

Remember what I said that last night whenever you feel yourself getting bitter against me. That was the truth of my feeling toward you, now & ever after.

Kiss Shane & Oona for me. I love them both dearly—and I will prove it in all the years to come. Good luck & happiness, Old Pal! Gene

---

237 • TO SHANE O'NEILL. ALS 4 pp. (Stationery headed: Hotel Wentworth / 59 West 46th Street / New York) [Harvard]

[early February 1928]

Dear Shane: I have been meaning to write you a letter for a long, long time but I have really been so busy going to rehearsals of my two new plays that have just opened that I honestly haven't had a chance. Or when I did have a few minutes to spare I was always so tired out that all I could do was to lie down and rest. So I know that you will forgive me. And now, just when I get through with those two plays I have to travel way across America to California to watch them putting on another new play of mine *Lazarus Laughed* in the city of Pasadena. I will go in swimming out there in an ocean I have never been in before—the Pacific. I hope it is as beautiful water as the water in Bermuda.

Do you go in swimming every day now? Or is it too cold for you? But you are such a big boy now that you shouldn't mind water that is 60° and you really ought to get Mother to let you swim every day because that's the only way you can get good practice and be able to swim the crawl as well as Eugene does. It may be too cold for Oona to go in now but it shouldn't be for you.

I saw Eugene the other night. He had dinner with me here at the hotel and then I took him and Jimmy Light to see a prize fight—or I ought to say prize fights because there were four of them and they were all very exciting although no one got knocked out. There was one man called Leo Lomski who fought a man called McTigue and beat him, and you tell Harold and Johnson for me to keep their eyes on Lomski because he is certainly a fighting fool and he will lick a lot of them before he gets through. Mother saw him fight too when she went with me when she was in New York.

Eugene is even bigger than when he was down this summer. He weighs 165 now. He told me to give you and Oona his love when I wrote to you.

You must write me a long letter sometime soon and tell me everything that you and Oona are doing because it will probably be a long time before I will be able to see you both again. But I will often think of you and I will miss you both very much. I often lie in bed before I go to sleep—or when I can't go to sleep—and I picture to myself all about Spithead and what you both have been doing all day and I wonder how you are—and then I feel very sad and life seems to me a silly, stupid thing even at best when one lives it according to the truth that is in one. But you are not yet old enough to know what that feeling is—and I hope to God you never will know, but that your life will be always simple and contented! But always remember that I love you and Oona an awful lot—and please don't ever forget your Daddy.

I am enclosing a check for fifteen dollars. Ten of it is to buy you a present with, and five is to buy Oona a present. You must both go to town with Mother and pick out whatever you want most.

Kiss Oona for me and tell her I love her—and tell yourself so, too.

Give my love to Harold & Helen & [illegible name] & Taber and give Johnson & Lilly and Nurse and everyone else I know my best wishes.

Don't forget your Daddy! All my love to you, dear son! Father

Friday / [February 3?, 1928]

Dearest Agnes: I sent a check to the Manhattan Storage people yesterday—so you ought to get the furniture before long now.

Your cable in answer to mine about the furniture & trunks left out at Ridgefield came last night. I will wire Bedini. The man who bought it has been after me to get the stuff out of his way now, if I will do him the favor, as he wants to start making repairs soon.

Now the following is important so please get me straight on it and do what must be done! The fire place andirons *were* (rightly or wrongly doesn't count now!) included in the deed and as soon as you get the stuff unpacked (I couldn't do anything about it here as the Man. Storage people had it all packed) you must have these articles repacked and sent back to Ridgefield! Otherwise I will have to buy him all new ones and you know how much that will cost! Will you please attend to this at once? I promised the man I would have you do so. He is a very decent chap and we don't want to pull anything that looks tricky on him.

I've asked Jimmy L. all about his Conn. affair. The time business was easy for him to get by but would be absolutely impossible for you for two years & a half yet. So count that out.[1] The best plan is absolutely the one you proposed and we agreed on.

A strange story has reached me via one of your dear-friends-to-your-face. It is that you said you had been advised to hang on, promise in a friendly way to do everything I desired for my happiness but never really do anything—that you said this course of action would upset my new life so that I couldn't work and would then give up and come back—and that you said this was what you were going to do. Naturally, I can't believe this. It would be hardly an act consistent with honor or the friendship we swore to each other. And it wouldn't be practical, either—for your own sake or the children's. For it would undoubtedly make it impossible for me to work—and then there would be no new plays and no income for anyone to live on—until you decided to keep your faith with me. And, as far as our personal relations are concerned, if you did such a thing deliberately to try to ruin what I know is now so surely my future happiness, I would hate you as bitterly as you would deserve—and who would blame me?

I am very happy now—deeply happy—at peace in a deep fashion I have never known before! You must realize this! I know I have found what I so horribly needed in order to live and move on. *I know now!* It is unthinkable that, knowing this, you should not keep faith. After all, I've been fair to you, Agnes.

I don't believe the story but I'll admit it has disturbed me. Hence, the above.

Marco is beginning to fall off a bit on advance sales for next week—which is not a good sign. *Interlude* is playing to practically subscribers only (at 2.50 a seat). There will be hardly anyone able to see it but subscribers—the Golden is so small—for six weeks yet. So out of my two successes I'm not liable to become rich. Working with the Guild has its advantages—but also its financial disadvantages. When you get a real hit you can't realize on it. The trouble with *Interlude* is that as soon as spring and balmy afternoons arrive no one will want to go into a theatre at 5:15—and I don't blame them. It's too bad the plays didn't get started earlier. My good luck always has a copper on it somewhere.

I have read and reread both your letters. I know that all this is pretty hard for you right now—this period of readjustment—and I am damned sorry. But it simply had to be. We

---

1. The O'Neills were considering the possibility of Agnes's getting a divorce in Connecticut.

were not happy, we were torturing each other into hatred, there was none of the old love left, and I know that in the long run, for you as well as me, we will look back and find it fortunate that we faced this fact while there was still a chance for both of us to begin again. I am certain that soon you will begin to see the vision of a new life stretching out before you, a life in which you will gain the things you really need to make you happy, which I could not give you.

But the first step in your readjustment must be a complete acceptance of the truth that the old life is absolutely, definitely and completely dead, and to banish its ghost from your memory. Only then can our new relationship of old close friends who wish to help each other really begin. From my end at least, I speak as one who is absolutely sure. Since you left N.Y. I have realized how absolutely sure I am with enormous conviction. Many things have happened inside me. *I know!*

Kiss Shane and Oona for me. I wish I could see them. Don't let them forget me. I love them a lot more than you have ever given me credit for. It is only that I am a bit unexpressive about what I feel toward them.

Good'bye for this time. All my loving friendship. *Start on your work as soon as you can!*
Gene

---

239 • TO AGNES BOULTON O'NEILL.   ALS 4 pp. (Stationery headed: Hotel Wentworth / 59 West 46th Street / New York) [Harvard]

Tuesday / [February 7?, 1928]

Dearest Agnes: Your letters and Shane's keep arriving in installments—some last night and another this a.m. I had already mailed a long letter to Shane. You had better explain to him that it was written before I received his.

I'm sorry you feel that way about my not having sent the notices of *S.I.* As a matter of fact, I never thought of it. I didn't get the papers the next day anymore than I did with *Marco*. I simply phoned to Terry Helburn and asked how the press was and she told me it was grand in general and that was that. Later I looked them over in the Guild press books. I haven't got them from the clipping bureau yet because they're holding them pending a check from me, as I already owe them for 100 and have forgotten to send a check. So you see. But *S.I.* was a triumph. The trouble with my triumphs is that there's always so much of my own living on my mind at the time I haven't got any interest left for plays. Do you remember *The Hairy Ape* opening night with my Mother's body in the undertaking parlor? "So ist das Leben," I guess. Or at least my "leben." "The power & the glory" always pass over—or under—my head. I was too busy worrying about what you were going to do—or not do—to help or hurt me in my present situation to be much interested in the fate of *S.I.* You see, there have been so many ugly rumors about what you said to this one and that about how you were going to "wait me out"—rumors not coming from any source supposedly hostile to you, either!— that I have felt anything but secure. It isn't that I don't trust you to keep your word—when you're yourself, the fine, honorable woman you are at bottom. But when you've had even a few drinks you are neither fine nor honorable—and I would be a fool if I didn't take into consideration that under such circumstances, with the foxy(?) advice of some of your lousy friends to egg you on (they meanwhile sneering behind your back and only too delighted to start a mess for all of us!), you might very well do—or not do—something that would burn me up with hatred and keep me from working—I naturally cannot work if I am constantly forced to buck society and live in an atmosphere of suspicion and concealment, of being legally one woman's and emotionally another's.

I repeat again: I trust you, the real you—but I don't trust your—our—alleged friends—and God knows I would be an ass indeed if I trusted John Barleycorn!

You must know that your proposal for me to come down for a week would be a bad thing! It can't be did! It would not be kind to you, or me, or the children. By the end of the week you and I might be hating each other again—look at your stay in N.Y.! No, Agnes, we must not see each other again for a long time—not until the "possessive" stuff has died out in each of us and we are able to meet as real friends and parents of our children. Please realize that! You know damn well it is true. We've got to bury our dead—to wipe out and pass on—before our real friendship can begin. The old destructive habits of thought and feeling have got to be erased from our reactions to one another. I would be doing you a great wrong—retarding the growth of your independent personality—if I came down. I'd like to see Shane & Oona but—this is better in the long run for them too.

I've got a lot more to write you and tell you of my future plans but it will have to wait for my next.

Kiss Shane & Oona for me! I'm damned sorry you are finding things so difficult—but I really can't believe you love me (except as a friend as I still love you) or have ever loved me for years. You could not possibly have done the things you did. You could never have touched a drink, for example. It would have choked you to death—if you really loved me. And now I am really loved I see only too damned clearly by contrast all you failed to give me. I am not blaming you. It was true of me, too. It is what life does to love—unless you watch and care for it. This time I am going to watch and care. And when you fall in love—as I am sure you soon will—you better bear that in mind, too.   All my loving friendship always!   Gene

---

240 • TO KENNETH MACGOWAN.   ALS 4 pp. (Stationery headed: The Berkeley / London, W.1) [Yale]

Feb. 22, 1928

Dear Kenneth: Well, we've been in London now for almost a week and I must confess—it is a confession for an O'Neill—that I certainly like this town better than any city I've ever been in. There is something so stable and solid and self-assuredly courteous about it. It's like a soothing bath for the nerves after the frazzle of New York. And I've been very much incognito. No one knows that a notorious Yank is in their midst. The "eminent dramatist" is very much on vacation and Eugene O'Neill, the man, is at last given his chance to spread himself and live. And, as in the story of the dinosaurus who only cohabits with his mate once in every thousand years, "Christ, how he does enjoy it!"

God, I wish I could tell you how happy I am! I'm simply transformed and transfigured inside! A dream I had given up even the hope of ever dreaming again has come true! I wander about foolish and goggle-eyed with joy in a honeymoon that is a thousand times more poignant and sweet and ecstatic because it comes at an age when one's past—particularly a past such as mine—gives one the power to appreciate what happiness means and how rare it is and how humbly grateful one should be for it. And dreaming it all over in these days when the dream has become flesh and flesh the dream, it really seems to my mystic side as if some compassionate God, looking back at Carlotta's unhappy life and mine, had said to himself, well, they deserve something from me in recompense for all my little jokes, they deserve each other if they have the guts to take the gift. And we did have—and here we are!

I know the tale of another's love is always sappy to a guy's ears—nevertheless I continue to impose mine on your friendship knowing that even if you think me quite "nuts" you will be glad I enjoy being that way! I felt freed the moment the boat left New York and although it was a rough trip and we spent most of the time in our cabins—(there were several on the passenger list who would have recognized us)—we managed to have a happy time of it. And these days in London have been perfect. To say that Carlotta and I are in love in the sense of any love I have ever experienced before is weak and inadequate. This is a brand new emotion and I could beat my brains out on the threshold of any old temple of Aphrodite out of pure gratitude for the revelation! It is so damn right in every way! We "belong" to each other! We fulfill each other! "The world is round and perfect. I am living a dream within the great dream of the tide——breathing in the tide I dream and breathe back my dream into the tide!"[1]

But you've had about enough of my raving, I suspect.

We're heading for the south of France on Sunday and will motor around until we find what we want either on the coast of France or Spain or Italy—a villa not too isolated and not too near, not too fancy and not too swank, where we have a car and a boat and so forth and be close enough to a town to mingle in when we need a change. We've got people—agents—in Paris already looking up all sorts of places and it will not take long, I think, until we are settled.

Then for *Dynamo*. I feel full of work and creative energy—new ideas have come—others are filling out in my mind. In short, old chummie, I bloody well burgeon a bit!

C/o Guaranty Trust, Pall Mall, London will be the address until I write you I'm settled. Drop me a line and let me know what you hear and all the dope on Langner's play.[2]

When we'll return to U.S. I don't know—and somehow I can't seem to care. The Guild, if they take them, can very well put on my stuff for a couple of years without me. Of course, a lot depends on what Agnes does or doesn't do—on whether she has the honor to keep the pledge we have always made to each other and the promise she made to keep that pledge when she was in N.Y. I think she will. She is fine and sound at bottom. But the influences she is under in Bermuda with that Phila. Social Register bunch of futile women with money is about as far removed from fundamental human beingism as one could get—and A. is easily swayed by the rich and the social. So one never can tell. But it doesn't matter much anyway as long as I can live and write where people mind their own business and approve of love without moral didacs. We may stay away for a long time in any event. Now I'm started I want to keep going. There's Greece & Egypt and the East—and South Africa where I've always wanted to go and where I need to go for the new negro play I've doped out and will write in the next few years—and the South Seas. There's a good bit of the old Gene O'Neill, A.B.[3]—his spirit refined and minus the spirits that kept it going—reborn in me. I *feel* life again—without fear this time. It isn't a battle now—it's the end of the war, I hope—and the dawn of a new appreciation and evaluation.

Well, all best to you—and Carlotta joins in. You have been a fine friend to us both—when friends to both were almost nil—and we both are deeply grateful. You must try and get over and see us this summer.

As for all my pseudo-friends, you will have my benediction when you hear any of them "viewing with alarm" if you infuriate them by saying you have heard from me and that for the first time in my life I am really happy! Adios, amigo! Write,   Gene

---

1. This quotation, slightly altered (for "round" read "whole"), is from a speech by Nina Leeds at the beginning of act 5 of *Strange Interlude*.

2. *These Modern Women*, which opened at the Eltinge Theatre on February 13, 1928, produced by Macgowan and Robert Rockmore.

3. Able-bodied seaman.

March 10th, [1928]

Dear Agnes: I just received the first letter I have gotten from you since leaving N.Y. four weeks ago. It was forwarded to the Guaranty Trust in London and by them to France. It seems to have been written without any knowledge that I had sailed from N.Y. I can't understand this as I wrote you a long letter the day before I left explaining the why and wherefore of my change of plans—why I'd decided not to go to California, etc. But I can't tell when your letter was mailed as the postmark is blurred out. It would help to make matters clearer if you would date your letters.

Two cables from you to the Wentworth also reached me—somewhat late!—by this same mail. The *Daily News* was after me before I left but I denied everything as usual. The notice they printed was a pretty snotty one from my end with its rot about our starving in the early days and our "frail" son, etc. but it certainly gives you all the sympathy as the pathetic deserted wife which I hope makes you as furious as it does me. But I suppose that's the yellow journal way of looking at it and it can't be helped. But to say you were nearly forty was the crowning insult of all.

I've been enjoying my visit to France, going from place to place looking for the right one to settle down in which I haven't found yet. But I'm in no hurry because I feel that if anyone had ever earned the right to a vacation I have. I'm quite happy just living and looking at things for a change. I'm now in Biarritz for a couple of days. It's a delightful place at this time of the year out of season. Later on, I hear it's expensive and jammed with society but now it's quiet and peaceful. I've had no permanent address to which to have mail forwarded until I told the Guaranty people to send stuff here for a few days. I came down from Paris slowly through the château district in Lorraine along the Loire and visited a number of the old châteaus and went through them. Wonderful places—and especially interesting to me because I happen to know French history so well.

Harry writes (forwarded from London by same mail) that a lawyer came to him saying you had cabled him but that he didn't seem to know what you wanted to know and so nothing happened. I think you can safely wait until you come up in April or May and then see Harry with your lawyer. I mean there's nothing for you to get excited or worried over as I left a separate account with plenty of money in it to take care of all your expenses, at the usual rate for the next six months, including your trip West. Of course, if you should be influenced to change your mind, why that will create an entirely new situation.

I have sent postals to Shane and Oona several times. Hope you got my letter from London. I'll let you know where I settle down—probably on the Mediterranean coast or in Majorca—as soon as I get put.

Your letter sounds happier. I'm glad. I hope you've started work. Of course, I won't sell Spithead as long as you want to live there. What do you think I am? Please have confidence in me. As long as you act like a friend toward me I will do anything you wish that I can afford. Everything will be taken care of. Send me my Trumingham and Smith bills, etc. Only be economical. I assure you my expenses over here are amazingly small. It will be wise to let me save some money out of this year's luck. As you know from the past, there are bad years that must be anticipated. With four children to support I have a right to save money. Yes, I include Barbara. After all I've done all that has been done in that line.

Kiss Shane & Oona for me. I miss them horribly at times. Don't let them forget me.

I am happy and quite sure of the lasting fundamental value of what I'm doing.   All deepest friendship always, dear!   Gene

242 • TO AGNES BOULTON O'NEILL.   ALS 4 pp. (c/o Guaranty Trust Co., / 50 Pall Mall, London) [Harvard]

[late March 1928]

Dear Agnes: I have just received, forwarded from London, your two letters to Harry about financial matters. After reading them I feel pretty hopeless about our reaching any friendly agreement since you seem to have determined on the policy of getting all you can out of me, regardless of my welfare or that of our children's future which depends, if you would only have foresight enough to see it, so much on my ability to save money in good years for the lean ones that inevitably have followed in the past when there have been no productions or the plays have been failures. I want to save money this year—(I am living very cheaply over here, thanks to a fifty-fifty basis and the big advantage of dollars in francs)—but if you are crying that you "*must*" have 2500.00 no less for back bills after I've just paid a thousand in back bills in New York I can see little hope of saving a cent at that rate. Moreover, if you keep this up on me, I'm not going to try to save. It would be too futile. Also, your attitude puts me in no right frame of mind to write any new plays. And if my work stops, my income won't be enough to keep one of us going, let alone four or five! I advise you to give this matter a little careful thought before you try "taking me for all I've got." Then if you want to sue, go ahead. Perhaps that's the best way—and the cheapest for me—for I have a pretty good side to my case to present to any court and, thank God, I'm now out of reach of all the cheap publicity that will be called forth by your action—and I can, if necessary, stay out of reach of it indefinitely over here. So don't think you can frighten me by threatening to sue. Outside of the fact that I should hate you for dragging such a nasty mess of notoriety around our children's ears, when, if you weren't so eager to get all you can, everything could be arranged quietly on a decent human basis, I don't care whether you sue or not. But I've cabled Harry to go down and see you and go over the back bills you've run up and do everything for you that is fair. But you've simply got to cut out running up bills regardless in the future. And you must not ask me to put any more money into Spithead. I can't and won't. I've already put too much into it. It's been the most expensive place that ever was built by anyone—and that's absolutely your fault since it was all left up to you. If I did what I want to do I'd advertise it for sale tomorrow. The only reason I don't is for your sake and the children's. You know that. And if you don't stop running up more bills for other than living necessities down there you'll force me to cable a notice to the Bermuda papers saying I won't be held responsible for such debts. If you're determined to act like an enemy, you can't expect me to take it lying down. I've got to put up a battle for some sort of financial security for myself in order to do my work.

I suspect that what may be in back of your head—thanks to the advice you seem to be following, for I cannot imagine you acting so unfairly on your own and going back on all you'd agreed on as to your expenses in your talk with me!—is that you think you can make me buy you into keeping your word as to what you promised you would do. Well, you can't. I don't give a damn now whether you go ahead with that or not. It will make no difference in my life over here—except to keep me in a state of mind where no new plays will be forthcoming to earn royalties for you to throw away.

I have received a letter by this same mail from a recent visitor to Bermuda who shall be nameless saying that she had heard the gossip down there that you had "gone to pieces," were drinking, and at least on the verge of becoming a bit promiscuous with your favors, if you hadn't already fallen. "Such a shame for my poor dear little children," the writer went on—and blamed me as much as you. Now, of course, I appreciate the malice in such letters beneath the ostensible friendliness and I don't believe this one—although if you're drinking I know that nothing is impossible! I simply pass it on to you to warn you that there must be such gossip and you would do well, whatever you choose to do, to keep it dark. I have no right to tell you not to have lovers, or not to drink—except in our children's names—nevertheless such letters, even when I discount them, give me a turn. For no matter what our differences are and have been, I still love and respect you as my partner of ten long years in which we both managed to remain fairly clean. And that I fell in love I cannot regard as any breach of good faith since, as long as you let me be, I was quite honest with you about it.

I'm sorry this letter sounds so bitter. I can't help it. I especially resent in the last letter I received from you over here—I've only got two so far—your implication that you are doing all the suffering. For Christ's sake, don't you think I suffer too? If you don't, Agnes, you're a damn fool! Sometimes—and often!—when I think of Shane and Oona I suffer like hell from a sense of guilt toward them, and a deep sense of guilt because I've made you suffer. You know damn well that I am a man who shrinks from the very notion of deliberately causing anyone sorrow. (Rages & fights and what one bitterly says then don't count.) It is in every line of my work. But what could I do? I did my damndest and fairest while I could. And I think, by God, that when you said "forgive me" that day at the hotel you saw the truth that you seem to be getting far away from now, the truth that at bottom you were a great deal more to blame than I was! I gave you every chance a man of honor could give, I fought and was willing to sacrifice myself, all I needed was understanding, sympathy and help in a time of deep emotional and spiritual turmoil. You were deaf and blind and dumb—(until it was too late and the irrevocable was an accomplished fact)—because you didn't want to hear or see or speak.

Think that over once in a while when you take to hating me and wishing me unhappiness!

Oh hell, I'll be fair about bills or anything else. You know that. I always have been generous enough to you and yours—even at times when I couldn't afford it. As for your plans for the future, do what and when you like. It doesn't matter. Life has become so complicated on all sides for me—I don't mean I'm unhappy but that I have to give up so much—all the past—for my happiness—that the one major complication is merely a symbol. And over here where Eugene O'Neill luckily has no news value, what's the difference? So go ahead at your own convenience. You will be fair, I know.   Gene

P.S. Kiss Shane & Oona for me. I wrote him yesterday and sent her a postal.

---

243 • TO HARRY WEINBERGER.   ALS 4 pp. (Villa Marguerite, / Guéthary, B.P., / France) [Yale]

April 8th [1928]

Dear Harry: I've been waiting to hear from you after your Bermuda trip but got a second letter from you today showing you were still in town on the 24th, so I might as well answer that and the one before it and get some things off my mind.

Firstly, I can't put it too emphatically to you that I consider any notion of a Conn. divorce as out of the question. You know you looked that up and found it would take a long time—3 years for desertion. Now time is just the most important element in all this for me—and for *us*. This present situation is all right enough as long as we stay hidden in out of the way towns in Europe but we can't live that way indefinitely; and if we venture around much

I am sure to be recognized. I was in London and in Paris. A London paper wrote about my being there and the Paris *Herald*[1]—which we get—has already had two notices about my being "somewhere in France." If we're caught living together here the Paris papers will take it up, cable it to U.S., and then there *will be* a scandal. For myself, I don't give a damn any more but it will make it hellish for Carlotta and prevent her for all time from getting the guardianship of her little girl.[2] So you see. She is the one who must be protected in this. Of course, it *would be possible* to hide out over here for years with a minimum chance of recognition—and this I would prefer doing to having Agnes blackmail me out of all I've got to give me a divorce. But the point is that from her last letter she has made all arrangement to go to Nevada, seems perfectly satisfied to do this, and plans to leave around the end of May— and I sure hope to Christ you didn't talk of Conn. to her but urged her on to Reno! I don't give a damn if it does cost a little more! I want that divorce at the earliest possible moment! This present situation is going to be positively lousy for us two when it comes time for us to get back in the world—if I want to be in New York next fall, etc.—and if Agnes will only carry out her plan it will settle everything in the best possible fashion for all of us. So kindly do your damndest to get her to do so.

As to publicity let me state again that I don't give a tinker's damn how much there is in the papers about Agnes getting a divorce *provided* there is no question of a correspondent. In fact, I would like nothing better than if Agnes would tell the papers—as Sinclair Lewis' wife recently did—that she is going to Reno to get a divorce because we have grown to be absolutely incompatible but that there is no question of a correspondent and the whole affair is entirely friendly. Every paper would carry that story and then that would be that, they'd see there was no chance of dirt, and they'd drop it. Divorce itself has damn little news value, if there's no correspondent. You know that. So why don't you suggest this plan to Agnes? Or shall I? It might solve this whole matter of publicity. We're only being hounded because they scent scandal and mystery. I'm all for taking the lid off the mystery and letting them see a plain everyday Reno divorce for incompatibility or what not. And the sooner the story of this comes out the better pleased I'll be—and the freer I'll feel. And as long as Agnes has definitely made up her mind to go to Reno why isn't it all right for her to come out openly and say so? I ask to know! So please get it out of your head that I'm afraid of publicity! I only don't want Carlotta mixed up in it. But for myself I'd rather have it come out now while I'm here than later on.

As for Spithead, keep it to bargain with. Tell Agnes if she won't sign that agreement, she can't have it. I'll sell it or rent it. *In no event* will I give it to her for life or guarantee her possession of it for more than five years. I've reconsidered. The situation is changed a bit since I last wrote you. For one thing, I have a letter from Agnes in which, although she isn't conscious of it, she makes some pretty damaging admissions which wouldn't listen well in a court. In fact, I should think, on the basis of that letter, I ought to be able to sue for divorce in any state myself. So if she wants to fight, I'll fight, tell her! I think I've got the goods on her— and I'm getting sick and tired of her high and mighty attitude about money! If she had a shred of pride she'd be ashamed of herself! I've not only given her everything she wanted for the past seven years but I've supported her child and staked every member of her family time and time again—7500 for this last item alone, at least.

But enough of that! However, remember about the letter. If she's going to sue or hold me up I'll send it on to you and you can tell me if, with it as evidence (it's all in her own

1. The *International Herald Tribune,* which was published in Paris.
2. Cynthia Chapman, the child of Carlotta and her second husband, Melvin C. Chapman, Jr. Cynthia lived with Nellie Tharsing, Carlotta's mother, in California.

handwriting) I can't start suit in Connecticut myself. And you can write her that this is the way I feel about it.

Here's something I wish to howl at you about old top! Madden writes me you said something to him about our marital troubles—or alluded to something of the kind—and told him you were going to Bermuda. A bad error! Never tell Madden anything! Remember that! He's a good guy in his way but a regular old maid for gossip. That's where the *World* man got his info, you'll find out. Marbury[3] is no fool. They couldn't pump her. Of course, Dick would deny it but that's undoubtedly (if you knew him) how it leaked. So give him no further confidences. I haven't given him any address but Guaranty Trust, London—that's how far I trust him.

I'm enclosing a check for 500.00 for you.

I'm working hard on *Dynamo* and it's coming along fine. Since I got A's letter that she was going to Reno, I've felt much more settled in mind for work. It's in that respect that her dodging the issue would hurt me—but in the long run it would hurt her too for she'd get no money.

And that's about all, I guess, for this time. Except to add that I'm still happy—a good deal more so now—for in this lonely, cut-off life in which we have to look to each other for everything Carlotta and I have stood the test, got to know each other better, and are more in love than ever! So there you are!

Why not tell the next reporter who calls that the last you heard from me I was in Prague and was bound eventually for Constantinople? I want attention directed away from France all I can. I think this is a good hunch.

I'm enclosing a letter to Agnes for you to mail from N.Y. I'm telling her in it that I'm on the Mediterranean.   All best!   Gene

P.S. Will you get a check book from Guaranty Trust (44th St) and one from Corn Exchange, Astor Place and send to me?

---

244 • TO AGNES BOULTON O'NEILL.   ALS 5 pp. (c/o Guaranty Trust Co., / Pall Mall, London) [Harvard]

[c. April 8, 1928]

Dearest Agnes: Your two letters reached me yesterday and I was certainly damned happy to know that you've gotten down to work on a thing that deeply interests you. It gives me more satisfaction than I can tell you to hear that you are writing again and confident and happy about it. That was the news that I have been looking forward to hearing. Now you are all right and on your own feet in your own life! That is exactly what you needed! If you had had that in the past few years we might have won out to final happiness together—but I realize it was exactly the fact of my being around that made it impossible for you! The irony of our fate, what? Well, when you come into your own as a writer—and I am absolutely sure you will if you hew to the line!—you can look back and bless the day I got out and left you free to do your stuff!

I shall look forward with the keenest interest to reading your script. It was rather a dirty dig you give me about my "fatal criticisms" of "write something else?" After all, you must acknowledge, if you are honest, that I have always done my best to encourage you to do your best and not to attempt easy things, or unimportant themes, or junk for money. I have

---

3. Elizabeth Marbury, one of Madden's partners in the American Play Company, at whose house in Belgrade Lakes, Maine, O'Neill had remet Carlotta in the summer of 1926.

always felt that was not only the artistically right thing but also, in the long run, the practical commercial thing. But that is all "old hat." You know what my beliefs are.

As for my own writing, I am now settled down temporarily (for the next month or so, that is—perhaps longer) here on the Mediterranean in a nice quiet little village and I'm hard at work on *Dynamo*. The play has developed a lot in my unconscious (or whatever it is) since I worked out the scenario and it looks grand to me and ought to evolve into a real "big one." I'm going to work slowly on it and try to avoid by careful writing the enormous amount of going over and condensing I had to do on *Interlude*, as I sure hate that end of the job and it takes too much out of me.

It's fine news about Shane and the school.[1] As you say, that's what he needs. I sent him a bushel of postcards while I was still on the move. Hope he got them all right. What I write on them I'm careful to compose so that the P.O. people will have nothing to gossip about, if they read it. I miss him and Oona like hell at times. Don't sneer! I love them as much as you do—perhaps more—in my oblique, inexpressive fashion. At any rate, they will find out I have been a good father—(as Eugene did)—when they are old enough to understand all that has happened and when they really come to know me and about me.

This reminds me: won't you please write to Gaga and give her some definite information about where she stands and what you want her to do?[2] I've just had a letter from her and she seems in a terrible state about our breaking-up and her own future. She writes that she's heart-broken because she knows she'll never see the children again, etc. It almost made me cry, honestly. She said she hadn't heard from you in a long time. I've sent her a hundred but it isn't money she needs. God damn it, Agnes, whatever her faults, we've both loved her, our children have loved her, and she's loved all of us, and stuck to us since Shane was born through thick and thin, and you can't hold her idiotic gossip against her when it's a case of wounding an old woman who has been a good friend to us, if there ever was one. You can't throw her aside as if she were an old rag that you'd used up and wanted to get rid of. Won't you please do something about this? If you think I've ever done anything for you, then I ask this as a favor! I'll pay whatever added expense she cost you. You know I can't do anything for her. It's being near the children she loves in what for eight years has been her home. For Christ sake, please write her. It's on my conscience and I feel like hell about it.

It sounds strange to hear you tell of all the interesting folk in Bermuda. "It was not like that in the olden days," what? I always miss the good breaks socially, eh? And I'll bet you are a good hostess, now that I'm not around to spoil the fun. In fact, when I remember the 2500 you *"must* have" for back bills (in your letter to Harry) I cannot doubt that you are a grand hostess. Also you must consider—and the guests must agree with you—that I am a grand "sugar daddy" to have in the background!

But let's avoid finances. As always, your tendency to be utterly careless with my money, tends to fill me with bitterness. As the wife of an artist, in that respect at least, you have always been a grand mate for a rich broker. My only prayer now is, may the broker appear— and soon! In the name of auld lang syne can't you find it in your heart to fall in love with a rich broker? I really think you owe it to me, Agnes—if not to the man, at least to the w. k. hard-working dramatist!

Joking aside, I hope you talked over everything with Harry—that he got down all right on the 26th and that we'll soon be able to finally sign up and both feel put. As for "Spithead," I will do anything agreeable to you about it provided you are agreeable to me on other things

1. Agnes had decided to send Shane to boarding school in Lenox, Massachusetts.
2. For health reasons, Mrs. Clark reluctantly had left Bermuda in the fall of 1927 and went to live in Provincetown, only to discover that she missed Shane and Oona so much that she wanted to return. She wrote Agnes of her interest in doing so but received no reply.

and don't crucify me. That is, I will neither rent nor sell it but give you entire use of it for as long as you reasonably wish provided I have permission to visit the children there. (I mean it might be arranged that when you wanted to come to N.Y. for a few weeks I might go down in your stead.)

Your plans for your trip in May and for the summer sound excellent to me. I think that country out there will be exciting and interesting for you—as much so as England and France and Spain have been for me. You love riding for one thing and you ought to get all you want of it there.

I'm sorry my letter from London in which I said I was happy sounded like "protesting too much" to you. As a matter of fact, I am as happy as I can be, being the sort of brooding person I am, and I feel growth inside me. I have my bad hours and days, naturally, but they are due to myself alone and to my obsession with the past which it will take me years to shake off. And there are memories I never want to shake off, no matter how much pain of regret for what might have been they cause me—for example, the other day I had a sudden clear vision of the day at the Happy Home when Shane was born, of my holding your hand, remember? And the early days at Peaked Hill come back. These sort I want to remember. It is only the poison and the hate I must forget—in justice to both of us and the nine years in which, speaking in general, we did our best.

How far we have come from Happy Home! How far, indeed! As far as the "indiscretion" and its results you write about. I hate to write about it and what I am saying I say without bitterness, only with sadness—but, for your own good, *mark well what I do say!* You have piled on indiscretion upon indiscretion! Don't you know that your letter—you always have had such an unfortunate vague memory for certain things!—gives me proof positive of adultery in your own handwriting? If you don't believe this, then kindly remember exactly what you wrote and the light will break on you. You have made the matter so brilliantly clear against yourself that no Judge would hesitate for an instant. Not that I ever intend to use it. I'm not threatening you. I'm your friend as long as you are mine. And it is your privilege to have had a lover or lovers. Certainly it would be ridiculous for me to object. But I do object and most emphatically and to the last ditch when, (notwithstanding that your own statement of the case proves the utter and entire impossibility of it!) (Remember what you wrote, please, and you'll see!) you have the unscrupulous effrontery to attempt to lay this thing at my door! You must have changed, by God, and hardly for the better spiritually—when you can do such a thing! But you might have remembered your dates—which you give explicitly!—better! Why, I wasn't even in the same country with you when this must have happened! Or did you write it deliberately to taunt me? If so, it misses its mark. I'm way beyond that point.

But enough of that! I swore I wasn't going to get bitter in this letter—and I'm not. Naturally, you're free to do as you please—but kindly count me out of the responsibility because I—just as naturally—won't accept it. After all, there is a limit to what you can expect of me! I'm not an utter ass!

Kiss the children for me. I hope it can be arranged so that I can see them before too terribly long. It all depends on you. I can't—and won't—come back to the U.S. until you've carried out your plan, even if I have to give up the idea of having any new play produced next season.   Work! Be happy!   Gene

P.S. I'm enclosing this to Harry to mail—quicker and safer.

PART FIVE

VOYAGER

1928–1931

*I've at last found a sustained plan of life, if
you get me, in which living will collaborate with
the writing instead of being always an obstacle
to be overcome and beaten under by writing.*
—*To M. Eleanor Fitzgerald, May 13, 1929*

On February 10, 1928, O'Neill once again became a traveler, leaving with Carlotta for Europe on a voyage that was both a flight and a quest. What they were attempting to avoid was a tabloid scandal that would vilify Carlotta and invade O'Neill's essential creative privacy. What they sought to find was peace, contentment in one another, and a world free of disturbance, where O'Neill's writing could seek out greater depth than he had yet found. *Lazarus Laughed* and *Strange Interlude* had pointed the new direction. Now he was ready to take up *Dynamo,* the first play of a planned trilogy intended to explore the dilemma of modern man trying to exist in a godless world.

Shortly before the separation from Agnes was known, Bio De Casseres had read O'Neill's palm and told him of the divorce and the new relationship. She promised him that after a period of great disturbance he would find the peace he sought. The disturbance was not far to seek, but it would be a considerable time before the promised contentment could be achieved.

Agnes did not behave according to the "code." Her claim of pregnancy revolted O'Neill, and when she, perhaps with an eye on the royalties of *Strange Interlude,* began to ask for a larger settlement than that on which they had originally agreed, O'Neill balked.[1] His attitude toward Agnes changed from one of persuasive reasoning to violent hatred. He impugned her personal habits, accusing her of drinking. He inveighed against her sexual morality and demanded that Weinberger set detectives upon her to catch her, as he put it, "in flagrante." Perhaps, he suggested to Weinberger, she had never been married to the Burton she claimed was her first husband and the father of her daughter Barbara. Or, if she had been married, had she been divorced? If not, were Shane and Oona illegitimate? Weinberger received letter after letter written in a distasteful frenzy. How much of it O'Neill really meant is hard to determine. He was an angry man, angrier than he had ever been before, and his anger was augmented by the guilt he felt at leaving his children. He wrote them, sending snapshots of himself and begging them not to forget "Daddy," and he was sentimentally concerned to ensure that Shane received the kayak that had given him so much pleasure at Peaked Hill Bar.

---

1. Louis Sheaffer records that the proposed settlement was to be between six and ten thousand dollars depending on O'Neill's annual income, plus the use of Spithead for life. See *O'Neill: Son and Artist* (Boston: Little, Brown, 1968), p. 280.

As Agnes delayed her trip to Reno and granted an interview to the tabloid press, O'Neill worked himself into an astonishing fury, in part justifiable, in part pure tantrum. The heart of the matter was that the divorce was invading his sanctum, which in a frenzy he sought to keep inviolate. The effort showed in certain follies in his external life. He laid false trails as to his whereabouts, at one point giving a traveling friend postcards to mail from a Baltic seaport to throw potential pursuers off the scent. His London accommodation address was used for all correspondence except for letters from a few close friends. Not all of these ruses were irrational. O'Neill was news and reporters prowled around, scenting scandal and making up false news reports, possibly with the intention of smoking him out of hiding.

In addition, he was in the old-fashioned sense "living in sin." To protect Carlotta from scandal was doubtless one of his concerns, but in his own character there was a reluctance to set his own unregularized sex life on display. Sometimes he asked his men friends not to bring their wives to visit for fear that the women would be embarrassed. George Jean Nathan and Lillian Gish, bound in a similar liaison, were welcome, but Eugene, Jr., was asked not to bring his girlfriend, and the new Mrs. Saxe Commins was not at first welcomed. Little by little the Puritan streak warmed, but at the beginning, he blamed Agnes's delay with the divorce for his inability to set his personal life in a respectable order.

A mixture of embarrassment and a long-held romantic desire to see the lands "beyond the horizon" may have motivated the lovers' voyage to the Orient. To Mike Gold on August 13, 1928, O'Neill wrote of his fear of becoming a "writing Robot" and of the rebirth of "the old romantic urge to travel." Yielding to the urge and putting the privacy of an ocean liner between themselves and their problems, O'Neill and Carlotta left for the Far East in October. The trip was not a success. O'Neill fell off the wagon with a spectacular splash, quarreled with Carlotta, and then became ill. Reporters found him and he was forced to ship out of Shanghai under an alias, James O'Brian. Relations with Carlotta deteriorated; she left him and sailed on a different ship for France, leaving her stolid Swedish maid, Tuve Drew, to keep a watchful eye on her man and to wire to her bulletins about his condition. As he gradually recovered and penitently reentered the land of the sober, a comedy of wireless messages was played out, until at Port Said, the two ships put in at the same time and O'Neill and Carlotta were reunited.

Despite their personal troubles, O'Neill welcomed the relative isolation with Carlotta and back in France began to work diligently at his new play, *Dynamo*, which was, he repeatedly asserted, "one of the ones." His faith in it was great, and because he felt unable to return to the United States with his marital problems unresolved, he sent it to the Theatre Guild to produce in his absence. It failed decisively. Inevitably, he laid his faulty writing to his troubled state of mind, which, he insisted, interfered with his inner vision. To this he added that his not being present at rehearsals in order to cut and rewrite as he usually did was an error. But the play's failure rankled, and he continued to try to understand why it had failed. At the heart of the matter perhaps he felt that the play, the first he had written in his new life, should have been great, an honor to their love. Its failure meant that somehow he had "wronged" Carlotta.

Agnes finally went to Reno; the divorce was granted on July 1, 1929, and on July 22, O'Neill's third marriage took place in Paris. Almost at once a new difficulty arose. *Strange Interlude* was made the occasion of a plagiarism suit by a woman who called herself Georges Lewys and who claimed that the play was stolen from her novel *The Temple of Pallas-Athene*. The suit was set aside once the case was presented, but it cost O'Neill time and money, not the least of which was the loss of the sale of the play to MGM Studios, where Lillian Gish was preparing to offer it as her first sound film.

There were, of course, rewards outside the domestic life. In Paris, Moscow, Berlin,

Vienna, and Stockholm his plays were produced with popular, if not always critical, success. Increasingly, translators applied for permission to introduce his work into their own languages. The possibilities of operas based on his plays were raised.

The couple settled into Le Plessis, a château near Tours, and quarrels and outer disturbances were set aside as O'Neill began to write a new play, *Mourning Becomes Electra*. He was to work the modernized Greek trilogy through six drafts for months on end,[2] determined that it be a play worthy of his marriage to Carlotta. He acknowledged her contribution by inscribing it to her and by thanking her for providing the "warm secure sanctuary for the man after the author's despairing solitudes and inevitable defeats."[3] Finally, for O'Neill, determined at all costs to put exterior disturbances from him, author and man became integrated in a firm marital relationship and the writing of a great work of theatrical art.

2. O'Neill's work diary concerning the writing of *Mourning Becomes Electra* is published in *The Unknown O'Neill: Unpublished or Unfamiliar Writings of Eugene O'Neill*, ed. Travis Bogard (New Haven: Yale University Press, 1988), pp. 394–403.

3. Cf. Eugene O'Neill, *Inscriptions: Eugene O'Neill to Carlotta Monterey O'Neill* (New Haven, Conn.: Privately printed, 1960), entry for April 23, 1931.

April 8th [1928]

Dear Terry: Your letter arrived some days ago and I was damn glad to hear from you— and tickled that the special edition of *S.I.*[1] pleased you. I feel that Horace did very well by it myself. It makes a handsome volume. And I hear by a letter from Bob Sisk[2] that the regular edition is selling like a young novel! Well, well, well! "Can such things be and overcome us like a summer cloud?" Evidently. He also tells me that there are still standees at the Golden. That trends on fanaticism, it seems to me. Myself, I wouldn't stand up 4½ hours to see the original production of the Crucifixion!

Well, I hate to tell you I told you so—but I did. I had great faith in *S.I.* even from the box office standpoint. I feel the same faith in *Lazarus Laughed,* if you can get someone for the lead who can do it. You'd be amazed to see the letters I get from all over on that play. It seems to give people new faith and religion and I firmly believe, if it is ever done the way the script reads, it will send people out of the theatre with a feeling of exaltation about life that will send them to that theatre in droves that will make the success of *S.I.* look paltry. I am certain that *Lazarus* fills a long felt spiritual want that everyone today is suffering from—want of faith in life. One significant thing is that the book, on its own and without being heralded or helped by production, had, before either *Marco* or *S.I.* were put on, a sale as large as the ordinary novel enjoys—and it had only been out a few months. You must confess this decidedly means something!

All of which leads me to the question, have you considered this play seriously? I wish you would. I feel that, in a way, its production will mean even more to the American theatre than that of *S.I.* did and, of course, I feel you're the only people who can really get away with it. Have you gotten any info. on the Pasadena production and Irving Pichel's performance?[3] If so, I wish you'd relay it on to me. The thing about *Laz* is that it is so much a producer's play, it has such unlimited opportunities for imaginative collaboration in that line that I should think an imaginative producer should be tempted to accept the challenge of it.

Besides which, I think it's a fine piece of writing, the best writing as writing I've ever done.

I'm hard at *Dynamo* but it's going to take much longer to write than I thought as the idea has developed tremendously both as to content and scheme of production (this latter I mean in imaginative flexibility—there will be only two sets but both will have to be solidly built). I am immensely elated over it—but, the point is, when will it be finished? Quién sabe? It won't be a play that either you or I would want done late in the year because, believe me, it will be so startling and different and intensely dramatic that it ought to be done in its own theatre as *S.I.* and *Porgy*[4] was and it ought to be done early for I'm sure it can run a full season on its own. Remember (wails the author) that I have already got almost as much family to support already as two ordinary authors—and it's the mere shank of the evening!

Another thing about timing the completion of *Dynamo* is that, while I am now going great guns on it by virtue of a lull in which I am enjoying peace and happiness, I cannot

---

1. In February 1928, Boni and Liveright published a signed limited edition (350 copies) of *Strange Interlude.*
2. Robert Sisk (1901?–1964), publicity man for the Theatre Guild.
3. Irving Pichel played Lazarus in the Pasadena Community production, which opened on April 9, 1928, and ran for twenty-eight performances.
4. Play by DuBose Heyward (1885–1940) and Dorothy Heyward (1890–1961) that the Theatre Guild produced in October 1927 and that later was adapted into the musical *Porgy and Bess* (1935).

foretell how long this so fortunate lull will last. (Of course what I am writing now is strictly confidential except for such as Maurice, Lawrence, Phil, etc. who already know the situation.) For I still do not know just exactly what is going to happen—and many things, which I cannot control, might happen so disagreeably (to put it mildly) that I would willy-nilly be thrown completely off my creative stride. This the lady in control of the situation by virtue of our marriage laws knows only too damn well—and it is a grand weapon! Whether she is going to try to use the situation to "take me for all I've got" by way of legal blackmail—a move which in self-preservation I would be forced to fight but which fight would make my situation particularly uncomfortable—remains to be seen. I deeply sympathize with the hero in Lawrence's play at times. It is wonderful—and disillusioningly revealing—to discover how soon an alleged broken heart becomes a financial transaction! However, all may be well and the fair and square thing for all concerned may be done. Or it may not. It all depends on whether the lady listens to the "wise" advice of her false worldly friends or not.

But enough of that! I didn't mean to bore you with any jeremiah about my domestic tribulations. It is only its possible influence on *Dynamo* I wish to make clear. I'll write you in some detail about certain aspects of *Dynamo* later—I mean not any story of it but merely hints as to its genre, etc.

Give my warm best to all the Committee. Tell Phil again how much I enjoyed working with him and how damn grateful I feel for his splendid job on *S.I.*—the most imaginative directing I've ever known. Tell Bob Sisk I'll write him soon. His long letters with all the news have certainly been a boon. I sure appreciate his courtesy in going to all that trouble. And tell Lynn & the rest of the cast that I hope they're half as satisfied with their work in *S.I.* as I am.

All best! Remember me to your husband. Write again when you have leisure. And do consider *Laz* seriously from all angles. It's worth it. Which of the Comm. are coming abroad this summer? I'll hope to see many of you.   Gene

P.S. Tell anyone who knows it among the bunch to keep this address strictly secret—or I might be let in for a lot of trouble. I have a villa here.

---

246 • TO HARRY WEINBERGER.   ALS 9 pp. (Villa Marguerite, / Guéthary, B.P., / France) [Yale]

April 22nd [1928]

Dear Harry: Your two letters arrived today and they have thrown me quite off balance. I had hoped that your trip to Bermuda would have more satisfactory results. As it is everything seems to be more complicated.

Well, at any rate, Agnes by her new ridiculous demands has removed from my mind any scruples that might remain there about fighting this thing out with her. I made her the offer of an extremely generous—as you agreed—agreement and, in her hoggishness she has seen fit to ask for more. Well, she can't have it and that's final! You would do well to point out to her that in the recent divorce agreement between Sinclair Lewis and his wife, she only gets one-fourth of his income and even that $1/4$ is never to be more than one thousand a month—and Lewis is a man whose income for the past ten years must have been at least three times as much as mine.

Now pay attention to what I am going to say, Harry, and please carry out my instructions because I've given this matter a great deal of thought and my decisions are final and not to be argued down.

In the first place, with the 1500 you took down to her and the 500 you cabled her, Agnes has now had 2000 for back bills. A month or so ago she wrote that that was all she needed—and it is all she is going to get. I will agree, however, to give you a check for two thousand more to be given to her *only* after she returns from Reno and I have a copy of the divorce decree. And this four thousand shall be considered as part of the ten thousand limit she may be entitled to next December.

When Agnes tells you she wants to play fair, she lies. Where money is concerned, as I know from many years of petty thievery on her part, she is absolutely a double-crosser and a hypocrite.

In the second place, I *will not* give her Spithead for life nor will I assure it to the children in any way, shape or form. Spithead is not hers nor theirs. It is mine. I have thirty-five thousand dollars sewn up in it—which would bring me in 2500 a year income if invested in stocks—and if I have a run of bad luck or am kept in a state of uncertainty—as at present—by her, in which work comes slowly or not at all, I will need the money from Spithead for my own living. *If* she gets the divorce, however—but not until then—I will guarantee that she can have the place for the next five years, that I will not sell it until after that time—and, if I don't need the money, she can live on there after that.

The point about Spithead is that her desire to live on there is inspired by pure snobbishness really and not by any desire for the children's welfare. The house is too big, the place cost too much to run, it is much too "swank" and if she weren't so idiotically set on keeping up what the Phila. Social Register people who are her neighbors regard as position in life, she'd see that the best plan for both her and me would be to sell out as soon as possible. Bermuda, furthermore, as everyone knows and I especially know to my cost, is the most expensive place in the world to live. Food is terrifically expensive. She will always be running into debt there, always appealing to me to get her out. She can't run that place on 500 a month and she knows it. And the children's schools there are notoriously bad—very British and no good as preparation for American colleges. She could live in France, for example (send Shane to school in Switzerland) like a king on what my agreement allows her.

This lady has got to be brought back to earth. In the months since I've left her she seems to have forgotten that I'm an artist whose income is uncertain, who has had to battle all the way as an artist who hews to the line has to in America. She's carrying on as if I were a bank president on a large fixed salary. Well, I'm going to wake her up if it's the last thing I ever do—and no matter at what cost to myself I'll "get" her in the end. I've never been played for a sucker yet and it's a late day to start. I'm a mild guy until someone steps on my toes once too often but when I have to battle, I can!

You are probably saying that I'm talking as if I hated her—and wondering why, so I'm going to tell you. I mentioned having received a letter from her which was important in this case. Well, in that letter she has the colossal nerve to tell me she's pregnant and doesn't know whether she'll have the child or not. She even specifies—(I'm not going to mince words!)—the exact date (Jan. 27th) on which she was last unwell. She has always been extra rattle-brained when it came to remembering dates and this slip-up was a fatal error for she forgot that she left N.Y. on the 14th of Jan. and that when this conception must have taken place I was not even in the same country with her! Neither, as a matter of fact, did I have anything to do with her when she was in N.Y. but she must be relying on the fact that she did, when she said she was too nervous to sleep in her own room, sleep in the next bed to me and she probably thinks she could get witnesses at the hotel to back that up. But I ask you if that isn't rubbing my nose in her dirt and whether I'm not right to get sore when she airily, not directly but by implication, tries to foist the parenthood of this affair on to me. As I said, I'm a mild man but there is a limit and being blamed for other men's children is that limit. I don't give a damn how many lovers she may have. That's her privilege, naturally. But I don't want them bringing O'Neills into being. I have my little Puritan prejudices!

But I won't bore you anymore with this unpleasing mess except to ask you just what the legal value of this letter is. It's in her handwriting on Spithead paper—exact date given, as I said. Would it be evidence of adultery in a divorce suit? If so, I'm in luck and I'll surely bring such a suit if she insists on riding me anymore. I've got to have peace of mind for my work and I can't when I have to look forward to a future in which such a woman, greedy and unscrupulous, is going to hang like a financial millstone about my neck! And if the letter isn't divorce evidence, it's wonderful publicity material and if she gets my back to the wall I'll use it. All this may sound harsh, Harry, and rough stuff but the plain facts in this case to me are that a woman, whom I took when she was nothing but a shabby hanger-on, an unsuccessful cheap fiction writer, with no status of any kind, with a child alleged to be born in wedlock (but no shred of proof of her having ever been married before was ever brought forward), that I married her under an agreement that I would never have to support that child (which I have always had to do, nearly), that she should pay 50–50 of all expenses (which she has never done) and that if ever either came to the other and said they were in love with someone else that automatically a divorce would be given and no alimony asked (and this she is now violating in both letter and spirit). When I married her I was already on the road to success, already recognized after two years of one-act plays in N.Y. That she ever helped me in my work is a grotesque fiction. She was always intensely jealous of my work as compared to what she could do. At times, even, she did her best to hamper it. And in the early days, when I was broke, my father supported us, my mother gave her the only decent furs and clothes she had ever had up to then, for she was brought up in the slackest, laziest kind of undeserving, merited poverty. And now this woman, to whom I have given three fine houses, who has thrown away my money so that I had to fight even her inefficiency and waste to save every cent I have saved (about ⅓ of what I should have saved!), this woman dares to take advantage of my being in love and wanting to marry, to try to blackmail me for all she can get while in the meanwhile she entertains her lover at my expense!

Oh no! It's a bit too thick! I am bitter and I am mad—so mad and so bitter that I'm in a state where I'll gladly blow up the works no matter who it crushes so long as it crushes her. I'm a good little hater when I'm driven to it. She had better watch her step. The thought of the children won't stop me because they're both too young to be hurt by it to any extent, and I can make up to them, later on when I get a chance, for all the folly she's brought on them.

Another idiotic claim of hers is that she stuck to me in spite of my old drinking. Well, drink never interfered with my working, my drinking has been greatly exaggerated, and she stuck because I was bread and butter and luxuries, because she liked to get drunk herself, and because when I drank she could feel a bit superior, a martyr. There were many times, indeed, when she urged me to drink and I would have stopped long before I did—in 1922 after my mother's death, for example—if it had not been for her. Few people realize this but it's very true.

But to get back to our onions. I won't alter the clause in regard to remarriage. God knows I'd like to see her married again to some man who would really show her where she gets off, but not to the extent of supporting him. I'm not subsidizing husbands for her, tell her.

As for all that bunk about her putting money in the bank for the children, etc. for God's sake don't let that fool you! You don't know her or how she's treated Barbara. She'd be more liable to take money out of their bank to buy herself something.

As for additional protection in case of my decease, she can't have it. I will make no will at any one's demands. My money is hard-earned and my own and I'll bequeath it to those of my children, past and future, who stick by me and to the woman who sticks by me. I shall certainly, in the light of what has happened and the way A's acting now, cut her entirely out of any will I make, in as far as I possibly can.

As for insurance, kindly don't bother sending me any data. I don't want to be insured and won't be. I've quite enough drain on income without having to pay heavy premiums. And I want to put all future money into stocks that I can keep near me out of her way and cash in at any time.

If I died as I am, without will, my children would be amply protected in as far as my money is concerned. My first duty to them is to insure my own ability, under the proper conditions, to function as a dramatist. And she is hurting them by trying to upset this.

You may say to yourself that this is all brave talking but what if she refuses to get a divorce unless I etc. Well, I've talked it all over with Carlotta and we don't give a damn whether she gets the divorce or not. If it's a case of my being blackmailed out of more than I can afford, of my life being made financially miserable, we'd rather do without. Moreover, we're quite willing to come out in the open and tell the world we're living together because my wife is charging too high for a divorce and trying to "take me." In fact, the way we feel now, we don't care how soon the tabloids get on the trail. It'll be a sensation for a couple of days in papers we'll never see and then it'll be over. The world is pretty used to artists' domestic radicalism. Here in Europe no one would raise an eyebrow. And as far as hurting the production of my plays, that's too silly! Outside of the Bible belt, where my stuff is never done anyway, it'd simply be good publicity. The crazier and more immoral they think you are, the more curious they are about your stuff. This is platitude.

Moreover, you can tell Agnes—and I want you to for, naturally, I can't write it to her—that if she doesn't accept the agreement as is, if she holds up the divorce, there are going to be no plays submitted for either publication or production until she does do so. I am in a fine position to carry out this threat or I wouldn't make it. Outside of the money I've got already over here and the stocks I can get over at a minute's notice, Carlotta has a sufficient income to keep us going more than comfortably over here for the rest of our lives. As for productions, I can get them in Germany, Czechoslovakia, & Russia just by having what I write translated. So I'm in a position to sit pretty and keep my income in the states down to royalties on old books—nothing much—and a few rents—less. We'll see how she'll thrive on that. Also if she keeps on acting nasty, I'll force the man to foreclose that mortgage on Spithead next year and that will evict her out of there quite effectively.

You must make up your mind, Harry, to change your attitude toward this case from now on (as my lawyer, I mean). We've tried the friendly stuff and it's failed. (Moreover, I wasn't aware of this pregnancy byplay when I promised to remain friendly.) You don't seem to think it has failed but from my point of view I've stopped being a friend. What remains to be settled is a peace between enemies—or a victorious warfare. I hate the memory of Agnes and I hope I'll never see her or hear of her again!

To return once more to an old subject, I reiterate that it's the continued secrecy, as if something dire were going on behind the scenes, that is keeping the newspapers warm, the idea that there is to be a great scandal and a correspondent. A simple divorce announcement from Agnes would kill all this, provided no correspondent were named. Or even if a correspondent were named. For Christ's sake, let's get it over with! I tell you I'll fairly force the news on the first newspaper man I meet that my wife is going to Reno for a divorce. It worked out all right for Sinclair Lewis, why shouldn't it with me? And anyway I've reached the limit of my ducking. It's a humiliating business. I've told the world all my life that if it didn't like what I did, it could go to hell, and it's degrading to me to sidestep now. I won't move nor change my name.

And again I reiterate, *don't discuss my affairs with Madden ever again!* He's my play-agent not my confidant, and he's a regular sieve for gossip.

The next reporter who calls you say that you've heard from me from Prague and I was going to Russia. That, at any rate, is good dope.

I'm going to give up work until this thing is settled. It's no use trying. I feel too bitter that a woman I've done so much for should try to double-cross me after I've been so generous. She's a skunk! And why write plays to give her money?

Please don't get any more money from Madden without letting me know what A. wants it for first. I'm writing Madden that I'll hold the Am. Play Co. responsible if they give any money to Agnes without my written authorization.

If Agnes should again refuse the agreement as is, I instruct you to withdraw it and tell her I'll hold out in future for Sinclair Lewis's terms—¼. Or let her sue in Conn. for a separation if she likes but tell her she won't get whatever they award her for very long. I'll see to it the stone is soon bloodless.

I want it made absolutely certain that Agnes gets no more money, except her 500 a month, until she leaves for Reno—(if she does)—and if she doesn't, that she gets only 250 a month for the children, as per the plan you suggested.

All best! Remember this is to be a battle from now on.

I'm enclosing letter to mail. Will you send Eugene check for 25.00 and charge to me—his birthday is May 4th.   Gene

---

247 • TO HARRY WEINBERGER.   ALS 3 pp. (Villa M[arguerite] / Guéthary, B.P. France) [Yale]

April 23rd [1928]

Dear Harry: Perhaps my too long letter of yesterday about Agnes was a bit hectic—I was all "het up." Nevertheless, today in cold blood my objections to her proposals still stand although I'm calmer about the hatred stuff.

What I'm writing to you now for is to again take up the publicity angle about which I feel very strongly that something must be done and done immediately! I've simply got to the limit of my power to go on with things as they are. I can't work any more or enjoy any peace of mind. It destroys all my energy, which is wasted in worry, to have the specter of that tabloid scandal hanging over my head like an unexploded bomb, and I've gotten to the point where I'm liable to go off at half-cock any moment and give the whole show away just in desperation to get it done and over with.

Now to me the remedy for all this is perfectly simple and it has a very good recent precedent in the Sinclair Lewis divorce which came off without scandal and with dignity—in spite of the fact that everyone knows that Lewis is living with a woman over here. And this happened because there *was never any secrecy* about the case! It was simply announced in the papers that they had separated, then that she was going to get a divorce on grounds of desertion, then that she'd gone to Reno, and nothing after that until the divorce was granted. Now if his case could be managed that way, why can't mine? I tell you again—and I know the newspaper game at least as well and probably better, since I once worked at it—I can't impress it on you too emphatically that it isn't any interest in a simple divorce without correspondents (which is nil no matter how public the person is, it's so common), that is keeping this story warm and keeping them on my trail here in Europe, it's the damned secrecy that is liable to ruin me! It's the secrecy that keeps the city editors saying "there must be something pretty rotten at the bottom of this O'Neill business or they wouldn't be so secret about it"—and they immediately think of all sorts of juicy grounds for separation and divorce such as came out in the Chaplin case—and they keep after the secret.

You may think it to my best interests to keep them in the dark but I'm convinced you're absolutely wrong and that this secrecy business will eventually result in my being sought out over here and involved in a terrible mess. It's all right to say change my name, move, disguise the mail, but I can't change my face and if I were discovered all that deception would only make me appear all the more guilty and make a dirtier story. Can't you see that? Now why can't you act as the lawyer for Lewis and his wife must have acted? Give out a simple statement as my lawyer that Agnes and I have definitely separated but that no third party is involved, that it is simply a case of our having grown incompatible and we have mutually agreed that it would be better for both of us if we lived apart. Then when they go to Agnes instruct her to corroborate this with the added information that she has decided to divorce me and is going out to Reno for that purpose—that there is no question of any correspondent, that we simply cannot hit it off together any more, etc. You can add to your statement that I'm traveling in Europe, you've heard from me in Prague, I'm probably going to Russia for *Laz* and then to Italy to finish *Dynamo*. By doing this you'll throw them all [off] my scent—not only that but you'll have ruined their story. After all, the city editors will say, it's only a divorce by agreement, there's no dirt in it, so what of it. They won't try to find me any more and, as in the Lewis case which was managed so well, nothing much will be published except for the bare facts.

Now please don't come back at me with stuff about my being a big story. So is Lewis— just as big as I am. As for Madden writing me about the Charlie Chaplin case, he's a damn fool. Chaplin's wife had charged him with ruining young girls, with every form of perversion—and he was guilty as everyone knows. There was every form of dirt to it. But in my case what is there to hide? Agnes isn't charging me with anything, not even with being in love with Carlotta. So what is there to be secret about—exactly what the city editors are wondering and what keeps them hot on my trail! There was a good reason for the secrecy while I was in N.Y. planning a get-away with C. but that's all over—and now secrecy is simply keeping me in dutch and on tenterhooks when you could so easily manage, as my lawyer, to set me free, get the facts out, and give me peace of mind to work in.

So I appeal to you as a friend to fix Agnes' end of this with her at once and get busy. And you might as well for I am determined, if you don't act for me, to act myself. I can easily release, ostensibly as quotes from a letter from me from Prague, a statement confirming our separation and saying I believe she intends to sue for divorce, through two or three perfectly safe and natural quarters—for example, Bobby Sisk up at the Guild who is a good friend and would be glad to do it with the utmost discretion for me.

The time for secrecy is over! The Sinclair Lewis case was open and above board and eminently dignified and successful. He hasn't been hounded over here, for that reason! Further secrecy in my case is useless and dangerous! When the wife makes no charges of dirt but only sues out at Reno on ordinary charges there is no scandal and no news value! Once this divorce—or separation—announcement is printed, the news is cold and no paper will bother trying to trace me or give a damn what I am doing! Witness the case of Lewis who is living in Berlin—and has been, by all accounts—quite openly with a woman he is in love with and who is the real cause of their divorce![1]

I underline all the above because it's so damned important to my immediate future and my work! So for Christ's sake, Harry, get busy on this—for I know I'm right! Give them the

1. Journalist Dorothy Thompson.

facts which are clean and to no one's discredit and they'll lay off. We're simply making them think this is a dirty, spicy case by ducking any more.   Gene

P.S. I'm enclosing a letter for Agnes for you to address as you say she's coming to N.Y.

---

248 • TO HARRY WEINBERGER.   WIRE. 1 p. ([Villa Marguerite / Guéthary, B.P., France]) [Yale]

May 1 1928

INSTRUCT MADDEN IMMEDIATELY HAVE PULITZER PRIZE MONEY[1] MADE OVER TO AUTHORS LEAGUE FUND FOR NEEDY AND ARRANGE THIS DONATION WITHOUT PUBLICITY THIS INSTRUCTION FROM PRAGUE YOU UNDERSTAND   GENE

---

249 • TO AGNES BOULTON O'NEILL.   ALS 2 pp. ([Villa Marguerite / Guéthary, B.P., France]) [Virginia]

[early May 1928]

Dear Agnes: Your letter came today. I'm sorry you gave the interview.[1] I think a simple divorce announcement would have been better, done the trick and killed their hope for a scandal. As it is, the mystery still remains to intrigue them—for they know damn well you're lying and they wonder what for.

But don't think I'm blaming you! I know you hadn't received my last letter about this same matter. Also I realize how you've been hounded. I'm damn sorry, Agnes, to have brought you into all this! But what could I do—or can I do? It was fate. But as soon as they know they're making all this fuss about just another Reno divorce, without correspondent or filth, they'll leave us all alone. Believe me, it is not nice for me to have to "hide out" on them, either! It's on my mind continually and I find it hard to get any work done. So for all our sakes, let's get all this settled at the earliest possible moment.

I'm sorry I wrote that severe last part of that letter about your "indiscretion." You shouldn't have given me such exact proof in the dates you gave me. But no matter. I suppose you've gone ahead with what you planned to do—and that ends the matter. I'll forget it. I don't want to have any bitterness in my memory of you. I want always to have your image in my mind as the Agnes I loved so entirely over so many years.

I object to your amendments to my agreement. I still feel the agreement is damned generous as I offered it and that your added demands (with the exception of the [illegible] for [back bills?])[2] are unjust and unnecessary. Surely you can trust me in [illegible] matter of Shane & Oona. Anybody else in question is financially independent and wants nothing from me. What are you afraid of? That I'll sell Spithead? I never will as long as you want to live there—(although I again say you're foolish. You [could?] live like a queen in France on 500 a month—or live in Czechoslovakia—and send Shane to school in Switzerland unless I go broke—and simply have to have money to live on myself and support you & Eugene & Shane & Barbara & Oona. After all, $45,000 is tied up in Spithead and that represents $1/2$ my worldly wealth and I don't get a cent of income from it! Please think of these things, if you

---

1. O'Neill won the 1928 Pulitzer Prize for *Strange Interlude*.

1. "O'Neill Divorce Rumors Scouted," *New York World,* April 27, 1928, p. 3.
2. Stains on this letter have necessitated conjectural readings.

want to be?] fair to me & yourself & the kids! My future, you realize, is yours, and theirs too, and you do no good in making my burden too heavy—for then I'll simply quit.

Get a lawyer, if you like. But please accept what I've offered you. I'll be generous in addition whenever I can. But don't try to force me. If I had wanted to be foxy with you—as you seem to want to be with me with your added demands—I'd have offered a good deal less in the first place and let you bargain up to what I wanted. But I didn't. I treated you honestly. I offered *more* than I felt I could afford!

But enough of finances. I hope you start on your trip soon. The sooner the better for both of us. They'll never let you alone around N.Y.

I sent via Harry a present for Oona's birthday. Hope she got it and enjoyed it.

What have you done about Gaga? Please at least write her! Don't be so damn cruel to that poor old woman who was our friend for so many years! It isn't like you! She writes me & I her but I'm no good for her. Have Shane write her! If he forgets her so easily, by God he's no real son of mine and I'm not going to write him again until I hear he has done so! I mean this! And he'll get nothing from me either. There is such a thing as being an ingrate—even when you're only eight!

All is well with me. I like Czechoslovakia. And I hope to get really down to work once this present mess of publicity clears away and you're on your way. However, if it keeps up much longer and you keep fighting for more money there isn't much chance of any *Dynamo* for the Guild next year. I can't perform miracles and I can only concentrate on one thing at a time.

And won't you be just too tickled to death to feel that you can—for the present anyway—hurt my work! A grand revenge! But maybe I wrong you. If so, I apologize. If we could talk together—our children's future, money agreements, etc.—everything would be all right and settled in half an hour, but as we can't, hence bitterness.

One last word—and one sincerely for your good! Don't over-drink in N.Y., and then vilify a certain lady! It only harms you. The very people you do it to are the first to sneer at you for a bum sport and yellow loser when your back is turned! This is *friendly* advice.   All good wishes! Find happiness! And work!   Gene

---

250 • TO HAROLD DEPOLO.   ALS 4 pp. (c/o Guaranty Trust Co., / 50, Pall Mall, London) [Virginia]

> (I'm still not "put" anywhere
> for any length of time. This
> is safest address)
> [postmarked May 9, 1928]

Dear Harold: Your letter, forwarded from London, reached me today and I was certainly damn glad to hear from you. It gets a bit lonely over here now and then, and a letter from an old friend in whom one can really trust through the good breaks and the bad is a real privilege and solace. But you know that. Not that I want to give the impression that I'm low in spirit or anything of the sort. On the contrary. But it *is* lonely at times, for naturally, under the circumstances for the present, a strictly segregated life is in order and even if there were any Yanks about that I knew I'd fight shy of them—which there aren't. I'm shifting about from spot to spot, working hard in a place that takes my fancy for a few days, then moving on to the next.[1] It's a new style of living for me but it's enjoyable and interesting, I love the

1. O'Neill kept his true whereabouts and activities from the DePolos because he believed they sided with Agnes.

country I've seen, and I'm getting quite a bit done on *Dynamo*. So what ho! For the rest, I'm happy except that I do miss the kids much more than anyone might think—and there are dark days and hours when the past rises up and all that might have continued on if Agnes and I had not both been so indifferently sure of each other's affection, so dumbly unaware of each other's need for expansion and growth and new understanding, rises up and smites me with remorse and regret. Which is to be expected—especially with me whom the past always haunts so persistently. But I make no moan. We who have had any real experience with life know that for everything real one gets in this vale of beefs one pays on the nail! And I have got something real! Believe that! You know I am no damn freshman in living and that I wouldn't shoot the piece for any untested illusion. You must have heard a lot of the gossipy dirt of Broadway relayed through Agnes—quite natural that she should believe it all—but I know you know women well enough to discount that—and know Broadway well enough. How shall one who has been a famous beauty, who comes of fine family and has always had money of her own and fought shy of theatrical folk outside of the theatre, escape any variety of calumny? It has never been done. I repeat again I am no fool—and I have never made mistakes about the real true being inside people's defensive exteriors. So—I only explain all this to you because I know you are deeply my friend and so might have apprehensions on my account—be confident that I have found a rare and precious thing, a thing tested by time and much suffering.

I'm glad you wrote me what you did about Agnes. Why should I take offense at your doing so? You are a gentleman and my old friend. You couldn't write anything that shouldn't be written if you wanted to. And you have also been a good friend to Agnes. Then again, I'm damn sure you've seen all this coming on for a long time—long before there was any question of any third person (the idea that a third person was a cause and not an effect is a joke!—but people love to blame others and not themselves!). You know, none better, what we have had to put up with in each other—and the handwriting has been on the wall for years. Speaking of my own end of it—while acknowledging that there is as much, if not more, for the other end in rebuttal!—as long as I could embark on a brain-drowning drunk once in a while the things one can't forget didn't pile up on me to any unbearable extent. I swallowed them with old J.B.[2] for a chaser of memory. But when I reformed they began to pile up into obtrusive prison walls. But no more of this. You have seen and you know what you know. And all's well if it ends well. But it's too bad for the kids' sake. However, what can one do? There is nothing so disastrous for kids as a home poisoned by a thinly-concealed bitterness and hostility. At least now they won't have that to suffocate them. And Shane had begun to be extremely—if secretively—sensitive to the undercurrents and he was worried by them, I know. Without seeming to take much notice of him I'm sure I know ten times more about what he's like inside than Agnes does—for he's very like me, God help him!

I thought of you in London when I found myself one day looking into a shop window with wonderful fishing tackle and discovered it to be Hardy's (if that's the right name—at any rate I recognized the name at the time).

I'm writing this from a villa I've taken for a month on the river near Prague. I don't speak any Czech but it doesn't matter, I like their country and am able to work in it. Prague is a damned interesting town. From here I may go on to Moscow if I hear *Lazarus Laughed* is to be done there soon. Or I may turn about and come back to Italy and finish *Dynamo* someplace on the water there. I've been around France a lot and down into Spain (for a week only). So you see I've kept moving. I like that. I'm sick of being so "put."

Write me when the spirit moves. I don't know when I'll be back. It all depends on how

2. John Barleycorn.

Agnes acts. If she does the fair thing that we had faithfully promised each other would be done if ever either of us fell in love with someone else, then everything should be settled by next fall—but believe me I won't return until this thing is settled! Just now she appears to be trying to "take me for all I've got"—legalized blackmail is a great thing! Of course, no new plays can be produced until I can return, but that will be her own fault. I've offered her a more generous agreement than Sinclair Lewis' wife got from him (and he has at least three times my income) and she still howls for more! Can you beat it? I ask you, since you know what she was and all I have done for her. Well, these little affairs do open one's eyes, what?

But no more of my domestic flurries. How was Bermuda this winter for you? Are you getting "fed up" with it yet? My long 9 mos. stretch there, what with other stuff that I did my damndest for my home's sake to fight down eating me, sort of finished Bermuda for me.

Adios and good luck! I'm enclosing a check hoping it may come in handy when you're getting settled at Lowell in case the breaks are bad. Don't break into any rash of haste to repay it—1940 will do. I'm prosperous for the nonce.

Love to Helen, Brush & Tabe when you write them—and, as ever, all my deep friendship to you! May we get a chance to meet again before too long. Until then, take care of yourself! And wish me luck in my new life! I've already got happiness!   Gene

P.S. I'm sending this along with other letters enclosed in a letter to Harry for him to mail in N.Y.—easier.

---

251 • TO THERESA HELBURN.   ALS 3 pp. (Villa Marguerite, / Guéthary, B.P., France) [Yale]

[June 10?, 1928]

Dear Terry: Firstly, keep the above address very much under your hat and warn anyone else around the Guild to whom I may have written it to do likewise. If it got abroad at all I might be let in for a lot of trouble. It must not be given to anyone no matter what their pretext. *Anyone!*

I've got a grand place here—quiet, woods & beach of its own—and the Pyrenees for a backdrop that is almost as good as Lee could contrive! Could one say more? And I'm in the pink—and enjoying life for a change. Also I'm hard at work on *Dynamo*—been at it for a couple of weeks. I'm working slowly, not letting myself do any rushing on, because I want to get the first draft as near to final form as possible and not have to go over it again and again as I did with *Interlude*—work which is tremendously wearing and lacks the interest of first enthusiasm. When it will be finished I dare not predict. The whole scheme for it has developed tremendously from the scenario and is still developing. It will have its own original flavor both as to setting and scope of physical action. This may not be very clear but I'd have to explain a book full to make it more definite. As an insufficient illustration I'd say the first part of the play derives from the method of simultaneous exterior and interiors I used with such revealing effect (at least, to me!) in *Desire Under The Elms*. The second part—the hydro-electric power plant—derives its method (use of sounds) remotely from *The Hairy Ape*. I use sounds very pronouncedly throughout the play as a definite dramatic motive— and, believe me, they will have to be done well and with crafty ingenuity. But nothing impossible! The trouble is we always let sounds go until the last minute and then throw them on, as it were, (boatrace scene, *Interlude*) when they ought to be rehearsed weeks ahead. And thereby we throw overboard what could be one of the most original and significant dramatic values modernity has to contribute to the theatre. Believe me, I know, because I've always called for significant sounds in my plays and got insignificant ones which destroyed their meaning in my theme. Even the tom-tom in *Jones* has never been what I meant at all although with a little extra expense and trouble it could be done perfectly.

But what ho! I seem to have taken up lecturing on the modern drama. To return to *Dynamo* I warn you that there is a gradually approaching thunder storm through the whole first part of the play that is a dramatic note in the composition and must be done as it *can* be done. Also during the second part we need in the background the continual metallic nasal purr of the generators—if you've ever spent a short time in a power house you know how essentially symbolic and mysterious and moving this sound, (which is like no other sound but itself), is. And I speak with great seriousness when I say that whoever is to do the sets and noises ought to pay a friendly call on the General Electric people and get them interested in giving expert advice.

There will be only two sets but each, of course, will involve solid construction work.

Pardon me if I go ahead laying down the "musts" when you haven't even seen the play yet, let alone taken it! Such are authors! But I have every confidence that if I do the writing as it ought to be done you'll have a play so dramatic and striking in treatment that you'll want it.

As for the dialogue, it is Interludism. Thought will be as prominent as actual speech, probably, but there will be much less of the cutting-in of the brief asides. *Dynamo*, for one thing, deals with more direct, less cerebral people. Phil, naturally, is the one to direct it, if he will. I'll never be sufficiently grateful to him for the grand job he did on *Interlude*.

One more thing and I'll be brief about it. I think *Dynamo* ought to be done as *Interlude* and *Porgy* were—that is, as a separate thing in its own theatre. I feel it will be big enough and original enough to demand that—also that, if done right when written right, it can run a season at least on its own. There's one thing I think the Guild will have to face—that there are, per se, plays for (original production in) repertoire and plays not for repertoire. (*Marco*, for example, is for r.)

Of course, I'm not wholly objective on this. Can't be. I have one wife, three children and one step-child dependent on me already—and it's the mere shank of the evening! Repertoire in the home life might starve on repertoire in the theatre! Of a certainty, I hear right now your come-back on that statement!—that I give up on my end. Tell it to God!

I'm tickled to death to hear via Madden that *M.M. & S.I.* are still bringing home the bacon. Give my fondest and gratefullest to Lynn and the rest of the cast! They sure did their stuff and I hope they're as satisfied as I am.

Again on *Dynamo*—the principal character (male) is eighteen in first part, nineteen in second—the girl a bit younger. There are six main—3 males, 3 females—characters and two (probably) almost walk-ons. That's all. I give you all these limits on *D* just so you'll know at least a bit of it when you talk tentatively of next season.

All best to you all! If any of you come to Europe be sure and come to visit! We'd love to have you. The only essential is that before and after you remember only that I'm living quite alone in another part of Europe. That's easy enough, isn't it? I may seem super-cautious but my affairs are by no means surely out of the woods yet, and for more than my own sake I have to watch my step.   Again, all good luck!   Gene

July 2nd. [1928]

Dear Harry: I have just received your letters with the publicity enclosed and am glad that stuff has broken. I am sure it will be cold turkey for the news boys from now on. Agnes' interview with O'Donnell[1] was spiteful and cheap in its underhand reference to Carlotta but that sort of stuff only shows her up to all real people as yellow and a bad loser and she hurts herself by it and not us.

You ask about the lady's first marriage. I can't tell you much because she was always more than vague—pretended to have forgotten all the details!—and I never pressed the point but let bygones be such although I never believed a word of it. Her tale is this, that in 1914 she went to England with her grandmother and in London met and married an English newspaper man named Burton just before the war broke out, and then he went and got himself killed in Belgium. What he was doing in that country she doesn't exactly remember but he wasn't in the army and he wasn't a correspondent. The whole story is pretty ridiculous, what? At any rate he got her with child before leaving and she came back to a Connecticut farm and had Barbara. That is all she has ever told me. She has no marriage certificate or any evidence whatever and I have never heard any of her family ever mention this marriage as even a fact of the past. On the other hand, there is very strong reason for suspecting that no such marriage ever took place. Barbara's father might be someone she met in England with her grandmother—that is, if she ever went to England at all!—but I strongly suspect he was a Polish farmer who lived near them at Cornwall Bridge, Conn. at that time and who she told me in an unguarded moment was her mother's lover while at the same time being in love with her. A nice mess, what? And people think my *Desire*, for example, is too sordid to be real! Perhaps this will also explain to you why I'm inclined to be bitter and want to fight it out with a lady to whom I contributed so much by marrying her, who has broken every promise on which that marriage was founded and who now is trying to put my future in hock to her for the rest of my life!

I suppose you will receive my letter with the counter-proposals to the Driscoll[2] agreement today. There is no use my cabling you until this is discussed. One point I am absolutely firm on, that if [she] wants Spithead she will have to accept one-fourth income; also I will not give her children any more than I give Eugene. And where is Barbara to come in? What she is after is to get enough so that I will have to support her too! A bit thick! I think a special clause should be inserted that any money used for Barbara's support and education must be deducted from allowance. I am paying for Barbara at the school now, for example. Point this out to Driscoll, that I am now supporting four children!

Do not let her bluff you about Carlotta's letters. She was very cagey in writing to me and there is nothing in any of them that goes beyond friendship and liking, otherwise I would not have left them around. But by all means have it agreed that all those letters be returned as well as all letters I ever wrote to Agnes; and have it provided that if she ever sells any letter of mine to her that she forfeits all rights under the agreement as far as she personally is concerned. This is very important.

As for the Columbus Avenue property, I don't want to do anything at all about it now. I would have to have her sign to sell it, wouldn't I? And she has a dower right in it, hasn't she? Tell me in your next if this can be got around in any way. If I could get a bang-up price for it

---

1. John O'Donnell, "Wife Will Grant O'Neill His 'Illusion' of Freedom," *New York Daily News*, June 21, 1928, pp. 3, 4.
2. Agnes's lawyer.

and didn't have to give any of it to her, I might sell. As for the long term lease, I wouldn't consider it unless I was offered a hell of a lot more absolute net than has been mentioned yet. As you say, I hold the key position up there and can afford to wait.

In regard to Rosenbach and the scripts, I wrote Horace some time ago that he had better hold off until my agreement with Agnes was an accomplished fact. I don't want to give her any more ammunition for demands. I have no objection to having any negotiations go forward—having him see the scripts for example—provided same can be kept absolutely dark.

Would there be any way of tracing down that alleged first marriage of hers that wouldn't involve large expense? I have a hunch that a private detective could gather more dope than sufficient in a few days spent among the natives of Cornwall Bridge who remember the Boulton regime up there where Agnes owned a small abandoned farm at the time (1913–14–15). Take this step by all means if you find this thing is getting down to cases. I am sure the whole secret is there. That is where Barbara was born. You must understand that I don't want to hurt Barbara. I think I have always been very decent to her. But I do want things to hold over Agnes' head—as she is holding my situation over my head—to show her how fatal a war can be to her future. Her friends have stuffed her with the idea that she has me by the balls or she would never have the guts to act as she is doing. I know her! And never let her forget that letter I have of hers about her late pregnancy! When she tries to pretend I had anything to do with that she is simply lying. She knows damn well I couldn't have.

And you might give this a thought: that it might be a good idea to get a good agency to put a man to trail A. when she is in N.Y.—and also in the country, for that matter, driving the car about. If she is staying with Mary Blair[3] in town then almost anything is liable to be happening. I have a strong hunch she could be caught in flagrante within the next month or so and if this could be managed it would give me a weapon that would enable me to dictate terms.

You say you have to wait to battle until the first blow is struck. I consider her interview to be a dirty unfair blow with all its inferences. And anyway the more knockout socks you have to bring into the ring with you, the better.

I repeat again that when you say their proposed agreement is my old one with only Spithead added you don't consider what that "only" means—forty five thousand in the place plus the furniture from Ridgefield that cost fifteen thousand and that it would again cost me—or her—the same amount to replace for a new home. To a man of my puny capital assets, this is a hell of a big only! Besides, if we were starting now under the present circumstances after all she's done meanwhile, I never would volunteer that old agreement. That is where I made one grand big mistake—a mistake she is now riding to the limit!

Tell Agnes that Carlotta is instructing her lawyer to get after her if she makes any more insinuations she can't prove! And, barring our discovery here, she can prove nothing. And even here I don't think there is anything legal on us. We are living under our own names and have never posed anywhere as man and wife or ever registered at any hotel as such. Carlotta has an old English lady's maid who can be said to be a companion. I am a visitor and have a separate guest room. So you see. Would this hold water?

I think I have about covered everything in your letters of the 21 and 22nd and you can now battle along for a while on my ultimatum. The point I want to stress again with you and want you to stress with her and her lawyers is that I am not foaming at the mouth for a divorce but am having quite a nice life of it as it is. Neither is any pressure being put upon me

3. Actress who played leading roles in the premiere productions of *The Hairy Ape* and *All God's Chillun Got Wings* and in the Broadway premiere of *Desire Under the Elms*.

by Carlotta. Now that we've made up our minds that we can live over here divorceless, and also travel about the world, everything has taken on new life and I'm beginning to work again. *But*, if she doesn't get a divorce as she promised on my terms, I'm sure going to see to it that her own future is going to be as insecure and unpleasant as I can possibly arrange it—and I'm willing to make a lot of personal sacrifices to that end for I am a good persistent long distance enemy when anyone gets deep enough under my skin.

I am enclosing checks to take my beloved frau up to the first of the year—and not another cent does she get out of me until that divorce is in, back bills or no back bills. By the way, she is lying, as usual, about the extent of my responsibility for those bills. I could not possibly have owed more than six hundred dollars worth of them, I have been figuring. She went ahead and deliberately had a lot of stuff done to the place without any authorization from me or my even knowing of it when she went down to Bermuda this winter.

Has she made any definite arrangements with her lawyers about their charge? I'll bet she hasn't and they will try and frisk me too!

Get it out of your mind that I am full of passion and hate these days. I've merely made up my mind that I won't stand for a trimming; that's all.

I'm also enclosing checks for Eugene up to first of year and one for Larkin.

Will you phone Miss Silcox of the Authors League and tell her I said it was O.K. to use my name on Committee. She will know what it is.

Give that private detective thing careful thought!

All best, Harry! Either she accepts my terms or some compromise close to them, or call the whole deal off and let's see what little game she'll start then.   Gene

P.S. Check for Eugene's allow. to 1st of year I made out to you.

There is a little over 5000 in the Corn Exchange at present, thanks to some stock play deposits made by Madden, as per my instructions. So you know where you stand.

---

253 • TO EUGENE O'NEILL, JR.   ALS 3 pp. ([Villa Marguerite / Guéthary, B.P., France]) [Yale]

> (Send letters to Harry W. and he'll forward. I'm not sure where I'll be for next few months.)
>
> July 3rd [1928]

Dear Eugene: I owe you an apology for not answering before this but when I haven't been hard at work on *Dynamo* I've been hopping about from place to place.

I was sure damned glad to get your letter and deeply grateful to you for it. It was a truly understanding letter. In short, it was exactly the letter I was hoping you would write and it made me feel very proud of you and close to you. I can say no more than that!

This is only a line because there's no news other than what was in my last. Agnes seems to be behaving rather cheaply about the situation—with her interviews to the tabloids, etc.—but women are nearly always rotten bad losers and I might have expected that sort of thing. However, I'm not so philosophical but that such undignified and ill-bred antics disgust me. She might just as well be a chorus girl yearning for publicity and a photo on the front page at any cost!

But we won't go into that. Each according to his or her lights, I suppose!

I'm enclosing a check for you to do whatever you like with by way of making the summer vacation more pleasant for you.

I'm doubtful of the wisdom of your going to Peaked Hill to visit the Lights—but do as you wish. I'm doubtful for the following reasons and maybe when you've heard them you'll be so forewarned and forearmed that it won't matter. In the first place, Jimmy drinks too much and when he drinks too much he talks too much about my private affairs. And Patti is a natural chatterbox, not maliciously but merely heedlessly. So I rely on you to choke them both off on that—to show them that one subject is absolutely barred as far as you are concerned or you can't stay with them. It isn't that I don't regard them both as true friends of mine—but friends have an idiotic habit of thinking they could run your life for you better than you can which sometimes causes more trouble than all one's enemies' malice.

All this applies more emphatically to P'town in general. Remember that, while I have a few good friends up there (John Francis, for example) there is more bitter envy and spite about my success among the multitude of artistic failures who infest the place these days than any place in the world, including the Algonquin hotel. You'll probably find lots of these bozos, if they get hold of you, trying to pump you or drop some poison in your ear—the women especially! Bear in mind that a certain lady has had and still has a wide reputation for her beauty and is consequently well hated by her sex. To add insult to injury, she comes of a good family, was educated abroad, and has always had an income of her own and was not dependent on the stage for a living. Actresses, especially bad ones, never forgive that sort of presumption—and P'town is crammed with bad actresses, profesh, amateur and the merely domestic. So just cut these ladies' (and he-ladies of which breed P'town is full) gab short. Any way you like. You can't insult them for there isn't the pride of a louse in the lot! And avoid their stupid booze parties. The point is they'd so like to involve you in something! Yes, it is a disagreeable place now from all I've heard! So when one's in the village, watch the old step and be canny!

But this sounds more like one of those good advice father letters than I care to have it. I don't want to foist good(?) advice on you. I know you are not the damn fool I was at your age! Thank God for that! I'm merely warning you of things that might crop up. I know you'll know how to handle them if they do.

Are you all set for Yale? Let me know all about it and if there is anything you need?

All love to you! Have a good summer!   Your   Father

---

254 • TO THERESA HELBURN.   TLS 3 pp. (Villa Marguerite, / Guéthary, B.P. / France) [Yale]

July 13th 1928

Dear Terry: I was very glad to get your card. I hope the Dolomites have pepped you up by this. Don't know anything about them but they sound peppy. I also found the Côte d'Azur very enervating the few days I was there, soon after I last wrote you—and damned boring! To me it doesn't hold a candle to the Côte Basque—but then I'm becoming quite a fan for the Basque country and its people and am getting more and more to think that it's here I may be destined to round out my days. I already have a deep feeling of home about it, even if my knowledge of French, let alone Basque!, is worse than elementary, although I can read it a bit. But they say the Basques come from the same stock as the original Black Irish to which I obviously belong, so maybe that's it.

I am now starting on the last third of *Dynamo*—it will be in three parts instead of two I wrote you about, but no additional set, the second part has same set as first—and I am quite stirred by it. Now here a point comes up and that is that whether you accept it or not I will not be able to get to N.Y. for any rehearsals next season. I have definitely made up my mind that now that I've dragged myself out of my old rut and taken a new lease on life and started traveling that I'm going to keep on. And I have already booked passage for the Far East the latter part of October. After some months there I am going to South Africa, a country I have always had a strong yen for because in the distant past I was pals with so many of its people, both British Africanders and Boers and really know a lot about it for one who has never been there.

But to return to my point: Should you want this play I am perfectly willing to have you put it on without my invaluable(?) assistance, provided I can have a session over here with you or Phil or, better, both before you leave. I have certain very important ideas about the doing of it, and the sets, which would have to be carried out to bring out the full values of the play—and I am sure you would immediately agree with the rightness of these notions. Of course, I could write them out in detail but you know that's never as good as talking them over. So what can we do about this? Where is Phil now? Could he come here for a visit, do you think? Could you? What are your plans? When are you going back? When are you going to be in Paris next? I expect to be there for a few days beginning the 30th of August.

Now I feel as fairly certain as one can be in such matters that you will want *Dynamo*. From a practical standpoint it [has] plenty of plot and the story is an extremely dramatic one. It is also obviously a play that is bound by its subject and treatment to stir up no end of controversy. There will be no worry about its not getting enough publicity, believe me! It hits at what is the matter with us religiously speaking, with our old Gods and our new sciences, from a psychological and symbolical angle that hasn't been touched before. All of its six characters are really dramatic but much more simple and direct people and more easily actable than in *Interlude*. And, finally, the sets along with the action as worked out in them will make an extremely arresting and original production.

So if you don't feel like signing on the dotted line right now, what more can I say? Of course, there's the writing. Well, I'm so close to it now I won't vouch for that more than to say that after I've been over the whole thing once, I'll be willing to stand by it.

I *am* in the devil of a pickle about one thing though—how to get it typed. There's no possibility of getting anyone to do it here. What would you suggest? I'd hate to leave it out of my hands for a moment. I could read it to you or Phil—or perhaps you could read it in my longhand—but that doesn't solve my problem, which is complicated by my complicated domestic situation and my not being able to let anyone come here whom I can't absolutely trust. Of course, I would prove my abysmal and undying faith in you by giving it in your keeping to take back and have typed! But then again, when you got it to N.Y. you might find a lot of it couldn't be made out—or there might be mistakes that couldn't be discovered—or something. Any suggestion you may have will be gratefully received!

My marital affairs have something to do with my resolve to travel—the only thing I'm grateful to the mess for. Things are at a deadlock. I cannot, out of pure self-preservation and in justice to my need for some sort of financial security to work in, agree to the exorbitant price for my freedom now being demanded. Both the other party concerned on this end and I have agreed that, under the circumstances, the only thing to do is to stick it out as is. It means staying out of the States until reason returns to the demander but, after all, I am happier in my present state over here than ever in my life before—so why not? To tell the truth, I am pretty sore and hurt by what has happened in the U.S. I feel as if I'd been walloped beneath the belt. This is the first time in my life—and a life which has known many intimacies with what the world calls crooks and outcasts—I have ever been double-crossed by anyone I trusted to come clean according to their word of honor. Well, I'll write it down to necessary experience, I suppose!   All best to you! Try and write me soon.   Gene

---

255 • TO LOUIS KANTOR (KALONYME).   ALS(X) 4 pp. ([Villa Marguerite] / Guéthary, [B.P., France]) [Lincoln Center]

August 2nd. [1928]

Dear Louis: Your note arrived this a.m. I don't know exactly what dope to give you for New York except to say that you saw me in Germany and I was flourishing as never before and also getting a lot of work done—that *Dynamo* was almost finished but I wasn't sure if I would submit it for production next season or not because I didn't want it to be produced without my cooperation, and the way A. is playing hold-out on me made it doubtful if I could get back to the States as I didn't want to return before I had been divorced and remarried. You can also state the truth that *Dynamo* is a production of some novelty and difficulty.

You can also deny with all possible emphasis the current lie that I left A. in poverty. She is spreading this for all the sympathy she can get. As a matter of fact I am still giving her the same household allowance she got when I was a member of the family. This, after all the tricks she's been pulling I regard as the last word in generosity! She has also pulled a lot of sob stuff about another more serious matter—among my alleged friends who seem to have fallen for it—which, if the tale reaches your ears, you will recognize because I told you the truth about it. How she could have carried her craving for sympathy so far is beyond me especially as she knows I have a letter in her own handwriting giving dates which clear me of all possibility of responsibility, even if her lying tale was true in other respects, which it isn't!

You can also say you know positively that she is deliberately trying to blackmail me legally out of an exorbitant amount as the price of my freedom—and the proof of this is her failure to take any steps about a divorce—in spite of our pledge when we married that either would give the other freedom for the asking and also the fact that I have done so much for her & hers which I was never supposed to do!

Finally, you can say that I have come to the conclusion that she is a pretty cheap contemptible human being and that all her letters to me have been returned unopened. All she ever wrote for was to do everything she could to keep me from working.

And that's about all! It's plenty and all true.

Also, I wish you'd drop in and see Harry and assure him of my happiness which now waxeth daily. Honestly, Louis, I never dreamed I could be so utterly satisfied with my life as I am these days! A. is certainly barking up the wrong tree if she thinks she has the edge of having me in a desperate hole.

I'm on the last part of *Dynamo*. I think it will be "one of the ones" all right and exceeding intriguing also from a production standpoint. It ought to be finished by Sept. 1st. As for my submitting it, I'm still hesitating and what I wrote in the first part of this letter is true. I think one day I'll let it go on without me, and the next, not. I'm going up to Paris on the 25th for a few days and hope to see some of the Guild crowd there and talk things over. Is it possible you may be in Paris around that time? I'd sure love to see you.

Remember to forget that incident of May![1] It had no meaning and was really a damned

---

1. O'Neill had gotten drunk with Kalonyme during the latter's visit to the Villa Marguerite in May.

good thing in its effect on my future, by way of a final K.O. to an old mistake. But how A. & Co. would love to get hold of it!

How are the old lamps? Has your stay on the Baltic helped any?[2]

(By the way, you saw me up on the Baltic, that's the dope.)

I'm enclosing some cards to mail from where you are.   All affectionate best!   Gene

Write when you know your own plans more definitely.

---

256 • TO NATHANIEL LIEF.[1]   ACS 1 p. (Card imprinted: Seebad Heringsdorf [Germany]; in O'Neill's hand: Guaranty Trust, / Pall Mall, / London) [N.Y.U.]

[postmarked August 6, 1928]

Dear Nat Lief: How's the shooting? Are you rolling around in that Rolls yet? Drop me a line. I see by a paper that the Luce and Dumb One has bumped off a legal daddy for herself. It must be her eyes.

I hear that there is much gab being peddled around about my being a base deserter & what not. That is all guff! "Hell hath no fury" etc.! The shoe is on the other hand! I have been double-crossed good & plenty in the U.S. and A new sensation! I don't like it! But we live & get got! But I'm happy as never before in spite of it.   E. O'N.

---

257 • TO MICHAEL GOLD.   ALS 3 pp. (Paris) [Detroit P.L.]

August 15th [1928]

Dear Mike: This is just a note which I hasten to scribble off in answer to yours which was forwarded to me here from the Guaranty Trust, London.

I'm enclosing the letter you want for the Guggenheim crowd. You didn't give me any dope on just who or what to address with those birds but I opine it's a Foundation. I've made it as strong as—well, as strong as I feel you deserve. Hope it will do some good. It's a damn shame you can't get fixed so you can devote all your time to your writing. You've got the stuff! So don't get discouraged! They can't keep a squirrel on the ground forever unless they chop down all the trees! If there's anything else I can do to help ever, let me know. C/o Guaranty Trust Co., 50, Pall Mall, London will always reach me. Sooner or later! I'm bound for the Far East this fall for a stay of some months—then to South Africa for a like period. If I decide to let *Dynamo* be done this season I'm going to take a chance on letting them go ahead with it without me. *Dynamo* will interest you, I think—both as to writing and scheme of production. It will, I imagine, bring all the pious scissor bills down on my neck in hobnailed droves. It is another attempt at a biography of a section of American soul.

It is good news that you are starting on a book of short stories. But why short stories—if you can help it? I ask this because I've often—ever since reading Gorki's books on his childhood and youth—thought, from my appreciation of your work and its quality, that you could do a wonderful thing on East Side life along the same lines taking your own life (as much or as little disguised as you wished) as the main thread on which to hang all the stories you like. Have you ever thought of this form? To me it seems to give so much more opportunity for life to live in than short stories. I've meant to write you this suggestion at

2. Kalonyme had serious trouble with his eyes and was trying various forms of treatment.

1. Brother of J. O. Lief, O'Neill's dentist; this is one of the cards O'Neill had Kalonyme mail.

least a half-dozen times, no kidding! It hit me hardest when I read an East Side sketch of yours in the *N.M.*[1] over a year ago. But you know how lazy one is about writing letters. Here it is at last, anyway. Think it over. But maybe you have. Outside of the artistic end, it stands a better chance of bringing home the bacon for you, you know. And, other things being equal, that deserves a thought. Books of short stories are lousy sellers.

Yes, all is high jake with me! I'm damned happy—in spite of much irritating news of lying tittle-tattle in New York and much endeavor on that end to give me "the works." But it will all come out in the wash. One doesn't bust out of a rut without getting bruised a bit— and I was in the heaviest and dumbest of ruts up to my neck! I'd become a writing Robot whose only living was in writing, since I'd given up life except as a formula I had to be resigned to. This sort of stuff would have been as fatal to my writing as it was to living if I'd stuck in it many years longer. Now I feel free and reborn in a sense. I've got back a lot of my old desire to see all things—the old romantic urge to travel—and all that stuff. Perhaps it's only my age. They say when you're teetering on forty you get that way. But I think it goes deeper than that. Also I've found love again. And that's always something!

What do you think of *Interlude*—I mean its doing a young *Abie's Irish Rose?*[2] Can you have the crust to pan me for a mystic when such miracles occur right on 57th Street? To say I am delightfully surprised is—well—

All best to you always, Mike. Drop me a line once in a while. As I say, it'll reach me eventually.   Your friend,   Gene

---

258 • TO HARRY WEINBERGER.   ALS 4 pp. (Villa Marguerite, / Guéthary, B.P. / France) [Yale]

Aug. 21st. [1928]

Dear Harry: Your letter of the 10th arrived yesterday but as I was on the last strokes of *Dynamo* I feared it might contain disturbing news and didn't read it until today. Yes, *Dynamo* is finished at last, and I am sure it is "one of the ones." So that's that! I feel quite proud of myself that, with all that has been done by my one-time frau deliberately to upset me, I've been able to produce as usual and know it is damn fine work. I'm getting it typed, then will go over it again and send it to Guild. This will all be completed sometime before I sail for Hong Kong on October 5th.

Your news about the agreement sounds fairly favorable except that I will never consent to giving each child (in case of remarriage) any more than I have given and give Eugene. It is an impudence that she should ask it. So the 40 a week stuff each is out. I am emphatically final in this decision. She simply wants me to keep Barbara.

Also I feel, as always, that if I give her Spithead she should only get $1/4$th of my income and I wish you would insist on this. I wrote Winston[1] to this effect too. However, an agreement, I suppose, is one thing and her getting me to pay up is another! She will be in the hole then. Believe me, whatever agreement I sign, if she ever gets more than six thousand a year out of me she'll have to go some!

There's no nonsense about my letting Hart foreclose on Spithead if she doesn't go to Reno. I'm going to do it. You wait and see.

1. The *New Masses*, a radical magazine to which Gold contributed frequently.
2. Play by Anne Nichols (1891–1966) that opened on May 23, 1922, and was for many years the longest-running show in Broadway history (2,327 performances).

1. Norman Winston had offered to try to mediate a settlement between O'Neill and Agnes.

I think you should have had Cornwall Bridge investigated long before this. Why delay when the time is precious with me? I am waiting for news from London. Lawyers are having the records at Somerset House (where every marriage in London is registered) gone over. I should hear soon now.

I remind you that there is little time. I'm leaving for the East Oct. 5th regardless. I'd like to get her off to Reno before then. So cable me whenever you want things hurried up. Once the steamer leaves Marseille I'll be out of touch with all this—and I'll want to be.

There must be a clause that she will never reopen the case.

All Carlotta's letters and mine to A. since I met C. must be returned.

I will sign no agreement that says I must pay the mortgage on Spithead! *This is absolutely final.* I would rather a million times have the mortgage foreclosed and lose all I've put into it (which I lose anyway!) than put another cent in it! *You better take this seriously, Harry, because I never meant anything more in my life!* If she wants Spithead, it is up to her to arrange for someone else taking over the mortgage.

I'm awfully afraid this agreement you're sending is not going to be one I can accept. You better pay more attention to matters I say emphatically in my letters I can't consider and not bother sending me agreements which are contrary to these.

I haven't sent the 2 Bermuda checks on purpose. I've decided to pay no bills there until she's in Reno. The more unpleasant everything gets for her in Bermuda, the better pleased I'll be! Let them attach Spithead! All the merrier!

Agnes is lying, as usual, when she says she has a letter saying I was splitting 50—50 with Carlotta. I simply wrote I was traveling on a 50—50 basis but mentioned no names. It might have been with any friend or friends.

In reading back over your letters today I discover a request at the end of one for the amount due on Oct. 1st. I never remember having read this. Probably got too sore thinking about A. or something. Sorry, old top! I could just as well have sent it before. But here it is now. The Am. P. Co. check was sent me by mistake.

I'll cable when I hear from London. Get busy on Cornwall! Get a detective, better! You'll keep postponing it.

I'm off for Paris tomorrow for a week's vacation.   All best!   Gene

P.S. I don't want to lease Columbus Ave. I may want to sell it once A's dower right in it is off.

---

259 • TO GEORGE JEAN NATHAN.   ALS 8 pp. (Paris) [Cornell]

August 26th [1928]

Dear Nathan: I've started to write you about a half-dozen times in the past few months but something always came up to switch me off of it. In a Paris *Herald* that I happened to pick up I saw where you had been over here and were sailing for home. Were you in France at all? I wish I had known you were coming. We might have been able to hook up someplace. There is nothing I would have liked better than to have had a long talk with you. So much water has flowed under so many bridges since I last saw you. Well, better luck next year!

I have spent most of my time (this is confidential, of course) in Guéthary near Biarritz down in the Basque country. Of course, there has been a lot of touring about but my headquarters, where I have written *Dynamo*, has been in Guéthary. I have a fine old villa there right on the sea. The Basque country and the Basques hit me right where I belong. According to present plans and inclinations it is there that I shall settle down to make a home for the rest of my days—and I feel that this time it's going to prove what none of my other attempts were—a real home! Europe has meant a tremendous lot to me, more than I ever hoped it could. I've felt a deep sense of peace here, a real enjoyment in just living from day to day, that I've never known before. For more than the obvious financial reasons, I've come to the conclusion that anyone doing creative work is a frightful sap to waste the amount of energy required to beat life in the U.S.A. when over here one can have just that more strength to put into one's job.

Dynamo is finished and is now in process of being typed. I want you to see a script of it as soon as possible. It is real stuff, I am sure—a good symbolical and factual biography of what is happening in a large section of American (and not only American) soul right now. It is really the first play of a trilogy that will dig at the roots of the sickness of today as I feel it—the death of the old God and the failure of Science and Materialism to give any satisfying new One for the surviving primitive religious instinct to find a meaning for life in, and to comfort its fears of death with. It seems to me anyone trying to do big work nowadays must have this big subject behind all the little subjects of his plays or novels, or he is simply scribbling around on the surface of things and has no more real status than a parlor entertainer. But more of this when we talk. The two other plays will be "Without Endings Of Days" and "It Cannot Be Mad." These two plays will be greater in writing scope than *Dynamo*—which has a direct primitive drive to it and whose people are psychologically simple, as compared to *Interlude*'s—and will give me a greater chance to shoot my piece as a writer—but *Dynamo*, believe me, has taken all I have to give as a dynamist of the drama, and it should make its power felt terrifically when once it is skillfully produced. I'm quite proud of it and anxious to get your reaction. It is going to bring all the pious sectarians down on my neck in hell-roaring droves, I prophesy—and should be as much argued about, I think, in its different way as *Interlude*. It will require some expert directing to get its full values across but I hope this will be safe in the hands of Phil Moeller. Unfortunately I won't be there to help and will have to take my chance on being present only in a detailed list of written instructions. The snarl in my domestic situation, with my wife still playing financial hold-out and making all sorts of impossible demands, has rather forced the decision on me of fighting shy of the U.S.A. for another year and continuing my travels. I am sailing for the Far East early in October—expect to be in India a bit, then settle down in Hong Kong for a spell of work, then to Java and way stations and so on down to South Africa for another settling down and more work, back to France in June. This ambitious scheme may vary in detail but the general plan of it will be carried out. I think this trip is going to give me a lot I need and I'm certainly looking forward to it.

The aspect of life has certainly changed for me in the past six months. For the first time in God knows how long I feel as if life had something to give me as a living being quite outside of the life in my work. The last time I wrote you I said I was happy. A rash statement, but I can make it again with tenfold emphasis! And, believe me, it has stood tests that would have wrecked it if it weren't the genuine article, for everything has been done from the outside that malice and revenge could dope out to ruin it! But it has come through finer and deeper and is the wealthier for all the knocks. As I approach my fortieth birthday I feel younger and more pepped up with the old zest for living and working than I've ever felt since I started writing. I may seem to slop over a bit about this but no one really knows into what a bog of tedium and life-sickness I was sinking. I was living on my work, as one does on one's nerves sometimes, and sooner or later my work would certainly have been sapped of its life because you can't keep on that way forever, even if one puts up the strongest of bluffs to oneself and the world in general. Now I feel as if I'd tapped a new life and could rush up all the reserves of energy in the world to back up my work. Honestly, to me it is a sort of miracle, so resigned had I become to being resigned to the worst, and you'll have to be indulgent to my wishing a bit of my pop-eyed wonder at it on you!

In addition to the plans for near future plays I've also done a lot of thinking on my idea for the Big Grand Opus.[1] It's too long for me to try to go into here but much of it when I see you. I want to give about three years to it—either one long stretch or, more probably, that amount of working time over a longer period with intervals of doing a play in between times. This G.O. is to be neither play nor novel although there will be many plays in it and it will have greater scope than any novel I know of. Its form will be altogether its own and my own—a lineal descendant of *Interlude,* in a way, but beside it *Interlude* will seem like a mere shallow episode! Does this sound ambitious? Well, my idea of it as it is growing in me certainly is aiming at stars and I only hope to God I have the stuff in me to do it right—for then it will be One of the Ones and no damn doubt about it!

So you see I'm feeling fairly fit when I'm dreaming of championship belts! I hear a lot of the boys in N.Y. are feeling very sad about the future of my work, fearing that it will be ruined by the fact that I had the guts to make a grab for happiness. I feel sorry for these melancholy ones whose wish is so obviously the father of their apprehension! They are going to be terribly disappointed! I wonder why the hell it is that even the people whom you would think were free from the banal dogmas of Main Street always believe that every artist's wife collaborated in his work and he couldn't have done it without her companionship (when more often he is driven to work to escape from her)? I'll be damned if I don't think it's the fool authors themselves who are responsible for this myth, what with their propitiatory dedications to their fraus stuck in the front of nearly every book one comes across.

I've also heard reliable gossip of much more serious rumors about what I have done and haven't. Of course, I expect this, knowing the original source of all such hooey. Some wives turn out that way and are only spiteful when they have promised to be sporting and come clean. But it's all rather nauseating. In all my life among all kinds—and a good part among the so-called worst kinds—of people, I've never been double-crossed before. Not because I couldn't be. I was always easy and wide open but I always found that men and women knew they could trust me so they never gypped my trust in them. This is a new experience. Frankly, I don't care for it. Somehow it reflects on a humanity that is already too reflected on for much faith. At first, I was a bit hurt by it but now I'm only peevish.

But enough of that! It's not worrying me much really and I don't know why I'm bothering you with it except that you may have heard said dirt and wondered what my reaction to it was.

I'm sending this letter by Louis Kalonyme. I'm also giving him a letter of introduction to you. He has been an intense and loyal admirer of yours for a long time and wants very much to meet you. He's an old friend of mine. You've probably seen a lot of his art criticism (and for one season, theatre) on *Arts & Decoration.* He's got real stuff in him but has had a rotten hard break from fate in that serious trouble with his eyes has kept him barging back and forth from one specialist to another in U.S., Germany & England. I've known Louis for six or seven years. He's a good guy. Well, that's about all about me, I guess.

I know this is a hell of a late date to be expressing my grateful appreciation of your article on the *Interlude* critics.[2] I meant to write you at the time but I was dodging around so much then.

1. "The Sea-Mother's Son"; see *Eugene O'Neill at Work: Newly Released Ideas for Plays,* pp. 180–82.

2. "The Theatre," *American Mercury* 14 (May 1928): 120.

I'm in Paris for a few days—then back to Guéthary for two weeks. You'd better address any letter care of Guaranty Trust Co., 50, Pall Mall, London.

All good wishes always,   As ever,   Eugene O'Neill

---

260 • TO EUGENE O'NEILL, JR.   ALS 6 pp. (c/o Guaranty Trust Co., / 50, Pall Mall, London) [Yale]

(you'd better use this address
as I'm leaving here soon)
[early September 1928]

Dear Eugene: Hope you got my cable all right. Consider it a lazy man's letter. Or, more kindly, a busy man's—for it's no lie to say I've been, and still am, busy getting *Dynamo* finished and typed and gone over so I can submit it to the Guild at the earliest possible moment. I expect now to have it mailed to them in about a week. Then will come a breathing spell which I'll be glad to reach for I'm dead tired and my brain is like a wrung sponge. The last part of *Dynamo* has been intensive work, there was so much to jam into such small space. The concentrated medium of the drama takes it out of one at such times. Well, at any rate, the play is written now and I feel it's "one of the ones," in spite of the usual reaction after a thing is finished of its seeming like a lot of junk.

Did I say I'd enjoy a breathing spell soon? Well, not so damn soon. There's packing and moving out of here and a million odds and ends to attend to. I won't really be able to sit back and rest until I get on the boat for China the first week in October.

Yes, I'm going to the Far East—sailing for Hong Kong and way stations the first week in October. I expect to spend some time in China, then go to Java and India for more or less short periods. After that—but here my plans are indefinite. It all depends on how things work out. I may go down the African coast and spend a couple of months in the Transvaal and Rhodesia. I've got to pick out a place in the East for two months' work and another place later on for another two months. The rest of the time will be given to travel. I'll be back here in France by the first of July at the latest. And, if you want to, I want you to plan to come over next summer and stay with me in this Basque country and see a lot of France (and Europe in general if you want to make trips around on your own). I'm planning now to make my permanent home here, once it's time to settle down again. I feel more at home here than I've ever felt anywhere before—more at peace and "belonging," even though I don't speak the language much. By the way, for Pete's sake go in a bit for French in the meantime. You'll be missing a lot if you don't—and there's no reason why you shouldn't come over here any summer you like from now on.

One reason I'm deciding to settle here is, of course, financial. You can live so much better here on so much less money.

I hope that by next spring all this present "hold-out" policy of Agnes' will be settled. If it isn't, well I know the situation here will be taken for granted by you. The didacs of a revengeful wife cannot be helped, I suppose—and may be expected, until she gets tired of being a bum sport. But, I sure hope to be divorced and remarried by then.

I hope you're going to like Yale and get something worth your while out of it. Enjoy your life there—that's the main thing (this sounds like all hell in the way of advice from a father!)—but give a thought once in a while to what you want to do with your life after college and, since you've got to work to stick there, try to give your work (your choice of it) some definite direction toward some goal. And do go out strong for that crew! I think the spirit one gets out of college athletics is a damn fine thing—provided, of course, one has the brains and character to keep the athlete part of one in its place, which you have. I've felt all my life that that was one value in life I cheated myself out of by my own perverse cussedness. I am under no illusions that I could ever have been a shining star at anything but it would have done me a hell of a lot of good inside—not to add, physically—if I had put myself through the self-discipline of trying to be. All of which sounds a bit confused. But you get me.

Another bit of brotherly—(for I always feel in such matters as if you were more a young brother than a son)—caution I want to hand you about college out of my fund of experience with college men is this: Don't get out of your own financial depth in the fellows you chum with. Nothing tends to have a worse effect on character than this (see all the psychologists!). I don't mean by this to avoid the rich because they're rich—as a matter of fact it's sons from families who have had money for generations who get along on moderate spending money—it's the heirs of the nouveaus who splurge. You know about what my status is—an up and down one with one flush year followed by one or two lean ones. For example, this year is grand while last year I was paying for Spithead and living on (mostly) the sale of securities that I'd bought when *Desire* was going strong. Perhaps I'm due for more continuous good luck in the future. I hope so—but you never can tell. The theatre, financially speaking, is always a gamble.

But I don't want you to think I'm crying poor. I have the deepest faith in your balance and good sense (which you can thank your Mother for as you certainly didn't get that virtue from me!) and I want you to know that anything you feel you need you can certainly have, without question, as long as I can give it to you. And you must feel it's your right to ask for it. You've got to come forward and not be modest. It will make it a lot easier for me. You see, it's a hell of a while since I went to college and I have no friends with sons there, so I'm completely out of touch with the current values of modern undergraduate life. I want you, as my son and for the sake of your own development in the four years, to hold up your end on your own proper level simply and with breeding and dignity. To give a sort of indicative example which may be revealing to you: I want you to have one fine, perfectly-fitting expensive suit of clothes where others will have three maybe but each minus the distinction. It will be less expensive for you & you'll be better dressed. This sounds like What the W. D. Man should W. but I'm no bug on clothes. The same dope goes for everything.

That being off my chest, let me say how proud I was you came off so well in the entrance exams. Keep up the good work. There is one aspect of college on which I have drastically changed my mind since I graced (at least "graced" is part of the word the Dean used, if I remember!) the campus of Old Nassau and that is the notion that one must not, under any compulsion, learn anything there. I believe now that it is rather good dope, and helps one to enjoy life, if one *does learn* as much as one can.

I'm enclosing a check to your Mother. This is extra, tell her, to use to help you in your first half term in any way you decide best between you. The usual check will, of course, be forthcoming, via Harry, the first of year. You can read her what I've said about college etc. and if she vetoes any of my "advice," consider it vetoed. She has more sense than I will ever have.

Write me your impressions of Old Eli after you've been there a bit. Call on Baker and William Lyon Phelps and President Angell and tell them who you are. It may help—if my Yale Litt.D.[1] counts for anything. They are all fine men and you'll like them. Also if you ever happen near William Brown, Dean of the Divinity School, introduce yourself. He was my sponsor that day. I think he expected to find me (being a divine) a cross between a gunman

1. O'Neill had received an honorary degree from Yale in 1926.

and the devil and was most edified by my surprising knowledge of theology and early Christianity (from the reading I'd done for *Lazarus*). But I liked him and think he liked me.

I'm sending you my itinerary for the trip—but you better always use c/o Guaranty Trust Co., 50, Pall Mall, London as address as I'll keep cabling them any change in plan and exact dates my whereabouts. Also Harry will know. Give your Mother Harry's address. Go to him in any sudden emergency.

And that's about all, I guess. I'll write you anything of interest from the East. I expect to get a lot from it as spiritual background for my future life and work. It's always called to me. When I was a sailor I was always aiming for there but never made it.

Be good and be happy! Give me a thought once in a while. I'm really profoundly proud and fond of you—after my fashion which is inarticulate about such things—and I know there is a rare feeling between us that ought to make both our lives richer as the years go by.

All love to you always!   Your   Father

---

261 • TO HARRY WEINBERGER.   ALS 2 pp. ([Villa Marguerite / Guéthary, B.P., France]) [Yale]

Sept. 6th [1928]

Dear Harry: Will you attend to the enclosed and have them switch the thing to N.Y. as you did the others?

I received yesterday a certificate from Somerset House, London. Only two Agnes Boultons were married in London from 1913–1917 inclusive. Neither married anyone called Burton and neither answers to A. in the data about birth, residence, etc., etc. So that's that. There's something damn queer behind this. A. has always acted funny about it. I want the truth for Shane's & Oona's protection. For all I know it may be bigamy. A. has always been damned crazy along certain lines.

Why do you talk about waiting until she sues? I want no public action on this—but I do want you to use it as a threat to make her act reasonable right now. I don't see why in God's name you don't just tell Driscoll the dope and demand that his client come forward with the truth! We now have a good weapon and you don't use it!

Certainly I want Winston to do his best but there are some demands of hers I simply can't give in to after the way she has acted toward me. She's got to be shown where she gets off!

You can tell Driscoll that I say my growing suspicion about her lying about this first marriage is why I became estranged from her and left her finally and that such would be my claim in court.   All best!   Gene

---

262 • TO GILMOR BROWN.[1]   ALS 2 pp. (Paris) [Yale]

(address)
c/o Guaranty Trust Co.
50, Pall Mall, London
Sept. 15th 1928

My dear Mr. Brown: I want to apologize most sincerely and conscience-strickenly for my rank discourtesy in not having written before to express my deep appreciation of your

---

1. Brown (1886?–1960), director of the Pasadena Community Theatre and of its April 1928 production of *Lazarus Laughed,* who also played Tiberius.

fine production of *Lazarus Laughed.* My only excuse for this unpardonable negligence is that I am a notoriously rotten correspondent at best and that since I left the States I have done hardly any letter writing at all.

I hoped, at the time I cabled you last winter, to be able to get out to California for the production. Later, conditions became such that this plan had to be abandoned and I suddenly made up my mind to come to Europe.

I assure you I shall never cease to regret my being forced to miss out on this. It was, I'm very much afraid, my only chance of seeing the play done in America. There are several possibilities, even probabilities, of its being done in Russia and Central Europe—but not a visible chance for any New York showing. Your organization seems to be the only one with the necessary amount of imagination and daring. Of course, the old Provincetown Player group (what remains of it) has the spirit for it but they lack the backing and the theatre.

Madden has sent me the photos. Kenneth Macgowan also sent me some. I find them extraordinarily impressive and interesting. Mr. Pichel's "Lazarus" and your "Tiberius" struck me particularly as hitting my nail on the head. I have heard from quite a few people whose judgment I respect who saw the play at Pasadena—and there was not one unfavorable comment. There were some criticisms about this point or that in the play itself but none on your production. Everyone I heard from felt it had marked a memorable achievement in the imaginative theatre the script cries for. Let me say again how damned sorry I am I couldn't see it.

In spite of my selfish disappointment, I want to congratulate your organization on its sound decision not to come to New York. I know from experience—none better!—that there is nothing more liable to corrupt the integrity of an art theatre, to reduce it from an unselfish compact group impulse to a disintegrated selfish striving of individuals, than bucking the uptown New York theatre game. The Theatre Guild is the only organization that has done this successfully without losing sight of its aim—and it took them many years of battling development in New York to accomplish this. So I certainly think you were wise. Your theatre needs no stamp of New York approval to give it authority.

Will you express to all those connected with the doing of *L. L.* my deep, if shamefully belated, gratitude? I hope you will find other things of mine in the future that you will want to do, and that the next time I'll be able to be there.

My sincere respects to you personally and all good wishes to the Pasadena Community Theatre!   Eugene O'Neill

---

263 • TO BENJAMIN DE CASSERES.   ALS 4 pp. (c/o Guaranty Trust Co., / 50, Pall Mall, London) [Dartmouth]

[postmarked September 15, 1928]

Dear Ben: I was damn glad to get your letter and damned gladder to know you felt the Introduction[1] was all right. Frankly, I felt uncertain about its pleasing you. I didn't think it did its subject justice. Writing in that form is so foreign to me that I know I don't express myself very well in it. I'm a very incoherent individual outside of the drama. But if you're pleased, that's that and I've got no kick against myself coming.

1. O'Neill wrote an introduction to De Casseres's *Anathema!,* a prose poem published in New York by Gotham Book Mart in 1928. It is reprinted in *The Unknown O'Neill: Unpublished or Unfamiliar Writings of Eugene O'Neill,* pp. 383–85.

Your article on the sissification of the stage[2] handed me a large and satisfactory chuckle. I'll bet you'll have a large section of infuriated fairies crawling your frame for that one. Also the ladies are not due to be thrilled with joy. The article on Shaw[3] is damn good too.

Dynamo is finished, typed and gone over and I've sent scripts off to the Guild and Madden. I've instructed Madden to have some copies of his made and to deliver one to you whenever you've a chance to read it. I'm much too near it just now—and suffering from the usual let-down—to have any clear view of it. But I do feel it's "one of my ones" and is a searching symbolical biography of a large section of [the] American soul. As it is the first play of a trilogy of such biography it can't be judged entirely for what I mean it to mean until the other two, dealing each with a different sort of American, are completed. The titles of the other two are "Without Endings Of Days" and "It Cannot Be Mad." (Keep these under your hat.) They'll be written in the more or less near future as they grow ripe. They're all mapped out now.

To return to *Dynamo* I feel my scheme of production—for which I've sent full drawings and suggestions to the Guild—will make a vividly dramatic impression in itself, if the sets and sounds are done as they should be done. And won't the Fundamentalist brethren be down on my neck in droves for my subject! Oh boy! But as they already think I'm a sort of minor AntiChrist, maybe they won't even be surprised. You never can tell.

I hope the Guild will do it—but again you never can tell. It's a treatment of a subject that you can never tell what reaction you'll get from any individual on it.

A general idea-title for the trilogy might be God Is Dead! Long Live—What? with science supplying an answer which to religion-starved primitive instinct is like feeding a puppy biscuit to a lion. Or something like that.

I'm doing much thinking on my grand major opus which will take me years to do— years with probably a play or two sandwiched in to change the subject for a bit. It's growing and growing in me and it fills me with a grand enthusiasm. It will have scope enough to contain all of life I have the guts to grasp and make my own. And it will not be like anything ever written before in its form and intensity. It would take a long letter indeed to even scratch at what I'm going to attempt so I won't try. Suffice it that compared to it *Interlude* ought to seem like a brief and paltry thing. It will have ten or more *Interludes* in it, each deeper and more powerful than *S.I.*, and yet it will all be a unit. Believe me, Ben, I'm going to bullseye a star with that job or go mad in the attempt. I'm going to do some preliminary work on it on my travels this winter—then write a play of the trilogy—then the next (the following) winter spend six months up in the Tyrol and go at the first parts of it with a vengeance.

My state of mind now? You can diagnose from the above. Never better! Never as good! I've found what I was looking for. I feel love and peace around me now to support me and give me strength when I'm weak. I won't have to do the whole thing of living, dreaming and working all by my own effort all the time any longer. I'll have more strength to give to my job. It's grand! I'm very happy! Can I say more?

Of course, I've been double-crossed and annoyed in every possible way and for a while it hurt my pride and shook my faith in human nature in its relation to me. Nobody ever "took me for a ride" before in anything but trifling matters. Even among prostitutes and bums whenever I laid myself open to "the works" and trusted them I found I got an even break.

But I'm all over that injury to my self-esteem as a regular guy. What the hell! I suppose I

2. "Broadway to Date—Place Any Dames! in the Drama, and Other Solemn and Satanic Opinions on the Current Stage," *Arts and Decoration* 26 (January 1927): 46.
3. "Broadway to Date—The Theatre Through the Holiday Season," *Arts and Decoration* 28 (February 1928): 55, 86.

should have expected it. I hear there are tall tales being told of my cruelty, parsimony and what not. Of course, they're all the bunk as anyone who really knows me or knows my family life in the past ought to be aware. Women have to get sympathy for themselves somehow—some women—and what is the truth but a viewpoint, after all. The queer point in this case is that I who didn't want to fight have been forced into a battle.

But I'm not worrying any more. It's forcing me further out of my old rut and that's a blessing.

I'm sailing for the Far East the first week in October—India and then China—Java and maybe South Africa toward the end. I'll be gone nine or ten months. I've always longed for this trip and I expect a lot out of it—inside me.

All best to you and Bio! Drop me a line once in a while and I'll promise to write you. (The address at top of letter will always reach me eventually.)

I feel ten years younger—and I'm off adventuring again! Praise be!   Your friend   Gene

---

264 • TO SHANE O'NEILL.   ALS 5 pp. (c/o Guaranty Trust Co., / 50, Pall Mall, London) [Harvard]

[late September 1928]

Dear Shane: I must ask you to forgive me because I haven't written to you in such a long time, but I have been so awfully busy finishing up my new play *Dynamo* and getting it typewritten and then going all over it again and correcting it that I haven't had time to write any letters. It was a hard job for me to find anyone to type it because where I was all the people speak German and only a very few of them know any English at all but finally I found someone to do it.

I have just been reading over your last letters—the ones you dictated to Gaga[1] and the one you wrote yourself which is fine writing and shows you must have studied hard and learned a lot in school since I saw you last. It must have been great fun when you went to the Aquarium and the Museum of Natural History and the Zoo. I used to have a nurse[2] like Gaga when I was a boy and after I went to boarding school I used to visit her every vacation when my Mother wasn't in New York and she used to take me to every one of those places every vacation so I got to know them all well. But now I haven't been to the Aquarium or the Museum or the Zoo in a great many years. Sometime when you and I are in New York together we'll have to go to these places and you can point out to me all the new things which have been added since I was a boy. They are all much bigger now than they were in those days. I liked the Zoo the best, didn't you? I liked watching the seals the same as you did—especially when the keeper came to feed them and he'd throw fish to them and they'd catch them in their mouths and never miss one catch! And I used to feed the bears pieces of cake we'd take out with us in a basket and put peanuts in the elephant's trunk when he'd reach out for them. But I never saw the elephant giving himself a bath. That must have been great fun! And it was funny what Oona said about him putting his tail in his mouth. But then an elephant is a funny made animal and you'd be liable to get all mixed up about which end of him was front, if you'd never seen one before or heard of one, as I suppose Oona hadn't. Did you go in the lion house where all the fierce lions and tigers and leopards are? I used to like the lions best of all animals because they are so beautiful looking and so strong. You

1. Shane and Oona saw Mrs. Clark and visited a zoo, aquarium, and museum during a trip to New York.
2. Sarah Sandy. See Louis Sheaffer, *O'Neill: Son and Playwright* (Boston: Little, Brown, 1968), pp. 55–56.

ought to hear one of them roar sometime as they do when they get mad. My brother, your Uncle Jim, who is dead, used to be able to make a noise just like a lion roaring and for a joke he used to go out to the Zoo and go up close to the lion's cage when the lion was asleep, and when the keeper wasn't looking your Uncle Jim would lean over close to the lion's ear and make the roaring imitation and the lion would wake up startled and jump to his feet mad as the dickens and wanting to fight and he'd start roaring, and then all the other lions and tigers and leopards would get mad too and start roaring, and the keeper would come running to see what was the matter but Uncle Jim would walk away as if he hadn't done anything and he'd be laughing to himself because he thought he'd played a great joke!

I was awfully glad to hear from your last letter that you like the school so much and that you've been going on picnics and having such a wonderful time in general. I'm pleased too that you've learned to swim so much better and I suppose by this time you could give Eugene or me a good hard race.

Tell Barbara I was awfully glad to get her letter and I think it was very nice of her to write to me.

I've been living in all sorts of houses since I came over here. The last one I was in was right on a beach like Peaked Hill or Campsea and I went in swimming every day. It was in Germany up on the Baltic sea and it was from there I sent you the postcard.

I'm sorry but I won't be able to come back soon although I miss you and Oona an awful lot and think of you all the time. I've got to go on a long voyage on a ship about some plays I want to write. I'm going to a place called India for a while, and to Java and to China and maybe after that I'll go way down to Africa and make a trip to Lake Tanganyika. It's right around there that lions and leopards live and it's India where tigers and elephants are but I don't suppose I'll see anything but tame elephants because I don't care about hunting much, especially when you're liable to get killed. But maybe I'll have a ride on top of a tame elephant. I'll write you letters about what I see and do and send you postcards.

I'm putting in this letter a check made out to Mother to buy you a birthday present— you can pick it out. I'll be way off when your birthday comes and I won't send anything from here because I'm afraid it would get smashed. But no matter how far off I am you'll know I'm thinking of you all that day and maybe one of my thoughts will fly through the air and you'll hear it and think of me. Let me know if you do.

Please write me. It will take a long time for letters to reach me but, if you use the address at the top of this letter, they will get to me sure sometime.

Kiss Oona for me. I'm writing her a letter too but not such a long one because she's only little compared to you. Give Barbara and Gaga my love.

Much deep love to you, my son, from   Your   Daddy

P.S. In a letter to Harry Weinberger I have told him to tell Mother that you are to have my bicycle for your next birthday, too. And for a Christmas present I give you my kayak and all the paddles and I give you & Oona together, each to own half, the St. Lawrence rowboat. Only you must promise never to use the kayak until you are much bigger, except in very calm weather right near shore when Mother says you can, because it is dangerous. And you must take care of Oona and not let her stand up in the rowboat, and promise to teach her how to row as soon as she is big enough. And, above all, you must promise to look after these boats and never let them scrape or bump into rocks and see that they are kept painted and kept in good condition—especially the kayak, which you must always remember your Daddy loves very much because he spent so very many happy hours in it and every time you go out in it you must think of him.

You must promise me all these promises, remember, and keep them because you would hurt me very much if you were lazy and careless about my presents when these presents have meant so much to me!

Much love again to you & Oona! Don't forget me!

---

265 • TO CARLOTTA MONTEREY. ALS 1 p. (Stationery headed: The Country Hospital / 17 Great Western Road / Shanghai) [Yale]

[c. November 25-30, 1928]

Dearest!   And God bless you! This in much haste to catch your coolie back.

I love you—always and forever!

Forgive me! I'll be a *good 'un* in future—do my damndest best to!

A million kisses, Blessed!   Good'night   Gene

---

266 • TO CARLOTTA MONTEREY. ALS 1 p. ("On boat returning from China to Europe"[1]) [Yale]

Dec. 1928

Dearest One: Please, for God's sake, don't make so much of last night! I honestly didn't do anything so horribly wrong—and I would have come out and walked this morning if you hadn't sounded so damned sore!

Please, Dearest! I'm not doing or going to do any of the things you think. Don't let a bad start entirely spoil this Christmas for us! When you know how entirely I love you!

I looked for you topside. I'll be there. Won't you come?   Your   Gene

---

267 • TO CARLOTTA MONTEREY. ALS 1 p. ([Singapore?]) [Yale]

Dec. 29, 1928[1]

Dearest: Come up. I don't know whether to dress or not.

I haven't been down or out because I woke up with an urge to write your "pome" and have been working on it.

A creative urge! What ho! But at the same time I feel down and funny. I've felt damn queer all day—and not for any ostensible reason.   Love!   Your   Gene

---

268 • TO CARLOTTA MONTEREY. WIRE 1 p. (S.S. COBLENZ) [Yale]

JANUARY 6, 1929

FOLLOWING MESSAGE GIVEN DOCTOR DEAREST FORGIVE ME BUT NEED YOUR HELP MORE THAN EVER BEFORE BECAUSE I AM HALF MAD WITH UTTER LONELINESS WITHOUT FRIENDS PLANS OR HOPES TUVA[1] HAS NEVER BEEN NEAR ME IT

1. This information and the date are supplied at the top of the letter in Carlotta's handwriting.

1. This date is supplied in Carlotta's handwriting.

1. Tuve Drew, a registered nurse who was serving as Carlotta's personal maid during their voyage. Carlotta left Mrs. Drew on the *Coblenz* when she left the ship in Ceylon and continued her trip home on the *President Monroe*.

WOULD BE A TREMENDOUS HELP IF YOU CABLE ME EVERY DAY I LOVE YOU AND I DESERVE THAT THE DOCTOR HAS MY PROMISE AND I WILL KEEP IT HOW ARE YOU I FEEL SO TERRIBLY WORRIED ABOUT YOU   GENE

---

269 • TO CARLOTTA MONTEREY.   WIRE 1 p. (S.S. COBLENZ) [Yale]

JANUARY 7, 1929

I KNOW DEAREST THE BEST MEDICINE IS THOU AND I AND KNOW YOUR GENOA PLANS AM FULL OF CONFIDENCE AND COUNTING DAYS DONT WORRY ABOUT ME   GENE

---

270 • TO CARLOTTA MONTEREY.   WIRE 1 p. (S.S. COBLENZ) [Yale]

JANUARY 7, 1929

GOOD NIGHT DEAREST ONE MORE DAY GONE   GENE

---

271 • TO CARLOTTA MONTEREY.   WIRE 1 p. (S.S. COBLENZ) [Yale]

JANUARY 7, 1929

RELY MY DOING EVERYTHING ALL RIGHT BUT MISS YOUR HELP LOVE TREMEN- DOUSLY HAVE HORRIBLE DESERTED FEELING DARLING AND THESE DAYS ARE LONGEST EMPTIEST IN MY LIFE   GENE

---

272 • TO CARLOTTA MONTEREY.   WIRE 1 p. (S.S. COBLENZ) [Yale]

JANUARY 8, 1929

POSSIBILITY COBLENZ MAY BE DELAYED PORT SUDAN SO WILL BE IN PORT SAID SAME TIME AS MONROE IF SO LET US ARRANGE TALK SOMEHOW IF ONLY FIVE MINUTES THIS WOULD MEAN EVERYTHING IN WORLD TO ME DEAREST ONE   GENE

---

273 • TO CARLOTTA MONTEREY.   WIRE 1 p. (S.S. COBLENZ) [Yale]

JANUARY 8, 1929

IT IS BEAUTIFUL BECAUSE YOU THINK SO I WILL BE THERE IF I HAVE TO SWIM GOOD NIGHT DARLING YOURSELF   GENE

---

274 • TO CARLOTTA MONTEREY.   WIRE 1 p. (S.S. COBLENZ) [Yale]

JANUARY 11, 1929

ITS HIDEOUS THIS LAST STRETCH OF HADES I MISS YOU SO GOOD NIGHT DEAR ONE   GENE

275 • TO CARLOTTA MONTEREY.   WIRE 1 p. (S.S. COBLENZ) [Yale]

JANUARY 11, 1929

OF COURSE I WANT YOU AND NEED YOU AS MUCH AS I LOVE YOU AND THE EXPERI-
ENCE YOU SPEAK OF WILL NEVER BE REPEATED I GIVE YOU BACK YOUR OWN
ADVICE FORGET THE PAST AND START BUILDING SOLIDLY FOR THE FUTURE
GENE

VERY ANXIOUS AFTER YOUR WIRE KEEPING PROMISE SPLENDIDLY KEEP UP HIS
COURAGE DONT WORRY   TUVE

---

276 • TO CARLOTTA MONTEREY.   WIRE 1 p. (S.S. COBLENZ) [Yale]

JANUARY 12, 1929

IMPOSSIBLE TO TELL YET ALL DEPENDS ON WHETHER YOU CATCH US I AM PRAYING
YOU WILL I WILL COME TO YOU IF ONLY FOR FIVE MINUTES ALL LOVE
DEAREST   GENE

---

277 • TO CARLOTTA MONTEREY.   WIRE 1 p. (S.S. COBLENZ) [Yale]

JANUARY 12, 1929

CHEER UP STILL A FAIR CHANCE COBLENZ PROBABLY NOT LEAVE PORT SAID UNTIL
MIDNIGHT MONDAY GOOD NIGHT SWEETHEART   GENE

---

278 • TO CARLOTTA MONTEREY.   WIRE 1 p. (S.S. COBLENZ) [Yale]

JANUARY 14, 1929

COBLENZ WONT PROBABLY SAIL BEFORE FOUR MORNING IF SAILS BEFORE
MONROE ARRIVES WILL WAIT ON SHORE ASK PURSER RESERVE BEST HE HAS GOT
LOVE   GENE

---

279 • TO SHANE AND OONA O'NEILL.   TLS 1 p. (Guaranty Trust Co., / 50, Pall
Mall, London) [Virginia]

[c. January 31, 1929]

Dear Shane and Oona: I have just received two of your letters that went all the way to
Shanghai in China but got there after I had left and then had to chase me all the way back
here. I sent you two letters written on the boat coming back and mailed from a place called
Balawan in Sumatra where we stopped three days. I hope you got them all right. I sent them
to New Preston in care of Mrs. Boulton and there were some postcards enclosed of Sumatra
which is a wild tropic colony owned by the Dutch and is one of the most interesting places I
have been to. There are lots of wild animals there and it is one of the places where the people
go who catch them and sell them to the Zoos.

It was a wonderful trip to the East and in spite of the fact that I was so sick for the last part
of the voyage out there and most of the time I was in Shanghai, I wouldn't have missed it for

a million dollars. I saw all kinds of strange places and met so many different kinds of people on the boats I was on and ashore in the towns that I feel as if I'd added a whole new world to my experience. I would have liked to have stayed away longer but I found that I couldn't seem to get to work out there—in most of the places the tropic heat took all your strength and ambition away—and that's why I am now back in Europe, to get on the job writing a new play[1] that I have already started although I've only been back here ten days.

But I won't say anymore about my trip now. I told you a lot in my other letters but most of the things I am saving to tell you when I see you again.

I was so glad to get your letters and to hear all the news about you and Oona. I suppose you have both grown so big now that I won't know you when I see you after being away so long a time. I think of you both a lot and sometimes I want to see you so much that I feel like taking the first boat to America—but I have such important business to attend to over here that I have to stay for a while longer. I hope you will both of you write to me soon after you receive this and I promise to answer your letters right away after this.

Did Gaga get the money I cabled Harry to send her? Tell her I am awfully sorry to hear she has been sick. Harry cabled me that Mother had been sick too. Tell Mother I am damned sincerely sorry. Tell her that when I was very sick in the hospital in Shanghai all the bitterness got burned out of me and the future years will prove this.

Kiss Oona for me and have her kiss you for me. I love you both very dearly. Don't forget me and let me know if there is anything you need or want especially and I will send you the money to get it.   Goodbye for this time; Write me soon.   Daddy

---

280 • TO EUGENE O'NEILL, JR.   TL[1] 2 pp. (Villa "Les Mimosas" / Boulevard de la Mer / Cap d'Ail, A.M. / France)[2] [Yale]

Feb. 5th 1929

Dear Eugene: Your letter just reached me! I've discovered by prying off the layers of the different addresses on it that it was first forwarded to Hong Kong (where we meant to stay but didn't) then on to Yokohama (where we meant to go but didn't) and forwarded by the National City Bank there back to Guaranty Trust in London and by them to me here when I informed them of my arrival. So it chased me for about twenty thousand miles—which is quite a run for a postage stamp! Lots of other letters seem to have done the same thing. It is partly my fault because I was too damn sick the last part of my trip out and most of the time in Shanghai to bother sending them my changes in plans. Well, anyway, it's here at last and I am damn glad to get it.

I'll save all the interesting details of my voyaging until I see you. They're much too much for a letter unless I wanted to write a young book. Suffice it that the whole trip, in spite of sickness and the lousy publicity I ran into, was a wonderful stimulating experience that I wouldn't have missed for a million. I met all kinds of people of all nationalities and I got the feeling from the East that I was after that made it real and living to me instead of something in a book. I'm full to the brim with all sorts of vivid impressions of sound, color, faces, atmosphere, queer experiences that pursued me—nothing of all this is sorted out in my mind yet, I'm still too close to it. The fact that I was weakened by illness and nerves really

---

1. *Mourning Becomes Electra.*

1. O'Neill apparently neglected to sign this letter.
2. On their return from the Far East, O'Neill rented a villa on the Riviera while he looked for a more permanent home.

helped in a funny way—it got me into such a highly sensitized state that every impression hit me with all it had and registered with full force. Everything seemed to be revealing itself for my benefit.

My sickness began in Singapore where I went in bathing around noon like an ass—I discovered that the tropics at twenty-one and at forty years are not the same—and that night I was suffering from a slight sunstroke and was still suffering when we came to Saigon in French Indo China, a poisonous place in more ways than one but fascinating in a queer sinister way. There I easily acquired the flu after another swim in a forest pool in the evening. So when we came to Hong Kong, still in the tropics, and found it sickly hot there too at that time I decided to move on to Yokohama but was so down when we hit Shanghai that I got off there and after a few days in a hotel pestered by reporters sniffing for a scandal, I went to a hospital with a threatened nervous breakdown piled on top of fever and a tomby cough. Once there, however, I began to get better and was out of it in ten days. So that's about all there was of that and is the basis of all the newspaper exaggerations. I was really good and sick but in no danger. And I haven't recovered my usual form even yet although a few weeks more here will do that trick.

The idiotic part of all the publicity both in China and Manila was that there have been some fakers in China getting away with murder impersonating well known people and the reporter boys were tipped off I wasn't Eugene O'Neill at all and they came around to show me up! The story that I was under the name of Reverend O'Brien on the *Coblenz* is, I regret to say, untrue. That is so hilariously amusing that I wish I had thought of it but the truth is I simply had them put me down as James O'Brien on the passenger list in order to make my get-away from Shanghai without any bands playing—for obvious reasons. And there you are! The whole affair was exasperating but would have handed me a laugh if it had not been for the constant danger of complications that would have injured other people.

But no more of my various adventures now. I'll give you them in detail when I see you.

And it's about all I have time for in the way of a letter just now—just to let you know how and where I am and that all is well with me. I came back here to work. Principal reason for leaving the East so soon and not going to Africa as I had planned was that I couldn't write a line there and felt the itch to get back on the job more powerful than any yen to keep going.

I'll write again soon. Let me hear from you when you're in the mood. Your letter was written so long ago that I'd sure like to hear if your first impressions of Yale have stuck. I was tremendously pleased and interested in what you write about the courses you are taking up and your crew work. Give me some more dope on all that.

Dynamo goes on in a few days and I am in an awful nervous stew about it thinking what I would have done in the way of cutting had I been at rehearsals, wondering about the casting, etc. Wearing, this! It's the last play I'll ever let go on without me, no matter what the result in this instance is.[3] See it if you get a chance and let me know about sets and acting.   All love to you always

P.S. Let me know if you need anything.

Later Feb. 11th

Harry just forwarded me your Mother's letter with yours enclosed. All hail to the raccoon coat! Am sorry to hear you were laid up during your holidays—tough luck! I'll write again soon. Tell your Mother I've written to the American Xpress to try and get her letter—but there are so many Eugene O'Neills wandering about I may not. Give a message to

3. *Dynamo* opened on February 11, 1929, at Broadway's Martin Beck Theatre and, after generally negative reviews, ran for fifty performances.

your grandmother that I was very glad to get her letter too—and will write when I get a chance.

---

281 • TO RICHARD MADDEN.   TLS 1 p. (Villa Mimosas, / Cap d'Ail, A.M., France)
[Yale]

March 11th [1929]

Dear Dick: Just a line to tell you that I think very well of the Livingston proposition for the translation of the plays into Italian and you can go right ahead with it. I would like very much to have them published in that country.

No, I am not going to reply to Nathan.[1] If I started replying to critics I'd give them too damn much satisfaction—and I hope I've got to the point where notices roll off my back like water off a duck. I know what I am trying to do better than any of them and I also know better just how near or far from my object I've come. *Dynamo* certainly isn't one of my biggest plays but it does definitely accomplish a certain object I had in mind and dispose, to my satisfaction at least, of its subject as part of a general plan of work. The only guilty feeling I have about it is that I knew damn well when I went over it the last time that I was in much too hectic and distraught—thanks to my domestic brawling—a state of mind to do a good job and I should never have allowed it to be put on this season, especially when I couldn't be around to do my stuff. Never again! But it's all my fault and I have only myself to blame if it's a flop. Perhaps I needed this lesson never to do it again! This implies no blame on the Guild, for I know they did their damndest—but no one can help my plays on as I can. It has been proven time and again although I've never received due credit in that respect.

Another reason why I wouldn't answer Nathan is that he is always only too ready to come out with the loud ballyhoo when he likes a thing and he certainly has my full approval when he doesn't like a play to pan it as heartily. I have my own opinion of his method, which I think is silly in this instance because anyone could make a fool of any play that way, but that's his business. He acknowledges—privately at any rate—that any play dealing in any way with religion is all wet to him. Also he didn't like either *The Hairy Ape* or *Desire*, certainly two of my finest, while he did like *Gold* and *The Fountain* (two of my worst). So what the hell?

Tell John Rumsey[2] that I fully appreciate all he had to say in his letter about the talky movie right commission on *"Anna Christie."* But as I had already written you my opinion on it and knew you would repeat same to him I haven't written him a letter that would simply have been a repeater. Give him my best regards.   All best, Dick.   Gene

P.S. Hope you've sent me statement for my income tax.

---

282 • TO ROBERT SISK.   TLS 2 pp. (Villa Mimosas, / Cap d'Ail, A.M., France) [Yale]

Mar. 11th [1929]

Dear Bob: Many thanks for your letter and for what you have done in spreading the glad tidings—and let me take this opportunity here and now also to express my gratitude for the

---

1. In his review of *Dynamo*, "A Non-Conductor," *American Mercury* (March 1929), Nathan criticized the play as "amateurish, strident and juvenile" and then quoted O'Neill's stage directions from act 1 to show how ridiculous the play was.
2. Madden's associate.

previous letters which I failed to answer. I had good intentions in that regard but so many things kept happening to me that I let all letter writing slide. By the way, the one you wrote about an article was forwarded back from the East and I never got it until much too late to do anything about it.

Judging by my returns from the clipping bureau, the critic boys seemed to have climbed my frame in hordes on the opus, *Dynamo*. Ah well, it is not the first time and, I hope, not the last—for when they begin accepting you without protest it's a sure sign that you're good and dead. And compared to what I had to take on *All God's Chillun* which, like *Dynamo*, was written around a controversial subject, this present panning is gentle and sweet. The eminent Broun, for example, called that the worst play ever written—then afterwards acknowledged that he had neither seen or read it! A rankly dishonorable guy, that Broun! To put it more cogently, a proper yellow son of a bitch! The history of his criticism of my stuff shows him up as a faker and liar of a particularly envious brand. Someday I may give it the air. I would have long ago if it were not that it is such a flattery to him to admit one even reads his stuff, let alone paying enough attention to it to answer it.

From Madden's reports of the last gross, it looks as if *Dynamo* would flop. Well, both the Guild and I have had flops before in our histories and I guess we'll both manage to stagger along after this dire blow. At any rate, I'm glad they felt it worth doing and, from all I've heard from private sources, it was certainly done well. But I am sorry I wasn't there. Perhaps I might have been of help in clearing it up in spots. It needs that, maybe. It certainly seems damn queer to me—although, knowing what most of the critics are, it shouldn't—that no one seems to have gotten the real human relationship story, what his mother does to the boy and what that leads to in his sacrifice of the girl to a maternal deity at the end—the girl his mother hated and was jealous of—that all that was the boy's real God struggle, or prompted it. This all fits in with the general theme of American life in back of the play, America being the land of the mother complex. I thought this was so plain in the play as almost to be too obvious. It is emphatically stated in every act—or so it seems to me. But not a damn one mentions it. They were so damned hot on the general religious theme that they couldn't see the human psychological struggle without which (I agree with them here) the play is fairly lifeless comment on an old hat question.

But perhaps this is all my fault—that what I see there I haven't made plain to others.

One thing I am sure of—it was a great mistake for me to have said anything in advance about a trilogy, or even to hint that it had anything to do with what was wrong with us, or to mention Gods, dead or alive, in any connection—in fact, to say anything whatever about subject matter, or treatment, or anything else. After this, I'll be mum. It was damn stupid and I ought to have known better. It is no question whatsoever, please know this, of your using, or Nathan using, stuff from my letters—it was just that I was plain dumb in urging that the trilogy dope be used on the program and thereby putting a false emphasis on the general idea when only one play was concerned. One lives and learns, let us hope. I was a boob.

But perhaps *Dynamo* tries to do too much in too little time and the issues get confused. Or perhaps—anything. Whatever it is I feel philosophical about it and that this flop will be all for the best in the end. I am sorry about the Guild end of it, however, and hope the production was not too costly and that they'll at least break even. Or maybe some miracle will happen and it will pick up. That has happened before with me. *"Anna Christie,"* for example, was a frightful financial frost for the first four weeks.

How do you think a revival of *"Anna C."* would do next year with Pauline Lord in the part, by the way? Give me your candid opinion. It has just occurred to me that it might be good dope.

I am hard at work but not on the second play of the trilogy—quite another idea that demanded I get busy on it without sticking to any old plan. The reaction on *Dynamo* had nothing to do with this. I was working at it long before *Dynamo* opened. It is not that I am off the trilogy but simply that this new one is what hits me most strongly right now. The trilogy plays can wait. In fact, it will be a good stunt to let them wait, all things considered.

Give my best to Terry and Phil and Lee and all. I have written Lawrence already. Tell Terry I know I owe her a letter and will get it off soon.

I am enclosing a couple of snaps that may or may not be of use—and, if not, that perhaps you might like to have anyway.   Many thanks and all good wishes always!
Eugene O'Neill

---

283 • TO BENJAMIN DE CASSERES.　　SL TLS 2 pp. (Villa Mimosas, / Cap d'Ail, A.M., France) [Dartmouth]

March 12th [1929]

Dear Ben:　　Oh come now, I don't think *Dynamo* is as bad as all that! I think you will find when all the dust blows over it will pretty well stand up for what I wanted it to be. That is, as it will appear in book form after I've revised the proofs.[1] I'll acknowledge there is something to be done to it in the way of emphasizing and cutting—and that may not at all be what the Guild did to the script. I don't know, as I haven't their cut version yet. I feel very guilty toward the play in this respect, that I let it out of my hands much too soon—before I had a chance to get the right perspective on it. Also, when I went over it the last time I was in a pretty hectic mental state from worry and I really was in no fit condition for the job. And I felt this unfitness at the time, that's the trouble—so I've no excuse. Also I had no right to let it go on without being there, no matter how good the Guild performance seemed. No one knows what I see in my stuff during rehearsals, or the changes I suggest or veto, because I have never been given any credit for it, but believe me no play of mine ever failed to gain immeasurably from my being around. Without handing myself any bouquets, I think I've a better theatrical eye and ear than most in the game.

The principal reason I don't agree with your criticism is that you don't agree with yourself. I have your letter written after you read the play and you call it "a masterpiece" up to the third act about which you had doubts. Now how can characters in what is a master-piece for two-thirds of it suddenly become "false, wooden, mannequins" etc. when you see them on the stage? Something must have happened that wasn't in the script you read, no? For surely you weren't handing me taffy in your former letter. It was your firm conviction. And you know as well as I do that every play that reads well ought to act well, unless it's a purely literary play and therefore not really a play. This is a truism as axiomatic as the stupidity of Heywood Broun. All stuff to the contrary is a laugh to anyone who knows the plays and the theatre of all time. It is without an exception. So there you are.

Understand that I am not insisting that *Dynamo* is as good as *Interlude* or *Lazarus* (which Nathan also thinks is piffle) or *Brown* or *Desire* or *The Ape* or *Jones*, but it does belong in the front second rank and that's about the best I could wring out of those characters and that subject matter. And please remember that it is part of a three play plan, the subjects of the other two being immeasurably more interesting to me. People have persisted in regarding the general theme for the three plays as the particular theme of *Dynamo*. This is, of course, my fault for having shot my mouth off about the theme for the three beforehand. A booby

---

1. *Dynamo*, heavily revised from the stage version, was published by Horace Liveright on October 5, 1929.

mistake! I must have been loony! I ought to know my onions and my critics better than that!

Read *Dynamo* when it comes out in book form and give me a third opinion—and don't let the general theme, which was secondary to me (as it will be in the other plays) blind you to the boy's psychological struggle which begins when he is betrayed by his mother and casts her off along with his father's God; and how he finally has to sacrifice the girl his mother hated to a maternal deity whom he loves sexually. His last words are—in my script—"Never let me go from you again! Please, Mother." Now that to me was three-fourths of my play—and yet not one damn single person seemed aware of this play of human relationships. They were all gunning after another shallower symbolism. My fault, perhaps, in giving the wrong steer myself. And yet to me that tragedy—very human and not abstract—is so emphasized in the play as almost to be too obvious. I certainly felt throughout that I was writing about human lives and not any abstract problem.

Well, I judge it's a flop and that's that—but it will come into its own someday just as *All God's Chillun* will. Wait and see. As for flops, I've had more than one and there is no gnashing of teeth hereabouts. A play's fate after I've written it—I mean, outside of my creation, the play in the book—is just roulette to me with a fat percentage in favor of the author losing *his* play either artistically or financially or both. So we takes our medicine graceful.

Re my explanation of my play in *Dynamo,* another word: Is not the boy's whole fight to repudiate his father's God humanly a fight to conquer his father? Isn't this plain in the second act scene between them? Isn't his feeling about his dead mother plain—the drag her influence from the grave immediately has on him so that a moment later he tries to kiss the girl and can't. That the dynamo is his mother that he has elevated by devious ways hidden from himself into God the Mother so that he can possess and be possessed by her, his electrocution of the Father God in her name, etc., seems to me to stand out in the play like red paint. How could anyone ever imagine, knowing the whole of my work, that I would write a play about the fight between a fundamentalist God and pseudo-Science? Why, unless I am stark nuts, the play obviously makes that banal conflict silly in the comic argument between Fife and the minister and in their specious mouthings throughout. Believe me, Ben, this play has been misunderstood as no other play of mine ever was except *God's Chillun.*

But to hell with post-mortems!

When will I return? Ask my wife! As soon as she deigns to grant me my liberty and I can marry again. But as I hear she really honestly intends to go to Reno soon, I will probably be back in the fall—then out to California to make a new home and adopt the West as my stamping ground for the future.

I finally got the copy of *Anathema!* forwarded from the East. Much gratitude to you! I shall treasure it—and not for my inadequate introduction either!

I've a million tales to tell you of my trip. It was grand!

I am working hard again and feel fine.

Ask Bio to try concentrating on my hand. I will hold it out and imagine her looking at it at eleven-thirty p.m. on April 1st (I pick that date because it's easy to remember). That will be six-thirty p.m. in New York. Are you set? I want to know when that peace is coming she promised me! Believe me, I can do with it!   All affectionate best to you both!   Gene

284 • TO OONA O'NEILL.   ALS 1 p. (c/o Guaranty Trust Co., / 50, Pall Mall, London / England) [Virginia]

March 14th '29

Dearest Oona: I am enclosing some pictures of me taken a short time ago that I think are pretty good and really look like me. I am sending them to you so you can look at them every once in a while and remember your Daddy. I have your picture on the table in my workroom where I write plays and I often look at it and wonder how you are and what you are doing and wish that I could see you. But that picture of you was taken over a year ago, I guess, and you must have grown a lot since then. When Mother takes some new ones of you please send me one. I would like to have it awfully much.

I am also enclosing a check made out to Mother to buy you a present with—anything you want.   I love you very much. Don't forget me!   Daddy

---

285 • TO SHANE O'NEILL.   COPY 2 pp.[1] (Guaranty Trust Co., / 50, Pall Mall, London / England) [Virginia]

March 14, 1929

Dear Shane   I am enclosing some snapshots that were taken a short time ago and that I think are very good. You can look at them every once in a while and then you will remember what I look like and not forget your Daddy. It is such a long time since I have seen you that I wouldn't blame you for forgetting me. Let us hope that I will see you before long now. I think of you every day and your picture is on the work table in my study where I can always see you. But you must have grown a lot since then. Someone wrote me that you were getting tall and still you kept broad-chested and strong for your age. I was very glad to hear that. It must be a fine school you are going to if you're in such fine shape. I hope you are studying hard too and learning a lot. You must write me a long letter sometime and tell me all about school.

I am here in Europe living right on the sea but it's too cold to go in swimming yet although it is warmer, I guess, than where you are. And right in back of the house are high mountains that I can walk all the way to the top of some days. And there are all kinds of boats on the sea near here, big steamers and sail boats and speed motor boats—like Bermuda only [more?] of them.

I am working hard starting a new play. I didn't work all the time on the trip to China, not because I was lazy but because the tropics took all the pep out of me, it was so darn hot! and then in China I was sick in the hospital part of the time.

You ought to write to Eugene at Yale sometime. He is rowing a lot, he writes me, and trying to be on the Freshman crew. I know he would like to get a letter from you. His address is 1111 Yale Station, New Haven.

I have been having a very quiet life since I returned here. I needed a rest because my trip to the East was just one excitement after another and, between that and sickness, I was all tired out. But the trip to China was worth it.

I am enclosing a check made out to you and you can endorse it yourself and then buy yourself a present with it. Don't get a silly present that will wear out quick but something you really need that will last. You better ask the Principal of the school just what you ought to get.   All love to you! Write soon and don't forget me.   Daddy

---

1. Although the copy of this letter is on two pages, it indicates that the original was three pages in length.

[March 17?, 1929]

Dear Bob: This is a postscript to the letter I wrote yesterday which must seem a bit dumb by way of reply to yours. The point is that your first letter got here two days after the second, so I hadn't heard anything of Kansas City minister, etc.

I appreciate your warning about people violating my confidences but, unless you're sure of your dope, I think you're up the wrong tree. I know there are some boobies—always were—who Gene me to their circle and pretend we're thick as thieves and that I never step without their advice. But the fact is that I haven't written to scarcely anyone since before I left for the East—for four months almost I never wrote a single letter. So I don't know where they get their dope. If by snide stuff in the paper you mean the *News*—all the stuff of that kind I've seen has been in that rag—then I can explain that. The man on the *News* who has kept that warm is, I believe, the brother-in-law of Driscoll who is my wife's lawyer. It was he who did that exclusive interview with her that was so catty. So maybe that's it. That baby doesn't need any confidences from me as long as his imagination works! Well, it's all in the game.

Thank you for telling me about the antics of Sinjin.[2] I have been wise to his imbecility for years now because in Bermuda I used to see the London *Observer* quite frequently. When the *World* cabled me to express my opinion on their choice I remained mum because they seemed so tickled at having bagged an Argus pheasant that I hated to call their attention to the fact that he was so obviously just another English sparrow—cocky and full of horseshit! To my mind, he is about the dullest commentator on the drama now writing English and I was of that opinion even in the days when he wrote a preface for my English publishers comparing me to Walt Whitman. He has written some of the damndest junk on plays that I have ever read. His trouble—and it is the trouble with Broun and so many of them—is that he's a disappointed playwright. In fairness to the Dramatists Guild every paper ought to fire from their drama department anyone who has written a play. The boys look at themselves in the mirror and then get so bilious with envy.

I hope the movie-talky bunch will be so stupid as to think they want *Interlude*. They've never been very stupid where I was concerned yet and I'm beginning to feel a bit put out about it.

Again much gratitude for your letters! They are a boon and a tonic to me—your sense of humor's keen perception of the relative values of things. Most of my friends write me as diffidently about the *Dynamo* notices as if they were breaking a death that would knock me prostrated and as if every critic were a Georg Brandes![3] It is sickening to be treated with such doleful tenderness as if I were the Pope's toe—me that was born on Times Square and not in Greenwich Village, and that have heard dramatic critics called sons of bitches—and, speaking in general, believed it—ever since I was old enough to recognize the Count of Monte Cristo's voice! The greatest burden I have to bear after each flop is the well-meant condolence chorus. They never reflect that a kick in the pants—especially when one feels one doesn't deserve it—is a grand stimulant.   Write some more!

1. This letter is not signed.
2. St. John Ervine, who had recently become drama critic of the *New York World*.
3. Brandes (1842–1927) was a Danish critic and literary historian.

March 25th [1929]

Dear Lawrence: Your letter arrived today and I hasten to reply. First and foremost: Won't you take time off when you're over here to pay us a visit? Be sure to! I enclose a note from Carlotta seconding this. We'd love to have you. Also we have a fine villa right on the Med. and it's grand here now. It will be a vacation for you and do you a lot of good! So do write or cable that you can and will come—and we'll meet you.

As for your giving out the stuff to the paper, it certainly was no blunder! It was grand dope and we're both grateful. It seems to have had the desired effect of giving the lady a prod, too, for she's now in Reno. She needed something like that to shame her. She was just dilly-dallying to be spiteful.

No one connected with the P.P. has written me knocking the *Dynamo* production. I'd take any such pans with a ton of salt, anyway. I'm quite resigned to it's being a failure—for many reasons. First, I'm sure now, from the reaction, that any play of mine that followed *Interlude* was almost bound to be—unless it enormously topped *Interlude* (a hard job but *Lazarus Laughed* could have, with its exultant spiritual message, if properly produced and acted).

Secondly, I blundered horribly in shooting off my mouth about a trilogy and the meaning of it. I didn't mean what is usually meant by trilogy, of course, and I didn't mean "message" or "solution" or anything definite. But it gave them all a clue as to how they should misinterpret and, as they were gunning for my next play, they seized on it eagerly. My own fault, though!

Secondly, I never should have let the play out of my hands so soon after completing it—contrary to my usual practice. Besides being in a distraught state of mind at the time I went over the script, I had no perspective on it. When I read it over—after settling here—too late—I was appalled by its raggedness and, in the third part, vagueness and complicatedness. It was in no shape for production. You will see what I mean when you read the book. I am doing a lot of work on the proofs—cutting a good deal more than Phil did and in different directions and pointing up the human story of Reuben's psychological mess over his father and his mother's betrayal and how he at last deifies and finds her again (the real plot of the play which no one seems to have seen in any of its implications but which I thought was obvious).

Thirdly, I should have been there and all I'm doing now would have been done at rehearsals. Or, more to the point, I should have held over the play until next season when I could be there. This is no beef against Phil, of course. I know he did a fine job with what was there—but he couldn't be expected to read my mind and rewrite from it!

No, I'm much to blame for the whole business and I deserve a kick in the pants! So feeling, I read even the envious bunk of Ervine & Broun with a humble spirit! But I am damn sorry the Guild was involved in the debacle. But you should have sent it back to me last fall for a little more work on it!

Fourthly, I think two big mistakes were made by the Guild—the orthodox Russian constructivist sets which my script *did not* call for (they are damned interesting in themselves but out of key with my play—a *Desire U. T. Elms* development) and the running of my definite scene structure in Parts One & Three into unbroken acts (I wanted *short* pauses but I *did want pauses* of darkness and my structure was built counting on them). Now I don't mean to say these mistakes were any primary cause for failure but I believe they were a *minor* contributing cause. But then again, it's my fault for not being there. So really I've got no complaints to hand in at all—so don't relay this on to Phil & the others. They would say quite rightly, what right have I—and I haven't any, as I know damn well. And many people have written me in praise of the production—all I mean is I like my script production better for that play.

And that's about all till we see you. Be sure and come! All best from us both!   Gene

P.S. I couldn't get to London—couldn't leave C. alone here and with her all sorts of complications might arise unless I hid—and I've had enough hiding. Can't afford take chances with solution so near.

---

288 • TO SISTER MARY LEO.   ALS 4 pp. (Villa Les Mimosas, / Cap d'Ail, A.M., / France) [Yale]

March 26, 1929

My dear Sister Mary Leo: Or should I have written "dear Adopted Grandmother?" Well, consider that said too! Although now that I am forty and have a son, (by my first marriage), of eighteen at Yale I begin to feel very much in the grandfather class myself! And your letters are so young in spirit they make me feel old by comparison!

I've owed you a letter for ages and am heartily ashamed of myself, particularly since I cannot honestly plead any excuse but my cussed laziness as a correspondent. But you'll forgive me, I know. Forgiveness is one of the things grandmothers just naturally are let in for!

Much gratitude to you for your beautiful letter. It is always a joy and a privilege to hear from you. When I read I feel myself receiving an emanation from your deep spiritual peace and security that is like a blessing to me. There is nothing I would not give to have your faith—the faith in which I was born and brought up (as a good O'Neill should be)—but since I may not know it, since belief is denied to me in spite of the fact that my whole adult spiritual life is that search for a faith which my work expresses in symbols, why then my thwarted search must have its meaning and use, don't you think, for whatever God may be? Perhaps they also serve who only search in vain! That they search—and not without knowing at times a black despair that believers never know—that is their justification and pride as they stare blindly at the blind sky! The Jesus who said "Why hast Thou forsaken me?" must surely understand them—and love them a little, I think, and forgive them if no Savior comes today to make these blind to see who may not cure themselves.

That you should have made the Stations of the Cross for me touches me deeply. I am sure it helped to give me the growing sense of calm and happiness which I have known here in France since my return from a restless trip to the Far East.

For I'm really not in the distressful state Mr. Skinner's criticism of *Dynamo*[1] would have me! I am more at peace with the world than I have ever been. But then Mr. Skinner—whom I like very much personally and whose critical abilities I respect—is a convert and converts are so damned arrant in jumping to the fore to defend a Faith that needs no defense! Haven't you found this so? They wear their Catholicism like a brand new self-conscious uniform—with a chip on its shoulder!

Yes, I've read *Henry Adams*[2]—some years ago but I remember it well. A great book! But so New England! And I've lived so much in New England in my past that all I want now is to forget it and be free of its Puritan pall!

1. Richard Dana Skinner, "Eugene O'Neill's Dynamo," *Commonweal* 9 (February 27, 1929): 389–90.
2. *The Education of Henry Adams* (1907), by Henry Adams (1838–1918).

To return to *Dynamo*, it failed to impress the critics because in the natural rhythm of things as they are in the New York "Show Business" (the medium in which my plays are *not* written but in which, unfortunately, they have to be produced), any play of mine was bound to stir up a reaction and fall flat after the huge and unexpected success of *Strange Interlude*. My only regret is that this reaction prevented anyone seeing the simple human psychological story of my play. They were all gunning after an elaborate thesis play—which *Dynamo* isn't! Of course, it's easier for critics to attribute an intention to you which you didn't have and then blame you for not having it! It saves a lot of thought on their part. This isn't the first time I've discovered that—nor will it be the last! *The Great God Brown* was another recent example—and *All God's Chillun Got Wings* an earlier one.

When I next go to the cathedral at Chartres—I go whenever I can—I will think much of you. There is Faith for you—in that cathedral!

I am enclosing a couple of snapshots which you may like to have. I hate my formal posed photos and wouldn't send you one if I had any, which I haven't. These really look like me.

My deep respectful affection to you always! Remember me in your prayers—and write me again when the mood is on you.   Your grateful adopted one,   Eugene O'Neill

---

289 • TO CARLOTTA MONTEREY.   ALS 1 p. ([Villa Les Mimosas / Cap d'Ail, A.M., France]) [Yale]

[March 27?, 1929]

Darling: I sit here and stare at the ring you gave me in commemoration of the birth of a new understanding between us[1]—that ring which is so undeniably the symbol of the deep spiritual truth we had wrung out of so much suffering and bitterness—and I am drowned in despair that dissension should have again sprung up between us.[2] And I am so bewildered by this ugly and mad thing, so appalled by its utter insanity, that I feel lost, defeated and done for. Why? Why? Why, in God's name! I love you! With all my soul and body I love you—with all the strength of my spirit! There is nothing I would not do to make you happy; and I have tried so hard to do so, thought always of only the one thing, to do all I could in every way I thought had bearing on the ultimate results to end this present situation in which we are forced by the world into an intolerable impasse.

And now when we are on the brink of achieving this, when the goal we have paid for so bitterly is in sight, when peace is measurably within our grasp, are we going to take the side of the world against each other and ourselves work the ruin?

Oh Dearest Heart of Mine, look at your Port Said ring and feel with me! That is the truth of you and me! Everything else—my petty considerations of self or yours—is a lie! That was born out of suffering! All else is the product of nerves and the small frets and worries of daily living. Friends? What have friends to do with Us? What has anyone to do [with] Us? Can anyone touch us? No, it is only you or I who can!

Oh, Darling One, isn't our love sufficiently proved to us, haven't we both sacrificed enough to it, so that we can feel it a rock on which to build our house at last? You said you would never doubt Us again!

1. When O'Neill and Carlotta were reunited in Port Said in January 1929, she gave him a ring.
2. O'Neill and Carlotta had quarreled over rumors of gossip and slander against Carlotta among O'Neill's friends in the United States.

I love you! I love you! You are my life and everything! And you love me! And everything else is a lie! And we are such God damned fools to torture each other so over the other things that have no meaning!   Your   Gene

---

290 • TO KATHLEEN JENKINS PITT-SMITH.   ALS 3 pp. ([Villa Les Mimosas,] / Cap d'Ail, [A.M., France]) [Yale]

address c/o Guaranty Trust Co., / 50, Pall Mall, London

May 9th. [1929]

Dear Kathleen: Just a few lines about Eugene and his trip. I won't attempt to answer the long, lost letter you enclosed now. Suffice it that I deeply appreciated one thing above all you wrote in it and will never forget it!

As for Eugene, I just sent him a check for 465 to cover his steamer ticket and tailor bill, etc. I sent him another check for 650 to cover his tour in Germany. Counting that as eight weeks it will be 80 a week which is more than enough for a student who isn't a damn fool American Tourist easy mark. I'm sorry I can't meet him in Cherbourg. I've been held up on the lease of the place in Touraine I'm taking and won't be able to move in until after his arrival—which means I've no place to take him to stay with me, as I'll have to remain down here, perhaps in a hotel, until I'm allowed to move up—and this is way out of his way. He will have to come to me after he's finished in Germany. I'll meet him in Paris.

It's really better this way, anyway. Confidentially, I prefer it for private reasons. I'm leading an irregular sort of existence now but by the time he's finished his tour I will be divorced and married again and he will have a regular home, and all the comforts of same, that he can feel is his home. The lady who will be my wife has met Eugene and likes him tremendously so he will be more than welcome with us. And I'd like him to get his first impressions of France in a fine house in the real non-tourist French countryside and not banging around with me in tourist hotels. So it will all work out much better this way.

I also gave him a few words of warning about money matters—telling him the truth that I'm embarking on an ambitious scheme of work that may mean years without a production—certainly two years—and while I hope it will add much to my artistic reputation internationally I have grave doubts about its financial results, and I'm now hoarding my money to prepare for a long lean season and give me the opportunity to do my stuff regardless for a few years to come. *Strange Interlude* was the kind of queer miracle that doesn't happen twice in a lifetime—and, at that, everyone nearly goes to see a novelty that became the fashion, and not to see my real play at all! So it really must be regarded as as much of a lucky financial accident as breaking the bank at Monte Carlo (which I haven't been so successful at!) would be. So I told Eugene to get all he can out of his German tour while the getting is good! Which was what I did when I treated myself to the trip to China.

All my good wishes to you! Let me know what you think of this new plan—or change of plan.   As ever,   Eugene O'Neill

P.S. I got Eugene's letter telling me his plans & his cable this a.m.

291 • TO BIO DE CASSERES.   ALS 3 pp. ([Villa Les Mimosas,] / Cap d'Ail, [A.M., France]) [Dartmouth]

address (I'm moving soon & don't
know definitely my new P.O. yet.)   >   c/o Guaranty Trust Co.,
                                                                  50, Pall Mall, London
                                                                  May 10th [1929]

Dear Bio: I have been going to answer your letter for some time but kept putting it off from day to day—as usual! Many ideas for future work have been emerging into my consciousness and my mind has been busy at the job of getting these ideas formulated clearly and tentatively planned out on paper.

Your letter with its benign prophecy was most welcome and helped much to encourage me—and it seems to me, in the light of the gradual clearing up of my domestic embroilment, and the plans I have made for my future, that you will just about hit the facts on the head as to time and the relief and peace that will then be mine. The "explosion" really didn't go bang until about the 1st of 1928 so that would postpone my release until July—which seems predictably right. You will remember you said that last night that not until I was 41 would the new era begin—and I think it will be at least then before all my affairs are smoothed out "for keeps" and my inner self freed from the dead, consciously alive in the new, liberated and reborn.

I am certainly planning ahead for peace and creative toil. We are taking a place in Touraine for three years—in the real French countryside in the beautiful valley of the Loire, the land of Rabelais and Balzac. It will be getting down to earth in a very simple true sense. There are many acres with the place—woods, grounds, streams and a large farm (run by the proprietor), the nearest town ten kilometers off, a wonderful old country house with grand furniture—and all for an annual rental that would be insane even to imagine in the U.S. So I feel "all set," and once planted there I expect to turn out fine stuff. And I expect *to live* as well as work—something I haven't achieved before to any satisfying extent without the aid of alcohol. I'm going to do my job on my own terms and let nothing or no one hurry or any consideration influence me to seek a production until I'm damn good and ready for it. I've written 18 plays (long) in the last eleven years. Too much! The time I spent driving myself to write the ones that should not have been written should have been spent perfecting the fine ones. But at that time I had to keep on writing, whether any genuine creative urge was there or not, in order to keep on living! Now I feel that soon I'll be able to be content just to live in the intermediate periods between creation. The East and Europe have taught me something, I think.

I'm not going to submit any play for production next year, and perhaps not the year after (this is confidential). America has had a bellyful of my stuff for a while—and from my end, I'm well fed up with the cheap fame and defame that began with *Interlude*. My craving now is for a spell of ease from newspaper notoriety.

So, as nothing will be calling me back to N.Y., you probably won't see me for a long time—unless you come over here, which I sure hope you will.

Give all my good wishes to Ben—and for yourself an equal amount. Remember me with affection as I always do both of you—and write me whenever the mood comes.   As ever,   Gene

P.S. Saxe Commins sailed back for N.Y. yesterday.[1] I suppose you will be seeing him. He has visited with me and can tell you all the news. A fine person, Saxe! And his wife is too.

---

1. Saxe Commins, who gave up his dental practice, and his new wife, Dorothy, spent a year in France and then returned to the United States, where he intended to start a new career as a writer.

> (address) This is always sure.
> c/o Guaranty Trust Co.,
> 50, Pall Mall, London
> May 11th [1929]

Dear Harold: Well, it sure was good to hear from you! I was beginning to think after such a long silent pause that you'd gone sour on me for some reason—and suspected that the perfidious frau might have been pouring some of her poison into Helen's ear which you might have taken without the ton of salt with which one should flavor that lady's stories! But let us say no more about it. I am glad I was wrong. But she has pulled so many rough lies about me to people that have come back to me that you can't blame me for being suspicious.

You sure seem to be having a full share of the bad breaks! It was a shock to hear that you had sold the Maine place. I remember it with affection and I know how much you thought of it. But what the hell is all this stuff about "failure" etc.? That doesn't sound like you! You're no failure! You've always played out your string to your utmost and always will! And you're hardly old and hoary yet even if a spell of break-down has made you feel that way! So cheerio! It's a long lane that has no turning and the breaks will come your way again, wait and see!

As for me and my doings, they would make a large volume and I can only give a brief outline here. After wandering around Europe and living in various spots, principally in France & Germany, I hied me to the Far East the end of last summer—Shanghai & way stations. And on that trip I got my share of tough breaks as to health! My persistence at my swimming racket was responsible. I got away with swimming in the noon sun in Ceylon but when I played a repeat in Singapore, right on the Line, it got me. I came back aboard with a cute "touch of sun"—and you know that makes you feel pretty sick and woozy. Then in Saigon in French Indo-China—a most interesting place but unhealthy as hell—I was so run down from my stroke that I naturally picked up the flu which was prevalent there. A nasty combine in sickeningly hot tropic weather! So when we got to Hong Kong, my destination, I was too sick to go ashore. At Shanghai I went to a hotel—and to bed. Then the newspapers got on my trail—and every other busybody in Shanghai. The Anglo-American colony there is like a rotten small town. My nerves were sun-shattered and gone and I still had the flu. The doctor, fearing I was going to crock completely, ordered me to the hospital where I spent two weeks. And that's how the reports of my dying came to be cabled to God's country. In reality I was all in but not seriously ill at all. To make matters worse, my friend had caught the flu from me and was sicker than I was. A pleasant time was had by all! The respectable Swedish married dame who was acting as a combination maid-secretary, although horribly shocked by events was nevertheless romantically thrilled by the adventure of it, and proved a brick, taking all the brunt of the notoriety barrage, and stood between us and the papers. In return they openly insinuated she was my mistress—a serious thing for her because she was happily married and had a husband and child in England. My mistress! You can't appreciate the joke of that but you would if you saw her! To show how bad it was, one of the big newspaper agency representatives lost his job for cabling back a palpably wild story about my being at death's door! It wasn't that I complained. I didn't care what stories they planted as long as a certain name was not dragged into it. And I found all of the paper boys good scouts personally—both in Shanghai and in Manila on the way back where they got after me again.

And now comes a sad tale! Prepare to weep! Whether it was sun-wooziness or what, I was introduced by a Frenchman to a swell gambling joint in Saigon and I bucked the wheel—and the game suddenly got me. I must have that Jim[1] strain in me after all. I went ga-ga—without benefit of a drop of booze, either, (I being still, to this day and forever after, teetotal). Well, I'll slide over the horrid details. I feel reluctant to admit having been so dumb, now the craze is long past. Suffice it I lost one hell of a pile there (in Saigon)—and, after I was out of the hospital, in the famous Wheel palace in Shanghai. I shudder even to think of how much I lost! *My system* is the bunk, take it from me! It made an enormous letter of credit into toilet paper in no time—and then some more I cabled for. Well, I didn't go absolutely broke. I suddenly woke up one day and quit. Can you beat it? Me!

But let's turn to more pleasant topics. Even writing the above confession down makes me seasick! Don't get the idea my trip East was total loss. On the contrary. It was a wonderful experience when I wasn't sick. I got a hell of a lot out of it—just as I have gotten and am getting out of Europe—and wouldn't have missed it for worlds.

As for my inner life, although Aggie's failure to keep her word with me until this late date has caused me no end of worry and trouble, I never felt half so happy and calm and conscious of the joy of being alive as I do now. I have found the right person for me and I love and am loved as I never have dreamed possible before. What more can one say? And I have changed a hell of a lot in many ways, Harold—in my whole outlook on life and my work. I've gained calm and poise and a sureness in living—a feeling of security, that the old hectic self-tortured days are past, never to return. It is a grand feeling—and, in the long run, my work is going to grow enormously from it, wait and see. I'm going to give more time to it, not be hurried and driven into over-production as I have been in the past. *Dynamo* was, in its way, a great lesson to me. I wrote the last part of it when my mind was muddled with worry, when I should have let the play rest. I sent it off to the Guild before I had any chance to get perspective on the play as a whole. My usual judgment was not there. I never looked at the script again until my return from the East. Then I saw—too late to do anything about its production—where it fell down, that I'd let my main human idea get messed up and lost in confusion at the end. (I've since held up the book and done a lot of work on the script.) So I feel its flop was my fault. Not the bunk of the critics. Those sad babies were only out to get back at me personally for *Interlude*'s success. What I mean is, I knew it failed as *my* work in the latter part.

I won't make that mistake again, believe me! I have some grand big ideas to carry out and they are not going to leave my hands until they are written up to their demands in every way.

But even if I had one all ready I wouldn't allow it to be produced next year. America has had a bellyful of my stuff for the time being—and I've had a bellyful of the cheap notoriety they call fame. We can both do without each other for quite a spell. It may be I won't want any production the year after either. At any rate, I'm simply going to work on without a care as to whether another play is ever produced or not. Living over here is cheap—(in some countries!). I've insured myself a couple of years' leeway. My principal expense will be alimony to that proud self-supporting lady who married me on a strictly fifty-fifty basis! It is to laugh! But I'm past bitterness of that score.

My reputation over here—in Scandinavia, Russia, Hungary, Germany, Czechoslo-vakia, France & England is growing all the time—many productions all over in repertoire—not much money in it, of course, but real artistic appreciation.

I've been working hard since my return—not a stroke in the East, of course—and have quite a bit on the first draft of a new one done—two acts.

---

1. James O'Neill, Jr., who was a heavy gambler.

So know that I'm happy and flourishing.

Carlotta M. and I are going to be married as soon as the final decree comes across from Reno. I suppose you know that. This means the final seal on my new peace. From then on I'll have a wife and a friend in one, who is back of me with everything in her every minute!

Well, I guess I'm boring you with this happy paean stuff—but I know you're one friend who will be glad of it. Certain of my so-called friends seem to resent that their dire predictions of disaster haven't come true and that I am happy! Human nature is sometimes fairly lousy stuff, what? Or maybe Aggie just poisoned their minds with her foul fairy tales. Quién sabe? I am not losing much sleep over it, one way or another.

Keep your pecker up as they say in Britannia! The breaks will turn! My love to Helen and the kids! How are they all? In the pink, I hope. Hope Helen didn't mind going to Madden. That seemed the simplest way—and surest, as I had no cash around at the time.

When will I come to visit the U.S. again? Don't know yet—not for quite a while—am making no plans for it yet—perfectly content over here—all depends on a lot of things.

All friendship always, as you know, Harold! Dig in again! You're too good a guy ever to let life lick you for long! Don't kid yourself any different!   As ever,   Gene

---

293 • TO M. ELEANOR FITZGERALD.   ALS 7 pp. (Nice) [Texas]

> May 13th [1929]
> (but I'm pulling out of
> here next week and the
> surest address is always
> Guaranty Trust Co.,
> 50, Pall Mall, London)

Dear Fitzie: I was damn tickled to get your letter! I had begun to think you had all forgotten my existence. Tell Jimmy that he still owes me a long letter, having never answered my effusive of last fall. When is he coming over? I saw by the Paris *Herald* that he had gotten a Guggenheim F'ship. I hadn't known he was out for one. Did Mike Gold get one? He wrote to me—last summer, I think—and I wrote to them giving him the biggest boost I could. Hope he copped. I am glad about Jimmy. It should give him a good chance to see what's doing over here—although, as far as I hear, nothing much is. Everyone I've met who has any authority to speak seems to think the European theatre is in a poor way—no plays and no directors of any startling ability. This doesn't include Russia. I haven't heard anything from there except a report that *All God's Chillun* had been done at the Kamerny. I wonder how they propagandized that! Lots of my stuff seems to be being done hither and yon—particularly in England. I believe they are putting on *Lazarus* at the Cambridge Festival theatre soon. Have you ever heard anything from Danchenko? I haven't.

Strange Interlude made quite a hit at the Royal theatre in Stockholm—financial as well as artistic. They are doing *Jones* there soon. *Interlude* also created a sensation of lauding and damning in Budapest—principally the former. It is going to be done in Berlin and Vienna soon. And so on. Nothing happens about stuff in France—for which I am sorry because I love France—but considering the present dry-rot of the French theatre, how could it? Needless to state, I haven't seen any of the above productions. My interest in the productions steadily decreases as my interest in plays as written increases. They always—with the exceptions you know—fall so far below or beside my intent that I'm a bit weary and disillusioned with scenery and actors and the whole uninspired works of the Show Shop. And where there is genuine inspiration and spirit, as in the P'town, there is nothing for it to work with (money, I mean) or in! Believe me, as far as production is concerned, I sigh for the old P'town days, the old crowd and zest. As it is I think I will wind up writing plays to be published with "No Productions Allowed" in red letters on the first page—for when I think of that dreary ordeal of disillusionment and compromise called rehearsals, with the best end in sight a "competent" production, I sure turn sick! The ideas for the plays I am writing and going to write are too dear to me, too much travail of blood and spirit will go into their writing, for me to expose them to what I know is an unfair test. I would rather place them directly from my imagination to the imagination of the reader—without benefit of the Lamb's Club, painted canvas, etc.

But I've said all this before, of course, so take it with a grain of salt.

I am particularly fed up with the cheap fame and notoriety *Interlude* has brought down on me—and the equally cheap defame that *Dynamo* was an excuse for. I'm deadly ill with being a public personage. And believe me I am planning my life ahead so that I'll damn well go back to my old private life of unpestered artist—if I have to hold back plays from production and publication until I'm forgotten to pull the trick. I'm capable of that now. Europe & the East have done a lot for my soul. I live now. I *can* live. I've learned a lesson— forty is the right age to begin to learn! And I think my new work is going to show more poise, more patience with itself to reach at perfection, more critical analysis of itself and contempla- tion, more time given it for gestation and genuine birth, more pains. I've gone off half- cocked too many times, driven on to drive myself to write at any cost to the writing, then to finish and be done with it and start something new. It's time I achieved a more mature outlook as an artist—and now I know I have. Perhaps a complete upheaval, a total revaluing of all my old values was necessary to gain that attitude. Well, I've certainly been through that! Divil a doubt! And wait for my new work—then you'll see. I've got some wonderful ideas to do—if I can do them. And it's my own fault if I can't. I've everything to back me up now—love of the kind I've always wanted, security and peace. I look forward confidently to years of undisturbed hard and difficult work—and a joy of living I've never known before to give me strength and patience to do that work to its utmost! I've at last found a sustained plan of life, if you get me, in which living will collaborate with writing instead of being always an obstacle to be overcome and beaten under by writing.

Dynamo doesn't count. When I read the script over on my return to Europe for the first time after I sent it to the Guild, I realized the last part was muddled and lousy and the whole play a big step backward from my best. But it's a wonder it is as good as it is. It was written at a time when I shouldn't have written anything. The whole perfidious Agnes mess was hounding me by every mail. I had to drive it out of my head each day before I could write. I was in a continual inward state of bitter fury and resentment. I drove myself to write because I felt it was time I turned out another play. Of course, I was blind to this at the time—not so damned blind, at that, for I had plenty of misgivings!—but I see it clearly now that I've regained my sanity again. I've worked hard at *Dynamo* for the book, putting back two scenes I'd originally planned for it and it is a much better play, revised throughout with the boy's psychological Mother-struggle-ending-in-a-girl-sacrificed-to-Mother-God brought out clearly. If I'd hung on to the damn script longer I could have done this before production— but I gave myself no time and when I read it over last Sept. before sending it off I simply couldn't keep my mind on it. I simply took a chance.

But what the hell! A play more or less is no great matter. One must fail in order to learn a little more about oneself from time to time. I don't give a damn about the production failing, except for the Guild's sake. I think if I'd written *Hamlet* after the success of *Interlude* it would have been condemned as bunk. And the quotes from my letters about the trilogy, which I meant as the spiritual kinship of three plays and not a trilogy in the usual sense at all, sounded very literal and gave a wrong impression. My fault, of course. I shouldn't have written such stuff. I made every fool mistake possible in the *Dynamo* affair. My brains were woolly with hatred. Thank God, all that is behind me and I've come through.

It might have been a blow at the time but you & Jimmy should thank me for putting the crusher on the repertory notion for the nonce. You'd have been caught in the wave of reaction and have had no fair chance. You realize that now, don't you? And I know you understand that I already felt guilty at not being there on *Dynamo* and I simply couldn't square it with my conscience to let even Jimmy take on an O'Neill rep. with O'Neill five thousand miles from the scene. And I didn't like the idea of people like Ross and the other man (I forget his name—Hurok?)[1] being in financial control. That's what I meant by "pikers." I felt one set-back and they'd exit and the O'Neill rep. would be doomed for many years.

I sure hope the P'town cops the necessary coin—but what will you do with Jimmy away? Who will direct?

As always, much love to you, Fitzie! You are deep in my affection ever! Let's hope we'll meet again before too long—over here, for I won't come back for a year and a half at least—perhaps longer. I love it here.

In my next letter I'll tell you something about the Far East voyage—a wonderful experience in spite of five weeks illness and newspaper meddling.

My love to Jimmy & Paddy[2] & all best to all I know.

I'm to be married in July, I hope, if Agnes doesn't change her mind in Reno. I am damned happy!   As ever,   Gene

---

294 • TO HARRY WEINBERGER.   ALS 2 pp. (Le Plessis / Saint Antoine-du-Rocher, / Indre-et-Loire, France) [Yale]

[early June 1929]

Dear Harry: I am reinclosing back to you the letter you sent care of me for Louis K.[1] I have no idea what his present address is—last I heard he was going to Spain. Moreover, I wouldn't want to forward it to him anyway as, for the present, I am keeping my exact address away from him.

R.E. the plagiarism suit[2]: There is this remote possibility that she may have sent her book to me—although I haven't the slightest memory of such a book ever being received. Lots of books used to be sent to me. Sometimes I even had Agnes or Agnes' sister type a reply for me to sign saying I'd read some book or script and adding some word of praise or encouragement when I'd never looked at the damn thing. I imagine all authors have pulled such foolish tricks for the sake of being pleasant or amiable—that is, until their amiability toward struggling unknowns gets knocked out of them by a suit like this. You might find out if Agnes remembers such a book as hers. She used to glance through these unknown offerings sometimes while I never wasted the time to glance at them.

---

1. Producers Sidney Ross and Russian-born Sol Hurok (1888–1974), who offered financial backing for an O'Neill repertory company under the artistic direction of James Light, with M. Eleanor Fitzgerald involved in the business management of the enterprise.
    2. Possibly Patti Light.

    1. Louis Kantor (Kalonyme).
    2. Georges Lewys, author of *The Temple of Pallas-Athene* (1924), claimed O'Neill had plagiarized her novel in *Strange Interlude*.

Understand though, that I regard this possibility as extremely remote. I certainly ought to remember that title if her book had ever been around the place—or if A. had ever mentioned it to me. Where does she claim she sent it—and when?

This damn suit frets the hell out of me! It isn't any doubt of the outcome but all the lousy publicity it entails in the English papers and the American papers in Paris—all coming just about the time the divorce news is due to break, with additional crazy stories about my having T.B. etc., just when I want to get married quietly and settle down in peace to work. It's hellish!

Who wants this garbage bath they are pleased to call fame? I'd like to give it away. It has always been about as welcome to me as an attack of hives, anyway! I've wasted almost as much energy ducking its annoyances as I've put in my work. I feel as pawed over by the sweaty paws of the public as a 4-bit whore—and correspondingly defiled! They—or their pandering press—can't touch my work, of course, but they can make me—as a private person—squirm with disgust.

But I am forgetting our old watchword of the Revolution—F--k 'em all!   As ever,
Gene

---

295 • TO STARK YOUNG.[1]   ALS 4 pp. (Stationery headed: Le Plessis / Saint-Antoine du Rocher / (Indre-et-Loire)) [Texas]

June 20th [1929]

Dear Stark: I know I am all sorts of an ungrateful son of a gun for not having answered your fine long letter before this! It was no lack of appreciation, believe me! Your letter was one of the very very few with real sympathy and understanding that have come my way since "God's Country" was left astern! And of that very few yours easily stands first in sensitive comprehension! So much thanks, Stark! In these days of a million malicious irritations proceeding from the homeland, your letter was a great bit of a blessing.

The principal reason for the delay in my reply is that we've been moving in the place here—really moving in to stay this time and not just unpacking trunks in another temporary shelter as has been the case previously—and I am just about getting adjusted to the new surroundings and beginning to feel at home. It is a beautiful place, Stark. All sorts of grand old woods and farm land—a fine old château with wonderful old carved wood furniture, including choir stalls originally from Langeais, ancient tapestries in the rooms downstairs—in short, it is quite perfect, and most important for me (inside) a great peace and calm broods over it all and time ceases to be a riveter's staccato of dots and dashes and becomes a flowing curved line. There is no life around but the life of the big farm that is part of the estate—cattle, sheep, ducks and chickens, wheat and hay fields. The proprietors run this, of course, and have all the responsibilities while we have all the benefit of feeling close to animals and the soil without the disillusionment of milking and praying for rain. I will not stun your ears with the incredibly small yearly rental we pay for all this grandeur. It is a bargain even for non-tourist France. We were lucky, that's all. The place has never been rented before. The owners are three sisters of the old provincial noblesse—the Vicomtesse of Something, the Marquise of Verdun, and another—really charming people when they get to know you and find you're not all barbarian, and seemingly quite pleased to have a writer for a tenant. They feel, I imagine, that it's a bit disreputably thrilling—although I hauled out my ribbon of

---

1. Young (1881–1963), critic, translator, and dramatist, whose play *The Saint* was produced by Mac-gowan, O'Neill, and Jones at the Greenwich Village Theatre in the fall of 1924.

With Carlotta in the fields near Le Plessis.

the National Institute of Arts and Letters (what ho!) to convince the eye of my sobriety and sound doctrine! But I'm really being unfair. They rushed off and bought *Strange Interlude* (they all read and speak English) and survived it without turning a hair, although confessing they had their own opinion of a woman like Nina.

I honestly love this place already and feel I'll get a lot of good work done here. It feels like home.

Yes, you are right in saying I've had about as much of a certain kind of success in *Interlude* as could be hoped for. You might add, as much as my stomach can stand! What a success! This plagiarism suit is the fitting final note of cheapness to wind up the whole affair! Still, I'd be a liar if I said the money wasn't welcome, even though I feel the play earned it under the false pretenses of a ballyhooed freak. It has, in a way, set me free.

What you suggest about the directions in *Dynamo* was always in the script—special emphasis that the dynamo looks like a great female idol & that the switches in the galleries remind one of many-armed Hindoo idols "tortured into scientific supplications." So you see. From photographs of the set I should say what Simonson gave was neither a real dynamo, which has mystery and intense, brooding life, nor an idol impression of a dynamo, but simply a dead show-shoppy imitation. Some art photographs of machinery I have seen show what can be done to preserve the life in machinery even in a realistic medium. Lee's dynamo was just scenery—and who but a scenic designer could ever adore scenery? However, I mean no malicious quips. Lee did a good job according to the conception he had and certainly the play, in its state at that time, was vague enough in outline. It is much better now.

I get your hint on the letter writing business. Certainly last summer I wrote a lot of damn fool ones to the wrong people. I was in an enraged and embittered state of mind over a betrayal of faith at the hands of a certain lady—legal blackmail & what not—and also at the barrage of lies coming from the same source. My letters were a sort of counter barrage aimed at the gossip spreaders. Childish stuff, of course. I know that now—but I was all emotion then and impulse to hit back, and had to explode or burst. I "sadly sympathize" with even the most envenomed reactions of the folk in my plays but in real life, alas, the sting of the double-cross always impels me to shout "son-of-a-bitch" and get down to the eye-gouging without delay! Hence many mistakes are made and the dignity of the creator gets much spotted with sawdust off the barroom floor!

Your working *The Colonnade* into a novel[2] interests me immensely. It strikes me as so rightly the thing for it! Not that it wasn't fine as a play. You know how very much I liked it. But, remembering it and the quality I liked so well that was uniquely your quality, I feel in a novel you'll have so much more opportunity to "do your stuff" with that theme. Certainly I look forward with pleasure—this phrase is literal here not polite cliché!—to reading it, and don't forget to send it to me.

The Three Fountains[3] arrived two days ago. Carlotta says to tell you she's reading it and "adoring it." She certainly talks enthusiastically about it. Did you get her letter of some time ago? I showed her yours to me and she has been raving on about the quality of your friendship ever since—immediately sat down to write you after reading it.

Yes, what you can do for me by sitting by is a hell of a lot! And it is what you have always done, really, in regard to my work and me—and it is at moments of change and crisis that one comes properly to value such friendship and learn gratitude!

Your opinion of my contribution to fundamentally poetic drama is the kind of reas-

2. Never published as a novel under the title "The Colonnade."
3. A collection of essays by Young on Italy (New York: Scribner's, 1924).

surance I long for from someone whose opinion I respect. It is what I like to think I have accomplished—what I have deeply fought for out of myself—but, at times, when no one seems to get that out of me I feel disheartened and all the rest of their praise for what I am not makes me laugh, not amusedly!

It's a keen disappointment to learn you're not coming over this year. I was hoping to have a chance to talk over my plans for future work with you. They are grand plans but whether I can do them as they should be done or not—quien sabe? But I'll have a go at it.

Here's hoping you may come over next spring! It should be beautiful here then. Carlotta adds her voice to this. And give our best to Bowman[4] and we hope he will be coming too. I'm sure you could work here, if you wanted to. It's that kind of place.

All best, Stark! Your letter meant a lot!   As ever,   Gene

---

296 • TO BARRETT H. CLARK.   ALS 4 pp. (Le Plessis / Saint-Antoine du Rocher / (Indre-et-Loire)) [Yale]

June 21st [1929]

Dear Clark: The above is my permanent address for the next years. Keep it much under your hat and make no exception to this rule. Incidentally, let me say that whenever you come over you will be most welcome here—and I hope you will come! It is a beautiful place and I know you would like it. Although I've only just moved in I already feel deeply at home here. It possesses the atmosphere of calm and peace and age and life long-rooted in the soil that is exactly what my spirit has been longing for for years. It is my growing certainty that I am going to get much good work done here—and that you are a very accurate guesser when you think that that work will [be] simpler, more compact, and less theatrical. At any rate, my plans and ambitions are directed ahead along those lines. I certainly admit that my worst plays have all been built around a germ idea that was in its essence theatre first and life secondarily. In justice to myself, I don't mean this in any meretricious "theatrical" sense; it simply means that my medium has at times taken the upper hand and become an end in itself and the slumbering director in me (son of the Count of Monte Cristo) has swamped the author. *Dynamo* was a good example of this. Was! Not so much so now. I've greatly simplified it. The only fault (in my estimation!) with *Lazarus* is that there is too much direction in the authorship. And a good example of the director aiding and abetting the author without obtrusion, the ideal combination for a modern dramatist, is *Desire Under The Elms*. The house there definitely takes part in the play and the revealing of the rooms enhances the drama as it actually would in real life, elm trees and all. It is such happy combinations I am going to insist upon from my imagination in future and rule out with suspicion any set or device that doesn't grow organically from the life in the theme. By straining the collaborative possibilities of the theatre I feel I've at last won to what is my own technique, and it now remains for me to simplify and clarify that technique of its abortive growths and its exhibitionism. Then I can concentrate on saying clearly what I want to say.

Many thanks for your long letter. I greatly appreciate what you have to say in rebuttal and I feel our differences of opinion don't really amount to much when you get down to it except an understandable misunderstanding of meaning on both sides.[1] But I must insist on

---

4. Architect William McKnight Bowman (1895–1966), who shared an apartment in New York City with Young.

1. In a letter of late May to Clark, O'Neill had given in great detail his responses to the 1929 revised and updated edition of Clark's *Eugene O'Neill: The Man and His Plays*.

what was really the only thing that "got my goat"—that you do make a direct accusative statement on the injurious fame stuff—and I hereby quote you chapter and verse, page 55, bottom of page: "That such fame has already done him some harm cannot be doubted, but I hardly think it can seriously alter his determination to pursue his own course in his own way." Come now! Acknowledge that's pretty definite, and that the qualifying clause with its "hardly think" is a bit weak in confidence. My point is my past work certainly merits anyone's absolute confidence that I'll go on as usual, and I don't believe any of that past work shows the ill effects of fame. Even *Dynamo*-as-produced did not err in that direction— rather the contrary.

But what the hell! Your letter blots all that out since I see you really don't feel that.

What you say about your arbitrary impregnation and delivery of a bouncing heir to my murdered gal is damned amusing![2] I've often caught my mind pulling just such tricks on me.

No, the plagiarism charge doesn't worry me much per se since the alleged resemblances, as published in the papers, seem to me to prove the lady must be unbalanced. They are really farcical. But it makes me boil with rage to think this neurotic blackmailer gets a million dollars worth of publicity for herself and her privately printed rubbish by deliberately slandering me! And I have no come-back and have to pay the legal piper too—since I suppose she has nothing—that's what galls! Surely our laws have little to do with justice! Such an injustice would be impossible anywhere else. I told Lenormand[3] about it and he was amazed that such a condition could exist. I wish there was some counter-suit I could bring. I feel very uncharitably toward that female and would like to get her. I haven't read her book yet and don't intend to. To pay 20 dollars for that privilege would be adding insult to abomination!

Much gratitude for your offer of help, as I cabled you!

All good wishes to you! We'll hope to see you over here someday!   As ever,
Eugene O'Neill

P.S. The London papers seem to have recently had me dying of T.B. in Switzerland (where I have never been!). How the hell such stories start is beyond me! This is the second time in a year I've been Camilled, but the first time (in Shanghai) I at least was sick of something while now I've never felt better! T.B. is so damned romantic to these murderous reporters evidently! But I wish they'd lay off butchering me because it's costly reassuring the anxious and disappointing the hopeful by cable! Somerset Maugham told me that some Maugham had run over a girl in his car on the Riviera and killed her and immediately every newspaper in England and the Colonies pinned it on him and he had a devil of a job clearing himself in the public eye! Nice, eh? Our slavery to the freedom of the press! Well, I'd rather be murdered by them than branded as a reckless killer, that's some consolation!

P.S. II I read Green's *Tread The Green Grass*[4]—and was disappointed. Maybe because that sort of thing leaves me cold but it bored me to death—seemed fantasy with diver's boots on.

---

2. O'Neill had pointed out to Clark that, in his book, he had predicted that "a child will be born of Reuben and Ada," when in fact at the end of *Dynamo* Ada is dead. Replying on June 5, Clark explained that, while he was watching the play unfold in performance, he guessed that Ada would have a child and then, while writing the book, remembered his "inspiration" and "my subconscious pride of prophecy took me back to the moment when I made the guess and for a second obliterated the facts in the case."

3. Henri-René Lenormand (1882–1951), French playwright, critic, poet, and novelist, whose plays are often compared to O'Neill's and with whom O'Neill became acquainted while in France.

4. Play (1929) by Paul Green (1894–1981), first produced in 1932.

297 • TO HARRY WEINBERGER.   ALS 7 pp. (Le Plessis / Saint Antoine-du-Rocher, / Indre-et-Loire, France) [Yale]

July 13, 1929

Dear Harry: Got your cable of the 10th (about having to send the decree to California) when I returned from Paris on the 11th. We had been up there having a lawyer fix up all the technicalities of our marriage and getting us duly posted according to French law. All is now set and everything waits on the arrival of the certified decree. The lawyer is arranging it skillfully so that there will be no chance of publicity until after the event—whenever we choose to announce it. I will send you a cable and you can give it out to the Associated & United Press & the N.Y. papers in general. We want the bare fact that we are married to get all the publicity possible, naturally, in the U.S.—but we don't crave the same attention over here since everyone in this district thinks we are married already.

As for the plagiarism case, one important thing has cropped up from this end. Nathan visited me and has offered to be a witness and do all he can—says he can spoil her arguments easily by citing many cases of plays produced or published before her book where hereditary insanity and eugenic babies figure. He remembered at once a play by the Hattons[1] on the eugenic theme. He also says he remembers my discussing the general idea of *Interlude* before her book came out—before I had ever gone to Bermuda—and I remember that now, too. It was around the time when I was finishing *Welded* and starting *Desire Under The Elms*—winter of '23–'24. Nathan, you will find, has a better memory and record of plays produced in America than anyone. He will be back in New York in about a month or so. He wants you to get in touch with him. Be sure and do so. He will make a very important witness. His reputation as dramatic expert is international. If it is charged he is prejudiced in my favor, it can be easily shown that he has panned many of my plays—successful ones, such as *Desire*, etc.

As for the charge about the asides, that is ridiculous on the face of it. I was merely following the universal practice of *all* playwrights before Ibsen, adapting it to a modern psychological image. It is realism without asides that is new in the theatre. Her lawyers will be only making asses of themselves to bring this up so I sure hope they do!

As for names of characters, I pick them regardless—from store signs, telephone directories, combinations of names of people I've known or heard of in the past, etc.—whatever happens to sound right. Darrell is a very common name in Bermuda both among whites and blacks. That's where I got that. Edmund was the name of my brother who died when a baby. Marsden is the last name of a guy I knew very slightly who had a camp for a couple of weeks on the beach near Peaked Hill. Leeds I simply took, as it occurred to me, probably suggested by the name of the town in England, since I thought of the Professor as descended from English provincial stock. Evans is a common enough name from Bob Evans down. Gordon is a name I've always fancied—incidentally was the 1st name of an old New London friend. The other first names—Nina, Sam, Charlie, etc. are as common as dirt.

This name similarity charge strikes me as an obvious absurdity that can only hurt her case. Do you mean to tell me any court is going to take such bare-faced framed stuff seriously? Why, it is obvious on the face of it that anyone stealing a plot would avoid all name similarity as he would the plague! He would pick names that had no connection whatever! It would be the first instinctive move to conceal all resemblance!

It strikes me that from the similarity stuff as published in the papers (I haven't received the official lawyer's stuff yet) you would have a right to complain to the court that the

1. Husband and wife team Fanny Locke Hatton (1870?–1939) and Frederic H. Hatton (1879–1946).

charges are obviously those of a neurotic, deranged mind and ask that a commission of alienists be appointed to examine the lady for sanity before the case should be considered. Have you thought of this? I mean it seriously. I had a talk with Harry Marks of the Gotham Book Mart in Paris (He came to see me about buying my original scripts, wants to see them, & I gave him a note to you) and he says he knows the Lewis[2] lady & her mother, that they are both bad eggs and crazy to boot, and that he will give you the names of various booksellers in New York who have something on her, etc. Be sure & see him.

There is a lot of stuff in your letter you don't make clear. In one to Riegelman you mention a "proposed settlement." Do you mean her lawyers have had the nerve to propose a settlement?

As for the paternity business in my own previous plays, I don't see so much to go on in *The First Man*. The obvious resemblance which I should think would have occurred to you, is in *Desire Under The Elms*. The mother there bears a child by Eben which the old man thinks is his and is proud of. In fact, there's a great deal of psychological similarity in this father-child episode in the two plays. As for hereditary insanity, that figures father-son in *Where The Cross Is Made & Gold*. Hereditary weakness father-child comes into *Beyond The Horizon*. Hereditary fears are the main stuff of *Emperor Jones*. Hereditary insanity father-granddaughter comes into *The Rope*, I think (I'll look this up). Insanity comes into *All God's Chillun* (fear of having a child that would inherit black skin) & *Ile*. Hereditary urge to the sea is a main theme of *"Anna Christie."* *The Great God Brown*—the boys & mother—is full of hereditary undertones. As also is *Lazarus Laughed* in the speeches of Tiberius & Caligula. In fact, it can easily be proved that the hereditary motive plays a great part in my work from the beginning. And a very plausible case might be deducted to show I stole *Interlude* from my own past work. Even to the form, for soliloquies are used in my plays years before *Interlude*—and soliloquy & aside belong equally to all theatrical technique from the Elizabethans down to Ibsen.

For witnesses I suggest the following should be asked to read book & play & testify
George Jean Nathan & possibly Mencken
Gilbert Gabriel & Stark Young
Krutch
Burns Mantle (he is important for many reasons)
Atkinson
Parker of the *Boston Transcript* (one of the best known in America)[3]
William Lyon Phelps of Yale (Head of English department)
Professor Baker of Yale (if he wouldn't be considered too prejudiced)
Professor Copeland[4] of Harvard English dept.
Clayton Hamilton
Walter Pritchard Eaton
Brander Matthews of Columbia
Henry Seidel Canby
Barrett Clark

And if you wanted a psychologist for good measure there is Doctor White[5] in Wash-

---

2. Gladys Lewis, the real name of Georges Lewys.
3. Gabriel was the drama critic of the *New York American*, Young of the *New Republic*, Joseph Wood Krutch of *The Nation*, Mantle of the *New York News*, H. T. Parker of the *Boston Transcript*.
4. Charles Townsend Copeland.
5. Psychologist William Alanson White (1870–1937), superintendent of St. Elizabeths Hospital in Washington, D.C., from 1903 until 1937, and one of Freud's earliest supporters in the United States.

ington—the best known in America who, I know, would be glad to help. The advantage of him is he knows me only slightly and I have never been his patient in any way. There is also Doctor Jelliffe.[6]

When I've read "The Crap-Can of Pallas Athaene" I'll let you know if I see any similarity to other books. (Of course, it is obvious she stole her asides from the drama from Elizabethan to Ibsen, which I acknowledge but which she seems to deny!) But I'm not so good at having a clear memory of books—except the very few that strike me—after I've read them. What you need here is the critical, editorial memory—minds like Nathan's, Clark's, Mencken's, Gabriel's, etc. Courtney Lemon[7] would be good on this. And Smith & Gross[8] over at Liveright's. But Nathan especially! His mind is an encyclopedia of past plays & plots. Be sure and get in touch with him as soon as you hear he's back! He will have valuable suggestions all around.

What do you mean in your 10th cable by "a year"? Do you mean to say it will be a year from now before this case comes to trial?

Do you know this damn suit has already cost me 35 thousand? Final arrangements had been made to sell *Interlude* as a talky for Lillian Gish for 75 thousand when this thing cropped up. Of course now it's all off—and there's little hope it will be taken up again for Gish will have to find a substitute and she may only do one talky. She had with difficulty got Schenck[9] to see *Interlude* (it's obviously a hard play to sell on account of censorship difficulties) and he was glad of this excuse, I guess, to drop it. I speak with authority for I've had several talks with Gish since she came to France.

Keep this under your hat!

Do you mean to say there is no way in law I can get back at this Lewis bitch who has done me all this injury? Then, by Jesus, I think I shall switch my citizenship to France, where an author amounts to something & has some rights at the earliest opportunity! I mean this!

The following is confidential: There is a possibility—only that!—that I might, through certain channels interest Henry Taft[10] in appearing for me with you in this suit. Don't you think his name and prestige, his high reputation for integrity, etc. would be a big asset? Let me know what you think? I won't do anything until I hear from you. And don't mention it to anyone.

What you say about "getting something" on the lady interests me much. By God, that's the stuff! That baby needs showing up! And from what Marks told me of her & her mother, it shouldn't be hard to dig up something. If you only get a good weapon she'll be glad to drop this case & publicly acknowledge her mistake. Her lawyer, Firestone,[11] is, according to Marks, a crooked shyster.

I think you will find she & her mother prepared the similarity stuff—perhaps with the help of some cheap writer, or quack psychologist (sounds like the latter to me). They've had experience in another suit. The California affair, according to Gish, was simply blackmail.

The news of Gaga's death[12] left me sick! I loved that old woman! She was grand to us in

---

6. Psychologist Smith Ely Jelliffe, cofounder, with Dr. White, of the *Psychoanalytic Review*.
7. Former dramatic editor of the New York *Call* and assistant editor of *Pearson's Magazine*, Lemon was a reader for the Theatre Guild from 1922 to 1930.
8. T. R. Smith, head of the editorial staff at Liveright's, and Pete Gross, another employee at the publishing firm.
9. Film producer Joseph Schenck.
10. Taft (1859–1945), noted lawyer and brother of President William Howard Taft.
11. Charles Firestone.
12. Fifine Clark had died on July 6, 1929.

our early years when I had nothing—loyal as hell to us! There is nothing I wouldn't have done for her! When Agnes cast her off a year ago last spring it was I who shamed her into taking her back. I sent money then to Gaga—300 altogether—and told her to appeal to me personally whenever she needed anything. I knew how Agnes has ill treated the poor woman for the past years since I've had a little money. Agnes, as we know, is a person without loyalty or gratitude. And I'm afraid she left Gaga to the mercies of a country quack. I could have got her into the Presbyterian hospital, I think, through the people I know there—just as I got Agnes' father, whom his loving family had left at the mercy of quacks (when he had a doctor at all!) to see the best T.B. man in New England and had him entered in New Haven hospital. But I came too late. The neglect had already done its work. And he died as Gaga has died!

I took your first cable that she was dangerously ill with a grain of salt. I know what a liar Agnes is when it comes to grafting money on some excuse. And the idea that I *owed* Gaga money is a lie! I sent her 300 to P'town as a gift—two hundred more later. Her back wages (which Agnes speaks of but which Gaga never mentioned in her letters to me since she knew the truth about them) were always supposed to be paid out of Agnes' household allowance. All this is simply an example of the same old lying spirit, neglect, laziness, shiftlessness, ingratitude for loyalty, etc. on A's part that I came to see so clearly as the years went on. Thanks be to Christ, that's over!—and she's out! Gaga's death brought it all back. If that old lady had ever told all she knew! But she never would have! She was too damn fine a character, she loved the children too much ever to retaliate on A. for all she went through—and I respect her and her memory for it! A fine, simple human being, generous, loyal, affectionate & self-sacrificing was Gaga! This life would be a paradise if we could say half that much about one-tenth of the rest of us!

I wired you to get money from Madden and do everything possible in the way of the needful in flowers, funeral expenses, etc. Let me know where she is buried—if in Province-town, will you drop a line to John Francis and ask him to find out if there is anything I can do? I would appreciate this very much, Harry. I feel damn badly about her death—as if I should have done more about her—but I just thought she was ailing as she had for spells often before. I couldn't imagine her dying—and when one has so many worries of one's own, one is inclined to forget other people's except when it's palpably serious. And I honestly believed Agnes was lying—and Gaga would have been the last one, knowing all she knew, to blame me for that suspicion!

I feel I've lost an old friend—one of the few real ones! But perhaps she had been lied over into hating me too. I'd hate to think that—but A. knew how I'd always defended Gaga from her meanness & malice, knew I loved her, and I wouldn't put it past her to have done all in her power to poison the old woman's mind against me. I remember on 2 distinct occasions when I interfered in Gaga's favor and Agnes said to me: "Either that old fool gets out of this house or I will!" And I answered with a truth she didn't appreciate "All right! That's fine! You get the hell out—and good riddance!" This was long before C. came on the scene—and yet they say C. came between us!

Pardon the reminiscing—but Gaga's death, I'm afraid, has made me feel a bit bitter in a certain direction again. But once more, thank God for Reno! Hurry up that decree!   As ever, Gene

298 • TO JOSEPH WOOD KRUTCH. ALS 4 pp. (Stationery headed: Le Plessis / Saint-Antoine du Rocher / (Indre-et-Loire)) [Library of Congress]

July 27th 1929

Dear Krutch: I was damn glad to get your letter but disappointed that you & Mrs. Krutch won't be over this season. Better luck next year! We'll look forward to having you, so put it down in the old date book!

I was sorry to hear you've had such bad breaks on your health but it's good to know you're getting on your feet again. I was pretty well washed out in Shanghai myself—after effects of sunstroke and flu from Singapore & Saigon—and I'll never forget my experience in the hospital there teetering on the verge of a nervous breakdown and lying awake nights listening to the night target practice of a Welsh regiment whose garrison was two blocks away, and to the beating of Chinese gongs keeping the devils away from a birth or a bride or a corpse or something devils like! It nearly had me climbing the walls of my room and gibbering a bit!

The recent reports of my dying of T.B. in Switzerland are bunk, of course. I never felt better than right now. Dear old T.B so irresistibly attractive to journalists! I'm sorry for their sakes I only had such a puny incipient touch of it so darn many years ago. But why be sorry? They'll keep on Camilleing me if I live to be ninety!

Nathan visited me over a week-end but outside of him I've seen no one—and am just as well pleased. Most of the people I want to duck seem to be in Europe but none of those I'd like to see.

What do you think of my plagiarism suit? It's a grand law we have when it comes to protecting authors! You couldn't get such a suit into the courts over here, but with us any old blackmailer can get away with murder—and I have no come back except paying lawyers no matter how much I win! The Universal Film Co. once paid this dame 500 for nuisance value to get rid of her and I guess her success in that suit spoiled her. She's got a grand lot of publicity out of me already, and she should worry, she can't lose no matter what happens. Hot stuff!

I've just sent back the last proofs of *Dynamo*. It's better, clearer, a different sort of play with all the confusion and fuzziness deleted, and the mysticism which had no real validity to me when I went over it. I like it better now—but not enough. I wish I'd never written it, really—and yet I feel it has its justified place in my work's development. A puzzle. What disappoints me in it is that it marks a standing still, if not a backward move. It wasn't worth my writing and so it never called forth my best. But a good lesson for me! Henceforth unless I've got a theme that demands I step a rung higher to do it, I'm going to mark time and play the country gent until such a theme comes. It wasn't that I didn't have such themes when I wrote *D*, but *D* was more developed in my mind as a play and seemed an easy choice. I'll have to beware of my theatrical penchant for writing plays when I feel I ought to be busy. Much too many plays and too few dramas are being written! I've written a few of those plays myself and they are blackballs in my own eyes. *D* is a just retribution on me who am always scornfully snorting that the reason no one does anything big in drama or novel now is that no one has the guts to shoot at something big and risk failure. There are no big themes chosen by our success-chasers. And that, in a nutshell, is to me the complete explanation of "what is wrong." They don't choose subjects for Art, they choose themes for writing!

Well no one can find fault with me on these lines on what I'm setting out to do now. It's an idea and dramatic conception that has the possibilities of being the biggest thing modern drama has attempted. Far the biggest! You have to go back to Greeks and Elizabethans to tie it. I say, most advisedly, "the possibilities." I don't promise by a long shot that after it gets ground down by my inadequacies it will possess any such lofty stature; but at least this time I'll have the satisfaction of knowing I failed at something big and thus be a success in my own spiritual eyes. If I fail! I have hopes, damn it!

Oh for a language to write drama in! For a speech that is dramatic and isn't just conversation! I'm so strait-jacketed by writing in terms of talk! I'm so fed up with the dodge-question of dialect! But where to find that language? Any suggestions on this question will be gratefully received.

Well, I've ranted on about enough. All best to you and Mrs. Krutch. Write when you're in the mood.   As ever,   Eugene O'Neill

P.S. The marriage finally came off—and impressively for us! We feel we've won—earned—this marriage—and we are most happy and secure about it. One can't wish for more than that.

I will be only too tickled to send you the scripts of all my new work before production. In future it's my intention to do just that in the case of the few critics whose opinions I respect. I think it's the only fair deal for all concerned—for how can any critic be expected to judge what the director, actors, designer contribute—or don't contribute!—to a play unless he has read it first?

But I won't have anything to show you for some long while yet. This new stuff of mine demands a lot of time—and is going to get it. How long remains to be seen but certainly there will be nothing of mine ready for production for a year or more.

---

299 • TO RICHARD MADDEN.   TLS 1 p. (Stationery headed: Le Plessis / Saint-Antoine du Rocher / (Indre-et-Loire)) [Yale]

Sept. 20th [1929]

Dear Dick: I have just got your letter about that Bucharoff guy.[1] He certainly must have his nerve and I think you had better sit on him good and hard and weed him out once and for all. You might point out to him that in the four years that have elapsed he has never once written me in answer to that letter of mine to say that he was going ahead with any work on any opera of any play, nor asked for terms or a contract or anything else. His claim is a joke. The notion of getting some soft movie money is driving him wild—though why he should think the right to attempt an opera should include movie and talky rights is beyond me. If he tries to make a contract for an opera for *Jones* the only thing we can do is to freeze him out on terms. I was willing enough that he should try to do an opera on some play or other at that time but the way he is acting now I am thumbs down on any proposition he may have to make.

The Pitoëffs[2] are doing *The Hairy Ape*, not *Strange Interlude*. It opens in Paris tomorrow night, I believe. I will see a performance later on. I have not been to any of the rehearsals because I am determined not to get involved with the show business in France. Bourgeois,[3] the translator, has been holding up the author's end. He claims Pitoëff is doing a very interesting job of it. I hope so although I can't see *The Ape* in French with French actors. However, if anyone in Paris is to do it, Pitoëff is the one. He has a very good reputation over here—he and his wife—and their theatre is certainly the most enterprising in France. I have

---

1. Simon Bucharoff (1881?–1955), composer, musical editor, and motion picture orchestrator.
2. Russian-born French actor, director, and translator Georges Pitoëff (1887–1939) and his wife, actress Ludmilla Pitoëff (1896–1951).
3. Maurice Bourgeois.

not written to you about this before because Bourgeois is going ahead under his old contract you made when he asked to translate *The Ape*. I don't know what his terms with Pitoëff are—the best he could get, I suppose. I know he could get no advance. The way I regard it is that it gives me another hearing in Paris, where they have never clamored after my stuff, and I couldn't afford to make any large demands at this time, especially with a play like *The Ape*. It is being done on a straight run, not repertoire. The royalty payments will be made through the American Play Co., of course.

I see by the Paris *Herald* that Boston and Providence have barred *Interlude*.[4] Dear old New England! Can't the Guild do anything to force this issue, I wonder? I am cabling you to see if you have any news. Is there any chance that *Interlude* will be barred it [in] any other of their subscription towns? It would be a shame if they stopped in Chicago.

All best to you!   As ever,   Gene

---

300 • TO CARL VAN VECHTEN.[1]   ALS 2 pp. (Stationery headed: Le Plessis / Saint-Antoine du Rocher / (Indre-et-Loire)) [Yale]

Sept. 30th [1929]

Dear Carl: The records arrived—and they are some camelias! As you expected the "Saint James Infirmary" is right in my alley! I am memorizing the words. Do you know Mr. Armstrong?[2] If so, give him my fraternal benediction. He is a darb.

"Empty Bed"[3] is grand—also my old favorites "Soft Pedal" & "Sing Sing" that Paul Robeson introduced me to.

Many, many thanks! It is good to have Bessie[4] around wahooing in the peaceful French evenings. She makes the ancestral portraits of the provincial noblesse shudder—or maybe it's shimmy!

Carlotta joins me in all best to Fania & you.

I'm hard at work. Are you? How is N.Y. these days? I see I've joined the Banned-In-Boston club of which I believe you're a member.[5]   Wa-hoo!   Gene O'Neill

---

301 • TO HARRY WEINBERGER.   TLS 1 p. (Stationery headed: Le Plessis / Saint-Antoine du Rocher / (Indre-et-Loire)) [Yale]

Oct. 5th 1929

Dear Harry: Your letters of the 24th and 19th and 14th arrived. I am glad you paid the things in connection with Gaga. You can also pay the storage charges on the furniture provided Agnes agrees to take it out at once. If you have not already sent the books that are there, then hold on to them until further notice. It occurs to me that there is no place to put them here at present as we are all stocked up with Carlotta's books. Keep them at the

4. The play was banned in Boston, according to the mayor, because it was "a plea for the murder of unborn children, a breeding ground for atheism and domestic infidelity, and a disgusting spectacle of immorality" (Sheaffer, *O'Neill: Son and Artist*, p. 341).

1. Van Vechten (1880–1964), novelist, music and dance critic, and photographer, and his wife, actress Fania Marinoff, were close friends of the O'Neills. Van Vechten was instrumental in the white recognition of black arts and letters in the 1920s.
2. Jazz trumpeter Louis Armstrong (1900–1971).
3. "The Empty Bed Blues."
4. Jazz singer Bessie Smith (1894–1937).
5. Van Vechten's *Nigger Heaven* was banned in Boston after its publication in August 1926.

Manhattan in my name—and my name alone, making it plain to the people there that no one can take them out but me. I would also get in touch with Bedini and pay him and get the trunk to the Manhattan. If he asks anything more about the old Star car, tell him to sell it for junk—or do anything he likes with it. Keep after Agnes to get the things from Bermuda. I don't want them sent over here yet but I do want to know they are safe in the Manhattan under my name. Don't let this slide. When is she going down there? I see by the papers that some drunk friend of hers ran the Dupont into trouble and she had to pay his large fine. Great stuff for the children, that! I can see where her alimony will be spent!

There is also a trunk of mine in storage in Winston's store, I believe. You might get in touch with him and say that it might be better to get this out of his way—it must be a nuisance to him—and send it to the Manhattan with the other stuff.

I am enclosing letters for Shane and Oona. I haven't addressed them because I thought she might have gone off to Bermuda before this mail got to New York.

You might make some pointed inquiries as to where Shane is going to school now, etc.—and where she is going to send him when she goes to Bermuda. It is about time his education was taken seriously and he settled down to one school. And you know damn well—or I do—that she is the type to let such things slide along in the most slip-shod way, if she isn't caught up on it. And I suppose I have something to say about it legally, haven't I? Or haven't I?

The Hairy Ape is playing in Paris but I haven't seen it yet—evidently an interesting production. All the French critics of the conventional type, and they are the most conventional in the world, were peeved by it—the patriotic ones condemned it as another example of the dreaded Yankee invasion of everything that was driving France to ruin—and the good critics were full of praise and interest. So there is much talk and the production has brought my name to the fore. How business is I don't know. I think it's too radical a product in every way for the dry-rot French theatre and theatre public to be anything but stunned by—and irritated in their abysmal smugness.   All best!   Gene

---

302 • TO GEORGE JEAN NATHAN.   ALS 3 pp. (Stationery headed: Le Plessis / Saint-Antoine du Rocher / (Indre-et-Loire)) [Cornell]

Nov. 12th 1929

Dear Nathan: Your letter arrived a few days ago and we were both damned glad to hear from you. We had just returned from Paris where we spent three weeks—I with a daily visit to the dentist all that time! Now my teeth are fixed for the present and I can concentrate on work. Which I have been doing since our return and I now feel I am at last off on the right foot. It should come with a rush from now on. All elaborate schemes have been cast aside and the aim now is to do this big job with the utmost simplicity and naturalness. I had gotten myself terribly messed up searching for new ways and means and styles—but the idea just wouldn't fit in with any of them. They only got in its way. So I'm going ahead and let it write itself! The result will probably be a modified, simplified *Interlude* technique. My plan is to work like hell, hold myself to doing an act a week at all costs, and get the first draft of the twelve acts in the three plays done by Feb. 1st. Then I'll set it aside for six months—take a trip somewheres and then write the first draft of another idea[1] that has grown ripe.

One thing that has made the preliminary work on this new trilogy extremely arduous has been the tremendous difficulty of seeing every character through all the situations in

---

1. Probably *Days Without End,* not written until 1933 and first produced in 1934.

different plays. With *Interlude* that was simple. They followed fairly straight lines of development in that work. But this is another story.

In Paris I saw Lenormand's *Mixture* and liked it quite well—a strong play that sort of
fizzles into anti-climax in the last two scenes. I like Lenormand himself immensely—a fine
sensitive artist. His wife, the Dutch actress[2] is also very much of a person. They are coming
down to visit us soon. I also met the Pitoëff's in Paris and liked them. She (Ludmilla) wants to
play *Desire Under The Elms* and I've given the translation rights to Madeleine Boyd (who
visited us here) and Strowski,[3] the Parisian critic, as collaborators.

And in Paris I saw my first "Talkie"—*The Broadway Melody*—and, think what you will
of me, I was most enthusiastic! Not especially at the exhibit itself, naturally, but at a vision I
had of what the "talky" could be in time when it is perfected. Looked at from the personal
angle I saw how its technique could set me free in so many ways I feel still bound down—
free to realize a real Elizabethan treatment and get the whole meat out of a theme. Not that
the "talky" folk are ever liable to let me realize any of these dreams but I think the day may
come when there will develop a sort of Theatre Guild "talky" organization that will be
able to rely only on the big cities for its audiences. As for the objection to the "talkies" that
they do away with the charm of the living, breathing actor, that leaves me completely cold.
"The play's the thing," and I think in time plays will get across for what their authors
intended much better in this medium than in the old. Also I believe a play written for the
"talkies" can have just as much literary value in printed form as any done for the regular
stage. And again I am certain plays can be written that could be played as written on either
the regular stage or as a "talky"—with a little help in the way of elasticity in the contrivings
of our stage scenic designers. At any rate, my inspirations on this subject have had one
practical result that I see the next play after the trilogy (an idea I set aside because I couldn't
see how to do it) as a stage play combined with a secure talky background to make alive
visually and vocally the memories, etc. in the minds of the characters. Keep this notion of
mine a secret, of course.

I am most eager to talk to Lillian about all this—after she has made *The Swan*[4]—hear all
about the inside of this new technique. Perhaps we can eventually get together on something
worth doing for both of us. Be sure to bring her here next summer!

Does my "talky" enthusiasm strike you as idiotic? Be frank and write me at some
length, when you've got the mood and the leisure, and let me know what you think, not of
the "talky" as is being done but as a medium for real artists if they got a chance at it.

Interlude got a bad spanking from the critical boys in Berlin. They say I have no roots
(being a Yank!) except in Ibsen and Strindberg, forgetting that that, if true, is equally true of
their own playwrights. One even objects to the play bitterly because I stole the aside from
Shakespeare! It is all too damn dumb! Judging from the stupidity of their comments, I think
Percy Hammond[5] would be a Georg Brandes in Berlin! But the thing that makes me especially sick about the discussion of this production and that of *The Hairy Ape* in Paris is the
evident fierce animosity to Americans as artists. They are forced to see our industrialism
swamping them and forcing them to bad imitation on every hand and it poisons them. They
are bound they'll die at the post rather than acknowledge an American has anything to show
them in any line of culture. It's amusing—and disgusting!—this clinging of theirs to their
last superiority out of the past!

2. Marie Kalff.
3. Boyd, a literary agent, and French critic Fortunat Strowski de Robkowa (1866–1952).
4. A 1930 United Artists comedy that was never filmed because when director Max Reinhardt with-
drew, Lillian Gish did also.
5. Drama critic of the *New York Herald Tribune*.

I see by the Paris *Herald* that Sinclair Lewis, Dreiser and I (in the order named) have been mentioned in the current Nobel Prize consideration—which mention is at least a step forward for us Yanks! (By the way, speaking of Sweden, when *Interlude* was done so successfully there no one mentioned my imitation of Ibsen & Strindberg, it remained for the non-Squarehead Berliners to discover that.) They say Thomas Mann is sure to get the award.[6] I hope so. He deserves it. I think his work, with a few exceptions, is great stuff, don't you?

Carlotta joins in all good wishes to Lillian & you. We are looking forward to your coming here next year. Don't let anything stop you!   As ever,   Eugene O'Neill

P.S. Where is your book?[7] We've never received one. Do you mean to say I'm going to have to buy it? If I don't get it soon, I will! That ought to shame you!

---

303 • TO RICHARD MADDEN.   TLS 2 pp. (Stationery headed: Le Plessis / Saint-Antoine du Rocher / (Indre-et-Loire)) [Yale]

Nov. 19th 1929

Dear Dick: I received your cable in answer to mine about the *Marco Millions*-repertoire doubt and I will await your letter explaining matters.

I have given Albert Coates[1] the right to make an opera of *The Hairy Ape*—telling him that I cannot make it absolutely final until the Bucharoff option expires. That covers things. Please get this Bucharoff guy out of the way as soon as possible. As you say, I was a damn fool ever to write him that letter—but at the same time I doubt if the letter would give him any rights if it came to court, seeing that he has never done anything about it and never even answered my letter or specified any play he wanted or was working on.

Coates wants to use the German translation for his words. His work is well known in Germany, for one thing, and he claims it is easier to set to music in German. I am quite agreeable to this. Does this mean that I will have to split my end with Freund, the translator, or what? What kind of a contract does one make under such circumstances? Of course, when it is time to give Coates a contract I will call on you. He is coming to visit me here toward the first of April when his London season is over and we will then work together on the thing. He seems like a fine guy from his letters and he certainly has a fine reputation as a director and a musician. So I think this is a good bet. What's your opinion?

I have given the rights to translate *Desire Under The Elms* and *The Long Voyage Home*, on the usual fifty-fifty basis, into French to a collaboration of Madeleine Boyd, whom you probably know, and Strowski, the French dramatic critic. That also seems like a good bet. Strowski hopes to get *The Long Voyage Home* on at the Comédie Française—which would be quite a kudo in French eyes although to mine, which have seen that illustrious troupe act, it means less than nothing. Ludmilla Pitoëff wants to do *Desire* and that's a fine bet. She is the best actress in France.

Considering the above, I think it best not to give the rights to do *Desire* in English in Paris to Saxe or anyone else. So if he still wants them stall him off. His troupe doesn't look good to me on paper and I doubt if he will accomplish anything here—and I don't want *Desire* murdered in Paris when I have a good prospect of getting a production with a fine actress in French in the not too distant future.

6. Mann did win the 1929 Nobel Prize for literature.
7. *Monks Are Monks* (New York: Alfred A. Knopf, 1929).

1. Coates (1882–1953), English conductor and composer.

Here are some financial instructions which I wish you would do me a favor to carry out carefully. Will you on the first of every month, *for six months only* beginning Jan. 1st 1930, give to Harry Weinberger a check for 833.33 (eight hundred and thirty-three dollars, 33 cents) for Agnes alimony? You can deduct it from the last *Interlude*'s royalty you collect before the first of each month. Please confirm this in your next letter to me so I will know it is all set. And thank you exceedingly for the trouble involved.

(I forgot to say when writing above of the French translation thing, that I will call you in as agent when it comes to a question of actual production. I was on the ground and could easily arrange the other stuff so there was no use bothering you. I really think *Desire* with Madame Pitoëff will have a fine chance of success in Paris.)

Tell me in your next how the stock market crash promises to affect the well-known show business—with particular reference to the *Strange Interlude* companies. I suppose it will do a lot of damage to the box office in general, once the inevitable after-effects of the smash set in. What happens after Pauline Lord ends her ten weeks with No. 2 Co.? Will the Guild try the South with it with some other actress? They better make all the hay with it this year while the sun is shining, what? How is business this year in general? I am no prophet but it looks to me as if the legit is in for a couple of very sad years, what with the crash of stocks and the encroachments of the Talkies.

I am working like the devil every day and getting along with my new work in fine style. It is going to be a real big thing, you will see, but there is a tremendous amount of labor involved on it. But it will be worth it. I haven't told anyone a thing about it—except bum steers—and I am not even going to tell you till you see the finished script. Not that I don't trust you to keep it dark but simply that my feeling now is that I will do no talking in advance, even to friends, but let the final job do all the speech making. I shot off my mouth too much in advance about *Dynamo* and it gave every one the wrong angle on the play. What you think you are going to do and what is finally accomplished are sometimes entirely different notions.

I see that Tessa[2] is in something new. Give my cheers for success to her.

I am feeling in the pink, after a three weeks session with the dentist in Paris, and enjoying the fall here. It is a grand part of the country and can't be beat for quiet—with Paris only five hours' drive away when one needs relaxation—but I am not going there again now until I finish my first draft of the whole work.

All best to you, Dick—and to Tessa. Write me a long one and give me all the dope on things theatrical. I see the *Times*—but I mean the inside dope.   As ever,   Gene

P.S. I wish you would send me a cable every week giving me the gross of the two *Interlude* companies as you used to—when you hear—deferred cable, of course.

---

304 • TO CARLOTTA MONTEREY O'NEILL.   ALS 2 pp. (Stationery headed: Le Plessis / Saint-Antoine du Rocher / (Indre-et-Loire)) [Yale]

Dec. 2nd '29
5 p.m.

Darling Fatbum: It again "rains in my heart as it rains" etc. I am most lonely and sitting here dreaming of you[1]—and it is pouring outside as it has been ever since lunchtime. I wrote

2. Madden's wife, Tessa Kosta (prima donna and musical comedy star) was appearing in a revival of the comic opera *The Fortune Teller* at Jolson's Theatre in New York.

1. Carlotta was in Paris for a short visit.

a wire to you soon after lunch and sent it off by Jacques. I imagine as he plodded through the muck on his bike that he did some morose pondering on the inconvenience of having a master who was in love with his wife to such a romantic extent. But no matter. I hope the wire was waiting for you on your arrival or got there soon after you, at least.

I did some more work after lunch, it being such a dismal day, and finished my fourth act. I wish that meant finishing the play, but now I've got to go back and redo a lot of the first and second acts. So the end of play one, which I think will be called "Homecoming," is still to be attained.

Then I went for a walk—not so pleasant but the air was good. And, having teaed and marmaladed, here I am.

What else shall I tell you? That I love you with everything in me? You know that. That I miss you terribly? You ought to know that too but I don't think you realize how much. It is as if I were one-half of a Siamese twins that had just been amputated apart! A lost feeling! The house is so big and still. I keep looking up expecting to see you sitting in the chair near me. I feel a hungry longing to reach out and touch your knee or your foot—or say "time for a caress!" and get up and put my arms around you and nuzzle in and kiss your neck—or sit on the cushion at your feet and feel your arms pressing me so tenderly against your breast—or simply look up when you're not looking, as I so often do, and think how beautiful and sweet you are and how lucky I am!

Good night, Beloved One! Kisses and kisses! I adore you!   Your   Gene

---

305 • TO LAWRENCE LANGNER.   TLS 3 pp. (Stationery headed: Le Plessis / Saint-Antoine du Rocher / (Indre-et-Loire)) [Yale]

Dec. 4th 1929

Dear Lawrence: I was damn glad to get your long letter with all the news. I often think of you and Armina[1] and wonder what's new with you and whether we are likely to see you over here next summer. We hope so. I am damn sure you would like this place and the country around it. We are enjoying the fall here even better than we expected. For one thing, the central heating really works—and that, I understand, is a miracle where French châteaus are concerned. And the weather is much milder than I had thought. True, it rains a lot but I don't especially mind that. I have rigged up a young gymnasium in one of the out buildings where I punch the bag, etc. I ride a bike a lot and walk and drive a car. Carlotta does likewise—all except the bag punching. And so we manage to have a pretty happy and healthy time of it. We don't feel the least bit lonely although we have been practically alone now for nearly two years. Which I'll say is proof enough of love, if it needed any additional proof! And we have a Victrola, and a radio that gives us symphony concerts from London and cheap vaudeville, and a dog, and two cages full of birds, some of which sometimes sing, and—but I should say we *had* a dog and are getting another. The one we had died of distemper recently and threw us into mourning for we had gotten very fond of him. I hear you had some bad luck with dogs you bought in London dying on you—but you probably hadn't had time to get really attached to them.

As for work, I am at it in my tourelle[2] every day from nine or quarter to, until lunch time at one-thirty and I am getting a lot done and hope to have the first draft of the whole opus

---

1. Armina Marshall (1899–), whom Langner married in 1925 and who was associated with him at the Theatre Guild.
2. The tower study in which O'Neill wrote.

finished by the middle of February, if my present gait keeps up. I worked on the preliminary doping out all last summer and then got off to a couple of bum starts that ate up time. Also there were interruptions like having to go to Paris for three weeks, every day of which I was in the dentist's chair. But now I am off on the right foot and well into it. It involves a lot of hard labor—more than there was in *Interlude*—but I think it will be worth it. No, I am not going to tell you what it's all about. Suffice it that it's the most ambitious thing I have undertaken. This doesn't mean that there is any elaborate new experiments in technique involved, or that I am trying to evolve a new language like Joyce. There isn't that about it. And I'm not coyly withholding the secret for any other reason except that, remembering my blundering about *Dynamo*, I simply have a reaction against saying a word about this in advance. I would rather wait until it is all done as well as I can do it and then let it do the talking for itself. Also I want to let it become exactly what it wants to be and not be forcing it into my preconceptions. It might very well turn out to be nothing like what I would describe it as at this stage of creation.

Did you see what the Berlin critics did to *Interlude*? My, oh my! But their bad intentions evidently misfired for the play has been running now nearly two months and the management assures me that it is one of the few hits this season in Berlin. I also get the same dope from outside sources that are reliable. Elisabeth Bergner made a terrific success as Nina and the rest of the cast is fine, I believe. She got all the credit for whatever the boys found good in the play. I wonder what they'd say if they knew that every gal who has played Nina, in the U.S., Sweden, Denmark, and Budapest, has also made a great hit. Three successes for *Interlude* out of three starts so far in Europe—Sweden, Budapest and Berlin—isn't so bad, what? I omit Denmark because I have no dope on that except that it caused the leader of the Conservative party in their parliament to make a public speech of his alarm and disgust, which sounds all to the good! You had better try London with it next summer while the going is good. It will probably drive the Limie critics into a fury but I think it might go—in fact, probably would go. What is your opinion?

To get back to the Berlin critical uproar I was accused of imitating every German dramatist they could drag up, including Schiller,[3] and then they threw in Ibsen, Strindberg, (the Scandinavians made no such accusation) and Shakespeare for good luck. One critic got real peeved because I had so obviously imitated Shakespeare—which is the finest compliment I have ever got. But his tone, as I got it via translation, seemed to indicate that he sniffed at the Bard as old hat. Another got mad because Charlie says in Act One that "Europe is dead, etc." He attributed that to my upstart Yankee effrontery mocking at the motherland of culture. In fact, what got under my skin was the obvious chauvinistic anti-Yank color to the critiques. It was the same in Paris with *The Hairy Ape*. They all began on the line of "this American playwright whom the naive Americans think can write, etc." and then let me have the anti-American "works." Some that praised me got around it by saying I was Irish. It is all very dumb and is making me feel very patriotic. The various Authors Leagues rant and sniff at the "Yankee invasion" as if they were a carpenter's union in Australia, and condemn us as barbarians while at the same time their highest-browed members say what Europe needs is more of our pep and electrical advertising! A grotesque spectacle, all this nonsense! I only hope my dear land appreciates the beatings I am taking in the first line trenches! (Pardon! I forgot Boston!)

And that's about all of my news. You asked me to suggest a good play to do. Why not Lenormand's *The Coward?* That is certainly a good play and you have it. Why hold it up? By the way, I have come to know Lenormand and his wife fairly well. I like them enormously.

---

3. Friedrich von Schiller (1759–1805), considered the foremost German dramatist.

But that doesn't effect my opinion on *The Coward* which I knew long before I knew him. I have also met the Pitoëffs and like them too. She is a fine actress, the best in France. She is going to do *Desire Under The Elms* in Paris as soon as it is translated. I think she will be grand in it.

I hear that the Wall Street crash has nicked almost everybody. What you say about it not affecting the theatrical business is too good to last, I am afraid. It is a good season to have subscribers back of you! What I am worrying about is how *Interlude* will fare on the road. It is too bad about *Karl and Anna*[4] but I hope the Rolland and Behrman plays[5] will come through in great shape. What are you going to do the rest of the season? You have a Paul Green play, haven't you? He has the stuff but I don't think much of the one[6] the Provincetown have announced. It seemed dreary to me—but I must acknowledge that it's the sort of material I am cold about when anyone writes it, so my opinion is biased. Folk fantasies always bore me stiff. Are you finally going to do the Turgenieff one.[7] That sounds good to me. And it's good to know you've acquired Barrett Clark—a nice fellow and he knows his onions and ought to be very valuable to the Guild.

Yes, I know the country around Wilton well. I remember looking at a house in Wilton before I bought Ridgefield. It is beautiful country but I think you are wise to confine yourself to week-end stays in the winter. Ridgefield always drove me to hard cider, acidosis, and the Old Testament in the weepy, muddy, slush-and-snow days. We will visit your estate yet— though when, God knows, for with all my kicks agin the European chauvinist culture snobs I certainly like living over here and we have this place for three years and are making no plans for any return visits yet awhile.

By all means send me *Lady Godiva*[8] when you are finished with the cutting. I remember your idea for it quite well and I am eager to see how you worked it out. I hope Cowl[9] finally decides to do it. It seems to me it is about time for her to be landing in something worth while or she will soon be hearing the fatal ten counted over her.

Well, that's about all. Let me hear from you again before too long—and visit us next summer. Carlotta joins in all best to you and Armina. Remember me to Phyllis[10] if she is with you, and to the stout son.   As ever,   Gene

P.S. My cheerio to Terry, Maurice, Phil, Helen,[11] Lee & Bob Sisk—and to Barrett Clark.

---

306 • TO CARLOTTA MONTEREY O'NEILL.   ALS 3 pp. (Stationery headed: Le Plessis / Saint-Antoine du Rocher / (Indre-et-Loire)) [Yale]

Dec. 4th '29
(after lunch)

My Darling: I have just finished reading your letters, Dearest. They have made my heart brim over with happiness! They are so beautiful—like you—they reach out to me like your arms, they press me against your heart! They are like passionate kisses on my lips! Oh, Dear

---

4. Play by Leonhard Frank that opened at the Guild Theatre on October 7, 1929.
5. *The Game of Love and Death* and *Meteor,* which opened at the Guild Theatre on November 25, 1929, and December 23, 1929, respectively.
6. *Tread the Green Grass.*
7. *A Month in The Country,* by Ivan Turgenieff (1818–1883), which opened at the Guild Theatre on March 17, 1930.
8. Written in 1927, this play was produced at the Westport Country Playhouse in the summer of 1933.
9. Actress Jane Cowl (1884–1950).
10. Langner's daughter from his first marriage.
11. Helen Westley.

One, I do love you so! And your letters make me feel so unworthy, make me conscious of how often I fail you—or seem to fail you—when I drift around moody with preoccupations about work or worrying about this or that unimportant irritation. But you must forgive this as only an eccentricity of me. For deep in my being, possessing my whole being, is always you! I never dreamed anyone could love anyone as much as I love you! The idea of life without you beside, in me, through me, part of me, would be impossible now. You are my life! And you must feel that even my work is a part of you too since it is the expression of the I who am you! If I am worried about it, over-anxious, it is because I do so want to justify myself in your eyes, to make you proud of me, to make you see how much you have done for me, to make the world see how much you have done for me! I feel *Dynamo*, in a sense, wronged us—not because critics panned it, that means nothing, they have panned some of my best stuff, but because I felt myself it was a step back, not a step forward, and so did not represent what you are to me.

Darling One, what are words? I can't tell you what is in my heart, you have to sense it there, you have to feel it in the symbol of my arm reaching out for you in the night, finding you and knowing peace and unity at last.

I had a bad night last night as you had the night before—kept waking up and had a hard job of getting to sleep. The bed seems strange without you. There is unrest in it. It, too, longs for the touch of your beauty, for the caress of your dear body that I adore so!

I worked hard this morning and got quite a lot done. The new conception of the first act interests me much. You will find it quite changed when you hear it. I have an entirely new conception of the lover of Christine.

Well, I guess I've now spoken about 20 words since you left! This is a talkative life without you!

You remember the letter you answered for me from the man in California who offered me a picture of my father. Well, it arrived today. It's one I haven't got, taken when he was quite young, and I'm damn glad to have it.

Please get yourself that present!

Good night, Darling One! I love you so much and miss you so! Two days gone now! Not long to wait! I'll be so damn glad to see you again! Kisses all over the body I love and on your hair and eyes and lips!   Your   Gene

---

307 • TO HARRY WEINBERGER.   TLS 2 pp. (Stationery headed: Le Plessis / Saint-Antoine du Rocher / (Indre-et-Loire)) [Yale]

Feb. 2nd 1930

Dear Harry: Your long letter arrived today and I am making haste to answer and take up one point that is most important to me—that is, that you say it may be necessary for me to come back and testify at this damn trial. I want to state right here and now and most emphatically that that's out! It will have to be a deposition! The foremost reason for this is that, as I have proven in a couple of my father's suits in the past, I make a damn bad witness. I hate the very idea of a court and as soon as I am in one I begin to foam at the mouth with fury. Using your lawyer sense you surely ought to realize that I am too nervous, I lose my temper too easily, I get bawled up and rattled under questioning, I think too slowly and speak too indistinctly to make any sort of a witness. The only result of my appearing on the lot would probably be to earn me a fine for contempt of court—especially when I feel that this case is such a lousy injustice. And, after all, why should I be put through this ordeal of hellishness for me—appearing—to furnish additional advertising for this blackmailing wench? You know very well how my coming way over from Europe for that case and appearing in the court for everyone to stare at will direct attention to it and give it a prominence it will not enjoy otherwise—not that it won't get enough as it is! It seems to me it would be a very unwise thing for me to appear to take it so seriously. There are plenty of good reasons you can give the court for my not being there—that I am finishing new work, which will be the truth, and can't let a charge that I regard as obviously absurd break into it—or that I am dying of tuberculosis—or what not. It's for you to figure out the best dope. But once and for all, come over I certainly will not on any account. Take that as final. I know myself and that I would do my case no good but harm as a witness. And, for the life of me, I don't see the necessity. If I swear to the truth before the proper authorities here, isn't that just as much truth as if I went on the stand? It will be a heap more dignified, make no mistake about that. And, I think any Federal judge who knows my reputation as a writer is liable to be inclined to take my written oath that I'm no literary thief as much as he would if he heard me stammering on the stand.

And here's another angle of the thing that gets my goat—Have you thought of the expense—absolutely unnecessary, as I don't plan to come back until a year or two from next fall—of our keeping this place running, as we would have to under the lease, while we came to America and paid all the expenses of the trip too. Carlotta would naturally want to come with me and I would want her to. It would certainly add five thousand, probably much more, to what this Lewis lady will cost me anyway. I think the suit is quite unjust enough without adding any further to the bill! And this would come just at the time when *Strange Interlude* had ended its career and there would be no prospect of a new play or new book for a year, probably two, to come and no income except what dribbles in from stock and the small amount from old book sales, maybe enough to pay alimony but that's all.

I have just had a thought for you to note—that is, bring out at the trial that I am one of three Americans who have ever been seriously considered for the Nobel prize—Dreiser, Lewis and I. You can prove this as it was so stated in the Swedish papers and copied in the Paris *Herald*. I think this is good dope. Also, curiously enough, I think the German write-ups of *Interlude* which panned it as being derived from Ibsen and Strindberg, and the technique from Schiller and Shakespeare, might do much to prove her case ridiculous.

Nathan should make a fine witness—and you can certainly get a host of others to testify with important names that the charge is ridiculous. Kenneth heard the plot of *Interlude*, I think, before her book ever was copyrighted.

You ask me about notes. Well, there are a lot tucked in with the script of *Interlude*, which is in three copy books. The notes are loose sheets. But what good would they be to you since they were written in '26 and '27. I have a further note—brief outline in a paragraph—in my old general notebook here—written in '24. But how could you prove I wrote it in '24 and not yesterday? From a legal aspect I don't see where notes could prove anything. Please enlighten me about this in your next.

This reminds me of your question of some letters back about what I have in the Chatham Phoenix safe deposit. You ought to know since I laid great emphasis on it at our last session together and gave you a duplicate key, which I hope to Gawd you haven't lost. My original scripts—all except *Dynamo*—are there. Your power of attorney ought to cover getting the original script of *Strange Interlude*, with notes tucked into it, if you need to look it over. It is in three black covered, red-edged account books.

I expect to finish the first draft of the new work about the middle of March. I have been working five to seven hours a day every damn day since the last of October—no going over, straight creative work—and I begin to feel a bit washed up although filled with elation at what I have got done. It is a terrific job. I hope I never tackle such another. I have never worked so hard in my life before at a stretch. And when the first draft is done, my job as I plan it will be only one-third finished, as I am going to make myself take an equal time going over it two times. In fact, what I plan practically amounts to writing the whole thing in long hand three separate times. I have come to the age when I am not going to be easily satisfied with what I do!

So, confidentially, there will be no production of mine next year, as I have told you before. My idea is to have two new plays absolutely ready by the fall of 1931 but not let anything out of my hands until then. Write, vacation, rewrite, let six months go by starting something else, then rewrite a third time. That is going to be my program from now on. I think results will prove it a good one. *Dynamo* taught me a lesson—with a kick, but it was worth it.

I have mislaid your letter with the agreements. I think five thousand maximum is too hard on me, considering it will fall due about six months after *Interlude* has closed. I thought what I proposed was fair enough. Give this a further thought. Why not make it four—and a thousand more if I have a play on, not in stock, or have made a talky sale in the last six months of '30.

All best. I am fine but dog tired and glad I am on the stretch of lap one.   Gene

---

308 • TO EUGENE O'NEILL, JR.   TLS 2 pp. (Stationery headed: Le Plessis / Saint-Antoine du Rocher / (Indre-et-Loire)) [Yale]

Feb. 20th 1930

Dear Eugene: I have been waiting to answer your last letter to Carlotta that was meant for both of us until I had finished the first draft of the huge job. Well, I finished it today. Thank God! It has been a terrific job and I have never worked so hard on anything before. But I am pleased with the results. Of course, there is the devil of a lot yet to do before the final result is reached—as much again and then some. When I will have the final version ready, quién sabe? Certainly not in time for any production next season. I am now going to Italy for a rest. I need it. I am all "washed up" and on edge and need a change of scene to get my mind off the obsession of this job that I have been living with night and day for the past four months.

Now as to your coming over: I am sorry to say that it doesn't look as if it would be possible this year. In the first place, the way things are stacking up, I simply cannot afford to stake you to the trip. There will be no play next year, *Interlude* will be finished, and I doubt if I will have more than enough income in the season of '30–'31 to pay alimony. And my expenses this past year, what with the divorce—a costly affair—and other stuff have been abnormally large. The pity is they promise to be even larger this coming twelve months. The damned plagiarism suit is due to cost me a pile of money. And so forth. You know that I will always give you a break and that I am not talking through my hat about this but have reason. But even laying aside the matter of expense, there are other matters. For one thing, there is a prospect that I may have to go to New York this summer about the suit. Then there is the eminent probability that Carlotta's mother and daughter will come for a visit—or if they don't that she will have to go to California to see them, in which case I will come to New York with her. You will understand that this family business has to be arranged in a sort of schedule with certain periods assigned to each party. You were over last year and it is her turn to shoot now. This doesn't imply that Carlotta wouldn't welcome you with shouts of joy no matter who was here—but the point is that we can't have too much of a crowd here at once. Carlotta couldn't stand the strain of the elaborate housekeeping entailed and if I was trying to work, which I will be, it would bawl me all up. So you see. That's the answer. So I think you will agree that it is only fair that you should stay where you are this summer. If there is anything special you figure out you want to do in the States in the summer, let me know and I will help you to the best of my ability. Another thing I feel strongly is this: You owe your mother a hell of a lot more than you do me in the way of giving you the background to become what you are, and I think you ought to take a good look inside yourself and figure out whether you don't owe her a bit more of your time, and whether you shouldn't see a lot of her during her vacation. You are an only child, you know, and that makes it a bit tough for her. I don't mean to do any lecturing but the above is worth a thought.

As for the other matter you brought up—that of bringing Betty[1] here—even if you had come over I wouldn't have advised that. What I am writing now is strictly between you and me, sabe? It is the fruit of whatever worldly sagacity various kicks in the pants, my own pants and others', have given me. Keep your love affairs free from all relatives and their homes if you want to avoid complications with your love or with your relatives or both. Why run the risk with your love of forcing it into human interrelationships where you never can foretell what the answer may be? For example, how do you know Betty would like me or Carlotta, or that we would like her? You may say that you know but that [is] only because *you* feel affection for all concerned. And if one dislike crept into this combination, then all the slumbering prejudices would awake and the complications would start—and spread! Ideally this sounds rather crass but practically all it amounts to is that everyone is human and more or less petty in small things no matter how nobly they may respond to soul-trying crises. My dope is emphatically that love should be kept on a pedestal and not made to run unnecessary risks, for it is very fragile and has a hard struggle to endure even with all the breaks one can give it. Family contact I rate as risk A One. Please understand me right. I respect your love for Betty and she sounds like a brick to me and I would sure like to meet her if I come to New York. Also understand that Carlotta has nothing to do with what I am writing and doesn't even know I am writing this. It is honestly for the sake of your preserving the glamour of your love that I am writing. It is for Betty's sake most of all. You shouldn't want her to be put in such a position, that's my notion. It might work out all right, but then again it mightn't and my whole idea is the practical one that when you are happy as it is why run any risks? If you were married it would be different—only because it would have to be different. But even in the case of marriage you have only to go back to your Mother and me. If families had been kept out of it we might have had a chance. I must confess, with the guy I was then, the chance was slim and she was probably well rid of me—but you never can tell how much family interference and prejudices had to do with it.

Well, that's off my chest. What I have written is far from clearly stated but I rely on you to get the gist of it and give me credit for good intentions even if you think I am all wrong in this particular case. One of the principal reasons for my caution, as I hope you will guess, is that your and my relationship is too fine for us to place it in a position where, through neither your fault or mine, it might be hurt or messed with. Put that one in your pipe and smoke it!

Well, there's no news except work. I have been writing every day for four months half the day and thinking about it the other half so there wasn't much chance for anything to happen.

Good luck and all love to you! Write me and let me know how everything is coming at Yale. I expect to be back here on the job in three weeks, or at most four. I hope this vacation will buck me up. I'm fagged out.   As ever,   Father

1. Elizabeth Green, whom Eugene O'Neill, Jr., would marry on June 15, 1931.

April 4th 1930

Dear Dolly: Well, your letter sure was a welcome surprise! I prize it the more highly since I have a guilty feeling I don't deserve it. I have a sneaking suspicion that I owe the Rippins a letter. Am I wrong? I hope so. But, at any rate, I know you are not the ones to hold it agin me. The fact is that I seem to drift into becoming a lousier and lousier correspondent as time goes on. When plays are finished I am too fed up with writing to write and while they are being written I feel too darn tired. But because I haven't written in so long proves nothing. It is not that I do not often think of you all and of the old days on Pequot Avenue when Friday used to present me with maimed rats in the middle of the night on my sleeping porch. Nor is it that I don't remember always with a deep warm sense of gratitude, your many kindnesses to me during that and other years. For I do—and that is not pleasant bunk but the most sincere truth!

You mention some of the old bunch but don't tell me anything of your family. I would rather hear that. How are they all? Well I sure hope and getting all the breaks. When you write again tell me all about them, remembering that I have been out of touch for years.

Yes, it sure would have done me proud—more or less!—to see the lights on Bank street. But I imagine that the talky of "*Anna Christie*" is all to the Garbo[1] and very little of the O'Neill left in it. So that rather pricks the bubble, what? I confess that I harbor no feverish desire to see said talky, though I do think the lady is damn good in her work.

As for all those dramas going on in New York simultaneously that time, the details let a bit of wind out of the newspaper yarn. As I remember two were being done gratis by Little theatres, one was a flat failure, and only the last, *Strange Interlude* was fulfilling my complete expectations. I hate to be disillusioning but——

You probably also noted two distinct stories during the past two years to the effect that I was dying of a lingering leprosy or T.B. or something—once in China, once in Switzerland. Well, I did have the flu in Shanghai, but not badly, but I have never even set foot in Switzerland let alone do any dying there. And so it goes. The newspaper boys will have their little story. Having been one once I appreciate their need but all the same it irks me to be a victim. The tale that I am over here for thirteen years is another fable. We have a lease on this place for two years more—three years in all—and that's the only basis for that fairy story.

This being notorious has its other burdens, too. As soon as they think you have made some money and might be tempted to buy them off as nuisances, the unknown scribblers begin to sue you for stealing their worthless works that you have never even seen. A lady nut, who properly ought to be in an asylum, is at present suing me for filching *Strange Interlude* from some unknown privately-printed bit of junk she wrote. Needless to state I never heard of her or her book before the suit was brought. But that doesn't stop her from getting untold advertising out of her suit and from it costing me a pile in lawyer's fees. She has nothing so I can't collect costs when I win. Such people never have anything.

This letter begins to sound a bit sad—but I want you to realize the other side of the silver lining—the all wet side. But don't think I am complaining. There is lots to make merry over. I never felt better in my life and was never happier. Can one say more? I like living over here a lot. We have a beautiful place and it is grand to work in. You can get a lot more for your money over here and life is more relaxed and less nervous and so more enjoyable. The non-

---

1. The second film version (the first was a 1923 silent film) of "*Anna Christie,*" starring Greta Garbo, was released in February 1930.

Prohibition side of it doesn't influence me, however, as it does most Americans, as I haven't had a drink of any sort in almost five years now. Whether we will decide to stay over here longer after our present lease is up is a question. Maybe so—but maybe by then we will have become homesick. I will be back for a visit anyway when my next play goes on in New York—perhaps next season but I doubt it. The thing I am writing now is the hardest I have ever attempted and it will take some time to get done the way it should be done.

Well, that's all my news except that I keep making excursions to different countries to see various of my plays done in different languages. And that my three children are flourishing from all I hear from them. My eldest son, Eugene, is one grand boy and I am quite proud of him. Not that I am not of the others but they are too young yet to tell how they will pan out. Eugene is a sophomore at Yale—spent last summer over here with us. He is six feet two and weighs one hundred and eighty-five. A large lad. But he has brains too. Is one of the highest students in his big class.

Also I am now really happily married for the first time.

And that's enough about me. But I thought you'd like all the news. Write me again when you feel in the mood. And give my friendliest and best to all the Rippins. As I hope all of you know, where any and all of you are concerned, you will always find me in the cheering section shouting for long life and happiness!   Yours as ever,   Eugene O'Neill

P.S. In case you may have seen a photo of us in a recent *Times* rotogravure in which I look like a decayed fish I am in self-defense sending you herewith a snapshot or two which really look like me.

---

310 • TO BARRETT H. CLARK.   TLS 1 pp. (Stationery headed: Le Plessis / Saint-Antoine du Rocher / (Indre-et-Loire)) [Yale]

April 27th 1930

Dear Clark: Many thanks for your letter. I was delighted to learn that there is still a chance of the Guild considering *Lazarus* favorably. I would want to simplify if it were ever done again, no matter who did it—in fact, would insist on it. Would want good music written, if possible, for the chanting of the crowd—you know, taking the Gregorian as supreme example—get a religious ceremonial aspect into the background of the play—give the principal events of Lazarus' second life the quality of a Stations of the Cross. I think your dope as to the immediate religious trend at this time is surely right. And I hope the Guild will see this too. You can quote this letter to them as evidence of my attitude.

The big question remains though—who could play "Lazarus"? None of the well-known regular actors, I am certain. They say Pichel made a damn fine job of it on the Coast. He has brains, ability and imagination and he approached the job in the proper spirit. On other lines I have thought of Paul Robeson, especially if he makes a good job of *Othello* which he is to do in London soon. He has the voice for it better than anyone I know, could do the laughter, has magnificent stage presence and can act. Also has brains and would know what the part meant. If only Lazarus was masked and everyone else without masks, the fact of his being a negro would not be too disconcerting. Give me your notion on this idea when you next write.

You can also confide to the Guild that I don't think there is much chance of new stuff being ready to submit for next season. I will have the second draft finished by the fall, I am sure, but then, as I wrote you before, I want to put it aside and let it rest before I go ahead with the final version, doing the first draft of another play in between times.

The second draft is coming along in great shape and I am enthusiastic. It is growing in every way all the time. My first draft stuck pretty closely to naturalism—that is, if you would call *Desire Under The Elms* naturalism which I certainly would not. But it is now sprouting out into a technique more uniquely belonging to me and my theme and I am highly excited with the possibilities. However, I don't want you to think that I am busting a button reaching out after something strange and new. It is really only a development and combination of methods I have successfully used before and feel absolutely at my own home in. I would like to tell you all about this enterprise, from soda to hock, but it can't be did in a letter. Keep the above confidential.

I will look forward to seeing Terry Helburn.   All best to you!   Eugene O'Neill

---

311 • TO HARRY WEINBERGER.   TLS 1 p. (Stationery headed: Le Plessis / Saint-Antoine du Rocher / (Indre-et-Loire)) [Yale]

April 30th 1930

Dear Harry: I will quote below the full text of the original note made in 1923 (fall) just before I started work on *Desire Under The Elms*. As I explained to you in my last letter this is the note I combined with my idea for a series of plays about a woman's life that I discussed, but never wrote down, with Nathan in the spring of 1923 when I came down from Ridgefield to see him just after I had finished *Welded*. I think Nathan should recall the date in connection with my giving him *Welded* to read.

This is the note you want: It is listed in my notebook under the title "Godfather" which is the first idea for a title I had:[1]

"Play of a woman whose husband (married just before he left—affair) is killed in war—aviator—falls in final practice—in flames—Shock of news. She becomes neurotic, hysterical, desperate, goes in for many love affairs—finally at 30, disgusted with herself and broken-down, longing for normality and health and, most of all, motherhood as a final peace, she marries a naive young man just out of college. Her affection for him is maternal—but mostly as the healthy father of her child. Then she discovers on visiting his home—his queer people—that insanity runs in his family. Causes a hatred in her for the very thought of having a child by him—dislike for him, feels he has cheated her. She meets classmate of his who has become doctor. (And also her husband begins to doubt himself because no child, to grow more incapable and childish.) She finally goes to him as patient—he is neurologist—and confesses everything. He takes a daring stand—for both their sakes, she must have child by someone else. Husband will never know. By whom? By him. They do this. She has son—falls in love with the doctor and he with her. Husband becomes very proud, capable, confident, successful. She has more children by the doctor. These children grow up instinctively hating the doctor, loving their mother and her husband. Especially the latter who clings to them as his backbone. They copy him, admire him, even look like him. The doctor fades into a small town practitioner. Finally in a fit of guilty desperation the wife, seeing her children more and more estranged, tells husband everything—except about insanity—but he cannot believe it, thinks it only her jealousy and neuroticism—even consults the doctor about her—the doctor denies. After many years the husband dies—65 or so—They, very old, marry. This finishes the estrangement of the children, grandchildren. Very old, the two wait for death to let them speak the truth."

And there you have it. You can see how the idea worked itself into the finished *Interlude*.

---

1. This entry is published in *Eugene O'Neill at Work: Newly Released Ideas for Plays*, p. 68.

The above is copied verbatim from my notebook. This notebook, by the way, has notes, some merely a few words like "life of Saint Paul" "Balaam's Ass—a satire," but most worked out in more detail, for *thirty-two plays* that I have never touched yet. This seems to me to be a good point to make if you can bring it out. A man with thirty-two ideas he hasn't used isn't going around stealing stuff.

Regarding the locked box in the safe deposit, I remember it now. It contains the scripts of all the earlier plays that were written on loose sheets and not in books. No need for you to look in that.   All best!   Gene

---

312 • TO ROBERT SISK.   ALS 6 pp. (Stationery headed: Le Plessis / Saint-Antoine du Rocher / (Indre-et-Loire)) [Yale]

August 28th 1930

Dear Bob: "Presumption" be darned! I was very glad to get your letter and I appreciate your point. But granting it applies in this particular case—which, for reasons to be related farther on in this letter, I don't believe—what the hell can I do about it more than I have done? *Only ten* people in all know anything about this play. All were close friends of mine and all were sworn to secrecy. Of these ten *only seven* know the story of the plot—the other three only knowing that it is a trilogy and not one play I have written, and some hints as to the technique employed. Of the seven who have heard the story *three* are on the Guild committee. Another is Nathan, another my then publisher, Liveright,[1] whom I felt was entitled to know. But not one of these ten has read a single line of the play—except for one speech (soliloquy-thought) that I read to Phil and Helen to show him a new method I was using for that particular detail.

"So what the hell, Bill, what the hell?" It isn't my fault if folks will romance and pretend that they're so privy to all my doings they can tell the world! It's my affliction and should call forth pity from you instead of censure! How anyone can say the play is a "magnum opus" and "reveals undreamt powers" when no one has read a line of it is beyond me. Or rather it isn't beyond me. It's American exhibitionism and the reverse English on the ballyhoo and I've known it for years. I'll bet some at least of the present gab traces back to people who hardly know me. I've heard tales of people going back and saying they were my guests here—like one of the family!—who couldn't get in except over my dead body. But there you are. And whenever you try to choke off such bunk, I've found by experience, you only give it an undue importance and make it worse.

All I have said about the work to anyone not included in the above-mentioned is that it was the most difficult job I've ever tackled and that explained why it was taking me so long—which you will recognize as what Byram had in the *Times*[2] and what I've told all the newspaper people. I wanted that to get around to counteract the bunk that I was over here living the life of Reilly in a château and racing cars, hurling my wealth about regardless, and forgetting to work, etc., etc. Quite a bit of such drivel got back to me.

As for the *Dynamo* episode, it doesn't apply here. *Dynamo* failed because it deserved to fail and would have failed anyway regardless of advance comment. It was a series of mistakes on my part, written when it shouldn't have been and with the wrong method, sent out of my hands prematurely, produced with the wrong method, damned exaggeratedly be-

1. Horace Liveright had recently been pushed out of the firm that continued to bear his name and been replaced by his head bookkeeper, Arthur H. Pell.
2. John Byram, "Mr. O'Neill Drops a Few Words About His New Play," *New York Times*, June 8, 1930, part 9, p. 1.

cause it followed *Interlude,* misunderstood through my fault in talking about a trilogy when only one play had been written—in fact, a mess of mistakes. But it would have survived even these mistakes—at least, from an artistic success standpoint—if it had had the stuff from me it should have had. That play was not the thing, that's all.

As for bringing my next play in quietly, you might as well give up that dream. It can't be done. I've had too much notoriety for too many years and *Interlude* topped all that and put me on a par with Peggy Hopkins![3] If I stopped producing for a number of years that would do it, of course, but it's hardly worth that abstinence. But let's hope they will discover another "best American dramatist" this season! That would help in more ways than one. I have been setting the pace for the pack for ten years now—artistically speaking—and it's gotten damn wearisome always breaking the wind. But such again is our dear Motherland. She will insist on "best" this and "best" thats—for artists as well as tree-sitters, with ensuing notoriety on the poor boob!

And the nature and technique of this present work—(which, secrecy or no secrecy, will be known all over at least three months before production after the first ham or hamess reads a script!!!)—will make it all too apparent that this is an ambitious attempt to do something bigger than I've done before. I honestly think talk at this early date will do a lot to prevent too much talk and expectation in the months immediately preceding production—will sort of weary people with the subject and take the edge of curiosity off. But maybe I'm all wrong.

To take up the reasons I promised you in paragraph one is simply to tell you in confidence about the work. It is a trilogy of three four-act plays—a real trilogy dealing with the same characters and continuing the same story, each play a complete episode in that story, a play-in-itself more or less but with suspense carrying over to the next and starting it. The title of the whole trilogy is *Mourning Becomes Electra*—the first play "Homecoming," 2nd "The Hunted," 3rd "The Haunted." It is founded—in the outline plot—on the old story of Agamemnon, Clytemnestra, Electra, Orestes on which the Greek dramatists wrote trilogies. I modernize this story to a psychological drama of human interrelationships, using no Gods or heroes, and interpret it with many variations and improvisations of my own. I locate it in a New England seaport town at the close of the Civil War. The King Agamemnon of the fable becomes Ezra Mannon, a General in the Union army. And so forth. I set it at that time to get costume and distance and yet keep it recognizably close to American life today.

Don't get the idea there is a lot of the Greek stuff in this. There isn't much as a matter of fact. I simply pinch their plot, as many a better playwright has done before me, and make of it a modern psychological drama, realistic and not realistic at the same time. I use the plot because it has greater possibilities of revealing *all* the deep hidden relationships in the family than any other—and because Electra is to me the most interesting of all women in drama. But I don't stick to the plot even. I only use some of its major incidents. The rest is my own.

As for technique, it is modified *Interlude* with thought in a new sort of obsessed, driving, monotonous rhythm—but no short asides as in *I.* And for all the principal characters I use half-masks, not as I've used them before although the idea is suggested in *Lazarus.* This is a Greek touch, if you will, although the masks themselves and the reason for their use is entirely un-Greek. My reasons for their use—there are many—are too long to go into here.

My suggestion as to how this trilogy should be done in the theatre—as I told Phil & Terry—is a first week of six performances—the whole thing done twice—then one play a week. It is so constructed, I hope, that anyone seeing any one of the plays would want to see the other two, and feel moreover he'd had his money's worth for one evening in the play he'd seen. This is a happy combination and I feel I've got it. It wasn't easy.

3. Notorious divorcée of the day.

But it's early yet to be talking about mode of production!

So now you know the outline, anyway, and you can see that, considering the story and unusual treatment of it, the work will have a sensational aspect for the public at large. Needless to say, it seems quite natural to me and not sensational at all, except as it turns out to be very fine or very bad! It stems directly from my past work.

And you can imagine how silent the actors or actresses who will read the script, and refuse to wear masks and stultify their personalities, will be about it to their critic friends! Then think of the time rehearsals will take even after a cast—and what a cast it will have to be!—is selected. I figure the whole cast will escape from the bag at least three months ahead of the opening and the sneers and great expectations will start their building up then anyway. So what difference does a little talk now make? I ask because, although such talk gives me a pain in the gizzard, I know damn well I can't stop it. The cheer leaders, you know, are as invulnerable a nuisance as the witty columnists and fairy detractors! But exactly who do you mean is doing the tall talking?

Another item about trilogy—only five sets in all, six big parts in cast. The Electra part—Lavinia in my plays—is much longer than Nina.

I'm now going over my second draft of the whole thing. I've written it over twice in 9 mos.—six plays in long hand! Christ how I've worked on the damn thing—and still must work! *Interlude* was easy compared to this one! I'm going to lay it aside for a rest soon and go off on a trip and forget it. Then I'll type and revise while typing. And then, for better or worse, that will be that! But this won't be until next winter.

I've dashed this letter off at odd moments today and yesterday. Yes, I know it reads like that! Now I read it over, it strikes me that, barring the details about the work, I might have compressed my reaction into a few words—to wit, that with an attempt so obviously ambitious when the facts, which cannot be kept secret, are made public, the talk doesn't matter so much. It all depends on the play. I am trying to do a big thing and I don't care who knows it, or who says so without knowing anything about it. I am always trying to do a big thing. It's only the joy of that attempt that keeps me writing plays. Otherwise I would quit for I really have little interest or enthusiasm for the modern theatre, and to write for success or notoriety, or even to write merely good plays wouldn't keep me on the job a minute. Shooting at a star may be hopeless in my case, time will tell, but it gives one a rich zest in being alive in oneself and putting up a battle about something or other. And so it is important to me, if to no one else.

Let 'em talk! After all, their talk is a challenge to do my damndest, and if the work has the stuff when it is finished nothing can keep it down—at least, not forever.

So, frankly, although I get your point and certainly appreciate your kindness in writing me about it, I don't really think the present gabble matters much—and I couldn't prevent it if it did. All I want to do is to keep the basic idea and method a secret for a good while yet—and then spill it myself before the actors get a chance to.

We're both very sorry you and your wife didn't get over to see us. Make it next summer!

Write me frankly if you think I'm wrong and why and where. Also your dope on the best way and when to let out information—granting the Guild will want it—and that it is a good trilogy! Much depends on this last!

Mrs. O'N. joins in all good wishes!   As ever,   Eugene O'Neill

P.S. You're dead wrong about *Interlude!* It didn't burst like a bombshell—except that a fine and original and unusual play is always a bombshell of a sort. There had been lots of talk about *Interlude* before it opened—extravagant talk, too! You just didn't happen to hear it. For example, Liveright ballyhooed it for six months before it opened—all over and to everyone! And there was Nathan's article in *Merc. & Woollcott's in V.F.* and Anderson's in the *Post.*[4] No, *The Emperor Jones & The Hairy Ape & The G. G. Brown & Desire U. T. Elms* were bombshells compared to which *Interlude* was a foreseen and expected event!

---

313 • TO JOSEPH MCCARTHY.   ALS 2 pp. (Stationery headed: Le Plessis / Saint-Antoine du Rocher / (Indre-et-Loire)) [Dartmouth]

Sept. 2nd 1930

Dear Mr. McCarthy: Your letter was forwarded and reforwarded until it is a wonder it ever reached me at all—but it did about a week ago. It certainly gave me great pleasure to hear from you and I deeply appreciate your appreciation of *Strange Interlude*. I am quite sure I remember you well from the Mt. St. Vincent days. Some of the boys who were there come back very clearly to me—and your speaking of the Kipling Jungle Book stories makes it all the more clear—and, of course, I remember the room-sharing. Do you ever think of Sister Martha who used to knuckle us on the bean? And Sister Gonzaga? They often come back to me.

A strange coincidence: When my Mother was buried from a church on East 28th Street in 1922 the priest who conducted the funeral service turned out to be a Mt. St. Vincent boy. I forget his name now, but I remembered him when he spoke of being there with me.

I am damned sorry to hear that "the breaks" have been so bad for you since the war, and I sure hope all that misfortune is behind you now and that the future will bring you everything you desire as a recompense. I can *really* sympathize with your T.B. experience because, as you may know, I spent six months in a sanitorium in 1912–13. I belong to the club, as you might say, although it has never bothered me since.

"Presumption" be darned! I am only too tickled that you think so well of your former roommate's work as to want a book! Roommates usually are inclined to be darned critical; so it's a great compliment! I'm sending you an autographed book under separate cover from here and asking my publisher to send you the rest of the set. I want you to have them directly from me in memory of our boyhood days together.

All good luck to you! Write me again to the above address if you're ever in the mood. I'm engaged on the most ambitious piece of writing I've ever tackled and shall remain over here until it is completed. When I come back to America we must arrange to get together sometime.

Again, all good wishes and thank you for writing!   With friendship,   Eugene O'Neill

---

314 • TO EUGENE O'NEILL, JR.   ALS 2 pp. (Stationery headed: Le Plessis / Saint-Antoine du Rocher / (Indre-et-Loire)) [Yale]

Sept. 2, 1928 [1930]

Dear Eugene: We have been flooded with visitors this July and August and I have kept on the job every morning in spite of their visitations. This explains why I haven't answered your long letter before this. When I had the time I was too tired, but I rarely had the time.

Your ambition to teach seems a fine one to me. My opinion about University professors

---

4. Alexander Woollcott, "Giving O'Neill Till It Hurts," *Vanity Fair*, 29 (February 1928): 48, 114; John Anderson, "Pieces of Eight-Thirty," *New York Post*, December 3, 1927, sec. 3, p. 10.

is exactly your own. I don't think much of the general run—the type—in America. They seem to me to be bloodless men who became professors for the same reason that other individuals of the same character become ministers and priests—and postmen and government clerks. The reason is a fear of life that would avoid all spirited contact and danger and seeks a cloistered, protected existence withdrawn from the life of its time. These men, as you know, turn everything they touch into dry rot and dust. I always grin with fury at what professors have done with the drama in their appreciation and critical tomes. They can manage to suck the blood even out of Shakespeare—because they are congenitally frightened of blood in anything and, as a protection, have made themselves blind to it!

But there's no use going into that. Your letter shows you know these birds and are in no danger of ever becoming one. On the other hand, I have the very highest respect for the real teacher, as I have for the real priest. At its finest, no calling can be more spiritually exalting or give greater inner rewards for a life of devotion and concentration on an ideal. So you can take it I am all for it. All I ask is that you be very sure of yourself first. Remember you could succeed in other walks of life. It will mean a sacrifice of other possibilities for you that it doesn't mean to most of those who elect to profess. You have got plenty of time to fight this out with yourself. Keep an open mind on your future until the last minute. I think you have made a damn fine choice and I hope you stick to it—but be sure!

As for helping you, you can rely on me to do all I can, you know that. How much I can depends on plays, of course. What with the alimony I am gouged out of, the income from my savings will just about keep me eating, if everything else stops. But I think you can count on enough to keep you eating too, if nothing more, even at the worst.

So that's that!

I'm glad you're pleased to have Peaked Hill. That place meant a lot to me—never as a home for a human being among his family, you understand, but as a solitude where I lived with myself it had infinite meaning. It is strange though, that of my best work only *Jones* was written there—and most of *Marco M.*

The trilogy, *Mourning Becomes Electra* comes on apace—and well it might for I have slaved on it as never on anything before. I'm just finishing going over the second draft of the three plays. Another draft, which I shall type myself and revise in that process, will come later on. Christ, what a job! I groan at times. Some days I think it's my finest and other days it seems I ought to hang it up in the suitable place in the toilet. I don't know what it is. Too on top of it to see the whole now. It's become nothing but a mess of fractious and balky details I'm kicking, coaxing, and worrying into the right alignment.

There's nothing much of news. It has been a lousy summer with gray and rain six days out of seven. Never saw such weather. The pool has been too chilly for comfort but a hot spell last week warmed it up.

Carlotta joins in all love to you! Write when you are in the mood! Good luck!   As ever,   Father

P.S. I am sorry about Bledsoe[1] but he was a damn fool to go ahead before he got a contract from Madden. I gave Gruenberg[2] the composer the opera rights to *Jones* six months ago—signed and sealed.

1. Jules Bledsoe (1898–1943), black actor and singer, who originated the role of Joe in *Show Boat* (1927).

2. Louis Gruenberg (1884–1964), Russian-born composer whose operatic version of *The Emperor Jones,* starring Lawrence Tibbett, opened at the Metropolitan Opera in January 1933.

Oct. 3rd 1930

Dear Frank: I was damn glad to get your letter. And encouraged to learn from the enclosed clipping that I'm a Mexican. Because I'm lighting out for a trip through Spain in a few days and maybe my native tongue will return from that hidden past. Which would be a help! But I'm afraid not. Did you note that Carlotta O'Neill of Madrid reminded her interviewer that the O'Neills were descendants of Kings? Ah! That's the true touch of the clan! It takes an O'Neill to be proud of royal blood these days! And to be frank and open about it and not sail under fake proletarian colors! But you wouldn't understand our regal dignity—being only a Shay, who were never much, God help them, but dukes or earls or trifles like that!

Funny coincidence: On the same mail with your letter came one from Cape Town, forwarded through Jonathan Cape. It was from some harp who works for the railroad down there and who claims I am his missing brother, born in Cape Colony. He sends me a photo of our mother to prove it—also a photo of me when I was young and ugly. That his name isn't even O'Neill doesn't bother this bird a bit—because he shows that mine isn't either! I was romantic and sensitive and proud as a youth, he tells me, and I threw up a good job to team up in a music hall act with a guy named O'Neill. Then he died. So, of course, as a good White Rat to a dead pal, I took his name. And my real name is Jim, not Eugene! I was, it appears, a great name snatcher and I copped Eugene after the death of a beloved younger brother, Eugene!

And so on far into the night of a seven page letter in which I have a lurid history until I finally stop writing home altogether years ago. Can you beat it? And he ends up by saying he is sorry to see by the African journals that I am dying of consumption! Perhaps the idea is that I should remember my origin in the will! At any rate, this bird seems in deadly earnest with his theory and I know he is going to think I am a renegade liar and cur when he gets a letter disillusioning him. It's a nutty one, what?—I thought it might amuse you.

I'm sorry to hear that Provincetown has gone bad on the old bunch. Rumor had reached me that things had changed up there so that it was no longer the same place. Well, one could see that on the cards the last two years I was there. But, as you say, there is still Truro. Is the Tiger Piss Inn still flourishing? I haven't had a drink in nearly five years! So help me! Booze was getting sick of me. After a long huddle with my liver and lights I decided to throw in the sponge—and mean it. Life since then has lacked the uproarious but I must admit I feel better.

I'm just finishing up the hardest job I've ever tackled. Expect it will be in final shape by the first of the year. Touraine is a grand place for quiet and work and I've been driving along at this for a year and a half now with damn few interruptions—which is a continuous labor record for me. I hope it's good stuff. Some days it seems so and others it don't. Quién sabe? (That Mexican touch!) At any rate, it's an ambitious stab and has been exciting to shoot at.

Outside of that, I'm well and happy, and that's about all the news. We will be coming back a year from this fall and expect to get a place in Maryland or Virginia—on tidewater. From what I hear that section is the best spot left in America to dig in and settle down. Europe is fine & this Touraine delightful—but not for too long. One gets fed up—and patriotic. I don't see expatriation as any answer to anything.

Give my best to Susan, Mary, Harry & the Guerins when you see them. I will look forward to getting your and Eben's book,[1] Frank! So don't forget to send it. And herewith my loudest cheers for its success!

Thank Dos Passos[2] for that photo. Damn nice of him! I've meant to write him but didn't know if he was in U.S or where. My best to Mike and Phyllis!

And all the breaks in the locker to you!   As ever,   Gene

---

316 • TO HARRY WEINBERGER.   ALS 2 pp. (Le Plessis / [Saint-Antoine du Rocher, / Indre-et-Loire]) [Yale]

Oct. 4th [1930]

Dear Harry: Just some dope on that gift of two original scripts to the Museum of the City of New York. Remember I spoke to you about it? I have just had a letter from Hardinge Scholle, director of the Museum, thanking me and asking that the scripts be turned over to him before the opening of the Museum in December. So I put it up to you to see that this is done. I am sending you under separate cover three small keys I have dug out of a trunk, one of which I hope will be the key to the box in the safe deposit box. Send these three keys back to me as soon as you have tried them out.

The scripts to be given to Scholle are, as I explained to you, those of the short play *Bound East For Cardiff*, my first play to be produced in New York, and that of *Beyond The Horizon*, my first long play to be produced, and my first Pulitzer Prize winner. (*Bound East For Cardiff* was also, if you remember, on the initial bill of the P. Players in N.Y.)

You will find these two scripts both in the small box, both written in pencil on both sides of loose sheet typewriter paper, held in clips. I have clipped on a title page to every script, I think, so you should have no difficulty picking them out.

Now for some additional dope. As I told you, it was my practice then to write out descriptions of scenes, characters, list of scenes, list of characters in a notebook. I *did not* incorporate these into my longhand script when writing the play but only afterwards when typing it. So to the *Beyond The Horizon* script, to make it complete, it will be necessary to add the pages containing this data out of my notebook of that time—a *black* book which you will also find in the small steel box. All you have to do is carefully cut the *Beyond The Horizon* pages from this notebook and clip them on to the play script, explaining to Scholle about it when you give the scripts to him. About *Bound East For Cardiff*, I don't remember whether I followed this procedure when it was written or not. That was way back in 1914. At any rate I know there is no record of it in any notebook.

Now is this all perfectly clear? If not will you write or cable for light? This is a damned important matter. If none of the keys open the box you will have to get a locksmith. Your power of attorney and this letter ought to cover that with the bank (Chatham Phoenix, 5th Ave at 55th St). Please get busy on this at once. Afterwards, if you think it advisable to help the plagiarism suit, you can either request Scholle not to announce the gift until the last minute before the Museum opens, or keep the two scripts in your safe until the end of November or so before officially turning them over for me. I imagine the first idea is quite safe and Scholle will be only too glad to respect any wishes I have about the announcement, provided he can have them for the grand opening.

1. *Here's Audacity! American Legendary Heroes* (New York: Macaulay, 1930), illustrated by Eben Given.
2. John Dos Passos (1896–1970), American novelist and playwright, whom O'Neill probably first met in Greenwich Village and later knew in Provincetown.

I think December will be just about the right amount of time before the suit, don't you?

Outside of the suit, this will be an excellent idea in helping to establish the sound value of the other scripts. And it is not a bad thing for the Museum, either! I am also giving them the old script of my father's of *Monte Cristo* but I've already sent that on. So the New York O'Neills will be well represented in the theatre section.

I'm off to Spain in a few days. Finished going over my second draft—it really amounted to a third draft—yesterday. Will type a final (I hope) fourth when I return—and that will be that. It seems to be rounding into fine shape!   All best!   Gene

---

317 • TO RICHARD MADDEN.   ALS 1 p. (Le Plessis, / Saint-Antoine du Rocher, / Indre-et-Loire, France) [Yale]

[c. October 5, 1930]

Dear Dick: Harry informs me that he has fixed everything up with Rumsey for you to take over the works and I hope it is all satisfactory to you.

Lenormand is not in France now. I tried to see him the last time I was in Paris. I will take up the matter with him later.

It is good to know you hope to get something binding out of Paramount on *Strange Interlude*. I couldn't take that deal seriously as long as I bound myself to sell and they weren't bound to anything. Remember the price must be 75000 absolute net! Tack on your commission to this and then tell them that is my price! But I honestly think we ought to get one hundred thousand. Can't you boost them? Can't you get Metro G. interested in it for Greta Garbo? I should think it would be great stuff for her, making Nina a Swedish foreign language Professor's daughter to cover her accent. Try it out on them on the excuse that I am eager to have her do it after seeing *"Christie"* (which I haven't seen, but no matter!).

Re Jasper Deeter.[1] It is all right for him to do my stuff in his own theatre without royalties provided he's still fighting against difficulties. But 5% on any outside productions!

Your cable re the Paramount deal bawled me up. First you cabled to hedge and not commit myself, then just the opposite. I imagined your second cable was sent for Rumsey's benefit.

Lillian Gish (this is confidential) cabled me *Interlude* was worth much more than the price offered and she was sure they would pay more if forced to. She judges from what she knows of the price paid for other things of like reputation.

I've finished my third draft of the whole opus. Am off to Spain now for a month's vacation. Will type the final edition when I return.

Carlotta joins in all best to Tessa & you!

Good luck!   As ever,   Gene

---

318 • TO THERESA HELBURN.   ALS 3 pp. (Stationery headed: Hotel du Rhin / 4 et 6, Place Vendôme / Paris) [Yale]

Oct. 6, 1930

Dear Terry: I have been meaning to write you about the *Strange Interlude* talky offer for some time. I got your cable but haven't done anything about the matter since then. What I

---

1. Member of the Provincetown Players who appeared in their 1920 premiere productions of O'Neill's *Exorcism* and *The Emperor Jones* and who in 1923 founded the Hedgerow Theatre in a Philadelphia suburb.

was principally trying to do was to pin Paramount down to a sale right now—that is get them legally to agree now that they would buy as soon as the suit is settled in our favor. Otherwise it seemed to me all their talk about buying something at some indefinite future date when the suit—and a possible appeal—will be finished, (if they did not change their minds in the meantime!) wasn't worth our binding ourselves when they bound themselves to nothing! We may get a better offer during that period. Or we may be able to jack them up to a bigger price if our U.S. comes out of the financial dumps. The suit won't come up until next year and I have no doubt the lady will appeal. How much longer an appeal will mean, God only knows. Plenty, I reckon!

I got in Paris today (damn these French pens!) after finishing going over my second draft. I did so much on this job it practically amounts to a third draft. We are off for a month's motoring in Spain now. When I come back I will type a fourth and (I hope) final draft.

(I'm through with the pen! It can't be done!)[1] This fourth draft will probably take two to three months. Then I will send you a copy and you can all see what you think. After that, I will have six or seven months leeway before next fall to lay it aside for a lengthy period and then go over it a fifth time if I feel that is necessary. This looks like a good scheme to me, and I ought to get a first draft of a new one done in that interval too, if the gods are good.

It seems in pretty darn good shape now to me but I am so close to it I can't see the whole for the parts. It's bad enough to try and see one play as a whole when you're close to it, but with a trilogy!—

Tell Phil I have thrown out my scheme for soliloquies—and most of the soliloquies. They were all right enough in themselves but I found they held up the play instead of helping it and I could well do without them. This was especially true in the first play. Soliloquies are more in the picture in the second and third plays—they are called out of the mood there instead of being thrust upon it.

All best to all of you! Hope the new season is treating you well. *Elizabeth & Essex* must have opened up by this time. How is *Green Grows The Lilacs* shaping up? Are you going to do *The Coward*?[2] As ever, Gene

---

319 • TO CARLOTTA MONTEREY O'NEILL. ALS 1 p. (Stationery headed: Le Plessis / Saint-Antoine du Rocher / (Indre-et-Loire)) [Yale]

Christmas 1930

Being no poet I would but string a sorry lyre for you, O Still Shadowy Eyes, if I attempted "that poem." So rather than shame myself before you I will fall back in paraphrase upon those lines which meant so much of you in the beginning and will always to the end of life mean to me a prophecy of beauty and charm and grace and passion so wonderfully fulfilled in our marriage and assure you that "your last kiss" will always "warm the air" and that never for me "will your eyes go out!"

"With all of me"—and an alligator bag! Your Gene

---

1. The remainder of this letter is written in pencil.
2. Theatre Guild productions of *Elizabeth the Queen* by Maxwell Anderson, which opened on November 3, 1930; *Green Grow The Lilacs* by Lynn Riggs (1899–1954), which opened on January 26, 1931; and *The Coward* by French playwright Henri-René Lenormand, which opened on July 15, 1935, at the Westport (Connecticut) Country Playhouse.

320 • TO CARLOTTA MONTEREY O'NEILL.   ALS 1 p. ([Hotel du Rhin / Paris])
[Yale]

Sunday night
[January 22?, 1931]

Dearest Own Wife: I am writing this soon after my return to the hotel and will send it out with the flowers tomorrow.

It seems so lonely in our apartment now! But you can imagine—and I am not going to burden you with any depressing news about how desolate I feel. Bad for you! So picture me as being as philosophical about it as can be and telling myself your absence will turn out to be a wonderful thing for you, will make you fat and well again—and therefore means our happiness! I have felt so sad lately seeing you look so worn out and unhappy—felt it was my fault, that I had failed you somehow. It will certainly buck me up tremendously when you come out of the hospital your old self again. So keep the old pecker up and carry on! Time does pass, you know, and even this three weeks, which seems like a million years to me now, will get itself past! Keep your mind on your job! Don't worry about me! I'm as comfortable here as I could be any place without you—which isn't saying much, of course!—and I'll keep my spirit cheery by the constant thought that you are getting well and that's my way to help you! So you get well, hear me! I'm very glad I have this work to do. It's luck really. Otherwise I *would* be lost!

I anticipate a dull evening with the composer gent![1]

God bless you! Kisses—and all my love!   Your   Gene

---

321 • TO SAXE COMMINS.   TLS 2 pp. (Hotel du Rhin / Paris, France) [Private]

January 24th 1931

Dear Saxe: I was tickled to death to learn by your letter of the 4th that you have landed with Liveright. Your work there ought to be very congenial, as I know you will like all the bunch there. I know how you must have felt at the other place.[1] One of those lads is a crook—as you know I have reason to know!—and I judge the other by the company he keeps. It was fine of Manuel[2] to use his influence with Liveright's in your behalf. Manuel, as I have always said since I first met him, is one rare person. His success with *Coronet* has pleased me more than anything I know of in a very long time.

Yes, there is something that you can do for me at Liveright's—and thus save a lazy man a letter. Alexander King has written to me—a very hectic sort of note—, in which he tells me he is dying of cancer of the kidneys, but he hopes to live long enough to finish the illustrations for *Lazarus Laughed*.[3] Well, somehow I suppose I ought to be awfully sorry, but something in the tone of the letter makes me believe that Alex has heard how down I am on his last illustrations for *"Anna Christie"* and that he is giving me a little sob story to work on my sympathies. People with cancer usually do not go writing letters about it to men they hardly know. Or if they do, they shouldn't.

---

1. Louis Gruenberg, who visited O'Neill to submit his *Emperor Jones* libretto to the playwright.

1. Commins's first job in publishing was with Covici-Friede.
2. Manuel Komroff, an editor at Liveright's, left to concentrate on his own writing after his novel *Coronet* (1930) became a best-seller.
3. King provided illustrations for limited editions of *The Emperor Jones* (1928), *The Hairy Ape* (1929), *"Anna Christie"* (1930), and died of a heart attack, at the age of sixty-six, in 1965.

At any rate, I want you to tell Pell I do not want King doing any more illustrations—and I especially don't want him doing *Lazarus Laughed*.

The O'Neill family has been having a run of hard luck. Carlotta is in the American hospital resting up after a bad attack of grippe and I have had it too, and I am here at the hotel getting most of my play typed and trying to rewrite a couple of acts that need it. I am anxious to get the damn thing off my chest now and hope within another month or so this will be done.

Much love from us both to you and Dorothy and Frances.[4] Good luck in the new job.   As ever,   Gene

---

322 • TO SHANE AND OONA O'NEILL.   TLS 1 p. ([Hotel du Rhin] / Paris, France) [Virginia]

Feb. 4th 1931

Dear Shane and Oona: I know I should have written you long ago to thank you for the two books you sent me for Christmas. I liked them very much and they came in very handy because I have been sick in bed with the grippe and have had nothing to do but read. They are very interesting books and just what I would have picked out myself if I had wanted to buy a nice Christmas present for myself.

I was so glad to know that your illness, Shane, was not so bad that you had to have an operation. You will have to look out for your old appendix and see that it does not kick up any more. I hope that neither you nor Oona have had the grippe. It seems to be all over the world now and I suppose a lot of people in Bermuda are sick with it too.

I suppose by this time you must have a lot of more fish in the pond than since you wrote me.

Do you like the boarding school in Bermuda? Do you think it is a good one to prepare you for going to college? I know it is an early date to be thinking of this, but still you cannot start soon enough in the right direction. I think you ought to go to a good prep school in the States when you get a little older.

I am glad you have a nice bicycle. I have one over here too, but it has been raining so much that I hardly ever get a chance to use it. The weather over here has been terrible.

Thank you ever so much for the two snapshots you sent me. You are certainly growing big and so is Oona. I shall put the pictures in a frame and keep them in my study so that I will always know how you look now and not the way I remember you.

All love to you both. I'll write to you again before long.   As ever,   Daddy

---

323 • TO JOSEPH MCCARTHY.   TLS 2 pp. (Stationery headed: Le Plessis / Saint-Antoine du Rocher / (Indre-et-Loire)) [Dartmouth]

February 18th 1931

Dear Mr. McCarthy: I meant to answer your first letter long before this—and now comes your second to remind me what a procrastinator I am. But I have been laid up with the grippe and also have been working like the devil putting the finishing touches on my new work. That is, I hope they are the finishing touches! One can never be sure. A month from now I may decide to rewrite the whole damn thing.

There is something in your first letter which surprises me very much. That is, when you

4. Frances Commins, Saxe and Dorothy Commins's daughter.

tell me you went from Mt. St. Vincent to De La Salle. For, as a matter of fact, so did I. How is it we didn't run into each other at De La Salle? I have forgotten what year I entered there but I was there for two terms—the first year as a day scholar and the second as a boarder. It is the De La Salle Institute on 59th Street that you mean, isn't it? We seem to be alumni of not one but two schools.

I was also greatly interested to know that you had been a reporter on the New Orleans *Picayune*. You have certainly knocked around a lot, as you say.

I was very pleased and flattered to hear that you had read all my plays again while you were sick—although they are pretty gloomy reading for one with a cold! But you are right in thinking that life at different times has given me "the works" and that this comes out in my work.

People who have not been through much themselves never really get what underlies my plays and never really understand them. I am damn glad that you do.

I have not read the book *Our Changing Human Nature*[1] which you refer to. Is it really good? If so I'll have to get it.

If you saw my brother in Chicago years ago in the condensed version of *Monte Cristo*, then you just missed seeing the worst actor that has ever been on the American stage—which was myself. Because I joined the company in New Orleans a week or so later. That is, I didn't join—I was sandbagged into becoming an actor. I was in New Orleans broke on the tail end of a bust which terminated in that city. My father happened to play there just as things were becoming desperate. I had seaman's papers but no ships seemed to be taking on anyone—at least not ships bound for New York where I wanted to return. I had not seen my father in about a year. I braced him for the fare north but he could not see it. He offered me a job in his company. It was a case of act or walk home, so I acted for the rest of the tour over the Orpheum circuit. I am proud to say that I preserved my honor by never drawing a sober breath until the tour had terminated. My brother and I had one grand time of it and I look back on it as one of the merriest periods of my life.

No, my brother is not alive. He died in 1923. Booze got him in the end. It was a shame. He and I were terribly close to each other, but after my mother's death in 1922 he gave up all hold on life and simply wanted to die as soon as possible. He had never found his place. He had never belonged. I hope like my "Hairy Ape" he does now.

My family were wiped out within three years. My father had died in 1920. There were only the four of us.

Thank you very much for your letter about *Strange Interlude* in London. It was received there much more favorably than I had expected. The English are usually very antagonistic to anything new in the theatre or anything at all that makes them think or feel. Whether it will run or not I do not know. I am inclined to doubt it.

I am leaving in a few days for the Canary Islands to get a little sun and warmth. The weather here has been incredible—raining every day since God knows when. Both my wife and I have had the grippe and are still suffering from the after-effects. And I am very tired and need a rest.

All good wishes to you. Your letters are a great pleasure to me, so write whenever the mood is on you.

With friendship,   As ever,   Eugene O'Neill

---

1. Book on psychology (1929) by Samuel D. Schmalhausen.

324 • TO GEORGE JEAN NATHAN.　　ALS 2 pp. (Hotel du Rhin / [Paris, France])
[Cornell]

April 7th 1931

Dear George:　　This is to be about the trilogy which I am sending you by this same mail. I won't mention that damned suit except to tell you how deeply grateful I am for what you did as a witness![1] It must have been a disagreeable ordeal for you and I appreciate accordingly! As for the "vain, conceited fellow," that was a damned clever bit. It was fortunate for me circumstances kept my stuff to a deposition. I am the world's worst actor in a courtroom scene as has been proven on the two occasions when I figured as a witness, to the detriment of my side, and was almost fined for contempt. I cannot retain my goat under a snooty lawyer's fire but lose my nerves and temper completely—which is duck soup for the enemy! The deposition let me keep the proper dignified poise. Why the hell they take testimony in these cases is beyond me. It is simply a case of two books and their sources, etc.

Your opinion of the trilogy will be anxiously awaited. It still needs the final trimming and toning down it will get before production or publication. Please allow for this in the reading. As you will see, no departures in technique are involved. *Interlude* soliloquies and asides only got in the way in this play of intense passions and little cerebration. The mask idea has also gone by the board. It simply refused to justify itself. It confused and obscured instead of intensifying. All that is left of it is the masklike quality of the Mannon faces in repose, an effect that can be gained by acting and make-up. The dialogue is colloquial of today. The house, the period costumes, the Civil War surface stuff, these are the masks for what is really a modern psychological drama which has no true connection with that period at all.

It has been one hell of a job! Let's hope the result in some measure justifies the labor I've put in. To get enough of Clytemnestra in Christine, of Electra in Lavinia, of Orestes in Orin, etc. and yet keep them American primarily; to conjure a Greek fate out of the Mannons themselves (without calling in the aid of even a Puritan Old Testament God) that would convince a modern audience without religion or moral ethics; to prevent the surface melodrama of the plot from overwhelming the real drama; to contrive murders that escape cops and courtroom scenes; and finally to keep myself out of it and shun the many opportunities for effusions of personal writing anent life and fate—all this has made the going tough and the way long!

And even now it's done I don't know quite what I've got. All I do know is that after reading it all through, in spite of my familiarity with every page it leaves me moved and disturbed spiritually, and I have a feeling of there being real size in it, quite apart from its length; a sense of having had a valid dramatic experience with intense tortured passions beyond the ambition or scope of other modern plays. As for the separate parts, each play, each act, some seem better than I hoped, some not so good. I don't know much about them anymore, they fade out into the whole.

And that's that. Let's hear your judgment.

A word about the chanty "Shenandoah" that runs like a theme song through the plays.

---

1. Nathan testified on March 16 at the end of the week-long plagiarism trial, characterizing his friend O'Neill as "a very stubborn fellow; very vain" who "seldom takes any suggestion concerning his plays"; a month later, the judge dismissed Miss Lewys's suit as "wholly preposterous" and ordered her to pay O'Neill $7,500, the Guild $5,000, and Liveright $5,000. As she had no money, none was collected.

You will have to hear it to understand the effect. It's the most haunting of all the old chanties—a yearning melancholy tune with a beautiful sad sea rhythm to it—a longing for escape.

I saw the trilogy announcement that leaked out. But that's all right. What I want to keep dark is the title of the whole thing—those of the separate plays don't matter, they reveal nothing. I want, if possible, to conceal the Greek plot foundation until the plays are given. I don't want people to come with Agamemnon & Co. in their heads expecting this or that to happen in a certain way. It would confuse and put a wrong emphasis on my use of the plot. Let the boys deduce the secret from the first play. That seems to me good showmanship. The accent will then be in the proper place. What are your ideas about this?

But I'm talking as if production were certain. I don't feel it is. What with the censorship howl and the difficulties of production, I have my doubts.

Carlotta has, I know, written Lillian all our news so I won't repeat. Our late experience on a small steamer in a hellish storm has made us veto the long California voyage I told you we'd decided on. We will come via N.Y. and to Cal. by rail. I hope we will hit N.Y. before you leave and get together there. I'll let you know definitely when we're coming as soon as we know. It depends on the time necessary to close up Plessis. We will leave most of our stuff here and will come back in the fall for a while. This, of course, is under the old hat. I don't want my former frau to know I'm in N.Y. until I've come and gone. I think I can frame it to get in without being noticed.

All affectionate best from us to you both!   As ever,   Gene

P.S. I am writing Saxe Commins, a very old and close friend of mine who is now working for Liveright, to phone you and call to get the script from you when you are *quite through* with it. I want him to read it and he will know who to show it to at Liveright's who can be trusted to keep mum. I have to work each script overtime because I've only three available for duty and two have to go to the Guild committee to insure quick action there.

And Saxe is a great worshiper of yours and I want you to meet him. He is a fine simple rare person. Carlotta likes him as much as I do—and that's a lot—and we know you'll like him.

---

325 • TO AGNES BRENNAN.   ALS 3 pp. (Stationery headed: Hotel du Rhin / 4 et 6, Place Vendôme / Paris) [Yale]

April 14th 1931

Dear Agnes: Your letter was certainly a most welcome surprise! I have thought of you and all the family very often in the years that have passed since we have seen each other, and wondered how you all were and what you were all doing. I am a rotten bad correspondent and that's my only excuse—a poor one, I'm afraid!—for your not having heard from me.

Your letter was a long time reaching me. For one thing, I have been away on a trip to the Canary Islands. And then the address you gave was a bit indefinite and the letter was sent to the French Authors' Society and they had to dig up my country address through my translator. From there it was reforwarded back to Paris where I am staying for a while.

As for the photograph, I will be only too delighted. It pleases me immensely to think you should want it. As soon as we are back in the country I will dig one up. If I find there isn't one there then I *promise* you the first time a new lot is printed you shall have one. You are in no special hurry for it, I know. And to make up for Claire's burglary (!) I am sending you an inscribed copy of *Strange Interlude*.

When you next see or write to your Mother be sure and give her my love and congratulations on her 91st birthday. I always remember with deep gratitude how kind she used to be to me when I was a boy and how I used to look forward to her visits at Pequot Avenue. It is a blessing for you that you have been able to keep her with you so long. How I wish my Mother could have lived! It has been lonely with my Father, Mother and Jamie all gone.

Your story about the man saying my Mother was a negress is about the limit! And believe me, since my name began to figure in newspapers as a dramatist, I've heard and read some strange lies about myself. For example, I still hear that I'm drunk all the time although everyone who knows me well knows I haven't even had a glass of beer in over five years! But that's all the penalty for having plays done. My bride has had to get pretty tough to stand it. I've been accused of everything but arson and someone will think of that soon!

Yes, I don't doubt Lillie would have thrown that fool overboard—and more power to her arm! The trouble is that by the time these lies get back to me they never can be traced to the person who started them. If they could, I would surely see to it he got bumped on the head with some very heavy object! But then—meaning no offense to your sex!—I think it is usually a female who starts the ball rolling. It is the ladies who bring most of the plagiarism suits against plays, I know. Witness that one who accused me of stealing *Strange Interlude* recently! She knew very well I had never seen or heard of her privately printed smut of a book and that she had no case, but she also knew there was a mess of publicity in it for her and her lawyers which would cost her nothing. So why not sue? The law in America doesn't protect playwrights against these racketeers. In any country in Europe such a suit against an author of standing would be impossible. It will cost me ten to fifteen thousand dollars legal expenses and I have no come-back whatever! I lose my money, win or lose, and she gets what she was after—her picture on the front page of all the papers! It's a queer world, and being an author isn't without its tribulations!

But I don't want to bore you with all my woes! After all, being a playwright has its good points, too. I've just finished a new play—or rather, a trilogy of them—that I've been working on the past few years. One sticks to it!

Give my love to Lillie and all the family. Tell Charlie he has all my good wishes for married bliss and, in spite of having been divorced twice, I can still recommend marriage in the highest terms! Hasn't Claire been married yet? If not, it must be because she has too many beaux to choose from! She was a beautiful girl the last time I saw her.

We are coming back to America before very long now—for a lengthy visit, at any rate. Our lease over here has still a year to run or we'd come back for good. We are both getting very homesick. Europe is fine but I don't see how any American can ever settle over here for good.

I'll look forward to seeing you and Lillie and everyone the first time I'm in New York for any period of time. It will be such a pleasure to see you all again—like old New London times!

How are all the Sheridans? When you see or write them please give them my love. I wanted to write Phil many times—but, as I say, I'm the world's worst correspondent.

Again, love and all good wishes!   Eugene

P.S. I'll be only too glad to autograph all my books you have—when I come to New York.

326 • TO THERESA HELBURN.   WIRE 1 p. (Paris) [Yale]

APR. 28, 1931

HAVE THOUGHT OF NAZIMOVA[1] WOULD BE GRAND IN SPITE OF ACCENT IF CAN BE DIRECTED TO ACT AS SHE DID FIRST IBSEN PRODUCTIONS AND CUT OUT HAM MANNERISMS ACQUIRED LATER STOP YOU KNOW BEST IF THIS IS POSSIBLE SO PROCEED ACCORDINGLY   GENE

1. Alla Nazimova (1879–1945), Russian actress who played Christine Mannon when *Mourning Becomes Electra* was produced by the Theatre Guild at the Guild Theatre on October 26, 1931.

PART SIX

LAUREATE

1931–1936

Perhaps I have sometimes been off the track, possibly
my use of masks and asides is artifice and bombast. . . .
But I fully believe that my long absorption in the
dualism of man's mortal soul has been worthwhile.
—*To John Mason Brown, November 18, 1934*

The O'Neills returned to New York on May 17, 1931, to prepare for the premiere of *Mourning Becomes Electra*. They lived in Northport, Long Island, while Carlotta readied an apartment at 1095 Park Avenue. The New York residence would not prove permanent, for once the play had its triumphant opening, they went south to Sea Island, Georgia, where they built a large house, named with a portmanteau coinage of their first names, "Casa Genotta."

In Sea Island, with Carlotta as his mainstay, O'Neill entered into the stable condition he had long sought—writing arduously and by way of relaxation swimming and fishing off his beach and occasionally visiting with friends. He accepted the position of associate editor on George Jean Nathan's magazine, *The American Spectator*, contributing three short essays titled *Memoranda on Masks*. He oversaw translations of his plays in several languages. When Liveright, his publisher, went bankrupt he considered the field carefully before signing with Bennett Cerf at the new Random House. As a condition of the agreement, he required that Cerf hire Saxe Commins as an editor—a fair return for Commins's efforts to extract O'Neill's rights and back royalties from the Liveright firm before it entered bankruptcy.[1]

He made new friends, notably Sophus Keith Winther, a novelist and professor of English at the University of Washington, whose critical study on O'Neill pleased its subject.[2] Of Danish descent—a fact that the Danish-American Carlotta approved—Winther was outspoken, belligerent, and amusingly irreverent about all sacred cows. Dudley Nichols, a former drama reviewer, Brooks Atkinson, the drama critic for the *New York Times*, Sean O'Casey, and Robert Sisk, the public relations man for the Theatre Guild, became special close friends. O'Neill felt no severe pinch at the hardships of the depression. His income, combined with that from a trust fund of Carlotta's, gave them ample money to build Casa Genotta and to support several persons. In addition to his alimony payments and the costs of schools for Shane, Oona, and Eugene, Jr., he made occasional small loans to Kenneth Macgowan and Saxe Commins and on a regular basis partly supported two friends from his Village days, Terry Carlin and Bill Clark, called Clarkie.

Taken as a whole the external world was as he wanted it, quiet and centered on his

---

1. Commins became editor-in-chief at Random House and an important figure in American publishing.
2. Sophus Keith Winther, *Eugene O'Neill: A Critical Study* (New York: Random House, 1934).

writing. Trouble, however, lay in the writing. Once established in Georgia, he began work on a new and difficult play. *Days Without End*, as it was finally titled, was the second play O'Neill had planned when he wrote *Dynamo*. The trilogy was given the working title of "Myths for the God-Forsaken," and its central exploration was the dilemma of modern man in a world where God was dead. Like *Dynamo*, the play refused to gel. In fact it gave him more trouble than any play he had written. He would fight it through seven drafts before it was complete, and it would remain a curiously undramatized study of a man's struggle to cast out the devil within and return to his Catholic faith. The use of two actors to play the separate halves of the protagonist was O'Neill's last device in the manner of his earlier experimental works.

Underlying the play's action were crucial autobiographical elements. O'Neill was a lapsed Catholic and in his inebriate days he often recited Francis Thompson's poem about a fugitive from God, "The Hound of Heaven." In him, something was changing. If the outer, experimental techniques were "artifice and bombast," perhaps the theological considerations concerning the "dualism of man's soul" were also outworn and forced as thematic material. In a letter to Kenneth Macgowan, written on his birthday, October 16, 1933, he speaks of a "sea change" having come over him and of the need to liberate himself from an "exhausted formula." He was speaking there of *Days Without End*, but that play did not provide the new beginning and the change of style he was seeking. Yet the considerations of lost faith refound in *Days Without End* turned his mind back to his personal past. At the same time the condition of his country, which during the depression was manifestly in danger of dying of its earlier greed, caused him to think back on its history and to remember what it had been in better days, even within the forty-five-year span of his own lifetime.

O'Neill's first reaction to the pressure of the religious play's problems was almost involuntary. He awoke one day with the outlines of an autobiographical comedy in his mind. He wrote *Ah, Wilderness!* rapidly and with great ease, and he found that once completed it required little revision. Its production in 1933 with song-and-dance man George M. Cohan as the father of a contented Connecticut household was one of O'Neill's brightest successes. It was also his first step toward openly autobiographical dramas.

The play's success did not relieve all the pressures building in him. The intensive work on *Days Without End*, the heat of the Georgia summer, and perhaps the painful return to aspects of his past in both plays brought him low in health. Frequently in the Georgia years, the entries in his work diary show that his health was turning on him: "Bad health mental and physical no work," or "Rest Cure no work."[3] Whether he wrote or not, however, his imagination was unfaltering. He conceived a series of plays on American historical themes, recounting the history of two families from pre-Revolutionary War times to the 1930s. The series, originally planned as a trilogy, grew rapidly from its inception to a mammoth eleven-play cycle. Yet the diary continued to note "depressed . . . very depressed," as he called the roll of the medicines he took to relieve various ailments. There seemed no relief. By September 1936, Casa Genotta was put up for sale. The diary entry for October 4 reads "will be glad to leave this place—hope we can sell it soon—climate no good for work half of year—and feel am jinxed here . . . still running temp." The O'Neills left the next day for New York City where he was to receive medical attention.

Another kind of attention was soon to invade his privacy and turn the world's eyes on him. At the invitation of Sophus Winther, the couple left New York City for Seattle on October 30. There on November 12, the world learned that he had won the Nobel Prize for

3. Eugene O'Neill, *Work Diary*, ed. Donald Gallup, 2 vols. (New Haven: Yale University Library, 1981), vol. 2, pp. 185, 189.

literature. He tried as best he could to stand out of the spotlight of his newest fame and refused to go to Stockholm for the award, writing instead a letter of acceptance that paid honor to his debt to Strindberg. On December 14, in company with Carlotta and her daughter, Cynthia, he motored south to San Francisco where the toll was finally collected. The work diary on December 23 records "feel very sick, weak & woozy . . . something all wrong, I'm afraid—getting to be god damned invalid!—it's revolting!" The day after Christmas he entered Merritt Hospital in Oakland, and on December 29 appendicitis with severe complications ushered in a long series of illnesses from which he never entirely recovered.

June 6th 1931

Dear Clark: Your letter, forwarded to California and then back here, has just reached
me. You see we had only planned to stay in New York a few days before going on to Frisco to
visit my wife's mother, so we had all French mail sent out there. Now all that plan has been
changed and here we still are and will be until next Wednesday. I've been wondering why I
hadn't heard from you via the Guild, and I suppose you've wondered why the hell I hadn't
had the decency to acknowledge your letter!

I am immensely pleased by your reaction to the trilogy. As for the exceptions you take I
know the one about the dialogue lacking point and being repetitious in spots is well taken.
But it should have been explained to you when you got the script that I am going over it
again this summer to correct just such defects. The present edition is not the final one for
production or publication.

I don't agree with your Freudian objection. Taken from my author's angle, I find fault
with critics on exactly the same point—that they read too damn much Freud into stuff that
could very well have been written exactly as is before psycho-analysis was ever heard of.
Imagine the Freudian bias that would be read into Stendhal, Balzac, Strindberg, Dostoievsky, etc. if they were writing today! After all, every human complication of love and
hate in my trilogy is as old as literature and the interpretations I suggest are such as might
have occurred to any author in any time with a deep curiosity about the underlying motives
that actuate human interrelationships in the family. In short, I think I know enough about
men and women to have written *Mourning Becomes Electra* almost exactly as it is if I had never
heard of Freud or Jung or the others. Authors were psychologists, you know, and profound
ones, before psychology was invented. And I am no deep student of psycho-analysis. As far
as I remember, of all the books written by Freud, Jung, etc., I have read only four, and Jung is
the only one of the lot who interests me. Some of his suggestions I find extraordinarily
illuminating in the light of my own experience with hidden human motives. But as far as
influence on my work goes he has had none compared to what psychological writers of the
past like Dostoievsky, etc. have had.

But here I am starting an argument that is too involved for my laziness at letter writing
to deal with!

What I want to write about is this: Let's get together and have a talk. Can you have
lunch with me here at one on Tuesday? Or Monday? Whichever is most convenient for you.
Wire me which—or else give me a ring around ten a.m. Monday. We are going out of town
on Wednesday—so try and make it either Monday or Tuesday.

Until then! All best! As ever,   Eugene O'Neill

P.S. Keep the above address confidential.

I thought I had your home address—will have to send this care French[1]—hope it gets to
you in time.

1. Clark was literary editor of Samuel French publications from 1918 to 1936.

328 • TO RICHARD MADDEN.   ALS 2 pp. (Northport, L.I.) [Yale]

June 15, 1931

Dear Dick: Your letter reached me this a.m. Regarding a date with Harris,[1] we are so busy getting put here that it is improbable I will be able to get to town before next week. In the meantime, I suggest you get in touch with him again and give him my reaction to his proposition as you have outlined it. This will help clear the ground before I see him.

Re a theatre to be called O'Neill: I am absolutely opposed to this at any time under any conditions! None of that stuff for mine! This is final!

Re his selection of plays to be revived: I think the choice of *Jones* is a mistake. *Jones* has been revived and revived since its original production. I don't think there would be any interest in another revival. I suggest *The Great God Brown* instead, by way of lending more variety to the selection and showing various aspects of my work. Remind Harris that *Brown* had a longer run in New York than *Jones* and attracted a larger public. Then there is *All God's Chillun Got Wings* to be considered. I don't think there would be the same outcry of race prejudice against that play now. It is a much finer play than it was ever given credit for being, as the high European opinion of it proves.

I quite agree that new talent for all my plays in any revival is imperative! Unless they are done with new blood and a fresh producing angle I don't think they would stand a chance. I don't get what Harris means by securing directors who have been identified with my productions. Wouldn't he direct them all himself? If not, frankly I am not interested in the idea at all. It is his direction only that makes the plan appeal to me—the hope that a fine director with real vision could bring out new values in the plays, give them a new vivid life in the theatre. None of them, as you know, was ever done up to its highest possibilities. Downtown we were always working under all sorts of handicaps which would not affect Harris. And *"Anna C."* under Hopkins became too much a vehicle for Lord to be true to my intent.

The choice of Bobby Jones is grand! I like to work with him better than with any man in our theatre. His direction of *Desire & Brown* downtown was fine stuff, —when you consider the handicaps he worked under no one could have done better.

But, everything else being O.K., there is one very important point to be considered— date of opening. I would not want any revival to precede the opening of the trilogy at the end of October (as planned now). That, in my decided estimation, would be bad for the trilogy and bad for the revival. So you better talk with Harris about this right away.

As for terms, that consideration can be taken care of later. We can easily agree on that, I think.

Write me when you have seen Harris and we can arrange a date for next week—if he finds what I have said herewith meets with his approval.

Also, as this repertoire matter does not seem to be confidential, I suggest you see Munsell[2] at the Guild and get—that is, get him to get, their reaction to it in relation to the trilogy.

All best! Our telephone no. here is 440 Northport.   As ever,   Gene

1. Jed Harris (1900–1979), Broadway producer and director, who was proposing an O'Neill repertory theatre.
2. Warren Munsell, business manager of the Theatre Guild.

329 • TO MAURICE WERTHEIM.   ALS 3 pp. (Northport, Long Island) [Private]

June 15th 1931

Dear Maurice: I am writing you to take up again the question of how best to open the trilogy. I have been giving the matter the devil of a lot of thought lately, and talked it out thoroughly with Bob Sisk, and the more I think the more decided my opinion becomes, looking at it from all angles, that my original idea of an opening week in which the whole work would be unveiled, two nights to each play, is the absolutely right scheme and the Guild's notion of starting week by week is all wrong.

Let's get down to cases: What do you gain by your scheme? One extra Sunday write-up, possibly; no more for you would be bound to get two by my plan since the first Sunday could cover only the first and second play and the following Sunday would have to cover the whole thing. You also gain an easier method of getting the trilogy on—and perhaps a week or two less of paid rehearsals. But my point here is that this *is* a difficult thing to produce and the *more difficultly* you produce it (as per *Interlude*) the greater the réclame and sensation will be—a big asset to start with! As for paid rehearsals, this drama is very obviously not one the Guild can afford to economize on in any way. It would not pay to do so, in the long run.

Here's what I think you lose: In a word, the driving impact of a trilogy concentrated in one week—a bigger *Interlude* in that sense! Week by week, it becomes an ordinary, unstartling episode—just three plays produced on three Mondays! You also lose—a very grave fault!—all the benefit of my careful construction of suspense from play to play. The week by week opening really ruins my trilogy, you know—for it *is* a trilogy and not three separate plays, and I want it seen and criticized as such. Once the whole thing is given in a week, then a week by week plan becomes justifiable. Then you will have the benefit of the smashing impact of that first week, of the whole work, to compel an interest in the public which can sustain suspense over weekly intervals. Do you get my point? I'm convinced when you have you and the rest of the Committee will agree.

As for the difficulty of getting an audience in for three nights that first week, I can't see it. After all, you give them a choice of two nights to see each play. I think you will find that first week will become "the thing to do," an occasion your subscribers will want to be in on. If they know far enough in advance, among the subscribers there ought to be more than enough who would make their dates for that week accordingly. As for the difficulty in rehearsing so that the trilogy can be given this way, I agree it is difficult. But, given proper time, it isn't any more impossible than *Interlude* was. And, in this case, we have everything to gain by doing the seemingly impossible and may well lose out by doing what is comparatively a commonplace stunt, done before with Shaw's *Methuselah*[1] with no great result.

It is well for the Guild not to lose sight of the greatest element in starting *Interlude* on the right road—doing what looked to be impossible!—daring and theatre guts!—originality with original material!

Think this all over and pass on this letter or a copy to the others. Remember especially that you owe me, in fairness to this work I have slaved at so long, that it should be given as near to three consecutive nights as possible—at least once in the beginning. It was written that way, and even my scheme for that preliminary week of two nights to a play is really a compromise. To follow with week by week is a tremendous compromise made to U.S. theatre conditions. But to cut out my first trilogy week altogether is really too big a compromise to ask of me!

---

1. The Theatre Guild had produced George Bernard Shaw's five-play philosophical treatise, *Back to Methuselah*, in 1922.

Again I pound my big point: The greatest chance of success the trilogy has is to hit New York a concentrated smash that will preserve the unity of the work as a whole, concentrate interest on the unusual sustained strength of the work as a whole, and not allow interest and suspense and enthusiasm to diffuse and peter out over a two and half weeks period with other plays opening all over the place in the intervals. In one week you can make the lasting impression that will carry on and count. In one week you can send two audiences full of press agents out to talk about the whole work so that future weekly audiences will have the expectation of the whole in their minds.

And that's that. I feel strongly about this. I *know*, not only from the artistic but also from the practical N.Y. theatre standpoint, that I am soundly right!

We are settled comfortably here in a small house easy to run, plenty of ground and privacy, a nice clean private beach to bake on. I am beginning to relax and rest already, after four days of it, and so is Carlotta. We were lucky to find it—just the place we needed. We both hope you and your wife will be able to get over and pay us a visit later on. We were too fagged out, as you undoubtedly realized, to take advantage of your invitation that time in New York.

Carlotta joins in all best!   As ever,   Gene

P.S. I Phone no. here is 440 Northport—if ever necessary.

P.S. II Shouldn't we hear from Phil soon? Gish will be back in N.Y. middle of July and we can then all of us see her possibilities.[2]

P.S. III Jed Harris is dickering with me about starting an O'Neill repertory season of 20 weeks this coming year. Seems serious about it. Of course, I'd try and hold that off until after the trilogy opened. Haven't seen Harris yet—all by letter & via Madden so far. I confide this to you so you won't think there is anything secret about it if you hear it from other sources.

---

330 • TO BROOKS ATKINSON.[1]   ALS 4 pp. (Northport, L.I.) [Lincoln Center]

Friday eve. / [June 19, 1931]

Dear Mr. Atkinson: Much gratitude for your letter and the script which reached me this noon. I deeply appreciate your writing me in such detail about your reaction to the trilogy and have read your criticisms of the separate plays with the greatest interest. Not that those were of the most importance to me. What I was after—and what pleased me most—was your favorable reaction to the whole work. For I flatter myself it *has* real "stature"—much more so than anything else I have ever done—and I am glad you share that opinion. It is, obviously, the most difficult and ambitious thing I have attempted, and it is a great satisfaction, after the two years of almost constant wearing labor devoted to it, to know that everyone of many different types of critical minds who have read it so far have felt the tragic force of the whole, although differing widely as to which play or part of a play they liked most or least.

Personally, I can't string along with your estimate. I like the last play the best. I feel it is the most my own, for one thing. The Electra figure in the Greek legend and plays fades out into a vague and undramatic future. She stops, as if after the revenge on her mother all was well and that was all of that. The Furies take after Orestes but she is left alone. I never could

2. O'Neill and the Guild considered Lillian Gish for the role of Lavinia Mannon in *Mourning Becomes Electra*, but, after auditioning her, decided against the casting.

1. Atkinson (1894–1984), theater critic of the *New York Times*, with whom O'Neill first became acquainted in September 1927 through Manuel Komroff.

swallow that. It seemed to me that by having her disappear in a nice conventionally content future (married to Pylades, according to one version of the legend!) the Greeks were dodging the implication of their own belief in the chain of fate. In our modern psychological chain of fate certainly we can't let her exit like that! She is so inevitably worthy of a better tragic fate! And I flatter myself I have given my Yankee Electra an end tragically worthy of herself! The end, to me, is the finest and most inevitable thing of the trilogy. She rises to a height there and justifies my faith in her! She is broken and not broken! By her way of yielding to her Mannon fate she overcomes it. She *is* tragic!

Another reason I like the last play best is that to me it contains the deepest inner drama—if you get me, for I'm putting it badly! It drags its drama out of fresh depths, and in a manner less externalized than in the other plays. It works more inwardly. The "anatomizing of Orin's soul" you object to is certainly not out of the "beaten path" of *my intent* in this drama. It is part and parcel of it! And his "intellectualization" in Act Three is the essential process by which he, being Orin, *must* arrive at his fate and view it so he can face it.

Your objection to the first play that it is less compact than the second is true enough. But consider the burden necessarily put upon that first play in getting the fate for the whole trilogy dug out of the past, the Mannon dead, and alive and psychologically motivated so as to be inevitable in the living characters! It is too complicated to be done truthfully by any dramatic short cut. I think, moreover, that all this is redeemed in compactness by the last two acts, Mannon's homecoming act and his death act, which are for me two of the most deeply moving in the whole work.

As for Aristotle's "purging," I think it is about time we purged his purging out of modern criticism, candidly speaking! What modern audience was ever purged by pity and terror by witnessing a Greek tragedy or what modern mind by reading one? It can't be done! We are too far away, we are in a world of different values! As Spengler[2] points out, their art had an entirely different life-impulse and life-belief than ours. We can admire while we pretend to understand—but our understanding is always a pretense! And Greek criticism is as remote from us as the art it criticizes. What we need is a definition of Modern and not Classical Tragedy by which to guide our judgments. If we had Gods or a God, if we had a Faith, if we had some healing subterfuge by which to conquer Death, then the Aristotelian criterion might apply in part to our Tragedy. But our tragedy is just that we have only ourselves, that there is nothing to be purged into except a belief in the guts of man, good or evil, who faces unflinchingly the black mystery of his own soul!

But what ho! I seem to be becoming rhetorical! I'll let you off on this with only the added comment, by way of illustration, that it was no easy job (and one I'm proud to have accomplished!) to contrive an approximation of Greek fate for my trilogy, (without benefit of Gods or morals but taken from the Mannon family itself), that a modern intelligent audience, as well as the author, could believe in! A modern psychological fate—the faith of an unbeliever in anything but man himself.

This letter is running away from me and I will end it with only a word more of comment on your criticism. You are probably right about the plays being a bit garrulous and complicated in spots. But I warned you the script was not final draft for publication or production. I will undoubtedly cut and simplify in my final going over—and in rehearsals when I *hear* the plays. Always do—or nearly always.

But damn it there is another thing you bring up which is on my mind. It was in a recent article of yours, too. About my sureness in dealing with simple people, etc. Well, it certainly is easier to deal with them, it certainly is a cinch to make a simple, uncomplicated, pictur-

2. Oswald Spengler (1880–1936), German philosopher and author of *The Decline of the West* (1918).

esque dialect "character" seem alive and real. I could have kept on writing plays about sailors and stokers and negroes and people like those in *Desire*, if I had wanted to. But it was too damned simple. There seemed to be more drama in the life of my time than dealing with such straightforward primitive folk could possibly take in—more significant drama—more in the rhythm of the meaning of contemporary life—more difficult—harder—more of a challenge to my egotism and ambition—in short, more of a reason for keeping on living and being a playwright! I had done my best by the old material. There seemed no use repeating. As I have demanded more scope of the theatre, so I felt the same urge to demand more scope of myself, to get a deeper, intenser, more comprehensive expression of self than dialect folk allowed me. Take any play of this trilogy and compare it to *Desire Under The Elms*, for example. Doesn't it say more about life—about the motives behind life, about the insides of people which constitute their *real* characters. I may now sacrifice externals to internals but more comes out of it, more mystery, more soul drama (one must use "soul" for lack of a better word). And yet I haven't sacrificed the primitive first causes. Rather what I do now is the struggle of the primitive to emerge in more complicated people, the drama of its thwarted, warped, revengeful, hidden emerging.

Well, anyway! What I really started out to say in this letter was I deeply regret not being able to go to the *Follies*[3] with you. I love the *Follies* and nearly all musical shows. But I have a dinner date that night and to spend the evening with the people. I am coming to town Tuesday night—motoring back here Wednesday night late. Can you have lunch with me at the Madison Wednesday at 1:30? Hope so, and we'll argue a bit. If you can come, will you wire me here when you receive this letter? If you can't, will you call me up at the Madison at one Wednesday and perhaps we can arrange to have a chat sometime late Wednesday afternoon. I don't know yet just what dates I'll have.

All best from Mrs. O'N. and myself. And again, much gratitude for your letter—even if I do seem to have so much to offer in rebuttal! Thanks for the casting hints—much!
Eugene O'Neill

---

331 • TO BROOKS ATKINSON.   ALS 2 pp. (Northport, L.I.) [Lincoln Center]

August 16th [1931]

Dear Atkinson: Any old time that suits your convenience. I expect to be in town quite frequently the latter part of the month and I'll try to get you via the *Times*—or you have a stab at getting me at the Madison—and we'll try to fix it so you can motor back here with me—after your moving is all over. How's that? Or later, if you prefer, after Sept. 1st (when rehearsals, the last I heard, are due to start). I will be coming out over week-ends and you may be able to join one of those. Or, if you can't find time to leave town, let's get together at the Madison. The important point is, let's get together somehow. I agree that a good deal may be accomplished by a revival of our discussion—from my selfish point of view, at least! The more of the inner workings and background of the writing of the trilogy I can set before you—and of my work in general—the better for me in the sense of my getting more value out of your criticisms, for or against. For although I am as intolerant as the next one when sure I am right (whether rightly or wrongly), still there are always points about any play where the impact of a fresh point of view gives rise to self-critical questionings and analysis of material that are of very great value. After prolonged work on a play I get so damned thoroughly identified with it that it's impossible to see or feel anything but the work as a

---

3. *The Ziegfeld Follies of 1931*, which opened at the Ziegfeld Theatre on July 1, 1931.

whole, its total effect. Defects in the parts, which have become simply blobs of familiar words, quite escape me. And criticism which might open one's eyes to muzzy spots and be of real service never comes until after the opening when, for better or worse, it's all over. That's *one of many* reasons why I'm always glad to have any critic (whose opinions I respect, and whose right to criticize the drama I admit) read my scripts before the openings. Unfortunately producers violently object to this. They want a surprise value at all costs. Also, between us, they know their acting and directing usually are judged better if the critic knows nothing of the play they are supposed (in most cases so mistakenly!) to interpret!

And so on and on when we get together!

Yes, it's a Cadillac 12! But lest this sound too opulent for a serious-minded *D*ramatist, let me hasten to explain I snared it second-hand. Only used 2000 miles, ironclad guarantee attached, looking brand new, over one thousand dollars off, who could resist this splendid gift of world depression? Not I, who have always been an A One snob when it came to cars and boats, which must have speed, line & class or "we are not amused." This snootiness dates back to early boyhood days. My father, the Count of Monte Cristo, always got me the classiest rowboat to be had, and we sported the first Packard car in our section of Conn., way back in the duster-goggles era. My brother and I once got this car up to a mite over 40. A great day—from which the car never fully recovered!

(It is the fact that M. Komroff has already shamelessly revealed himself to you as another car-bug-author that gives me nerve to make above confession!) All best to you.   Eugene O'Neill

P.S. The bound revised galleys of *M.B.E.* will be ready in about ten days. I'd like to have Gabriel read them, too—but, as I remember, he had some objection to reading *Interlude* before production. Has he still? If with you, will you ask him? Of course, he'd keep it under the old hat, the situation (mine) being a bit ticklish, what with producers' wishes & various other complications. Damn it, I think in future I'll publish before production, no matter who it hurts.[1]

---

332 • TO THERESA HELBURN.   ALS 1 p. ([New York, N.Y.]) [Yale]

Thursday eve. / (before leaving for Northport)
[August 20, 1931]

Dear Terry: I told Lillian the truth, the whole truth and nothing etc. She is a game sport and took it in fine spirit. But it was a tough job for me! It's too damned bad! But we were all right about it.

I hereby withdraw my objection to Anderson[1] and bow to your judgment who know more about her than I do. Go get her if you can. The Ann Harding thing won't come to anything, I know. She's sure to be tied up or want a million a week. Still, we might wait for her return wire—(if she answers at all!).[2]   As ever,   Gene

1. *Mourning Becomes Electra* was published by Horace Liveright, Inc., on November 2, 1931.

1. Judith Anderson (1898–), who had succeeded Lynn Fontanne as Nina Leeds in the original Broadway production of *Strange Interlude* and who eventually played Lavinia Mannon in the touring company of *Mourning Becomes Electra*.
2. Ann Harding, then a leading dramatic actress in films, wanted to play Lavinia but was unable to obtain a release from her movie contract.

333 • TO BROOKS ATKINSON. ALS 1 p. (Northport, [L.I.]) [Lincoln Center]

Sunday / [September 19?, 1931]

Dear Mr. Atkinson: Well, I will string along with you on that third play to this large extent, that when I listened to it in rehearsal last week I immediately *heard* what I hadn't seen—that over considerable crucial sections it wobbled about and lost its line and stumbled over its own feet. Also it still needed cutting throughout and pointing up. So I have been working like hell ever since on it—rewritten a good deal of Act Two, etc., etc.—and it is now shaping up much better. I'll probably do still more this coming week. By heck, it's going to do its stuff by the time I'm through with it if I have to break a mental leg!

So much for humble admission! *Nevertheless* I still am convinced your fundamental objection as to its laboratory character is all wrong. Even in the version you've just read, and with no Lavinia except a girl from the Guild office staff reading, in spite of its imperfections it came out as moving, sound, theatre-of-the-theatre drama. So keep your mind open on this subject and on the opening night of this "Haunted" I promise you a convincing surprise! Wait 'n' see!

The second play comes out in grand shape, as you foresaw. It would. It has all the breaks, compared to the two others. It is the direct action one of the trio—carries no burden of exposition, etc., etc., involves only direct motivation. The first play also stands forth—(as well as the 2nd, considering exposition)—but its first act still needs condensing and working over, which I am doing. I promise you a surprise on this one, too.

In short, you're in for a better three evenings[1] than you anticipate! (Don't think I'm trying suggestion hypnosis on you! These be my honest prophetic visions merely.)

Yes, the *Charterhouse of Parma*[2] is sure one of the few Ones! Marvelous stuff! Imagine any present day novelist handling that story! But don't let's get morbid unhealthy thoughts!

Mrs. O'Neill joins in all best. I'm now off for a swim. Back to N.Y. tonight—and more rehearsals. We've at last got a Lavinia with the emotional guts to carry the role. (I hope we've got her!) Name Alice Brady. Will give her her chance to come through at last with what she showed she had in *Bride Of The Lamb*.[3] Confidential yet, this. How does this hit you?) Eugene O'Neill

---

334 • TO EUGENE O'NEILL, JR. ALS 2 pp. (1095 Park Ave., [New York]) [Yale]

Friday eve. / [January 8?, 1932]

Dear Eugene: I wasn't so surprised at the bad news! When I read about that bank folding up I sort of surmised you might have been among the casualties! Sure thing, you can have the second 1200 now. As for opening an account for you at my bank (Guaranty Trust) I'll see—write to them tonight. Formerly they would not take a checking account unless you agreed never to let it get below one thousand—which wouldn't do for you—but maybe the depression has chastened their spirit. If they will take it, I'll tell them to notify you, send you card for signature, etc. If they're cold, I think Carlotta can fix it at her bank which is just as

---

1. Despite earlier plans to produce the three plays on successive evenings, the trilogy was played in its entirety in one evening.
2. Novel (1839) by French writer Henri Beyle (1783–1842), whose pen name was Stendhal.
3. A play by William Hurlbut (1883–?) starring Brady that had opened at the Greenwich Village Theatre on March 30, 1926.

sound. One way or the other you will hear you have an account somewhere within the next few days. Meanwhile, to keep the home stew boiling, I am enclosing a dividend check endorsed over to you. It ought to be good so you needn't hesitate about cashing it. A grand surprise to me, this one was! It represents a small share in a cattle ranch in Montana your romantically-investing Grandfather left me. I thought those cows had all perished of hoof-and-mouth disease long ago!

Re the German plan,[1] it sounds good to me and I leave it entirely up to you. But maybe you had better postpone signing up definitely until you see what happens about reparations, etc. next spring (that is, if you can). Because if France continues to play Shylock, a revolution in Germany, which will upheave the Universities along with everything else, is as possible as not.

Carlotta's Mother & daughter are on here. I like them both very much. Her mother goes back to the Coast tomorrow or next day, and C. takes Cynthia to her school in Conn. on Sunday. You and Betty will like Cynthia when you meet her. She's a fine kid!

Shane & Oona have also been calling on us (their mother has an apt. in N.Y. now). Lawrenceville has improved Shane a lot already and I feel he is all set now for a few years to come. Oona I hadn't seen since I came back and I was very anxious about what she'd be like. But it's all right. She's very much O'Neill in spite of the environment she's been up against, and a nice shy quiet little girl. I'm very pleased about this, as you may imagine.

The Greek book is sound stuff—although some of the moral interpretations he manages to inject into it here and there could only have occurred to anyone during the Victorian era.   All best from us to Betty & you!   Father

---

335 • TO EUGENE O'NEILL, JR.   ALS 2 pp. (Stationery headed: "The Cloister" / Sea Island Beach / Georgia) [Yale]

May 13th 1932

Dear Eugene: This is going to be short & sweet because, to be frank about it, the fact that I will be seeing you in near future gives a lazy letter writer a good excuse to be lazy!

Am enclosing a check for a combined birthday and graduation present. I had hoped to make this a full "gran'," as the boys call it, but the outlook has blued over considerably of late—for various depressing reasons I won't touch on here—and enclosed seems now the utmost the traffic will bear in addition to what we agreed on for later on.

I am damned sorry I won't be present at your graduation. But I sure will be around in spirit (in full Litt. D. regalia!) beaming as a proud parent beams! And, not to flatter my dramatic talent, I'm sure in my imagination I'll put on a more moving show—for me!—than the actual event. For you know me. Anything in the way of a public occasion so bedevils me with heebie-jeebies that I am incapable of getting the right focus on it, and I would only be a sort of befuddled burden on your hands. Anyway, and above all, it is most fitting and just that your Mother should have this to herself—and I hope she comes as near to bursting with pride as is possible without bursting!

And I'm proud, too. You know that. I've said it before and between each time of saying it you give me added reasons to say it. Which makes it a damn satisfying life for me as a father!

You're a fine person and I know a fine life is before you. You make me soundly ashamed of all the years I wasted in stupidity, and whose loss as a background for culture is a handicap

1. Eugene was planning to go to graduate school in classical studies at the University of Freiburg.

that will always make my road tougher to travel. But, at the same time, you cure my remorse threat; for the realization that you are achieving where I fell flat sort of gives me a compensating thrill of achievement! (No hard feelings, you understand! My envy makes me proud, that's the notion I seek to convey!) So go on, and God bless you! And be assured, for all I am worth to you, I am always behind you!

Carlotta joins in love to Betty and you. She will call you up from New York, I imagine. She's leaving here, to go up and pack,[1] on Monday. She will be there until the 28th or 29th. I'm at work with gusto on the new play.[2] Feel like a reborn guy after ten days swimming, sun, & fresh air. New York apart. dwelling is not for me! I was a fool ever to attempt it.

The house is coming along fine and will be a beauty. Betty and you are going to like it a lot here—and I'm sure looking forward to your visit.   Again, love!   Father

---

336 • TO RICHARD MADDEN.   ALS 2 pp. (Stationery headed: "The Cloister" / Sea Island Beach / Georgia) [Yale]

Friday Night—May 13th [1932]

Dear Dick: I wired you this eve. to call off the *Desire* proposition[1] as, after careful consideration, I saw little in favor of it and much against it.

First and foremost, I evidently haven't made clear to you, as I hoped I had, that any proposal, which involves my association again with any of the old P.P. group who gave me the double-cross when I went to Europe, is out as far as I'm concerned. They owed me loyalty, after all I'd done for them; they pretended to be my friends, and as soon as my back was turned gave me the knife. They chose which side of the fence they were on, then! Let them stick to it—for my side is barred to them now! There are some things I will neither forget nor forgive! I don't believe, generally speaking, in letting personal issues enter into business—but this is an enduring exception to that rule. So please remember in future, will you, and it will avoid further explanation.

(The above is, of course, strictly between you and me! You can always stall them off on excuse that I don't want whatever play it is revived at the time.)

And I *don't* want *Desire* revived now, right on top of *Electra*. They have too many points of similarity, and together tend to overemphasize one side of my work in the public mind.

Another objection: Unless I mistake you this would be a summer revival. No summer revivals for mine!

Still another: Don't like cast. MacKellar is all washed up. And even at her best she would be lousy in this part—couldn't play it.

Still another: As long as there *is* a chance of the Guild reviving *anything* of mine I want to hold off on *everything* else (in N.Y.)—at least until after their revival is produced.

Still another: Not enough advance, not a high enough royalty scale, considering the management which carries no prestige or authority.

Still another: I think in the future, for a revival under A One management, we would be able to get Walter Huston,[2] if it were planned far enough ahead. And that's worth waiting for!

---

1. The O'Neills were planning to move to Sea Island and were building a house there.
2. *Days Without End.*

1. Former Provincetown Players director James Light and set designer Cleon Throckmorton (1897–1965) sought O'Neill's permission to revive *Desire Under the Elms* with Helen MacKellar starring as Abbie.
2. Huston had originated the role of Ephraim Cabot in the 1924 production.

And other objections which occurred to me and have slipped my mind now.

Oh, here's something: Why Light and Throck for *Desire,* anyway? Light had absolutely nothing to do with the original production at the G.V. Bobby Jones directed it, with my cooperation. He also designed the set—so why Throck? These birds get themselves connected with past productions of my stuff they were only superficially, if at all, mixed up in.

And that's all of that. I simply can't see either money or glory in this proposition—only a failure.

Your *Thirst* inquiry thrilled me! If we could unload that one on the screen, what manna from heaven, eh? I hope you got hold of a copy of the book without having to buy it! It's a rare collector's item—I haven't any myself!—and was at one time selling at 75 dollars a copy, though I suppose the depression has knocked that down some.

Feel in the pink again—swimming, boating, everything fine here. Have started work with gusto on my new play.

Carlotta joins in all best to Tessa & you!   As ever,   Gene

---

337 • TO CYNTHIA CHAPMAN.   ALS 1 p. (Stationery headed: "The Cloister" / Sea Island Beach / Georgia) [Yale]

May 16th 1932

Dearest Cynthia: I am so darned sorry I won't see you again before you leave[1]—but, things being as they are, I think it is up to me to stay down here and stick on the job, now that I am working again.

Getting to know you has meant a great deal to me, for I have learned to respect and admire you for yourself, quite apart from my stepfatherly affection for your mother's daughter. I want you to know I sincerely feel this, and for you to feel my home is always yours to come to, whenever you wish, by right of the love I bear you!

So that's that! We'll get together before too long, I am sure of that. In the meantime I won't forget—and don't you! All love & luck to you! You are a brave girl and a true one! Be true to yourself and everything will be yours in time that your heart desires! I am proud to be your stepfather!   Gene

---

338 • TO SAXE COMMINS.   ALS 2 pp. (Stationery headed: "The Cloister" / Sea Island Beach / Georgia) [Private]

May 22nd 1932

Dear Saxe: Your letter was misaddressed and didn't reach me till today. There's no "Atlanta" about it—only the above.

About that jack: Don't be a nut! I'll be "uneasy" if you think of paying it before 1942. Otherwise uneasiness on that score won't visit me. Forget it, Saxe! I tore up your meticulously businesslike note long ago. No such things exist between you & me. And I really owe that money to you for your services as Doctor Commins in Rochester long ago. So, in fact, in short, and finally, go to hell with your damned nonsense! I'm your friend, ain't I? That used to mean what's mine is your'n—and I'm old-fashioned.

It's rotten about your having to take a cut—but I suppose it's on the cards these days.

---

1. After completing the year at prep school in Connecticut, Cynthia Chapman, Carlotta's daughter by her second husband, Melvin C. Chapman, Jr., was returning to California for the summer.

Wait until this income tax the great minds at Wash. are contriving takes its cut at me next year—and we can go out with tin cups together! However, I'll have this home down here—and it's a peach!—paid for—and there are plenty of free fish, shrimp, & oysters around.

Carlotta is now in N.Y. doing the final packing. She is going to call you up, I know. If she hasn't by the time you get this, beat her to it. She's working herself to death to get it over and get back here, I'm afraid. Longest time we've ever been separated. I miss her like hell!

I feel fine again—sea & sun—New York is bum stuff for me. Hard at work on my new one—good start on 1st draft—it looks like a real one, this play.

Thanks for the snap of your child. The depression is going right over her head, I should say from appearances! Give her my love. And Dorothy. I'll try to listen in on her last broadcasts[1] after our radio gets here.

And all blessings be on her and the anxiously-awaited one![2] Dorothy is a grand, brave human being and you are a lucky guy!

All love to the three-four of you!   As ever,   Gene

---

339 • TO CARLOTTA MONTEREY O'NEILL.   ALS 3 pp. (Stationery headed: "The Cloister" / Sea Island Beach / Georgia) [Yale]

May 25th 1932 / (Wednesday night)

Darling Mistress Fatbum: Worked today satisfactorily, although there is little progress on paper, mostly thinking out. Swim as usual. Then up to house. Hundreds of new plants & bushes have arrived on the scene—or so it seems—and are waiting to be set in, both in yard & patio. The Ford motor steam-roller broke down just toward closing time, and that means a delay in rolling down the drive, I'm afraid, because four bolts snapped clean off in its innards and it seems it will be some job to get it fixed again. But the mover's trucks will have plenty of unpacked (unrolled) shell to drive in on (it's all spread out, waiting to be rolled)—so they won't be affected. Another delay (on the living room) is that the makers in Pittsburgh have wired the curved glass for the upper panes on big windows won't be sent till Friday—by express. However, if they keep their word, it ought to be here Monday a.m. and be in by the time you arrive—only a couple of hours work to get it in.

So much for unexpected hold-ups. For the rest, everything goes forward. The man for the rubber tiling for your bathroom (if I mistake not) is getting busy. They are painting the upstairs floors—dark but not too dark. I thought the effect was damn good. Wooden screens are almost all in—sea side of patio wall at last white now (looks fine from beach). Fountain finished. Outside of windows nearly all painted. Outside my galleon windows painted. And a thousand carpenter's odd jobs which you hardly notice but which eat up time are getting out of the way.

Your three letters mailed Monday arrived—and were, as usual, the big, desirable event of the day. Why do you say you hesitated to phone Sunday night because you knew I hated it? Not with you at the other end, I don't! If you knew how thrilled and delighted I was! Haven't you discovered that I love you yet, Foolish One?

"A pat for the fat one," you write. But I am afraid to give it—almost—he is so touchy these days and sensitive from thinking so constantly of you! But I'll do it. "Here! Carlotta, your Beloved One, sends you this pat. Here now! Don't get so excited! What?" He says, "a

---

1. Dorothy Commins, an accomplished concert pianist, was participating in a radio series devoted to the history of piano music.

2. Saxe and Dorothy Commins were expecting their second child; when he was born, on July 1, 1932, he was named Eugene after O'Neill, who was his godfather.

Casa Genotta, Sea Island, Georgia.

pat! Is that all?" "Well," I warn him, "it's just as well for you that was all she sent. As it is, you'll never let me get to sleep tonight!" I'm afraid he's too greedy where you are concerned, he wants everything of you, so ever-wonderful and an ever-renewed revelation of beauty are you to him!

And to me! Soul & body & all of me lives in you! Mistress, I desire you, you are my passion, and my life-drunkenness, and my ecstasy, and the wine of joy to me! Wife, you are my love, and my happiness, and the word behind my word, and the half of my heart! Mother, you are my lost way refound, my end and my beginning, the hand I reach out for in my lonely night, from my ghost-haunted inner dark, and on your soft breasts there is a peace for me that is beyond death! Daughter, you are my secret, shy, shrinking one, my pure and unsoiled one, whom the world has wounded and who still looks with bewildered, hurt eyes at the world and at her wound and cannot understand; but I cuddle you in my arms, and you are blood of my blood and flesh of my flesh, and over your comforted, sleeping head against my heart I swear my oath at life, that my life shall be between you and all wounds and hurt hereafter!

(Well, you wanted a poem and the above has the right feeling of one, although in prose, and crude enough at that, God help me! But IT's TRUE!—the very truth of my truth, and of what you mean to me!—and for that virtue I pardon its defects and love it, and hope you, too, feeling its truth, will love it. And don't you dare, even for one fleeting suspicious fraction of a second attribute any least word of it to an author's considered writing! I'd be horribly hurt if you did! For it just gushed out of me sitting here at this letter, thinking of you and of what sorry stuff my life had been made before you came to me, and of all your love had done to weave a beautiful pattern out of your beauty into that sorry stuff, and given it a basic harmony of design, and a line reaching forward. So believe my "pome" born spontaneously from my heart! Please, Dear!)

Good night, Sweetheart! Only five days more! Take care of yourself for my sake! And kiss my soft warm one for me! (But, come to consider it, that would be rather difficult—so simply tell her for me to consider herself kissed—and kissed and kissed!) And he sends a message to say to her that outside of her arms life simply isn't worth living! Your lover,   Gene

P.S. (Just finished reading over this letter. My God, who reading it would credit me with being your five-year-old lover—and 3 year old husband to boot! Really, Sweet One, I blushed for myself at some of my—er—unveiled remarks!—so immodestly your lover!—I actually ALMOST blushed!—but, God, how proud I was, too!—and how wonderful it seemed to "get that way!")

---

340 • TO DUDLEY NICHOLS.[1]   ALS 3 pp. (Stationery headed: "The Cloister" / Sea Island Beach / Georgia) [Yale]

May 29th 1932

Dear Mr. Nichols: I'm damned glad you didn't throw that letter away permanently! Because reading it gave me a deep satisfaction and pleasure that I would not like to have foregone. A fair number of letters come my way about this or that in connection with my work, but most of them are silly stuff, as you may guess, and it is almost never I receive one from anyone whose judgment I give a damn about. Such letters as yours, which convince me

1. Nichols (1895–1960), critic and writer, who had contributed a long and appreciative introduction to the 1928 Modern Library edition, *The Emperor Jones, The Straw.*

by their sincerity that my plays have left an enduring mark on people of imaginative perception and spiritual insight, are about the finest reward I could wish! Better even than reward, encouragement! And this latter is often sorely needed. For despite acceptance by the notoriety that is modern fame—(and because of it, even though one remains uninfected!)—it is sometimes difficult to "pull up one's socks" and go on. One gets weary and bewildered, among the broken rhythms of this time one misses one's beat and line of continuity, one gets the feeling of talking through a disconnected phone, foolishly, to oneself.

So, you see, much gratitude for your letter is in order—and most certainly is felt by me! Not that I can preen my vanity up to the point where I may unblushingly second your high opinion of what I have accomplished. But it's a heartening challenge to keep on trying to justify such an opinion. And it's the dream that I may sometime say what must be said as it must be said that keeps me going—Showshop or no Showshop!

Funny, your writing me at this particular time about affirmation. I am changing inside me, as I suppose one always does, or ought to do if there is growth, when one has passed forty, and even the most positive affirmative Nay! of my past work no longer satisfies me. So I am groping after a real, true Yea! in the play I'm now starting—a very old Yea, it is true, in essence, but so completely forgotten in all its inner truth that it might pass for brand new. Whether I will be able to carry the writing of it up to Yea! remains to be seen.

This play is, incidentally—and most confidentially!—a development from my old idea for the second play of the *Dynamo* trilogy. So what you say about *Dynamo* came at a timely time!

Also, some days before your letter arrived, I was making first notes on an idea that had suddenly come to me—a really tremendous affirmative conception for an opus magnus![2] But it must wait until I feel grown up enough to write it—if ever. I'm certainly not fool enough to think I'm capable of it yet—but I'll keep hoping!

All of which rambling on about my aims and ambitions I hope you'll feel your letter brought on your head—and not attribute to monomania!

Yes, Revolution seems beside the real mark to me, too. So many Revolutions there have been since the Greeks, and Man's soul has grown dumber and dumber. If he even had more to eat that might be something—but he still seems to be giving starvation a battle. As for Russia, wait until they have to stand the ordeal of success. Just now, on the way up to some somewhere, it's all so exultantly easy for them.

I can't imagine what happened to *Electra* No. 2.[3] I saw the last rehearsal before they opened their road season and they really gave an excellent performance. Reed was no Nazimova, of course, but she wasn't poor by any means. Abel was certainly no Earle Larrimore (whom I think has done the finest work of them all) but he was anything but bad. And Judith Anderson I thought extremely good and better than Brady in many places. The grind of the road, I suppose, got them.

All good wishes to you. I'll hope to see you in N.Y. when next I go up. It will all depend on work as to just when that will be. I told you Fall in my last letter, but I may stick on my job here longer at a stretch than that. But remember that what I said about if you get down this way at any time always holds good.

I know the New Milford neighborhood. It's beautiful country. You will get a lot out of living there, I think.

---

2. "Testament for Tomorrow," *Eugene O'Neill at Work: Newly Released Ideas for Plays,* pp. 234–35.

3. After its tour, the road company of *Mourning Becomes Electra,* with Florence Reed (1883–1967) as Christine, Walter Abel as Orin, and Judith Anderson as Lavinia, reopened the play on Broadway on May 9, 1932, but it lasted for only sixteen performances.

Write again when you're in the mood. And don't stick me on no Messiah pedestal! I'd never dare meet you then and be a witness to your devastating disillusion!
Eugene O'Neill

---

341 • TO FREDERIC I. CARPENTER.[1]   ALS 2 pp. (Sea Island Beach, / Georgia)
[Private]

[postmarked June 24, 1932]

My dear Mr. Carpenter: Thank you very much for your letter and the kind appreciation of my work you express in it.

As for your question regarding Oriental ideas, I do not think they have influenced my plays at all. Certainly, not consciously. Many years ago I did considerable reading in Oriental philosophy and religion, however, although I never went in for an intensive study of it. I simply did it in order to have some sort of grasp for the subject as part of my philosophical background. The mysticism of Lao-tzu & Chuang-tzu[2] probably interested me more than any other Oriental writing.

No, I had no intention of embodying any of "Maya" in Nina.

"Nina, cara Nina" is simply a characteristic literary quip of the type of novelist Marsden is supposed to be. Of course, it is his echo of *Anna Karenina*,[3] mixed with a flair for exhibiting a foreign language endearment. He's that sort, is Charlie!

No, there's no contact with *Tamar*.[4] As a matter of fact, though I know and like most of Jeffers' other work I have never read *Tamar*.

All good wishes to you.   Yours very sincerely,   Eugene O'Neill

P.S. I haven't read *Emerson and Asia*[5] yet—but will.

---

342 • TO ROBERT SISK.   ALS 2 pp. (Sea Island Beach, Ga.) [Yale]

July 4th 1932

Dear Bob: It was damned good to hear from you. I've been meaning to drop you a line ever since we migrated—so has Carlotta—but what with my working on the new play and Carlotta doing an efficient, ever-watchful job on completion of the house and moving in, we've kept postponing your letter.

I'm damned sorry you are having such an uncomfortable time of it with R.K.O.[1] The damned fools! They seem to take a perverse satisfaction in giving the works to everyone of value they entice to them. It sure sounds like the prize racket! Well, two years in jail isn't so damned long. (Pardon these easy words of comfort!) You can serve that standing on your head—especially when you've got them paying so well. And by way of philosophical solace I suggest Jack Sharkey's slogan when someone asked how it felt to have the crowds boo him: "Fuck 'em! I'm getting their dough!"

---

1. Critic and English teacher at the University of California, Berkeley, whose many years of research on O'Neill and Oriental philosophy culminated in his *Eugene O'Neill* (New York: Twayne, 1964; rev. ed., 1979).
2. Lao-tzu (c. 604–531 B.C.), Chinese philosopher and founder of Taoism; Chuang-tzu (fl. fourth century B.C.), Chinese philosopher and teacher, exponent of Lao-tzu.
3. Novel (1875–77) by Leo Tolstoy.
4. *Tamar* (New York: P.G. Boyle, 1924), a collection of poetry by Robinson Jeffers (1887–1962).
5. Carpenter's Ph.D. dissertation, which was published under this title (Cambridge, Mass.: Harvard University Press, 1930); he apparently sent O'Neill a copy.

1. Sisk had left the Theatre Guild and gone to Hollywood as a screenwriter.

But that is all bunk, of course. I really appreciate what you must be going through and you have our deepest sympathy. Still, in self-defense, be as hard-boiled about it as you can and don't let it get under your skin any more than you can help.

Your news that the film of *Interlude*[2] promises to be a smash sounds good. Not that I really give a damn what they've done to it, but a success may mean the sale of other plays. And, crassly and frankly, outside of money the films simply don't exist for me, and nothing they do or don't do seems of the slightest importance to my work as a playwright on its own proper plane.

Which reminds me that I've just sold an extremely lousy one-act thriller (which Holbrook Blinn was once going to do when he was running Grand Guignol at the Princess back in 1914), from my punk first volume *Thirst*. The play is called *Recklessness*. Educational Films bought it. Paid five thousand net. Which I thought was a good price for a forgotten dud of one-act. It seemed like unexpected manna from heaven. What is your opinion?

I'll leave the ravings about our new home to Carlotta when she writes you. Suffice it that I agree with all she can say. We are very happy about it. It really is a peach of a place. First home I've ever built. All the others I got ready made. So it's a new proud thrill.

July 10th

Well, this letter seems to be one of those weekly installment affairs! My excuse is that we're full up with visitors—Eugene, Jr. & his wife & Shane—and I've been on the hop leading fishing and swimming parties—and talking parties. Also, it has been most hellishly hot—no breeze for some days, and that is a rare occurrence on this beach. But I don't seem to mind the heat here as I did in Bermuda summer. It doesn't take it out of you.

Speaking of visitors, Munsell & wife & son, dropped in a few days ago, en route to New Orleans, and had lunch with us. They appeared to like the place, although the exterior of our château still looks a bit seedy with only one coat of white, through which the brick color emerges in rashy blotches, and the landscape people are still working on the grounds. It is really extraordinary what these latter have accomplished in such a short time. Most of what was bare sand with a few pines is now the good start of fine lawns with clusters of palms, oaks, bays, myrtle, tamarisk, oleander, etc., all of them sprouting and making themselves at home.

When can Mrs. Sisk and you come see us? Or if she can't leave the child, when can you? We'd love to have you any time you can make it, you know that. If you could get away in the fall, it would be a pleasanter change then. Just now it's hot—like everywhere else.

I had been working steadily ever since we came down until my sons appeared—and will take up again as soon as they leave around the 15th. Have finished Acts One & Two and the first two scenes of three in Act Three of "Without Endings of Days." There will be four acts, as now schemed—although possibly Scene Three of Act Three may develop into an act, making the total five. The play will be regular length, of course. I am extremely interested in the way it has developed so far and think it promises to be a real one. But there's a hell of a lot of work ahead before I reach the finished product. This is all first draft, of course.

Well, I guess that's about all. Never felt better. This Sea Island is my kind of place. Carlotta is tired out by the job of getting settled—but otherwise fit and in love with this home she's made for us. So all is well with us.

Our best to the three of you!   As ever,   Eugene O'Neill

P.S. And remember to come see us the first chance you get!

2. MGM's film version of *Strange Interlude*, starring Norma Shearer, Clark Gable, Ralph Morgan, and Robert Young, opened in August 1932.

July 30th 1932

Dearest Cyn: Well, I have been meaning to write you many times in the past couple of months—it has been so darned nice of you to write me and your letters have made me very happy. But I've been busy on the new play. And outside of that I've been just lazy! Which isn't much to offer in the way of an excuse—but you will understand and forgive me, I know. Candidly, as a correspondent I'm acknowledged to be one of the world's bummest!

It must have been grand on Lake Tahoe. I've always wanted to go there. Got that urge years ago when I first read Mark Twain's *Roughing It*. He camped there with some friends way back around 1865—started a forest fire there by accident. There is a lot about that neighborhood and the boom days of the Comstock lode silver mining in the book. Twain lived through all that crazy exciting time in Nevada. He was a newspaper reporter in Virginia City—or Silver City, I forget which. *Roughing It* is a description of all his experiences in the early Western days. You ought to read it sometime. I think you would be interested, knowing that country as you do.

I'm sorry you never had a ride in my Gar Wood 28–40. Not that I ever had much of a ride in it myself! It, too, was a pip—but too much of a pip! Seventeen gallons of gas per hour it devoured! I began to hear that old sweet song "Over The Hills To The Poorhouse!" I was really lucky to be able to sell it almost at once, for practically what I paid for it. It would have been a white elephant down here where it's usually too rough to use a speedboat except on inland passages where you have to know as much as a pilot to avoid the numerous shifting mud and sand banks. But it was a pip! We made the 100 miles from Jacksonville in two hours and forty minutes, slowing down for bad spots and everything.

The swimming is grand, although the water has become almost too warm. You could lie in it all day and night without ever feeling chilly. I do quite a bit of surfboarding when the waves are right. That's great fun, isn't it?

As for the fishing, I do a lot. Had fine luck a couple of days but since then nothing much. It isn't really the right season just now. But I expect to try and get a real-sized shark on rod and reel soon and that means a tough battle. There's any amount of sharks around but they never seem to bother people. At least, there's no record of anyone ever having been nailed by one around here.

As for work, well, that's proceeding along the usual route of days when I think it's fine stuff, followed by days in which I feel it's too lousy for words, and that I better quit play-wrighting and become a poor but deserving plumber, or something! But that's all in the life of an author. It's always that way. You puff and sweat and groan inwardly, and like yourself and hate yourself, and after a long time, just when you're reaching for the insect powder to take a good gob and put yourself out of misery, the darn thing somehow gets finished and you realize you've really done something good and get quite fond of yourself again. Or you realize it's punk—and you start to rewrite the whole thing.

Forgive my shedding these few tears over my sad author's lot! But, feeling you are kind and sympathetic, I couldn't resist it. Authors just love to beef! Your Mamma can tell you all about that! She watched my ups and downs while *Mourning Becomes Electra* was in process of becoming. She simply hides the insect powder—or I guess doesn't even bother to hide it anymore (which is insulting, don't you think?)—and goes on with her super-efficient home management. Your Mamma is sure a demon housekeeper! I expect any day that she's going to grab me absent-mindedly and have me varnished, vacuum-cleaned, and polished with floor wax before I have a chance to resist! Every time Blemie[1] sees an ad for Sapolio or Dutch Cleanser he shudders with dread!

Much love to your Grandmother! And to you! Write whenever you're in the mood. I love to hear from you, you know. It makes you part of our home here—where I hope you will surely come to visit us before too long.   Again, much love! Keep well and happy! Gene

---

344 • TO GEORGE C. TYLER.   ALS 2 pp. (Sea Island Beach / Georgia) [Princeton]

Sept 3rd 1932

Dear Mr. Tyler: Your letter hits me at the worst possible moment. If only this had come at the time you saw me at the apartment, I could have, and would have, responded gladly, but now I am up a tree with everybody else. My situation now is that all the *Electra* money has gone into the house I've built down here, with a balance still owing, and I'm cash broke and borrowing myself to keep me over until *Electra* opens up again—praying that it will stay out when it does open! Beyond that, my savings from other years are represented by real estate that can't be sold for what it is mortgaged for, and some dividendless securities that I couldn't realize on without taking a four-fifths to nine-tenths loss on the original investment. In short, my story is the story of everyone today. I go into these details because I feel I owe you an explanation—and because I feel damned badly about having to return a negative reply to your letter, and I want you to believe it's the flesh and not the spirit that is weak. To make matters worse, although I'm writing a new play, it won't be ready for production next season; so there is only the road tour of *Electra* to rely on—and you know that's very problematical. And the money I will get from that—if I get it!—is mortgaged in advance, for the first months, at least—to next year's direful Income Tax—and to alimony and children's schools! I don't expect to be on my feet again for a year and a half—even if I get all the breaks and "Prosperity" shows some signs of revival.

I repeat again I hate like hell to write you this! And I *do* hate to! But facts are facts. What I can't, I can't.

You say something about "humiliating" in your letter. For God's sake, don't feel that about such a request *to me!* Feel as if you were asking a nephew something you had a perfect right to ask him! And please also feel that I am answering in the same spirit of familiar frankness.

There's just one chance I might be able to come to the front a little later—and that is if the talky of *Strange Interlude* is so successful that it encourages the film people to buy something else of mine. But this is such a pitifully thin hope that I feel guilty about even mentioning it to you. I've sold only two plays to them so far—"*Anna Christie*" years ago and *Strange Interlude* a year & a half back—and a forgotten one-act play for which I got nothing, to a small independent. They are all scared to touch my stuff. However, there's always the chance——

All good wishes from Mrs. O'Neill and me!

Again, I am damned sorry!   As ever, affectionately,   Eugene

---

1. Nickname of the O'Neills' beloved Dalmatian, Silverdene Emblem.

Oct. 11, 1932

Dear Harry: The enclosed letter from Madden of March 3rd 1931 explains the total of 1930 income.

The 1000 for rental is $\frac{1}{3}$ rental of Le Plessis—$\frac{1}{3}$ of 75000 francs = 25000 francs = $1000 approx.

The $4500 claimed for business entertaining at Le Plessis was my wife's estimate taken from the house keeping books kept by our butler there—(in French, of course). No, we haven't got the books now. Why should we have saved them? What the hell would they have proved, anyway—even if the investigator knew French and the French system of keeping house? How could anyone tell just how much extra was for business entertaining? And if I'd been the crook the Income Tax people always seem to think, I would have had the butler keep a separate padded item showing entertainment expense for any amount I liked—and sworn to before a notary, too! No, in honesty, this item can only be an estimate by the wife of the family who, in our case, pays all bills, etc. And Carlotta's estimate is moderate. Why, one extra item alone must have run to two thousand or more—wine, beer & spirits. We naturally had to keep a complete stock at the Château always on hand—of fine wines, particularly. And this was entirely an extra expense because neither Carlotta nor I ever drink anything but water!

Tell the Income Tax man to have a heart! After all, they ought to be able to estimate that the amount claimed is not unreasonable in proportion to my income nor the tax I paid. I was living abroad for the time I did principally to consolidate my position as the only American playwright who has ever been seriously accepted by Europe. In a way, I was sort of representative of American culture—and had to act accordingly. Among the people entertained at the château were: Klein of the Kunstler Theatre (director of) Berlin—Wettergren director of the Royal Theatre, Stockholm—(*Strange Interlude* was done at both these theatres)—Baron de Rothschild, owner & director of the Pigalle Theatre, Paris (where *All God's Chillun & Desire* were given)—Tairov of the Kamerny Theatre, Moscow, & his wife & leading actress, Alice Koonen—Gruenberg, the composer of *Emp. Jones* opera—three of the Directors of the Theatre Guild—George Jean Nathan—Lillian Gish (who was then dickering for talky rights of *Strange I.*)—Maurice Bourgeois, my French translator—Bati, director (then) of the Champs Elysées Theatre in Paris—Génner, of the Odéon Theatre in Paris that gave *Emperor Jones*—Henri Lenormand, the French playwright & his wife, a Dutch actress (who did *Ile*)—the director of the Gate Theatre in London—the partner of Jonathan Cape, my English publishers—my Hungarian translator Thérese Renner—

And so on and so forth. I can string out the list endlessly if it is so desired.

As for the expenses for the car (I used it on all trips everywhere—never train) I claimed $\frac{1}{2}$ total expenses of car, including chauffeur's salary. My wife, who paid him and looks after all servants accounts, gave me this item from the chauffeur's book. No, we haven't the book. But the car was a big de luxe Renault Reinastella and you can easily see this is reasonable considering the traveling done. This $\frac{1}{2}$ chauffeur, his expenses, & expenses car and gas came to $1021.24, my notes show. The rest of the amount claimed on car consists of $\frac{2}{5}$ths of its cost = $1840.00. You will remember I made no claim in '29 for $\frac{1}{5}$th cost and you advised me I could therefore claim $\frac{2}{5}$ths for 1930.

All Madden's statements come to me with his 5% already deducted—which explains discrepancy between what you got from Liveright and his statement of it in his letter enclosed.

I enclose a letter from you which explains my claim for loss on mortgage sold you. I also enclose a form filled out by Moran which explains New London property items.

I also enclose my pencil calculations when making out tax re my different business trips for European productions and expenses thereof for myself & secretary. I figured these out on a reasonable and fair estimate of $25 per day hotel expenses and $20 per day to cover all outside that & extra entertaining. The biggest item here is the six week trip in Spain. This, as I've explained, was partly to supervise production of *"Anna Christie"* in Madrid but mostly to gather material and atmosphere for a play dealing with Philip II & Don Juan of Austria on which I am still at work (the play, I mean).[1] I did not figure this out on the 25 hotel, 20 extra per day as with the others but took it directly from the damage shown on my letter of credit. Have I the letter of credit? No, they take those from you when finished.

The extra four hundred on legal fees was to Du Vivier. As you can testify, he was helping on the Paris end with the plagiarism suit and conferred with you in Paris during the summer of '30. This was the first item paid him. The balance came under last year's return.

You will note from one of the pencil pages of the tax calculations I enclose that I clean forgot to deduct for books bought during year—part of an author's trade expense if anything is. This would have amounted to from 500 to 1000 surely, judging from other years.

Kindly point out to the Income Tax man that I had not then—and have not now—fled with my capital into tax exempt securities, as most people have. But I will unless they give me some sort of decent break on reasonable expenses which can't be proven except by a fair consideration of the legitimate expenses a man in my position has to undergo.

One extra item on the penciled traveling expenses—in May—a dinner to the Kamerny troupe in Paris (270.00)—27 people—who were playing *Desire & All God's C.* there. I cheated myself on that. It came to much more.   All best!   Gene

P.S. If they want me to make affidavit on this (material in this letter) I'm perfectly willing—only please send letter back to me for reference in that case.

But what does my oath at the bottom of return mean, then?

P.S. II I also enclose full Moran statement on property for you if you need it.

---

346 • TO EUGENE O'NEILL, JR.   ALS 3 pp. (Sea Island Beach, / Georgia) [Yale]

Nov. 11th 1932

Dear Eugene: Don't say it! I know! But honestly I have been working more intensively than ever before and have felt too lazily drained out after the stint each day to get started on a letter. This is an explanation, not an excuse. This "Endings Of Days" is sure beating my brains out! I have a first draft of it which I am now revising—but am not satisfied even with the revising done so far. There will be a hell of a lot of work still to do on it. Whether I'll get it in final shape in time for production next fall begins to look a bit doubtful—unless some fortunate inspirations boost me along. In addition to "Endings Of Days" I also dashed off a first draft of another play in September.[1] It came on me all of a flood and working every day 8:30 to five or six I got the whole thing off my chest in one month. It's no idea you have ever heard me talk of—and is quite different from anything I have ever done. It came so easily that I'm scared of it—afraid to go back and read it—even so diffident that I'll save telling you the details until I go back and find I like it. Of course, I know I'll find a lot to do on it even if it

1. See *Eugene O'Neill at Work: Newly Released Ideas for Plays*, pp. 229–34.

1. *Ah, Wilderness!*.

turns out worth while. As for whether I will ever allow it to be produced, granted it's good, that will be another difficult decision to make. It could so easily be absolutely spoiled by a performance that was the slightest bit off key.

Anyway, you see my boast about hard labor is no spoofing. There is little else of news with us. September proved a month of rotten weather here—hot, windy, and oppressive— and most of October, which they say is usually fine here, was almost as bad.

A road Co. of *Electra* is out but liable to close any week as the business has been rotten— same story here everywhere in every line!—and they haven't been making expenses so far. The Guild is hoping now that election is over things may improve a bit—but I doubt it. That's what everyone in these U.S. is doing, hoping against hope and kidding themselves along with very little, or no, basis in fact for their wish-fulfillment dreams. Anyway, if *E* dies on me it is going to be very, *very* sad!

You've heard all about the election, of course. It was a Democratic landslide, as everyone expected—but more so. Which seems to mean beer in the near future—which, unfortunately, means nothing to me. Outside of this, I doubt if the substitution of Democratic crooks and windbags for the Republican brand will put any chicken in anybody's pot.

It's fine to know you and Betty are getting so much out of life over there. Be sure to snatch everything you can out of it—because if things keep blowing up over here—well!

The China book sounds grand! But pass it up if it's at all expensive. The time has come when we must all pull in the belt.   Carlotta joins in much love to you both!   Father

P.S. They're talking of doing *Electra* in Berlin, Deutsches Theatre, sometime this season. I've given translator & Fischer Verlag a battle over every item in contract, telling them plainly to agree or go to hell, I didn't give a damn if I never had another play done in Germany. So they agreed! They're not used to Yankee authors talking that way and refusing to accept German production as an honor. But I've had my bellyful of their snide "show shop" tricks—cheaper than any encountered in the American theatre—and I meant what I said.

P.S. II—A more pleasant bit of news I'd forgotten. I was asked to be a member of the Irish Academy being organized by Shaw & Yeats & Robinson, etc.—and accepted. Of course, I'm "associate" because not Irish born. But this I regard as an honor, whereas other Academies don't mean much to me. Anything with Yeats, Shaw, A.E., O'Casey, Flaherty, Robinson in it is good enough for me. Joyce refused to join—hates Academies. Dunsany also refused because sore he was asked to be "associate." The rule is you must have been born in Ireland & treated Irish subjects to be a full member. Dunsany fails on the latter count. Still & all I think little Ireland will have an Academy that will compare favorably with any country's. At any rate, I'm pleased about all this.

---

347 • TO ARTHUR MCGINLEY.[1]   ALS 1 p. (Sea Island Beach, / Ga.) [Private]

Dec. 10th 1932

Dear Art: Just a line in haste in answer to your letter which reached me this p.m. The enclosed is the best I can do. I am in a tough spot myself what with the beating I have taken in investments, along with everyone else—just about cash broke. All I got from *Electra* last year is sunk in the house we've built down here—all I'm getting now from *E*. is mortgaged to Income Tax. And I have large alimony & four children being educated, and no new play ready for a long while yet. So you see. I'm not crying poor on you. Just a frank explanation.

---

1. Boyhood friend of O'Neill from New London, who had become a sportswriter.

There is no one I would rather be of service to than you. The fact that we haven't been able to get together much of late years makes no never mind in the status of my old friendship, I hope you know that.

I had heard rumors about Tom[2] giving J.B. a hard battle. It's good news that he's admitted he's licked. He'll be all right now.

Yes, for Pete's sake, hang on to the old job! A man with one seems just about to be a millionaire these days. A hell of a time, this, what?

I remember the argument with Phil[3] but thought it happened in Dondero's. I wouldn't have made any such crash later on. The Old Man and I got to be good friends and understood each other the winter before he died. But in the days you speak of I was full of a secret bitterness about him—not stopping to consider all he took from me and kept on smiling.

Will baseball take you down this way this spring? Or isn't there any more Hartford baseball? If you do come be sure and spend a few days with us en route. I won't be going to N.Y. for God knows how long. Too damned expensive.

Good luck!   As ever,   Gene

---

348 • TO EUGENE O'NEILL, JR.   ALS 4 pp. (Casa Genotta, / Sea Island, Ga.) [Yale]

Jan. 14th 1933

Dear Eugene: Your two letters arrived all right and I was darned pleased to hear so at length from you. Also, as you know, the books came through unscathed—I mean, as you know through Carlotta's letter to Betty. Many thanks! The book you sent me is a valuable addition to the library, and Carlotta was immensely pleased with hers.

You are wrong in thinking that I have not written plays before where they came all in a flood without long preparation, as this new one of last September did. Several of my best were done just that way. I wrote *The Emperor Jones* in ten days, *The Hairy Ape* in three weeks, *Desire Under The Elms* in a little over five (with an intermission caused by work with the *Welded* production). As you say, there really is no rule that I can see except that as you grow older you take more pains (generally speaking) and take less for granted—also you choose more complicated themes and prefer characters of more involved, modern, "civilized" psychology and less obvious, more suppressed and hidden motives. But the taking of pains over subtle details is a prominent factor. I've spoiled several good themes in the past by an intolerance about rewriting, an injudicious cocksureness, an impatience to get on with the next. As it happens, though, this Sept. opus deals with very simple people and it may very well prove to be all right as is, as *Jones, Ape & Desire* did. It has very little plot. It is more the capture of a mood, an evocation [of] the spirit of a time that is dead now with all its ideals and manners & codes—the period in which my middle 'teens were spent—a memory of the time of my youth—not of *my* youth but of the youth in which my generation spent youth—there is very little actually autobiographical about it except a few minor incidentals which don't touch the story at all. The title, in strict confidence, is *Ah, Wilderness!*

I've put "Without Endings Of Days" aside—and for a long time, I think. In spite of all my intense labor on it, it simply refused to work itself out as a satisfyingly expressive whole. I finally got nervous indigestion out of my frustrated battle with it—and threw up the sponge for the time being. A case in point where infinite pains and concentration availed nothing! Pending some revealing gush of inspiration, said drama is out! I was most dejected about this

2. Tom McGinley, Art's brother, who was a heavy drinker.
3. Possibly Phil Sheridan, another New London friend.

for a time but now I feel relieved and full of new ideas, as if an old man of the sea had been removed from my back. And I've started a new one about which I'm very enthusiastic, "The Life Of Bessie Bowen" being the interestingly unplaylike title for this one. The play, I hope, will emphasize and give much meaning to that title.

When I get *Ah, Wilderness!* typed I will send you a copy. It's not a play one can explain. Moreover I haven't looked at it since I finished. Don't get the impression I feel I may not *like* it. I have an immense affection for it. But whether it is enough of a play to carry across what I mean in it in a theatre is something I'm not deciding for a long while yet. Perhaps if I give you the subtitle you will sense the spirit of what I've tried to recapture in it "A Nostalgic Comedy of the Ancient Days when Youth was Young, and Right was Right, and Life was a Wicked Opportunity." Yes, it *is* a comedy—and not in a satiric vein like *Marco M.*—and not deliberately spoofing at the period (like most modern comedies of other days) to which we now in our hopeless befuddlement and disintegration and stupidity feel so idiotically superior, but laughing at its absurdities while at the same time appreciating and emphasizing its lost spiritual & ethical values.

But, hell, that doesn't say what I mean. It's in the mood of the play, as you'll see when you read it. The point is it's new ground for me. Hence, in spite of my affection for it, my uncertainty about it as play. But what pleasure I got out of writing it! It was such a change from the involved and modern and tragic hidden undertones of life I usually go after. It's about the last play they would ever suspect me of writing. And, really, let me confess it, I think it's pretty damned good, too—and even if no one agrees I'm afraid they can never convince me!

What you say about the German translations is damned interesting and illuminating. Thank you for going into such detail. I had the *Electra* translation gone over by a German shark in N.Y. The first version was very poor, the shark said, so it was refused and sent back to the translator for rewriting. This was done and it is now pronounced a fine job. I thought you would have enough work on your hands without taking that on. I'll send you a copy when I get one.

Coming to finances, I may be forced to give you a cut next year. But no good anticipating trouble. Did I tell you in my last *Electra* had closed? Didn't make much difference. I was getting practically nothing from it, anyway. But it's all out and nothing in from now on—until God knows when. And it would do no good to have a play on in N.Y. now. There is no business. The theatre here is in frightful shape as a business. I don't know what in hell they will do if it keeps on much longer. Even the big hits in N.Y. are cutting prices, etc., etc. Everyone seems desperate. So even if I have a play ready for next year—which I very much doubt now—it can't be counted on for anything. Between alimony & income tax, Federal & State, the overhead is something ghastly, that's the big trouble!

Emperor Jones as opera with Tibbett playing it at the Met. seems to be the season's sensation in the theatre line! Fact! People woke up to *Jones* again, it seems. I couldn't hear it for static over the radio but the critics say it is play with incidental music rather than opera. And they all rave over Tibbett's acting & voice. Which pleases me. I always knew any good actor, white or black, could make a hit in *Jones*. It's simply realistic superstition to think only a coon can play it. It's one of the surest fire parts in modern drama.

The "Leonenberger" sounds grand! Send us a snap of one, will you? If times get better you might bring me back one on your final return. Just now, even Blemie eats too much!   Much love from us to you & Betty.   Father

349 • TO RICHARD MADDEN.   WIRE 1 p. (Sea Island Beach, Ga.) [Yale]

[March 17, 1933]

UNITED ARTISTS PROPOSITION RECEIVED STOP TELL HORNBLOW TO STOP JOKING HE KNOWS BETTER THAN THAT STOP I NEVER HAVE WRITTEN LEGITIMATE PLAYS FOR ACTORS OR ACTRESSES LET ALONE SCREEN TREATMENTS AND THEY COULD NOT INTEREST ME IN REWRITING ANYTHING OF MINE TO FIT A TALKIE PRIMA DONNA FOR EIGHT HUNDRED AND FIFTY BILLION DOLLARS IN HOARDED GOLD STOP IF THEY WANT TO BUY DESIRE OR TREATMENT OR BOTH THE PRICE IS SAME AS FOR JONES BUT NET STOP OTHERWISE LETS DROP THE SUBJECT PLEASE QUOTE THIS WIRE VERBATIM TO UNITED ARTISTS REGARDS=   GENE

---

350 • TO EUGENE O'NEILL, JR.   ALS 4 pp. (Casa Genotta, / Sea Island, / Ga.)
[Yale]

May 13th 1933

Dear Eugene: Your letter must have picked a slow boat. It did not reach me here until this a.m.

Do I think your plans denote incipient insanity in the family? Far, far from it! I approve in toto! I am immensely pleased by the whole tenor of your letter. Let me confess with shame that I had underrated the soundness of your judgment—or, more exactly, overrated your fascination for things German—and was afraid you might have fallen under the youthfully enthusiastic spell of the Hitler hokum. Temporarily, I mean. I knew you would see through it before very long. Anyway, from this confession, you can imagine that I read your letter with inner shouts of acclaim. My own opinion of the Nazi movement is that it is the prize clowning of this doleful era of moronic antics! The stupidity of it is simply beyond belief— the incredible misunderstanding of the psychology of other peoples and the boomerang effect of that blunder! Really, it's hard to have any patience with the Germans now. They are worse than the Bourbons at never learning from experience. Here, after years of effort by their sensible leaders—and helped by the miserly gluttony of France—the world was all set to think pro-German—and now, smash!—the world remembers the War and regrets its failure to move on to Berlin when it had the chance and administer a more crushing beating! Well, well! Pighead is the word!

I appreciate that you have been in a very irritating position as a foreign student among a lot of intolerant Nazis. Ever since the Nazis began to act up Carlotta & I have done a lot of uneasy wondering about your & Betty's status under the new regime. I only hope you keep your temper until you're safely over the frontier!

The Iceland expedition is a grand idea! I feel a decided personal interest in it. I don't know if you remember—perhaps I never told you—but around the time I did my adaption of "The Ancient Mariner" I was seriously contemplating a similar, but more ambitious, attempt with the Saga of Eric the Red, inspired by the same interest you express in your letter for the Vineland-Discovery of America background. But I was stopped by the uninteresting, colorless (from a dramatic point of view) translation, as I recollect, and by my total ignorance of the Icelandic music which I wanted to weave into it. But it remains a grand idea—and perhaps, with help from you, I may be able to go ahead with it sometime.

The return to Yale is the right line. I have a very deep feeling nowadays—in fact, ever since my years in France—that this is the destined time for America to fall back upon itself in a cultural sense, to cease running to Mama & Papa Europe whenever it feels spiritually wounded by its own crudity, to realize appreciatively and with pride that the adolescent attitude has become a pose, that *it is* adult if it will only examine itself. We laid so much emphasis in the past few decades on what we lack, that we became entirely blind to what, under the sordid surface, we were daily gaining, as well as the worth of the scorned traditional past in American History. Naturally, I don't mean we should begin to cultivate the narrow nationalistic egotism which is the sure boastful sign of an inferiority complex (Nazi!) but merely that it is time we acquired the poise and dignity of a people who are self-possessed, sure of their equality among the other nations, quietly confident, not needing to be jingo. (I have done a bit of study in American History this winter and this has helped much in making me understand these U.S.—and myself as American.)

To get down to the trials of the depression, I would say that, in spite of going off the gold standard, etc., things here are really better. At any rate, the spirit is better. Roosevelt, whatever mistakes he may make, is a man with guts who is honestly facing the facts and acting upon them—no flabby, spineless Hoover!—and the country is back of him so far, in spite of politics. He is immensely popular and Congress, willing or no, has not yet had the nerve to buck that popularity and obstruct him with "special interest" intriguing. How long this happy state will last, quién sabe? And how all the stupendous plans for farm relief, etc., etc. will work out, no one can predict. The country is hopeful now on the basis that these schemes *will do* the trick. But if it turns out that they fail to improve matters—and they are all frankly experimental—then we will have a reaction to much worse depression than any known yet—and probably a demand for uncontrolled inflation that no government can resist.

Re your finances: I deeply appreciate your fine spirit about the cut. You are grand stuff, Eugene. But it won't be necessary for you to draw in the old belt so drastically—unless improbable and unforeseen disasters intervene. You can count on 1200 for next year. I've had a bit of good luck in selling *Emperor Jones* to the Talkies.[1] No great price, but with all the companies in bankruptcy or near it, as good as could be expected. The good luck was marred somewhat by the banking crisis coming up just around payment date with the result that instead of cash down I had to compromise on so much down, balance next Jan. 1st, or lose the sale. Will I ever get that balance? Well, some of it, anyway—perhaps! But I'm grateful for the sale which helps a lot in planning the near future on what I did get. I want, if possible, not to have any play produced next season either. Conditions in the N.Y. theatre are frightful and will be until general conditions change for the better. I want to wait and give this time to happen. The new plays will be difficult to "get over" and they will need all the breaks possible. Bucking present conditions sets a play an almost impossible task.

Speaking of plays and your letter in answer to mine about *Ah, Wilderness!*, my failure to answer that was not due to thinking you had misunderstood me but simply to slaving on the 5th draft of "Without End of Days" which I finished about two weeks ago. It's now being typed. This 5th version is a great improvement on the others but I don't think it is yet what I want it to be. I'll read it over in a couple of months and see. Involves a new technical method—a sort of Faust-Mephistopheles in one person idea, modern psychologically conceived, the damned self being masked, the two selves speaking as from one individual, the unmasked self being the only one the other people in the play see—or hear, even when it is the masked self who speaks. This is just to give you a general idea.

What you said about the generations in that letter was damned interesting, even though *Ah, Wilderness!* does not bring up any comparison except by remote implication and contrast.

1. The United Artists film version of *The Emperor Jones*, starring Paul Robeson, with a screenplay by DuBose Heyward, opened in September 1933.

No, it is purely a play of nostalgia for youth, a sentimental, if you like, evocation of the mood of emotion of a past time which, whatever may be said against it, possessed a lot which we badly need today to steady us. I mean, not the same thing, that's dead; but the inner reality of that thing conceived in terms of life today. The good idea of the simple old family life as lived by the typical middle class hard working American of the average large-small town which is America in miniature—the coming of the new radical literature of that day to youth (Shaw, Ibsen, Wilde, Omar Khayyam, etc.)—that's what I've tried to do in the play. A play about people, simple people of another day but real American people. But you will see better than I can explain when you read it. *And* a comedy! It's damned funny (at least to me!). But it makes me weep a few tears, too!

To get back to finances, I will see that the three hundred you want gets to Iceland the early part of June—or, perhaps, before that. Let me know as soon as you receive it so I'll know. I'll have the Guaranty Trust in N.Y. attend to it.

I think you are wise to postpone the Greek trip and hold it out as a future reward to yourself. It will make it all the more valuable to you when it comes. And I ought to be able to help you on it then if things recover here.

Casa Genotta is beautiful now and we are certainly proud and happy in our home. You would be amazed the way the grounds have taken hold and burgeoned. Everything seems to have been here for years.

A final word at parting! Between us, Son—and meaning no offense and no desire to muscle in on such a personal issue!—I hope to Christ you have decided to dish your Prussian hair bob! Every time I look at your pre-bob photos I am puzzled as to how one with such an appreciation for the Greek feeling for life could deliberately disfigure his physical good looks in the name of post-Goethe Germania! (How Goethe would loathe that hair brush style, by the way!) And the utilitarian excuse I can't go, either! Combing the old locks once in a while is not my notion of sweated labor! Of course, this is rank impertinence and I will love you just the same, bristle bean or not, but still I do hope to Christ—!

If you don't believe me, I'll leave it to Betty's honest opinion. I don't know what she thinks but I'm sure she agrees!   Carlotta joins in much love to you both!   Father

P.S. We're going up North—to mountain lake, somewhere—from mid-August to October 1st to get a change from this climate at its most enervating time. Feel you need to do that every other year when you live here. So that will fit in well with your return. We'll be able to see you both at New Haven or N.Y. on our way back. Fini!

---

351 • TO CYNTHIA CHAPMAN.   ALS 2 pp. (Stationery headed: Casa Genotta / Sea Island / Georgia) [Yale]

May 21st 1933

Dearest Cynthia: Well, hopeless to make excuses for the long delay in answering your letter! I won't try. I'll rely on the fact that you must have become resigned to what a shiftless correspondent I am by this time and that, in the kindness of your heart, you make due allowance for congenital failings!

I'm treating myself to a bit of vacation just now. Finished the fifth draft of the play I've been working on two weeks or so ago. Since then, much swimming and fishing and lazing in the sun. Am having the play typed now and won't look at it again for a month or more. Then I'll read it and try and figure out just how much work has still to be done on it and whether it will be ready for production next season or not.

Or I may decide it's rotten and burn it up! You never know! I have the first draft of another new one finished, too—and an outline of still another. So there is no lack of material to go on with.

Last week was spring cleaning with us—packing away winter stuff and getting out the light wear—and your mother surpassed herself! Blemie and I spent the week in corners here and there trembling to the roar of vacuum cleaners and floor polishers.

Our latest personal contact with the depression is that my publishers, Liveright, have gone bankrupt. It's a merry world! Luckily, I have a contract by which I am released from them in case they bust. But, of course, the royalties owing me I will never get—and now I have the worry of picking a new publisher who will stay sound. Plenty of offers, of course, but it takes a lot of careful scrutiny to make the right choice.

Beer muscles? Well, look out and be sure it's muscle! As I remember the ultimate effect of beer—oh, those dear, dead, ancient days!—it ran more to fat than muscle. Though not on me. *Nothing* can put fat on me! It's the old story of them as wants it can't get it. But beer means nothing in our lives in Georgia; even if my hat had not long ago been withdrawn from that ring. Georgia & I are still bone dry! Which rhymes like a W.C.T.U. slogan.

Think of you? Of course I do—and often. You don't realize how much I appreciate having you for a step-daughter and admire your fine qualities and soundness of character—as a person, quite outside of your being my "step" anything. And I sure hope we will all get together this summer and I will have the pleasure of seeing you again. It all depends now on finances—the universal question mark these days. The breaks lately have been bad and it's really impossible to predict a month ahead, even, whether one can do what one plans to do or not. However, here's hoping!

I'm glad Gus[1] is all you desire in the way of Romeo! From what I've heard he sounds like fine stuff and I hope to meet him someday.

Give my love to your Grandmother—and remember I am, even when most lazily silent as to letters, always your loving step-father—and your devoted friend always, which makes it more so.

A favor! Send me a snapshot of yourself when you get one you like.   Love!   Gene

---

352 • TO GEORGE JEAN NATHAN.   ALS 2 pp. (Stationery headed: Casa Genotta / Sea Island / Georgia) [Cornell]

May 31st 1933

Dear George: I have practically settled that I will go with Random House as soon as a few things get ironed out. To me their proposition is particularly attractive and presents an exceptional setting. I don't want to go with a big firm with a large mixed list but to place my stuff where it will be concentrated upon. Random House, with its sure fire commercial background of The Modern Library, and its other background of the Random House fine books, will have no one but Robinson Jeffers and me as a starter on the new selected trade list they are starting. And Jeffers is the kind of company I am proud to be in.

I needn't add that they are offering me all I was after financially—and then some. And, what is most important to me, they are giving Saxe Commins a fine job on a three year contract. I have been holding out for this—was determined the Liveright mess was not going to throw Saxe out on a cold, unemployed world. As you know, he is one of my oldest and

---

1. Augustus Barnett, whom Cynthia Chapman, age sixteen, married later in 1933.

most loyal friends and I want to do all I can to help him. He has two kids and he and his wife have been putting up such a courageous battle with the breaks constantly coming against them. So I've wanted to seize my opportunity to make sure that they get a good break at last. He will be getting a real chance in the right spot at Random House—where, with most of the other publishers, he would be out of it as far as real opportunity goes, even if I could make them take him on.

Another important point is that according to the report on the financial status of every publisher that has made me an offer (which I had the Guaranty Trust Co. make for me) Random House is in an exceptionally sound position as compared with even the most favorably situated of the others.

So you see. I think you will agree with me that my choice is a good one and based on a pretty sound survey of the field. I've been doing nothing for a month but look over publishers' lists—and God, what strings of junk most of them put out!—and read the financial reports from the Guaranty and Madden and Saxe's dope. I think with Random House I will feel my stuff is at home—and darned if I felt that about any of the others! Also I like Cerf[1] and know we can work together—especially with Saxe there in personal charge of my end as part of his Random House job.

It's damned good news to hear, via your note to Carlotta, that you've about decided to pay us that visit! Fine! There's a lot I want to tell you, too lengthy for a letter, and a lot I want to ask your advice about.   As ever,   Gene

P.S. Thanks for your information about the royalty guarantee form of contract! But, thinking it over, I have decided I don't need it when I have the security I am getting in Random H. contract.

---

353 • TO BENNETT CERF.   TLS 3 pp. (Stationery headed: Casa Genotta / Sea Island / Georgia) [Columbia]

June 4th 1933

Dear Mr. Cerf,   There is one important thing all wrong with the contract, and that is due to the fact that we never cleared up between us the matter of advance on new books, after I offered to guarantee you three new plays—a stipulation which was not included in my old tentative contract, where I assumed that five thousand was to be advanced only on my first new play to be published. The point now is that the advance as applied to three new plays is one thousand less than I would have received from Liveright under my old contract with them—and that, you must admit, is hardly fair. What I suggest, therefore, is that the five thousand advance down apply only to the first new play, a like amount to be paid on each new play thereafter when you accept the script for publication.

I would not make this demand if I were not absolutely sure myself—and confident that you are equally sure, from the evidence of figures on past sales—that you cannot possibly lose on this arrangement, or even have to wait more than a brief period after publication for the amount advanced to be earned.

There is another clause which, because of the special conditions existing in my case, I think inadvisable from your interest as well as mine—the clause covering my paying the cost of changes in script, over ten percent. Now that is perfectly all right with me provided I don't submit a final script to you until the end of rehearsals—which, of course, would mean delay

1. Bennett Cerf (1898–1971), former vice-president of Liveright and cofounder, with Donald Klopfer, of Random House.

in publication. But if publication simultaneous with production is desired, with galleys set up by the time rehearsals start, then I must be allowed a free hand to incorporate in the galleys any changes or cuts that rehearsals reveal as valuable to the play.

I know this clause is part of the usual contract and I agree that it is fair as regards novels, etc., but in the case of a play when publication at the same time as production is an asset to the publisher, it seems to me a mistake—for I can't, in justice to my work, call a script final until rehearsals are well along. Liveright gave me this privilege. Saxe can tell you exactly how it worked out with *Electra*—and remember in that case, it was really three plays that were being rehearsed in rotation, which made it difficult. With one play, undoubtedly the final draft will be ready earlier—and none of my next three plays will be more than average length—at least, I'm absolutely sure neither of the first two will be.

Outside of these two items, the contract looks okay to me—pending, of course, whatever Weinberger may have to suggest in a final going over.

There are some notions that have occurred to me re the best scheme for getting out the new edition of the old plays, but this can wait until I see you again, either on my way North in August or back in October.

We're glad you enjoyed your visit here. It certainly was a pleasure for both of us to have you. Come again!

All good wishes,   Very sincerely,   Eugene O'Neill

---

354 • TO OONA O'NEILL.   ALS 1 p. (Stationery headed: Casa Genotta / Sea Island / Georgia) [Virginia]

June 9th 1933

Dear Oona: Thank you so much for your nice letter, and for the picture which I am having framed to hang on the wall of my bedroom. You could not give me anything that would please me more. You look so happy and healthy—and pretty! I am so proud of being the father of such a fine girl!

I will hope to see you this fall on my way back from the Adirondacks, where we expect to spend August & September—which, as in Bermuda, are unpleasantly sweltering down here.

It is all right for Shane to visit here in the summer, because he is so much more grown than you, but I am afraid the sudden change to this climate would not be a good thing for you until you are a little older.

Much love to you—and again thank you for the picture!   As ever,   Daddy

---

355 • TO HARRY WEINBERGER.   ALS 2 pp. (Stationery headed: Casa Genotta / Sea Island / Georgia) [Yale]

June 11th 1933

Dear Harry: The extra 15 for Terry[1] is okay with me. I've been thinking about him a lot. The ideal thing for him—between us, for I know he'd be offended by the suggestion—would be a Home—not charity but a decent place where I could pay a reasonable amount monthly and know he was getting real care. And I'm sure he'd have a better time in such a place, once he was "put" there. It will have to come to that in the end. I read the copy of wire you

---

1. Terry Carlin, who died in Boston in late 1933.

enclosed without enthusiasm. It may solve his problem for three months or so—then he'll be out in the world again. What he needs now is the security of a final settlement. And I distrust Bohemian charity. Truro means booze—and a little more booze and what mental control he has left will be gone and he'll be a total wreck. However, I suppose nothing can be done about it, knowing him.

Try and pry that Book of Month money from Liveright—the total of it.

Hot as hell here—and I read how N.Y. is the same.   Yours in a sweat,   Gene

---

356 • TO SOPHUS KEITH WINTHER.   TLS 3 pp. (Stationery headed: Casa Genotta / Sea Island / Georgia) [Tao House]

July 7th 1933

Dear Mr. Winther,   I have read your book[1] and am most enthusiastic about it. Congratulations on a splendid job. It impresses me as a searching critical analysis, finely conceived and soundly carried out. What particularly strikes me is that you have so illuminatingly revealed the relationship of the plays to the mental and spiritual background of their time, and shown that background as inseparable from the work—something no one else has so far troubled to do except sketchily, yet which is so essential to any true comprehension of what I have attempted to accomplish. I am also delighted with the way you dispose of the "gloomy," "pessimistic," "one-sided" nonsense which has always greeted every play of mine until it has become a meaningless cliché of criticism which uses catchwords to defend itself from understanding. Then again, your appreciation of the meaning of *Lazarus Laughed* is especially grateful to me because I have always regarded it as one of my best, and been disappointed that no one yet has had the courage to produce it in New York, and it has had to depend for a hearing upon the reading public. This is unfortunate, because it is so essentially a drama which must be seen and heard to bring out its best values.

I am deeply grateful to you for your book. It says so many things about aspects of my work that have been overlooked in previous estimates,—things I have always wanted said. It is truly comprehensive. After reading it, I know anyone with intelligence will read or see the plays, past or to come, with a fresh understanding and a new standard for valid criticism. I can say no more—except thank you.

We are going to New York in three weeks and I will then bring your script to the attention of my new publisher—Random House—and see what is possible in that direction. You may rely on me to do my damndest. I have a play agent who also collects book royalties but no literary agent into whose hands I could put it.

In reading, I thought I noticed an error here and there—for instance "son" where you meant "wife" in one spot—that sort of thing—nothing important.

Naturally, there are a few points where I don't agree with you—something you say about the danger of mysticism, for example. To me the danger lies more in no mysticism. We tend complacently to regard the unknown as non-existent because it is unknown to us—but drama should keep a place for intuitive vision or it loses an inherent, powerful value.

And what you say about mental telepathy in *Desire* and *Electra*. I hadn't defined it to myself as that, but I certainly believe that under special, stress conditions of extreme passionate tension, where one person is emotionally "tuned in" on another, so to speak, that some sort of super-awareness is possible at a crucial moment. Or call it due to an extraordinary

---

1. *Eugene O'Neill: A Critical Study* (New York: Random House, 1934), the manuscript of which Winther had sent to O'Neill for his comments.

intensification of the functions of the senses—one hears a sound too low for ordinary hearing, etc. That science has not got this in its card index seems to me simply because it is obviously barred from ever sitting in on such rare occasions. But, after all, as I interpret the latest scientific-mystical dogmas, we seem to become more and more merely other electrical plants, and, accepting that, emotional thought transference strikes me as much less incredible than my radio set!

I mention the above, not by way of criticism, but because the points brought up are extremely interesting to me. I am a great believer in all we don't know about ourselves, but inclined to skepticism about what we think we know.

Again, my grateful appreciation—and all good wishes to you.   Cordially,   Eugene O'Neill

---

357 • TO PAUL HYDE BONNER.[1]   TLS 3 pp. (Stationery headed: Casa Genotta / Sea Island / Georgia) [Princeton]

July 12th 1933

Dear Paul,   I have read the play and it is certainly damned interesting. You have aimed high, attempted a most difficult thing, and you ought to feel tremendously encouraged over the result. It is surprisingly free of those missteps of inexperience which almost invariably mar the first plays of any author. The dialogue is excellent, has the right "heard" rather than "read" quality; the characterization is sound and consistent psychologically. I am sure not only that the play reads well but that it would act well. And the underlying theme of the play is deeply intriguing intellectually and emotionally moving.

But my feeling is you still have a lot of work to do before you submit it for production. As I read I became conscious of a weakness in dramatic architecture, in inner unity. I do not mean architecture in the "well made play" sense, of course. What I have in mind is found in the plays of Tchekov as well as Ibsen's. It is a clear dramatic revelation of the relationship of all the parts to the whole—a close interweaving of all threads to sustain and bring out the main underlying theme, whether that theme concerns a group of people or is concentrated on one character. In reading your play I felt a looseness of construction, a wavering about, a diffusion of interest as if, while your main theme was clear in your own mind, in the play the several stories of human interrelationships were alternately concentrating interest on themselves *as themselves* rather than as harmonious parts building up into and illuminating a central conception.

Which may sound confusing but I know you will get what I'm driving at. The play needs closer knitting together, dramatic pointing up and sharpening of outline, in order to get over at its full value what you are trying to express about life. I think if you will put it aside for a few months to get perspective, then read it over with the question in your mind right from page one of Act One, what is my main theme and how am I building up to it, you will see just what to do about this. You will discover just where you get in your own way. (Believe me, I speak from experience!)

There are several purely technical points about which my theatre experience leads me to have misgivings but I won't bore you with those now. They don't touch the essential quality—are a matter of stagecraft, easily corrected (if found to be true) without affecting anything fundamental in your play.

---

1. Bonner (1893–1968), former textile executive who later became successful as a writer of novels of intrigue.

I think you rely on your Easter Island monolith to do too much for you. Dangerous!

So much for carping! Don't take my objections as too valid. I'm a fellow playwright, setting up no claims as critic, and the best I can do is to report my reactions on your play as I would see its faults if it were mine. But this is hardly a sure criterion for infallible judgment! However, I would not be honest with the friendship I feel for you if I didn't give you these personal objections. Also, I know you want frankness. But don't let anything I have said discourage you or you *will* be mistaking my judgment. I repeat again, you have aimed high, you have tackled a hell of a hard one, and you should feel damned proud of the result!

I hate to be hard-hearted but if the drop in the dollar brings you and Lilly to Sea Island then, says I, there's a lot to be said for inflation. You know, just to show what a morbid guy I am, I've often thought of that angle—and hoped it would! You and I will purchase a shrimp boat (on the cuff!) and start in to earn an honorable living while Lilly and Carlotta see who can grow the biggest yams.   Our affectionate best to you both,

Eugene O'Neill   (Gene)

(The above formality being a letter-signing habit slip)

P.S. How about script? Shall I retain for future reference in case you want to make some queries—or send to England?

---

358 • **TO DUBOSE HEYWARD.**   ALS 2 pp. (Wurzburg Camp / Faust, N.Y.) [Private]

August 7th 1933

Dear Mr. Heyward: Much gratitude for your letter—which, by the way, has had a lot of chasing to do before it caught me up here.

It does not need your letter to tell me that you put your best into *Jones*—and I hope I need not assure you that your best is good enough for me, and then some! I know I am going to be particularly pleased with this picture. It was my intention to see it last week when we were in New York, but we landed in the midst of that damnable heat wave and Mrs. O'Neill and I were so knocked out that we did not leave our rooms in the hotel except when we absolutely had to. Georgia seemed like a nice cool summer resort during those oven-like three days! But I will see the picture as soon as I return to N.Y. for rehearsals.

Oh, I can easily credit your experience with the censorship. The same sort of thing happened with *"Anna Christie"* & *Strange Interlude*. And Mr. Hays,[1] who cheers with senile lechery when that dainty Mae West sings "I like a guy wot takes his time" has barred *Desire Under The Elms* forever from the films! (Meaning no slur at Mae, you understand. I think she's grand.) And in England the censorship made them change the title *Strange Interlude* to *Strange Interval*—why no one in England could discover, but apparently on moral grounds! Crazy? You said it! But it's almost a comfort to know England is even more idiotic!

I'm damned pleased to know Robeson came through so well. I did have misgivings about him.

Again, thank you for your kindness in writing. When we are back at Sea Island, after the battle of rehearsals is over, we certainly hope Mrs. Heyward and you will find time to pay us a visit. I sure felt that time you were there that you and I would be great friends if we ever had the chance of getting acquainted. So here's hoping we'll get together!   Cordially, Eugene O'Neill

---

1. Will H. Hays (1879–1954), American lawyer and politician. As president of the Motion Picture Producers and Distributors of America (1922–45) he instituted a production code for motion picture censorship (1930), generally known as the Hays Code.

359 • TO LAWRENCE LANGNER.   ALS 3 pp. (Wurzburg Camp, / Faust, N.Y.) [Yale]

August 7th '33

Dear Lawrence: The more I have considered it from all angles the more convinced I become that the best showmanship is to do *Ah, Wilderness!* first. Psychologically speaking, we will thus break the continuity of "O'Neill" plays in the public mind and be able in a sense to start again on them with *Days Without End* after the surprise of *Ah, Wilderness!* has made them temporarily forgotten. In this way we will avoid the reaction after *Mourning Becomes Electra* which would be harmful to *Days Without End* (as *Dynamo* on top of *Interlude*)—the direct comparison, get me, the natural inclination to feel that after a big trilogy like *Electra* with so dramatic a Greek tragic plot, etc. a play of love and religious faith like *Days Without End* can't be so much, is a let down in interest. But with *Ah, Wilderness!,* it will be obvious to even the dumbest theatre goer that no such comparison can apply, it is in another class entirely, demanding a fresh approach and unique hearing. Don't you agree? But once *Ah, Wilderness!* has broken the spell of comparisons with *Electra,* I think we can do *Days Without End* as soon as we like and be sure that its hearing will also be from a fresh standpoint.

Another thing: *Days Without End* is nothing if not controversial, especially in its Catholic aspect. It is sure, fail or succeed, to arouse much bitter argument. It will be well hated by the prejudiced who won't see the psychological study end of it but only the general aspect. And, technically too, there will be much argument pro & con. Now I feel strongly that such a post-production atmosphere, if *Days Without End* were done first, would be fatal for *Ah, Wilderness!* All the boys would take out on it the resentments and bewilderments they had gotten from *Days Without End* and *Ah, Wilderness!* is too gentle and sentimental a thing to buck a too hostile world.

Give all this careful thought, all of you, and I know you'll agree.

I've made the change back to Catholicism and the priest uncle in *Days Without End*—and it sure is more definitely alive that way. Am sending off this revised script to be retyped.

Beautiful lake, this—a cool welcome change for a while from Georgia sea level summer (not to add the N.Y. summer of last week!). All our best to Armina & you!   As ever, Gene

P.S. I hope *Lady Godiva*[1] turned less wooden for you!

P.S. II There is one thing about *Days Without End* I want you all to note: I expect to cut quarter to half hour out of it in rehearsals. It is much too long.

---

360 • TO LAWRENCE LANGNER.   ALS 3 pp. (Wurzburg Camp, / Faust, N.Y.) [Yale]

Aug. 8th 1933

Dear Lawrence: Thinking it over, I'm afraid my letter of yesterday re which play should be done first sounded a damned sight more definite on the matter than I really am. As a matter of fact, I waver and feel one way about it one day and another the next. There is a lot to be said on both sides, and I've been saying it all to myself until I'm quite gaga and confused and my opinion is worthless. All I know is that any play of mine that immediately follows *Electra* is in a bad spot—no matter how good it is; and I'm so close to both these two plays that I really don't know just how good or bad either of them is. This is particularly true in the

1. Langner's play that was being produced at the Westport Country Playhouse.

case of *Ah, Wilderness!* which is so out of my previous line. Has it got something finer to it than its obvious surface values—a depth of mood and atmosphere, so to speak, that would distinguish it from another play of the same genre, the usual type? I felt it had when I wrote it. (Nathan, for example, says most emphatically yes.) But now, frankly, I'll be damned if I can trust myself to judge. I simply don't know. It's up to you Guilders to decide. Has it charm and humor and tender reminiscence enough to disarm the people who will feel that dramatically it is a terrible let-down after *Electra?* Ask me another! I certainly don't know the answer—but it's important some—should guess it before long.

But why go on in this strain? I'm only writing you to tell the Guild that, frankly, I've thought myself into a state of confusion on the issue of productions of these two opuses and, for the nonce, you-alls will have to furnish all the bright ideas. At present, *Ah, Wilderness!* and *Days Without End* are just a few hundred typewritten pages to me. This mist will lift, but it's a dense fog just now.[1]

Am fishing enthusiastically each day but so far the fish seem quite unaware of it.

Best from us to Armina & you!   As ever,   Gene

P.S. Sent you a wire today re my notion how to classify plays in any publicity announcement. Think you'll agree.

P.S. II Send script *The Pursuit Of Happiness*[2] to above address. (I mention this because I've forgotten whether we gave you this address as is above or Wolf Lake.)

P.S. III I want to apologize, Lawrence, for wishing all my hunches and perplexities on you when I know you have so much on your own mind with your own work. But I've calculated that my letters and wire would reach you when the stress was over. Hope I was right. I bobbed up from Ga. at an unfortunate time for everybody, myself included, but it couldn't be helped, and I knew if I waited with my scripts until later it would only put the Guild in more of a mess re plans for next season.

---

361 • TO PHILIP MOELLER.   ALS 2 pp. (Wurzburg Camp, / Faust, N.Y.) [Texas]

August 19th '33

Dear Phil: This to supplement Carlotta's letter of yesterday in which she told you we'd surely be down Thursday. I will expect you to have the choicest samples of acting talent on view that ever were viewed. *Fresh* talent! This play sure needs a little Abbey Theatre simplicity from its cast to live in life as well as the Show Shop! But you realize that as well as I do.

I'm so damned pleased you liked the play so well! Personally, quite outside of any opinion as to its claim to worth as a play, I have a very great affection for it because for me it is a true evocation of a mood of the past, of an American life that is dead.

Re casting again, I still can't see Helen as the mother. She is too well known and striking a personality as Helen Westley, too generally recognizable as herself. I'm afraid in this play of a family, she would stand out too disproportionately where she ought to merge in—through no fault in her acting, you understand, but simply because she is Helen Westley, so familiar to Guild audiences. I don't agree with you that what we want in this play are *strong* personalities. What we want are *fresh* personalities, new blood!

---

1. *Ah, Wilderness!* opened on October 2, 1933, at the Guild Theatre; *Days Without End* opened on January 8, 1934, at the Henry Miller Theatre.
2. Play by Langner and Armina Marshall Langner, written under the pen names of Alan Child and Isabelle Louden, that was produced by Laurence Rivers, Inc. It opened at the Avon Theatre on October 9, 1933.

So I'm thumbs down on Nugent,[1] too! I'd rather give Travers[2] a chance. My God, aren't there any *new* people in our theatre? I'm going to tell you here and now what I feel is the one weakness of the Guild—stereotyped casting, not digging up new talent as other managements seem to do, always depending on old standbys. It's certainly a justifiable policy in difficult emotional plays like *Electra,* (I am the first to admit that), where those who can possibly act the parts can be counted on one's fingers. But *Ah, Wilderness!* should be easy to cast with fresh faces that will help remove it from the routine theatre. Aren't all these Summer theatres bringing out any new talent, for God's sake?

Re "Richard," I needn't tell you that no fairies need apply—nor anyone who isn't all American male boy. It would be fatal.

How about Guy Kibbee for "Sid." Can he be got? He's well known, I admit, but he *has something!* I've never heard that Nugent was anything but another adequate ham—and, as such, he's been on view to N.Y. audiences for God knows how long!

That's why I suggested Fania[3] as "Lily"—because she isn't the hackneyed actress type for the role and so might get over the living "Lily" to an audience—might *act,* in other words.

Don't think of this play as a New England play!!! It isn't, you know, in any essential respect—and near-to-New-York Connecticut never was real New England, as any New Englander will tell you. It could be laid in the Middle or Far West with hardly the change of a word. There are no colloquialisms in it, I think, that aren't general American small town. It could be New York state with no change, or N.J. or Penn. I happened to have my old home town of New London in mind when I wrote—couldn't help it—but New London, even in those days was pretty well divorced from its N.E. heritage—*was* lower Conn., in fact, with New York the strongest influence.

Well, that's about all of this! Except to say that I know we're going to have a lot of fun doing this play—if we get a cast to work with!—and I know you can direct it as no one else could.

Try to think up as many fresh people as you can, won't you? I'm hopelessly out of touch there, you know, and all depends on you & Terry.

I hope Bobby can do the sets. No one could touch what he can give it.

Re Helen again, you know I feel as you do about Fania, that I love her and there's no one I'd rather have in my stuff, but somehow I can't see her personality losing itself in the Miller family.   All best from Carlotta & me! See you soon!   Gene

---

362 • TO "AH, WILDERNESS!" COMPANY.   WIRE (draft) 1 p. (Stationery headed: The Madison / Madison Avenue at 58th Street / New York) [Yale]

[October 2, 1933]

Co   Sorry, deeply sorry I am not with you but there is a certain peculiar oil in opening nights that invariably poisons me[1] stop even at this distance I already feel in a very delicate condition stop Good luck to all of you tonight   E.O'N

1. J. C. Nugent.
2. Henry Travers.
3. Fania Marinoff.

1. Reference is to Nat Miller in act 2 of *Ah, Wilderness!*: "there's a certain peculiar oil in bluefish that invariably poisons me."

363 • TO GRACE RIPPIN. ALS 2 pp. (Sea Island Beach / Georgia) [Boston U.]

[postmarked October 16, 1933]

Dear Dolly: Rule One: Never believe reports, newspaper or otherwise, about me or my work, or pay any attention to what anyone says. Such stuff is nearly always inaccurate and misleading. Always read the play or see it! The idea that your Mother is in *Ah, Wilderness!* is absurd—and, as you will see when you read the play, there is no "rooming house" in it and no "Pequot Ave.," or anything pertaining to New London that would not equally pertain to any other Connecticut coast town. I was very careful about that because I was writing about general types of people of that period in any large small-town, and not particular persons. And I make it a point never to put real people I have known into my plays. All my characters are my own fabrication. They may have certain points about them which resemble, at times, certain traits in persons I have known, but the whole character is never true to that of any actual person.

Another thing: The time of *Ah, Wilderness!* is 1906, which was before I ever knew a Rippin!

The only two things in the play which are actual facts out of my past are two things in the dinner scene which were true about my Father.

So you see! Nothing in it—but don't hold me or my play responsible for all the gab that gets around about it. Read the play and see for yourself, that's the answer! What has set them all off is that I call the play "A Comedy of Recollection," but I meant recollection of general family life, etc. of that period, as contrasted with today, and *not* recollection of any specific family. The "Millers" in my play are like thousands of families in America of that time.

It was good to hear from you again.

Give my fondest to your Mother—and much love to you & Emily and all the clan! If I ever get up your way I certainly will hie me to 416! As ever, Gene

---

364 • TO KENNETH MACGOWAN. TLS 4 pp. (Stationery headed: Casa Genotta / Sea Island / Georgia) [Yale]

[October 16, 1933]

Dear Kenneth, I have been waiting to write you until the hectic period of *Ah, Wilderness!* production passed and we got temporarily put down here again.

First, many thanks for the check. But I hope you didn't put any strain on the bankroll to do it. You remember our agreement that you were not even to think of repaying me until all other obligations were off your chest and you felt on easy street. You know, if I were ever hard pinched, I would let out a frank howl to you for assistance. Things looked bad for a while last winter, what with the hole my "sound conservative investments" had dumped me into, and my alimony overhead (which depression leaves undepressed!) but they never quite had me completely down. And now *Ah, Wilderness!* has gone over, all's well again. I explain all this because I don't want you ever to have me on your mind—that way—and get that debtor feeling which is so fatal to old friendship. And now that's said again, let's forget it.

I hoped you liked my nostalgic adventure into comedy in *Ah, Wilderness!* I think it should hand you many reminiscent grins. You will remember those good old days as well as I, and you must have known many Miller families. I had a grand time writing it—also a grand time rehearsing, for the cast, taking it all in all from bits to leads, is the best I have ever had in a play. They really make it live very close to what I imagined it. A most enjoyable experience in the theatre, all told—and how the damn thing moves young, middle-aged and old! It's astonishing. And a proof to me, at least, that emotionally we still deeply hanker after the old solidarity of the family unit.

Days Without End, the mask, pseudo-Faustian, "modern miracle play" opus goes into rehearsal about December first. I want it to open as soon after Christmas day as possible because then, if ever now, you catch people in a frame of mind to remember their past or present religious background. I think this play will interest you, psychologically as well as technically, and the ending astonish you a bit, coming from me. It was an end I resisted (on personal grounds) but which finally forced itself on me as the one inevitable one.

These two plays will, I know, set you to wondering what sea change has come over me. The truth is that, after *Electra* I felt I had gone as far as it was in me to go along my old line— for the time being, at least. I felt that to try to top myself in various other phases of the old emotional attitude would be only to crucify my work on what had become for the time an exhausted formula. I felt a need to liberate myself from myself, so to speak—to see and express, if possible, the life preserving forces in other aspects which I knew from experience to be equally illustrative of the fate in human beings' lives and aspirations. In short, I felt the justice in the criticism that my plays in toto were too one-way and presented only one side of the picture, and that, if only to bring out that tragic side by contrast, I ought to express the others. And now, whatever the fate of *Days Without End*, I'm damned glad I did, for I feel immensely freer inside myself and better able to digest *all* the demands that future work may entail.

Well, well, there I go again giving you an earnest, heartfelt earful. Like old times, what? But then a guy ought to have some rights to express himself on his 45th birthday. In which connection, I must assert as no self-deluding lie but as a fact, that I'm damned if I don't feel a hell of a lot younger, body and spirit, than I did at 35 or 25. And there's a reason—*Carlotta*.

Your fear that our Adirondack jaunt might have been T.B. inspired was baseless. I never felt better—and T.B. has always been the least of my worries. If that had been on the cards, I would have been just too dead ten or fifteen years ago. What happened was we had a chance to rent a beautiful camp there for almost nothing and jumped at it. You see, the climate down here is very much like Bermuda—fine for ten months but August and September are oppressively hot and hard to take. So we'll probably go North someplace every year at that time. I hope sometime you'll get a chance to visit us here. Carlotta has designed a really beautiful home for us. She has a marvelous flair for that—and for keeping it running right. At last I know the meaning of home. And don't we both love it!

Sometime, if you're ever in the mood and have the leisure, I wish you'd write me about your experiences on the Coast, and what, if any, are your hopes that something real may finally come thro' out there.[1]

You mention a letter re *The Hairy Ape*. No such ever reached me.

Ever see Dr. Hamilton? If so, my warm greetings to him.

All best, Kenneth, and to your wife and the kids. I hope we'll have a chance to get together again before too long. In the meantime, drop a line.   As ever,   Gene

P.S. Bobby, of course, did a marvelous job on *Ah, Wilderness!* You should see the costumes and rooms and the beach scene.

---

1. Macgowan had gone to Hollywood and was working for RKO Studios.

365 • TO LAWRENCE LANGNER.   ALS 4 pp. (Stationery headed: Casa Genotta / Sea Island / Georgia) [Yale]

Oct. 29th 1933

Dear Lawrence: Your letter arrived this morning. Funny coincidence! A letter of mine to Warren Munsell, written just after I heard finally from Bobby, tells him to tell you all that. I *have* reconsidered about Lee and want him to do *Days Without End.* Said letter I sent off two days ago and it must have hit N.Y. this a.m. So you see. "Great minds," what? Must be mental telepathy.

My feeling contra Lee was never more than a hunch that he was not in sympathy with the mystic undertones of the play—could not be because he looks toward sociological solutions. Or, at least, that's my notion which may be all wrong. Not, you understand, that I think everyone connected with this play should be devout Catholics, any more than its author is. But my feeling about the sets is that they must somehow have, without one ever being conscious of it except in that last church scene, the quality of being merely background for the psychological-religious drama in John Loving's soul—should never attract notice as being something in themselves. And I felt that someone not in sympathy with the spiritual content of the opus would instinctively try to make the sets *his thing* rather than a collaboration in my thing. And when Lee wrote me that he hoped I wouldn't insist on naturalistic sets I immediately had visions of Expressionism, Constructivism, what not—all wrong for this play.

However, I admit he is right in believing the sets should not be as naturalistic in their numerous details as my book descriptions. They should be *vaguely* naturalistic, if you get me. The office should be any office of any kind of business man—so placeless that one second after the curtain is up no one sees the set or recognizes it in any way as anything but a vague background. The same applies to all the rooms in the apartment. In only the last scene in church should the set itself, in dramatic contrast to those before, become a vivid, beautiful striking thing—for there it is a character in the drama, so to speak.

In a word, what I want throughout is the simplest, most unobtrusive simplicity, done with the right color and atmosphere. We must keep the drama with lights but never, except in that last scene, with sets. It's a cinch, really. The only difficult thing will be to get Loving's mask just right, for looks & speech, and to have the exactly right crucifix for the end. I want none of your sadistic Spanish Christs who give you the horrors, but a Resurrection Christ who will express "the Resurrection & the Life" John Loving finds in Him at the end—a spiritual exaltation transcending human suffering—an idealized exultant human God.

No, that isn't such a cinch!

I'm writing all this so you can relay it on to Lee when he returns, if you'll do that little thing.

I'm especially anxious to have your sympathetic backing on this particular play, not only because it's a tough one to get over and is bound to arouse a lot of antagonism, but because I want to lean over backwards in being fair to it and getting it the best breaks. For, after all, this play, like *Ah, Wilderness!* but in a much deeper sense, is the paying of an old debt on my part—a gesture toward more comprehensive, unembittered understanding and inner freedom—the breaking away from an old formula that I had enslaved myself with, and the appreciation that there is their own truth in other formulas too, and that any life-giving formula is as fit a subject for drama as any other.

I'm now doing a bit of rewriting on the first act and probably will do more elsewhere. But not along the lines Phil suggested! God forbid! He had an awfully wrong slant on it when he talked of it that day.

Has anything been done about Jane Cowl or Digges[1] yet?

Well, having got that earful on *D.W.E.* off my chest, what's the latest on *A School For Husbands*[2] and *The Pursuit Of Happiness?* They certainly both got off to a fine start. I hope they're both building right along.

I note what you say about the six months of continual labor. Yes, you sure have been the most versatile gent in our theatre! I don't see how you carried it off—and kept right on looking weller and weller. About two weeks of that and I'd be on the parrot's perch whispering sweet nonsense into Polly's ear—nuts complete! Well, you made everything you did stick, and you ought to be feeling damned pleased with Mr. & Mrs. Langner.

Our affectionate best to you both! We look forward to seeing you in N.Y. Or why not fly down here some day in the meanwhile and surprise us—if you need a rest? The weather has been poor so far, I must admit, but it's due for a change.

Again, cheerio!   As ever,   Gene

---

366 • TO PHILIP MOELLER.   ALS 2 pp. (Stationery headed: Casa Genotta / Sea Island / Georgia) [Texas]

Oct. 30, 1933

Dear Phil: From what I heard of *Wilderness* over the radio[1] last night—*that last scene*—I gather Essie & Nat *still* don't know their lines! A most disgraceful, slovenly exhibition, between you and me, what with going up in lines, extemporizing with gaps and waits and hems and haws, mixing up names, etc. On the level, Phil, I think it's up to you, to protect the Guild and my play, to insist on the discipline of line rehearsals until *what I wrote as I wrote it* is again set.

I'm not referring to the cuts made for the radio. I knew just where those were, having consented to them for the occasion, and don't count them as gaps.

I hope this radio last scene was no indication of the way it's given nightly in the theatre—(although certainly it points to a general laxness somewhere)—or, believe me, *Ah, W* won't continue a big hit for long! Audiences will begin to walk out on it—and I would be the last to blame them!

You will admit I don't beef often—but this is certainly justified. For God's sake, get after that last scene—as I wrote it! Make them learn *MY* lines!   All best!   Gene

---

367 • TO BENNETT CERF.   AL[1] 2 pp. (Sea Island, / Ga.) [Columbia]

Nov. 6, 1933

Dear Cerf: No, I *certainly cannot consent* to your trying to get any advance endorsements of *Days Without End* from high dignitaries of the Church![2] In fact, I feel so strongly on this point that if you do, I shall have to oil up the family automatic and surge forth and eliminate you from our midst! It is the very last thing I would want done! It would throw my whole

---

1. Dudley Digges; neither he nor Jane Cowl were cast in *Days Without End.*
2. A comedy in two acts with ballet interlude adapted in rhyme by Arthur Guiterman and Lawrence Langner from Molière's *L'Ecole des maris* (1661), which was produced by the Theatre Guild and opened at the Empire Theatre on October 16, 1933.

1.The play was broadcast on October 29, 1933, on "Mobilization for Human Needs."

1. The signature at the end of this letter appears to have been cut off.
2. *Days Without End* was published by Random House on January 17, 1934.

intention in writing the play into a misleading, false emphasis. It is a play about a Catholic. It is an attempt to express what I feel are the life-preserving depths in Catholic mysticism—to be fair to a side of life I have dismissed with scorn in other plays. BUT it is also a psychological study whose psychological truth would be the same, essentially, if a Buddhist or a Greek Orthodox hero were involved. *It is not Catholic propaganda!* If, after it comes out, the Church wants to set the seal of its approval on it, well that's up to them. But I don't give a damn whether they do or not—and I certainly will not make the slightest move to win that approval in advance.

So much for my personal angle—as your suggestion affects my feeling about the integrity of my work. But putting that all aside and considering only the practical angle, I still think you are all wrong. I don't think you know the prelates, and their feeling about my work, and the use of Church themes in the theatre, as well as I do. It's an even chance your scheme would get the play denounced in advance instead of lauded! Also, these same prelates are no fools and they would look on a publisher's attempt to use them as press agents with a very intolerant eye. No! As far as the Church is concerned, hands off! Let the play speak for itself without any advance comment on that part of its subject from you or the Guild or me. And then let the Church like it—or lump it.

For your advance publicity, you have plenty of dope to use without mentioning Catholicism—interesting dope—"a new departure in technique"—"a new use of the mask"—"a modern Faustian drama"—"a modern miracle play"—etc. But, for God's sake, lay off the Catholic stuff! I repeat again, from my creative standpoint, this play, if pro-Catholic, is only incidentally so. It means much more than that meaning to me, and I can't have my meaning distorted by false emphasis from my own camp before the play even appears. There will be enough distortion of all kinds read into it by critics and public, God knows, without that.

And lastly, I'm still working on the play and revising—have just sent two acts to Saxe to retype in their new form—and I don't want anyone to read it now until I finally call it finished!

All best! See you soon—and I'll then give you a thousand other reasons why I know your suggestion, from all standpoints, is bad stuff.

P.S. I can't impress on you too strongly how emphatically I feel on this point! Please appreciate this so there will be no misunderstanding!

---

368 • TO LAWRENCE LANGNER.   ALS 2 pp. (Sea Island, [Georgia]) [Yale]

Nov. 8, 1933

Dear Lawrence: I am tickled to death that you're on the production committee—and herewith hasten to take up a few points:

Re D. Digges—too bad, but I had a hunch he would not look favorably on playing second fiddle to Earle[1] and the others. Can't O'Neill[2] be wooed from the Coast?

Re Jane C.—the more I consider it the less impressed I am by this casting. You know what J. is—a starry ham, if there ever was one—no Cohan who will play the game.[3] She will certainly try her sentimental, tearful best to steal the show from Earle, and as the wife is a

---

1. Earle Larimore (1899–1947), who played John in *Days Without End*.
2. Possibly Henry O'Neill.
3. Stage star George M. Cohan (1878–1942), who appeared in *Ah, Wilderness!*, altered his highly individual acting style to fit in with the ensemble.

sympathetic role, and "John" will have to fight every second to get across, this would create difficulties. Thinking of the balance of the play, a star as "Elsa" seems to me top heavy unless you have a bigger star as "John." You see what I mean. I'm trying to think now in terms of average audience reaction, not of the written script. We don't want to do any casting which might make that last act seem anti-climax.

Re the script: I have done and am still doing a lot of cutting and revising to clarify and simplify. So the Guild need not have any scripts typed until they get my new one—only have to junk them. I'm having new acts one & two typed now. Will have the others finished before long.

Re the mask: The sooner Lee can get hold of Larimore and get started on it, the better. It's new ground, you know, and I imagine a lot of experimenting will have to be done before the right result can be reached. But we need that right result to work with as early in rehearsals as possible because without the mask how can either Phil or I get any idea of how Loving will *sound* and *look.* I know I can't get any workable knowledge of what may need revision about him until I see and hear him.

Re rehearsal time: Can't we get Equity to allow five weeks on this on the just grounds that it's experimental and enormously difficult? We *need* at least that, you know we do. Or, at any rate *I* know *I* do for my end because a preliminary week out of town is no help to me and never will be. I can't see or react with an audience around. The Pittsburgh week of *Ah, W* and my attendance at that performance taught me nothing whatsoever I didn't already know except to transpose *one speech* on account of a laugh—which I could just as easily have done from my hotel in N.Y. on information from Phil. The cuts I made were made in N.Y. before I left for Pittsburgh—as soon as Fogle long-distanced me the opening time—and my seeing the show in Pittsburgh did not affect my judgment in that respect. After all, you know where a script can be cut, if absolutely imperative, and where it can't be cut, time or no time, without watching a sticks audience react! And there will be no laughs to allow for in *D.W.E.!*

All this is to make clear again my personal reactions re opening out of town. Such weeks may help the cast to work in the needed dress rehearsals which were neglected during rehearsals—but my working dress rehearsals have to be without audience or I can't work.

A favor! Will you have someone let me know the minute you decide what date rehearsals start? The earlier I know, the easier for me to make plans.   All our affectionate best to you & Armina!   Gene

---

369 • TO GEORGE MIDDLETON.[1]   ALS 3 pp. (Stationery headed: Casa Genotta / Sea Island / Georgia) [Library of Congress]

Nov. 12, 1933

Dear George: First let me get off my chest what Carlotta has, I believe, already told you in her letter—how very much I liked *Hiss! Boom! Blah!*[2] My congratulations on a fine piece of work! And thank you for your kindness in sending the book!

I've been doing some last hard work on *Days Without End* or I would have answered your letter sooner. Your week of O'Neill sounds to me like too damned much O'Neill in a week! I'll have to confess the criticism of the picture of *Jones* goes over my head. I haven't

1. Middleton (1880–1967), prolific playwright, who was a founder and president of the Dramatists Guild.
2. Play by Middleton, published in 1933 by Samuel French but not produced until April 17, 1936.

seen it. Somehow I can't get up any interest in talking pictures. I was beginning to be quite intrigued by the old silent films—so much so that I made treatments of *The Hairy Ape & Desire Under The Elms* (which, of course, no one would do!)—and then came the Talkies and I gave up.

It's grand that *Electra* interested you so much—but I'm particularly pleased *Ah, W.* hit you in a soft spot. I have a deep personal affection for that play—a feeling toward it that is quite apart from any consideration of it as a piece of dramatic writing by me as playwright.

I'll be only too delighted to send you a photo. Tickled to death you want it! As for the Players, I'd rather not, if you don't mind. In spite of the fact that I have a number of friends in that Club,³ I must confess I have anything but a friendly feeling for the organization. I can never forgive nor cease to resent the fact that when my father died of all the Clubs & Societies of which he was a member the Players was the only one which absolutely ignored his death—sent no flowers, no word, nothing. My mother was deeply hurt and my brother & I were furious. As well we might be! For my father had been a friend of Booth's,⁴ had played with him, and was one of the Club's oldest members! You must admit it was a pretty snide lousy thing to do. Perhaps this will strike you as petty—but it's the way I feel.

Carlotta asks me to ask you just where she can write your wife. Will you be in N.Y. while we're up for rehearsals?—Dec. 1st to early Jan. (probably). If so, we must all get together.

Carlotta joins in all best to you both.   As ever,   Eugene O'Neill

---

370 • TO SEAN O'CASEY.¹   TLS (Stationery headed: The Madison Hotel / Fifteen East Fifty Eighth Street / New York)

[December 15, 1933]

My dear Sean O'Casey,   I have been meaning to drop you a grateful line ever since I finished reading your *Within The Gates*. It is a splendid piece of work. My enthusiastic congratulations to you! I was especially moved—and greenly envious, I confess!—by its rare and sensitive poetical beauty. I wish to God I could write like that!

All who admire your work here—and there are a lot of us!—are hoping the play may be placed with the right management to give it the New York production it deserves. And when it is produced I hope you may come to this country and that while you are here you and Mrs. O'Casey will find time to visit Mrs. O'Neill and me in our home in Georgia.

I have just seen the English edition of *Within The Gates* and I deeply appreciate your generous reference to *Mourning Becomes Electra*.² If anything about that play has suggested anything which was of the slightest service to *Within The Gates* I am only too flattered and I like my trilogy all the better for it!

Good luck to you! My admiration for your work—and all personal good wishes! Eugene O'Neill

P.S. For years, every time I've read a new play of yours I've meant to write to you to this same effect—and my only excuse for not having done so is that where letters are concerned I am the laziest man on earth!

3. The Players, a theatrical social organization.
4. Actor Edwin Booth (1833–1893), a charter member and first president of the Players.

1. O'Casey (1880–1964), Irish playwright, author of *Juno and the Paycock, The Plough and the Stars,* as well as *Within the Gates* (1933). The text of this letter is taken from *The Letters of Sean O'Casey, 1910–41,* ed. David Krause (New York: Macmillan, 1975), vol. 1, pp. 482–83.
2. In his "Notes for Production" for *Within The Gates,* O'Casey acknowledged that he derived the idea of

371 • TO "DAYS WITHOUT END" COMPANY.   WIRE 1 p. ([New York]) [NYPL]

JANUARY 9, 1934

CAST THIS IS TO THANK ALL OF YOU FOR YOUR SPLENDID WORK FOR WHICH I SHALL NEVER CEASE TO BE GRATEFUL STOP DONT LET THE BAD NEWSPAPER RE-VIEWS BOTHER YOU STOP YOU KNOW I TOLD YOU TO DISCOUNT THEM IN AD-VANCE STOP THIS PLAY WAS NOT WRITTEN FOR THAT TYPE OF MIND BUT I KNOW YOU WILL FIND HERE AS IN BOSTON A STEADILY GROWING AUDIENCE OF THE INTELLIGENT AND UNPREJUDICED WHO WILL KNOW WHAT THE PLAY IS ABOUT AND APPRECIATE YOUR GRAND WORK IN MAKING IT LIVE STOP THIS IS A PLAY WE CAN CARRY OVER THE CRITICS HEADS STOP SO CARRY ON WITH CONFIDENCE IN THE FINAL RESULT AND MAKE THEM LIKE IT STOP ARE WE DOWNHEARTED NO WE WILL GET THEM IN THE END STOP AGAIN MY GRATITUDE TO YOU ALL = EUGENE ONEILL

---

372 • TO HAROLD MCGEE.[1]   AL (draft) 2 pp. ([Casa Genotta, Sea Island, Ga.]) [Yale]

[early February? 1934]

Dear Harold: I'm tickled to death to know you liked *D. W. E.* so well. It is cheering to hear from those who did—who weren't soured on it in advance by the critical crap which couldn't see the play because of its subject matter. Same like when we did *All God's Chillun*, remember?—all the pseudo-liberal moderns giving their narrow guts away in a gush of hysterical, bigoted bilge, thinly concealed as objective criticism. Well, oh well! It's no unex-pected blow. I foresaw that angle of it all the time I was writing the play, and the boys sure ran true to form and didn't disappoint me! My faith in the play remains unshaken by such nonsense. They successfully killed it for this country—tor the present, anyway—but it will come into its own in other countries just as *All God's Chillun* has.

I note that you were not moved to the point of reembracing the Faith. Well, no more have I been, although to judge from the chatter that reached me in New York, you'd think I was on the verge of joining the Trappist Monks! Which leads me to fear that any day now I may be arrested for attempted rape on my sister, confession of which is so obvious as Orin in *Mourning Becomes Electra*. That I never had a sister shouldn't matter to the folks who think I'm all of John-Loving in *Days W. E.* and who so easily ignore that for one item of similarity of experience there are ten dissimilar items which have a great part in the psychological working out of the play to its inevitable end.

But what the hell.

I know all about the Players. My Old Man, who knew Booth well and played with him on numerous occasions, was one of the oldest Player members when he died. But, frankly, Harold, I'm off of clubs. They're out of my orbit, I'm practically never in New York except for rehearsals and I'd never make use of them then. So what the hell's the use? I just can't see it, much as I appreciate your kindness in offering to put me up. But if I ever change my mind, I'll remember your letter and send out a call to you to make good on it.

---

a front curtain, which would appear "between the opening of the play and the scenes following," from O'Neill's suggestion of a front curtain for *Mourning Becomes Electra*.

1. McGee (1900–1955) was a member of the Provincetown Players and a director at the Experimental Theatre.

You better postpone the return to our theatre until it shows some signs of health again.
Sure, Carlotta remembers you and joins me in all best—and give mine to Bert.   As ever,

---

373 • TO WILLIAM BUTLER YEATS.[1]   WIRE (draft) 1 p. (Stationery headed: Casa Genotta / Sea Island / Georgia) [Yale]

[c. February 12, 1934]

Only too delighted have Abbey Theatre produce *Days Without End*   Eugene O'Neill

---

374 • TO WARREN MUNSELL.   TLS 2 pp. (Stationery headed: Casa Genotta / Sea Island / Georgia) [Players]

Feb. 18th 1934

Dear Mr. Munsell,   The bad news re *Days Without End*[1] is no more than I expected. I was only hoping against hope. The public for that play—and by public I mean all those (believers or unbelievers) who are sensitive enough to feel some spiritual significance in life and love—are not easy to lure into the theatre. They simply are not interested in the modern theatre. And the barrage of idiotic reviews which greeted the opening killed whatever chance there might have been of getting them in. Not that it was much of a chance at best. I never had any illusions when writing this play that, except by a "modern miracle," it could be a popular success. If ever there was an art for art's sake labor, it was mine in *Days Without End!* And for me it is a success. Also, I know it will come into its own in other countries where the Catholic foreground will be taken matter-of-factly and not give critics the self-consciously modern, blind jitters. There, they will be able to see what it's all really about. As Madden has probably told you, William Butler Yeats—no Catholic—cabled me he and the Abbey Theatre people want to produce it immediately. If a poet like Yeats sees what is in it, all my hard work on it is more than justified.

Will you tell the Committee how very much I appreciate all the Guild has done to stand back of this opus. I feel the more grateful for this fine attitude of every one concerned because I know most of you did not see eye to eye with me on either the play's statements or its implications. But at least you all saw that if it was not *your* truth it still could be *a* truth—and, what the hell, I want no more than that, I'm not interested in converting anyone to anything—even if I knew *the* truth!

What you say about the slump of *Ah, Wilderness!* is a blow. But, what with the taxi strikes and zero weather, wasn't everything bound to slump? It should pick up if anything does. I'd hate to have it go out of town this season. It should be good for all next season on the road—if you have Cohan sewed up for then, which you have, haven't you? I think, with Cohan, it can play towns after the film[2] does—or simultaneously—and do finely. Certainly if a road show was ever made to order *Ah, Wilderness!* (with Cohan) is it.

I don't get the Coast thing with Rogers.[3] When would it be—in summer? I'm all against

---

1. Yeats (1865–1939), Irish poet and playwright, who was one of the directors of the National Theatre Society Limited (Abbey Theatre).

1. *Days Without End* closed after fifty-seven performances.
2. The MGM film version of *Ah, Wilderness!* starring Wallace Beery, Lionel Barrymore, Mickey Rooney, Aline MacMahon, Spring Byington, and Bonita Granville, opened in December 1935.
3. Will Rogers, who was to star in a second company of *Ah, Wilderness!* on the West Coast.

it unless we can get a large guaranty that would make it as worth our while as the regular company touring there.

All best to everyone!   Very sincerely,   Eugene O'Neill

---

375 • TO WILLIAM E. BROOKS.   TLS 1 p. (Stationery headed: Casa Genotta / Sea Island / Georgia) [Private]

March 5th 1934

Dear Doctor Brooks,   My deep gratitude to you for your kind letter with its sensitive appreciation of *Days Without End!* It is especially gratifying to me in view of the narrow-minded hostility and anti-religious prejudice which recently greeted this play when it was seen on the stage in New York.

As for your questions, I do believe absolutely that Faith must come to us if we are ever again to have an End for our days and know that our lives have meaning. All of my past plays, even when most materialistic, are—at any rate, for me—in their spiritual implications a search and a cry in the Wilderness protesting against the fate of their own faithlessness.

Again my gratitude for your letter.   Faithfully yours,   Eugene O'Neill

---

376 • TO RICHARD MADDEN.   TLS 2 pp. (Stationery headed: Casa Genotta / Sea Island / Georgia) [Yale]

March 8th 1934

Dear Dick,   Re Golding Bright's[1] remarks on the Abbey Theatre, they are stupid Limey nonsense. The Abbey is so much better than any company they could get together in London that there is no comparison, and I will be only too glad to give them an option on British rights, provided their production of the play in Dublin is successful. Will you kindly cable or write Bright to this effect? The Abbey's terms for the Dublin production are O.K. with me.

Re Tairov,[2] by all means, send him my address he asks for—and write the special letter to Russian Society of Playwrights called for in Rubinstein's letter to you. Beyond that, there seems nothing to do on the Russian situation.

The Jolson broadcast[3] is a bit of velvet all right. It will be amusing to hear what he does with it. I hope Brutus Jones won't burst into "Mammy!"

The Coast *Ah, Wilderness!* with Rogers sounds O.K., although I think Munsell should have asked 1000 weekly guarantee. Am I not supposed to be consulted on such arrangements before they are settled? I should have held out for 1000 guarantee on a 10% of gross business. It's fair enough.

When would this tour start? Is it a summer affair? Who wants *The Rope* for a film?

All best, Dick—   As ever,   Gene

---

1. English play agent.
2. Alexander Tairov, founder and producer of Moscow's Kamerny Theater.
3. Al Jolson was planning to do his own self-edited radio version of *The Emperor Jones* on the Kraft Music Hall.

May 1st 1934

Dear Mr. Winther,   I think what you have written about *Days Without End*[1] is searchingly intelligent and fine and agrees well with the integrity of your analysis of my work as a whole. My congratulations! I am immensely pleased by it.

There is only one suggestion for a revealing addition to your comment. You do not take into consideration my explanatory sub-title to the play (which is on the jacket but was, unfortunately, omitted by oversight from the book itself) "A Modern Miracle Play"—and this is extremely important if one is to understand my intention. For just as I meant *Mourning Becomes Electra* to be a modern psychological treatment of the Greek theme, I planned *Days Without End* as a modern psychological handling of the old medieval Catholic, Faustian theme of a man with a damned soul which he has given to his devil as he cursed and denied his God. And the germ of the treatment of the theme which underlies *Days Without End* can be found in my notes on masks, published in the first numbers of the *American Spectator*, in which I wrote—"Or take Goethe's *Faust*, which, psychologically speaking, should be the closest to us moderns of all the classics. Here I would have Faust unmasked and Mephistopheles wearing throughout the mask of Faust————————Is not the whole of Goethe's truth in symbols of the spiritual meaning of our time just that Mephistopheles and Faust are one and the same—are Faust?"

As for further pattern in the play, his God is God of Love (very important, this)—he denies Him—he gives his soul to hatred of love (and fear of life, unfaith, death-longing)—he seeks substitutes but never can believe—finally he finds love again on temporal plane (wife) so the demon in him he has given his soul to must destroy and deny this (adultery) because it leads back to faith, must desire to murder it (kill wife) as part of own death-longing.

The above is merely a sketchy indication of a few of the many psychological and spiritual ramifications of my design. If you knew the amount of time and labor I spent working all this out (considering its length I worked harder and longer on this play than on any before) you would appreciate how eager I am for this aspect of it to be understood by the few. I never in my wildest dreams hoped it would be understood by the general public. And I foresaw all the time I was writing it the critical outburst against it in New York, altho' I didn't think they would be so cheaply wise-guy as they were. I thought it would run about six weeks. It lasted seven. So I was one to the good! If ever I wrote a work-for-work's-sake play, *Days Without End* is it. New York critics dwell in a too pseudo-sophisticated, self-consciously modern, wise-crack atmosphere to be able to judge objectively a play which treats religious faith as a psychological problem of to-day—now—for us—and does not treat it as a sentimental anachronism or a quaint conception of childlike, primitive negroes.

Days Without End challenged and insulted their superiority complexes in this respect—and they reacted like bigoted, priest-burning, Puritan atheists! Also my play treats adultery seriously—as a sin against love—and how could the first-night intelligentsia of New York countenance that!

Generally speaking a great mistake has been made, I think, in identifying John Loving too much with the author. True, as you put it, I have certainly made use of a lot of my

1. Winther had added material on O'Neill's most recent play in order to make his forthcoming book, *Eugene O'Neill: A Critical Study*, as current as possible.

spiritual gropings in recounting his past. But, to anyone who knows me, the points of dissimilarity in the characters are more numerous than the resemblances. There is a lot of the spiritual conflict of several other people I have known—not only former Catholics but Protestants—in John Loving, especially as regards his struggle after the play gets started in the present.

Please don't take it for granted on the evidence of the New York criticisms you have read that the play does not act well. Take it from me, it does. Did you read H. T. Parker's criticism in the *Boston Transcript?*[2] He was the best of all our newspaper critics and surely could not be charged with any Catholic bias. (He was, I believe, a complete agnostic.) His article would give you a true impression of the reaction in Boston (a New England non-Catholic Theatre Guild subscriber audience). *Days Without End* went over finely there. It is, at present, going over finely to a totally different Catholic public in Dublin, Ireland, at the Abbey Theatre. It is shortly to be given to Protestant publics in Holland and Sweden. And I am confident it will be rec'd with intelligent interest in all countries in Europe within the next year or two. They are a bit older over there. They can critically consider a play dealing with the subject of religious faith without being afraid that understanding it might lay them open to the charge of not really being up-to-date intellectuals!

As for the end of the play it seemed to me the one inevitable end for the character of John Loving, once he is faced with the loss of love again through his wife's death (her murder by Loving). It is, I think, if looked at psychologically, the inevitable end—or if looked at mystically, also mystically inevitable. And that was my aim throughout the play, to keep my theme mystically true as an old miracle play and psychologically true as a *modern* miracle play.

But the end hardly means that I have gone back to Catholicism. I haven't. But I would be a liar if I didn't admit that, for the sake of my soul's peace, I have often wished I could. And by Catholicism I don't mean the Catholic church as a politically-meddling, social-reactionary force. That repels me. I mean the mystic faith of Catholicism whose symbols seem to me to approach closer than any other symbols to the apprehension of a hidden spiritual significance in human life.

Mrs. O'Neill joins me in all best to you and Mrs. Winther. Very sincerely,   Eugene O'Neill

---

378 • TO DONALD PACE.[1]   TLS 4 pp. (Stationery headed: Casa Genotta / Sea Island / Georgia) [Bowdoin]

May 7th 1934

Dear Mr. Pace,   Your *Lightning* model is a very beautiful piece of work indeed and I am tremendously pleased with it. The way you have done all the details on deck (the cannon is grand stuff!) and aloft is extraordinary. It seems to me a finer job, in its details, than your *Flying Cloud.* I can't say more by way of appreciation than that.

But I confess there is one thing relative to scale and authenticity I want to ask you about.

2. "In New Vein—The New Play from O'Neill," *Boston Evening Transcript,* December 28, 1933, p. 13.

1. Builder of ship models who had a shop and studio at 33 West Forty-second Street in New York and was making some models for O'Neill.

Are you sure you have the length-over-all, from knight-heads to taffrail, of this model correct to scale? I noticed immediately that this model was no longer over-all than your *Flying Cloud*—approximately 28 inches, which approximates the *Flying Cloud*'s length of 225 to 230 feet as given in Clark's *Clipper Ship Era* and Carl Cutler's *Greyhounds of the Sea* (altho' Richard McKay's book gives 235 over-all for this ship).[2] Now I had expected your *Lightning* model to be longer than the *Flying Cloud* one, since, according to all three McKay, Cutler and Clark books she was 243 or 244 feet over-all—that is approximately $2^1/_2$ inches longer than your model is, as I have measured it. Whose figures did you work from on this model? Were they those of the Museum (Webb, was it?) you told me about? Does this mean that the figures in these books are wrong? Are you sure that the Museum is correct and the books incorrect?

I ask these questions in no spirit of criticism of your work. I merely want final information as to the right dope so I can judge by one standard. For instance the Clark, Cutler and McKay books agree in giving the length over-all of the *James Baines* as 266 feet and so I am expecting your model to be approximately 33 inches long from taffrail to knight-heads.

Another thing. In two of these books the main yard of the *Lightning* is given as 95 feet (twelve inches in your scale) but your main yard is only ten and a fraction inches. (They also state the main yard of the *Baines* was 100 feet.)

You won't mind my going into this matter so at length, I know. You see, one of my greatest interests in selecting these models is to have before me, comparatively, the changes in McKay design in his fastest ships, to have them all on tables side by side. So I want to have figures on these dimensions and rig that will check with the figures you work on. What are your figures for the *James Baines* and the *Sovereign of the Seas?*

Thank you for your good wishes re the Coast production of *Wilderness* with Will Rogers. From what I hear it went over very well.

So you used to be a vaudevillian, did you? Well, so was I—for some months on the Orpheum circuit in 1912. So we're fellow White Rats!

Much gratitude for the *Great Republic* picture. I'm glad to have it. And I would like very much indeed to have the Currier and Ives print you speak of. It is damned kind of you to send me these things which I would never run across myself.

Mrs. O'Neill wrote you that she has made me a present of the *Lightning* and sent you her check for its full cost. So you can apply the advance I paid you on the *Lightning* on to the junk.

The crate will be expressed back to you to-day.

What was it you wanted to explain to me about the lettering on the stern of the *Lightning?* I don't know where I could find a "letter man" hereabouts.

This is too long a letter for a guy who has been ordered to rest and let correspondence alone. In closing, let me again state that my questions re dimensions and scale are not intended as any disparagement of your model which I am delighted with and proud to own. But I do want to know authoritatively just which figures I should disregard as inaccurate and which regard as valid. Otherwise, I'm up a tree on my comparisons of the models.

All good wishes to you.   Very sincerely,   Eugene O'Neill

2. Arthur Hamilton Clark, *The Clipper Ship Era* (New York: G.P. Putnam's, 1910), Carl Cutler, *Greyhounds of the Sea* (New York: G.P. Putnam's, 1930), Richard McKay, *Some Famous Sailing Ships and Their Builder, Donald McKay* (New York: G.P. Putnam's, 1928).

379 • TO LEE SIMONSON.   AL (draft) 3 pp. (Stationery headed: Casa Genotta / Sea Island / Georgia) [Yale]

[May? 1934]

Dear Lee: No I won't cut a single damned line. That's final. I could not and keep an honorable conscience about my relationship to my work. For my conscience still insists on telling me that my plays belong primarily to the Theatre and not to the Show Business. Also I have a great personal affection for *Ah, Wilderness!* (as a whole in which no part is greater than the whole) and I want to keep that affection.

Besides, I think this whole question is much fuss about nothing. The answer is, ring up at 8:15 or 8:10 on the road next season. A Guild production—of a play by me—with Cohan—which has run a full season in New York—and particularly a play with the inherent road appeal of *Ah, W*—can ring up at 8 if it has to.

I'm feeling a bit better physically—have gained 17 pounds—but mentally and nervously I'm still way below par. It was lucky I got due warning in time or I would have cracked up in one of our most adequate nervous breakdowns. I'm under orders to forget new work for an indefinite period. And I must say it's most gratefully soothing—the forgetting—for I'm fed to the teeth with the damned theatre.

One lesson this experience has taught me: Never again two productions in one season! It was all right in the old days when I restricted my job to the written play and never went to more than four or five rehearsals or allowed myself to get too involved in the inevitable compromises and distortions of production. But now, what with attendance at all rehearsals plus out-of-town training openings, I find even one production pretty trop. You understand, I know, I am casting hereby no invidious reflections at the Guild. I mean the whole theatrical game which the Guild, willy-nilly, has to compromise with in order to exist. Bucking it always drives me to secret inner rages and hatred which exhaust my spiritual vitality. I take my theatre too personally, I guess—so personally that before long I think I shall permanently resign from all production and confine my future work to plays in books for readers only. The game isn't worth the candle. If I got any real spiritual satisfaction out of success in the theatre it might compensate. But I don't. Success is as flat, spiritually speaking, as failure. After the unprecedented critical acclaim to *Mourning Becomes Electra* I was in bed nearly a week, overcome by the profoundest gloom and nervous exhaustion. Even the reception of *Days Without End* didn't do that to me. In fact, by contrast, it was invigorating because it made me mad!

So what? Well, pardon my wishing on you the above distressful autobiographical items. Only want you to understand what painfully lies behind my feeling about cutting, etc.

All best to you both—and the child—from us both.   As ever,

---

380 • TO RICHARD MADDEN.   TLS 4 pp. (Stationery headed: Casa Genotta / Sea Island / Georgia) [Yale]

May 28th 1934

Dear Dick,   I have rec'd your letter and Mr. Rumsey's re the stolen letters.[1] The more I hear of this dishonorable affair, the sorer I am getting—and I tell you frankly that the person

---

1. Some letters O'Neill had written to Madden had been offered for sale in a book dealer's catalog.

I am principally sore at is you. My letters to you were not only confidential business letters—that alone would be bad enough!—they were also the confidential personal letters of a friend. That you should shove them in a general file for any clerk to paw over, read, or steal, that you should not have placed enough value on them as to keep them in a private confidential file, strikes me as an unpardonable breach of business ethics as well as a betrayal of friendship. It is incredibly grotesque, to say the least, that my agents would seem to be the only people to whom my letters—some of them longhand letters, at that!—are worthless trash to be saved by boys in the office as souvenirs!—without even asking my permission!

This affair has nothing to do with Saxe—nothing to do with Random House. Please leave them out of it. It also has nothing to do with Harry except in so far as I instruct him what steps I want him to take as my lawyer.

But it has a great deal to do with the continuation of my connection with you and The American Play Co. as agents. And my friendly personal relationship with you. For, as I have instructed Harry, I hold you and The American Play Co. responsible for those letters. I insist that, as your decent, honorable obligation to me, you take every possible step to recover every letter that was stolen and sold. I have instructed Harry to cooperate with you in this but to remember that this is your job not mine. It isn't your letters that were stolen from me—it's mine that were stolen from you. And I must insist that in view of what has happened, some plan be worked out between you and Harry for future disposal of my old letters that will protect me. I suggest that each year the old ones that have passed the legal age-limit for which you must hold them, should be returned to me to be destroyed. And I want all letters, past, present, or to come, kept from now on in a confidential private file to which only you, Rumsey, or Miss Rubin[2] would have access.

Surely, both you and Rumsey must see the common sense necessity and justice of this. You cannot treat my correspondence as simply that of one of your authors—unless you willfully blind yourself to a fact that any bookdealer in town could tell you, that my letters are collector's items, have a cash value both here and abroad. Very few living authors' have. I am, willy-nilly, a special case in this respect. No, Brown certainly cannot have any of those letters. In holding them out, without asking your or my permission, when his instructions were to destroy them, he was, in my regard, just as guilty of theft as the crook who sold the others.

I cannot impress on you too forcibly how damned seriously I take this whole affair. I tell you frankly the continuance of our business and personal relationship depends upon how seriously you prove to me you take it. God damn it, put yourself in my place for a moment. How would you like your letters containing private personal affairs as well as confidential business details to be hawked around bookshops to be read by anyone and quoted in catalogues? I think you would hit the ceiling just as I am doing and demand adequate protection from your agents for the recovery of such stolen goods and for the trustworthy safeguarding of all other past and *all* future correspondence!

I'm sorry Mr. Rumsey is so upset. But I assure you neither you nor he are one half as damned upset as I am. For it is *my* private business affairs and personal confidences to a friend that has been hawked around, not yours. And as for nerves, I'm in the process of trying to recover from a threatened nervous breakdown, and episodes like this, which help to destroy what little faith I have left in the honorable obligations of friendship in business, don't help me toward recovery a damned bit!   Gene

---

2. Jane Rubin, Madden's secretary and his successor upon his death in 1951.

381 • TO SHANE O'NEILL.   AL (draft) 2 pp. ([Casa Genotta, Sea Island, Ga.]) [Yale]

[June 12, 1934][1]

Dear Shane: For a boy not yet fifteen I must say you have very large ideas! No, of course I won't give you the four hundred dollar outboard. I can't afford it and you ought to know I can't. It's about time you realized I am an author and not a millionaire business man. You are old enough now to begin to have some sense and face a few facts and not get exaggerated notions of my wealth. I cannot afford to keep a motorboat myself although I would like to have one. I think you have a lot of nerve to ask for such an expensive present.

Even if could afford it, I tell you frankly you wouldn't get it. If you want presents, let me see you do a little work for them first. So far your record at Lawrenceville seems to prove that you do no studying at all and that the fifteen hundred dollars I pay for you there is a waste of money. I'm beginning to think you would be a darned sight better off if you went to public school where you would not learn expensive tastes you are—and will be—in no position to afford.

Let's get this straight between us once and for all so there will be no future misunderstandings. When you show you have some brains and dig down and get to work, then I will be willing to do things for you I can afford, outside of the money I pay your mother for your education, etc. But until you do this, don't expect anything from me except the usual birthday and Christmas presents or you will be disappointed.

In short, you have got to prove to me in these coming years that you are not lazily expecting something for nothing but are willing to work for it. Otherwise, you will get nothing. Is that clear? And, believe me, you will find out I mean it! I've been doing a lot of serious thinking about you and I've come to this decision.   Love to you & Oona.

---

382 • TO AGNES BRENNAN.   TLS 1 p. (Stationery headed: Casa Genotta / Sea Island / Georgia) [Yale]

June 14th 1934

Dear Agnes,   I am presuming on our relationship and friendship to take up with you a certain matter which has, by accident, been brought to my attention. A rumor has reached me that you and the family are temporarily embarrassed by taxes, etc. soon coming due—a matter of $300.00—. Is this true? If so, I hope you will permit me to advance that amount to you and take the load off your mind.

Now I know the Brennans are proud but please don't be angry with me for intruding like this, or feel that you would be under the slightest obligation by accepting this loan. When you wrote me once before I was, unfortunately, in no position to be able to do anything. Nevertheless, I have always felt guilty because I had to fail you then. So I would regard it as a privilege to be of this slight assistance now.

On the chance that the rumor is true and that you will permit me to help, I am—(to save time and worry for you)—enclosing a check for $300.00—. If what I have heard is a lie, you can return it. But, in any event, please take this letter in the spirit in which it is written—one of frank friendship.   Carlotta joins me in love.   Eugene

---

1. Date supplied in Carlotta O'Neill's handwriting.

383 • TO RICHARD DANA SKINNER.   AL (draft) 6 pp. ([Casa Genotta, Sea Island, Ga.]) [Yale]

[July? 1934]

Dear Dana: It's fine to know the book is making such good progress.[1] You make me feel like a guilty lily of the field with all this talk of work—a wilted lily just now, the thermometer verging on one hundred hereabouts!

The dates given for my plays in the books are cock-eyed in spots—my fault—I'm a lazy, what-of-it guy about such matters and did not proof read them originally and never made corrections since.

Of course, some plays were written in one year, rewritten into their published and stage-produced form in a later year—usually this meant only a condensation, without any change in essentials.

I enclose a list with dates and some explanatory comments which should make all clear to you.

Love from us both to all the Skinners.   As ever

Published Plays
1913 (Fall)–1914 (Winter)—The Five One-Act Plays in *Thirst* (published by Badger, Boston, 1914)
1914 (Spring)—*Bound East For Cardiff* (Very important, this play! In it can be seen—or felt—the germ of the spirit, life-attitude, etc. of all my significant future work—and it was written practically within my first half-year as a playwright, before I went to Baker, under whose influence the following year I did nothing $^{1}/_{10}$th as original. Remember in these U.S. in 1914 *Bound East For Cardiff* was a daring innovation both in form & content)
1914 (Fall)–15—Baker—nothing significant
1915 (Fall)–1916 (Winter)—Greenwich Village—nothing
1916 (Summer—Provincetown—start of P. Players)—wrote *Before Breakfast* & short story "Tomorrow" (published *Seven Arts* in 1917)
1917 (Winter—Provincetown)—*In The Zone; Ile; The Long Voyage Home; Moon Of The Caribbees*
1917 (Summer) A short story (never published) about stokers, etc. in which was germ idea of *Hairy Ape*—also this summer came the idea for *Beyond The Horizon*
1918 (Winter)—*The Rope; Beyond The Horizon* (Summer)—*The Dreamy Kid; Where The Cross Is Made* (Fall)—First draft of *The Straw*
1919 (Winter)—*Chris* (never published, produced by Geo. Tyler out of town & closed—the play from which *"Anna Christie"* developed) (Spring)—Final draft *The Straw*
1920—(Winter)—*Gold* (Summer) *"Anna Christie"* (Fall) *Emperor Jones* & *Diff'rent*
1921 (Winter)—*The First Man* (Spring & Summer)—First draft of *The Fountain* (Last of this year & first week of '22, as I remember) *The Hairy Ape* (written in 3 weeks)
1922 (Summer)—Final draft *The Fountain* (Fall)—One-half of *Welded*
1923 (Winter)—Finished *Welded* (Summer)—Preliminary work and one scene of *Marco Millions* (Fall) *All God's Chillun*
1924 (Winter & Spring) *Desire Under The Elms* (Summer) Finished *Marco Millions* (in its original two part, two-play form, each play short full-length)

---

1. Skinner was working on a critical study of O'Neill's plays, later published as *Eugene O'Neill: A Poet's Quest* (New York: Longmans, Green, 1935).

1925 (Winter)—Final draft *Marco Millions*, condensed into one play—*The Great God Brown* (Fall) *Lazarus Laughed*, half of a first draft.

1926 (Winter & Spring)—*Lazarus Laughed*, final draft (except for some cutting & condensing in 1927) (Spring & Summer) First half of *Strange Interlude*

1927 (Winter, Spring, Summer)—Final draft *Strange Interlude*

1928 (Spring, Summer)—*Dynamo*

1929 (Spring) to 1931 (Spring)—*Mourning Becomes Electra*

1932 (Spring, Summer)—1st 2 drafts *Days Without End* (September)—Wrote *Ah, Wilderness!* (Fall) 3rd draft *Days W.E.*

1933 Final 4 drafts *Days W. E.*

---

384 • TO HARRY WEINBERGER. ALS 2 pp. (Stationery headed: Casa Genotta / Sea Island / Georgia) [Yale]

Nov. 3rd 1934

Dear Harry: Thanks for the clippings. But don't wish the Nobel on me! It honestly doesn't mean anything to me—in fact, I've just about made up my mind to refuse it if it does come my way. My strong personal hunch is that it's a jinx (except for old men), that it puts you on a spot, and that I've been made into a too-respectable, stuffed-shirt eminent literary personage already without the Nobel piled on it.

I'm sending you the *Monte Cristo*-Fechter version under separate cover.

As for balance your retainer I'll have to ask you to wait a couple of weeks—unless you're in dire need. Ever since Aug. 1st and the Big Dole I've had nothing but expenses coming up, and in spite of 3 weeks *Ah, W* returns so far I'm still in a weak cash position.

Meanwhile, too, you may pry something out of Reliance Pictures which will cover the retainer. All best! Gene

---

385 • TO JOHN MASON BROWN.[1] TLS 2 pp. (Sea Island, Georgia) [Harvard]

November 18, 1934

Dear Friend and Critic: If there is something of the Great God Brown in your astral attitude, I should be the last to complain. We of the serious theatre recognize that you can serve us best by taking your stand remote from the crowd and criticizing us in the aspect of eternity. Our friend Elmer Rice[2] might not admit this; but I, in spite of your charge that I take myself too seriously, don't hesitate to say that I value your rather severe strictures and wish I might convince you that I am on the right track.

You tickle my pride by choosing Marlowe to address me,[3] but if I could do so without arrogance, I would say that the analogy seems a little forced. I like to believe, though I think I have never said it publicly, that art is a continual reaching out—sometimes only a groping in the dark, playing footsie with coy ideas, but sometimes coming clear in the light of some

---

1. Brown (1900–1969), theater historian and critic, who served as theater critic for the *New York Post* and the *Saturday Review of Literature*. Like O'Neill, he studied playwriting with George Pierce Baker in English 47 at Harvard.

2. Rice (1892–1967), playwright and novelist, author of, among many other plays, *The Adding Machine* (1923) and *Street Scene* (1929).

3. "Christopher Marlowe to Eugene O'Neill," in Brown's *Letters from Greenroom Ghosts* (New York: Viking, 1934), pp. 71–116.

transcendent ultimate meaning. Marlowe was not a searcher in this sense; he was a dreamer and a glorious swaggerer. He had no need to search, for his dreams were what he chose to make them; and even if he had lived to write as many plays as Lope de Vega[4] or Owen Davis, you can hardly imagine that he would have developed much further—as a technician, yes; but not in his knowledge of the human soul.

It is this that I earnestly seek. Perhaps I have sometimes been off the track, possibly my use of masks and asides is artifice and bombast—just as Marlowe's mighty line was often the same. (You newspaper critics must know the temptation to fill a few lines with good hot air when the messenger is waiting on your doorstep.) . . . But I fully believe that my long absorption in the dualism of man's mortal soul has been worth while.

Only lately, as you know, my life has been simplified by finding a great body of established belief which recognizes this dualism—the Catholic Church. In my new sense of the shapeliness of life within the pattern set by a beneficent Creator and confirmed by His servant the Church, I think I can become the dramatist that I wish to be. One of my recent plays taught me, shall we say, that I cannot serve God and Mannon. I am ready now to go forward with the former, and forget my false dynamic gods and my nostalgia for the idea of a godless Fate. We shall see where this will lead me.

Believe me truly grateful for your interest in my work, and for your flattering praise of what you like in it. It is more than our common memory of 47 that should give us reason to understand each other.   Faithfully,   Eugene O'Neill

---

386 • TO HARRY WEINBERGER.   TLS 1 p. (Stationery headed: Casa Genotta / Sea Island / Georgia) [Yale]

November 27th 1934

Dear Harry,   Re Clarkie:[1]

Clamp down on him or he'll begin to think your office is the home of Santa Claus and every day is Christmas. Put the chill on the next time he calls and tell him I can't afford perpetual philanthropy as I have too much overhead already. You see what I mean. It's all right to hand him a boost occasionally but when he tries to ride it into the ground, it's not. Otherwise he'll never try to work—or even try to get help from anyone but me. I know this from past experience. I've had to put the curb on him several times before. So just tell him to have a heart and lay off me for a while.   All best,   Gene

---

387 • TO NELLIE G. THARSING.[1]   ALS 1 p. (Stationery headed: Casa Genotta / Sea Island / Georgia) [Private]

Nov. 28th 1934

Dear Mother: Thank you immensely for the throw-over! It is a beautiful piece of work and, incidentally, just exactly what I need when I'm working in the window-seat of my study in winter. It is most kind of you to have thought of this gift—and I know how long and hard you must have worked on it. Believe me, I appreciate it, and will appreciate it more and

---

4. Félix Lope de Vega Carpio (1562–1635), Spanish dramatic poet and author of approximately 1,800 plays.

1. Bill Clark, onetime circus daredevil, whom O'Neill met in Greenwich Village in 1915–16 and whom he helped financially for many years.

1. Carlotta O'Neill's mother.

more as time goes on and it becomes the warm, comfortable companion of winter working days—a constant reminder of your kindness!

From what Carlotta tells me of your letters I judge you are well on the road to recovery from your illness. That's grand! And I am glad to report that I'm emerging from the after-effects of my near nervous breakdown last April. So mutual congratulations are in order, I think. We'll show 'em all yet that we're still there with the old pep, won't we?

Tell Cyn that I feel a guilty dog for not having written in so long. It is not from lack of thought of her, or lack of gratitude for her thought of me, but simply that, at best, I am a perfectly lousy correspondent and since last April I have been, if possible, even lousier! But *I will* write to her soon now. It's grand that she is so happy in her marriage. If I were her real, instead of just her step-father, I could not be a bit happier at knowing she has found happiness!

Again, deep gratitude for your so-welcome gift—and, as ever, much love to you! Gene

---

388 • TO LEÓN MIRLAS.[1]   TLS(X) 4 pp. (Stationery headed: Casa Genotta / Sea Island / Georgia) [Private]

December 19th 1934

My dear Mr. Mirlas,   Thank you for your fine letter and for your kindness in sending me your critical essay and the original designs for the settings of *The Great God Brown*.

Your critical essay I have read with the keenest appreciation. You have shown in it a sympathetic understanding of *The Hairy Ape* and *The Great God Brown* which is immensely gratifying to their author! But what is most satisfying is that you have revealed an insight into the spiritual overtones of these plays—(their most important value to me, naturally!)—which I have, unfortunately, only too rarely discovered in even the most appreciative critical commentaries from Europe or the United States. So thank you again for the privilege of reading your essay! Please do me the favor of conveying my gratitude to Mr. Mirabelli for his courtesy in letting me have original designs. They are extraordinarily interesting and will have a favored place in my collection of original designs and photographs of productions from all over the world. I wish I could have seen them realized on the stage in your production.

I am sending you under separate cover copies of *Ah, Wilderness!* and *Days Without End*. The first is a simple comedy—a nostalgic sentimental recollection of the days of my youth, of the typical family life of that time in the typical town of our States—of the customs and morals of those days as contrasted with what exists to-day. *Days Without End* is an attempt to transform some of the values of the old miracle play, and the old Faustian-damned soul legend, into a psychological mask drama of modern life. It was a flat failure when produced in New York a year ago but has since then been successfully done in Ireland, Holland and Sweden. And is now scheduled for production in various other countries. In New York it was entirely misunderstood by the critics, as I expected it would be, for a play that even mentions any religion these days is doomed in advance—especially doomed if the religion happens to be Catholicism. They took the easy line of attack that I must have gone back to Catholicism

---

1. Mirlas (1907–), Russian-born Argentinian critic, translator, and short-story writer, who translated virtually all O'Neill's plays for production and publication in Argentina and who wrote two books on O'Neill, *El teatro de O'Neill: estudio de su personalidad y sus obras* (Buenos Aires: Claridad, 1938) and *O'Neill y el teatro contemporaneo* (Buenos Aires: Editorial Sudamericana, 1950).

and the play was Catholic propaganda—and then let their pseudo-sophisticated prejudices shriek anathemas. It was all very adolescent and hysterical. Of course, the simple fact is I chose Catholicism because it is the only Western religion which has the stature of a real Faith, because it *is* the religion of the old miracle plays and the Faustian legend which were the sources of my theme—and last and most simply because it happens to be the religion of my early training and therefore the one I know most about. As for propaganda, I need not tell you that my plays never have been, and never will be, interested in converting anyone to anything except the possibility of the drama as an art. In *Days Without End* it interested me, by way of a change, and as a compensation for a perhaps too one-sided attitude, to show the reverse side of the picture and reveal a modern man who is forced back to his old God and thereby regains his lost soul in what is truth for *his* particular ego—not *The* Truth, for I have no *The* Truth to offer, but merely a play of human life and this man's truth in it.

Pardon the dissertation! I only explain at such length because I shall be interested to hear your reactions to this play and I want you to know what I was trying to do in it, whether I succeeded in the attempt or not. It was a most difficult play to write, to try to condense the various motives into one drama of ordinary length.

With all good wishes for the New Year,   Very sincerely,   Eugene O'Neill

---

389 • TO WARREN MUNSELL.   AL (draft) 4 pp. (Stationery headed: Casa Genotta / Sea Island / Georgia) [Yale]

[late December 1934 or early January 1935]

Dear Mr. Munsell: It's bad news about Cohan—very bad indeed. Let's hope Terry can persuade him to see reason. For I have no new play ready and had been counting on *Ah, Wilderness!* to run out this season, at least.

I want to take strong exception, however, to the Guild's idea that if Cohan drops out the play must automatically close. I can't see that, and I think such an attitude of forlorn quitting before an outworn star-system dogma that the star's the thing is unworthy of everything the Guild is supposed to mean in the American theatre. After all, the Guild is a producing medium for fine plays first and foremost, isn't it—and only rarely and accidentally just another actor or actress exploiting organization? I feel most strongly that for the Guild to close such a valuable property as *Ah, Wilderness!* has proved itself to be—(not only in the East with Cohan but in the West with Rogers and everywhere in Europe it has so far been done, without any Cohan or Rogers)—without making the slightest attempt to see if it can't keep on running on the road with someone else playing the father, is outrageously unfair to me. I think the Guild owes it to every author of one of its big N.Y. successes to see to it that such a play has every possible chance to live out its full life on the road as long as that play splits even and costs the Guild no loss. I believe *Ah, Wilderness!* can go on, with Fred Stone, say, or someone else—not as profitably as with Cohan, perhaps, but still profitably, or, at least, breaking even. I may be wrong in this but the Guild owes my play and me and the cast the chance to prove I may be right. And, more importantly, it owes itself as the most important artistic producing unit in our theatre, the duty not to let star actors or actresses dictate to it— especially when in my plays which have made a star or two in their time, and revived one or two pretty dead ones, but have never yet depended on one.

Another point in your letter which I don't see is the disappointment you express about the first two Chicago weeks. Surely, unless I've forgotten all I started to learn about show business in my cradle, the three weeks before Christmas are always progressively down anywhere in the U.S. And I'm damned if I consider 11,000 per for those weeks (including Cleveland) as so bad at a 2.50 (2.00 matinee) top, in an era of extreme theatrical depression. How many producers of straight plays in N.Y. during those three weeks didn't wish to God their plays were doing that? Not many, from the reports!

As always, this letter is to the rest of the Guild as well as to you—and comes out frankly with what I feel as I know you-alls would wish me to.

At the end of your letter bearing such evil tidings you said Happy New Year! You have a cruel idea of a joke!

But just to show there's no hard feelings, Happy New Year right back at you.   Sincerely,

---

390 • TO MRS. GEORGE PIERCE BAKER.[1]   ([Casa Genotta, Sea Island, Ga.])

Jan. 20, 1935

Dear Mrs. Baker: Your kind letter took a great load off my mind. Ever since I sent that to the *Times*,[2] I've been laboring under a guilty feeling that it was unforgivably inadequate. I did try hard to make it a message of my very deep feeling of gratitude and sadness, and emphasize the greatest gift one human being can give another—the courage to believe in his work and go on—a gift which Mr. Baker gave to me, as he did to so many others. What I will always remember first about him is not the teacher but the man, the charm of his personality, his ability just by being himself to convey faith to you, and understanding sympathy, and friendship. Many men can teach but only a fine, rare few can be in themselves an education in faith for others!

But I am a clumsy writer indeed when it comes to anything but dialogue, and I was afraid my word had bungled expressing any of this. However, now that I know you found worth in what I wrote, that's all I care about.

Again, my deepest sympathy—and, always, all good wishes to you.   Cordially yours,   Eugene O'Neill

---

391 • TO HARRY WEINBERGER.   WIRE 1 p. ([Casa Genotta, Sea Island, Ga.])
[Yale]

JANUARY 29, 1935

GIVE BENNY[1] MY CONSENT TO GO AHEAD WITHOUT CHARGE STOP DONT AGREE WITH YOU THINK BENNY VERY AMUSING GUY AND BELIEVE KIDDING MY STUFF EVERY ONCE IN A WHILE HAS VERY HEALTHY EFFECT AND HELPS KEEP ME OUT OF DEAD SOLEMN ILLUSTRIOUS STUFFED SHIRT ACADEMICIAN CLASS =   GENE

---

1. The text of this letter is taken from *George Pierce Baker: A Memorial* (New York: Dramatists Play Service, 1939), pp. 21–22.
2. Baker died on January 6, 1935; O'Neill's tribute, "Professor George Pierce Baker," appeared in the *New York Times*, January 13, 1935, sec. 9, p. 1.

1. Jack Benny (1894–1974), comedian, who apparently was seeking permission to do a parody of one of O'Neill's plays (possibly *Ah, Wilderness!*) on his weekly radio show.

392 • TO ROBERT SISK.   TLS 2 pp. (Stationery headed: Casa Genotta / Sea Island / Georgia) [Yale]

March 1st 1935

Dear Bob,   I hasten to reply to yours of the 23rd with its encouraging tidings re *Hairy Ape*. First, as to the silent film treatment I made years ago to show Lasky.[1] The last copy I possessed of this Madden sent to Kenneth Macgowan a year or so ago. Kenneth wrote me for it. He must still have it around as it was never returned—so you can probably get it from him. However, don't put much importance on it. I dashed it off over night to submit to Lasky for Jannings[2] who wanted to do a film of the play. As I remember it, it was not so hot although there might be interesting suggestions as to trend of plot. But I would much rather turn you and Nichols[3] loose on the play fancy free. It goes without saying I have absolute confidence in you—and this also applies to Nichols—and I would make no stipulation whatever as to treatment, even if you'd let me. By all means, get my old 'script from Kenneth, if you like. Let Nichols go over it and see if there's anything in it he cares to use. But if there isn't, that's all right with me.

Don't be backward about the business angle with me for I don't feel anything of that and will be absolutely frank with you. I quite agree it would be unwarrantable to expect a *Wilderness* or *Interlude* price. I figure the *Hairy Ape* value on what I got for *Emperor Jones*. I figure it worth considerably more than *Jones* because it has no solid South in this country with thumbs down in advance and because it is much more widely known internationally than *Jones*. The *Ape* has been given practically everywhere and still appears in repertoire in Europe now and again. Also there is a personal angle in my price idea as compared with *Jones*. I owned all picture rights to *Jones*, while with the *Ape*, altho' I control ³/₄, Arthur Hopkins owns ¹/₄ interest which I gave him when he brought the *Ape* from the Provincetown up to the Plymouth. Now what I've figured on getting is a close approximation to $25,000.00 clear for my end—which means, with Hopkins' interest, and Madden's commission added, that the price I've had in mind for the *Ape* rights is $37,500.00—that is, one-half the *Wilderness-Interlude* price. And $7,500.00 more than I got for *Jones*.

I've given you the above calculations in detail so you would know exactly how and why I figured what I feel to be a fair valuation, based principally on *Jones* actual sales value in the Spring of '33, right after the Banking crisis, the low of the depression. Let me know frankly what your reaction is.

Well, I'm wildly enthusiastic just now on the new Work[4] I'm on. I've been at plans and preliminaries for the past two months—switched from what I had started on to this. It's honestly the most ambitious conception I've ever had. There's years of the devil's own work to it—but it is really without precedent and has the possibilities of greatness in modern drama. I'll write you the outline later on and you'll see for yourself I'm not exaggerating.

My best to Nichols—and Kenneth,—if you see him,—and Carlotta joins me in much friendship to all the Sisks.   As ever,   Gene

1. Movie producer Jesse Lasky.
2. Emil Jannings (1886–1950).
3. Dudley Nichols, who was now a Hollywood producer and screenwriter.
4. O'Neill's multiplay cycle, eventually called "A Tale of Possessors Self-dispossessed."

393 • TO ROBERT SISK.   TLS 2 pp. (Stationery headed: Casa Genotta / Sea Island / Georgia) [Yale]

March 15th 1935

Dear Bob,   Thank you for your letter which arrived yesterday, and for the two scripts which arrived to-day. I'll read them during the first between-acts intermission I come to in the detailed scenarios I'm making for the sections of the new work.

My only word to you and Nichols re the treatment for the *Ape* is one which I believe may be of value both from an artistic and also a showman's standpoint. Keep in mind always what I was trying to do in writing the play—the method. It isn't Expressionism. It isn't Naturalism. It is a blend—and, as far as my knowledge goes, a uniquely successful one. "Yank" is a living recognizable human being but he is also a symbol in a sort of modern Morality Play. Try to keep the "difference" of the play, its unique theatre quality. Make it something as entirely novel among film plays as it was among legitimate dramas when it was first produced. As plain realism, you would have nothing but just another story of a stoker.

I am thinking of the picture now just as I would think about a play for the legitimate theatre. I can't think any other way. But I *do* know my theatre—any kind of theatre!—and I know any audience is always compelled by the fresh approach, the unique—provided it is well done and has the blood and power of living life in it. The reason for the failure of most "difference" in the theatre is that it is almost invariably difference for its own sake— trivial or bizarre or pretentiously arty or perverse—it lacks the guts and passion of life to convince and give it life—it is not the courageous breaking into individual expression of the creative imagination, but the stunt of an exhibitionistic mind.   Carlotta joins me in all best,   Gene

---

394 • TO ROBERT SISK.   TLS 3 pp. (Stationery headed: Casa Genotta / Sea Island / Georgia) [Yale]

March 21st 1935

Dear Bob,   Just got your letter of the 19th. You haven't said yet whether you got any action from Kenneth on my silent script or not. I only mention it because you speak about getting more story and, as I remember the script, it might possess a few valuable hints along that line—hints, you understand, for as I've said, as a whole it was probably lousy. I remember, for one thing, that it logically carried on the Steel-Yank feud to Pittsburgh—or any steel town. Yank, after his frustrated I.W.W. experience, resolves he'll blow up steel all on his own. So, with this idea in mind, he gets a job in the Nazareth works and you see him there working for steel. He steals dynamite and sets it off. But again, a fiasco and frustration. All his attempt does is to blow down a section of wall—and immediately an army of workers rebuilds the wall up before his eyes (an expressionistic touch). In the mental and spiritual despair following this blow he wanders at night to the outskirts of the town where the millionaire steel owners' estates are and he gets in to the girl's father's place. A big fiesta is taking place there celebrating the engagement of Mildred. She, bored by her fiancé and everything else, wanders forth into the night and in the garden comes upon Yank. He remembers his threat to throw her in the furnace, picks her up and runs back to the works with her and is about to pitch her into a blast furnace when he discovers she isn't scared, she is having the one big thrill of her life, she is laughing at him. Then as he hesitates, she bends down (he is holding her over his head) and kisses him. This finishes him. He lets her down. Then, before all the assembled multitude of mill workers who have run up, she slaps his face scornfully, turns her back on him and walks off. All his fellow workers jeer at him and he is too beaten even to fight them. It is this final frustration and humiliation which sends Yank out to wind up in the Zoo with the Gorilla.

Told thus, in strict realistic terms, it all sounds bald—but built up on the plane of the play it might lead toward a real something. Of course, my idea in the screen story, was to build up the attraction-repulsion, hate-lust thing between Yank and Mildred, to make her even more of a bitch.

I thought I'd get this off to you and Nichols right away in case there's anything in it for you, and you haven't the script.

A suggestion which is not in script: Why not start Yank's boyhood and horrible home-life (a hint of which is in play, you'll remember) in the slums of the same steel town where Mildred's Steel King Father has his estate—some link between them of attraction-repulsion as children or adolescent—so that in the end you complete a circle which is, in a way, fated from the beginning.

Other matters I'll leave for another letter.   Carlotta joins me in all best for you and Cepha.   Gene

---

395 • TO SHERWOOD ANDERSON.[1]   TLS 2 pp. (Stationery headed: Casa Genotta / Sea Island / Georgia) [Newberry]

April 24th 1935

Dear Sherwood,   I am so glad to know you enjoyed your visit here. It was all too brief for me, too. I felt as you did that there was a devil of a lot I wanted to say but that it was too long a story to start then. Well, here's hoping that something will take you and Mrs. Anderson this way again before too long—or that sometime you will have the leisure and the urge to hop in your car and come down just to visit us. I needn't say you will always be welcome. Or, again, maybe I can take advantage of your invitation to Marion after I break the back of this outsize opus. Anyway, no matter how, I hope we can, and will soon, get together again. Because I've never lost the sense I had when I first read your work, and which was confirmed when I first met you years ago, that there was spiritual kinship between us—and so, the foundation of lasting friendship.

What you said at the last of your note is darned kind, and coming from you it means the hell of a lot to me. Thank you.

Mrs. O'Neill joins me in all good wishes to you and to Mrs. Anderson.   Very sincerely yours,   Gene

---

396 • TO ROBERT SISK.   TLS 4 pp. (Stationery headed: Casa Genotta / Sea Island / Georgia) [Yale]

July 3rd 1935

Dear Bob,   This is a late reply to your last but we have been having a long round of family visitors, followed by Nathan, and I've been working all along too—so not much spare time.

1. Anderson (1876–1941), short-story writer and novelist, who was living in Marion, Virginia, at this time.

By the way, speaking of George, he said many fine things of your *Informer* film.[1] He liked it immensely. How has it come out at the box office? I've had a dismal hunch that they might have trouble getting folks interested in Irish stuff. And I know damned well that the better the stuff the less you can expect any support whatever from the Irish in the U.S.A.!

As to the new project, I'll sketch it briefly for you. (To go into detail would take a book!) It's a cycle of seven plays portraying the history of the interrelationships of a family over a period of approximately a century. The first play begins in 1829, the last ends in 1932. Five generations of this family appear in the cycle. Two of the plays take place in New England, one almost entirely on a clipper ship, one on the Coast, one around Washington principally, one in New York, one in the Middle West. As to titles, the *Electra* pattern will be followed—a general title for the Cycle, and one for each play. Each play will be, as far as it is possible, complete in itself while at the same time an indispensable link in the whole (a difficult technical problem, this, but I think I can solve it successfully). There will, of course, be much less hang-over of immediate suspense from one play to another than in *Electra*. Each play will be concentrated around the final fate of one member of the family but will also carry on the story of the family as a whole. In short, it is a broadening of the *Electra* idea—but, of course, not based on any classical theme. It will be less realistic than *Electra* in method, probably,—more poetical in general, I hope—more of *Great God Brown* over and under tones, more symbolical and complicated (in that it will have to deal with more intermingling relationships)—and deeper probing. There is a general spiritual undertheme for the whole cycle and the separate plays make this manifest in different aspects.

And so on. I won't give you any more of that nature because prophecies on that score at this stage are subject to contradiction when actual writing comes. I'm only telling you from the way it shapes up in scenario. I've written detailed scenarios running to 25000 words each of the first three plays, finished the outline but not the scenario of the fourth, and am now working on the outline of the fifth. I won't start actual dialogue on the first play until I've completed the scenarios of all—that means, late next Fall at the rate so far.

No religion to any of the plays except very incidentally as minor realistic detail.

The family is half Irish, half New England in its beginnings. But the New Englanders are a bit different from any I've tackled before—and so are the Irish.

How to produce? Nothing decided yet. The best scheme might be at the rate of two per season, keeping the past ones going, along with the new ones, in some sort of repertoire arrangement. A strictly no star company. The idea would be to build a repertoire company for this cycle.

And that's about all the dope up to date. I'll keep you posted on developments as I move along.

I probably won't let the first play be produced until I've got three plays finished and a first draft written of the remaining four. The Guild expect to do the first two season after next but it's doubtful if I'll be far enough along by then.

Some of the above information appeared in the statement Crouse[2] sent out. But a lot did not. So please keep it under your hat. I sent out that statement to contradict a damn fool rumor in the papers that I was writing a nine-play autobiography! That would be enough to set everyone agin me—and I'd be the last to blame them!

---

1. *The Informer*, a film about betrayal during the 1922 Irish Rebellion starring Victor McLaglen (who won an Academy Award for his performance); Sisk was instrumental in bringing it to the screen despite the apathy of RKO executives.
2. Russel Crouse (1893–1966), head publicist of the Theatre Guild and later a major playwright and coauthor of *Life With Father* (1939), among other plays and musicals.

"Sole flaw in our arrangement?" The sole flaw in yours is that you don't fly down here on one of your trips to New York. Wouldn't take long, you know. New fast planes land Savannah, from there private plane takes you and lands you here St. Simon's Island in half an hour. Or take bus Savannah to Brunswick, two hours. Do it next time.

Don't go cold on the *Hairy Ape* thing, darn you! There ought to be a really fine picture there.

Carlotta joins me in all best to you and Cepha and Miss Sisk.   As ever,   Gene

P.S. You said you were sending some *Informer* notices. You didn't did you? Because, if so, they never got here.

---

397 • TO CYNTHIA CHAPMAN BARNETT.   ALS 1 p. (Stationery headed: Casa Genotta / Sea Island / Georgia) [Yale]

August 13th 1935

Dear Cyn: Just a line—and the enclosed by way of birthday greeting.

I won't bore you here with any discourse on this and that. We can have a long talk when I see you. Suffice it for now that I admire your will to be true to yourself and your courage in making a clean-cut, uncompromising decision.[1] You have the stuff! You will come through all right! So pull up your socks and stick it out!

And believe that just as your mother understands and stands behind you, so do I—and that goes for the years to come as well as now! I am proud of you, and darned fond of you, too—in fact I think you're just about the top in daughters!   Much love to you!   Gene

---

398 • TO HARRY WEINBERGER.   WIRE 1 p. ([Casa Genotta, Sea Island, Ga.]) [Yale]

DECEMBER 23, 1935

LETTER TO SHANE FROM HIS MOTHER ADDRESSED TO FLORIDA MILITARY ACADE-MY HAS BEEN FORWARDED HERE ALTHOUGH HE IS NOT DUE HERE UNTIL THE TWENTY EIGHTH STOP IN THESE KIDNAPPING DAYS IT SEEMS TO ME EITHER HIS MOTHER OR HIS SCHOOL SHOULD HAVE SOME IDEA OF HIS WHEREABOUTS NOW WHICH EVIDENTLY NEITHER OF THEM HAVE STOP WILL YOU GET IN TOUCH WITH HER AND MAKE HER CHECK WITH SCHOOL ON THIS =   GENE

---

399 • TO PHILIP HORTON.[1]   TLS 2 pp. (Stationery headed: Casa Genotta / Sea Island / Georgia) [Yale]

February 11th 1936

Dear Mr. Horton,   There are no recollections of mine about Hart's life that would be worth a damn to you. For, although our friendship extended over several years, I saw comparatively little of him. I lived in Connecticut then, while he was either living in New

1. Carlotta's daughter was divorcing her husband.

1. Critic and writer whose biography of Crane, *Hart Crane: The Life of an American Poet*, appeared in 1937.

York or away some place, and on the occasions when we did meet in town we were both almost invariably blotto.

As for my impression of him, what can I tell you except what you will hear from all who knew him—that while his was a super-sensitive, tortured personality he was at the same time a simple, likable human being—that no one with any imagination could fail to sense the real, creative flame in him, or doubt that he was a true poet driven to expression by a fierce passion for beauty.

I'm sorry but I have no letters from Hart. All the letters in my files up to 1928 were left in Bermuda and were subsequently lost, or destroyed, or stolen.

The Introduction mix-up was this: Horace Liveright wrote me that Hart had submitted *White Buildings* to him, but that he felt the poetry was too confused and difficult to have any sale at all, unless it had some news-name to explain it. Now those were the days when *Desire Under The Elms* had recently been almost pinched by the cops, and the masks in *The Great God Brown* had caused a lot of promiscuous conversation, so I was mildly notorious. Hence Horace had a publisher's hunch and decided he would only publish if I would write a critical introduction, and that he had told Hart so. Hart wrote me, too, confirming this ultimatum of Liveright's. Well, of course, I then told Horace I would. But, later on, after I'd tried to make a start on the introduction, I became convinced that I was not fitted for the job and would only make a mess of it—that, to do Hart justice, it should be written by some poet or critic with a knowledge of the whole trend of modern poetry, and the significance of Hart's work in relation to that trend. I wrote Horace to this effect, and also told him, that from his sales angle, (granted his idiotic belief that my boosting could help a book of poetry at all, which I knew was publisher's nonsense!)—I could do a lot more good by writing a sincere statement for the jacket of the impression Hart's work made on me than by faking a critical introduction. Well, Horace finally saw it that way, and Tate consented to do his fine introduction, instead of the punk one I would have done, and I did the jacket—and that's that.

And that's about all I can give you. Please forgive the delay in this reply. But the January seventh dating of your letter must be an error, isn't it? It never reached me until a week ago, forwarded from Random House.

Good luck to your biography!   Very sincerely yours,   Eugene O'Neill

---

400 • TO THERESA HELBURN.   TLS 2 pp. (Stationery headed: Casa Genotta / Sea Island / Georgia) [Yale]

April 7th 1936

Dear Terry,   That this is a pretty tardy reply to your letter does not signify that I was not delighted and flattered by it. It merely means I'm a damned lazy correspondent and try never to write a letter to-day that I can put off until to-morrow.

There is a word of warning in regard to planning ahead that I feel bound to repeat now, in justice both to the Guild and me. Don't begin to plan for the production of the Cycle, except in a very general way, until you receive finished plays from me to plan on. Don't expect first drafts. I hate letting anyone see first drafts. Mine are intolerably long and wordy—intentionally so, because I put everything in them, so as not to lose anything, and rely on a subsequent revision and rewriting, after a lapse of time with better perspective on them, to concentrate on the essential and eliminate the overweight. But to a person reading a first draft, that draft is the first impact of the play on them, and it is apt to be a very misleading impact indeed. My first drafts always bore me for long stretches, so I can hardly expect them to do less for other people. And being bored by a first draft would be a disheartening approach to this Cycle for the prospective producer.

And don't rely on receiving the first plays at any definite future date, for though I may do some speculating about the matter, I cannot honestly even tell myself just when it will be. It depends on so many things which cannot be foretold. For example, the old subconscious might get on the job in great shape, and I might find myself in a surge of creative energy where I could keep going on, in first draft, from one to another until five or six or even all eight were written. In which case, as you will appreciate, I would be insane to pause for any interruption—especially such an exhausting interruption as production is for me, followed always by a long period of blank uncreativeness. It would be much better in the long run, from both our standpoints, for me to go on without a break, even if it meant a delay of one or two years. It would be much better, from your angle, if, from the start, you had all eight to base a company on.

All of which sounds like handing you a large package of uncertainty to go on with. But the ill of uncertainty is inherent in authorship—at least, my kind of authorship. You're always dependent on factors in yourself you cannot control but which control you, and your prophecies, optimistic or pessimistic, have an ironic habit of changing sides on you before the game is finished.

I'll read the play you sent down during the first pause I come to between acts—or plays. I suppose you're in no hurry to have the script back.

It was grand to have you and Maurice[1] here. Come again—only be sure and make Oliver[2] accompany you the next time. Tell him we've got a wall, too, and he can go out and add a foot or two on that whenever the mania seizes him.

Carlotta joins in best to you both—and Blemie sends a sweet kiss to Blunder!   Sincerely, Gene

---

401 • TO EUGENE O'NEILL, JR.   TLS 3 pp. (Stationery headed: Casa Genotta / Sea Island / Georgia) [Yale]

June 20th 1936

Dear Eugene,   It was good to get your letter. I would have written you, only you said in your wire you were writing, so I waited to learn all the details of your good news. And it sure is good news! But, as I wired you, I was by no means astonished, or anything like that, that you had done so nobly, for your somber premonitions had not impressed me as being liable to coincide with the facts when they appeared. I know such dreary forebodings too damned well. They are the familiar spirits of this branch of the O'Neills—one of the baneful heritages you get from me, I'm afraid. I've been enjoying more than my usual share of them lately, too, what with this Cycle of plays stretching out into a future of seemingly endless hard labor. It looks now as if there would have to be still another play—a ninth which will carry me back to 1770 as a starter.

What you write about the exams is damned interesting and I am glad you told me so much about the oral. Of course, I knew there was one, but had no idea it was such a

---

1. Maurice Wertheim.
2. John Baker Opdyke, Helburn's husband, who was known as Oliver.

formidable inquisition. I can imagine how you felt when you paced the hall waiting for the verdict!

As for the job,[1] from what you tell me, that assuredly is a grand bit of good fortune! And the salary is more than I ever thought you would get to start with.

Speaking of money, you know, I hope, that if ever you get in a tough spot I can always manage to come across with something, although, as you may guess, the next couple of years will be lean ones unless that rarity for me, a Movie-rights purchase, comes up. I want to tell you frankly what my exact situation is. Whatever income I have from investments is more than abolished by the alimony dole. That means that as far as my half of Carlotta's and my household expenses, etc. is concerned I am living on capital and will be for the next two years or more, for I do not expect to be able to release any new play for production or publication before then. Royalties on books bring in something but comparatively little. Stock, amateur performances' royalties don't amount to much because my plays are difficult to cast and seldom attempted. Foreign productions continue to be flatteringly constant—but are done in repertoire for a few performances at a time, and with half to a translator, tax, etc. the return to me in dollars is negligible, or less. I had hoped something from the London production of *Ah, Wilderness!* by the Irish Group Theatre, but in spite of a unanimously enthusiastic critical reception, no one is going to see it and it has possibly closed by this.

So that's about the situation—and it is due to grow steadily worse instead of better, pending the appearance of my new work. I tell you all this not to cry poor, you understand, but to present the hard facts.

I am determined, if I go broke in the process, not to release any play of the Cycle until I have at least three or four in final form, and more in first draft. This is essential to me because the emphasis with me is naturally on the work as a whole, not on its separate parts. It is also essential for the stage production of the work as a whole that the Guild have several plays to plan on as a starter—for they intend to get together a special repertoire company just to do this Cycle, and when it comes to tying up actors and actresses for three or four years, in these days of Talkie temptation, you've got to show them parts in several plays that make it to their advantage to sign up. You can't do it on one or two plays with a vague promise of good parts in plays not yet written, no matter who the author. The plan, as I guess I've told you before, is to do two plays a season.

So you see how this Cycle has me involved in a hell of a lot of labor—and costly time—before I can expect any returns of any kind. You will also appreciate that I have many low days of O'Neill heebie-jeebies when I feel very old and tired, and doubt myself and my work, and wonder why in hell something in me drove me on to undertake such a hellish job when I might have coasted along and just written some more plays, as a well-behaved playwright does.

But enough of that.

I foresaw that you would probably get some tart retorts from the Middle-West on your article. Mid-Westerners are very sensitive people—that is, in one respect.

Love to you and Betty from us—and a sweet kiss from Blemie to Cabot.   Father

---

1. After passing his Ph.D. oral examination at Yale, Eugene O'Neill, Jr., accepted a position in the classics department at Yale.

August 12th 1936

Dear Lawrence,   Your letter to Garland[1] is fine and dandy, and hits the nail on the head, and much gratitude to you for writing it, and for sending me a copy. That ought to be that. If it had been a question only of the *Variety* article, I would have agreed with you and Warren that it should be ignored. After all, who cares for *Variety?* But Garland taking it up means all the Scripps-Howard papers in the long run, and put too much of a spot-light on it to let it pass without denial.

But I hope you yourself don't believe the Cycle is "an American life" in any usual sense of the word, or you're going to be disappointed. I mean, I'm not giving a damn whether the dramatic event of each play has any significance in the growth of the country or not, as long as it is significant in the spiritual and psychological history of the American family in the plays. The Cycle is primarily just that, the history of a family. What larger significance I can give my people as extraordinary examples and symbols in the drama of American possessiveness and materialism is something else again. But I don't want anyone to get the idea that this Cycle is much concerned with what is usually understood by American history, for it isn't. As for economic history—which so many seem to mistake for the *only* history just now—I am not much interested in economic determinism, but only in the self-determinism of which the economic is one phase, and by no means the most revealing—at least, not to me.

As for inside dope on the progress on my work, I have the second play[2] in good shape—beyond first draft—I can call it pretty well completed, unless I have to make minor changes in it later because of things in the other plays. The first play[3] I have in first draft—but, damn it, it is two-plays long and will have to be entirely rewritten to condense it—or if it can't be condensed, then I may have to add still another first play, making nine in all!

Try a Cycle sometime, I advise you—that is, I would advise you to, if I hated you! A lady bearing quintuplets is having a debonair, carefree time of it by comparison.

We are grateful for your renewed invitation to Langnerlane Farm but I think we'll again have to postpone. I'm going good on the work just now—in fact, haven't missed a single day on the job since the first of March—and I want to stick with it.

I was glad to note by your first letter that you are both satisfied with the results of your Westport season.[4] I'd like to see Savo in the Molière.[5] But how about the Le Gallienne-Hamlet scheme?[6] Is anything to come of that? It struck me as an extraordinarily interesting idea—and one that should be successful in every way.

Our love to you both—and again thank you for your letter to Garland.   As ever, Gene

P.S. A hell of a hot oppressive summer here. Carlotta and I are neck and neck toward the Olympic and World's sweating record! We just continually drop and drip.

    1. Robert Garland, critic of the *New York World-Telegram,* whose "Theatre Guild Finds G.B.S. Too Expensive—Also Reported to Have Decided That O'Neill Must Stand on Other Feet," *New York World-Telegram,* August 7, 1936, p. 6, reported that the Guild would no longer produce O'Neill.
    2. *A Touch of the Poet,* completed in 1942 but not produced until 1957.
    3. "And Give Me Death," also called "Greed of the Meek," destroyed in 1943.
    4. The Langners had produced a season of summer theater in Westport, Connecticut.
    5. Jimmy Savo starred in *The Would-Be Gentleman* at the Westport Country Playhouse.
    6. Actress Eva LeGallienne (1899–) did eventually appear as Hamlet in a production of the play but it

[August 1936]

Dear Harold: It was fine to hear from you again. But your letter came too late. I had the day before wired the Suffren theatre people[1] my permit for them to bring their production of *Jones* to New York—provided they agreed to my terms, which were pretty stiff. I haven't heard from Madden yet what has happened about this.

Frankly, I don't think a revival of *Jones* with Robeson, no matter how well done, would have a chance at this time. Paul in *Jones* is too familiar, too old hat. It's too soon after his appearance in the film version. I think the only chance a revival would have now would be with some new personality in the role, which would bring new public curiosity about it. That's the reason I was willing to give my okay to Ingram.[2] I'd heard he had gotten grand notices and I knew he'd attracted a lot of interest in the *Green Pastures* film. Of course, if he's as bad as you say—and I know you know what you're talking about—then it seems pretty hopeless. But then, all revivals, no matter who's in them, are pretty hopeless in the New York theatre of today. I turn down propositions for revivals of different plays every season because I have no faith or interest in them, and because I'm always hopefully saving those plays for some future time when a real repertoire theatre may come into being. But *Jones* isn't one of the plays I've been holding out simply because I regarded it as too recently filmed and familiar to have any revival interest for so many years to come that it wasn't worth considering.

Well, that being that, how the hell is yourself? Grand and getting every break, I hope. If what I heard from a recent visitor to Provincetown is true, you couldn't pick a lousier spot for a vacation. He said it had developed into a combination of Old Fairies Home and Montparnasse tourist Bohemia with a strong dash of Coney Island on July 4th.

Me, I am slaving and sweating—and do we sweat in Georgia in August!—at this cycle of eight plays I'm trying to do. Have two of them in first draft—but it's a long road yet. I think after I finish this toughest of all my jobs, I shall feel I've said all I ever want to say, and turn in all the old torn medals and newspaper wreaths and call it a day and relax for the rest of my life.

In closing I want to tell you how deeply I appreciate your friendship in writing me as you did. As for trusting you to do *Jones* I know of no one I'd trust more with it, and I know you won't think any other idea had anything to do with my conviction that a *Jones*-Robeson revival would be just a waste of time and money and doesn't interest me.

Carlotta joins me in all best to you—and give my best to Bert.

---

404 • TO KENNETH MACGOWAN.   ALS 3 pp. (4701 West Ruffner Street, / Seattle, Wash.) [Yale]

Nov. 15 '36

Dear Kenneth: The past couple of days have been pretty hectic—dodging the radio & newsreel baloney, when they refused to take no for an answer, & etc.—or I would have

---

did not open until August 23, 1937, at the Cape Playhouse in Dennis, Massachusetts, and Langner was not involved in the production.

1. Robert F. Cutler's County Theatre in Suffren, Long Island, New York, opened a revival of *The Emperor Jones* on August 10, 1936, with Joshua Logan directing.
2. Rex Ingram, who starred in the County Theatre production of *The Emperor Jones* and who had played De Lawd in the 1936 film version of Marc Connelly's play *The Green Pastures*.

acknowledged your wire ere this. I needn't tell you, I hope, that your message was among the few that meant most. I know your friendship is sincerely pleased at my good luck.

And quite apart from congrats over the Nobel, I was damned tickled to hear from you again. Thought you'd forgotten me. You owe me a letter from way back—or am I wrong again? No, I'm sure I'm not. I've sort of kept in touch with your doings through Bob Sisk, and I've been damned glad to hear what a fine thing you are making of it out here. I can guess what peace of mind that must bring you, after all the years of financial worry and uncertainty, in which the so-called Legit. rewarded your work so miserably and thanklessly. And this Nobel thing makes me think back—(only I often do, anyway)—and remember the days when your friendship was such a constant encouragement, and when you worked so hard and unselfishly to help put my work across, and I want to tell you now, again, of the gratitude I always will feel. You are one of the finest guys and one of the best friends I have ever known, Kenneth, and I rate it a damned shame and loss that circumstances in the past few years have placed us so far apart in these U.S. that we never get a chance even to say howdy to each other, let alone work together any more. I often dream of what a grand break it would be if you and Bobby and I could get together again, and start again in New York on our own with a resurge of the old spirit to prompt us. I don't notice much of that spirit in the present New York theatre—in fact, not any. The dreams there seem to be "all wet." Maybe I'm getting aged and crabbed but there seems nothing left—outside of the Radical propaganda on 14th street—which has any definite ambition toward any goal. Of course, there are plenty of compromisers who straddle the fence, and try to be both this and that, and end up by being neither. But I don't know of one producing group that has the guts to hew to the line as we did. And so, outside of my job of writing plays, I've just about lost all interest in the theatre.

Perhaps all this strikes you as a bit too mournful and dejected. And maybe it is. Truth is, I'm worn out physically and badly need a complete rest. I worked on my damned cycle constantly every day for seven months without one day off—all through an extra scorching Georgia summer—and by the end of Sept. I was a wreck and about ready to feed the hookworms. Carlotta was also climate-sunk. So we've decided to sell the Sea Island mansion and give Dixie back to Tin Pan Alley. And to look for a home in a more salubrious clime—once the Ga. one is sold. We came here for a complete climate change—and a rest—and for me to "get" the background of all this part of the country for use in cycle. But principally for a rest. And now comes the Nobel—and no chance of rest for a while, what with all plans up in the air. So it is not an unmixed blessing. In fact, so far, I'm like an ancient cab horse that has had a blue ribbon pinned on his tail—too physically weary to turn round and find out if it's good to eat, or what.

We may take that steamer ride you suggest sometime, but not for the nonce we can't. I'm waiting for word from Sweden and can't move until all about that is settled. And then there's the climate. Boy, what we crave now are cold, and gray skies, and be damned to sun and warmth!

Carlotta joins me in all best to you! And my best to all the other Macgowans!   As ever,   Gene

P.S. I'm bound to be here for the next two or three weeks—so write, if you can find time, and let me know all of what's what with you.

405 • TO JAMES E. BROWN, JR.[1]   AL (draft) 2 pp. ([4701 West Ruffner St., Seattle, Wash.]) [Yale]

[late November 1936]

My dear Mr. Brown: Enclosed you will find the speech you suggested.[2] I have never been a guest of honor, or made a speech in my life, and I've only written about two of them before this, but I hope this one is adequate. Certainly, I can assure you that I've never written anything truer or more sincere than the acknowledgment therein of my debt to Strindberg. It is no mere artful gesture to please a Swedish audience. It's a plain statement of fact and my exact feeling, and I am glad of this opportunity to get it said and on record.

I want to thank you again for your courtesy in cabling me. To tell the truth, I am completely at sea as to just what may be expected of me under the circumstances, and I know of no one who is able to advise me, especially in this part of the country where I am a stranger. At the same time, I realize the Swedes are apt to be as punctilious about correct procedure as we are careless, and naturally, the last thing in the world I would wish would be to offend them in any way. It is unfortunate that I cannot get to the festival, but this Prize caught me entirely unawares, in the midst of all sorts of involvements—the principal one being the state of my health.

I was all shot to pieces from overwork, and was ordered out here last month for a complete change of climate and absolute rest and to forget that such a thing as a play existed. Somehow, the Nobel sort of makes me remember—so, in that respect, coming at this particular time, the Prize is not altogether an unmixed boon. The point is I am not physically or mentally up to the strain of being a guest of honor at a festival just now, even if other circumstances permitted my going. I would simply crack up badly. So I hope all those connected with the festival will accept my statement of the impossibility of my attending in good faith and not put it down to arbitrary temperament or something of that sort.

Again, allow me to thank you for your courtesy. I shall look forward to the pleasure of meeting you and thanking you in person when I do get to Stockholm.   Y. v. s.

---

406 • TO RUSSEL CROUSE.   TLS 2 pp. (4701 West Ruffner Street, / Seattle, / Washington) [Yale]

November 25th 1936

Dear Russel,   Your letter with clippings enclosed just reached us and we are very grateful for both of same. From what I have happened to see, and hear of, the Press has certainly given me a grand deal and I'm immensely gratified thereat. And the Irish Free State has congratulated me officially—that is, its Washington ambassador has, as adding, along with Shaw and Yeats, to the credit of old Ireland. So what could be more perfect?

Of course, I do still—unfortunately—subscribe to the International Clipping Bureau, in order to keep cases on foreign production and publication, and when I see what the bloody Limeys and Frogs have to say, for instance, I may not feel so uppish. I can foresee plenty of very superior and crappy cracks indeed!

I enclose herewith, for your edification, a copy of the speech, limited to a few minutes,

---

1. Third secretary of the American embassy in Stockholm, Sweden.
2. For the text of O'Neill's acceptance speech, which was delivered for him by Brown, see *The Unknown O'Neill: Unpublished or Unfamiliar Writings of Eugene O'Neill*, pp. 427–28.

which I am making (by proxy of a representative from the U. S. Legation) at the Nobel banquet in Stockholm on Dec. 10th. Let me know what you think of it. It is probably lousy, for God knows as a writer of speeches I am almost as bad as I am as a speaker of them—and that is superlatively punk! The first section is, you will note, replete with more than a little amiable phonus bolonus about my American colleagues—though why the hell I should be so amiable, I don't know, for few, if any, of them have ever had the decency to admit that my work had ever meant a thing to American drama or to them, or that my pioneering had busted the old dogmas wide open and left them free to do anything they wanted in any way they wanted. (Not that many of them have had the guts to try anything out of the ordinary— but they could have.)

Re this Nobel award, for example, I have rec'd congratulations from all over the world, including cables from dramatists such as Hauptmann, Pirandello, Lenormand, etc. but none from home front playwrights with the exception of Ned Sheldon, Sam Behrman,[1] George Middleton and your esteemed self. Verily, as I have always said—perhaps too loudly to expect appreciation—my U.S. colleagues are, speaking in general, cheap shit-heels!

But I couldn't very well tell the Swedes that, could I? Not over the banquet plates. It wouldn't be nice. So instead, I pour coals of bilge on the noggin of ingratitude, and give them both barrels of the old akamarakus!

The Strindberg part of the speech, however, is no "telling the tale" to please the Swedes with a polite gesture. It is absolutely sincere—and could be checked up with what I wrote for the program of the first bill[2] when the reorganized Provincetown started its career under Kenneth's, Bobby Jones' and my directorship with a production of Strindberg's *Spook Sonata* (at my suggestion). And it's absolutely true that I am proud of the opportunity to acknowledge my debt to Strindberg thus publicly to his people.

Outside of craving your opinion on the speech itself, I would also like your slant on the advisability of your releasing copies of it to the A.P., U.P., I.N., and New York papers just after it is made in Sweden on Dec. 10th. I mean, of course, let 'em know you have it in case they should want it to quote from. My point about this is that, if I am to be quoted, I'd like it to be exact and not have my poor speech at the mercy of the memory of banquet reporters, their imaginations aflame with Swedish punch. My proxy from the U.S. Embassy—if what I've heard of U.S. Embassies be true—is quite likely to be cockeyed, too, and prefer his version to mine. He may say Sandow or Shipman instead of Strindberg—and then where would I be? Anyway, write me what you think.

Physically, I am still in the punk with the nerves all shot—. Was beginning to relax and rest out here when the Nobel bomb burst. There hasn't been much chance to relax since. Not that I'm complaining, you understand.

Carlotta joins me in all fondest to you. We rejoice at the good standee news concerning *Red, Hot and Blue,*[3] and we shall be very hurt if you don't take us for a ride in your new Rolls the next time we hit New York. In fact, here's wishing you two Rolls and a pink Duesenberg cabriolet!   As ever,   Gene

1. S. N. Behrman (1893–1973), graduate of Baker's English 47 and author of *The Second Man* (1927), *End of Summer* (1936), and many other plays.

2. "Strindberg and Our Theatre," published in the Provincetown playbill for January 3, 1934, and reprinted in *The Unknown O'Neill: Unpublished or Unfamiliar Writings of Eugene O'Neill*, pp. 387–88.

3. Musical comedy by Cole Porter (1891–1964), Howard Lindsay (1889–1968), and Crouse, which opened October 29, 1936, at the Alvin Theatre.

407 • TO SINCLAIR LEWIS.   TLS 1 p. (4701 West Ruffner Street, / Seattle, / Washington) [Yale]

November 25th 1936

Dear Red,   I needn't tell you how much I appreciated your note of congratulation on the Nobel. It means a lot—and what you said to the Press, too. So much very sincere gratitude to you!

Yes, it's a damned shame Gorki never got the prize. When he died I wrote a tribute for the Soviet magazine in New York which exactly expressed my opinion that he had been the top of all living writers.[1]

Again, thank you for your note. It was damned kind of you. And all the best of good wishes always to you and your work!   Very sincerely,   Eugene O'Neill

---

408 • TO SIDNEY HOWARD.[1]   TLS 1 p. (4701 West Ruffner Street / Seattle, / Washington) [California]

November 26th 1936

Dear Sidney Howard,   Your letter, forwarded, just reached me out here, and I am certainly grateful for it. It's damned fine of you to write what you did, and I will always remember your letter as one of the most gratifying things the Nobel award has brought me.

As for your dire threat to ruin Nobel majesty with my letter about Lewis' rescue work in Fall River, all I can say is, go to it with my grateful blessing! This being Eminent, even if it's only for a few days, is a most godforsaken pain in the neck. The idiocies the radio and newsreel confidently expect of you, for example, are a severe drain on the sense of humor, even after you've at length convinced them that no means no.

I had a grand note from Lewis. And what he said to the Press pleased me immensely. A fine guy! I'm so glad now that I was honestly so glad for him when he got the award.

Speaking of Lewis, do you know the result of the Academy election? I don't. My ballot reached me on the first mail forwarded out here and I sent it on at once, a week to spare, so it must have been received on time. Here's hoping Lewis made it![2]

Carlotta joins me in good wishes—and again, much gratitude for your letter!   Sincerely, Eugene O'Neill

---

1. Maxim Gorky (1868–1936), Russian dramatist and novelist, whose play *The Lower Depths* (1902) is often compared to O'Neill's *The Iceman Cometh*; O'Neill's tribute is reprinted in *The Unknown O'Neill: Unpublished or Unfamiliar Writings of Eugene O'Neill*, p. 425.

1. Howard (1891–1939), dramatist and graduate of Baker's English 47, whose plays include *They Knew What They Wanted* (1924), *Lucky Sam McCarver* (1925), and *The Late Christopher Bean* (1932).
2. Sinclair Lewis, in his address accepting the Nobel Prize for literature in 1930, had harshly criticized the American Academy of Arts and Letters; as a result, he was not nominated for the Academy until 1936, when he narrowly failed to be elected. He was, however, elected in 1937.

409 • TO THEODORE DREISER.[1] TLS 1 p. ([4701 Ruffner St.,] Seattle, / Washington) [Pennsylvania]

December 3rd 1936

Dear Dreiser,   Your letter on the Nobel award is damned fine and generous of you, and I want you to know how deeply I appreciate it and what pleasure it gives me. You are one of the very few I really wanted to hear from.

And it will mean a hell of a lot to me if you will believe that the feeling behind my reference to you[2] was, and is, and always will be absolutely genuine. For I can say to you with entire sincerity and truth, from my head and heart both, that I would take a great deal more satisfaction in this prize if you were among those who had had it before me. As it is, I have a sneaking feeling of guilt—as if I had pinched something which I know damned well should, in justice, be yours.

Again, thank you for your letter.   Very sincerely,   Eugene O'Neill

1. Dreiser (1871–1945), author of *Sister Carrie* (1900) and *An American Tragedy* (1925), among other novels.
2. O'Neill had apparently commented favorably about Dreiser to the press.

PART SEVEN

HEIGHTS

1936–1945

Bum health is my only real block—the periods
when there just isn't the vitality for the grind
of intensive day after day labor. When you live
through the play you write, you have to have a
lot of reserved life untapped.
—*To Eugene O'Neill, Jr., April 28, 1941*

During the decade that O'Neill lived in California, at the greatest personal cost he brought his work to its fulfillment. At Tao House, the home he and Carlotta built near San Francisco, he wrote *The Iceman Cometh, Long Day's Journey into Night, Hughie, A Moon for the Misbegotten,* and drafts of the eleven-play cycle "A Tale of Possessors Self-dispossessed," of which only *A Touch of the Poet* and an unrevised typescript of *More Stately Mansions* remain. The Tao House plays have given him title to being a world dramatist, and they are the result of the many years of arduous imaginative inventing that would finally allow him to express his truth completely. In these plays, the exterior and interior beings seem conjoined. The sanctuary that Carlotta created for him in the California hills was undisturbed. It was pleasingly rural and remote from the turbulence of show business. Carlotta guarded it well, so that when he went through the doors that shut off his study from the rest of the house, nothing could intrude on the creative silence.

Whether the cycle would ever have been completed is a question that anyone reading the few remaining notes and story outlines left undestroyed can reasonably ask. In plan the plays encompassed almost the entire course of the history of the United States, and a pageant of characters moved across the vast stage in a vivid display of love and hate and greed. O'Neill's theme was a bitter assertion: to gain the world, the United States had sold its soul. The Harford and Melody families were to demonstrate this in their unceasing search for power. Dynastic recounting was familiar in the work of many novelists, but to write a work of such scope for the stage was new, and the problems presented in composition and production were nearly insuperable.

Writing the cycle was a labor more intensive than anything else O'Neill had undertaken. Each play grew to enormous length. Scenarios of many thousands of words when developed in dialogue grew to drafts longer than *Strange Interlude* or *Mourning Becomes Electra.* "They get that way in spite of me," he lamented to Arthur Hobson Quinn.[1] He fended off inquiries from the Theatre Guild directors about production, refusing to discuss the possibility until several plays were completed and the whole plan firm. Day after day when his health permitted, he sat in the silence of his study working on the outlines, scenarios, and drafts of the massive drama. In effect, at Tao House he disappeared from the public's view.

1. Letter to Arthur Hobson Quinn (letter 481).

Productions of his earlier plays were few and what there were failed. His most telling appearance as a playwright was through Dudley Nichols's script for John Ford's film of the four one-act plays about the *S.S. Glencairn*. O'Neill lived, so it seemed, only to wrestle with the cycle through exhausting years of creative labor. Something of his father's work ethic kept him at his desk, but at the heart of the effort was his own need, the emotional habits of his entire life. For those whose lives were not so ordered by the need of work, he showed contempt. If he were responsible for them, as he felt responsibility for Shane and Oona, he cast them out of his life when they failed him.

In the end, the knotted narrative of the cycle became a Gordian, and he turned from it in weariness, putting it aside to write the great autobiographical plays that crowned his career. These finished, there was silence. The exterior man proved incapable of sustaining the relentless pressure of the inner force. He was cared for by a respected Oakland physician, Charles A. Dukes, but there was no permanent remedy for the often uncontrollable tremor he developed. He understood the tremor to be caused by Parkinson's disease, but he also remembered it as a lifelong, minor affliction, perhaps inherited from his mother. As memories of the past formed the subject of his final works, so the physical past caught up with him, shaking his hand so badly that at times he could write nothing. He could not type or dictate. His way of composing had been with a pencil in microscopically small handwriting, more etched than penned. To write in the tiny script, a psychological necessity that was his ultimate gesture toward privacy, was made impossible by the invading tremor.

At Tao House, beyond the study, he found a calm and civilized world of walled gardens, orchards, and livestock in golden pastures. His prize bantams lived in a stout chickenhouse protected against predators from the acreage surrounding the property. In the hills, he and his beloved Dalmatian, Blemie, could walk in a wilderness. Old friends and members of Carlotta's family came, but not in numbers. It was an ordered world that centered on his needs—while it lasted a peaceable kingdom.

Like any demi-Paradise it did not last. Shane came and proved likable. Oona, on a visit to reacquaint herself with her father, was "charming." Eugene, Jr., progressed as a faculty member in classics at Yale, publishing scholarly articles and co-editing with Whitney Oates, a Princeton professor, the two-volume *Complete Greek Drama*, a work that made available to a wide public the corpus of Greek plays.

Then Shane fell into difficulty with his schooling. O'Neill, contrary to his understanding with Agnes, was not always consulted or even informed where Shane was to be entered into school. Expensive preparatory schools did not profit Shane. He thought perhaps his father would set him up as a breeder of horses. He would study art. He would go into the movies. Slowly, he began the fatal drift downward that would lead him to suicide in 1977.

Oona, who had become a friend of Gloria Vanderbilt at school at Brearley, began to move in the heady circles of New York café society. For O'Neill her charm quickly faded when she was named by the public relations flacks of the Stork Club "debutante of the year" for 1942–43. O'Neill, feeling that his name had something to do with the award of the dubious honor, became infuriated with his daughter and with Agnes, whose guidance of the seventeen-year-old girl appeared lax. In 1943, after Oona went to Hollywood and married Charles Chaplin—then involved in a notorious paternity suit—O'Neill would no longer acknowledge her.

The life of Eugene, Jr., who was his father's pride, also began to show signs of coming apart. During the Tao House years, he divorced his second wife. A third marriage also ended in divorce. When the war came, he left his position at Yale, sought and failed to find important war work, and entered radio and television broadcasting. He began to drink heavily. The omens were not of the best for a continuation of such academic success as he had earlier achieved.

The coming of World War II capped the troubles of O'Neill's exterior existence. Tao House lies halfway up the western slopes of the rim of hills that fringe the eastern side of San Francisco Bay. Even today it is not easily accessible. With gasoline rationing, with servants, including Herbert Freeman, O'Neill's handyman and chauffeur since Sea Island, leaving to enlist or to enter war work, with O'Neill's and Carlotta's illnesses increasing in severity, life at Tao House became untenable. The life-support systems of the house gave way, and the O'Neills were forced to sell it. In 1944, they moved to San Francisco. The following year they went East as the Theatre Guild prepared the premiere of *The Iceman Cometh*.

410 • TO JANE MALMGREN.[1]   ALS 1 p. (Stationery headed: Samuel Merritt Hospital / Oakland, California) [Private]

Sunday / Jan. '36 [1937]

Dear Miss Malmgren: Many thanks for your so beauteous, rhymes or no rhymes, poem—and so gorgeously illustrated, too! And much gratitude for the gifts! I sure like their infinite variety!

But don't insinuate this institution resembles the Mannon mansion in *M.B.E.!* That is too depressing a thought—for, as I remember, the male inmates didn't have much luck there, but lost considerably more than their appendixes (if that's the right plural correctly spelled, which I doubt).

Seriously, much gratitude for your appreciation of my plays, and all good luck to you at U.C., and to your ambitions.   Eugene O'Neill

---

411 • TO CARLOTTA MONTEREY O'NEILL.[1]   WIRE 1 p. ([Samuel Merritt Hospital,] Oakland, Calif.) [Yale]

FEBRUARY 26, 1937

ONLY TO SAY THAT IF YOU FEEL ANY STRANGE PUFFING AND BLOWING FROM THE BACK OF THE TWENTIETH CENTURY AND OVERLAND DONT BE ALARMED IT WILL ONLY BE ME PUSHING REMEMBER REST ALL YOU CAN ALL MY LOVE SWEETHEART =   GENE

---

412 • TO CARLOTTA MONTEREY O'NEILL.   WIRE 1 p. ([Samuel Merritt Hospital,] Oakland, Calif.) [Yale]

FEBRUARY 28, 1937

HEARING YOUR VOICE AGAIN A THOUSAND MILES NEARER WAS WONDERFUL STOP KEEP THINKING OF THIS AS A HAPPY REUNION JOURNEY AND THE DAYS WONT SEEM SO LONG ONLY TWO DAYS MORE WHEN YOU RECEIVE THIS GOOD NIGHT AND GOOD REST DARLING AND ALL MY LOVE =   GENE

---

413 • TO CARLOTTA MONTEREY O'NEILL.   WIRE 1 p. ([Samuel Merritt Hospital,] Oakland, Calif.) [Yale]

MARCH 1, 1937

HOPE YOU RECEIVED WIRE FLOWERS OMAHA WIRE CHEYENNE AND FLOWERS OGDEN STOP THIS COMING DAY AND NIGHT WILL SEEM LIKE WORLDS LONGEST TO ME ALL MY LOVE =   GENE

---

1. A young drama student at the University of California in Berkeley who sent a poem to fellow patient O'Neill, who had had an appendectomy, in which she compared the neo-Grecian façade of Merritt Hospital, reproduced on the letterhead of the hospital stationery, to the Mannons' home in *Mourning Becomes Electra*, which had recently been produced at the University of California.

1. While O'Neill remained hospitalized, Carlotta went east, after the sale of Casa Genotta, to pack their belongings. As she returned to California by train, he arranged for bouquets of roses and a barrage of telegrams to be delivered en route.

[early March 1937]

Dear Mr. Pearson,   I just got out of the hospital a few days ago, after two and a half months there, and, frankly, I will have to ask you to give up the idea of my writing that footnote for *Lazarus Laughed*, because I simply don't feel up to it. I am not even supposed, for months yet, to answer letters which have the remotest connection with work. And what I asked Eugene to tell you was that if, when you wanted the footnote, something fresh and interesting occurred to me to say about *Lazarus Laughed*, I would be glad to do it—but, otherwise, not. Well, I'm now in the low state of mind of convalescence where the mere thought of writing anything about anything exhausts me, and I want to forget that such things as plays exist.

As for what impelled me to write the play, that is a long story starting way back in my boyhood in Catholic schools when I first heard the legend of the dead man brought back from death, and it took a peculiarly deep and fascinated hold upon my imagination. Years later, when I first began writing, I considered as a one-act play the return from death scene. Later, I felt a long play about his second life was the thing I must do. All this was before I knew Andreyev's work. So I think any footnote about the influence of Andreyev's story² would be misleading and put a false emphasis on what would be seen to be incidental if the whole story of the conception of *Lazarus Laughed* was told. But I'm not up to writing that story now, and I would not wish to be quoted unless I could tell it in its entirety.

I am sorry to disappoint you on this but I know you will understand.

Much gratitude for your congratulations on the Nobel award and all good wishes to you. I feel I know you, too, from hearing Eugene speak of you with such friendship. That has helped me to be perfectly frank with you in this letter—but, believe me, it makes disappointing you a good deal harder.   Very sincerely yours,   Eugene O'Neill

---

April 26th 1937

Dear Miss Flanagan,   I have written Mr. Madden regarding the proposed cycle, as outlined in your letter, and asked him to see you and explain my objections or doubts about three of the productions. As I wired you, I am enthusiastic about the plan as a whole—and this letter is only to tell you how grateful I am to the Play Policy Board of the Federal Theatre for approving such an extensive program of my work. It is particularly gratifying coming at this time when illness has, for the past six months, forced me to drop all work on my new series of plays, and I am now facing a long period of convalescence and rest in which any

---

1. Pearson (1909–1975), Yale English professor and friend of Eugene O'Neill, Jr., who included *Lazarus Laughed* in the *Oxford Anthology of American Literature* (New York: Oxford University Press, 1938), which he edited with William Rose Benét.
2. "Lazarus" by Russian playwright, novelist, and short-story writer Leonid Nikolayevich Andreyev (1871–1919).

1. Flanagan (1890–1969), director of the Federal Theatre Project of the Works Projects Administration, who negotiated a lump sum payment of royalties for fourteen of O'Neill's plays, which received forty-two productions throughout the United States by various Federal Theatre groups.

activity connected with plays is forbidden. It gives me a reassuring feeling that while I'm forced to be idle, at least my work will be working, and so I won't feel too much of a loafer!

Again, my grateful appreciation.   Yours very sincerely,   Eugene O'Neill

---

416 • TO EUGENE O'NEILL, JR.   TLS 2 pp. (2909 Avalon Avenue / Berkeley / California) [Yale]

May 10th 1937

Dear Eugene,   I was delighted to get your letter with all its news. To treat the big tidings first, ever since I saw in the papers that the divorce had gone thro', I had been expecting to hear from you about marriage.[1] Well, after reading your description of Janet, all I can say is that you are a damned lucky guy, and you have every reason to feel that this time the God of things as they ought to be is giving you all the breaks. For the rest, I need not tell you that you and Janet have my deepest wish and hope for lifelong happiness. May your marriage be as happy for both of you as Carlotta's and mine has been for us! I know you know I could not think of any better wish than that.

Regarding a wedding present, I am sure you will feel I have done about all I can afford, under present circumstances, in helping you to be free for this marriage. But what I want to add to that is the promise of a trip out here for you both to visit us as soon as we get our new home built. This means a year from this coming summer. We have already bought the land, a farm of a hundred and fifty acres in the hills overlooking the whole San Ramon Valley—a wonderful site with the most beautiful view imaginable—and we are now busy going over plans for the house with an architect. Unless there is some unforeseen delay work on the house should start sometime in July. We only have this place we are in now until the first of June—then we move out to another house in the country near Lafayette which we have rented for the six months in which our home will be building. This last is a nice place with twenty acres of ground, but the house itself is small—and, frankly, we are too unsettled to invite you out this summer! All our stuff is in storage and we will be more or less camping out until we are able to move into our own place.

I know you will understand our position. And there is another more important angle. My health is still not what it ought to be. I am very much in the convalescent stage and I have to go to doctors for treatment twice a week. Improving all the time, but it is a slow process and the Docs say I will not really feel myself again before the end of the year at earliest. At present I go along for a week or so of feeling better, then I have a couple of days when I sink back and feel punk again. This is the usual convalescent rhythm, of course, but it is very irritating and boring and depressing to the spirit, particularly as all work is forbidden and compulsory rest does not come easy. But I do see the absolute necessity of sticking it out this time and not making the mistake of the past few years. If I had had more sense about it then, I would never have gotten to the state of low vitality where my system was an easy mark for every sort of infection. It behooves me to behave this time—and no maybe about it, or I am liable to join the permanent invalid class.

To jump from my ills to yours, I am getting Californian enough to blame your colds on the New Haven climate—that is, I would if it were not for the fact that nearly everyone in Frisco and Oakland seemed to be down with the flu last winter. As for your tremor, the only thing that I ever found that did any good for mine was to cut out smoking. That helps quite a

---

1. After his divorce from Elizabeth Green, Eugene married Janet Hunter Longley, the daughter of a Yale mathematics professor.

bit—but whether it helps enough to be worth foregoing the pleasure of tobacco is something else again. The whole matter of tremors seems to be something doctors know little about, judging from my experience. I have had mine ever since I can remember, long before I had even smoked my first cornsilk cigarette, let alone dissipated any, and my mother had suffered from the same complaint, and told me her father had had it too. It seems to me the only thing is to regard it as a heritage of God knows how long a line of people with high-strung nerves, and bear the embarrassing discomfort of it as best one may.

It is grand news about your getting a raise, and that the University is showing such quick appreciation of your work in so many ways. Best of all is your enthusiasm for your labors there. I think now you would be a fool to consider leaving Yale for any Western university. You are all set there now for a brilliant career, and it would be tempting fate to move and start all over establishing yourself elsewhere, no matter how favorable the opening appeared.

Well, I guess this is about enough for one letter. Again, my congratulations—and my love to Janet and you—and all parental blessings and wishes for happiness!   As ever, Father

P.S. I send no message from Carlotta because she is writing you.

---

417 • TO BARRETT H. CLARK.   TLS 2 pp. (Stationery headed: Lafayette / Contra Costa County / California) [Yale]

September 14th 1937

Dear Clark,   By all means use my *Times* article on Baker. I am all for the idea of the pamphlet. As for the additional material Mrs. Baker has, if that means my letters to her after his death, then I am willing they should be used. It is entirely up to her. On the other hand, if it includes my letters of many years to him, I would like to have a look at copies of them first. You know how it is, I may have taken confidential insulting cracks at people or institutions that I would by no means agree with now, or want published to cause gratuitous bad feeling even if I did still agree.[1]

It's a long time since I've written you, so here goes with some personal news. My health has improved greatly during the summer. It's about time! My appendicitis operation last Christmas certainly started a continuous variety show of ailments. It was like chain smoking. As one died out, it started another. Two and a half months in hospital didn't stop the old relay. It went merrily on after I got out. I won't bore you with details. Suffice it that the low of them all was in hospital when an abscess in my inside burst and so poisoned me that they had to inject everything but T.N.T. to keep me from passing out for good. A tight spot. And the whole experience not a damned bit funny. By late spring I had begun to feel hopeless—thought I never would be well enough to work again. Of course, I brought it all on myself by disregarding many warnings during the past few years, but that was no consolation whatever.

But now, as I've said, I begin to feel something like myself. Have begun to flirt with my Cycle of plays again—with many fresh ideas and angles, including still another play which carries the beginning back to 1775, and will make nine plays in all. There will be nothing of *Ah, Wilderness!* or *Days Without End* in this Cycle. They were an interlude. The Cycle goes

---

1. *George Pierce Baker: A Memorial* included O'Neill's *New York Times* tribute, his January 8, 1935, telegram and January 20, 1935, letter to Mrs. Baker, and brief excerpts from a May 5, 1926, Baker to O'Neill letter and from a May 21, 1926, O'Neill to Baker letter.

With Carlotta in the courtyard of Tao House, Danville, California.

back to my old vein of ironic tragedy—with, I hope, added psychological depth and insight. The whole work will be a unique something, all right, believe me, if I can ever finish it. As you will appreciate, the technical problem alone is overpowering—of keeping each play a unit in itself while at the same time making it a vital part of the whole conception. I have to think in terms of nine plays, and a continuity of family lives over a space of 150 years, while I am writing each play. But given time and health I can do it. What I would like to do is not have any productions until the whole thing is finished. Outside of the financial aspect, productions are only nerve-racking interruptions to me—"show business"—and never have meant anything more. The play, as written, is the thing, and not the way actors garble it with their almost-always-alien personalities (even when the acting is fine work in itself). But whether circumstances will permit my abstention from production for such a long time remains to be seen. The present status of the Cycle is one play, (the third now) in good shape, needing only revising; another play,[2] (formerly the first, now the second) in a first draft as long as *Interlude,* needing complete rewriting. All the rest well thought out and scenarioed with much detail. And eight hundred million notes—more or less!

I am going easy on work yet, however, and warily, because I still must watch my step and not risk a slide backwards. But by the first of the year I hope to be ready to really drive ahead.

By that time we hope, barring strikes, to move into our new home, now building. We have a beautiful site in the hills of San Ramon Valley with one of the most beautiful views I've ever seen. This is final home and harbor for me. I love California. Moreover, the climate is one I know I can work and keep healthy in. Coastal Georgia was no place for me. Working through two long successive stifling summers down there did more than any other one thing to bring on my recent complete crack-up.

We hope you will get out this way sometime and visit us in our new home.

In closing, my deep gratitude for your tribute.[3] I hope I'll continue to deserve it.

All good wishes from us both to you and Mrs. Clark,   Very sincerely,   Eugene O'Neill

---

418 • TO KENNETH MACGOWAN.   ALS 3 pp. (Lafayette, / Contra Costa County, / California) [Yale]

Sept. 20th '37

Dear Kenneth: Well, I have honestly been meaning to write you for the past three months—ever since we settled out here. We rented this place—about the only one we could find for rent that was at all right—for six months, which will probably run into seven (the 1st of the year) before our new home, now building, is ready to move into. The house here is nothing to rave about but there are twenty-two acres of garden and orchards (maintained, thank God, by the owner and not us!) which are grand. Also, principal item to me, a pool. On the whole, not bad, though much too costly. We have spent an enjoyable summer, and my health, I am glad to report, is much improved. But until the first of the year, the Docs still warn me I must go easy—and this time, believe me, I am obeying orders.

However, pending the time when I can really buckle down, I have been doing some flirting with my Cycle and find myself full of fresh angles and ideas. One of these brilliant

---

2. "Greed of the Meek."

3. Possibly the updated edition of Clark's *Eugene O'Neill: The Man and His Plays* (New York: McBride, 1936).

inspirations, more's the pity, is for still another play, making nine in all, and taking the opening curtain back to 1775. It looks very good indeed in outline and I am afraid it simply can't be left out. So the job ahead becomes just that much more of a job. But, given health and time, I know I can do it—and if done as it ought to be this Cycle sure will be a final something! Then I shall retire and spend my declining days composing limericks.

Our new home is going to be a beauty. The property—158 acres—is in the hills of the San Ramon Valley, with one of the finest views I have ever seen. Construction is going ahead—so far without strikes to hold it up. Roof will be on in about four weeks. Carlotta is in a whirlwind of activity doing this and that and the other and generally bossing everything. She has a wonderful flair for home making—not to mention home running—and I think this is going to be her masterpiece. She says to tell you she is fixing up a guest room that will be sure to please you, and for you to remember there is always welcome for you inscribed on its threshold. So don't forget!

One of the best things about this new place is that it is absolute country and yet only three-quarters of an hour motor ride from Frisco—that is, after the new tunnel opens up through the Berkeley hills next month.

Meanwhile, if you get up to Frisco in the near future, we have no guest room here but will send the car in for you and take you back, if you can find time to visit. We are only a half hour from Frisco here.

Well, that's all my news, I guess—except that I've sent to London for a book for you—*Masks Of The World* by Joseph Gregor, director of the theatrical art section of the National Library in Vienna—translation from German. It has some fine colored plates. I just got my copy and I thought, after a look, that you'd like one in your library, too. But it won't reach you for a few weeks. I'm telling you about this beautiful present so prematurely because I don't want you to go buying it yourself before you heard from me.

Bobby[1] came out here with Felton Elkins three or four days ago and we had a fine visit. He looked fine and was the same old Bobby. It was grand to see him.

We have seen quite a bit of Felton and his wife. They drive over almost every week. He has been a big help to us in many ways—the same contractor who built his house is building ours—etc. I have always liked him, as you know, and, if I remember right, you did, too—and I like him even better now that he is older and has cut out booze. (There is no one detests liquor in others more than a reformed tank!)

Much affection from us both, Kenneth. I suppose you're working your head off but drop a line when you get the chance. And be sure and let us know whenever you are going to come to Frisco.   As ever,   Gene

---

419 • TO HARRY WEINBERGER.   TLS 2 pp. (Stationery headed: Lafayette / Contra Costa County / California) [Yale]

Sept. 24th 1937

Dear Harry,   Yours of Sept. 21st to hand. I enclose herewith check to that wench for $700.00—for Shane's school, plus $500.00 dole due Oct. 1st.

I have read with more than a little irritation the quote from her letter. With its drivel about "background of culture," "social background," "right attitude toward life"—all this from a tramp of a Boulton!—it would be particularly ludicrous if it were not so exasperating. Where Shane ought to go is, like Eugene did, to a public school where he wouldn't be

1. Robert Edmond Jones.

coddled like a mental case—or to a good strict college prep school of the more democratic sort where they expect you to study seriously and fire you if you don't.

But it's her racket and I refuse to concern myself. I'll pay for him till he's 21, as long as our agreement states I must. After that, I am through—and when I say through, I mean through!

During all the time I was in hospital, I never rec'd one word from him or from Oona. Birthday and Christmas presents I have never failed to send Shane. He practically never even acknowledges them. (Oona does—sometimes.) So I am stopping all presents henceforth. Until, if ever, he realizes that he will get from me exactly the treatment he gives, I am not going to ask him to visit us or communicate with him in any way.

Much more than I object to these brats' attitude toward me of grabbing all they can get without troubling themselves to be grateful, I object to their attitude toward Carlotta. She has gone out of her way to be kind, always remembering their birthdays and Christmas—and sends them presents in between, too, which is more than I do. Shane never writes to thank her, Oona does sometimes but often not.

In short, I feel my dear little ones are nothing to be proud of, or take pleasure in—unlike Eugene—and unless they change drastically, I am off them for life. There is too much greedy parasitic Boulton in their blood—I am afraid—not to add Boulton stupidity in their brains! All best from us, Gene

P.S. Doesn't Georgia's failure to send word by Sept. 15th mean that the earliest year of their claim is now ruled out by time limit?

---

420 • TO HARRY WEINBERGER. TLS 1 p. (Stationery headed: Lafayette / Contra Costa County / California) [Yale]

Sept. 27th 1937

Dear Harry, The enclosed calls for investigation. Have you the deed for this plot among my things you have? Julian Moran[1] never sent it to me that I can remember. Know I haven't got it now. I do remember he made a lump payment, on my authorization, for perpetual care. By whom, I don't know. Nor do I remember who else is buried in this plot, if any. My Mother's Mother, I think. I've always had an aversion to visiting graves.

Another thing, I don't know what sort of stones are over my Father, Mother, and Brother. Julian Moran once wrote me about erecting an immense monument—sent me a design costing over five thousand. I thought this was nonsense and said so. Couldn't afford it, anyway. Told him simple stones were more dignified, in any case. Don't remember now whether it was a question of my brother's grave that he brought up the family tomb matter or not. Don't know what he did about it finally. In fact, I know practically nothing about this plot.

What I suggest is a day's trip to New London to investigate. If you can't go, can't you send your nephew[2] or someone to call at St. Mary's Cemetery Office and get dope—also ride out to Catholic Cemetery, locate plot and note down all details of what kind of stones over whom, condition of plot, etc. etc. You remember what a lazy, do-it-to-morrow slob Moran was. He never made any reports to me on this matter except that one time about the monument and paying for perpetual care. And there is no one I know in New London now that I could get to do it. All best, Gene

1. New London lawyer who handled O'Neill's parents' and brother's estates after their deaths.
2. Harold Wayne, Weinberger's law associate.

[early October? 1937]

Dear Shane: Your letter arrived a few days ago. Yes, I received the letter you sent to Sea Island last spring. I did not answer it because I was sore at you. And I still am sore—and with good reason. You may not remember it but for nearly three months last winter I was in a hospital seriously ill and during all that time I did not receive one damned line from either you or Oona. You can't have the excuse that you did not know. The news of my illness was sent out by the Associated Press, United Press, etc. to papers all over the country. So, later on, was the fact that the Nobel Prize medal had to be presented to me in the hospital at Oakland. I received letters and wires of sympathy from all over, even from strangers. From my own children—except Eugene—nothing. And yet you knew, even if you didn't get the Oakland address from the papers, that you could always reach me care of Harry Weinberger.

Now if you think that is any way to act, or that I am going to stand for your acting like that and still feel any affection for you, you are badly mistaken. Oona has some excuse. She is still only a kid. But you are old enough to be responsible for your actions—or lack of them— and I hold you responsible. I expect the same sort of respect and consideration from you that I received from Eugene when he was your age. If you give it, there is no reason why the relationship between you and me should not develop into as fine a one as that between Eugene and me has been for years and still is. Quite outside of our being father and son, Eugene and I are friends, as man to man, which is a thing few fathers and sons manage to achieve. And that's what I want to be to you—a friend. But if you show no friendship toward me, if you prove by your actions you are indifferent whether I live or die, except when you want something from me, then you must admit I would be a poor sap and sucker to waste my friendship on you, simply because you happen to be my son.

I am giving you this straight from the shoulder because it is time you and I came to a frank understanding. It is time you realized that in this life you are going to get from others exactly the same treatment you give to others. If you take me for granted, and think you can treat me as no friend of mine would dare to treat me without losing my friendship forever, why then I warn you you must be prepared to lose my friendship forever, too.

So think it over. It is up to you. If you want to be my son in more than name, you will have to learn to act with a little more decent consideration and gratitude—not to add, respect. It isn't difficult, you know. Eugene has done it without it breaking his back. All you have to do is get it in your head that you can't expect something for nothing, even from fathers.

Well, that's that. If you are the boy I still hope you are, despite evidence to the contrary, then this letter should make you think, and so much good will come of it for us both. If you are not—well, then it's just too bad.

Carlotta is glad you liked the Japanese robe. And we are both happy that you are so pleased with the new school.[1] It sounds grand. And it's your good luck to be away from that damned hookworm Florida joint. That country, with its rotten debilitating climate did more than anything else to wreck my health and lead to the long stretch of hospital and illness I went through last winter and spring. I am feeling fine again now and will be able to start hard work again, I hope, by the first of next year—or when we move into the new home we are building in the San Ramon Valley (near Oakland) which will be finished sometime in

1. After two years at Florida Military Academy, Shane was sent for his senior year to the Ralston Creek School in Golden, Colorado.

January. At present, we are living in a small rented house. I like California immensely. Carlotta joins in love to you.

---

422 • TO RICHARD MADDEN. WIRE 1 p. ([Lafayette, Contra Costa County, California]) [Yale]

OCTOBER 18, 1937

UNDER NO CIRCUMSTANCES WILL I PERMIT PRODUCTION NEGRO ADAPTION OF HAIRY APE STOP IT IS STUPID AND RIDICULOUS STOP PLEASE PUT IT EMPHATICALLY TO FLANAGAN I WILL NOT TOLERATE ANY ADAPTIONS STOP PLAYS MUST BE DONE AS WRITTEN AND ONLY JONES AND ALL GODS CHILLUN CAN BE GIVEN BY NEGROES IN FUTURE STOP I AM NOT INTERESTED IN FREAK THEATRE WHERE WHITE PLAYS ARE FAKED INTO BLACK PLAYS STOP IF NEGROES CANNOT ACT WHITE PARTS AS WHITES HAVE PLAYED NEGROES THEY SHOULD NOT BE IN THEATRE STOP PLEASE MAKE THIS STRONG SAY UNLESS THEY AGREE NOT CHANGE ONE WORD IN ANY PLAY YOU ARE AUTHORIZED GIVE THEM LEGAL NOTICE OF TERMINATION OF CONTRACT STOP THEIR SCHEDULE OF PRODUCTION IS FAR FROM THEIR CYCLE OF LAST SPRING AND I AM ENTIRELY FED UP WITH THEM = GENE

---

423 • TO ROBERT SISK. TLS 2 pp. (Stationery headed: Lafayette / Contra Costa County / California) [Yale]

October 18th 1937

Dear Bob, We are happy to learn from your letter of the fine break on the woman's prison picture.[1] Here's hoping you can ooze out that director—without spraining your punting foot!

I'm tickled with your tidings about Irving Berlin's willingness to do honor to Rosie.[2] If she doesn't hand him a laugh, I miss my guess. And you've never seen her either, have you? Boy, you have missed something! It was a great moment in my life when she first burst on my sight in Wurlitzer's remotest storeroom in all her gangrenous-green, festooned-with-rosebuds beauty. There sure must have been an artist soul lost to the world in the New Orleans honkey-tonk—or bordello—she came from.

It will be grand to meet Berlin. I've always wanted to. Have always heard he was one of the finest guys extant. I hope Crouse will be about to join the fiesta—and to prompt, for he seems to know all the words of all the old songs.

If we get to Frisco we'll act on your recommendation of *Stage Door*.[3] But we're so busy these days with the house, etc. I don't know about Frisco. When it is shown in Oakland will be easier.

Carlotta is reading *The Raven*. I haven't got to it yet. Our best to you, Cepha, and Miss Sisk. Gene

---

1. *Condemned Women*, produced by Sisk, which opened in April 1938.
2. A player piano, a gift to O'Neill from Carlotta.
3. Play (1936) by George S. Kaufman and Edna Ferber (1887–1968), the film version of which opened in October 1937.

424 • TO SHANE O'NEILL. AL (draft) 2 pp. ([Lafayette, Contra Costa County, Calif.]) [Yale]

[c. October 16, 1937]

Dear Shane: The carved walrus tusk arrived yesterday. It is a beauty and I don't know of anything I would rather have had as a present. I've never seen one just like it before. It will look fine on my desk and be very useful as a paper weight. So much gratitude to you! I certainly appreciate your having remembered my birthday with such an unusual gift—and also with your letter which arrived two days ago.

The folder about the ranch came yesterday, too. Judging from it and the description in your letters, it must be a very interesting place and, under a tutoring system, you ought to settle down and do some real studying. You will have to, won't you, if you expect to enter college soon. But are you going to college? You have not told me. If you are, what university have you chosen? Let me know about this when you write again.

I hope you can come and visit us when our new home—in the San Ramon Valley about an hour's ride from San Francisco—is finished. We can't invite you for Christmas because it won't be finished before the middle of January—and this rented house we're in now is so small we can't have any visitors. Anyway, Christmas is the rainy season here and you wouldn't like it. But how about next Spring vacation?

Carlotta joins in love to you—and again my thanks for your birthday letter and the grand present.

---

425 • TO HARRY WEINBERGER. TLS 2 pp. (Stationery headed: Lafayette / Contra Costa County / California) [Yale]

November 12th 1937

Dear Harry,   Re the copy of the letter about Shane and college, I have some very emphatic remarks to make:

When Shane says I do not want him to go to college, he is lying. I have always wanted him to do exactly as he wished in this respect. Why, in my last letter I asked him if he were going, and to tell me what university he had chosen!

As for Duke, however, or any other Southern College, I am absolutely opposed. I haven't lived in the South for five years without learning a lot about the effect of the atmosphere in the Tin-Pan-Alley, Fair Dixie—nor without hearing and seeing a great deal of Southern college students and grads. Sea Island in summer was infested with them. Their colleges have the very lowest cultural and ethical standards of any in this country. And, unless I am badly misinformed, Duke does not rank high even in the South! They tell me they give football players a Ph.D.—in addition to their weekly salary, of course!—if they know their A.B.C.s.

I think it would be encouraging every lazy weakness Shane has to send him there. Unless a miracle happened, he would come out after four years of wasted time a drunken hookworm. Please make it as strong as you can that I am absolutely thumbs down on this. In fact I feel so strongly about it that I refuse all responsibility for him at any future time if she sends him there.

My suggestion is that he stay where he is an extra year, work hard, and enter a university of high standing in the Northeast,—Harvard, Yale, or any other of the first rank—preferably Yale where Eugene could and would be of help to him—not Princeton, where my record would be the reverse of helpful, psychologically. At such a college, he would get his chance. Whether he got anything valuable out of it, would be up to him. But at Duke, unless he possesses an iron will and latent talents so brilliant as to succeed in spite of every environmental handicap—which I doubt—he would be getting no chance.

After all, a year more of prep school would not disgrace him. He would be entering college just before he is twenty—(two years from this fall)—and there are plenty of students at the best colleges who don't get in before that age.

Southern Colleges, it must be remembered in justice to them, are run for Southerners to prepare them for Southern life. If, for example, Shane's ambition is to run a gasoline—and corn whiskey—filling station in the Carolina sticks, then Duke is surely the spot to instill the proper culture for it—or if he wants to raise tobacco or cotton. Duke should be the Alma Mater for all tobacco growers!   All best to you,   Gene

---

426 • TO EUGENE O'NEILL, JR.   TLS 1 p. (Stationery headed: Lafayette / Contra Costa County / California) [Yale]

December 10th 1937

Dear Eugene,   The enclosed copy of a letter from the head of Shane's present school—a tutoring place—to his mother (relayed to me by Harry Weinberger) explains itself. You are mentioned because I had said that you had told me if Shane got into Yale, you might help him with a bit of advice now and then if he displayed any inclination to do some work.

The lady was willing for him to take the lazy way and go to Duke. I put my foot down, said a Southern University would be a waste of time and probably turn him out at the end of four years a hookworm, unfit for anything in the way of work.

So you see what the shooting is about. It will be a great favor if you will read the enclosed letter from his principal carefully and let me know at your earliest what you would advise for him. Shane is a nice kid, as you know, and I want him to have the best chance he is capable of taking. If you think it would be too difficult for him to make Yale entrance requirements by 1939 under the circumstances, where would you advise him to go in the East or Midwest?

I'm taking this opportunity to enclose a Christmas check. It's for you both—to get something you want for your home.

I'm feeling pretty fit and starting to work hard again on the monstrous Cycle. We will move into our new home around January first. It's only about eight miles from here. Will be moving in before it's really finished, but we want to save a month's rent and they can complete the job after we're in. It's a grand spot. You will love it, both of you, I know.   Merry Christmas and love to you both from us.   Father

P.S. A wee check from me too—with love—for you and Janet.   Carlotta

---

427 • TO THERESA HELBURN.   TLS 3 pp. (Stationery headed: Tao House / Danville / Contra Costa County / California) [Yale]

February the 13th 1938

Dear Terry,   No, absolutely no hope for any play next season. I don't want even to think of production until I have four or five of the nine finished, and (if I can do it without winding up in the Poorhouse or the Home for the Aged and Infirm) I'd like to wait until all nine are completed. This last is the ideal, of course. Then we really could engage a repertoire company for the whole Cycle—show the actors and actresses we want parts that would make it worth their while, out of pure self-interest, to tie up for several seasons under our conditions. No stars, of course, but show the young and ambitious their chance to become stars through this Cycle. No featured names, unless we ran into some with the right spirit of cooperation. Do this Cycle very much as if we were starting a new Guild or Provincetown Players, that's my idea. Keep it as far away from the amusement-racket theatre and all Broadway connotations as we possibly can. Treat it as it should be treated from its very nature, as a special unique thing. That's the only way to do it. It's not only the one right way to produce it, artistically speaking, but it's sound, practical showmanship. I'm very obdurate on this point. In fact, to be blunt, I won't allow it to be done any other way.

But when will I be ready with even the minimum of four or five plays—let alone the full nine? I don't know and I can't predict. So much depends on my health, for one thing. I did manage to finish the first draft of another play—the new No. One of the nine—last Summer and Fall and early Winter. This makes three I now have in first draft. But two of these are still far from what I want them to be and have to be rewritten. The other—No. Three—is in pretty good shape for a first draft and won't need much work.

Here's how health comes into it: For the past two months neuritis—a new ill in my repertoire—has been giving me hell. The Docs think it's due to teeth. I had a wisdom tooth yanked out three days ago, badly abscessed. I'm to have four more out in a short time. Oh, I know this dental racket begins to sound like a gag on my part. It seems every time I've been in New York for ages I've spent most of the time at the dentist's. But it's the painful truth. Thank God, after the present purge, I won't have many of my own left for the boys to work on, and can look forward to comparative peace, dentally speaking. And financially speaking. The amounts I've contributed to dentists in the past ten years would astound you.

The point is that between neuritis and the upheaval of moving into a new house which wasn't finished on schedule, (and still isn't entirely finished) I've had to drop work for the past month and a half. These are the things that make predictions hopeless, that you can't foresee.

Another thing, writing one of the units in this Cycle is a much more complicated business than doing a single play, or half of *Strange Interlude* or one of the *Electra* trilogy. Often I start a work-day writing dialogue for the play I'm on, and wind up writing suggested notes on a scene in the eighth or ninth play! Of course, this will all be very valuable in the later stages but it does eat up time and energy and slow up progress on the immediate job.

The Walter Huston-Rosalind Russell stuff is nonsense. I don't even know who Rosalind Russell is. A film harness, I presume. Only basis for the rumor, as far as I can make out, is that when Walter *and his wife* paid us a visit last summer, I did speak of the Cycle *in a very general way,* and they said they'd like to be associated with its repertoire company, and I said fine, if it turned out there were the right parts for them, etc. It was all very vague—and I had hoped I made it clear I would give no thought to any definite casting until the plays were finished. Not that Walter might not be a good bet. He's a fine actor in the right parts, a fine guy, and he has the right spirit. But I can't know about it yet. As for la Russell, she was never mentioned. Walter may have spoken to her, advising her it might be a future opportunity, if she could make it. And then she told her press agent and he did the rest. At least, that's how I figure it.

I hope that this letter makes the situation regarding the Cycle clear to you. Until you see the completed plays—four or five or the whole nine—just forget it. I've never been able to think about theatre production until my job of the written play was done, and I can't now.

I don't know what you mean by the Guild's "second acting company that will alternate with Lunt productions." Is this a new Guild plan? You must remember in writing me that I'm quite out of touch with the current New York theatre, except where I hear haphazard by letter from this friend or that, and that the Frisco and Oakland papers we see give much space to films and radio and practically none to legit.

By all means come and visit us—and bring Oliver this time. We ought to be comfortably settled here by mid-May even with further delays. But you'd hate it right now. It's been raining, believe it or not, every day for the past eighteen days, breaking every weather bureau record and driving the Chambers of Commerce into violent hysterical weeping— and also holding up all the finishing touches on our home.

Our love to you and Oliver—and again much gratitude for the grand bedspread! As ever, Gene

---

428 • TO HARRY WEINBERGER.   TLS 2 pp. (Stationery headed: Tao House / Danville / Contra Costa County / California) [Yale]

March 8th 1938

Dear Harry,   Enclosed, herewith, one-half your fee, as per usual.

The tax returns you sent had one error—an unpardonable insult from a Northern California point of view. You addressed my Federal returns to Los Angeles instead of to San Francisco. You can bet I erased that in a hurry! They would have fined me ten million dollars!

The new home has run way over estimated costs and, what with the general financial outlook so dreary, Carlotta and I are feeling very low. Also the weather has broken all California records in lousiness. Also, neuritis continues to plague me. Had one tooth out two weeks ago and am to have four more out next week. This bad health stuff is a rotten bore. It busts up my working entirely. I only have to tear up the stuff I force myself to do when I'm under the weather. It just won't come right unless I feel reasonably fit. Rotten nerves I don't count. I've always had those. But piling other ills on top of the rotten nerves gets me groggy. I haven't yet learned to take that extra punishment and go on regardless.

Re that design you sent me from McNeel for the cemetery plot. Altho' $650.00 seems high, I guess you better tell them to go ahead with it and we will do without the separate grave markers. But certain changes must be made. For one thing, O'NEILL is spelled with one L on their design. For another, I want O'NEILL on TOP with list of the five dead *underneath*. I DON'T want any space left for those to come, because no one else will ever be buried there. I am the last of this pure Irish branch of the O'NEILLS—my children are a weird mixture, racially speaking,—and I certainly would rather be thrown down the sewer than be planted in New London. I want to be buried wherever my home happens to be when I die.

Here's the design on the monument as I want it———

O'NEILL

James O'Neill, actor, Born 1846 Died 1920
Ella Quinlan O'Neill, his wife, Born 1857 Died 1922
James O'Neill, 2nd, their son Born 1878 Died 1923
Edmund O'Neill, their son, Born 1883 Died 1885
Bridget Quinlan, mother of Ella O'Neill, Born 1829 Died 1887[1]

---

1. Birth and death dates for Edmund O'Neill and Bridget Quinlan are supplied in ink to the text of this typewritten letter, presumably by Weinberger or someone in his office.

This is simple and clear with no chance for mixing up who's who. It simply follows pattern of cast of characters in a play, which is absolutely appropriate for an actor's family.

How can we check on these McNeel people to see they do this job as specified? Are they absolutely reliable? Years of birth and death for my mother's mother, and my brother, who died before I was born, they can get from the head stones now on plot—then destroy those headstones. Or maybe you have that data in your files from that letter the priest wrote to you that you sent me and I sent back to you.   All best from us,   Gene

---

429 • TO SHANE O'NEILL.   TLS 1 p. (Stationery headed: Tao House / Danville / Contra Costa County / California) [Virginia]

March 25th 1938

Dear Shane,   I am enclosing check to cover your trip here. You better come by what they call an intermediate fare instead of plain day coach. It is no fun sitting up in a day coach all night and missing sleep. On an intermediate ticket you can get a berth by paying extra.

The information I get from the Oakland railroad station is that a round trip ticket, intermediate, from *Golden* to *Oakland* is $49.95 and $5.50 extra for berth. I'm adding five to the total—for meals—sixty in all.

Be sure to send us a wire a couple of days in advance letting us know *exact day and hour* you will arrive at *Oakland, Sixteenth Street Station.* Remember it's the *Sixteenth Street Station,* and we will meet you.

Carlotta joins me in love to you. It will be grand to see you again.   Father

If anything goes haywire our telephone is *DANVILLE 107.*

Thanks for your letters!   Carlotta

---

430 • TO KENNETH MACGOWAN.   AL (draft)[1] 2 pp. ([Tao House, Danville, Contra Costa County, California]) [Yale]

[April 1938]

Dear Kenneth: I am going to be absolutely frank, as I know you would want me to be. A visit *with Edie*[2] simply would not work. Carlotta feels too bitter and enduring a resentment. She will never forgive those among my supposed friends who took the attitude, when we went off together, that I was being hooked by an unscrupulous floosie, and believed as Gospel every rotten thing they could of her. For that matter, I don't feel very forgiving myself. And we had too many reliable reports of what Edie said, and of her great sympathy with Agnes, to have any doubt where she stood. And when you add to this the antagonism which she and Carlotta just naturally feel toward each other, anyway— No, it wouldn't be a pleasant visit. At best, there might be a joking veneer on the surface but the atmosphere would be poisoned.

And so. It's one of those things. I'm damned sorry it is—but it is. And I know you will understand and agree with me that it's much wiser to be realistic about it. You also know, I

1. This letter survives in draft only and may never have been sent.
2. Edna, Macgowan's wife.

hope, that Carlotta has a very genuine and deep affection for you—and you know my feeling. There is no one in the world we would rather have with us than you.

The above, of course, is strictly confidential between us. And, believe me, it wasn't easy to write.

Thanks for the mask snaps, which I enclose back to you herewith. They are damned interesting. I have no snaps of my few—and my prize drum!—but I hope you will come and see them.

It's fine news about Peter[3] and Harvard. Shane has just been here on a visit and Eugene is coming this summer. Shane, with three years of a hookworm Southern prep. school against him, won't make a University for another year. Then, I think, he'll go to Colorado—the best in the territory between East & Coast, so Eugene assures me. He is at a combination of ranch and tutoring school at Golden, Colorado now and has gone heavily horsey, cowboy boots and all—has learned to break horses and is a fine rider. He's getting a job on a ranch this summer as a wrangler. What he will eventually choose to do, God knows, but for once in his life he's genuinely self-confident and enthusiastic—about horses and stock-raising, not scholastic pursuits, I might add.

Yes, I am hard at the Cycle again—have been ever since the neuritis that gave me hell all winter let up a month or so ago. Almost gone now. Five teeth out eventually stopped it. Thank God, I have few left now to cause trouble! Have you ever had neuritis? Well don't, if you haven't. It's the most demoralizing, nerve-wracking pain I know of.

Carlotta joins me love to you.   As ever,

---

431 • TO HANS OLAV.[1]   TLS 1 p. (Stationery headed: Tao House / Danville / Contra Costa County / California) [Private]

May 13th 1938

Dear Mr. Olav,   Your letter, forwarded, has just arrived. I hope the following, written in haste so as to reach you in time, will serve your purpose. I need not add that I regard it as an honor to pay tribute to Ibsen's memory.

(I cannot remember, as Mr. Shaw does, the impact of the first appearance of Ibsen's plays in English. I was too preoccupied with being born just then. But I do remember well the impact upon me when I saw an Ibsen play for the first time, a production of *Hedda Gabler*[2] at the old Bijou Theatre in New York—and then went again and again for ten successive nights. That experience discovered an entire new world of the drama for me. It gave me my first conception of a modern theatre where truth might live.

Not long ago I read all of Ibsen's plays again. The same living truth is still there. Only to fools with a superficial eye cocked to detect the incidental can they have anything dated or outworn about them. As dramas revealing the souls of men and women they are as great to-day as they will be a hundred years from now.)   Very sincerely,   Eugene O'Neill

---

3. Macgowan's son.

1. Editor of the Norwegian-American newspaper *Nordisk Tidende*, which published a special Ibsen tribute in honor of the 110th anniversary of his birth on June 2, 1938. The article included a photocopy of O'Neill's letter as well as one from George Bernard Shaw.

2. This production starred Alla Nazimova, who later created the role of Christine Mannon in *Mourning Becomes Electra*.

432 • TO EUGENE O'NEILL, JR.　　TLS 1 p. (Stationery headed: Tao House / Danville / Contra Costa County / California) [Yale]

April 22nd 1938

Dear Eugene,　　Just a line to tell you that it's all right about transportation. You know I said that would be on me a year ago when I invited you. Find out what the cost will be and let me know. They have raised the rates, damn 'em, but if you can arrange for a round-trip ticket which would give you the privilege of stopover time for your Reno and your Montana stays, it might save a lot—and money is a consideration these days.

My neuritis has about left me, thank God. It gave me a hell of a Winter. Now I'm hard at work again trying to make up the lost time.

Here's hoping your marital misadventure[1] will untangle as easily as you expect and you won't be nailed for alimony at the last moment. And here's looking forward to your visit with us.　　Carlotta joins me in love,　　Father

---

433 • TO SHANE O'NEILL.　　TLS 1 p. (Stationery headed: Tao House / Danville / Contra Costa County / California) [Virginia]

May 30th 1938

Dear Shane,　　I meant to answer your letter before this but have been working so hard I've postponed it from day to day.

Thanks for the snap shots. Your late horse looks so gentle and friendly. It's a shame he had to cut up with such suicidal results. In the other snap, you sure look like the old rodeo cowboy! You must have learned a lot of riding since you came West.

Regarding a new horse, I'll wait for your further reports. It's up to you. But I think, if you're going East, it would be foolish to buy one until you returned. You don't know what might happen when you weren't there to watch. And aren't you likely to find a better bargain at the end of the Dude Ranch season than now when it's just about to start?

I'm sorry you can't take that job this summer. It would be fine stuff for you. But, under the circumstances, I agree that the wisest thing is to get in Colorado as soon as you can. I'm glad you went to look over the University and liked it. First impressions of a place have a habit of enduring and proving themselves right.

Yes, the swimming pool is officially opened and I was going in every day until we struck a chilly spell of weather three days ago.

Blemie has been very sick with an intestinal disease. A few nights back we were afraid he might be on his last legs. But a good Vet. has pulled him around and he appears pretty well again.

Carlotta joins me in love to you, and all cheers for your making Colorado U. in the Fall.

Let me know when you're going East and when you will return. I enclose a bit of help on your allowance.　　Father

---

1. Eugene was in the process of divorcing his second wife.

434 • TO EUGENE O'NEILL, JR.   TLS 1 p. (Stationery headed: Tao House / Danville / Contra Costa County / California) [Yale]

July 10th 1938

Dear Eugene,   Just a line to say I've just finished looking through your two volumes,[1] which Saxe sent me. It's a splendid thing you and Oates have done—one of those jobs you rarely meet, of which you can honestly say to yourself that it would be a great loss if it had not been done. A bit of an Irish bull, that last, but let it go, you see what I mean. Anyway, I hope you are as proud of yourself for doing it as I am of you.

Random House has done well by you, don't you think? I certainly do. They are fine books for any library.

Carlotta joins in love—and here's looking forward to seeing you.

Let me know about the transportation—or [are] you going to wait and collect from me here?   As ever,   Father

---

435 • TO LAWRENCE LANGNER.   TLS 3 pp. (Stationery headed: Tao House / Danville / Contra Costa County / California) [Yale]

August 2nd 1938

Dear Lawrence,   This is a hell of a time to be answering your letter! My apology. I've meant to "tomorrow" every day but I've been working hard, and it's been hot, and by the time late P.M. came around I'd feel too damned languid.

And all the delay is not my fault. Your letter took a long time reaching us. For Pete's sake, tell the Guild stenographers that we left Seattle a year and a half ago. Both a letter of Terry's and yours have been addressed there and it's a wonder I ever got them. This ought to be corrected because you might sometime want a quick answer to something important, and blame me when you didn't get one.

A recent letter of Madden's informs me some paper carried a report I was leasing the Broadhurst Theatre to put on the Cycle myself. Did you see it? Of all the bloody nonsense I ever heard that is the worst—as I know the Guild knew. I simply can't explain how all this stuff about a break between the Guild and me ever started. And who the mysterious house-guest of the original rumor was. We've only had two—for the day only—since we moved in—Cerf and Crouse. In discussing the Guild with both I probably said I thought your movie-casting policy was all wrong, and unworthy of the Guild, and that I wouldn't have any stars in the Cycle if it were never produced. But I've said the same to you. I may have said I was glad not to be produced until the Guild got a new start on a new angle. But hell again, I'd tell any of you that, too. And anyway, such remarks are immaterial because I haven't enough ready yet to be even thinking of production.

Now I know Crouse would never repeat a word of what I said, and Cerf, even if he let drop a word casually, before he thought, would never distort it. My only answer is that some of the newspaper boys unfriendly to the Guild got hold of a casual remark and then made a dinosaur out of a bacillus. I had hoped my wire to Joe Heidt[1] would squelch this stuff for

---

1. *The Complete Greek Drama* (New York: Random House, 1938), edited by Eugene O'Neill, Jr., and Whitney J. Oates, a classics professor at Princeton University.

1. Press agent for the Theatre Guild.

good. But evidently someone, for some reason, is determined to pound it regardless of denials or any verification whatever.

Can you picture me leasing the Broadhurst to embark on a producing career? Two preliminary steps would be necessary before that could happen. No. 1, I would have to be adjudged insane and committed to an asylum. No. 2, I would have to escape.

All I can suggest is that you tell Joe Heidt he has my full authority every time such a report appears immediately to quote a new wire from me in denial. You realize, I hope, that I never see any of these press tales. No clipping service except International, (to keep tab on foreign productions), and no Eastern papers. *San Francisco Chronicle,* that's all, and you know how little Eastern theatre gossip it carries. So don't think I am aware of what goes on because I'm not. Unless someone writes me.

(Continued in our next—the above was written a week ago) I am very much interested in your plans for an Acting Company. That's the stuff! If the Guild had to scrap everything and start all over again at the Garrick as a fresh adventure, I would be a lot more whole-heartedly with you than I ever have in your late opportunist movie-casting days. For in my opinion, Lawrence—and you know I speak as a friend—the Guild has richly earned a kick in the pants. The relentless picking on everything you've done lately by the critics may have been arbitrarily unjust—even vindictive—but the resentful feeling that prompted their injustice was justified. Ever since several Guild directors got bored with 52nd Street and went Hollywood, you have been steadily getting farther away from the spirit of all the old Guild represented, all that made it a distinctive and distinguished leader in the American Theatre—all that made it a commercial success, for that matter! You became in spirit and intent—to all appearances, anyway—just another manager star-casting with an eye on the box office and playing the racket according to the stale old rules that the mere existence of the Guild in the old days had proved shoddy and stupid. I think the feeling behind all the adverse criticism was one of being betrayed—that you'd sold out on them—and of resentful disillusion.

Well, to hell with it! God knows I don't join the anvil chorus with any relish. You know that. But it seems to me you rationalize too much away—by "you" I mean every Guilder I've talked to or heard from in several years—and evade the main underlying truth. You won't know real regeneration until you do face it, I think. You should have stuck to your old ideal, win, lose or draw, bondholders or no bondholders. You wouldn't have lost. Even if you had, you wouldn't have lost inside yourselves—or "face" with your supporters. After all, an ideal is something. Or we ought to lie to ourselves that it is, anyway, for life's sake, because if it isn't, what the hell is anything?

I may be doin' you-alls wrong, Kid, but the above is my honest feeling, and I'd suggest as a symbolic, regenerative rebirth ceremony that the six original members of the Committee hold a secret commemorative meeting in which you all sit around and meditate in silence for an hour, and then rise as one and give each other a good boot in the tail—the ladies being accorded full equal rights in this!

Re *Lazarus Laughed,* no, I never made a version without choruses—only said that for production I'd cut out the chorus leaders with the double-sized masks. Yes, I think that play has something to say today that might find ears. But it ought to be done on the scale it calls for to get the effect I imagined. But why don't you try an experimental reading with a chorus of ten good voices,—more, if you can manage—five men and five women, off stage, or experiment with loud speakers off stage? You have my permit to trim down the chorus stuff. There's too much of it.

I had a hell of a Winter with neuritis. Boy, you can't work with that pain in you! Or I can't. In my writing arm, too. But all gone now for some time. I've been working hard since the first part of April. On Fourth play.[2] Expect to finish it—first draft—in another month or so. The status of the Cycle then will be three plays in first draft, one, two and four—(Nos. 1 and 2 needing a lot of rewriting)—and No. 3 in fairly finished shape except for one scene.

We are hoping to see you and Armina here at your earliest opportunity. It's really a beautiful spot. And the house—well, you know Carlotta's genius for that.

Meanwhile, all affectionate best from us to you both—and cheers to the Guild—and here's hoping Miner[3] is the right man (I've heard fine things about his work)—and pardon my more-in-sorrow-than-in-anger lambasting of Guild errors. I never make any, of course, or I wouldn't speak. Well, well, well! It must be the climate.   As ever,   Gene

---

436 • TO SHANE O'NEILL.   AL (draft) 3 pp. ([Tao House, Danville, Contra Costa County, California]) [Yale]

[early October? 1938]

Dear Shane: This is a hell of a time to be asking my advice, when you are already at Lawrenceville! Why didn't you write me this summer? Until I received your two letters this week, I naturally thought you were coming back to the ranch school early to try and make University of Colorado this fall—or, at latest, a year from now—as you had written me you intended. What is the truth about you and the ranch school, anyway? It is nonsense for you to expect me to believe you suddenly decided it was no good. When you were here, you said it was a fine school. So what is the truth? Were you fired or what?

Your big mistake was in not having the guts to stay in Colorado and take that ranch job you said you could get, and stand on your own feet. It would have done wonders for you in giving you self-respect and independence.

However, to the devil with post mortems! You want to know what I think of the Lawrenceville idea. I think Lawrenceville is all wrong for you now. You have gotten too far behind. Anyway, Lawrenceville is only valuable if you are prepping for a Class A Eastern university—which it would be foolish for you to attempt at this late stage of the game, with their difficult entrance requirements.

And I don't think it would do you any good to change to another private school. What for? They are all more or less the same, and you have been to too many private schools already. What might do you good is a real change of atmosphere to a public school—get a high school diploma, as you suggest. Once you have that, you could decide whether you really want to go to some college that accepts high school diplomas for entrance, or whether you want to go to work (*and* can get a job!).

It's all very well to tell me you would like to get out and be on your own, but those are vague words. Get out where? Be on your own how? I'll take your ambition seriously only when you tell me just what line of work you want to do and show me you can get a job at it— and *do* get a job at it! After all, no one has stopped you from getting a job during the summer, I imagine. If you are as eager to be on your own as you say, you would have done so.

So my advice, considering the circumstances as you report them—and your letters are the only reports on you I ever receive—is for you to get a high school diploma, and then decide what you want to do—and can do. Public schools are just as good as private—a damned sight better, in many respects. You know, don't you, that Eugene did nearly all of his schooling at public schools?   Carlotta joins in love to you.

2. *More Stately Mansions*, never given a final revision and not produced until 1962.
3. Worthington Miner (1900–1982), director, playwright, and producer, who had recently joined the executive board of the Theatre Guild.

437 • TO HARRY WEINBERGER. TLS 1 p. (Stationery headed: Tao House / Danville / Contra Costa County / California) [Yale]

October the 11th 1938

Dear Harry, Your letter at hand with the enclosures from That Woman and from Law-renceville. Despite my antagonism for her and all she stands for, I agree with her on this. You can write her that I appreciate it is bad stuff for Shane to have me advising him in opposition to her plans. It enables him to find a good excuse for doing nothing and evading all responsibility, and he is foxy enough to see this. *But* remind the lady—and *strongly!*—that she had not informed me of her plans by writing you, although it is a condition of our agreement that I must be so consulted. She has continually broken the agreement in this respect—in the cases of both children.

Tell her I thought from the only information received, Shane's letters, that he had given up all idea of Colorado University. He never mentioned it. That was what put me off Lawrenceville. Lawrenceville has no value unless a boy is going to College. High School is much better Prep for holding down the only kind of job Shane could expect to get. Also, of course, he said nary a word in his letters about the true reason for his passion for High School—the girl business.

Finally, assure her that if Shane writes me for any more advice, I will simply refer him to her. But I do expect, as per agreement, that she keep me informed in advance, by writing you, what her plans are. All best from us, Gene

---

438 • TO SHANE O'NEILL. TLS 1 p. (Stationery headed: Tao House / Danville / Contra Costa County / California) [Virginia]

October the 21st 1938

Dear Shane, I would have replied to your letter sooner but I have been laid up for a week with rheumatism. I was delighted to get your birthday letter and the two grand ties. Many thanks. They are just the kind I like and I certainly appreciate the gift. But you mustn't feel you must spend your money to make me presents. It's enough to get a letter and know you think of me on these occasions. Not that I'm not darned glad to have the ties, you understand.

Replying to the first of your letters, if you wrote me this summer about not being able to get in Colorado this Fall, I never rec'd any such letter. Now that you are set at Lawrenceville, what you ought to do is forget the High School idea, and dig in and do some hard work and earn a college diploma. You can do it if you are willing to make the effort. You have the brains. And, after all, you said in your previous letter that you liked Lawrenceville as a school, and it's a fact that a diploma from there means more than a High School one. So make up your mind to get all you can out of Lawrenceville, and stop feeling sorry for yourself. Don't you know you are being given a better break than nine out of ten boys in this country get? It's not silly, as you say, for you to stay at Lawrenceville, now that you're there. On the other hand, it would be extremely silly for you to change to High School now, even if it was possible. You have been to too damned many schools already. For God's sake, stay put this time until you get into college! No school is any good, unless you do some hard work. If you do the work, any school is good. That's the whole answer to the school question.

I'm enclosing a check for your birthday—and again, my grateful thanks for the ties! Carlotta joins me in love to you.   As ever,   Father

---

439 • TO HARRY WEINBERGER.   TLS 1 p. (Stationery headed: Tao House / Danville / Contra Costa County / California) [Yale]

Feb. 27th 1939

Dear Harry: Your two letters about Shane have arrived. I answer them myself, (and never mind the typing) because my secretary has just returned from a week in a San Francisco hospital where she had an operation on her right eye. Operation seems to be a complete success but we can't tell finally until a month or so when she has used the eye a bit. It will be kept bandaged for some time to come. As you can imagine, I have been some worried, and off work completely. And still am. A damned serious business, this cutting eyes, even when absolutely necessary. Carlotta has been very brave about it. The operation was extremely painful but she never complained. She has to wear, for the present, a goggle arrangement with just a tiny peep hole for the sound eye to see through, straight ahead. And she has to have a nurse out here with her for some time.

Re Shane, I am disgusted but not surprised. I knew the Lawrenceville thing would not work. A waste of money, as you say. The only thing to do is let him take a job. With no coddling and no help from anyone. Put him entirely on his own. Let him learn by experience, the tougher the better, what he will be up against in competitive life. That might put some guts in him. But what's the use of talking?

The whole point is that Shane is a Boulton and just naturally dumb and shiftless, like all the rest of them, where education and books are concerned. Not one of them ever got through any school! It's a fact! And it is a fact about him, no matter how the professors try to gloss it over, or his mother evades it. The alibi she is now trying to cook up about his eyesight is nonsense. I have seen him read cheap magazines by the hour without ever thinking about eyesight. So do not humor her, and involve me, by making any suggestions to her about taking him to a New York specialist. In fact, don't make any suggestions to her about him at all. Simply acknowledge her letters and let it go at that. I have said all I have to say to Shane and he knows exactly how I feel about everything he is doing, or not doing. Now it is up to him to do as he pleases. He is no baby. He will be twenty soon. The one thing I am determined to avoid above everything is to give her any excuse to wish any part of her responsibility on me. She has gone ahead always without consulting me until after the event, and I refuse absolutely to involve myself in the future. He will be twenty-one in a year and a half and, then thank God, I will be let out of even the financial responsibility for him in our agreement. I look forward to that day! Meanwhile, I have done all, and a good deal more, for him than he has deserved to have done, without ever receiving the slightest sign of gratitude or appreciation. I am through—until such time as he proves himself not to be a parasitic slob of a Boulton. As he is now, son or not, he simply does not interest me as a human being. Nor as a son. And that is the attitude I want you to take as my representative.

How about the old Income Tax? As Cane[1] will have told you, Carlotta and I have decided to split the marriage exemption as we did last year. Get it out here soon, will you?

All best, Harry! Enclosed the dole to the invertebrate trollop.   Gene

---

1. Melville Cane, Carlotta's lawyer.

440 • TO ROBERT E. SHERWOOD.[1]   TLS 1 p. (Stationery headed: Tao House / Danville / Contra Costa County / California) [Harvard]

March 12th 1939

Dear Robert Sherwood,   I will be only too pleased to inscribe the books for the Instituto Cultural Argentino Norteamericano. Added to the considerations you mention, I have a warm sentimental memory spot for the Argentine—even though my career down there terminated with the benches along the Paseo Colon in Buenos Aires as the best I could do in bedrooms.

So you met Dr. Mirlas. I wrote him a few days ago. I am glad to hear your good opinion of him. From his letters I judged him to be just what you say. But I am naturally a bit prejudiced in his favor!

It's darned good of you to send *Abe Lincoln In Illinois*. We were going to get it from Random House. All I've heard about it makes me eager to read it. It's a grand thing for us all that you should have done it at this particular time, and that it is such a great success.

Thank you for the good wishes about my health. I'm fairly fit now and working hard, but for two years and a half I had an exasperating time—one of those middle-aged swooning spells when the past catches up with you, and you seem to fall apart in sections, with one ill merely the unpleasant prologue to another. No matter how philosophically reconciled you attempt to be, it does keep interrupting work. Lately it has been Carlotta's turn for bad luck. She is just out of the hospital after an eye operation—a most successful one, I am happy to say.

Carlotta sends her love to you. We hope, if you and Mrs. Sherwood ever get out this way you will pay us a visit. We are only fifty minutes drive from San Francisco and yet it is real country with no suggestion of suburbia—and the most beautiful country I've ever seen, at that.

All good wishes to you.   Very sincerely,   Eugene O'Neill

---

441 • TO THERESA HELBURN.   TLS 1 p. (Stationery headed: Tao House / Danville / Contra Costa County / California) [Yale]

April 3rd 1939

Dear Terry,   Yes, Madden wrote me about the Hammerstein-*Marco* thing.[1] Too bad. Have you ever thought of *The Fountain* as an operetta? In my opinion, it would lend itself more readily than any of my stuff to light musical adaption.

Another play to think of in musical connection is *The Hairy Ape*. Coates, the conductor, was once going to make an opera of it. He didn't. I mention this to show you that the idea had occurred to a famous musician. But I'm not thinking of grand opera now but of something more like *Porgy and Bess*.[2] Give this idea a little pondering, will you? With the right composer, it could work out into a most striking and out of the ordinary rut affair. And very timely. Because I think we are all a bit sick of answers that don't answer. *The Hairy Ape* at

---

1. Sherwood (1896–1955), dramatist, whose plays include *The Petrified Forest* (1935), *Idiot's Delight* (1936), and *Abe Lincoln in Illinois* (1938).

1. Playwright, lyricist, and producer Oscar Hammerstein II (1895–1960) apparently had suggested the idea of a musical version of *Marco Millions*, a project which never materialized.

2. Opera (1935) by George Gershwin (1898–1937) and DuBose and Dorothy Heyward.

least, faces the simple truth that, being what we are, and with any significant spiritual change for the better in us probably ten thousand years away, there just is no answer.

Carlotta's eye operation was a great success and she is fine.

I'm damned delighted to hear the Barry play[3] is a success for you! It's about time the Guild's luck changed and you had a decent break. But if you've ever played roulette—it's a gambling game like the show business but less disreputable!—you all ought now to be heartened by the thought that after a long consecutive run in the red, it sure keeps coming black when it once changes!

Carlotta joins me in love to you and Oliver.   As ever,   Gene

---

442 • TO GILBERT SELDES.[1]   AL (draft) 3 pp. ([Tao House, Danville, Contra Costa County, California]) [Yale]

[c. April 6, 1939]

Dear Gilbert Seldes: My suggestion is, you have a long talk with Madden and explain all the details of your proposition to him. I am so far away and understand so little of the whole set-up of television production, that this seems the best way to tackle this, to save your time and give you a quick decision.

I hope you know I want to cooperate with you, that I would feel confident [that] with you in charge the best would be done with my stuff that could be done. *But* there are buts. I want you to understand. If I had a play on in New York, or there was any prospect of a production in the near future, I would tell you to go ahead, regardless. But I want, if I can, to finish all of the Cycle of plays I'm writing before releasing the first of them for production, and that means years to come. So it is up to me to conserve all possible financial resources— and television rights come under that head. My fear is that early experimentation with my stuff may kill its value, that the wise thing is to hold off until television is perfected.

Then, too, I feel I have already proved my interest in television experimentation, and done more than my bit of collaboration by practically giving away plays to be televised in England. In addition to *Emperor Jones,* there was *Ah, Wilderness!* and *Marco Millions* and they are going to do *The Hairy Ape* (I believe).

Or if you were proposing in behalf of a new television company, which was struggling to make its way, it might be different. But there is no reason, except the customary niggardliness toward authors, why a corporation like Columbia cannot damned well afford to include a fair royalty to the writer among its production costs, even in the experimental stages. The lads who control Columbia will make fat profits from television later on, but it's five million to one in my book that they won't be asking the suckers who gave them something for nothing to take any cut whatever of that profit!

What I think would be fair to me is some arrangement guaranteeing a certain number of productions of each play within a year, and also guaranteeing a minimum total royalty for these productions whether all of them were given or not.

All best to you. I hope we can get together on this. If not, well I know you will understand my position, and that I cannot afford just now not to be a bit implacable on the matter of royalties.   V.s.y.

3. *The Philadelphia Story* by playwright Philip Barry (1896–1949), which, starring Katharine Hepburn and Joseph Cotten, opened on March 28, 1939, at the Shubert Theatre.

1. Seldes (1893–1970), author, critic, and one of the earliest and most influential writers on the popular arts in America, who had joined the Columbia Broadcasting Company in 1937 as director of television.

443 • TO HENRY T. NETHERTON.[1]   TLS 1 p. (Stationery headed: Tao House / Danville / Contra Costa County / California) [California]

May the 9th 1939

Dear Mr. Netherton,   I will be glad to contribute one hundred dollars for the first prize in The Berkeley Playmakers' next one-act play contest—or, as a part of that prize, if you should decide to make it more.

But no Eugene O'Neill tacked on it! My one condition is that you announce it simply as a prize given by The Playmakers and that I shall not be mentioned in any way whatsoever. I have stubborn long-standing scruples on matters like this, and a rule that is hardened against persuasion. If you want a name for the prize, I suggest that of George Pierce Baker. As The Playmakers are an outgrowth of his classes at the University of California in 1924, it would be a fine thing for your theatre to help keep his memory alive. Nothing would please me more because I had a deep affection and respect for Professor Baker.

However, please believe this last is merely a suggestion. I don't want you to think I am tying a lot of strings to such a small contribution.

But on the one condition I did make, you can consider me as more adamant than adamant!

With all good wishes to you and The Playmakers,   Very sincerely,   Eugene O'Neill

---

444 • TO GEORGE JEAN NATHAN.   TLS 2 pp. (Stationery headed: Tao House / Danville / Contra Costa County / California) [Cornell]

May the 13th 1939

Dear George,   Many thanks for the clipping. Ah, Wilderness, those dear old days when you and I were little convent boys together! Remember how Sister Mary used to paddle your behind to the chime of the Angelus and never miss a beat? Life was so simple then.[1]

I was sorry to read your report on the new O'Casey play.[2] I suppose these lousy times make it inevitable that many authors get caught in the sociological propaganda mill. With most of them it doesn't matter. They have nothing much to lose, and the sociological attack helps them by giving a lot of shallow stuff a phony partisan importance. But O'Casey is an artist and the soap box no place for his great talent. The hell of it seems to be, when an artist starts saving the world, he starts losing himself. I know, having been bitten by the salvationist bug myself at times. But only momentarily, so to speak, my true conviction being that the one reform worth cheering for is the Second Flood, and that the interesting thing about people is the obvious fact that they don't really want to be saved—the tragic idiotic ambition for self-destruction in them.

However. O'Casey, I'm betting, will soon get a sick bellyful of the Comrade Church after he's seen through the power-greed of a sufficient number of its communicants.

The only important news with us is that Carlotta's operation was a complete success. Her eyes are in better shape now than they ever have been. I've been working steadily, without yet taking the rest I'd promised myself. Going back over the third play lately to make some changes that will hook it up more closely with the fourth. That's the devil of this job,

---

1. Founder and producing director of the Berkeley Playmakers, a semiprofessional theatre group in Berkeley, California.

1. Nathan's and O'Neill's mothers were in convent school together at St. Mary's Academy in Notre Dame, Indiana.
2. *The Star Turns Red.*

the amount of time spent on such revision. It's a sort of special, additional task for a playwright. No one who confined himself to writing single plays could ever imagine how much extra thought and labor are involved. Sometimes, I feel sick about it, the constant driving on while seeming, in the light of final completion, to be making no progress. Still and all, I do keep pretty damned interested, for it is an arousing challenge, and the stuff is there, if I have the stuff to make it mine.

How about your plans for Europe? Have you decided yet? We are still hoping you may come here.

Love from us, George. It will be grand to see you again, whenever it is.   Always yours, Gene

---

445 • TO EUGENE O'NEILL, JR.   TLS 1 p. (Stationery headed: Tao House / Danville / Contra Costa County / California) [Yale]

May the 17th 1939

Dear Eugene,   All I can say is, I get a confident feeling from your letter, and from all you have written Carlotta, that you are maturely sure of yourself this time and have a right to be. And from all you have told us of Sally,[1] I should say it will be your own damned fool fault if you do not find enduring happiness and peace with her. So, my benevolent patriarchal blessing on both your noggins!

Tell Sally I rely on her to have you hog-tied and branded for life! I know she will agree with me that in future this marrying has simply got to cease!

As for the honeymoon railroad fare item, you can count on me. Let me know when you want me to send it. I will not pretend that the breaks are so lucky at present that I can toss this off like the late "Bet-a-Million" Gates at a faro table. But neither can I howl that it will drive me in the Poorhouse. I would afford it, anyway, even if I couldn't.

It will be grand to welcome you and Sally here.   Love to you both,   Father

---

446 • TO RICHARD DANA SKINNER.   AL (draft) 3 pp. ([Tao House, Danville, Contra Costa County, California]) [Yale]

[June 1939]

Dear Dana: Your guilty conscience beat mine to it. I've been saying to myself for the past six months, it's about time I dropped Dana a line. I'd have come to the point, too, unprodded, although when it's a question of letter writing, I've become practically an expert at the mañana game.

Carlotta and I hail the appearance of Elizabeth Ellery Raymond![1] It is hardly the best of all possible worlds she enters but let's hope by the time she is old enough to recognize her plight, it may have taken a turn for the better. We are damned sorry to hear of the tough time Ellie has had. Well, anyway, when she and I next meet we can discuss our operations, and what is more delightful? Speaking of operations—and you can't stop me once I'm started!— Carlotta had an extremely serious one on her right eye a couple of months ago. It proved a great success and her vision now is better than it has ever been.

1. The third wife of Eugene, Jr.

1. Skinner's first grandchild.

I knew from John Pell's[2] letters how well you were doing with the new Company,[3] but I am glad to hear from you more of the details. Grand news, Dana! I know you know how pleased I am.

Regarding your plans for the summer, you put me on the spot. I cannot hope for the next World War, and yet I would like the chance to see some or all of the Skinners out here. Isn't our San Francisco Fair an inducement? Oh, I know you have a similar jamboree in your neighborhood, but we have Sally Rand and her Nude Ranch in ours. You haven't forgotten Sally, I hope. Well, then.

The Cycle of plays? The score is four down and five to go. However, of the four, two—the first and second—are still in first draft and, for reasons too complicated for a letter, it is better not to try and finish them until I have gone on much farther with the whole thing. A matter of keeping them in their right place so they won't anticipate too much of what must appear again when the curve completes its circle. That will do for an explanation, although it doesn't tell all the story. A devilish job, this Cycle! It involves problems of adjustment between parts and whole for which there is no precedent in playwrighting. And how this element, which I only dimly foresaw, or I might never have attempted the thing, devours time and labor! Rewriting and then rewriting some more! I work and work and time passes while, in relation to the whole work, I seem to stand still. Most discouraging, at times, like being on a treadmill. And then, the attempt to get a deeper, more revealing, more complicated motivation into character—to get at all the aspects of the inner strength of opposites in the individual which is fate—keeps me constantly overreaching the medium. Confidentially, of the four plays written so far, three were double length or over! Which means I have really written seven plays, judged by length and labor. I say "were double length" because one, the fourth play, I am bringing down to normal. Only the third one wrote itself as naturally an ordinary length play. This is all most deplorable! I don't want any of them to be double length, except the last which will have to be, and I'm damned if I'll let them get away with it! So you see how it is. Yet I'm not really complaining. It's all extremely interesting and stimulating, and I'm glad of the excuse to have a long creative vacation from the Broadway theatre racket. As you know, the glamour of the Showshop and the fascination of casting and rehearsing and performing were never glamorous or fascinating to me. To put it mildly! I didn't tour with *Monte Cristo* the first seven years of my life for nothing!

But I would like a vacation from the Cycle and I may try writing a single play which is quite outside its orbit. Have quite a few ideas I like. So far, however, the Cycle just won't let me concentrate on anything else. It evidently doesn't approve of vacations of that sort—or any sort!

I'm again going to plague you to plague Margaret[4] to plague her sister for information on the business of the Irish woman in the Cycle who becomes a nun. At present, I've had to leave her indefinite now, because I can't find out where to discover the information. Here are facts again: Middle aged Irish woman. Only child, daughter, marries, goes away. Husband dies. She feels guilt because for love of him she let him make her give up practice Catholicism. With no more worldly responsibilities wants give rest of her life to God, enters convent. Time she would enter 1832. A fine unselfish character but ignorant peasant. Could not enter any teaching order, of course. It comes to this: What order, established in the U.S. in 1832 could she enter and in what capacity? Surely, there must be a book I could get, listing all orders in the U.S., when first established here, what conditions are for entering, etc. But I

2. O'Neill's stockbroker.
3. Townsend-Skinner & Co., Inc., a New York City firm specializing in economic research.
4. Margaret Hill Skinner, Skinner's wife.

cannot seem to obtain it. No one seems to know. I was thinking that Margaret's sister would know, if anyone does.

By your letterhead, I judge E. Carroll Skinner[5] has become one of your most valuable associates. Give her our affectionate felicitations. And to Peggy,[6] although I regret to note she is letting herself in for the bedevilments of a literary career, take it from a bedeviled one. And our love to Margaret and you & Ellie and the grandchildren.   As ever,

---

447 • TO OONA O'NEILL.   TLS 2 pp. (Stationery headed: Tao House / Danville / Contra Costa County / California) [Virginia]

July the 14th 1939

Dear Oona,   You will have to forgive me for not having written sooner. Now I seem to owe you three letters, for your third just arrived to-day. Well, this will have to do for three in one!

One thing that made me delay was that we had to get our schedule of visitors straightened out. We have only one guest room, as Shane has probably told you. So a mix-up in dates would be bad. What further complicated matters was that up to the time I received the letter you wrote just before your school closed, we had not heard from you for so long we had concluded you had given up the idea of coming. So we went ahead with plans for friends who wanted to visit. As nearly all these people live in the East, and have to plan such a long trip far in advance, it isn't a case where you can ask them to change dates later on.

And there were other complications which I will explain when I see you. What I want to tell you now is how much I want to see you and how happy I am that you wish to come. But on account of the arrangements we had made before we heard from you, it can't be before August the twentieth. Anytime that suits you after that. I hope this will be all right for you and that it will not interfere with any other plans you have made for your summer, and that you can arrange to stay a week or ten days with us.

I am glad you like swimming. We have a good pool. Be sure to bring your suit. I promise you the water *is* warm.

I was delighted to learn about the fine work you have done in music and that you passed all your exams. Evidently you had no need to be doubtful about the Latin exam. French, Latin, English and Algebra were always easy for me in my prep school days. And I actually passed a German exam as part of the entrance requirements for Princeton, which is hard to believe now when I can scarcely read a word of it! It was things like Physics and Chemistry that used to get me down. I hope when you come to tackle them you don't have the trouble I did.

As for the fare for your trip, I insist on paying that. Just find out from your mother before you leave how much it is and I will give you a check to take back to her.

If you happened to see a report in the New York papers that I was coming East for the theatre celebration at Provincetown, pay no attention to it. Somebody made up that story and there is no truth in it.

Yes, it is about time you and I got together again. It has been too long since the last time![1]

---

5. Eleanora Carroll Skinner, Skinner's second daughter.
6. Margaret Hill Skinner, Skinner's third daughter.

1. O'Neill had last seen his daughter in 1931.

Carlotta joins me in love to you—and here's looking forward to the great happiness of seeing you!   Daddy

P.S. Please tell Shane I got his fine letter and I will answer it within the next couple of days without fail.

---

448 • TO SHANE O'NEILL.   TLS 2 pp. (Stationery headed: Tao House / Danville / Contra Costa County / California) [Yale]

July the 18th 1939

Dear Shane,   I wrote Oona a couple of days ago to tell you to expect an answer to your letter soon and here it is.

My feeling, that Harry spoke to you about—and by the way, I didn't tell him to say anything to you—was based on the fact that you had let me hear so little from you at Lawrenceville. But forget it. I appreciate a lot the frankness of this last letter of yours and I hope you will always write me in just that spirit. What you say of your feeling a new understanding had sprung up between us on your last visit was exactly what I felt. Which made it doubly hard to comprehend why later on you went ahead with a complete change in your plans without consulting me and were all booked for Lawrenceville by the time I heard from you.

My advice on the subject of raising horses would not be much use to you. I don't know anyone in that game, what conditions or prospects are, or anything else about it. All I know is that if you want to get anywhere with it, or with anything else, you have got to adopt an entirely different attitude from the one you have had toward getting an education. In plain words, you've got to make up your mind to study whatever you undertake, and concentrate your mind on it, and really work at it. This isn't wisdom. Any damned fool in the world knows it's true, whether it's a question of raising horses or writing plays. You simply have to face the prospect of starting at the bottom and spending years learning how to do it. The trouble with you, I think, is that you are still too dependent on others. You expect too much from outside you and demand too little of yourself. You hope everything will be made smooth and easy for you by someone else. Well, it's coming to the point where you are old enough, and have been around enough, to see that this will get you exactly nowhere. You will be what you make yourself and you have got to do that job absolutely alone and on your own, whether you're in school or holding down a job.

After all, parents' advice is no damned good. You know that as well as I. The best I can do is to try to encourage you to work hard at something you really want to do and have the ability to do. Because any fool knows that to work hard at something you want to accomplish is the only way to be happy. But beyond that it is entirely up to you. You've got to do for yourself all the seeking and finding concerned with what you want to do. Anyone but yourself is useless to you there.

I'm glad you got the job on the party-fishing boat. It's a start in the right direction of independence. The more you get to know of independence the better you will like it, and the more you will get to know yourself and the right aim for your life.

What I am trying to get firmly planted in your mind is this: In the really important decisions of life, others cannot help you. No matter how much they would like to. You must rely only on yourself. That is the fate of each one of us. It can't be changed. It just is like that. And you are old enough to understand this now.

And that's all of that. It isn't much help in a practical advice way, but in another way it might be. At least, I hope so.

I'm glad to know of your doing so much reading and that you're becoming interested in Shakespeare. If you really like and understand his work, you will have something no one can ever take from you.

We are looking forward to Oona's visit. I appreciate your writing about her as you did. It is so long since I have seen her. Too long. Ordinarily I would have been coming East every year or two to put on new plays and would have seen her then. But a Cycle of nine plays is another matter. It brings up complications that keep me tied down to the job, especially as I have not yet caught up on my schedule from the delay my long illness of two years ago caused.

Don't talk of dry spell! We know all about that! We had hardly any rain last winter and now we live in dread our springs will get so low before the summer ends that a lot of the stuff we have planted around the house can't be watered and will have to die. It's rotten. Natives tell us there was less rain this year than at any time for forty years.

Carlotta joins me in love to you. Let me know as soon as you have any definite plans for the immediate future. And keep your chin up! You will be all right as soon as you get yourself organized along one set line.   As ever,   Father

---

449 • TO HARRY WEINBERGER.   TLS 2 pp. (Stationery headed: Tao House / Danville / Contra Costa County / California) [Yale]

July the 22nd 1939

Dear Harry,   I ought to have acknowledged your letters before this but I have been enjoying one of my intermittent sinking spells for the past three or four weeks and have felt generally punk.

I'm glad you've got the Joisey Lilly[1] to see the light on school tuition. I've written Oona and Shane. We can't have Oona out until late August because she hadn't written in so long we decided she didn't want to come, and went ahead with plans for other visitors. But that is as good a time here as any other.

I wrote Shane a long letter which I hope will mean something to him. Not the usual fatherly crap, but pointing out he's got to find himself by himself, for no one can help him in that.

No, don't do anything on the eye specialist stuff. Shane needs alibis taken from him, not handed him. If there was anything really wrong with his eyes, they would have spotted it at Lawrenceville. He never complained of eyes to me, or seemed to have any difficulty reading what he wanted to read. And don't make any suggestions about buying a horse farm for him on a year or so experience. Hell, he'd have to work hard for many years before he'd be able to work successfully on his own. The whole trouble with him is he's had too much handed him for nothing. He's got to wake up—to make himself wake up. I think he would, too, if he could get away from her, and everyone else, and find the pride of being independent. The Vet idea seems bunk to me. It means years more of books and teachers, and something in him resists that, and will continue to sabotage it. What he evidently wants is a job, if I can believe his last letter.

No, I won't go over your play and blue pencil it. I think you have done exceedingly well in your revision. All I suggest is that *you* go over it with a sharp eye for rhetorical hackneyed stilted expressions—like "upstanding men," "cry out aloud," say—which make your char-

1. Agnes Boulton O'Neill.

acters sound too stuffed and banal. If *you* do this, you'll learn. If I did it, you wouldn't—I mean, wouldn't learn to do it yourself.

The big handicap of this play is that while it's damned interesting to those interested in the subject, it will simply bore those who are not. Of course, everybody *ought* to be interested but that gets you nowhere.

Get more feeling of natural easy familiar conversation into your characters' talk where it fits the mood. People, even then, must have said "it's" occasionally instead of "it is," "there's" instead of "there is," "can't" instead of "cannot," etc. You simply have to learn to tell *by ear* which would be right in what sentence—which emphasis you need. Go over it with the idea in mind not of reading words on paper but of listening to your people say it! All the best from us! Gene

P.S. Your script is being sent under separate cover. The Stefan Zweig book[2] just arrived. Many thanks for your thought of us.

---

450 • TO SHANE O'NEILL. TLS 2 pp. (Stationery headed: Tao House / Danville / Contra Costa County / California) [Virginia]

August the 22nd 1939

Dear Shane, I have been waiting to answer your letter until the drawings came. They did not arrive until yesterday. My judgment isn't worth much in such things but I would say they indicated you had a latent talent that would be worth trying out. Always provided, of course, that you like drawing well enough to dig in and really work hard at it. The illustration game, like every other, is tough for a newcomer to break into, and you've got to steel yourself to keep on and not be stopped by the disappointments you will inevitably encounter before you can make a success of it.

At any rate, my advice is to go on with this study until you can prove to yourself what you've got. I agree with you that a job in a business office, even if you could get one, is not for you. And I also agree that taking a Vet course would be a long waste of time. If you were interested enough in that angle to make good at it, you would have no doubts about it. As for the short story idea, I think you are wise in feeling you don't belong in that, either.

No, go on with your drawing and get really interested in illustration work. Put the horse-raising plan out of your head for the present. You won't get anywhere, you know, if you try aiming for two goals at the same time. You've got to concentrate on one objective. If I were you I would think of illustration work as the thing you want to do, with horse-raising as a future sideline, and not vice versa. It will be time enough to regard horse-raising as the main issue when you have succeeded at the thing which will make the farm you dream about possible.

Besides, to be frank, you don't strike me as being as keen on this horse-raising business as you believe. If you loved horses as much as you think, you would rather start working in a stable on a breeding farm than do anything else in the world—and to hell with the money end of it, as long as you had enough to eat! How the devil can you ever expect to learn how to raise horses unless you start at the bottom? Do you think you know enough now, on the basis of having gone for a few months to a ranch prep school in Colorado? That is nonsense. What right have you, in experience, to own and run a horse-farm? Little more right than I have to own and run an automobile factory! You would only make an abject failure of it

---

2. Perhaps the new edition of Zweig's play *Jeremiah* (1917), published to mark the first American production of the play by the Theatre Guild on February 3, 1939.

through ignorance and lack of experience. Of course, if you can earn enough money at something else so you can afford a farm as a hobby, and to hire a manager who would run the farm for you until, after many years, you learned from him how to run it yourself, that's another matter—but a very expensive matter!

The trouble with you on the horse-raising idea is you again choose the easiest way. You want to start at the top with your own farm and horses, as if you already knew the business without ever taking the trouble to learn it!

But enough of that. I hate bawling you out. All I really wish to say in this letter is that my advice for the immediate future is to concentrate on the illustration work. It's a good career, and you may have the right stuff to succeed at it.

We are looking forward to Oona's visit. I will certainly be happy to see her again.

Carlotta joins in love to you. Let me know how you get on with your drawing. I am extremely interested to see what you will do with it. It may be the answer you are looking for.   As ever,   Father

P.S. Your drawings are being returned to you under separate cover.

---

451 • TO KENNETH MACGOWAN.   TLS 1 p. (Stationery headed: Tao House / Danville / Contra Costa County / California) [Yale]

Sept. 10th 1939

Dear Kenneth,   I should have written long since to thank you for the records, which I am delighted to have in the collection. But August was a hectic month with us. A family month. First came Eugene on a visit with a new bride. A stalwart stout young woman. All right in her way—which is all-too-familiar Connecticut small city type—but, from my angle, a rather disappointing daughter-in-law. (Boy, you don't know the half of the family racket yet! Wait till the progeny begin introducing their brides and their bridegrooms!) On the top of their leaving us, Carlotta's son-in-law[1] (a hell of a nice guy) became seriously ill and had to be taken to the hospital. Lastly, Oona flew out for a visit. This turned out to be a bright spot. I was very apprehensive, not having any idea what she might be like. But Carlotta and I were both delighted with her. She is really a charming girl, both in looks and manners. And she has intelligence, too. So, (knocking on wood) hurrah for that!

Then came the War and ears glued to the radio. And all the time I've been trying to keep on with the job.

I imagine this European tragic mess has got your goat as badly as it has mine. Jesus, the incredible, suicidal capacity of men for stupid greed! That's about the only comment I can find to make, remembering all that has been done from 1918 to date.

Your tale of Ivan Kahn's reformation is damned amusing. I envy him his turkey gobbler. In those Ridgefield winters, apple jack, hard cider and acidosis frequently led me into intimate converse with a rat in the wall regarding cosmic matters. But the bastard didn't know any answers. He only asked questions.

I hope to God this war business will not ruin that Rockefeller Foundation opportunity! Love from us, Kenneth, and let us hear from you.   As ever,   Gene

---

1. Roy Stram, Cynthia Chapman's second husband.

With Oona at Tao House.

452 • TO SHANE O'NEILL.   AL (draft) 1 p. ([Tao House, Danville, Contra Costa County, California]) [Yale]

[c. September 10, 1939]

Dear Shane: This is just a line to reply to the money end of your letter. I am mailing Harry a check for two hundred to send to your mother. She can discuss with him the details of how she wishes the two thousand paid for Oona and you. I didn't approve of the idea of Harry being delegated to give you so much each week. Harry's services cost me money and I can't afford now to hire him to be a weekly paymaster. I owe him money now. Your mother will have to make some other arrangement.

Yes, the European mess is hell. I hope with you that we won't be dragged into it, but if it lasts long enough I am afraid we will be. I remember too well the way the attitude of the public here was gradually changed by events in the last war.

Carlotta and I enjoyed Oona's visit immensely. She is charming and lovable.

I hope you mean it when you say you really intend to work this time. This is a damned serious crisis in the life of everyone on earth, whether they have the sense to know it or not. You have got to prove to yourself you can grow up and take your own life seriously. Or you will never be able to face the future with courage—a future which, even with the luckiest breaks, is bound inevitably to be damned tough for all of us.

Love to you and Oona, and thank her for her letter to me.   As ever,

---

453 • TO GEORGE JEAN NATHAN.   TLS 2 pp. (Stationery headed: Tao House / Danville / Contra Costa County / California) [Cornell]

October the 1st 1939

Dear George,   Many thanks for the copy of your broadcast.[1] Anna Held[2] having forgotten somehow to give me that pink garter you mention, I shall treasure your essay side by side with a picture of Bonnie Magin in tights which I once clipped from the *Police Gazette*[3] in an aspiring prep school moment.

As for the dedication of *Encyclopedia Of The Theatre* to me,[4] my deep gratitude, George. I am honored and delighted.

I note in a recent *Newsweek* article you speak of my having finished the fifth play of the Cycle. I wish I had! The truth is I haven't even started the fifth yet. Madden, I know, is responsible for handing you this bum steer. He wrote me some time ago he had spoken to you of the great progress I had made on the Cycle. I explained at great length, when he was here, just how I stood, that the fifth play was the one I would tackle next, but he evidently got it bawled up.

Just between us, I haven't done a lick on the Cycle in several months. It had me worn to a frazzle and stale as hell. I'd been working on it continuously, practically every day, since I recovered from my stretch of illness two years ago. So I decided to forget it for awhile and do

---

1. Possibly the April 23, 1939, radio broadcast on NBC of the New York Drama Critics Circle award ceremony at which Nathan spoke.
2. Held (1878–1918), flirtatious actress, who starred in numerous musical comedies and vaudeville shows of the late nineteenth and early twentieth centuries.
3. *National Police Gazette*, a pulp magazine which specialized in crime and confession stories and in pinups.
4. Published by Alfred A. Knopf in 1940, Nathan's dedication read, "To Eugene O'Neill, After Many Years."

one play, or maybe two, that had nothing to do with it. Which I've done, and I expect to finish a draft of one[5] in about two weeks. I will then go over it and get it in final shape. So it's on the cards that you will be getting a script for your valued judgment before many moons have passed. It looks good to me. At any rate, it has been an interesting time writing it. I'm not going to tell you a word about it, not even the title. I want you to read it without any advance information as to what kind of play it is, or anything.

Keep this very much under the hat. All I've let out to Cerf or the Guild or Madden, is that I had several ideas for plays outside the Cycle which I *might* do later *if* I could forget the Cycle for a while. And that's as far as I wish any authorized rumor to go. The reason is, I don't know when I will want to publish or produce this play, or any additional separate plays I may write. I may want to keep them to myself for years—until financial pinch forces my hand. Every time I think of making that trip East to face casting, rehearsals and all the rest of the game, I feel a great bored weariness and reluctance, as if I'd had quite enough of that for one life. Anyway, my point about secrecy is that if my publishers, producers, and agent knew I had anything finished, they would be on my neck all the time with this or that persuasive argument, and I want to duck that.

After this play is finished, I may go back to the Cycle and start the fifth play. Or I may do a second separate play. I have a fine idea for one that is much on my mind. But it's no good prophesying now. It all depends how the spirit moves then.

I suppose, with all the rest of us, this European mess has given you the jitters. It has certainly convinced me that only pessimists are not morons, and that only a blithering near-sighted idiot could desire to live very long in the future.

Carlotta joins me in love and Blemie, now a patriarch of twelve but still going strong, sends you a Dalmatian Heil!   As ever,   Gene

---

454 • TO CARLOTTA MONTEREY O'NEILL.   ALS 1 p. (Stationery headed: Tao House / Danville / Contra Costa County / California) [Yale]

Christmas 1939

Own Beloved: Again and forever, all my love, Darling, and my gratitude for the beauty and peace that your love has given me—and a million poems I am not poet enough to write to your eyebrows and your eyes and your nose and your lips—and your etcetera!   Your Gene

---

455 • TO HARRY WEINBERGER.   TLS 1 p. (Stationery headed: Tao House / Danville / Contra Costa County / California) [Yale]

January the 11th 1940

Dear Harry,   I've been fighting off a cold or I would have answered your letter at once.

I don't agree with you that a wire from me to be read at this Finland Relief meeting of the Stage and Artist Committee would have any meaning. That is, not unless it was accompanied by a substantial contribution, and I simply cannot afford that now, especially as I have already contributed to a Finnish Fund out here.

In cases like this, the old axiom of "put up or shut up" strikes me as particularly valid. And I heartily distrust things like this Algonquin luncheon. Theatrical people always man-

5. *The Iceman Cometh.*

age to use such occasions to get a bunch of publicity for themselves. There is a lot of acting and loose emotional talk with damned little concrete benefit ever resulting from it.

Don't get me wrong. I'm all for Finland,[1] even to the extent of wishing our government would break off all relations with Russia and outlaw the Communist Party in this country as a foreign-controlled, traitor organization. I'm all for wiring Senators and Congressmen to have the Government support Finland in every possible way. But Algonquin luncheons of Show Shoppers, in any cause or on any pretext, strike me as the last word in futility. The tragic plight of Finland is too damned serious a matter to be mixed up with such frivolous gestures. I'm honestly surprised you let yourself get roped in on it. You know damned well all such doings carry no weight whatsoever in Washington—and the only help that can really help Finland is the help from the United States.   All best from us,   Gene

---

456 • TO LAWRENCE ESTAVAN.[1]   COPY (Stationery headed: Tao House / Danville / Contra Costa County / California)

Jan. 15th 1940

Dear Mr. Estavan,   Thank you for sending me a script of the Theatre Research Project's monograph on my father. I have read it with great interest, naturally, and it seems to me you have done a fine job with it. I realize, too, that you were working under great difficulties because the material you had to draw upon was so meager in many respects.

I cannot be of much help to you about his old days. My father kept few records of his family or career, and most of what he had kept was lost after his death. Nor did he ever go in for much reminiscing about the past. All I remember him telling about his San Francisco experiences was the Passion Play episode,[2] and Belasco told me much more about that than he did.

But I will be glad to reply as best I can to your queries, and also point out any inaccuracy in your monograph where I am sure my own information is the real fact, or nearer to it than yours.

Your first query—Can't answer that one. I know little about my father's parents. Or about his brothers and sisters. He had two older brothers, I think. I remember him saying one brother served in the Civil War—an Ohio regiment, I suppose—was wounded, never fully recovered and died right after the war. He had three sisters, all dead now, whom he never saw except when a theatrical tour brought him to the Middle West where they lived.

Second query—My brother, James Jr., was born in San Francisco on Sept. 10, 1878. (In your monograph you have him on the scene before this.) I am not sure but I think he was born at the home of some San Francisco friend of my father's, not in a hospital or a hotel.

Third query—My brother died in November 1923, a year after my mother's death. (There was also another brother, Edmund, born in St. Louis in 1883. He died before I was born when he was under two years old.)

Fourth query—My time on the stage with my father was limited to a couple of months

1. On November 30, 1939, Soviet planes bombed Helsinki and other Finnish towns, opening the Russo-Finnish War.

1. Assistant District Supervisor for the Writers' Program of the Works Project Administration in Northern California, who supervised the research and writing of *History of the San Francisco Theatre, Volume 20: James O'Neill* (1942), a draft of which he sent to O'Neill. The text of this letter is taken from the published monograph (pp. 115–21).

2. After a short run, amidst protests from religious and civic groups, the 1879 San Francisco production of *The Passion* was closed by the police and the cast briefly jailed.

as assistant manager of *The White Sister,* and another two months as an actor in the vaudeville version of *Monte Cristo.* Said version, let me add, was a horrible hash-up of the play, its general frightfulness reaching a high spot in the formidable lousiness of my acting. I had a small part but I couldn't have been worse if I'd been playing Hamlet.

Fifth query—You will have to excuse me on this one. If I started on anecdotes about him I would have to write a book, because he had many extraordinary contradictory sides to his character. I can't think of any one or two anecdotes that would give you a true picture. The father in my play *Ah, Wilderness!* is like him in some aspects but totally unlike him in others.

Sixth query—There was no business in which he dropped a fortune. He owned an interest in a small mail order company (where I worked for a time after a year at Princeton), which was caught in the panic of 1907 and failed a year later. But it did not break him, by any means. The truth is, he did lose a fortune, and a big one, during his whole career, but *Monte Cristo* enabled him to afford his losses. He was an easy mark for anyone with a spare gold mine, zinc mine, coal mine, silver mine, pieces of real estate, etc.—and he rarely guessed right. But he never went into anything so heavily it could ruin him.

Seventh query—The vaudeville version of *Monte Cristo* did not play in San Francisco. At that time there was a fleeting vogue in vaudeville for big dramatic condensed-play star acts, and naturally O'Neill in *Monte Cristo* was one of the first they wanted and they paid my father a lot of money to do it.

Eighth query—I can't remember much about the *Monte Cristo* movie. All I know is, it was one of the first twenty-five cent admission, Famous Player feature films using a play and star from the legitimate stage.

Ninth query—William Connor and George Tyler were his oldest friends in the theatre. Although he had many friends, I can't remember any of them who could really be called a crony of his.

Tenth query—I have no information about Mrs. Platt[3] except she lived in St. Louis, not Cincinnati.

Eleventh query—My father's parents were extremely poor, from his story. When he was only ten years old he had to start working in a machine shop for fifty cents a week.

Twelfth query—No relation. My mother's people came from New Haven, Connecticut, originally, then moved to Cleveland.

Thirteenth query—My answer to query nine covers all I know on this. Except add Nate Salisbury, Buffalo Bill's old partner.

Fourteenth query—I can't answer this. No memory of ever having heard anything about it.

Fifteenth query—This I have answered before. I was never in San Francisco on those tours.

Notes on monograph—My father's date of birth—He was born in 1846, really. And his birthday was Oct. 14th, not Nov. 15th. Like all actors he cut his age for publication. Only one year, however. The date you use from the *Dictionary of American Biography* is all wrong.

Another error in the monograph is on page 113 where you mention the plays of mine he had seen. He never saw *Thirst;* and *Gold* was not produced till the year after his death. *Bound East for Cardiff* and *The Long Voyage Home* were among plays he saw at the Provincetown that he liked. But his principal satisfaction was when my first long play to be done, *Beyond the Horizon,* was produced on Broadway by John D. Williams in the winter of 1920 and won the Pulitzer Prize that spring.

Again on page 113—The story you quote about his coming down to the Provincetown

3. James O'Neill's sister.

Theatre to direct *Before Breakfast* is, to put it kindly, somewhat exaggerated. There was no question of his directing. I got him down to make suggestions on the acting. He made some I didn't agree with, but also some I thought were fine and which the actors were glad to follow. As for "Freudian Pattern," the only comment I have on that is Nuts!

Page 113—My father never owned any property in Maryland, nor a large farm anywhere.

Here is some further data which might interest you: Date of the vaudeville *Monte Cristo*, season 1911–1912.

My father's family emigrated to the United States when he was eight years old, according to what he told me.

My father and mother were married on June 14th 1877 at Saint Ann's Church in New York City. Their wedding certificate is one of the few records of my parents in their early days that I possess.

I have an old San Francisco program, Baldwin's Theatre, Sept. 24th 1879—"Grand Gala Night—Occasion Extraordinary!—visit to this theatre of General Grant on the occasion of the farewell benefit of Miss Nina Varian." First on the bill was a scene from *Romeo and Juliet* with Varian as Juliet and Lew Morrison as Romeo. Next came "The Double Male Quartette!" Finally, Sardou's play *Diplomacy!* in compliment to General U. S. Grant, with my father heading the cast in the role of Captain Julian Beauclerc.

I hope these fragments of information, which are all I can think of, may be of some use to you. I wish I had more to offer, but as I've said, I have practically no records of his San Francisco days, very little in general about the time before I was old enough to take notice, and in the following years I was off at school, or wandering about, or living away from my family a lot of the time.

All good wishes to you and again thank you for your courtesy in sending me the monograph script.   Very sincerely yours,   Eugene O'Neill

---

457 • TO SHANE O'NEILL.   TLS 2 pp. (Stationery headed: Tao House / Danville / Contra Costa County / California) [Virginia]

January the 18th 1940

Dear Shane,   I am sorry to learn from your last letter about the picture you were going to send that you ruined working on it in electric light. Tough luck for you—and for us. We would like to have seen it.

Don't let the fact that you have discouraged fits about your work worry you. That's all in the game. I have always spent a lot of time while writing a play cursing myself because I couldn't make it all I wanted it to be. The time to get suspicious of yourself is when you begin to be satisfied with everything you do. Then you're finished, whether you know it or not.

What sort of book is this *Fare to Midlands*,[1] you mention? I am interested to know about it. It is true that George Bellows[2] and another artist and I spent a month in the winter of 1909 on a farm my father owned near Zion. If you could call it a farm! I don't believe anyone ever raised much on it. My father took it over in payment of a debt he couldn't collect. Bellows and Keefe[3] and I did our own cooking and everything, and damned near froze to death. They painted and I wrote a series of sonnets, bad imitations of Dante Gabriel Rossetti.

---

1. A local history of central New Jersey by Henry Charlton Beck (New York: E. P. Dutton, 1939).
2. Bellows (1882–1925), known best for his paintings of sporting scenes and landscapes.
3. Edward Keefe.

I knew Bellows well in those days. We roomed together for a time in a studio in the Lincoln Arcade Building at 65th and Broadway. Last I ever heard from him was in Bermuda in 1925 when we lived at "Campsea." He wrote asking me if he could paint my portrait when I returned to New York. Although I've always hated posing, I would have been tickled to death to have him paint me, but before I had a chance to answer his letter I read in the paper where he had died suddenly, from a burst appendix, as I remember. I always thought a lot of Bellows, both as an artist and a man, although I had not seen him for a long time before his death. He was a damned fine person.

The Education of Henry Adams is a grand book. I'm glad you are reading it. Why don't you read up on American politics of that time? You would find them interesting, I know, particularly the Civil War years when Adams' father was Ambassador to Great Britain.

There's not much news with us. It's rained a lot lately, thank God. We certainly needed it. And I'm working hard as usual. And the chickens are flourishing and so is Blemie, although he begins to show signs of old age.

By the way, what is the matter with that sister of yours? She wrote us around Christmas she was sending us pictures of herself but nothing like that has ever arrived.

Carlotta joins me in love to you.   As ever,   Father

---

458 • TO BARRETT H. CLARK.   TLS 1 p. (Stationery headed: Tao House / Danville / Contra Costa County / California) [Yale]

February the 5th 1940

Dear Clark,   In reply to your letter of July [January] 29th, you can tell Mr. Ross of Fisk University[1] that I cannot let him do *Mourning Becomes Electra*. You can let him down easy by saying I don't allow amateurs to do it—which, for that matter, is the truth, barring some unlikely, super-favorable occasion.

Just between us, there is something ludicrous to me in the idea of a negro Mannon family. And I think men like Ross should be directing all their energy to encouraging their people to create an American negro drama—plays written, acted and directed by negroes— and not waste time making tenth rate productions of white plays. It's only by following that line that they will ever get anywhere. Don't you agree? I stopped the Federal Theatre from allowing negroes to do anything but my negro plays for this reason.

I'm feeling fine, thanks—better than any winter since we have been on the Coast—no neuritis, thank God!—and have been getting a lot of work done, although I've been loafing for the past few weeks while enjoying a visit from Saxe Commins.

Mrs. O'Neill joins me in all good wishes.   Very sincerely,   Eugene O'Neill

---

459 • TO GEORGE JEAN NATHAN.   TLS 2 pp. (Stationery headed: Tao House / Danville / Contra Costa County / California) [Cornell]

February the 8th 1940

Dear George,   If you recall various of my reminiscences, you will recognize in this play a lot of material I have talked about using ever since you've known me. But never until a year or so ago did it take definite line and form as a play in my mind, its many life histories interwoven around a central theme.

---

1. An all-black school in Nashville, Tennessee.

All of the characters are drawn from life, more or less, although not one of them is an exact portrait of an actual person. And the scene, Harry Hope's dump, is a composite of three places.[1]

The plot, if you can call it that, is my imaginative creation, of course, but it has a basis in reality. There was a periodical drunk salesman, who was a damned amusing likable guy. And he did make that typical drummer crack about the iceman, and wept maudlinly over his wife's photograph, and in other moods, boozily harped on the slogan that honesty is the best policy.

The story of Parritt has a background of fact, too. The suicide really happened pretty much as shown in the play. But it was not the man the character of Parritt is derived from who bumped himself off that way. It was another person and for another reason.

The script probably still needs pruning in stage directions and tightening here and there. Not much, however, and I don't feel like doing it now. The play will always have to be too long, I think, from the ordinary production standpoint. But to hell with that angle. I'm not giving a thought to production. In fact, I hate to think of it being produced—of having to watch a lot of actors muscle in their personalities to make strange for me these characters of the play that interest me so much—now, as *I* have made them live!

Again, for God's sake, keep this play under your hat. No one but you and Cerf and Saxe Commins know it exists. Saxe is the only one who has read it. He typed the revised first draft during his visit with us. As for Bennett, I told him when he was here, but only after he had pledged absolute secrecy, and on the strict understanding that he should not mention publication until I did, if he had to wait ten years. One reason I told Cerf was because I want him to have one script buried in his safe, in case of accident—and in case I need the advance on the book.

You know if Madden and the Guild got wise I had finished this play what pressure arguments and pleadings would put me on a spot. The trouble is, they are personal friends as well as agents and producers. Otherwise, a go-to-hell rebuttal would be simple.

Besides the fact that I want to keep on now doing the only work that interests me in the theatre—writing—and that a production always throws me off work, sometimes for six months, there is a physical reason why I now dread the New York casting, rehearsal strain. Although my health is good, I am not the same as I was before my long illness, and never will be again. Even here, in the most peaceful healthy environment, I get sudden set-backs of complete exhaustion when I have to stay in bed for several days. (I am enjoying one right now—am writing this in bed.) I'm honestly afraid of what such an attack would do if it caught me in New York at the ragged end of production strain. I might come out of it an invalid for years, or even the rest of my life. This is no kidding. And what the hell production, no matter how successful, would be worth that, particularly in these times when nothing seems of less importance than whether another play is produced or not produced—or written, or not written, for that matter!

Well, I hope you like *The Iceman Cometh*. Including the title, which I love, because it characteristically expresses so much of the outer and the inner spirit of the play. I really admire this opus, George. I think it's about as successful an attempt at accomplishing a thing comprehensively and completely in all aspects as I've ever made. And I feel there are moments in it that hit as deeply and truly into the farce and humor and pity and ironic tragedy of life as anything in modern drama.

---

1. Saloons O'Neill frequented in his years in New York (1911–12, 1915–16)—Jimmy the Priest's (James J. Condon's, 252 Fulton Street), the Hell Hole (Tom Wallace's Golden Swan on Sixth Avenue), and the Garden Hotel bar on Madison Avenue near the old Madison Square Garden.

What ho! There's nothing like being one's own severest critic, eh?

Carlotta joins in love to you.   As ever,   Gene

P.S. Play is written in exact lingo of place and 1912, as I remember it—with only the filth expletives omitted. If you catch any slang you think doesn't belong in that time, let me know.

---

460 • TO RICHARD MADDEN.   TLS 2 pp. (Stationery headed: Tao House / Danville / Contra Costa County / California) [Yale]

February the 23rd 1940

Dear Dick,   Your letter re Eddie Dowling[1] and *The Straw* has just arrived. I can't form any opinion until I know definitely what he means by fixing it up to give it a fresher, more modern outlook. If it means any rewriting, to place the play in the present time, that is out. For one thing, I haven't enough interest in the play, even if I could afford the time off from my present work to do it. Another thing, I am sure many of the details of T.B. treatment must have radically changed since the period of the play and I know nothing about present day sanitariums. Further, the play was written wholly within the spirit of its time and it is always a bad mistake to attempt altering that, because it can't be done successfully. Lastly, you know I have little faith that any revival in New York of any play, no matter who is in it, will be a success—and *The Straw* is not one of my best plays.

Between us, I don't get Dowling's point in wanting to play Stephen himself. *The Straw* is the girl's play absolutely, and any chance of success it might have would depend on who played Eileen and how she played it.

I will wait to hear further details from you as to just what Dowling has in mind. But frankly, I don't see anything in a *The Straw* revival that would make it worth my while to do any revising on it. All I've ever thought the script needed was a general pruning and cutting. It's too gabby. Otherwise, it is what it is, for better or worse, a play I wrote at a certain time, pretty good, considering, but something that no longer interests me.

Another thing: You know the advance I expect on revivals. I hardly think Dowling would see his way to pay it.

You understand, I mean no doubt of Dowling's ability as actor or director. On the contrary, I share your conviction that he would be a splendid Stephen. But what is Stephen? No Stephen, however fine, can carry *The Straw*.

I'm still waiting for a *Glencairn* contract from Lyons[2]—and beginning to feel a bit uneasy at the delay.

Have you got any *Desire* royalties from Bright yet?   All best from us,   Gene

P.S. Note enclosure. Please tell the gentlemen the rights are not available. Thank you.

---

1. Broadway actor, director, producer, and playwright who had recently been highly acclaimed as the director and star of William Saroyan's *The Time of Your Life* (1939) and would later direct the 1946 Theatre Guild premiere production of *The Iceman Cometh*.

2. O'Neill's four *S. S. Glencairn* one-act plays had been optioned for a film, the negotiations being handled in California by the Lyons Agency.

461 • TO DUDLEY NICHOLS.   TLS 2 pp. (Stationery headed: Tao House / Danville / Contra Costa County / California) [Yale]

April the 27th 1940

Dear Dudley,   I've just finished reading the 'script and I most sincerely congratulate you on the fine job you have done.[1] You have preserved the flavor and spirit of the original plays wonderfully well. As for the things you mention in your letter—like the tarpaulin and anchor touches—I am all for them. I believe a picture of a play should concentrate on doing those things which the stage cannot do. Then a balance can be struck in which the picture medium brings fresh drama to the play to take the place of the stuff which belongs to the stage and cannot be done as well in pictures. So the more of such enhancing additions, the merrier, as far as I am concerned. And believe me, although I see as few pictures as I see stage productions, I can appreciate and feel the purely visual drama of your 'script, and think of *The Long Voyage Home* solely as a new unified picture drama, forgetting the four one-act plays written for the stage.

There are a few things which bother me. They relate to facts. Undoubtedly you and Ford[2] have checked on them and I must be wrong. But here goes. One extremely important one, because if it isn't fact, you will have everyone on your necks. You have the ship loading shells and high explosive from the U.S. Now isn't it true our Neutrality Act doesn't permit us to sell arms or munitions, the only exceptions allowed being planes and plane parts, etc.?

The other things have to do with ship stuff. You have a mess room steward doing a steward's job and bunking in the forecastle. And you haven't any bo'sun on your tramp. It's true no bo'sun appears in my plays but he is mentioned. In the plays there is no situation where there might not be a reason for his never being in the scene, but in the picture he would *have* to be around directing the men at times. Query No. 3: Twenty-five percent bonus for crew? Is that what they get in this war?

These are picayune queries, I admit, prompted by what I once knew of tramp steamer conditions, etc. Well, here's a suggestion that may give you a few extra shots. As I remember *In The Zone*, it conveys no suggestion of a double lookout (at least), which a ship would probably have at such a time. One man on the forecastle head, one in the crow's nest. It gives you a chance to add crow's nest stuff, particularly dramatic in a storm when you get a tremendous effect of the roll up there. And here's a memory. When due for a crow's nest watch in a storm, the man about to relieve would wait in the door to the forecastle alleyway while a wave dashed over the forecastle head. Then as the wave receded down the deck, timing it just right, he would sprint for the ladder up the mainmast to the crow's nest—the idea being to get there and start climbing before the next sea came over and caught him. The same thing, in reverse, then happened with the man he relieved who came down and then sprinted for the forecastle door.

But never mind this query and suggestion stuff! The important thing I want to say in this letter is how much I like your adaption and how grateful I am to you and Ford. I can see the grand picture it will be. In fact, I now visualize some of your effects a good deal more clearly than I remember the details of the plays on the stage!

But I wish you two weren't so goddamned non-commercial. Because I have a new love interest angle which would bring box office queues ten miles long. You remember the Yank-anchor scene? Well, have him go over the side down to the anchor. And what do you think

1. Nichols wrote the screenplay of the film *The Long Voyage Home*.
2. John Ford, who directed the film.

he finds caught on one of the flukes? A blonde! And by her panties! It seems she has fallen off a yacht—or something. Well, you have to admit this is a new way of getting the gal on the boat. And then— But hell, what's the use of talking to a coupla guys like you what ain't got no practical theatre sense. Go on and make a fine picture, if you're that nuts!

On this elevated spiritual plane I close. Mrs. O'Neill joins me in all best to you and Sean O'Fearna[3]—and again, much gratitude to you both.   Cordially,   Eugene O'Neill

P.S. I. May I keep the 'script or do you need it on the job?

P.S. II. By all means, fly up for a visit if you get a chance, but don't feel you ought to because your 'script needs explaining or because I want to wish any suggestions on you.

---

462 • TO BENNETT CERF.   TLS 2 pp. (Stationery headed: Tao House / Danville / Contra Costa County / California) [Columbia]

May the 16th 1940

Dear Bennett,   Your letter of May 13th just arrived. I heard from Nichols several days ago but the war news has had me so infuriated—and disintegrated, with all kinds of emotional conflicts tearing me apart—that I simply could not think about anything else.

Nichols' attitude, as expressed in a long letter, is that he really has no standing since a screen writer signs over all his rights in his script. It is not his property. It belongs entirely to the studio. When Wanger[1] put this publication up to him, he felt that Wanger had a right to his consent since he, Nichols, had signed a contract knowing exactly what it meant. The studio had dealt fairly with him, paid him well, and he felt he owed it that much loyalty. But he told Wanger it was really up to me to decide. Nichols, you see, is put on a hot spot. He wants to do whatever I want, while at the same time he knows he has no legal right whatever in the matter. He has to pass the buck to me.

Well, here's what I think—and I'm trying to keep what I believe to be the best interests of everyone concerned in mind—yours, Nichols', Wanger's, (I really have a lot of respect for Wanger), Ford's and my own. Now Nichols' script, as it is, was never meant to be read by anyone but screen technicians, as he states himself. Furthermore, it is not the final picture that will be seen on the screen. It is constantly added to or cut or readapted as the picture is being made. Now I believe—and so does Nichols—that, under these circumstances, a script to be published should represent in every detail the final picture, and should be rewritten a bit to make it something for the layman to read and not just a working script for technicians.

So my final stand is, if the script is rewritten along such lines—it wouldn't be any tremendous job—and *is* the final picture, I consent to its publication. Otherwise I don't. Because to publish a script which was never meant for publication, and is not the picture the public sees, seems to me a meaningless publicity stunt, for Wanger Productions, Inc.—and even as that, a mistaken hunch.

And there's still another angle. I'm no hog but it does occur to me, what do I get out of this? This script is an adaption of my play. Would the Theatre Guild ask me to let them have a play of mine published just to advertise their production? If they did, they would at least have the argument that I had a royalty interest in the production's financial success. But I have no such interest in Wanger's picture. I sold outright and I did not get any tremendous

3. Ford's real name was Sean Aloysius O'Feeney, but his family's name in Ireland was O'Fearna, which Ford's parents changed when they emigrated to America before he was born.

1. Walter Wanger, producer of *The Long Voyage Home,* who had proposed that Random House publish Nichols's screenplay.

price, either. I like Ford, and I like what I know of Wanger, but I haven't seen the final picture yet and I don't know whether I'll like it or not. Until I see exactly what has been done, I don't think Wanger has any right to ask me for concessions, free-gratis, which are not in my contract. Do you?

What you said about the war news: Yes, it is hard to keep on working. I'm not even trying now. I've found it's impossible. It doesn't seem of the slightest importance. The tragedy for France is what hits me most deeply. Next to the U.S. it is the country I know and love best. If ever the Germans drive to the country around Tours where Carlotta and I lived, we shall feel as if they were in our own garden.

My evening prayer now is, may every son of a bitch of a Nazi have his guts blown out!— and may every lousy politician in Washington who now plays politics with this crisis suffer the same in years to come! If democracy is wiped off the face of the earth it ought to have engraved on its tomb not "murdered by foreign dictators" but "murdered by its own politicians." Well, cheerio—and all our best! Gene

---

463 • TO ROBERT G. DAWES.[1] COPY 1 p. (Tao House / Danville / Contra Costa County / California) [Museum of City of N.Y.]

June the 3rd 1940

Dear Mr. Dawes, About the two *Monte Cristo* scripts, there seems to be a misunderstanding. They are both scripts of the plays as done by my father. Whatever differences there may be between them is due to changes and cuts he made at different times. The one at the Museum is the older script. I suggest, if you have a chance, you compare the version Mr. Clark will give you with the one in the Museum and see if you prefer the latter. If so, I will be grateful to Mrs. Seymour if she will accept this letter as my permission to you to copy the script there.

I appreciate your assurance that in the production you are planning the "Hoboken" angle will be prohibited. If I hadn't trusted you in that, I'd have refused permission. The deliberate kidding approach to old melodramas is pretty stale stuff now. It belongs to the radio comedian. *Monte Cristo*, produced as seriously as it used to be, will be amusing enough to a modern audience without any pointing for laughs. And, played seriously, it should also have an historic interest for the student of Americana, as the most successful romantic melodrama of its time, and one of the most successful plays of all time in America. For over twenty years my father took it all over this country, to big cities and small towns, in a period when nearly every place on the map had a theatre. The same people came to see it again and again, year after year. This is hard to believe, when you read the script now, even considering the period. The answer, of course, was my father. He had a genuine romantic Irish personality—looks, voice, and stage presence—and he loved the part. It was the picturesque vitality of his acting which carried the play. Audiences came to see James O'Neill in *Monte Cristo*, not *Monte Cristo*. The proof is, *Monte Cristo* has never had much success as a play at any time, either here or abroad, except for the one dramatization done in this country by him. He bought that outright for very little, because no one believed there was any money in it.

I'm afraid you'll find in producing it that *Monte Cristo* without a James O'Neill is just another old melodrama, better than most of them, but with little to explain how it could ever have had such an astonishing appeal for the American public.

All good wishes to you, Very sincerely, Eugene O'Neill

1. Professor of dramatic arts and speech at Ohio University, Athens, who was planning to do a production of *Monte Cristo*.

464 • TO BENNETT CERF.   TLS 1 p. (Stationery headed: Tao House / Danville / Contra Costa County / California) [Columbia]

June the 15th 1940

Dear Bennett,   Meant to reply to your letter of June 11th immediately but have been too damned depressed by the news of the debacle in France.[1]

I agree with you about the new three volume set. The only thing to do is to postpone it. Before your letter we had heard from Saxe about the evacuation of the bookstores by all paying customers. I leave the decision on when it will be best to publish the set entirely to your judgment.

Yes, I believe, too—remembering the last war—that there may be a crazy period of brief war and preparedness prosperity. And after that the deluge in which this country will be forced to become an American version of the Totalitarian State. It can't be helped. There seems no other way to preserve our security as a nation. And, of course, we can tell ourselves we are still a democracy, just as the Russians kid themselves Stalinism is the proletariat delivered from bondage into ideal liberty!

As for Mussolini, I have always believed that compared to him Al Capone was a good citizen and an honorable gentleman, and even Hitler an honest man. The Duce is a figure for contempt—and no one has a greater contempt for him than Hitler, as he will discover. Pah! A Wop ham and heel! I keep for him my favorite Arab curse: "May wild jackasses of the desert piss on the grave of his grandmother!"

All best from us,   As ever,   Gene

---

465 • TO GEORGE JEAN NATHAN.   TLS 2 pp. (Stationery headed: Tao House / Danville / Contra Costa County / California) [Cornell]

June the 15th 1940

Dear George,   It's too bad the jury duty stuff has upset your plans for a visit out here, but Carlotta and I will keep hoping you can make it at a later date. Any time you like will be all right for us, so do your damnedest to fit it in. We would sure love to have you here. There is so much to talk over, before all the world we've lived in vanishes in this debacle. And there isn't much time left.

You ask about my health. Well, now that swimming time is here again, and thanks to a series of shots I have been taking for low blood pressure, I am pretty fit again—physically. But mentally, spiritually, and creatively I feel like a dead clam—a nerve-ridden, dead clam, if you can imagine such a paradoxical bivalve. Haven't been able to write a line for the past couple of months, or take the slightest interest in work. After I finished *The Iceman Cometh* I started another non-Cycle play, "Day's Journey into Night"—not concerned with the present world's crisis, as the title might indicate, but the story of one day, 8 A.M. to midnight, in the life of a family of four—father, mother and two sons—back in 1912,—a day in which things occur which evoke the whole past of the family and reveal every aspect of its interrelationships. A deeply tragic play, but without any violent dramatic action. At the final curtain, there they still are, trapped within each other by the past, each guilty and at the same time

---

1. On June 14, 1940, German troops occupied Paris.

innocent, scorning, loving, pitying each other, understanding and yet not understanding at all, forgiving but still doomed never to be able to forget.

But hell, I'll tell you about it when I see you. What I started to say was, I finished the first draft of Act One (five acts in it) and then got physically washed up. On top of that, the debacle in Europe, and I became totally demoralized and have been unable to concentrate on anything but war news ever since. So there the play rests, and God knows when I'll go back to it. Hardly now, when Paris has fallen and we may soon hear they are fighting for Tours, which is like an old home town to us, as you know. Perhaps Le Plessis will be blown to pieces! This war is hitting us where we belong, so to speak.

And yet, what can one do as a person, remembering the United States first, beyond subscribing to Red Cross and Relief Funds, and what is that? And what can one do as an author who tries to remain an artist? Forget history, forget philosophy, forget the last war and what it did to this country, forget that it was the stupid, double-crossing greed and fear of democratic politicians—(particularly the swinish British Tories whom the O'Neill in me loathes, anyway)—that conspired with Hitler to create Nazi Germany, forget all this and everything else a free intelligence should remember, because one loves France in spite of its politicians? And then feel it one's duty to devote one's work to a hymn of hate? Well, although I hate Nazism as bitterly as anyone, I can never do that to my work.

But I envy authors who can honestly voice in work of genuine integrity, a belief in salvation through any sociological idealism. Or through Holy Wars. But such faiths are not for me. Or any other faith, I'm afraid, except a profound pessimism, convinced of the futility of all faiths, men being what they are. All I know is, if we must reinvent a God here in America, it had better be a God infinitely more noble than the State, democratic or otherwise. Or else!

My main selfish worry is that now the Cycle recedes farther and farther away, until I cannot imagine myself ever going back to it. It isn't that anything which is happening or may happen can affect the truth of the main theme of the Cycle. Quite the reverse! It proves it! It is I who am lacking, who have been affected to the point where I cannot believe the Cycle matters a damn, or could mean anything to any future I can foresee. And if I become finally convinced it is not in me to go on with it, I shall destroy all I have done so far, the completed plays and everything else down to the last note. If it cannot exist as the unique whole I conceived, then I don't want it to exist at all.

Well, it isn't considerate of me to be wishing this load of woe on you. I know you have enough troubles of your own right now. But the jury duty is a blessing in disguise, isn't it? — I mean, it compels you to forget war news for a while.

Love from us and here's hoping again we will have you here later on.　　As ever,　　Gene

---

466 • TO OONA O'NEILL.　　TLS 2 pp. (Stationery headed: Tao House / Danville / Contra Costa County / California) [Virginia]

July the third 1940

Dear Oona,　　I imagine you have come to the conclusion that I am the worst correspondent in the world! Well, it's true, I guess. But don't take my negligence in this respect to mean I haven't thought of you, because I have. A lot. And my intentions regarding letter writing have been of the best. I always promise myself that to-morrow without fail— But somehow to-morrow keeps on being to-morrow. Well, now it's to-day at last, anyway.

Shane told me when he was here that you probably would not return to Warrenton, so your news about that is no surprise. I have heard about Brearley.[1] It has a fine reputation and I hope you will stick there and not make any more changes.

I am delighted you came out so well in your exams because that means you must have done some hard work. That's the stuff! In these times, when the future is so uncertain for all of us, even a girl as young as you are must look ahead seriously and realize that she may have to face life as a young woman with no one able to help her—except herself!

I know Shane has told you all the news about this ranch so I won't go into that. There is nothing much that is new, anyway. Everything is about the same as when you were here. It's true that for a couple of months I was feeling pretty rotten. On top of finishing another play—which always leaves me worn out and sunk, anyway—I had an attack of low blood pressure and then got the flu, which didn't help matters. None of this was serious, however. Just darned uncomfortable and making me unfit for work. The war news, also, has affected my ability to concentrate on my job. With so much tragic drama happening in the world, it is hard to take the theatre seriously. But I am beginning to snap out of this demoralization. The only thing is go ahead and do your stuff, as long as you can, no matter what happens. But it is discouraging to feel that the Cycle I have been writing will have little meaning for the sort of world we will probably be living in by the time I finish it. A period of universal unrest and change is a bad period for serious creative work which is not propaganda of some sort. Not to add that conditions in the theatre will be so bad that it is doubtful if anyone will dare to produce it as it should be produced—and it *must* be done my way, or I won't let it be done at all.

Well, never mind that. Those are my worries, and there's nothing you can do about them, so why wish them on you.

To change to a pleasanter subject, we would be only too happy to have you come out here in the late summer, if you'd like to. It would have to be after September first, however, because we expect to be away a part of August, which part we don't know definitely yet. But how can you come, if you have to tutor? Much as I'd love to see you, I think the important thing, for your own sake, is to enter Brearley as well prepared for it as you possibly can be, and let nothing interfere with that.

Well, think this all over and write me when you return from Bermuda.

Carlotta sends her love to you. I think of you a lot and love you a lot and am very proud of you.   As ever,   Daddy

P.S. Yes, that Fats Waller "Your Feets Too Big" is a very, very beautiful thing!

---

467 • JOHN FORD.   WIRE 1 p. ([Tao House, Danville,.Contra Costa County, California]) [Indiana]

JULY 6, 1940

MY CONGRATULATIONS ON A GRAND DEEPLY MOVING AND BEAUTIFUL PIECE OF WORK. IT IS A GREAT PICTURE AND I HOPE YOU ARE AS PROUD OF IT AS I AM. CARLOTTA IS EQUALLY ENTHUSIASTIC. OUR ONE DISAPPOINTMENT TONIGHT WAS THAT WE MISSED SEEING YOU AGAIN. ALL CHEERS TO YOU AND MUCH GRATITUDE   GENE

1. After two years at a private school, Warrenton Country School, in Warrenton, Virginia, Oona O'Neill attended the Brearley School in New York City.

July 14th 1940

Dear Eugene,   Many thanks for sending us the review from the *American Journal of Philology*.[1] I am delighted to have it to add to the other things you've sent me. Although, generally speaking, it finds me densely ignorant, there is one point you make I wish could penetrate the skulls of modern critics—that in order to pass adequate aesthetic judgment a critic must first have some idea of what the author attempted to do. However, I suppose if any modern critic took such arduous mental pains he would be tossed out of the union and branded an escapist!

Your long letter of some weeks back should have been answered long ago, but ever since the Nazi blitzkrieg started I had sunk deeper and deeper into a profound pessimistic lethargy. I had had a spell of poor health before that, low blood pressure and two bouts of flu, and that didn't help. Until recently my mind was absolutely unable to concentrate on work or anything but war news. I hadn't written a line since I finished a play in January. The invasion of France hit me harder than I would ever have dreamed it could—an intensely emotional reaction inspired by memories of Le Plessis, and the years Carlotta and I spent there—a second country kind of loyalty. Well, that's futile now. The battle of Britain I can take more philosophically. Of course, if Ireland is invaded, I shall probably volunteer at once—or might if I was sure the great majority there wouldn't welcome the Nazis with howls of joy! Remembering the Black and Tan atrocities committed by the British not so many years ago, it would hardly be surprising. One might even call it justice.

I'm back on the job again now, and I can look back with great gratification on the play I finished in January. It is really one of the very best things I have ever done.

It's grand to know you are so satisfied with your past years work. Your description of what you did on the Ph.D. thesis sounds like one terrific job. I hope, in spite of what looks like a damned precarious regimented, war-demoralized near future in this country, that when it is published, it will receive the recognition it deserves. But I doubt if the work of any of us can escape being adversely affected in one way or another. I've had to put my Cycle on the shelf—and God knows when, if ever, I will take it up again. You simply cannot go on with a work which needs a long secure future to complete, and which must assume a world to which it could spiritually belong. Or at any rate, I cannot, the way I now feel.

So you went out to Gaylord Farms? I am glad to hear Doc. Lyman is still up and doing. He did a good job on me all right. I've had my troubles since then but never a vestige of anything connected with T.B.—although I wouldn't be surprised to hear that legend (literary and theatrical) has it that because I'm living in California I am slowly dying of it. T.B., since Keats, Stevenson and Camille, has been *such* a *romantic* ailment for whores and writers.

I think your hives must be hereditary. If so, even bad whiskey won't cure them, but suddenly when you're around forty, they will disappear for keeps for no reason whatever. That's what mine did.

Carlotta joins me in much love to you and Sally.   As ever,   Father

---

1. Review of Grace Lucile Beede's *Vergil and Aratus: A Study in the Art of Translation, American Journal of Philology* 61, no. 3 (1940):377–79.

July the 17th 1940

Dear Lawrence,   I've just rec'd from Dick Madden a clipping from the *Times* about a new play of mine called *The Iceman Cometh* and I want to tell you it's true, more or less, although just how the report leaked out I can't guess. As far as I know, only three people have read it. It is one of the two ideas for plays outside the Cycle I mentioned having that time you phoned—and long before that in one of my letters. Reason I haven't written you any more about it is that I judged from your last two letters there was a chance you and Armina would be out here. Then you could read it here. The same applies to Terry. She said in her last letter she might be out this summer.

One reason I haven't sent you or Terry a script is that there are only two in existence. I have one and I sent the other to Bennett Cerf to lock in the Random House safe for safekeeping—but not for publication. Don't blame Bennett for not telling you or Terry. I made him promise to keep it dark from everyone, bar none. Frankly, I did not want you to see it yet—in New York. I was afraid you would want to produce it right away and I don't want the strain of any production now. There are other good reasons against it, too. On the other hand, if you or Terry happened out this way, as you thought you might, then I could give you the script to read with the proviso that production was out for the present, and do all my explaining why at the same time. But the idea of trying to do all this in letters simply had me stopped. Hence the secrecy. To tell the truth, like anyone else with any imagination, I have been absolutely sunk by this damned world debacle. The Cycle is on the shelf, and God knows if I can ever take it up again because I cannot foresee any future in this country or anywhere else to which it could spiritually belong.

Well, to hell with that. I'm writing this to explain my past few months secrecy re the completion of *The Iceman Cometh,* and to say if you and Armina, Terry and Oliver, want to read this opus you can get the script from Bennett. I'm writing to release him from his pledge of secrecy as far as you and Terry are concerned. But give it back to Cerf to lock up in the safe afterwards, and *please don't* let anyone else see it. Remember only two scripts exist and it's no time to let too many people, even in the Guild, really know about it yet. And forget about any production.

I'm working again on something—not the Cycle—after a lapse of several months spent with an ear glued to the radio for war news. You can't keep a hop head off his dope for long!

The crushing of France hit Carlotta and me hard for sentimental reasons in addition to the larger aspects of the disaster. When Tours was lost we felt almost as badly as if Danville, California, had fallen.

We regret you and Armina didn't make it out here. Keep on trying! And love from us to you both.   As ever,   Gene

P.S. Let Terry read this, too, will you? I sure am economical about letters, and I owe her one!

P.P.S. I particularly don't want Lunt of your Committee to get hold of the script. You will remember what Fontanne did with the *Strange Interlude* script and the mess that caused.

470 • TO CARLOTTA MONTEREY O'NEILL.   ALS 1 p. (Stationery headed: Tao House / Danville / Contra Costa County / California) [Yale]

July 22nd 1940

Darling Wife: Here's congratulating myself for the blessing of you these eleven years!

Time falters, civilization disintegrates, values perish, the old beauty becomes a gutter slut, the world explodes, the income tax rises, the years grow heavy on us and Blemie—

But still! There is love that does not die, and there is your ✴ which is the most beautiful and charming ✴ in the world—so what the hell!   Your   Gene

---

471 • TO LAWRENCE LANGNER.   TLS 1 p. (Stationery headed: Tao House / Danville / Contra Costa County / California) [Yale]

August the 11th 1940

Dear Lawrence,   Many thanks for your letter regarding *The Iceman Cometh*. I'm damned pleased you liked it so well. Personally, I love it! And I'm sure my affection is not wholly inspired by nostalgia for the dear dead days "on the bottom of the sea," either! I have a confident hunch that this play, as drama, is one of the best things I've ever done. In some ways, perhaps *the* best. What I mean is, there are moments in it that suddenly strip the secret soul of a man stark naked, not in cruelty or moral superiority, but with an understanding compassion which sees him as a victim of the ironies of life and of himself. Those moments are for me the depth of tragedy, with nothing more that can possibly be said.

However. I'd better not start a dissertation on my idea of what modern tragedy should express or this letter will become a young book.

Remember I wrote you that Armina was to read the play, too, if she wants to. It's not a woman's play, superficially speaking, but there are some who won't let the surface keep them from feeling what's beneath it, and I know Armina is one.

No word from Terry yet. We are still hoping she may turn up.

My enthusiastic congratulations on your idea for a National Inventor's Council.[1] And I mean, enthusiastic! It strikes me as the best idea I've heard since preparedness became the critical issue. I hope to God the thrice-damned and accursed dogs of politicians don't snarl it up for you in their stupid, contemptible, partisan racket!

Love from us to you and Armina.   As ever,   Gene

---

472 • TO THORNTON WILDER.[1]   TLS 1 p. (Stationery headed: Tao House / Danville / Contra Costa County / California) [Yale]

September the 29th 1940

Dear Mr. Wilder,   By all means! I have had for many years a deep admiration for Joyce and it will be a privilege to sign the letter of recommendation. He deserves the Nobel and should have had it long ago instead of some of us others who were lucky.

---

1. Langner was one of the organizers of the National Inventors Council of the U.S. Department of Commerce and served as its secretary from 1940–58.

1. Wilder (1897–1975), dramatist and novelist, among whose works are the Pulitzer Prize winning novel *The Bridge of San Luis Rey* (1927) and the Pulitzer Prize winning plays *Our Town* (1938) and *The Skin of Our Teeth* (1942).

It will be a favor if you will tell Padraic and Mary Colum for me that, if Joyce does not receive the award, and they wish to raise funds to help him, I will regard it a further privilege to contribute the most I can.

Thank you for your kind word to me in your letter to Mrs. O'Neill. I appreciate it the more because of my sincere respect for the fine work you have done.   Very sincerely yours,   Eugene O'Neill

---

473 • TO SHANE O'NEILL.   TL 1 pp. (Stationery headed: Tao House / Danville / Contra Costa County / California) [Virginia]

[October 25, 1940]

Dear Shane,   Many thanks for your birthday letter. The present you mention hasn't arrived yet. I am looking forward to it, and here's my gratitude in advance. Whatever it may be, I will be delighted to have it as a proof of your remembrance.

Not having heard from you in so long, I concluded that you didn't want to write because you could not report that you had made any step along the road to independence, but were going along in the same old rut. It's good to know you have a job now and I hope this means that you really have started to find yourself—and own yourself! I don't want to do any more advising. I said all that can be said when you were out here, and I hope it didn't go in one ear and out the other. As far as I am concerned, it is now up to you. You've got to find the guts in yourself to take hold of your own life. No one can do it for you, and no one can help you. You have got to go on alone, without help, or it won't mean anything to you. You will be twenty-one in a few days. It will be a good day for you to spend a few hours alone having a frank talk with yourself, and considering this and that and the other. A better day than New Years to make some good resolutions—and then keep them!

I'm sorry to report the record you and Oona sent arrived broken. You didn't pack it tightly enough, and it must have received a jolt en route that cracked it in half. But many thanks, just the same.

I agree that a change to apprentice iron worker would be a good deal more interesting work than carpentry. My opinion hasn't changed that a shipyard job where you could eventually work into ship designing, in which your talent for drawing would be an asset, might be *the* right thing for you. What happened to that small shipyard job you were promised which you wrote me about months ago—the one where the Navy tugs were to be built? Did it quit on you—or did you quit on it?

Have you ever thought of enlisting in the Navy? A couple of years in that branch of the service might do you a lot of good. You can learn any one of a lot of trades while you're serving, if you want to learn one. And I know you'd like the Navy a lot better than the Army, into which you are liable to be drafted within the next couple of years. You better do a lot of serious thinking on this matter.[1]

---

474 • TO OONA O'NEILL.   TLS 1 p. (Stationery headed: Tao House / Danville / Contra Costa County / California) [Virginia]

October the 25th 1940

Dear Oona,   As I've just written Shane, the record you sent arrived broken. Too bad. It was not packed tightly enough and some bang it received cracked it in half. Was it intended

---

1. The rest of this letter is missing.

as your present on my birthday? Your letter is vague on that point. Anyway, many thanks for sending it.

It is good to learn you like the new school so well. I hope you will stay in this one.

The Long Voyage Home is an exceptional picture with no obvious Hollywood hokum or sentimental love bilge in it. I like very few pictures but I did like this one. John Ford, who directed it, is one of the best directors in the game—and, incidentally, a most likable man personally. And Dudley Nichols, who wrote the screen adaption, also did a good job. Between them, they managed to keep the spirit of my plays in spite of the changes they had to make—bringing the story up to the present war, etc.—and the handicaps under which everyone in the picture business has to work.

Shane wrote me he has seen the picture and liked it. Did you go with him?

I am working hard and feeling fine. We had our first good rain since last April today. But the real rainy season won't start until December. After that there is plenty, and I don't look forward to it. However, for all the year round climate you can't beat this part of the country, so I am not kicking.

Carlotta joins me in much love to you.   As ever,   Daddy

---

475 • TO KENNETH MACGOWAN.   TLS 3 pp. (Stationery headed: Tao House / Danville / Contra Costa County / California) [Yale]

November the 29th 1940

Dear Kenneth,   Many thanks for the copy of your "open letter."[1] I'm damned glad you sent it because I quit clipping bureaus many years back—except foreign, to keep cases on production over there (when there was an over there!)—and I might never have seen it.

I like it a lot. I agree with you on the general excellence of the picture and with the exceptions you take to that general excellence. The opening sex wallop of Hollywood bumboat tarts rubbing their prats agin the tropic palms left me faintly nauseated. And there were a few other touches that struck me as not belonging. But they are not important and I haven't, and wouldn't, mention them to Ford or anyone but you, because the picture as a whole is so damned good, and such a courageous thing for a producer to do, especially at this time.

Nichols' work, as you say, is a grand job. He deserves equal credit with Ford. And the photography is splendid. All in all, I was enormously pleased.

So much for the picture part of your open letter. The memory of the old P.P. days part moved me to a sad nostalgia. There was a theatre then in which I knew I belonged, one of guts and idealism. Now I feel out of the theatre. I dread the idea of production because I know it will be done by people who have really only one standard left, that of Broadway success. I know beforehand that I will be constantly asked, as I have been asked before, to make stupid compromises for that end. The fact that I will again refuse to make them is no consolation. The fact that I will have the final say on everything is also no consolation. The fact that I like these people personally and the relationship is always friendly and considerate, is no consolation. The big fact is that any production must be made on a plane, and in an atmosphere to which neither I nor my work belongs in spirit, nor want to belong; that it is a job, a business within the Showshop, a long, irritating, wearing, nervous, health-destroying ordeal, with no creative enthusiasm behind it, just another Broadway opening—the Old Game, the game we used to defy in the P.P. but which it is impossible for me to defy now,

---

1. Macgowan apparently had sent an open letter to a publication praising *The Long Voyage Home*.

except in my writing, because there is no longer a theatre of true integrity and courage and high purpose and enthusiasm. There are just groups, or individuals, who put on plays in New York commercial theatres. The idea of an Art Theatre is more remote now, I think, than it was way back in the first decade of this century, before the Washington Square Players or the P.P. were ever dreamed of.

The above is not the usual beef of fifty-two years old against the decadence of the times. It seems to me plain simple fact. After all, the times *are* obviously decadent, and the condition of the theatre reflects them. To have an ideal now, except as a slogan in which neither you nor anyone else believes but which you use out of old habit to conceal a sordid aim, is to confess oneself a fool who cannot face the High Destiny of Man!

The above all sounds much too pessimistic. I don't mean too pessimistic about the times. One couldn't be that, God knows. But about my own mood. So long as I shun production and live here with Carlotta, doing my job of writing plays, I rate myself the most fortunate of men. Especially since I am certain the two plays I've done outside the Cycle in the past year and a half belong among the very best things I've ever written. In some ways I believe they are better than anything I've done before. The last of them *Long Day's Journey Into Night* I finished quite recently. It isn't even typed yet.

Would you like to read *The Iceman Cometh?* If so, I have a script I can send you. I certainly want you to read it because I know it will interest you. But pick your own time. If you are being harassed and overworked right now so that you're worn out at the end of each day, I know you won't want to tackle it. And I wouldn't want you to, because it's long and it needs close to three hours' concentration. I want you to read it when you can give all to it, so to speak. Which I know is what you would wish. I've been hoping you might be able to pay us a visit and stay a couple of days. Then when you were rested I would have dumped the script in your lap.

It's rotten luck about your Five Year Plan, and I realize from my own experience that it is hard to take it philosophically as a part of a general fate which everyone shares. Me, I've abandoned the idea of future security, and stopped thinking beyond a few months ahead, because even if this country escapes with the best break on the inevitable, we are all certain to be taxed out of a great part of whatever income we get. Even tax exempt securities won't be exempt in a few years. They can't be, and ought not to be.

The best news in your letter is that you hope to quit Hollywood within a year. I don't want to butt in with any unsolicited opinion but it seems to me you ought to do that—at any cost, even if you have to gamble on the future, and use part of your capital each year. After all, capital can no longer be regarded as capital in any security meaning it used to have, while individual freedom is becoming more valuable and rare every day, especially when one is over fifty and the horizon begins to creep up on you. "Shoot the piece" should be the motto of all us Fiftyites—shoot it before it's too late!

Well, I began this feeling I owed you two letters but it looks now as if I felt I owed you five! That's what comes from writing trilogies and cycles. You get so damned long-winded.

Make yourself come up for a visit, darn you! It would do you good. And do me good. Tell the bastards you're sick or something! After all, it's only two hours or so by plane.

Much love from us.   As ever,   Gene

476 • TO WILLIAM AGAR.[1]   TLS 1 p. (Stationery headed: Tao House / Danville / Contra Costa County / California) [Princeton]

February the 5th 1941

Dear Mr. Agar,   You are right. The appeal to President De Valera is *not* easy to sign. I have fought it out with myself and I find I cannot sign it. My final conviction is that we Irish Americans owe it to the Irish people not to attempt to influence their decision by any means whatsoever. It is they who will be massacred by German bombers if they commit this act of war. If we could promise our country would fight as an ally of Ireland and defend her independence we might have a right to make this appeal, but as things are I feel we have no right.

I hope you can believe that it is also hard for me not to sign this appeal. I appreciate the points you make. I agree with most of them. No dead hand from the past bothers me, although I was reared with a hymn of hate for England the predominant lullaby. It is simply a matter of conscience.

All good wishes to you.   Very sincerely,   Eugene O'Neill

---

477 • TO RALPH E. WHITNEY.   TLS 1 p. (Stationery headed: Tao House / Danville / Contra Costa County / California) [Private]

March 11th 1941

Dear Mr. Whitney,   Your letter, forwarded from Random House, has just arrived.

I made one voyage as an A.B. on the American Line in the summer of 1911. It was a longer experience than the usual voyage, however, because the *New York,* on which I shipped, was laid up for repairs in Southampton and I worked on her there for several weeks before being transferred to the crew of the *Philadelphia* for the return trip.

The atmosphere of *The Hairy Ape* does not derive from any one Line or ship. The connection with the American Line is that the leading character of the play was suggested in part by a friend of mine, a Liverpool Irish stoker, who lived, when ashore, at the same waterfront dump—Jimmie the Priest's—that I did, and who was on the *New York* when I sailed on her. But during the time I knew him he had also shipped on Cunard and White Star liners—even on ye old Fall River Line! He committed suicide later by jumping off a liner in mid-ocean—to the bewilderment of everyone who knew him, for there never lived a more self-assured, self-contented guy, seemingly. As for the terrific heat driving him temporarily nuts, which sometimes happened with stokers in those days, that was hard to believe of him because he had always proudly thrived on it. I can't remember now whether it was an American Line ship he took the last jump from or not. It well may have been.

Well, this isn't much information for you but I hope it's enough to serve your purpose. Incidentally, I still have my A.B. discharge certificate from the *Philadelphia*—one of my most treasured possessions, since it is the only memento of my sailor days that didn't get lost, strayed or stolen.

All good wishes to you.   Very sincerely,   Eugene O'Neill

---

1. Agar (1894–1972), geologist and worker in the cause of international peace who at this time was directing publicity for Fight For Freedom, Inc., and had asked O'Neill to sign an open letter to Prime Minister Eamon De Valera of the Irish Free State urging him to bring his country into the war and thus end it more quickly.

478 • TO HELEN HAYES.[1]   WIRE 1 p. ([Tao House, Danville, Contra Costa County, California]) [Lincoln Center]

MARCH 17, 1941

MY GRATEFUL CONGRATULATIONS FOR YOUR SPLENDID PERFORMANCE IN THE STRAW. DESPITE ITS FAULTS I HAVE ALWAYS HAD A SENTIMENTAL SOFT SPOT FOR THIS PLAY WHICH NO ONE LIKED WHEN IT WAS PRODUCED ON THE STAGE AND SO I APPRECIATE ALL THE MORE YOUR MAKING IT LIVE OVER THE AIR. ALL GOOD WISHES AND THANK YOU FOR YOUR KIND WORD ABOUT ME =
EUGENE ONEILL

---

479 • TO SHANE O'NEILL.   TLS 2 pp. (Stationery headed: Tao House / Danville / Contra Costa County / California) [Yale]

April 18th 1941

Dear Shane,   Your letter is comprehensible to me only if I assume that you have decided to forget every word I said to you when you were here a year ago. And it is pretty evident by what you haven't done in the past year that you did not think any of my advice worth taking. Well, that is your privilege and I am not questioning your right to decide for yourself, but on the other hand you have no license to ask my help as long as you continue to live as you are living.

There is no use in my repeating all I said to you last year. You certainly remember the points I emphasized, because I know damned well you realized then that what I said was true. It is even truer now, considering the disastrous way the world crisis has developed since then. That's one thing I can't understand about your letter. You seem to have no realization of what is going on in the world. You write as if these were normal times, in which a young man of twenty-one could decide exactly what job he should choose as offering him the pleasantest prospect for a normal peacetime career. Don't you know the country will almost certainly be in the war soon? Don't you know that those who became twenty-one since the draft law passed will soon be included in the draft? Don't you know that if this country gets into the war, it will probably go on for years, and that no one can possibly predict what conditions will be like even a year from now? The one sure thing is that for years to come the big opportunities for young men will be in one of the branches of the United States Service or in the industries directly connected with the Defense Program.

Until you show you have some conception that all this affects you—as it affects me and every person in this country—and that you are making some decision which faces realistically the crisis we are all in, I simply don't know what to say to you. But I am absolutely certain that planning to start a career in the movies at this time is no answer to anything. In fact, at any time, I would not regard it as an answer for you. The farther you stay away from any job that has to do with the theatre, the better off you will be. And I certainly will not give you a letter to Kenneth Macgowan. It wouldn't do you the slightest good, anyway. I happen to know something about Kenneth's job. It is extremely specialized and he has nothing to do with hiring anyone.

What happened to the job you were to get in Texas? Or was that just a phony tale?

1. Hayes (1900–), actress, whose "Helen Hayes Theater" broadcast excerpts from *The Straw* on March 16, 1941.

I don't like to pan you but it is a big disappointment that after all the talk a year ago you have done so little to make yourself independent.

My health has been extremely poor during the past winter. It was the lowest I've felt since I was laid up in '37. The fact that the weather has been lousy, with record rains, had something to do with it. And, naturally, like everyone else with any sense or imagination, I'm worried as hell about the future—which doesn't help any.

Carlotta joins me in love to you and please give our love to Oona. I owe her a letter and will write before long.   As ever,   Father

---

480 • TO EUGENE O'NEILL, JR.   TLS 2 pp. (Stationery headed: Tao House / Danville / Contra Costa County / California) [Yale]

April the 28th 1941

Dear Eugene,   I am delighted to learn about the promotion. My sincerest congratulations! It is a deep pleasure and pride and satisfaction to know you are progressing steadily and that your fine work is appreciated. Work you know is your work, which belongs to you! That's the best thing about it. It seems to me I so rarely meet anyone who *knows* that the work he does *is* his work, a part of him, and not an extraneous support for his living. Even with people who are extremely successful, I feel this. Their work is an exterior job, not an inner necessity. They may possess a pleasant affection for it but no love and pain. I feel you love yours—in its deeper aspects, I mean, the devotion to knowledge and culture.

I hope you will be able to come out here this summer. There are a lot of things I'd like to say—and hear. I'm a louse not to have written you in so long. I meant particularly to tell you ages ago how deeply moved I was by the letter you wrote way back around my last birthday. "Deeply moved" is right, not merely words! It was a grand letter to get from a son. I kept waiting for a mood in which I could answer as it should be answered, but the mood continued consistently indigo all winter. Poor health plus world crisis pessimism—but mostly poor health—the lowest prolonged period since my crack-up in '37. The weather was no help. For three months or more it rained four out of every five days, or more, and the flu epidemic closed the schools, etc.

This health business wouldn't bother me so much if it did not affect work. I've been able to get little done since last December except a lot of notes and outlines. However, the stride seems to be coming back now, with sun and warmth. And my work is one of the few things I don't feel depressed over. In the past two years I've written two plays I'm really enthusiastic about: *The Iceman Cometh* and *Long Day's Journey Into Night*. They will rank among the finest things I've ever done, I know. But they—particularly the second—are emphatically not plays I want produced or published at this crisis-preoccupied time. They could not be understood. Not their real meaning or truth. *The Iceman Cometh* might be a big success, if done well, but it would be for its least significant merits and its finest values would be lost, or dismissed because the present psychology would not want to face them. Moreover, conditions in the New York theatre are a mess, from all I hear, and due to grow increasingly worse. My health isn't up to bucking the strain of that kind of battle, even if there were no other reasons for remaining unproduced. So I'm staying patly aloof, and ignoring all Theatre Guild persuasions.

In addition to the two plays, the Cycle, although on the shelf, is still very much alive. I constantly make notes of fresh angles I get on individual plays, or on the nine as a whole, and these will be a big help when I return to it. I've also written detached outlines for four new plays outside the Cycle (one, a comedy)[1] which look damned good to me. So you see, crisis or no crisis, I don't feel blocked at all in my work, no matter what my intuitions are about its lack of timeliness! Bum health is my only real block—the periods when there just isn't the vitality for the grind of intensive day after day labor. When you live through the play you write, you have to have a lot of reserve life on tap.

I enclose a check for your birthday. Again, much paternal pride and congratulations! And love to you and Sally.   As ever,   Father

---

481 • TO ARTHUR HOBSON QUINN.   TLS 2 pp. (Stationery headed: Tao House / Danville / Contra Costa County / California) [Pennsylvania]

April 30th 1941

Dear Mr. Quinn,   Although I was never directly influenced by Wagner's theory of the union of the arts, I was undoubtedly greatly influenced indirectly through Strindberg and Nietzsche. I was also in my formative years an enthusiastic admirer of the French symbolists and pre-symbolists Sister Vincentia mentions—still am, for that matter. So I would say Sister Vincentia's idea is sound as far as I am concerned. The outline of her thesis[1] is extremely interesting. It will be a favor if you tell her how impressed I am and give her my good wishes. I mean, of course, if you think it would be any encouragement to her. Anyone who can take such an intelligent and imaginative interest in the arts deserves every encouragement— particularly in these tragic days.

You won't see a new play of mine soon, I'm afraid, although I have written six in the past six years. Four of them are the first four in my nine-play cycle, Tale of Possessors Self-Dispossessed. The individual titles of these first four plays are: "Greed of the Meek," "And Give Me Death," A Touch of the Poet and More Stately Mansions. They take the cycle from 1775 to 1843. The next play, "The Calms of Capricorn,"[2] begins in 1857. I've done some dialogue on it but not much. When I got that far, around two years ago, I found I had gone stale. So I decided to take a vacation by writing a play which had nothing to do with the cycle. Not long after that the war broke out, and with the world exploding into revolution it seemed imperative to devote all my energy to writing some plays I had long wanted to write which could be finished, and did not depend, like the cycle, on years of dubious and incalculable future.

I've written two plays since then, The Iceman Cometh and Long Day's Journey Into Night. Finished them and am now writing another.[3] I wouldn't call any of the four cycle plays I have mentioned finally finished. Three of them are oversize—really double length plays like Strange Interlude. Which is all right, except that they get that way in spite of me and my plans for them, and I don't want them to be!

The two non-cycle plays I am most enthusiastic about. They are, I am sure, two of the finest plays I have ever written.

As for production, I never intended to permit any of the cycle plays to be given until I had finished all nine. And I don't want the non-cycle ones done now. It is no time for them.

---

1. "The Visit of Malatesta"; the other three probably are "The Last Conquest," Hughie, and "Blind Alley Guy." See Eugene O'Neill at Work: Newly Released Ideas for Plays, pp. 298–370. Of the four, only the one-act Hughie—first produced in 1958—was completed.

1. Sister M. Vincentia Burns, "The Wagnerian Theory of Art and Its Influence on the Drama of Eugene O'Neill," Ph.D. diss., University of Pennsylvania, 1943.

2. The Calms of Capricorn: A Play Developed from O'Neill's Scenario by Donald Gallup, with a Transcription of the Scenario (New Haven: Ticknor & Fields, 1982).

3. Probably Hughie.

Another reason is my health which has been poor since my serious general crack-up in '36–'37—especially poor this last winter. New York, casting, rehearsing, all the job of producing, has always ruined me nervously and thrown me off work for months, success or no success. At this time—when perhaps there is so little time left for the free writer even in this country—it seems the only wisdom is to concentrate on what is most important and get as much as I can write written. Producing can always wait. It needs me—I would not trust anyone to produce in my absence—but it could do without me. If I were dead, it could still go on. So why risk health, which I need for writing, on the relatively unimportant? At any rate, that is the way I look at it now.

Well, I have presumed on your much appreciated interest in my work to wish a heap of information on you. To paraphrase a slogan of that Belle of the Twenties, the late Texas Guinan, "Never give a playwright a break or he'll take advantage of you."

Always, all good wishes to you.   Very sincerely,   Eugene O'Neill

---

482 • TO LAWRENCE LANGNER.   TLS 2 pp. (Stationery headed: Tao House / Danville / Contra Costa County / California) [Yale]

[c. July 10, 1941]

Dear Lawrence,   Your two notes just arrived. There isn't a chance in a million you can interest Lionel Barrymore in an *Ah, Wilderness!* revival, but I am glad you wrote him. You never can tell.

No, I don't think Cohan is an all wrong idea. On the contrary. A revival with him would have real sentimental audience value. Trouble is, he never would know the lines now. It was bad enough for him before. It would be a completely ad lib performance—but so would Barrymore's, probably, if he tackled it.

Don't think I ruled out Huston and Carey[1] absolutely. All I meant was that there could be better choices from a popular, color standpoint. I'm going to drop a line to Bob Sisk and see if he has any hunch on what picture personality would be right for the part—and might be willing. I'll let you know if he has any ideas.

Here's a hunch on another revival possibility. I've just received a letter from Madden saying David Selznick is starting a six or eight week season at the Lobero Theatre, Santa Barbara. He wants *"Anna Christie"* for week with Ingrid Bergman as Anna. If she makes hit, he wants to bring play to San Francisco for several weeks. All this, I suppose, is to build up Ingrid. However, who knows, she may be fine. It's hard for any capable actress to be really bad as Anna. I suggest you give this a thought—and, if possible, have someone out here look over her Santa Barbara performance for you. I specify Santa Barbara because I've asked terms for San Francisco which may stop Selznick on that idea. I don't intend to let him use *"Anna Christie"* as a build-up vehicle for Ingrid without paying for it. But if she is good a New York revival with her might fit with your season, and Selznick might be eager to cooperate. If this strikes you as something, talk with Madden and he can keep you in touch with developments.

Don't forget *Desire Under The Elms*. There, I think, if you can get the right woman—and Huston—is a good chance for a real hit revival.   Love from us,   Gene

P.S. A 14 inch depth for boxes would be better—12 inch isn't enough for two of the scripts. Many thanks! It is damned kind of you to trouble about this.

1. Harry Carey (1878–1947), actor, who played Nat Miller in the 1941 Theatre Guild revival of *Ah, Wilderness!*

483 • TO RICHARD MADDEN.   TLS 1 p. (Stationery headed: Tao House / Danville / Contra Costa County / California) [Yale]

July the 27th 1941

Dear Dick,   In reply to your letter of the 23rd, re *"Anna Christie,"* this is the first time you have told me that Cheryl Crawford[1] was interested in a New York revival with Bergman. It was I who suggested to Langner that this might be a possibility for the Guild revival season. This being the case, I think you ought to tell Langner just what the situation is and have Crawford talk it over with the Guild. Langner was going to have someone see Bergman in the part out here—and decide on the basis of how good an "Anna" Bergman acts.

Whether Crawford produces it, or the Guild, or the two in combination, the terms are $1500.00 advance, 10% of gross and minimum guarantee of $500.00—

Re *The Fountain*, you are right in thinking I would not be interested in preparing a libretto, no matter how good Weill's and Anderson's[2] suggestions might be. Couldn't do the job, even if I had nothing else to do. It's not my racket and I know nothing about it. And long ago I lost whatever interest I ever had in *The Fountain*. I couldn't work on it now. So thank Anderson and Weill for me but tell them it can't be done. I warned you that getting Anderson into it wouldn't turn out. In his place, I know I wouldn't be interested.

Regarding a possible librettist, I suggest you call up Russel Crouse—tell him I asked you to—and ask him who he thinks would do a good job on it. He knows, or used to know, everyone in that line and he might have a damned good idea which you could pass on to September.

Re *Ah, Wilderness!*—radio, is Du Pont now the only possibility? Not so long ago, you wrote me there was still a chance of General Electric wanting it for Mazda bulbs. Is this out, now?

You have heard from Sam Lyons that he wired from Los Angeles a new Mayer-*Hairy Ape* offer. Still not good enough. Too little cash down. How come it is Sam and not Arthur Lyons I hear from? Is Sam now in charge of the Coast office?   All best,   Gene

---

484 • TO THERESA HELBURN.   TLS 2 pp. (Stationery headed: Tao House / Danville / Contra Costa County / California) [Yale]

July the 29th 1941

Dear Terry,   Apologies for not replying to your letter sooner. It wasn't that it didn't interest me. I am enthusiastic about your idea for a film of *Mourning Becomes Electra* with Hepburn and Bette Davis and Pascal[1] directing. However, I doubt if any of the major companies will dare touch it. The fools! They could easily handle the brother-sister thing in the last part by suggestion, as father-daughter was done in *The Barretts of Wimpole Street* picture—that is, if the Hays office is the obstacle.

Our one chance for a film of *Mourning Becomes Electra* is the independent companies—a good reliable independent—with us gambling on a moderate cash payment and a percent-

---

1. Crawford (1902–1987), Broadway producer and director.
2. Kurt Weill (1900–1950), German composer and playwright, and Maxwell Anderson, who collaborated on several musical plays, including *Knickerbocker Holiday* (1938) and *Lost in The Stars* (1949), were apparently interested in adapting *The Fountain* into a musical.

1. Gabriel Pascal (1894–1954), who directed the 1941 film of Shaw's *Major Barbara*.

age of gross, less distribution cost. There seems to be a lot stirring among independents now. Two are dickering with me for the rights of *The Hairy Ape* and *Desire Under The Elms* and it looks as if both deals might go through. *The Long Voyage Home,* as you know, was an independent film, done by Ford and Cooper, and Walter Wanger in on it to some degree. In spite of it being a no plot, no sex, no slop, honest picture, it has made good money for all concerned—not Hollwood wow millions but good money just the same. This on the word of Bob Sisk who took pains to find out what results were.

A Mr. September has been doing a lot of dickering with Madden regarding your notion of a couple of years ago, a musical of *The Fountain.* For Radio City theatre. But I hear now his backers have gone bad on him and the deal is off. Why don't you consider this again? Not as a Guild affair, necessarily, but as something the Guild would have an interest in with someone else putting up the money. *The Fountain,* with right music and beautiful setting, done well, would be shrewd showmanship right now, I think (and I can be objective about it because I don't give a damn about *The Fountain* as a play). The musical could be perfect escape medium with a little mysticism, a little poetry, a little nice melancholy, and a little romance. Also a sound story. Also the Latin-American angle. Give this a thought.

When thinking of a woman for *Desire Under The Elms* revival, think of Beatrix Lehmann, the English actress—and tell Lawrence to. She is rated the best actress in England and made a great hit in the part in London two years ago—and toured the provinces successfully in it afterward, war or no war. She also made a great hit as Lavinia in *Mourning Becomes Electra.* She must be good from all reports—exceptionally talented. She could get the right New England accent in rehearsal, I am sure. And there are Anglo-American angles which might make her a big asset right now. The critics would feel Allied-bound to give her the Big Hello, if you know what I mean. Let me know what you think.

It's true I'm in an "exciting rhythm" of having had a lot of good ideas for new stuff in the past six months, but not of getting down to hard concentrated work on any of it. The flesh has been weak. Not long after Lawrence and Armina were here I faded out to a state where I could hardly swim—and that's pretty bad because swimming comes easier for me than walking. Now I'm getting shots of thiamin and they seem to do the trick and I feel somewhat alive again.

Love from us to you and Oliver.   As ever,   Gene

P.S. Carlotta will drop in on a Bergman-*"Anna Christie"* matinee in Frisco, tell Lawrence. It's too much for me. I couldn't sit through it without getting heebie-jeebies and wondering why the hell I ever wrote it—even if Joan of Arc came back to play "Anna."

---

485 • TO LAWRENCE LANGNER.   TLS 1 p. (Stationery headed: Tao House / Danville / Contra Costa County / California) [Yale]

August the 7th 1941

Dear Lawrence,   Frisco reaction to Bergman-*"Anna Christie"* appears enthusiastic from all I can gather. Carlotta will see it Saturday next.

Let's settle on Carey for *Ah, Wilderness!* More I think of it, more I believe he is best available.

Here's a suggestion from Bob Sisk which I think is red hot: A revival of *The Hairy Ape* with Victor McLaglen as Yank and *John Ford* to direct it. Ford could do a grand job, I think— if he would, and Bob thinks he could be persuaded. Also he has proved he can get the best out of McLaglen and make him a fine actor. Remember *The Informer* film?

The Hairy Ape is ripe for revival. It is, spiritually speaking, a surprisingly prophetic play. Not superficially, about labor conditions, although the C.I.O. is offspring of the I.W.W. One Big Union idea (which no one seems to realize), but about Man, the state we are all in of frustrated bewilderment. Also we have certainly failed to "belong" and then unlocked the cage and turned the Gorilla loose. Etc. Etc. The symbol and real meaning of the play would be much clearer now than when it was done. Very few got it then. And I think its Expressionistic treatment (sets, etc.) would be better understood, and not considered as a stunt, as in 1922.

Also, the fact that the play dates in its details, goes back in time, is all to the good. It gives an audience perspective. They can see the real play which is dateless, without any pro or con C.I.O. or Communistic or Republican party prejudices, if you get me.

I'm enthusiastic about this. Give it your best thought, you and Terry.   As ever,   Gene

---

486 • TO LAWRENCE LANGNER.   TLS 2 pp. (Stationery headed: Tao House / Danville / Contra Costa County / California) [Yale]

August 24th 1941

Dear Lawrence,   Your idea of Tallulah[1] for *Desire Under The Elms* is brilliant and I am all for it. She would be grand. And Bickford[2] is a fine notion for *The Hairy Ape*. I'm sure he would do a good job. As for your doubts about Ford, from all I've heard of him—and from meeting him myself—I'd say he never lets his binges get between him and any job he regards with enthusiasm. The question is, will he regard a stage *Hairy Ape* with enthusiasm? I know he would a film of the play. I think you can trust him to make his decision on the basis of whether he feels he can do some remarkable direction with the play. If not, he won't touch it. If so, it's a fair bet his contribution might be remarkable. Direction from a striking pictorial angle, if sets were made to fit the scheme of direction, would add to the play's effectiveness.

Re *"Anna Christie"*-Bergman, the road idea (I repeat) seems good stuff, but we must do a lot of cogitating before okaying New York, even if she can play there. The fact is *"Anna Christie"* is the stalest of all my plays—stale from much use, and stale because it is the most conventional playwrighting of anything I've done, although its subject matter was damned unconventional in our theatre of 1921. You will note I did not include it when picking representative plays for my *Nine Plays* book,[3] despite its success. The chief value I set on it is the character of old Chris. It is a play written about characters and a situation—not about characters and life. Contrast it with *The Iceman Cometh,* which, God knows, is full of characters. Well, that's not fair. *The Iceman* is worth a hundred *"Anna Christie"*s. Take one of my flops, like *Dynamo. Dynamo* may step on its own feet dramaturgically speaking (and I'm not so sure it does, at that, because 1929 criticism is no test. Any play which mentioned God, either favorably or unfavorably, unless as a childish, humorous, ignorant negro myth, in that year of disgrace was automatically a poor play in any critic's book) but *Dynamo is* written about characters plus life.

Well, to hell with that. You get my meaning. And from the Guild revival angle, it will be pointed out in acid that you couldn't possibly make two more conventional choices than *Ah, Wilderness!*[4] and *"Anna Christie"* from my work. It's true, too.

---

1. Tallulah Bankhead (1903–1968).
2. Charles Bickford (1891–1967).
3. *Nine Plays by Eugene O'Neill* (New York: Liveright, 1932).
4. The only Theatre Guild revival that materialized was of *Ah, Wilderness!* starring film star Harry Carey, which opened on October 2, 1941, and, despite good notices, closed after twenty-nine performances.

We are damned sorry to learn your sickness was really bad.

Never mind. Next time we meet you can tell me all about your intestines, and I'll tell you all about my gall bladder, and liver, and low blood pressure and pyloric spasms, and we'll both be too interested to listen to each other, and hour after pleasant hour will pass unheeded, and we'll forget income taxes, and if anyone asks us about the war we'll say, "what war?" There's nothing like having a real good ailment. It's one thing that never bores you, or leaves you at a loss for a word. I'm sure if one of the Knitting Women had called to Louis XVI as he ascended the guillotine, "Well, Capet, how're the old kidneys lately?," he would have waved the headsman aside and begun a serious conversation as follows, "Well, not so good, Sister. You may not believe me, but last night I had to get up and urinate no less than eleven times. I never get a wink of sleep any more. I don't know how I stand it." At this point the headsman would have interrupted with a little anecdote about his arthritis, and all the Knitting Women would have told of their hot flashes, irregular menstrual periods, varicose veins, flatulence, flat feet and what not. Danton would have muscled in with a long harangue on the horrible hangover he had yesterday morning. Robespierre would have addressed the mob for two hours on the new pills he was taking to get rid of his pimples. The Revolution would have been forgotten. Louis would have become the Well Beloved again—a Royal Pal. The Bourbon dynasty would have been saved. In fact, I think the quickest way to stop Hitler is for some Allied agent, disguised as a good listener, to ask him, "Well, Adolph, how are the old hysterics lately?" Hitler will promptly ask for an armistice in which to start the tale properly, and then sue for peace at any price in order to gain leisure to relate all his symptoms.

Fantastic, you say? Not a bit of it. Nerves are the most absorbing ailment of all. There is practically no limit to their symptoms. As I know. Why, listen, Lawrence, only last night I woke up suddenly in a cold sweat. Everything was shaking. I thought, my God, an earthquake! But it wasn't. It was me. And then—

But I better stop or I'll be writing you a brand new farce. You know me, Pal. Always, as I've said, writing about character plus life!

Love from us to you and Armina—and Terry and Oliver.   As ever,   Gene

---

487 • TO ANNE SHOEMAKER.[1]   TLS 1 p. (Stationery headed: Tao House / Danville / Contra Costa County / California) [UCLA]

November the 17th 1941

My dear Miss Shoemaker,   It was a great pleasure to get your note. I had meant to drop you a line years ago when you first played "Essie." Because I remembered *The Great God Brown* so well, and your grand work in it, and I thought there could hardly be a greater contrast than those two O'Neill ladies, and I knew you must be amused when you thought of it. I meant to write you this time, too, when I learned you were playing "Essie" again, but I'm afraid I'm one of those well-intentioned-and that's all-correspondents.

It's too bad the *Ah, Wilderness!* revival met such a dismal box office fate. Not that it was a stunning surprise. I don't expect much of revivals, and *Ah, Wilderness!* has been done to death since the original production—movie, radio, stock and amateur theatres. But I did believe, after the splendid New York notices, that it could run profitably there for eight weeks or so. Who wouldn't have thought the same? Well, let's blame it on the war.

---

1. Actress who played Essie Miller in 1934 and in the 1941 revival of *Ah, Wilderness!* and who originated the role of Cybel in the 1926 premiere production of *The Great God Brown.*

I often remember *The Great God Brown* production. Those were exciting days in the theatre. It seemed that something fine was being born, an American theatre which might survive on its own courageous merits and be independent of commercial show business. I will always believe the eight months run of a play as difficult and deep-searching as *The Great God Brown* was the greatest miracle the New York theatre has ever achieved. There is something to be said for the Mad Twenties. They were sometimes crazy in the right way.

Again, my gratitude for your "Cybel"—and for your "Essie," which I know I would have appreciated just as much, if I had seen it. And here's hoping we may work together again sometime.

All good wishes to you.   Cordially,   Eugene O'Neill

---

488 • TO SILVIO BEDINI.[1]   TLS 1 p. (Stationery headed: Tao House / Danville / Contra Costa County / California) [Private]

December the 14th 1941

Dear Mr. Bedini,   I remember well your father and mother—and the little boy who played with Shane.

In reply to your first query, the quotation is from a little book called *The Illumined Way,* written by a Hindu mystic.[2] That is, as I remember. I haven't the book now. I painted it on the rafters of a flat over Francis' grocery store where I lived in 1916–'17—not in the house I afterwards owned at Peaked Hill Bar.

As for Hart Crane, I consider him one of the few modern American poets who possessed real genius. There are no anecdotes I can give you. I only met him at intervals during '23–'24, and most of the times I did see him we were both cockeyed.

All good wishes to you, and to your father and mother.   Very sincerely yours, Eugene O'Neill

---

489 • TO HARRY WEINBERGER.   TLS 3 pp. (Stationery headed: Tao House / Danville / Contra Costa County / California) [Yale]

January the 19th 1942

Dear Harry,   Your letter of January the 16th at hand.

I've decided that any further discussion of changes in the present agreement had better be postponed until after the new tax law is passed and I can figure out where I stand—what percentage of my income taxes will take, and what alimony I can afford to pay in future, present agreement or no present agreement.

The trouble with the current discussions is that they are continuations of pre-war dickering. My situation, under 1942 tax, will be drastically changed for the worse. Six thousand alimony plus 1942 taxes might add up to nearly all my income!

Then there is the matter of War Bonds. I feel it's my duty to have Pell change a

---

1. Son of the couple who were the caretakers of the O'Neills' Brook Farm estate in Ridgefield, Connecticut, and who, while on a visit to Provincetown, found a painted inscription in a room where O'Neill had lived.

2. A book by Mabel Collins Cook (1851–1927) subtitled *A Guide to Neophytes, Being a Sequel to "Light on the Path"* (Palmyra, N.J.: Yogi Publication Society, 1903). Actually, the lines O'Neill wrote on the rafters in Francis's Flats were taken from *Light on the Path* (Chicago: Yogi Publication Society, n.d. [before 1885]), also by Mabel Cook. See Louis Sheaffer, *O'Neill: Son and Playwright,* pp. 385–86.

considerable part of my securities into War Bonds in the near future. That means much less fixed income—and it's that income which pays my alimony.

Also I think it is wise to keep my hands free to apply for relief from the Reno court on the whole alimony set-up in the present agreement—especially the fixed minimum—if I am forced to by the new taxes and can't get relief any other way. I have a hunch a great many alimony suckers are going to apply for relief—and are going to get it. Don't you agree? The future tax set-up will make it imperative.

The only change in the present agreement I would be willing to concede right now is my last proposal: If she marries in 1942 she can have what she wants concerning Spithead—*if* and only *if!*—and, in return, for this concession, if she doesn't marry, she agrees I can deduct taxes from alimony income, provided Congress doesn't allow *full* deduction of alimony.

The joker in this last proposal of hers, even if she agreed to the changes you want, is that it leaves me burdened forever with six thousand a year unless she marries, whereas now she is guaranteed only $5250.00—Oona will come of age in a few years—or quite probably marry before that time. Then the lady will only get $4500.00. If I had movie sales to boost income to 30,000.00, the deductions from her ten thousand would be 1200 for Shane (plus Oona's school) or $2400 after Oona comes of age or marries. So I would not be gaining much by the agreement proposed now, even where it is supposed to relieve me a lot. But movie sales are improbable—and so highly taxable, what's the use? And productions are out entirely. I don't want any in such times at any price. It would be wasting the plays, and I like them too much for that. So take it as almost certain my income will be $18000.00 or less. Let's figure on last year's alimony income under the proposed arrangement. It was $14000.00—Deduct $6000, leaves $8000. Present Federal tax on $14,000.00 for married guy, one dependent—$2277. The coming taxes will double that, they say,—$4500 approximately. That leaves me $3500.00. Deduct State tax, and property tax, leaves $2750.00, say. Deduct Oona's school from that and what have you, except almost nothing, for me to live on? So where am I getting a break from her? I'm $750 better off under the present agreement. And don't you believe the Reno court will, if I have to appeal to it, see sense in my figures and my request for a New Deal of 1/4 income up to $20,000.00, say, with a minimum of $300.00 a month. Or some similarly reduced arrangement? Give this your earnest consideration.

I hope to hell you do get out to the Coast in February or March. Not only would we enjoy welcoming you here again, but it would be grand to have a chance to talk this out. Doing it long range by letter is bum stuff, and I always overlook this angle or that.

It's grand about the Nathan case!

And I hope you have a good rest (and don't buy any more real estate) in Florida.

My health is punk, and my mental health worse, if you want the truth. The war has me sunk as far as working is concerned. My mind is in Pearl Harbor, the Philippines, Singapore, etc.

All best from us—and be sure you ride that anti-trust suit out here!   As ever,   Gene

P.S. In brief, here's how I sum up all the situation re the lady: If she wants to get married badly enough,[1] I have her over a barrel and she'll eventually accept my Bermuda bribe. If she doesn't, I'll never get any real alimony relief from her and will eventually have to try the Reno court. And there you are. Only time will tell.

---

1. Agnes Boulton O'Neill did not remarry until 1947.

490 • TO EUGENE O'NEILL, JR.   TLS 2 pp. (Stationery headed: Tao House / Danville / Contra Costa County / California) [Yale]

February the 2nd 1942

Dear Eugene,   I've been unpleasantly preoccupied with the yearly ordeal of preparing Federal and State income tax returns, or I would have replied to your letter sooner. The bad news is plenty bad this year. The only consolation is, it isn't half as bad as it will be next year—and that's the hell of a consolation!

Your article on the *Troades*[1] is grand stuff! I agree it is the best thing you have ever done, and I am delighted it was received so enthusiastically when you read it at Hartford—an astonishing triumph for you, considering that any approval of a pacifist play these days has such a barrier of suspicion and prejudice to overcome. Thank God, you had an intelligent audience which did not read an intent to weaken morale into your analysis! A most hopeful proof that there is a great difference between American reaction in this war and the last one. We don't have to believe this time that war is a glorious thing, and victory in battle a final settlement of all the issues involved. In the last war, if you had read such a paper, you would have been denounced as a hireling of the Kaiser, and been punished with the loss of your job, probably.

You've got me wrong on my attitude toward histrionics. No one approves more of the right kind in the right place. It's the ham variety I detest—the phony and obviously pumped up, the putting on an act, exhibitionism which has nothing behind it but wind and a stupid vanity. Unfortunately, most of the histrionics one sees or reads about fall into this category, and it is in life and not in the theatre that the worst examples are found. Witness that primest low ham of all time, Mussolini! Or take the average Congressman or Senator—if that isn't asking too much!

I'm glad you continue to remember *Long Day's Journey Into Night* with fine appreciation. As I told you when you were here, it and *The Iceman Cometh* are to me the most completely satisfying things I have written. I can't reproach myself that either should have been done better. I know they couldn't be—by me or anyone else. Each achieves my highest aim for it—and my aim was high. *Long Day's Journey Into Night* is the finer drama, but *The Iceman Cometh* is fine drama, too. They each demanded the best I had to give, and I'm damned happy I didn't let either of them down.

Last week I finished the first draft of a new play, *A Moon For The Misbegotten*. A good title, eh? I wish I could report the first draft lived up to it, but it does not. Much work to do before it will be anything. A case of too much war on the brain. Pearl Harbor exploded when I was starting the most difficult part. After that I dragged through the rest. It is an extremely simple play with only three characters, and almost plotless from the usual dramatic structure standpoint, so it takes a lot of doing. However, I'm enthusiastic about the idea and eventually I hope to make it what it should be. Just now I'm too sunk in spirit, what with war and rainy season blues and physical ailments, to feel up to it.

Much gratitude for the Christmas present book! It is an interesting piece of work and a fine companion volume for the others you've given me.

Love to you as ever—and again, congratulations on your *Troades* article—and even on your histrionics! I am sure The Count of Monte Cristo, looking down from Heaven—where, since his arrival, all but one of the holy candles have been extinguished—smiled benignly and said, "Well done, Lad! Well done!"   Father

1. "The Prologue of the *Troades* of Euripides," *Transactions and Proceedings of the American Philologic Association* 72 (1941):288–320.

Eugene O'Neill, Jr.

491 • TO HARRY WEINBERGER.   TLS 2 pp. (Stationery headed: Tao House /
Danville / Contra Costa County / California) [Yale]

May the 12th 1942

Dear Harry: Replying to your letter of May 7th, I want to make clear exactly how I feel about Oona's adventure into stupid exhibitionism.[1] I consider it unpardonable that she should make such a cheap, silly spectacle of herself as an ad for a Night Club racket—and the interview she gave out was tops in empty-headed, nitwit bad taste and vulgarity. So dumb, too, from the standpoint of her own interest. All it earned her was criticism and dislike from anyone who amounts to anything. She will never live it down. At this particular moment in our history, people are justly sore at the antics of the frivolous, and a glamour Deb. trading on her father's name to get into the papers, is a damned irritating news item when everyone is worried to death about serious matters.

I'm afraid the young lady is mentally and spiritually a Boulton. Could one say worse?

I have not written to her and don't intend to. She knows my reaction without my telling her. She has not dared to write me. And I do not want to hear from her, nor see her again until she has proved she has come out of this silly, brainless stage and may amount to something as herself and not as my daughter.

Hollywood would be her finish. It is the worst place on earth for a silly young girl. It destroys them overnight, almost. Handled by unscrupulous racket agents who are always looking for someone with publicity value to promote, regardless of what happens to the victim eventually, she could probably cash in on one picture, and that would probably mean the end forever. She has never shown the slightest talent for acting, and the very fact of being my daughter, which would get her unearned publicity at first, would help to kill her afterwards.

No, if she goes to Hollywood, it will be absolutely against my wishes. So much so, that if she does, I will never write to her or see her again as long as I live! I mean this, Harry,—just as I meant it about her mother. I don't want that kind of daughter. She could mean nothing to me but disgust. I would rather have a Red Cross Nurse or a worker in an aircraft factory for a daughter than a million glamour Night Club debs or movie floozies. I've reached the point where I'm entirely fed up with the Boultons, even those who have my blood in them.

If you see the lady, make this clear—and strong. If Hollywood is in, then I'm out—*forever!* As ever,   Gene

---

492 • TO EUGENE O'NEILL, JR.   TLS 3 pp. (Stationery headed: Tao House /
Danville / Contra Costa County / California) [Yale]

June the 1st 1942

Dear Eugene: Yours is a tough letter to answer. Tough because my love for you—and I mean love—is as real as my respect for the work you have done and are doing. It is like acid always burning in my brain that the stupid butchering of the last war taught men nothing at all, that they sank back listlessly on the warm manure pile of the dead and went to sleep, indifferently bestowing custody of their future, their fate, into the hands of State departments, whose members are trained to be conspirators, card sharps, double-crossers and secret betrayers of their own people; into the hands of greedy capitalist ruling classes so

---

1. The Stork Club, New York's noted night spot, had chosen Oona O'Neill as "Debutante No. 1" of the year.

stupid they could not even see when their own greed began devouring itself; into the hands of that most debased type of pimp, the politician, and that most craven of all lice and job-worshippers, the bureaucrats.

I could go on from there, extensively and eloquently, and give you an Anarchist diatribe against the State which, published, would earn me fifty years in Leavenworth—or deportation to Ireland!—but what I started to say was how I loathe the stupid waste of your becoming involved in this[1] at the risk of your life, because of the stupidities of the past twenty-five years.

But I agree with you that you should be, and that your decision is right. Because now the one issue we must all keep in mind, dismissing all others, however idealistic, as immaterial for the duration, is as simple and primitively clear as the issue in a Prohibition gang war—kill or be killed, crush or be crushed. There is no longer any possible choice. We have got to win the war and win it by a complete extermination of the Japanese and Prussian military caste. It is the only language those gentry can understand—and their people can understand— that they be shown up before their own people and the world not as superior-race heroes but as completely vanquished and inferior at their own game. We left the Germans at the close of the last war with too many "outs." War was still a thing that always was fought outside Germany. Their army was not beaten, they could say. It was still the unconquerable army. Only the home front collapsed. So, militarily speaking,—above all, psychologically speaking—they were still the superior warrior race. I hope to God the same mistake is not repeated this time. We must not stop until their beloved total war is totally crammed down their throats and their racial inferiority (speaking in their terms) whines for mercy. It will be time enough then to remember Humanitarian principles. And I believe that then world peace— except for minor wars, of course—will be assured for—well, maybe as long as fifty years.

But to hell with that. The main thing I want to say is that I think you are wise to aim at liaison work, and keep after it now before it's too late. You would certainly be most valuable to the Service in that line, and I should think one of their greatest needs would be men with knowledge of Icelandic and Iceland. They must be hard to find. Be sure and let me know any progress on this. I shall be waiting anxiously. Iceland is no picnic, certainly, but it's better than South Pacific Islands like New Guinea, the Solomons, etc. where, when we attack, enemy number one will be blackwater fever, number two, tropical malaria, with the Japs a bad third in deadliness.

I've been really sick the past month and more—still am—can't work—nothing. Trouble is, any infection that starts spreads to the weak spots left by my '37 crack-up and I go all wrong. I'm also bewildered by what my financial set-up will be under new taxes, if Congress doesn't allow alimony deduction. I will have practically no income, no matter what I earn. If compulsory 10% savings become law, as they must before long in one form or another, I will have nothing at all. I've just refused an offer for *The Hairy Ape* film rights with a ten thousand advance because I wouldn't get a nickel out of that ten. Incredible, isn't it? I don't mind the taxes. We ought to pay them. But I do hate this democratic matriarchate law which makes me pay double or triple the tax on my *real* income that others have to pay—while an utterly lazy worthless woman does no work, lives as usual, war or no war, and pays no tax at all! She also refuses me any relief, knowing I have no legal recourse under our agreement. Some doll! I wish I could give her to a Nazi concentration camp! And she seems determined to make Oona as worthless as she is. Well, let's be philosophical. Every man's life contains at

---

1. Eugene, Jr., had applied for a commission in the Intelligence Corps; eventually, he was rejected for all military service.

least one bitch. I suppose I ought to be proud in a way, for she is undoubtedly the prize specimen of them all.

Much love from us—and much gratitude for your letter—and write soon about developments. As always, Father

P.S. I'm giving Yale Library original long hand scripts of:

Marco Millions
Great God Brown
Lazarus Laughed
Strange Interlude

Carlotta will give them *Dynamo* and *Days Without End*. She's already given *Electra*. Then Yale will have all except *Ah, Wilderness!* of what might be called my 3rd period work. I'm giving Princeton Library all of 2nd period—*The Straw* to *Desire Under The Elms* (I can never get over my affection for Old Nassau. It's a neurosis!). All first work to Museum of the City of New York. Then it will all be kept within short distance so that anyone sufficiently interested won't have too much trouble. *The Iceman Cometh*, etc. will eventually go to Yale, I think.

I'll be glad to be rid of these scripts. I never look at them anyway—or do anything to care for them, and they need that if they are to last.

As to whether my work justifies all this preserving, quién sabe? Long before the time any final judgment can be passed on that, I'll be much too dead to care. Maybe the world will be, too. However, as long as the Yale and Princeton Libraries want the stuff, they're welcome to it. Perhaps, as a just man, I should have asked Harvard if it wanted any, but I'm not a just man where Harvard is concerned (early Princeton influence, perhaps). I just don't like the damned place.

---

493 • TO NORMAN HOLMES PEARSON.   TLS 2 pp. (Stationery headed: Tao House / Danville / Contra Costa County / California) [Yale]

June the 18th 1942

Dear Norman Pearson: Much gratitude for your fine letter! It is grand to know my work means so much to you, and that you are enthusiastic about the gift of the scripts to the Yale Library. As I wrote Mr. Knollenberg,[1] I, for my part, am only too delighted that the Library considers them worth preserving. So we are all pleased—and that's something to cheer about in a world which, to put it mildly, is not at present burgeoning with a bumper crop of pleasure!

Still more gratitude for what you say of Eugene. I am, as you may guess, so proud of him and what he has done, that praise for him practically makes me behave like a besotted fond parent!

I hope you will like *The Iceman Cometh*. Not to put on the fake modesty stuff, I consider this play one of the best I have ever written. In many respects, it is the most satisfying work of all, up to that date—(it was finished two and a half years ago)—because it leaves me with no feeling that I fell down on the job in one way or another, that it should be much better, that I failed to realize my highest hope for it. For me at least, *The Iceman Cometh* is all I wanted it to be—reveals everything I hoped it could reveal—and *is* fine drama.

To get back to the scripts, I'm afraid neither Mrs. O'Neill nor I understand exactly what you mean by "under the same restrictions as were set for the *Electra* scripts." The Library may

1. Bernhard Knollenberg, librarian at Yale University.

treat the scripts I sent the same as it treats the *Electra* scripts and disregard whether they are actual gifts at the moment or not—make them accessible to serious scholars whenever Mr. Knollenberg thinks advisable.

Regarding the matter of accessibility to scholars. I'd like to quote from a letter I've written Mr. Boyd,[2] the Princeton Librarian, on this subject: "No objection to making the scripts accessible to serious scholars whenever you like. But, as an act of mercy, will you caution such scholars against writing me and asking questions—because I probably won't know the answers. I mean this seriously. When I was getting these scripts together to send you, I discovered how very little I remembered about these plays, and now that you have all the records I had to prod memory, my mind will be practically a blank. Nothing is so dead and quickly forgotten by a playwright as his past work, once it has been produced on the stage. At least, that has been my experience. Probably because the play as written and the play as produced, no matter how excellently or successfully, can never be the same. One's memory of the play and its characters, and of the produced play with its acted characters, become confused and cancel each other out. Besides, you have already begun to think of the next play, and you want to forget everything but that. So whatever memory does linger on grows more and more blurred and is apt to be both unimportant and inaccurate."

I quote this because it also applies to the Yale scripts—my poor memory, I mean—and if scholars can be discreetly discouraged from thinking I can be appealed to as an all-remembering oracle, it will save them a lot of disappointment, and me a lot of fruitless brain gouging. Of course, I don't mean this as an implacable blanket rule. Where the case is exceptional, I will be glad to do my damnedest to help.

All good wishes from us—and again, thank you for your letter.   Very sincerely, Eugene O'Neill

---

494 • TO GEORGE JEAN NATHAN.   TLS 1 p. (Stationery headed: Tao House / Danville / Contra Costa County / California) [Cornell]

June the 19th 1942

Dear George: Under separate cover, I am sending you a script of the one-act *Hughie*— the only one of the series titled "By Way Of Obit" I have so far completed. You will remember I threatened to send you this soon after I finished it a little over a year ago, but I didn't have it typed for a long time, and then didn't go over it for months after that. It is really only recently that I've had a clean typed copy.

I've forgotten how much or little I explained about this series—there will be seven or eight of them if I ever manage to get them all done. *Hughie* is a good example of the technique. In each the main character talks about a person who has died to a person who does little but listen. Via this monologue you get a complete picture of the person who has died—his or her whole life story—but just as complete a picture of the life and character of the narrator. And you also get, by another means—a use of stage directions, mostly—an insight into the whole life of the person who does little but listen.

These plays are written more to be read than staged, although they could be played. But to hell with more explanation. You'll get it all reading *Hughie*.

Some of them will be based on actual characters I've known—some not. *Hughie* isn't. The Night Clerk character is an essence of all the night clerks I've known in bum hotels— quite a few! "Erie" is a type of Broadway sport I and my brother used to know by the dozen

2. Julian P. Boyd.

in far-off days. I didn't know many at the time the play is laid, 1928, but they never change. Only their lingo does. As for "Erie's" slang, I've tried, generally speaking, to stick to the type's enduring lingo, and not use stuff current only in 1928 but soon discarded. Being too meticulously timely is not worth the trouble and defeats its purpose, anyway.

I'm fond of *Hughie* myself. I'll bet Ring Lardner would have liked it. And here's hoping you do.   Love from us.   Gene

P.S. —*Hughie* is the last in time of all. They range from 1910–1928.[1]

---

495 • TO NORMAN HOLMES PEARSON.   TLS 1 p. (Stationery headed: Tao House / Danville / Contra Costa County / California) [Yale]

July 30th 1942

Dear Norman Pearson: I'm immensely gratified that *The Iceman Cometh* made such an impression on you. As I wrote you, I cannot be becomingly modest about this play. It is as deeply moving to me as it is ever likely to be to anyone, and I unhesitatingly give myself a pat on the back for it.

I'm delighted to know you found it satisfies every demand both as a tensely-developing dramatic story and as a life symbol. This, of course, has been my intent in many plays, but it did not always come off. Even in titles I have tried for that double meaning—which explains why many people, without realizing the reason, find a lot of them so striking. They hit the subconscious as well as the conscious.

What you say of the wholeness of each character—the life story in each—is another thing I like about this play. *The Iceman Cometh* is, I think, the only play with seventeen fine parts. Which makes casting a problem. It needs seventeen fine actors! It can't ever have them in our theatre because fine actors won't play small parts, however good, and no management could afford their salaries, anyway. So the best I can hope for—as many times before in my experience—is that the parts are strong enough to "carry" mediocre acting and make it look good.

Yes, I am particularly proud of the picture one gets of the women who never appear— the living influence even of those who are dead. Parritt's mother, Hickey's wife, Hope's wife, and at the last even Jimmy Tomorrow's wife makes a brief but illuminating entrance in his speech about her. They are all characters of the play to me.

Well, now you've read the play, I know you will understand my refusal to produce it in these times. It is not only my poor health, which might be wrecked by the strain and land me in a hospital again. It's that I know what is important to me in the play could not be seen or heard now. It might well succeed on its outer story and dramatic structure values, but its inner life would be suppressed or ignored. Would have to be—indeed, perhaps ought to be, because now we need an unquestioning faith in all pipe dreams, however irrational, lest we be defeated in spirit and thrown into the sty of final "realistic" opportunism, where God is a murderous blind hog, and there is no dream, and The Iceman cometh like a thief in the night, and we wearily welcome him because there is no longer a kick in any booze whatever.

Again, my gratitude for your appreciation. It means a lot.   Very sincerely,   Eugene O'Neill

---

1. O'Neill destroyed the outlines and notes for the seven other plays in this series.

September the 28th 1942

Dear Harry: Replying to your letter of Sept. 24th re Oona and the Neighborhood Playhouse dramatic school, if I am not legally bound to acquiesce, I don't acquiesce—for the following reasons:

1st Because I am unalterably opposed to her going on the stage at any time. For someone who possesses great talent, it is a fine career, but I am convinced from what I know of her—and from reports I got from Maplewood[1]—that she has little if any talent for acting. Actresses are born that way, not made.

2nd Because I believe if she had really serious ambition, she would have the sense to know that the way to learn to act is to get a job in the theatre, however small, and prove you have ability. It isn't to go to an acting school.

3rd Because I am convinced her wanting to go to this school is simply another typical Boulton trick to avoid real work or study. She can be lazy there (people never get fired, I am sure) and continue to trade on my name, as she has already done cheaply and shamelessly.

4th Because I am certain she wants to go on the stage, thinking it is the easiest way and my name will be a great help. That is stupid. It won't be a help. It will mean she will have all the breaks against her. (Particularly after all the bad advertising she has got.) She will be spotlighted from the start—and a spotlight at the start is a terrible handicap to overcome. It practically takes geniuses to do it. Oona is no genius but merely a spoiled, lazy, vain little brat who has, so far, by her actions only proven that she can be a much sillier and bad-mannered fool than most girls of her age.

5th Because I had a brother once who took the easy way of going on the stage and trading on his father's name. He became a third-rate actor—a nice lazy job, when you've got a job, and have someone to support you when you haven't. He ended up in tragedy, embittered, with his life wasted and ruined. The pity of it was, he had a fine brain. I loved him and I can never forget the easy start that murdered the life he might have had. On the other hand, I never traded on my father's name. I always resented being regarded as Monte Cristo's son. Once in New London when I worked on the newspaper there, I said before some people (who still remember it) "Someday I won't be known as his son. He will be known as my father." Only a boast, then, of course, but it had the right spirit behind it, and it came true. Eugene has proven that same spirit can come true. He has never traded on my name. He has made himself a name as a classical scholar that I never could have attained. The trouble with my two Boulton children, who seem to be so much more Boulton than O'Neill, is that they lack that pride. They want to do as they damned please and yet at the same time remain dependent babies, with everything handed to them—life a perpetual breakfast in bed, so to speak.

6th Because my own wish about Oona—which, of course, doesn't count—is that she should wake up and realize we are in a war—and what a war! It's no time for Americans of her age to aspire to theatrical or movie careers. What is less dramatic or important now than the Broadway Showshop when one thinks of Stalingrad or the Solomons? Christ, why doesn't she train to be a Red Cross nurse, if she wants training that means something? Or war work of any genuine hard-working kind. (Not the social variety.) That kind of experience

---

1. Oona played a small role in a summer stock production of *Pal Joey* in Maplewood, New Jersey.

might make a real woman of her. New York and Broadway yearnings are apt to make her a tart.

7th Because I cannot afford anything I am not forced to afford. My last alimony year income, please point out to the lady, is no indication of my 1942 income—nor are '41 taxes '42 taxes. It took in the *Ah, Wilderness!* revival in the fall of '41, a flop but it did bring in extra money. I will be lucky if 1942 income goes over eleven thousand. Let her figure out what I get, with her alimony and taxes deducted. Tell her to use Spithead money to finance Oona's career on the stage. After all, the property is half Oona's, or will be.

Well, what the hell, Harry. I don't know why I've written at such length, except that I want you to know my attitude thoroughly. I think this dramatic school business is simply more laziness, more sly evasion, more talentless pretense, more parasitism, more prideless begging and grafting, more weak failure to face the world and the war—or, for that matter, to face oneself in any world of decent values—in short, pure Boultonism. I'll take no more of it than the law allows, thank you.

Enclosed is check for the revised dole. No, I can't report I am any better. I feel lousy plus.   All best from us.   Gene

P.S. I have recently done some work for the Merchant Marine, at their request. Will write you about it later.

---

497 • TO L. F. GITTLER.[1]   COPY 1 p. (Stationery headed: Tao House / Danville / Contra Costa County / California) [Yale]

Oct. 23rd '42

Dear Mr. Gittler: Afraid this is too long or not what you want anyway. If so, forget it, and count me out. I did my sincere best. Quote:

As an ever grateful American recipient of the high honor of a Nobel award, it is inspiring to know that the Nobel Prize Committee will continue to function with courageous independence despite the hatred and threats of Nazi barbarism. The Nazis have long hated the Nobel award. They realize that these awards are symbols of the aspiring spirit of free cultures, and of a future international brotherhood of man within the spirit of a universal free culture. This makes them a danger to Nazi ambition. In Germany culture has been assassinated. Only a debased slave-science, devoted exclusively to research in murder, and the contemptible literature of hate and fear propaganda, are permitted to exist. What the Nazis know they must do to succeed finally in their bloody, brain-spattered destruction of civilization is to murder all free cultures throughout the entire world. This annihilation is the sweet mystic dream of their Leader, whom they adore as the modern pagan son of God—a little maggot of a man, a tenth-rate writer who could hardly hope to win a Nobel Prize unless one was bestowed in recognition of supreme human baseness, who has at last found his true avocation as the greatest mass murderer in history.

It is against this intolerably hideous and sadistic leader-dream of a world deformed and tortured, lashed back into a past of ignorant serfdom, its culture dead and spat upon, that the United States of America is waging war. Our allies are all the men and women in Scandinavia and in every country of the world who love liberty and detest slavery. Many of these countries have been conquered by force from without and the vilest treachery within. Others may still share their fate of Martyrdom. But the free men and women of Europe, whose allies

1. Official of the Special Events Section of the Office of War Information.

and friends we are, cannot be conquered in spirit. They know a terrible day of reckoning will come for their oppressors. They know that victory and the death of the evil dream, and of all who dreamed it, are certain. The free in spirit of this world cannot fail to win. They will win because the longing of the human spirit for the dignity and self respect of freedom is imperishable and unconquerable. All things, including leaders, have their day and pass, but the aspiring soul of Free Man remains, and will remain as long as there is Man. Eugene O'Neill

---

498 • TO JAMES T. FARRELL.[1]   TLS 1 p. (Stationery headed: Tao House / Danville / Contra Costa County / California) [Pennsylvania]

November the 23rd 1942

Dear Mr. Farrell: Have been laid up or I would have answered your letter of November 12th at once.

Needless to tell you what I think of the action of the American Library Association in placing *Studs Lonigan* on their list and then, after the British government had okayed their choice, withdrawing it. It is a lousy bit of work, the same old racket of would-be censorship which always attempts to use wartime or post wartime to grab a little power. I know the game well, having had many experiences with censorship or attempts at it both in this country and several foreign ones (including Great Britain).

Last night I received a note from Mr. Henle of The Vanguard Press, requesting a comment from me. I am sending him one, although it is difficult for me not to fly off the handle and do more harm than good.

Two things make me more than ordinarily sore: First, I was for a while, as long as I could afford it, a dues paying supporter of the A.L.A. I thought they stood for something helpful to fine writing. Second, I have a great admiration for *Studs Lonigan*. It is a splendid piece of work.

Always, good luck to you and your work.   Very sincerely,   Eugene O'Neill

---

499 • TO HARRY WEINBERGER.   TLS 2 pp. (Stationery headed: Tao House / Danville / Contra Costa County / California) [Yale]

Dec. 3rd 1942

Dear Harry: Your letter re the Income Tax people's argument on *The Long Voyage Home* sale has just arrived. I feel more than ever that their intention to reverse the Department's ruling, which has always applied in the past, is a dishonorable trick that takes advantage of war conditions to make me the goat. If they want a new interpretation of the law, fine. That is their privilege. But in justice, they should announce this first and set a deadline, so that authors would know where they stand and figure accordingly. The injustice to me is that Ford offered me a choice between a cash down sale, and a 10% of profit proposition. I accepted the cash down because I was afraid—as you will remember—that any royalty basis, even for outright sale, might be questioned by the Revenue Tax people; whereas *I knew* from the Department's past rulings on cash down sales, that the 20000 would be regarded as a capital asset sale. The injustice is that if I had accepted the 10% royalty deal, the money

---

1. Farrell (1904–1979), novelist and short-story writer, known best for his *Studs Lonigan* trilogy (1932–35) of life among Irish Catholics in Chicago's South Side.

would have been spread over several years, and that would have saved me a big sum (if they are going to look upon the 20000 paid in one year as income). Also, I would have made more money, since *The Long Voyage Home* profits were close to 300,000, and it is still being shown in Australia, South Africa, etc.

It is an ironical thing—and shamelessly dishonorable and stupid—that they should choose to make a case of the one American playwright who has made very little money, comparatively, out of movies (when there are so many playwrights who have made fortunes out of film rights)—the one American playwright who is a Nobel prize winner and has never written or worked for pictures—and all over a film which is honest and fine, rated as one of the best ever, artistically, which was not done as money-making trade goods—and, *above all*, which proved to be a wonderful propaganda film, glorifying the sacrifice and heroism of merchant marine sailors and doing a lot for British-American friendship. The film was acclaimed in Great Britain as well as here. The point is that at a time when no one else was doing anything for merchant marine seamen, and few doing anything for British-American amity, this fine film version of my plays did do a lot.

To change the subject, Oona was out on the Coast recently—may still be for all I know. She made the trip sponging on some rich girl friend.[1] Wrote me from Omaha on the way out to say she'd like to see me *to tell me what she intended to do*—no word of excuse or apology for all her cheapness in the eight months she had not written me. Then she wrote Carlotta from the St. Francis in San Francisco, before she had heard from me, saying she had to go South with her friend but might be up north later. I had written her a letter to knock her ears down, but had no address to mail it to. Then a month later, she wrote Carlotta from Sacramento, again saying she'd like to see me. I wrote telling her I had no wish whatever to see the kind of daughter she had proved herself to be, and unless she changed and got some intelligence and sense of responsibility, I never wanted to see her again. Imagine her joyriding about the country regardless in these clogged transportation times—and at a rich friend's expense!

Well, that's that. I'm telling you all this so you will know the facts, in case her idiot mother tries some tale on you. Please *don't* see Oona. I meant all I said in my letter to her, and *I want it left at that*. It was a kick in the pants she richly deserved. If she's an all-Boulton fool it will have no effect. If she had any latent guts or pride, it may have a good effect in the long run when she eventually realizes what a nitwit public nuisance she has been.

Enclosed is the lady's dole. I suppose she won't find her daughter at home much, now the money is low. Well, she ought to understand thoroughly that type of character.

Carlotta joins me in all best!   As ever,   Gene

P.S. Here is an argument for the Income Tax people that looks good to me. You say their theory is that a play is part of my stock in trade. Suppose I was a chain grocery store creator who sold part of my controlling stock in the company's common and preferred stock two years or more after I created the company (getting backing for it just as a playwright gets backing for plays or films, by giving an interest in the property to the backer or manager). Would the money I received from the sale of the stock be regarded as income, or as a sale of part of my capital assets? The latter, of course. Or suppose I sold one of the chain stores, after owning it ten years or more?

---

1. Carol Marcus, for whom Oona acted as a chaperone on Marcus's trip west to visit William Saroyan. Saroyan was in basic training in Sacramento.

December the 16th 1942

Dear Dudley: Coincidence: The day before your letter arrived we mailed you a
Christmas card (Connecticut address) on which I wrote "Why don't we hear from you?" So
your letter was warmly welcomed. We had guessed that you must be passing through a
trying period of readjustment to the war—like all the rest of us—and had heard from Bob
Sisk about the Hemingway movie job and also heard or read of your working with Renoir.[1]
But all that was some time ago. We didn't know if you were still in Hollywood.

I am delighted to learn how satisfied you are in the collaboration with Renoir, and that
R.K.O. really kept hands off the film you've just made, and gave you authority and freedom.
That is practically a miracle, isn't it? Here's hoping they don't suffer a change of mind and
revert to type. Film making can be something fine. Only a fool would deny that. But, as in the
theatre, it can only happen when imaginative creative minds have a chance to use the
medium without interference.

But enough of that. I'm merely agreeing with what you know. And all I really want to
say is that I think you were wise to make a final decision and concentrate on what you know
you want to do.

Regarding *Desire Under The Elms*, I hope you may finally be in a position to do that. I
needn't tell you it would be a great joy to leave it in your hands. There is only one hitch. If I
get a decent offer for it (financially speaking) in the near future, I would have to accept for
purely financial reasons. Things are none too good with me in that respect. It will be a tough
battle to survive this war and have anything left. However, there is no offer for *Desire* and
probably won't be, so what the hell am I talking about.

Russel Crouse has just written me from New York he saw in one of the dramatic
columns that Boris Karloff was being considered for a film version of *The Hairy Ape*.[2] Have
you heard any talk of this in Hollywood? I know nothing about it, but then I might not be
approached until whoever is interested had everything else lined up. Of course, I don't pay
any attention to theatrical column rumors, but sometimes they are true. And this one has a
certain plausibility as a shrewd showmanship notion. Karloff, so Crouse, who ought to
know, assures me, is really a fine actor, when not swamped in junk pictures, and an
intelligent man.

No, *The Iceman Cometh* would be wrong now. A New York audience could neither see
nor hear its meaning. The pity and tragedy of defensive pipe dreams would be deemed
downright unpatriotic, and uninspired by the Atlantic Charter, even if the audience did
catch that meaning. But after the war is over, I am afraid from present indications that
American audiences will understand a lot of *The Iceman Cometh* only too well.

If this indicates that I am an optimist about a United Nations victory, but a pessimist
about any intelligent, greedless peace, that's it, exactly. The so-garrulous liberal intelligentsia of this world always naively forget that a peace is made by and of men, and if men
have changed at all spiritually since the last war, it is for the worse. Also, war uses up all the
self-sacrifice human nature can spare. Peace is an exhausted reaction to normal. As Marco

1. Nichols wrote the screenplay for the 1943 movie version of Hemingway's *For Whom the Bell Tolls* and
for two films directed by Jean Renoir, *Swamp Water* (1941) and *This Land Is Mine* (1943), the second of which
he also coproduced.
2. *The Hairy Ape* was not made into a film until 1944, when United Artists produced it with William
Bendix starring as Yank.

tells the Kaan in *Marco Millions:* "I've never read much in any history about heroes who waged peace." If there are any noble-minded statesmen or diplomats in the world to-day who can be relied on to make an unselfish peace and then keep on waging it, I don't see them. They all seem to believe any end justifies any means—and the end to that is total ruin for man's spirit. Whether there is social revolution or not, it won't matter a damn. What have you left when you turn over a manure pile—but manure?

Well, that's not so cheery, I better stop. Your description of your household retainers is damned amusing. You certainly don't lack the proper religious environment!

My health has been rotten for over a year and Carlotta has had her troubles, too, with arthritis and a bad back. But she is a wonder—manages to do a hell of a lot of housework and still remains cheerful, although she loathes it. We have only a cook now—and lucky to have her. Freeman is in the Marines and we have no one outside but the farmer. I can't drive a car any more and Carlotta never could. So we are more or less marooned—even before gas rationing. We get the hardware man from Danville to drive us to Oakland when I have to go in for treatments every two weeks. All of which sounds tougher than it is. Now we're used to it, we manage all right and it's no great hardship.

As for work, Pearl Harbor caught me enthusiastically writing new non-cycle play, *A Moon For The Misbegotten.* After that, I couldn't concentrate. Managed to finish the first draft but the heart was out of it. Haven't looked at it since. There is a fine unusual tragic comedy in *A Moon For The Misbegotten* but it will have to wait until I can rewrite the lifeless post-Pearl Harbor part of it. All I've been able to do in the past ten months is rewrite one of the Cycle plays, *A Touch Of The Poet,* and do a little work on "The Last Conquest" (the World-Dictator fantasy of a possible future, and the attempted last campaign of Evil to stamp out even the unconscious memory of Good in Man's spirit—you will remember I sketched the idea to you the last time you were at Tao House). But again in this play, I soon feel my creative impulse blocked by the hopeless certainty that it could not be understood now, or its possibilities admitted—more than that, a feeling in myself that, until this war, which must be won, is won, people should concentrate on the grim surface and not admit the still grimmer, soul-disturbing depths. I censor myself, so to speak, and with this shackle added to recurring spells of illness and mental depression— In short, "The Last Conquest" remains for the most part in scenario, although it constantly haunts me.

Of course, this is no way for the free creative spirit to act. Its answer to war should be that of Archimedes: "Get out of my light. Your shadow is disturbing my problem." Should be, in theory. But this total war is different. It is, unfortunately, really *total* and no answer can evade it.

Carlotta joins me in all best. We would like to see you, but I guess there is no possibility of that. Even if you had to come to San Francisco, I don't see how you could get out here. Thirty miles each way and we are on *A* gas ration—and thumbing a ride has become practically impossible, so I'm told!

Let me hear from you whenever you're in the mood.   As ever,   Gene

---

501 • TO SOPHUS KEITH WINTHER.   TLS 3 pp. (Stationery headed: Tao House / Danville / Contra Costa County / California) [Tao House]

December the 26th 1942

Dear Sophus: Merry Christmas![1] Your and Eline's card arrived yesterday. It made us glad and sad—sad because your Duncan brought back so many memories of Blemie, whose

1. O'Neill wrote across the top of this letter, "Written Christmas day."

ghost still benignly haunts Tao House. Two days ago we waded through the mud out to his grave beneath the pines at the foot of the hill to place a Christmas wreath on it, hoping he would look down from the Paradise of Ten Billion Trees and Unrationable Dog Biscuits and pity us. We are glad you have a Dalmatian. They are much more sensible than any other breed of dog I know—and I've known many breeds. Unlike the English Bulldog or bull terrier, for example, or the French poodle, or the German Gestapo dog, they never drool or yap or whine about the white dog's burden of Empire, or their supremely rational culture, or the enlarged yard space due a superior race of mutts. Unlike the Irish Wolfhound, they don't bay beautifully at the misty moon about "the cry of the hounds on the hills of old Ireland." I never heard Blemie mention Dalmatia except as a certain section of land where his ancestors happened to be when they were born. And, of course, Dalmatians are not only superior to other dogs, they are like all dogs, infinitely less stupid than men.

Pessimistic fantasy, perhaps, but somehow I feel pessimism appropriate on this feast of peace and good will, when there is no peace on earth, nor any good will behind the surface even between allies—or what's worse, between the factions in our own country.

What particularly gripes me is the growing ruin of the class between Big Business and Unionized Labor—the small business man, shop keeper, white collar worker, professional man, small farmer, etc. We see so many instances of that in this neighborhood. The people who are the finest type of American are pushed to the wall, while the lousiest type uses Defense work to get rich quick as lazily as possible, hoping the war will go on indefinitely. Of course, some of this ruin of the Forgotten Class may be necessary in total war, but I am convinced there is also a deliberate plan by a Washington clique to use the war to smash this class—in order to achieve the true democracy of the future, when without this class democracy cannot live!

To me, who remember the last war so well, with its ghastly betrayal of the dead, there seems to be in this one a recurrent pattern which I am bitterly afraid will be revealed only too clearly when the peace-making arrives. Again, the peace will be made in secret conference by alleged statesmen and diplomats—that is, by political and professional liars, double-crossers, and greedy international crooks. The peoples will be ruined, war-weary and exhausted. Britain will try to play her old balance of power game and Russia will play the same game against her. And our naive politically-appointed representatives, who will know as little of the realities of Europe as they have ever troubled to know in the past, will be sold twenty gold bricks in the first twenty minutes, have their watches stolen, their pockets picked, and their bright idealistic blue prints thrown down the crapper. After which, with shining grateful faces (but without their pants) they will emerge and announce proudly to press and radio: "The self-sacrificing spirit of the United States of America completely dominates the Peace Conference. This indeed marks the birth of a new era of universal brotherhood among nations." Meanwhile the cops will be removing (temporarily) from the Conference a Serb who has just bitten off a Croat's ear, a Hungarian and a Roumanian who have just finished an amicable chat about Transylvania by stabbing each other—and etc. wherever you put your finger on a map of Europe.

I am sorry if I have said anything to affront your faith in an upward spiral of mankind. Because I myself believe that perhaps a million years from now it may begin to dawn on Man (only when he has a crying jag, I fear) that he has been a damned fool. But I hope you put your upward spiral in hock during the next peace conference. Otherwise, you will surely be rudely goosed by the hard facts behind the flimflam, and fall and maybe severely fracture your tamborine. As Rabelais said, or would have said if he thought of it, you can't build Utopia out of turds! It is one of my favorite maxims.

It seems to me the only realistic way this war can be regarded is as a grim battle in which we must crush or be crushed. That's a good enough war aim for me—to crush Germany and Japan as utterly as they would like to smash us, and no humanitarian foolishness about their peoples not being to blame. Every people is to blame for its government. And no garrulous liberal slogans and window dressing. The only thing I fear is that our bungling, power-grabbing bureaucrats and politicians may make victory cost us so much more than it need cost us of personal liberty and independence, which won't or can't be restored to us, that our material victory over outside enemies may be also a bitter, inner self-defeat which will set the stage for revolution here.

But hell, I would write you a book if I went into all that is in my mind about this. I'll save it till we meet again.

The Guggenheim stuff arrived two days ago. I done my damnedest for you and mailed it back yesterday.[1] But don't count on my sponsorship having much influence there, because I don't believe it has.

I say nothing of my work because there is little to say. Rewrote one of the Cycle plays, that's about all, since I saw you last. I've been too ill physically, or too war-minded—one or the other or both. Every time I really get interested, something or other disturbs, and I go dead. My Parkinson's disease is much worse—some days can't write because can't control hand, fingers. Annoying, to say the least.

We are just about entirely marooned on our hill, now. *A* gas ration cards, Freeman gone, etc. I just manage to make my "must" trip to the Oakland urologist every two weeks. But we're used to the readjustment now and all's well. I love the dopes who go around boasting how cheerfully they endure their *hardships*—or even complaining about them! A little trip to the Solomons—no Japs included, just climate and living conditions—would do them a lot of good.

Our fondest to you and Eline. We sure miss seeing you. And our best to Duncan. He looks like a grand pal.   As ever,   Gene

---

502 • TO JULIAN P. BOYD.   TLS 2 pp. (Stationery headed: Tao House / Danville / Contra Costa County / California) [Princeton]

January the 28th 1943

Dear Mr. Boyd: Your letter was most welcome. No, I was not accusing you of base ingratitude but only of being a mañana correspondent—a failing for which I have the deepest sympathy, being one myself. In fact, one reason I welcome your letter so heartily is because it prods me into writing you what I have intended to write for the past several weeks, and that is that the scripts are now the property of the Princeton Library and no more custody about it. If any formal document to this effect has to be signed, send it on. But I should think this letter would be enough.

I am glad to hear the exhibition is being set up. It will be a favor if you let me know how it goes. I am curious because I cannot imagine anyone being much interested during war-time—and Princeton is practically an Armed Forces' camp now, isn't it?

No objections to your using the George Tyler letters—that is, if I have your assurance that there are no sharp cracks in them about actors or actresses now alive. (As I remember the miscasting of the two plays Tyler produced, there well might be!) Such cracks are remembered, passed on, and finally appear in theatrical gossip columns, and someone's

---

1. O'Neill wrote a letter in support of Winther's application for a Guggenheim Fellowship.

feelings are hurt, even though it dates back twenty years or more. I would not want that to happen.

No objection to the announcement and description of the exhibit. Or the illustration. As I wrote you before, all I wish to avoid is any public announcement about the gift. For example, it would be perfectly all right with me if you had someone write an article on the scripts for your *Library Gazette*. In that article it could be stated the scripts are a gift. This idea occurs to me because the Yale Library suggested such an article on its scripts and I consented. In that way the news leaks out eventually to everyone who is really interested without ever becoming news in a newspaper sense.

I have looked through my files and cannot find a letter from Mencken. I never had more than two or three letters from him, as I remember, because even in the old *Smart Set* and *American Mercury* days, it was Nathan who always wrote me. The Mencken letters I did have were in the files I left in my Bermuda house when I went to Europe in 1928. I never recovered these files. They were either destroyed or stolen.

As for the larger handwriting in the Tyler letters, one explanation is, I made myself write larger in letters so they could be read easily. And my handwriting was naturally a bit larger, anyway, when I wasn't absorbed in creative work. The more concentrated and lost to myself my mind became, the smaller the handwriting. At least, this seemed to be the general rule then. But if you ever look over the early one-act sea play scripts at the Museum of the City of New York, you will find the handwriting large by comparison with later work. The minute style grew on me. I did not wish it on myself, God knows, because it made it so hard to get my scripts typed—forced me to type a lot of them, which was a damned nuisance. I always hated typewriting and was very bad at it. Of late years, I can't write anything but minute, but there is a physical reason for that—the curse of Parkinson's disease—it's easier to control tremor in minute writing. And that's all I know on the handwriting business.

I am delighted to know you found the scripts interesting when you examined them. One thing about them is sure. They certainly are not ordinary exhibits, in these days when practically every author types or dictates his originals. Which I wish I could but can't.

Mrs. O'Neill joins me in all good wishes.   Very sincerely,   Eugene O'Neill

---

503 • TO ROBERT SISK.   TLS 4 pp. (Stationery headed: Tao House / Danville / Contra Costa County / California) [Private]

February the 22nd 1943

Dear Bob: The O'Neill household has been much upset lately or this reply would have been sooner. Carlotta had a bout of flu and just escaped pneumonia. And my Parkinson's disease has been getting much worse—which is inevitable, even if there was no war strain to encourage it. Some days I can't write—can't physically, I mean—my hands won't behave. And we have been badly bitten by cook-troubles. A recent one, who lingered for two weeks, turned out to be a loony—a definite psychopathic case—and were we glad to get her off the premises! Living in the country these days is no cinch, from so many angles, but when we think of how much more difficult it is in the East we're delighted to be here.

It is grand to hear you are so satisfied with your work at Metro. *Faculty Row* certainly ought to be a hit—with O'Neill on the blackboard, how can it miss? (many thanks for the ad!)—and I particularly like your idea for the O'Brien kid.[1] You should have a lot of

---

1. MGM did not produce a film with the title *Faculty Row*; child actress Margaret O'Brien starred in MGM's *Lost Angel,* which was produced by Sisk and opened in April 1944.

amusement doing that one. I have a suggestion you might think worth working in. It's taken from life and the old days of Provincetown. A certain radical lady writer there had a prodigy child (male) a bit older than your girl star, who had read the *Encyclopedia Britannica* from cover to cover. Fact! More horrible still, he possessed an abnormal memory, and he persisted in interrupting ignorant adult discussions on any topic, correcting errors, and giving the old *Britannica* facts. A most obnoxious child, intensely loathed by one and all!

By all means, keep plugging on the Frank Morgan film theme in other films. That is really true propaganda for democracy. I am surprised and pleased that it drew cheers from an audience. A darned hopeful sign of awakening! The trouble is, as I harped on in *Lazarus Laughed,* men cheer and then forget everything but the things they should forget. I am afraid the peace after this war will be another outstanding proof of that.

Much gratitude for your offer of help in our isolation, but we are like you, nothing to complain about. Yes, I, too, read in the papers about how frightful it is for us rationed civilians. The beefers had better save their beefs. They ain't seen nothing yet.

Re my daughter, you can't prove she is in Hollywood by me. I have heard from her only once since she relinquished education in favor of Stork Club glamour. She wrote tersely to state she wanted to see me to tell *me* what *she* intended to do. Strangely enough, while I admire youthful independence, this did not strike me as the correct approach after nearly a year's silence, considering various interviews she had given out, her general conduct during that time as reported to me, etc. In fact, I was extremely fed-up and wrote her a sound spanking reply. Since which, communication lines are severed, so to speak. If she has the notion of becoming a film glamour girl, she has never divulged such ambition to me. But it is probable, I suppose—the easiest way to exploit my name for dough and publicity, her advisors will figure. In my letter I told her I would rather have a Red Cross nurse or a munition plant worker for a daughter than ten million glamour nitwits. I fear that didn't take very well. From her letter, I judge she has never heard of the war, or of taxes, or even of the alimony that supports her.

It is one of those things, Bob—her mother's spoiled little girl, and the only right I've had was the right to be vetoed. I bore you with the above information because I'd like you at least to know the truth down there in case she does land a job. It will be no case of my being estranged from the young lady just because she wants to break into films, as they may believe is a good publicity angle, but for sundry other matters which had to do with her past conduct toward me.

About *Long Day's Journey Into Night,* I still have no script I could send. No one has read it. Carlotta has had so much housework to do for a long time—we keep only a cook (when we can get one!) and the secretary work is out. Besides, it is certainly no play for now, for many reasons, so why bother?

In the past year I've rewritten one of the Cycle plays *A Touch Of The Poet,* did some work on another non-Cycle play, "The Last Conquest" and am now rewriting the play (non-Cycle, too) which got blown apart by Pearl Harbor, *A Moon For The Misbegotten.* But everything moves slowly—bad health interruptions, and, of course, war preoccupation—and post-war apprehensions!—giving me on many days the old "what's-the-use" apathy.

Yes, I have a grand idea for a picture, "The Last Conquest" play I've mentioned above. In many ways it *could* be done much better in a film than on the stage. Also, it *could* be the most significant picture ever made—my opinion, of course. But hold everything! You couldn't get anyone to touch it with a two mile pole. To prove this here's something about it: Time, the future, a century or so hence. The seemingly inevitable has happened. There is one universal Collectivist World State. The realistic life-conception that men are only what they seem has triumphed completely and given birth to a State religion. The State is the Mother Goddess with temples and statues everywhere and an immense bureaucratic priesthood. But the main figure in the State is Her Son, Divine but also a man, the Leader, the Savior of Mankind, the World Dictator. His principal minister and adviser—and *his* ruler, really,—is Satan in the form of a man, a former magician, hypnotist, and ventriloquist. All men, including the Elite ruling caste, have become slaves to Divine Leader and the State—but believing that the slavery of the citizen is the natural state of man they are contented. Man has no value in himself, but merely as a citizen of the State.

In short, Evil, as symbolized by Satan, has won a complete and final realistic victory—that is, seemingly. Men no longer have souls. Good is simply unscrupulous opportunism. The Will to Power has enslaved the world and crushed the spirit from men. Hope is dead. All has been conquered. Satan feels his job on earth is really finished. But there is still one thing to do. There still exists in the minds of men, thrust back in the subconscious because the law does not permit thought about it, a dim memory of an old unrealistic legend concerning a savior of ancient times. The danger in the legend is that it contained a prophecy he would come back to earth a second time. So Satan advises the Leader to let him undertake The Last Conquest which will erase forever from men's minds this hidden memory of Christ (Good). The danger is slight, of course, but still it does exist and it should be liquidated. And the way to do this is to attack first, as always,—to fake the Second Coming, to repeat all the main incidents of Christ's former career on earth but turn it into a farcical pageant which will make everyone laugh with scorn. The memory must be murdered by sneering laughter. As for how to fake Christ himself, Satan is a wonderful wood carver, too. He shows a life size figure of Christ to the Divine Leader and his council of Ministers, Satan's colleagues. As for making the figure speak, Satan is the greatest of all ventriloquists, and he knows everything Christ said before, and all he has to do is to use these words because they will sound so ridiculous now. He makes the figure of Christ appear to say, as an example, "Love ye one another." Grotesque! In the Omnipotent World State the first principle of realistic self-preservation is to hate and fear your neighbor, because, like yourself, what is he but a greedy animal?

Etc. That's all in Prologue. First scene of play, the Mount of Temptation in which Christ is offered the world if He will give up His soul. When He refuses, all the citizens of the world gathered (by decree) on the plains below let out a roar of incredulous laughter. To refuse all in exchange for what doesn't exist! Evidently, an imbecile!

Well, you get the idea. And Satan does *not* win in the end. In fact, strangely enough, he does not really want to win—that is, part of him does not. He is a complicated proud character and—

In the play, only the Divine Leader-World Ruler and His Minister of Spiritual Affairs (Satan) are men—that is, until the final of two last Calvary Scenes. All the other ministers are ventriloquist dummies. So are any other individual figures—bureaucratic priests of the State Goddess in the Temple scene, etc. The citizens of the State are mostly painted on drops. (So appropriate! I feel like that already!) Satan will be a wonderful part if I ever finish this opus—so wonderful no actor could ever memorize all the lines in four weeks, let alone play it— So that saves me any worry about production.

Of course, what I've given you is such a bare sketch that it really conveys little. Seriously, I think the idea hits the real disease of the world, of which the last world war and this one and the ones to come are and will be but symptoms. It might be subtitled "Propaganda Against Realism." Governments now *all* act as if any end justified any means, in peace as well as war, and call that realism—and I'm sure all the boys on Alcatraz agree with them! The end of that credo is death in life—for nations as well as individuals. What to do about it?

I don't know. I have no faith and no answers—only a hope. But, by Christ, I do see the question and I don't let myself evade it, although that would make life and wars a lot easier to take and death less desirable.

But I drift. Now you've got this colossal idea, just drop it in Mr. Goldwyn's or Mr. Mayer's lap, forward their check for a hundred grand and start shooting. Of course, they may land in Leavenworth with us when it dawns on Washington that I mean a possible future United States State, too. But what the hell, we will all have each other.

All affectionate best from us to you and Cepha.   As ever,   Gene

---

504 • TO AGNES BRENNAN.   TLS 2 pp. (Stationery headed: Tao House / Danville / Contra Costa County / California) [Yale]

June the 19th 1943

Dear Agnes: I thought that property had already been sold for taxes. I gave it up as a worthless piece of junk years ago, and felt it was silly to bother paying the taxes.

You ask if there is anything you can do about it. Well, here's a proposition you can pass on to Lil, if she believes there is any chance of selling. I'm enclosing a check for the taxes due, so she can pay them as my duly authorized agent. Then if she can find any buyer for the place, she and I will split fifty-fifty on whatever she gets for it. She will deserve this commission because, judging from past experience, it will be a miracle if she finds a buyer. Jules Moran never got the faintest nibble, and I have never received an offer.

But, tell Lil, the last thing I want would be for her to take this on as something I wished on her. Unless she feels pretty sure there is a chance of selling it, I don't want her to bother with it. If, on thinking it over, she feels—as well she might!—that it wouldn't be worth the trouble she can return the check and I will let them sell it for taxes. One way or another I would like to be rid of it. Owning real estate, except one's home, is no game for an author.

I would not mention this at all if your letter did not say Lil thought the place might be salable now.

News from us is mainly doleful, so I will make it brief. We are alone here now except for the farmer who comes—when he can—to cultivate the land. No servant. Can't get one. The last cooks we had—for brief periods—not only could not cook but there was something wrong with each of them. One was a real lunatic—and I mean really cuckoo. We were sure relieved to get her out of the house before she decided it would be nice to set fire to it! Carlotta does the cooking now and makes a fine job of it, although it is new work for her. I wipe dishes and work outside attending to chickens, etc. Well, such is war and we are not kicking, but what makes it tough is that her health is bad and so is mine. She has had a run of bad luck lately—arthritis, then a terrible dose of poison oak, and now a strep throat. I have two incurable ailments to keep me amused, one being Parkinson's disease, which is not fatal but gets steadily worse and is damned unpleasant. Some days I cannot control my hands, so I cannot write or typewrite—and I've never been able to dictate creative work. However, I continue to work (shorter hours) and have a lot done—some of the best things I've ever written—which will see the light when the right time comes.

You, of course, have read of the latest antics of my daughter, Oona, and I am sure you share my opinion of them. The young lady and I severed relations some time ago—because of many things. When she last was here with us—two years ago—she appeared to be developing into an intelligent, charming girl. But in New York with her mother to advise her, she suddenly changed into a silly, cheap publicity grabber. That Stork Club glamour girl racket—a phony advertising-the-Club affair—went to her head. She couldn't see that all they wanted was to use her news value as my daughter, and didn't give a damn about her. That has been her line ever since—using "O'Neill's daughter" to get any kind of display no matter how vulgar and stupid—and finally ending up in this typical Hollywood scandal and marriage with a man as old as I am (probably older, for what actor gives out his real age).[1] Of course, he's rich, and that is the answer, or one of the answers. I need not tell you, I know, that you are never going to hear of our entertaining Mr. and Mrs. Chaplin, or of their entertaining us. Enough is enough!

Love to you and all the Brennans.   As ever,   Eugene O'Neill

---

505 • TO JAMES T. FARRELL.   TLS 2 pp. (Stationery headed: Tao House / Danville / Contra Costa County / California) [Pennsylvania]

July the 28th 1943

Dear Mr. Farrell: I waited for "The Odyssey In Dublin"[1] to arrive before replying to your letter. (Mail to the Coast is a bit erratic these days.) It is a revealing piece of work—about the most interesting and credible analysis I have read. It makes me want to reread *Ulysses*, something I haven't done since around the time Damon's brochure was printed, 1929. Until I do, I won't know if I agree with your criticisms of the pamphlet. Much of Joyce's novel has become blurred in my memory. There are some parts of it I always found terrifically boring, greatly as I admired most of it—parts that seemed to me all out of proportion to their importance—the series of imitations of English prose styles, for example.

Your point that no critical analyst has dealt sufficiently with the Irish aspects of Joyce is certainly true. They seem to understand so little of Irish history, political and religious—little of the Irish past in Joyce. They do not see how distinctively Irish the pride of Stephen Dedalus is—and how old it is. And so they cannot feel the depth of *Irish* tragedy in the dying mother—Stephen's pride drama. They examine it as if it were a scene from Ibsen or Strindberg illuminated by Freud.

Speaking of the Irish past, I want to recommend a book published in the U.S. some six months ago, *The Great O'Neill* by Sean O'Faoláin. If you haven't already read it, you will find it worth your while. It is a biography of Hugh O'Neill but also a study of Irish history in Elizabethan times. I learned from it a lot of Irish past I had mislearned before. You know what most Irish histories are like—benign Catholic benediction-and-blather tracts, or blind jingo glorifications of peerless fighting heroes, in the old bardic fashion. Hugh O'Neill, as O'Faoláin portrays him in the light of historical fact, is no pure and pious archangel of Erin, but a fascinatingly complicated character, strong proud and noble, ignoble shameless and base, loyal and treacherous, a cunning politician, a courageous soldier, an inspiring leader—but at times so weakly neurotic he could burst openly into tears (even when sober!) and whine pitiably that no one understood him. In short, Shakespeare might have written a play about him. He was worth it—one of the most interesting men of his time, and one of the most intelligent and successful of all the Elizabethan age power-grabbers.

Will you thank Foster Damon for me when you write him and tell him how much I appreciated his inscribing "The Odyssey In Dublin" and how much I liked it. I knew him by name well in the old days but cannot remember meeting him. Which proves nothing

---

1. Oona O'Neill (age eighteen) married Charles Chaplin (age fifty-four) on June 16, 1943.

1. An article by S. Foster Damon that appeared in *Hound and Horn* (October–December 1929); Farrell apparently sent O'Neill a copy of the essay.

because whenever I was in New York then my memory wasn't so good—probably due to something I ate.

All good wishes to you and Hortense Alden,[2] and again many thanks for sending me Damon's brochure.   Sincerely yours,   Eugene O'Neill

---

506 • TO SEAN O'CASEY.   TLS 2 pp. (Stationery headed: Tao House / Danville / Contra Costa County / California) [Private]

August the 5th 1943

My dear Sean: This is a hell of a late reply to your May letter, but the O'Neill household has suffered so many upsetting ordeals in the past two months that, while promising myself I would surely write you to-morrow, when to-morrow arrived I always felt too dull and depressed to attempt it. Carlotta has been ill with bad arthritis. This has made it particularly hard for her because she is now doing all the housework and cooking. Impossible to get a servant. I can't be of much help, except as dishwiper, what with my ailment. The matter of merely keeping the home fires burning is a problem when it is complicated by inexperience and illness. If we were both a bit younger and physically fit it would be easy enough.

It seems silly even to mention our troubles when civilian life in this country is such a bed of roses compared to what people have to endure, sick or not, in so many other countries. But my tale of woe does explain why I have done little or no work recently. Too tired the flesh and spirit—and too damned many worrying interruptions of one kind or another to nag at the mind and distract concentration.

All I've done since Pearl Harbor is to rewrite one of the plays in my Cycle. *A Touch Of The Poet*—(an Irish play, incidentally, although located in New England in 1828). This is the only one of the four Cycle plays I had written which approached final form. The others will have to be entirely recreated—if I ever get around to it—because I no longer see them as I did in the pre-war 1939 days in which they were written. I have also (in the past two years) written a non-Cycle play entitled *A Moon For The Misbegotten*. In this, too, the important characters are Irish, although it is less remote in time (1923) than the Cycle play. Beyond these two plays—and they both still need a final touch of condensation—I've messed around with another play, "The Last Conquest," but haven't got beyond writing the Pro-logue and a scenario of its eight scenes. It kept dying on me, after each brief burst of enthusiasm. In many ways it could be better done as a picture than a stage play—that is, if Hollywood ever could treat a subject of depth and integrity with depth and integrity—which, of course, is a fantastically impossible notion.

You would like *The Iceman Cometh*, I know. It was written after I stopped going on with the Cycle in '39 and is one of the best things I have ever done. And the play I wrote immediately after it, (in 1940) *Long Day's Journey Into Night*, is *the best*. No one, except Carlotta, has read this play yet. I have a strong feeling against letting anyone see it now. For that matter, no one has seen the two Irish plays I've mentioned. Because they are still in longhand, and my secretary (Carlotta) has had to resign as such for the duration (except for letters). She simply has not the strength or time to keep on that job, too. Typing my longhand is tough work. A magnifying glass is part of the necessary equipment. I couldn't hire anyone else to do it, even if there were anyone to hire.

I'm delighted to know you saw the *Mourning Becomes Electra* production in London and

---

2. Actress who became Farrell's second wife in 1941.

liked it. I saw all the press comments on it, of course. And they sent me a lot of photographs. Beatrix Lehmann looked the part of Lavinia more than Alice Brady who played it in New York. But I doubt she could have given as fine a performance. Alice, at her best, was hard to beat.

As for the envy you felt about the play, hell, don't you know I want to bite off one of your ears in jealous fury every time I think of—well, of *The Plough and The Stars,* to mention only one of several.

The next time you write, tell me about yourself and your recent work. (God knows I have wished a bellyful of information about mine on you in this letter, and you ought to retaliate!) I've read *Purple Dust,*[1] of course, and there was grand stuff in it for me. Madden wrote me several times he hoped he had found a good producer for it but, if he succeeded, he never told me and I have been so entirely out of touch with the New York theatre, I wouldn't know unless he or George mentioned it to me.

Carlotta joins me in love to you. And much gratitude for your letter. It bucked up my spirit a lot. Here's hoping we may have an opportunity to get together again in New York, as we did once when there was no war.   Very sincerely,   Eugene O'Neill

---

507 • TO J. J. DOUTHIT.   TLS 1 p. (Stationery headed: Tao House / Danville / Contra Costa County / California) [Dartmouth]

November the 30th 1943

Dear Mr. Douthit: Your letter should have been answered sooner, but I've been ill.

I've racked my memory but can't recall a Steven Simkovitch in connection with the "Garbage Flat," or in any other connection. However, this does not mean I didn't know him and know him well. There were many good drinking companions in those days I knew only by their nicknames. If I ever heard their real names, I promptly forgot them.

But I must take exception to Mr. Simkovitch's story. The "Garbage Flat" I remember fondly and vividly. I ought to. I christened it. And there were only three tenants—Terry Carlin, Jack Druilard and I. No Howard Scott. No Steven. Of course, we had many visitors. Steven probably was one of them. Must have been, since he evidently knew the dump. Druilard, who was momentarily—and miraculously—"in the bucks," at least to the extent of a month's rent, acquired the flat for us, unfurnished; and it continued to be unfurnished except for piles of sacking as beds, newspapers as bed linen, and packing boxes for chairs and tables. Also, it remained unswept. Toward the end of our tenancy, there was a nice even carpet of cigarette butts, reminding one of the snow scene in an old melodrama. And—well, in short, the name I gave it was by no means in any way a libel.

So I'm afraid the Simkovitch tale was a fiction based remotely on fact.

For more facts, the time was Spring of 1916 and the flat was located on Fourth Street between Washington Square and 6th Avenue. It was not a basement. Carlin died ten years ago, unknown to fame, but one of the grandest guys I have ever known. Druilard, the last I heard of him, and it was many years ago, was a newspaper reporter.

Many thanks for your letter. It brought back amusing times in times which are far from amusing.

Good luck to you!   Very sincerely,   Eugene O'Neill

---

1. Play first produced in Ireland in 1940 but not premiered in New York until 1956.

508 • TO LAWRENCE LANGNER. TLS 2 pp. (Stationery headed: Tao House / Danville / Contra Costa County / California) [Yale]

December the 31st 1943

Dear Lawrence: First, about the recording device.[1] I am damned grateful for the trouble you are taking. As you describe it, it might be a great help, especially later on when this cursed ailment gets worse, as it is bound to do.

Regarding Spencer Tracy, any visit now or for some time to come is out. Because this household is groggy and not up to visitors. The man who works for us is sick. The cook has flu—a really bad case. Temp. 105 for a while with pneumonia threatening. She won't be on the job again for weeks. This means Carlotta is again doing the cooking, and all the other work she does, *plus nursing and cooking for the cook!* She is all in and on the verge of cracking. So am I, from worrying about her. And we are marooned. Carlotta's daughter is sick, too— can't help. Even the doctor is laid up. And there is nothing we can do but stick it out. The only lucky break is that so far (I knock wood!) Carlotta and I have escaped flu, which isn't to say either of us is bloomingly healthy. We keep loaded up with sulfa, aspirin, etc., to ward off the worst if we do get it, and that doesn't make one feel very cheery. Also I have to keep on the sedatives. It's that, or jump out of my skin.

No, I'd sure like to meet Tracy, because I admire him, but this is no time, as I know he'd be the first to understand. Too much is on our necks.

The Great God Brown might be a good bet for him—to play Brown, of course. He'd be fine in the first part, before Dion's death, and fine in the last part. The trouble is—for a star—that a lot of the best of the play is Dion's. *Strange Interlude* is Nina's play—always has been here and in Europe. You can't get away from it. That's the way it's written. I can't see Tracy in *Marco*, either—nor see a *Marco* revival except with music to give it a fresh angle.

My best bet for Tracy would be *Lazarus Laughed.* Now give heed to this and reread it carefully in the light of what that play has to say to-day. "Die exultantly that life may live," etc. "There is no death" (spiritually) etc. Also think of the light thrown on different facets of the psychology of dictators in Tiberius and Caligula. Hitler doing his little dance of triumph after the fall of France is very like my Caligula.

As far as the unreal-realistic paraphernalia of the masked mobs, chorus, etc. is concerned, forget that. We'll throw all that out. Use only a few people, the rest all offstage sound—unseen choir effect. *Boris Godunov* as a hint of the method. Oh yes, I mean with music. No one but Chaliapin could ever do Lazarus' laughter, but it could be done by the actor starting to laugh and then have his laugh carried on and up by exultant music so that you get the feeling the music is his laugh. You see what I mean. Who to do the music? Hell, there must be someone. And Tracy could get the spiritual quality of Lazarus over, because he could believe in it. Or so I believe.

Anyway, Tracy or not, the above is an idea for a play with music which might really be something. As for sets, everything simplified to a few symbolic details—Roman Empire dominant—one enormous column—a massive wall—a distant aqueduct—temple—a throne—positions changed for each scene—and that's all. These are only hints to give you the general idea in my head—a method of removing *Lazarus Laughed* from the super-expensive production and colossal overhead class and keeping only what really matters.

Think it over. You might also get Tracy to read it with this idea in mind.

Masks, except in *The Great God Brown*, were my mistake. My idea of what they could be made to do was sound enough. I still believe in it. But you need an artist whose life work is to

---

1. Langner had given O'Neill a Sound Scriber, an early recording device.

make masks for the stage. And then you need time to train actors to use them. With no such artist, and no time, the best thing to do is forget it. At that, *The Great God Brown*, produced in four weeks with the sheriff on the doormat, ran for eight months in New York, all but five weeks of that time uptown. Fact! I've just looked it up. I shall always regard this as the one miracle that ever happened in the New York theatre! It strikes me the Mad Twenties were sometimes mad in the right way, and that we should pray we may become that mad again, and not remain insane the way we are now, and have been ever since.

Well, I ramble. Here's wishing you and Armina a fluless New Year. It was sure grand to see you.   As ever,   Gene

P.S. I might even find a better new title for *Lazarus Laughed*—simplified version.

---

509 • TO EUGENE O'NEILL, JR.   TLS 2 pp. (Stationery headed: Tao House / Danville / Contra Costa County / California) [Yale]

January the 28th 1944

Dear Eugene: Not exactly the felicitous moment to reply to your two unanswered letters. I've just finished collecting data to send to Harry for my income tax returns, and the mind, if any, is black as Icelandic landscape. For example, all I seem able to think about, by way of reaction to your threat of a grandchild, is a dismal assembly line of diapers endlessly passing through a din of outraged yells. You and Sally will pardon this, I hope. My heart is really in the right place—just drained of all emotion for the nonce by the strain of being a good paid up citizen of the State. I could bear the paying up cheerfully if the Washington priesthood would only make the documents they demand we sign a bit more understandable. As it is, I feel as if I were paying dues as a member of the Isis cult while being denied any clue to the mystery.

Your letters since you returned to New Haven—the ones to Carlotta, too—have pleased me a lot. Because of the spirit in them. You sound reborn and aspiring—as one to whom a future with meaning and a goal beckons. It is such a comfort and relief—and an inspiration—to read such letters these days. I am so fed up reading or listening to propaganda cheeriness, intermixed with dire warnings, and hearing people talk about post-war in a hopefully hopeless fashion. No one could be more pessimistic than I am about man's fate during the next hundred years, but what the hell, true pessimism says Kismet and grins ironically, it does not drool dolefully. And it admits that in any future the individual *can* make his own satisfying fate.

Your idea of a new method of teaching Greek—or rather of applying the new method used in teaching modern languages to Greek—surely is exciting. It ought to do the trick, I think—get the old prejudices out of the student mind that Greek is an old dead language, impossibly difficult and not worth the tough job of learning it except to some one who wants to be a professor. Psychologically, the mere knowledge that Greek is being taught successfully as if it were French, or Spanish, or Russian should do a lot to change the student's attitude.

What has happened on the Indiana University possibility, if anything? I feel, New Haven climate notwithstanding, it would be a mistake for you to make a change until after the War. Who can tell now what conditions anywhere will be like then? Stay put and wait and see seems the wise dope—especially when you are satisfied with *your work* where you are.

As Carlotta has told you, this rancho is now, definitely and finally, up for sale. The game of keeping it going has become too much for two people in poor health and depleted incomes. A home loses its charm when you begin to feel it owns you, and not you, it—when you have to live from day to day in continuing dependence on other people. Etc. Peace won't alter the impossible conditions much, if at all. Not here on the Coast. They may well be worse! And if we don't get out from under now, we might find ourselves stuck with the place later on when we couldn't give it away. That is our great dread.

As for plans after we do sell—and selling at the right price will be no cinch, we'll need a little luck—we haven't made any plans except to stay in Frisco until the German part of the war is over. After that, quién sabe? No, no Concord stuff. That was just a literary fantasy of mine!

Much gratitude for the books. Haven't got around to reading them yet but will soon.

About the notebook. I find myself sentimentally reluctant to part with it. I'll wait a while.

Love from us to you and Sally.   As ever,   Father

---

510 • TO GEORGE JEAN NATHAN.   ALS 2 pp. (1075 California Street, / San Francisco / (Apart. 1006)) [Cornell]

[March 5, 1944]

Dear George: This is not the letter I promised you—or, at least, not in the detail it should be. It is mainly to give you our present address. The "news" I was going to write you was that our place was for sale. Well, we had luck—found a buyer quickly—got out at a good price— what we put into it, which is saying a lot.

It had become a case of the place owning us, and it was crushing both of us. Carlotta, particularly, since most of the burden fell on her. We had loved it but we were getting to hate it because we were slaves to it—always living in daily uncertainty and insecurity. Well, I'll go into details about all this later.

We left a week ago—were fortunate to find this apartment here. Intend to stay here until at least the German part of the war is over. Carlotta, worn out, started relaxing by catching some infection. Now she's in bed. Taking sulphur. Her condition was serious last night—trained nurses here, etc.—temp. 104! She's better tonight, thank God!

All is sold, automobiles, furniture, everything except books! It's a relief to be free of possessions.

More anon. I hope you can read this. I loaded up with bromide & chloral to get my hand steady enough to give you a break. Carlotta won't be able to type for some time.

Much love from us, George—and please forgive my not writing you sooner. The hell of wanting to write a long letter is that you keep putting it off.   As ever,   Gene

P.S. I'm all shot nervously—but otherwise holding up. The past four weeks of selling, packing, moving, etc. have been a great upheaval and strain.

P.S. II Just got a wire telling me of Harry Weinberger's death. It hits me hard. Twenty-eight years of friendship. It started with his doing work for me for nothing—as he did for so many. There was a lot of extraordinary fineness in Harry that few people ever gave him due credit for. I shall miss his ever loyal and generous friendship. I only hope he knew the depth of my affection for him—and I feel sure he did.

511 • TO HAROLD WAYNE.   ALS 1 p. (Apartment 1006 / 1075 California Street, / San Francisco) [Yale]

[March 5, 1944]

Dear Harold: Your wire telling me of Harry's death arrived some hours ago but I am still knocked out by the shock. Carlotta has been seriously ill ever since we moved in here and I'm terribly worried about her. The news about Harry just about finished me. After I got the wire at the door I took it to my room to open and kept reading it over and over in a stunned daze. I couldn't believe my eyes. I'd heard from him only a week or so ago. I couldn't think of him as gone. And when I finally did realize the truth, I cracked up completely and sobbed my head off. No one, I think, knows how damned fond I was of Harry. I ended my wire to you by saying I loved him. That is the simple truth, backed up by twenty-seven years of friendship which began when he did some work for me for nothing, knowing I had nothing, as his generosity did so often for so many others who needed help but had nothing. My great hope, now that he is gone, is that he realized the depth of my friendship for him, that he knew if things ever got tough and down to cases with him, and every other friend in the world had failed, I would never have failed him, no matter what, any more than, if the reverse were true, he would have ever failed me. I think he knew this, I hope to God he did! Because more than anything else, friendships like that give life value, and recompense for all its double-crossing opportunism and meannesses.

He, my friend, can never be dead to me. I don't forget easily. His friendship will live in my mind and heart as long as I live. And just that long will I continue to be grateful for it.

In my wire I said I was sure you knew how completely I shared your grief. So this is no letter of condolence to you. I feel as though someone ought to write me one for having lost such a friend. No, take this as my sharing my deep sorrow with you, and all who knew him well and loved him.

Give my kindest greetings to your wife—and write when you can and tell me more about how he came to die so suddenly.   Eugene O'Neill

---

512 • TO ROBERT EDMOND JONES.   AL (draft) 2 pp. ([1075 California St., San Francisco, Calif.]) [Yale]

[April 9, 1944][1]

Dear Bobby,   I don't need to tell you I'm delighted about the *Emperor Jones* revival in the fall. Don't know Canada Lee's work, but I'll take your word for it that he can do a fine job. I *do* know what you can do with the production, that you will be able to forget all the other productions and make this your imaginative own, as if it were a new play being produced. That is what is needed.

Perhaps Carlotta and I will be back in the East by the time this happens. I hope so but can't tell yet because it depends on various unpredictables. As you know, we sold our home. It was time. We had become slaves to the damned place and it had worn us to a frazzle. Carlotta, particularly. She had been ailing and the final job of packing and getting out in a hurry finished her. When we moved in here, she became seriously ill and remained so for several weeks. She's better now but far from well.

1. Date supplied in Carlotta O'Neill's handwriting.

We don't own anything now except the books in storage—no house, no furniture, no automobiles or tractor, no fields to be cultivated, no chickens to be tended, no roads to be mended or orchards to be pruned, no lawn to be watered or flowers to be reared, no hedge to be trimmed, no meals to be cooked or dishes to be washed! We got rid of everything—and at a fine price, no sacrifice, that's the best part of it. So although neither of us has recovered from the strain yet, we do feel free. You can have no idea what we have been through in the past two years, especially the last year. Some of it seems funny now in retrospect but it was far from amusing when it happened.

Returning to your letter, if you want one of my plays for a curtain raiser, I would suggest *Where The Cross Is Made*—a very tentative suggestion. I suggest it for atmospheric and symbolic reasons, and because it hasn't been done in New York since P. Player days, and has never had a really fine production—never had the right direction in acting or scenic effect to project its weird ghostly quality. I think of it as a possible opportunity for you. Also, I'm thinking not of the play as now printed but of a properly cut version. When I last looked at it—long ago—it struck me as much too talky for its own good, as getting in its own way. But I did feel the stuff was there, unusual atmosphere and story—good theatre. It interested me a lot more than most of my one-acters. Give it a look, imagining a cut version, and tell me frankly how you feel.

Love from us.   As ever,

---

513 • TO EUGENE O'NEILL, JR.   TLS 2 pp. (1075 California Street—San Francisco—California) [Yale]

April the 28th 1944

Dear Eugene: Been meaning to write you ever since Sunday. We heard the "Invitation to Learning" program[1] and were both enthusiastic. Your voice and diction registered finely and your "radio personality" certainly gets across to the listener. Congratulations! To the program, too. It is a damned interesting one, if last Sunday's is an example of every week. I agree with you that there will be tremendous educational possibilities when television gets going. For that matter, there are right now whenever the singing ad stuff gives them a chance. I think it's a grand hunch for you to dig in on this. Announce anything you have to, say I—even if you have to be accompanied by one of those little hymns to Doctor Hollywood's Vitamin Wheat Bread! And keep us posted, so we can be all ears. Announcing a good hot jazz band would have my enthusiastic support.

I'm delighted you met Art McGinley and that you went out to his home for dinner. I met his wife and step-daughter for a moment in New York—in '33, I guess. Liked them but can hardly say I know them. I sure do know Art, although I haven't seen him in years, and he certainly is a grand guy, one of my closest pals for many years. If he really told you all about the old days, you must have had an amusing and educational time. He and I got in some of the craziest stunts together. Sometimes it was his alcoholic inspiration and sometimes mine, but it was always nuts. Did he tell you of the time at Francis' flats in Provincetown when he was visiting Terry Carlin and me, and we sent him to town to buy some hootch (his money), and on his return he got to the top of the last flight of stairs where we were eagerly awaiting. He had a quart under each arm and a straw hat on. To our horror, he wavered and plunged back down the stairs, through the window at the foot of the stairs taking it with him, and

---

1. Eugene, Jr., had recently taken a job as an announcer on WABC's weekly radio show; he later became a panelist on the program.

wound up on the roof of Francis' store. He pulled himself together, still sound in wind and limb, still with a quart under each arm and his straw hat on, and marched up the stairs to us. It was a deeply moving moment and Terry and I were profoundly touched. As Terry remarked with feeling: "Well, thank Christ, the whiskey didn't break its neck!"

Get Art alone sometime and tell him I release him from any pledge of silence. Then you'll hear something!

I'm damned sorry about his arthritis. Thank God, that's one of the things I haven't got, but I know what it can do—the hell Carlotta suffers from it, for one example.

Art is one of the best sports writers in the country—has a grand sense of humor and real wit—a damned sight better than most of the well known New York sports writers. He could have made the Big City time if he had wanted, I'm sure of it, and I think he was wise to stay clear of the always tense, cut-throat competitive game that goes on in New York sports writing.

Much love from us. Carlotta is better but still not herself.   As ever,   Father

---

514 • TO MARK VAN DOREN.[1]   TLS 2 pp. ([1075 California St., San Francisco, Calif.]) [Princeton]

May 12th 1944

Dear Mr. Van Doren: I was greatly pleased to receive your letter and to know your Committee believes the original scripts I recently discovered can be of real service. That's all I want to know. It salves all my sentimental pangs.

So, via my old friend Saxe Commins of Random House, who has instructions to deliver them to your Committee, I am sending the script of my first play, the one-acter, *The Web* and also another item I dug up which I imagine, perhaps mistakenly, should have considerable rarity-interest, the original script of the only short story ever to be published and also the only script of a short story in existence. I wrote three or four in that same period—*The Hairy Ape* began as a short story—but the scripts were later destroyed. "To-morrow," which I am sending you was published in *The Seven Arts* in 1917, when Van Wyck Brooks, Randolph Bourne, Waldo Frank were among the editors. As a short story—well, let's not go into that, but I thought it was pretty devastating stuff at the time, and so evidently did Van Wyck Brooks, Waldo Frank, etc., although I doubt if they were as overwhelmed by its hideous beauty as I was.

I hope the Committee approves my choice. The other one-act plays I will, as I said in my last letter, hold for later War Bond drives, but you can consider them as pledged to you.

I've attached to each script a signed page with whatever brief explanation (in longhand) I thought necessary for the enlightenment of the purchaser.

I'm glad Julian Boyd is Chairman of your Manuscript Committee. Through my correspondence with him, and his knowledge of the Princeton scripts, he will be on to the idiosyncrasies of the early play scripts—no numbering of pages written on both sides, etc. In *The Web*, however, I think there is a dodge, peculiar to the very first plays—no title page, no list of characters—which will be a new angle even for Mr. Boyd.

To be sure the pages were in order I had to read *The Web* again, and I want to tell you, Mr. Van Doren and Gentlemen of the Committee, that if ever a man felt he was enduring hardship in the line of duty, I was certainly that gent! I love it but I sure don't like it!

---

1. Van Doren (1894–1972), poet and critic, who was then with the Office of War Information and had asked O'Neill to donate manuscripts for a War Bond drive.

I am so glad you liked Eugene.[2] I am damned proud of him. And I'm selfishly grateful for his learning because I can always learn so much from him. It is grand to have a son who is an education instead of one who makes you doubt the value of education.

All good wishes. Very sincerely, Eugene O'Neill

---

515 • TO R. W. COTTINGHAM.[1] AL (draft) 5 pp. ([1075 California St., San Francisco, Calif.]) [Yale]

[May 12, 1944][2]

Dear Mr. Cottingham: Much gratitude for your courtesy in letting me see the biography for the A.P. reference files.

As for "absolute accuracy," I am sure the Nobel Prize I received was *not* any two-year amount. The prize for literature in any one year at that period was worth that much. The amount of the prize varies—I suppose, according to the income from Nobel's gift—but, as I understand it, there is never a doubling two years' prizes into one. This would obviously be unfair.

Your list of plays includes two one-acters, *The Moon Of The Caribbees & Before Breakfast* but does not name the others included in my books. In the order of writing the complete list is *Bound East For Cardiff, Before Breakfast, The Long Voyage Home, In The Zone, Ile, The Rope, The Dreamy Kid* and *Where The Cross Is Made*—all written before 1920. I suggest the list of one-act plays be separated from the long plays to distinguish between them.

I know it is not my business to attempt any censorship of your biography, and I am not, but I want to register a protest against your quote from my friend, Barrett Clark's book. He has written much fine sensible criticism of my stuff, but the exaggerated statistics on the deaths, etc. in my plays is one of those startling statements which, when examined, prove nothing. To make a good case, he includes the earliest, most immature stuff, attempts at plays written when I was still trying to become a playwright. That these would-be plays were ever published is my misfortune. But published or not, anyone can see they are merely preliminary amateurish-melodramatic junk and should no more be considered as adult works than diapers should be rated as trousers.

Well, there is a lot more I could say—such as dragging in Shakespeare and the Greek dramatists as my illustrious masters in mass-murder and driving folks mad, and doing a spot of statistics on their works but I don't believe statistics ever prove anything except what the statistician wants to prove, and I will spare you and get back to inaccuracies: On page three, it was *Beyond The Horizon,* produced on Broadway in 1920, and *not Emperor Jones* (produced at the Provincetown Playhouse downtown the following year)[3] which first established me and also won the Pulitzer. A simon pure uncompromising American tragedy, which a Broadway manager dared to produce on Broadway was surely an epoch-making event in those days—and that it actually kept going from February to the end of the season was another tremendous upset.

This reminds me that I can give you an absolutely true anecdote which, as far as I know, is fresh and hasn't been written and rewritten into a lying legend. In 1920 I had honestly

2. Van Doren met Eugene O'Neill, Jr., through the "Invitation to Learning" program, which Van Doren moderated.

1. West Coast employee of the Associated Press.
2. Date supplied in Carlotta O'Neill's handwriting.
3. O'Neill is in error here; *The Emperor Jones* premiered on November 1, 1920.

never heard of the Pulitzer Prize, or if I had, hadn't listened. So when a wire reached me in Provincetown saying I had won it, my reaction was a disdainful raspberry, "Oh God, a damned medal! And one of those presentation ceremonies! I won't accept it." (I have never been fond of medals or ceremonies.) Then a wire from my agent arrived which spoke of a thousand dollars and no medal and no ceremony. Well, I practically went delirious! I was broke or nearly. A thousand dollars was sure a thousand dollars! It was the most astoundingly pleasant surprise I've ever had in my life, I think.

If the above doesn't suit your purpose, dismiss it, and no hard feelings.

Another inaccuracy on page three: *Bound East For Cardiff was the first play* I read to the Provincetown Group. They produced an earlier play of mine later that summer called *Thirst*. No doubt some of the Group did think that one pretty frightful. I would be the last to quarrel with their opinion.

Mourning Becomes Electra is in twelve acts, four to each play.

I think there is one fact you have omitted which has definite news value. In the years since my plays first attracted attention, I have had several offers to work in Hollywood, some of them fantastically munificent. I have always declined. I have never even been in Hollywood or Los Angeles. This doesn't mean that I have any prejudice against pictures. It merely means that the screen has never interested me as a medium. So why work at something which doesn't interest me when I have always had work on my hands which does interest me and has also paid me well? It is as simple as that—common sense, although some people seem to regard it as a mad—and even inexcusable—eccentricity!

There is one thing I think you ought to mention in a biography, however brief, since it is undoubtedly my most valuable contribution as an *American* dramatist: The undeniable and acknowledged fact is that it was my work which first awakened the outside world to the fact that an adult American drama existed which could be considered as something beyond mere theatrical entertainment, and criticized as an art, as the work of the best European playwrights was criticized. My plays have been translated into many languages and produced all over the world. A couple of years ago, for an extreme example, *The Hairy Ape*, translated into Bantu, was played in South Africa by a company of Zulus before an audience of their own tribes.

Another example: I recently met a Czech refugee who knew my work as few Americans know it, yet had not read a line of it in English or attended a production in English—had seen a lot of the plays at theatres in Prague, read others in Czech translations.

I hope this does not sound like vain boasting because what I want to say is that it isn't important, except to me, that someone by name, O'Neill, did this. It was my luck to be the first, that's all. What is important for the international recognition of American drama is that an American dramatist did manage to break through the old European sadly superior attitude toward the American theatre, and awaken an interest in the work of our serious playwrights which had not existed before.

I hope this letter may be of some help. If I can be of any further assistance, let me know.   All good wishes to you,

---

516 • TO LAWRENCE LANGNER.   TLS 2 pp. (1075 California Street / San Francisco 8 / California) [Yale]

May the 13th 1944

Dear Lawrence: Well, the Sound Scriber has been set up, and I think it is a wonderful machine, and again I want to say how damned grateful I am to the Guild for such a grand present. I can't test it out on the main job of creating with it, simply because I just am not in a creative vein at present. The coming invasion[1] is too much on the heart and brain. I can't think of much else. But I have tested my end of the Sound Scriber on the play form—read spots of *The Iceman Cometh* and *Long Day's Journey Into Night* into it. The result is quite surprisingly effective, considering I am neither a ham nor even an articulate speaker. The voice that comes back fascinates me. It is not my voice and yet it reminds me of someone. (I'm not relying only on my evidence, because one might not really know what one's voice is really like.) It has an impressive ghostly quality and I do succeed in making each word on it clear.

I'll go on with this and when practice makes me wise to the microphone, I expect to get fine results, worth while keeping as personal records. I want to try a few poems, written during the past three years when that mood for poetry writing, which rarely seizes me, did compel me to write it down. They have no titles except "Fragments,"[2] and I'll never try to publish them, but I think records of them in the ghostly voice which is and is not my voice might give them just the right quality.

This, you will agree, is the best kind of practice. It has a mood of fresh creation, even though it is stuff already written. By the time I am ready to create again, I ought to be all set.

Carlotta is still too ill to do anything on her part of the machine, but the man who installed it made her use it a bit, so she knows how, anyway.

The Sound Scriber came at a good time. Old Doc. Parkinson's favorite disease has been giving me hell. It moves in rhythms of better and very bad—the very bad accompanied by extreme mental depression and insomnia. I haven't got to sleep till three, four or five, even, for a week. Sedatives don't work. They are water off a duck's back. But the insomnia part is not as bad as it sounds, although there come nights when I don't sleep one wink—and I mean, not a single wink. But I've learned not to fight it. When I know it's one of those nights, I just get up again and say, "All right, you bastard, let's stay up all night. You loved to do it in the old days, so why not now?" Then I tiptoe to the kitchenette and make a lot of coffee, the idea being, if I'm going to stay awake, I'll damned well do it right. Funny thing, sometimes after drinking quarts of coffee I've lain down—and fallen asleep! But alas, that was around daylight. I like to sit by the window and watch dawn come over the city. It's the only time of day I've ever liked any city—when it is silent and appears deserted. Which is peculiar because I really like people, all kinds of people—that is, as individuals. As crowds, parties, States, God how I loathe them for [a] stupid, brutal, ignorantly selfish, cruel, mean, greedy, unspeakable swinish mob who soil the earth by being alive on it!

Well, the above was meant to lead up to something but it went astray. I was going to say the worst part of Parkinson's in the bad spells is the inner shakes which are so much harder to take than the outer—when you feel it inside all over your body until even your brain seems to do the shimmy. It was like that a couple of days ago when I read into the mike of the Sound Scriber a favorite bit of mine from *The Iceman Cometh*—Act Three, the brief passage between Hickey and Larry when Larry is forced to admit, while refusing to admit, that his saving dream that he is finished with life and sick of it and will welcome the long sleep of death is just a pipe dream. When I played the record back and listened to the voice that was my voice and yet not my voice saying: "I'm afraid to live, am I?—and even more afraid to die! So I sit here, my pride drowned on the bottom of a bottle, keeping drunk so I won't see myself shaking in my britches with fright, or hear myself whining and praying, 'O Blessed Christ, let me live a little longer *at any price!* If it's only for a few days more, or a few hours

1. The Allied invasion of Normandy, which took place on June 6, 1944.
2. See *Poems: 1912–1944*, pp. 102–12.

even, let me still clutch greedily to my yellow heart this sweet treasure, this jewel beyond price, the dirty, stinking bit of flesh which is my beautiful little life!'"—well, it sure did something to me. It wasn't Larry, it was my ghost talking to me, or I to my ghost—and what with the Parkinson's and all, (except, unfortunately, no more a bottom of any bottle, except of ineffective sedatives, or a pot of coffee) I found myself wondering. It really was quite a moment of strange drama. So you see, even the little I've tried your gift, I've discovered dramatic uses for it the makers never dreamed of—and I'll probably keep on discovering them.

Much love from us to you and Armina—and again my thanks for the gift. I'm honestly quite fascinated by it—in a way entirely foreign to its purpose, of course—at least, so far. I would be!   As ever,   Gene

---

517 • TO THERESA HELBURN.   TLS 3 pp. (1075 California Street, / San Francisco) [Yale]

May 16th 1944

Dear Terry: About the prospect of an independent purchaser for *Mourning Becomes Electra* film rights, it depends on whether any method can be found (considering taxes plus a sliding scale of alimony) which will make it worth my while, and also be legally impregnable against the commando raids of Federal Revenue agents. Otherwise, what's the use? I've never liked having distorted pictures made of my plays, and the picture medium has never interested me. I thought long ago when I saw *Caligari*[1] that there could be a genuine, original art form developed along that line. Talking pictures seem to me a bastard which has inherited the lowest traits of both parents. It was the talkless parts of *The Long Voyage Home*—the best picture ever made from my stuff—that impressed me the most.

But let's get back to the tax situation. The first method of an outright sale is out. The new ruling of the Department made a year ago is that all sales of film rights are taxed as income whether the sale be outright or not. I know all about this because the Revenue bandits also made their new ruling retroactive—in my opinion, as shameless a swindle as has come out of Washington under the New Deal, and that is sure saying a lot! I know about it because I was nicked three thousand bucks and more *last year* on my *1940* return because my outright sale of *The Long Voyage Home* rights was declared to be ordinary income, and not taxed as sale of capital asset.

Your second suggestion of a percentage of profits deal doesn't appeal to me either. I won't gamble on a picture. As a leasing, there are possibilities, perhaps. I don't know. An expert tax lawyer would have to decide. Perhaps the tax expert for the Dramatists' Guild would know. Lawrence could ask him. There is no theatrical tax expert here I could tap.

As for price, considering the inflated Hollywood prices for any sort of material to-day, I think we should not sell for anything less than $150,000.00.

So you may understand what my feeling is about a film sale of a favorite play I know Hollywood will distort, let's consider *The Hairy Ape*. It remains one of my favorites. I have an enduring affection for it—always will have—and an enduring respect for it as drama, the more so because so few people have ever seen what it is all about. But let that go. I sold it because, with Tao House and ranch overhead on my neck, I had to sell it or sell some of my securities whose income—pays the alimony! And I sold it cheap—for what the purchaser offered, practically,—because I figured if I held out for a fair price, between taxes and

---

1. *The Cabinet of Dr. Caligari.*

alimony *increased* by the sale, I would get *less than two thousand more* out of double the price I got! But the important point is not price or taxes. I didn't really want to sell because I knew no one in Hollywood had the guts to film *my play*, do it as symbolic expressionism as it should be done, and not censor it into imbecility, or make it a common realistic stoker story. I remember that its first stage production was one of my most satisfying times in the theatre. I remember Wolheim was practically perfect as "Yank," and was also a pal of mine. I don't want to have that memory spoiled. So when I tell you *I am not* going to see the film—nor read one word written about it—nor even ever admit that it exists, I sure mean it! But all the same, I will always feel guilty. The memory of what *The Hairy Ape* is, was, and should be, will, in a sense, be spoiled for me. The picture, even if financially a hit, will be soon forgotten, and the play will remain as if no picture had ever touched it. But still, I will always regret.

About *Mourning Becomes Electra*, I am sure Hepburn would be splendid as "Lavinia." The rest I'm afraid would be a dreadful hash of attempted condensation and idiotic censorship—as the *Strange Interlude* film was.

How about General Mannon's speeches about war, death, etc. and what Orin has to say of war when he returns? Would those be ruled out as morbid pacifism or something? Yet to me these contain an implication, at least, of deep spiritual truth. Do you remember when Orin says to Lavinia in Act III of "The Hunted": —"I had to kill another in the same way. It was like murdering the same man twice. I had a queer feeling that war meant murdering the same man over and over, and that in the end I would discover the man was myself!"

But I'm getting away from the point—and also, getting to the point where I wonder if we ought to sell *Mourning Becomes Electra* at any price.[2] After all, it was a splendid Guild production—your high spot, as a *theatre*, I think—a great Guild achievement against great odds—an event that was a high example of the combined acting, producing, and writing art of the American theatre—so compelling that in the depths of the Depression this tragic trilogy brought packed houses to the theatre in late afternoon for weeks at a six dollar top! (*Strange Interlude* was produced in boom days.) And to me, it is also a high spot. It did more than any other single play to win the Nobel Prize. In every capital of Europe where it was done before the war it was an event. And it still goes on, despite the war, 13 years after your production, and will go on. Only a year ago, it was produced in Lisbon and later revived there—a great success. People came to the theatre in the early evening, something they'd never done before except for Wagnerian opera. It has been done in Switzerland since then. Now they want to do it in Madrid. It is no boasting but plain fact that, no matter what exceptions are taken here or there by this or that critic for this or that reason, it is generally regarded in Europe as the high point in American dramatic writing. Well, all that belongs to the Guild, too. And whether people of this country give a damn about it or not—and they don't—it belongs to their culture. Furthermore, you of the Guild and I are—well, being you're a lady, I won't say growing old but at least entering the period when one begins to select, if one can, some memories of one's work in life worth cherishing and keeping untarnished.

Do we want to let Hollywood debase (as it must, being at heart, even with the best intentions, merely a commercial mob amusement racket) the *Mourning Becomes Electra* in our memories, the achievement that had great significance, whereas the picture will have none?

Am I being sentimental? The Guild will probably think so, since I notice that *Mourning*

2. *Mourning Becomes Electra* was not made into a film until 1947, when Dudley Nichols produced, directed, and adapted it for RKO, with Rosalind Russell, Michael Redgrave, Raymond Massey, Katina Paxinou, and Kirk Douglas starring.

Becomes Electra is not even included in the list at the bottom of your letter paper—presumably a list of your greatest achievements, box office or no box office. You omit *Mourning Becomes Electra* although any international jury composed of critics of dramatic art would tell you it is the most significant modern play you have ever produced since the Guild began. Why, Christ, compared to it, a lot of the plays on your list are, as far as fine drama is concerned, merely things to hang on a hook in a backwoods privy! The jury I speak of would, I know, agree to that judgment with enthusiasm.

Well, the above has rankled for a long time. Now you have it. It doesn't matter a damn, I admit, except that I can hardly be expected to see it as an expression of loyalty to my finest work—or, what is worse, loyalty to yourselves for the important work you have done for American drama and an American theatre (as distinct from the Showshop Business).

Well, I better stop this letter. I don't seem able to stick to the subject. I certainly intended no bitter protests when I started it. I guess the *Hairy Ape* film has soured my disposition. I so deeply regret having sold that play, need or no need, to be boy-and-girled by the Amusement Racket. God knows what a distortion will come of it! The bitterest thought is that with guts, courage, and imagination, a grand, strange, unusual picture could be made of it. Well, it's too late for regrets now. But I want to avoid any such regrets about *Mourning Becomes Electra*.

Carlotta joins me in love to you and Oliver. She is still ill but picking up a bit.   As ever,   Gene

---

518 • TO ARTHUR HOPKINS.   AL (draft) ([1075 California St., San Francisco, Calif.]) [Yale]

[June 5, 1944][1]

Dear Arthur: It was grand to hear from you. Many and many a time in the past years since my serious illness in '36–'37, I've said to myself, I'm going to write Arthur. (Cross my heart, this is the truth!) Not on any particular subject but in general about the way I felt, and know you must feel, about the disappointment of seeing the spirit of the American theatre forget the hope of the Twenties of theatre for art's sake and drift into all sorts of blind alleys— theatre for sociology's sake, partisan politics' sake, provincial patriotism's sake, etc. But as it was to be a long letter, I, of course, kept putting it off and it never got written. Now it will have to wait until I can talk to you. This, I hope, won't be too long. We have sold our home— too much on our necks now that Carlotta, too, is ill—and plan to return East as soon as we can. How soon depends on certain unpredictables which have to be settled up, so I can't predict definitely, but certainly before the end of the year, I should say.

Polly in "*Anna Christie*" again[2] certainly brings back a host of pleasant memories. I wish I could have heard her in it, but if your programs reach the Coast yet, I've heard nothing of it. I don't think it is just a man of 55 looking back on the good old days. There *was* a spirit then that has been lost. There *were* uncompromising idealists with a real love for what the American theatre might become. If there are any such left—with a few exceptions to prove the rule—then I never hear from them. All are from Showshop people, and mark that angle as they may with idealistic phrases for my beguiling, that angle is all they can conceive of as theatre. Not that I have any prejudice against Showshop as such, God knows, any more than

---

1. Date supplied in Carlotta O'Neill's handwriting.
2. Pauline Lord had been featured in a radio adaptation of "*Anna Christie*," broadcast May 17, 1944, on "Arthur Hopkins Presents."

I have against pictures, but there should be a theatre, too, recognized as separate and an attempt at art, and not judged by the same standards, or by any propaganda standard.

Your libel on me enclosed in your letter is too flattering for me to start suit, I've decided. You can go as far as you like in this same vein, and expect no trouble from me.

Madden writes me that *The Hairy Ape* film will be released in August. I shall give it a wide miss. My memories of Wolly in the original production are too close, and the play remains one of my favorites. The movie is bound to be a mess. How could they even touch the meaning of the play—ever, but especially in these days—in a mass entertainment trade? I won't blame them for anything they've done—considering the circumstances—but damned if they'll make me look at it. My consolation about pictures of my stuff, and my justification regarding my stand of refusing to work on a picture or have anything to do with it, but leave the entire responsibility to the producer are that I find the pictures are soon forgotten but the plays remain as if no picture had ever touched them. *The Hairy Ape* should remain around for some time, asleep, perhaps, but alive. I hope so, anyway. It deserves to, I think. When you read it now, it has a lot of spiritual prophecy in it which has come true and will come truer. The releasing of the gorilla, for example, is a poor final attempt at belonging in life, and a poor revenge for not belonging, because it leads only to death.

However, this begins to sound like a sales talk for a faith, citing a horrible example, and as I never did and never shall belong in one any more than "Yank" could, I better shut up.

The *Times* write-up gave your program a fine send-off and I sure hope you will have a great success with it. I don't know enough about radio to have any idea what the long range possibilities may be. Certainly your idea is a fine one and should go on and on. The thing I have felt all wrong about stage plays translated into radio is that they were condensed by people who didn't know the play, and didn't know how to condense, anyway—didn't make use of the radio medium to help them condense. I know that your direction can do all this.

I'll postpone telling you anything of my work since last production until I see you. Too long for letters. Considering handicaps, the record isn't so bad. Among the plays are two I rate at the very top, *The Iceman Cometh* and *Long Day's Journey Into Night*. The reasons I haven't produced are also too numerous and complicated for a letter. They were—and are—valid—for me, at least.

Carlotta joins me in all best to you. And again, my deep gratitude for all you did for me. That, believe me, I have never forgotten nor ever can forget.   Affectionately,

---

519 • TO ROBERT EDMOND JONES.   AL (draft) ([1075 California St., San Francisco, Calif.]) [Yale]

[July 2, 1944][1]

Dear Bobby: Oh hell is right! I am bitterly disappointed about the *Jones* thing. In spite of the fact that I had a hunch it wouldn't happen. They never do, I've found. Usually, with proposed revivals, I say no—or if I say yes, I don't give a damn whether they happen or not. But I knew you would do something fine with *Jones*—and fresh, as the two grand ideas for effects in your letter prove. Also, I thought I might see it because we hope to be in the East before year's end.

Your letter arrived a week before Madden's. I waited to find out what excuse would be offered for not getting financial backing. Madden says rising racial friction has scared people on a negro star play. This sounds nonsense to me. *Jones* isn't that type of play. If a negro

1. Date supplied in Carlotta O'Neill's handwriting.

Othello can get by with Desdemona, the friction hasn't spread from the tough district to the theatre. My idea is that the Chester-Elkins' sister combination simply is not reliable. I don't know Chester. He may be. I never met Felton's sister, either—but I've heard plenty about her, and I'd say she was one of those ladies who are sure things will happen because they insist they must happen. Perhaps I wrong her. As for her using her own money, no, not if she's like Felton. His income must have been fairly enormous during our Provincetown-Greenwich Village theatre days. Well, you know how much he backed us, even when he had a job with us! I liked Felton, saw good things in him no one else seemed to see, always felt he was a victim of a silly but implacably destructive fate from the day he was born. But one of his worst defects I discovered back in Harvard days—and quick. He was a tightwad except where his personal indulgence and vanity was concerned. He could cry poor on a waiter's tip with two grand in his wallet.

I'm damned sorry your work on *Jones* is wasted. But keep it, for God's sake. There will come a time. And I'll say no to all *Jones* revival projects unless they take you in on it. Also *Desire*, as per your wish and mine. Also *Brown* (but no one in these "realistic" days will ever revive *Brown*).

Nothing new on the Guild notion of a *Desire* revival. Probably won't be. They just toss off such ideas, probably to keep me cheerful and interested. It doesn't work. I am neither.

Speaking of color friction plays, I need not tell you no one ever wants to revive *All God's Chillun*, the only play that ever dared touch the real tragedy and fate of it. But it will soon be done at the Royal Theatre in Stockholm—or revived—I forget if they ever did it before in Sweden. And *Mourning Becomes Electra* was recently revived in Lisbon. Its two productions there are the only times Lisboners have ever gone to the theatre in early evening except for Wagnerian opera—which is something, considering Latins' daily habits and that it is for an American play. Also *Desire* is still being done—for the fourth year—in the provinces in England—and so are *Ah, Wilderness!* and *"Anna Christie"* touring about there. So war or no war, the plays do go on, hither and yon.

Love from us,   As ever,

---

520 • TO EUGENE O'NEILL, JR.   TLS 1 p. ([1075 California St., San Francisco, Calif.]) [Yale]

July 9th 1944

Dear Eugene: The "Invitation to Learning" broadcast on Cicero's *Orations* was of great interest to me. Although anyone who believes the newspaper and publicity man's legends about me—which give the general impression I was born drunk in Jimmy the Priest's and raised to manhood in the Hell Hole—would never credit it, I really liked Latin in Prep. school, especially Cicero, and was good at it—used to be able to reel off parts of his *Cataline* by heart. This liking Latin was regarded as a startling mental defect by one and all of my fellow students—as I suppose it would be in school to-day. Which is all beside the point except to demonstrate that I could remember enough of Cicero's *Orations* to take an intelligent interest.

What I didn't like was what I thought was a bit too much pointing out resemblances between those days and these—the "timely" discussion stuff. I recently read some pseudo-serious article which compared Roosevelt to Tiberius Gracchus from an historical standpoint of economical determinism and philosophic Instrumentalism (that is, evidently). It made me want to puke. It was so profoundly slick and superficial. What I got from it was that there had once been a United States of America called by the inhabitants for convenience sake, Rome, and at a certain economic spot in its agricultural destiny, there arose Tiberius Franklin Gracchus, the son of a certain farmerette in Kansas, known as Corny to friends and traveling salesmen for the McCormick Reaper Company—

But I seem to be getting as mixed up as the author left me—so let's drop it and give T. Franklin Gracchus, tribune of Tammany Hall, back to the Roman people.

As a closing word on the broadcast, let me commend your natural graciousness as chairman, as it registered to me over the wire. But perhaps I was biased.

We are still in a poor way—Carlotta still ill and I have lately had one of the bad spells of Parkinson's, pretty tough. I am convinced doctors know very little about this disease, except symptoms, one of which is that it customarily follows a rhythm, no one knows why, of ups and downs, the downs being accompanied by acute mental depression as well as increased shakes. The other day my hands without warning jerked a cup of coffee all over the surrounding landscape, and suddenly I burst into weeping, not because I'd spilt the coffee but impelled by the same nervous impulse, as it were. As I've never been addicted to nervous weeps, no matter what the strain or (in the old days) how much booze was in me—I am terribly upset by such exuberant blues, and if the docs didn't say these things were all part of the game, I would feel more than slightly nuts. As it is, I try to be merely disgusted with myself.

Much love from us,   As ever,   Father

---

521 • TO EUGENE O'NEILL, JR.   TLS 2 pp. (1075 California Street / San Francisco 8 / California) [Yale]

August 13th 1944

Dear Eugene: I must confess that I missed your *Marius The Epicurean* broadcast. Same old story. I set the alarm, woke up enough to turn it off, then was asleep again before I could grab the impulse to get out of bed. I had not fallen asleep until 4 A.M. The program really comes at a tough time for me because I so rarely fall asleep until 2, 3, or 4, and don't have breakfast until around ten. It's a pity the program cannot be transcribed and given on the Coast at a better time. So many people miss it who would like to hear it—not because they're still asleep like me, but because it hits practically every Sunday morning household at the wrong moment, for one reason or another—I mean the wrong moment for a program that requires undivided attention.

However, it *can* be done. I've proved that once. And the next time I'll surely make it.

No, normally, I'm not much for weeps, nerves or no nerves. I had to learn to control them at an early date—see *Long Day's Journey Into Night*—or I would have become a futile fountain. So I naturally reacted toward the other extreme in self defense, and acquired an admiration for gambler's dead pan—an ancient universal code which antedates Stoic philosophy, I am sure, and has nothing to do with Anglo-Saxon Icebergs, since you used to be able to see all races practicing it at Monte Carlo, and you can find shining examples of it in French History, Irish History, etc.

On the other hand, to split fifty-fifty with you, I admit you can find shining examples of manly weeping, too. And I really agree (mentally) with what you say about "Nature's mechanism," etc. There have been so many times when I wanted to weep—and couldn't.

About Roosevelt-T. Gracchus, more when we can talk it out. I evidently was not clear in my letter. What I object to is the too-easy, superficial comparisons, where everything is made to fit into a petty angle of contemporary partisanship. (I'm thinking now of the junk I burlesqued.) Teaching, when you have time to develop a comparison in depth is one thing.

Remarks during a fifteen minute radio program where the comparison is not the subject is another thing. After all, the subject was Cicero's *Orations*. What would have interested me would have been to show the importance of *Oratory* in Cicero's time and the period in our history when the orations, not speeches, of our Senators had a comparable importance—the pre Civil War period of Webster, Hayne,[1] Calhoun, etc. I can remember when I was a kid in school—before prep. school—there were still elocution classes in which oratory was taught, and the famous oration of Webster was liable to be murdered with gruesome gestures by almost any senior as a bright spot of Commencement Exercises. Although I was a mere child at the time, the horrible spectacle of these seniors flinging their menacing fists about wildly in the general direction of South Carolina, is with me still.

I cite the above boyhood reminiscence to show you how long those orations remained alive—and with them the respect for oratory as oratory.

You seem to have got me down as a Roosevelt hater. I never said he was a nonentity. That would have been too stupid. It's true I feel contempt for his sly hypocritical politician's tricks, and his willingness to grab votes from any stinking sty, such as the Kelly machine in Chicago, when he should publicly denounce and refuse such help. But that's politics, a squalid game with squalid rules, and he's a politician, playing the game according to the rules, and playing it cunningly and unscrupulously like the *great politician* he is. Of course, if he were a great *man* he would refuse to play according to such rules. Wilson did—and he wasn't so great, merely great compared to Roosevelt—and, of course, to the majority of our Presidents who were nothing much of anything.

On the other hand, I admire Roosevelt for the guts and courage he has shown in overcoming his physical handicaps, and for the way he has borne the terrible, killing responsibility of a War Commander. Occasionally, in this role, he attains the semblance of genuine stature and dignity. But, all the same, if I were voting this fall, I'd vote for Norman Thomas[2] whom I believe to be by far the most honorable and intelligent man of the three.

But what the hell, the above is idle conversation. I really do not give a damn who is elected. It will not matter in the long run—or in the short run, for that matter. Dewey, if he gets in, will have the sense to go with the tide. Old Guard Republicanism is dead—a good deal deader than the Old Guard Democracy of the South will ever be while you or I live.

Carlotta is still going to doctors. One thing they have discovered for certain is that she has a strong wheat allergy which is the cause of the bad throat she has had for six months— and by bad I mean really *bad*. But her other ills are cured or clearing up. She has had one hell of a time of it, one thing on top of another. She joins in much love to you. As ever,   Father

---

522 • TO MRS. GUYMAN.[1]   AL (draft) 2 pp. ([1075 California St., San Francisco, Calif.]) [Yale]

[August 19, 1944][2]

Dear Mrs. Guyman,   I remember well the dissertation on my work which you sent me when I was living in France.

1. U.S. Senator Robert Young Hayne (1791–1831).
2. Thomas (1884–1968), Socialist leader, and perennial Socialist Party candidate for President. In 1944, he was running against Republican Thomas E. Dewey, governor of New York, and incumbent Franklin D. Roosevelt.

1. Possibly married name of Margarete Weiss, whose 1928 Vienna University dissertation, "Die Dramen Eugene O'Neills," is the only Vienna dissertation on O'Neill before 1936.
2. Date supplied in Carlotta O'Neill's handwriting.

Be angry? Forgive you because in your dire straits and despair you have appealed to me? I assure you it is a privilege to be able to help, and the fact that I have never met you means nothing. From your letter, I know how you have suffered and are suffering and that is enough. Also, for your appreciation of my works, I owe you a debt of gratitude. And I do feel that, knowing my work, you do know me—the best of me.

It would be an impertinence to offer you sympathy. I am an American civilian who has the luck to be safe and far away. But perhaps I have enough sensitiveness and imagination to *feel* a little of how terrible life can be to one in your situation, who has been through what you have been through.

I hope the amount enclosed[3] may be of some assistance—at least help you to stop work for time enough to recover your strength.

There is this consolation: The war in Europe cannot last much longer. You may soon be able to return home to Vienna. The Nazi domination seems about finished—defeated every-where in battle and beginning to devour itself in Germany.

It is, as I have said, an impertinence for me to offer you words of consolation. But I do, nevertheless. Keep up your courage a little longer. The long and horrible night is passing for you. I hope the peace to come will mean peace to you personally in every way—and happiness.

Forgive me if this is not the long letter I should write you. I am ill. My health has been bad for several years. I have been able to do little work in the past two years.

Let me know if you need any further help. I would send you more this time but I am not among those whose means has been increased by the war. Quite the contrary!

All good wishes to you—and remember, keep up your courage! It will not be long.   Yours v. s.

---

523 • TO EUGENE O'NEILL, JR.   TLS 1 pp. ([1075 California St., San Francisco, Calif.]) [Yale]

September 11th 1944

Dear Eugene: Thanks to Carlotta, who made coffee and gave me a big cup of it, black, I was wide awake and mentally alert by the time the broadcast began—in fact, so alert that I wanted to jump right across the Continent into the midst of your group and ask with that legendary Irishman of American humor: "Is this a private fight or can I get into it?"

But it's just as well I couldn't because I know they don't permit one to call anybody a goddamned fool on the air. To me it appeared you were the only one who possessed intelligence and had read Spengler without prejudice. Your opponents seem to have come to the debate with a firm determination to do their bit in the war effort by refusing to admit that Spengler was anything but a charlatan, and that scholarship was a fake when it happened to be German. I expected any moment to hear McKittrick say (dourly) that Spengler's books should be burnt—and Goethe's, too, for that matter!

Well, many thanks for letting me know about the broadcast. Rage and all, it aroused me mentally and did me a lot of good. My intellectual existence these days is that of an unusually torpid clam who, like Gerard de Nerval's pet lobster, doesn't bark, but unlike that famous lobster, does *not* know the secrets of the sea. (I admit it is hard to imagine a torpid clam who is a nervous wreck, but it will be worth your while if you can do it. I'm sure Lewis Carroll would have been delighted to welcome one into Wonderland! The clam could have joined in

---

3. At the end of the letter Carlotta O'Neill wrote, "sent £25/0/0."

the chorus of Beautiful Soup while he dreamed of Presidential Candidates' solemn oaths and the sacred pledges of diplomats.)

What I liked most about the broadcast was that you had the courage at this time to express your appreciation of Spengler's work, although you disagree with parts of it—as who doesn't. You will hardly become more popular among dried-up Academic circles as a result—but I guess that will not cause you to lose much sleep.

We hope to be in New York by the middle of November or thereabouts. *If* we can get on the Streamliner, etc. which I think we can. So it won't be long before I see you. I'll be glad to be back in the East. Not that I like New York. But neither do I like any city except Paris. It's just that I need a change badly, and all my old friends are in New York. I've missed not seeing them in so long. As for our plans after New York, that can wait until I see you.

Again, congratulations on your part of the Spengler broadcast. And if you chance to see Doctor McKittrick, will you kindly wish him the best of "Romantic Dooms" with my compliments.   Much love from us.   Father

---

524 • TO CARL VAN VECHTEN.   TLS 1 p. (1075 California Street / San Francisco) [Yale]

October the 19th 1944

Dear Carl: Many, many thanks for the birthday greeting! It sure was a welcome note of warmth. We are both blue at having to postpone the return East until April.

I celebrated the day by visiting a really swell columbarium. California, as is well known, leads the world in the swellness of its columbariums designed, apparently, to keep the dead lively, cheerful and constantly amused. I had intended to price a few snappy urns, just by way of safeguarding my future, but as neither the curator of the dump nor I could hear each other above the roaring of ten thousand savage canary birds and the horrid gush of innumerable fancy fountains, it all came to nothing. In fact, I left the place swearing I'd live forever to spite those damned canaries, and that my next pet bird would be a buzzard.

So here's looking forward to seeing you in the spring—and much love to you and Fania from us.   As ever,   Gene

---

525 • TO ELIZABETH SHEPLEY SERGEANT.   TLS 2 pp. ([1075 California St., San Francisco, Calif.]) [Yale]

December 4th 1944

Dear Elsie: Your letter arrived to-day and I hasten to reply with our latest news—which will probably convince you that if we have minds, we have difficulty in making them up! Our plans again are changed, and this time finally. We are *not* going to New York in April. We are going back to Sea Island, Georgia. The more I have thought of New York, the more I have asked myself what for, why spend a lot of money we cannot afford when it means nothing to us except seeing a few friends who will probably be glad to visit Sea Island to see us after the German war ends. I hate New York and all cities (except Paris) and I loathe hotels, as you know. I don't want to produce or publish anything now, and I don't want to fight against persuasion to do so.

Also, although I love my memories of New England (New London & Cape Cod, as I *first* knew it *alone*) I'm afraid I might loathe it now simply because it had changed, was not my memory of what was all so far away and long ago in another world.

Why Sea Island, you may ask and not Chesapeake Bay? Because the all year climate is better, and because we want to go where we have friends, acquaintances, people we know we can rely on when we build our last home. Because everyone connected with Sea Island Company was always courteous and eager to help us in every way. In the Chesapeake Bay region, we would have to start all over again amongst strangers. We sold our old home at Sea Island because we had become too blind to its virtues and too impatient of its minor defects. We wanted a change—and the house was too large for two people—too much upkeep. So was the one we built out here. We *will not* make that mistake again!

So our plan is to go to Sea Island around April first and rent a place to live in until conditions give us a chance to build.

God, if you knew how I long to get back to and in the sea. One thing our ranch in the San Ramon valley taught me was that no matter how beautiful the hills and woods and meadows, and a valley of orchards with fertile earth, I can admire it objectively but not in any deep spiritual sense. I don't belong. I am not it and it is not me. Beach grass is the only verdure I really understand, dunes are my hills, the beach-sun is my only sun and the sea is the symbol of the mystery of the life to which I belong, and has been that for me since I was a small boy. Sometimes in a moment of sun-beach-sea, or on the sea, I have lost myself, all identity, and become one with the rhythm of life itself. But more of that when I see you.

The point now is, when and how do we see you? If you do decide to go to New Mexico in January, and could come to San Francisco on your way, and have friends here you could stay with (San Francisco is one of the most war crowded cities in the U.S.) that would be fine for me. I would give you scripts to read—and all the time you wanted because I haven't done a line of work in a long while. It came to a point where sickness, worry, and uncertainty kept piling one on top of another month after month until my creative urge just balked, said "all is vanity, including your plays, past and present, and I am fed up with you and your woes, so good bye and kindly scatter my ashes down the nearest drain." Then it died. Or perhaps, like Little Nell, it's only sleeping. Frankly, after ten months cooped up in a city apartment, I can't seem to care a damn which it is. Of course, it's really the height of luck we have the apartment, and I know I'm ungrateful about it, and my grousing out of order. The worst part of Parkinson's disease to me is the fits of extreme melancholia that go with it. God knows I have had enough of Celtic Twilight in my make-up without needing any more of the same. And this isn't the same. It isn't sadness. It's an exhausted horrible apathy.

Here's hoping the New Mexico way may work out. Otherwise, we will have to wait for more planning until we reach Sea Island. I can't send you scripts because I have only my working copies with me. Extra scripts are in storage, in any one of 100 boxes of books! They were sent to New York long ago. Other scripts I have with me are originals or rewritten 1st typed copies. You couldn't read them. My handwriting is indecipherable, even if I could send them away. As for Random House, they have only a copy of *The Iceman Cometh*. I'll write Saxe Commins to loan you that if you wish—I say loan because it is really their copy.   Much love from us,   Gene

---

526 • TO BARRETT H. CLARK.   TLS 2 pp. (1075 California Street—San Francisco 8—California) [Yale]

December 15th 1944

Dear Clark: I have heard of Professor Mabie's[1] work, and someone sent me a pamphlet about the theatre when it was finished, so I also have a memory of that.

1. E. C. Mabie, professor and head of the Department of Speech and Dramatic Art as well as director of the University Theatre at the University of Iowa, Iowa City.

Yes, he may do *Strange Interlude* and you can put it on your available list.[2] I haven't read the play since it was produced, save for excerpts here and there, but I don't think much of it will "date" that is really important, and certainly Nina's reactions to her aviator lover's death should be closer to to-day's audience than the '28 one of forgetfulness and the Big Boom.

An important point Mabie should know is that, unless my memory is wrong, the play as printed in my books is longer than the Theatre Guild acting script. I made cuts for time, also because some dialogue was condensed for the stage but I thought it should be retained as in the original for a reader of the book. I've done this with quite a few of my plays. On the other hand, I made too many cuts in *Mourning Becomes Electra* and let too many of them (but not all) stay in the book. It was a fuller, better play in its final written version, I think. And so with *Ah, Wilderness!* It was a better portrayal of a family in its final written version. I never thought then of having a star in it. Even in its present book version with the cuts, it has always been given in Europe with the boy as the main figure—and successfully.

Who has an acting script of *Strange Interlude?* I don't know. Perhaps the Guild. As long as the play is going to be freed for amateur production, your office should have, if possible, copies of the Guild production version. It would be interesting, I think, for a man like Professor Mabie to have both the book and acting script. He could leave out cuts or put them in, as he desired.

The story of my cut version of *Lazarus Laughed* is fable. It's true I've thought of different ways it might be cut and simplified—for example, cut my complicated mask scheme—no double-sized mask idea for Chorus—all crowds done by off stage sound effects—cuts in the repetitious chants and all these given to the Chorus—many of the minor characters cut out—concentration on Lazarus, Tiberius, Caligula, etc. with Chorus background—music to sustain Lazarus' laughter and that of others, as if this music sprang from their laughter, went along with it, dominated it, and finally became pure music with no voice or voices left.

Well, you get the idea. Take all the pageantry of my immense "Imaginative Theatre" stadium out. Make it simple, all to be put on in a modern large theatre, the symbolic story of Lazarus' brief second life on earth, and the message he brought back from the tomb.

There's no chance of my doing this now. I'm too ill. I haven't done any work in a long time, although there is a lot waiting to be done. I can't take any interest in it. But tell Professor Mabie that if his theatre wants to try it along the lines set forth above, he has my permission. I think it is just the kind of job they ought to try. It's hard and it's technically creative.

They would have my general conception of what ought to be done, but it is up to them to do it. Also, they would be working on something practically virgin, something Broadway never touched, the kind of thing their theatre should stand for, an American play of the spirit, and a play which should have a message now when death and the meaning or meaninglessness of life are so close to us. There is also a lot of the murder madness and death realism of Tiberius and Caligula in Hitlerism—very much so!

Well, anyway, tell Professor Mabie of this offer. I'd like to hear his reaction.

All best from us.   As ever,   Eugene O'Neill

P.S. I believe I told you my scheme re *L. L.* before in a letter written early this year or late last year. If you have it in your files you might find a lot of other suggestions. As I remember it was in more detail.

---

2. Clark was executive director of the Dramatists Play Service, which leased plays to nonprofessional theaters.

527 • TO LAWRENCE LANGNER. AL (draft) 1 p. ([1075 California St., San Francisco, Calif.]) [Yale]

[January 22, 1945][1]

Dear Lawrence: Frankly, I feel too ill to see anyone but old friends now, much as I would like to meet Mr. Kazan[2] under more pleasant conditions. Anyway, I thought it was agreed long ago that Eddie Dowling was my "must" for *The Iceman* to play Hickey and also direct if he can do both jobs. No foreign director can really direct *Iceman* for an American production. It's simply impossible. (I'm presuming Kazan is a foreigner.) Finally, I don't wish play produced in near future, so discussing it now would be futile, no matter with what director. Love to you and Armina from us.

---

528 • TO EUGENE O'NEILL, JR. TLS 2 pp. ([1075 California St., San Francisco, Calif.]) [Yale]

January the 23rd 1945

Dear Eugene: The fog must have been over me, and for longer, because here I am just thanking you for the books. They are damned interesting and I am delighted to have them.

Yes, I saw the book-review in the *Times*[1] and liked it a lot. I shall be looking forward to the others. They do take their time there. Arthur Hopkins wrote me of an article of his that was forthcoming in the magazine section,[2] but it did not forthcome until six weeks or so later.

I hope the radio job in New York gets signed and sealed. As in Show Business, you can't believe a thing until it is. If you knew all the glowing proposals brought to Madden each year, on this and that, that never get beyond words, or achieve a backer.

Since the end of the war seemed in sight, I've had a lot of requests for translation rights in France, Spain, Italy. The queer thing is that two of them—from France and Rome—are for *Lazarus Laughed:* Why, I wonder. It isn't that they have used up the other well-known plays in these countries. By comparison with most other European countries, France and Italy have done little or published little. Anyway, I hope the Rome publication comes eventually to a production. In that setting it could be something. The editor, I am informed, is violently anti-Fascist, which probably means Communist. But in Moscow the Moscow Art Theatre was ordered not to do it. Too mystic. Many years ago, it is true, and the fashion of sociological faith changes. Still it adds to the mystery. Probably the true answer is that none of these guys have read the play!

I'm glad to know that Shane is all right, and has a job he enjoys. What I don't know is why he started a feud with me. The last time he visited I thought we were closer than ever before. Afterwards, he wrote me from New York and I replied to the address he said would always reach him. That was around Christmas '41, I guess, anyway, the winter before his

---

1. Date supplied in Carlotta O'Neill's handwriting.
2. Elia Kazan (1909–), Turkish-born stage and film director, actor and novelist, who directed Thornton Wilder's *The Skin of Our Teeth* in 1942 and later went on to direct stage premieres of Tennessee Williams's *A Streetcar Named Desire* (1947) and Arthur Miller's *Death of a Salesman* (1949).

1. "Homeric Hexameters," *New York Times Book Review*, November 5, 1944, pp. 3, 25. The other reviews by Eugene, Jr., were "The Attic Pattern," *New York Times Book Review*, January 28, 1945, pp. 7, 20; and "Values from Above," *New York Times Book Review*, February 25, 1945, p. 20.
2. "Looking Toward a People's Theatre," *New York Times Magazine*, July 30, 1944, p. 17.

sister was ruinously promoted by her mother and the press agent for the Stork Club as a Glamour Girl.

Well, my trying to have any influence on the two of them was foolish. The dice were loaded. I felt that all the time. They yesed me and then did what Mama told them—which, of course, was the opposite. Natural enough, I suppose, but the results not so good. I'm glad if you've seen Shane since the last publicity about his mother broke out, and he approved all right. Not a pretty picture to have one's mother in tabloids (even out here) accused of pursuing in simple nudity a fifth rate motion picture hack writer, at a drunken party.[3] I pitied Shane, but for me it seemed merely a fitting curtain for a dirty Hollywood farce. But, of course, that is not the final curtain. There will be more of the same constantly cropping up from some source or the other—an Oona-Chaplin divorce,[4] etc. Well, to hell with it. As ever much love from us. Father

---

529 • TO EUGENE O'NEILL, JR. TLS 2 pp. (1075 California Street / San Francisco 8 / California) [Yale]

May 7th 1945

Dear Eugene: It was grand to get your long letter of March 28th and I am glad you are through with New Haven and settled so luckily in New York. I remember King Street well, also Varick and Houston. But the best news is that you are now wholly liberated, intellectually and emotionally, from your wife. More importantly, that you have enough evidence against her to keep her from bothering you, and you can be legally untied whenever you wish. Be sure of the *legal* end of that. Otherwise she might fool you.

What makes you think I would disapprove of your present arrangement?[1] On the contrary, my blessing on it. I had several of such and, looking back, find no regret and no one hurt, except in A's case where the essentially irregular and free led me into the *bonds* of matrimony.

No, I haven't heard from Shane in any way, nor do I expect to. He is like me but also very different from me, as far as a relationship with a father goes. There was no other influence pulling me away from my father. My family's quarrels and tragedy were within. To the outer world we maintained an indomitably united front and lied and lied for each other. A typical pure Irish family. The same loyalty occurs, of course, in all kinds of families, but there is, I think, among Irish still close to, or born in Ireland, a strange mixture of fight and hate and forgive, a clannish pride before the world, that is peculiarly its own.

Well, there is nothing like that in Shane's past. He has a background all torn apart, without inner or outer decency, the Boulton background—a laziness, a grafting, in which nothing is ever finished, a slow decay, spite, unscrupulousness, envy, ridiculous social aspirations, a hatred of anyone who succeeds. Bohemianism at its nasty silliest— Well, you've heard me say all this before. I repeat, because it is Shane's background and explains (to me, at least) a lot of his negativity. Thanks to an alimony background, he could always lean on it and did. And this move to Hollywood is another step away from me—and a bad

---

3. Agnes Boulton O'Neill had fallen in love with a married man, many years her junior, named Morris Kaufman, whose wife sued him for divorce, accusing him of committing adultery with Agnes in New York and Hollywood. When the divorce was final, Agnes married Kaufman.

4. When Chaplin died in 1977, he and Oona had been married for thirty-four years and had eight children.

1. Eugene, Jr., was living with Ruth Lander, an artist's agent.

influence for him. The Chaplin-Hollywood atmosphere—well, you can guess. It's possible Shane might *be given* a job in the technical side of pictures that may fascinate him. But the influences will be all against his coming up here.

Your radio news is good—that is, you manage to keep in it and at it, and never let yourself be forgotten. It seems to me that a talk with Richard Madden, my old play agent, might help you. As far as radio and movie stuff is concerned, he is associated with the Lyons Agency, one of the biggest on the Coast for film and radio actors and also in New York for radio material and people. Madden could introduce you to them. It would be no case of using my influence because I haven't any with Lyons. They haven't sold anything for me. And you have had experience in radio, which should make it worth their while taking you on as a client.

Think this over. A good, reliable agent costs you ten percent but he may be worth all he gets and more in helping you help yourself *commercially,* and you can always veto anything he digs up that you don't like. Madden has been my agent since 1919, and looking back over everything I am certainly glad he has. He is an old friend now as well as an agent.

"Forgive me for overstepping the bounds?" Nuts! I am in debt to you for giving me a clear picture which I could not obtain from anyone else. And will act accordingly, if I ever get a chance. But, frankly, I am a bit fed-up with a son who so deliberately takes the other side, although he is nearly 26, still acts as if a Hearst Paper's sob-interview with Agnes (drunk) in 1928–'29 was the well of Truth.   Much love from us.   Father

P.S. In talking of Lyons agency, I'm looking at it from the hard-boiled commercial way they would look at you.

---

530 • TO MR. MAXWELL.   AL (draft) ([1075 California St., San Francisco, Calif.])
[Yale]

[May 8, 1945][1]

Dear Mr. Maxwell: Your letter was delayed a lot in forwarding and this reply by sickness. I have never indulged in the luxury of a secretary, although Mrs. O'Neill functions as such at times. But she has been ill, too.

In the matter of tearing up plays, you should regard that as a good omen in that you have the guts for self-criticism which few playwrights practice. I've destroyed about ten or so myself, and this does not count my first publication (*Thirst* and other plays) which I wish had never been published, and about five in the *Complete Works* that I would gladly see in the ashcan.

Tell you how I work, get an idea, develop it, etc. Well that *is* a tall order because there are so many examples of different methods. For example *Emperor Jones.* I first heard of the legend applied to President Sam of Haiti, from a man with Sells Circus who had traveled there. He gave me a President Sam coin as a pocket piece. Well, about two or three years later, it came back as a play idea (revolutionary for its time) and I wrote it in ten days—no scenario, just a few notes in preparation. *The Hairy Ape* I dashed off too, without much preparation in about ten days. It was derived remotely from a stoker who had been a friend of mine on and off shipboard ten years before. These were "easy" plays—They just came to me. And two others I cannot explain at all—*Desire Under The Elms & Ah, Wilderness!* I had not the vestige of their idea in my note book. I simply awakened with these plays in mind. A brief scenario of *Desire Under The Elms* and I began writing dialogue, as if I'd pondered over this

1. Date supplied in Carlotta O'Neill's handwriting.

play for months. *Ah, Wilderness!* was just as easy, but here I had some memories to help me. Of these (contrary to legend) few were autobiographical. The idea that *Richard* in the play resembles me at his age is absurd. I was the exact opposite.

Other plays, like *The Great God Brown, All God's Chillun Got Wings*, required more working out. *The Great God Brown* was in my notebook for some time before it took form as an Expressionistic play which has little resemblance to the original notes. *All God's Chillun Got Wings* also was only a note for some time. In my note book, I write a line or so about anything that strikes me as a basis for a future play—a character, or an incident, a memory, a story I hear or read, any fragment— Most of these never develop (in the unconscious or wherever it is such germination happens) into ideas for plays. Some of them do.

But with most plays my experience has been (*Strange Interlude, Mourning Becomes Electra*) that my original note becomes a lot of notes, then germinates into a detailed scenario—then waits—finally becomes a first draft of a play which sometimes follows the notes, and sometimes does not. I have the 1st draft typed and again wait. Then a second draft. And so on until I feel I have put all I have to give into the play—and had cut all I felt was unnecessary, etc.

Well, I doubt if this is of any use to you. There are as many ways as playwrights. You'll find your own. I hope the play in New York gets produced, but don't be too disappointed if it isn't. It's a tough gamble, the Broadway racket, even for the experienced show-business, trade playwrights. For a good serious play, the odds against are large indeed. But one or two do break through every season. So it isn't impossible. And don't burn stuff up too quickly. Let it wait. You may find that a new angle will transform it overnight into a play you want to write which has rich significance to you. You can never tell.

Here's wishing you all the luck. And don't get discouraged. I'll give you a true example of my beginner's luck. In 1914 I sent my first two long plays to a New York manager, one of the biggest there. He was also a friend of my father's. You would have thought I had an "in." But I waited and waited. I wrote letters. But nothing happened. Then his firm went bankrupt and at the end of two years, the Receiver finally sent my plays back—in the exact package I had wrapped them in so hopefully. The package had never been opened! I'll bet you never tie that for a discouraging kick in the pants! However, the producer was right although he didn't know it. The two plays were much better unseen and unheard. I destroyed them later on. So it was all for the best in the end.   Again, all best to you.

---

531 • TO MR. HOLLIS.   AL (draft) ([1075 California St., San Francisco, Calif.]) [Yale]

[May 20, 1945][1]

Dear Mr. Hollis: Many thanks for your letter of May 11th. The big trouble with me now is that all my records except those you have sent here are in storage and have never been catalogued. So I don't remember exactly what I've already got. And in thinking of a song in the 1910–20 period, or 1900s, or even 1920–30 I can't remember what year the tune appeared. By way of guidance, the collection is especially weak in 1910–1920, and, of course, before that when the cylinder record prevailed which I don't want.

Of the ones you mention from the new record collection you discovered I would like all the Al Jolson, Frank Tinney if he has any, Nora Bayes, and "The Song Is Ended," "Wistful and Blue" & "Sam, the Old Accordion Man." I have quite a few of Etting[2] already. Re the

1. Date supplied in Carlotta O'Neill's handwriting.
2. Ruth Etting (1907–1978), blonde torch singer best known as a nightclub performer, who also appeared in several Broadway shows.

Hoosier Hot-chas, if you could send them all to me, I imagine there would be a lot I would want because they revive so much forgotten popular stuff. The same applies to Frank Novak and his Rootin-Tootin Boys, about as terrible an aggregation of orchestra and chorus as ever drenched the air, but somehow I love them because I remember the tunes played by just such orchestras, 5th rate Ted Lewis, and joining in choruses myself which contain just as many flats.

A favorite ditty of mine was "Minnie, the Mermaid"—date, sometime in '20's, I guess. You see, for the popular song collection, I like also the idiotic songs that once made me laugh in my lager & ale.

Among other items that come back in memory in connection with this or that in the past, and were popular in their day and must have been recorded, are Irving Berlin's "I Love A Piano" (around 1916)—"I Love The Ladies" (not Berlin—around 1914) "That Mysterious Rag" (Berlin—around 1913) "At The Devil's Ball" (Berlin—around 1913); Jolson's Mason Dixon Line song—and above all "Don't Blame It All On Broadway" (a beautiful lament and apology for the Big Stem. When sung with upturned eyes by a well-stewed waiter endowed with the proper adenoids, it positively wrung you to pieces!)

Well, I hope the above helps a little—and again all good wishes and thank you for your searching in my behalf.   Sincer.

PART EIGHT

ENDING

1945—1952

I do not offer you anything but my love,
my heartbreak, my need of your love.
—*To Carlotta O'Neill, January 19, 1948*

The Iceman Cometh, hung about with a certain solemnity occasioned by O'Neill's return to the stage, was received with respect but without the full understanding and acclaim it would generate ten years later in the revival staged by José Quintero, starring Jason Robards as Hickey. The production of *A Moon for the Misbegotten* that followed was poorly cast and directed, and it closed before coming in to New York. Its failure ended O'Neill's life in the theatre. The tremor grew worse, his walking less steady, and his physical condition generally made work impossible. Carlotta like her husband had developed serious illnesses. Her condition was aggravated by sedative bromides into near paranoia. She became hostile and suspicious of O'Neill's activities, on one occasion arranging that some of his manuscripts should "disappear," on another going so far as to have private detectives shadow him.

Early in 1948, Carlotta left O'Neill. Unattended in the New York apartment, he fell and broke his shoulder. During the period of hospitalization that followed, certain of his friends, notably Saxe Commins, urged him to separate permanently from her. The Comminses were prepared to make room for him in their Princeton home, but theirs was a misdirected kindness. O'Neill's devotion to Carlotta was complete, and he wrote her on February 10, 1948, deploring the hell they had been through and begging her not to leave him. She returned, and in April they moved to Boston. Shortly thereafter they bought and refurbished a home in Marblehead Neck, Massachusetts.

Around them a tragic familial story was weaving its course. Shane, drinking heavily, began to take drugs and attempted suicide. He had married and had a son, Eugene O'Neill III. The baby, born in 1945, suffered crib death the following year. In 1948, Shane was arrested on a charge of heroin possession. Like Shane, Eugene, Jr., had broken his step. Thrown out of radio and television jobs because of his heavy drinking, divorced for a third time, he lived without an objective, much as Shane had always seemed to do. He became dependent on his father for support. On September 25, 1950, he slashed himself with a razor and bled to death.

At the dark center of his world was O'Neill's inability to write. Occasional relief from the tremor enabled him to pen a letter to an old friend, but he had nothing, really, to recount except the reiterated story of the cost of remodeling the new house and the failure of the experimental drugs he was taking. The plays he had yet to write were locked within him forever.

In February 1951, a quarrel with Carlotta had frightening consequences. He plunged outdoors, slipped on the rocks by the sea, and broke his leg. Carlotta, dangerously ill, offered him no help. The two were hospitalized, she in a mental hospital. O'Neill was moved from Massachusetts to a hospital in New York where again his friends tried to separate the pair. The attempt was useless. O'Neill returned to Carlotta as soon as he was able, his love for her as unalterable as hers for him.

What was left of their lives together was spent in the Hotel Shelton in Boston. Its walls closed around the final silence. There, after the publication of *A Moon for the Misbegotten*, O'Neill made Carlotta his literary executrix, a trust she held with loyalty and competence during the remainder of her life, ensuring that his literary remains were in order and that his most important plays received the best productions possible. Shortly before he died, she helped him destroy the drafts and scenarios of the cycle and other unfinished work so as to ensure that no one else would attempt to complete what he could not. Only the completed cycle play, *A Touch of the Poet*, and a typescript of the unrevised *More Stately Mansions* survived. O'Neill died on November 27, 1953, and was buried at Forest Hills Cemetery in Boston. Carlotta died on November 17, 1970. Her ashes are buried by his side.

532 • TO RANDOM HOUSE.   COPY 1 p. ([Barclay Hotel, New York, N.Y.])
[Columbia]

November 29, 1945

Gentlemen: I am this day depositing with you, on condition that it not be opened by you until twenty-five years after my death, a sealed copy of the manuscript of an original play which I have written, entitled *Long Day's Journey Into Night*.

I should like to have you publish this play under the same terms as those set forth in our agreement dated June 30, 1933 (in which you are referred to under your former corporate name of "The Modern Library, Inc.") as amended and extended, except, however, in the following respects:

1. Publication shall not take place until twenty-five (25) years after my death.

2. No advance shall be payable prior to said publication date, at which time an advance of Five Thousand Dollars ($5,000) shall be paid.

3. Copyright in the United States and in Canada shall be taken out in your name.

4. Where the term "Author" is used in our prior agreement, it shall, after my death, apply to my Executors or Administrators, to whom all payments hereunder shall be made.

If the foregoing terms are acceptable to you, will you kindly sign and return to me the enclosed copy of this letter.   Sincerely yours,   Eugene O'Neill

ACCEPTED: November 29, 1945.
RANDOM HOUSE, INC.   By (signed) Bennett A. Cerf

---

533 • TO CARLOTTA MONTEREY O'NEILL.   ALS 1 p. ([35 East 84th St., New York, N.Y.]) [Yale]

July 22nd 1946

Sweetheart: With the same old love deep in my heart I felt for you on that day in Paris, 1929!

I wish you could say the same, forgiving as I forgive, all the mistakes and injuries done one to another through thoughtlessness or lack of understanding.

In justice, as everyone but ourselves seems to know, our marriage has been the most successful and happy of any we know—until late years.

Here's for a new beginning! All my love and thanks. Sweetheart—   Your   Gene

---

534 • TO DUDLEY NICHOLS.   TLS 1 p. ([35 East 84th St., New York, N.Y.]) [Yale]

22 August 1946

Dear Dudley: About the shanty records, Carlotta has just finished telephoning to the Gramophone Shop, and has found out about a place where records can be re-pressed with small harm to the originals—or with luck, with no harm at all. So we will see about doing this and let you know. I hate to trust some one from RKO's New York office with these records, which are now so terribly hard to get.

As far as his picture goes, Glenn Ford looks all right, but I can't tell much from that. I take your word that he has all the stuff to do Orin.[1]

1. Michael Redgrave played Orin in the film of *Mourning Becomes Electra*.

Also I hope we'll get Mason for either Brant or the General.[2]

Certainly I would be willing to let you compete with any bids that might be offered in the future for film leases, with your proposed independent set-up. No, there will never be any question of my wanting my own productions. You overestimate my wealth, and I never invest money in the theater. This explains why I have some money rather than none at all. You don't want to see me out in front of St. Patrick's with my dark glasses and my little fox terrier and my large tin cup, do you? Or do you think that would make a good picture?

I remember your telling me over the phone some time ago that there might be humorous touches connected with Katina's[3] pictures. These went down great with me, but were taken seriously by another member of the family, so I am in the doghouse, and so are you, and so is Mrs. M.   All good wishes. I am still speaking to you.   Gene

---

535 • TO PATRICIA NEAL.[1]   COPY 1 p. (35 East 84th Street, [New York, N.Y.]) [Private]

[November-December 1946]

Dear Pat Neal: I was delighted to hear that you liked *The Iceman Cometh.*[2] It was charming of you to take the time to write and tell me so. It was also good news to hear of your success.[3] This was no surprise to me as I know you will, one day, be one of our best.

All best. Keep up the good work!   Very sincerely,   Eugene O'Neill

---

536 • TO CARLOTTA MONTEREY O'NEILL.   ALS 1 p. ([35 East 84th St., New York, N.Y.]) [Yale]

Dec., '46

To Carlotta—   Though I have seemed ungrateful and unaware and lost at times, that was only the surface irritation. But deep in my heart I have never forgotten all you have meant to me and been to me, have loved you as much and needed you.

I am sorry for the unhappiness I have caused you. How unhappy it has made me, you have seen and know.

Let us forget and forgive, Darling, as now for a time we have forgotten and forgiven. We have love still, Sweetheart. We [have] the chance of a new life!   I love you!   Gene

---

2. Probably James Mason, who was not in the movie; Leo Genn played Adam Brant and Raymond Massey played the "General," Ezra Mannon.
3. Katina Paxinou, Greece's foremost actress, who played Christine in the film.

1. Neal (1926–), actress whom O'Neill had seen on stage at the Westport (Connecticut) Country Playhouse, the summer theatre run by the Langners, and who later became a stage and screen star.
2. The Theatre Guild production of *The Iceman Cometh,* directed by Eddie Dowling and starring Dudley Digges, E. G. Marshall, and James E. Barton, opened on October 9, 1946, and ran for 136 performances.
3. Patricia Neal had scored a personal success in Lillian Hellman's *Another Part of the Forest,* which opened on November 20, 1946.

In New York for the rehearsals of *The Iceman Cometh*.

537 • TO FATHER WILFRID PARSONS.[1]　WIRE 1 p. ([35 East 84th St., New York, N.Y.]) [Georgetown]

MARCH 21, 1947

= DEAR FATHER PARSONS I AM ONLY TOO PLEASED TO GIVE YOU A STATEMENT TO BE ISSUED PRIOR TO THE OPENING OF THE ICEMAN COMETH I AM AND ALWAYS HAVE BEEN OPPOSED TO RACIAL DISCRIMINATION OF ANY KIND AND I ASSURE YOU I WILL INSIST ON A NON DISCRIMINATION CLAUSE IN ALL FUTURE CONTRACTS. SURELY MY PAST RECORD AS A DRAMATIST AND A PRODUCER HAS SHOWN WHERE I STAND ON THIS ISSUE =　= EUGENE ONEILL

---

538 • TO TOM PEDI.　TLS 1 p. ([35 East 84th St., New York, N.Y.]) [O'Neill Center]

July 8th 1947

Dear Pedi:　I had meant to answer your letter every day since I received it but have been feeling so rotten that I have kept postponing it.

Your letter meant a lot to me. As you say, there are times when something nice happens. Your letter was one of those things.

I am delighted that you got so much out of playing in *The Iceman Cometh*—and I can say in return that I certainly got a lot out of your portrayal of Rocky. It was exactly right. Rocky lived and was real just as I had imagined him.

Again, much gratitude for your fine letter. I will let you know, later, when I am feeling better, about your coming here to have a talk. Just now I am all shot and planning to go to the country if I can.

Always good luck!　Sincerely,　Eugene O'Neill

---

539 • TO CYNTHIA CHAPMAN STRAM.　ALS 2 pp. ([35 East 84th St., New York, N.Y.]) [Yale]

August '47

Dear Cyn:　Again many happy returns—and judging from your last letter you are enjoying life now and have a fixed goal to work toward. So I'm confident that my hope for happy days, long overdue, (the days I mean!) will not turn out to be just one of those hopes. This time I know they won't.

Gerry[1] looks grand in the picture you sent. Some laddie! He sure has sprung up from the time I last saw him. A good prospect for a future all-American end!

Give Roy my best, and tell him I haven't forgotten I owe him a letter. Now that my ability to write in long hand has improved—that is, it *is* possible on many days, I'll be better on the correspondence.　Love and a hug to the best of stepdaughters!　Gene

---

1. Washington, D.C., priest and member of the Committee for Racial Democracy in the Nation's Capital who asked O'Neill for a statement regarding the policy of the National Theatre, where *The Iceman Cometh* was playing, not to admit blacks.

1. Gerald Stram, Cynthia's son by her second marriage, to Roy Stram.

540 • TO CARLOTTA MONTEREY O'NEILL.   ALS 1 p. ([35 East 84th St., New York, N.Y.]) [Yale]

Dec. 28, 1947

My Sweetheart: As on so many birthdays since 1928, I want again to give you my love, and my great need of your love, which is my life.

Please do not sneer at this, for it is the one truth that counts, that can support us in our old age against the sneers of the world.

I do not offer you anything but my love, my heartbreak, my need of your love—and my apology that I should have forgotten your card at Christmas. I paid for that in tears.

I love you, Carlotta, as I have loved you, as I always will!   Gene

---

541 • TO CARLOTTA MONTEREY O'NEILL.   ALS 1 p. (Stationery headed: Penthouse 35 East 84th Street New York 28) [Yale]

[January 19, 1948]

Darling: For the love of God, forgive and come back. You are all I have in life. I am sick and I will surely die without you. You do not want to murder me, I know, and a curse will be on you for your remaining days.

I love you and I will! Please, Darling!   Your   Gene

---

542 • TO RUSSEL CROUSE.   TLS 1 p. (Stationery headed: Doctors Hospital / East End Avenue at 87th Street / New York 28, N.Y.) [Yale]

February Third Nineteen Forty Eight

Dear Russel,   I'd love to see you any time in the evening beginning next week. By then I ought to be able to cook up a smile of welcome or sing to you faintly, "Oh Come and Be Sweet To Me Kid."   Cordially   Gene

---

543 • TO CARLOTTA MONTEREY O'NEILL.   ALS 1 p. (Stationery headed: Doctors Hospital / East End Avenue at 87th Street / New York 28, N.Y.) [Yale]

February 10th 1948

Darling: Please, O Dear God, let this anniversary of our setting out together not make you think of a flop! You have been life to me, and the greatest beauty and joy, and without you I am nothing!

Please, Sweetheart, I have been through hell and you have. I could never act again as I have acted.

I love you, Darling, Darling. I love you! I love you! I am yours. Don't leave me!   *Your* Gene

544 • TO MELVILLE CANE.   ALS 1 p. (Doctors' Hospital, [New York, N.Y.])
[Columbia]

April 9th '48

Dear Mr. Cane: Since Mrs. O'Neill has forbidden any direct communication with her, I send the enclosed to give to her. I know she would only tear up a note from me, anyway. Nevertheless, will you tell her from me that I love her and always will.

When things were all patched up for the moment on a basis of truth, you wrote a beautiful letter which summed up the whole situation. It was, and is, my thought to a word. It is disgraceful, that a marriage rightly estimated for fifteen years to be a model of mutual respect, and help, and love, should end up in bitter recrimination over nothing, suspicion over less, and loss of temper by *two* sick people.

Excuse my being emotional, if I have been! In a case like this, I don't see how anyone ever understands any of the true issues.   Cordially,   Eugene O'Neill

---

545 • TO SAXE COMMINS.   ALS 2 pp. (Stationery headed: The Ritz-Carlton / Boston 17, Massachusetts) [Private]

July 26 '48

Dear Saxe: Much gratitude for the inscribed book.[1] I feel as if I'd read it already, you've told me so much about it, but I know I will have a new pleasure in reading it.

The big news with us, which I meant to write you long ago, is that we had the good luck to get in first on the sale of a house *right on the ocean* near Marblehead—first sale of waterfront property in its vicinity for many years. Carlotta bought this out of her reserve fund. It is a tiny house with little rooms, the upstairs ones with sloping eaves—built in 1880. Reminds me of the first home my father bought in New London, also on the waterfront when I [was] a kid. We both love this new place. Of course, a lot has had to be done to modernize it—as to kitchen, etc. and to thoroughly insulate it for an all year round home—our last. Everything to cut down overhead and make it a cinch to run with just a cook. No car. We won't need one. The aim is to simplify living and gain as much security for our old age as is possible. I feel I shall be able to write again, and again have some roots—of seaweed—with my feet in a New England sea. It is like coming home, in a way, and I feel happier than in many years, although we are still stuck here in a hotel impatiently awaiting the completion of the work on the place.

As to health, we are both much better and will be better still when we are in our home. My arm isn't right yet and won't be for six months, they say, but it steadily improves. No swimming this summer, of course. But next year—! The tremor is better, too, but I'm just cursed with it for life, I guess, and the best to hope for is to circumvent it. This letter, for example, is written during a good spell and it's not so bad, eh? And why complain when the world itself is one vast tremor.

All best to you, Dorothy & the kids.   As ever,   Gene

P.S. Remember me to Bennett, Haas, Klopfer.[2]

1. *Basic Writings of George Washington,* edited and with an introduction by Saxe Commins (New York: Random House, 1948). Commins's inscription read, "To Gene, through all the years with unchanging love and devotion, always Saxe, July 9, 1948."
2. Robert Haas and Donald Klopfer, Bennett Cerf's partners at Random House.

546 • TO WINFIELD E. ARONBERG.[1]   ALS[2] 2 pp. ([The Ritz-Carlton, Boston, Mass.]) [Yale]

Sept. 12th 1948

Dear Bill:—   The income tax quarterly payment has been mailed.

As for the letter from Shane you were entirely right in not forwarding it to me. I wish you would write and make it as strong as you can that he cannot ever expect money from me. He has his interest in Spithead and he must make all appeals to his mother. And he might try going to work for change. Or his wife[3] might.

Please, also, try to make him understand the truth that I have very little money now myself. And can afford no gifts, nor loans, to anyone.

This business of re-building an old summer place, small as it is, for all year 'round occupancy, has proved an incredible drain. Not only did it use up all Carlotta's securities ($48,000.00) that she had in her account with Pell, but, also, $15,000.00 of my cash (for the second payment) and now, for the third & last payment, I have had to sell $10,000.00 of my securities in my Pell account,—& we have to mortgage the place to clean up the final payments. It will cost more than either of the two, fine, large, brick houses we built before the war!

(You might add, if you think it wise when talking with Shane, that we can't even afford a car! *Which is true.*)

Still, we *had* to have a home, at any cost, and it is beautifully situated, & promises a place of peace & tranquility for our old age. Also, we are constantly hearing of people who are in as bad a fix or worse, who are trying to build homes.

As for the new husband-wife ruling for next year's income tax returns, Carlotta says for her part of it, to please get in touch with Mr. Melville H. Cane, 25 West 43rd St.—

With all good wishes—   Very sincerely,   Gene

Address after the 17th of Sept.
Point o'Rocks Lane
Marblehead Neck
Massachusetts
Please give this to *no one.*

---

547 • TO DUDLEY NICHOLS.   ALS 2 pp. (Stationery headed: Point o'Rocks Lane Marblehead Neck, Massachusetts) [Yale]

Dec. 4th 1948

Dear Dudley: Your letter of Nov. 26th arrived here two days ago. This is our home—our last since we can never afford to have another, or stand the strain of another moving—the terrible sheer physical strain of it. It is a grand *little* place perched on a point of rocks with the old Western Ocean beating on these rocks right below my study window as I write you. There is peace here for me, and for Carlotta, too—after all the five years of cities, apartments, hotels—fifty years in jail they seem, as I look back on them. The interior of our rebuilt house is as charming as only Carlotta can make one. And now at last, with everything to the last

---

1. Lawyer who had been Harry Weinberger's associate and was now handling O'Neill's legal affairs.
2. This letter is written in Carlotta O'Neill's handwriting and signed by her husband.
3. Catherine Givens, whom Shane had married on July 31, 1944.

book in place (or nearly so) we can sit back and rest a while, and I can hope to start writing plays again.

This letter is not a fair sample of my handwriting. It is too good, (aided by medicine), but I *can* write again fairly legibly without aid for more than a few lines—a thing I haven't been able to do for years. The damned tremor, as a whole, is worse all over—legs are bad, etc. but I seem to have regained some control over my hands. You can't know how much that means to me! But I better knock wood! The damned thing has nothing predictable. One good thing is, there is a lot of research into tremors going on in Boston now. They are waking up to the fact that there may be a lot of tremors contained in the old word Parkinson's—or that is what I get from their talk.

The above was written yesterday p.m. Now it's the following morning and I am writing without any nerve sedative to steady my hand. Not so bad, what? But it's slow work with a lot of concentration required.

The things you say about Hollywood decay are equally true in the "legit," from the little I hear. There is nothing one can do about it. It's simply one symptom of a world-wide passing into an existence without culture—the world of mob-destiny. Kismet! And to hell with it!

I haven't seen the cut version of *M.B.E.* and never will. And I ducked seeing the beautiful musical mess derived from *Ah, Wilderness!*[1] I hear and hope it is a financial flop of the worst sort.

We are so sorry to learn of Esta's "allergy," but it's fine news to know she is well now. Judging from Carlotta's experience, "allergy" is just the name for another quack's racket. Your father sure said the last word on how best to conserve one's health!

I hope you are able to make the film you speak of all on your own without any interference whatever.

Last but not least, I want to tell you how much your *poem* moved me. Congratulations! It is fine work!

My hand is petering out on control, so I'll put a stop on this strain on your eyesight. Love from us to you both. Carlotta will write Esta soon. At present she is in bed recovering from a terrific cold. Yes, *cold!* Not virus Z, nor one, or two, or three, or four, or five-day Flu, or any of the pet names the Docs cook up to make things sound dangerous and mysterious and worth ten bucks more per visit. I confidently predict that in a few years some eminent research shark is going to discover, with the aid of a ten ton microscope, a new and violent virus with fourteen legs and four balls causing a totally new disease called "Pain-In-The-Arse Piles." Merciful Allah, will all us suckers go for that one! We will all be telling each other: "Now I know what has ruined my life!"

(I better exit on that)   As ever,   Gene

---

548 • TO CHARLES O'BRIEN KENNEDY.[1]   ALS 2 pp. (Stationery headed: Point o'Rocks Lane Marblehead Neck, Massachusetts) [O'Neill Center]

Dec. 6th 1948

Dear Charlie: Much, much gratitude for the photo of the old Barrett House![2] I know of no gift which could have pleased me more! I had thought that there might exist some old

1. *Summer Holiday,* a 1948 film musical, starring Mickey Rooney, Gloria de Haven, Walter Huston, and Agnes Moorehead.

1. Director and playwright who directed the Provincetown Players premiere production of *Diff'rent* (1920) and was a friend of O'Neill's thereafter.
2. New York hotel in which O'Neill was born.

photo of Longacre Square, showing the Barrett House, but never dreamed of one of the hotel itself.

As for the guy leaning against the lamp post, of course he had a bun on. I remember seeing him there the day after I was born. You forget that there were men in those days and when they decided it was fitting they should go on a drunk, *they went on a drunk!* Not like the weaklings of today, who after ten days of weak mixed drinks have to have an animal trainer bed them down in Bellevue and gently subdue their menagerie visions! In the old days when I was born, a man—especially one from Kilkenny—went on a five year drunk and finished by licking four cops, and then went home to raise hell because dinner was late.

—(Business of filling pen)—

Yes, I received the photo of my father and Brandon Tynan,[3] and I should have acknowledged it months ago. Only excuse is we were in the furor of getting this house rebuilt and moved into. So much work we had to do ourselves, and neither of us fit to do it—but we did it and here we are recovering from deep fatigue but with *a home* again after five years of cities, apartments, hotels—peace again with the ocean beating on the rocks almost underneath my study window—in a small house just big enough for us two.

I'm getting so I can control my hand better and I hope soon to be really at work again. On the other hand (pardon the mixture) the tremor in the rest of my frame is much worse, particularly my legs. But hell, I'm pleased by that change. I might want to write a few more plays—the ideas are ready—but I've always hated walking.

Will you thank Brand Tynan for me for his kindness in writing on the back of the photo. I certainly appreciated it—although the long delay would not indicate.

Carlotta joins me in wishing you all the best there is! Merry Christmas! As ever,   Gene

---

549 • TO CARLOTTA MONTEREY O'NEILL.   ALS 1 p. ([Point o'Rocks Lane, Marblehead Neck, Mass.]) [Yale]

For Carlotta—Dec. 28th, 1948

"When I am old,
    And all Love's ancient fire
Be tremulous and cold:
    My Soul's desire!
Remember, if you may,
Nothing of you and me but yesterday,
When heart on heart we bid the years conspire
    To make us old."

With love forever, Darling!   Your   Gene

3. Actor with whom James O'Neill, Sr., starred in *Joseph and His Brethren* in 1913–14.

550 • TO EUGENE O'NEILL, JR.   ALS 2 pp. (Point o'Rocks Lane, / Marblehead Neck, / Marblehead, / Mass.) [Yale]

[late December 1948 or early January 1949]

Dear Eugene: Much gratitude for the Christmas present—although it put me to the blush because I had failed to send you one. The truth is Carlotta and I, still up to our ears in debt on this place, had sent out word that there would be no Christmas in the O'Neill house this year and please send no presents. I forgot to notify you—and I am damned glad to have the Gerard Manley Hopkins volume and get to know him at last. I like the poems immensely.

As to why I have not written you in so long, it is really nothing more than a sick man's reason, making a slow recovery from nervous shock and a badly twisted arm. In Boston, a long hotel sojourn in which I went twice [a] week to Doc. Ober, the daddy of all the great bone specialists, for treatments. This was entirely successful. My arm and shoulder are practically perfect now except for heavy work of lifting, etc.

As for the Parkinson's, I have to report the reverse. It has gone more to my legs, I weave around unless I use all my will power. I've been a guinea pig for several of the new concoctions which are alleged to help some people but all they do is make me much sicker. The last I tried for three days worked for the first day—no tremor—but the second day the tremor was back and I began to pass into a strange state of benumbed sickliness I can't describe. The third day my eyes looked like a maniac's, bright as polished ebony encased in reddish eyeballs, I could hardly see, and so sick and feeble I had to cut out the cure. I also swore my guinea pig days were over for good!

The one hope is that, at last, a lot of medical work is being done on tremors—or so they say—and not to leave one name, Parkinson's to cover the whole field of tremors and let [it] go at that, as incurable!

Well, this letter, believe it or not, has taken two days to write and an amount of energy and fatigue that would astound you. I try to kid people along in the few other letters I've written. No one likes to get gloomy [illegible] letters. And it bores oneself, too, writing them.

My hand is beginning to lose control. Other news—little house, fine & restful—no one around in winter—Ocean the same as ever—"mother & lover of men."   Much love to you and Ruth.   Father

---

551 • TO WINFIELD E. ARONBERG.   TLS 3 pp. (Stationery headed: Point o'Rocks Lane Marblehead Neck, Massachusetts) [Yale]

February the fourth 1949

Dear Bill: We have discovered that the date of our coming to live in this house (Sept. 15th '48) is the date for our residence in Massachusetts. Carlotta has learned that Cane has some clients here whose income tax he looks after so he must know the laws of Massachusetts, which could be a help to you if you cared to take advantage of his experience in that line.

I received a long letter from Eugene, in reply to one I wrote thanking him for a book of poems he sent me for Christmas. He wants me to back that loan for another year, and, of course, I have to do it. It is not that I begrudged helping him *then*, it is just that my finances—

our finances—have changed so radically, that what was easy then is a big burden of worry and uncertainty now.

I don't think Eugene has any idea what our financial set-up is now. He doesn't seem to realize that the good old days are over. Carlotta took everything she had (sold all her securities and bonds) to go into this house. Prices, as you know, are ridiculously high. I had to add $15000.00 to her $50,000.00 and then she had to take out a $20,000.00 mortgage before we could move in. My income from Pell is very small. And, Carlotta's income, from her trust, pays for our cook and a few things she needs, now and then. I am sure we are the only couple in Massachusetts that does not own a car!

I feel that it is about time for Eugene to sit down and think things over very seriously. He is nearly forty years old. And he must make up his mind that he will get nothing from me and that it is necessary to find some job, and remain on that job, to plan for his future. I am not well. My tremor gets worse every day. I will never write another play and there is no use kidding myself that I will. As to production, I do not want anything produced. I mean anything new. These Hollywood directors would distort everything I intended—and cheapen my work. And I am too tired, too ill, to go through a production myself. Carlotta and I each have an incurable, crippling sickness. We want and need peace—surely we deserve it.

And now, Bill, I must say something to you that I find most difficult. I can't afford paying you on our present arrangement. It will have to be on each individual piece of work you do for me. There will be no more production, no more alimony, just income tax and little things that may come up. I do hope you understand. It just has to be that way.

Another thing, writing letters is a difficult thing for me to do. And particularly letters of a personal type. Therefore, Bill, I beg of you to get hold of Eugene and tell him what is in this letter. He must know the position Carlotta and I are in.

The *Mourning Becomes Electra* money, due me this summer, will have to go in Pell's account to keep it up to the figure where the income is sufficient for the housekeeping bills— and in case either of us become seriously ill.

Carlotta joins me in the best of good wishes.   As ever,   Gene

P.S. Another thing. Income from radio, stock, books will go down with a bang in this year and thereafter with nothing new coming up—foreign, too.

---

552 • TO EUGENE O'NEILL, JR.   ALS 1 p. (Stationery headed: Point o'Rocks Lane Marblehead Neck, Massachusetts) [Yale]

[postmarked March 7, 1949]

Dear Eugene: Just a line. Hand not so good, as you see. Enclosed is the note, signed where it ought to be, I hope!

Nothing more now. This is too much effort. Hope you can read it.   Much love to you.   Father

Dear Eugene:

Just a line. Hand not so good, as you see. Enclosed is this notes, signed where it ought to be, I hope!

Nothing more now. This is too much effort. Hope you can read it.

Much love to you.

Father.

O'Neill's last letter to Eugene, Jr., shows the painful deterioration of his handwriting.

553 • TO CARLOTTA MONTEREY O'NEILL. ALS 1 p. ([Point o'Rocks Lane, Marblehead Neck, Mass.]) [Yale]

X'mas 1949

To "Mama"—and still as over all the years, "Sweetheart" and "Darling" and "Beloved Wife" and "Friend," too!—in these days of sickness and toil (on your part) and despair— Well, there is always us, there is still love, My Own!   Your   Gene

P.S. The enclosed is for the French affair.[1]

---

554 • TO EUGENE O'NEILL, JR. TLS 1 p. (Stationery headed: Point o'Rocks Lane / Marblehead Neck / Massachusetts) [Yale]

February the 25th 1950

Dear Eugene: Just a line to thank you for your letter it was good to hear from you.

No news, except both of us more crippled. Carlotta's arthritis very bad. Nothing to do about it. I have one of the best neurologists in this country. He is completely frank—they know nothing at all about the cause or cure of tremors! But they have lots of pills which do help a few people's shakes. On the other hand, they make a lot of other people sick and they have to stop taking them. I have tried four of these different drugs and each time the result was very bad. And it was no unique bad reaction. Other patients suffered the same.

No, I don't think the idea of dropping in here this summer is good. In fact, it's bad. But to drop in Salem,[1] *arranging a meeting before hand,* is better for everyone concerned.

Enclosed is the Note which I have endorsed.   Love to you—   Father

---

555 • TO WINFIELD E. ARONBERG. ALS[1] 2 pp. (Stationery headed: Point o'Rocks Lane / Marblehead Neck, Massachusetts) [Yale]

Oct. 26th 1950

Dear Mr. Aronberg:—   Enclosed you will find the funeral bills & check.[2] Gene seems to think it is better this way as he promised to pay the bills!

I don't see how any more shocks can come from the Pitt-Smith Clan. (Gene is not over the shock of that yet.) And, if Shane goes in for any more stupidities—could you not write to me & let me break the news with as little shock as possible. I, personally, don't see why Gene should be dragged into Shane's mode of life. Of course, he has to sign papers for the sale of Spithead—but after that!

If we were dead he'd have to get on somehow—let him begin now.

Gene joins me in good wishes.   Sincerely,   Carlotta Monterey O'Neill   Gene

---

1. O'Neill enclosed money for the purchase of a handbag.

1. Salem Hospital, Salem, Massachusetts, which O'Neill visited regularly for treatments.

1. This letter is written in Carlotta O'Neill's handwriting and signed by both her and her husband.
2. Eugene O'Neill, Jr., committed suicide on September 25, 1950.

556 • TO FRANK MEYER.[1]   TLS 1 p. (Stationery headed: Point o'Rocks Lane / Marblehead Neck / Massachusetts) [Yale]

November the 20th 1950

Dear Mr. Meyer: Your letter was a great pleasure to me; and to learn that Eugene had wanted me to have his Ph.D. diploma warmed my heart. Would you please send it here to our home—and thank you for your trouble.

I would ask you to come to see me but my health has been very poor since Eugene's death. When I am better again I will write to you, and, perhaps, we may meet some day.

Again, many thanks, and all good wishes.   Sincerely,   Eugene O'Neill

---

557 • TO CARLOTTA MONTEREY O'NEILL.   ALS[1] 2 pp. (Stationery headed: Salem Hospital / Salem, Massachusetts) [Yale]

Feb 8th 1951

My dearest,   I had my leg put in a cast last night.

I am coming along all right. I received a telegram from Parallee Havre saying Dad[2] was dead. Have been trying to remember name of florist in San Francisco and have finally located by [illegible]. So I will wire him. This is a great blow to both of us. I should be able to get around on a crutch within a few days.

And I know you will progress rapidly under the treatment. All is not lost and we have much to look forward to—write me as soon as you can.

I feel dreadfully lonely for some word from you.   With all my love,   Gene

Berkeley California Landscape 60741
(Parallee's number)

---

558 • TO CARLOTTA MONTEREY O'NEILL.   ALS[1] 2 pp. (Stationery headed: Salem Hospital / Salem, Massachusetts) [Yale]

[February 9?, 1951]

My Dearest: I am so overjoyed by learning through Dr. Mayo's & Dr. Horwitz's[1] phone calls, on my own, that you have had steady progress and you will be soon well again. I have made progress too, and with the help of two men can walk a few steps on stilts, with one man on each side of me.

---

1. Longtime friend of Eugene, Jr., who was his neighbor in Woodstock, New York.

1. This letter was apparently dictated by O'Neill to a nurse at Salem Hospital, who also signed it for him.
2. Harold (Dad) and Parallee Havre, neighbors and good friends of the O'Neills in Berkeley, California.

1. This letter was apparently dictated by O'Neill to a nurse at Salem Hospital, who also signed it for him.
2. Frederic B. Mayo, the O'Neills' personal physician, and William H. Horwitz, a staff psychiatrist at Salem Hospital.

I've had some visitors. Bobby Jones, Lawrence Langner and Aronberg.

Doris tells me that you are worrying about money and what you are going to do. There is certainly no question about money—there will be plenty of that. If you will write to me we can make advanced plans about that.

There never was a situation that love and money couldn't conquer.   All my love sweet heart!   Gene

---

559 • TO BENNETT CERF.   TLS 1 p. (Stationery headed: Hotel Shelton / 91 Bay State Road • Boston 15, Massachusetts) [Columbia]

June the 13th 1951

Dear Bennett: Thank you so much for sending me the 'scripts, notes, etc.[1] I am trying to find out how I stand and clean up a lot of confusion. As soon as they arrived Carlotta rushed to the phone to let you know so you wouldn't worry. No, I do *not* want *Long Day's Journey Into Night*. That, as you know, is to be published twenty-five years after my death—but never produced as a play.[2]

I would be very grateful to you if you would have sent to:

Ernst, Cane and Berner

25 West 43rd Street

New York 18

New York

a complete list of all my copyrights and renewals—with dates and numbers. Mr. Pincus Berner will look after my affairs from this date forward.

Again, my deep thanks and gratitude for the trouble I have caused you.

With the best of good wishes,   Sincerely,   Gene

---

560 • TO CARLOTTA MONTEREY O'NEILL.   ALS 1 p. ([Hotel Shelton, Boston, Mass.]) [Yale]

[July 22, 1952]

To darling Carlotta, my wife, who for twenty-three years has endured my rotten nerves, my lack of stability, my cussedness in general—,

This token of my gratitude and awareness—a poor thing—a play she dislikes, and which I have come to loathe—dating back to 1944—my last.[1]

I am old and would be sick of life, were it not that you, Sweetheart, are here, as deep and understanding in your love as ever—and I as deep in my love for you as when we stood in Paris, Première Arrondissement on July 22, 1929—and both said faintly, "Oui!"   Your Gene

---

1. At O'Neill's direction Cerf sent him scripts and other papers that he had deposited with Random House in 1948.

2. Carlotta O'Neill in 1956 released *Long Day's Journey* to Stockholm's Royal Dramatic Theatre, where it opened on February 2. It was published by Yale University Press on February 20, 1956. It opened on Broadway on November 7, 1956, and earned for O'Neill his fourth Pulitzer Prize.

1. This message is inscribed in a copy of *A Moon for the Misbegotten* (New York: Random House, 1952) on the occasion of the O'Neills' twenty-third wedding anniversary.

INDEX

We have listed here only the proper names, the titles of books, magazines, and song, and addresses to which O'Neill refers. It has not always been possible to include the full names of the persons to whom he refers. The last names of "Lefty Louie" and "Chuck" are lost in the mists of time. A missing envelope may make one of the names of an addressee undiscoverable, and, although we have provided many first names where O'Neill does not give them, we have left a number that appear to have only passing importance undiscovered. For the most part, we have also omitted casual closing references such as the oft-repeated "Kiss Shane and Oona for me."

The index provides an informal table of contents by listing in boldface after the names of recipients of letters the page numbers on which letters so addressed can be found. Thus the first three entries after "Atkinson, Brooks" are page numbers of letters sent to him. The subsequent entries are references to him in other letters.

Denton, Mr.: 267
Demuth, Charles: 75
Desire Under the Elms: 139, 187, 188, 189, 192,
  193, 194, 195, 198, 202, 207, 210, 213, 218,
  238, 248, 252, 254, 273, 300, 302, 314, 325,
  327, 331, 344, 346, 347, 354, 355, 366, 370,
  387, 391, 395, 405, 406, 408, 410, 416, 418,
  428, 438, 449, 502, 521, 522, 530, 537, 561,
  570
De Valera, Eamon: 564
Diff'rent: 142, 146, 148, 149, 151, 170, 171, 438
Digges, Dudley: 425, 426
Dillingham, Charles: 201
Diogenes: 11
Dixon, Thomas: *The Clansman,* 17
Dodge, Delphine: 236, 262
Dodge, Mabel: 137
"Don't Blame It All on Broadway" (song): 572
Dos Passos, John: 373
Dostoevsky, Feodor: 386; *The Brothers Karamazov,*
  183
Douthit, J. J.: **547**
Dowling, Eddie: 502, 568
Dramatic Mirror, The: 83
Dreamy Kid: 95, 438
Dreiser, Theodore: **458;** 75, 355, 361
Drew, John: 208n
Drew, Tuve: 288, 320
Driscoll, Mr.: 302, 315, 330
Druilard, Jack: 547
Dublin Drama League: 230
Du Bois, Dr. Eugene: 241
Duke University: 473
Dumas, Alexandre, père: *The Count of Monte Cristo,*
  12; *The Lady of Monsoreau,* 12; *The Three Mus-*
  keteers, 12
Dunsany, Lord Edward John Moreton Drax Plun-
  kett: 101, 407
Durban, South Africa: 79, 170
Duvivier, Mr.: 406
Dynamo: 3, 189, 259, 260, 278, 283, 288, 290,
  291, 299, 300–01, 304, 306, 307, 308, 309,
  310–11, 317, 318, 325, 326, 327, 328, 331,
  332–33, 337, 339–40, 343, 344, 345, 350, 356,
  358, 361, 362, 367, 384, 400, 522

Eames, Clare: 179
Eaton, Walter Pritchard: 60–61, 347
Ebel, August: 28n, 70
Ebel, Bartley: 28n
Egerton, George: 128n
Eldridge, Florence: 198, 211
Elkins, Felton: **69;** 49, 53, 63, 69, 104, 468
Elkins, Josephine: 63, 67
Ell, Christine: 73n, 105, 144
Elliott, William: 143
Ellis, Mary: 211
Emperor Jones, The: 5, 76, 138, 140, 142, 143, 145,
  147, 149, 160, 162, 164, 165, 166, 169, 170,
  176, 188, 193, 195, 205, 210, 219, 230, 248,
  260, 300, 327, 338, 347, 370, 371, 387, 405,
  408, 409, 410, 411, 428, 431, 444, 453, 471,
  485, 551, 554, 560–61, 570
"Empty Bed Blues" (song): 352
Encyclopedia Britannica: 542

"Eric the Red" (play idea): 178
Erlanger, A. L.: 63
Ervine, St. John: **116, 145;** 116, 251, 330, 331;
  John Ferguson, 95, 96; *Jane Clegg,* 116; *Mixed*
  Marriage, 145
Estavan, Lawrence: **497**
Etting, Ruth: 571
Everyman Theatre: 145, 166, 170
Experimental Theatre, The: 140

Farnum, William: 91, 92, 94, 104, 190
Farrell, James T.: **535, 545;** *Studs Lonigan,* 535
Fechter, Charles: 138n, 439
Firestone, Charles: 348
Federal Theatre: 463
Finnish Relief Fund: 496–97
First Man, The: 4n, 139, 150, 162, 347, 438
Fisk University: 500
Fitzgerald, M. Eleanor (Fitzie): **168, 338;** 76, 177,
  182, 184, 191, 194, 229, 233
Flagg, Marian: 11, 18
Flaherty, Liam: 407; *The Informer,* 447
Florida Military Academy: 448
Flying Cloud (ship model): 433–34
Flame: 73
Flanagan, Hallie: **463**
Fog: 1, 8, 75, 79
Fogle, Mr.: 427
Fontanne, Lynn: 119, 266, 267
Forbes, James: *The Travelling Salesman,* 20
Ford, Colin: 29, 42, 49, 50, 53
Ford, Glenn: 575
Ford, John: **508;** 521, 522
Forrester's (New London rooming house): 40
47 Workshop, The: 9, 70, 79, 89, 170
Fountain, The: 139, 150, 160, 161, 166, 171, 174,
  177, 188, 190, 196, 198, 209, 215, 325, 438,
  520, 521
"Fragments": 556
France, Anatole: 116
Francis, John: 78n, 305, 349, 524, 552–23
Frank, Leonhard: *Karl and Anna,* 359
Frank, Waldo: **78;** 75, 553
Frazer, James: *The Golden Bough,* 150, 200
Frederick, Pauline: 143, 152
Freeman, Helen: 115, 211
Freeman, Herbert: 538
French, Samuel: 386
Freud, Sigmund: 192, 247, 386
Freund, Mr.: 355
Friday (cat): 364
"Full Many a Cup": 27, 35

Gabriel, Gilbert: 347–48, 392
Galsworthy, John: 139, 198; *Justice,* 70
Garbage Flat, New York City: 547
Garbo, Greta: 364, 374
Garland, Robert: 452
Garden Hotel, The ("The Hell Hole"): 98, 117
Garwood 28–40 (motor boat): 403
Gaul, George: 94, 207
Gautier, Judith: 128
Gaylord Farm Sanatorium: 8–9, 25, 76, 180
Gayney, Dr.: 157
Génner, Mr.: 405

Gering, Marion: 224
Gerry, Elbridge: 190
Gershwin, George: *Porgy and Bess,* 484
Gest, Morris: 183, 188, 201
Gile, Dr.: 252
Gilpin, Charles: 142, 170, 177
Gish, Lillian: 218, 253, 256, 259, 262, 288, 348, 354, 374, 389, 392, 405
Gittler, L. F.: **534**
Glaspell, Susan: **186;** 9, 80, 82, 110, 111, 115, 140, 168, 185–86; *Bernice,* 95; *Chains of Dew,* 169; *The Inheritors,* 149; *Woman's Honor,* 103
Glover, T. R.: *The Conflict of Religions in the Early Roman Empire,* 200
"Godfather" (play idea): 366
Goethe, Johann Wolfgang von: 412, 564; *Faust,* 432
Gold: 94, 104, 122, 130, 133, 137, 139, 143, 146, 147, 148, 149, 152, 155–56, 210, 325, 347, 438
Gold, Mike: **177, 193, 206;** 198, 211, 288, 308, 338; *Battle Hymn,* 177n; *Fiesta,* 198, 206, 211; *Hoboken Blues,* 206; *The Life of John Brown,* 177n
Goldberg, Isaac: **205**
Golden Swan, The: 99, 106
Goldman, Emma: 75
Goldwyn, Samuel: 544
Goodman, Edward: **82;** 169
Goodman, Jules: 60–61
Goodman, Lucy (Mrs. Edward): 82
Goodman, Philip: 184
Goodman Theatre: 224
Gorelik, Mordecai: **224**
Gorki, Maxim: 457; *The Lower Depths,* 36, 206
Gramophone Shop, New York City: 575
Grand Guignol: 402
Grant, Ulysses S.: 499
Gray, Thomas: "Elegy Written in a Country Churchyard," 23
Great God Brown, The: 139, 140, 188, 198, 199, 200, 201, 208, 210, 211, 213, 217–18, 221, 225, 228, 246, 248, 250, 327, 333, 347, 370, 387, 441, 449, 523–24, 530, 548–49, 561, 571
Great Republic (clipper ship): 434
"Greed of the Meek" (play idea): 467, 518
Green, Morris: 196, 211
Green, Paul: 258; *Tread the Green Grass,* 345, 359
Greenwich Village: 144
Greenwich Village Players, The: 79, 88
Greenwich Village Theatre, The: 189, 196, 198, 208, 213
Gregor, Joseph: *Masks of the World,* 462
Griesser, Marjorie: **166**
Gross, Pete: 348
Groton, Conn.: 22, 33, 60
Gruenberg, Louis: 371, 376, 405
Guggenheim Foundation: 540
"Guilty Are Guilty, The" (play idea), 204
Guyman, Mrs.: **563**

Haas, Robert, 580
Hackett, James C.: 95
Hayne, Robert Young: 563
Hairy Ape, The: 5n, 139, 140, 141, 161, 162, 166, 167, 170, 171, 173, 174, 182, 188, 193, 195,

209, 210, 211, 233, 248, 252, 254, 258, 273, 276, 300, 325, 327, 351, 353, 354, 355, 358, 370, 378, 408, 423, 428, 438, 441, 444, 445–46, 448, 484, 515, 521, 522, 529, 537, 553, 555, 557–59, 560, 570
Hale, Ruth: 146
Hamilton, Clayton: **124;** 23, 26, 70, 347
Hamilton, Gilbert V.: 217, 223, 243, 253, 257, 423; *A Research in Marriage,* 217
Hampden, Walter: 201, 207
Hammerstein, Oscar, II: 484
Hammond, Percy: 354
Hapgood, Hutchins (Hutch): 100
"Happy Home," Provincetown, Mass.: 285
Harding, Ann: 392
Harkness, Edward S.: 214
Harland, Henry: *My Friend Prospero,* 15, 17; *The Cardinal's Snuff Box,* 17
Harrigan, William: 198
Harris, Jed: 387, 389
Harris, Sam: 201
Harvard football team: 31, 32, 36
Harvard University: 9
Hasenclever, Walter: *Menschen,* 184; *Jenseits,* 184
Hatton, Fanny Locke and Frederic H. Hatton: 346
Hauptmann, Gerhardt: 146, 190
Havre, Harold: 588
Havre, Parallee: 588
Hayes, Helen: **516;** 101, 103, 112, 116, 121, 123–24, 126, 127, 137, 138
Hays, Will H.: 418, 420
Hazleton, George C. and Ritter Brown: *The Whirlwind,* 105
Helburn, Theresa: **147, 290, 300, 305, 374, 382, 392, 441, 449, 473, 484, 520, 557;** 4, 147, 149, 190, 218, 253, 276
Held, Anna: 495
"Hell Hole, The." *See* Golden Swan, The
Hewlett, J. Monroe: 102
Hemingway, Ernest: 537
Henle, Mr.: 535
Hepburn, Katharine: 520, 558
Heywood, DuBose: **418;** *Porgy,* 290, 301
Hiebert, Daniel: **70;** 28n, 133
Hill, Frederick P.: 262
Hills, Grace Dupree: **194**
Hitler, Adolph: 506, 523
Hogarth, Leona: 211
Hohl, Arthur: 207
Holladay, Adele: 106
Holladay, Louis: 73, 106n
Holladay, Paula (Polly): 106n
Hollis, Mr.: **571**
Holloway, Baliol: 269
"Homo Sapiens" (play idea): 178
Hong Kong: 336
"Honor Among the Bradleys": 130
Honduras: 18–20, 79, 170, 173
Hoosier Hotshots, The: 572
Hopkins, Arthur: **559;** 5, 84, 88, 95, 103, 140, 147, 159, 161, 162, 169, 171, 188, 190, 201, 224, 242, 244, 256, 261, 267, 387
Hopkins, Peggy: 368
Hornblow, Arthur: 410
Horton, Philip: **448**

Horwitz, Dr. William H.: 588
Houdini, Harry: 17
Howard, Sidney: **457**
Huber, family: 236, 241, 262
Hughie: 518, 531–32
Hugo, Victor: *The Laughing Man,* 14
Hull, Henry: 207
Hurlbut, William: *Bride of the Lamb,* 393
Hurn, Mr.: 241
Hurok, Sol: 340
Huston, Walter: 196, 395, 474, 519

Ibsen, Henrik: 146, 346, 354, 355, 358, 361, 382,
   412, 477; *Hedda Gabler,* 52, 477; *Rosmersholm,*
   151
Iceman Cometh, The: 2, 496, 500–02, 506, 510,
   511, 514, 517, 518, 522, 526, 530, 537, 546,
   555, 556–57, 560, 566, 568, 576, 578
Ile: 75, 80, 82, 83, 170, 405, 438, 554
In the Zone: 4n, 79n, 82, 84, 87, 88, 130, 166, 170,
   171, 188, 201, 438, 503, 554
Informer, The (film): 447, 521
Ingelow, Jean: *High Tide on the Coast of Lincolnshire,*
   12
Ingram, Rex: 453
"Invitation to Learning" (radio program): 552, 561
Ireland: 509, 519
Irish Academy: 407
Irish Players, The: 128, 199
Irving, Henry: 196
"It Cannot Be Mad" (play idea): 311, 317

Jacques: 357
James Baines (ship model): 434
Jannings, Emil: 444
Jarboe, Mr.: 262
Jeffers, Robinson: 413; *Tamar,* 401
Jelliffe, Smith Ely: 348
Jessner, Leopold: 166
Jewett Players: 48
Johnson, Mr.: 274
Jolson, Al: 431, 571, 572
Jones, A. L.: 196, 211
Jones, Henry Arthur: 148
Jones, Nina: 70, 104
Jones, Robert Edmond: **551, 560;** 5, 9, 137, 140,
   150, 161, 168, 171, 173, 183, 186, 187, 190,
   196, 198, 201, 207, 208, 243, 244, 256, 266,
   267, 387, 396, 421, 424, 435, 454, 456, 468,
   551, 589
Jonson, Ben: *The Alchemist,* 200
"Josephine Song." *See* "My Yosephine"
Joyce, James: 358, 407, 511, 545; *Ulysses,* 265
Jung, Carl: 247, 386

Kahn, Ivan: 493
Kahn, Otto: 89, 218
Kaiser, Georg: *Gas Trilogy,* 224
Kalff, Marie: 354
Kalonyme, Louis. *See* Kantor, Louis
Kantor, Louis: **146, 307;** 190, 312, 340
Karloff, Boris: 537
Kaufmann, George S. and Edna Ferber: *Stage Door,*
   471
Kauser, Alice: 185–86

Kauser, Benjamin: 185–86
Kazan, Elia: 568
Kamerny Theatre: 184, 238, 405
Keats, John: 265
Keefe, Edward: **156**
Keith, Robert: 207
Kelly, Margot: 190
Kelly, Mr.: 253
Kennedy, Charles O'Brien: **582;** 142n, 161, 182
Kenton, Edna: **185;** 140, 183, 184, 186
Khayyam, Omar: 412
Kibbee, Guy: 421
King, Alexander: 376
King, Dr.: 114
Kinkead, Cleves: *Common Clay, The,* 49
Kipling, Rudyard: *The Jungle Book,* 370
Klaw, Marc: 63
Klauber, Adolph: 169
Klein, Mr.: 405
Klopfer, Donald: 580
Knollenberg, Bernhard: 530
Knowles, Sheridan: *Virginius,* 190
Kommer, Rudolph K.: 212, 229
Komroff, Manuel: **200;** 259, 376, 392
Koonen, Alice: 405
Kosta, Tessa (Mrs. Richard Madden): 356
Kruger, Otto: 156
Krutch, Joseph Wood: **247, 350;** 141, 218, 347

Lafayette, Calif.: 467
Lamb's Club: 111, 201
"Lament for Beatrice": 50
Langner, Armina Marshall: 4, 5
Langner, Lawrence: **149, 164, 243, 331, 357, 419,**
   424, 426, 452, 479, 510, 511, 519, 521, 522,
   548, 555, 568; 4, 76, 94n, 139, 145, 147, 236,
   250, 253, 259, 262, 266, 327, 558; *Lady Godiva,*
   359, 419; *The Pursuit of Happiness,* 420, 425; *A*
   School for Husbands, 425
Lao-Tze: 401
Lasky, Jesse: 444
Larkin, Mr.: 262
Larimore, Earle: 266
"Last Conquest, The" (play idea): 533, 512–13,
   546
Lawrenceville Academy: 394, 437, 481, 482, 490
Lawson, John Howard: *Processional,* 194; *Roger*
   Bloomer, 181, 194
Lazarus Laughed: 140, 198, 201, 204, 205, 206–07,
   208, 213, 214, 215, 217, 218, 224, 225, 228,
   229, 232, 234, 242, 244, 245, 245–46, 254, 257,
   266, 269, 273, 274, 290, 299, 316, 327, 331,
   338, 344, 347, 365, 377, 439, 463, 480, 530,
   548, 567, 568
LeClercq, Arthur: 138n
Lee, Canada: 551
Lehmann, Beatrix: 547
Lefty Louie: 99, 106
Le Gallienne, Eva: 452
Leiber, Fritz: 177
Lemon, Courtney: 348
Lenormand, Henri: 345, 374, 405, 456; *The Cow-*
   ard, 358–59, 375; *Mixture,* 354
Le Plessis, France: 2, 289, 335, 341
Leo: 106

Woollcott, Alexander, 112, 161
World War II: 493, 506–07, 528–29, 533
Wycherly, Margaret: 142, 145

Yale University: 530
Yeats, William Butler: **430;** 407, 455
Yeats, Mrs. William Butler: **230, 231**
"You n' Me": 49

Young, Roland: 179
Young, Stark: **341;** 251, 347; *Colonnade,* 343; *The Saint,* 190, 198; *The Three Fountains,* 343

Ziegfeld Follies: 391
Zimmern, A. E.: *The Greek Commonwealth,* 20
Zoo, New York City: 318
Zweig, Stefan: 492